THE OXFORD HANDBO

INTERNATIC
BUSINESS
STRATEGY

THE OXFORD HANDBOOK OF

INTERNATIONAL

BUSINESS

STRATEGY

Edited by

KAMEL MELLAHI, KLAUS MEYER,
RAJNEESH NARULA, IRINA SURDU,

and

ALAIN VERBEKE

OXFORD
UNIVERSITY PRESS

OXFORD

UNIVERSITY PRESS

Great Clarendon Street, Oxford, OX2 6DP,
United Kingdom

Oxford University Press is a department of the University of Oxford.
It furthers the University's objective of excellence in research, scholarship,
and education by publishing worldwide. Oxford is a registered trade mark of
Oxford University Press in the UK and in certain other countries

Published in the United States of America by Oxford University Press
198 Madison Avenue, New York, NY 10016, United States of America

British Library Cataloguing in Publication Data

Data available

Library of Congress Control Number: 2020945949

ISBN 978–0–19–886837–8

Printed and bound by
CPI Group (UK) Ltd, Croydon, CR0 4YY

Preface and Acknowledgments

Every cause has an effect, and, conversely, every event or action is preceded by a cause. From a scientist's perspective, determinism is reflected in Newton's laws of motion: objects do not simply change their state without some intervention, and these interventions provide a complete explanation of what becomes the new state of the object.

This has been an incredibly comforting line of thought to my younger self, as it implied that all I needed to do was to select the precise method of mediation to alter outcomes. It proved useful as an engineer, and, when migrating to the social sciences, I was under the impression that I merely needed to acknowledge that there are more complex and opaque interactions between causes. In brief, until about ten years ago, I continued to find solace in the very simple adage that "everything has a reason."

Alas, once I turned my mind to philosophy, my happy reliance on this light form of determinism seems to have been naïve. To my incredible consternation, philosophers have long argued that, if all actions have causes that preceded them, by extension, humans have no free will. If this were so, all future events are already destined to occur, and therefore, resistance was futile.

To claim that managers have agency to shape the long-term positioning of their organizations—what we call strategy—is, for the hard-core determinist, an example of human hubris. I will leave the reader to consider this conundrum, one that has occupied the minds of intellectual giants such as Aristotle, Omar Khayyam, Gottfried Leibnitz, Pierre-Simon Laplace, Karl Popper, and Neils Bohr. I and my fellow editors invite you to join their august company.

At a more granular level, one has to wonder: Is this book simply a fait accompli? Did Irina really propose the idea, or did greater forces prompt her to do so? Was the ready acceptance by the other editors a predictable outcome, based on some long-forgotten incident in our individual childhoods, perhaps? My temporally constrained simple-mindedness fails to identify the obvious motivations of our four dozen contributors who also (possibly) had no choice but to seize this (life-changing) opportunity.

I leave the reader to chew on these metaphysical aspects of the outcome (the chapters in this volume) and their causal antecedents. I also ask you to consider the rich irony that we have chosen to publish a volume on (international business) strategy despite our collective and individual lack of agency.

It is important, especially, to express our gratitude to the numerous people who have contributed to making this book a success. Their motivations are less obvious; and seem to the untrained observer to be acts of selfless charity. Sabreena Zaman, doctoral student at the Henley Business School, kindly assisted with copyediting the chapters. We also want to acknowledge the Academy of International Business (AIB), the *Journal of International Business Studies*, and the John H. Dunning Centre for International Business for providing us the facilities (and refreshments) to host an author's workshop during the AIB Meeting in Copenhagen in July 2019. Dana Minbaeva and Larissa Rabbiosi of the Copenhagen Business School were our most kind and generous hosts. Last, but not least, Mads Emil Wedell-Wedellsborg, another brilliant Henley doctoral student, provided support with the workshop.

Hubris it may well be, but we are steadfast in our belief that managers can influence outcomes in international business. On the other hand, we embrace causal determinism when it comes to the entirely predictable high quality of the work included here, a consequence predestined by the intellectual abilities of our contributors. We, in turn, are honored to have had the privilege to edit this volume, as The Fates have no doubt always envisioned.

Rajneesh Narula
(on behalf of Kamel Mellahi, Klaus Meyer, Irina Surdu, and Alain Verbeke)

Contents

PART I FOUNDATIONS OF INTERNATIONAL BUSINESS STRATEGY

PART II CORE ISSUES IN MODERN INTERNATIONAL BUSINESS STRATEGY RESEARCH

PART III GOVERNANCE STRUCTURES IN INTERNATIONAL BUSINESS STRATEGY

PART IV DYNAMICS OF INTERNATIONAL BUSINESS STRATEGY

PART V NEW DIMENSIONS
OF INTERNATIONAL
BUSINESS STRATEGY

LIST OF FIGURES

LIST OF TABLES

LIST OF CONTRIBUTORS

Ulf Andersson is Professor at Mälardalen University, Sweden and Adjunct Professor at BI Norwegian Business School.

Ari Van Assche is Professor of International Business at HEC Montréal and holds a Professorship in Pedagogical Innovation for Economic Diplomacy.

Simone R. Barakat is Professor of Strategy at Universidade Anhembi Morumbi, São Paulo, Brazil.

Gabriel R. G. Benito is Professor at BI Norwegian Business School, Oslo, Norway.

Stephen Brammer is Dean of the School of Management at the University of Bath, UK.

Keith D. Brouthers is Professor of Business Strategy at King's Business School, King's College London, UK and a Fellow of the Academy of International Business.

Luciano Ciravegna is Associate Professor at King's College London, UK, Department of International Development and INCAE, Costa Rica.

Kieran M. Conroy is Assistant Professor of International Management at Queen's University Belfast Management School, UK.

Alvaro Cuervo-Cazurra is Professor of Global Strategy at Northeastern University, US.

Teresa da Silva Lopes is Professor of International Business and Business History and Director of the Centre for Evolution of Global Business and Institutions, at the University of York, UK.

José Guilherme F. de Campos holds a PhD in Management from the School of Economics, Management and Accounting, University of São Paulo (USP), Brazil.

Maria A. De Villa is Professor of Strategy at Universidad EAFIT, Colombia.

Pavlos Dimitratos is Professor of International Business at the University of Glasgow Adam Smith Business School, UK.

Isibor Jerry Ebeigbe is a Postgraduate Researcher in International Business at the University of Leeds, UK.

Saul Estrin is Professor of Managerial Economics and Strategy and the founding Head of the Department of Management, London School of Economics, UK.

Mats Forsgren is Professor Emeritus of International Business at the Department of Business Studies, Uppsala University, Sweden.

Anthony Goerzen is the D.R. Sobey Professor of International Business at Smith School of Business of Queen's University.

Lars Håkanson is Professor of International Business at Copenhagen Business School, Denmark.

Ulf Holm is Professor of International Business at the Department of Business Studies at Uppsala University, Sweden.

Geoffrey Jones is the Isidor Straus Professor of Business History, at the Harvard Business School, Harvard University, US.

Liena Kano is Associate Professor of Strategy and Global Management at the Haskayne School of Business, University of Calgary, Canada.

Philip Kappen is Associate Professor of International Business at the Department of Business Studies, Uppsala University, Sweden.

Jing Li is Associate Professor of International Business and Canada Research Chair in Global Investment Strategy at Beedie School of Business, Simon Fraser University, Canada.

Dana Minbaeva is Professor of Strategic and Global Human Resource Management at the Department of Strategy and Innovation, and the Vice-President for International Affairs at Copenhagen Business School, Denmark.

Ram Mudambi is the Frank M. Speakman Professor of Strategy at the Fox School of Business, Temple University, US.

Kamel Mellahi is a Senior Manager at Dubai Chamber Centre for Responsible Business. Prior to joining the Dubai Chamber, he held professorship positions in Strategic Management at Warwick Business School, the University of Sheffield and the University of Nottingham, UK.

Klaus Meyer is Professor of International Business at Ivey Business School, Western University, Canada.

Giulio Nardella is Assistant Professor of Strategy and Responsible Business, School of Business and Economics, Loughborough University, UK.

Rajneesh Narula is the John H. Dunning Chair of International Business Regulation at the Henley Business School, University of Reading, UK.

Renato J. Orsato is Professor at the São Paulo School of Management (EAESP) at Getulio Vargas Foundation (FGV), Brazil, and Visiting Scholar at INSEAD, France.

Pinar Ozcan is Professor of Entrepreneurship and Innovation at Oxford University's Saïd Business School, UK.

Bent Petersen is Associate Dean and Professor in International Business at the Copenhagen Business School, Department of International Economics, Government and Business, Denmark.

Olga Petricevic is Assistant Professor at the University of Calgary, Canada.

Alicia Rodríguez is Assistant Professor at Carlos III University of Madrid, Spain.

Elizabeth L. Rose is Professor of International Business at the University of Leeds, UK and Adjunct Professor of Business Policy and Strategy at the Indian Institute of Management Udaipur, India.

Grazia D. Santangelo is Professor of Strategic and International Management at Copenhagen Business School, Denmark.

Christian Schwens is Professor of Business Administration and Head of the Endowed Chair for Interdisciplinary Management Science at the University of Cologne, Germany.

Daniel M. Shapiro is Professor of Global Business Strategy and former Dean of the Beedie School of Business, Simon Fraser University, Canada.

Carlos M. P. Sousa is Professor of Marketing and Business Strategy at Molde University College, Norway.

Irina Surdu is Associate Professor of International Business Strategy at Warwick Business School, University of Warwick, UK.

C. Annique Un is Associate Professor of International Business and Strategy at Northeastern University, US.

Alain Verbeke is Professor of International Business and holds the McCaig Chair in Management at the Haskayne School of Business, University of Calgary, Canada and Editor-in-Chief of the *Journal of International Business Studies*.

Qun Tan is Associate Professor of the Department of Marketing at Xiamen University, China.

David J. Teece is the Thomas W. Tusher Professor in Global Business and the Director of the Tusher Center initiative for the Management of Intellectual Capital, Haas School of Business, University of California, Berkeley, US.

Eric W. K. Tsang is the Dallas World Salute Distinguished Professor of Global Strategy at the Naveen Jindal School of Management, University of Texas at Dallas, US.

Lawrence S. Welch was an honorary Professor at the University of Melbourne, Melbourne Business School, Australia. Lawrence Welch passed away on the 21st of September 2020.

Basak Yakis-Douglas is Associate Professor of International Business Strategy at King's Business School and an Associate Fellow at Saïd Business School, University of Oxford, UK.

Wenlong Yuan is the Stu Clark Chair in Entrepreneurship and Innovation at the Asper School of Business, the University of Manitoba, Canada.

Ivo Zander is the Anders Wall Professor of Entrepreneurship at the Department of Business Studies, Uppsala University, Sweden.

Florian B. Zapkau is Assistant Professor of International Business at the School of Business and Economics, Vrije Universiteit Amsterdam, the Netherlands.

INTRODUCTION

KAMEL MELLAHI, KLAUS MEYER,
RAJNEESH NARULA, IRINA SURDU, AND
ALAIN VERBEKE

THE international business (IB) strategies of multinational enterprises (MNEs) are of interest to academics, managerial practitioners, and policymakers alike. Indeed, the MNE has been the main subject of interest for IB scholars since the 1970s when scholars shifted their focus from examining the competitiveness of nations from a predominantly economic perspective, to appreciating the importance of the firm and how resources are allocated within the firm. The growth of the firm is discussed in relation to its, often distant, home and host contexts. The MNE has become ever more important in the study of strategic management decisions as nowadays most firms are MNEs, and these MNEs operate in institutional contexts, which vary widely and may significantly influence strategy effectiveness. The modern MNE is "a coordinated system or network of cross-border value-creating activities, some of which are carried out within the hierarchy of the firm, and some of which are carried out through informal social ties or contractual relationships" (Cantwell, Dunning, & Lundan, 2010: 569). This drives a move from context-aware to context-rich studies in management and strategy research.

The field of IB strategy is a thriving field of scholarly inquiry and we hope that this volume will further broaden and deepen our understanding of MNEs' strategies and operations. At least three factors contribute to the growth of the field of IB strategy.

First of all, the field is constantly looking to revisit its core theoretical foundations and assumptions (Buckley, 2019; Cuervo-Cazurra & Narula, 2015; Mellahi, Frynas, Sun, & Siegel, 2016; Narula, 2012; Rugman & Verbeke, 2003; Rugman, Verbeke, & Nguyen, 2011). This is reflected in the calls for research in IB journals such as *Journal of International Business Studies*, *Journal of World Business*, *International Business Review*, *Multinational Business Review*, and *Global Strategy Journal* on the challenges associated with radical potential of nascent technologies, rapidly changing political risks, global value chain sustainability, or global human resource and talent management challenges.

MNEs are some of the most complex firms because they need to learn about, and manage, these grand challenges at home and abroad Grosse & Meyer, 2019).

Second, the field addresses important problems that different types of firms are facing, including the challenges arising from the liability of newness for new ventures, the resource constraints characteristic of smaller firms (Dimitratos, Amorós, Etchebarne, & Felzensztein, 2014), or the role of state ownership in emerging market MNEs' international strategies (Li, Meyer, Zhang, & Ding, 2018; Meyer, Ding, Li, & Zhang, 2014). These are challenges that require firms to upgrade their extant reservoirs of resources and capabilities, so as to be able to manage changing institutional and social environments and compete with diverse local and foreign competitors. MNEs that are unable to upgrade their resources and capabilities successfully may be forced to retrench from international operations and, in the worst of cases, may cease to exist.

Third, IB strategy is a field where theory continuously seeks to meet practice (Narula, 2006; Narula & Verbeke, 2015). Of interest to IB strategy scholars are the complexities and uncertainties firms need to address in international markets, especially when making large-scale resource allocation decisions. These are rarely clear-cut and simple to resolve, and certainly do not always fit the theoretical models developed to address them. Therefore, scholars must be clear about how they can enrich our field-specific arsenal of concepts, models, and theories, which should have the capacity to handle the complexities and uncertainties associated with strategizing in international markets (Mellahi et al. 2016; Narula, 2020; Verbeke, 2020).

The present volume includes twenty-three chapters, divided into five parts. Part I discusses the achievements and limitations of the conceptual foundations of IB strategy, whereas Part II delves deeper into the application of these foundational views on core IB strategy topics. Part III focuses on the differences in motivations and decision-making processes between smaller and larger firms, private and state-owned, emerging or developed market MNEs. Part IV provides an analysis of dynamic IB strategy decisions, which require a revisiting of traditional theories and models. Finally, Part V provides an analysis of areas of MNE decision-making that are increasingly important for practitioners and academics alike. The links between international strategy and the social responsibilities of the MNE, as well as the deployment of effective and ethical human resource practices in international markets are such examples.

In order to put together this volume, we selected authors who, in our view, have made a significant contribution to our understanding of the IB strategies of the MNE that will continue to remain relevant. Further, we also invited strategic management scholars to reflect on how issues related to strategy are enacted in an IB context. We are grateful to all the authors for their insightful depiction of extant works and challenging propositions for future research directions.

In Chapter 1 of this volume, Rajneesh Narula, Alain Verbeke, and Wenlong Yuan start by explaining the foundations of IB strategy upon which most theoretical perspectives are built. In doing so, the chapter introduces the seven foundational concepts in IB strategy in a unifying framework. These include refinements of traditional ideas about the role of firm-specific advantages (FSAs) and country-specific advantages (CSAs) as well as the generic behavioral characteristics of economic actors engaged in international strategizing. In a modern international context, differences between home and host market and institutional environments often require artful orchestration of knowledge bundles (Verbeke, 2009). Further, decision-making and execution require both access to sufficient information and the capability to process this information—yet, information is incomplete, resulting in an imperfect assessment of current and even more so future situational and environmental contexts (Kano & Verbeke, 2015; Verbeke, 2009; Verbeke, Ciravegna, Lopez, & Kundu, 2018). Bounded reliability, reflecting the scarcity of effort to make good on open-ended promises (Verbeke & Greidanus, 2009) is proposed in this chapter as a more managerially relevant behavioral assumption.

Chapter 2 makes a compelling case for why history does, in fact, matter. Geoffrey Jones and Teresa da Silva Lopes skillfully explain how history can help us understand the changing role of the MNE, in light of external changes such as the growth of political nationalism. Although "grand challenges" facing MNEs are often labeled as "new," the authors note that we may still learn from history. Differences in data sources and methodologies used are discussed, presenting opportunities for interdisciplinary collaboration.

Chapter 3 proposes that MNE research and practice require a more focused and explicit capabilities-based perspective to capture the complexities of competing internal, organizational alternatives and their effect on IB strategizing. David Teece and Olga Petricevic also explain why the uncertain conditions in the IB environment demand superior firm-level capabilities for the MNE to achieve long-run competitive advantage and evolutionary fitness. The authors use the dynamic capabilities approach to unpack the sources of firm-level competitive advantage in the presence of changing external conditions. The chapter concludes with valuable propositions around how future empirical studies may be able to operationalize dynamic capabilities.

Chapter 4 zooms in on a key dimension of IB strategy, namely location. As one of the pillars of John Dunning's "eclectic paradigm" (Dunning, 1980), location strategies are important because the location options available to MNEs are great, while the management and control of international operations in different locations has become increasingly complex. The move from natural resource-seeking to knowledge-seeking investment, and the evolution in how MNEs orchestrate their global value chains reflects this complexity. Ram Mudambi focuses on how locational dynamics driven by MNE strategies have so rapidly changed the global profile of many industries.

Part II analyzes the core issues in IB strategy research. Chapter 5 starts with a much-loved topic in IB strategy. The chapter provides an overview of progress in international entry mode research since the highly cited review by Brouthers and Hennart (2007) in order to understand whether new and different theories have gained traction, new methodologies are being applied, and whether we have gained a better understanding of the link between mode choice and performance. Florian B. Zapkau, Christian Schwens, and Keith D. Brouthers express their disappointment that, although we have some theoretical development in the area, new methodologies are scarce and the performance implications of international entry mode choices specifically, remain, at the point at which the Handbook was written, largely unknown.

Overall, we know that, while unique knowledge and proprietary innovation remain important to international competitive advantage, the performance and survival of MNEs, depend on their continued ability to upgrade and renew these advantages, as competition, imitation, and environmental change erode their value. Chapter 6, authored by Lars Håkanson, Philip Kappen, and Ivo Zander, focuses on strategic knowledge creation in MNEs, and the processes through which geographical patterns of international R&D have evolved, along with the structures, systems, and processes through which MNEs have sought to govern and coordinate these activities. Internationalization processes are also the focus of Chapter 7, where Grazia D. Santangelo offers an overview of the Uppsala model starting from its original formulation (Johanson & Vahlne, 1977) to its revision (Vahlne & Johanson, 2017) providing a stimulating and open-ended debate on the relationship between market knowledge and commitment. In line with the idea that theoretical models and concepts must be debated and revisited to remain relevant, Eric W. K. Tsang tells us more in Chapter 8 about how to appropriately integrate and combine theories to effectively explain dynamic IB strategies.

Part III explains that the heterogeneity observed in IB strategic behavior stems from the size, origin, governance, and other characteristics of the firm. Chapter 9 provides a synthesis on the literature on small MNEs such as international new ventures, where Isibor Jerry Ebeigbe and Elizabeth Rose discuss the characteristics of new ventures—proactive, entrepreneurial, innovative—can inform our understanding of IB strategy. Chapter 10 focuses on what Pavlos Dimitratos refers to as the "real" international entrepreneurial firm, namely the micro-multinational, which employs deeper forms of internationalization including contractual joint ventures and wholly owned subsidiaries and is truly risk-taking in its international strategizing. In Chapter 11, Liena Kano, Alain Verbeke, and Luciano Ciravegna provide insights from family firm research, with a particular focus on the microfoundational drivers of family managers' decision-making such as socio-emotional wealth. The infusion of family-business specific constructs into the study of IB strategy is elegantly executed. Chapter 12 adds to this discussion by critically reviewing the novelty—if any—of the international strategies of emerging-market multinationals, and describing new theoretical concepts resulting from analyzing these firms. Advancement in the area is expected to come from understanding these firms by studying their home market environments. Alvaro Cuervo-Cazurra, Alicia Rodríguez, and C. Annique Un focus specifically on four strategies—frugal innovation, contractual innovation, upgrading escape, and institutional escape—used by emerging-market firms to become MNEs. Further, many of these emerging-market firms are state owned, which is why the emergence and importance of state-owned MNEs (SOMNEs) has generated considerable academic and policy interest. In Chapter 13, Saul Estrin, Jing Li, and Daniel M. Shapiro examine the theoretical perspectives and empirical evidence about

SOMNEs and discuss the boundary conditions that limit what they referred to as "the liability of stateness," with reference to hybrid forms of ownership and political and institutional arrangements that exist in emerging markets.

Part IV explores the dynamics of IB strategy post initial entry into international markets. MNEs establish subsidiaries that develop their organizational dynamics and within the constraints of the parent firm develop their own strategies (Meyer, Li, & Schotter, 2020). In Chapter 14, Gabriel R. G. Benito, Bent Petersen, and Lawrence S. Welch start by explaining that mode choices go beyond the initial entry and, as firms switch from one mode to another, or use combinations of modes, more dynamic and complex choices emerge, which may not be adequately explained by the usual static approaches to international entry mode choice. Chapter 15 goes on to explain that when firms set up international subsidiaries, these may become embedded in their local host market environments. Ulf Andersson, Mats Forsgren, and Ulf Holm build on their seminal works (Andersson, Forsgren, & Holm, 2001, 2002) on the relationship between network embeddedness and the evolution of MNE subsidiary roles. Maria A. De Villa argues in Chapter 16 in favor of combining insights from the corporate political strategy and IB strategy literatures to understand the political strategies of MNE subsidiaries and their outcomes, in terms of achieving legitimacy in the host country and boosting performance. In turn, when MNE subsidiaries underperform, some may exit foreign markets; this is the subject of Chapter 17, where Carlos M. P. Sousa and Qun Tan offer alternative behavioral lenses through which to understand divestment behavior, including attribution theory. Chapter 18 follows up to illustrate and explain that, of those MNEs that exit foreign markets, some re-enter. Irina Surdu explains that decisions such as re-entry depend on the manner in which the past experience (in this case, the exit) is framed and perceived by decision makers; the author highlights the importance of behavioral concepts that complement rationality-based assumptions about dynamic MNE strategies (Surdu, Mellahi, Glaister, & Nardella, 2018; Surdu, Mellahi, & Glaister 2019; Surdu & Narula, 2020).

Finally, Part V invites the reader to explore new dimensions of IB strategy. These reflect the growing pressures that MNEs are facing in their home as well as host markets. Chapter 19 discusses the strategic implications of digitalization for the MNE; the rationale is that firms entering new markets with digital technologies depend less on mediators and may control the delivery of their products or services, while new entrants gain advantages from exploiting digital platforms. Pinar Ozcan and Basak Yakis-Douglas lay out how the classic principles of international competitive strategy are transformed in today's markets due to digitalization, providing suggestions about how MNEs can respond to these transformations. Chapters 20, 21, and 22 offer different approaches to examine the social and environmental responsibilities of the MNE. Chapter 20 expresses the view that the conversation around the corporate social responsibility (CSR) and corporate social irresponsibility (CSI) of firms should be front and center in the IB strategy discipline; Giulio Nardella and Stephen Brammer articulate major perspectives on CSR and CSI, ranging from "the right thing to do" to "the profitable thing to do." Chapter 21 emphasizes the increased social pressure placed on MNEs to "do the right thing" and manage global value chains responsibly; Anthony Goerzen and Ari Van Assche extend the dynamic capabilities approach to explore the global value chain governance strategies of lead MNEs and the contextual differences that influence the resources and capabilities required to improve global value chain performance. In Chapter 22, very insightfully, Renato J. Orsato, Simone R. Barakat, and José Guilherme F. de Campos discuss the opportunities that firms have to profit from sustainability strategies. Eco-efficiency strategies can reduce costs and environmental impacts, and lead to differentiating products and services on the basis of ecological prerogatives. In addition, new value propositions can arise from innovative business models and market developments. Finally, in Chapter 23, Kieran M. Conroy and Dana Minbaeva explore human resource management policies and practices, with a focus on the challenges for MNEs of having to manage increasingly diverse workforces and the impact thereof on successful MNE strategy implementation.

This collection is a complete *Handbook of International Business Strategy* that should serve as a knowledge repository for strategy scholars and contemplative MNE managers. Each of the chapters provides insightful future research directions as well as implications for management and policy. As editors, we express our hope that the core insights from this Handbook will stimulate the next generation of IB strategy scholars to pursue research in this area and to collaborate with practitioners. Such collaboration will be a key pre-condition for crafting models and theories that can adequately capture the evolving complex realities of modern IB functioning.

References

Andersson, U., Forsgren, M., & Holm, U. 2001. Subsidiary embeddedness and competence development in MNCs- a multi-level analysis. *Organization Studies*, 22(6): 1013–1034.

Andersson, U., Forsgren, M., & Holm, U. 2002. The strategic impact of external networks— subsidiary performance and competence development in the multinational corporation. *Strategic Management Journal*, 23: 979–996.

Brouthers, K. D. & Hennart, J. F. 2007. Boundaries of the firm: Insights from international entry mode research. *Journal of Management*, 33(3): 395–425.

Buckley, P. 2019. The role of international business theory in an uncertain world. In Tulder, R., Verbeke, A., & Jankowska, B. (Eds.), *International Business in a VUCA World: The Changing Role of States and Firms (Progress in International Business Research*, Vol. 14). London: Emerald. https://doi.org/10.1108/S1745-886220190000014002.

Cantwell, J., Dunning, J. H., & Lundan, S. M. 2010. An evolutionary approach to understanding international business activity: The co-evolution of MNEs and the institutional environment. *Journal of International Business Studies*, 41(4): 567–586.

Cuervo-Cazurra, A., & Narula, R. 2015. A set of motives to unite them all? Revisiting the principles and typology of internationalization motives. *Multinational Business Review*, 23(1): 2–14.

Dimitratos, P., Amorós, J. E., Etchebarne, M. S., & Felzensztein, C. 2014. Micro-multinational or not? International entrepreneurship, networking and learning effects. *Journal of Business Research*, 67(5): 908–915.

Dunning, J. H. 1980. Toward an Eclectic Theory of International Production: Some Empirical tests. *Journal of International Business Studies*, 11, 9–31.

Grosse, T., & Meyer, K. E. 2019. *Oxford Handbook of Management in Emerging Markets*. Oxford: Oxford University Press.

Johanson, J., & Vahlne, J.-E. 1977. The international process of the firm: A model of knowledge development and increasing foreign market commitments. *Journal of International Business Studies*, 8(1): 23–32.

Kano, L., & Verbeke, A. 2015. The three faces of bounded reliability: Alfred Chandler and the micro-foundations of management theory. *California Management Review*, 58(1): 97–122.

Li, J., Meyer, K. E., Zhang, H. & Ding, Y. 2018. Diplomatic and corporate networks: Bridges to foreign locations, *Journal of International Business Studies*, 49(6): 659–683.

Mellahi, K., Frynas, J. G., Sun, P., & Siegel, D. 2016. A review of the nonmarket strategy literature: Toward a multi-theoretical integration. *Journal of Management*, 42(1): 143–173.

Meyer, K. E., Ding, Y., Li, J., & Zhang, H. 2014. Overcoming distrust: How state-owned enterprises adapt their foreign entries to institutional pressures abroad. *Journal of International Business Studies*, 45(8): 1005–1028.

Meyer, K. E., Li, C. & Schotter, A.S. 2020. Managing the MNE Subsidiary: Towards a Multilevel and Dynamic Research Agenda, *Journal of International Business Studies*, 51: 538–567.

Narula, R. 2006. Globalisation, new ecologies, new zoologies, and the purported death of the eclectic paradigm. *Asia Pacific Journal of Management*, 23: 143–151.

Narula, R. 2012. Do we need different frameworks to explain infant MNEs from developing countries? *Global Strategy Journal*, 2: 188–204.

Narula, R., & Verbeke, A. 2015. Making internalisation theory good for practice: The essence of Alan Rugman's contributions to international business. *Journal of World Business*, 50: 612–622.

Narula, R. 2020. Policy opportunities and challenges from the Covid-19 pandemic for economies with large informal sectors. *Journal of International Business Policy*, https://doi.org/10.1057/s42214-020-00059-5.

Rugman, A. M., & Verbeke, A. 2003. Extending the theory of the multinational enterprise: Internalization and strategic management perspectives. *Journal of International Business Studies*, 34(2): 125–137.

Rugman, A. M., Verbeke, A., & Nguyen, Q. T. 2011. Fifty years of international business theory and beyond. *Management International Review*, 51(6): 755–786.

Surdu, I., Mellahi, K., & Glaister, K.W. 2019. Once bitten, not necessarily shy? Determinants of foreign market re-entry commitment strategies. *Journal of International Business Studies*, 50: 393–422.

Surdu, I., Mellahi, K., Glaister, K.W., & Nardella, G. 2018. Why wait? Organizational learning, institutional quality and the speed of foreign market re-entry after initial entry and exit. *Journal of World Business*, 53: 911–929.

Surdu, I., & Narula, R. 2020. Organizational learning, unlearning and re-internationalization timing: Differences between emerging-versus developed-market MNEs. *Journal of International Management* (forthcoming).

Vahlne, J.-E. & Johanson, J. 2017. The internationalization process 1977–2017: The Uppsala model 40 years later. *Journal of International Business Studies*, 48(9): 1087–1102.

Verbeke, A. 2009. *International Business Strategy*. Cambridge: Cambridge University Press.

Verbeke, A., Ciravegna, L., Lopez, L. E., & Kundu, S. K. 2018. Five configurations of opportunism in international market entry. *Journal of Management Studies*, 56(7): 1287–1313.

Verbeke, A., & Greidanus, N. 2009. The end of the opportunism versus trust debate: Bounded reliability as a new envelope-concept in research on MNE governance. *Journal of International Business Studies*, 40(9): 1471–1495.

Verbeke, A. 2020. Will the COVID-19 Pandemic Really Change the Governance of Global Value Chains?. *British Journal of Management*, 31(3): 444–446.

PART I

FOUNDATIONS OF INTERNATIONAL BUSINESS STRATEGY

CHAPTER 1

···

THE THEORY OF INTERNATIONAL BUSINESS STRATEGY

···

RAJNEESH NARULA, ALAIN VERBEKE, AND WENLONG YUAN

INTRODUCTION

···

OVER the last fifty years, the field of international business (IB) has evolved from an international economics perspective, revolving around national competitiveness, to also address more managerially oriented questions on geographically dispersed value creation and related stakeholder management. IB strategy focuses on the effective and efficient matching of the multinational enterprise's (MNE) internal strengths and weaknesses, with external opportunities and challenges across national borders. The intent of IB strategy is to create economic value, while satisfying stakeholder goals. The most efficient means to create value and to cater to stakeholder demands typically vary across geographic space (Narula & Verbeke, 2015; Verbeke, 2013).

The key opportunities and challenges across borders drive IB strategy choices, especially larger-scale, discrete decisions with major resource allocation implications for the firm. Such decisions include inter alia foreign direct investment (FDI) location and operating mode choices, the transfer of knowledge across borders and the governance of subsidiary entrepreneurship (Rugman, Verbeke, & Nguyen, 2011; Narula, Asmussen, Chi, & Kundu, 2019). Several theoretical approaches have been developed to explain MNE international strategy in the realm of larger-scale resource commitment choices associated with risk and uncertainty, such as modes of operation in particular international markets, and the timing and scope of internationalization (Forsgren, 2013; Kano & Verbeke, 2019). The analysis of such decisions has increasingly integrated insights from the resource-based view of the firm, the dynamic capabilities perspective, and institutional theory, among others (Narula et al., 2019). These have all coalesced into internalization theory, which, in its broader sense has become a generally accepted theory of the MNE. It provides an analytical framework that now underscores much of IB strategy research (Narula et al., 2019). It is a key foundation for the analysis of the MNE's international expansion trajectories, and it represents a credible lens for analysis of broader MNE strategic decisions.

In this chapter, utilizing this theoretical lens, we unpack and discuss the key building blocks for analysis of the MNE's international expansion strategy. We start with an overview of the historical evolution of the relationship between the MNE's resources and capabilities—which may constitute firm-specific advantages (FSAs)—and the broader factors embedded in the firm's home and host market environments—which may constitute a source of country-specific advantages (CSAs). We then introduce a framework that brings together the traditional foundations of IB strategy theory with more recent extensions developed during the past two decades (Kano & Verbeke, 2015, 2019; Narula & Verbeke, 2015; Verbeke, 2009; Verbeke & Greidanus, 2009; Verbeke & Yuan, 2005). We end with three applications of our proposed framework to illustrate the relevance of these ideas for IB strategy.

The Evolution of Firm-Specific and Country-Specific Advantages

Early contributions to modern IB strategy built upon macro-level factors, in line with international trade theory, but added a focus on firms overcoming or taking advantage of market imperfections. Although scholars such as Vernon (1966) and Dunning (1958) recognized the importance of firms, their initial focus was on country factors and CSAs. Hymer (1960) conceptualized the requisite fundamental shift from country-level analysis of MNE activities, to the analysis of MNEs commanding what are referred to as FSAs (at the time being the equivalent of ownership advantages). Such FSAs supposedly explain why particular firms choose to internalize and can be successful across national borders, despite the additional costs of doing business abroad.

Seminal works in internalization theory (Buckley & Casson, 1976; Hennart, 1982; Rugman, 1981) further extended Hymer's thesis, but moved away from that author's market-power interpretation of FSAs, toward an efficiency-based one. They proposed that MNEs exist because internal organization is a more efficient governance mechanism to transfer, exploit, and deploy proprietary resources, as compared to using transactions in external markets. Such external markets are fraught with information asymmetries and potentially unreliable business partners, and with governments imposing additional, unnatural market imperfections discriminating against foreign firms. MNEs thus choose to internalize markets for intermediate products because of their efficiency properties. MNEs were expected to replace inefficient transactions in external markets when the costs of organizing the equivalent interdependencies inside the MNE were lower than arm's length transactions in external markets.

Internalization-based rationales continue to be used to explain IB strategies and their performance outcomes. Each version of internalization theory is ultimately concerned with governance design as well as comparing the efficiency properties of alternative institutional arrangements. Rugman's (1981) approach is particularly relevant to IB strategy, given its strong management-oriented focus (Narula & Verbeke, 2015). Rugman built on the empirical fact that "MNEs do exist and do control economic activities across borders, thereby engaging in location choices and governance choices that appeared to be determined largely by the nature of these firms' FSAs" (Narula & Verbeke, 2015: 613).

Building upon the concept of FSAs, we propose that the core challenge for IB strategists is to craft linkages and alignment between the MNE's reservoir of FSAs and the CSAs (also known as location advantages) of home and host countries, as presented in Figure 1.1 (Narula & Verbeke, 2015; Rugman & Verbeke, 1992). In this context, FSAs represent the distinct resource bundles and capabilities held by an MNE (whether owned or otherwise controlled) that confer competitive advantage in the marketplace against rivals. All MNEs—small or large, private, public, or state-owned, from emerging or developed markets—command at least some firm-specific resources and capabilities that they seek to leverage in order to gain a competitive advantage in international markets. In turn, CSAs derive from locational characteristics such as natural resources, institutional strengths, or the purchasing power of consumers in particular countries. MNEs need to organize themselves internationally and make difficult choices among alternative strategic options when deploying their resources and capabilities to capitalize on favorable configurations of host CSAs (e.g. easily accessible cheap labor; knowledge spill-overs accruing to participants in local clusters; a large market for the firm's outputs; etc.). The interaction between firm-specific and country-specific factors broadly influences how MNEs develop IB strategies.

More specifically, combining FSAs and CSAs (both of which can be either strong or weak relative to those of other firms and countries respectively), leads to four combinations to predict MNE strategies (Hillemann & Gestrin, 2016). In the case of strong

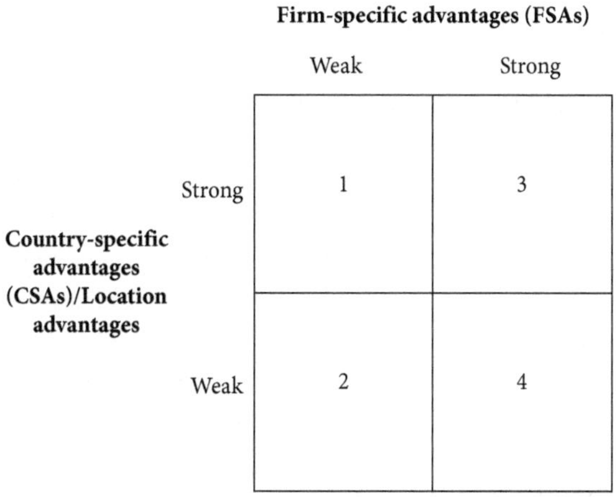

Firm-specific advantages (FSAs)

		Weak	Strong
Country-specific advantages (CSAs)/Location advantages	Strong	1	3
	Weak	2	4

FIGURE 1.1 The "classic" FSA–CSA framework.

Source: Collinson and Rugman (2011), Rugman (1981).

home CSAs and weak FSAs, international expansion is primarily based on country factors, such as natural resources, with the MNE's own resources and capabilities being somewhat less important for competitive advantage. When firms lack strong home country-specific and firm-specific resources, they do not have a clear source of competitive advantage to rationalize international expansion; in such cases, internationalization represents a flawed decision, likely to result in failed international operations. When both home CSAs and FSAs are strong, international expansion will, in most cases, still require the firm to recombine its extant resources and capabilities, with country-specific factors—that is, requisite resources to operate successfully in the newly entered host countries. Lastly, in the case of weak home CSAs and strong FSAs, MNEs rely largely on their own strengths for competitive advantage, without much contribution of country factors; this will typically occur in the case of proprietary but easily marketable, technology-driven products for which there is global demand.

In practice, it is the specific nature of FSAs and CSAs that together determine the form and competitiveness of the MNE's international operations (Rugman & Verbeke, 1992: 762). As illustrated by the left-hand side of Figure 1.2, FDI will occur when external markets for the MNE's FSAs are inefficient; for example, markets for knowledge that, if efficient, would have led to contractual agreements in quadrants 3 and 4, on the right-hand side of Figure 1.2. Quadrant 3 reflects a variety of market contracting arrangements whereby the MNE's and local economic actors' resource bundles can easily be transacted. Quadrant 4 reflects the case of, for instance, technology purchasing from the MNE by a local firm, which itself commands resource bundles that cannot be purchased in the external market.

Quadrant 1, on the left-hand side, suggests a wholly owned subsidiary, since the requisite additional resources in the host country for the MNE to operate successfully can be acquired in efficient markets. Quadrant 2 suggests inter-firm collaboration (e.g. through an equity joint venture). Even so, critical decisions on the actual entry mode choice may need to take into account additional complexities associated with operating internationally. Consider, for example, the following scenario in quadrant 2 of Figure 1.2: an MNE with FSAs taking the form of patent-circumventable knowledge that can easily be copied and acquired by a local firm acting as a joint venture partner, in a host country with weak protection of intellectual property rights. In this instance, the comparatively most efficient strategic decision may actually be to forego an operation in this host country, in spite of say low labor costs, the presence of a skilled workforce, and the unique complementary skills, for example, in distribution, of the potential joint venture partner. On the surface, the nature of each firm's resources suggests that FDI and a joint venture arrangement could be pursued. But the possible unreliability (as a result of unenforceable safeguards in the legal system) of the needed local joint venture partner, who would bring essential, complementary resource bundles to the table that cannot be purchased in external markets, could severely affect the perceived location advantages of the host country considered.

Apart from the complexity and uncertainty described above that are driven by macro-level institutional features, the revised matrix shown in Figure 1.2, seeks to provide a

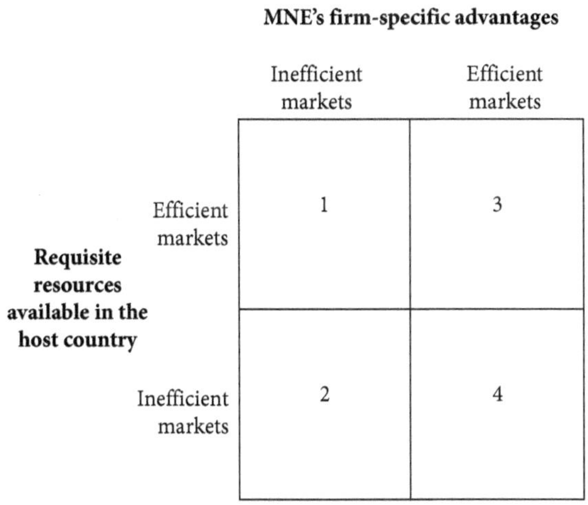

MNE's firm-specific advantages

FIGURE 1.2 The "revised" FSA–CSA framework.

Source: Hillemann and Gestrin (2016), Grøgaard and Verbeke (2012), and Hennart (2009).

basic tool to explain how MNEs organize transactions across borders, by combining transaction cost economics and resource-based view thinking (Chi, 2015; Narula & Verbeke, 2015). The notion of FSAs not only includes proprietary know-how related to production processes and final products, but also transactional advantages in terms of efficient internal coordination and control systems, thereby combining the emphasis on valuable resource bundles from the resource-based view, with the requirement for comparative governance efficiency from transaction cost economics (Coase, 1937; Williamson, 1985). The resource-based view of the firm emerged in the 1980s, following the development of internalization theory, with the work of Penrose influencing Rugman's earlier works (Chi, 2015). Our point is that the revised FSAs-CSAs matrix integrates resource-based and transaction cost-based drivers of IB strategy. More recently, progress in resource-based view thinking on issues such as tacit knowledge and competitive advantage, and in transaction cost economics on issues such as bounded rationality and complementary behavioral assumptions, have shaped IB scholars' further refinement and extension of theory, to analyze IB strategy.

A UNIFYING FRAMEWORK OF IB STRATEGY: SEVEN THEORETICAL CONCEPTS

Scholars examining IB strategy choices made by MNEs have tended to emphasize distinct concepts that constitute the foundations for their individual theories. However, such differences often represent variations on a limited number of central concepts and themes, many of which are discussed and updated in subsequent chapters of this

Handbook. In light of this conceptual diversity, Verbeke (2009) identified seven founda-tional blocks of IB strategy, which incorporate theoretical developments on resource recombination (Hennart, 2009; Teece, 2014; Verbeke & Yuan, 2010) as well as behavioral assumptions (Kano & Verbeke, 2015, 2019; Verbeke & Greidanus, 2009). Relevant IB strategy research requires a finer-grained analysis as to how various types of FSAs and CSAs are actually bundled, by taking into account the entrepreneurial judgment and behavioral assumptions underlying these processes. The seven building blocks shown in Figure 1.3 are the following:

(1) non-location-bound (or internationally transferable) firm resources and capabilities;
(2) location-bound (or non-transferable) resources and capabilities;
(3) location advantages;
(4) complementary resources and capabilities of external actors;
(5) resource recombination;
(6) bounded rationality; and
(7) bounded reliability.

The first four concepts included in the framework—non-location-bound resources, location-bound resources, location advantages, and complementary resources—represent a refinement of traditional ideas around what constitutes a source of FSA. Here, a distinction is made between two types of MNE internal resources as a function of their non-location boundedness, and two types of external resources as a function of their general accessibility to economic actors operating in a particular location. These elements will jointly condition the MNE's international expansion trajectory. The fifth concept—resource recombination—emphasizes the importance of recombining resources in novel ways and the necessity of incorporating the role of entrepreneurial judgment; whereas the sixth and seventh concepts—bounded rationality and bounded reliability—reflect the generic behavioral characteristics of economic actors engaged in purposive economic organization, in this case, related to MNE functioning. These behavioral characteristics require economizing governance to reduce the impact of information problems and commitment failures, thereby supporting the MNE's value creation, from developing new knowledge to delivering products in the marketplace. In the following section of this chapter, we explain each of these concepts in more detail.

Traditional Components in IB Strategy Research

The purpose of distinguishing between non-location-bound FSAs, location-bound FSAs, location advantages, and complementary resources of external actors is to provide greater detail concerning the relationship between the firm and its external environment, as compared to traditional internalization theory rationales (Narula & Verbeke 2015).

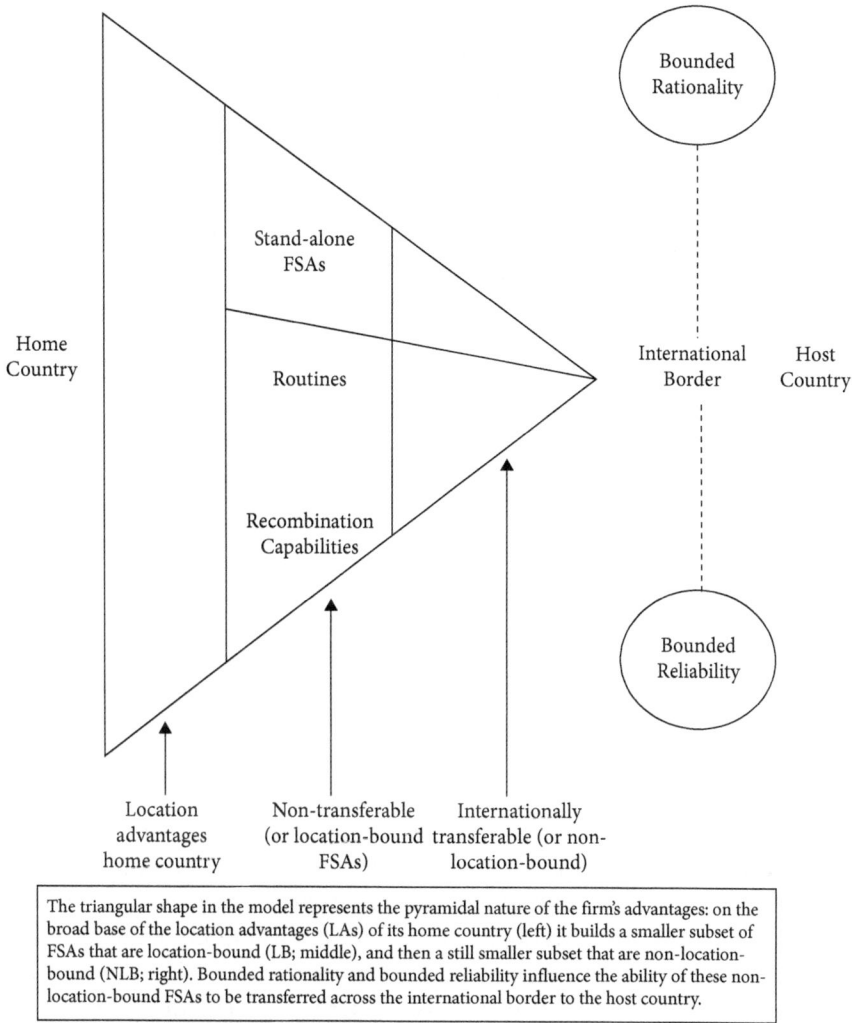

The triangular shape in the model represents the pyramidal nature of the firm's advantages: on the broad base of the location advantages (LAs) of its home country (left) it builds a smaller subset of FSAs that are location-bound (LB; middle), and then a still smaller subset that are non-location-bound (NLB; right). Bounded rationality and bounded reliability influence the ability of these non-location-bound FSAs to be transferred across the international border to the host country.

FIGURE 1.3 Core concepts in IB strategy.

Source: Verbeke (2009).

Firm-specific resources and capabilities are critical to the MNE's success in the market-place, and include physical resources, financial resources, human resources, upstream knowledge, downstream knowledge, administrative (governance-related) knowledge, and reputational resources. Although outsiders may not always fully understand the nature and uniqueness of these strengths relative to rival companies, because of ambiguity and information asymmetries (King, 2007), benchmarking exercises should, in principle, help the MNE's senior management to identify these strengths. With regards to the complementary resources of external actors, we should note that firms mostly require access to additional resources not generally available in open markets but held by specific firms, to operate successfully abroad. Since external actors hold these resources, efficient contracting or broader collaborative agreements with these actors will be instrumental to the MNE's success abroad.

From a firm's perspective, location advantages can be present at the input and output side, and range from conventional production factors such as the quality and quantity of labor inputs to the size and growth rate of the market for final products. Location advantages thus include the entire set of location-related, external resources and market opportunities that the MNE can build upon or tap into. The relevant resources and market opportunities are accessible primarily by firms operating in these locations and must be compared with the resource and opportunity bases of other locations. Here, we assume that these resources and opportunities become less and less accessible to "distant" companies, especially those without local operations. Typical examples of location advantages include abundant natural resources, a superior educational system, as well as a sophisticated and demanding local market (Narula & Santangelo 2012). MNEs often take advantage of favorable home environments to build their human resource base or to engage in home country innovation. The geographic scope of location advantages can vary widely, ranging from a particular country, part of a country (such as a concentrated industry cluster), or spanning country borders. For example, a favorable tax regime or general business incentives may benefit all firms operating in a specific country, while location advantages from economic clusters often accrue only to firms operating within the boundaries of the cluster. In some cases, location advantages, such as those created by regional trading and investment agreements, may reach beyond country borders.

Importantly, the firm-specific resources and capabilities that confer an advantage vis-à-vis rivals and location advantages can be closely related. Location advantages can make significant contributions to a firm's resource base, especially when a particular location offers a somewhat privileged access to resources, such as direct access to a highly educated workforce or a disciplined judiciary that will strictly enforce intellectual property rights protection. For example, key resources such as brand names and patents confer value only if the prevailing intellectual property rights regime protects such proprietary knowledge. This also means that fully realizing the economic value conferred by location advantages will require firms to align judiciously their proprietary resources with these location advantages. For example, easy access to cheap labor at home does not in itself guarantee low-cost production that would be competitive in a given industry; low-cost production will also require deploying the appropriate production technology and an organizational apparatus focused on achieving cost efficiencies. It should therefore be noted that location advantages do not offer an equal boost to all firms with local operations.

Recombination Advantages as a Higher-Order FSA

The fifth concept, recombination, is central to our current analysis of IB strategy (Verbeke, 2009). With rivals competing fiercely to win market share, even the most powerful firms on the *Fortune Global 500* list often find that their most important strengths are not stand-alone elements, such as physical, financial, or human resources; nor strengths granted by patents and brand names. Instead, their key strengths are their routines (managerial practices) and recombination capabilities, which incorporate much of the MNEs' valuable knowledge. A lot of mainstream IB research has traditionally focused on internationally transferable practices as the cornerstone of international corporate success, with such routines allowing for resource combinations in predictable and stable, that is, repeatable patterns. However, in complex and dynamic international contexts, the differences between domestic and foreign environments, and the idiosyncratic nature of stakeholder demands in each host country, often require novel orchestration of resource bundles (Rugman, Verbeke, & Nguyen, 2011; Narula, 2014; Collinson & Narula, 2014; Narula et al., 2019). The MNE thereby becomes viewed as a repository of resource bundles that need continuous adaptation across borders. New processes and products result from melding extant bundles of resources with new ones. Here, superior recombination capabilities are becoming a major source of strength for the MNE.

We propose that, in any MNE, successful resource recombination requires three preconditions to be fulfilled (see also Verbeke & Yuan, 2010). First, resource recombination requires the deployment of entrepreneurial skills to identify and respond to new productive opportunities. Entrepreneurial judgment constitutes the core of the MNE's recombination capability, and individuals in MNEs must therefore act as entrepreneurs to create novel ways of deploying resources. Second, resource recombination necessitates the presence of slack resources (i.e. unused productive resources), which can be released from routinized activities for new usages (Verbeke & Yuan, 2007). The importance of organizational slack beyond what is needed for current, efficient operations aligns with Penrose's (1959) thesis that emphasizes a minimum threshold quantity of available managerial services to permit firm growth, especially in new markets. As MNEs do not have unlimited resources at their disposal, routinizing current businesses is one way of releasing managerial resources for new business activities. Third, resource recombination reflects a type of higher-order firm-specific capability. The MNE must not only combine its existing resources reliably but also recombine resources in creative ways, usually by including both existing resources and newly accessed resources. In some cases, the MNE may also need to forego standard managerial practices to act upon new business opportunities. Although strong routines often play a critical role in the MNE's capability exploitation, as they allow sharing crucial knowledge across borders to achieve economies of scope, they can be detrimental to the MNE's recombination endeavors. The creative melding of new resources in a host environment with existing resources almost by definition leads to deviations from "proven" managerial practices. New practices can create inconsistencies and frictions among various units inside the MNE, thereby requiring a careful balancing act by senior management at the corporate head office between promoting established, firm-wide practices and allowing the requisite tailoring thereof as a response to new cross-border opportunities, in order to achieve competitive advantage.

Bounded Rationality

Bounded rationality refers to the information problems managers face in their decision-making processes and reflects "scarcity of mind" in purposive action. The concept was popularized by Simon (1982), and it often functions as a major theoretical assumption in management theories (see Williamson, 1985). Thus far, with few exceptions (notably, Verbeke & Yuan, 2005), scholars have done little to adapt and extend the bounded rationality concept in the context of IB strategic decisions.

So, what does bounded rationality mean for an IB strategist? We know that strategic decision-making and execution require both access to sufficient information and the capability to process this information. Bounded rationality means that information problems can arise in both areas. First, given environmental complexity and dynamics, any information about the MNE's environment and its operations is necessarily incomplete, especially when this information relates to future states of environmental parameters. Incomplete information can impede successful international expansion and result in frictions in the MNE's internal operations when available information is unevenly distributed. Second, even with abundant and correct information, executives in the MNE still face issues of processing the information, such as selecting which information they view as most relevant, and making judgment calls on its implications for the MNE's operations. For MNEs, operating in multiple geographic markets with varying levels of complexity and uncertainty exacerbates the bounded rationality problems that would typically arise in a domestic setting, thereby complicating strategic choices. We will now use two business scenarios in the MNE context to illustrate the significance of bounded rationality problems.

The first bounded rationality scenario is associated with the optimal entry mode choice when senior executives in the MNE contemplate international expansion. They can choose among different options, such as setting up a wholly-owned subsidiary (whereby the firm transfers resources and capabilities from the home country to its foreign affiliate), licensing (whereby the firm transfers technology or manufacturing related resources and capabilities to foreign licensees), and establishing a joint venture (whereby the focal MNE and another company both transfer resources to a new, joint operation that will combine these complementary resources in creative ways). But which entry mode should MNE executives choose to create the comparatively highest economic value, while satisfying stakeholder demands? The answer depends on these executives' judgment on four issues.

The *first* issue is related to property rights. If licensees and joint venture partners can access and successfully absorb the MNE's firm-specific resources and capabilities through experiential and observational learning, these may become less valuable to the MNE. *Second*, licensees and joint venture partners may not uphold the same quality standards (broadly considered) as the MNE, thereby potentially resulting in negative responses from a variety of MNE stakeholders, especially shareholders, customers, and workers. *Third*, if the MNE chooses FDI, it will deploy its extant reservoir of FSAs in a new institutional setting, whereby elements such as work practices, cultural values, and government policies can be very different as compared to those prevailing in the home country. The MNE therefore needs to determine whether its extant resources and capabilities truly constitute FSAs when transferred to the host country, and to what extent this reservoir of resources and capabilities may need to be augmented. For example, past experience abroad that led to competitive success may be of little value when the newly entered host country is cognitively distant from earlier international markets. *Fourth*, if recombining resources in novel ways is required in international expansion, different entry modes, such as full internalization, licensing, joint ventures, and other types of arrangements with outside actors, will lead to diverging (but difficult to predict) development trajectories of the MNE's resource base and its future sources of competitive advantage vis-à-vis rivals. These four issues represent significant bounded rationality challenges in the realm of the entry mode decisions.

A second bounded rationality scenario concerns the difference in perspective between decision makers at home and abroad. Senior managers in the home country and those in the host country may select different parts of the available information as relevant to strategic decisions (Verbeke & Yuan, 2005). Managers' roles in the MNE, and their functional and institutional experience, can lead them to prioritize certain types of information over other ones. Even if senior managers from the head office in the home country and those in foreign subsidiaries were to prioritize the same facets of available information, they may still differ in how they interpret this information, because of differing experiences and hierarchical position in the firm, and the specificities of the institutional environment in which they operate. This divergence in judgment suggests that head office and subsidiary managers may function with alternative mental models and develop different perspectives about both current and future states of the MNE and its environment, even when being able to access and process the same sets of information. Direct interaction between subsidiary managers and local customers, suppliers, media outlets, and other local sources of information, can help these managers be better attuned to present and coming changes in local demand and supply conditions, as well as macro-level trends. Such local engagement also helps subsidiary managers to build mental models as insiders, reconstructing external information, and framing issues, as the basis for immediate responses to changes in the host market where they operate. Subsidiary managers typically have a more optimistic perspective about the potential of the host country where they work, and about their own capabilities to respond to local environmental dynamics.

Bounded Reliability

Bounded reliability and bounded rationality are complementary concepts. While bounded rationality is concerned with the difficulties in accurately assessing present or future circumstances, bounded reliability is about how actors may sub-optimally undertake specified tasks, thereby leading to incomplete fulfillment of promises (Verbeke, 2009). Put simply, bounded reliability refers to the scarcity of effort to make good on open-ended promises. Although agents may promise to pursue a particular outcome ex ante, such expressed intentions do not always carry through, which ultimately results in the failure of achieving the promised goal. Firms thus introduce enforcement mechanisms or safeguards to detect and avoid bounded reliability challenges, and to punish the reneging on promises. Bounded reliability has three major sources (Kano & Verbeke, 2015).

The first major source of bounded reliability is opportunism, that is, self-interest seeking with guile (Williamson, 1996). Agents may look for ways to shirk through false promises, or through reneging on promises ex-post. The IB, case-based literature describes numerous examples of economic actors, such as suppliers, customers, or employees, in the firm acting opportunistically, with the propensity for opportunistic behavior being triggered or amplified by the complexities and uncertainties character-izing the multinational context of the business involved (Verbeke et al., 2018; Hillemann, Verbeke, & Oh, 2019).

The second major source of bounded reliability is benevolent preference reversal, whereby agents make initial promises in good faith, but their preferences change over time. Different from opportunism where the intent to cheat is central, agents experien-cing benevolent preference reversal do not mean to harm the associated party to which they made promises. Benevolent preference reversal often arises in the behaviors of senior managers in MNEs, and manifests itself either through "good faith local prioritization" or through "scaling back on over-commitments."

"Good faith local prioritization" refers to the situation whereby inter alia subsidiary managers promise to act in good faith, but over time switch their efforts from serving the stated organizational/global preferences to local preferences, often at the expense of organizational goals. For example, subsidiary managers may promise to respect the decisions of corporate headquarters and implement specific investment projects. However, these promises may not carry through, as local investment opportunities may subsequently appear more promising, offer more intrinsic satisfaction, and give immedi-ate rewards to subsidiary managers through improved relationships with local partners and recognition by corporate headquarters for local achievements. The incentives to stick with approved head office decisions may be low, if any punishment for non-fulfillment of commitments is delayed in time and the headquarters' monitoring apparatus suffers from severe information asymmetries.

In the realm of "scaling back on over-commitments," economic actors can be over-confident in their capacity to deliver on open-ended promises. Various elements are typically associated with such overconfidence bias: agents may behave impulsively when making an initial promise, in order to impress superiors; they may make fallacious projections based on best-case scenarios rather than average-case scenarios; they may discount known risks; and they may overestimate their ability to control possible environmental changes. All these elements—frequently observed in managerial practice— may force agents ultimately to scale back on their overcommitment.

The third main source of bounded reliability is identity-based discordance. Here, agents make initial promises to pursue particular outcomes and engage in patterns of behavior supposed to benefit the organization, but then either regress to old patterns of behavior and the pursuit of obsolete goals or engage in patterns of behavior that amount to divided engagement. With divided engagement, the conflict among different individuals and groups in the organization unintentionally has a negative impact on organizational performance. Individuals and groups work against each other, because they fail to see the "larger picture." Both with regression and divided engagement, the failure to make good on open-ended promises can be traced back to the agents' identity, for example, in terms of dominant norms and past experiences (Verbeke & Fariborzi, 2019). An example of the former would be the unwillingness of a subsidiary manager, in spite of promises to the contrary, to implement new, head-office imposed state-of-the-art monitoring and reporting practices in the subsidiary because of the perceived proven success of past practices. An example of the latter would be managers of different subsidiaries fighting against each other, with exploration-oriented subsidiary managers seeking resources to invest in new product lines and exploitation-oriented ones focused solely on existing product lines, but with both groups convinced that they are serving the MNE's goals.

Bounded rationality challenges in the MNE are caused by insufficient information and information processing capacity, and also by the fact that different individuals in the organization will select and judge particular information facets in idiosyncratic ways. In contrast, bounded reliability originates from quite different sources. In the case of opportunism, agents' behavior is caused by strong-form self-interest, even when they have access to sufficient information and have a good information processing capability. In the case of benevolent preference reversal, agents make the same mistakes repeatedly, even when they again know in advance the predictable outcomes of these mistakes, but there is no strong-form self-interest at play in these reversals. Strong-form self-interest is also absent in identity-based discordance, which reflects individuals being internally conflicted or having conflicts with others because of their identity, even though the intent is to serve the organization as well as possible.

But benevolent failures to make good on commitments can ultimately lead to opportunism. For example, an individual may commit an action of "good faith local prioritization," with well-intentioned promises made to the corporate head office, but then replacing corporate projects with local projects when allocating scarce resources. When it comes to performance appraisal, this individual may behave opportunistically, by reporting inaccurate and incomplete information to cover up performance gaps. Moreover, short-term and emerging long-term preferences and behaviors of the same individual may differ. A subsidiary manager may be committed to keeping promises in the short term, but good faith local prioritization can then emerge in the longer run, thereby creating long-term conflicts between headquarters and subsidiaries. We should note that bounded reliability first materializes at the individual level—with boundedly reliable individuals being either internal stakeholders (such as employees) or external contracting partners (e.g. suppliers, licensees, etc.)—but unreliability can be contagious and spread into teams, business units such as subsidiaries, and sometimes even infect the entire organization. This occurs when external stakeholders become victims of large-scale commitment failures from an organization, as exemplified by the Volkswagen emissions scandal that became public in 2015.

MNEs can implement various governance mechanisms to reduce unreliability or mitigate its effects (Verbeke & Greidanus, 2009; Kano & Verbeke, 2015). Examples of such governance mechanisms include contractual safeguards, joint goal development, multi-level decision-making routines and training, to reduce the negative effects of opportunism, "good faith local prioritization," "scaling back on over-commitments," and "identity-based discordance," respectively.

New Insights from Applying the Unifying Framework of IB Theory

The abovementioned seven components provide a unifying framework for understanding and guiding IB strategies of the MNE. With the MNE as the focal unit of analysis, this framework can be applied to examine a broad range of topics, including both the management of the multinational network (i.e. internal governance), and the interactions of the MNE with the broader macro-environment and external stakeholders (i.e. externally oriented governance). In what follows, we explain how the framework can be used to understand the internal functioning of the MNE and the interactions between the MNE and its environment.

Implications of Macro-Environmental Factors for the MNE: An Analysis of Host Country Location Advantages

A significant factor in influencing location advantages is the distance between host and home countries. There have been two popular but contrasting perspectives about distance. One proposes the death of distance (see Friedman, 2005). This perspective argues that the world is shrinking and has become relatively homogeneous, thanks to the progress in information technologies and global communications. The assumption is that elements such as web-based sales, seamless global supply chains, and instant communication within and between firms will gradually eliminate barriers of time and space. As a result, a truly global marketplace will emerge, offering unlimited access to MNEs with global expansion ambitions.

There is a strong consensus among IB and economic geography scholars, however, that distance still matters (Mudambi, Narula, & Santangelo, 2018). As such, focusing solely on macro-level measures of market size and growth typically leads to overestimating host market attractiveness (Ghemawat, 2001; Rugman & Oh, 2008). Four types of distance—cultural, administrative (or institutional), geographic (or spatial), and economic—affect the risks and additional costs of new market entry. The debate concerning the role of distance reflects the conflicting views about the transferability of

FSAs across borders. The argument for a homogeneous world assumes that resources and capabilities that constitute an advantage in the home country can be easily exploited in other markets regardless of distance.

In contrast, scholars who recognize the role of distance emphasize the limited transferability, deployability, and exploitation potential of FSAs across borders. Here, bounded rationality problems faced by senior managers may bias their perceptions of the international profit potential of the MNE's extant reservoir of FSAs. They may overestimate the non-location boundedness of firm advantages and underestimate the difficulty of accessing host country location advantages or complementary resources of host country economic actors. Because of the influence of distance, macro-level parameters, such as industry growth rates and consumer disposable income, may not constitute accurate proxies for the attractiveness of host markets.

Applying the unifying framework to investigate the role of distance leads to new insights that the conventional sides in the debate have neglected. First, though the degree of macro-level distance may be critical for the MNE's success/failure in a foreign market, macro-level distance is not equivalent to the actual distance challenges facing individual firms. In other words, macro-level and micro-level distance reflect different levels of analysis, and the distance challenges for a particular firm when entering a host country may be much lower than the distance between the two countries. For example, given the enormous cultural, administrative, geographic and economic distance between the US and Taiwan, a consumer goods company from the US would not ordinarily consider Taiwan as an attractive market. Rather, countries such as Canada, Mexico, and some EU countries may be more attractive based on a distance-adjusted, country-level market analysis. However, if several senior executives of the US firm have Taiwanese roots, the firm may have FSAs in hand to access the Taiwanese market. This hypothetical example demonstrates that, because of individual firms' differential resource reservoirs, each will need idiosyncratic levels of investment in location-bound FSAs to exploit opportunities in a foreign market. A macro-level foreign market analysis neglects firm-level specificity, even after taking into account the macro-level distance between countries.

Second, MNEs have several options to address high-distance locations. They may choose to reduce their geographic scope and operate only in low-distance locations, as suggested by Ghemawat (2001), but they can also develop recombination capabilities to overcome distance barriers. For example, MNEs may increase the cultural and functional diversity of their senior management team, thereby commanding multiple cognitive bases to estimate more accurately and address more effectively the potential cultural and functional challenges associated with international expansion in particular locations. MNEs can also develop a human resource reservoir with experience-based business knowledge and cultural affinity to manage risks and uncertainties associated with high distance. For some established MNEs that have many decades of international experience in foreign markets, macro-level distance may not matter at all when the target host country has a low level of distance with countries where the firm already has mature affiliates. In this case, what will count is the "added" distance between the target host country and the MNE's existing operation closest to the host country, rather than the distance from the home country (Hutzschenreuter, Voll, & Verbeke, 2011).

Third, the debate about the impact of distance tends to view firm-specific resource bundles and capabilities as being developed in the home country and subsequently transferred to other markets. Extant perspectives thus neglect the role of motivations to enter host countries, including high-distance ones, whereby one motivation may precisely be to develop new FSAs (Makino, Lau, & Yeh, 2002; Narula, 2014). When MNEs look to transfer and exploit their bundles of internationally transferable resources and capabilities in foreign markets and face restricted access to the location advantages and complementary resources in high-distance host countries, they may choose to reduce their geographic scope. However, when MNEs seek to enter foreign markets to utilize the host location environment to develop new FSAs (e.g. in the case of strategic resource-seeking investment), a high-distance location may present more abundant learning opportunities than low-distance locations, even though entry costs may indeed be high. Using the unifying framework allows us to understand that confining the MNE's geographic scope to low-distance countries neglects the importance of MNE strategic motivations and the potential, unique contributions of high distance locations in creating new FSAs.

Understanding MNE Management: Combining FSAs and CSAs in a Multinational Network

Traditionally, MNEs viewed host country subsidiaries simply as recipients and distributors of company knowledge and products, with strategic decision-making and control residing primarily in the home country corporate headquarters. In this traditional organizational design, significant distance between corporate headquarters and foreign markets/ subsidiaries can lead to enormous bounded reliability and bounded rationality challenges, because senior managers at the head office may not fully understand subsidiaries' potential to create value for the firm. Headquarters become isolated and oblivious to changing conditions in key international markets. Moreover, this traditional design neglects subsidiaries' potential to develop unique capabilities through autonomous activities, thereby enhancing the MNE's existing resource bundles (Birkinshaw & Hood, 2001).

Recognizing the problems associated with the abovementioned traditional approach to MNE management, scholars have proposed that corporate managers should assign differentiated roles and responsibilities to foreign subsidiaries (Rugman, Verbeke, & Yuan, 2011). By selectively decentralizing elements of strategic decision-making and control, companies can optimize the deployment and exploitation of their extant resource base, while supporting the development of new resources and capabilities in their multinational subsidiary network. Scholars have proposed and empirically examined alternative approaches to assign roles and responsibilities to foreign subsidiaries, with Bartlett and Ghoshal (1986) being the most influential model.

More specifically, Bartlett and Ghoshal (1986) offer normative guidelines for senior management to assign differentiated roles to subsidiaries, based on two dimensions. The first dimension is the strategic importance of the market where the subsidiary is located; for example, in terms of technological innovation, demand sophistication, and market size. The second dimension represents the strength of each subsidiary's resource base; for example, in terms of R&D, manufacturing capabilities, sales and marketing, or any other strength that may contribute to competitiveness. Based on these two dimensions, subsidiaries can be classified as follows:

(1) the black hole (weak in distinctive internal resources and capabilities, but located in a strategically important market);
(2) the implementer (weak in distinctive internal resources and capabilities, and located in a strategically less important market);
(3) the strategic leader (commanding strong capabilities in a strategically important market); and
(4) the contributor (commanding strong capabilities in a strategically less important market).

From the perspective of our unifying framework, the Bartlett and Ghoshal (1986) typology provides a useful perspective on FSA development, by emphasizing the roles of both host country location advantages and specialized subsidiary resources in this development process. Even so, their version of FSA development does not recognize valuable autonomous subsidiary initiatives, sometimes pursued in spite of narrow charters allocated to a subsidiary. In this context, senior executives at corporate headquarters may lack knowledge/experience to recognize and support bottom-up subsidiary initiatives, especially if these come from peripheral subsidiaries that have been assigned lesser roles in the MNE's network. Thus, the challenge for senior management in the MNE is not simply to choose which subsidiaries should fulfill particular roles, and then to assign charters for FSA development. Rather, the main challenge is to identify potentially valuable knowledge, regardless of its origin (Verbeke & Yuan, 2005). Several best practices have been put forward to promote autonomous subsidiary initiatives, including mechanisms such as allocating seed money to new initiatives, formally requesting proposals, using subsidiaries as incubators (with these exploration-oriented subsidiaries being located away from units that only exploit extant knowledge), and creating internal subsidiary networks for cross-pollinating ideas (Birkinshaw & Hood, 2001).

Furthermore, Bartlett and Ghoshal's (1986) typology neglects the critical distinction between upstream (input) markets and downstream (output) markets when assessing the strategic importance of host country environments. The authors focused mainly on the output market, with relatively limited attention devoted to input market features, such as the quality of the local environment for R&D knowledge development or the presence of specialized labor. Similarly, subsidiaries' strengths at the upstream end (e.g. in technology development and sourcing) may be very different from their strengths at the downstream end (e.g. in marketing and distribution). The strategic

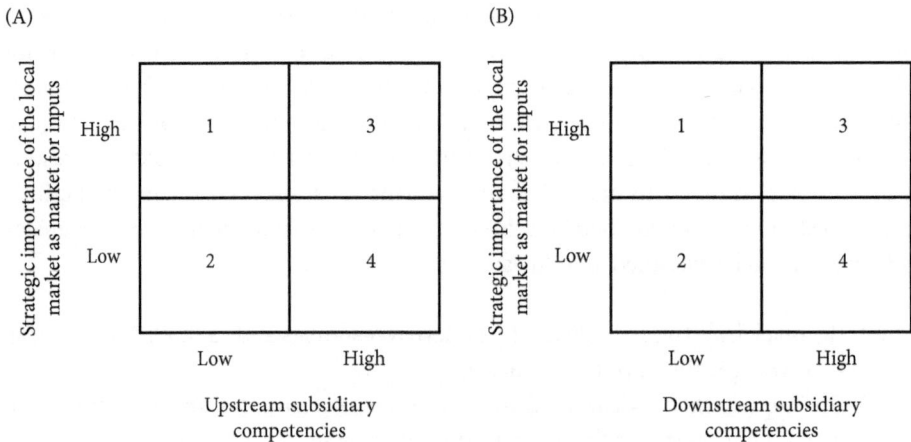

FIGURE 1.4   Unbundling subsidiary roles in Bartlett and Ghoshal (1986).

Source: Verbeke (2009).

motivation of an MNE's foreign expansion usually focuses on either the input market or the output market. In addition, either downstream FSAs or upstream ones, but not both, will typically matter in international expansion projects. We thus extend the Bartlett and Ghoshal (1986) typology by differentiating between (a) the strategic importance of the host country—that is, its location advantages in the input versus the output market—and (b) the subsidiary's strengths in upstream versus downstream activities, as illustrated in Figure 1.4.

Quadrant 1 of Figure 1.4 (A) describes subsidiaries with weak upstream capabilities but operating in a strategically important input market. One example is that of subsidiaries unable to acquire advanced technological expertise in important technology clusters such as Silicon Valley because they lack absorptive capacity and requisite local network relationships. Another example is that of plants set up to manufacture and sell products on the basis of home country technologies, but unable to capitalize on location advantages provided by a supposedly low-cost country such as China because they were established in a comparatively high-cost region of the country. This quadrant also includes instances where poor recombination capabilities in upstream activities result in subsidiaries' failure to utilize input-side location advantages, even though such location advantages are often viewed as generally available to firms operating in the country. Quadrant 2 of Figure 1.4 (A) includes subsidiaries with weak, distinct upstream capabilities in a strategically less important market. The host country environment is viewed as relatively unimportant to the MNE's future competitiveness at the input market side, and the absence of distinct subsidiary competences makes it difficult for the subsidiary to perform a role in the MNE that would stretch beyond the host country. Some upstream activities such as R&D may therefore be absent altogether. Quadrant 3 in Figure 1.4 (A) reflects subsidiaries with strong upstream capabilities in strategically important input markets. For example, there may be a favorable environment that provides strong location advantages in terms of the presence of a sophisticated technology cluster, low-cost labor, and other input factors, and subsidiaries are equipped with appropriate upstream capabilities to capitalize on such location advantages. This quadrant is the most desirable context for foreign subsidiaries that want to augment their role and extend their charter within the MNE. Examples of subsidiaries in quadrant 3 include many R&D centers in Silicon Valley and manufacturing plants in low-cost countries such as India and China. Finally, quadrant 4 represents subsidiaries with strong upstream capabilities but operating in a strategically unimportant input market. Although the input market may lack factors such as advanced technology or abundant low-cost labor, the subsidiary's efficient sourcing, manufacturing or other upstream capabilities compensate for the unfavorable input market and make the subsidiary an important contributor to the MNE's competitiveness. For major Japanese automakers, North America as an input market does not contribute much to their competitiveness, but their subsidiaries' adoption and further improvement of modular production methods, the keiretsu-style management approach and other proven best practices have made these Japanese subsidiaries core manufacturing centers that contribute greatly to their parent firm competitiveness. This example also highlights the key difference between subsidiary roles in Figure 1.4 (A) and (B). Japanese subsidiaries in the US are largely contributors in the input market, positioned in quadrant 4 of Figure 1.4 (A), but are often also strategic leaders in the output market, meaning quadrant 3 in Figure 1.4 (B). In this case, the same host country market is strategically important for selling outputs and comparatively unimportant for providing inputs, but the subsidiaries in that country command strong upstream and downstream capabilities.

This rethinking of the Bartlett and Ghoshal (1986) typology on the basis of the unifying framework provides two key insights for conducting future scholarly work on MNE strategic management. First, it allows highlighting the potential of subsidiaries in defining their own roles, as a result of their location advantages and their own development of new FSAs through creative resource recombination. Second, it suggests adding a value chain analysis when examining FSAs and location advantages. Such value chain analysis would allow focusing on the precise sources of firm-level competitiveness (particular resource combinations and resource recombinations), thereby refining the assessment of which internal capability components and external location-related resources and opportunities matter most.

Understanding the Interaction between the MNE and External Providers of Complementary Resources: The Case of Strategic Collaboration

MNEs set up strategic collaborative agreements such as equity joint ventures and non-equity alliances for a variety of reasons. In international joint ventures, local partners often contribute reputational assets, a deep knowledge of how to navigate non-market forces, and other location-bound firm-specific resources. These resources are complementary to the MNE's extant reservoir of FSAs and can facilitate local responsiveness. The essence of such strategic collaboration is that the requisite complementary resources cannot be easily procured from external markets through contracting. In the case of joint ventures, both the MNE and the local partner normally take an equity stake in the venture. Resolving governance and resource bundling challenges then requires agreement between the partners, who should use a going concern lens, rather than a mere contracting view.

If a joint venture was set up to overcome both trade and investment barriers, and high economic distance to a host country, then economic liberalization (meaning the removal of these trade and investment barriers), combined with local learning in the venture will gradually decrease the foreign MNE's incentives for strategic collaboration. This will be the case especially if the MNE is capable of learning more rapidly and more effectively than the local joint venture partner. For example, Kale and Anand (2006) observed in their study on joint ventures in India, that with ongoing liberalization in the 1990s, many foreign MNEs no longer required local partners. These firms became increasingly familiar with overseas markets and as a result of growing cross-border integration of markets for goods and services, the resource complementarity as a key motive for joint ventures between MNEs and local partners often disappeared. The abolishment of regulations requiring foreign investors to enlist joint venture partners was critical in this regard, since requisite complementary resources could now be purchased in external markets or had in many cases been absorbed by the MNE through learning within the joint venture.

The objectives of the MNE and those of the local partner can be important for the longer-term stability of the venture (Fang & Zou, 2010). If both the MNE and the local partner aim to acquire critical firm-specific resources from each other, a learning race may ensue, meaning that, whoever extracts the desired resources most rapidly, will tend to be motivated to dissolve the alliance (Martinez-Noya & Narula, 2018). Alternatively, if firms combine their resources to create synergies, then strategic collaboration may create new sources of competitive advantage. If these sources of competitive advantage are deeply embedded within the collaborative structure itself, as is the case with global airline alliances such as Star Alliance and Oneworld, the motivation to remain in the alliance may be very high. Here, individual alliance partners, whether large international carriers or more local airlines, may not be able to forego the collaboration and exploit the newly created sources of competitive advantage outside of the alliance (e.g. common flight reservation systems; efficiencies from joint purchasing of inputs; sharing of airline lounges for passengers; etc.).

Our unifying framework suggests that, given capability gaps in an MNE's resource and capabilities reservoir, and difficulties in accessing requisite resources in external markets, strategic collaboration, including joint ventures, may be the preferred option for successful entry in a host market. Here, the key challenges for the MNE will be accessing the local partner's complementary location-bound FSAs and the bundling or recombination thereof with the MNE's FSAs. The MNE can thereby expand internationally without having to develop itself the requisite complementary resources and capabilities, a task that is sometimes impossible to achieve in the short to medium term (e.g. if establishing a wholly owned subsidiary is prohibited by law or local economic actors dominate distribution channels and can deny access to foreign entrants). The creative combination of MNEs' non-location-bound advantages and the partners' location-bound advantages may create new FSAs instrumental to value creation. At the same time, MNE senior management must ensure that strategic collaboration does not lead to unwanted knowledge appropriation, whereby the collaboration could result in creating a competent local competitor when the alliance dissolves. From the local partner's perspective, the challenge is to continue making distinct, valuable contributions to the partnership, so as to reduce the likelihood that MNE learning would make the strategic collaboration superfluous.

The unifying framework also suggests that alliance formation can take various forms. In Figure 1.5, the vertical axis represents alliance formation and full ownership as two alternative entry mode options, whereas the horizontal axis describes the alliance's purpose in terms of what type of FSAs are targeted for development.

Quadrant 1 in Figure 1.5 reflects an MNE's FDIs in a subsidiary. The goal is for the subsidiary to develop location-bound FSAs, typically geared toward facilitating

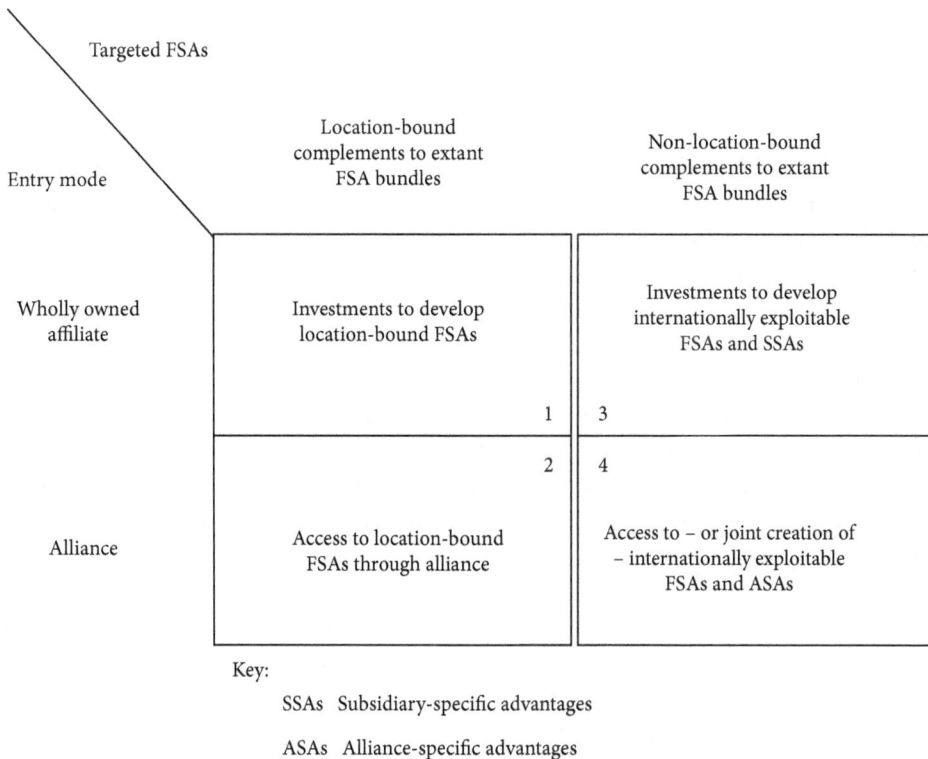

FIGURE 1.5 MNE foreign market penetration via wholly owned affiliates versus alliances.

Source: Verbeke (2009).

local responsiveness. Quadrant 3 describes the MNE pursuing a more ambitious strategy of establishing a subsidiary that should develop non-location-bound FSAs as well as subsidiary-specific advantages (SSAs). The latter refer to strengths that are deeply embedded in the subsidiary and provide the MNE a distinct source of competitive advantage, but one that cannot simply be transferred and replicated elsewhere in the network. In other words, SSAs lead to products and services that can be profitably sold internationally, but the exploitation of these SSAs may be tied to the subsidiary's location and to its embedded resource base (Rugman & Verbeke, 2001). Subsidiaries positioned in quadrant 3 represent "strategic leaders," as discussed in the Bartlett and Ghoshal (1986) model. However, units with strong SSAs are not necessarily perceived as good corporate citizens by the MNE head office, because of their partly autonomous development trajectory within the MNE network. Quadrants 2 and 4 are related to alliance formation. In quadrant 2, an MNE forms an alliance with a local firm when other entry-mode choices are not available, whether as a result of government restrictions on MNE activities or local actors commanding ownership and control over requisite complementary resources that cannot be purchased in external markets. The joint effects of trade and investment liberalization, and MNE learning may shift the MNE's preferred strategy to quadrant 1. This dynamic perspective suggests that an alliance can be an unstable and intermediate option, and that it will be replaced by wholly owned affiliates when MNE learning and external institutional changes make this possible.

Quadrant 4 in Figure 1.5 describes the case of alliance partners trying to develop new non-location-bound advantages through the alliance. In some cases, these firms may be engaged in a learning race. Here, each firm involved in the strategic collaboration tries to learn as much as possible from the partner and may also try to reduce partner access to—and learning from—its own knowledge base. In case one firm wins the learning race, the winner will have little motivation to maintain the alliance, leading to alliance instability. Alternatively, if the alliance develops advantages with international exploitation potential, but ones that cannot easily be exploited by partners individually outside of the alliance, a different outcome is likely. In this instance, the alliance partners cannot simply exit and benefit from the learning that occurred. As noted above, the airlines participating in global alliances pool and recombine their resources to create advantages at the alliance level; this also means that individual firms cannot appropriate such advantages if they were to leave the alliance. Quadrant 4 thus highlights the existence of alliance-specific advantages (ASAs), which are different from endogenous FSAs (originating inside the firm) and exogenous location advantages (originating outside the firm, in its external environment). ASAs are embedded in the alliance and can be exploited internationally only by the alliance. ASAs are often tacit, dispersed across several alliance partners and context-specific (e.g. in the realm of the airline industry, it is typically a government agency that allocates slots to airlines in airports, thereby often benefiting local incumbents). The alliance's governance trajectory and technological development path shape the essence of ASAs, which can typically not be appropriated by individual alliance partners. These characteristics of ASAs enhance the stability and longevity of an alliance in quadrant 4. As ASAs rely on the structural and systemic bundling of the strengths from individual partners, dissolving the alliance would lead to the loss of such advantages for all parties.

Our proposed framework allows in-depth analysis of the complex processes that unfold, when alliance partners aim to combine their respective FSAs in the context of international strategic collaboration. Moreover, the analysis extends the unifying framework by identifying the relevance of ASAs. Unlike the case of conventional "transferable" and "appropriable" FSAs, a single firm cannot appropriate ASAs, though these may be deployable across locations, because they are structurally distributed across alliance partners.

CONCLUDING REMARKS

IB strategy essentially revolves around creative resource recombination across borders. Many of the MNE's supposed FSAs developed in its home base may not be internationally transferable, deployable, or profitably exploitable. Some of these FSAs may simply be location-bound, but even distinct resource bundles and capabilities that are transferable abroad may need melding with host country resources to create competitive advantage vis-à-vis rivals. Here, entrepreneurial judgment is required to orchestrate the MNE's evolving portfolio of FSAs. An important question for MNE entrepreneurs in this regard is whether the MNE's governance choices are conducive to economizing on bounded rationality and bounded reliability, and whether these governance choices are optimal for value creation and satisfying stakeholder demands in distant markets. This question should always be asked in a comparative institutional sense, that is, vis-à-vis real-world alternatives.

Resource recombination in foreign markets by definition involves complementary resources available in these host environments. These resources can come in different forms. First, some complementary resources are freely available and generally accessible as exogenous CSAs. Second, other complementary resources may be priced efficiently in external markets and can be procured easily. Third, a last category of complementary resources is more difficult to access because of imperfect markets, and it is here that IB strategy is most critical. Crafting mutually beneficial resource combinations with host country actors may not be easy, especially when non-market forces are in play. In some cases, it may not be possible to combine extant MNE FSAs with requisite complementary resources in the host environment, namely if the latter are accessible only by domestic incumbents, or by particular foreign investors with extensive slack resources, a long experience in high-distance institutional environments, or privileged relationships with non-market actors. Non-market institutions may de facto eliminate entry opportunities for foreign MNEs, and IB strategy is therefore as much about saying "no" to foreign investment options as it is about selecting optimal governance solutions to permit effective resource recombination. Only by understanding whether requisite resource recombination is feasible, and how it changes across host environments and over time, and contributes to MNE performance outcomes, can scholars grasp the essence of IB strategy.

References

Bartlett, C. A., & Ghoshal, S. 1986. Tap your subsidiaries for global reach, *Harvard Business Review*, 64: 87–94.

Bartlett, C. A., & Ghoshal, S. 1989. *Managing across Boarders*. Boston, MA: Harvard Business School Press.

Birkinshaw, J. & Hood, N. 2001. Unleash innovation in foreign subsidiaries, *Harvard Business Review*, 79: 131–137.

Buckley, P. & Casson, M. 1976. *The Future of the Multinational Enterprise*. Basingstoke and London: Macmillan.

Chi, T. 2015. Commentary: Internalization theory and its relation to RBV and TCE. *Journal of World Business*, 50(4): 634–636.

Coase, R. H. 1937. The nature of the firm. *Economica*, 4(16): 386–405.

Collinson, S. C., & Narula, R. 2014. Asset Recombination in International Partnerships as a Source of Improved Innovation Capabilities in China. *Multinational Business Review*, 22(4): 394–415.

Dunning, J. H. 1958. *American Investment in British Manufacturing Industry*. London: Allen & Unwin.

Fang, E., & Zou, S. 2010. The effects of absorptive and joint learning on the instability of international joint ventures in emerging economies. *Journal of International Business Studies*, 41(5): 906–924.

Forsgren, M. 2013. *Theories of the Multinational Firm: A Multidimensional Creature in the Global Economy*. Cheltenham: Edward Elgar.

Friedman, T. L. 2005. *The World is Flat: A Brief History of the Twenty-First Century*. London: Macmillan.

Ghemawat, P. 2001. Distance still matters: the hard reality of global expansion, *Harvard Business Review*, 79: 137–147.

Grøgaard, B., & Verbeke, A. 2012. Twenty key hypotheses that make internalization theory the general theory of international strategic management. In A. Verbeke & H. Merchant (Eds.), *Handbook of Research on International Strategic Management*. Cheltenham: Edward Elgar.

Hennart, J. F. 1982. *A Theory of Multinational Enterprise*. Ann Arbor, MI: University of Michigan Press.

Hennart, J. F. 2009. Down with MNE-centric theories! Market entry and expansion as the bundling of MNE and local assets. *Journal of International Business Studies*, 40(9): 1432–1454.

Hillemann, J., & Gestrin, M. 2016. The limits of firm-level globalization: Revisiting the FSA/CSA matrix. *International Business Review*, 25(3): 767–775.

Hillemann, J., Verbeke, A., & Oh, W. Y. 2019. Regional integration, multinational enterprise strategy and the impact of country-level risk: The case of the EMU. *British Journal of Management*, 30(4): 908–925.

Hutzschenreuter, T., Voll, J. C., & Verbeke, A. 2011. The impact of added cultural distance and cultural diversity on international expansion patterns: A Penrosean perspective. *Journal of Management Studies*, 48(2): 305–329.

Hymer, S. H., 1960. *The International Operations of National Firms: A Study of Direct Foreign Investment*. Doctoral dissertation, MIT.

Kale, P. & Anand, J. 2006. The decline of emerging economy joint ventures: The case of India. *California Management Review*, 48: 62–76.

Kano, L., & Verbeke, A. 2015. The three faces of bounded reliability: Alfred Chandler and the micro-foundations of management theory. *California Management Review*, 58(1): 97–122.

Kano, L., & Verbeke, A. 2019. Theories of the multinational firm: A micro-foundational perspective. *Global Strategy Journal*, 9(1): 117–147.

King, A. W. 2007. Disentangling interfirm and intrafirm causal ambiguity: A conceptual model of causal ambiguity and sustainable competitive advantage. *Academy of Management Review*, 32(1): 156–178.

Makino, S., Lau, C. M., & Yeh, R. S. 2002. Asset-exploitation versus asset-seeking: Implications for location choice of foreign direct investment from newly industrialized economies. *Journal of International Business Studies*, 33(3): 403–421.

Martinez-Noya, A., & Narula, R. 2018. What more can we learn from R&D alliances? A review and research agenda. *BRQ Business Research Quarterly*, 21(3): 195–212.

Mudambi, R., Narula, R., & Santangelo, G. D. 2018. Location, collocation and innovation by multinational enterprises: a research agenda. *Industry and Innovation*, 25(3): 229–241.

Narula, R. 2014. Exploring the paradox of competence-creating subsidiaries: balancing bandwidth and dispersion in MNEs. *Long Range Planning*, 47(1–2): 4–15.

Narula, R., Asmussen, C. G., Chi, T., & Kundu, S. K. 2019. Applying and advancing internalization theory: The multinational enterprise in the twenty-first century. *Journal of International Business Studies*, 50(8): 1231–1252.

Narula, R., & Santangelo, G. D. 2012. Location and collocation advantages in international innovation. *Multinational Business Review*, 20(1): 6–25.

Narula, R., & Verbeke, A. 2015. Making internalization theory good for practice: The essence of Alan Rugman's contributions to international business. *Journal of World Business*, 50(4): 612–622.

Penrose, E. 1959. *The Theory of the Growth of the Firm*. New York, NY: Wiley.

Rugman, A. M. 1981. *Inside the Multinationals: The Economics of Internal Markets*. New York, NY: Columbia Press.

Rugman, A., & Oh, C. H. 2008. Friedman's follies: Insights on the globalization/regionalization debate. *Business and Politics*, 10(2): 1–14.

Rugman, A., Verbeke, A., & Yuan, W. 2011. Re-conceptualizing Bartlett and Ghoshal's classification of national subsidiary roles in the multinational enterprise. *Journal of Management Studies*, 48(2): 253–277.

Rugman, A. M., & Verbeke, A. 1992. A note on the transnational solution and the transaction cost theory of multinational strategic management. *Journal of International Business Studies*, 23(4): 761–771.

Rugman, A. M., & Verbeke, A. 2001. Subsidiary-specific advantages in multinational enterprises. *Strategic Management Journal*, 22(3): 237–250.

Rugman, A. M., Verbeke, A., & Nguyen, Q. T. 2011. Fifty years of international business theory and beyond. *Management International Review*, 51(6): 755–786.

Simon, H. A. 1982. *Models of bounded rationality and other topics in economics Collected Papers* (Vol. 2). Cambridge, MA: MIT Press.

Teece, D. J. 2014. A dynamic capabilities-based entrepreneurial theory of the multinational enterprise. *Journal of International Business Studies*, 45(1): 8–37.

Verbeke, A. 2009. *International Business Strategy*. Cambridge University Press.

Verbeke, A. 2013. *International Business Strategy* (2nd ed.). Cambridge University Press.

Verbeke, A., Ciravegna, L., Lopez, L. E., & Kundu, S. K. 2018. Five configurations of opportunism in international market entry. *Journal of Management Studies*, 56(7): 1287–1313.

Verbeke, A., & Fariborzi, H. 2019. Managerial governance adaptation in the multinational enterprise: In honour of Mira Wilkins. *Journal of International Business Studies*, 50(8): 1213–1230.

Verbeke, A., & Greidanus, N. 2009. The end of the opportunism versus trust debate: Bounded reliability as a new envelope-concept in research on MNE governance. *Journal of International Business Studies*, 40(9): 1471–1495.

Verbeke, A., & Yuan, W. 2005. Subsidiary autonomous activities in multinational enterprises: A transaction cost perspective. *Management International Review*, 45(2): 31–52.

Verbeke, A., & Yuan, W. 2007. Entrepreneurship in multinational enterprises: A Penrosean perspective. *Management International Review*, 47(2): 241–258.

Verbeke, A., & Yuan, W. 2010. A strategic management analysis of ownership advantages in the eclectic paradigm. *Multinational Business Review*, 18(2): 89–108.

Vernon, R. 1966. International Investment and International Trade in the Product Life Cycle. *The Quarterly Journal of Economics*, 80(2): 190–207.

Williamson, O. E. 1985. *The Economic Institutions of Capitalism*. New York, NY: Simon and Schuster.

Williamson, O. E. 1996. *The Mechanisms of Governance*. New York, NY: Oxford University Press.

CHAPTER 2

INTERNATIONAL BUSINESS HISTORY AND THE STRATEGY OF MULTINATIONAL ENTERPRISES

How History Matters

GEOFFREY JONES AND TERESA DA SILVA LOPES

INTRODUCTION

THE phenomena of globalization and deglobalization, and the consequent shifts of power and wealth that they are producing, have caught the attention of governments and policy makers in recent years (*Financial Times*, 2016). However, this topic of globalization and the evolution of the strategies followed by multinational enterprises (MNEs) have been foundational topics of research in international business (IB) and business history (BH) (Dunning, 1958, 1974; Wilkins & Hill, 1964/2011; Wilkins, 1970, 1974). Nonetheless, and with the notable exception of Alfred D. Chandler whose studies of the M-form of organization were famously diffused to Europe by McKinsey consultants during the 1960s, the impact that both disciplines have produced beyond academia remains limited (Chandler, 1962). This chapter aims to explain how history matters to studies in IB strategy, by providing the ideal complement to IB research. It proposes that the two disciplines IB and BH should collaborate, and this provides an opportunity to increase their economic and also social and cultural impact. The combination of large databases, theory, and models with studies that provide a nuanced understanding of individual firms and the differences between firms, the complexity of the economic and political environment, and the growing role of the entrepreneur, have the potential to offer a significant contribution.

IB and BH have long analyzed the country and firm-specific factors that explain the changing boundaries of firms and their international competitiveness. These include, but are not limited to the political economy; industry dynamics; the level of experience and stages of internationalization of MNEs; organizational forms and coordination mechanisms; governance with regard to ownership and management; strategic intent and the ability to transfer resources and the resulting spillovers; the role, autonomy, and evolution of subsidiaries; socially responsible and sustainable initiatives; the characteristics of the entrepreneurs and managers of MNEs; and the long-term impact of MNEs. Both disciplines draw on international and comparative analyses and on IB concepts and theories, and also those of adjacent disciplines, such as economics, geography, and sociology.

In turn, we can identify significant differences in terms of the methodologies used. First, the manner in which IB and BH apply existing theory differs. While IB scholars use theory to test assumptions that lead to the development of new theory, business historians typically conduct inductive research. They draw on IB theory in their search for patterns and generalizations, which helps refine it. Second, how the two disciplines deal with the concept of time is also distinct. While IB scholars are increasingly interested in dynamic decisions and changes over time, the time periods that they analyze tend to be relatively short, and their approach is atemporal and ahistorical. In contrast, business historians can often look at long periods of time and create periodizations, dividing larger time frames into smaller units, marked by significant events or turning points to organize the analysis (Lopes, Casson, & Jones, 2019).

Third, the sources and evidence that IB scholars use in their research are also distinct, in that they typically draw on samples extracted from large firm-level or industry-level databases. This is driven by the employment of social science methodology focused on illustrating casualty. Business historians, in turn, draw on archival-based research, including interviews—among other primary sources—and stress that firms differ, and those differences influence how they make decisions. As such, historians tend to also put a greater emphasis on human agency. Apart from acknowledging the complexity of the multifaceted aspects of the business enterprise with multinational activity, business historians recognize the power of "contextual intelligence" in shaping the boundaries and strategies of the MNE over time and in embedding individual actors across time and space (Khanna, 2014). Additionally, business historians are equally interested in discontinuities as well as continuities of firms and industries in their explanation of IB strategy. They tend to place greater emphasis on the political context in which multinational strategies are pursued, which include the key role that political factors and regulation often play in strategic organizational outcomes (Jones, 2002; Jones & Khanna, 2006; Lopes, 2020; Wilkins, 2001, 2015, 2016).

Calls for a fruitful dialog between IB and BH extend back for decades (Hertner & Jones, 1986). However, even after the appeal by Jones and Khanna in 2006, published in the *Journal of International Business Studies*, for IB scholars to bring history back to international business (Jones & Khanna, 2006), limited progress has been made. Although "history matters" has almost become a platitude, how it matters remains a work in progress, as does how it can contribute to studies such as the ones presented in this volume about IB strategy. This chapter first provides a long-term view of globalization and the concurrent evolution of the MNEs and their prevailing strategies. There is a well-established literature in BH about the evolution of global business in the long run, including overviews provided by Wilkins (1970, 1974, 1998c), Jones (2005a, 2013, 2014, 2019a, 2019b), and Fitzgerald (2015). Drawing on this research, this chapter highlights the prevailing strategies of firms with multinational activity over each of the globalization waves, and how they evolved in the long run. The third section emphasizes the recent research in IB history with regard to the strategy of MNEs and highlights some topics where there is potential for fruitful dialog with IB. The chapter ends with a discussion of how history matters more than ever in IB, and how this disciplinary dialog has great potential to produce research that is not only academically relevant but is also of meaningful in today's business world.

GLOBALIZATION WAVES AND MNES' PREVAILING IB STRATEGIES

First Global Economy and Management of Geographical Distance: 1840–1929

Multinational activity gained prominence from the mid-nineteenth century, when the first wave of global integration took place. This period, between 1840 and 1929, was characterized by accelerated growth and investment as well as radical transformations associated with large movements of knowledge, capital, and people. Rapidly falling transport and communications costs, symbolized by the advent of steamships, railroads, and the telegraph, and western imperialism, which forcibly opened up the African and Asian markets to foreign firms, were at the heart of this globalization wave (Bordo, Taylor, & Williamson, 2003; Jones, 2005a). The majority of foreign direct investment (FDI) took the form of resource-seeking investments. This reflected that the industrialized west required a growing number of primary commodities and food from the rest of the world. For instance, United Fruit Company (US) created large-scale banana plantations throughout Central America on the basis of concessions obtained from corrupt local governments. In response to the perishability of the banana fruit, the company internalized the entire value chain, creating transport and infrastructure companies to transport bananas (e.g. the Great White Fleet) and distribution companies to market them in the US. By 1914, United Fruit controlled two-thirds of all bananas sold in the US (Jones, 2005a; Wilkins, 1970).

Natural resources and food were also the concern of thousands of "free-standing" firms—the "born global" (BG) firms of their generation—which conducted little or no business in their home economies, primarily in Europe (Wilkins and Schröter, 1998). This was just one of the multiple innovative organizational forms created during this period in response to risks and costs associated with operating internationally (Lopes et al., 2019).

A smaller stream of multinational activity was identified in the manufacturing sector. Firms based in the US and Western Europe primarily invested in other developed markets, in response to growing tariff rates later in the nineteenth century. A remarkable example is the Singer Sewing Machine Company (US), which became one of the world's first manufacturing multinationals when it opened a factory in Glasgow, Scotland, in 1867. The company pioneered selling to the base of the pyramid, which was achieved through building a direct salesforce and offering customers credit to buy their relatively expensive machines. Singer's sewing machines became one of the world's first global consumer goods. By 1914, the company accounted for 90 percent of all sewing machines sold in the world and was the largest modern business enterprise in countries such as Russia (Jones, 2005a; Wilkins, 1970).

A recurring pattern was already evident in this period. Firms such as United Fruit had few linkages with the local economy and the overall social and economic impact in the host countries was not positive. Knowledge transfer worked best when foreign firms went to a country with the appropriate institutional arrangements, human capital, and entrepreneurial values to absorb transferred knowledge, much of which was tacit and not readily codified (Bruland & Mowery, 2014).

This wave of globalization was impressive, but it was not sustainable due to the impact of the exogeneous shocks that followed. World War I changed the nature of the international political economy. German firms had most of their international assets expropriated, and the Russian Revolution in 1917 was followed by the expropriation of all foreign capitalist assets, including the vast businesses owned by companies such as Singer Sewing Machines and oil companies such as the Shell Group. The war was followed by macroeconomic instability and growing tariff barriers. The Wall Street Crash in 1929 shut down the global economy, which became characterized by high tariff barriers and extensive capital controls.

Deglobalization 1929–1979: MNE Resilience

In the period between 1930 to 1979, the high levels of economic integration achieved earlier reverted to mid-nineteenth-century levels. The Great Depression and its aftermath of exchange controls and tariffs, the highly destructive impact of World War II, and the era of the Cold War, which saw capitalist enterprises excluded from large areas of the world such as the Soviet Union and China, all worked to reduce the scale of the MNE. In developed western countries, however, barriers to trade and investment began to fall with the formation of cross-country agreements such as the 1947 General

Agreement on Tariffs and Trade (GATT) and the establishment of the European Economic Community (EEC) in 1957, and with further reductions in transportation and communication costs (Dunning & Lundan, 2008; Jones, 2005a; Wilkins, 1974). MNEs proved resilient in the context of such hostile political and economic developments, but they also adopted new organizational forms. During the interwar years, there was a spread of collaborative arrangements, such as international cartels. US MNEs were prevented from formal participation by anti-trust laws, but often engaged informally. A notable example is the world lamp cartel, which controlled three-quarters of world output of electric lamps between the mid-1920s and World War II. US-based General Electric was not a formal member but controlled the strategy of the cartel through various devices (Reich, 1992), because cartels were viewed as powerful actors in the transfer of knowledge and intellectual property across borders (Fear, 2008).

After World War II, cartels faced many challenges as US anti-trust policies became more aggressive and were exported to other countries; although they persisted in certain industries, such as airlines and diamonds. The high levels of political risk in the non-western world—brought about by newly independent countries that sought to restrict foreign ownership and pursue interventionist policies—led MNEs to focus on investing into developing economies. They also pursued strategies that relied less on equity for investment and more on long-term contracts and debt. World trade in commodities was increasingly handled by giant commodity trading firms, such as Cargill, the grain trader and largest private company in the US (Broehl, 1992, 1998). A number of the most important trading companies, including André & Cie., Philipp Brothers, and Marc Rich, were either based in Switzerland or used Swiss-based affiliates to book most of their transactions. Switzerland offered a low tax environment and corporate secrecy, with the added benefit of not belonging to the United Nations. Philipp Brothers and Marc Rich in particular flourished as developing countries nationalized mines, plantations, and oilfields (Jones & Storli, 2017). The new companies provided export markets for now state-owned enterprises, functioned as investment banks to fund capital investment, and engaged in bribery of local business elites.

More conventional multinationals engaged in market-seeking investments, which continued to exist and expand during these decades. Coca Cola employed a franchise model to globalize its brand at a fast pace after World War II (Ciafone, 2019). Another example was the Anglo-Dutch consumer goods multinational Unilever. Created by a merger completed in 1929, Unilever was one of the largest European MNEs. It became highly diversified by operating in industries such as food and spreads, home and personal care, and animal foods, and also ran a vast trading company in the African continent. By the 1970s, Unilever was active in almost every country in the non-Communist world; the company localized its management in the developing world, enabling it to navigate the era when many governments (e.g. India and Turkey) pursued anti-foreign business policies and insisted on large local ownership stakes (Jones, 2005b; Jones, 2013).

While most western multinationals withdrew from the developing world, others stayed. In 1947, the US department store chain Sears started a successful business in Mexico, a country that had only a decade earlier banished foreign oil companies and was widely regarded as nationalistic. Sears localized its business strategy to appeal to the Mexican consumer and worker, embodying policies based on profit-sharing, pensions, and low-priced meals as per the traditions of the Mexican Revolution (Moreno, 2003).

New Global Economy, 1979–2008: Disaggregation of MNE Activities within Global Value Chains

The role of business in the growth and dynamics of the second global economy was considerable. A resurgence of globalization was driven by the re-opening of China to global business in 1978, followed by the collapse of the Soviet Union and the end of the Cold War a decade later, as well as a surge of deregulation and privatization in Western economies, starting with the US and UK in the 1980s. The creation of the World Wide Web in the 1990s marked the beginning of sharply falling communications costs previously associated with international investment.

MNEs' key firm-specific advantages (FSAs) during this period were their ability to effectively focus on the core business and disaggregate their activities within global value chains. The organization of production became less hierarchical and more flexible, relying on more collaborative, network-type relations between different actors within value chains. Transport innovations, such as container ships, enabled western MNEs to transfer assembly facilities to low-cost countries. Orchestration through planning and contracting by the parent firm, replaced ownership as the main means of coordination over productive resources in different markets. A prominent example was the well-known US consumer electronics company Apple, which, in the late 1990s, began outsourcing its assembly business to Foxconn (a Taiwanese-based company). Foxconn had a close relationship with the local government in Zhengzhou, China, which provided them with access to cheap land and forced labor to build Apple's equipment. Foxconn manufactured 90 percent of iPhones in 2016 (Jones, 2019a).

Emerging-market multinational enterprises (EMNEs), based in Asia or Latin America, also began to expand globally from the 1980s (Kosacoff et al., 2007; Thite, Wilkinson, & Budwar, 2016). A large subsection of these EMNEs were state owned, including highly successful Gulf airlines such as Emirates and Qatar, while other EMNEs had close relationships with their home governments. In China, state support enabled highly competitive local firms to emerge in high-technology sectors. Examples include Huawei, the internet networking firm, and wind and solar energy firms such as Xinjiang Goldwind. The number of Chinese firms in the global top ten turbine manufacturers went from zero to four between 2006 and 2010 (Buckley, Voss, Cross, & Clegg, 2011; Jones, 2019a).

New Deglobalization since 2008: The Rise of Political Risk

The financial crisis caused a shock to the global economy starting a new period of turbulence that disrupted the linear growth of globalization leading to what may be viewed as a new era of globalization. The world financial crisis was partly the result of three decades of the financialization of capitalism, enabled by the deregulation of financial services. The financial crisis resulted in a severe economic downturn, but more fundamentally, it provoked a change of sentiment about the benefits of liberal global capitalism. Whereas tariff levels remained stable, governments implemented protectionist non-tariff measures. There was a surge in micro-protectionism, a widespread adoption of local content rules, public procurement discrimination against foreign firms, export taxes and quotas, and trade distorting subsidies. In this new global context, populist and nationalist governments came to power in countries such as Brazil, Turkey, and the Philippines but also made it into European governments in the UK, Hungary, and Poland. Donald Trump's assumption of the US Presidency in 2017 was followed by a surge of trade protectionist and anti-immigrant rhetoric, as well as the withdrawal from the Trans-Pacific Partnership (TPP) trade agreement and the Paris climate change agreement signed in 2015 (Jones, 2014, 2017).

The new era of deglobalization is important for the IB strategies of MNEs because of the challenging political and economic environments that have characterized this era. Some emerging market firms that had gone global during the heady days of the second global economy experienced managerial and financial challenges. These included Indian multinational companies, such as Tata and Arcelor Mittal, which struggled to manage their acquisitions in major (western) markets. As in previous eras of deglobalization, MNEs sought to accommodate nationalistic governments. For instance, in 2016, following the Brexit vote, the UK government promised the Japanese automobile manufacturer Nissan special incentives should Brexit negotiations result in trade barriers that would hinder the company's sales into the EU. By 2019, the reconfiguration of global value chains appeared to be well underway (Jones, 2019c).

THE DIALOG BETWEEN IB AND BH

There have always been different strands of research in BH. These rely on the level of generalization business historians aim to achieve with their research, and the disciplines and theories they draw upon to achieve such generalizations (Friedman & Jones, 2011; Lopes, 2020). These disciplines may range from economics and IB, to geography and sociology, or business historians may rely on a combination of these (Casson, 1986; Friedman & Jones, 2011). As BH lacks a distinctive methodology beyond rigorous engagement with empirical evidence, business historians are in the position where they may act as "hubs," as they are more open to collaborating with researchers from different disciplines in order to produce interdisciplinary research.

The history of multinationals and global business has a long pedigree in business history. The topic is featured extensively in core journals such as *Business History Review* and *Business History and Enterprise & Society*. There is also a large monograph literature (e.g. Cox, 2000; Haueter & Jones, 2017; Hausman et al., 2008; Hertner & Jones,

1986; Jones, 1986, 1988, 2000, 2005a, 2005b, 2018; Jones & Schröter, 1993; Teichova & Cottrell, 1983; Teichova et al., 1986; Lopes, 2007; Lopes & Casson, 2007; Wilkins, 1970, 1974, 2001). These studies draw on carefully researched archives and analyze IB strategies over long periods of time, and engage with core IB theory, such as internalization theory (Buckley & Casson, 1976; Hennart, 1982; Rugman, 1981; Rugman & Verbeke; 2003).

Traditionally, researchers focusing on the history of the MNE are concerned with the drivers of FDI and use theory to help build generalizations. Research on FDI decisions remains relevant today, as new types of multinationals and multinational activities have attracted the attention of scholars; for example, EMNEs, BG firms, and global value chains (Barbero, 2014, 2018; Buckley & Verbeke, 2016; de Villa, 2016; Hesse & Neveling, 2019; Jones & Lluch, 2015; Lopes, 2019). While internalization theory continues to be applied in BH research, extensions are also being proposed to take into account differing historical contexts and time periods. Additionally, a wider variety of challenges and impacts—not only economic but also political, technological, and environmental—are also being investigated as topics of research in IB history. Many of these relatively recent publications have been collaborations between business historians and IB scholars (Bucheli & Kim, 2012, 2015; Casson & Lopes, 2013; Gao, Zuzul, Jones, & Khanna, 2017; Jones & Pitelis, 2015; Lopes & Casson, 2012; Lopes et al., 2019). These papers provide a basis for what can become a very fruitful dialog between IB and BH.

In this following section, we provide some indication around how this dialog between IB and BH may develop in the future. Drawing on the case of deglobalization, we discuss how historical evidence can be an important basis on which to speculate the way in which MNEs may respond to new political risks in the present. Further, we explain how the use of a combination of data sources can become a useful approach to uncover phenomena that appear absent from large databases. In doing so, we hope to provide an illustration of how business historians and IB scholars can jointly develop and enrich IB theory.

Deglobalization—What We Can Learn from the Past

We propose that the quality of contemporary debates about deglobalization can be much enhanced by paying greater attention to historical evidence. For example, the result of the referendum in the UK in 2016 (in which a small majority of the voters recommended their country exit from the EU) led to widespread expectations that many MNEs would divest or reduce their investments in the country. This was plausible as business historians had long identified that inward investment was attracted by a nation's ability to serve as an export platform to other markets (see for instance, Jones & Bostock, 1996). The IB literature has also suggested that when markets become highly risky, MNEs should either avoid those markets or consider withdrawal when problems arise (Fitzpatrick, 1983; Simon, 1982, 1984).

However, there is historical evidence showing that many MNEs choose to stay in foreign markets, even when environmental conditions become adverse and increase the risks associated with their business investments. In such instances, risk management strategies used are those of prevention and mitigation, apart from avoidance and withdrawal (Casson & Lopes, 2013). Firms often use prevention strategies, which involve taking steps to counter a potential problem before it occurs; or mitigation strategies, which involve reducing the impact of a problem once it has occurred. In the UK example, leaving the EU may lead us to witness MNEs follow a variety of risk management strategies—some may change their organizational designs to be able to better identify and manage risks; others may partially or fully withdraw from the market. For example, EasyJet is already creating an innovative headquarter (HQ) design in order to avoid withdrawal and remain in the UK market as well as continue operations within the rest of Europe. By setting up an Austrian HQ, EasyJet sought to obtain an Austrian license, which will enable the MNE to operate flights within the EU after Brexit. The new organizational design would allow EasyJet to become a Pan European aviation group, with three airlines based in Austria, Switzerland, and the UK, all controlled by EasyJet PLC, listed on the London Stock Exchange. Apple's recent attempt to reduce its dependency on Chinese suppliers was related to a combination of both business and political risks. In order to maintain efficiencies at different levels of the value chain, Foxconn has sought to reallocate some of the value chain to India and Vietnam in order to reduce the impact of US–China tensions on Apple (*Financial Times*, 2019).

An illustration of a mitigation strategy aimed at dealing with a combination of business and political risks is the case of Cisco in China. Cisco helped build the Chinese internet during the 1990s and facilitated the government's desire to monitor and censor the Web when it undertook the CN4 upgrade in 2004 (Jones & Grandjean, 2018). However, just over a decade later, the company had lost its dominance of the Chinese internet market and put most of its remaining business into a joint venture with Chinese company Inspur. This development was prompted by revelations by former US National Security Agency contractor Edward Snowden that US technology firms' products had been used by the American government to spy on China. The Chinese government ordered the state bureaucracy and state-owned companies to buy more local equipment, while drafting strict regulations for foreign equipment makers and accelerating investment in domestic technology. Meanwhile, the US has systematically worked to restrict the operations of Chinese MNEs such as Huawei (the world's largest maker of telecoms equipment) on alleged security grounds (*Forbes*, 2015).

Historically, we can find numerous cases that provide evidence of similar risks impacting on MNEs' risk management strategies. This is important for business and policy makers who are able to use this historical data to speculate how companies may respond to risk. Take, for instance, the case of the German MNE Beiersdorf during the twentieth-century deglobalization (Jones & Lubinski, 2012; Reckendrees, 2018). The interwar period (1919–1938) was characterized by the spread of nationalistic and fascist regimes in different parts of the world. This meant that MNEs were received with hostility in foreign markets. Subsequently, the spread of the Communist regime, and the policies of newly independent postcolonial governments resulted in further expulsions and hostility toward foreign firms.

Corporate strategies of MNEs during this period ranged from seeking strong local identities to divert nationalistic pressure, to participating in coups to overthrow foreign governments perceived as hostile. Prevention and mitigation strategies often implied the elaboration of innovative organizational structures for international activities, designed to circumvent potentially hostile government interventions. Beiersdorf was a leading pharmaceutical and skin care company based in Germany when they found themselves exposed to political risks due to being under Jewish ownership and management, and because their main competitive advantages comprised of their brands and trademarks. In response to political risk, Beiersdorf created an organizational design known as "cloaking," which involved hiding their assets abroad from their own government. During the interwar period, Beiersdorf created companies in Switzerland and the Netherlands to prevent risk in light of World War II potentially starting. From 1933 and throughout the Nazi regime, Jewish managers were sent to the Netherlands and, to further conceal the fact that it was a Jewish company, Beiersdorf carefully aligned its marketing activities with the beauty ideals of the new regime.

Other adaptation strategies followed. As part of its cloaking strategy to prevent risks, the MNE separated its affiliates from the German HQ, through the creation of a ring structure, where Amsterdam was placed in the middle of the ring structure. The core company in Amsterdam was responsible for purchasing the most important raw materials, for ensuring quality control, and for jointly organized research, advertisement, and general administration. An annual fee had to be paid by the other ring firms to finance this central organization. In most countries, such as Switzerland, France, and the US, Beiersdorf's affiliates primarily held the trademarks (and only at times plants and equipment), whereas the actual business was conducted by independent partner companies. The Beiersdorf affiliate and the partner firm shared profits equally. The parent company in Germany received a license fee based on turnover. Contacts with Beiersdorf Germany were limited to the fee and the purchase of such raw materials and products that could not be manufactured abroad. As a consequence, Beiersdorf was henceforth composed of two legally separated pillars, namely the German business and the foreign business. The German parent company sought to retain its managerial influence by establishing an "administrative committee." The parent company also funded the advertising campaigns of the ring firms and sought to drive strategic planning through regular meetings of the committee with the ring firm directors.

The initial motives for the ring structure, then, were a diverse mixture of mitigation and prevention of political and business risks, partly shaped by past experiences and partly by perceived future threats. The foundations of the ring structure attempt to revitalize the lost foreign business, secure tax advantages, and, in particular, enable capital transfers in an environment of rising foreign exchange controls. This was reinforced by Nazi regulations concerning German-owned foreign companies that, starting with 1936, were required to remit to the German central bank (Reichsbank) all funds not essential to ongoing operations as well as all future "surplus" funds, with the central bank also determining what actually constituted a surplus. At the same time, foreign affiliates, especially in the Netherlands, Switzerland, and US, were expected to retrieve lost trademarks, which Germans were not allowed to repurchase. While these strategies were quite successful in the short term, in the long term they failed to protect most of Beiersdorf's foreign assets from expropriation. Therefore, factories and key trademarks were mostly lost in the different markets in which the company was operating. It took many years for the MNE to rebuild the lost brands and develop their IB strategy.

Complementing Sources of Evidence

IB scholars have a general preference for the use of large quantitative databases, often to the detriment of qualitative research (Verbeke, Coeurderoy, & Matt, 2018). Given the availability of some widely used and accepted sources and databases, IB research has, to some extent, been limited to a narrow range of topics, such as the role of technology, R&D, branding, and marketing on the international strategies of the MNE. These approaches to use widely available single data sources have moved IB scholars further away from BH methodologies (Verbeke & Kano, 2015). In a relatively recent article on the future of IB research, Verbeke et al. (2018) make an appeal for IB scholars to use more detailed sources of data. Their argument is that IB researchers face the trade-off between using large data with disappointingly poor globalization information, and small samples with much better corporate globalization information, and agree on the virtues of an increase in collaborative research with business historians (Verbeke et al., 2018).

With regards to their approach to data collection, business historians are known for their willingness to use different, and occasionally unconventional, data sources in their research. These can range from company archives, to oral histories, the analysis of artifacts, diaries of entrepreneurs, court cases, or registration data of patents and trademarks. This research can often help complement information obtained through the use of more conventional statistics, and broad datasets collected at one point in time about the MNE and its foreign investments.

A few notable examples of how business history methodologies can enrich our understanding of MNEs' IB strategies are as follows. During the 1980s, Wilkins showed that foreign investment data from the UK does not reflect the extent of investment in physical assets abroad. Specifically, the author found that thousands of companies registered in England and Scotland during the nineteenth century did not quite fit the expected model of "multinational enterprises" (Wilkins, 1986, 1988, 1998a, 1998b). The so called "free-standing firm" was based in the UK, yet it had all business operations and management located in the host country. Furthermore, their management strategy was not subordinated, and they were not coordinated by a parent company based in the UK. These firms undertook only foreign operations, they were registered in countries with advanced stock markets, and then transferred capital across markets (see also Hennart, 1994). More recently, Lopes et al. (2018) highlighted another type of "disguised" foreign investment, not accounted for by FDI statistics. Drawing on trademark registration data, the authors found that the textiles industry in markets such as Brazil owes much of its development to investments made by expatriate entrepreneurs, who were found to set up local businesses and register their firms and trademarks as if they were local entrepreneurs. The analysis of the trademark data, through examining the entrepreneurs and the types of textile brands and firms they created, shows that they were in fact expatriates who used foreign technology, marketing, and management techniques, as well as international networks, for the procurement of certain materials and the distribution of their goods. These entrepreneurs often relied on foreign sources to fund their businesses and tended to employ home country managers (see Lopes et al., 2018).

Extending Theory Using History: The Case of Internalization Theory

As mentioned previously, one of the distinctive features of business historians relates to the fact that they have shown that globalization is non-linear, and MNE trajectories are unique. Therefore, existing theories in IB often do not apply to the history of business. Many examples can be found historically in the strategies and HQ designs adopted by firms with international activities. Classic internalization theory argues that if a market becomes risky, the firm should divest or change its mode of operation in that market (Buckley & Casson, 1976). However, this is not what actually happens in practice, neither historically nor in the present day (Casson & Lopes, 2013). Many firms change their strategies and structures in order to remain in such environments. This resilience to high-risk environments is a key FSA of EMNEs investing in other emerging markets or in other high-risk environments (e.g. Matthews, 2006; Verbeke & Kano, 2015).

To deal with new or unexpected imperfections in host markets, MNEs often choose to keep the same mode of operation and either change the design of their HQs by distributing all or part of their functions (legal, financial, or strategic) across different markets. MNEs can also change the type and role of the entrepreneur used to provide or source local knowledge in the host country (for instance, by hiring a local manager or an expatriate entrepreneur). Historical evidence shows that some MNEs changed only one aspect of their international strategy and others all of them (Lopes et al., 2019).

A dialog between business historians and IB scholars with regards to the design of MNE HQs has the potential to map the typologies of HQs across sectors and identify the typologies of motivations for the relocation of strategic functions of HQs by home country and host country. It can also link that analysis to the performance of the MNE with a view of having more efficient and strategic structures to support survival in the long term (Rugman & Verbeke, 2003). By looking in-depth at the nature of firms, a dialog between IB scholars and business historians also has the potential to identify different configurations of specific entrepreneurial roles in foreign operations, in relation to particular organizational designs and distribution of HQ roles. Additionally, by integrating a more macro analysis with in-depth archival and interview-based research, this collaborative research may also help formalize the use of an integrated approach for internalization theory, with the potential of it becoming more applicable to different time periods, geographies, firm sizes, and contexts.

The integrated approach, as proposed by Lopes et al. (2019), is an illustration of that. This approach integrates several topics that have been dealt with separately by IB theory (see Figure 2.1). It considers the role of the entrepreneur in the sourcing of knowledge and the accessing of complementary assets, and the design and functions of HQs. This analysis of entrepreneurial roles and the distribution of HQ roles is combined with internalization theory to explain unconventional or innovative organizational forms of MNEs. The proposed integrated approach follows the classic internalization theory (Buckley & Casson, 1976) but also includes several extensions provided over time by Rugman (1981), Hennart (1982, 1991, 1993), Casson (1987, 1990), Rugman & Verbeke (1992, 2003, 2008); Buckley & Casson (2009), Verbeke (2003, 2009), Narula &Verbeke (2015), and Casson et al. (2016), among others.

Figure 2.1 is three dimensional. On the *first* dimension, the innovative entrepreneur chooses the location and internalization strategy of the corporation, which ranges from markets to hierarchies, and includes other hybrid modes such as subcontracting, franchising, and licensing. The second dimension relates to the type of entrepreneur chosen for sourcing local knowledge in the host country (e.g. local entrepreneur, expatriate entrepreneur, secondee). The type of expatriate could include an alien migrant, permanent resident expatriate or a temporary resident expatriate, for instance. On a *third* dimension, the innovative entrepreneur chooses the design of the HQ, which can range from co-locating all the HQ functions (legal, financial, and strategic) in one country, to

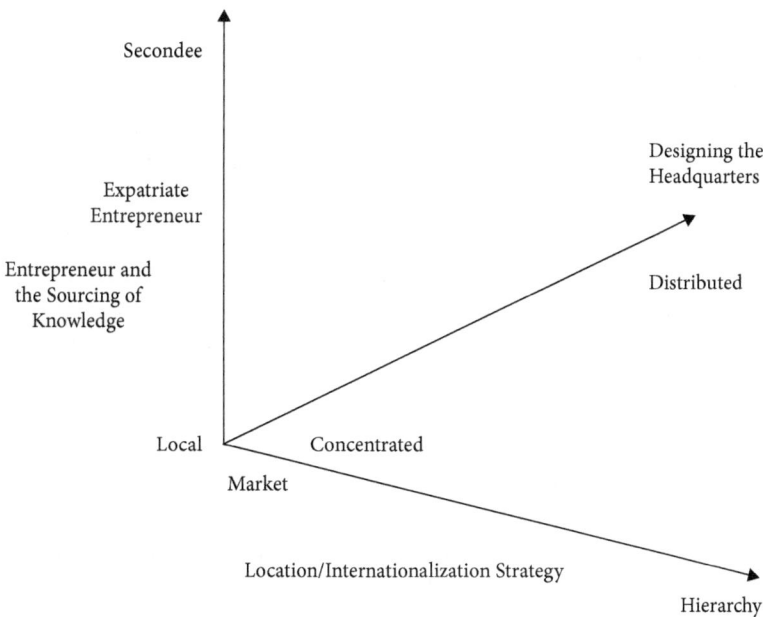

FIGURE 2.1 An integrated view of internalization theory.

Source: Lopes, Casson, & Jones (2019).

distributing these across distinct markets. Other options exist, of course. For example, the legal and financial functions could be concentrated in one country, with only the strategic function being distributed.

An integrated research approach may translate into inserting the entrepreneurship literature more into IB theorizing and taking into account not only the firm and the complexity of its environments but also the increasingly important role of the entrepreneur. This approach provides a systematic analysis of MNE decisions, which resembles real-world decision-making processes and may, perhaps, be more likely to be understood and adopted by business practitioners and policy makers.

CONCLUSION: HOW HISTORY MATTERS

The history of MNEs helps elucidate the idea that many IB challenges, are often unexpected, and the business strategies employed to deal with such challenges are somehow "new." These are, in many cases, the replication of events and strategies used by MNEs in the past, adapted to different economic, political, social, and technological contexts. Since the mid-nineteenth century, the world economy has known two waves of globalization and two periods of disintegration. In each globalization wave MNEs had different rationales to investing abroad, ranging from natural resource seeking, to market seeking or efficiency seeking. The roles of HQs varied between the centralization of all decisions (financial, strategic, and legal), only passing operational decisions to subsidiaries, to decentralization, depending on the context and FSAs of each MNE. During the first globalization wave, decentralization meant that firms with multinational activities had to deal with geographical distance and often high-risk environments. By the twenty-first century, decentralization was associated with the ongoing disintegration of global value chains and management of efficiencies. The main role of the MNE's HQ became the coordination of complex networks of inter-firm and intra-firm transactions.

The dialog and collaboration between scholars from both IB and BH can provide fruitful insights to both the corporate world and policy makers about managerial problems and how they change over time. Business historians can gain from more dialog with IB scholars, with the aim of integrating theory in their empirical explanations and increasing the impact of their research. As IB aims to become a more relevant discipline to practitioners on topics such as globalization and deglobalization, it needs to simultaneously consider the role of context and the role of the entrepreneur.

The detailed study of the evolution of IB and the strategies followed by firms with multinational activities also provide insights at different levels of institutional analysis: the country and region level, the industry, the firm level, the entrepreneur, and the product/brand. All these different levels can be very useful to help refine theory and to understand IB strategy. Business historians are able to highlight precisely what were the trends and patterns followed by MNEs, and what strategies worked in which contexts. The key advantage is their ability to conduct longitudinal and empirical studies on MNE strategies over long periods of time. As business historians are not preoccupied with implying causality like their IB counterparts, they are often freer to experiment with, and explore, different sets of MNE issues, including the long-term social and cultural impact of multinationals.

References

Barbero, M. I. 2014. *Multinacionales latinomericanas en perspectiva comparada, teoría e historia.* Cátedra Corona, Universidad de los Andes, 23.

Barbero, M. I. 2018. Introduccion las nuevas multinationales: Entre historia y la teoria. *Anuario Centro de Estudios Economicos de la Empresa y el Desarrollo*, 10(10): 11–30.

Bordo, M. D., Taylor, A. M., & Williamson, J. G. 2003. *Globalization in Historical Perspective.* Chicago, IL: University of Chicago Press.

Broehl, W. G. 1992. Cargill: *Trading the World's Grain.* Hanover, NH: University Press of New England.

Broehl, W. G. 1998. *Cargill: Going Global.* Hanover, NH: University Press of New England.

Bruland, K., & Mowery, D. C. 2014. Technology and the spread of capitalism. In Neal, L., & Williamson, J. G. (Eds.), *The Cambridge History of Capitalism.* Cambridge: Cambridge University Press.

Bucheli, M., & Kim, M-Y. 2012. Political institutional change, obsolescing legitimacy, and multinational corporations. *Management International Review*, 52(6): 847–877.

Bucheli, M., & Kim, M-Y. 2015. Attacked from both sides: A dynamic model of multinational corporations' strategies for protection of their property rights. *Global Strategy Journal*, 5(1): 1–26.

Buckley, P. J., & Casson, M. 1976. *The Future of the Multinational Enterprise.* London: Macmillan.

Buckley, P. J., & Casson, M. 2009. The internalisation theory of the multinational enterprise: A review of the progress of a research agenda after 30 Years. *Journal of International Business Studies*, 40(9): 1563–1580.

Buckley, P. J., & Verbeke, A. 2016. Smiling and crying curves in international business. *International Business Review*, 25(3): 749–752.

Buckley, P. J., Voss, H., Cross, A., & Clegg. J. 2011. The emergence of Chinese firms as multinationals: The influence of the home institutional environment. In Pearce, R. (Eds.) *China and the Multinationals: International Business and the Entry of China into the Global Economy.* Northampton, MA: Edward Elgar.

Casson, M. 1986. General theories of the multinational enterprise: Their relevance to business history. In P. Hertner & G. Jones (Eds.). *Multinationals: Theory and History.* Aldershot: Gower.

Casson, M. 1987. *The Firm and the Market: Studies in Multinational Enterprise and the Scope of the Firm.* Oxford: Blackwell.

Casson, M. 1990. *Enterprise and Competitiveness.* Oxford: Clarendon Press.

Casson, M., & Lopes, T. d. S. 2013. Foreign direct investment in high-risk environments: An historical perspective. *Business History*, 55(3): 375–404.

Casson, M., Porter, L., & Wadeson, N. 2016. Internalization theory: An unfinished agenda. *International Business Review*, 25(6): 1223–1234.

Chandler, A. D. 1962. *Strategy and Structure.* Cambridge, MA: Harvard University Press.

Ciafone, A. 2019. *Counter-Cola. A Multinational History of the Global Corporation*. Oaklan, CA: University of California Press.

Cox, H. 2000. *The Global Cigarette*. Oxford: Oxford University Press.

de Villa, M. A. 2016. From multilatina to global latina: Unveiling the corporate level international strategy choices of grupo Nutresa. *AD-Minister*, 29: 23–57.

Dunning, J. H. 1958. *American Investment in British Manufacturing Industry*. London: George Allen and Unwin.

Dunning, J. H. (Ed.) 1974. *Economic Analysis and the Multinational Enterprise*. London: Praeger.

Dunning, J. H., & Lundan, S. M. 2008. *Multinational Enterprises and the Global Economy*. Northampton, MA: Edward Elgar.

Fear, J. 2008. Cartels. In Jones, G., & Zeitlin, J. (Eds.), *The Oxford Handbook of Business History*. Oxford: Oxford University Press.

Financial Times. 2016. The tide of globalization is turning. 6 September.

Financial Times. 2019. Why the world's tech factory faces its biggest tests. 10 June.

Fitzgerald, R. 2015. *The Rise of the Global Company: Multinationals and the Making of the Modern World*. Cambridge: Cambridge University Press.

Fitzpatrick, M. 1983. The definition and assessment of political risk in international business: A review of the literature. *Academy of Management Review*, 8(2): 249–254.

Forbes. 2015. Cisco seeks partnerships to revive its China business amid geopolitical headwinds. 24 September.

Friedman, W., & Jones, G. 2011. Business history: Time for debate. *Business History Review*, 85(1): 1–8.

Gao, C., Zuzul, T., Jones, G., & Khanna, T. 2017. Overcoming institutional voids: A reputation-based view of long run survival. *Strategic Management Journal*, 38(11): 2147–2167.

Haueter, N. V., & Jones, G. 2017. Risk and reinsurance. In Haueter, N. V., & Jones G. (Eds.) *Managing Risk in Reinsurance: From City Fires to Global Warming*. Oxford: Oxford University Press.

Hausman, W. J., Hertner, P., & Wilkins, M. 2008. *Global Electrification: Multinational Enterprise and International Finance in the History of Light and Power*. Cambridge: Cambridge University Press.

Hennart, J.-F. 1982. *A Theory of Multinational Enterprise*. Ann Arbor, MI: University of Michigan Press.

Hennart, J.-F. 1991. The transaction cost theory of the multinational enterprise. In C. N. Pitelis, & R. Sugden, R. (Eds.), *The Nature of the Transnational Firm*. London: Routledge.

Hennart, J.-F. 1993. The swollen middle: Why most transactions are a mix of "market" and "hierarchy." *Organizational Science*, 4(4): 529–547.

Hennart, J.-F. 1994. Free-standing firms and the internalisation of markets for financial capital: A response to Casson. *Business History*, 36(4): 118–31.

Hertner, P., & Jones, G. 1986. *Multinationals: Theory and History*. Aldershot: Gower.

Hesse, J.-O., & Neveling, P. 2019. Global value chains. In Lopes, T. d. S., Lubinski, C., & Tworek, H. (Eds.) 2019. *The Routledge Handbook on the Makers of Global Business*. London: Routledge.

Jones, G. 1986. *British Multinationals: Origins, Management and Performance*. Aldershot: Gower.

Jones, G. 1988. Foreign multinationals and British industry before 1945. *Economic History Review*, 41: 429–53.

Jones, G. 2000. *Merchants to Multinationals*. Oxford: Oxford University Press.

Jones, G. 2002. Business enterprises and global worlds. *Enterprise and Society*, 3(4): 581–605.

Jones, G. 2005a. *Multinationals and Global Capitalism: From the Nineteenth to the Twenty-First Century*. Oxford: Oxford University Press.

Jones, G. 2005b. *Renewing Unilever: Transformation and Tradition*. Oxford: Oxford University Press.

Jones, G. 2013. *Entrepreneurship and Multinationals: Global Business and the Making of the Modern World*. Northampton, MA: Edward Elgar.

Jones, G. 2014. Firms and global capitalism. In L. Neal, L., & J. G. Williamson, J.G. (Eds.), *The Cambridge History of Capitalism*. Cambridge: Cambridge University Press.

Jones, G. 2017. *Profits and Sustainability: A History of Green Entrepreneurship*. Oxford: Oxford University Press.

Jones, G. 2018. *Varieties of Green Business: Industries, Nations and Time*. Northampton, MA: Edward Elgar Publishing.

Jones, G. 2019a. International business and emerging markets in historical perspective. In R. Groose, & K. E. Meyer (Eds.), *The Oxford handbook of management in emerging markets*. Oxford: Oxford University Press.

Jones, G. 2019b. Origins and development of global business. In T. d. S. Lopes, C. Lubinski, & H. Tworek (Eds.) 2019. *The Routledge handbook on the makers of global business*. Aldershot: Routledge.

Jones, G. 2019c. The Great Divergence and the Great Convergence. In T. d. S. Lopes, C. Lubinski, & H. Tworek (Eds.) 2019. *The Routledge handbook on the makers of global business*. Aldershot: Routledge.

Jones, G., & Bostock, F. 1996. US multinationals in British manufacturing before 1962. *Business History Review*, 70(2): 207–256.

Jones, G, & Grandjean, E. 2020. John Chambers, Cisco and China: Upgrading a golden shield. *Harvard Business School Case*, 318–158, rev. April.

Jones, G., & Khanna, T. 2006. Bringing history (back) into international business. *Journal of International Business Studies*, 37: 453–68.

Jones, G., & Lluch, A. (Eds.) 2015. *The Impact of Globalization on Argentina and Chile: Business Enterprises and Entrepreneurship*. Northampton, MA: Edward Elgar.

Jones, G., & Lubinski, C. 2012. Managing political risk in global business: Beiersdorf 1914–1990. *Enterprise & Society*, 13(1): 85–119.

Jones, G., & Pitelis, C. 2015. Entrepreneurial imagination and a demand and supply-side perspective on the MNE and cross-border organization. *Journal of International Management*, 21(4): 309–321.

Jones, G., & Schröter, H. G. (Eds.) 1993. *The rise of multinationals in Continental Europe*. Aldershot, UK: Edward Elgar Publishing.

Jones, G., & Storli, E. 2017. Marc Rich and global commodity trading. *Harvard Business School Case*, 813–020, rev. December.

Khanna, T. 2014. Contextual Intelligence. *Harvard Business Review*, 92(9): 58–68.

Kosacoff, B., Forteza, J., Barbero, M. I., Porta, F., & Stengel. E. A. 2007. *Globalizar desde Latinamérica. El caso Arcor*. Buenos Aires: McCraw Hill.

Lopes, T. D. S. 2007. *Global Brands: The Growth of Multinationals in the Alcoholic Drinks Industry*. New York: Cambridge University Press.

Lopes, T. D. S., & Casson, M. 2007. Entrepreneurship and the development of global brands. *Business History Review*, 81(winter): 651–680.

Lopes, T. D. S. 2019. Transaction costs in the international trade of port wine. *Entreprises et Histoire*, 94: 164–185.

Lopes, T. D. S. 2020. The nature of the firm—and the eternal life of the brand. *Enterprise & Society, Forthcoming.*

Lopes, T. D. S., & Casson, M. 2012. Brand protection and globalization of British business. *Business History Review*, 86(2): 287–310.

Lopes, T. D. S., Casson, M., & Jones, G. 2019. Organizational innovation in the multinational enterprise: Internalization theory and business history. *Journal of International Business Studies*, 50(8): 1338–1358.

Lopes, T. D. S., Guimarães, C. G., Sais, A., & Saraiva, L. F. 2018. The "disguised" foreign investor: Brands, trademarks and the British expatriate entrepreneur in Brazil. *Business History*, 60(8): 1171–1195.

Matthews, J. A. 2006. Dragon multinationals: New players in 21st century globalization. *Asia Pacific Journal of Management*, 23(1): 5–27.

Moreno, J. 2003. *Yankee Don't Go Home*. Chapel Hill, NC: University of North Carolina Press.

Narula, R., & Verbeke, A. 2015. Making internalization theory good for practice: The essence of Alan Rugman's contributions to international business. *Journal of World Business*, 50(4): 612–622.

Reckendrees, A. 2018. *Beiersdorf—The Company Behind the Brands Nivea, Tesa, Hansaplast & Co.* Munich: Verlag C. H. Beck.

Reich, L. S. 1992. General Electric and the world cartelization of electric lamps. In A. Kudo and T. Hara (Eds.) *International Cartels in Business History*. Tokyo: University of Tokyo Press.

Rugman, A. M. 1981. A test of internalization theory. *Managerial and Decision Economics*, 2(4): 211–219.

Rugman, A. M., & Verbeke, A. 1992. A note on the transnational solution and the transaction cost theory of multinational strategic management. *Journal of International Business Studies*, 23(4): 761–771.

Rugman, A. M., & Verbeke, A. 2003. Extending the theory of the multinational enterprise: Internalization and strategic management perspectives. *Journal of International Business Studies*, 34(2): 125–137.

Rugman, A. M., & Verbeke, A. 2008. Internalization theory and its impact on the field of international business. In J. J. Boddewyn (Eds.) *International Business Scholarship: AIB Fellows on the First 50 Years and Beyond—Research in Global Strategic Management*. Bingley: Emerald.

Simon, J. D. 1982. Political risk assessment: Past trends and future prospects. *Columbia Journal of World Business*, 17(3): 62–71.

Simon, J. D. 1984. A Theoretical perspective on political risk. *Journal of International Business Studies*, 15(3): 123–143.

Teichova, A., & Cottrell, P. L. 1983. *International Business and Central Europe, 1918–1939*. Leicester: Leicester University Press.

Teichova, A., Levy-Leboyer, M., & Nussbaum, H. 1986. *Multinational Enterprise in Historical Perspective*. Cambridge: Cambridge University Press.

Thite, M., Wilkinson, A., & Budwar, P. 2016. *Emerging Indian Multinationals. Strategic Players in a Multipolar World*. Oxford: Oxford University Press.

Verbeke, A. 2003. The evolutionary view of the MNE and the future of internalization theory. *Journal of International Business Studies*, 34(6): 498–504.

Verbeke, A. 2009. *International Business Strategy*. Cambridge: Cambridge University Press.

Verbeke, A., Coeurderoy, R., & Matt, T. 2018. The future of international business research on corporate globalization that never was . . . . *Journal of International Business Studies*, 49(9): 1101–1112.

Verbeke, A., & Kano, L. 2015. The new internalization theory and multinational enterprises from emerging economies: A business history perspective. *Business History Review*, 89(3): 415–45.

Wilkins, M. 1970. *The Emergence of Multinational Enterprise: American Business Abroad from the Colonial Era to 1914*. Cambridge, MA: Harvard University Press.

Wilkins, M. 1974. *The Maturing of Multinational Enterprise: American Business Abroad from 1914 to 1970*. Cambridge, MA: Harvard University Press.

Wilkins, M. 1986. Defining a firm: History and theory. In P. Hertner & G. Jones (Eds.), *Multinationals: Theory and History*. Aldershot: Gower.

Wilkins, M. 1998. The free-standing company, 1870–1914: An important type of British foreign investment. *Economic History Review*, 41(2): 259–282.

Wilkins, M. 1998a. Multinational enterprises and economic change. *Australia Economic History Review*, 28(2): 103–134.

Wilkins, M. 1998b. The free-standing company revisited. In M. Wilkins & H. Schröter (Eds.). *The Free-Standing Company in the World Economy*. Oxford: Oxford University Press.

Wilkins, M. 1998c. Multinational corporations: An historical account. In Kozul-Wright R., & Rowthorn R. (Eds.) *Transnational Corporations and the Global Economy*. London: Palgrave Macmillan.

Wilkins, M. 2001. The history of multinational enterprise. In Rugman, A., & Brewer, T. L. (Eds). *The Oxford Handbook of International Business*. Oxford: Oxford University Press.

Wilkins, M. 2015. The history of multinationals: A 2015 view. *Business History Review*, 89(3): 405–14.

Wilkins, M. 2016. Business and borders: Capitalism. Speech at the American Historical Association (8 January).

Wilkins, M., & Hill, F. E. 1964/2011. *American Business Abroad—Ford in Six Continents*. New York: Cambridge University Press.

Wilkins, M., & Schröter, H. G. (Eds.) 1998. *The Free-Standing Company in the World Economy*. Oxford: Oxford University Press.

CHAPTER 3

....

CAPABILITY-BASED THEORIES OF MULTINATIONAL ENTERPRISE GROWTH

....

DAVID J. TEECE AND OLGA PETRICEVIC

INTRODUCTION

....

IN this chapter we argue that traditional approaches to modeling the growth of the multinational enterprise (MNE) that focus on costs and efficiencies are too narrow to adequately and comprehensively address what accounts for MNE heterogeneity and subsequently the financial performance, growth, and innovation of multinational firms. This is especially evident in today's era of deglobalization (Witt, 2019) and fragmentation of the economic global order (Petricevic & Teece, 2019), which are significantly amplifying the uncertainty associated with operating in international markets; this global fragmentation demands firm-level capabilities for achieving long-run competitive advantage and evolutionary fitness. Traditional, economic-based approaches to explaining the growth of the MNE, with their roots in the works of Coase (1937), Kindleberger (1969), Buckley and Casson (1976), or Williamson (1975) among others, focused on governance and growth via internationalization. Following this stream of work, the MNE was defined mainly in terms of its ownership of assets in international markets. Past work focused on the existence of (inefficient) markets, and in so doing, assumed away any significant role for managers, leadership, learning, differential technologies, entrepreneurship, capabilities, and other sources of cross-firm heterogeneity. However, firms are not only efficiency-seeking entities. The growth of the firm is dependent on the quality of its management and its ability to combine resources in ways that markets cannot (Ghoshal, Bartlett, & Moran, 1999; Penrose, 1959). Hence, traditional approaches that suppress entrepreneurship, assume equilibrium, mute managers, and ignore leadership cannot advance our understanding of the formation of firm-level competitive advantage and MNE growth (Teece, 2014).

With intellectual roots in explaining the internalization of knowledge-based, intangible advantages to overcome market failures (Hymer 1960/1976), and by leveraging Dunning's (1977) eclectic paradigm, internalization theory emerged as a generally accepted MNE theory. Several important contributions have developed from this intellectual lineage, highlighting internalization and the role of firm-specific advantages (FSAs) as a mechanism to explain MNE decisions for foreign market entry, such as how to serve the target markets, and to what extent the network of the MNE can transform and leverage firm advantages to compete on a rugged, international business (IB) landscape. As also noted in Chapter 1, one of the most important contributions of internalization theory in the context of contemporary theories of the MNE has been the explication of FSAs vis-à-vis country-specific advantages (CSAs) (Rugman, 1981). This was later extended to contrast non-location-bound FSAs with location-bound FSAs (Rugman & Verbeke, 1992) and ultimately advanced our thinking on the role of idiosyncratic FSA bundles (Rugman & Verbeke, 2003), which have the potential to evolve dynamically and facilitate MNE expansion and governance choices. The contribution of internalization theory, with its focus on unique bundling of firm resources and capabilities, is a powerful mechanism (and an important, early antecedent to the capability-based thinking) in considering how MNEs should leverage their resources or core competencies to facilitate international growth trajectories and options. Scholarly contributions rooted in internalization theory are therefore a compelling reminder that sole focus on pursuing efficiency at the expense of leveraging MNE-specific advantages and capabilities can stifle international growth opportunities (Buckley, 2016; Narula, 2014; Verbeke & Kano, 2016).

While foundational thinking has provided a robust theoretical infrastructure, today's global realities and the changing view of the MNE, require a more focused and explicit capability-based perspective. In particular, we posit that contemporary theories of the MNE require tools and frameworks that simultaneously account for the uncertainties that firms face in their external environments and complexities of competing internal, organizational alternatives, in order to understand the role of capabilities in managing both external and internal uncertainties. We present the dynamic capabilities approach to understanding MNE growth (Teece, 2007, 2014, 2018) as a multidisciplinary perspective on the nature of the MNE, and a tool to analyze the characteristics of individual firms and the sources of firm-level competitive advantage in the presence of changing external conditions. Dynamic capabilities encompass the distinct routines (and routine bundles) and culture that characterize an organization, but also the non-routine actions of entrepreneurial managers and expert talent that help organizations grow, adapt, and prosper. Dynamic capabilities are also embedded in "signature" organizational routines and processes rooted in an organization's unique history. A dynamic capabilities approach therefore supports a richer understanding of the distinctive characteristics of MNEs (Cantwell, 2014; Teece, 2014).

In developing our reasoning in support of capability-based thinking, we start by explaining the changing nature of the IB strategy landscape, as well as the evolving views about the nature of the MNE. Then, we present the core building blocks of capability-based thinking in managing the MNE growth. We conclude the chapter by offering some thoughts on how our work on capability-based thinking could be applied and examined in future empirical and theoretical scholarly efforts.

THE CHANGING NATURE OF THE IB LANDSCAPE

The increase in global interconnectedness accompanied by revolutionary technological developments significantly influenced the value-creating activities of MNEs in the last few decades. It led to an unprecedented, albeit unequally distributed, rise in cross-border investments, transfer and adoption of advanced technologies, diffusion of best managerial and industry practices, and improvements in firm-level governance to many parts of the world (Verbeke, Coeurderoy, & Matt, 2018). Technological developments also brought on the emergence of new players, such as "springboard" MNEs (Luo & Tung, 2018), "dragon" MNEs (Mathews, 2017), emerging-market MNEs (EMNEs) (Hennart, 2012; Ramamurti, 2012), and micro-MNEs (Dimitratos, Amorós, Etchebarne, & Felzensztein, 2014), all of which often challenge traditional conceptualizations of the role of firm-specific resources and capabilities in the decision to internationalize. Viewing the MNE growth through the traditional internalization lens typically suggests that firms undertaking foreign direct investment (FDI) activities exploit ownership advantages and other types of proprietary assets (Dunning, 2001; Hymer, 1960, 1976; Vernon, 1966), or idiosyncratic bundles of country-specific and firm-specific resources (Rugman & Verbeke, 2003) when implementing growth strategies in international markets. However, the growth strategies of the emerging "new players" often include non-traditional, non-market-based, and non-proprietary resources and capabilities (Bhaumik, Driffield, & Zhou, 2016), and may often even focus on resource acquisition (instead of leveraging) as the FDI motive (Wang, Hong, Kafouros, & Wright, 2012). Such behaviors contrast the traditional views of MNE growth via (1) *asset exploitation* and (2) *asset augmentation* (Narula & Dunning, 2000; Meyer, 2015).

Furthermore, the existing rules of global competition are increasingly evolving. We see the emergence of hypercompetition, next-generation competition, and multi-invention contexts (D'Aveni, 1994; Teece, 2012). At the same time, entirely new rules of global competition are being invented. Most notable are recent developments related to the "rise of the rest" (Amsden, 2001: 2), namely countries that once occupied the periphery of the global economic system, such as emerging or developing economies (Benito & Narula, 2007). Their rise and economic expansion, accompanied by the emergence of neo-techno nationalism, innovation mercantilism, and systemic, state-led interventionism (Petricevic & Teece, 2019; Nager, 2016), has led scholars to suggest that our traditional frameworks and approaches require rethinking and upgrading in the presence of these developments (see Hernandez & Guillén, 2018; Witt, 2019).

At the same time, the global economic order is increasingly becoming fragmented and bifurcated, while its underpinning structural characteristics are being reshaped (Lundan, 2018; Ozawa, 2019; Witt, 2019). This is not just presenting a change in the locus of economic power on a world stage (Kobrin, 2017). It is a change in the mechanisms and underlying norms and values that have, thus far, governed the global economic order and guided MNE activities and behavior. One notable phenomenon is the rise of the "rule of rulers" (Jannace & Tiffany, 2019) in the form of strategic interventions of some nation states (in particular China), with the goals of disrupting and tilting the economic and innovation trajectories on a global scale. Perhaps, to some extent, the governance of the global system has become an increasingly difficult to predict variable for the MNE's IB strategizing (Ozawa, 2019).

External developments are significantly transforming the IB environment and causing cascading effects on the ability of MNEs to develop and deploy their firm-specific resource and capability bundles to navigate the newly emerging structure(s) and norms of the global system. As a result, all companies (new, old, domestic, or multinational) likely face "deep uncertainties" and require quick adaptation to these complex and turbulent external environments (Teece, Peteraf, & Leih, 2016). MNEs need to understand how to carve growth trajectories under volatile, uncertain, complex, and ambiguous external, environmental conditions. In this era of structural and perpetual change, MNEs are required to re-evaluate their approaches for developing and upgrading the bundles of their resources and their dynamic capabilities for navigating this uncertain landscape. External pressures, as we discuss in the next section, are often coupled with an increasingly evolving view of the nature and the role of the MNE.

Contemporary Views of the MNE

As the dynamics underpinning the evolution of the IB system resemble characterizations of a "rugged" rather than "flat" business landscape (Ghemawat, 2003), the views of the nature of the MNE have also gradually shifted to portraying the MNE as "a gestalt par excellence—which is an entrepreneurial focal firm that seeks to capture co-created value by purposefully *engaging with* and *shaping the value creation and co-creation process* in its entirety at home and across borders" (Pitelis & Teece, 2018: 527). This view of the MNE suggests that internalization only partially explains the gestalt of the MNE. In addition to internalizing, MNEs also "*orchestrate* the global process of value and wealth creation and capture" (Pitelis & Teece, 2018: 527). MNEs have increasingly taken on the shape of an internally differentiated interorganizational network (Ghoshal & Bartlett, 1990) that encompasses subsidiaries, customers, suppliers, partners, regulators, and other ecosystem players. MNEs are also embedded in multiple types and dimensions of contexts (Asakawa, Park, Song, & Kim, 2018; Ferraris, 2014; Meyer, Mudambi, & Narula, 2011). Thus, orchestration and integration of ownership and location advantages or FSAs–CSAs (e.g., Dunning & Lundan, 2008; Narula, 2014; Rugman & Verbeke, 2003;

Pitelis & Teece, 2010, 2018) is a key foundation of any contemporary theory of the MNE. We argue that orchestration is an entrepreneurial function of market creation and cocreation that forms the basis for, and facilitates, an MNE's IB strategies.

This view of the MNE requires upgrading of theoretical lenses and frameworks to accommodate MNE capabilities for orchestrating increasingly complex global value chains (Gereffi, 2018) as well as global innovation activities (Parrilli, Nadvi, & Yeung, 2013), in addition to orchestrating the increasingly complex networks of its subsidiaries (Dellestrand & Kappen, 2012; Narula, 2014; Luo, 2005). The locus of advantage for an MNE therefore emerges from capabilities required to manage and orchestrate networks, platforms, clusters, and knowledge connectivity on a global scale (Alcácer, Cantwell, & Piscitello, 2016; Cano-Kollmann, Cantwell, Hannigan, Mudambi, & Song, 2016; Meyer, Mudambi, & Narula, 2011). Some contemporary portrayals of the MNE invoke images of the "global factory," that is, "a structure through which multinational enterprises *integrate* their global strategies through a combination of innovation, distribution and production of both goods and services" (Buckley, 2009: 131). Others suggest that "MNEs means *augmenting* existing or creating new advantages via *recombining* resources and capabilities *across networks* of foreign subsidiaries" (Matysiak, Rugman, & Bausch, 2018: 227). In essence, "[t]he modern MNE has to be a *'meta-integrator,'* able to leverage knowledge within and between the different constituent affiliates of its international network, which requires efficient internal markets and well-structured cross-border hierarchies" (Narula, 2017: 215). Thus, the modern MNE becomes the locus for creating and leveraging knowledge, resources, networks, and products/services and for capturing value from these orchestrated and integrated processes globally.

Emerging portrayals of the MNE, in turn, require a shift in the assumptions guiding our work. Specifically, these assumptions are shifting from the early views that markets exist (albeit inefficient) to the view that markets can be created or cocreated and that MNEs play a key role in this process (Pitelis & Teece, 2010; Teece, 2014). Furthermore, MNEs are agile and coevolve with the environments in which they operate and compete (Lundan & Li, 2019). Knowledge, learning, and (technological) innovation (Hutzschenreuter & Matt, 2017; Kogut & Zander, 1993) are the driving mechanisms facilitating this process. Ultimately, MNEs are profoundly heterogeneous in their abilities to navigate the treacherous IB terrain, which "is one of the most important lessons from history" (Jones, 2005: 289).

Given the changes in the external and internal environments of the MNE, and the foundational conceptual work on internalization theory, it emerges that capability-based approaches are central to developing the "theory of the MNE," instead of the MNE being a special case of the "theory of the firm" (Cantwell, 2014; Dunning & Lundan, 2008; Narula, 2014; Luo, 2000; Pitelis & Teece, 2018; Rugman & Verbeke, 2003; Tallman & Fladmoe-Lindquist, 2002; Teece, 2014/2019). Specifically, Teece (2014) has argued that "[b]oth governance and entrepreneurship/capability perspectives are needed to shed light on the nature of the MNE" (Teece, 2014: 9). In this vein, Narula and Verbeke (2015) later suggested that developments in the internalization theory, in fact, anticipated the dynamic capabilities approach. We will further illuminate the dynamic capabilities perspective and its use in IB strategy.

DYNAMIC CAPABILITIES AND MNE GROWTH

Around the same time as the advancements in internalization theory started to evolve in IB, strategic management scholars began to acknowledge and explicitly address the importance of dynamic processes, including the acquisition, development, and maintenance of differential bundles of resources, knowledge, and capabilities over time, to explain heterogeneity in firm performance and growth trajectories (e.g., Henderson & Cockburn, 1994; Kogut & Zander, 1992; Szulanski, 1996). The dynamic capability perspective emerged as the anchoring perspective, which refers to "the firm's ability to integrate, build and reconfigure internal and external competencies to address rapidly changing environments" (Teece, Pisano, & Shuen, 1997: 516). However, despite its intellectual proximity to the notion of FSAs in the context of the MNE, considerations such as how resources and capabilities are developed, how they are orchestrated and integrated within the firm, and how they are released have generally remained underexplored in the IB strategy literature.

The dynamic capabilities perspective adopts a process-oriented approach (and more recently, a configurational approach) with specific focus on achieving "evolutionary fitness" between the MNE and its external environment (Teece, 2007, 2014, 2018; Wilden, Devinney, & Dowling, 2016). Specifically, dynamic capabilities act as *a buffer* between firm resources and the changing external business environment, and as *an engine* that mobilizes and reconfigures bundles of organizational routines, resources, and assets, thereby maintaining the sustainability of the firm's competitive advantage, even under conditions of "deep uncertainty." Notably, Wu (2010) examined 253 Taiwanese firms facing highly volatile environments and found that firms possessing dynamic capabilities were able to more effectively enhance their competitive advantages in the presence of such uncertainty. Similarly, by studying large firms from four countries in Latin America, Cuervo-Cazurra, Ciravegna, Melgarejo, and Lopez (2018) found that firms that have developed uncertainty management capabilities at home are better able to navigate the host market internationalization challenges. The institutional diversity that MNEs have experienced fosters broader learning, stimulates more frequent search for new solutions, widens the repertoire of possible responses to new threats and opportunities, and promotes novel designs of global value chains, all of which impact the development of dynamic capabilities in MNEs (Cuervo-Cazurra et al., 2018; Lundan and Li, 2019). Dynamic capabilities emphasize the allocation, development, deployment, and renewal of assets and resources that are required for alignment of the MNE with its changing environments.

Indeed, the dynamic capabilities approach is building on the general premises of the resource-based view (RBV) of the firm and the idea of sustainable competitive advantage

(Barney, 1991). However, it differs from RBV on a number of dimensions. For example, the nature of rents in RBV is Ricardian (based on the premise of owning and controlling superior assets and resources), while the dynamic capabilities perspective highlights the Schumpeterian (i.e., entrepreneurial) rents, which flow from the innovation-based competition and "creative destruction," highlighting the firm's ability to reconfigure and transform itself and even, to some extent, shape its environment. Teece et al. (1997) and later Teece (2007, 2014, 2019) offer compelling arguments on how economic-based models (e.g., monopolistic approach, game-theoretic perspective, industrial organization models) fail to account for rents that are generated from adapting, learning, entrepreneurial actions, organizational heritage, and signature processes in reconfiguring organizational routines and assets to position the MNE to respond to shifting environments, and in doing so, to create long-run advantage and competitive flexibility. In particular, Luo (2000) emphasizes capability upgrading as an essential component to the evolutionary development of sustainable advantage and for creating new bundles of resources that foster MNE growth and expansion. By studying upgrading of capabilities in an technologically advanced subsidiary, after it had been acquired by an EMNE, He, Khan, and Shenkar (2018) demonstrate how the learning process underpinning the upgrading of capabilities is induced and shaped by firm strategies and characteristics.

Furthermore, while RBV focuses on the imitable resources, the dynamic capabilities perspective highlights the importance of inimitable processes, positions, paths, signature process, and organizational heritage (which we will elaborate on further). In contrast to the premise of the RBV related to resource picking in strategic factor markets, the dynamic capabilities perspective focuses on *capability building* (Makadok, 2001). This shifts the focus from exploitation (in RBV) to *exploration* (in dynamic capabilities); similar to the notion of MNEs augmenting existing and creating new advantages by dynamically recombining and leveraging non-location-bound FSAs, CSAs, and location-bound FSAs.

Building Blocks of the Dynamic Capabilities Perspective

Generally, dynamic capabilities constitute an organization's capacity "to purposefully create, extend, and modify its resource base" (Helfat et al., 2007: 4) by capturing its future ability "to perform a task in at least a minimally acceptable manner" (Helfat et al., 2007: 5). This distinction is clearly articulated in Winter's definition of "ordinary" or "zero-level" capabilities as the "how we earn a living now" capabilities, and "dynamic capabilities" as "those that operate to extend, modify or create ordinary capabilities" (2003: 992). Ordinary capabilities allow firms to achieve best practices and lend themselves to being measured and benchmarked, ultimately making them vulnerable to replication. There is a broad consensus in the literature that "dynamic" capabilities contrast with "ordinary" capabilities, with the former being concerned with the process of change, cocreation, and coevolution, which is idiosyncratic and entrepreneurial in nature. Following the example of the differential calculus, Collis (1994) illustrates the point that *dynamic* capabilities govern the *rate of change* of ordinary capabilities.

Specifically, "ordinary capabilities are about doing things right, whereas dynamic capabilities are about doing the right things, at the right time" (Teece, 2014: 23). By elaborating on "the right things," Teece (2014) identifies investments in new products, processes, and business models that are in alignment with the firm's external environments at home and abroad, and in a constant, dynamic state of calibration.

Others have suggested that dynamic capabilities are "second-order competencies" (Danneels, 2012: 43) or "regenerative capabilities" (Ambrosini, Bowman, & Collier, 2009), which create "flow" in the "stock" of organizational resources, and therefore enable the firm to engage in a process of Schumpeterian competition (Danneels, 2012). This is especially relevant for the MNEs operating in today's turbulent and uncertain environments, and facing bifurcated global governance, which resembles Schumpeter's observation that successful companies are required to stand on the ground that is crumbling beneath them (McCraw, 2007). As we argued earlier, the "ground" that MNEs stand on today is not only crumbling but is fundamentally being reshaped and has taken on new dimensions.

Hence, dynamic capabilities induce the ongoing variation among organizations with respect to "how well they perform an activity" (Helfat & Winter, 2011: 1244). Thus, dynamic capabilities enable aggregation and coordination of different types of *routines* and *routine bundles* (Parmigiani & Howard-Grenville, 2011; Winter, 2003). Di Stefano, Peteraf, and Verona (2014: 308) view a dynamic capability as an "organizational drivetrain" that relates, mobilizes, and deploys a complex root system of routines.

We explain that the building blocks of dynamic capabilities that enable this dynamic orchestration and deployment of a firm's reservoir of routines lie in the firm's *processes, positions and paths* (Teece et al., 1997). The *processes* include managerial and organizational processes, such as coordination and integration. The *positions* refer to the firm's current strategic posture, or its endowment of asset positions, such as technological assets, financial assets, reputational assets, structural assets, institutional assets, or organizational boundaries. The *paths* are strategic alternatives available to the firm, which can be in the form of path dependencies (i.e., the repertoire of routines that may constrain its future activities) or technological opportunities that may influence the rate and the direction of its future technological activities. Thus, dynamic capabilities "act simultaneously both as a constraint on and as an enabler of" an MNE's internationalization strategies and trajectories (Teece, 2014: 24).

Furthermore, Teece (2007) suggested that dynamic capabilities can be disaggregated into three distinct clusters of organizational capacities: (1) to *sense* and *shape* opportunities and threats, (2) to *seize* opportunities (and neutralize threats), and (3) to maintain competitiveness through enhancing, combining, protecting, and, when necessary, *reconfiguring* the business enterprise's intangible and tangible assets. Sensing is an inherently entrepreneurial activity that involves exploring technological opportunities, probing markets, and scanning the elements of the business ecosystem. Seizing is the process of acting upon identified opportunities, such as the implementation of business models to meet customer needs, shape markets and/or market outcomes, and capture value. Reconfiguration (or transformation) is the realignment of the organization's resources and assets and it draws on management leadership skills. The main argument is that the development and exercise of these three clusters of capacities lies at the core of the MNE's success (and failure). Hence, scholars have proposed that dynamic capabilities tend to enable an organization to sustain its "evolutionary fitness" (Helfat et al., 2007: 7) and "achieve new forms of competitive advantage" (Teece et al., 1997: 513). For MNEs operating in uncertain and dynamic IB environments, there is a need to evolve in order to sustain their competitiveness, but also an opportunity for the MNE to shape the environment in which it operates.

The element of dynamic capabilities that involves shaping (and not just adapting to) the environment is entrepreneurial in nature, and often requires *dynamic managerial capabilities* underpinned by human capital, social capital, and managerial cognition (Adner & Helfat, 2003; Helfat & Martin, 2015; Kor & Mesko, 2013). To identify and shape opportunities, firms must constantly scan, search, and explore across technological and geographical boundaries, both "local" and "distant" (March & Simon, 1958). Entrepreneurial managers (Augier & Teece, 2009) and entrepreneurial actions (Teece, 2012) are key facilitators of this process. Based on Helfat and Martin's (2015) review of empirical studies, managers vary greatly in their influence on organizational change and overall organizational performance.

For example, firms search by probing their environments for information and their discoveries facilitate changes in organizational routines and processes (Greve & Taylor, 2000). Managers allocate resources to search activities as a response to environmental changes and shape the configuration of routine clusters inducing heterogeneity across organizations in terms of their search routines (Vissa, Greve, & Chen, 2010). Seizing of identified opportunities requires proper resource allocation. Although this argument may seem intuitive, the process is far from being straightforward (Coen & Maritan, 2011). The managerial challenge is to balance firm endowment of non-location-bound FSAs, CSAs, and location-bound FSAs and organizational capabilities in order to determine when and under what conditions there is potential of reaching higher performance outcomes from investing in new versus existing FSAs and capability bundles, and how to establish global linkages for their transfer and allocation (Lorenzen & Mudambi, 2013).

Applying this thinking to the MNE, Teece (2014: 18) expands on the three clusters of processes and managerial orchestration explicated in his 2007 paper to specifically highlight:

(1) identification and assessment of opportunities at home and abroad (corresponding to sensing);
(2) mobilization of resources globally to address opportunities, and to capture value from doing so (corresponding to seizing); and
(3) continued renewal (corresponding to transforming).

Thus, dynamic capabilities for MNE growth rely on *"signature" processes* and *"signature" business models*, rooted in the MNE's organizational heritage and supported by organizational history, experience, culture, and creativity. While much of the existing literature has emphasized the leveraging, upgrading, and transforming of dynamic capabilities, recent studies have also started to demonstrate the explicit value of buffering and preserving of the signature processes, especially during internationalization (Arikan, Koparan, Arikan, & Shenkar, 2019).

Furthermore, the "evolutionary fitness" that the MNE achieves through its dynamic capabilities depends on "how well the dynamic capabilities of [that] organization match the *context* in which the organization operates" (Helfat et al., 2007: 7, emphasis added). This is especially relevant for MNEs that operate and cross different cultural, geographic, institutional, regional, subnational, or supranational contexts, and face different political regimes, regulatory structures, or social and cultural norms. By highlighting how integrating dynamic capabilities with internalization theory can generate further insight into the MNE's ability to achieve evolutionary fitness in cross-border activities, Matysiak et al. (2018: 244) suggest that: "the purpose of MNEs' sensing, seizing, and transforming is to achieve (ever new) resource–capability recombinations that confer competitive advantages in the form of non-location bound FSAs, country-specific advantages, and location-bound FSAs in dynamic industry and country environments." For example, the study by Li, Easterby-Smith, and Hong, (2019) found that dynamic capabilities of MNEs in high-velocity markets (emerging markets) rely extensively on combined knowledge from global and local "situation-specific" knowledge.

More recently, a configurational approach for conceptualizing dynamic capabilities has emerged (Wilden et al., 2016). It is increasingly being recognized that dynamic capabilities are configurations and interaction of many system elements, comprising of the community of organizations, institutions, individuals, customers, suppliers, complementors, regulatory authorities, standard-setting bodies, and subsidiaries, to name a few. These elements reside and interact across different levels in the dynamic capability development and deployment. Thus, Teece (2018) suggests that an *ecosystems* view of dynamic capabilities is required to properly account for dynamics embedded in this framework.

The building blocks of the dynamic capabilities perspective that have been discussed here suggest that the essence of the MNE's competitive advantage comes from its ability to develop, amalgamate, and astutely orchestrate entrepreneurial actions, and its signature processes rooted in its organizational heritage. We argue that dynamic capabilities are important because they can enable MNEs to adapt to, cocreate, and even shape, the changes in markets, technologies, and the general business environment.

APPLYING A DYNAMIC CAPABILITIES PERSPECTIVE FOR MNE GROWTH

Scholarly effort in IB strategy has been devoted to the development of more precise conceptualizations of dynamic capabilities (e.g., Al-Aali & Teece, 2014; Augier & Teece, 2007; Lessard, Teece & Leih, 2016; Luo, 2000; Pitelis & Teece, 2010; Prashantham & Floyd, 2012; Sapienza, Autio, George, & Zahra, 2006; Teece, 2014; Weerawardena, Mort,

Liesch, & Knight, 2007). The general observation that dynamic capabilities are "complex, structured, and multi-dimensional" (Winter, 2003: 992) continues to persist, which poses challenges to applying and empirically investigating their impact. Consequently, dynamic capabilities have remained impervious to measurement and observation (Grant & Verona, 2015). One way to make dynamic capabilities actionable is to make them empirically accessible.

So (how) can we measure dynamic capabilities? Dynamic capabilities have been conceptualized and portrayed as a collective construct. In general, collective constructs cannot be observed directly but, instead, their existence has to be inferred from more observable entities. Collective constructs are defined and conceptualized in terms of their structure and their function (Morgeson & Hofman, 1999). The structure of any given collective construct can be viewed as a series of interactions, interdependencies, or event cycles between its component parts. Their function refers to the causal outputs or effects. Consequently, we have been observing the causal output and effects of dynamic capabilities (e.g., Drnevich & Kriauciunas, 2011; Protogerou, Caloghirou, & Lioukas, 2012), which enabled us to gain some insight into their realized function (Fainschmidt, Pezeshkan, Frasier, Nair, & Markowski, 2016). For example, a recent meta-analysis by Fainschmidt et al. (2016) suggests that (higher-order) dynamic capabilities are more strongly related to firm performance (vis-à-vis lower-order ones), and that this relationship is stronger for firms in developing economies (providing additional support for the context-dependency characteristic of dynamic capabilities).

Recent studies have started to develop conceptual explanations of the more difficult to observe microfoundational, multidimensional, and multilevel nature of dynamic capabilities (Helfat & Peteraf, 2015; Hodgkinson & Healey, 2011; Teece, 2007; 2014; Salvato & Rerup, 2011). These developments suggest that "dynamic capabilities" constitute a broader "umbrella" concept under which diverse but interrelated components (Teece, 2007; Winter, 2003) and processes (Schreyögg & Kliesch-Eberl, 2007) are collected and configured (Wilden et al., 2016). Consequently, scholars have embarked on the quest to better identify the structural characteristics of the dynamic capabilities construct. For example, using data on Irish manufacturers' adaptation to an environmental regulation regime, Hilliard and Goldstein (2019) measure dynamic capability using widely observable search routines. Others are comparing the effects of reconfiguration and restructuring on firm performance in dynamic environments, finding that reconfiguration activities (comprised of adding, splitting, merging, transferring, or deleting of units inside the firm) achieves greater fit with dynamic environments than organizational restructuring of managerial/executive roles (Girod & Whittington, 2017).

However, the sources of dynamic capabilities may not only reside inside the firm (Teece, 2012). Instead, dynamic capabilities may in part co-evolve through interactions with ecosystem partners. The study by Giudici, Reinmoeller, and Ravasi (2018) found that dynamic capabilities can be cocreated relationally with other members of an innovation network. Notwithstanding the value of these more recent contributions to the dynamic capabilities literature, scholars continue to insist on the more systematic inquiry into how multiple components emerge within the firm and through that firm's interactions with the broader ecosystem to form the structure of the dynamic capabilities construct. These issues become especially salient when considering the variety of relational and boundary-spanning activities and the multiple IB contexts in which MNEs operate and compete.

As discussed earlier, dynamic capabilities induce variation among organizations respective to "how well they perform an activity" (Helfat & Winter, 2011: 1244). This raises interesting questions about the structural differences among different firms' dynamic capabilities for achieving the functional objective of growth and gaining or sustaining heterogeneous performance outcomes over time (Morgeson & Hofmann, 1999). Decomposing the higher-order collective phenomenon of dynamic capabilities into a set of smaller component parts (Teece, 2007) and across contexts (Johns, 2006) would make them more easily observable (Godfrey & Hill, 1995), measurable, and conducive for monitoring (Schreyögg & Kliesch-Eberl, 2007). Morgeson and Hofmann also note that "constructs with similar functions may have dissimilar structures" (1999: 255). The study by Petricevic and Verbeke (2019) constitutes an initial effort to decompose dynamic capabilities into structurally distinct subsets: two subsets being more macro-oriented (i.e. sensing and seizing opportunities within networks) and the other two more micro-oriented (i.e. sensing and seizing opportunities within specific alliances). They argue that each of these subsets has a different structure of underlying routine and firm-specific advantage bundles, which depends on the context (i.e., alliances vs. networks) in which these capacities are being deployed. They explore how these different subsets (independently and interdependently) drive the firm's overall effectiveness in sensing and seizing external opportunities for innovation. They further illustrate the point that context provides boundary conditions for dynamic capabilities (Helfat et al., 2007) and plays a large role in determining the structure of the collective construct (Johns, 2006; Morgeson & Hofmann, 1999). A study by Grøgaard, Colman, and Stensaker (2019) identified three clusters of recombination capabilities (i.e., legitimizing, leveraging, and launching capabilities), which underpin the MNE's ability to sense, seize, and develop its organizational flexibility. As MNEs operate in contexts that cross many boundaries, it will be critical for future studies to further conceptualize and operationalize the distinctive and interactive effects of different contextual variables on non-location-bound location and non-location-bound FSAs and dynamic capabilities.

Recent configurational and ecosystem views of dynamic capabilities (Teece, 2018; Wilden et al., 2016) require explicit considerations of systems of interactions and change over time (Bergh & Fairbank, 2002; Pettigrew, Woodman, & Cameron, 2001) in any future empirical approaches to operationalizing dynamic capabilities. The resulting, observable causal output of dynamic capability is more than just the sum of its interlinked routines (Schreyögg & Kliesch-Eberl, 2007). This would not only require more empirically sound adoption of multilevel modeling techniques (MLMs) (Peterson, Arregle & Martin, 2012) but also greater consideration of cross-level effects and incorporating more than just two levels into an MLM analysis (Vandenberg, 2020), in addition to adopting multipronged (or mixed method) approaches by combining quantitative and qualitative empirical techniques.

One approach that has been recently adopted in studying complex IB strategies and different configurations of variables is fuzzy-set Qualitative Comparative Analysis (fsQCA) (e.g., Li & Bathelt, 2019; Misangyi et al., 2017; Verbeke, Ciravegna, Lopez, & Kundu, 2019). This approach is particularly suitable for empirically analyzing dynamic capabilities as it enables configurational analysis of the causal relationships between a group of antecedent conditions and an outcome of interest (Fiss, 2011). Kent (2005: 226) argues that fsQCA "sits midway between exploratory and hypothesis-testing research." As such it bridges quantitative and qualitative examination and lends itself to a more nuanced analysis of the IB strategy phenomena (Aguilera-Caracuel, Fedriani, & Delgado-Márquez, 2014). One strength of the fsQCA is its ability to address causal complexity as it facilitates the evaluation of cases as configurations of conditions, rather than assessing the net effect of each variable on outcomes (Ragin, 2008). It enables CSAs identifying multiple causal recipes linked to a particular outcome, which is particularly relevant for studying MNEs' dynamic capabilities. An additional advantage of using fsQCA vis-à-vis traditional variance decomposition methods is its ability to handle small data samples (see Ragin, 2008 for more details).

Another approach to examining dynamic capabilities is the use of more sophisticated qualitative case study designs (Welch & Piekkari, 2017), ranging from greater leveraging of semi-structured interviews and observations in study design (Giudici et al., 2018; Heaton, Lewin & Teece, 2019) to extended case analyses (Daneels, 2012), historical longitudinal analysis (Leih & Teece, 2016; Grøgaard et al., 2019), or comparative case study methodology with purposeful sampling (Arikan et al., 2019). Case studies are generally defined as "an empirical inquiry that investigates a contemporary phenomenon within its real-life context; when the boundaries between phenomenon and context are not clearly evident; and in which multiple sources of evidence are used" (Yin, 1994: 13). One important merit of qualitative case studies lies in their capability of explaining complex connections between phenomena and their contexts (Dubois & Gadde, 2014). For example, purposeful sampling allows for selection of cases that best enhance understanding of the research phenomenon in contrast to cases selected to serve abstract theorizing. From an MNE's perspective, it is particularly relevant to develop a greater understanding of the context-dependency of dynamic capabilities, which carefully designed qualitative approaches would enable us to do generating more nuanced insights.

Taken together, the explication of diverse sets of building blocks of dynamic capabilities and their complex, configurational nature implies that serious, thoughtful, sophisticated, and innovative methodological reconsiderations are required to advance research on dynamic capabilities.

Concluding Remarks

In this chapter we have provided an overview of the dynamic capabilities framework as a starting point to examine success factors that undergird MNE growth trajectories when operating in structurally different host locations. Dynamic capabilities have heterodox, interdisciplinary, and eclectic foundations. As such, dynamic capabilities are "an overarching framework within which studies of firm behavior from a variety of perspectives can coexist under the broad umbrella of inquiry into how firms manage internal and external resources to build sustainable competitive advantages under deep uncertainty" Teece (2016: 213). Faced with pervasive deep uncertainties, distinct organizational capabilities will enable MNEs more than ever to achieve evolutionary fitness and, at least to some extent, shape their environment.

References

Adner, R., & Helfat, C. E. 2003. Corporate effects and dynamic managerial capabilities. *Strategic Management Journal*, 24(10): 1011–1025.

Aguilera-Caracuel, J., Fedriani, E. M., & Delgado-Márquez, B. L. 2014. Institutional distance among country influences and environmental performance standardization in multinational enterprises. *Journal of Business Research*, 67(11): 2385–2392.

Al-Aali, A., & Teece, D. J. 2014. International Entrepreneurship and the Theory of the (Long-Lived) International Firm: A Capabilities Perspective. *Entrepreneurship Theory and Practice*, 38(1): 95–116.

Alcácer, J., Cantwell, J., & Piscitello, L. 2016. Internationalization in the information age: A new era for places, firms, and international business networks? *Journal of International Business Studies*, 47(5): 499–512.

Ambrosini, V., Bowman, C., & Collier, N. 2009. Dynamic capabilities: An exploration of how firms renew their resource base. *British Journal of Management*, 20: S9–S24.

Amsden, A. H. 2001. *The Rise of "theR": Challenges to the West from Late-Industrializing Economies*. New York, NY: Oxford University Press.

Arikan, I., Koparan, I., Arikan, A. M., & Shenkar, O. 2019. Dynamic capabilities and internationalization of authentic firms: Role of heritage assets, administrative heritage, and signature processes. *Journal of International Business Studies*, 1–35.

Asakawa, K., Park, Y., Song, J., & Kim, S. J. 2018. Internal embeddedness, geographic distance, and global knowledge sourcing by overseas subsidiaries. *Journal of International Business Studies*, 49(6): 743–752.

Augier, M., & Teece, D. J. 2007. Dynamic capabilities and multinational enterprise: Penrosean insights and omissions. *Management International Review*, 47(2): 175–192.

Augier, M., & Teece, D. J. 2009. Dynamic capabilities and the role of managers in business strategy and economic performance. *Organization Science*, 20(2): 410–421.

Barney, J. 1991. Firm resources and sustained competitive advantage. *Journal of Management*, 17(1): 99–120.

Benito, G. R., & Narula, R. 2007. States and firms on the periphery: the challenges of a globalizing world. In G. R. Benito, R. Narula (Eds.), *Multinationals on the Periphery*. London: Palgrave Macmillan.

Bergh, D. D., & Fairbank, J. F. 2002. Measuring and testing change in strategic management research. *Strategic Management Journal*, 23(4): 359–366.

Bhaumik, S. K., Driffield, N., & Zhou, Y. 2016. Country-specific advantage, firm-specific advantage and multinationality–Sources of competitive advantage in emerging markets: Evidence from the electronics industry in China. *International Business Review*, 25(1): 165–176.

Buckley, P. J. 2009. The impact of the global factory on economic development. *Journal of World Business*, 44(2): 131–143.

Buckley, P. J. 2016. The contribution of internalisation theory to international business: New realities and unanswered questions. *Journal of World Business*, 51(1): 74–82.

Buckley, P. J., & Casson, M. C. 1976. *The Future of the Multinational Enterprise*. London: Palgrave Macmillan.

Cano-Kollmann, M., Cantwell, J., Hannigan, T. J., Mudambi, R., & Song, J. 2016. Knowledge connectivity: An agenda for innovation research in international business. *Journal of International Business Studies*, 47(3): 255–262.

Cantwell, J. 2014. Revisiting international business theory: A capabilities-based theory of the MNE. *Journal of International Business Studies*, 45(1): 1–7.

Coase, R. 1937. The nature of the firm. *Economica*, 4(16): 386–405.

Coen, C. A., & Maritan, C. A. 2011. Investing in capabilities: The dynamics of resource allocation. *Organization Science*, 22(1): 99–117.

Collis, D. J. 1994. Research note: how valuable are organizational capabilities? *Strategic Management Journal*, 15(S1): 143–152.

Cuervo-Cazurra, A., Ciravegna, L., Melgarejo, M., & Lopez, L. 2018. Home country uncertainty and the internationalization-performance relationship: Building an uncertainty management capability. *Journal of World Business*, 53(2): 209–221.

D'Aveni, R. A. 1994. *Hypercompetition: Managing the Dynamics of Strategic Maneuvering*. New York, NY: Free Press.

Danneels, E. 2012. Second-order competences and Schumpeterian rents. *Strategic Entrepreneurship Journal*, 6(1): 42–58.

Dellestrand, H., & Kappen, P. 2012. The effects of spatial and contextual factors on headquarters resource allocation to MNE subsidiaries. *Journal of International Business Studies*, 43(3): 219–243.

Di Stefano, G., Peteraf, M., & Verona, G. 2014. The organizational drivetrain: A road to integration of dynamic capabilities research. *Academy of Management Perspectives*, 28(4): 307–327.

Dimitratos, P., Amorós, J. E., Etchebarne, M. S., & Felzensztein, C. 2014. Micro-multinational or not? International entrepreneurship, networking and learning effects. *Journal of Business Research*, 67(5): 908–915.

Drnevich, P. L., & Kriauciunas, A. P. 2011. Clarifying the conditions and limits of the contributions of ordinary and dynamic capabilities to relative firm performance. *Strategic Management Journal*, 32(3), 254–279.

Dubois, A., & Gadde, L. E. 2014. "Systematic combining"—A decade later. *Journal of Business Research*, 67(6), 1277–1284.

Dunning, J. H. 1977. Trade, location of economic activity and the MNE: A search for an eclectic approach. In B. Ohlin, P. O. Hesselborn, & P. M. Wijkman (Eds.), *The International Allocation of Economic Activity*. London: Macmillan.

Dunning, J. H. 2001. The eclectic (OLI) paradigm of international production: past, present and future. *International Journal of The Economics of Business*, 8(2): 173–190.

Dunning, J. H., & Lundan, S. M. 2008. Institutions and the OLI paradigm of the multinational enterprise. *Asia Pacific Journal of Management*, 25(4): 573–593.

Fainshmidt, S., Pezeshkan, A., Frazier, M. L., Nair, A., & Markowski, E. (2016). Dynamic capabilities and organizational performance: A meta-analytic evaluation and extension. *Journal of Management Studies*, 53(8): 1348–1380.

Ferraris, A. 2014. Rethinking the literature on "multiple embeddedness" and subsidiary-specific advantages. *Multinational Business Review*, 22(1): 15–33.

Fiss, P. C. 2011. Building better causal theories: A fuzzy set approach to typologies in organization research. *Academy of Management Journal*, 54(2): 393–420.

Gereffi, G. 2018. *Global Value Chains and Development: Redefining the Contours of 21st-Century Capitalism*. Cambridge: Cambridge University Press.

Ghemawat, P. 2003. Semiglobalization and international business strategy. *Journal of International Business Studies*, 34(2): 138–152.

Ghoshal, S., & Bartlett, C. A. 1990. The multinational corporation as an interorganizational network. *Academy of Management Review*, 15(4): 603–626.

Ghoshal, S., Bartlett, C. A., & Moran, P. 1999. A new manifesto for management. *MIT Sloan Management Review*, 40(3): 9–20.

Girod, S. J. G., & Whittington, R. 2017. Reconfiguration, restructuring and firm performance: Dynamic capabilities and environmental dynamism. *Strategic Management Journal*, 38(5): 1121–1133.

Giudici, A., Reinmoeller, P. and Ravasi, D. 2018. Open-system orchestration as a relational source of sensing capabilities: Evidence from a venture association. *Academy of Management Journal*, 61(4): 1369–1402.

Godfrey, P. C., & Hill, C. W. 1995. The problem of unobservables in strategic management research. *Strategic Management Journal*, 16(7): 519–533.

Grant, R. M., & Verona, G. 2015. What's holding back empirical research into organizational capabilities? Remedies for common problems. *Strategic Organization*, 13(1): 61–74.

Greve, H. R., & Taylor, A. 2000. Innovations as catalysts for organizational change: Shifts in organizational cognition and search. *Administrative Science Quarterly*, 45(1): 54–80.

Grøgaard, B., Colman, H. L., & Stensaker, I. G. 2019. Legitimizing, leveraging, and launching: Developing dynamic capabilities in the MNE. *Journal of International Business Studies*, 1–21.

He, S., Khan, Z. and Shenkar, O. 2018. Subsidiary capability upgrading under emerging market acquirers. *Journal of World Business*, 53(2): 248–262.

Heaton, S., Lewin, D., & Teece, D. J. 2019. Managing campus entrepreneurship: Dynamic capabilities and university leadership. *Managerial and Decision Economics*, 41(6): 1126–1140.

Helfat, C. E., Finkelstein, S., Mitchell, W., Peteraf, M., Singh, H., Teece, D., & Winter, S.G. 2007. *Dynamic Capabilities: Understanding Strategic Change in Organizations*. New York, NY: John Wiley & Sons.

Helfat, C. E., & Martin, J. A. 2015. Dynamic managerial capabilities: Review and assessment of managerial impact on strategic change. *Journal of Management*, 41(5): 1281–1312.

Helfat, C. E., & Peteraf, M. A. 2015. Managerial cognitive capabilities and the microfoundations of dynamic capabilities. *Strategic Management Journal*, 36(6): 831–850.

Helfat, C. E., & Winter, S. G. 2011. Untangling dynamic and operational capabilities: Strategy for the (N) ever-changing world. *Strategic Management Journal*, 32(11): 1243–1250.

Henderson, R., & Cockburn, I. 1994. Measuring competence? Exploring firm effects in pharmaceutical research. *Strategic Management Journal*, 15(S1): 63–84.

Hennart, J. F. 2012. Emerging market multinationals and the theory of the multinational enterprise. *Global Strategy Journal*, 2(3): 168–187.

Hernandez, E., & Guillén, M. F. 2018. What's theoretically novel about emerging-market multinationals? Journal of International Business Studies, 49(1): 24–33.

Hilliard, R., & Goldstein, D. 2019. Identifying and measuring dynamic capability using search routines. *Strategic Organization*, 17(2): 210–240.

Hodgkinson, G. P., & Healey, M. P. 2011. Psychological foundations of dynamic capabilities: Reflexion and reflection in strategic management. *Strategic Management Journal*, 32(13): 1500–1516.

Hutzschenreuter, T., & Matt, T. 2017. MNE internationalization patterns, the roles of knowledge stocks, and the portfolio of MNE subsidiaries. *Journal of International Business Studies*, 48(9): 1131–1150.

Hymer, S. H. 1960/1976. *The International Operations of National Firms: A Study of Foreign Direct Investment*. Cambridge, MA: MIT Press.

Jannace, W., & Tiffany, P. 2019. A new world order: The rule or law, or the law of rulers? *Fordham International Law Journal*, 42(5): 1379–1417.

Johns, G. 2006. The essential impact of context on organizational behavior. *Academy of Management Review*, 31(2): 386–408.

Jones, G. 2005. *Multinationals and Global Capitalism: From the Nineteenth to the Twenty-First Century*. New York, NY: Oxford University Press.

Kent, R. A. 2005. Cases as configurations: Using combinatorial and fuzzy logic to analyze marketing data. *International Journal of Market Research*, 47(2): 205–28.

Kindleberger, C. P. 1969. *American Business Abroad: Six Lectures on Direct Investment*. New Haven, CT and London: Yale University Press.

Kobrin, S. J. 2017. Bricks and mortar in a borderless world: Globalization, the backlash, and the multinational enterprise. *Global Strategy Journal*, 7(2):159–171.

Kogut, B., & Zander, U. 1992. Knowledge of the firm, combinative capabilities, and the replication of technology. *Organization Science*, 3(3): 383–397.

Kogut, B., & Zander, U. 1993. Knowledge of the firm and the evolutionary theory of the multinational corporation. *Journal of International Business Studies*, 24(4): 625–645.

Kor, Y. Y., & Mesko, A. 2013. Dynamic managerial capabilities: Configuration and orchestration of top executives' capabilities and the firm's dominant logic. *Strategic Management Journal*, 34(2): 233–244.

Leih, S., & Teece, D. 2016. Campus leadership and the entrepreneurial university: A dynamic capabilities perspective. *Academy of Management Perspectives*, 30(2): 182–210.

Lessard, D., Teece, D. J., & Leih, S. 2016. The dynamic capabilities of Meta-multinationals. *Global Strategy Journal*, 6(3): 211–224.

Li, P., & Bathelt, H. 2019. Headquarters-subsidiary knowledge strategies at the cluster level. *Global Strategy Journal*, 10(3): 585–618.

Li, S., Easterby-Smith, M., & Hong, J. F. 2019. Towards an understanding of the nature of dynamic capabilities in high-velocity markets of China. *Journal of Business Research*, 97: 212–226.

Lorenzen, M., & Mudambi, R. 2013. Clusters, connectivity and catch-up: Bollywood and Bangalore in the global economy. *Journal of Economic Geography*, 13(3): 501–534.

Lundan, S. M. 2018. From the editor: Engaging international business scholars with public policy issues. *Journal of International Business Policy*, 1(1): 1–11.

Lundan, S. M., & Li, J. 2019. Adjusting to and learning from institutional diversity: Toward a capability-building perspective. *Journal of International Business Studies*, 50(1): 36–47.

Luo, Y. 2000. Dynamic capabilities in international expansion. *Journal of World Business*, 35(4): 355–378.

Luo, Y. 2005. Toward coopetition within a multinational enterprise: A perspective from foreign subsidiaries. *Journal of World Business*, 40(1): 71–90.

Luo, Y., & Tung, R. 2018. A general theory of springboard MNEs. *Journal of International Business Studies*, 49(2): 129–152.

Makadok, R. 2001. Toward a synthesis of the resource-based and dynamic-capability views of rent creation. *Strategic Management Journal*, 22(5): 387–401.

March, J. G., & Simon, H. A. 1958. *Organizations*. New York, NY: John Wiley & Sons.

Mathews, J. A. 2017. Dragon multinationals powered by linkage, leverage and learning: A review and development. *Asia Pacific Journal of Management*, 34(4): 769–775.

Matysiak, L., Rugman, A. M., & Bausch, A. 2018. Dynamic capabilities of multinational enterprises: the dominant logics behind sensing, seizing, and transforming matter! *Management International Review*, 58(2): 225–250.

McCraw, T. K. 2007. *Prophet of Innovation. Joseph Schumpeter and Creative Destruction*, Cambridge, MA: Harvard University Press.

Meyer, K. E. 2015. What is "strategic asset seeking FDI"? *Multinational Business Review*, 23(1): 57–66.

Meyer, K. E., Mudambi, R., & Narula, R. 2011. Multinational enterprises and local contexts: The opportunities and challenges of multiple embeddedness. *Journal of Management Studies*, 48(2): 235–252.

Misangyi, V. F., Greckhamer, T., Furnari, S., Fiss, P. C., Crilly, D., & Aguilera, R. 2017. Embracing causal complexity: The emergence of a neo-configurational perspective. *Journal of Management*, 43(1): 255–282.

Morgeson, F. P., & Hofmann, D. A. 1999. The structure and function of collective constructs: Implications for multilevel research and theory development. *Academy of Management Review*, 24(2): 249–265.

Nager, A. 2016. Calling out China's Mercantilism. *The International Economy*, 30(2): 62–64.

Narula, R. 2014. Exploring the paradox of competence-creating subsidiaries: balancing bandwidth and dispersion in MNEs. *Long Range Planning*, 47(1–2): 4–15.

Narula, R. 2017. Emerging market MNEs as meta-integrators: the importance of internal networks. *International Journal of Technology Management*, 74(1/2/3/4): 214–220.

Narula, R., & Dunning, J. H. 2000. Industrial development, globalization and multinational enterprises: new realities for developing countries. *Oxford Development Studies*, 28(2): 141–167.

Narula, R., & Verbeke, A. 2015. Making internalization theory good for practice: The essence of Alan Rugman's contributions to international business. *Journal of World Business*, 50(4): 612–622.

Ozawa, T. 2019. A note on Dani Rodrik, "Populism and the economics of globalization." *Journal of International Business Policy*, 2(2): 182–193.

Parmigiani, A., & Howard-Grenville, J. 2011. Routines revisited: Exploring the capabilities and practice perspectives. *Academy of Management Annals*, 5(1): 413–453.

Parrilli, M. D., Nadvi, K., & Yeung, H. W. C. 2013. Local and regional development in global value chains, production networks and innovation networks: A comparative review and the challenges for future research. *European Planning Studies*, 21(7): 967–988.

Penrose, E. T. 1959. *The Theory of the Growth of the Firm*. New York, NY: John Wiley & Sons.

Peterson, M. F., Arregle, J. L., & Martin, X. 2012. Multilevel models in international business research. *Journal of International Business Studies*, 43(5): 451–457.

Petricevic, O., & Teece, D. J. 2019. The structural reshaping of globalization: Implications for strategic sectors, profiting from innovation, and the multinational enterprise. *Journal of International Business Studies*, 50(9): 1487–1512.

Petricevic, O., & Verbeke, A. 2019. Unbundling dynamic capabilities for inter-organizational collaboration: The case of nanotechnology. *Cross Cultural & Strategic Management*, 26(3): 422–448.

Pettigrew, A. M., Woodman, R. W., & Cameron, K. S. 2001. Studying organizational change and development: Challenges for future research. *Academy of Management Journal*, 44(4): 697–713.

Pitelis, C. N., & Teece, D. J. 2010. Cross-border market co-creation, dynamic capabilities and the entrepreneurial theory of the multinational enterprise. *Industrial and Corporate Change*, 19(4): 1247–1270.

Pitelis, C. N., & Teece, D. J. 2018. The new MNE: "Orchestration" theory as envelope of "Internalisation" theory. *Management International Review*, 58(4): 523–539.

Prashantham, S., & Floyd, S. W. 2012. Routine microprocesses and capability learning in international new ventures. Journal of International Business Studies, 43(6), 544–562.

Protogerou, A., Caloghirou, Y., & Lioukas, S. 2012. Dynamic capabilities and their indirect impact on firm performance. *Industrial and Corporate Change*, 21(3): 615–647.

Ragin, C. C. 2008. *Redesigning Social Inquiry: Fuzzy Sets and Beyond*, Wiley Online Library.

Ramamurti, R. 2012. What is really different about emerging market multinationals? *Global Strategy Journal*, 2(1): 41–47.

Rugman, A. M. 1981. *Inside the Multinationals*. London: Croom Helm.

Rugman, A. M., & Verbeke, A. 1992. Multinational enterprise and national economic policy. In P. J. Buckley and M. Casson (Eds.), *Multinational Enterprises in the World Economy: Essays in Honour of John Dunning*. Aldershot: Edward Elgar.

Rugman, A. M., & Verbeke, A. 2003. Extending the theory of the multinational enterprise: internalization and strategic management perspectives. *Journal of International Business Studies*, 34(2): 125–137.

Salvato, C., & Rerup, C. 2011. Beyond collective entities: Multilevel research on organizational routines and capabilities. *Journal of Management*, 37(2): 468–490.

Sapienza, H. J., Autio, E., George, G., & Zahra, S. A. 2006. A capabilities perspective on the effects of early internationalization on firm survival and growth. *Academy of Management Review*, 31(4): 914–933.

Schreyögg, G., & Kliesch-Eberl, M. 2007. How dynamic can organizational capabilities be? Towards a dual-process model of capability dynamization. *Strategic Management Journal*, 28(9): 913–933.

Szulanski, G. 1996. Exploring internal stickiness: Impediments to the transfer of best practice within the firm. *Strategic Management Journal*, 17(S2): 27–43.

Tallman, S., & Fladmoe-Lindquist, K. 2002. Internationalization, globalization, and capability-based strategy. *California Management Review*, 45: 116–135.

Teece, D. J. 2007. Explicating Dynamic Capabilities: The Nature and Microfoundations of (Sustainable) Enterprise Performance. *Strategic Management Journal*, 28(13): 1319–1350.

Teece, D. J. 2012. Next-generation competition: New concepts for understanding how innovation shapes competition and policy in the digital economy. *Journal of Law, Economics and Policy*, 9 91): 97–118.

Teece, D. J. 2014. A dynamic capabilities-based entrepreneurial theory of the multinational enterprise. *Journal of International Business Studies*, 45(1): 8–37.

Teece, D. J. 2016. Dynamic capabilities and entrepreneurial management in large organizations: Toward a theory of the (entrepreneurial) firm. *European Economic Review*, 86: 202–216.

Teece, D. J. 2018. Dynamic capabilities as (workable) management systems theory. *Journal of Management & Organization*, 24(3): 359–368.

Teece, D. J. 2019. A capability theory of the firm: an economics and (strategic) management perspective. *New Zealand Economic Papers*, 53(1):1–43.

Teece, D. J., Peteraf, M., & Leih, S. 2016. Dynamic capabilities and organizational agility: Risk, uncertainty, and strategy in the innovation economy. *California Management Review*, 58(4): 13–35.

Teece D. J., Pisano G., & Shuen. A. 1997. Dynamic capabilities and strategic management. *Strategic Management Journal*, 18(7): 537–533.

Vandenberg, R. J. 2020. Multilevel models in international business research: A commentary. In L. Eden, B. Nielsen, & A. Verbeke (Eds.), *Research Methods in International Business*. London: Palgrave Macmillan.

Verbeke, A., Ciravegna, L., Lopez, L. E., & Kundu, S. K. 2019. Five configurations of opportunism in international market entry. *Journal of Management Studies*, 56(7): 1287–1313.

Verbeke, A., Coeurderoy, R., & Matt, T. 2018. The future of international business research on corporate globalization that never was. *Journal of International Business Studies*, 49(9): 1101–1112.

Verbeke, A., & Kano, L. 2016. An internalization theory perspective on the global and regional strategies of multinational enterprises. *Journal of World Business*, 51(1): 83–92.

Vernon, R. 1966. International trade and international investment in the product cycle. *Quarterly Journal of Economics*, 80(2):190–207.

Vissa, B., Greve, H. R., & Chen, W. R. 2010. Business group affiliation and firm search behavior in India: Responsiveness and focus of attention. *Organization Science*, 21(3): 696–712.

Wang, C., Hong, J., Kafouros, M., & Wright, M. 2012. Exploring the role of government involvement in outward FDI from emerging economies. *Journal of International Business Studies*, 43(7): 655–676.

Weerawardena, J., Mort, G. S., Liesch, P. W., & Knight, G. 2007. Conceptualizing accelerated internationalization in the born global firm: A dynamic capabilities perspective. *Journal of World Business*, 42(3): 294–306.

Welch, C., & Piekkari, R. 2017. How should we (not) judge the "quality" of qualitative research? A re-assessment of current evaluative criteria in International Business. *Journal of World Business*, 52(5): 714–725.

Wilden, R., Devinney, T. M., & Dowling, G. R. 2016. The architecture of dynamic capability research identifying the building blocks of a configurational approach. *Academy of Management Annals*, 10(1): 997–1076.

Williamson, O. E. 1975. *Markets and Hierarchies: Analysis and Antitrust Implications*. New York, NY: Free Press.

Winter, S. G. 2003. Understanding dynamic capabilities. *Strategic Management Journal*, 24(10): 991–995.

Witt, M. A. 2019. De-globalization: theories, predictions, and opportunities for international business research. *Journal of International Business Studies*, 50(7): 1053–1077.

Wu, L. Y. 2010. Applicability of the resource-based and dynamic-capability views under environmental volatility. *Journal of Business Research*, 63(1): 27–31.

Yin, R. K. 1994. *Case Study Research: Design and Methods* (2nd ed.). Newbury Park, CA: Sage Publications.

....

CHAPTER 4

LOCATION AND INTERNATIONAL STRATEGY FORMATION
A Research Agenda

....

RAM MUDAMBI

INTRODUCTION

....

LOCATION is one of the pillars of the classic OLI (ownership, location, and internalization) paradigm (Dunning, 1980), the broad tent that has provided an envelope for a great deal of theorizing for international business (IB) scholars. In the early decades of research, location was treated as subordinate to decisions around how to control international operations. At the end of the twentieth century, Dunning (1998) brought it back into the academic debate, and since that time, it has attracted increasing scholarly interest.[1]

The early IB literature categorized multinational enterprise (MNE) location drivers under two broad headings, namely: (1) market seeking and (2) asset seeking. These motivations for international operations may be related to the firm's value chain, as elaborated later in this chapter. The crux of this body of literature is that MNEs undertake foreign direct investment (FDI) either to sell output into foreign markets (i.e. market-seeking drivers) or to produce output to sell globally (i.e. asset-seeking drivers).

Market-seeking FDI, involving production for local sale, is the original form of FDI, and in the corporate variant recognizable to IB scholars dates back to at least the nineteenth century (notably, Jones, 1994). Much of the traditional activities of subsidiaries evolved within such units that were charged with adapting products developed in the home country to international host markets. Through the early twentieth century a great deal of market-seeking FDI occurred within the framework of global imperialism, that is, investments where the home country was the colonial metropole. As the two largest

---

[1] A pedagogical presentation of this analysis appears in Dunning & Lundan (2008). For recent discussions on "L" advantages see Mudambi et al. (2018) and Narula et al. (2019) among many others.

colonial powers, the United Kingdom and France were the prime home countries for FDI-related activities during this period.

IB activity suffered a major collapse in the period between World War I and the launch of the Bretton Woods system following World War II. Bretton Woods marks the beginning of the modern era of MNE location that continues to the current time. The major shifts in the institutional regimes of IB—that include the dismantling of the imperialist system and the collapse of the communist bloc—widened the arena within which MNE activities could be undertaken.[2] MNE market-seeking location strategies have continued to follow population and purchasing power.

Asset-seeking FDI distinguished between different types of assets (Dunning, 1980). The term "assets" is used here to be synonymous with "resources" in the sense of the resource-based view (see also Narula & Santangelo, 2012). IB strategies focusing on, for instance, natural resources, differed from those aimed at gaining access to human resources. These theoretical developments also emphasized the importance of recognizing whether assets (resources) were strategic, that is, crucial for the firm's market survival, or otherwise.

This chapter maps out the changes in the manner in which scholars theorize and study the MNE's location drivers and subsequent location choices. MNE location decisions are also important for economic development because MNE investment has long been a significant channel through which less developed countries can advance (Amuzegar, 1982; Barro, 1991; Kader, 1980). Despite the potential positive effects of FDI, which include local knowledge spillovers, we also point out circumstances in which FDI benefits may not be realized. This is particularly the case when MNE FDI gives rise to the emergence of a "dual" economy (Lewis, 1954; see also Narula, 2018) wherein its benefits fail to diffuse locally.

MNE location strategies are becoming increasingly important at present because the location options available to firms are greater, while the management and control of international operations in different locations is becoming increasingly complex (Awate & Mudambi, 2018; Kumaraswamy et al., 2012; Meyer et al., 2011; Mudambi et al., 2017; Narula, 2018). The move from natural resource-seeking to knowledge-seeking FDI, and the evolution in how MNEs orchestrate their GVCs, reflects this complexity. In the second part of the chapter, we zoom in on how these locational dynamics—driven by MNE strategies—have changed the global profile of many sectors beyond recognition in a time scale that is dramatically compressed by historical standards.

LOCATION DRIVERS: PAST AND PRESENT

The early IB literature took its cues from international economics (Kemp & Long, 1984), development economics (Bromley, 1985), and economic geography (Bridge, 2008), so that natural resources dominated the discussion of asset-seeking location (e.g., Behrman, 1981).

---

[2] Chapter 2 discusses these institutional shifts and their implications in more detail.

Based on the early successes of the Organization of Petroleum Exporting Countries (OPEC), and the increases in the per capita incomes of many of its members especially in the Middle East, many economists concluded that natural resources could be the basis for economic development (Kader, 1980). For instance, a notable study of the Kuwaiti economy points to the "growth of the domestic economy and the massive increase in the purchasing power of the Kuwaiti people" (Markandaya & Pemberton, 1985). Later, empirical studies cautioned that "human-capital variables indicate that the oil countries are typically less advanced than would be suggested by the level of per capital GDP" (Barro, 1991), so that oil wealth was recognized to be somewhat of a mixed blessing. By the twenty-first century, it was increasingly clear that even this assessment was optimistic. Natural resources were characterized as an impediment to development within two inter-related streams of literature: a narrower, more technical stream that has been labeled the "Dutch disease" (see Bruno & Sachs, 1982) and a broader body of work under the umbrella of the "natural resource curse" (see Wick & Bulte, 2009). This research acknowledges that the natural resource sector injects a stream of wealth into the local economy by attracting FDI from advanced-country MNEs. However, it demonstrates that these operations also impose severe allocative costs.

More specifically, the MNEs in the extractive sectors in developing countries tend to be significantly more advanced than the rest of the local economy. Hence, they are able to pay higher wages and thus attract the best human resources (as well as other market resources) away from other domestically focused, less technologically advanced sectors. This implies that the high productivity and wages of the extractive MNE sector are sustained at the cost of reducing productivity in the economy's non-tradable sectors. Further, the higher incomes of those working in, and with, the extractive MNEs drive up the local prices of most goods and services, ranging from food staples to housing, often immiserating those in the rest of the domestic economy. The "Dutch disease" label refers to this re-allocative effect of FDI location in the pursuit of natural resources.

Furthermore, asset-seeking FDI—such as that related to the pursuit of natural resources—is increasingly associated with the emergence of the "dual economy" (Narula, 2018). The dual economy captures the contradictions that may arise when a sector that is modern and high in knowledge intensity operates within an economy that is mainly comprised of traditional sectors whose knowledge intensity is low (Lewis, 1954). In such a setting, asset-seeking FDI undertaken to obtain natural resources has traditionally operated in "enclaves" with few linkages into the domestic economy (see Phelps et al., 2015). Hence, while the local operations of MNEs are often technologically sophisticated, knowledge spillovers tend to be very limited.

Thus, asset-seeking FDI in the pursuit of natural resources is expected to exacerbate local income inequality, but more importantly, it stunts the development potential of the rest of the economy. This is because the host economy's most valuable resources are locked up in enclaves and used by their current MNE tenants. These enclaves are mainly satellites of the advanced-economy home countries of the MNEs. This is a notable avenue through which the modern MNE shapes the characteristics of the locations in which it operates (Mudambi, Li et al., 2018). Development economists have long recognized that the contributions of FDI to development depend crucially on the extent of its "linkages" with the rest of the domestic economy (e.g., Dolan & Tomlin, 1980). The enclave nature of FDI in natural resource sectors precludes linkages to the domestic economy beyond direct employment and demand for low knowledge local inputs. Therefore, the benefits stemming from FDI in natural resource sectors may well be outweighed by the costs (Hirschman, 1977).

Examples of MNEs in extractive industries that operate enclave economies abound in the literature and are particularly plentiful in countries that have failed to develop. In Papua New Guinea, considerable "support is found for the proposition that such projects tend to perform as enclaves, having only weak direct links with host national economies" (Emerson, 1982). More recent evidence from Burkina Faso in Africa indicates that while MNEs in enclave economies have few economic and business linkages to the local economy, they are deeply enmeshed in the local political system (Cote & Korf, 2018). This combination is unlikely to be conducive to economic development.

In short, far from being a blessing, natural resources began to be seen as a curse. The possession of natural resources created an incentive structure within which foreign MNEs were encouraged to minimize local linkages and help create or reinforce local elites of rentiers rather than entrepreneurs. It is hardly surprising that not one of the countries that successfully developed their economies and joined the ranks of the advanced nations (mainly from East Asia) were natural resource rich. The natural resource curse represents an important research opportunity for IB scholars. It is certainly true that natural resource rich countries are a varied group and that some have felt the effects of the "curse" more seriously than others. Future research could focus on the country factors that ameliorate the effects of the curse with a view to designing policies that could turn it into a blessing.

Advanced Location Drivers

Empirical estimates of the root source of MNE value creation have traced it to knowledge-based intangibles—R&D knowledge and marketing knowledge (Morck & Yeung, 1991). The rising knowledge intensity of the world economy (King, 2004) along with the entry of aggressive emerging-economy MNEs (EMNEs) has increased the extent of innovation-based competition (Cano-Kollmann et al., 2016). While MNEs in extractive industries continue to make FDI decisions based on the location of natural resources, these sectors' shares of global and even emerging-economy gross domestic product (GDP) have shrunk to the point where they are no longer central to the agenda of economic development or even to the study of MNE strategy.

MNEs' search for knowledge assets now dominates their location strategies (Lewin et al., 2009). Leveraging these assets requires MNE subsidiaries to become locally embedded (Andersson et al., 2002; Ryan et al., 2018; Santangelo, 2012). By definition, this involves developing deep local linkages with the inevitable associated knowledge spillovers.[3] The rapid development that occurred within the class of countries that are now referred to as the "emerging economies" and the rise of peripheral countries in Western Europe, such as Ireland, have been often related to the operations of MNEs in knowledge intensive sectors.

The extant IB literature has paid a great deal of attention to knowledge linkages within the MNE at the level of the organization. Indeed, one of the most well-developed literatures within IB relates to knowledge flows within headquarter–subsidiary relationships. This literature is operationalized at the level of the MNE's subunits and studies what have been referred to as "organizational pipelines" (Bathelt et al., 2004). However, I would like to emphasize that a key aspect of MNE knowledge-based competition and location strategies is the role of the other generic linkage form, namely personal relationships that are operationalized at the level of the individual manager or employee (Lorenzen & Mudambi, 2013). This form of knowledge linkage within the MNE has received much less attention from IB scholars.

In their search for sophisticated human resources, advanced-economy MNEs are increasingly recognizing that they have a key linking asset within their organizational boundaries: their migrant employees, many of whom studied in advanced-economy universities before entering into employment in their adopted countries. MNEs are now tapping these high-skilled employees to return (often temporarily) to their original home countries to become the managers and decision makers of their competence-creating subsidiaries located there (Choudhury, 2015; Marino, Mudambi, Perri, & Scalera, 2020). In the process, they begin a symbiotic process that has been called "brain circulation" (Saxenian, 2005) and is now a key driver of the global innovation system.

A particularly fruitful avenue for future research would be to integrate Saxenian's (2005) theory of brain circulation with the role of migrants and diasporas in MNE knowledge processes (Barnard et al., 2019). This would require bringing together country-level migration policies on the one hand and the employment of migrants by MNEs on the other. Early work in this area has raised some exciting possibilities (Choudhury & Kim, 2019).

LOCATION IN A WORLD OF GLOBAL VALUE CHAINS

The rise of global value chains (GVCs) was one of the primary factors motivating scholars to begin integrating the IB strategy and economic geography literatures (see Beugelsdijk et al., 2010). This integration process has yielded many valuable insights and

---

[3] For an in-depth discussion on the likelihood and effects of MNE subsidiary knowledge spillovers, see Chapter 15.

advanced our understanding of the location dimension of IB strategy. At a very basic level, it has related location to the value chain, recognizing that market-seeking strategies are positioned at the downstream end, whereas asset-seeking strategies tend to be positioned further upstream (Mudambi, 2008). GVC analysis emphasizes that the key unit of analysis is no longer the product or the industry but the activity that the MNE conducts in an international location (Grossman & Rossi-Hansberg, 2008; Mudambi, 2008). As firms' value propositions have become increasingly "fine-sliced" over the last three decades or so, MNEs have new strategic options open to them. They are able to match activities with locations at a much more fine-grained level, resulting in a location footprint that brings their global value creation closer to its theoretical maximum (Mudambi & Puck, 2016). The world of GVCs has supplanted the Ricardian world so that locations are now matched with activities rather than goods or industries.

Advanced economies are home to the knowledge-intensive activities that appear at the two ends of the value chain—R&D at the upstream end and marketing at the downstream end. Emerging economies tend to compete for, and often win, the lower knowledge activities in the middle of the GVC. Orchestrating MNEs (typically based in advanced economies) tend to control high knowledge-based activities, and participatory firms (often located in emerging economies) tend to carry out low knowledge-based activities. However, as I will discuss in the next section on dynamics, this global "division of labor" is changing.

GVC Dynamics

This static location picture of the global outline of the GVC is only the *status quo ante*. GVCs are subject to continual dynamic forces that change their locational contours over time. Emerging economy firms that undertake low knowledge activities in the middle of the GVC view their operations as learning "labs." Virtually all of them have the strategic objective of moving up the value chain to higher knowledge, higher value activities. Moving up the value chain has been dubbed a "catch-up process" (Mudambi, 2008), a firm-level manifestation of an economy-wide phenomenon (Abramovitz, 1986). While some have expressed doubts about the feasibility of such catch-up strategies by emerging-market firms (Buckley, 2009), the empirical reality is that catch-up is occurring on a scale that is unprecedented in MNE history. The rise of EMNEs is testament to the reality of this upsurge (Awate et al., 2012; Cuervo-Cazurra, 2012; Kumaraswamy et al., 2012; Mudambi et al., 2017). Many EMNEs are now emerging as significant global players in a wide range of industries ranging from automobiles to telecommunications, to software and business consulting. An important consequence of working in GVCs is that many EMNEs are upgrading their business processes as well as their social processes, including workplace safety and workers' rights (Narula, 2019). The IB literature on catch-up processes has focused relatively less attention on this form of upgrading, so it is a fruitful avenue for future research.

Research within IB strategy now assesses both the activities sited in emerging economies by advanced-economy MNEs (Lamin & Livanis, 2013) as well as the activities sited in advanced economies by EMNEs (Awate et al., 2012, 2015). The former are processes whereby advanced-country MNEs "reach in" to tap knowledge resources in emerging markets. The latter are processes whereby EMNEs "reach out" to tap knowledge resources in advanced economies (e.g., Perri et al., 2017). Recent research on "reaching in" and "reaching out" processes has uncovered a surprising characteristic of the global innovation system: even the group of advanced countries is beginning to split into innovation leaders and innovation followers (Berman et al., 2020).

At present, there are conflicting findings in the literature regarding the concentration of value creation and the role of technology in this context. Florida (2005) presented data demonstrating that knowledge creation based on basic science and applied science (patents) is characterized by extreme concentration in knowledge hotspots, so that the world is "spiky." In contrast, Mithas and Whitaker (2007) studied employment and wages in the United States and found little evidence that information technology led to increased concentration. A potential resolution may be that Florida (2005) focuses on innovation and knowledge creation while Mithas and Whitaker (2007) analyze production. There is certainly evidence that the global knowledge creation landscape is becoming increasingly concentrated as the overall knowledge intensity of the global economy rises (King, 2004; Cano-Kollmann et al., 2016).

Economists have known since the time of Adam Smith that a key outcome of rising technology intensity is increased specialization. We have some evidence of such global specialization along two dimensions. First, global innovation systems are becoming increasingly anchored in a small set of locations and these locations are unique to every industry. Thus, Detroit, Stuttgart, and Munich have increased their innovation profiles within the global automotive industry (Hannigan et al., 2015); and Boston, San Francisco, and London have increased their innovation share in the global pharmaceutical industry (Gautam & Pan, 2016). Second, the leading innovative centers in every industry are becoming complementary rather than competitive with one another. In all global industries, MNEs are leading the charge to minimize duplication, so that knowledge hotspots specialize not only by industry but also by activity (Kao, 2009). In other words, knowledge hotspots are becoming increasingly complementary as MNEs focus particular specialized activities in particular locations. New York is becoming more complementary with London in financial services as the former has become more specialized in securitization while the latter has focused more deeply on international finance (Clark, 2002). The evidence for both these dimensions of industry specialization and activity specialization is far from complete. Therefore, both of these represent fruitful avenues for future research.

LOCATION WITHIN GLOBAL PRODUCTION
AND INNOVATION SYSTEMS

The international location strategies of advanced economy MNEs and EMNEs give rise to changing location profiles over time. Thus, the activities undertaken in emerging-economy locations such as Shanghai and Bangalore today are significantly different than activities undertaken in those same locations in the 1990s (Hannigan & Mudambi, 2015). The extent of knowledge intensive activities in many emerging economy locations now rivals that in even the apex knowledge hotspots in advanced economies. Thus, locations' positions within global production and innovation are constantly changing over time (Awate & Mudambi, 2018). This means that some areas move toward greater centrality, while others are pushed toward the margins.

I emphasize that the processes by which locations gain, maintain or lose centrality in these global systems is the outcome of MNE strategies. Mobile firms search for the requisite resources in immobile locations in the same manner in which bees seek to obtain nectar from flowers (Cano-Kollmann et al., 2016). Over time, spillovers from knowledge-intensive MNE activities result in some host locations becoming richer pools of knowledge and thus attractive for further investment. Since MNEs are network firms that integrate knowledge from geographically dispersed locations, technological change implies that their optimal portfolio of locations may also change over time. More specifically, we know that the manner in which an MNE alters its portfolio of locations depends, to a large extent, on its current location footprint (Hutzschenreuter et al., 2007; Hutzschenreuter et al., 2011). This is because its activities typically involve integrating complex flows of knowledge, goods, and services from a wide variety of geographical locations and budgetary and managerial bandwidth considerations mean that these can only be altered in a path-dependent manner (Meyer et al., 2011; Santangelo et al., 2016). Hence, embeddedness in a local context can become difficult. In fact, Chapter 21 provides a useful overview of the challenges associated with MNEs orchestrating their complex GVCs. The authors emphasize the conditions under which MNEs may struggle to orchestrate (and thus control) their GVC activities in a manner in which their interests and those of local firms are aligned.

These locational dynamics—driven by MNE strategies—have changed the global profile of many sectors beyond recognition in a timescale that is dramatically compressed by historical standards. As locations in emerging markets rapidly become more technologically advanced, they have, in some cases, supplanted locations in advanced economies, especially in mature industries. As a consequence, income levels in many emerging-market knowledge hotspots are approaching those in advanced economies.

The world of the twentieth century was generally one of local labor markets and local value chains wherein incomes were largely determined by geography—low knowledge individuals in high income countries enjoyed standards of living far above those of high-knowledge individuals in low-income countries. Falling spatial transaction costs (Mudambi et al., 2018) have led to the replacement of local value chains with GVCs, a process that has been facilitated by technology (mainly information technology). In the process, low-knowledge individuals in high-income countries have seen their living standards stagnate and even decline over the last few decades. These economic realignments have given rise to serious stresses and strains in global political systems. Indeed, they are one factor underpinning the current global rise of populism (Mudambi, 2018) and they are, at root, the outcome of MNE location strategies. Policy design to ameliorate and diffuse the current tensions that have arisen, especially in high-income advanced economies, may be one of the most important realms for future IB research.

References

Abramovitz, M. 1986. Catching up, forging ahead and falling behind. *Journal of Economic History*, 46(2): 385–406.

Amuzegar, J. 1982. Oil wealth: A very mixed blessing. *Foreign Affairs*, 60(4): 814–835.

Andersson, U., Forsgren, M., & Holm, U. 2002. The strategic impact of external networks: Subsidiary performance and competence development in the multinational corporation. *Strategic Management Journal*, 23(11): 979–996.

Awate, S., Larsen, M., & Mudambi, R. 2012. EMNE catch-up strategies in the wind turbine industry: Is there a trade-off between output and innovation capabilities? *Global Strategy Journal*, 2(3): 205–223.

Awate, S., Larsen, M., & Mudambi, R. 2015. Accessing vs. sourcing knowledge: A comparative study of R&D internationalization between emerging and advanced economy firms. *Journal of International Business Studies*, 46(1): 63–86.

Awate, S., & Mudambi, R. 2018. On the geography of emerging industry technological networks: The breadth and depth of patented innovations. *Journal of Economic Geography*, 18(2): 391–419.

Barnard, H., Deeds, D., Mudambi, R., & Vaaler, P. 2019. Migrants, migration policies, and international business research: Current trends and new directions. *Journal of International Business Policy*, 2(4): 275–288.

Barro, R. 1991. Economic growth in a cross section of countries. *Quarterly Journal of Economics*, 106(2): 407–443.

Bathelt, H., Malmberg, A., & Maskell, P. 2004. Clusters and knowledge: Local buzz, global pipelines and the process of knowledge creation. *Progress in Human Geography*, 28(1): 31–66.

Behrman, J. 1981. Transnational corporations in the New Economic Order. *Journal of International Business Studies*, 12(1): 29–42.

Berman, A., Marino, A., & Mudambi, R. 2020. The global connectivity of regional innovation systems in Italy: A core-periphery perspective. *Regional Studies*, 54(5): 677–691.

Beugelsdijk, S., McCann, P., & Mudambi, R. 2010. Place, space and organization: Economic geography and the multinational enterprise. *Journal of Economic Geography*, 10(4): 485–493.

Bridge, G. 2008. Global production networks and the extractive sector: Governing resource-based development. *Journal of Economic Geography*, 8(3): 389–419.

Bromley, D. 1985. Resources and economic development: An institutionalist perspective. *Journal of Economic Issues*, 19(3): 779–796.

Bruno, M., & Sachs, J. 1982. Energy and resource allocation: A dynamic model of the "Dutch disease." *Review of Economic Studies*, 49(5): 845–859.

Buckley, P. 2009. The impact of the global factory on economic development. *Journal of World Business*, 44(2): 131–143.

Cano-Kollmann, M., Cantwell, J., Hannigan, T. J., Mudambi, R., & Song, J. 2016. Knowledge connectivity: An agenda for innovation research in international business. *Journal of IB Studies*, 47(3): 255–262.

Choudhury, P. 2015. Return migration and geography of innovation in MNEs: A natural experiment of knowledge production by local workers reporting to return migrants. *Journal of Economic Geography*, 16(3): 585–610.

Choudhury, P., & Kim, D. 2019. The ethnic migrant inventor effect: Codification and recombination of knowledge across borders. *Strategic Management Journal*, 40(2): 203–229.

Clark, G. 2002. London in the European financial services industry: Locational advantage and product complementarities. *Journal of Economic Geography*, 2(4): 433–453.

Cote, M., & Korf, B. 2018. Making concessions: Extractive enclaves, entangled capitalism and regulative pluralism at the gold mining frontier in Burkina Faso. *World Development*, 101: 466–476.

Cuervo-Cazurra, A. 2012. Extending theory by analyzing development country multinational companies: Solving the Goldilocks debate. *Global Strategy Journal*, 2(3): 153–167.

Dolan, M., & Tomlin, B. 1980. First World–Third World linkages: External relations and economic development. *International Organization*, 34(1): 41–63.

Dunning, J. 1980. Toward an eclectic theory of international production: Some empirical tests. *Journal of IB Studies*, 19(1): 1–31.

Dunning, J. 1998. Location and the multinational firm: A neglected factor. *Journal of IB Studies*, 29(1): 45–66.

Dunning, J., & Lundan, S. 2008. *Multinational enterprises and the global economy*. Cheltenham: Edward Elgar.

Emerson, C. 1982. Mining enclaves and taxation. *World Development*, 10(7): 561–571.

Florida, R. 2005. The world is spiky. *The Atlantic Monthly*, October: 48–51.

Gautam, A., & Pan, X. 2016. The changing model of big pharma: Impact of key trends. *Drug Discovery Today*, 21(3): 379–384.

Grossman, G., & Rossi-Hansberg, E. 2008. Trading tasks: A simple theory of offshoring. *American Economic Review*, 98(5): 1978–1997.

Hannigan, T. J., Cano-Kollmann, M., & Mudambi, R. 2015. Thriving innovation amidst manufacturing decline: The Detroit auto cluster and the resilience of local knowledge production. *Industrial and Corporate Change*, 24(3): 613–634.

Hannigan, T. J., & Mudambi, R. 2015. Local R&D won't help you go global. *Harvard Business Review* online, June 25. Available at: https://www.researchgate.net/profile/Ram_Mudambi/publication/281462497_Local_RD_Won't_Help_You_Go_Global/links/55e9b0f208aeb6516264a000/Local-R-D-Wont-Help-You-Go-Global.pdf.

Hirschman, A. O. 1977. A generalized linkage approach to development with special reference to staples. *Economic Development and Cultural Change*, 25: 67–98.

Hutzschenreuter, T., Pedersen, T., & Volberda, H. 2007. The role of path dependency and managerial intentionality: A perspective on international business research. *Journal of International Business Studies*, 38(7): 1055–1068.

Hutzschenreuter, T., Voll, J., & Verbeke, A. 2011. The impact of added cultural distance and cultural diversity on international expansion patterns: A Penrosean perspective. *Journal of Management Studies*, 48(2): 305–329.

Jones, G. 1994. The making of global enterprise. *Business History*, 36(1): 1–17.

Kader, A. 1980. The contribution of oil exports to economic development: A study of the major oil exporting countries. *The American Economist*, 24(1): 46–51.

Kao, J. 2009. Tapping the world's innovation hotspots. *Harvard Business Review*, 87(3): 109–115.

Kemp, M., & Long, N. 1984. The role of natural resources in trade models. *Handbook of International Economics*, 1: 367–417.

King, D. 2004. The scientific impact of nations. *Nature*, 430: 311–316.

Kumaraswamy, A., Mudambi, R., Saranga, H., & Tripathy, A. 2012. Catch-up strategies in the Indian auto components industry: Domestic firms' responses to market liberalization. *Journal of International Business Studies*, 43(4): 368–395.

Lamin, A., & Livanis, G. 2013. Agglomeration, catch-up and the liability of foreignness in emerging economies. *Journal of International Business Studies*, 44(5): 579–606.

Lewin, A., Massini, S., & Peeters, C. 2009. Why are companies offshoring innovation? The emerging global race for talent. *Journal of International Business Studies*, 40(6): 901–925.

Lewis, W. A. 1954. Economic development with unlimited supplies of labor. *The Manchester School*, 22(2): 139–191.

Lorenzen, M., & Mudambi, R. 2013. Clusters, connectivity and catch-up: Bollywood and Bangalore in the global economy. *Journal of Economic Geography*, 13(3): 501–534.

Marino, A., Mudambi, R., Perri, A., & Scalera, V. 2020. Ties that bind: Ethnic inventors in multinational enterprises' knowledge integration and exploitation. Research Policy, online advance. doi.org/10.1016/j.respol.2020.103956.

Markandaya, A., & Pemberton, M. 1985. Medium-term planning in oil-based economies: A case study of Kuwait. *OPEC Review*, 9(4): 351–368.

Meyer, K., Mudambi, R., & Narula, R. 2011. Multinational enterprises and local contexts: The opportunities and challenges of multiple embeddedness. *Journal of Management Studies*, 48(2): 235–252.

Mithas, S., & Whitaker, J. 2007. Is the world flat or spiky? Information intensity, skills, and global service disaggregation. *Information Systems Research*, 18(3): 237–259.

Morck, R., & Yeung, B. 1991. Why investors value multinationality. *Journal of Business*, 64(2): 165–187.

Mudambi, R. 2008. Location, control and innovation in knowledge intensive industries. *Journal of Economic Geography*, 8(5): 699–725.

Mudambi, R. 2018. Knowledge-intensive intangibles, spatial transaction costs and the rise of populism. *Journal of International Business Policy*, 1(1–2): 44–52.

Mudambi, R., Li, L., Ma, X., Makino, S., Qian, G., & Boschma, R. 2018. Zoom in, zoom out: Geographical scale and multinational activity. *Journal of International Business Studies*, 49(8): 929–941.

Mudambi, R., Narula, R., & Santangelo, G. D. 2018. Location, collocation and innovation by multinational enterprises: A research agenda. *Industry and Innovation*, 25(3): 229–241.

Mudambi, R., & Puck, J. 2016. A global value chain analysis of the "regional strategy" perspective. *Journal of Management Studies*, 53(6): 1076–1093.

Mudambi, R. Saranga, H., & Schotter, A. 2017. Mastering the "make-in-India" challenge. *MIT Sloan Management Review*, 58(4): 59–66.

Narula, R. 2018. An extended dual economy model. *International Journal of Emerging Markets*, 13(3): 586–602.

Narula, R. 2019. Enforcing high labor standards within developing country value chains: consequences for MNEs and informal actors in a dual economy. *Journal of International Business Studies*, 50(9): 1622–1635.

Narula, R., Asmussen, C. G., Chi, T., & Kundu, S. K. 2019. Applying and advancing internalization theory: The multinational enterprise in the twenty-first century. *Journal of International Business Studies*, 50(8): 1231–1252.

Narula, R., & Santangelo, G. D. 2012. Location and collocation advantages in international innovation. *Multinational Business Review*, 20(1): 6–25.

Perri, A., Scalera, V., & Mudambi, R. 2017. What are the most promising conduits for knowledge inflows? Innovation networks in the Chinese pharmaceutical industry. *Industrial and Corporate Change*, 26(2): 333–355.

Phelps, N., Atienza, M., & Arias, M. 2015. Encore for enclave: The changing nature of the industry enclave with illustrations from the mining industry in Chile. *Economic Geography*, 91(2): 119–146.

Ryan, P., Giblin, M., Andersson, U., & Clancy, J., 2018. Subsidiary knowledge creation in co-evolving contexts. *International Business Review*, 27(5): 915–932.

Santangelo, G. D. 2012. The tension of information sharing: Effects on subsidiary embeddedness. *International Business Review*, 21(2): 180–195.

Santangelo, G. D., Meyer, K. E., & Jindra, B. 2016. MNE subsidiaries' outsourcing and insourcing of R&D: The role of local institutions. *Global Strategy Journal*, 6(4): 247–268.

Saxenian, A. 2005. From brain drain to brain circulation: Transnational communities and regional upgrading in India and China. *Studies in Comparative International Development*, 40(2): 35–61.

Wick, K., & Bulte, E. 2009. The curse of natural resources. *Annual Review of Resource Economics*, 1(1): 139–156.

PART II

CORE ISSUES IN MODERN INTERNATIONAL BUSINESS STRATEGY RESEARCH

CHAPTER 5

....

A REVIEW OF INTERNATIONAL ENTRY MODE RESEARCH

2007–2018

....

FLORIAN B. ZAPKAU, CHRISTIAN SCHWENS,
AND KEITH D. BROUTHERS

INTRODUCTION

....

AN international entry mode or mode of operation refers to the organizational structure a firm chooses when entering a foreign market (Brouthers & Hennart, 2007).[1] Most often, this research explores the initial entry into a new foreign market, whereas fewer studies investigate subsequent mode changes or performance implications of entry mode choices. Multinational enterprises (MNEs) can select among alternative modes ranging from non-equity (i.e. direct/indirect exporting, contractual agreements) to equity modes (i.e. joint ventures and wholly owned subsidiaries) (Pan & Tse, 2000). The former modes require no direct resource commitment to the foreign market (but also imply lower control over foreign market activities), whereas the latter require foreign direct investments (FDIs) (but facilitate greater control over the foreign operations) (Sanchez-Peinado & Pla-Barber, 2006). When engaging in FDI, MNEs have additional choices available to them such as engaging in international acquisitions or setting up new foreign entities themselves (i.e. greenfield establishments) (Klier, Schwens, Zapkau, & Dikova, 2017). The strategic choice of an initial international entry mode has considerable performance implications and is often difficult to reverse (Benito, 2005; Zhao, Ma, & Yang, 2017).

[1] Acknowledgment: The authors thank Julia Haaß and Yorick Waardenburg for their support with the data collection in this project.

Given the importance of the international mode decision, it is not surprising that a multitude of studies have investigated MNEs' choices from various theoretical lenses and with different methodologies over the last decades. Recent mode choice literature reviews (e.g. Laufs & Schwens, 2014; Schellenberg, Harker, & Jafari, 2018; Surdu & Mellahi, 2016) and meta-analyses (e.g. Giachetti, Manzi, & Colapinto, 2019; Morschett, Schramm-Klein, & Swoboda, 2010) have documented the advances in this research area. The growing maturity of the research field even prompted the question of whether further studies are still needed in view of the rather marginal theoretical and empirical progress achieved in recent years (Shaver, 2013). However, notable scholars continue to advocate that several entry-mode-related questions remain unanswered (Hennart & Slangen, 2015). In particular, disagreement still exists in crucial areas such as the differentiation of modes into conceptually distinct categories (e.g. Meyer, Wright, & Pruthi, 2009), the antecedents of international entry mode choices (Morschett et al., 2010), and their performance implications (Giachetti et al., 2019; Zhao et al., 2017). Undoubtedly, international entry mode choice research has made considerable progress. However, the large body of literature also causes a lack of clarity regarding the field's current state, making it difficult for researchers to identify relevant knowledge gaps and for practitioners to yield meaningful insights for evidence-based international entry mode choices.

In this chapter, we systematically review the current state of international entry mode research. Our point of departure is Brouthers and Hennart's (2007) review article, which summarized the—at that time—emerging field and presented promising areas for future research. Our objective is to take stock of the progress that has been achieved since 2007 and uncover areas where our understanding of the international entry mode decision requires additional research. To this end, we follow up on Brouthers and Hennart's (2007) suggested directions for future international entry mode research and investigate whether:

(1) prevalent theories (i.e. transaction cost economics (TCE), resource-based view (RBV), institutional theory, and Dunning's Ownership, Location, and Internalization (OLI) framework) have been deepened;

(2) new and different theories (such as a strategic decision-making perspective or stakeholder theory) have gained traction;

(3) new and different methodologies (such as experiments and simulations) have found their way into the field; and

(4) we have gained a better understanding of the link between entry mode choices and international performance.

This chapter makes an important contribution to knowledge because our systematic literature review clarifies the current state regarding several key areas in international entry mode research. In turn, this approach provides a better understanding of the antecedents, outcomes, and boundary conditions of MNEs' international entry mode choices against the backdrop of Brouthers and Hennart's (2007) review article.

We determine areas where progress has been made and where shortcomings still exist, hampering our understanding of this important strategic decision. We identify future directions of scholarly inquiry to map out topics where we, indeed, still need more entry mode studies.

Entry Mode Theory and Review Methodology

When Brouthers and Hennart (2007) reviewed the entry mode literature they focused on empirical work published in academic journals between 1980 and 2006 and identified over 120 studies. They noted that, starting with the mid-1990s, interest in entry mode research began to increase and the rate of publications on this topic continued to grow in the 2000s. Their review was a first attempt at summarizing this growing but disparate literature and providing a way forward. The authors identified important trends and made key recommendations on how to move the literature forward. These recommendations constitute the focus of our review.

The first gap Brouthers and Hennart (2007) identified was the need to deepen the understanding of existing theories. Their review identified four main theoretical approaches (TCE, RBV, institutional theory, and the OLI framework) predominantly used in entry mode research, while also recognizing that other theories were gaining scholarly interest. Brouthers and Hennart (2007) noted that despite the prevalence of studies drawing on one or more of these four theoretical approaches, our understanding and application of them could be improved. Many of the assumptions underlining TCE, RBV, institutional theory, or the OLI model had not been explored empirically and boundary conditions were not well understood. The other concern in this area had to do with firm strategy and how the strategy a firm is pursuing in a particular market (its motive for entry) influences the mode of operation it should adopt, since this strategy can influence the need for learning and the type of resources that are to be exploited. Differences in strategy might necessitate different theoretical lenses to explain mode choice.

Second, Brouthers and Hennart (2007) suggested that researchers might improve our understanding of mode choice through the application of new theoretical approaches and frameworks. More specifically, they recommended looking at the impact of individual managers, management teams, and intrafirm power and politics. Few studies had, at the time, included the influence of decision makers on the entry mode decision, hence, ignoring a potentially influential element of the decision process. Their recommendations were to examine managerial trust and risk propensity, the decision-making process, and the trade-offs managers face in internal negotiations. Further, they suggested that organizational culture may play a critical role in entry mode choices but that its role was, at the time, unexplored. The manner in which MNEs' objectives in international entry (profit maximizing vs. stakeholder goals) influence the "best" mode choice was of interest, but had also remained underexamined.

Third, Brouthers and Hennart (2007) zoomed in on the use of research methods. They noted that different research questions require different methods; for example, not all entry mode choice studies require samples from multiple home and host countries because the use of the wrong sample can restrict the ability of researchers to add to knowledge in a coherent manner. They proceeded to explaining that research exploring home country issues should seek to keep host countries constant by using only one host country (and vice versa). A similar logic can be applied to studies exploring technological know-how; in such studies, there is the need to restrict samples to single industries to determine if a specific technology has an influence on strategic decisions such as entry mode choices. Other methodological issues included in the 2007 review were:

- the need to use longitudinal data to explore what happens before or after a mode is established;
- the inclusion of measures of MNEs' willingness and ability to learn;
- and the use of experiments or simulations to investigate what occurs during the decision process.

The final gap identified by Brouthers and Hennart (2007) in the early literature was the link between theory-based mode choice and subsidiary performance. At the time of their review, Brouthers and Hennart (2007) only found a few studies looking at the relationship between mode choice and performance, of which only one (Brouthers, Brouthers, & Werner, 2003) accounted for endogeneity using the Heckman method outlined in studies such as Shaver (1998). The authors emphasized that more studies are needed to correct for endogeneity in the mode choice decision to determine if, and when, different international entry modes provide better performance outcomes to MNEs.

With these four recommended areas for future research as our starting point, we investigate the empirical entry mode research that has been published since the highly-cited 2007 review in an attempt to identify how new research has addressed the gaps identified by Brouthers and Hennart (2007) and added to our knowledge of international entry mode choices. We identified, appraised, and synthesized studies that met pre-defined inclusion criteria consistent with our research questions (Petticrew & Roberts, 2006; Tranfield, Denyer, & Smart, 2003). To ensure replicability, we established a systematic stepwise procedure consisting of: (1) definition of article inclusion criteria, (2) article search, and (3) article appraisal. Two research assistants supported us in searching relevant entry mode studies.

To be eligible for our review, articles were required to meet the following inclusion criteria. First, consistent with Brouthers and Hennart (2007), articles had to examine the antecedents and/or performance implications of a firm's decision on the mode of operation when entering a foreign market (i.e. the international entry mode choice). Regarding equity entry modes, our review focuses only on the ownership decision (i.e. foreign market entries with partial or full ownership) and excludes articles on the establishment mode choice (i.e. the choice between setting up a greenfield or the acquisition of an existing firm abroad) since a number of current reviews already look at this topic (Dikova & Brouthers, 2016; Klier et al., 2017). Second, articles had to be published between 2007 and 2018 (inclusive) to be eligible for our review. Third, we considered only articles in peer-reviewed journals, as they provide more validated knowledge and have fewer restrictions in terms of article availability (Podsakoff, MacKenzie, Bachrach, & Podsakoff, 2005) and excluded entry mode studies published in books or book chapters (e.g. Meyer & Wang, 2015), conference presentations and proceedings, working papers, or dissertations. However, we included articles from all available English language peer-reviewed journals, not only from top-tier publication outlets. Fourth, as per Brouthers and Hennart (2007), we considered only quantitative empirical articles for our review, as such work allows for a summative assessment facilitating integration into a comparable body of research (Petticrew & Roberts, 2006). In turn, we excluded conceptual papers (e.g. Hennart & Slangen, 2015) and papers relying on qualitative data to address international entry mode issues (e.g. Kontinen & Ojala, 2011), even though these papers might provide new and interesting insights. Fifth, relevant articles had to consider the international entry mode choice as part of their theoretical framework (and not merely e.g. as a control variable). Sixth, we considered only articles that analyzed the international entry mode choice at the firm level.

In the next step, we performed a keyword search on Google Scholar and ABI Inform (ProQuest) using search terms such as: *market entry mode, entry mode choice, international entry mode, non-equity mode, equity mode*, and combinations thereof. This keyword search yielded 419 potentially relevant articles. Then we searched the literature sections of prior review articles (e.g. Laufs & Schwens, 2014; Schellenberg et al., 2018) and meta-analyses (Giachetti et al., 2019; Morschett et al., 2010; Zhao et al., 2017) published since 2007. This step provided another sixty-four articles. Our initial literature search therefore yielded 483 potentially eligible articles published between 2007 and 2018.

After careful appraisal of these articles, the authors decided whether to include or exclude each article based on the abovementioned inclusion criteria. A total of 138 articles on international entry mode choices were included in our final review sample.

Progress Since 2007

Our review covered a wide range of journal outlets (Table 5.1). Of the 138 articles identified, an increasing number focused on small and medium-sized enterprises (SMEs) (compared with the 2007 review): thirty focused exclusively on SMEs, twenty-eight on large MNEs, and twenty-two utilized combined samples of large and small firms, with the remaining studies being less explicit about the type of sampled firms. A wide range of industries have been included in these studies namely general manufacturing (twenty-four studies), services (three studies), and combined samples with both manufacturing and

Table 5.1 Top journals publishing entry mode research (2007–2018)

Journal	Number of articles
International Business Review	23
Journal of International Business Studies	12
Journal of World Business	10
Management International Review	9
International Marketing Review	6
Journal of International Management	4
Journal of Business Research	3
Journal of International Marketing	3
British Journal of Management	2
Journal of Management	2
Journal of Management Studies	2
Strategic Management Journal	2
Total number of articles	**78 (out of 138)**

Note: Journals with at least two relevant articles.

service firms (eighty-three studies). Brouthers and Hennart (2007) noted that most studies examined the choice between wholly owned subsidiaries and joint ventures although sixteen different mode types had been considered overall. The choice between shared and full ownership remains the most studied entry mode decision, with around half of the studies in our sample examining what motivates MNEs to choose between joint ventures and wholly owned subsidiaries.

The first issue identified in Brouthers and Hennart (2007) focused on deepening our understanding of existing theoretical approaches. Although many of the papers we reviewed utilized the same four theories/frameworks (see Table 5.2) as in the original review (i.e. TCE, RBV, institutional theory, and Dunning's OLI), we found that there is now comparatively more emphasis on institutional theory and the RBV and less theoretical development building on the OLI framework. TCE continues to be the most prevalent theoretical framework in international entry mode research. Only few studies (e.g. Dadzie, Owusu, Amoako, & Aklamanu, 2018; Liang, Musteen, & Datta, 2009; Sanchez-Peinado, Pla-Barber, & Hébert, 2007) differentiate among MNE strategies by examining their motivations—market-seeking versus resource-seeking—and how these motivations subsequently influence entry mode choices.

Some scholars seek to advance our understanding of existing theories by identifying and testing moderators and how these may influence well-established relationships. For those using the RBV, progress has been made in several ways. For example, Brouthers, Brouthers, and Werner (2008b) explore how institutional distance increases/decreases the value of resource-based advantages as firms internationalize. Chiao, Lo, and Yu (2010) investigate how perceived institutional differences influence the relationship between RBV-related factors and entry mode choice for emerging market firms. Dikova and Van Witteloostuijn (2007) use TCE to look at both the establishment and entry

Table 5.2 Traditional and new theoretical perspectives used in entry mode research

Theoretical perspective	Brouthers & Hennart (2007)	Our review (2007–2018)
Traditional perspectives		
Transaction cost theory	48	45
Dunning's OLI framework	19	7
RBV	10	21
Institutional theory	10	30
Cultural and other distances	15	19
New perspectives		
Agency/upper echelons theory		6
Family firms (socio-emotional wealth)		8
Network theory/social capital		7
Organizational learning		9
Real options theory		3

Note: Some articles employed more than one theory.

mode choice as a sequential decision process. Maekelburger, Schwens, and Kabst (2012) explore the use of knowledge safeguards (experience, networks, and imitation) and institutional safeguards (property rights protection and cultural proximity) as a means to protect specific assets. Kuo, Kao, Chang, and Chiu (2012) investigate how transaction costs influence family and non-family firms differently. In the same vein, proponents of institutional theory have looked for nuances in their analysis of the relationship between institutions and entry mode choice. Notably, Hernández and Nieto (2015) study the direction and magnitude of institutional differences on mode choice. Meyer, Ding, Li, and Zhang (2014) explore how state ownership influences an MNE's reaction to institutional pressures in a way that differs from privately owned firms.

The second main area recommended to researchers was in the application of new theories. Brouthers and Hennart (2007) suggested, for example, that applying theoretical approaches such as upper echelons theory and organizational culture frameworks might lead to new insights. As noted in Table 5.2, while many of the same theories are still being used, some new theoretical approaches have also been explored by entry mode researchers; even so, organizational culture frameworks have yet to be considered. With regards to the influence of decision makers, Datta, Musteen, and Herrmann (2009) and later Lai, Chen, and Chang (2012) build on agency theory to look at the influence of the board of directors (characteristics) on entry mode choice. Nielsen and Nielsen (2011) explore top management team characteristics using upper echelons theory, while Pinho (2007), Xie (2014), and Laufs, Bembom, and Schwens (2016) draw on insights from upper echelons theory to study chief executive officer (CEO) characteristics and mode choice.

Other newly introduced theories include socio-emotional wealth, organizational learning, network theory, and real options theory. Several scholars use arguments from socio-emotional wealth theory primarily to explore international entry mode choices of family firms (e.g. Kao & Kuo, 2017; Kuo et al., 2012; Pinho, 2007; Pongelli, Caroli, & Cucculelli, 2016; Yamanoi & Asaba, 2018). Organizational learning theory was introduced to gain a greater understanding of how past actions (especially mode decisions) impact future mode choices (e.g. Schwens, Zapkau, Brouthers, & Hollender, 2018; Swoboda, Elsner, & Olejnik, 2015). Network theory (e.g. Filatotchev, Strange, Piesse, & Lien, 2007; Maekelburger et al., 2012; Rhee, 2008) has been used to improve our understanding of managerial connections with others outside the firm and how these connections influence mode choice. Finally, real options theory (e.g. Brouthers, Brouthers, & Werner, 2008a; Cuypers & Martin, 2010) was introduced as a theoretical perspective to deal with aspects of uncertainty explored without theory in older mode studies identified by Brouthers and Hennart (2007).

Applying new methodologies was also a key recommendation in Brouthers and Hennart (2007). Experiments or simulations can be used to manipulate different variables to help uncover the cognitive trade-offs managers face when considering mode choices. Longitudinal data can be used to determine what happens before and after mode selection. However, we could identify only a few studies using experiments or simulations to explore mode choice (e.g. Kraus, Ambos, Eggers, & Cesinger, 2015). Our review also indicates that very few studies have looked at longitudinal data and initial mode choice (Chen & Chang, 2011; Paul & Wooster, 2008). Other studies like Puck, Holtbrügge, and Mohr (2009) have chosen to explore mode changes with single surveys that account for different points in time. Brouthers and Hennart (2007) championed the use of only one home or host country when exploring country effects; in our review we found that well over half the studies appeared to heed this advice (see Table 5.3). Specifically, fifteen studies focused on one home and one host country (especially Taiwan–China). Another eighteen studies used a single host country but multiple home countries (the most popular host country being China). Many studies (i.e. seventy-four studies) included only one home country (the most popular home country being Spain) but multiple host countries. One critical issue with many of these studies is that they still use "distance" measures to explore institutional differences between countries even though with a single country focus such measures have significant shortcomings (Brouthers et al., 2016).

Finally, when Brouthers and Hennart (2007) reviewed existing mode choice research there were few studies looking at the performance implications of using theoretically selected modes. In the meantime, new research on the performance implications of different mode choices has been published, which is also reflected in two recent meta-analyses on this topic (Giachetti et al., 2019; Zhao et al., 2017). In total, our review found over twenty new primary studies exploring performance issues that overall yield mixed insights. Only one new study examined mode survival (Papyrina, 2007). Studies like Ogasavara and Hoshino (2007) and others (e.g. Hollender, Zapkau, & Schwens, 2017; Johnson & Tellis, 2008; Morresi & Pezzi, 2011; Ripollés & Blesa, 2012) compare performance (or stock market reactions) between different types of modes and/or ownership structures, but do not account for the endogeneity of mode choice. In contrast, very few

Table 5.3 Home and host countries included in the reviewed studies

	Single host country	Multiple host countries
Single home country	Total: 15 studies of which Taiwan v. China (6) Japan v. USA (2) China v. Germany (2) Japan v. China Japan v. Brazil USA v. Brazil Sweden v. Germany Italy v. China	Total: 74 studies of which Spain (18) China (12) USA (10) Germany (9) Taiwan (6) Japan (5) Italy (5) Finland (3)
Multiple home countries	Total: 18 studies of which China (6) Korea (2) Turkey (2) Ghana Italy Mexico Mongolia Norway Russia UK USA	Total: 26 studies

studies (e.g. Brouthers et al., 2008a; Brouthers et al., 2008b; Kim & Gray, 2008) incorporate an alignment perspective. Building on the concept of mode fit, this last set of research accounts for endogeneity by looking at the alignment between theoretically predicted modes and the selected mode of operation.

Deepening Prevalent Theories

Our review revealed that the literature made some progress toward a more fine-grained understanding of the boundary conditions under which prevalent theories like TCE or RBV help explain international entry mode choice. Particularly notable are those studies that seek to combine knowledge from different theoretical approaches to deepen our understanding of the boundary conditions involved in the mode choice decision. Yet, based on our review, we find that more work is needed to deepen prevalent theories.

Few studies examine the underlying assumptions behind these main theories or test complete theories. TCE studies, for example, often fail to test the relationship between asset specificity and uncertainty despite the fact that Williamson clearly notes that opportunism (a main assumption in this theory) only comes into play when dealing with high asset specificity in the presence of uncertainty (Williamson, 1975). Even basic issues around what constitutes asset specificity have not been explored. Williamson (1998) suggests that there are six forms of asset specificity (physical assets, human assets, site specificity, dedicated assets, brand name capital, and temporal specificity), but most studies only consider physical specificity. The measurements of these variables are also under question; a notable example is that the most commonly used asset specificity measure—a firm's R&D ratio—does not actually reveal whether the technology used in a certain country is highly asset specific or not. We have similar concerns with other perspectives like the RBV where, again, the R&D ratio is often used to measure firm-specific resources, or institutional theory where culture (or cultural distance) is used to measure the cognitive pillar of the institutional environment. These measurement issues limit our ability to understand entry mode decisions and they need to be resolved to advance the research agenda.

We encourage future research to work on making further improvements on (1) the measures we use in these key theories, (2) testing the underlying assumptions behind these theories, and (3) exploring the boundary conditions of these theories by combining them with other theoretical perspectives. More specifically, when it comes to the measurements used, it is important that future research works on developing new, more accurate, measures instead of relying on past (and often weak) constructs. The development of new measures often entails a rethink of basic ideas and enables a better understanding of the assumptions underlying a theory. As has already been mentioned, scholars using TCE might start by using improved measures of asset specificity (e.g. by gathering direct measures from managers or by measuring asset specificity at the foreign subsidiary level) and examining the different forms of asset specificity beyond physical asset specificity. Firms often employ different types of asset specificity when expanding abroad and with few exceptions these other forms have been largely ignored.

To address issues dealing with the underlying theoretical assumptions, one way forward would be to study the motive or strategy behind an international entry. The four main theories are based on the idea of market-seeking activities of foreign investors. Yet often, international entry is undertaken for other reasons like resource acquisition, low cost production/procurement, or tax/financial benefits. These different motives will influence not only which theoretical lenses should be applied but also how the variables discussed in the theory would influence mode choice. Lack of understanding of the motive of entry might explain the mixed results obtained when applying the same theory with different categories of firms. Since most studies do not explicitly discuss the expansion motive (or measure it), it is difficult to determine how TCE, RBV, or institutional factors should be regarded.

Finally, when exploring theoretical boundaries, researchers need to think carefully about the assumptions underlying each theory and how/why these assumptions might change as the firm internationalizes or moves from one foreign location to another.

Here, research may benefit by introducing theoretical approaches like social network theory along with institutional theory because social networks might help firms overcome some of the uncertainties created by institutional distance. Firms with greater (or better) networks in the target market or region might have an advantage over firms without such network members. This is consistent with past research that shows how network membership impacts internationalization decisions (Zimmerman, Barsky, & Brouthers, 2009). Scholars may also combine the dynamic capabilities perspective with the RBV, since dynamic capabilities are the capabilities a firm has that allow it to change its routines and processes; this is relevant here because internationalization strategies often require MNEs to change in order to remain successful post entry.

New Theories

Our literature review revealed that some progress has been made by applying new theoretical lenses to explain mode choice. In this regard, studies seem to have taken up the call by Brouthers and Hennart (2007) to put the decision maker and the top management team into the center of their examination of mode choice by drawing on, for example, upper echelons and agency theories. Given that it is individuals who ultimately make the strategic choices, we suggest that a detailed examination of the impact of managers and management teams is particularly pertinent to make progress in the mode choice literature. For example, we still know relatively little regarding how the personality (e.g. narcissism, overconfidence, risk attitude) or heuristics and biases of the main decision maker(s) affect an MNE's international mode choices. To follow this thread, we propose multiple areas for future research.

The role of the main decision maker may vary depending on the governance structure of the firm. For example, in family firms, where management and ownership are often concentrated in one role, the role of the main decision maker (and his/her embeddedness in the top management team) may be different compared to large stock-listed companies (Zapkau, Schwens, & Kabst, 2014), which may ultimately lead to different strategic choices in terms of entry mode. Theoretical lenses that specifically account for non-financial factors such as the desire to maintain family values, identity, legacy, or influence (e.g. socio-emotional wealth or stakeholder theory) may be useful to advance current knowledge in mode choice research.

In terms of new theories, Brouthers and Hennart (2007) encouraged research on intrafirm power and politics. However, our review of the literature revealed no studies following this thread. Yet, the relevance of research concerning intrafirm power and politics is not limited to general management and organization science research (for a review of this literature see Fleming & Spicer, 2014), but it is also particularly pertinent for the mode choice literature (Dörrenbächer & Gammelgaard, 2016). Future research warrants more detailed observations of how micro-political and power-related issues (e.g. headquarter-subsidiary power distributions) determine a firm's choice of an international entry mode.

Lastly, theories such as real options or organizational learning have begun to attract attention among mode choice researchers and we believe these theories to be particularly useful to gain a better understanding of how MNEs learn to deal with the exogenous and endogenous uncertainties surrounding mode choices. Ipsmiller, Brouthers, and Dikova (2019) provide a helpful framework and guide to the real option literature. We further emphasize that real options reasoning may help explain whether the initial formation of a joint venture is the best strategy to reduce uncertainty, allowing for a subsequent full acquisition. Further, learning theory may be particularly useful in the area of international mode choice to explain phenomena like re-entry commitment strategies (Surdu, Mellahi, & Glaister, 2019), or the limits of learning, based on location-bounded concepts (Schwens et al., 2018). In turn, scholars also need to study an MNE's ability and willingness to learn as part of their research on learning and mode choice.

New Methodologies

Our review also took stock of the progress made in terms of applying new methodologies that allow for examining different types of research questions or studying phenomena at different points in time. We identified only a few studies that draw on longitudinal data. While we are aware of the difficulties associated with obtaining such data, we encourage future research to expand their efforts toward obtaining and using longitudinal datasets. A recent study by Surdu et al. (2019) shows the potential that longitudinal data have for answering new and different types of research questions, including those that pertain to how organizations learn over time and change their initial entry strategies.

Likewise, studies employing methodologies such as experiments or simulations remain scarce (for an exception see Kraus et al., 2015). We repeat the call by Brouthers and Hennart (2007) for more research applying such methodologies. Given that every methodology has some inherent limitations, we think it would be particularly useful to triangulate different research methodologies to obtain more robust evidence in future entry mode research. For example, studies drawing on cross-sectional primary data often face difficulties in terms of issues like endogeneity, reverse causality, or common methods bias. Supplementing primary data with experimental evidence or secondary data may help with overcoming data limitations (Zellmer-Bruhn, Caligiuri, & Thomas, 2016). Likewise, simulation studies may help substantiate the underlying theoretical mechanisms that studies draw upon. Chandrasekaran, Linderman, and Sting (2018) outline how simulation methods can enhance empirical data.

Mode Choice and Performance

Our review of the new mode choice literature failed to find much progress in the area of performance implications of international entry mode choices. But as Brouthers and

Hennart (2007) emphasize, if mode selection does not lead to enhanced performance, why should MNEs concern themselves with this strategic decision? It is important for future mode choice studies to not just choose appropriate samples, investigate new theories, and control for important strategic differences; these studies can add significantly to knowledge if they also explore the relation between mode choice decision models and subsequent MNE performance. Furthermore, while looking at firm performance may be relatively more convenient due to the availability of firm-level data, mode choice may only have a small impact on overall MNE performance, depending on the level of international activity and the strategic importance of the market entered, among other factors. In turn, international mode choice might be a dominant factor in explaining foreign subsidiary performance. Thus, future research can advance the entry mode agenda by developing new subsidiary performance measures and linking these to theoretically derived mode choice models.

New Research Challenges to Address

In addition to the research areas Brouthers and Hennart (2007) pointed at (and that are still relevant according to our assessment), we provide some further recommendations that emerged from our review. First, research might focus on the cooperative and competitive orientation of the firm and its decision makers and how this orientation impacts mode choice. The emerging field of coopetition research, for example, has long highlighted that more than half of cooperative alliances are formed between competitors in various industries (Harbison & Pekar, 1998). The rivalrous and relational forces underlying coopetition lead to several potentially relevant research questions. For instance, under which boundary conditions is it more favorable for MNEs to opt for contractual agreements as opposed to joint ventures when entering international markets in a joint collaborative effort with a competitor? Further, there are questions about the role of competitors in entry mode choice decisions. Do the number and type of competitors in a market influence the mode of entry into a foreign market? The dynamics of competition, and how these dynamics influence an MNE's international mode strategies are understudied.

Second, future research could examine the digital economy and how the emergence of new technologies has impacted the modes that are available to multinational firms. Research on e-commerce development has examined mode choices (e.g. Singh & Kundu, 2002) but more work is required in this area as technologies advance and firms/customers become more familiar with these technologies. For example, mobile technologies offer entry opportunities that were difficult to anticipate a few years ago. Gaining access to a whole new group of potential customers through these technologies offers new challenges for firms including greater competition, but it also provides opportunities to acquire new customer groups, skills, and resources. The internet has enabled managers to easily gather data on foreign markets (e.g. institutional structures, customs of doing business), to identify and locate potential customers or customer groups, and to learn about competitors and their products and strategies. Firms with more advanced digital technology skills (such as big data analytics or artificial intelligence—AI) might have an advantage in terms of the knowledge and subsequent learning about international markets and make different mode choice decisions. We propose that future mode choice research can make a significant impact by helping us gain a better understanding of how digital technologies lead to different mode decisions.

Finally, future research might focus on how the entrepreneurial orientation of the MNE (manager) influences the mode used in new foreign markets. For example, notable works such as Covin (1991) have long suggested that firms tend to range from conservative to entrepreneurial and that this managerial/firm orientation influences their strategy and performance. In the same way, MNEs may differ not only in respect to the resources that they have and their perceptions of institutional distances between markets but also in how entrepreneurial they are (Ripollés, Blesa, & Monferrer, 2012). Combining entrepreneurship theory with other, more established, international business (IB) strategy theories such as TCE, RBV, or institutional theory might help scholars understand why MNEs are seen to react differently to the same international opportunities, which is often reflected in their entry mode choices.

Concluding Remarks

Over the past few decades, international mode choice has attracted substantial research attention. In this chapter, we analyzed the international entry mode choice literature in order to take stock of how the field has progressed since Brouthers and Hennart (2007) first reviewed this emerging area. We identified 138 journal articles publishing quantitative empirical studies between 2007 and 2018, indicating that the field is still vibrant and continues to grow. Our aim was to understand what progress has been made on the four main issues raised by Brouthers and Hennart (2007) and to identify what aspect of mode choice researchers can focus on to advance our understanding of this key MNE decision.

Our investigation revealed that some progress has been made in terms of deepening prevalent theories and probing into new theories. Despite these achievements, we identified areas where more work is required to advance this research agenda. By drawing on the progress that has been made and by deepening extant theories and applying new theories and methodologies, future entry mode scholarship faces various challenges and research opportunities. We propose, however, that these challenges and opportunities have the potential to significantly advance our understanding of how MNEs make this very important strategic decision and to yield implications for other major strategic decisions pertaining to IB (and beyond).

References

Benito, G. R. G. (2005). Divestment and international business strategy. *Journal of Economic Geography*, 5(2): 235–251.

Brouthers, K. D., Brouthers, L. E., & Werner, S. (2003). Transaction cost-enhanced entry mode choices and firm performance. *Strategic Management Journal*, 24(12): 1239–1248.

Brouthers, K. D., Brouthers, L. E., & Werner, S. (2008a). Real options, international entry mode choice and performance. *Journal of Management Studies*, 45(5): 936–960.

Brouthers, K. D., Brouthers, L. E., & Werner, S. (2008b). Resource-based advantages in an international context. *Journal of Management*, 34(2): 189–217.

Brouthers, K. D., & Hennart, J.-F. (2007). Boundaries of the firm: Insights from international entry mode research. *Journal of Management*, 33(3): 395–425.

Brouthers, L. E., Marshall, V. B., & Keig, D. L. (2016). Solving the single-country sample problem in cultural distance studies. *Journal of International Business Studies*, 47(4): 471–479.

Chandrasekaran, A., Linderman, K., & Sting, F. J. (2018). Avoiding epistemological silos and empirical elephants in OM: How to combine empirical and simulation methods? *Journal of Operations Management*, 63: 1–5.

Chen, M.-Y., & Chang, J.-Y. (2011). The choice of foreign market entry mode: An analysis of the dynamic probit model. *Economic Modelling*, 28(1–2): 439–450.

Chiao, Y.-C., Lo, F.-Y., & Yu, C.-M. (2010). Choosing between wholly-owned subsidiaries and joint ventures of MNCs from an emerging market. *International Marketing Review*, 27(3): 338–365.

Covin, J. G. (1991). Entrepreneurial versus conservative firms: A comparison of strategies and performance. *Journal of Management Studies*, 28(5): 439–462.

Cuypers, I. R. P., & Martin, X. (2010). What makes and what does not make a real option? A study of equity shares in international joint ventures. *Journal of International Business Studies*, 41(1): 47–69.

Dadzie, S. A., Owusu, R. A., Amoako, K., & Aklamanu, A. (2018). Do strategic motives affect ownership mode of foreign direct investments (FDIs) in emerging African markets? Evidence from Ghana. *Thunderbird International Business Review*, 60(3): 279–294.

Datta, D. K., Musteen, M., & Herrmann, P. (2009). Board characteristics, managerial incentives, and the choice between foreign acquisitions and international joint ventures. *Journal of Management*, 35(4): 928–953.

Dikova, D., & Brouthers, K. (2016). International establishment mode choice: Past, present and future. *Management International Review*, 56(4): 489–530.

Dikova, D., & Van Witteloostuijn, A. (2007). Foreign direct investment mode choice: entry and establishment modes in transition economies. *Journal of International Business Studies*, 38(6): 1013–1033.

Dörrenbächer, C., & Gammelgaard, J. (2016). Subsidiary initiative taking in multinational corporations: The relationship between power and issue selling. *Organization Studies*, 37(9): 1249–1270.

Filatotchev, I., Strange, R., Piesse, J., & Lien, Y.-C. (2007). FDI by firms from newly industrialised economies in emerging markets: corporate governance, entry mode and location. *Journal of International Business Studies*, 38(4): 556–572.

Fleming, P., & Spicer, A. (2014). Power in management and organization science. *The Academy of Management Annals*, 8(1): 237–298.

Giachetti, C., Manzi, G., & Colapinto, C. (2019). Entry Mode Degree of Control, Firm Performance and Host Country Institutional Development: A Meta-Analysis. *Management International Review*, 59(1): 3–39.

Harbison, J. R., & Pekar, P. (1998). *Smart Alliances: A Practical Guide to Repeatable Success*. San Francisco, CA: Jossey-Bass.

Hennart, J.-F., & Slangen, A. H. (2015). Yes, we really do need more entry mode studies! A commentary on Shaver. *Journal of International Business Studies*, 46(1): 114–122.

Hernández, V., & Nieto, M. J. (2015). The effect of the magnitude and direction of institutional distance on the choice of international entry modes. *Journal of World Business*, 50(1): 122–132.

Hollender, L., Zapkau, F. B., & Schwens, C. (2017). SME foreign market entry mode choice and foreign venture performance: The moderating effect of international experience and product adaptation. *International Business Review*, 26(2): 250–263.

Ipsmiller, E., Brouthers, K. D., & Dikova, D. (2019). 25 Years of Real Option Empirical Research in Management. *European Management Review*, 16(1): 55–68.

Johnson, J., & Tellis, G. J. (2008). Drivers of success for market entry into China and India. *Journal of Marketing*, 72(3): 1–13.

Kao, M.-S., & Kuo, A. (2017). The effect of uncertainty on FDI entry mode decisions: The influence of family ownership and involvement in the board of directors. *Journal of Family Business Strategy*, 8(4): 224–236.

Kim, Y., & Gray, S. J. (2008). The impact of entry mode choice on foreign affiliate performance: The case of foreign MNEs in South Korea. *Management International Review*, 48(2): 165.

Klier, H., Schwens, C., Zapkau, F. B., & Dikova, D. (2017). Which resources matter how and where? A meta-analysis on firms' foreign establishment mode choice. *Journal of Management Studies*, 54(3): 304–339.

Kontinen, T., & Ojala, A. (2011). Social capital in relation to the foreign market entry and post-entry operations of family SMEs. *Journal of International Entrepreneurship*, 9(2): 133–151.

Kraus, S., Ambos, T. C., Eggers, F., & Cesinger, B. (2015). Distance and perceptions of risk in internationalization decisions. *Journal of Business Research*, 68(7): 1501–1505.

Kuo, A., Kao, M.-S., Chang, Y.-C., & Chiu, C.-F. (2012). The influence of international experience on entry mode choice: Difference between family and non-family firms. *European Management Journal*, 30(3): 248–263.

Lai, J.-H., Chen, L.-Y., & Chang, S.-C. (2012). The board mechanism and entry mode choice. *Journal of International Management*, 18(4): 379–392.

Laufs, K., Bembom, M., & Schwens, C. (2016). CEO characteristics and SME foreign market entry mode choice: The moderating effect of firm's geographic experience and host-country political risk. *International Marketing Review*, 33(2): 246–275.

Laufs, K., & Schwens, C. (2014). Foreign market entry mode choice of small and medium-sized enterprises: A systematic review and future research agenda. *International Business Review*, 23(6): 1109–1126.

Liang, X., Musteen, M., & Datta, D. K. (2009). Strategic orientation and the choice of foreign market entry mode: an empirical examination. *Management International Review*, 49(3): 269–290.

Maekelburger, B., Schwens, C., & Kabst, R. (2012). Asset specificity and foreign market entry mode choice of small and medium-sized enterprises: The moderating influence of knowledge safeguards and institutional safeguards. *Journal of International Business Studies*, 43(5): 458–476.

Meyer, K. E., Ding, Y., Li, J., & Zhang, H. (2014). Overcoming distrust: How state-owned enterprises adapt their foreign entries to institutional pressures abroad. *Journal of International Business Studies*, 45(8): 1005–1028.

Meyer, K. E., & Wang, Y. (2015). Transaction cost perspectives on alliances and joint ventures: Explanatory power and empirical limitations. In J. Larimo, N. Nummela, & T. Mainela (Eds.), *Handbook on International Alliance and Network Research*. Cheltenham: Edward Elgar.

Meyer, K. E., Wright, M., & Pruthi, S. (2009). Managing knowledge in foreign entry strategies: A resource-based analysis. *Strategic Management Journal*, 30(5): 557–574.

Morresi, O., & Pezzi, A. (2011). 21 years of international M&As and joint ventures by Italian medium-sized listed firms: Value creation or value destruction? *Research in International Business and Finance*, 25(1): 75–87.

Morschett, D., Schramm-Klein, H., & Swoboda, B. (2010). Decades of research on market entry modes: What do we really know about external antecedents of entry mode choice? *Journal of International Management*, 16(1): 60–77.

Nielsen, B. B., & Nielsen, S. (2011). The role of top management team international orientation in international strategic decision-making: The choice of foreign entry mode. *Journal of World Business*, 46(2): 185–193.

Ogasavara, M. H., & Hoshino, Y. (2007). The impact of ownership, internalization, and entry mode on Japanese subsidiaries' performance in Brazil. *Japan and the World Economy*, 19(1): 1–25.

Pan, Y., & Tse, D. K. (2000). The hierarchical model of market entry modes. *Journal of International Business Studies*, 31(4): 535–554.

Papyrina, V. (2007). When, how, and with what success? The joint effect of entry timing and entry mode on survival of Japanese subsidiaries in China. *Journal of International Marketing*, 15(3): 73–95.

Paul, D. L., & Wooster, R. B. (2008). Strategic investments by US firms in transition economies. *Journal of International Business Studies*, 39(2): 249–266.

Petticrew, M., & Roberts, H. (2006). *Systematic Reviews in the Social Sciences: A Practical |Guide*. Oxford: Blackwell.

Pinho, J. C. (2007). The impact of ownership: Location-specific advantages and managerial characteristics on SME foreign entry mode choices. *International Marketing Review*, 24(6): 715–734.

Podsakoff, P. M., MacKenzie, S. B., Bachrach, D. G., & Podsakoff, N. P. (2005). The influence of management journals in the 1980s and 1990s. *Strategic Management Journal*, 26(5): 473–488.

Pongelli, C., Caroli, M. G., & Cucculelli, M. (2016). Family business going abroad: the effect of family ownership on foreign market entry mode decisions. *Small Business Economics*, 47(3): 787–801.

Puck, J. F., Holtbrügge, D., & Mohr, A. T. (2009). Beyond entry mode choice: Explaining the conversion of joint ventures into wholly owned subsidiaries in the People's Republic of China. *Journal of International Business Studies*, 40(3): 388–404.

Rhee, J. H. (2008). International expansion strategies of Korean venture firms: Entry mode choice and performance. *Asian Business & Management*, 7(1): 95–114.

Ripollés, M., & Blesa, A. (2012). International new ventures as "small multinationals": The importance of marketing capabilities. *Journal of World Business*, 47(2): 277–287.

Ripollés, M., Blesa, A., & Monferrer, D. (2012). Factors enhancing the choice of higher resource commitment entry modes in international new ventures. *International Business Review*, 21(4): 648–666.

Sanchez-Peinado, E., & Pla-Barber, J. (2006). A multidimensional concept of uncertainty and its influence on the entry mode choice: An empirical analysis in the service sector. *International Business Review*, 15(3): 215–232.

Sanchez-Peinado, E., Pla-Barber, J., & Hébert, L. (2007). Strategic variables that influence entry mode choice in service firms. *Journal of International Marketing*, 15(1): 67–91.

Schellenberg, M., Harker, M. J., & Jafari, A. (2018). International market entry mode–a systematic literature review. *Journal of Strategic Marketing*, 26(7): 601–627.

Schwens, C., Zapkau, F. B., Brouthers, K. D., & Hollender, L. (2018). Limits to international entry mode learning in SMEs. *Journal of International Business Studies*, 49(7): 809–831.

Shaver, J. M. (1998). Accounting for endogeneity when assessing strategy performance: does entry mode choice affect FDI survival? *Management Science*, 44(4): 571–585.

Shaver, J. M. (2013). Do we really need more entry mode studies? *Journal of International Business Studies*, 44(1): 23–27.

Singh, N., & Kundu, S. (2002). Explaining the growth of e-commerce corporations (ECCs): an extension and application of the eclectic paradigm. *Journal of International Business Studies*, 33(4): 679–697.

Surdu, I., & Mellahi, K. (2016). Theoretical foundations of equity based foreign market entry decisions: A review of the literature and recommendations for future research. *International Business Review*, 25(5): 1169–1184.

Surdu, I., Mellahi, K., & Glaister, K. W. (2019). Once bitten, not necessarily shy? Determinants of foreign market re-entry commitment strategies. *Journal of International Business Studies*, 50(3): 393–422.

Swoboda, B., Elsner, S., & Olejnik, E. (2015). How do past mode choices influence subsequent entry? A study on the boundary conditions of preferred entry modes of retail firms. *International Business Review*, 24(3): 506–517.

Tranfield, D., Denyer, D., & Smart, P. (2003). Towards a methodology for developing evidence-informed management knowledge by means of systematic review. *British Journal of Management*, 14(3): 207–222.

Williamson, O. E. (1975). *Markets and Hierarchies: Analysis and Antitrust Implications*. New York, NY: Free Press.

Williamson, O. E. (1998). Transaction cost economics: how it works; where it is headed. *De Economist*, 146(1): 23–58.

Xie, Q. (2014). CEO tenure and ownership mode choice of Chinese firms: The moderating roles of managerial discretion. *International Business Review*, 23(5): 910–919.

Yamanoi, J., & Asaba, S. (2018). The impact of family ownership on establishment and ownership modes in foreign direct investment: The moderating role of corruption in host countries. *Global Strategy Journal*, 8(1): 106–135.

Zapkau, F. B., Schwens, C., & Kabst, R. (2014). Foreign direct investments and domestic employment of German SMEs: The Moderating Effect of Owner Management. *Journal of Small Business Management*, 52(3): 451–476.

Zellmer-Bruhn, M., Caligiuri, P., & Thomas, D. C. (2016). From the Editors: Experimental designs in international business research. *Journal of International Business Studies*, 47(1): 399–407.

Zhao, H., Ma, J., & Yang, J. (2017). 30 years of research on entry mode and performance relationship: a meta-analytical review. *Management International Review*, 57(5): 653–682.

Zimmerman, M. A., Barsky, D., & Brouthers, K. D. (2009). Networks, SMEs, and international diversification. *Multinational Business Review*, 17(4): 143–162.

CHAPTER 6

STRATEGIC KNOWLEDGE CREATION IN MULTINATIONAL ENTERPRISES

LARS HÅKANSON, PHILIP KAPPEN, AND IVO ZANDER

INTRODUCTION

THE nature, management, and effects of knowledge creation in multinational enterprises (MNEs) have attracted a large and varied literature, reflecting their importance not only for the strategy and management of MNEs themselves, but also for society at large. Of special interest has been the observation that MNEs may obtain and develop innovative capabilities not only in their countries of origin but also in host countries. This insight originally added to the academic interest in the phenomenon, because it conflicted with the inherited theoretical tenet that MNEs base their international expansion on capabilities developed in response to conditions in their domestic markets.

Knowledge creation and innovation in MNEs occur in all functional areas, but to keep the topic within manageable bounds, this chapter has a narrower focus on activities conventionally denoted "research and development" or R&D. The delimitation reflects both the empirical importance of R&D undertaken by MNEs, and the theoretical significance attached to it in extant literatures. MNEs control between two thirds and three quarters of the world's industrial R&D resources (UNCTAD, 2005) and spend, on average, ten times more on R&D than on advertising, for example (Govindarajan, Rajgopal, Srivastava, & Wang, 2019). Their decisions about where, how, and for what purposes these resources are deployed are of fundamental economic, political, and cultural importance, not only for the countries in which they are directly active, but, at times, for the world as a whole. These decisions are also central to MNE international business (IB) strategy and involve complex managerial challenges, both issues that have been the object of much scholarly attention (see Papanastassiou, Pearce, & Zanfei, 2020 for a recent review). The latter types of decisions are at the core of the following discussion, which deliberately assumes a managerial and MNE-centered perspective, leaving out important aspects of MNE R&D activities, such as their relationship to foreign direct investment (FDI) theory or their broader societal impact through technology transfer and so called "spill-over" effects.

The aim of this chapter is to provide a historically grounded perspective on MNE knowledge creation and innovation. The arguments are presented in three sections. The first of these outlines the prevailing view of strategic MNE knowledge creation, founded on the notion that, in recent decades, MNEs have internationalized R&D on unprecedented scales. Aided by advancements in information and communication technologies, both formerly centralized R&D structures and more loosely coordinated ones have been replaced by interconnected networks of geographically dispersed R&D centers, enabling modern day MNEs to create, assimilate, integrate, and exploit new knowledge on a global scale. This ability constitutes not only a major competitive advantage but, in some narratives, provides the very raison d'être for the MNE as an organizational form (Kogut & Zander, 1992, 1993; Noorderhaven & Harzing, 2009). This influential perspective has inspired much insightful research and scholarly commentary, but its selective focus on large, resourceful R&D units in some of the most established MNEs, we suggest, has created an exaggerated and often distorted impression of the scale, nature, and importance of international R&D and other knowledge-creating activities in MNEs.

Addressing some of these shortcomings, the following section attempts to provide a more nuanced historical view of the evolutionary dynamics that have shaped the structures, systems, and procedures of international R&D activities in MNEs from different countries and industries. It outlines and contrasts the "emergent" or "evolutionary" patterns characteristic of twentieth-century European and US MNEs, both with the more deliberate and cautious strategies pursued by Japanese MNEs and with the strategic approaches taken by many MNEs from emerging economies, such as China and India. In each case, the resulting structures have been (and remain) subject to continuous change, reflecting both developments in the IB environment and evolving internal needs and aspirations of the MNEs themselves. We present this historical perspective as a counterpoint to the one implicit in much of the inherited literature, where observed R&D structures are often seen as expressions of a natural and strategically driven development toward an ever more perfect realization of the knowledge-based advantages conceived of as the *sine qua non* of the multinational corporation (Magee, 1981; Teece, 1981).

The closing of the section summarizes our arguments and outlines how MNEs have tried to exploit the opportunities while dealing with the frictions associated with the knowledge-creating structures arising from combinations of emergent and deliberate decision sequences (Mintzberg & Waters, 1985). These responses have varied between MNEs of different origins, as determined by the time of entry into the world economy, the state of technology and competition, institutional conditions, existing organizational structures and administrative heritages, and the power of new information processing capabilities. The objective is to highlight, on the one hand, a few areas where available findings and insights seem to rest on rather solid empirical ground, and to suggest, on the other, fruitful avenues for future research on the strategy and organization of knowledge-creating activities in MNEs—an ever-evolving target. These suggestions and challenges are outlined in the chapter's final section.

THE RECEIVED VIEW ON MNE KNOWLEDGE CREATION

Theoretical Origins

The knowledge-creating activities of MNEs have attracted much attention in two major strands of IB literature. The impetus for this interest came from empirical observations in the early 1980s that—contrary to the received wisdom at the time—MNEs oftentimes perform R&D not only in their countries of origin but also in host countries, and that, at times, foreign innovative activities are quite considerable.

For FDI theory and the economic theory of the MNE, this phenomenon called for amendments to the dominant view that emphasized the exploitation of competitive advantages developed in response to home country conditions as the driving force of FDI and firm internationalization. The wish to obtain new and/or complementary knowledge began to be seen as an important, perhaps even dominant, category of "asset-seeking" FDI (Dunning, 2000). This inspired a wide range of research, with the aim to describe and explain the geographical patterns of MNEs' foreign R&D activities, as evidenced in R&D employment or patent records. This new focus was strengthened by the interest of researchers studying the impact of FDI in home and host nations. In home countries, there was concern that MNEs were relocating knowledge-intensive activities abroad, reducing employment of skilled scientists and engineers in their domestic markets, thereby undermining home country competitiveness. In contrast, host countries often welcomed and encouraged the setting up of local R&D laboratories, as a mechanism believed to promote technology transfer and "spill-overs" to the local economy. At times, but in recent decades less often, concerns were raised that scarce local technical experts were engaged in activities serving the interests of foreign MNEs, rather than those of the countries hosting them. While resulting in many important insights and significant findings, the inadvertent effect of this stream of research has been the creation of an exaggerated image of the relative importance of foreign R&D, overemphasizing the magnitude and impact of the international knowledge-creating activities in MNEs, as compared to that undertaken in their countries of origin.

In the literature on strategy and management, the significance of international R&D relates to its role in explaining the rise and international competitiveness of MNEs. Perhaps the first explicit articulation of this idea was in Vernon's (1979) early "armchair speculation" of the characteristics of the "global scanner," at a time when evidence had just appeared regarding foreign subsidiary R&D and the role of foreign sources of technology:

> Communication is virtually costless between any two points of the globe; information, once received, is digested and interpreted at little or no cost. Ignorance or uncertainty, therefore, is no longer a function of distance; markets, wherever located, have an equal opportunity to stimulate the firm to innovation and production; and factory sites, wherever located, have an equal chance to be weighed for their costs and risks.   (Vernon, 1979)

Vernon's conceptualization of the global scanner can be read as a radical elaboration of Perlmutter's (1969) seminal discussion of the "geocentric firm," as the mature endpoint of the organizational evolution that successful MNEs undergo, leaving behind the earlier "adolescent" stages of ethnocentrism and polycentrism. The implicitly teleological interpretation adopted by Perlmutter—MNEs evolve in predetermined ways because this is what allows them to fulfill their full potential—has continued to influence the subsequent literature. It was prominently echoed, for example, in the early studies on the evolution of organizational structures in MNEs conducted within the Harvard Multinational Enterprise Project (Franko, 1976; Stopford & Wells, 1972; Yoshino, 1976). Based on Chandler's (1962) seminal work and the associated "strategy–structure paradigm," successful MNEs were found to be converging toward "global organizational structures" as a means to cope with the information processing requirements arising from increasingly ambitious and complex international strategies. Similarly—although sometimes emphasizing the role of "administrative heritage" and country-of-origin effects (Bartlett, 1986)—subsequent research on strategic processes in MNEs saw them moving toward a "network model" (variously named "heterarchy," "horizontal," "multi-focal," or "transnational"). As Westney (2019) has noted, "the assumption of convergence from variety toward a single 'ideal type' (in both the Weberian and the normative senses) of the MNE" has continued to influence the literature until this day.

The Network Model

Formulated over three decades ago in the seminal works of Bartlett (1986), Hedlund (1986), and Prahalad & Doz (1987)—as well as in the influential text by Bartlett and Ghoshal (1989)—the network model has obtained near paradigmatic status in IB strategy research. A central feature of the network model is the view that MNEs' international networks provide means to promote learning and innovation that are not available to purely domestic firms, a view furnishing the lens for much of the subsequent study of R&D and knowledge creation in MNEs.

Unfortunately, these early works did not acquire the status of *exemplars* in the Kuhnian sense (Kuhn, 1962). Paradigmatic acceptance of the model was largely confined to its conceptual aspects; the empirical methods of longitudinal, detailed sociological observation of MNE organizations on which the early studies were based, did not inspire much following. Along with a fair amount of theoretical contributions, extant empirical research in the area has mostly been of a quantitative nature, testing and expanding on elaborations of the network model based on information collected in questionnaire surveys or patent data (e.g. Almeida, 1996; Frost, 2001; Feinberg & Gupta, 2004). In early studies describing and analyzing the extent and nature of international R&D (Cordell, 1971; Håkanson, 1981, 1983; Pearce, 1989), units engaging in advanced, innovative knowledge creation appeared as interesting exceptions. Subsequent research has tended to highlight and further explore precisely these outliers, not because of their empirical significance but because of their theoretically interesting implications (Birkinshaw, 1997; Birkinshaw & Fry, 1998). In consequence, relatively little is known about the nature and management of more mundane, day-to-day knowledge creation and exchange in MNEs. By the same token, little interest has been devoted to the importance, role, and management of R&D undertaken in home country locations, which in all but a few MNEs accounts for the overwhelming share of the total amount of R&D activities.

In contrast to the work in the Chandlerian tradition, the network conceptualization of the MNE tended to emphasize the indeterminacy of structural responses, abandoning both the notion that appropriate organizational structures can be derived from particular strategies, and the role of information handling capacity as a key driving force for organizational change. Its focus was on the growing complexity of the strategic challenges confronting MNEs—such as the need for a "dual focus" on simultaneous global integration and local adaptation, or the role of learning and experimentation to upgrade and maintain competitive advantages—and on the nature of the processes required to meet them. For a time, advances in information technologies encouraged a revival of the matrix organization as a means to resolve these often conflicting demands, but faith in this structural solution waned. While emphasizing the need for flexibility and multidimensionality, the network view provided no clear structural implications:

> the heterarchical firm does not worry too much about logical inconsistency, but instead focuses on practical coherence. The structure is flexible over time: at a certain moment, global product management is most important; next year perhaps integration of total R&D resources is paramount. The flexibility and multidimensionality goes beyond what is possible in a formal matrix organization, which often tends to rigidify rather than—which is the intention—allow fast and flexible response.   (Hedlund & Rolander, 1990)

In consequence of the network views' disinterest in structural properties of MNEs, and of the empirical methodologies adopted, extant research provides little by way of a holistic understanding of the role of R&D and knowledge creation in MNEs. Its focus has been on a few main themes, all derived from the basic assumptions of the network model.

The Role and Evolution of Foreign R&D

Whereas the early literature tended to emphasize the heterogeneity and variety in terms of the tasks and "roles" of foreign R&D units (Håkanson, 1981, 1983; Pearce, 1989; Ronstadt, 1978), more recent research has tended to pass over such differences, adopting instead more universal narratives regarding the role and evolution of international R&D networks. A central tenet of these narratives is the belief that MNEs can obtain superior competitive advantages through their ability to "tap into" foreign sources of scientific, technological, and market knowledge. The key issues concern foreign subsidiaries' ability to identify and absorb relevant local knowledge, and to transfer that knowledge internally within the MNE organization to the units that can best profit from it.

According to one influential narrative, successful foreign subsidiaries over time accumulate financial, human, and technical resources, as well as political clout and autonomy, enabling them to move along an evolutionary path from routine technical support, over local adaptation of products and processes, into design and proper product development for regional or global markets (e.g. Birkinshaw & Hood, 1998; Pearce & Papanastassiou, 1999). This evolution is associated with a gradual deepening of the subsidiary's "external embeddedness"—intensive and trustful interaction with relevant stakeholders such as local customers, suppliers, and universities—and with strong "internal embeddedness"—coordination and knowledge exchanges with headquarters (HQs) and peer subsidiaries elsewhere in the world. In this process, the technological capabilities initially transferred from the parent organization play an important role as stepping-stones into new technological fields, as they may be recombined both with internal resources available elsewhere in the MNE and with external resources tapped from the local environment. While the narrative recognizes the importance of local networks and the role of parent company technology, it sees entrepreneurial initiative on the part of foreign subsidiary managers as a main driving force, at times lending the evolution of international R&D networks a somewhat haphazard, serendipitous character. The MNC becomes depicted as a highly politicized federative arena, where sophisticated foreign subsidiaries compete for attention, influence, and resources (Andersson, Forsgren, & Holm, 2007; Birkinshaw, Bouquet, & Ambos, 2007; Mudambi & Navarra, 2004). This stream of literature places HQs in the passenger seat, largely drifting along to wherever foreign subsidiaries take them.

A contrasting perspective sees the evolution of international R&D networks as the outcome of strategic deliberations on the part of central MNE managers. Here, foreign R&D locations are selected either on their ability to provide access to critical markets, market trends, and technical developments, or because they offer opportunities to employ technical and scientific expertise at salary levels below those prevailing at home (e.g. Reddy, 1997; Kumar, 2001). To the first category belong R&D establishments in foreign industrial clusters, where geographical proximity is thought to provide privileged access to the "buzz" of tacit, state-of-the-art knowledge not available elsewhere (Malmberg, Sölvell, & Zander, 1996; Bathelt, Malmberg, & Maskell, 2004). Especially in

MNEs from emerging economies, it also includes investments in R&D facilities aiming to employ specialized technical expertise not available at home. In this narrative, international R&D networks are rationally designed, carefully coordinated systems, orchestrated to develop and exploit technical and market knowledge in ways not available to domestic firms.

Common to both these perspectives is their neglect of mergers and acquisitions, empirically a major mechanism and driving force for R&D internationalization. Mergers and takeovers have been important especially in industries undergoing international concentration and consolidation; however, in many MNEs, they have also been an important means of diversification, in terms of both new product-market combinations and access to supplementary knowledge assets. The significance of mergers for R&D internationalization depends on the particular circumstances and underlying motives. In horizontal mergers, acquired R&D capabilities are often redundant from the point of view of the acquiring firm, since they duplicate ones it already possesses. In such cases, the aim is often to scale down and close acquired R&D units in ways that do not cause too much disruption and reputational damage with local authorities, other stakeholders, and remaining employees. At other times, mergers and acquisitions aim to access complementary knowledge assets and technical resources, in the hope that, when successfully combined with existing ones, they will help develop valuable new innovation capabilities. Here, acquiring firms often confront difficult challenges in the organizational integration of engineers and scientists in acquired R&D units into existing structures, typically a process over several years, and often with disappointing outcomes (Birkinshaw et al., 2000; Håkanson, 1995).

These seemingly irreconcilable narratives of the nature and evolution of MNEs represent competing attempts to summarize and interpret observed evolutionary patterns in R&D internationalization, which have varied both over time and between MNEs of different national origins. As will be elaborated, each in isolation captures only one part of the complexity of these processes, the understanding of which requires a more contextually informed perspective.

PATTERNS OF MNE KNOWLEDGE CREATION AND INNOVATION

The evolution of innovation and knowledge creation in MNEs displays significant variations not only across countries and industries but also between individual firms, all but impossible to capture in detail. Nevertheless, the following account attempts to outline some broad developments in the internationalization of R&D among MNEs from the countries that have received most scholarly attention. This empirical heritage is closely related to the theoretical heritage, both biasing research findings to a rather narrow sample of MNEs from few select countries and regions.

European and US MNEs

In line with classical theories of the MNE, the majority of European and US MNEs expanded internationally by exploiting firm-specific advantages (FSAs) developed in the home country (Jones, 1996). These advantages typically involved novel technological capabilities and associated products or services (Hymer, 1976), and they were essential for overcoming the liabilities of foreignness encountered during the initial attempts to enter unfamiliar foreign markets (Zaheer, 1995).

In their international expansion, European and US MNEs were primarily looking either to secure the supply of necessary inputs and raw materials, or to extend the market for their products (Dunning, 1983; Wilkins, 1988). Both resource-seeking and market-seeking motives reflected the desire to ensure or enhance corporate profitability, sometimes complemented by other, but in most cases secondary motives, such as the wish to improve efficiency by locating activities in foreign countries offering especially favorable conditions to perform them, or to strategically monitor competitors in international oligopolistic industries (Knickerbocker, 1973). As a rule, foreign units functioned as an extended arm of the home country parent, providing sales support and, when needed, local adaptation of products and services. Over time, and especially in major markets, foreign operations were expanded to include local manufacturing, and technical service to local customers and local adaptation of products and processes sometimes developed into more substantial R&D capabilities. As foreign units became increasingly more embedded in their local business environments, some started developing products and services aimed at local, and sometimes regional, markets (Blomkvist, Kappen, & Zander, 2010). However, in only a handful of cases did these capabilities make significant technological and financial contributions to the overall MNE group (Blomkvist et al., 2012; Rugman & Verbeke, 2009).

The great majority of European and US MNEs remained dependent on the home country for their technological renewal (Patel, 1995; Dunning & Lundan, 2009; Belderbos, Leten, & Suzuki, 2013). However, both incidentally and by deliberate design, some also became more extensively engaged in strategic knowledge asset seeking in their international operations (Dunning, 1993, 2000; Awate, Larsen, & Mudambi, 2015). Extending the occasional use of listening posts into market and technological developments in select foreign countries, some MNEs began searching for functional expertise or the strengthening of parts of their value-adding activities (Chesnais, 1988; Cantwell, 1995). At times, mergers and acquisitions were undertaken with the deliberate aim to acquire technological capabilities and products believed to offer better growth prospects than those of the company's current business portfolio (Dunning & Narula, 1995). However, the bulk of the accumulation of foreign R&D capabilities resulted from horizontal foreign mergers and acquisitions undertaken during the post-war restructuring of industries. In horizontal foreign acquisitions, the addition of foreign R&D resources was often the incidental result of the pursuit of other strategic goals (Håkanson & Nobel, 1993; Ronstadt, 1978). At times, such added R&D capacities were a welcome supplement to existing ones; more often, they were scaled back and eventually disbanded (Gerybadze & Reger, 1999; Håkanson & Kappen, 2016).

While European and US MNEs experienced similar overall patterns of internationalization, some distinctive differences are notable. Internationalization of European MNEs, especially from small domestic markets, was typically rapid, with foreign sales through both exports and local production within few years accounting for dominating shares of the total. These developments were accentuated during the interwar period, when political unrest, increasing nationalism, and rising trade barriers encouraged the setting up of foreign manufacturing activities as well as the transfer and build-up of associated technical and marketing capabilities. In contrast, US MNEs typically maintained a focus on the large domestic market, sometimes extended to include Mexico and selected Latin American countries, and tended to adopt a more cautious and carefully planned approach to the internationalization of technological capabilities. The internationalization of R&D in European firms was less deliberate, often emerging from the entrepreneurial initiatives among rather autonomous foreign subsidiaries, on the one hand, and the incidental addition of foreign R&D laboratories through mergers and acquisitions, on the other. In consequence, by the early and mid-1990s the international R&D networks in many European MNEs had become increasingly unwieldy and cumbersome to manage. Thereafter, a period of consolidation appears to have set in (Gerybadze & Reger, 1999), the effects of which remain to this day.

The continuing incremental growth of foreign technological capabilities, fueled by the increasing use of foreign acquisitions in globally concentrating industries, led to a gradual transformation of the R&D structures of both European and US MNEs. Toward the end of the 1980s foreign operations had come to account for more than one third of total R&D activities in MNEs from several European countries (including Sweden, Belgium, the Netherlands, the UK, and Switzerland), with significantly less pronounced developments among MNEs from some larger economies, such as Germany, Italy, and France (Cantwell, 1989, 1992; Zander, 1994). Although departing from rather dissimilar R&D structures, European and US companies tended, in the following decades, to evolve in a similar fashion. US MNEs had typically developed quite centralized organizational structures, with home country hubs controlling transfers to foreign units of domestically developed technological advancements, in European ones, foreign subsidiaries often enjoyed a higher degree of autonomy, and R&D networks were typically only loosely controlled. However, by the end of the millennium, many, both US and European MNEs, had developed multicentered R&D structures, with some foreign units playing prominent roles (Gassmann & Von Zedtwitz, 1999). Among US MNEs, one-way communication and technology transfer from home country to foreign units shifted toward more complex flows of knowledge across dispersed units within the MNE network; among European MNEs, the formerly uncoordinated and sometimes haphazard knowledge exchanges were replaced by formal systems of communication, coordination, and control. In consequence, R&D cooperation between home and foreign units increased (Frost & Zhou, 2005). Although this was still the exception rather than the rule, it sometimes involved joint innovation projects among several and geographically dispersed MNE units (Hedlund & Ridderstråle, 1995).

From the 2000s onwards, both European and US MNEs became interested in expanding or establishing R&D operations in emerging economies, such as China and India (Walsh, 2007; Asakawa & Som, 2008; Bruche, 2009; Dunning & Lundan, 2009). This was sometimes a continuation of traditional evolutionary processes (Chen, 2007; Baskaran & Muchie, 2008), strengthened by local government demands for more advanced local operations as a precondition to market access. A major motive was also the wish to access pools of highly qualified technical and scientific expertise, often available at salaries dramatically below those prevailing in Western Europe and the US (Gammeltoft, 2006; Lewin, Massini, & Peeters, 2009). As a rule, R&D units established by western MNEs in emerging markets were initially set up to undertake mainly routine testing and other ancillary technical tasks (UNCTAD, 2019). In some cases, however, these units managed to develop valuable unique competences, obtaining mandates as centers of excellence for the whole MNE (Andersson & Forsgren, 2000; Cantwell & Mudambi, 2005).

Japanese MNEs

Increasingly prominent from the 1960s onwards, the internationalization of Japanese MNEs and their foreign R&D activities was different (Dunning, 2009). At the outset, many Japanese MNEs benefited from comparatively low labor costs at home, but labor cost advantages started to dissipate already in the 1970s and could not be sustained by moving manufacturing to neighboring countries (Yoshino, 1974). In response also to various forms of tariff and non-tariff protectionist measures, Japanese MNEs broadened their international activities and capabilities to include a combination of large-scale, advanced manufacturing, distinctive organizational traits and processes, and gradually enhanced technologies (Franko, 1983; Aoki & Dore, 1994; Collinson & Rugman, 2008). The reliance on broad-based, unique and difficult-to-imitate sources of competitive advantage became particularly important in major foreign markets, most prominently the US market (Yoshino, 1974; Yonekura & McKinney, 2005).

For many Japanese MNEs, the development of more advanced foreign technological capabilities was linked to a deliberate effort to access and assimilate foreign technological knowledge (Belderbos, 2003; see also Shimizutani & Todo, 2008), either through joint ventures with foreign MNEs entering the Japanese market, or by seeking to tap into foreign sources of technical and scientific expertise (Methé & Penner-Hahn, 1999). Although many of the drivers for R&D internationalization mirrored those in European and US MNEs (Granstrand, 1999; Belderbos, 2003), Japanese MNEs were typically much more reluctant to expand R&D activities abroad (Reger, 2002; UNCTAD, 2005; Von Zedtwitz, 2005). A characteristic feature was the establishment as "listening posts," especially in the form of small R&D units in geographical proximity to major universities in the UK and the US (Gassmann & Von Zedtwitz, 1999; Granstrand, 1999;

Asakawa, 2001a, 2001b; Lam, 2008). Their aim was to access cutting-edge technological advancements that could then be transferred to home country units. To this end, they were often granted high degrees of autonomy to further their embeddedness in local scientific communities (Lehrer & Asakawa, 2003). Over time, several such R&D centers expanded their research domains, but some also experienced a shift in focus from basic to applied R&D (Asakawa, 2001a; Song et al., 2011). However, already by the late 1990s, many foreign R&D units had become more strongly integrated in the overall MNE organization, in the process gradually losing some of their previously attained autonomy (Asakawa, 2001b).

Emerging-Market MNEs

While European, US and Japanese MNEs dominated throughout most of the twentieth century (Wilkins, 1988; Dunning, 1983), emerging-market MNEs (EMNEs) started to make a more significant mark on the global economy from the 1990s and onward (Dunning, 2009; Guillén & Garcia-Canal, 2009). While some of these MNEs had existed for a long time, their foreign operations had historically been associated primarily with low-cost and undifferentiated products (Lecraw, 1977), primarily targeting other developing or emerging economies (Lall, 1983; Wells, 1981, 1983). Much of this changed in the new millennium, especially with the emergence and international expansion of MNEs from countries such as South Korea, Taiwan, Brazil, China, and India.

Many EMNEs internationalized by linking into the global value chains of already established MNEs, often as part of explicit catching-up and learning strategies (Hobday, 1995; Mathews, 2002a, 2002b; Buckley, 2009). Over time, many developed competitive advantages extending well beyond initial low-cost advantages to include, for example, organizational and business model innovations (Williamson, Ramamurti, Fleury, & Fleury, 2013). The strive to gradually advance up the value chain included the acquisition of firms in developed economies (Elia & Santangelo, 2017), not only to capture established brand names, markets, and networks of suppliers and distributors but also to obtain first-hand access to state-of-the-art technology, management, and marketing expertise (Deng, 2007). Similar to the earlier experience of Japanese MNEs, the internationalization of many EMNEs thus involved a distinctive exploration and learning component.

Relatively little is known about the internationalization of R&D activities of EMNEs, and existing evidence suggests considerable variation in the extent to which these MNEs apply domestically developed and acquired foreign-based technological capabilities (Williamson et al., 2013). EMNEs from Asia have often systematically upgraded their technological capabilities, especially by means of foreign acquisitions (Hobday, 1995; Lee & Lim, 2001; Chaturvedi & Chataway, 2006; Celly, Prabhu, C., & Subramanian, 2013; Awate et al., 2015; Brandl & Mudambi, 2015), sometimes complemented by the establishment of overseas R&D outposts (Lee & Lim, 2001; Bonaglia, Goldstein, & Mathews, 2007). Among Chinese MNEs, the most well-researched MNEs from emerging economies (see Alon, Anderson, Munim, & Ho, 2018 for a recent review), both greenfield establishments and foreign acquisitions have played a role in obtaining and exploiting advanced technological capabilities (Child & Rodrigues, 2005; Hong & Sun, 2006; Deng, 2007; Di Minin, Zhang, & Gammeltoft, 2012). Other investments aimed at the upgrading of technological capabilities have included the establishment of foreign listening posts, design institutes, and R&D centers (Deng, 2007; Fan, 2006). The increase in foreign R&D activity among Chinese MNEs also includes M&As aimed at defending home market positions by tapping into existing supplier and customer relationships, accessing established brands, and generally building stronger future market positions (Von Zedtwitz, 2005; Hong & Sun, 2006; Deng, 2007, 2009; Rui & Yip, 2008; Di Minin et al., 2012).

Whatever the motives, some observations suggest that the technological insights gained by an increasing number of foreign units will ultimately become fused with domestic R&D activities in the home country (Di Minin et al., 2012; Meyer, 2015; Anderson et, 2015). However, the extent to which Chinese MNEs—and MNEs from other emerging economies—will integrate technological knowledge in foreign units is still to be revealed. In some, such transfers may be limited by foreign units enjoying excessive degrees of autonomy (Lehrer & Asakawa, 2003); in other cases, there may not be sufficient absorptive capacity at home to effectively assimilate the knowledge residing in foreign units (Methé & Penner-Hahn, 1999). On the balancing side, this challenge seems to be universal to a broader set of MNEs as studies show that acquired units tend to be less integrated (Blomkvist et al., 2018) and differ in their knowledge trajectories in comparison to greenfield investments (Blomkvist et al., 2014).

Pathways and Intent in MNE Strategic Knowledge Creation

As outlined, the paths toward increasing R&D internationalization have differed considerably over time and between MNEs from different countries and industries, reflecting the outcome of both "emergent" and "deliberate" strategies (Mintzberg & Waters, 1985). In European and US MNEs, early internationalization strategies were typically of a market-seeking nature, based on the exploitation of FSAs initially developed domestically. The internationalization of R&D often followed an *evolutionary* pattern, moving from technical support to gradually more advanced forms of engineering and development. Especially in European MNEs from small domestic markets, where foreign subsidiary managers tended to enjoy a high degree of autonomy, these developments did not always reflect strategic deliberations by HQ managers but were often the result of entrepreneurial initiatives by foreign subsidiary managers. In US MNEs, corporate HQs tended to exercise stronger control over foreign operations. Investments in foreign R&D activities were typically undertaken only after careful review and central authorization, reflecting a more strategic approach, which was later adopted also by many European MNEs (Gerybadze & Reger, 1999).

In both US and European MNEs, exploration of opportunities in technologies and markets new to the firm were often somewhat *serendipitous*, resulting from individual entrepreneurial initiatives of foreign R&D staff and subsidiary managers, or from the unexpected discovery of technological capabilities in horizontal acquisitions undertaken to strengthen positions in existing markets and industries. As a rule, however, the dominating share of the R&D effort remained at home, close to the head office and major production units. Knowledge-creating foreign subsidiaries, pursuing advanced foreign R&D at the frontiers of technology, have remained the exception rather than the rule even among MNEs with comparatively extensive foreign R&D operations (Blomkvist et al., 2018).

In contrast to the evolutionary and, at times, rather haphazard patterns characteristic of early R&D internationalization in European and US MNEs, the internationalization of R&D in Japanese companies and, later, MNEs from emerging economies, often proceeded in a more deliberate and strategic manner. The more strategic approach to the internationalization of R&D was to a large extent dictated by their late entry into the world economy, and the associated need to rapidly catch up with established MNEs from developed economies. Japanese firms initially often employed "listening posts" not only to access and improve existing capabilities, but sometimes also to *arbitrage* foreign technological developments by combining them with internal capabilities at home. MNEs from many emerging countries, including China and India, have tended to strategically use mergers and acquisitions to upgrade and strengthen their technological capabilities, sometimes diversifying into ones unrelated to their original core businesses.

The pathways taken by MNEs in the development and organization of their strategic knowledge capabilities have been determined by a complex interaction between a wide range of factors: the state of the world economy when they initially internationalized, institutional conditions in home and host countries, competition and technological change in their respective industries, and their organizational and administrative heritages (Zander & Mathews, 2010). In view of this complexity, the patterns summarized above constitute only coarse descriptions at a rather high level of abstraction. MNEs of different national origins, internationalizing at different times, and active in different industries have developed very different responses to vastly different conditions. However, the literature on knowledge creation in MNEs is yet to account for the relevant contingencies and organizational outcomes more compellingly, while at the same time it needs to consider how the organization and management of MNE knowledge-creating activities continues to be a moving target.

In recent decades, the economic, institutional, and technological changes commonly subsumed under the title "globalization" have facilitated the establishment and acquisition of R&D units in foreign countries, while revolutionizing the possibilities for control, coordination, and information exchange between geographically dispersed units. These forces have also fundamentally affected the location and configuration of other functions, most dramatically, the design of international supply chains, altering the structural properties of MNEs, and the interactions not only within international R&D organizations but also between R&D and other MNE functions. In recent literatures, much attention has been given to the role of information technology in connecting internal (and external) actors in MNE innovation processes, but very little to the organization designs into which those technologies are incorporated.

The disaggregation and dispersal of value chains, originally phenomena primarily affecting production (Buckley, 2014), are increasingly shaping all functional areas and implemented all the way from the bottom of the organizational hierarchy to HQs (Nell, Kappen, & Laamanen, 2017). In many MNEs, country foreign subsidiaries are no longer primary organizational units, as decision-making has increasingly shifted toward regional or worldwide systems of functionally organized entities (Mees-Buss, Welch, & Westney, 2019). While these developments promise simplicity by virtue of centralization and decreasing dependency on fully fledged foreign subsidiaries, they may also limit local discretion to pursue entrepreneurial initiatives, which have been, historically, a source of knowledge creation and innovative dynamism.

The forces favoring globalization and international integration have not gone unimpeded. In the past decade, a deliberalization movement has gained momentum (Verbeke, Coeurderoy, & Matt, 2018; Witt, 2019; World Bank, 2020), with nationalistic policies and increasing protectionism. Should these tendencies take the overhand, the consequences are difficult to foresee—they could fuel the call for centralization of the MNE's strategic knowledge creation activities, while also heralding the return of multidomestic MNE structures as they existed in the interwar period of the past century. Added to these developments on the firm and spatial level of analysis are global trends of digitalization and sustainability, which are sure to influence both the internationalization process (Coviello, Kano, & Liesch, 2017) and activities performed abroad (Chakrabarty & Wang, 2012). These and other dynamics at both firm and country levels make it seem highly unlikely that contemporary and "modern" MNEs have reached a common ideal type configuration. On the contrary, empirical research is called for into the plethora of developments, and detailed systematic study of the internal organizational processes of MNEs with different histories and characteristics becomes highly relevant. There are good reasons to assume that the forces shaping the structures and processes of strategic knowledge creation differ depending not only on present day forces and influences but also on MNEs' temporal and geographical origins and ensuing administrative heritages.

FUTURE RESEARCH

The history of MNEs from the developed economies is comparatively well researched, and it is clear that they have gone through periods of significant change over the past century. The solidification of the received view of these MNEs and their approach to strategic knowledge creation has nevertheless curtailed attempts to critically examine its pervasiveness and also to explore what important changes may have occurred over the past two decades. European, US, and Japanese MNEs have not stopped evolving since the turn of the century. Structural changes brought about by technological advancements and the redesigning of global value chains have no doubt fundamentally affected how their R&D activities are organized and managed. Yet, the recent evolution of knowledge creation in these MNEs is still largely undocumented (Papanastassiou et al., 2020) and it offers fertile ground for future research in a number of areas identified below.

One of these areas concerns contemporary trends in the internationalization of R&D. Since the 1990s and early 2000s (UNCTAD, 2005), there have been few systematic studies of the evolution of foreign R&D in European, US, and Japanese MNEs. We know quite little about whether historical trends of gradually increasing shares of foreign R&D have been sustained, or whether international expansion has come to a standstill or even declined during more recent periods (perhaps as the result of an increasing proportion of open innovation). Also, studies that document both levels and shifts in the relative proportions of "research" and "development" in foreign R&D could cast useful light on the current state and trajectory of MNE knowledge creation. One particularly relevant issue is the development of R&D activities obtained through foreign mergers and acquisitions—what factors and deliberations determine whether to close down or retain acquired R&D units, and to what extent do they become integrated with activities taking place in other parts of the MNE? We know little about current practices in the management of international R&D and how these practices may have co-evolved with changing MNE structures. Further research is necessary to establish if the processes of centralization and specialization that have been observed in some leading MNEs (Mees-Buss et al., 2019) are also shared by others, and how such changes have affected their capacity to create and leverage knowledge created in foreign subsidiaries.

Second, we know little about current developments in knowledge creation among EMNEs, especially firms originating in countries other than China and India. There is much more to be learned about the internationalization of R&D among these MNEs, their underlying strategies, the role played by foreign subsidiaries in the upgrading of technological capabilities, and the systems and processes that are put into place to transfer, coordinate, and integrate knowledge creation between home and foreign units. Most extant accounts suggest a long-term desire to ultimately integrate knowledge developed in acquired foreign units with the knowledge held at HQs in the home country, indeed, recent studies suggest an overall positive effect from international R&D on home country R&D among Indian MNEs (De Beule & Somers, 2017). Yet, how the process is managed and the extent to which knowledge transfer and integration can indeed be effectuated, remains to be documented.

In contrast to European and US MNEs, whose R&D capabilities grew and evolved within the confines of the developed economies, emerging MNEs are unique in that they evolve more distinctively along two parallel tracks—one that draws on "good enough" technology and products for the emerging economies (Gadiesh, Leung, & Vestring, 2007), and one that is driven by access to the more advanced technological capabilities residing in the developed economies. How EMNEs balance this two-pronged approach to international expansion, and how it has affected the development and management of foreign R&D, remains to be understood in greater detail.

While relatively much attention has been given to strategic investments to access technological capabilities in foreign countries, the more evolutionary developments that can be expected among subsidiaries in the developing economies, and how these subsidiaries are managed, are two of many interesting issues that stand open for further investigation.

Conversely, we know little about how European, US, and Japanese MNEs deal with products that represent the bulk of demand in the developing countries, and how they manage the inherent tension between attributes of products developed for emerging and developed economies (Govindarajan & Ramamurti, 2011). The evolution of R&D investments in emerging economies (Zhang & Pearce, 2010; D'Agostino & Santangelo, 2012; Jha, Dhanaraj, & Krishnan, 2018) and how MNEs from the developed economies can deal with and manage the organizational implications of "superstar subsidiaries" (Blomkvist et al., 2012, 2014) in countries such as China and India are two interrelated issues that deserve particular attention.

For all types of MNEs, the integration of R&D across geographically dispersed units has remained a void in our understanding of their knowledge-creating activities. The implicit assumption has been that the emergence of increasingly advanced and capable foreign subsidiaries must mean that MNEs have developed ever more perfect ways of integrating and combining knowledge across these subsidiaries, but systematic empirical evidence on the issue is scarce indeed. Case-based evidence and cross-sectional studies have generated a rudimentary understanding of MNE innovation that involves geographically dispersed units (Bartlett & Ghoshal, 1990; Hedlund & Ridderstråle, 1995; Frost & Zhou, 2005; Ambos & Schlegelmilch, 2004; Bergek & Bruzelius, 2010), but little is known about the commonness of such innovation projects and their relative contribution to the overall technological renewal of the MNE. Answering these questions is of fundamental importance for understanding the nature of MNE knowledge-based competitive advantages, and how these evolve over time and shifting conditions in the broader IB environment.

Concluding Remarks

This chapter discussed the processes through which geographical patterns of international R&D have evolved, by zooming in on the structures, systems, and procedures through which both developed-market MNEs and EMNEs have sought to govern and coordinate these activities over time. We point to several gaps in the literature predominantly around the recent evolution of knowledge creation in both these types of MNEs. To effectively address these substantial lacunae in our understanding of strategic knowledge creation in MNEs, it would be particularly useful to again undertake the type of predominantly qualitative and detailed comparative case studies of MNEs successfully carried out several decades ago (Prahalad & Doz, 1987; Bartlett & Ghoshal, 1989; recent examples include Zeschky, Daiber, Widenmayer, & Gassman, 2014;

Mees-Buss et al., 2019). Although such an approach often requires difficult-to-obtain access to managers' time and to sensitive information, the rewards to researchers who take on the challenge, we argue, will be plentiful. Knowledge creation and innovation in MNEs and their ability to adapt to competition and changing environmental circumstances have been and will remain central issues in IB strategy research.

REFERENCES

Almeida, P. 1996. Knowledge sourcing by foreign multinationals: Patent citation analysis in the U.S. semiconductor industry. *Strategic Management Journal*, 17(S2): 155–165.

Alon, I., Anderson, J., Munim, Z. H., & Ho, A. 2018. A review of the internationalization of Chinese enterprises. *Asia Pacific Journal of Management*, 35(3): 573–605.

Ambos, B., & Schlegelmilch, B. B. 2004. The use of international R&D teams: An empirical investigation of selected contingency factors. *Journal of World Business*, 39(1): 37–48.

Anderson, J., Sutherland, D., & Severe, S. 2015. An event study of home and host country patent generation in Chinese MNEs undertaking strategic asset acquisitions in developed markets. *International Business Review*, 24(5): 758–771.

Andersson, U., & Forsgren, M. 2000. In search of centre of excellence: Network embeddedness and subsidiary roles in multinational corporations. *Management International Review*, 40(4): 329–350.

Andersson, U., Forsgren, M., & Holm, U. 2007. Balancing subsidiary influence in the federative MNC: A business network view. *Journal of International Business Studies*, 38(5): 802–818.

Aoki, M., & Dore, R. 1994. *The Japanese Firm: Sources of Competitive Strength*. Oxford: Oxford University Press.

Asakawa, K. 2001a. Evolving headquarter-subsidiary dynamics in internal R&D: The case of Japanese multinationals. *R&D Management*, 31(1): 1–14.

Asakawa, K. 2001b. Organizational tension in international R&D management: The case of Japanese firms. *Research Policy*, 30(5): 735–757.

Asakawa, K., & Som, A. 2008. Internationalization of R&D in China and India: Conventional wisdom versus reality. *Asia Pacific Journal of Management*, 25(3): 375–394.

Awate, S., Larsen, M. M., & Mudambi, R. 2015. Accessing vs. sourcing knowledge: A comparative study of R&D internationalization between emerging and advanced economy firms. *Journal of International Business Studies*, 46(1): 63–86.

Bartlett, C. A. 1986. Building and managing the transnational: The new organizational challenge. In M. E. Porter (Ed.), *Competition in Global Industries*. Brighton, MA: Harvard Business School Press.

Bartlett, C. A., & Ghoshal, S. 1989. *Managing across Borders: The Transnational Solution*. London: Hutchinson.

Bartlett, C. A., & Ghoshal, S. 1990. Managing innovation in the transnational corporation. In C. A. Bartlett, Y. Doz, & G. Hedlund (Eds.), *Managing the Global Firm*. London: Routledge.

Baskaran, A., & Muchie, M. 2008. Foreign direct investment and internationalization of R&D: The case of BRICS economies. *Diiper Research Series Working Papers*, 7.

Bathelt, H., Malmberg, A., & Maskell, P. 2004. Clusters and knowledge: Local buzz, global pipelines and the process of knowledge creation. *Progress in Human Geography*, 28(1): 31–56.

Belderbos, R. 2003. Entry mode, organizational learning and R&D in foreign affiliates: Evidence from Japanese firms. *Strategic Management Journal*, 24(3): 235–259.

Belderbos, R., Leten, B., & Suzuki, S. 2013. How global is R&D? Firm-level determinants of home-country bias in R&D. *Journal of International Business Studies*, 44(8): 765–786.

Bergek, A., & Bruzelius, M. 2010. Are patents with multiple inventors from different countries a good indicator of international R&D collaboration? The case of ABB. *Research Policy*, 39(10): 1321–1334.

Birkinshaw, J. 1997. Entrepreneurship in multinational corporations: The characteristics of subsidiary initiatives. *Strategic Management Journal*, 18(3): 207–229.

Birkinshaw, J., Bouquet, C., & Ambos, T. C. 2007. Attention HQ. *Business Strategy Review*, 17(3): 4–9.

Birkinshaw, J., Bresman, H., & Håkanson, L. 2000. Managing the post-acquisition process: How the human integration and task integration processes interact to foster value creation. *Journal of Management Studies*, 37(3): 395–426.

Birkinshaw, J., & Fry, A. 1998. Subsidiary initiatives to develop new markets. *Sloan Management Review*, 39(3): 51–61.

Birkinshaw, J., & Hood, N. 1998. Multinational subsidiary evolution: Capability and charter change in foreign-owned subsidiary companies. *Academy of Management Review*, 23(4): 773–795.

Blomkvist, K., Kappen, P., & Zander, I. 2010. Quo vadis? The entry into new technologies by foreign subsidiaries of the multinational corporation. *Journal of International Business Studies*, 41(9): 1525–1549.

Blomkvist, K., Kappen, P., & Zander, I. 2012. Superstar subsidiaries of the multinational corporation: In search of origins and drivers. In M. Andersson, C. Karlsson, B. Johansson, & H. Lööf (Eds.), *Innovation and Growth: From R&D Strategies of Innovating Firms to Economy-wide Technological Change*. Oxford: Oxford University Press.

Blomkvist, K., Kappen, P., & Zander, I. 2014. Win, place, or show? How foreign market entry strategies contribute to the technological growth of the multinational corporation. *Long Range Planning*, 47(1–2): 16–31.

Blomkvist, K., Kappen, P., & Zander, I. 2014. Superstar inventors—Towards a people-centric perspective on the geography of technological renewal in the multinational corporation. *Research Policy*, 43(4): 669–682.

Blomkvist, K., Kappen, P., & Zander, I. 2018. Who is in and who is out? Integration of technological knowledge in the multinational corporation. *Industrial and Corporate Change*, 28(3): 437–457.

Bonaglia, F., Goldstein, A., & Mathews, J. A. 2007. Accelerated internationalization by emerging markets' multinationals: The case of the white goods sector. *Journal of World Business*, 42(4): 369–383.

Brandl, K., & Mudambi, R. 2015. EMNCs and catch-up processes: The case of four Indian industries. In A. Cuervo-Cazurra & R. Ramamurti (Eds.), *Understanding Multinationals from Emerging Markets*. Cambridge: Cambridge University Press.

Bruche, G. 2009. The emergence of China and India as new competitors in MNCs' innovation networks. *Competition & Change*, 13(3): 267–288.

Buckley, P. J. 2009. The impact of the global factory on economic development. *Journal of World Business*, 44(2): 131–143.

Buckley, P. J. 2014. International integration and coordination in the global factory. In P. J. Buckley (Ed.), *The Multinational Enterprise and the Emergence of the Global Factory*. London: Palgrave Macmillan.

Cantwell, J. A. 1989. *Technological Innovation and Multinational Corporations*. Oxford: Basil Blackwell.

Cantwell, J. A. 1992. The internationalization of technological activity and its implications for competitiveness. In O. Granstrand, L. Håkanson, & S. Sjölander (Eds.), *Technology Management and International Business: Internationalization of R&D and Technology*. Chichester: Wiley.

Cantwell, J. A. 1995. The globalisation of technology: What remains of the product cycle model? *Cambridge Journal of Economics*, 19(1): 155–174.

Cantwell, J., & Mudambi, R. 2005. MNE competence-creating subsidiary mandates. *Strategic Management Journal*, 26(12): 1109–1128.

Celly, N., Prabhu, J. C., & Subramanian, V. 2013. Innovation by Indian EMNEs. In: P. J. Williamson, R. Ramamurti, A. C. C. Fleury, & M. T. L. Fleury (Eds.), *The Competitive Advantage of Emerging Market Multinationals*. Cambridge: Cambridge University Press.

Chakrabarty, S., & Wang, L. 2012. The long-term sustenance of sustainability practices in MNCs: A dynamic capabilities perspective of the role of R&D and internationalization. *Journal of Business Ethics*, 110(2): 205–217.

Chandler, A. D. 1962. *Strategy and Structure: Chapters in the History of American Industrial Enterprise*. Cambridge, MA: MIT Press.

Chaturvedi, K., & Chataway, J. 2006. Strategic integration of knowledge in Indian pharmaceutical firms: Creating competencies for innovation. *International Journal of Business Innovation and Research*, 1(1–2): 27–50.

Chen, Y.-C. 2007. The upgrading of multinational regional innovation networks in China. *Asia Pacific Business Review*, 13(3): 373–403.

Chesnais, F. 1988. Multinational enterprises and the international diffusion of technology. In G. Dosi, C. Freeman, R. Nelson, G. Silverberg, & L. Soete (Eds.), *Technical Change and Economic Theory*. London: Pinter Publishers.

Child, J., & Rodrigues, S. B. 2005. The internationalization of Chinese firms: A case for theoretical extension. *Management and Organization Review*, 1(3): 381–410.

Collinson, S., & Rugman, A. 2008. The regional nature of Japanese multinational business. *Journal of International Business Studies*, 39(2): 215–230.

Cordell, A. J. 1971. *The Multinational Firm, Foreign Direct Investment and Canadian Science Policy*. Science Council of Canada, Special Study.

Coviello, N., Kano, L., & Liesch, P. 2017. Adapting the Uppsala model to a modern world: Macro-context and microfoundations. *Journal of International Business Studies*, 48(9): 1151–1164.

D'Agostino, L. M., & Santangelo, G. D. 2012. Do overseas R&D laboratories in emerging markets contribute to home knowledge creation? An extension of the double diamond model. *Management International Review*, 52(2): 251–273.

De Beule, P., & Somers, D. 2017. The impact of international R&D on home-country R&D for Indian multinationals. *Transnational Corporations*, 24(1): 27–55.

Deng, P. 2007. Investing for strategic resources and its rationale: The case of outward FDI from Chinese companies. *Business Horizons*, 50(1): 71–81.

Deng, P. 2009. Why do Chinese firms tend to acquire strategic assets in international expansion? *Journal of World Business*, 44(1): 74–84.

Di Minin, A., Zhang, J., & Gammeltoft, P. 2012. Chinese foreign direct investment in R&D in Europe: A new model of R&D internationalization? *European Management Journal*, 30(3): 189–203.

Dunning, J. H. 1983. Changes in the level and structure of international production: The last one hundred years. In M. Casson (Ed.), *The Growth of International Business*. London: George Allen & Unwin.

Dunning, J. H. 1993. *Multinational Enterprises and the Global Economy*. Wokingham: Addison Wesley.

Dunning, J. H. 2000. Regions, globalization, and the knowledge economy: The issues stated. In J.H. Dunning (Ed.), *Regions, globalization, and the knowledge-based economy*. Oxford: Oxford University Press.

Dunning, J. H. 2009. The key literature on IB activities: 1960–2006. In A. M. Rugman (Ed.), *The Oxford Handbook of International Business*. Oxford: Oxford University Press.

Dunning, J. H., & Lundan, S. 2009. The internationalization of corporate R&D: A review of the evidence and some policy implications for home countries. *Review of Policy Research*, 26(1–2): 13–33.

Dunning, J. H., & Narula, R. 1995. The R&D activities of foreign firms in the United States. *International Studies of Management & Organization*, 25(1–2): 39–74.

Elia, S., & Santangelo, G. D. 2017. The evolution of strategic asset-seeking acquisitions by emerging market multinationals. *International Business Review*, 26(5): 855–866.

Fan, P. 2006. Catching up through developing innovation capability: Evidence from China's telecom-equipment industry. *Technovation*, 26(3): 359–368.

Feinberg, S. E., & Gupta, A. K. 2004. Knowledge spillovers and the assignment of R&D responsibilities to foreign subsidiaries. *Strategic Management Journal*, 25(8–9): 823–845.

Franko, L. G. 1976. *The European Multinationals: A Renewed Challenge to American and British Big Business*. Stamford: Greylock Publishers.

Franko, L. G. 1983. *The Threat of Japanese Multinationals: How the West Can Respond*. Chichester: Wiley.

Frost, T. S. 2001. The geographic sources of foreign subsidiaries' innovations. *Strategic Management Journal*, 22(2): 101–123.

Frost, T. S., & Zhou, C. 2005. R&D co-practice and "reverse" knowledge integration in multinational firms. *Journal of International Business Studies*, 36(6): 676–687.

Gadiesh, O., Leung, P., & Vestring, T. 2007. The battle for China's good-enough market. *Harvard Business Review*, 85(9): 81–89.

Gammeltoft, P. 2006. Internationalisation of R&D: Trends, drivers and managerial challenges. *International Journal of Technology and Globalisation*, 2(1–2): 177–199.

Gassmann, O., & Von Zedtwitz, M. 1999. New concepts and trends in international R&D organization. *Research Policy*, 28(2–3): 231–250.

Gerybadze, A., & Reger, G. 1999. Globalization of R&D: Recent changes in the management of innovation in transnational corporations. *Research Policy*, 28(2–3): 251–274.

Govindarajan, V., Rajgopal, S., Srivastava, A., & Wang, Y. 2019. R&D spending has dramatically surpassed advertising spending. *Harvard Business Review*. https://hbr.org/2019/05/rd-spending-has-dramatically-surpassed-advertising-spending. Accessed November 3, 2019.

Govindarajan, V., & Ramamurti, R. 2011. Reverse innovation, emerging markets, and global strategy. *Global Strategy Journal*, 1(3–4): 191–205.

Granstrand, O. 1999. Internationalization of corporate R&D: A Study of Japanese and Swedish corporations. *Research Policy*, 28(2–3): 275–302.

Guillén, M. F., & Garcia-Canal, E. 2009. The American model of the multinational firm and the "new" multinationals from emerging economies. *Academy of Management Perspectives*, 23(2): 23–35.

Håkanson, L. 1981. Organization and evolution of foreign R&D in Swedish multinationals. *Geografiska annaler, Series B, Human Geography*, 63(1): 47–56.

Håkanson, L. 1983. R&D in foreign-owned subsidiaries in Sweden. In W. Goldberg (Ed.), *Governments and Multinationals*. Cambridge: Oelgeschlager, Gunn & Hain.

Håkanson, L. 1995. Learning through acquisitions: Management and integration of foreign R&D laboratories. *International Studies of Management and Organization*, 25(1–2): 121–157.

Håkanson, L. & Kappen, P. 2016. Live and let die: A survival analysis of foreign R&D Units in Swedish MNCs. *International Business Review*, 25(6): 1185–1196.

Håkanson, L. & Nobel, R. 1993. Foreign research and development in Swedish multinationals. *Research Policy*, 22(5–6): 373–396.

Hedlund, G. 1986. The hypermodern MNC—A heterarchy? *Human Resource Management*, 25(1): 9–35.

Hedlund, G., & Ridderstråle, J. 1995. International development projects—Key to competitiveness, impossible, or mismanaged? *International Studies of Management & Organization*, 25(1–2): 158–184.

Hedlund, G. & Rolander, D. 1990. Action in heterarchies: New approaches to managing the MNC. In C. A. Bartlett, Y. Doz, & G. Hedlund (Eds.), *Managing the Global Firm*. London: Routledge.

Hobday, M. 1995. East Asian latecomer firms: Learning the technology of electronics. *World Development*, 23(7): 1171–1193.

Hong, E., & Sun, L. 2006. Dynamics of internationalization and outward investment: Chinese corporations' strategies. *The China Quarterly*, 187: 610–634.

Hymer, S. 1976. *The International Operations of National Firms: A Study of Direct Investment*. Cambridge, MA: MIT Press.

Jha, S., Dhanaraj, C., & Krishnan, R. T. 2018. From arbitrage to global innovation: Evolution of multinational R&D in emerging markets. *Management International Review*, 58(4): 633–661.

Jones, G. 1996. *The Evolution of International Business: An Introduction*. London: Routledge.

Knickerbocker, F. T. 1973. *Oligopolistic Reaction and the Multinational Enterprise*. Cambridge, MA: Harvard University Press.

Kogut, B., & Zander, U. 1992. Knowledge of the firm, combinative capabilities, and the replication of technology. *Organization Science*, 3(3): 384–397.

Kogut, B., & Zander, U. 1993. Knowledge of the firm and the evolutionary theory of the multinational corporation. *Journal of International Business Studies*, 24(4): 625–645.

Kuhn, T. S. 1962. *The Structure of Scientific Revolutions*. Chicago: University of Chicago Press.

Kumar, N. 2001. Determinants of location of overseas R&D activity of multinational enterprises: The case of US and Japanese corporations. *Research Policy*, 30(1): 159–174.

Lall, S. 1983. *The New Multinationals: The Spread of Third World Enterprises*. Chichester: Wiley.

Lam, A. 2008. Transnational learning and knowledge transfer: A comparative analysis of Japanese and US MNCs' overseas R&D laboratories. In C. Smith, B. McSweeney, & R. Fitzgerald (Eds.), *Remaking Management: Between Global and Local*. Cambridge: Cambridge University Press.

Lecraw, D. 1977. Direct investments by firms from less developed countries. *Oxford Economic Papers*, 29(3): 442–457.

Lee, K., & Lim, C. 2001. Technological regimes, catching-up and leapfrogging: Findings from the Korean industries. *Research Policy*, 30(3): 459–483.

Lehrer, M., & Asakawa, K. 2003. Managing intersecting R&D social communities: A comparative study of European "knowledge incubators" in Japanese and American firms. *Organization Studies*, 24(5): 771–792.

Lewin, A. Y., Massini, S., & Peeters, C. 2009. Why are companies offshoring innovation? The emerging global race for talent. *Journal of International Business Studies*, 40(6): 901–925.

Magee, S. P. 1981. The appropriability theory of the multinational corporation. *Annals of the American Academy of Political and Social Science*, 458(1): 123–135.

Malmberg, A., Sölvell, Ö., & Zander, I. 1996. Spatial clustering, local accumulation of knowledge and firm competitiveness. *Geografiska Annaler, Series B, Human Geography*, 78(2): 85–97.

Mathews, J. A. 2002a. *Dragon Multinational: Towards a New Model of Global Growth*. New York, NY: Oxford University Press.

Mathews, J. A. 2002b. Comparative advantages of the latecomer firm: A resource-based account of industrial catch-up strategies. *Asia Pacific Journal of Management*, 19(4): 467–488.

Mees-Buss, J., Welch, C., & Westney, D. E. 2019. What happened to the transnational? The emergence of the neo-global corporation. *Journal of International Business Studies*, 50: 1513–1543.

Methé, D. T., & Penner-Hahn, J. D. 1999. Globalization of pharmaceutical research and development in Japanese companies: Organizational learning and the parent-subsidiary relationship. In S.L. Beechler & A. Bird (Eds.), *Japanese Multinationals Abroad: Individual and Organizational Learning*. New York, NY: Oxford University Press.

Meyer, K. E. 2015. Process perspectives on the growth of emerging economy multinationals. In A. Cuervo-Cazurra &R. Ramamurti (Eds.), *Understanding Multinationals from Emerging Markets*. Cambridge: Cambridge University Press.

Mintzberg, H., & Waters, J. A. 1985. Of strategies, deliberate and emergent. *Strategic Management Journal*, 6(3): 257–272.

Mudambi, R., & Navarra, P. 2004. Is knowledge power? Knowledge flows, subsidiary power and rent-seeking within MNCs. *Journal of International Business Studies*, 35(5): 385–406.

Nell, P. C., Kappen, P., & Laamanen, T. 2017. Reconceptualising hierarchies: The disaggregation and dispersion of headquarters in multinational corporations. *Journal of Management Studies*, 54(8): 1121–1143.

Noorderhaven, N. & Harzing, A.-W. 2009. Knowledge-sharing and social interaction within MNEs. *Journal of International Business Studies*, 40(5): 719–741.

Papanastassiou, M., Pearce, R., & Zanfei, A. 2020. Changing perspectives on the internationalization of R&D and innovation by multinational enterprises: A review of the literature. *Journal of International Business Studies*, 51: 623–664.

Patel, P. 1995. Localised production of technology for global markets. *Cambridge Journal of Economics*, 19(1): 141–153.

Pearce, R. D. 1989. *The Internationalisation of Research and Development by Multinational Enterprises*. Basingstoke: Macmillan.

Pearce, R. D. & Papanastassiou, M. 1999. Overseas R&D and the strategic evolution of MNCs: Evidence from laboratories in the UK. *Research Policy*, 28(1): 23–41.

Perlmutter, H. V. 1969. The tortuous evolution of the multi-national corporation. *Columbia Journal of World Business*, 4(4), 9–18.

Prahalad, C. K., & Doz, Y. 1987. *The Multinational Mission: Balancing Local Demands and Global Vision*. New York, MA: The Free Press.

Reddy, P. 1997. New trends in globalization of corporate R&D and implications for innovation capability in host countries: A survey from India. *World Development*, 25(11): 1821–1837.

Reger, G. 2002. Internationalisation of research and development in Western European, Japanese and North American multinationals. *International Journal of Entrepreneurship and Innovation Management*, 2(2–3): 164–185.

Ronstadt, R. C. 1978. International R&D: the establishment and evolution of research and development abroad by seven U.S. multinationals. *Journal of International Business Studies*, 9(1): 7–24.

Rugman, A. M., & Verbeke, A. 2009. Location, competitiveness, and the multinational enterprise. In A. M. Rugman (Ed.), *The Oxford Handbook of International Business*. Oxford: Oxford University Press.

Rui, H., & Yip, G. S. 2008. Foreign acquisitions by Chinese firms: A strategic intent perspective. *Journal of World Business*, 43(2): 213–226.

Shimizutani, S., & Todo, Y. 2008. What determines overseas R&D activities? The case of Japanese multinational firms. *Research Policy*, 37(3): 530–544.

Song, J., Asakawa, K., & Chu, Y. 2011. What determines knowledge sourcing from host locations of overseas R&D operations? A study of global R&D activities of Japanese multinationals. *Research Policy*, 40(3): 380–390.

Stopford, J. M., & Wells, L. T. 1972. *Managing the Multinational Enterprise: Organization of the Firm and Ownership of the Subsidiaries*. New York, NY: Basic Books.

Teece, D. J. 1981. The market for know-how and the efficient international transfer of technology. *Annals of the American Academy of Political and Social Science*, 458(1): 81–96.

UNCTAD. 2005. *World Investment Report: Transnational Corporations and the Internationalization of R&D*. New York, NY and Geneva: United Nations.

UNCTAD. 2019. *World Investment Report: Special Economic Zones*. New York, NY: United Nations.

Verbeke, A., Coeurderoy R., & Matt, T. 2018. The future of international business research on corporate globalization that never was … *Journal of International Business Studies*, 49: 1101–1112.

Vernon, R. 1979. The product cycle hypothesis in a new international environment. *Oxford Bulletin of Economics and Statistics*, 41(4): 255–267.

Von Zedtwitz, M. 2005. International R&D strategies in companies from developing countries—The case of China. *Globalization of R&D and Developing Countries*. New York, NY and Geneva: United Nations.

Walsh, K. A. 2007. China R&D: A high-tech field of dreams. *Asia Pacific Business Review*, 13(3): 321–335.

Wells, L. T. Jr. 1981. Foreign investors from the third world. In K. Kumar & M.G. McLeod (Eds.), *Multinationals from Developing Countries*. Lexington: D. C. Heath and Company.

Wells, L. T. Jr. 1983. *Third World Multinationals: The Rise of Foreign Direct Investment from Developing Countries*. Cambridge, MA: MIT Press.

Westney, D. E. 2019. Changing MNEs, *Japan MNE Insights*, 6(2): 1–7.

Wilkins, M. 1988. European and North American multinationals, 1870–1914: Comparisons and contrasts. *Business History*, 30(1): 8–45.

Williamson, P.J., Ramamurti, R., Fleury, A., & Fleury, M. T. L. 2013. *The Competitive Advantage of Emerging Market Multinationals*. Cambridge: Cambridge University Press.

Witt, M.A. 2019. De-globalization: Theories, predictions, and opportunities for international business research. *Journal of International Business Studies*, 50(7): 1053–1077.

World Bank. 2020. *World Development Report 2020: Trading for Development in the Age of Global Value Chains*. Washington, DC: World Bank.

Yonekura, S., & McKinney, S. 2005. Innovative multinational forms: Japan as a case study. In A. D. Chandler & B. Mazlish (Eds.), *Leviathans: Multinational Corporations and the New Global History*. Cambridge: Cambridge University Press.

Yoshino, M. Y. 1974. The multinational spread of Japanese manufacturing investment since World War II. *The Business History Review*, 48(3): 357–381.

Yoshino, M. Y. 1976. *Japan's Multinational Enterprises*. Cambridge, MA: Harvard University Press.

Zaheer, S. 1995. Overcoming the liability of foreignness. *Academy of Management Journal*, 38(2): 341–363.

Zander, I. 1994. *The Tortoise Evolution of the Multinational Corporation—Foreign Technological Activity in Swedish Multinational Firms 1890–1990*. Stockholm: Institute of International Business, Stockholm School of Economics.

Zander, I., & Mathews, J. A. 2010. Beyond heterarchy—Emerging futures of the "hypermodern" MNC. In U. Andersson & U. Holm (Eds.), *Headquarters Role in the Contemporary MNC*. Cheltenham: Edward Elgar.

Zeschky, M., Daiber, M., Widenmayer, B., & Gassman, O. 2014. Coordination in global R&D organizations: An examination of the role of subsidiary mandate and modular product architectures in dispersed R&D organizations. *Technovation*, 34(10): 594–604.

Zhang, S., & Pearce, R. 2010. Sources of technology and the strategic roles of MNE subsidiaries in China. *Multinational Business Review*, 18(3): 49–72.

....

CHAPTER 7

INTERNATIONALIZATION PROCESS PERSPECTIVE

Revisiting the Link Between Market Knowledge and Market Commitment

....

GRAZIA D. SANTANGELO

INTRODUCTION

UNDERSTANDING how to plan the internationalization process (IP) effectively is critical for international business (IB) scholars and managers alike. Thus, it is not surprising that research investigating this process has developed along a distinctive stream in the IB field. Initiated by the pioneering article of Johanson and Vahlne (1977), which developed the IP (known also as Uppsala) model, and further revitalized by the latest revision of the model (Vahlne & Johanson, 2017), the interest on firm internationalization has manifested in a growing number of studies analyzing the IP in relation to consolidated firms, international new ventures, born globals (BGs), and family firms (Coviello, 2006; Ellis, 2011; Knight & Liesch, 2016; Pukall & Calabrò, 2014), as well as to firms originating from emerging markets (Hertenstein, Sutherland, & Anderson, 2017; Luo & Tung, 2007; Meyer & Thaijongrak, 2013) and those targeting these markets (Meyer & Gelbuda, 2006; Santangelo & Meyer, 2011).

A core issue in the IP model and in the discussion that it has generated over time is the relationship between the firm's knowledge and commitment about foreign markets and its path of internationalization. In particular, the discussion revolves around the nature of the process depicted in the IP model as mainly incremental and gradual. Over time, this view has been challenged (see Forsgren, 2002) and attention has been drawn on the non-linearity and discontinuity of the process around how firms acquire foreign market knowledge when they first internationalize (Pedersen & Shaver, 2011; Santangelo & Stucchi, 2018), how their commitment toward internationalization progresses over time (Benito, 2005; Benito & Welch, 1997; Nachum & Song, 2011; Santangelo & Meyer, 2011), and how their internationalization dynamics evolve (Santangelo & Meyer, 2017).

This chapter discusses the IP perspective by focusing on the salient points that have animated this debate. It revisits the debate on the IP to ultimately address the following questions:

- How do firms acquire knowledge in different phases of the IP?
- How do internationalization dynamics evolve over time and what is the underlying mechanism?

How we address these questions bears critical implications for the strategy-making of MNEs at different stages of their IP. The discussion focuses on internationalization through foreign direct investment (FDI), defined as an "international investment that reflects the objective of a resident in one economy (the direct investor) obtaining a lasting interest in an enterprise resident in another economy (the direct investment enterprise)" (IMF, 2003). FDI, among the internationalization modes through which firms can expand abroad (e.g. indirect and direct exports, outsourcing, licensing) is a higher-commitment mode requiring substantial resources and, consequently, entailing higher risk (Kumar & Subramanian, 1997). Firms engaging in FDI for the first time (i.e. first-time internationalization) experience different challenges than those having already passed this hurdle (i.e. subsequent internationalization). Thus, first-time and subsequent internationalization are likely to be different processes with distinctive challenges. For firms striving to become international, the acquisition of knowledge that could ease their first-time internationalization is vital. Firms that have already become MNEs are, instead, more eager to learn about how their commitment towards internationalization can be effectively adjusted in response to, for instance, environmental changes. With subsequent internationalizers, the focus is on the evolution of the internationalization dynamics and the underlying mechanism that firms strive to cope with.

In this chapter, I propose that addressing questions about knowledge acquisition over time and internationalization dynamics, is critical to outline specific lines of inquiry that can inform the future research agenda on the firm's IP. In doing so, I also discuss the current research on the relationship between market knowledge, firms' resource commitment to internationalization, and performance. I conclude this chapter with directions for future research, which are set to provide timely recommendations on how the contingencies identified in the debate on the IP model may inform future lines of inquiry on the acquisition of market knowledge for first-time and subsequent internationalization. This will be useful to scholars and managerial decision makers concerned with the evolution of the dynamics of the IP over time.

The IP Perspective

The IP model is the general framework used for interpreting the firm's internationalization. The model has been initially proposed by Johanson and Vahlne (1977) and continuously revised over the last forty years. These different revisions had the objective to enrich and extend the initial formulation of the model with the introduction of new constructs and the adoption of new perspectives from other research fields in order to offer an updated understanding of the IP. In what follows, an overview of the IP model and its most salient revisions are discussed before weighing in on the debate that the model has stimulated over the last few decades.

An Overview of the IP Model

The IP model—rooted in Penrose's (1959) *Theory of the Growth of the Firms* and Cyert and March (1963) *Behavioral Theory of the Firm*—revolves around experiential learning, which is the basis for commitment decisions toward internationalization; that is, firms are expected to commit their resources toward internationalization based on their degree of prior experiential knowledge. The model depicts internationalization as a sequential process where state variables (i.e. "market commitment" and "market knowledge") influence change variables ("commitment decisions" and "current activities") in an iterative process. Thus, the firm's internationalization is the result of cumulative actions and this reflects on entry mode choice as well as on the sequence of foreign countries firms enter. In terms of entry mode choice, internationalization progresses along an "establishment chain" with firms moving from exports to contractual modes and eventually to equity modes of servicing foreign markets (Andersen, 1997; Johanson & Vahlne, 1977). The cumulative and incremental nature of the process also reflects in the way firms expand geographically. In the logic of the IP model, firms internationalize over time by entering successively more "psychically" distant countries. They are expected to start internationalizing in neighboring countries and eventually enter more distant host locations. Overall, the basic structure of the model, grounded in the distinction between state and change variables, has remained preserved across the different revisions. Instead, the labels of the state and change variables have been revised over time to account for diverse aspects of the IP that could help update our understanding of this process and the factors it is contingent on.

In their 2009 revision of the IP model, the authors add "recognition of opportunities" to the "knowledge" concept, and bring into the model the business network view (Forsgren, Holm, & Johanson, 2005) by adding "relationship" to commitment decisions in order to clarify that "commitment is to relationships or networks of relationships" (Johanson & Vahlne, 2009). The relevance of relational aspects reflects in the centrality of the concept of "insidership." A firm's network position and knowledge, which enables recognition of opportunities, influences relational commitment decisions and "learning, creating and trust building," which are the outcomes of firm current activities. Thus, insidership in the relevant network(s) is a necessary condition for successful internationalization, and firms failing to establish trustworthy relationships are expected to suffer from what is referred to as a liability of outsidership, which severely affects their IP.

In later revisions of the model (Vahlne & Johanson, 2013, 2017), new perspectives are introduced. Vahlne and Johanson (2013) introduce ideas from dynamic capabilities theory, the theory of entrepreneurship, and the theory of management of uncertainty. In particular, in this version of the model, knowledge is relabeled in terms of different types of dynamic capabilities, which relate to opportunity recognition, internationalization, and networking. The relational aspects of commitment decisions are now accounted for in terms of reconfiguration of resources and redesign of coordination systems across the firm's internal and external networks. Thus, dynamic capabilities, including networking capabilities, facilitate the management of international operations within and across firms. Vahlne and Johanson (2017) make a further effort to enrich the model by bringing in perspectives developed in other research areas. Specifically, they frame the IP model within an evolutionary theory perspective. The model still revolves around state and change variables with the emphasis now placed on the latter (i.e. now relabeled "commitment process" and "knowledge development processes"). Experiential learning remains the driver of the model and is now explicitly anchored to the evolutionary economic perspective (Nelson & Winter, 1982). Calling upon the concept of "history dependency" (Cyert & March, 1963), the 2017 model further emphasizes that learning is based on experience and occurs under conditions of risk and uncertainty and partial ignorance across all internal and external units. Thus, "knowledge development processes...are occurring continuously, thereby changing the state variables" (Vahlne & Johanson, 2017) (i.e. "capabilities" and "commitment/performance" in this version of the model). The nature of the firm's IP remains essentially gradual and incremental; this is an assumption that has been preserved in later versions of the IP model.

The Debate around the IP Model

The debate revolving around the IP model challenges the view that the IP is mainly gradual and incremental pointing also to non-linearities and discontinuities of this process. MNEs can revise their commitment decisions toward internationalization and, as a result, increase or decrease their international operations (Benito, 2005; Benito & Welch, 1997; Nachum & Song, 2011; Santangelo & Meyer, 2011); and move quickly over multiple stages or even jump stages (Pedersen & Shaver, 2011; Santangelo & Stucchi, 2018). Benito and Welch (1994) were among the first to highlight that learning and capability building influence the change of international operations following an iterative process. Meyer and Gelbuda (2006) illustrate the relevance of feedback effects on the outcome of one cycle of actions on the actions of the next cycle. A number of works study the IP in terms of step function to account for the discontinuous increase and decrease of commitment over time (e.g. Clarke & Liesch, 2017; Meyer & Thaijongrak, 2013; Pedersen & Shaver, 2011; Santangelo & Meyer, 2011). The representation of the IP in terms of step function has been also recommended to explicitly account for the time dimension (Meyer & Thaijongrak, 2013), as illustrated in Figure 7.1.

These ideas have been reflected in a number of studies showcasing that the nature of the IP is contingent on several relevant factors. First, the stages of internationalization may vary across industries (Malhotra & Hinings, 2010) depending on the industry's

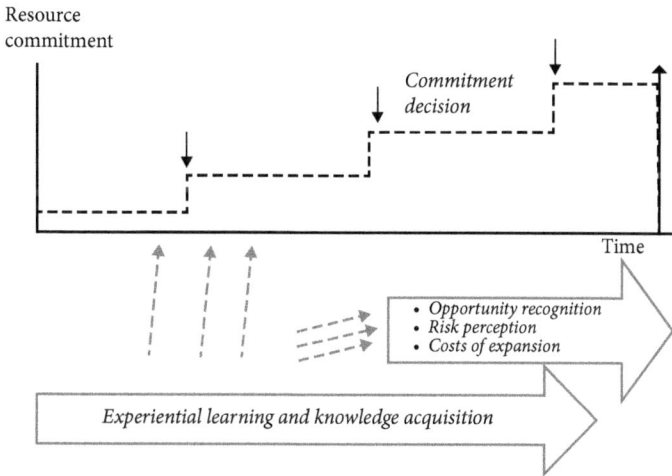

Resource
commitment

*Commitment
decision*

Time

• *Opportunity recognition*
• *Risk perception*
• *Costs of expansion*

Experiential learning and knowledge acquisition

FIGURE 7.1 The longitudinal dimension of the internationalization process (adapted from Meyer & Thaijongrak, 2013).

underlying technology, with firms in specific industries being able to "jump" over some of the IP stages. The IP of, for example, iBusiness firms is more condensed although effort and local knowledge remain important to succeed in these markets (Brouthers, Geisser, & Rothlauf, 2016; Siddiqui & Li, 2017). The adoption of advanced manufacturing technologies in specific industries offers another example. Technologies such as 3D printing enable global market presence with lower resource commitments than ever before (Laplume, Petersen, & Pearce, 2016). Also, digitalization widens the variety of international transactions and the number of parties involved, making firms more exchange-oriented than production-oriented, as in the 2017 IP model. As a result, digitalization amplifies the learning opportunities from third parties as well as the challenges associated with the governance of the transactions with these parties. Thus, MNEs' learning and commitment decisions across industries do not necessarily proceed gradually and incrementally (Coviello, Kano, & Liesch, 2017).

Second, there are contingencies that explain the "pace" and development of the IP relates to firm-specific factors (Forsgren, 2002; Pedersen & Petersen, 1998; Petersen, Pedersen, & Lyles, 2008). Here, firms are heterogeneous in their perception of the gap between the knowledge possessed and that needed to successfully operate in a new market (i.e. knowledge gap). Firms are also expected to perceive differently the increase or decrease in these international knowledge gaps following the launch of a foreign market venture. Intra-firm network relationships and the transfer of knowledge within a network can help to fill the knowledge gap (Hutzschenreuter & Matt, 2017). Yet, learning remains costly and different firms show a diverse ability to establish the requisite capabilities to learn and successfully manage international expansion, with their IP proceeding in wave-like patterns rather than incrementally (Håkanson & Kappen, 2017).

Third, a set of contingencies that have been identified in relation to the "pace" and development of the IP can be traced back to managerial learning, and cognitive capabilities.

Dynamic capabilities that are built and nurtured by internationally oriented entrepreneurial founders, for instance, explain the fast pace of internationalization of BG firms (Weerawardena, Mort, Liesch, & Knight, 2007). Also, as managers take action in relation to internationalization, their initial expectations are updated through learning, and thus, the motives for expanding abroad will change over time. This is important, because, unlike in the IP model that implicitly features "selling abroad" as the main internationalization motive, Cuervo-Cazurra, Narula, & Un (2015) have pointed to other motives such as "buying better," "expanding abroad," and "escape." Shifts from one motivation to another can influence increasing or decreasing of commitment toward foreign operations as well as their pace.

Fourth, contingencies influencing the nature of the IP may also relate to the firm's external context and inform cross-country differences. In the IP model, the context where firms operate has been traditionally accounted in terms of "psychic" distance between the home and host country, with firms progressively expanding into more psychically distant countries (Johanson & Vahlne, 1977). Starting with the 2009 revision, the inclusion of the business network perspective in the model has enabled us to account for the context beyond the concept of cross-country "psychic" distance. Specifically, the 2009 revision of the IP sets a landmark by viewing the home context as a web of network relationships that eases learning, trust, and commitment building toward internationalization. Firms can start their IP by learning from the experience of their own customers and or suppliers about foreign markets. Thus, network relationships in the firm's home context enable them to identify and exploit internationalization opportunities. Along the same lines, in connection with a firm's internationalization dynamics, Santangelo and Meyer (2017) speculate that a more (less) munificent domestic business ecosystem provides resources that increase (decrease) the likelihood that a firm path-breaking (path-continuing) internationalization may lead to outstanding performance (very large losses). However, recent research has highlighted the dark side of domestic business networks, which constitutes a double-edged sword to the geographic scope of firms with the "dark" side narrowing down firms' geographic scope and raising the opportunity costs of maintaining foreign operations (Iurkov & Benito, 2018, 2019). Consequently, the development of the IP is contingent on a variety of motives related to managerial prior expectations and learning about the firm and the conditions of operations at home and abroad.

Another stream of research has accounted for the role of context in the IP, with particular attention given to institutional frameworks. These studies are grounded in institutional theory, which states that institutions regulate economic activities in different ways across different countries (North, 1990) and thus, institutional actors may influence the formulation and implementation of IB strategies (Meyer, Estrin, Bhaumik, & Peng, 2009; Peng, 2003; Tsui-Auch & Möllering, 2010; Vaaler, Schrage, & Block, 2005). Based on this premise, this stream of research has investigated how institutions can facilitate or inhibit the firm's IP and the associated perceived host market risk. Most of these studies have focused on internationalization into and/or from emerging countries because the institutional framework in these country contexts is markedly different from those in advanced economies (Khanna & Palepu, 1997, 2010; Meyer & Peng, 2005; Wright, Filatotchev, Hoskisson, & Peng, 2005). Institutions in advanced economies are typically supportive of firm internationalization with country-specific advantages (CSAs) contributing to the upgrading of firm-specific advantages (FSAs) and facilitating foreign expansion (Rugman & Verbeke, 1992). Exporting firms from emerging markets where the institutional framework is weaker, are, in turn, discouraged from investing directly abroad (Welter & Smallbone, 2011). On the graduality of the IP, Santangelo and Meyer (2011) corroborate their theory with empirical evidence on how institutional voids and institutional uncertainty in emerging markets affect the implementation of MNE strategy, and thus accelerate or slow down the IP. Specifically, they explain that institutional voids increase rigidities in markets and organizations, and thus reduce the likelihood of commitment decrease. Instead, institutional uncertainty induces investors to design their strategies for flexible responses, and thus, enhances the chance for entrepreneurial opportunity recognition and commitment increase. In the context of small and medium-size enterprises, Akbar et al. (2018) also show that institutional voids have a negative direct effect on entry mode escalation but not on resource escalation.

Extant research has also looked at *changes* in environmental conditions. In particular, Santangelo and Meyer (2017) discuss the role of volatility of the home institutional context in MNE internationalization dynamics. Namely, the authors propose that home institutional volatility may either favor the development of core rigidities, and thus increase the likelihood that firms aligning their commitments to their past internationalization will experience very large losses or exit, or it may favor the development of flexible strategies, which increase the likelihood that commitment decisions breaking with past internationalization will lead to outstanding performance. In relation to a more general type of uncertainty, Figueira-de-Lemos and Hadjikhani (2014) add that, when environmental changes are perceived as detrimental, firms tend to decrease their tangible assets and commit in a more intangible way. On the opposite, when changes to the environment are perceived as beneficial, firms follow an incremental path of commitment, generally through investing in tangible resources.

Furthermore, the role of the context has been discussed from an economic geography perspective in response to the calls for more multidisciplinary IB research (Beugelsdijk & Mudambi, 2014; Mudambi, Narula, & Santangelo, 2018). In response to this call, Santangelo and Stucchi (2018), for instance, suggest that the challenges the organizations face when dealing with domestic subnational geography may eventually facilitate building coordination and control capabilities that can be reused when expanding internationally for the first time. When dispersing operations within the home country, organizations need to develop effective remote management templates to coordinate, integrate, and monitor their domestic operations, and ease intra-organizational coordination and knowledge sharing. These capabilities are then useful to coordinate and control operations beyond national borders.

These debates have spurred two main lines of research along which the discussion on firms' IPs has unfolded. The first line of research concerns the relationship between market knowledge, commitment decisions toward internationalization, and firm internationalization. In this context, the ultimate aim is to understand (1) how firms acquire market knowledge for first-time and subsequent internationalization, and (2) why they change their commitment toward ongoing operations in a given host country. A second line along which the discussion on the IP has unfolded concerns the identification of a clear mechanism explaining the different internationalization paths organizations can embark on. Here, the discussion revolves around the relationship between firm commitment decisions toward internationalization and the company's success or failure, with the ultimate aim to understand how the diverse paths of internationalization may influence MNE performance and survival. Each of these two lines of research is further discussed in the next section.

Market Knowledge, Commitment Decisions, and Firm Internationalization

The incremental and gradual nature of the process of internationalization as proposed in the IP model, has been challenged in connection with both first-time and subsequent international operations. First-time commitment may occur despite the lack of cumulated foreign market knowledge. Firms offering an internet-based platform or adopting business models relying on virtual communities (Brouthers et al., 2016) as well as new ventures (Coviello, 2006; Pukall & Calabrò, 2014) typically leapfrog over various phases of the process when they first expand abroad. The leap-frogging of emerging market firms has also been regarded as another example of firms jumping stages of the IP and following instead a springboard approach to internationalization (Luo & Tung, 2007). Emerging market firms (particularly Chinese firms) have managed to be among those who internationalize rapidly; this is because these firms do not prioritize psychically proximate countries and adopt high-risk, high-control entry modes such as international acquisitions. These examples of MNEs are at odds with the conventional IP model and pose the question of how these firms have acquired the necessary knowledge for first-time internationalization. Responses to this question have come from two different perspectives, both of which I discuss below.

The big step hypothesis argument offers a cost-related perspective (Pedersen & Shaver, 2011). From this perspective, first-time international expansion is the result of a managerial choice about an initial large ad hoc investment designed to create the architecture, systems, and managerial mindsets that would enable the firm to handle cross-border activities. From this perspective, internationalization is a discontinuous process with first-time internationalization being drastically different from subsequent internationalization. A firm initially incurs large fixed sunk costs to intentionally develop the required formal and informal management systems supporting the management, integration, and control of international operations. Having taken the first step in developing these formal and informal management systems, the firm "does not have to make the same level of investment, should it expand its international operations to other countries" (Pedersen & Shaver, 2011), but it will, over time, be exposed to the more limited costs associated with adapting these existing systems to each subsequent host country market.

An additional response to the question of how firms acquire knowledge for first-time internationalization closely relates to the effort of Vahlne and Johanson (2017) to frame the IP within evolutionary theory, with an increased emphasis being placed on learning. In this learning-focused perspective, first-time internationalization is the result of an exaptation (Santangelo & Stucchi, 2018). This is a concept that originates from evolutionary biology (Gould, 1980, 1991) and has been applied first in evolutionary economics (Dew, Sarasvathy, & Venkataraman, 2004) and subsequently in organizational learning and management research (Cattani, 2005; Marquis & Huang, 2010). The process of exaptation relates to features adopted for a particular purpose in a specific environment, that are then used for a different purpose in a different environment (Gould & Vrba, 1982).

In the context of the firm's IP, firms can exapt (re-use) capabilities initially developed for a specific purpose in the home context to the international context to expand abroad. Organizations that run geographically dispersed businesses in the domestic market can develop capabilities to manage geographically dispersed corporate units and reuse them to engage in cross-border acquisitions. Thus, coordination and control capabilities initially developed for a specific purpose (i.e. managing domestic geographical dispersion) in a specific environment (i.e. the home context) are exapted (re-used) to a different environment (i.e. the international context) for a different purpose (i.e. acquiring and integrating external resources). However, these capabilities over time lose relevance as firms acquire first-hand international market knowledge (Santangelo & Stucchi, 2018).

The prediction of a gradual and incremental internationalization of the IP model is also challenged by cases of firms revising their commitment toward ongoing operations and consequently accelerating or slowing down their internationalization. Lego, for instance, revisited their decision to offshore production activities, which drove them to subsequently reduce their internationalization commitment and slow down the pace of internationalization (Møller Larsen, Pedersen, & Slepniov, 2010). Research looking into these organizational cases has suggested that the explanatory power of the IP model can be enlarged by framing changes in firm internationalization commitments within the Mintzberg and Waters (1985) logic of strategy formation (see Santangelo & Meyer, 2011). Namely, strategy changes reflect the deviation of "realized" internationalization strategies from the strategy intended at the outset. These deviations can be a response to different stimuli such as the environment, which "dictates patterns either through direct imposition or though implicitly pre-empting organizational choices" (Mintzberg & Waters, 1985). In emerging market contexts, for instance, institutional voids and uncertainty are likely to trigger deviations between intention and outcome, with foreign firms increasing or decreasing their commitment such that the realized strategy deviates from the strategy intended at the outset. Thus, firms may increase as well as decrease their commitment toward a foreign market in response to host country institutional uncertainty and institutional voids, respectively (Santangelo & Meyer, 2011).

COMMITMENT DECISION, FIRM'S PERFORMANCE AND INTERNATIONALIZATION DYNAMICS

A further line of research along which the discussion around the IP model has unfolded concerns the dynamics of the IP. A critical point in this discussion is the lack of a clear mechanism linking the diverse internationalization paths, which an MNE can embark on as a result of their commitment decisions, and of their organizational performance.

The relationship between the path of internationalization and MNE performance (e.g. profitability) has been shown to be non-linear (García-García, García-Canal, & Guillén, 2017) mainly because we expect there to be a limit to an MNE's ability to reap the benefits of internationalization. This non-linearity has been traced back to the non-linear association between resource commitments and exposure to risk. A change (increase or decrease) in internationalization commitment may lead to a higher as well as lower risk (Clarke & Liesch, 2017; Figueira-de-Lemos, Johanson, & Vahlne, 2011). More recently, proponents of examining the IP model through an evolutionary theory lens, have made an effort to link internationalization and firm performance by linking the internationalization path resulting from diverse MNE commitment choices to MNE exposure to risks (Santangelo & Meyer, 2017). In particular, an increase in a firm's commitment toward internationalization may yield a higher risk but the nature of this risk would be different depending on the type of internationalization path pursued by the firm. These relationship dynamics are illustrated in Figure 7.2.

In Figure 7.2, resource commitment is related to time, and the historical path of resource commitment of the industry is used as a benchmark for decision makers. Following this rationale, firms expanding at a faster pace would face a higher risk of overstretching their capabilities when increasing their resource commitment (firm A in Figure 7.2). In turn, firms internationalizing at a relatively slower pace would face a higher risk of falling behind (firm B in Figure 7.2). Both types of firms may be exposed to higher risk, meaning that the relationship between resource commitment and risk is non-linear with higher risk associated to both low (firm B) and high (firm A) commitment, as illustrated in Figure 7.3.

Higher risks can yield higher returns, and thus outstanding performance, but they may also lead to significant losses and eventually to an MNE exiting the market. Drawing on evolutionary thinking, Santangelo and Meyer (2017) suggested that the more the firm's commitment toward internationalization is novel at any point in time compared to what the firm had done in the past (i.e. path-breaking internationalization), the higher the risk to overstretch firm capabilities, and thus the higher the probability of

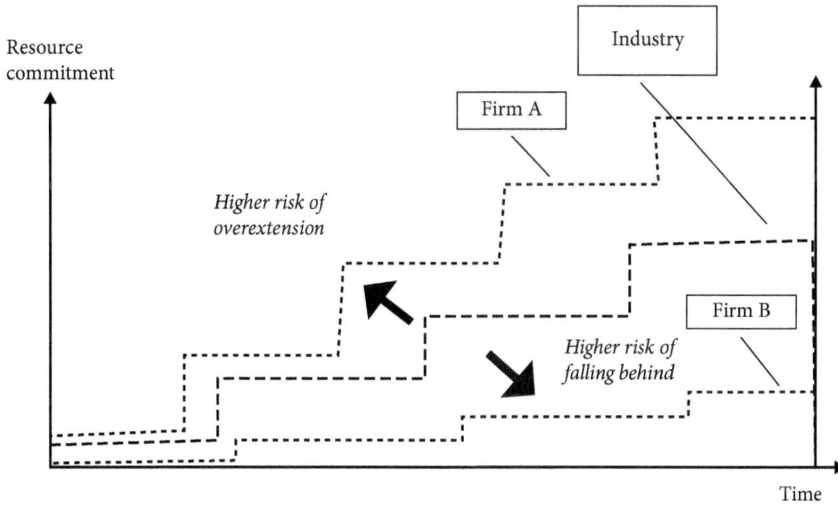

FIGURE 7.2 Dynamics of resource commitment and associated risks (adapted from Santangelo & Meyer, 2017).

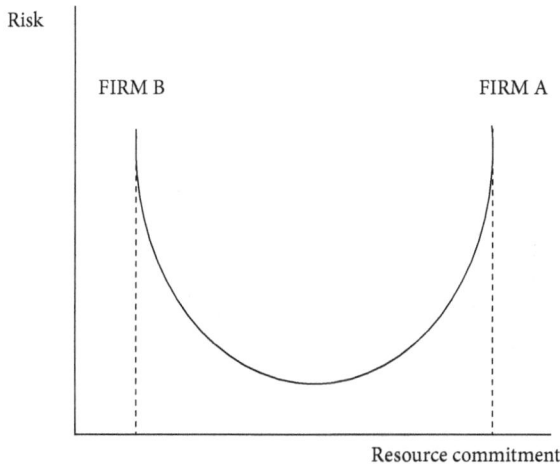

FIGURE 7.3 Relationship between risk and resource commitment.

the firm becoming among the best or worst performers in its industry. The more a firm's commitment is aligned to the firm's past internationalization (i.e. path-continuing internationalization), the higher the risk of falling behind, and hence the higher the probability of the firm not becoming one of the highest performers. Yet, in a stable environment, path-continuing internationalization may also become a low-risk strategy, and thus increase the probability of survival. In terms of the graphical representation of Figure 7.2, the resource commitment of firm A is likely to be path-breaking and that of firm B path-continuing. The nature of the risks associated with the resource commitment of firm A and firm B is likely to differ, with critical implications for MNE performance. Thus, it is very important to understand the mechanism underlying a firm's internationalization dynamics and how these diverse internationalization paths influence MNE performance and survival.

The implications of path-breaking and path-continuing strategies for MNE performance depend on the firm's evolving environment, because it is relative to its environment that an organization needs to be "fit" (Carroll & Harrison, 1994); therefore, the market selection mechanism (e.g. profits) typically assesses the fit between the MNE's commitment decisions and its environment. Market selection eventually determines whether commitment decisions along a specific internationalization path would lead to outstanding performance or large losses and exit. This means that the relationship between MNE commitment decisions and performance is not deterministic but exposed to chance; higher and lower risk internationalization paths may result, at different points in time, in different performance outcomes depending on the MNE's response of the market (Winter, 1971). It is because MNEs adjust their internationalization strategy in response to their market environments that we observe gradual, discontinuous, and often non-linear internationalization dynamics.

Setting the Research Agenda on the IP

The discussion on the relationship between market knowledge, commitment decisions, internationalization dynamics, and subsequent performance outcomes can be further advanced by bringing into the discussion key contingencies identified in the debate around the IP model. While firm-specific contingencies have been accounted for by extant research, industry-specific, manager-specific, and context-specific factors still need to be analyzed. I, therefore, see opportunities for future research to explore these factors to ultimately address the insights that have resulted from the debate on the IP model.

How Do Firms Acquire Knowledge in Different Phases of the IP?

The discussion on the relationship between market knowledge, commitment decisions, and firm internationalization has revolved around the acquisition of knowledge for first-time and subsequent internationalization from cost-based and learning-based perspectives. Industry-specific factors have been controlled for in research adopting a learning-based perspective with no specific arguments developed, however, on the role these factors may play in the firm IP. Industry-specific factors have been, instead, overlooked in work adopting a cost-related perspective. Yet, in the digital age, cross-industry differences, which are related to the opportunities and challenges that digitalization offers, open up to a number of research questions that can advance the two perspectives. In particular, the following set of research questions may help guide future research in this area:

(1) Would the adoption of digital technologies compress the time between the large ad hoc initial investment and subsequent international investments across industries?

(2) Would it shorten the time in which exapted capabilities are relevant for subsequent internationalization?

(3) Would the adoption of these technologies reduce the cross-industry divide in different phases of the IP?

Manager-related factors are another contingency that can be fruitfully considered to advance the cost-based and learning-based perspectives. In particular, we require more consideration of the internationalization motives related to managers' expectations and learning about the firm as well as related to the conditions of operations at home and abroad. Along these lines, the following research questions can be explored:

(4) Would the decision on the large ad hoc initial investment required to acquire knowledge for first-time internationalization be contingent on the specific internationalization motives resulting from managerial prior expectations and learning capabilities?

(5) Would the ability to exapt capabilities that enable the acquisition of knowledge for first-time internationalization be contingent on specific internationalization motives?

(6) Would the initial investment decision and exaptation process be contingent on the international orientation of the entrepreneurial founder of the internationalizing firm?

A further set of contingencies the IP literature has considered refer to the role of environmental conditions and the changes in these conditions over time. Since the 2009 revision of the IP model and the subsequent literature that emerged from it, environmental conditions (e.g. business ecosystems and business networks) have been suggested as a critical factor. What we are yet to understand is:

(7) How does the bright and dark side of domestic business networks play out in first-time internationalization in the cost-based and learning-based perspectives?

(8) Would the decision of a large ad hoc initial investment for first-time internationalization be contingent on the extent of a firm's embeddedness in its domestic business network?

(9) Would the ability of the firm to exapt capabilities to acquire knowledge for first-time internationalization vary depending on the extent of firm's embeddedness in these networks?

(10) Would the extent of a firm's embeddedness in these networks make the relevance of exapted capability for subsequent internationalization last longer? Or, would it shorten the time before a subsequent international expansion after a large initial ad hoc investment?

The consideration of environmental contingencies in terms of institutional voids and uncertainty may also be useful in shedding light on additional avenues for research. Possible research questions that arise are:

(11) Do home country institutional voids and uncertainty accelerate or slow down the firm's decision of an initial large ad hoc investment toward internationalization?
(12) Do they accelerate or slow down the exaptation of capabilities to acquire the knowledge needed to pass the first internationalization hurdle?
(13) In host countries with severe institutional voids and uncertainty, does the relevance of exapted capability for subsequent internationalization last longer?
(14) How do changes in environmental conditions both at home and abroad affect a firm's decision toward a large ad hoc initial investment, and later on, its learning through exaptation?

How Do Internationalization Dynamics Evolve Over Time and What is the Underlying Mechanism?

Past literature has identified the novelty of the internationalization path of the firm and market selection as critical aspects in defining the evolution of firm internationalization over time. Yet, the contingencies of the process of internationalization identified in the debate around the IP model have been left out from this discussion or, at best, only conceptual arguments have been suggested. This leaves plenty of opportunities for future research to test and further refine these arguments. Bringing industry-specific factors into the IP discussion may help shed light on the likelihood that some firms would embark on novel internationalization paths and potentially have greater chances of surviving market selection. In relation to the uneven opportunities and challenges that digitalization offers across industries:

(1) Would path-breaking (versus path-continuing) commitments toward internationalization be more appealing in some industries rather than others?
(2) Would they be more likely to lead to outstanding performance and greater chances of surviving market selection?

Contingencies related to manager-specific factors may also enlighten future IB strategy research. Hence, there may be benefits to providing answers to questions such as:

(3) Is the evolution of firm internationalization dynamics contingent on the international orientation of entrepreneurial founders?

(4) Does the performance associated with more or less novel internationalization paths depend on the international orientation of entrepreneurial founders of the internationalizing firm?

(5) Does the decision to embark on a path-breaking (versus path-continuing) internationalization vary depending on the motives that managers identified based on their expectations and learning about the firm and the conditions of operations at home and abroad?

(6) Are the risks that the different paths yield in terms of performance and market survival more severe depending on the internationalization motives that managers identify?

Additional contingencies that may lead the way to further avenues for research relate to environmental factors. In particular, domestic business ecosystems and business networks may play a critical role in the evolution of MNE internationalization dynamics. The extent of an MNE's embeddedness in these networks may either favor MNE experimentation toward more novel paths of international commitment or have an inertial effect on these firms. A set of research questions may help explore such ideas:

(7) Would the bright or dark side of domestic business network prevail on the evolution of MNE internationalization dynamics over time?

(8) Would the firm's embeddedness in a domestic business network alleviate or exacerbate the risks associated with the internationalization path the firm has embarked on? Further, would it contribute to MNE performance and survival in the market?

Consideration of environmental factors related to institutional voids and uncertainty may add further nuances to this line of research around the effect of MNE environments. In particular, fruitful avenues of research can be exploited by addressing the following questions:

(9) Are commitment decisions toward more or less novel paths of internationalization contingent on the extent of institutional voids and uncertainty in the home/host context? If so, how?

(10) Do greater institutional voids and uncertainty in the home/host context enable firms to deal with the risks associated with their internationalization path, thus, enabling them to outperform competitors and survive market selection?

Also, institutional change has been identified as a critical contingency in the firm IP. The questions that now arise are:

(11) Would MNEs shift from more to less novel internationalization paths or vice versa in response to environmental changes or would they stick to less novel paths in response to these changes? And how would MNEs manage the risks that this choice will yield with regards to their market performance and market survival?

Concluding Remarks

The chapter reflects on the IP perspective by critically discussing the relationships between market knowledge, commitment decisions, and firm internationalization, as well as how internationalization dynamics evolve over time to influence the MNE's performance. These ideas have been central to the evolution of the IP model, which was initially proposed by Johanson and Vahlne (1977), but also to the debate that the model has animated over time in the IB strategy arena. The bulk of the debate has related to the graduality of the process of internationalization depicted in the IP model, which continues to be challenged by relatively newer studies pointing predominantly to the non-linear and discontinuous nature of the IP.

In this chapter, I revisited the evolution of the IP model, including key studies debating its relevance. The chapter then leverages on this discussion to outline the developments related to the relationships between market knowledge and commitment, and those related to the relationship between commitment decisions, MNE performance, and internationalization dynamics. In particular, the discussion on the relationship between market knowledge, commitment decisions, and firm internationalization offers insights on *how firms can acquire knowledge for first-time and subsequent internationalization.* The discussion on the relationship between commitment decisions, firm performance, and internationalization dynamics sheds some light on *how internationalization dynamics evolve over time and what the underlying mechanisms are* by elucidating the role of novelty and market selection in a firm's internationalization path. The discussion highlights the diverse risks that different internationalization paths may yield as well as the role of market selection in ultimately determining MNE international performance and market selection. Finally, I elaborate on why, by bringing into our theorizing and empirical analysis the contingent factors that may influence internationalization decisions, we may advance research on the IP. To this end, for each line of research, the role of the different external and internal contingencies is discussed, and research questions are developed to set a research agenda on the IP.

Acknowledgments

The author is grateful to the coeditors of the Handbook, Gabriel Benito, and the participants in the Oxford Handbook of International Business Strategy Chapter Development Workshop held in Copenhagen on June 22, 2019, for insightful comments and suggestions.

References

Akbar, Y., Balboni, B., Bortoluzzi, G., Dikova, D., & Tracogna, A. 2018. Disentangling resource and mode escalation in the context of emerging markets. Evidence from a sample of manufacturing SMEs. *Journal of International Management,* 24(3): 1–14.

Andersen, O. 1997. Internationalization and market entry mode: A review of theories and conceptual frameworks. *Management International Review*, 37: 27–42.

Benito, G. R. G. 2005. Divestment and international business strategy. *Journal of Economic Geography*, 5(2): 235–251.

Benito, G. R. G. & Welch, L. S. 1994. Foreign market servicing: Beyond choice of entry mode. *Journal of International Marketing*, 2(2): 7–27.

Benito, G. R. G. & Welch, L. S. 1997. De-internationalization. *Management International Review*, 37(2): 7–25.

Beugelsdijk, S. and Mudambi, R., 2014. MNEs as border-crossing multi-location enterprises: The role of discontinuities in geographic space. In J. Cantwell (Ed.), *Location of International Business Activities*. London: Palgrave Macmillan.

Brouthers, K. D., Geisser, K. D., & Rothlauf, F. 2016. Explaining the internationalization of iBusiness firms. *Journal of International Business Studies*, 47(5): 513–534.

Carroll, G. R. & Harrison, J. R. 1994. On the historical efficiency of competition between organizational populations. *American Journal of Sociology*, 100(3): 720–749.

Cattani, G. 2005. Preadaptation, firm heterogeneity and technological performance: A study on the evolution of fiber optics, 1970–1995. *Organization Science*, 16(6): 563–80.

Clarke, J. E. & Liesch, P. W. 2017. Wait-and-see strategy: risk management in the internationalization process model. *Journal of International Business Studies*, 48(8): 923–940.

Coviello, N. E. 2006. The network dynamics of international new ventures. *Journal of International Business Studies*, 37(5): 713–731.

Coviello, N., Kano, L., & Liesch, P. W. 2017. Adapting the Uppsala model to a modern world: Macro-context and microfoundations. *Journal of International Business Studies*, 48(9): 1151–1164.

Cuervo-Cazurra, A., Narula, R., & Un, C. A. 2015. Internationalization motives: Sell more, buy better, upgrade and escape. *The Multinational Business Review*, 23(1): 25–35.

Cyert, R. M. & March, J. G. 1963. *A Behavioral Theory of the Firm*. Englewood Cliffs, NJ: Prentice-Hall.

Dew, N., Sarasvathy, S. D., & Venkataraman, S. 2004. The economic implications of exaptation. *Journal of Evolutionary Economics*, 14(1): 69–84.

Ellis, P. D. 2011. Social ties and international entrepreneurship: Opportunities and constraints affecting firm internationalization. *Journal of International Business Studies*, 42(1): 99–127.

Figueira-de-Lemos, F. & Hadjikhani, A. 2014. Internationalization processes in stable and unstable market conditions: Towards a model of commitment decisions in dynamic environments. *Journal of World Business*, 49(3): 332–349.

Figueira-de-Lemos, F., Johanson, J., & Vahlne, J. E. 2011. Risk management in the internationalization process of the firm: A note on the Uppsala model. *Journal of World Business*, 46(2): 143–153.

Forsgren, M. 2002. The concept of learning in the Uppsala internationalization process model: A critical review. *International Business Review*, 11(3): 257–277.

Forsgren, M., Holm, U., & Johanson, J. 2005. *Managing the Embedded Multinational— A Business Network View*. Cheltenham: Edward Elgar.

García-García, R., García-Canal, E., & Guillén, M. F. 2017. Rapid internationalization and long-term performance: The knowledge link. *Journal of World Business*, 52(1): 97–110.

Gould, S. J. 1980. *The Panda's Thumb*. New York, NY: Norton.

Gould, S. J. 1991. Exaptation: Tool for an evolutionary psychology. *Journal of Social Issues*, 47(3): 43–65.

Gould, S. J. & Vrba, E. S. 1982. Exaptation—a missing term in the science of form. *Paleobiology*, 8(1): 4–15.

Håkanson, L. & Kappen, P. 2017. The "Casino Model" of internationalization: An alternative Uppsala paradigm. *Journal of International Business Studies*, 48(9): 1103–1113.

Hertenstein, P., Sutherland, D., & Anderson, J. 2017. Internationalization within networks: Exploring the relationship between inward and outward FDI in China's auto components industry. *Asia Pacific Journal of Management*, 34(1): 69–96.

Hutzschenreuter, T. & Matt, T. 2017. MNE internationalization patterns, the roles of knowledge stocks, and the portfolio of MNE subsidiaries. *Journal of International Business Studies*, 48(9): 1131–1150.

IMF. 2003. *Foreign Direct Investment Trends and Statistics—A Summary*. Policy Papers. IMF.

Iurkov, V. & Benito, G. R. G. 2018. Domestic alliance networks and regional strategies of MNEs: A structural embeddedness perspective. *Journal of International Business Studies*, 49(8): 1033–1059.

Iurkov, V. & Benito, G. R. G. 2019. Change in domestic network centrality, uncertainty, and the foreign divestment decisions of firms. *Journal of International Business Studies*, 49(8): 1033–1059.

Johanson, J. & Vahlne, J.-E. 1977. The international process of the firm: A model of knowledge development and increasing foreign market commitments. *Journal of International Business Studies*, 8(1): 23–32.

Johanson, J. & Vahlne, J.-E. 2009. The Uppsala internationalization process model revisited: From liability of foreignness to liability of outsidership. *Journal of International Business Studies*, 40(9): 1411–1431.

Khanna, T. & Palepu, K. 1997. Why focused strategies may be wrong for emerging markets. *Harvard Business Review*, 75(4): 41–48.

Khanna, T. & Palepu, K. 2010. *Winning Strategies for Emerging Economies*. Cambridge, MA: Harvard Business School Press.

Knight, G. A. & Liesch, P. W. 2016. Internationalization: From incremental to born global. *Journal of World Business*, 5(11): 93–102.

Kumar, V. & Subramanian, V. 1997. A contingency framework for the mode of entry decision. *Journal of World Business*, 32(1): 53–72.

Laplume, A. O., Petersen, B., & Pearce, J. M. 2016. Global value chains from a 3D printing perspective. *Journal of International Business Studies*, 47(5): 595–609.

Luo, Y. & Tung, R. L. 2007. International expansion of emerging market enterprises: A springboard perspective. *Journal of International Business Studies*, 38(4): 481–498.

Malhotra, N. & Hinings, C. R. 2010. An organizational model for understanding internationalization processes. *Journal of International Business Studies*, 41(2): 330–349.

Marquis, C. & Huang, Z. 2010. Acquisitions as exaptation: The legacy of founding institutions in the U. S. banking industry. *Academy of Management Journal*, 53(6): 1441–1473.

Meyer, K. E., Estrin, S., Bhaumik, S., & Peng, M. W. 2009. Institutions, resources, and entry strategies in emerging economies. *Strategic Management Journal*, 30(1): 61–80.

Meyer, K. E. & Gelbuda, M. 2006. Process perspectives in international business research. *Management International Review*, 46(2): 143–164.

Meyer, K. E. & Peng, M. W. 2005. Probing theoretically into Central and Eastern Europe: Transactions, resources and institutions. *Journal of International Business Studies*, 36(6): 600–621.

Meyer, K. E. & Thaijongrak, O. 2013. The dynamics of emerging economy MNEs: How the internationalization process model can guide future research. *Asia Pacific Journal of Management*, 30(4): 1125–1153.

Mintzberg, H. & Waters, J. A. 1985. Of strategies, deliberate and emergent. *Strategic Management Journal*, 6(3): 257–272.

Møller Larsen, M., Pedersen, T., & Slepniov, D. 2010. *Lego Group: An Outsourcing Journey*. London: Ivey Publishing.

Mudambi, R., Narula, R., & Santangelo, G. D. 2018. Location, collocation and innovation by multinational enterprises: a research agenda. *Industry and Innovation*, 25(3): 229–241.

Nachum, L. & Song, S. 2011. The MNE as a portfolio: interdependencies in MNE growth trajectory. *Journal of International Business Studies*, 42(3): 381–405.

Nelson, R. R. & Winter, S. 1982. *An Evolutionary Theory of Economic Change*. Cambridge, MA: Harvard University Press.

North, D.C., 1990. A transaction cost theory of politics. *Journal of Theoretical Politics*, 2(4): 355–367.

Pedersen, T. & Petersen, B. 1998. Explaining gradually increasing resource commitment to a foreign market. *International Business Review*, 7(5): 483–501.

Pedersen, T. & Shaver, J. M. 2011. Internationalization revisited: The big step hypothesis. *Global Strategy Journal*, 1(3–4): 263–274.

Peng, M. W. 2003. Institutional transitions and institutional choices. *Academy of Management Review*, 28(2): 275–296.

Penrose, E. 1959. *The Theory of the Growth of the Firm*. New York, NY: Wiley.

Petersen, B., Pedersen, T., & Lyles, M. A. 2008. Closing knowledge gaps in foreign markets. *Journal of International Business Studies*, 39(7): 1097–113.

Pukall, T. J. & Calabrò, A. 2014. The internationalization of family firms: A critical review and integrative model. *Family Business Review*, 27(2): 103–125.

Rugman, A. M. & Verbeke, A. 1992. A note on the transnational solution and the transaction cost theory of multinational strategic management. *Journal of International Business Studies*, 23(4): 761–771.

Santangelo, G. D. & Meyer, K. E. 2011. Extending the internationalization process model: Increases and decreases of MNE commitment in emerging economies. *Journal of International Business Studies*, 42(7): 894–909.

Santangelo, G. D. & Meyer, K. E. 2017. Internationalization as an evolutionary process. *Journal of International Business Studies*, 48(9): 1114–1130.

Santangelo, G. D. & Stucchi, T. 2018. Internationalization through exaptation: The role of domestic geographical dispersion in the internationalization process. *Journal of International Business Studies*, 49(6): 753–760.

Siddiqui, N. A. S. & Li, S. 2017. CAGE in cyberspace? How digital innovations internationalize in a virtual world, *AIB Conference*. Dubai.

Tsui-Auch, L. S. & Möllering, G. 2010. Wary managers: Unfavorable environments, perceived vulnerability, and the development of trust in foreign enterprises in China. *Journal of International Business Studies*, 41(6): 1016–1035.

Vaaler, P. M., Schrage, B. N., & Block, S. A. 2005. Counting the investor vote: political business cycle effects on sovereign bond spreads in developing countries. *Journal of International Business Studies*, 36(1): 62–88.

Vahlne, J.-E. & Johanson, J. 2013. The Uppsala model on evolution of the multinational business enterprise–from internalization to coordination of networks. *International Marketing Review*, 30(3): 189–210.

Vahlne, J.-E. & Johanson, J. 2017. The internationalization process 1977–2017: The Uppsala model 40 years later. *Journal of International Business Studies*, 48(9): 1087–1102.

Weerawardena, J., Mort, G. S., Liesch, P. W., & Knight, G. 2007. Conceptualizing accelerated internationalization in the born global firm: A dynamic capabilities perspective. *Journal of World Business*, 42(3): 294–306.

Welter, F. & Smallbone, D. 2011. Institutional perspectives on entrepreneurial behavior in challenging environments. *Journal of Small Business Management*, 49(1): 107–125.

Winter, S. G. 1971. Satisficing, selection, and the innovating remnant. *Quarterly Journal of Economics*, 85(2): 237261.

Wright, M., Filatotchev, I., Hoskisson, R. E., & Peng, M. W. 2005. Strategy research in emerging economies: Challenging the conventional wisdom. *Journal of Management Studies*, 42(1): 1–33.

CHAPTER 8

....

MULTI-THEORETICAL APPROACHES TO STUDYING INTERNATIONAL BUSINESS STRATEGY

....

ERIC W. K. TSANG

INTRODUCTION

....

BUSINESS phenomena are complex. Adding an international dimension to managers' decision matrices complicates the matter further. Theories created by management researchers usually focus on certain aspects of a phenomenon only. For instance, transaction cost economics (TCE) argues that managers make contracting decisions in a transaction–cost–economizing manner (Williamson, 1985) while neglecting the value that can be generated by different governance modes (Zajac & Olsen, 1993). Therefore, Anderson and Gatignon's (1986) analysis of the choice of foreign market entry modes based on a transaction cost framework is biased in this respect. Another example is that when Pouder and St. John (1996) discuss the competitive behavior of firms located in hot spots—fast-growing geographic clusters of competing firms—they identify six different theoretical perspectives, each of which focuses on different aspects of the phenomenon. There is little overlap between these perspectives in terms of what they focus on.

With the growth in the number of management researchers in general, and international business (IB) researchers in particular, more and more theories have been created over the years. More than half a century ago, Koontz (1961) used the term "management theory jungle" to describe the proliferation of theories. The "jungle" surely has significantly expanded. Concomitant with this development is the tendency that researchers work in silos, trying to protect the turf of their favorable theories (Donaldson, 1995). As pointed out by Van de Ven (1989):

> we now have many theories competing with each other to explain a given phenomenon. Proponents for each theory engage in activities to make their theory better by increasing its internal consistency, often at the expense of limiting its scope.

Over time, boundaries between the different camps of theorists become insurmountable (Aldrich, 1992), resulting in *the blind men and the elephant* syndrome. These scholarly camps engage in debates concerning the explanatory power of their theories (e.g. Ghoshal & Moran, 1996; Williamson, 1996). McKinley and Mone (1998) sarcastically comment that "there is more consensus among organizational employees and other organizational participants about the nature of organizations than there is among organization theorists." One way to counter this unhealthy development is to encourage more studies that adopt a multi-theoretical approach. This chapter discusses such an approach in the context of IB strategy research.

To start with, it is important to be explicit about the philosophical perspective adopted in the chapter. Philosophy is connected with empirical research in at least two ways, namely ontologically and epistemologically. What researchers believe about the nature of the phenomena that they study reflects their ontological commitment. While ontology is about the entities that constitute reality, their categorization and relations, epistemology is concerned with the way researchers acquire, propose, and justify their knowledge claims. The two are intimately related in that researchers' ontological commitment often influences their epistemological orientation. Their ontological and epistemological stances together affect the method they regard as legitimate in conducting empirical research, and the way they interpret research results. This chapter is based on the version of realism proposed by Roy Bhaskar and Rom Harré, which is commonly referred to as critical realism. Realism is based on two basic philosophical theses. First, a reality independent of human perception and cognition exists. Second, this reality has its own inherent order (Fay, 1996). Bhaskar (1978) draws a sharp distinction between scientific concepts, laws, theories (what he calls the *transitive* objects of knowledge), and the structures and mechanisms of the world to which our theories refer (the *intransitive* objects of knowledge); the latter are considered to be intransitive because they exist independently of our knowledge of them. Following Sayer (1992), structures are defined as sets of internally related objects and mechanisms refer to ways of acting. Objects are internally linked in a structure when their identity depends on them being in a relationship with the other components of the structure.

The chapter is organized as follows. The next section discusses the nature of theory and clarifies some terminology—distinguishing "theory" from "model" and "paradigm." Some explanations are then proposed for the relatively few multi-theoretical studies that exist in IB strategy research. This is followed by a discussion of the functions of a multi-theoretical approach with specific examples; the examples are selected based on the extent to which they can adequately illustrate the various functions. The chapter ends with suggestions about how to appropriately employ a multi-theoretical approach.

THEORY AND ITS RELATED TERMS

What is a theory? From a realist perspective, a theory refers to a representation of the structure of the enduring system in which events occur as phenomena, and by which they are generated (Harré, 1970). One of the key functions of theory is to provide answers to "why" questions. As Sutton and Staw (1995) rightly say, "data describe which empirical patterns were observed and theory explains why empirical patterns were observed or are expected to be observed." In science, theories are created for the purpose of explaining phenomena of interest by imposing order on unordered human experiences (Dubin, 1978). Bunge (1997) calls for adopting "mechanismic explanation," which describes the cogs and wheels of the causal process through which the event in question was brought about (Hedström & Ylikoski, 2010). Even if we only focus on predictions, which are often considered another major function of theory (see Friedman, 1953), we need to understand the mechanism underlying a theory's predictive power so that we can effectively make use of the normative implications of the theory (Tsang, 2006). It should be noted that the same prediction can be derived from different mechanismic explanations, but the same mechanismic explanation should point to the same prediction under the same or very similar circumstances.

The managerial implications of an explanation are formulated based on the mechanisms related to the explanation. Hodgson (2004) highlighted that, in the domain of management research, "a faulty explanation would be likely to lead to faults in corporate strategy and in the design of governance structures." For instance, let's suppose that lower survival rates of foreign direct investments (FDIs) in culturally distant countries are explained by the employment of a large number of expatriate managers, who are then less able to cope with various cultural idiosyncrasies in the host country compared to local managers and so fail to manage the business effectively. As a result, the performance of the FDI operation suffers. In this case, one likely recommendation is to reduce the number of expatriate managers and to hire more local managers. If that explanation is flawed, the recommendation will not help improve survival rates.

"Theory" is a term that has been used widely but imprecisely by management researchers in general, and IB researchers in particular. Worse still, there are two terms that are often used interchangeably with "theory," namely "model" and, in some studies, "paradigm." Among others, Bunge (1998) proposes a useful distinction between a theory and a model:

> Theoretical models differ from theories in two respects. First, models have a narrower range (or reference class) than theories; to use Merton's expression, models are "theories of the middle range." ... Second, unlike theories, theoretical models need not contain explicitly any law statements.

A well-known model in IB research is the Uppsala internationalization process (IP) model proposed by Johanson and Vahlne (1977) more than four decades ago. They subsequently elaborated the mechanism related to their model (Johanson & Vahlne, 1990). According to Bunge's (1998) distinction and given the nature of their model, the authors may also call the process model a theory.

The term "paradigm" was made popular in the academic literature by Kuhn's (1962) landmark work, *The Structure of Scientific Revolutions*. Unfortunately, the term has been used—or abused, to be more precise—by management researchers in various ways. The term paradigm was first brought to the attention of management researchers probably by Burrell and Morgan's (1979) seminal work, *Sociological Paradigms and Organizational Analysis*. They use the term to "emphasise the commonality of perspective which binds the work of a group of theorists together in such a way that they can be regarded as approaching social theory within the bounds of the same problematic" (Burrell & Morgan, 1979). They propose four paradigms: functionalist, interpretive, radical humanist, and radical structuralist. They use the term paradigm with a broader meaning than "theory" as each paradigm includes a few theories.

The subsequent developments of the term paradigm become chaotic. Although some management researchers follow Burrell and Morgan's (1979) definition and use of paradigm closely (e.g. Schultz & Hatch, 1996), others use paradigm and theory interchangeably. For example, Donaldson (1995) distinguishes between structural contingency, institutional, population ecology, resource dependence, agency, and transaction cost theories. He considers each theory a paradigm and uses the terms theory and paradigm interchangeably. Similarly, in analyzing the paradoxical nature of cooperative and competitive strategies, Clarke-Hill et al. (2003) advocate a multiparadigm approach that combines strategic positioning, the resource-based view (RBV) and game theory. Following Lewis (2000), they define paradigm as "a way of thinking about phenomena based on distinct epistemological and methodological assumptions" (Clarke-Hill et al., 2003), which is very different from the abovementioned definition of theory. It is more appropriate to regard strategic positioning, the RBV and game theory as theories (in particular, if game *theory* is not a theory, it should not be called "game theory" in the first place.) The most notable use of the term paradigm in IB is probably John Dunning's eclectic paradigm of international production. His use of paradigm is remotely related to the central meaning of paradigm intended by Kuhn—exemplar, which refers to "the concrete accomplishments of a scientific community" (Eckberg & Hill, 1979). As such, it would be more appropriate for Dunning to use the term theory or model instead. In fact, Dunning (2001) admitted that he initially called his contribution the "eclectic theory." This confusion of terminology is not surprising because even Kuhn (1962) himself failed to clearly define paradigm and Masterman (1970) found that he had used the term with at least twenty-one different meanings.

It is also necessary to distinguish between "interdisciplinary" and "multi-theoretical" studies. Some scholars use the former, such as Dunning's (1989) call for a more interdisciplinary approach to the study of IB in his 1988 presidential address at the Academy of International Business annual meeting. This call was later echoed by Wright and Ricks

(1994). By interdisciplinary, he refers to "a holistic and integrated approach to a study of IB and its constituent subject areas, the primary purpose of which is to advance our understanding of the former as a discipline in its own right" (Dunning, 1989). In his discussion, he mentions disciplines such as economics, finance, management, and marketing. There are two main differences between this meaning of interdisciplinary approach and the multi-theoretical approach discussed in this chapter. First, the terms theory and discipline have very different meanings. A discipline can have many theories and a theory can be used by scholars in multiple disciplines. For instance, TCE was first proposed by Coase (1937) in the field of microeconomics and later spread to a number of disciplines (including IB), while economics has many theories other than TCE. Second, Dunning's emphasis is on encouraging scholars from different disciplines to engage in IB research, rather than taking the perspective of more than one theory in a single study. An interdisciplinary IB study can be based on one theory. Yet, our focus has been on employing more than one theory in a single study.

In sum, I point to the confusion that exists concerning the use of the terms theory, model, and paradigm. To avoid this confusion, the following discussion will only use theory based on its above-stated definition. Moreover, the discussion is about multi-theoretical, not interdisciplinary, approaches.

RELATIVELY FEW MULTI-THEORETICAL STUDIES

About two decades ago, in reviewing the research on the internationalization of smaller firms, Coviello and McAuley (1999) found that a single theoretical framework dominated the empirical studies they reviewed and concluded that, in order to enhance our understanding of the phenomenon, scholars required a multi-theoretical approach. Yet, empirical studies on that topic in particular, and in IB strategy in general, very seldom adopt such an approach. There are at least three plausible reasons.

The first reason is related to the training of a typical IB scholar. Although doctoral programs in North America usually require students to read major theories in management, which includes IB, strategy, entrepreneurship, and organizational behavior, doctoral programs in Europe or Asia are often less extensive in this respect. Even in North America, after students have passed their comprehensive exams, they start working on their dissertations usually basing their theoretical assumptions on one main theory. Needless to say, it is a time-consuming endeavor to trace the development of a theory, understand the details of its arguments, and generate sound hypotheses based on that theory. Within the time frame of finishing a dissertation while also submitting manuscripts to journals, it is easier to master one theory than multiple ones. Economies of scale matter a great deal during this critical stage of doctoral training. Moreover, the saying "jack of all trades, master of none" often rings in students' ears. In fact, their dissertation committee chairs may advise that with regards to job interviews, where applicants are often expected to benefit from showing that they are experts in one theory rather than having shallow knowledge of various theories. This is important because being successful in the job market is the primary concern of most doctoral students.

A related reason is that the tenure clock (particularly for North American universities) is not conducive to learning new theories or research methods. Junior scholars are under tremendous pressure to perform well in the classroom and to publish the required number of journal articles for obtaining tenure. The dissertation is usually one main source of generating such journal submissions. In other words, a single-theory researcher will remain as such during at least the first five to six years of that individual's career. While this may be an astute career strategy for these scholars, it might, over time, hinder our field as a whole. Having successfully overcome the tenure hurdle, scholars may not be motivated to work on other theories especially if they have already established their reputation as an expert of a particular theory. They could become concerned that diversifying into other theories will dilute their professional image.

A third plausible motivation is that promotion and tenure decisions are usually based on journal instead of book publications. Publishing in leading journals thus becomes more competitive over the years. Unlike books, journal articles are much shorter. Within the space constraint, authors have to clearly elaborate their arguments. Keeping other factors constant, it is usually easier to develop a coherent theoretical framework with in-depth discussions using one rather than multiple theories. Further, authors may deem it imprudent to cast the theoretical net too widely, fearing that reviewers would evaluate their manuscript as too broad and consisting of trivial results (see Klein, Tosi, & Cannella, 1999). Indeed, many journal reviewers tend to consider incoherent arguments or trivial findings a valid reason for rejecting a manuscript. As such, authors may perceive that a paper adopting a multi-theoretical approach carries a relatively higher risk.

FUNCTIONS OF MULTI-THEORETICAL APPROACHES

The previous section discusses some of the difficulties faced by IB researchers when adopting a multi-theoretical approach. Yet, such a multi-theoretical approach may potentially serve important functions that help advance the IB strategy field both empirically and conceptually. This current section covers five such functions. The first two—capturing the essence of complex strategic decisions and providing a more complete explanation of outcomes—are specifically related to the complexity of phenomena studied by IB and management researchers, while the remaining three—compensating for the explanatory deficiency of a single theory, exploiting the complementarity of theories, and testing conflicting explanations—are mostly concerned with the limited scope and focus of a theory.

Capturing the Essence of Complex Strategic Decisions

Most of the phenomena studied by IB researchers are the result of complex decisions. When managers make such decisions, they naturally consider a variety of factors. Yet a theory is limited in scope and unable to cover most of these factors, implying that researchers have to bring in multiple theories in order to arrive at a more comprehensive explanation. For example, in their study of US executives' assessments of international joint venture (IJV) opportunities in China, Reuer, Tyler, Tong, & Wu (2012) use four theories, namely RBV, TCE, real options theory (ROT), and information economics. They justify their approach by arguing that "managers are likely to draw upon decision criteria from multiple theories, although they are also boundedly rational, so what information they actually prioritize when assessing IJV partners is important to address" (Reuer et al., 2012). In other words, given the multiplicity of factors that managers have to consider when evaluating IJV opportunities, adopting a single theoretical lens will likely miss some of these factors in their decision processes. Using an experimental technique known as policy capturing, they surveyed sixty top US executives to examine how executives cognitively weigh criteria from the four theories when assessing IJV opportunities in China. Their results indicate that all the four theories highlight criteria that are important for these executives' assessments of potential Chinese IJVs.

Whereas Reuer et al. (2012) chose to collect data directly from managers (which is relatively uncommon), most IB researchers use existing archival databases or compile their own databases. For instance, in their study of foreign market re-entry commitment strategies after initial entry and exit, Surdu, Mellahi, & Glaister (2019) constructed their database principally from two secondary data sources, namely Factiva (Dow Jones) and LexisNexis (Reed Elsevier). The authors make use of both organizational learning and institutional change theories to formulate their hypotheses. Their results suggest that both theories are explanatory, relevant, and complementary: (1) the experience of exit as a result of unsatisfactory performance affects how re-entrants learn from their past experiences and subsequently adjust their re-entry strategies and (2) institutional dynamics complement organizational learning considerations when firms formulate re-entry strategies. A further example is Gaur, Kumar, & Singh's (2014) study of the shift from exporting to FDI by emerging economy firms. Their sample consists of Indian firms derived from the Prowess database of the Center for Monitoring the Indian Economy. They integrate RBV and institutional theory to develop hypotheses about the conditions under which firms are more likely to make this shift and further internationalize their operations. Their results indicate that "both institutional and firm-specific resources, individually and jointly, help firms make the shift from exports to FDI" (Gauer et al., 2014).

Providing a More Complete Explanation of Outcomes

In addition to studying phenomena related to strategic decisions, IB researchers are often interested in explaining why certain outcomes of such decisions, such as profitability or survival of FDI, occur. An excellent example of such a study is that by Child, Chung, & Davies (2003) who conducted a survey of Hong Kong firms managing operations in mainland China. They argue that there are two main categories of factors affecting the performance of such cross-border units in a transition economy. The first category consists of factors that are beyond managerial control, including underdeveloped institutions, fragmented markets, backward technologies, and state interference, while the second category refers to managerial action, such as selection of investment locations, transfer of resources, assignment of expatriates, and development of trust with local partners. The former factors correspond to the natural selection view that performance is determined by environmental circumstances, and within that view, industrial organization (Porter, 1980) and population ecology (Hannan & Freeman, 1989) are two of the most thoroughly researched theories. The latter factors constitute the core of strategic choice theory, which emphasizes the role played by managers in shaping conditions and processes both within and outside the firm (Child, 1997). Child et al. (2003) bring in contingency theory that attempts to resolve the tension between environment and managerial action as determinants of firm performance. Contingency theory is concerned with the "fit" between environmental conditions and the structures and strategies that managers adopt in their firms and proposes influence to both environment and managerial action through their congruence (Donaldson, 2001).

In this previous example, the authors develop hypotheses based on each of the three theoretical perspectives, with the aim of providing a test of their relative explanatory power. Their results indicate that all three perspectives have significant explanatory power, supporting Capon, Farley, & Hoenig's (1996) view that a more integrative framework consisting of a variety of factors is needed if business performance is to be better understood and more fully explained. From a realist perspective, there are many factors affecting a cross-border unit's performance through different causal mechanisms. For example, a strategy of assigning more expatriate managers to the unit will impact on performance in a way that is different from a host government policy giving tax incentives to the unit. Since different theories tend to emphasize different sets of factors—such as managerial versus institutional factors—it may often be beneficial to employ more than one theory in order to arrive at a more complete explanation of a phenomenon's outcomes.

Compensating for the Explanatory Deficiency of a Single Theory

The abovementioned two functions probably cover most of the multi-theoretical studies in the IB and management literature. However, there are, at least, three additional functions of multi-theoretical research. One is related to the limited explanatory scope of a single theory. While a single theory is adequate for explaining one aspect of the phenomenon, it may fail to explain another (potentially important) aspect. One major reason is that the plausible mechanisms related to the latter are not within the explanatory domain of the theory. For instance, Kogut (1991) develops a version of ROT that explains the formation of joint ventures as an option to expand in response to future market and technological developments. A joint venture partner possesses a real option because it is able to simultaneously limit its downside losses to an initial, limited investment amount and to position itself to expand in case circumstances turn out to be favorable. An acquisition of the venture indicates the exercise of the option, and the timing of the acquisition is triggered by a product market signal suggesting an increase in the venture's valuation.

In a relatively more recent study, Iriyama and Madhavan (2014) draw on ROT to study the conditions under which an IJV partner is likely to acquire its counterpart's equity stake upon a market signal of further opportunities; or sell its equity stake to the counterpart upon a market signal of fewer opportunities. Their longitudinal dataset consists of changes in equity share distributions in IJVs formed by Japanese automotive suppliers during the period of 1986–2003. A complication is that in a two-partner joint venture, each partner has the related real option and inter-partner equity shifts are basically a zero-sum game: one partner's equity acquisition is another partner's equity divestment (Iriyama & Madhavan, 2014). ROT cannot provide an explanation for the dynamics of such equity shifts in IJVs, which are likely to be influenced by partner characteristics. Iriyama and Madhavan (2014) incorporate organizational learning theory, arguing that a partner's prior experience affects how likely it is that the multinational enterprise (MNE), or the local partner, can adjust their IJV ownership stake in their own favor upon the emergence of market signals. During the initial stage of an IJV operation, the local partner may be more capable in interpreting market signals and negotiating favorable equity shifts with the foreign partner. As the latter's host country experiential learning accumulates, it can more effectively evaluate market signals, bargain with the local partner, and shift ownership in its favor. Such learning-based mechanisms have been outside the scope of ROT.

Another example is Bai, Tsang, and Xia's (2018) study of initial public offering (IPO) location choice between home country and foreign country based on the population of Chinese private issuers during the period 2005–2014. Their core research question is: How do CEOs' undergraduate educational experiences influence their firms' decision to list in a foreign or domestic capital market? A natural starting point is upper echelons theory. Yet, one serious limitation of the theory is that it does not take into account that some experiences have longer-lasting influence on an individual than others. A unique characteristic of their study is that the time gap between a CEO's undergraduate education and the firm's IPO event can be more than three decades long. Hence, to provide a mechanismic explanation that links the two events together, the authors bring in imprinting theory, to argue that CEOs' educational experiences have imprinting effects on their IPO location preferences; in that CEOs with prestigious domestic degrees tend to list their firms in mainland China whereas CEOs with foreign degrees tend to list them overseas.

Exploiting the Complementarity of Theories

Since theories usually focus on certain aspects of a phenomenon, there is a possibility that two theories may provide a more holistic explanation than either one in that the aspects covered by the theories are complementary to one another. For example, as mentioned at the beginning of this chapter, TCE focuses on the cost aspect of selecting governance modes. As such, the TCE logic explains the formation of joint ventures in terms of market failure for intermediate inputs, asset specificity, and high uncertainty over specifying and monitoring performance. Putting more emphasis on the benefit side of a governance mode, RBV regards joint ventures as a means of exploiting and developing a firm's resources. Note that cost and benefit are complementary aspects of a governance mode. Ignoring either aspect may lead to flawed conclusions. For instance, an MNE may choose to form an IJV with a local firm, instead of a wholly owned subsidiary, despite the fact that the former option incurs significantly higher transaction costs than the latter. TCE scholars may interpret this governance mode as inefficient and conclude that a decision error was made by the MNE. However, the local partner may be able to generate value, such as providing access to distribution channels, new customers and institutional actors, all of which may be missing when a wholly owned subsidiary is established. We should take into account such values when evaluating the MNE's decision. Hence, the mechanism driven by cost considerations and that driven by value considerations can affect MNE governance choices. Notably, Tsang (2000) exploits the complementarity of TCE and RBV theories. He first compares the two theories' rationales for forming joint ventures and then integrates both into a more holistic perspective with respect to explaining joint venture formation. By so doing, the author produces a deeper explanation that "uncovers the inner workings of the relevant causal mechanism" (Marchionni, 2008).

Furthermore, two theories may be complementary with respect to explaining the same phenomenon by proposing different mechanisms. Unlike the case discussed earlier, here each theory is sufficient in explaining the phenomenon. Combining both theories shows the possibilities of different mechanisms at work. Using data from the global automotive industry from 2002 to 2008, Lampel and Giachetti (2013) study the performance of international manufacturing diversification. They identify the complementarity of TCE and RBV on this issue. Briefly stated, TCE scholars argue that internationally diversified manufacturing firms can gain competitive advantages by exploiting market imperfections (e.g. differences in national and human resources) and also gain the increased flexibility and greater bargaining power resulting from a multinational production network and from greater economies of scale and scope. However, spreading manufacturing operations over multiple countries will sooner or later lead to higher governance and transaction costs that gradually negate the advantage of internationalizing manufacturing. RBV research, in contrast, suggests that firms pursuing international manufacturing diversification have the advantage of transferring their resources (e.g. engineering know-how and patented production processes) to new activities rather than selling or renting these resources on the open market. Yet, as firms continue the process of building their manufacturing operations globally, the whole value chain becomes increasingly complex. More managerial resources have to be spent on coordinating and monitoring these geographically dispersed manufacturing operations, resulting in reduced efficiency. In sum, both TCE and RBV predict that the relationship between such diversification and performance is curvilinear (i.e. inverted U-shaped) although each theory proposes a different mechanism. Lampel and Giachetti's (2013) results support the curvilinear relationship between international diversification and MNE performance.

Testing Conflicting Explanations

The last function of multi-theoretical approaches is to resolve conflicting explanations. The causal mechanisms proposed by different theories may often lead to contradicting predictions. This is not surprising since each theory proposes a somewhat distinct set of mechanisms, and some mechanisms of a theory may give rise to outcomes that are different from those derived from another theory under certain circumstances. There is a need to examine which theory's prediction is better supported in a given context.

A notable example is the study of international diversification and joint ownership control conducted by Chung et al. (2013). Their sample consists of Japanese subsidiaries located in the five countries directly impacted by the 1997 Asian Financial Crisis: Indonesia, Thailand, South Korea, Malaysia, and the Philippines. The authors contrast between risk diversification theory (RDT) and ROT, each of which proposes distinct motivations for international diversification and for subsidiary divestment in crisis-stricken countries. According to RDT, since countries have less than perfectly correlated economic cycles, investing in overseas operations enables an MNE to offset increased risk in one country by the potentially reduced risk in other countries, resulting in more stable corporate earnings (Rugman, 1979). As an MNE's global portfolio of subsidiaries becomes more diversified, decision makers may believe the firm is close to being fully diversified internationally for maximum efficiency and be more prepared to divest its underperforming subsidiaries. This divestment decision would be more easily justified for subsidiaries located in crisis-stricken countries. By contrast, ROT argues that MNEs benefit from internationally dispersed subsidiaries by having the right, but not the obligation, to shift value chain activities to countries that are more favorable when conditions in any one country become less favorable (Chung, Lee, Beamish, & Isobe, 2010). In the case of competitive devaluation in crisis-stricken countries, such as the example of the Asian Financial Crisis, a globally diversified MNE can take advantage of its ability to shift value chain activities to these countries due to their exchange rate depreciation, lower factor costs, and other favorable trade conditions. Thus, there is a real-options driven motivation to retain ownership of overseas subsidiaries for their future flexibility. In other words, the two theories generate opposite predictions based on the same initial conditions: RDT predicts that the greater the extent of an MNE's international diversification, the more likely the firm will divest its subsidiaries in crisis-stricken countries, whereas ROT predicts a lower likelihood of divestment. In addition to this pair of competing hypotheses, Chung et al. (2013) propose a set of competing views with respect to the moderating effect of join ownership control on subsidiary divestment. Their overall findings point toward supporting the predictions of ROT.

Some Suggestions

Despite the empirical and conceptual functions of multi-theoretical approaches, studies based on more than one theory are still relatively few in the IB strategy literature. This section offers several suggestions to not only promote a multi-theoretical approach but also highlight some precautions for researchers who choose to adopt this approach in the future.

Promoting Multi-Theoretical Studies

As discussed, many IB researchers are trained to be single theory experts. If researchers are not well-versed in more than one theory, they are not likely to study phenomena through a multi-theoretical lens. Thus, there is a need to plant the seed in doctoral training so that a long-lasting imprinting effect can be made on the next generation of researchers (Marquis & Tilcsik, 2013). To achieve this objective, one way of organizing doctoral seminars is that all students are required to attend the same set of seminars that cover the major areas of IB and management research, regardless of a student's chosen specialization in his or her dissertation. This is the seminar arrangement of the doctoral program in the author's school. A key benefit is that students are not only exposed to a variety of theories but also required to have a reasonably good understanding of the theories in order to pass the seminars and the comprehensive exam that is based on the seminars. In addition to stressing multi-theoretical reasoning in doctoral seminars, dissertation committee chairs should encourage their students to practice it when conducting dissertation research. A dissertation committee may consist of experts of different theories. Like other skills, multi-theoretical reasoning can be difficult to learn but it is likely to improve with practice. It may also be a worthwhile investment by doctoral students before they embark on their academic careers upon graduation.

Secondly, if one is not familiar with a theory that is allegedly related to the phenomenon under study, learning the theory in a rush may not be feasible. Learning may also be constrained by the tenure clock. Collaboration with a scholar who is an expert of that particular theory is a better option. Such collaborations also help to break down theoretical silos and stimulate integrative and holistic thinking, which is likely to benefit researchers in the long term. Researchers also become more familiar with different theoretical lenses and schools of thought through discussion and mutual learning in the collaboration process.

Thirdly, as gatekeepers, journal editors and reviewers play a critical role in promoting multi-theoretical studies. Editors may explicitly state their preference for such studies. As the saying goes, "whenever there is demand, there will be supply." When reviewers evaluate a journal submission, whether conceptual or empirical, they may look out for multi-theoretical opportunities that will strengthen the theoretical foundation of the manuscript and encourage authors to think beyond the constraint of the theory proposed in the manuscript. For empirical papers, it is often an onerous task for authors to collect additional data in order to incorporate another theory into their study. That said, it is possible that they can add new variables to test the theory based on the data they have already collected. A caveat is that authors should by no means be coerced into adopting a multi-theoretical lens. Their intellectual autonomy and freedom should be respected (Tsang, 2014). If authors are able to provide sound reasons as to why a single theory is sufficiently appropriate in the context of their study, their view should be accepted. In short, a frank and open-minded communication between editors, reviewers, and authors is needed to advance this research approach.

Reconciling Inconsistent Core Assumptions

When researchers consider including more than one theory into their study, they should understand not only each theory's proposed causal mechanism related to the phenomenon under investigation but also its core assumptions. Every management theory has core assumptions of how people behave. Such behavioral assumptions are about the major causal relationships postulated by a theory (Mäki, 2000) and are key elements of the mechanismic explanations offered by the theory (Tsang, 2006). For instance, a core behavioral assumption of TCE is opportunism, defined as "self-interest seeking with guile" (Williamson, 1975). The degree of opportunism manifested by the parties involved affects the transaction costs associated with a governance mode, which then influence the governance choice (Wathne & Heide, 2000).

When researchers attempt to use more than one theory in constructing their arguments, they first have to examine whether any of the theories have conflicting core assumptions. For instance, the agency and stakeholder views of the firm have significant differences alongside several dimensions (see figures 1 and 2 of Shankman (1999) for a summary). In particular, managers are perceived by agency theory as egoistic and morally hazardous, while, by stakeholder theory, they are perceived as enlightened, self-interested, and with an objective of balancing the interests of all major stakeholders. Researchers who attempt to include these two theories in a single study will face an uphill task of reconciling their conflicting assumptions. They may have to argue, for example, that managers behave in accordance with agency theory in certain contexts and with stakeholder theory in others. Although this is in practice a possibility, given the complexity of human psychology (Sternberg & Ben-Zeev, 2001), putting forward a convincing argument may be challenging. A similar caution applies to, say, TCE and stakeholder theory because like agency theory, the former has a far less charitable assumption about human nature than the latter. Unless one is an expert of multi-theoretical reasoning, this kind of theory combination had better be avoided.

Instead of integrating theories that have conflicting core assumptions to explain a phenomenon, a better approach may be to compare their explanatory power. For example, Ryan and Schneider (2003) skillfully examine the implications of the escalation in institutional investor power and heterogeneity for agency theory and stakeholder theory separately. The authors proceed to discuss the merits and limitations of each theory in explaining their phenomenon of study. Although the conceptual paper by Ryan and Schneider (2003) is not in the international business strategy domain, their approach may be used as inspiration.

Addressing Levels Issues

Business phenomena are multilevel, with individuals working in teams, teams working within organizations, and organizations operating within an industry environment, which, in turn, is part of an even larger socio-political context of a country. To add one more level, IB studies also investigate phenomena within or across clusters of countries, such as Ronen and Shenkar's (1985) classification of eight clusters of culturally similar countries. The topic of levels issues is complicated and beyond the scope of this chapter (see Klein, Dansereau, & Hall, 1994; Rousseau, 1985; St. John, 2005 for details). What should be noted here is that researchers adopting multi-theoretical approaches are more likely to encounter levels issues than those working with single theories, because different theories aim at explaining phenomena at different levels. While some multi-theoretical studies manage to include theories such as TCE and RBV (Tsang, 2000) or RDT and ROT (Chung et al., 2013) that are at the same level, other studies do not pay sufficient attention.

When discussing mixed-level research, it is important to distinguish between three different levels, namely level of theory, level of measurement, and level of statistical analysis. Level of theory refers to the target (e.g. individual, group, organization, country) that a researcher intends to describe or explain (Klein et al., 1994), and is "the level to which generalizations are made" (Rousseau, 1985). Level of measurement refers to the source of the data and "the unit to which data are directly attached" (Rousseau, 1985), such as psychological data being at the individual level and corporate cultural data at the firm level. Lastly, level of analysis refers to the treatment of the data when statistical procedures are applied.

Although the definition of each of the three levels should appear clear and straightforward, ambiguities do arise occasionally in IB research. For example, while there is consensus that cultural distance is a country level construct, there are debates about the level of a closely related construct—psychic distance. Sousa and Bradley (2006) argue that "it is the individual's perception of the differences between the home country and the foreign country that shapes the psychic distance concept." Different members of the same organization can perceive different degrees of psychic distance with respect to the same foreign country. Accordingly, psychic distance is an individual level construct and should be measured as such by, for example, cognitive mapping (Stöttinger & Schlegelmilch, 1998). This argument has merit in that many management decisions associated with psychic distance, such as the decision to export to or set up an operation in a foreign country, are made based on the manager's perception at the moment of decision making (Dow & Karunaratna, 2006). But there are thorny methodological difficulties, such as surveying a manager's perception immediately prior to the decision in question. To overcome these difficulties, Dow and Karunaratna (2006) propose to split psychic distance into a sequence of related macro-level factors, which are measured at the country level and are called "psychic distance stimuli." Examples of stimuli include culture, language, education, and religion. The relationship between the two conceptualizations of psychic distance is that psychic distance stimuli "create the climate within which a manager's cognitive processes operate, and therefore frame the conditions within which managers form their perceptions and make their decisions" (Dow & Karunaratna, 2006). The choice between the two conceptualizations depends on whether the objective is to explain MNE behavior or a population of firms within a country.

Problems related to levels issues arise when any pair of the three levels is incongruent. In particular, difficulties often occur because of the misalignment between the theoretical level of a construct and the level at which it is measured (St. John, 2005). Consider, for instance, Child et al.'s (2003) study. The three theoretical perspectives are at the individual and environmental levels whereas the authors collected all their data through a survey of business executives. There is an inconsistency in terms of the levels of theories and the level of measurement. As they acknowledge, "the measurement of the variables has been based on executives' perceptions" (Child et al., 2003). They admit this inconsistency as a major limitation of their study. A better alternative is that they supplement their survey data with objective measures of some environmental variables, such as market attractiveness, intensity of competition, and legal support. The latter data should be available at the provincial or city level. This step will also address the problem of common method variance arising from the fact that each questionnaire was answered by only one representative of a sample firm. In contrast, Surdu et al.'s (2019) study of foreign market re-entry commitment strategies addresses levels issues more appropriately. The study employs organizational learning and institutional change theories, the former being at the firm level and the latter at the country level. They take host market-specific experience as an indicator of organizational learning and measure it at the firm level by the number of years the focal firm operated in the specific host market between initial entry and market exit. As to host country institutional change, they use the Economic Freedom of the World Index, which derives an overall institutional score for each of the approximately 100 nations and territories and measure institutional change by the difference of the indexes at t − 1 of exit and t − 1 of re-entry. Therefore, each of the two variables is measured at the appropriate level.

Among the three levels, level of theory is more fundamental and determines the other two. For instance, if psychic distance is conceptualized as managerial perceptions that affect decisions, then the construct has to be operationalized at the individual level.

This in turn determines the data collection and analysis procedures. The key is to align the three levels and check for any incongruences. When a study involves more than one theory, this step of alignment has to be conducted for each theory separately.

Beware of Ockham's Razor

Despite the valuable functions of a multi-theoretical approach, researchers should beware of the principle of parsimony, a.k.a. "Ockham's razor," which is often considered an important standard for judging the quality of a theory. Basically, parsimony is a theoretical virtue. Barnes (2000) distinguishes between two different but inter-related principles of parsimony: anti-quantity and anti-superfluity. The former stipulates that theorists "posit as few theoretical components as possible in the construction of explanations of phenomena," while the latter advises theorists to "avoid positing superfluous components—components which are not required for the purpose of explaining the relevant data" (Barnes, 2000). Although Ockham's razor is usually used to evaluate competing theories, it sheds light on multi-theoretical studies. According to the two principles of parsimony, when including more than one theory in a single study, researchers should try to minimize the number of theories used and to make sure that none of the theories are superfluous in terms of explaining their data.

Lampel and Giachetti's (2013) study is somewhat problematic in this respect. As discussed, they draw on both TCE and RBV to derive the main hypothesis about the curvilinear relationship between manufacturing diversification and firm performance and arrive at a conclusion that both theories predict an inverted U-shaped relationship. They also derive two hypotheses about the moderating effects of product diversification and co-location of manufacturing and sales activities in the same geographic market based on the two theories. In so doing, they provide richer conceptual arguments proposing multiple causal mechanisms. However, a serious problem of the study is that the empirical section does not test any of these mechanisms. They used archival data that consist of the number of vehicles produced and sold in fifty-eight countries by thirty-eight automakers with headquarters in fifteen different countries from 2002 to 2008. Their statistical analysis is based on a reduced model format (see Tsang, 2006), excluding the variables related to the causal mechanisms that link the independent variables and the dependent variable together. It serves little purpose for them to use both theories to develop their hypotheses because none of the mechanisms proposed by either theory are, in fact, tested in the empirical part. Since either theory is sufficient to explain their data and using both does not improve the empirical results, they have violated the principles of parsimony. One way to show the necessity of using both theories is by adopting what Tsang (2006) calls a structural model in their empirical section consisting of two sets of variables: one directly related to TCE and the other to RBV. Then a case can be made that including both sets in the statistical analysis generates better results in terms of, say, variance explained or model fitting than just including either set. Child et al. (2003) show in their table 4 that adding each of the three theoretical perspectives to their analysis significantly increases the variance explained, providing a sounder empirical justification for their multi-theoretical framework.

Concluding Remarks

The complexity of IB strategy phenomena and the limited scope of any single theory indicate the potential for multi-theoretical approaches to offer more comprehensive explanations of MNE international strategies. However, multi-theoretical studies remain relatively few due to deficient doctoral training, individual career considerations, and constraints of the journal review process. This is an unfortunate situation because multi-theoretical approaches have at least five useful functions that together may significantly advance future research. Undoubtedly, multi-theoretical reasoning is often a challenging task. Yet, it is high time IB or management researchers took up this challenge.

References

Aldrich, H. E. 1992. Incommensurable paradigms? Vital signs from three perspectives. In M. Reed & M. Hughes (Eds.), *Rethinking Organization: New Directions in Organization Theory and Analysis*. London: Sage.

Anderson, E., & Gatignon, H. 1986. Modes of foreign entry: A transaction cost analysis and propositions. *Journal of International Business Studies*, 17(3): 1–26.

Bai, X., Tsang, E.W. and Xia, W., 2018. Domestic versus foreign listing: Does a CEO's educational experience matter? *Journal of Business Venturing*, 35(1): 105906.

Barnes, E. C. 2000. Ockham's razor and the anti-superfluity principle. *Erkenntnis*, 53(3): 353–374.

Bhaskar, R. 1978. *A Realist Theory of Science*. Hassocks: Harvester Press.

Bunge, M. 1997. Mechanism and explanation. *Philosophy of the Social Sciences*, 27(4): 410–465.

Bunge, M. 1998. *Social Science under Debate*. Toronto: University of Toronto Press.

Burrell, G., & Morgan, G. 1979. *Sociological Paradigms and Organizational Analysis*. Aldershot: Ashgate.

Capon, N., Farley, J. U., & Hoenig, S. 1996. *Toward an Integrative Explanation of Corporate Financial Performance*. Boston, MA: Kluwer.

Child, J. 1997. Strategic choice in the analysis of action, structure, organizations and environment: Retrospect and prospect. *Organization Studies*, 18(1): 43–76.

Child, J., Chung, L., & Davies, H. 2003. The performance of cross-border units in China: A test of natural selection, strategic choice and contingency theories. *Journal of International Business Studies*, 34(3): 242–254.

Chung, C. C., Lee, S. H., Beamish, P. W., & Isobe, T. 2010. Subsidiary expansion/contraction during times of economic crisis. *Journal of International Business Studies*, 41(3): 500–516.

Chung, C. C., Lee, S. H., Beamish, P. W., Southam, C., & Nam, D. D. 2013. Pitting real options theory against risk diversification theory: International diversification and joint ownership control in economic crisis. *Journal of World Business*, 48(1): 122–136.

Clarke-Hill, C., Li, H., & Davies, B. 2003. The paradox of co-operation and competition in strategic alliances: Towards a multi-paradigm approach. *Management Research News*, 26(1): 1–20.

Coase, R. H. 1937. The nature of the firm. *Economica*, 4(16): 386–405.

Coviello, N. E., & McAuley, A. 1999. Internationalization and the smaller firm: A review of contemporary empirical research. *Management International Review*, 39(3): 223–256.

Donaldson, L. 1995. *American Anti-Management Theories of Organization: A Critique of Paradigm Proliferation*. Cambridge: Cambridge University Press.

Donaldson, L. 2001. *The Contingency Theory of Organizations*. Thousand Oaks: Sage.

Dow, D., & Karunaratna, A. 2006. Developing a multidimensional instrument to measure psychic distance stimuli. *Journal of International Business Studies*, 37(5): 578–602.

Dubin, R. 1978. *Theory building*. New York: Free Press.

Dunning, J. H. 1989. The study of international business: A plea for a more interdisciplinary approach. *Journal of International Business Studies*, 20(3): 411–436.

Dunning, J. H. 2001. The eclectic (OLI) paradigm of international production: Past, present and future. *International Journal of the Economics of Business*, 8(2): 173–190.

Eckberg, D. L., & Hill Jr, L. 1979. The paradigm concept and sociology: A critical review. *American Sociological Review*, 44(6): 925–937.

Fay, B. 1996. *Contemporary Philosophy of Social Science: A Multicultural Approach*. Oxford: Blackwell.

Friedman, M. 1953. *Essays in Positive Economics*. Chicago, IL: University of Chicago Press.

Gaur, A. S., Kumar, V., & Singh, D. 2014. Institutions, resources, and internationalization of emerging economy firms. *Journal of World Business*, 49(1): 12–20.

Ghoshal, S., & Moran, P. 1996. Bad for practice: A critique of the transaction cost theory. *Academy of Management Review*, 21(1): 13–47.

Hannan, M. T., & Freeman, J. H. 1989. *Organization Ecology*. Cambridge, MA: Harvard University Press.

Harré, R. 1970. *Principles of Scientific Thinking*. Chicago, IL: University of Chicago Press.

Hedström, P., & Ylikoski, P. 2010. Causal mechanisms in the social sciences. *Annual Review of Sociology*, 36: 49–67.

Hodgson, G. M. 2004. Opportunism is not the only reason why firms exist: Why an explanatory emphasis on opportunism may mislead management strategy. *Industrial and Corporate Change*, 13(2): 401–418.

Iriyama, A., & Madhavan, R. 2014. Post-formation inter-partner equity transfers in international joint ventures: The role of experience. *Global Strategy Journal*, 4(4): 331–348.

Johanson, J., & Vahlne, J. E. 1977. The internationalization process of the firm—A model of knowledge development and increasing foreign market commitments. *Journal of International Business Studies*, 8(1): 23–32.

Johanson, J., & Vahlne, J. E. 1990. The mechanism of internationalisation. *International Marketing Review*, 7(4): 11–24.

Klein, K. J., Dansereau, F., & Hall, R. J. 1994. Levels issues in theory development, data collection, and analysis. *Academy of Management Review*, 19(2): 195–229.

Klein, K. J., Tosi, H., & Cannella, A. A. 1999. Multilevel theory building: Benefits, barriers, and new development. *Academy of Management Review*, 24(2): 243–248.

Kogut, B. 1991. Joint ventures and the option to expand and acquire. *Management Science*, 37(1): 19–33.

Koontz, H. 1961. The management theory jungle. *Academy of Management Journal*, 4(3): 174–188.

Kuhn, T. S. 1962. *The Structure of Scientific Revolutions*. Chicago, IL: University of Chicago Press.

Lampel, J., & Giachetti, C. 2013. International diversification of manufacturing operations: Performance implications and moderating forces. *Journal of Operations Management*, 31(4): 213–227.

Lewis, M. W. 2000. Exploring paradox: Toward a more comprehensive guide. *Academy of Management Review*, 25(4): 760–776.

Mäki, U. 2000. Kinds of assumptions and their truth: Shaking an untwisted F-twist. *Kyklos*, 53(3): 317–336.

Marchionni, C. 2008. Explanatory pluralism and complementarity. *Philosophy of the Social Sciences*, 38(3): 314–333.

Marquis, C., & Tilcsik, A. 2013. Imprinting: Toward a multilevel theory. *Academy of Management Annals*, 7(1): 195–245.

Masterman, M. 1970. The nature of a paradigm. In I. Lakatos and A. Musgrave (Eds.), *Criticism and the Growth of Knowledge*. Cambridge: Cambridge University Press.

McKinley, W., & Mone, M. A. 1998. The re-construction of organization studies: Wrestling with incommensurability. *Organization*, 5(2): 169–189.

Porter, M. E. 1980. *Competitive Strategy*. New York, NY: Free Press.

Pouder, R., & St. John, C. H. 1996. Hot spots and blind spots: Geographical clusters of firms and innovation. *Academy of Management Review*, 21(4): 1192–1225.

Reuer, J. J., Tyler, B. B., Tong, T. W., & Wu, C. W. 2012. Executives' assessments of international joint ventures in China: A multi-theoretical investigation. *Management and Organization Review*, 8(2): 311–340.

Ronen, S., & Shenkar, O. 1985. Clustering countries on attitudinal dimensions: A review and synthesis. *Academy of Management Review*, 10(3): 435–454.

Rousseau, D. M. 1985. Issues of level in organizational research: Multi-level and cross-level perspectives. *Research in Organizational Behavior*, 7: 1–37.

Rugman, A. 1979. *International Diversification and the Multinational Enterprise*. Lexington, KY: Lexington Books.

Ryan, L. V., & Schneider, M. 2003. Institutional investor power and heterogeneity: Implications for agency and stakeholder theories. *Business & Society*, 42(4): 398–429.

Sayer, A. 1992. *Method in Social Science: A Realist Approach*. London: Routledge.

Schultz, M., & Hatch, M. J. 1996. Living with multiple paradigms the case of paradigm interplay in organizational culture studies. *Academy of Management Review*, 21(2): 529–557.

Shankman, N. A. 1999. Reframing the debate between agency and stakeholder theories of the firm. *Journal of Business Ethics*, 19(4): 319–334.

Sousa, C. M., & Bradley, F. 2006. Cultural distance and psychic distance: Two peas in a pod? *Journal of International Marketing*, 14(1): 49–70.

St. John, C. H. 2005. Multi-theoretical mixed-level research in strategic management. *Research Methodology in Strategy and Management*, 2: 197–223.

Sternberg, R. J., & Ben-Zeev, T. 2001. *Complex Cognition: The Psychology of Human Thought*. New York, NY: Oxford University Press.

Stöttinger, B., & Schlegelmilch, B. B. 1998. Explaining export development through psychic distance: Enlightening or elusive? *International Marketing Review*, 15(5): 357–372.

Surdu, I., Mellahi, K., & Glaister, K. W. 2019. Once bitten, not necessarily shy? Determinants of foreign market re-entry commitment strategies. *Journal of International Business Studies*, 50(3): 393–422.

Sutton, R. I., & Staw, B. M. 1995. What theory is not. *Administrative Science Quarterly*, 40(3): 371–384.

Tsang, E. W. K. 2000. Transaction cost and resource-based explanations of joint ventures: A comparison and synthesis. *Organization Studies*, 21(1): 215–242.

Tsang, E. W. K. 2006. Behavioral assumptions and theory development: The case of transaction cost economics. *Strategic Management Journal*, 27(11): 999–1011.

Tsang, E. W. K. 2014. Ensuring manuscript quality and preserving authorial voice: The balancing act of editors. *Management and Organization Review*, 10(2): 191–197.

Van de Ven, A. H. 1989. Nothing is quite so practical as a good theory. *Academy of Management Review*, 14(4): 486–489.

Wathne, K. H., & Heide, J. B. 2000. Opportunism in interfirm relationships: Forms, outcomes, and solutions. *Journal of Marketing*, 64(4): 36–51.

Williamson, O. E. 1975. *Markets and Hierarchies: Analysis and Antitrust Implications*. New York, NY: Free Press.

Williamson, O. E. 1985. *The Economic Institutions of Capitalism*. New York, NY: Free Press.

Williamson, O. E. 1996. Economic organization: The case for candor. *Academy of Management Review*, 21(1): 48–57.

Wright, R. W., & Ricks, D. A. 1994. Trends in international business research: Twenty-five years later. *Journal of International Business Studies*, 25(4): 687–702.

Zajac, E. J., & Olsen, C. P. 1993. From transaction cost to transaction value analysis: Implications for the study of interorganizational strategies. *Journal of Management Studies*, 30(1): 131–145.

PART III

GOVERNANCE STRUCTURES IN INTERNATIONAL BUSINESS STRATEGY

CHAPTER 9

....

INTERNATIONAL NEW VENTURES

Do They Really Matter?

....

ISIBOR JERRY EBEIGBE AND ELIZABETH L. ROSE

Introduction

....

FIRMS that internationalize[1] rapidly and soon after their establishment certainly do not constitute a new phenomenon. Wilkins (1988) described the "free-standing companies," which were established in the nineteenth century and flourished until World War I; in modern international business (IB) strategy research, these firms would be classified as international new ventures (INVs). The Finnish International Business Operations (FIBO) database (e.g., Luostarinen, 1994) includes evidence of INVs that were established in Finland in the early 1700s. A century earlier, the English East India Company, alongside similar competitors from other Europeans countries, was also an INV (e.g., Robins, 2012).

That said, while rapid- and early internationalizing firms have existed for hundreds of years, they are no longer rarities. This relative explosion in numbers is consistent with the burgeoning literature dealing with various aspects of such firms' internationalization strategies. Improvements in information and communication technology (ICT) have been critical to this development. The growing availability of fax machines in the 1970s and early 1980s made immediate, information-rich international communication widely available, making it much more feasible for even fledgling businesses to sell their goods and services outside the borders of their home countries. More recently, the ubiquity of internet access facilitates cross-border reach at much lower cost, greatly

---

[1] We take "internationalize" to refer to any strategy that includes the generation of revenue in a country in which the firm is not headquartered. This can include any entry mode, from exporting to foreign direct investment (FDI).

reducing the barriers faced by fledgling firms (e.g., Arenius et al., 2005). Advances in ICT have been game-changers with respect to physical distance, making it feasible for a New Zealand-founded entrepreneurial firm like Icebreaker (a company that produces merino wool clothing) to internationalize rapidly and become a global player in the international outdoor clothing market.

The technology-enabled enhanced access to international markets has particularly important implications for start-ups in two types of home countries: small and open economies (SMOPECs) and emerging markets. SMOPEC-based firms have long experienced strong push incentives to target international markets early, given the limited market size (and therefore growth potential) at home (e.g., Hallbäck & Gabrielsson, 2013); it is no coincidence that much of the INV literature pertains to examples from countries such as Australia, Denmark, Finland, New Zealand, Norway, and Sweden. The ICT-related implications for emerging-market entrepreneurial firms have also been particularly important. As many such firms have turned to international markets more recently, they have been able to embed the newer communications facilities into their internationalization strategies (e.g., Nowiński & Rialp, 2013). In India, examples range from information technology (IT) giant Infosys (an INV when it was founded in 1981) to small start-ups with virtually no capital requirements, such as the business founded by high school students to provide internet-based fitness consulting to clients in Kenya, benefiting from the ever-growing power and availability of smart phones that provide extensive internet access at reasonable cost. In Sub-Saharan Africa, organizations such as IROKO—one of Nigeria's largest internet and entertainment companies—have leveraged technology-enabled access to offer a wide range of African entertainment to international markets.

In this chapter, we propose that there are often aspects of IB strategy that are specific to small, entrepreneurial firms that internationalize early in their existence. There are two fairly straightforward comparison groups: large multinational enterprises (MNEs) and small- and medium-sized enterprises (SMEs) that internationalize later in their history. The most widely addressed comparison in the literature is between INVs and large MNEs, often with a focus on the Uppsala model (e.g., Johanson & Vahlne, 1977) that is widely applied to explain the gradual internationalization patterns observed among large MNEs.[2] INVs, by definition, internationalize in a matter that is anything but gradual, at least in the early years of their internationalization (e.g., Oviatt & McDougall, 1994; Knight & Cavusgil, 1996). In addition, the INVs' smaller size and newness are typically associated with more limited resources within the firm (e.g., Zahra, 2005); these include intangible, firm-specific knowledge and experience resources. As such, they are likely to adopt different approaches to procuring the resources needed for internationalization, focusing more on access (which may be temporary) as opposed to ownership. In this way, INVs may rely heavily on being embedded in business networks and ecosystems, to support their international activities. Their newness and size also dictate the use of a

---

[2] Chapter 7 provides a detailed overview of the use and misuse of the Uppsala stage model of internationalization thus far.

more niche product or market strategy. These attributes make the comparison of INVs and large MNEs tricky and unsatisfactory.[3]

The comparison between INVs and other SMEs, while arguably more salient, is less explored (for an exception, see Gerschewski, Rose, & Lindsay, 2015). We argue that examining the differences that may exist between INVs and other SMEs allows for a deeper understanding of the different motivations for, drivers of, and outcomes from international strategy; this means comparing firms that are actually comparable with respect to size and resources. Smaller size has both challenges and benefits. Challenges include limited resources and liabilities of newness (e.g., Zahra, 2005) and outsidership (e.g., Johanson & Vahlne, 2009), while benefits pertain to organizational agility (e.g., Autio, Sapienza, & Almeida, 2000). We propose that comparing INVs with their relatively more similar counterparts, that is, SMEs, enables us to identify which firm attributes and relationships are specific to INVs, as opposed to the broader category of smaller MNEs of which they are part.

Theoretically, considerations of the internationalization of INVs bring together the fields of IB, entrepreneurship, and strategic management, and can shed light on issues that are more difficult to investigate in larger MNEs. Notably, studying INVs involves an emphasis on the entrepreneurial founder and/or top management, in terms of personal attributes and experiences, resources, and motivations for international expansion (e.g., Bloodgood, Sapienza, & Almeida, 1996; Coviello, 2015). While the linkages between the decision maker and organizational outcomes can be extremely difficult to identify in large firms, due to the inherent organizational complexity, they may be clearer with rapidly internationalizing SMEs such as INVs. Research into INVs also allows for a clearer understanding of how a firm may learn—rapidly—about operating across national borders, in terms of both specific international markets and designing internationalization strategies in general.

The remainder of this chapter proceeds as follows. First, we review the progression of key existing research pertaining to the IB strategies of INVs. Then, we discuss how INV research offers insights about IB strategic choices that should be generalizable to a wide range of internationally active firms. This includes a discussion of how extant theories could be enhanced by drawing on insights from current INV studies. Finally, we offer some further suggestions about how future research into INVs can be developed.

THE INV LITERATURE AND ITS DEVELOPMENT

The literature on INVs dates back to the work of McDougall (1989). Comparing domestic and INVs, the study by McDougall (1989) found that international new ventures which "from inception, engage in international business," had founders

---

[3] It is also important to note that not all MNEs are large firms. See Chapter 10, which discusses the internationalization strategies of micromultinational enterprises (mMNEs).

who were internationally oriented, and that these firms seemed to have structures and strategies that differed substantially from those of domestic new ventures, thus enabling them to expand internationally very early in their histories. Despite the prevailing focus on large MNEs at the time, among both academics and managers, these insights into the INV phenomenon attracted attention and subsequently led to an increase in research into new ventures with surprisingly aggressive international strategies.

Notable among these studies is the work of Jolly, Alahuhta, and Jeannet (1992), who identified a set of small exporters who engaged in foreign direct investment (FDI) virtually from their establishment. Rennie (1993) later studied and discussed export firms that competed across national borders soon after being founded (referring to them as "born global" (BG) firms).[4] Building on the Jolly et al. (1992) description of a new set of venture types, the seminal work of Oviatt and McDougall (1994) highlighted the increasing role of firms that were young and actively participating in international markets, describing them as deriving "significant competitive advantage from extensive coordination among multiple organizational activities, the location of which are geographically unlimited." Oviatt and McDougall (1994) noted that, despite a long history, INVs had been largely overlooked in the academic literature, and argued against the utility of incremental stages-based models of internationalization for explaining INVs' early venturing into international markets. In essence, studies published in the early 1990s introduced research into the emergence of the INV phenomenon and inquiry into these firms' characteristics and antecedents of internationalization. We also identified some comparative studies of these and other types of small or new ventures (e.g., Jolly et al., 1992; Knight & Cavusgil, 1996; Oviatt & McDougall, 1994; Rennie, 1993). For instance, Oviatt and McDougall (1994) and Knight and Cavusgil (1996) documented evidence of the internationalization patterns of INV firms that challenged extant theories pertaining to the internationally active firm. These seminal works set the scene for subsequent studies to combine IB-related theoretical frameworks with discussions grounded in entrepreneurship-led research for examining the IB strategies of INVs.

The 1990s, which still concerns what we refer to as the early work on INVs, created the foundation for the development of subsequent research pertaining to these firms' underlying characteristics, their strategies in international markets, and the determinants of their international performance, sometimes in comparison with other types of organizations (e.g., Bell, 1995; Bloodgood et al., 1996; Madsen & Servais, 1997; McAuley, 1999; Oviatt & McDougall, 1995). In the second half of the 1990s, scholars began to focus on INVs' involvement in networks to enable early and rapid internationalization. For example, Coviello and Munro (1995, 1997) investigated the internationalization processes (IPs) of software firms that were expanding quite rapidly and observed that these firms' links with established networks could affect the markets targeted and entry modes adopted. Coviello and Munro (1995, 1997) specifically found that both formal and informal

---

[4] The literature has yet to reach agreement on terminology: firms that internationalize soon after being founded tend to be referred to as either "INVs," "BGs" and/or "early internationalizing firms." In this chapter, we refer to these as INVs without necessarily engaging in this (thus far, unfruitful) debate.

networks affected not only market selection and entry modes but decisions about product development and market diversification as well. Their findings also suggest that there are changes in firms' approaches to network relationships as they move through the IP, and that performance, particularly in high-priority markets, likely depends on the development and subsequent restructuring of network relationships, with the goal of attaining more control over them. These and other studies concluded that the early internationalization of INVs was facilitated by such network relationships (e.g., Casson, 1997; Coviello & Munro, 1995, 1997; Reuber & Fisher, 1997; Madsen & Servais, 1997).

INV Research in the 2000s

By the early 2000s, the proliferation of internationally active SMEs had encouraged the growth of research on INVs, on the basis that globalization and advances in ICT were enabling SMEs to aggressively seek and pursue international opportunities soon after their formation (Autio et al., 2000; Luostarinen & Gabrielsson, 2006; Ruzzier et al., 2006). Some research also focused on the impact of the external environment on new ventures' cross-border activities, highlighting the nature of firms' openness to markets. Etemad (2004) reported on a theoretical framework for internationalizing SMEs, arguing that firms, rather than basing their international status solely on features such as the easy movement of goods and services across borders, can internationalize by tapping into specific regional clusters more rapidly than their competitors, and/or competing in high-end markets that are already integrated into the global economy. Other studies along these lines have highlighted factors outside the immediate control of internationalizing SMEs that have the potential to drive early cross-border venturing; these include market liberalization, advances in ICTs, market growth, and the global integration of firms within an industry (e.g., Etemad, 2004; Loane & Bell, 2006; McDougall, Oviatt, & Shrader, 2003; Servais, Madsen, & Rasmussen, 2006). Research has addressed a range of determinants, including the age of the firm at initial internationalization (Autio et al., 2000; Oviatt & McDougall, 2005), the founder's entrepreneurial character and available resources (Luostarinen & Gabrielsson, 2006; McDougall et al., 2003), and network processes and social capital (Chetty & Campbell-Hunt, 2004; Coviello, 2006; Sharma & Blomstermo, 2003).

For instance, Autio et al. (2000) shed light on the growth of the entrepreneurial firm, highlighting the importance of the time between founding and the initiation of international engagement, thereby informing research on the learning advantage of newness (see also Zahra, Zheng, & Yu, 2018; Zhou, Barnes, & Lu, 2010). The learning advantage of newness contrasts with the notion of organizational inertia that seems to interfere with the abilities of mature firms to adapt to the changes associated with expanding into foreign markets. The logic is that learning becomes more difficult for firms as they grow older, which may hinder their capacities to derive full advantage, especially non-financial, from international growth. In a larger, more mature organization, unlearning deeply embedded habits may be difficult, owing to well-established foreign business practices.

Newer and smaller firms may be more inclined—and able—to pursue international opportunities, due to their inherently flexible operational practices and more restricted allegiance to domestic stakeholders, including political and network affiliations; the resulting agility encourages—and facilitates—more rapid learning, which may yield stronger business growth in international markets (see Autio et al., 2000). The benefit of rapid learning is posited to emanate from a pattern of behavior that is developed from many new ventures' proactive disposition toward expanding into multiple markets in a short timeframe (e.g., Kropp, Lindsay, & Shoham, 2006; Oviatt & McDougall, 2005; Zhou, 2007).

INV founders' resources, and their inclination toward being risk-accepting, proactive, and innovative, have also been discussed in the literature (e.g., Luostarinen & Gabrielsson, 2006; McDougall et al., 2003). In addition, there is evidence that the prior experience of founders and/or top management teams tend to facilitate INVs' early expansion across national borders (e.g., Acedo & Jones, 2007; Casillas, Moreno, Acedo, Gallego, & Ramos, 2009; Luostarinen & Gabrielsson, 2006; McDougall et al., 2003). For example, McDougall et al. (2003) observed that INVs tend to have highly experienced international teams that pursue aggressive strategies and know to emphasize high quality and excellence in service delivery, thus enabling the firms to compete globally within integrated industries. The entrepreneurial founders' international experience may also form dynamic capabilities, which are viewed as critical for supporting early internationalization (cf. Weerawardena, Sullivan Mort, Liesch, & Knight, 2007).

Research on network processes and social capital in the context of internationalization and performance also became prominent in the early 2000s (e.g., Andersson & Wictor, 2003; Fernhaber & Li, 2013; Nowiński & Rialp, 2016). Building on the earlier works by Coviello and Munro (1995, 1997), scholars recognized the need to expand on network research to develop theories and concepts that are specific to INVs (e.g., Sharma & Blomstermo, 2003; Yli-Renko, Autio, & Sapienza, 2001). There is evidence that network relationships enable social capital that can be utilized to generate mobility for the entrepreneurial firm. In particular, Sharma & Blomstermo (2003) explained that a firm's access to market knowledge prior to its first international market entry and its selection of entry mode may stem from its network relationships. Researchers adopting the perspective of developing social capital via network relationships have also explored the role of social ties in internationalization (e.g., Coviello & Cox, 2006; Ellis, 2000; Yli-Renko, Autio, & Tontti, 2002), the effect of network changes and alterations over time (Coviello, 2006), and the utility of network capabilities in augmenting entrepreneurial behavior (Mort & Weerawardena, 2006).

INV researchers have employed a variety of theoretical frameworks to understand IB strategy, in an attempt to extend the conversation beyond large MNEs to discussions about young, resource-constrained firms that internationalize quite rapidly. These include resource-oriented theories, such as the resource-based view (RBV) of the firm (e.g., Knight & Cavusgil, 2004), organizational learning (e.g., Autio et al., 2000), and the knowledge-based view (e.g., Gassmann & Keupp, 2007). Considering BG firms, Knight and Cavusgil (2004) highlighted the crucial nature of organizational knowledge for supporting internationalization efforts and performance in foreign markets, noting that an innovative inclination and the ability to rearrange combinations of relevant knowledge equips the firms to offer products that meet customer demands and expectations, and that this, in turn, enhances the potential for stronger international market sales. This paper assisted in directing INV research thinking toward the RBV (e.g., Rialp & Rialp, 2007), which emphasizes the firm's resources and capabilities (Barney, 1991; Grant, 1991), and the further application of the entrepreneurship perspective to studies on rapid internationalization (Jones et al., 2011), while also helping to open up research incorporating the international entrepreneurial perspective to a range of phenomena (e.g., Covin & Miller, 2014; Kuivalainen et al., 2007).

Learning is also an important aspect of firms' venturing across borders and is observed to be a key source of advantage for INVs, in terms of enabling and maintaining international growth soon after founding (see De Clercq, Sapienza, Yavuz, & Zhou, 2012). It has been noted that INVs' rapid international expansion is, in part, a function of the ability to draw on a strong knowledge base (e.g., Oviatt & McDougall, 1994; Park & Rhee, 2012; Yeoh, 2004) bolstered by the acquisition, adoption, and absorption of new knowledge (e.g., Casillas et al., 2009; Fletcher & Harris, 2012; Prashantham & Floyd, 2012). Entrepreneurial behavior (e.g., Zhou et al., 2010) and managerial and network capabilities (e.g., Chetty & Campbell-Hunt, 2004; Kungwansupaphan & Siengthai, 2014) have been posited to contribute to effective learning in INVs. Similarly, the firm's orientation—entrepreneurial, technological, and learning—is expected to be related to, and potentially drive, its knowledge development, cross-border decision-making, and the extent and scope of its internationalization (e.g., Baum, Schwens, & Kabst, 2011; Bunz, Casulli, Jones, & Bausch, 2017; Knight & Cavusgil, 2004; Sapienza, De Clercq, & Sandberg, 2005; Zhou, 2007).

In addition to considering the INV's age at its initial internationalization as a knowledge development factor (e.g., Autio et al., 2000), the timing of specific venturing across borders, as it pertains to the firm's learning processes, has also been investigated (e.g., Blomstermo, Eriksson, & Sharma, 2004; Ripollés et al., 2012). Despite conflicting insights with respect to the impact of entry timing on INV learning, this line of work points toward the dynamics of learning and the importance of firms undertaking constant modifications in the pursuit of organizational goals, including the acquisition of *new* knowledge (e.g., Ripollés et al., 2012; Schwens & Kabst, 2009b; Zou & Ghauri, 2010) and the utilization of limited resources (e.g., Baum, Schwens, & Kabst, 2015) to mitigate risk and safeguard survival (Bunz et al., 2017; Chandra, 2017). The network perspective, in particular, is used to explain various learning outcomes for INVs, including knowledge gains (e.g., Fuerst & Zettinig, 2015; Schwens & Kabst, 2009a), opportunity seeking and exploitation (e.g., Chandra, Styles, & Wilkinson, 2012), and the development of new capabilities (e.g., Evers, Andersson, & Hannibal, 2012; Khavul, Peterson, Mullens, & Rasheed, 2010). Various aspects of the learning process have been considered (e.g., Zahra, Ireland, & Hitt, 2000; Zou & Ghauri, 2010). For instance, Zahra et al. (2000) noted that international diversity—in terms of geographic scope and aspects of the host country's technological and cultural environments—and mode of entry can affect the extent of technological learning for new firms; this effect depends on firm-level routines that determine the INV's expansion and its capabilities for exploiting technological learning (Tuomisalo & Leppäaho (2018) offer a systematic review of research pertaining to INV learning).

Another interesting (we argue) line of inquiry is that related to how these entrepreneurs make decisions; that is, their inclination to create international opportunities by seeking to interpret, adjust, create products, and understand markets using the logic of effectuation (Sarasvathy, 2001). Studies utilizing effectuation theory to explain INV behavior highlight a spontaneous and unplanned decision-making process, in contrast to the more systematic causation approach that is often adopted by entrepreneurs in setting up firm activities and venturing across borders (e.g., Harms & Schiele, 2012; Nummela, Saarenketo, Jokela, & Loane, 2014). Harms and Schiele (2012) concluded that entrepreneurs tend to adopt more effectuation than causation in their efforts toward timing of internationalization; that is, by internationalizing early. Nummela et al. (2014) explained that spontaneity and systematic decision-making can go hand-in-hand for firms, but that their relative prominence is reliant on (un)certain market conditions and the individual inclinations of managerial decision makers.

So, are INVs Important for Our Understanding of IB Strategy?

One fundamental question is whether or not INVs actually represent a different "species" of firms, relative to other internationally active firms. Much of the literature seems to assume that this is the case. However, we suggest that this view may be overly narrow. Even a cursory look at examples of INVs makes it clear that many of the traditional assumptions about these firms—that they are exporters that operate in high-technology industries and lack knowledge about IB strategy—do not necessarily reflect reality. While exporting is common among these firms, there is ample evidence that they employ other entry modes; for example, Gerschewski et al. (2015) reported that 29 percent of the firms in their sample reported entering their first markets using an entry mode other than exporting. INVs can be found across a wide range of product and service categories, and it is not credible to assume that all, or even most, INV founders are novices with respect to undertaking business across national borders; there is evidence that many INVs are established by serial entrepreneurs who have considerable expertise with conducting IB (e.g., Karra, Phillips, & Tracey, 2008). While INVs generally face resource constraints (e.g., Knight & Cavusgil 2004), they are not alone in that regard. Even their documented vulnerability to being subject to buffeting by global forces does not make them unique, as this is certainly not the sole domain of newly internationalizing firms.

Our review of the literature suggests that previous research pertaining to INVs has focused heavily on topics such as the importance of networks for accessing resources (e.g., Coviello & Munro, 1997; Chetty & Campbell-Hunt, 2004), internationalizing as part of a larger supply chain (e.g., Yli-Renko et al., 2001), processes for learning about cross-border business (e.g., Schwens & Kabst, 2009b; Pellegrino & McNaughton, 2015), developing and deploying social capital (e.g., Yli-Renko et al, 2002), and leveraging entrepreneurial orientation (e.g., Knight & Cavusgil, 2004). There is no reason to believe that these issues pertain to INVs alone, and not SMEs that internationalize later in their existences. Rather, it can be argued that these are issues that pertain, albeit in varying degrees, to internationally active firms of any size. While SMEs—including INVs—are likely to rely heavily on networks as sources of key resources (e.g., Fuerst & Zettinig, 2015), there are few large MNEs that are so completely vertically integrated that, in the increasingly competitive and interconnected global economy, they do not engage in network associations in the process of internationalizing their supply chains. Anti-globalization sentiments and pressures to engage in socially responsible activities, among other motivations, mean that large MNEs also need to develop competences related to the development and deployment of social capital.[5] Firms of any size that do not focus on continuous learning, especially with regard to international markets, put themselves at a competitive disadvantage. In a similar vein, the benefits associated with entrepreneurial orientation of managers are not limited to smaller firms.

Certainly, INVs have some specific characteristics (see Knight & Cavusgil, 1996), but we would argue that they are interesting to study not because they represent a different "species" of firm, but rather because they represent a special case of firms that undertake IB strategies. Essentially, INVs can be viewed as extreme cases that serve as boundary conditions for some of the theoretical frameworks that are used to make sense of IB strategy. Understanding more about how the theoretical frameworks function at these boundary conditions offers the opportunity for stronger testing and theoretical development. We introduce four examples in which INVs offer an excellent setting in which to refine and even enhance current theoretical assumptions, namely:

(1) the RBV;
(2) microfoundations, psychic distance, and liabilities of foreignness;
(3) organizational learning; and
(4) the relationship between inward and outward internationalization.

The RBV of the Firm

The nature of INVs means that research pertaining to them tends to be quite explicit in its recognition of both uncertainty and resource constraints and the impacts that these constraints may have on decisions pertaining to IB strategy. Because INVs tend to lack slack, with respect to finances and other resources (e.g., Knight & Cavusgil, 2004;

---

[5] Chapter 21 provides a detailed discussion of the capabilities that firms require in order to successfully manage and orchestrate the partners in their global value chains.

Rialp & Rialp, 2007), they are considerably more vulnerable to uncertainty than the resource-rich MNEs that are more often the context in which the RBV is applied and tested. This makes the deep understanding of resources and their utilization especially salient. INVs' often fluid approach to tapping into networks alliances in order to access the resources that are necessary to support international strategy also encourages a broadening of the boundaries of the firm within the RBV (see Fernhaber & Li, 2013).

Microfoundations

A distinctive aspect of research into INVs—and in the field of international entrepreneurship more generally—is on individuals as decision makers. This is consistent with the recent emphasis on microfoundations in IB and strategy research (Felin, Foss, & Ployhar, 2015), whereas, traditionally, strategic decisions have tended to have been treated as emanating from "the firm" or "the group" (e.g., the top management team). The focus on the individual in the INV literature is facilitated by the fact that the research is undertaken in the context of smaller firms, in which the actual decision makers are more readily identifiable. Research pertaining to individual decision makers is particularly important, given that the entrepreneurs who found and/or drive the firm can provide detailed understanding of the firm's internationalization behaviors (Coviello, 2015). Focusing on, and having access to, the entrepreneurial decision maker allows for more explicit identification of processes, pathways, and key decisions. The access also offers the potential of observing real-time (or close to real-time) decision-making regarding internationalization, with fewer levels of hierarchy through which to filter interpretations. In this way, studying INVs should allow the broader IB strategy literature to benefit from a clearer understanding of who is making strategic decisions pertaining to international activities—along with how and why these decisions are made and, of course, their subsequent implications.

The ability to focus on the actual decision makers also offers the potential to develop deeper insights into the determinants and impacts of psychic distance and liabilities of foreignness, both of which are individual-level constructs that tend to be measured at the firm level in the IB strategy literature. For example, psychic distance is notoriously difficult to measure, which means that researchers tend to fall back on available country-level data, or stylized facts about top managers (e.g., languages spoken, educational background, international travel) to operationalize a construct that actually depends heavily on the past experience and tacit knowledge associated with the individual decision maker (for early work on this, see Beckerman, 1956).

Organizational Learning

The ways in which firms learn about internationalization, embed that understanding within the organization, and utilize it in strategic decision-making are issues of key interest to IB strategy researchers. Studying such issues involves subtleties that are difficult to isolate in the context of a large MNE. Deep investigation of aspects associated with learning and knowledge development should be considerably more feasible in INVs, given their less complicated organizational structures and internal relationships (see Pellegrino & McNaughton, 2015 for an example of this approach). Cavusgil & Knight (2015) note the importance of the organizational learning perspective for explaining how small ventures—including INVs—capture, develop, share, and improve knowledge and, in turn, enhance performance in the face of specific pressures. This theoretical lens can be used to understand the links between individual learning(s) of the entrepreneurial founder and/or top management and the collective knowledge of these smaller firms, as well as how knowledge pertaining to IB strategy develops over time. The rationale behind this is that investigating questions associated with how such learning occurs within INVs, and how learning undertaken by specific individuals is then shared within the firm, can shed light on the learning processes that occur in larger firms as well. This is particularly important as most MNE research studies either individual learning drivers or process or firm learning drivers, and processes without a clear link between when and how the knowledge of individual decision makers becomes part of organizational routines, thus becoming, to some extent, firm-level knowledge.

Inward and Outward Internationalization and the Domestic Context

While experience with inward internationalization (e.g., importing) has long been posited to facilitate outward (e.g., exporting) internationalization (e.g., Luostarinen, 1979; Welch & Luostarinen, 1993), limited work has been done to investigate such a relationship empirically. INVs, especially those that have internationalized recently, offer an ideal context in which to study the inward–outward internationalization connection, which may allow managers opportunities to learn about cross-border business in a lower-risk situation; this may be especially pertinent for emerging- and developing-market firms for which information and engagement with MNEs may be less readily available (the Helsinki or product-operations-market (POM) model of Luostarinen (1979) may provide a particularly useful theoretical framework for such research). Studying INVs may also allow for the development of deeper understanding pertaining to how, when, and why firms de-internationalize (e.g., Benito & Welch, 1997); the underlying assumption of most IB strategy research is that outward internationalization proceeds along a trajectory, rather than involving expansion and retrenchment and, in some cases, re-entry.

The domestic context affects organizations' international strategies in many ways that are difficult to capture adequately using the secondary measures that dominate quantitative work in IB strategy. The ability to connect with actual decision makers in INVs may prove useful for understanding these subtleties. For example, many nations offer strictly domestic firms the opportunity to gain useful skills pertaining to internationalization without crossing national borders; a Canadian firm that aims to serve the entire country must be able to operate across two languages and multiple cultures—and the situation is considerably more complex for firms in countries such as India. Such differences (e.g., with respect to language and culture) within the home market may allow firms to acquire relevant knowledge in their domestic operations that then becomes valuable for IB venturing. It is reasonable to assume that such domestic experience will play a role in the firm's approach to internationalization, and young INVs represent an excellent environment in which to understand this phenomenon.

What Do We Need to Progress?

We hope to have convinced the reader that INVs are interesting firms to study in their own right, in addition to allowing researchers to develop deeper insights into issues that apply to a broader range of firms that undertake business internationally. As extreme internationalizers with respect to age and, often, speed, INVs also present an excellent opportunity to consider how many of the theoretical frameworks that are used in IB strategy research perform near their boundaries; this has the potential to put some of the theories to stringent tests of appropriateness. We suggest some methodological and theoretical issues that, when addressed in more depth, should enhance our understanding of how INVs internationalize—which should have positive spillovers for our understanding of a wider collection of firms that undertake business across national borders.

First of all, the literature on INVs suffers from a lack of agreement regarding some key operational definitions (see Coviello, 2015; Zander, McDougall-Covin, & Rose, 2015). In addition to the fact that these firms are known by a variety of names (e.g., INVs, BGs, early internationalizing firms), there is little agreement about how to identify INVs, in terms of age at internationalization, the requisite proportion of overseas sales and the extent of international coverage (e.g., "global" vs. one other country). Part of the challenge arises from context-dependence. SMEs, in general, are defined differently in various countries and regions. The European Union identifies an SME as having fewer than 250 employees and an annual turnover not exceeding EUR 50 million, and/or an annual balance sheet total not exceeding EUR 43 million. In India, the definition has been linked to investment levels, with a distinction between the manufacturing and service sectors, although the government is now in the process of moving to a simpler definition based on turnover that is below Rs 250 crore, which is approximately EUR 3.2 million. New Zealand defines SMEs as firms with fewer than 50 employees.

Second, on top of definitional issues, researchers vary with respect to how they define two key attributes of INVs: the time to first internationalization and the proportion of foreign sales within a set timeframe. While many use the US-oriented Knight and Cavusgil (2004) classification of three years, post-establishment, to internationalization and 25 percent of foreign sales within three years, this practice is far from uniform. For example, Zou and Ghauri (2010) and Gassmann and Keupp (2007) consider INVs as having had foreign engagement within their first six and ten years, respectively, and the ratio of foreign to total sales employed in classifying these firms is broadly in the range of 5–25 percent (see also Zhou et al., 2010). We emphasize that this lack of uniformity with regards to operationalization underscores the still-developing nature of INV research (Coviello, 2015), which is why part of this definitional variation is understandable. The process of initiating IB depends on diverse aspects. Geography comes into play; for example, internationalizing from a home base within the European Union is a different sort of decision to internationalizing from a home base in a remote location such as New Zealand. The young firm's home-country economic situation (e.g., developed vs. emerging vs. developing) and the nature of its access to venture capital affect its ability to internationalize early, as does the nature of what it is selling (e.g., products vs. services) and its means of distribution (e.g., physical vs. virtual). Still, the adoption of specific definitions does not seem to be driven by these contextual issues, and thus the lack of a universally accepted definition is arguably a barrier to research progress, as, at the very least, it precludes effective cross-study comparisons.

Third, beyond the important issue of operational definitions, the INV literature would benefit from continuing to build on the empirical research that has motivated it from the start. In-depth qualitative work—especially case-based research—may allow researchers to develop new insights into INVs' IP, as opposed to performance outcomes. This offers the potential for nuanced understanding of strategic decision-making and issues of timing that can then be applied to other types of firms. With respect to quantitative research, more carefully constructed comparisons between INVs and firms that internationalize later will enable the development of a deeper understanding about what findings are actually specific to INVs.

Fourth, like much of the body of research pertaining to IB strategy, the INV literature relies heavily on empirical observation, and the fact that it is still a young field means that there is considerable scope for theoretical development. As a subset of the field of international entrepreneurship, the study of INVs draws on the theoretical bases used in IB, strategy, and entrepreneurship. We therefore propose that deeper engagement with the psychology and sociology literatures may assist in the development of a better understanding of individual entrepreneurs' perspectives on decision-making and dealing with the risk and uncertainty associated with undertaking international expansion, over and above the risk and uncertainty inherent in starting up a new business, along with how these firms' internationalization strategies are developed from the context of their home environments. In addition, the IB strategy literature offers potential avenues. It may be helpful to move on from emphasizing deviations from the Uppsala model (e.g., Johanson & Vahlne, 1977), even with its more recent adaptations (e.g., Johanson & Vahlne, 2009), and consider other models of internationalization that may provide valuable insights into INVs' internationalization; one notable such example is Luostarinen's (1979) underutilized model, that is, the Helsinki or POM model (see also Luostarinen & Gabrielsson, 2006). Developed at about the same time as the Uppsala model and based on a more detailed categorization of international entry strategies, the Helsinki model is explicit about the potential for firms to internationalize—and de-internationalize—using considerable flexibility with respect to both location and entry mode. This flexibility and multidirectionality may provide a better fit to the realities of INVs' international strategies.

Concluding Remarks

While the IB strategy literature has long had the MNE as its focus, the literature on INVs has grown tremendously since McDougall (1989) first introduced this concept. Our position in this chapter is that INVs, while certainly interesting in their own right, also provide a useful setting in which to study broader issues pertaining to MNE IB strategy. This is because INVs' smaller size and less complex organizational structures, with more identifiable decision makers, should make it more feasible for researchers to truly understand their internationalization drivers and choices. We anticipate that studying INVs may yield more general insights into flexible approaches to accessing and utilizing resources, along with how learning related to internationalization is embedded within organizations. Such research also offers the potential to contribute to the microfoundations focus that is growing in the IB strategy literature, while extending our understanding of key issues such as psychic distance, liabilities of foreignness, and the impact of the firm's domestic context. The necessity for INVs to operate without much slack also makes them useful for advancing research pertaining to de-internationalization and, more broadly, the relationship between inward and outward internationalization.

References

Acedo, F. J., & Jones, M. V. 2007. Speed of internationalization and entrepreneurial cognition: Insights and a comparison between international new ventures, exporters and domestic firms. *Journal of World Business*, 42(3): 236–252.

Andersson, S., & Wictor, I. 2003. Innovative internationalisation in new firms: Born globals—the Swedish case. *Journal of International Entrepreneurship*, 1(3): 249–275.

Arenius, P., Sasi, V., & Gabrielsson, M. 2005. Rapid internationalisation enabled by the internet: The case of a knowledge intensive company. *Journal of International Entrepreneurship*, 3(4): 279–290.

Autio, E., Sapienza, H. J., & Almeida, J. G. 2000. Effects of age at entry, knowledge intensity, and imitability on international growth. *The Academy of Management Journal*, 43(5): 909–924.

Barney, J. 1991. Firm resources and sustainable competitive advantage. *Journal of Management*, 17(1): 99–120.

Baum, M., Schwens, C., & Kabst, R. 2011. A typology of international new ventures: Empirical evidence from high-technology industries. *Journal of Small Business Management*, 49(3): 305–330.

Baum, M., Schwens, C., & Kabst, R. 2015. A latent class analysis of small firms' internationalization patterns. *Journal of World Business*, 50(4): 754–768.

Beckerman, W. 1956. Distance and the pattern of intra-European trade. *The Review of Economics and Statistics*, 38(1): 31–40.

Bell, J. 1995. The internationalization of small computer software firms: A further challenge to "stage" theories. *European Journal of Marketing*, 29(8): 60–75.

Benito, G. R. G., & Welch, L. S. 1997. De-internationalization. *MIR: Management International Review*, 37: 7–25.

Blomstermo, A., Eriksson, K., & Sharma, D. 2004. Domestic activity and knowledge development in the internationalization process of firms. *Journal of International Entrepreneurship*, 2(3): 239–258.

Bloodgood, J. M., Sapienza, H. J., & Almeida, J. G. 1996. The internationalization of new high-potential U.S. ventures: Antecedents and outcomes. *Entrepreneurship Theory and Practice*, 20(4): 61–76.

Bunz, T., Casulli, L., Jones, M. V., & Bausch, A. 2017. The dynamics of experiential learning: Microprocesses and adaptation in a professional service INV. *International Business Review*, 26(2): 225–238.

Casillas, J. C., Moreno, A. M., Acedo, F. J., Gallego, M. A., & Ramos, E. 2009. An integrative model of the role of knowledge in the internationalization process. *Journal of World Business*, 44(3): 311–322.

Casson, M. 1997. Entrepreneurial networks in international business. *Business and Economic History*, 26(2): 811–823.

Cavusgil, S. T., & Knight, G. 2015. The born global firm: An entrepreneurial and capabilities perspective on early and rapid internationalization. *Journal of International Business Studies*, 46(1): 3–16.

Chandra, Y. 2017. A time-based process model of international entrepreneurial opportunity evaluation. *Journal of International Business Studies*, 48(4): 423–451.

Chandra, Y., Styles, C., & Wilkinson, I. F. 2012. An opportunity-based view of rapid internationalization. *Journal of International Marketing*, 20(1): 74–102.

Chetty, S., & Campbell-Hunt, C. 2004. A strategic approach to internationalization: A traditional versus a "born-global" approach. *Journal of International Marketing*, 12(1): 57–81.

Coviello, N. E. 2006. The network dynamics of international new ventures. *Journal of International Business Studies*, 37(5): 713–731.

Coviello, N. E. 2015. Re-thinking research on born globals. *Journal of International Business Studies*, 46(1): 17–26.

Coviello, N. E., & Cox, M. P. 2006. The resource dynamics of international new venture networks. *Journal of International Entrepreneurship*, 4(2): 113–132.

Coviello, N. E., & Munro, H. J. 1995. Growing the entrepreneurial firm: Networking for international market development. *European Journal of Marketing*, 29(7): 49–61.

Coviello, N. E., & Munro, H. J. 1997. Network relationships and the internationalisation process of small software firms. *International Business Review*, 6(4): 361–386.

Covin, J. G., & Miller, D. 2014. International entrepreneurial orientation: Conceptual considerations, research themes, measurement issues, and future research directions. *Entrepreneurship Theory and Practice*, 38(1): 11–44.

De Clercq, D., Sapienza, H. J., Yavuz, R. I., & Zhou, L. X. 2012. Learning and knowledge in early internationalization research: Past accomplishments and future directions. *Journal of Business Venturing*, 27(1): 143–165.

Ellis, P. 2000. Social ties and foreign market entry. *Journal of International Business Studies*, 31(3): 443–469.

Etemad, H. 2004. Internationalization of small and medium sized enterprises: A grounded theoretical framework and an overview. *Canadian Journal of Administrative Sciences*, 21(1): 1–21.

Evers, N., Andersson, S., & Hannibal, M. 2012. Stakeholders and marketing capabilities in international new ventures: Evidence from Ireland, Sweden, and Denmark. *Journal of International Marketing*, 20(4): 46–71.

Felin, T., Foss, N. J., & Ployhar, R. E. 2015. The microfoundations movement in strategy and organization theory. *The Academy of Management Annals*, 9(1): 575–632.

Fernhaber, S. A., & Li, D. 2013. International exposure through network relationships: Implications for new venture internationalization. *Journal of Business Venturing*, 28(2): 316–334.

Fletcher, M., & Harris, S. 2012. Knowledge acquisition for the internationalization of the smaller firm: Content and sources. *International Business Review*, 21(4): 631–647.

Fuerst, S., & Zettinig, P. 2015. Knowledge creation dynamics within the international new venture. *European Business Review*, 27(2): 182–213.

Gassmann, O., & Keupp, M. M. 2007. The competitive advantage of early and rapidly internationalizing SMEs in the biotechnology industry: A knowledge-based view. *Journal of World Business*, 42(3): 350–366.

Gerschewski, S., Rose, E. L., & Lindsay, V. J. 2015. Understanding the drivers of international performance for born global firms: An integrated perspective. *Journal of World Business*, 50(3): 558–575.

Grant, R. 1991. The resource-based theory of competitive advantage: Implications for strategy formulation. *California Management Review*, 33(3): 114–135.

Hallbäck, J., & Gabrielsson, P. 2013. Entrepreneurial marketing strategies during the growth of international new ventures originating in small and open economies. *International Business Review*, 22(6): 1008–1020.

Harms, R., & Schiele, H. 2012. Antecedents and consequences of effectuation and causation in the international new venture creation process. *Journal of International Entrepreneurship*, 10(2): 95–116.

Johanson, J., & Vahlne, J. E. 1977. The internationalization process of the firm—a model of knowledge development and increasing foreign market commitments. *Journal of International Business Studies*, 8(1): 23–32.

Johanson, J., & Vahlne, J. E. 2009. The Uppsala internationalization process model revisited: From liability of foreignness to liability of outsidership. *Journal of International Business Studies*, 40(9): 1411–1431.

Jolly, V. K., Alahuhta, M., & Jeannet, J. P. 1992. Challenging the incumbents: How high technology start-ups compete globally. *Strategic Change*, 1(2): 71–82.

Jones, M. V., Coviello, N. E., & Tang, Y. K. 2011. International entrepreneurship research (1989–2009): A domain ontology and thematic analysis. *Journal of Business Venturing*, 26(6): 632–659.

Karra, N., Phillips, N., & Tracey, P. 2008. Building the born global firm: Developing entrepreneurial capabilities for international new venture success. *Long Range Planning*, 41(4): 440–458.

Khavul, S., Peterson, M., Mullens, D., & Rasheed, A. A. 2010. Going global with innovations from emerging economies: Investment in customer support capabilities pays off. *Journal of International Marketing*, 18(4): 22–42.

Knight, G. A., & Cavusgil, S. T. 1996. The born global firm: A challenge to traditional internationalization theory. *Advances in International Marketing*, 8: 11–26.

Knight, G. A., & Cavusgil, S. T. 2004. Innovation, organizational capabilities, and the born-global firm. *Journal of International Business Studies*, 35(2): 124–141.

Kropp, F., Lindsay, N. J., & Shoham, A. 2006. Entrepreneurial, market, and learning orientations and international entrepreneurial business venture performance in South African firms. *International Marketing Review*, 23(5): 504–523.

Kuivalainen, O., Sundqvist, S., & Servais, P. 2007. Firms' degree of born-globalness, international entrepreneurial orientation and export performance. *Journal of World Business*, 42(3): 253–267.

Kungwansupaphan, C., & Siengthai, S. 2014. Exploring entrepreneurs' human capital components and effects on learning orientation in early internationalizing firms. *International Entrepreneurship and Management Journal*, 10(3): 561–587.

Loane, S., & Bell, J. 2006. Rapid internationalisation among entrepreneurial firms in Australia, Canada, Ireland and New Zealand: An extension to the network approach. *International Marketing Review*, 23(5): 467–485.

Luostarinen, R. K. 1979. *Internationalization of the Firm: An Empirical Study of the Internationalization of Firms with Small and Open Domestic Markets with Special Emphasis on Lateral Rigidity as a Behavioural Characteristic in Strategic Decision Making*. Helsinki School of Economics, Dissertation, Series A: 30, Helsinki School of Economics: Helsinki.

Luostarinen, R. K. 1994. Internationalization of Finnish firms and their response to global challenges, research for action, *Forssa: WIDER Report*, UNU/WIDER.

Luostarinen, R. K., & Gabrielsson, M. 2006. Globalization and marketing strategies of born globals in SMOPECs. *Thunderbird International Business Review*, 48(6): 773–801.

Madsen, T. K., & Servais, P. 1997. The internationalization of born globals: An evolutionary process? *International Business Review*, 6(6): 561–583.

McAuley, A. 1999. Entrepreneurial instant exporters in the Scottish arts and crafts sector. *Journal of International Marketing*, 7(4): 67–82.

McDougall, P. P. 1989. International versus domestic entrepreneurship: New venture strategic behavior and industry structure. *Journal of Business Venturing*, 4(6): 387–400.

McDougall, P. P., Oviatt, B. M., & Shrader, R. C. 2003. A comparison of international and domestic new ventures. *Journal of International Entrepreneurship*, 1(1): 59–82.

Mort, G. S., & Weerawardena, J. 2006. Networking capability and international entrepreneurship: How networks function in Australian born global firms. *International Marketing Review*, 23(5): 549–572.

Nowiński, W., & Rialp, A. 2013. Drivers and strategies of international new ventures from a Central European transition economy. *Journal for East European Management Studies*, 18(2): 191–231.

Nowiński, W., & Rialp, A. 2016. The impact of social networks on perceptions of international opportunities. *Journal of Small Business Management*, 54(2): 445–461.

Nummela, N., Saarenketo, S., Jokela, P., & Loane, S. 2014. Strategic decision-making of a born global: A comparative study from three small open economies. *Management International Review*, 54(4): 527–550.

Oviatt, B. M., & McDougall, P. P. 1994. Toward a theory of international new ventures. *Journal of International Business Studies*, 25(1): 45–64.

Oviatt, B. M., & McDougall, P. P. 1995. Global start-ups: Entrepreneurs on a worldwide stage. *The Academy of Management Executive*, 9(2): 30–44.

Oviatt, B. M., & McDougall, P. P. 2005. Defining international entrepreneurship and modelling the speed of internationalization. *Entrepreneurship Theory and Practice*, 29(5): 537–553.

Park, T., & Rhee, J. 2012. Antecedents of knowledge competency and performance in born globals: The moderating effects of absorptive capacity. *Management Decision*, 50(8): 1361–1381.

Pellegrino, J. M., & McNaughton, R. B. 2015. The co-evolution of learning and internationalization strategy in international new ventures. *Management International Review*, 55(4): 457–483.

Prashantham, S., & Floyd, S. W. 2012. Routine microprocesses and capability learning in international new ventures. *Journal of International Business Studies*, 43(6): 544–562.

Rennie, M. W. 1993. Global competitiveness: Born global. *The McKinsey Quarterly*, (4): 45–52.

Reuber, A. R., & Fischer, E. 1997. The influence of the management team's international experience on the internationalization behaviors of SMEs. *Journal of International Business Studies*, 28(4): 807–825.

Rialp, A., & Rialp, J. 2007. Faster and more successful exporters: An exploratory study of born global firms from the resource-based view. *Journal of Euromarketing*, 16(1–2): 71–86.

Ripollés, M., Blesa, A., & Monferrer, D. 2012. Factors enhancing the choice of higher resource commitment entry modes in international new ventures. *International Business Review*, 21(4): 648–666.

Robins, N. 2012. *The Corporation that Changed the World: How the East India Company Shaped the Modern World*. London: Pluto Press.

Ruzzier, M., Hisrich, R. D., & Antoncic, B. 2006. SME internationalization research: Past, present, and future. *Journal of Small Business and Enterprise Development*, 13(4): 476–497.

Sapienza, H. J., De Clercq, D., & Sandberg, W. R. 2005. Antecedents of international and domestic learning effort. *Journal of Business Venturing*, 20(4): 437–457.

Sarasvathy, S. D. 2001. Causation and effectuation: Toward a theoretical shift from economic inevitability to entrepreneurial contingency. *The Academy of Management Review*, 26(2): 243–263.

Schwens, C., & Kabst, R. 2009a. Early internationalization: A transaction cost economics and structural embeddedness perspective. *Journal of International Entrepreneurship*, 7(4): 323–340.

Schwens, C., & Kabst, R. 2009b. How early opposed to late internationalizers learn: Experience of others and paradigms of interpretation. *International Business Review*, 18(5): 509–522.

Servais, P., Madsen, T. K., & Rasmussen, E. S. 2006. Small manufacturing firms' involvement in international e-business activities. In S. Zhou (Ed.), *International Marketing Research (Advances in International Marketing* (Vol. 17). Bingley: Emerald Publishing.

Sharma, D. D., & Blomstermo, A. 2003. The internationalization process of born globals: A network view. *International Business Review*, 12(6): 739–753.

Tuomisalo, T., & Leppäaho, T. 2018. Learning in international new ventures: A systematic review. *International Business Review*, 28(3): 463–481.

Weerawardena, J., Sullivan Mort, G., Liesch, P., & Knight, G. 2007. Conceptualizing accelerated internationalization in the born global firm: A dynamic capabilities perspective. *Journal of World Business*, 42: 294–306.

Welch, L. S., & Luostarinen, R. K. 1993. Inward-outward connections in internationalization. *Journal of International Marketing*, 1(1): 44–56.

Wilkins, M. 1988. The free-standing company, 1870-1914: An important type of British foreign direct investment. *Economic History Review*, 41(2): 259–282.

Yeoh, P. L. 2004. International learning: Antecedents and performance implications among newly internationalizing companies in an exporting context. *International Marketing Review*, 21(4/5): 511–535.

Yli-Renko, H., Autio, E., & Sapienza, H. J. 2001. Social capital, knowledge acquisition, and knowledge exploitation in young technology-based firms. *Strategic Management Journal*, 22(6–7): 587–613.

Yli-Renko, H., Autio, E., & Tontti, V. 2002. Social capital, knowledge, and the international growth of technology-based new firms. *International Business Review*, 11(3): 279–304.

Zahra, S. A. 2005. A theory of international new ventures: A decade of research. *Journal of International Business Studies*, 36(1): 20–28.

Zahra, S. A., Ireland, R. D., & Hitt, M. A. 2000. International expansion by new venture firms: International diversity, mode of market entry, technological learning, and performance. *Academy of Management Journal*, 43(5): 925–950.

Zahra, S. A., Zheng, C., & Yu, J. 2018. Learning advantages of newness: A reconceptualization and contingent framework. *Journal of International Entrepreneurship*, 16(1): 12–37.

Zander, I., McDougall-Covin, P., & Rose, E. L. 2015. Born globals and international business: Evolution of a field of research. *Journal of International Business Studies*, 46(1): 27–35.

Zhou, L. 2007. The effects of entrepreneurial proclivity and foreign market knowledge on early internationalization. *Journal of World Business*, 42(3): 281–293.

Zhou, L., Barnes, B. R., & Lu, Y. 2010. Entrepreneurial proclivity, capability upgrading and performance advantage of newness among international new ventures. *Journal of International Business Studies*, 41(5): 882–905.

Zou, H., & Ghauri, P. N. 2010. Internationalizing by learning: The case of Chinese high-tech new ventures. *International Marketing Review*, 27(2): 223–244.

CHAPTER 10

....

IT'S NOT (ONLY) THE INTERNATIONAL NEW VENTURE BUT (ALSO) THE MICROMULTINATIONAL, DAFTIE!

Reconsidering the Unit of Analysis in International Entrepreneurship

....

PAVLOS DIMITRATOS

INTRODUCTION

....

THE international entrepreneurship (IE) literature hitherto has focused on the activities of international new ventures (INVs)—also referred to as "born globals" (BGs)—which are those small firms that internationalize rapidly following their inception and often continue their subsequent internationalization at a fast pace. The activities of INVs have dominated the IE field as early and fast internationalization has been at the forefront of research since McDougall's (1989) seminal article that challenged the incremental pace of the firm's international growth. The implicit assumption is that INVs have been considered to be the most entrepreneurial internationalized firms.

Implicit in this literature is that, INV behavior is characterized by high levels of entrepreneurial orientation operationalized through innovativeness, proactiveness, and risk attitude (Miller, 1983; Miller & Friesen, 1982). Specifically, innovativeness relates to the proclivity of the firm to introduce novel products and services; proactiveness refers to the firm's tendency to initiate strategic moves and act ahead of competition; and risk attitude refers to the propensity of the firm to engage in venturesome projects. This conceptualization of the three entrepreneurial orientation dimensions may be viewed to be transferred into the international context in a "concept travelling" capacity (George & Marino, 2011). This can be problematic because, although INVs are considered to be entrepreneurial, there is essentially no empirical evidence that suggests that their international entrepreneurial orientation (IEO) is strong.

In one of the early definitions, McDougall and Oviatt (2000) link IE (but not INVs!) to strong entrepreneurial orientation by proposing that IE is the combination of the three dimensions in an international context, which creates value to the firm. As Covin and Miller (2014) more recently note, IEO is typically captured through innovativeness, proactiveness, and risk-taking in the international context (see also Dimitratos, Lioukas, & Carter, 2004; Freeman & Cavusgil, 2007). IEO mirrors a set of organizational behaviors that may overcome obstacles in the internationalization process of the firm (Jones & Coviello, 2005).

In this chapter, I propose that IEO is an important theme for both theory and managerial practice. An untested conjecture in the IE literature is that it equates the firm's fast entry into international markets to strong IEO characteristics of that firm. To corroborate, in a review of the INV area, Aspelund, Madsen, and Moen (2007: 1435) observe that "[m]ost authors mention international entrepreneurial orientation as being a decisive factor for the establishment of INVs." This remains a largely unproven proposition. It is further unclear in this stream of research whether being an INV is an antecedent, predecessor, or even the same concept as IEO. As Covin and Miller (2014) stress, there are often tautological relationships in IEO research. Moreover, IEO is oftentimes treated as a unitary concept failing to distinguish between its three different dimensions. Not all IEO characteristics may have the same effect on internationalization (Dai, Maksimov, Gilbert, & Fernhaber, 2014). I challenge the prevalent view that IEO and INVs are interlinked notions and that all INVs are entrepreneurial. These are unproven propositions that have received little, if any, empirical support, and hence may be unwarranted or even misleading causal relationships. From a managerial perspective, better understanding the nature of entrepreneurial orientation in an international context is increasingly relevant, given the recurrent evidence that an entrepreneurial firm is routinely linked to long-term organizational success (Rauch, Wiklund, Lumpkin, & Frese, 2009) and subsequent international performance (Schwens et al., 2018).

If we follow the argument that INVs may not always be so entrepreneurial, we should acknowledge that the failure to grasp the characteristics of different international entrepreneurial firms and the manifestations of entrepreneurial orientation in an international strategic context inhibits theory development. Covin, Green, and Slevin (2006: 80) observe that "intellectual advancements pertaining to entrepreneurial orientation will likely occur as a function of how clearly and completely scholars can delineate the pros and cons of alternative conceptualisations of the entrepreneurial orientation construct and the conditions under which the alternative conceptualizations may be appropriate." Consequently, we lack an appropriate conceptualization of the entrepreneurial orientation dimensions in the international business (IB) setting, which, I suggest, is strongly linked to the ambiguity around the nature and degree of entrepreneurial orientation among internationalized small firms (which may not be INVs).

This chapter advances the argument that the real international entrepreneurial small and medium-sized enterprises (SMEs) may not be the INVs but the so-called micromultinational enterprises (mMNEs). Moving away from the INV notion, Dimitratos, Johnson, Slow, and Young (2003: 165) define the mMNE as that "small- and medium-sized firm that controls and manages value-added activities through constellation and investment modes in more than one country." An example of an mMNE is Miracle Company, an Egyptian medical supplies medium-sized firm. It specializes in more than sixty-five soft orthopedic rehabilitation and medical support products. Its customers include orthopedic, pediatric orthopedics and spine surgeons, pharmacies, hospitals, distributors, surgery centers, physical therapists, athletic trainers, and healthcare professionals. The firm sells its products in Egypt and more than thirty-six foreign countries through networks of agents and distributors; while it also has a subsidiary in the US. mMNEs can be entrepreneurial firms that acknowledge the benefits of expanding internationally via advanced entry modes. These benefits encompass superior international customer service to collect exceptional feedback on market conditions (Lu & Beamish, 2001). Therefore, this chapter proposes that the mMNE is likely to be a type of entrepreneurial firm deserving close attention in IE.

Specifically, I put forward the claim that the INV is related to only one of the three dimensions of IEO, namely proactiveness. I also propose that the mMNE, which employs deeper forms of internationalization including contractual joint ventures and wholly owned subsidiaries, is a key international entrepreneurial firm. mMNEs pertain to risk propensity of IEO, which ought to be the salient dimension in the IE area since it encapsulates perceptions of expected return from the investment undertaken. The third dimension of IEO, namely innovativeness, captures entry into foreign markets and may refer to both INVs and mMNEs (and indeed all internationalized SMEs).

This chapter is structured as follows. The next section discusses some of the key studies on internationalized small firms, which involves INVs, mMNEs, and the IEO dimensions. The section following that examines entrepreneurial orientation in the IB strategy setting and aims to provide a conceptualization of entrepreneurialness for IB activities, by also explaining why this conceptualization matters. The last two sections of the chapter provide limitations of my ideas and concluding remarks.

An Overview of the Internationalized Smaller Firm: INVs, mMNEs, and the Role of IEO

The INV and its activities has been the main topic of interest in the IE area (e.g. see the comprehensive literature review by Jones, Coviello, & Tang, 2011) because early and fast internationalization has prevailed in the field over other types of internationalized SMEs. Generally the resource-based view and the network perspectives have been the influential theoretical perspectives in the IE area, underlining the core competencies and collaborating capabilities, respectively, which INVs should nurture and strengthen in order to achieve prompt and speedy internationalization (the necessary "means" in this literature) and ultimately successful internationalization (e.g. Cavusgil & Knight, 2015). That aside, the IE field has reached a stage of maturity to the point that, lately, the field has witnessed reviews on specialized topics, always in the context of INV activities, such as learning mechanisms of those firms in foreign markets (Tuomisalo & Leppäaho, 2019) or their effectuation processes in relation to international opportunity identification and pursuit (Karami, Wooliscroft, & McNeill, 2019). In the INV literature, the main focus remains to identify the differences and enhancements that speedy internationalization entails vis-à-vis the incremental and slow internationalization that the stage model had proposed over than four decades ago (Johanson & Vahlne, 1977).

Despite the prevalence of the pace of internationalization in this area, the mode of internationalization (exporting, licensing, joint ventures, wholly owned subsidiaries) is considered to be a key aspect characterizing the internationalization of the firm. On this issue, Zahra and George (2002) propose that market selection (where), speed (how fast), and entry mode (how) are also the three main aspects of interest in IE research. Not unexpectedly, mode of internationalization has been investigated in this IE literature under the prism of solely INV activities and strongly linked to speed of entry (e.g. Puthusserry, Khan, & Rodgers, 2018; Verbeke, Zargarzadeh, & Osiyevskyy, 2014).

However, recent studies present evidence on the activities of the mMNE and argue that these activities should be distinguished from those of the sole exporting firm. The mMNE literature does not take the INV as its starting point of analysis (Jones et al., 2011) for the main reason that mode of entry and the associated level of resource commitment abroad are monumental decisions for the survival and growth of the firm. As such, it is disentangled from the timing to international marketplace decision. Entry mode is an important strategic decision that determines the degree of resource commitment to the foreign market in relation to the risks the firm will bear in the host country and the level of control a firm can exercise over its foreign activities (Dimitratos et al., 2003; Prashantham, 2011). Entry mode further forms a competitive strategy pillar for the firm (Zahra, Ireland, & Hitt, 2000).

There are few, yet increasingly more and more, empirical studies on mMNEs, which accentuate the importance of factors such as suitable organizational attributes (Allison & Browning, 2006; Dimitratos et al., 2003; Dimitratos, Johnson, Ibeh, & Slow, 2009; Stoian, Dimitratos, & Plakoyiannaki, 2018), close networking arrangements (Dimitratos, Amorós, Etchebarne, & Felzensztein, 2014; Dimitratos, Johnson, Plakoyiannaki, & Young, 2016; Prashantham, 2011; Stoian, Rialp, & Dimitratos, 2017), and transaction cost considerations (Vanninen, Kuivalainen, & Ciravegna, 2017). All these factors may affect the probability of the firm to select deeper forms of foreign engagement, and so, become an mMNE. Most importantly, in the mMNE literature, timing to international markets and international mode are viewed as two different dimensions or axes, which can produce a two by two matrix, wherein incremental exporters, rapid exporters, incremental mMNEs, and rapid mMNEs make up the four quadrants of that matrix: it is evident that

INVs should be removed from the mMNE category, the former category referring to the timing dimension while the latter category to the mode criterion.

IEO as a Key Concept in IE Research

In this chapter, I seek to examine the differences between INVs and mMNEs through better understanding IEO, which is a major entrepreneurial notion of interest. Therefore, I identify some of those notable articles that have examined and discussed the entrepreneurial orientation dimensions in the IE context.[1] I discuss in this section their key findings regarding the different dimensions of IEO.

The literature search identified only a few articles that examined entrepreneurial orientation dimensions for internationalized firms. Deng, Jean, and Sinkovics (2018) allude to entry modes in their investigation and define INVs as those firms that feature an innovative, proactive, and risk-taking organizational culture, yet they do not measure this assertion directly. Zhou, Barnes, and Lu (2010) find that through a proactive, risk-taking, and innovative behavior, young INVs are better able to configure resources to upgrade the knowledge and network capabilities that give rise to learning advantage of newness-related performance. Cavusgil and Knight (2015) further note that early internationalizing firms have deeper capacity for innovation and their ability to serve customers in innovative ways, but they do not examine the other two dimensions of IEO. Kim, Basu, Naidu, and Cavusgil (2011) find that BGs have high median levels of innovativeness and innovativeness leads to enhanced financial performance.

The literature on mMNEs is significantly scarcer. These studies, however, capture the importance of operation modes in understanding mMNE strategies and their determinants. For instance, Stoian et al. (2017) directly compare mMNEs and exporting firms to provide evidence that higher levels of innovative behavior in the international arena are associated with increased commitment to international operations. In a similar comparative analysis between mMNEs and exporters, Dimitratos et al. (2014) report that higher levels of propensity for risk-taking, innovativeness, and proactiveness of the internationalized firm correlate to a stronger chance of the firm becoming mMNE. In short, there is scant evidence that indicates that INVs exhibit high levels of (primarily) innovativeness, but also proactiveness and risk attitude compared to incremental internationalizers. However, there seems to be increasing evidence that mMNEs exhibit higher IEO levels than exporters. It is further remarkable that, overall, most of the examined studies report activities of exporting firms rather than mMNEs, a finding also previously confirmed by Slevin and Terjesen (2011).

---

[1] To ensure a reliable method in the selection of studies used, we consulted the *Academic Journal Guide (AJG)* list; as such, 4*, 4, and 3* rated journals in appropriate fields to the research area, i.e. IB area, entrepreneurship and small business management, and general management were searched for relevant articles. The research included the use of designated keywords that were identified to have relevance to this field. The keywords used were "international new venture," "born global," "international entrepreneurship," "micromultinational," "entry mode," and "speed of entry."

Consequently, I draw the reader's attention to three main findings from this literature search. First, it appears that the INV may not necessarily be an entrepreneurial firm as operationalized through the three IEO dimensions. In other words, speed to international markets should not necessarily be equated to high levels of entrepreneurialness. The INV can even be an "accidental internationalizer" that, due to its business model, sells niche products to spatially dispersed customers and acts primarily upon IB opportunities (Hennart, 2014). I propose that the claim that all INVs are entrepreneurial firms may be ill-founded: this is a statement that has received cursory empirical testing in the literature and should at least be discounted.

Second, the relevant IE studies that have been published thus far involve predominantly examinations of exporting firms, hence the mode of internationalization has been neglected (oftentimes not even reported) and can be an important dimension when analyzing entrepreneurial firms venturing abroad. Third, the limited evidence that compares mMNEs and exporters indicates that mMNEs score higher on the IEO dimensions. In the next section, I theorize how the three IEO dimensions can apply to international entrepreneurial firms bringing the INV and mMNE dimensions into this conceptualization.

A Proposed Reconceptualization of IEO

In the IE area, Covin and Miller (2014) have contemplated on the distinctiveness of entrepreneurial orientation in the international context and its differences with its domestic counterpart. This debate overlaps with recent discussions in the entrepreneurship field on the nature of entrepreneurial orientation dimensions (e.g. Anderson et al., 2015). There can be low or no correlations between the three entrepreneurial orientation dimensions (Kreiser, Marino, & Weaver, 2002), which is a compelling reason to explore the manifestations of IEO at the individual dimension level (rather than the unitary construct—see also Rauch et al., 2009). Following the rationale of Covin and Miller (2014), I aim to provide a conceptualization of the entrepreneurial orientation dimensions in the international marketplace, which will identify their special characteristics in the global setting.

IEO Dimension One: Innovativeness

Innovativeness not only deals with the ability to introduce new products and the radicalness of these introductions, but also with entry into new markets. This is closely connected to the assertion that creation of new markets may be considered innovativeness in an international context (see Covin & Wales, 2019). In a related vein, globalization has been synonymous to new entry into international markets (Slevin & Terjesen, 2011). Entrepreneurship is about the opportunity pursuit and quest for new combinations, that is, a new enterprise (Davidsson & Wiklund, 2001). In general, I claim that innovativeness per se predominantly entails value creation through resource recombinations in inward or outward internationalization activities, which also extends to entry into new geographic markets. Simply put, internationalization and selection of foreign markets on their own reflect high levels of innovativeness. Hence, both INVs and mMNEs are innovative firms as a result of their international activities.

IEO Dimension Two: Proactiveness

As to proactiveness, the aspect of being ahead of competition forms an indispensable part of this entrepreneurial aspect. I posit that being fast in the international market-place perfectly relates to proactiveness since INVs aim to capture opportunities abroad ahead from competitors. Since the launch of the INV term, these organizations have been viewed to be the juxtapositions of incremental or gradual SME internationalizers that are cautious in their moves abroad (Oviatt & McDougall, 1994). Incremental internationalizers are comparatively more sluggish, slow, cautious, or reactive in capturing segments of the foreign market (Hennart, 2014; Prashantham, 2015). INVs can establish first-mover advantages in their specialized niches, which oftentimes may be spread across different countries (Simon, 2009). Whereas the prevalent belief in the IE area has been that INVs are necessarily entrepreneurial firms, I moderate this argument by asserting that INVs are primarily proactive toward their rivals. A US medium-sized INV producing sophisticated popcorn machinery will choose to export fast to Canada, Europe, and Australia to pre-empt local US competitors who are chiefly interested in the domestic market. Essentially, INVs may not be only innovative organizations since they have internationalized their operations but also proactive firms due to their strategizing to be ahead of competition. Also important is that Covin and Miller (2014) find that proactiveness is an IEO dimension that may affect international performance considerably in related studies. Nevertheless, INVs are likely to score low in terms of risk proclivity, particularly if they are merely exporters.

IEO Dimension Three: Risk Attitude

This third entrepreneurial orientation characteristic is a key entrepreneurial aspect that I emphasize in this chapter. I claim that risk attitude is that dimension of IEO that has erroneously received lesser attention than it should have had in the fields of IB, strategy, and IE. Only if the firm commits significant resources abroad, will it assume risk that may threaten its growth or even survival: this is unavoidably the most crucial aspect of the internationalized small firm's activities. The establishment of substantial resource commitments through advanced modes refers to the realized and significant risk that firms incur. mMNEs through their deep modes of internationalization seek geographical closeness to foreign clients to tap into new market opportunities. These firms seldom have the human, financial, and production resources to invest in such advanced modes, hence becoming mMNEs constitutes a sizable cost to them, which typifies their IEO. A Scottish biotech firm that forms a contractual joint venture (rather than exporting) in the US to exploit opportunities in the American continent assumes considerable potential risk through this advanced mode. This risk would be even higher had a wholly owned subsidiary been established. The substantial level of investment abroad that mMNEs engage in renders risk proclivity the most salient IEO dimension because risk threatens the survival and affects the long-term performance of the firm. The top management team of a firm with a strong risk proclivity are likely to commit high levels of resources to advanced modes. If successful, these modal strategies will render them advantages of closeness to foreign clients, provision of sophisticated customer services, access to sophisticated market information, and intimate attendance to foreign competitor and other stakeholder demands, as the emerging literature on mMNEs suggests. mMNEs are innovative since they have international operations but also risk takers due to their deeper forms of resource engagements, that many of them become involved in.

In their article, Anderson et al. (2015) indicated that managerial attitude toward risk is a necessary and distinct component that makes up the higher-order entrepreneurial orientation construct. Innovativeness and proactiveness together form the other component of entrepreneurial orientation. This argument alludes to the uniqueness of the risk attitude dimension vis-à-vis proactiveness and innovativeness, a proposition with which other empirical findings appear to concur (Block, Sandner, & Spiegel, 2015; Dai et al., 2014). The prevalence of risk proclivity is further corroborated repeatedly by findings in the economics literature (Herranz, Krasa, & Villamil, 2015; Kan & Tsai, 2006). The underlying assumption in all these writings is that, unless an individual or organization has a strong tendency to undertake risks, the other two entrepreneurial dimensions are not even likely to show up in their behaviors or activities. In essence, risk attitude should be the *sine qua non* of IEO. By the same token, I claim that mMNEs, because of strong risk proclivity are likely to be the most international entrepreneurial firms. INVs, which are distinguished by high levels of proactiveness (and innovativeness), may be moderately entrepreneurial firms, especially if it they are only exporters. Following this argumentation, the mMNE is a risk-taking and innovative firm; if it is also an INV, it will feature all three IEO dimensions and be a highly entrepreneurial firm. However, the existence of strong levels of risk proclivity on their own may render it the most entrepreneurial type of internationalized SME.

Further, the idea of risk that mMNEs are expected to undertake is also more nuanced. Although I posit that mMNEs take on significant levels of risk given their limited resources, risk is a relative term that reflects the expected returns from the foreign direct investment (FDI) undertaken for a given firm toward capturing a particular foreign opportunity (e.g. Levy, 1994). For instance, this may mean that, an SME that wishes to invest a sizable level of resources for a contractual joint venture abroad faces a higher relative risk if funds come solely from savings of the broader family that owns this enterprise than that of the SME that spreads funding across a combination of family savings, venture capital and subsidy sources, although the two investments may be of equal absolute level. Moreover, risk should be viewed in light of the particular value of the return that the mMNE will expect, meaning that it is the overall risk/return profile of the foreign project that this firm will anticipate and consider (e.g. Brophy & Guthner, 1988).

I propose that there are considerable implications stemming from my reconceptualization of the IEO concept. As to theory, first and foremost, the literature should avoid the sole study of speed associated with INVs. INVs and proactiveness refer to only one of the three IEO dimensions and quite likely not the most significant ones, especially when the long-term strategy of the firm is to grow and become an mMNE. mMNEs and risk attitude appear to be more salient and can significantly enrich the IB strategy and entrepreneurship research agendas.

Relatedly, risk attitude and risk management must widely be investigated in relation to mMNEs. Theoretical perspectives such as the resource-based view that has centered around the fast-internationalized firm should examine the objectives, resources, and capabilities of the mMNE that is managed by risk-taking decision makers determined to commit a substantial level of resources abroad. By the same token, the social capital theory, another prevalent perspective in the field of IE, should examine the different contractual equity and non-equity alliance forms through which mMNEs expand abroad. Likewise, the choice between the wholly owned and partially owned subsidiary (i.e. contractual joint venture) for a small multinational could be determined by different criteria than those for a large multinational. Intertwined with this argument is that, transaction cost and real options theories that focus on the multinational enterprise (MNE) mode choices should receive a major share of attention.

Lastly, there are important policy implications to this research. Policy makers keen on supporting international entrepreneurial firms would better identify and assist mMNEs, which bind substantial resources in the foreign marketplace through their risk-taking behavior, rather than focusing merely on the behavior of INVs.

FUTURE RESEARCH DIRECTIONS

I proposed a reconceptualization of entrepreneurial orientation in the international setting. I posited that innovativeness principally manifests itself on internationalization and foreign market selection, proactiveness on fast entry abroad, and risk attitude on foreign mode choice. Based on this conceptualization, all internationalized firms will be innovative since they have sought new market entry (or sourced foreign inputs). Additionally, INVs will be proactive vis-à-vis their incremental internationalized competitors, and mMNEs will be risk takers as compared to exporting firms. I have further argued that risk propensity is likely to be the most salient IEO dimension because it can influence the survival and performance of the internationalized small firm. INVs, if they are exporting firms, will not inevitably exhibit strong levels of risk proclivity and IEO. It then follows that the risk attitude dimension of IEO and the choice of operation mode should be more central to this body of research.

My reconceptualization is not free of limitations. I outline three in this section and invite future research in this area. First, I argued in favor of the distinctiveness of the IEO dimensions and the prevalence of risk attitude in IE. Risk and risk management have also received a significant level of attention in the IB and strategic management literatures (e.g. Miller, 1992). In this literature, an argument advanced is that the three entrepreneurial orientation dimensions are closely interrelated, and it then becomes difficult to distinguish the several of their manifestations. For example, Shrader, Oviatt, and McDougall (2000) find a trade-off between foreign market revenue exposure, host country risk, and entry mode commitment for INV activities. Also, risk has several dimensions (Miller, 1992) such as the likelihood and magnitude of risk, which may affect international operations differently (Dimitratos et al., 2016). This also pertains to the relative risk and the risk/return discussion outlined above. Nevertheless, the argument that risk attitude and the mode choice of the mMNE entails critical costs and risks, and due to this should prevail in the debate concerning the entrepreneurial nature of the internationalized firm, is valid, and relevant to IE scholarship and practice. My argumentation does not preclude the correlation of the three dimensions but rather suggests that risk attitude is the most significant dimension because of its strongest possible effect on the performance of the internationalized smaller firm.

Second, although I posited that each of the three IEO dimensions becomes apparent in mainly three different aspects of internationalization, overlaps between these manifestations are likely to occur. For instance, innovativeness apart from internationalization and foreign country selection may be observed in new product offerings even of minor nature that INVs and mMNEs are likely to offer to foreign clients. When the INV strives to be ahead of competition, it also assumes some risk as it is exposed to challenging cultural and institutional settings. INVs perceive lower likelihood of risk toward international opportunities than gradual internationalizers (Dimitratos et al., 2016). Similarly, when the mMNE undertakes risk, it is also likely to seek to pre-empt competitors that have not invested in such high commitment modes. Indeed, it appears that the three dimensions of IEO are chiefly reflected on the different aforementioned internationalization aspects, as discussed in this chapter, yet other manifestations of IEO are likely to appear in the activities of internationalized firms.

Third, one should not disregard the temporal character of IEO dimensions. There is solid evidence suggesting that entrepreneurial orientations can change over time as the organization develops and grows (Wales, Monsen, & McKelvie, 2011). This finding has also been confirmed in internationalized small firm activities (Gabrielsson, Gabrielsson, & Dimitratos, 2014). If the firm de-internationalizes from some or all its foreign markets, its innovativeness levels will fall. Similarly, if, after its initial rapid entries, the firm internationalizes at slower pace, its proactiveness levels will decline. Also, if exporting modes are pursued following the initial establishment of subsidiaries, its risk attitude will diminish. The temporal character of all these IEO dimensions pertains to the dynamic nature of international opportunities, which has been highlighted in the IB, strategy, and entrepreneurship literatures in recent years (Reuber, Dimitratos, & Kuivalainen, 2017). This means that IEO characteristics are likely not to be stable throughout time, and processual research into its evolving and idiosyncratic stages should take place.

CONCLUDING REMARKS

To sum up, in this chapter I advance the argument that the IE literature has provided single emphasis to the INV as if this was the sole international entrepreneurial firm. Based on existing literature, I propose that there is scant empirical evidence to substantiate the proposition that INVs are distinguished by strong IEO dimensions. Moreover, given the prevalence of exporting firms in the IE literature, most INVs can, indeed, score low in terms of risk proclivity, a salient IEO dimension. I argue in favor of a reconceptualization of IEO wherein INVs predominantly exhibit strong proactiveness toward competition. In addition, I suggest that mMNEs that expand through high commitment modes of operation deserve more attention due to their strong risk attitude. High risk propensity should be considered more carefully when studying the IEO dimension and investigation into mMNEs ought to be of paramount significance in the IB strategy and entrepreneurship fields.[2]

REFERENCES

Allison, M. A., & Browning, S. 2006. Competing in the cauldron of the global economy: Tools, processes, case studies, and theory supporting economic development. *International Journal of Technology Management*, 332(3): 130–143.

Anderson, B. S., Kreiser, P. M., Kuratko, D. F., Hornsby, J. S., & Eshima, Y. 2015. Reconceptualizing entrepreneurial orientation. *Strategic Management Journal*, 36(10): 1579–1596.

Aspelund, A., Madsen, T. K., & Moen, O. 2007. A Review of the foundation, international marketing strategies, and performance of international new ventures. *European Journal of Marketing*, 41 (11/12): 1423–1448.

Block, J., Sandner, P., & Spiegel, F. 2015. How do risk attitudes differ within the group of entrepreneurs? The role of motivation and procedural utility. *Journal of Small Business Management*, 53(1): 183–206.

Brophy, D. J., & Guthner, M. W. 1988. Publicly traded venture capital funds: Implications for institutional "fund of funds" investors. *Journal of Business Venturing*, 3(3): 187–206.

Cavusgil, S. T., & Knight, G. 2015. The born global firm: An entrepreneurial and capabilities perspective on early and rapid internationalization. *Journal of International Business Studies*, 46 (1): 3–16.

Covin, J. G., Green, K. M., & Slevin, D. P. 2006. Strategic process effects on the entrepreneurial orientation-sales growth rate relationships. *Entrepreneurship Theory and Practice*, 30(1): 57–81.

[2] The author acknowledges the research assistance of Mahtab Shabbir (Adam Smith Business School, University of Glasgow) in the IEO literature search of this book chapter.

Covin, J. G., & Miller, D. 2014. International entrepreneurial orientation: Conceptual considerations, research themes, measurement issues, and future research directions. *Entrepreneurship Theory & Practice*, 38(1): 11–44.

Covin, J. G., & Wales, W. J. 2019. Crafting high-impact entrepreneurial orientation research: Some suggested guidelines. *Entrepreneurship Theory & Practice*, 43(1): 3–18.

Dai, L., Maksimov, V., Gilbert, B. A., & Fernhaber, S. A. 2014. Entrepreneurial orientation and international scope: The differential roles of innovativeness, proactiveness, and risk-taking. *Journal of Business Venturing*, 29(4): 511–524.

Davidsson, P., & Wiklund, J. 2001. Levels of analysis in entrepreneurship research: Current research practice and suggestions for the future. *Entrepreneurship Theory and Practice*, 25(3): 81–99.

Deng, Z., Jean, R. J. B., & Sinkovics R. 2018. Rapid expansion of international new ventures across institutional distance. *Journal of International Business Studies*, 49(8): 1010–1032.

Dimitratos, P., Amorós, J. E., Etchebarne, M. S., & Felzensztein, C. 2014. Micro-multinational or not? International entrepreneurship, networking and learning effects. *Journal of Business Research*, 67(5): 908–915.

Dimitratos, P., Johnson, J. E., Ibeh, K. I. N., & Slow, J. 2009. Core rigidities of micromultinationals: The Scottish experience. In M. V. Jones, P. Dimitratos, M. Fletcher & S. Young (Eds.), *Internationalization, Entrepreneurship and the Smaller Firm: Evidence from around the World*. Cheltenham: Edward Elgar.

Dimitratos, P., Johnson, J. E., Plakoyiannaki, E., & Young, S. 2016. SME internationalization: How does the opportunity-based international entrepreneurial culture matter? *International Business Review*, 25(6): 1211–1222.

Dimitratos, P., Johnson, J., Slow, J., & Young, S. 2003. Micromultinationals: New types of firms for the global competitive landscape. *European Management Journal*, 21(2): 164–174.

Dimitratos, P., Lioukas, S., & Carter, S. 2004. The relationship between entrepreneurship and international performance: The importance of domestic environment. *International Business Review*, 13(1): 19–41.

Freeman, S., & Cavusgil, S. T. 2007. Entrepreneurial strategies for accelerated internationalization of smaller born globals. *Journal of International Marketing*, 15(4): 1–40.

Gabrielsson, M., Gabrielsson, P., & Dimitratos, P. 2014. International entrepreneurial culture and growth of international new ventures. *Management International Review*, 54(4): 445–471.

George, B. A., & Marino, L. 2011. The epistemology of entrepreneurial orientation: Conceptual formation, modeling, and operationalization. *Entrepreneurship Theory & Practice*, 35(5): 989–1024.

Hennart, J. F. 2014. The accidental internationalists: A theory of born globals. *Entrepreneurship Theory and Practice*, 38(1): 117–135.

Herranz, N., Krasa, S., & Villamil, A. P. 2015. Entrepreneurs' risk aversion, and dynamic firms. *Journal of Political Economy*, 123(5): 1133–1176.

Johanson, J., & Vahlne, J. E. 1977. The internationalization process of the firm–A model of knowledge development and increasing foreign market commitments. *Journal of International Business Studies*, 8(1): 23–32.

Jones, M. V., & Coviello, N. 2005. Internationalisation: Conceptualising an entrepreneurial process of behaviour in time. *Journal of International Business Studies*, 36(3): 284–303.

Jones, M. V., Coviello, N., & Tang, Y. 2011. International entrepreneurship research (1989–2009): A domain ontology and thematic analysis. *Journal of Business Venturing*, 26(6): 632–659.

Kan, K., & Tsai, W. 2006. Entrepreneurship and risk aversion. *Small Business Economics*, 26(5): 465–474.

Karami, M., Wooliscroft, B., & McNeill, L. 2019. Effectuation and internationalisation: A review and agenda for future research. *Small Business Economics*, 53: 1–35.

Kim, D., Basu, C., Naidu, E., & Cavusgil, T. 2011. The innovativeness of born-globals and customer orientation: Learning from Indian born-globals. *Journal of Business Research*, 64(8): 879–886.

Kreiser, P. M., Marino, L. D., & Weaver, K. M. 2002. Assessing the psychometric properties of the entrepreneurial orientation scale: A multi-country analysis. *Entrepreneurship Theory and Practice*, 26(4): 71–93.

Levy, H. 1994. Absolute and relative risk aversion: An experimental study. *Journal of Risk and Uncertainty*, 8(3): 289–307.

Lu, J. W., & Beamish, P. W. 2001. The internationalization and performance of SMEs. *Strategic Management Journal*, 22(6–7): 565–586.

McDougall, P. P. 1989. International versus domestic entrepreneurship: New venture strategic behavior and industry structure. *Journal of Business Venturing*, 4(6): 387–399.

McDougall, P. P. & Oviatt, B. M. 2000. International entrepreneurship: The intersection of two research paths. *Academy of Management Journal*, 43(5): 902–906.

Miller, D. 1983. The correlates of entrepreneurship in three types of firms. *Management Science*, 29(7): 770–791.

Miller D., & Friesen P. H. 1982. Innovation in conservative and entrepreneurial firms: Two models of strategic momentum. *Strategic Management Journal*, 3(1): 1–25.

Miller, K. D. 1992. A framework for integrated risk management in international business. *Journal of International Business Studies*, 23(2): 311–331.

Oviatt, B. M., & McDougall, P. P. 1994. Toward a theory of international new ventures. *Journal of International Business Studies*, 25(1): 45–64.

Puthusserry, P., Khan, Z., & Rodgers, P. 2018. International new ventures market expansion through collaborative entry modes: A study of the experience of Indian and British ICT firms. *International Marketing Review*, 35(6): 890–913.

Prashantham, S. 2011. Social capital and Indian micromultinationals. *British Journal of Management*, 22(1): 4–20.

Prashantham, S. 2015. *Born Globals, Networks, and the Large Multinational Enterprise: Insights from Bangalore and Beyond*. London; Routledge.

Rauch, A., Wiklund, J., Lumpkin, G. T., & Frese, M. 2009. Entrepreneurial orientation and business performance: An assessment of past research and suggestions for the future. *Entrepreneurship Theory and Practice*, 33(3): 761–787.

Reuber, A. R., Dimitratos, P., & Kuivalainen, O. 2017. Beyond categorization: New directions for theory development about entrepreneurial internationalization. *Journal of International Business Studies*, 48(4): 411–422.

Schwens, C., Zapkau, F. B., Bierwerth, M., Isidor, R., Knight, G., & Kabst R. 2018. International entrepreneurship: A meta–analysis on the internationalization and performance relationship. *Entrepreneurship Theory and Practice*, 42(5): 734–768.

Shrader, R. C., Oviatt, B. M., & McDougall, P. P. 2000. How new ventures exploit trade-offs among international risk factors: Lessons for the accelerated internationalization of the 21st century. *Academy of Management Journal*, 43(6): 1227–1247.

Simon, H. 2009. *Hidden Champions of the Twenty-First Century: The Success Strategies of Unknown World Market Leaders*. New York: Springer.

Slevin, D. P., & Terjesen, S. A. 2011. Entrepreneurial orientation: Reviewing three papers and implications for further theoretical and methodological development. *Entrepreneurship Theory and Practice*, 35(5): 973–987.

Stoian, M. C., Dimitratos, P., & Plakoyiannaki, E. 2018. SME internationalization beyond exporting: A knowledge-based perspective across managers and advisers. *Journal of World Business*, 53(5): 768–779.

Stoian, M. C., Rialp, J., & Dimitratos, P. 2017. SME networks and international performance: Unveiling the significance of foreign market entry mode. *Journal of Small Business Management*, 55(1): 128–148.

Tuomisalo, T., & Leppäaho T. 2019. Learning in international new ventures: A systematic review. *International Business Review*, 28(3): 463–481.

Vanninen, H., Kuivalainen, O., & Ciravegna, L. 2017. Rapid multinationalization: Propositions for studying born micromultinationals. *International Business Review*, 26(2): 365–379.

Verbeke, A., Zargarzadeh, M. A., & Osiyevskyy, O. 2014. Internalization theory, entrepreneurship and international new ventures. *Multinational Business Review*, 22(3): 246–269.

Wales, W., Monsen, E., & McKelvie, A. 2011. The organizational pervasiveness of entrepreneurial orientation. *Entrepreneurship Theory and Practice*, 35(5): 895–923.

Zahra, S. A., & George, G. 2002. International entrepreneurship: The current status of the field and future research agenda. In M. A. Hitt, R. D. Ireland, S. M. Camp, & D. L. Sexton (Eds.), *Strategic Entrepreneurship: Creating an Integrated Mindset*. Oxford: Blackwell.

Zahra, S. A., Ireland, R. D., & Hitt, M. A. 2000. International expansion, technological learning and new venture performance. *Academy of Management Journal*, 43(5): 925–950.

Zhou, L., Barnes, B. R., & Lu, Y. 2010. Entrepreneurial proclivity, capability upgrading and performance advantage of newness among international new ventures. *Journal of International Business Studies*, 41(5): 882–905.

CHAPTER 11

INTERNATIONALIZATION OF FAMILY FIRMS

When Is a Managerial Focus on Socio-Emotional Wealth Effective?

LIENA KANO, ALAIN VERBEKE, AND
LUCIANO CIRAVEGNA

INTRODUCTION

FAMILY firms form an essential part of the global economy. They represent the most ubiquitous type of businesses, are important players in the international arena (Family Firm Institute, 2017), and are major contributors to economic growth, wealth creation, job generation, and competitiveness (De Massis, Di Minin, & Frattini, 2015). In fact, some of the world's largest and oldest multinational enterprises (MNEs) are family firms (Casillas & Pastor, 2015; *The Economist*, 2014). These family MNEs—the internationally operating firms where the founding family is involved in critical decision-making through ownership, leadership, or both (Bennedsen & Foss, 2015)—are the focus of this chapter.

The significant role played by family firms in the world economy has attracted attention from international business (IB) scholars. Family firm internationalization is a growing (yet fairly small) field of research, addressing principally how certain features of family governance impact family firms' international expansion. Despite the increasing scholarly interest in family firm internationalization, the field remains fragmented. Extant studies focus predominantly on determining whether family firms are more or less internationalized than their non-family counterparts, and can be divided into two major camps: studies exploring family firms' reluctance to internationalize (e.g. Gomez-Mejia, Makri, & Larraza-Kintana, 2010), and studies emphasizing features of family governance that facilitate internationalization (e.g. Miller, Le Breton-Miller, Lester, & Cannella, 2007).

A more nuanced question, explored in this chapter, is as follows: Do family firms internationalize differently in terms of their specific international strategic choices, such as their choices of markets, entry modes, value chain organization, resource allocation, partnership arrangements, or internal organization of operations in host markets? Further, how does family firm heterogeneity impact their internationalization trajectories? Are there any family firm-specific barriers to successful internationalization, and how can family firms overcome them? Why are some of the world's oldest, most successful MNEs family owned, yet only 12 percent of all family firms survive the second generational transition (PWC, 2016)?

We attempt to answer these questions by linking IB theory—namely, internalization theory (Buckley & Casson, 1976)—with the rich literature on family firms. The infusion of family business-specific constructs into the study of internationalization is helpful because IB scholars, who often use economics-based theories (comparative institutional analysis; transaction cost economics; internalization theory) to explain family firm international strategy, tend not to focus on affective elements of family-type governance (central to much family firm research). Linking predictive IB theory with a nuanced treatment of the family ownership element, characteristic of the family business literature, has a significant potential to enhance our understanding of family firm internationalization.

Researchers in both IB and family business fields agree that family firms possess unique features that shape their international strategies (Hennart, Majocchi, & Forlani, 2019). These features include family-based asset specificity (Verbeke & Kano, 2012) and associated resource benefits and constraints, as well as idiosyncratic decision rules vis-à-vis international strategy. The latter are reflected in two broad concepts. First, family firms are characterized by the presence of socio-emotional wealth (SEW), meaning that they are influenced by non-economic objectives and preferences of their owners, such as keeping the firm in the family, providing jobs for future generations and building a family-related reputation in the community (Berrone, Cruz, Gomez-Mejia, & Larraza-Kintana, 2010; Miller, Wright, Le Breton-Miller, & Scholes, 2015). It has been argued repeatedly that family firms may pursue international strategies that carry the lowest likelihood of SEW loss (Gomez-Mejia et al., 2010). Second, family firms have an inherent propensity for what is referred to as the bifurcation bias (Kano & Verbeke, 2018; Verbeke & Kano, 2012), that is, a dysfunctional decision rule that de facto favors family-based ("heritage") assets and routines over those assets and routines that do not have a direct connection to the family ("commodity"). In this chapter, we specifically propose that the combination of SEW and (absence of) bifurcation bias in family firms determines internationalization features of these firms, and helps explain both their international competitive success and their divergence from efficient international governance and consequent failure in host markets.

The remainder of the chapter is organized as follows. We start with summarizing extant literature on family firm internationalization, with a particular focus on constructs/perspectives relevant to our analysis, namely SEW and bifurcation bias. Next, we briefly review internalization theory. We then discuss the dynamics of international governance decisions in family firms. We conclude by summarizing our integrative perspective and identifying several avenues for future research in this area.

FAMILY-CENTRIC DRIVERS OF INTERNATIONALIZATION

Family firm internationalization has been studied from a wide variety of theoretical perspectives, including agency theory (Lien & Filatotchev, 2015), the resource-based view (Graves & Thomas, 2006), the social capital perspective (D'Angelo, Majocchi, & Buck, 2016), internalization theory (Hennart et al., 2019; Kano & Verbeke, 2018), the Uppsala model (Pukall & Calabrò, 2014), SEW (Gomez-Mejia et al., 2010), and stewardship theory (Calabrò, Torchia, Pukall, & Mussolino, 2013). These conceptual lenses are based on different, and sometimes contradictory, assumptions. It is not surprising that the literature lacks consensus concerning the role of the family in firms' international governance, strategy, and performance.

Most extant studies have attempted to determine whether family firms are characterized by a level and speed of internationalization different from non-family firms, but the empirical results have been inconclusive. Recently, scholars have even argued that the issue of whether family firms are more or less internationalized than non-family ones is an empirical and conceptual non-starter (see Kano & Verbeke, 2018). This contention is supported by Arregle, Duran, Hitt, and van Essen's (2017) large-scale meta-analysis, which convincingly demonstrates the lack of association between a firm's ownership and international scale. Further, most extant work on family firm internationalization has performed analysis at the firm level, rather than the level of the individual or the level of the family. The micro-foundations of family firm internationalization therefore remain poorly understood, which, we argue, is problematic given that family managers' behavior is likely to be subject to unique drivers and biases (Kano & Verbeke 2018; Verbeke & Kano, 2012).

Despite the high degree of theoretical pluralism observed in the family firm internationalization literature, most extant studies have been conducted from a family business perspective (with SEW being the most frequently adopted conceptual lens), with IB-centric theoretic approaches notably underrepresented. Among IB perspectives, the Uppsala model (Johanson & Vahlne, 1977, 2009) has been the most utilized, often in conjunction with the SEW perspective. Generally, however, these perspectives have been adopted to argue that family firms are inherently risk-averse and internationalize in a stepwise manner (e.g. Kontinen & Ojala, 2010)—a finding that is empirically contested (see for instance, Boers, 2016). TCE and internalization theory have been adopted in several studies, mainly to explore entry mode choice (e.g. Sestu & Majocchi, 2020), but have not been widely utilized in family firm internationalization research. To the best of our knowledge, the economizing properties of family governance are yet to be explored. Consequently, we link internalization theory with extant family firm research to explore how credible assumptions about the behavior of family firm managers can explain family MNEs' international strategic governance. In what follows, we discuss the micro-level constructs employed in the family firm literature, which may be relevant to strategic decision-making in an international context.

Family firm scholars have identified five core dimensions of SEW: (F) family control and influence; (I) family members' identification with the firm; (B) binding social ties; (E) emotional attachment to the firm; and (R) renewal of family bonds to the firm through dynastic succession (Berrone, Cruz, & Gomez-Mejia, 2012). Together, these dimensions of SEW (labeled "FIBER") are argued to explain unique international strategies of family firms,[1] in that these firms are likely to choose international configurations that carry the least threat to a particular FIBER dimension prioritized by the family. Although the SEW perspective provides a fine-grained lens to understand the behavior of family firms, it has no predictive capacity in terms of internationalization, and does not incorporate long-term efficiency considerations with regards to the way in which these firms govern their international operations. Consequently, SEW does not explain governance choices of large family firms whose international strategic configurations are indistinguishable from those of non-family MNEs (Carr & Bateman, 2009).

Most recently, IB scholars have suggested that family firms' internationalization behavior can be explained by their inherent propensity for, and ability to economize against, bifurcation bias (Kano & Verbeke, 2018; Majocchi, D'Angelo, Forlani, & Buck, 2018). A biased firm may hold an inflexible long-term attachment to its perceived heritage assets, while ascribing a short-term, substitutable status to perceived commodity assets, regardless of the actual value of these assets for the economic future of the firm. Bifurcation bias may affect important international governance decisions in the family firm, for example, the choice between internalization and outsourcing, by interfering with an assessment of the economizing properties of internalization versus outsourcing in relation to factual (vs. perceived) characteristics of operations associated with each decision.

The concept of bifurcation bias overlaps with, but is distinct from, SEW. All family firms are argued to possess some degree of SEW, which does not necessarily impact international activity decisions in a negative manner. Further, while family firms are inherently more susceptible to bifurcation bias than their non-family counterparts, they are not always bifurcation biased (Verbeke & Kano, 2012), nor do all biased firms exhibit the same level of bifurcation bias. Importantly, a firm focused on SEW is not always

---

[1] We recognize that the FIBER framework also suffers from a number of shortcomings, namely that the identified dimensions overlap, are difficult to measure directly, and are not often exhaustive of family firm priorities (Miller & Le Breton-Miller, 2014). Yet, for the purpose of our discussion, FIBER serves to underscore the multidimensional nature of SEW, which is treated in most extant studies as an umbrella term to account for the affective endowment of family firms (see also, Cruz & Arredondo, 2016). Though imperfect, the FIBER construct allows us to conduct a finer-grained discussion of the potential impact of SEW on internationalization research, whereby, we propose, specific dimensions of SEW can tentatively be linked to distinct internationalization outcomes for the firm.

bifurcation biased. In the presence of strong bifurcation bias, different components of SEW are likely to be prioritized de facto and guide international strategy decisions; here, dysfunctionality can be expected in the long term. In the absence of bifurcation bias, SEW-related choices can be assessed based on their compatibility with efficient governance, as proposed by internalization theory proponents.

INTERNALIZATION THEORY OVERVIEW

Internalization theory (Buckley & Casson, 1976; Hennart, 1982; Rugman, 1981) is concerned with firm-level international governance choices and their sustainability over time.[2] The latest version of the theory, hereafter referred to as *new* internalization theory or NIT (Hennart, 2009; Rugman & Verbeke, 1992, 2004; Verbeke, 2013), focuses on ongoing economizing and capability-creation properties of the MNE's entire structural and managerial governance system. According to NIT, the purpose of MNEs is to develop, exploit, and augment their firm-specific advantages (FSAs) across international borders. The nature of FSAs, together with the nature of the home and host locations, ultimately determine the international governance choices of MNEs.

When transferring their FSAs to host countries, MNEs will, over time, choose the most efficient governance approaches to cross-border transactions. For each international transaction or class of transactions, the MNE must make three types of governance decisions:

(1) whether transactions are internalized or externalized;
(2) how interface with the external environment should be organized for externalized transactions; and
(3) how internalized transactions should be organized within the MNE.

On balance, the most efficient governance mechanisms are those that allow the MNE to achieve comparatively superior management on three dimensions, for any given transaction:

(1) *reducing bounded rationality,* or the limits on managers' ability to process and act on important information (Simon, 1961);
(2) *reducing bounded reliability,* or the limits on managers' ability to fulfill open-ended promises (Kano & Verbeke, 2015); and
(3) *adapting extant structures and practices for the novel resource recombination at hand,* inter alia through maintaining a supportive entrepreneurial context

---

[2] It is beyond the scope of this chapter to provide a lengthy, detailed overview of the core foundations of internalization theory. For an introduction to the theory, please see the early works of Buckley and Casson (1976), Hennart (1982), and Rugman (1981).

conducive to new expressions of value creation (Grøgaard & Verbeke, 2012; Verbeke & Kenworthy, 2008).

For the remainder of the chapter, we define "efficient governance" as governance that best facilitates the abovementioned economizing and value generation related objectives. The underlying assumption of NIT is that firms not making international governance decisions on the basis of comparative efficiency will suffer losses and will eventually switch to efficient governance forms.

An alleged limitation of NIT is that its exclusive focus on firm-level economic efficiency constrains its applicability to situations where non-economic motivations are central to actors' decision-making (Hillemann & Verbeke, 2015; Rugman, 1983). It has also been suggested that internalization theory has a limited capacity to model tension and conflict typical of family firms (Reuber, 2016), and leaves no room for the integration of behavioral aspects (Pukall & Calabrò, 2014). We argue that NIT does, in fact, incorporate behavioral aspects through its explicit micro-foundational assumptions, but also agree that, much like the earlier version of internalization theory, NIT does not fully take into account family-owned MNEs' propensity to be guided by SEW considerations. For instance, a NIT-informed prediction would be that family firms where non-efficiency motives drive international strategy, will fail to internationalize successfully. And yet, empirically, we know that many of the oldest and most successful MNEs in the world are, indeed, family firms (*The Economist*, 2014). NIT does not explicitly account for the success of firms whose governance arrangements are chosen based on SEW criteria. Kano and Verbeke (2018) address the paradox of family firms' success (in spite of their tendency to make affect-based decisions) by suggesting that family firms that manage to economize on bifurcation bias behave like any other firm and internationalize according to the efficiency logic. However, what remains unclear is how SEW may influence the international strategy of unbiased family firms, and whether unique, family-centric considerations can, in fact, contribute to economizing and value creation objectives of international governance.

Governance Properties of SEW Endowment

Scholars advancing a "facilitative" perspective of family firm internationalization suggest that family firms can leverage their unique features, embedded in FIBER dimensions—family control and influence; identification of family members with the firm; binding social ties; emotional attachment; and dynastic succession—to support their international activities. Here, the pursuit of FIBER can promote development of valuable and internationally relevant advantages such as a loyal and stable workforce (Verbeke & Kano, 2010), patient capital (Chrisman et al., 2015), significant latitude in decision-making

(De Massis et al., 2014), committed leadership (Fernandez & Nieto, 2006), and advanced relational capabilities (Ward, 2004). In this section, we explore how each distinct FIBER dimension can facilitate efficient internationalization by enhancing economizing and entrepreneurial properties of governance. Our arguments are summarized in Table 11.1.

Table 11.1 Economizing and value-creating properties of SEW dimensions (FIBER)

	SEW lens	NIT lens	
FIBER dimension	Economizing on bounded rationality	Economizing on bounded reliability	Facilitating a supportive context for value creation
F. Family control and influence	• Reduces complexity of decision-making through centralization/ enables easier information access	• Reduces identity discordance among geographically dispersed units	• Strategic flexibility facilitates quick entrepreneurial response to competitive changes • Reduced transaction costs enable investment into new FSA development
I. Identification with the firm	• Reputation mitigates transaction uncertain-ties in host markets	• Safeguards transactions by signaling firm's reliability to external actors/customers • Enhances family managers' motivation to succeed in internationalization	• Stimulates focus on quality/promotes development of FSAs such as quality control/ improvement processes, product design • Strong reputation facilitates easier access to capabilities of external actors
B. Binding social ties	• Facilitate information exchange/reduce information asymmetries	• Provide informal/ relational safeguards for external transactions • Compensate for institutional weaknesses in the realm of IP/asset protection • Foster customer loyalty/ safeguard against predatory practices	• Enable customization through coopting customers into product development/adaptation • Enhance innovation by promoting spontaneous joint practice and exchange of technical information among units
E. Emotional attachment	• Facilitates information exchange with external partners by promoting stability of external relationships	• Introduces a self-enforcing economizing mechanism against imperfect effort/ improves reliability of transactions within the firm • Safeguards external transactions by promoting stability of relationships	• Promotes pride in end products/fosters innovation and continuous improvement

SEW lens	NIT lens		
R. Renewal of family bonds to the firm through dynastic succession	• Safeguards against myopia in decision-making	• Safeguards against imperfect effort by prioritizing quality/ allowing sufficient time for proper execution of projects • Safeguards external transactions through mutual long-term investments • Signals long-term reliability to host country regulators/governments	• Patient financial capital facilitates FSA development/innovation • Managers are encouraged to pursue entrepreneurial initiatives/are not pressed for short-term returns

F: Family Control and Influence

The founding family's capacity and desire to exercise control over the firm—either through direct involvement in management, dominant ownership position, or personal influence—is one of the defining characteristics of family firms (Berrone et al., 2012). Control is a baseline dimension of SEW: without the ability to exercise control, the family will not be able to pursue its overall SEW objectives. Centralization of control grants managers flexibility and enables speedy decision-making in the realm of internationalization (Chen, Hsu, & Chang, 2014; Fernandez & Nieto, 2006). Concentrated decision-making reduces complexity and facilitates a homogenous distribution of information among decision-makers (Mitter, Duller, Feldbauer-Durstmüller, & Kraus, 2014), and thus safeguards against bounded rationality. Further, concentration of control reduces potential conflict over resource allocation between headquarters and subsidiaries, and safeguards from identity-based discordance that may arise among various, geographically dispersed units of the organization (Kano & Verbeke, 2015). Miller and Le Breton Miller (2005) empirically demonstrate that concentration of control enables family firms to build long-lasting relationships with international stakeholders; these relationships further serve as informal safeguards against bounded reliability in host markets. Reduced complexity decreases transaction costs and potentially frees up resources for investment in development of new FSAs. Finally, decision autonomy allows family managers to quickly respond to competitive changes in both home and host countries and to pursue local entrepreneurial opportunities. International success of such family MNEs as the French tire producer Michelin and the German pharmaceutical giant Merck is often attributed to the controlling families' discretion to decide on markets and investments, without the need for lengthy consensus-building and outside pressures for short-term returns (*Economic Times*, 2017; Le Breton-Miller & Miller, 2006; Leleux & Glemser, 2009).

However, unconstrained prioritization of control can lead to serious governance challenges in host markets. Complexity of international operations requires family firms to alter management structures (Alessandri, Cerrato, & Eddleston, 2018) in ways that facilitate value creation from international transactions, but are also likely to reduce family control. Desire for sustained control may lead to a reluctance to enter new markets, to a rejection of external investors, and/or to a greater perceived need to protect assets through internalization. As a result, family firms that seek to maintain control (above other considerations) may select governance arrangements that are suboptimal in terms of their economizing and value creation properties, or forego international markets altogether. This was observed at different points in the internationalization of Suzuki, the Japanese automotive producer. For nearly four decades, Suzuki was led by Osamu Suzuki[3] (Inagaki, 2016). In 2009, Suzuki entered into a partnership with Volkswagen (VW), the leading German automotive producer, with the objective of gaining access to advanced drive train technology, needed to defend the firm's market share in the US and Europe. When VW attempted to increase its ownership of Suzuki (Firstpost, 2014), the latter exited the partnership; Mr. Suzuky was quoted as saying: "I don't want you to misunderstand: Suzuki is not becoming a 12th brand for Volkswagen. I don't want other folks telling me how to do things" (*Automotive World*, 2011). The failed partnership contributed to Suzuki's exit from the US market, associated primarily with the lack of suitable products (Tabuchi, 2012).

I: Identification with the Firm

Identification with the firm refers to the firm's identity being closely tied to the identity of the founding family and its members. This identification is frequently (but not necessarily) reinforced by an overlap between the family's name and that of the firm (De Massis et al., 2018), and typically implies a strong emphasis on nurturing the firm's reputation (Berrone et al., 2012). In fact, some empirical research suggests that family firms benefit from a stronger reputation compared to firms with dispersed ownership (Deephouse & Jaskiewicz, 2013).

Reputation is a valuable FSA that helps firms mitigate uncertainties in foreign markets (Gao, Zuzul, Jones, & Khanna, 2017), thus providing a safeguard against bounded rationality. Favorable reputation can also safeguard international transactions by signaling reliability to host country actors, such as customers, suppliers, distributors, and regulators, particularly when hybrid forms of governance are involved. When family managers' self-worth is tied to the business, they may be intrinsically motivated to ensure that the firm successfully plans and executes international projects (Dutton, Dukerich, & Harquail, 1994; Memili, Misra, Chrisman, & Welsh, 2017), which decreases the probability of imperfect effort. Finally, favorable reputation facilitates easier access to complementary capabilities held by external actors (Kano, 2018).

---

[3] Osamu Suzuki, formerly known as Osamu Matsuda, was adopted into the family. Adult adoption is a common custom in Japan to guarantee the survival of family firms. Before stepping into his lead role, Osamu married into the firm's founding family and took the Suzuki family name.

The family's identification with the firm can entail pride in the firm's products or services, or an "attachment to a substantive (i.e., nonfinancial) mission or craft that the family has long embraced" (Le Breton-Miller & Miller, 2006). This attachment often takes the form of a focus on quality, as a way of advancing the firm's reputation—a phenomenon observed in, for example, Italian confectionary company Ferrero's relentless search for the best-quality ingredients and recipes for its chocolates. Family firms' "craft mentality" (see Hennart et al., 2019) potentially results in internationally transferable FSAs, such as product design or quality assurance processes. Worldwide success of the iconic luxury brand Hermes, for example, is attributable to the family's commitment to superior quality and uncompromised craftsmanship, whereby the family name itself has become "synonymous with enduring quality and luxury" (see Bennedsen & Fan, 2014). At the same time, excessive concern for reputational asset dissipation may prevent family firms from engaging in international diversification (Gomez-Mejia et al., 2010), because reputation can be at risk in complex cross-border activities, where the firm relies on partners and suppliers whose actions are difficult to anticipate and monitor (Kano, 2018). In other words, unconstrained pursuit of the family's identification with the firm may interfere with effective pursuit of cross-border entrepreneurial opportunities and/or lead the firm to prioritize opportunities that are perceived as less risky—a behavior observed in many family firms, particularly small and medium-sized enterprises—SMEs—(Calabrò & Mussolino, 2011; Sciascia et al., 2012).

B: Binding Social Ties

Research acknowledges that family firms generally possess a larger social capital endowment (Zahra, 2003) than firms with dispersed ownership. Family-based social ties become established over a long term and permeate both the family and the firm domains (Habbershon, Williams, & MacMillan, 2003). These social ties are "binding" in that they are stable, continuous, mutually reinforcing and inter-dependent (Stadler, Mayer, Hautz, & Matzler, 2018), and the continuity of succession enables family firms to maintain and exploit their social networks more effectively (Le Breton-Miller & Miller, 2006; Sirmon & Hitt, 2003). Due to their complexity and embeddedness, these ties are difficult for competitors to imitate (Stadler et al., 2018), and may be exploited for the purpose of international expansion—specifically, to aid economizing and value creation when managing complex networks. Relational capital developed by the family can facilitate exchange of information (safeguard against bounded rationality). Relational capital can also act as an informal safeguard against the bounded reliability of external partners (Kano, 2018), and compensate for the weakness of local institutions, for example, by providing protection against property expropriation (Schmitz, 1999) when the family develops relational ties with regulators. One example is Gianni Agnelli—former head of the Agnelli family and the majority owner of the Fiat Group, an iconic Italian automaker—who, through his personal relationships with the world's political elites, enabled Fiat to strike deals in such challenging markets as the USSR, when few other western companies had operations in that market, and none could do so without sanctions imposed by the US government (Tagliabue, 2003).

Social ties foster buyer loyalty, and thus may safeguard against customer defection toward established host country or international competitors (Hennart et al., 2019). Social ties can also facilitate innovation by coopting customers into product development and customization, and by encouraging spontaneous joint practice among geographically dispersed units. As an example, Swedish furniture manufacturer IKEA's long-term, cooperative relationships with its international partners facilitated smooth and efficient logistics in IKEA's global value chain (Ivarsson & Alvstam, 2010).

That being said, indiscriminate prioritization of extant social ties can become problematic, particularly when existing relationships are focused predominantly on the home community (which is often the case). Further, family firms that prioritize social ties may seek international configurations that allow them to utilize existing social networks, or to establish reciprocal bonds with partners deemed trustworthy—either "kin-controlled firms" (Memili, Chrisman, & Chua, 2011) or other family firms (Swinth & Vinton, 1993). In practical terms, this means that social ties can guide the choice of markets (e.g. following a known distributor to a particular host market), as well as "make or buy" decisions (e.g. outsourcing an activity to a trusted supplier). These configurations may limit the firm's access to host resources that reside with non-kin partners and threaten efficient contracting. Family firms tend to attach a socially constructed meaning of reliability to family governance (Reuber, 2016), which becomes problematic when the actual reliability of family-owned partners/subcontractors is weak.

E: Emotional Attachment

In family businesses, the boundaries between the family and the firm are often blurred (Berrone et al., 2010), which results in an emotional attachment of the family to certain aspects of the business, such as products, brands, relationships, locations, and heritage routines. If properly channeled, emotional attachment can safeguard against bounded reliability by discouraging shirking/perfunctory contribution. Emotional attachment is considered the reason why family managers invest more of their time and effort than non-family ones into managing the firm, a phenomenon captured by the concept of stewardship (Corbetta & Salvato, 2004; Davis, Allen, & Hayes, 2010). Stewardship of family members, as one of the expressions of emotional attachment, can be seen as a self-enforcing mechanism to economize on bounded reliability within the firm. Emotional attachment of family members to various dimensions of the firm typically spreads to social links outside of the firm (Kepner, 1983; Pongelli, Calabrò, & Basco, 2019), and thus promotes stability of the firm's external relationships (Miller & Le Breton-Miller, 2014), facilitating access to host country knowledge and safeguarding transactions with host country partners. Emotional attachment may also promote entrepreneurial action by fostering pride in the firm's products and a focus on developing impactful innovations and pursuing continuous product and process improvement. Notable examples include

Italy's Illycaffè S.p.A.'s mission to sell "the best coffee in the world" (Hennart et al., 2019), or Michelin's decades-long quest to develop a radial tire, which has become a modern standard for safe and pleasant travel (Miller & Le Breton-Miller, 2005).

Yet, uncontrolled emotional attachment to operations or assets may impact boundaries of the firm, in that it may lead family firms toward excessive internalization of heritage activities in host markets (Kano & Verbeke, 2018). Emotional attachment to heritage locations (e.g. a desire to create jobs in local communities) may prevent the firm from achieving cost efficiencies through offshoring. Internal governance structures and incentive systems may also cater to emotional needs of the family (e.g. by delegating authority of heritage activities to "chosen" family members/linking incentives to heritage practices). Family-owned French car manufacturer Peugeot, for example, rejected a non-family CEO's suggestion to relocate operations to low-cost countries and insisted on keeping large operations in France. Peugeot's failure to achieve cost efficiencies of offshore production, which its competitors benefited from, resulted in substantial losses and a brush with bankruptcy in 2012 (Fainsilber, 2014).

R: Renewal of Family Bonds to the Firm through Dynastic Succession

Dynastic succession has implications for the time horizons of strategic decisions made for the business (Berrone et al., 2012). Long-term orientation, resulting from the focus on transgenerational continuity, represents one of the key advantages of family firms over firms with dispersed ownership (Miller & Le Breton-Miller, 2005) and can support efficiency of international governance in a number of ways. Namely, longer time horizons curb managers' myopia (economizing on bounded rationality) and lead them to prioritize quality of all business activities, which, in turn, facilitates successful internationalization (James, 1999; Memili et al., 2017). Long-term orientation also signals reliability to external partners, whereby repeated transactions and mutual, asset-specific investments into partnerships safeguard continuous exchange (Williamson, 1996). Longer time horizons allow family MNEs sufficient time to accumulate host country knowledge, thus facilitating development of relevant capabilities in host markets. The initial international successes of US-based confectionary conglomerate Mars and Italy's Ferrero have been linked to their founding families' patient approach to R&D, whereby products targeted for international markets were developed, customized, tested, and perfected before launch. This approach de facto traded off short-run profitability for long-term success based on intricate knowledge of host markets (Brenner, 1992; Sanderson, 2017). Finally, long-term orientation, if institutionalized throughout the MNE, stimulates subsidiary entrepreneurship, because managers are not held accountable for short-term returns (Carney, 2005) and, instead, have the discretion "to pursue substantive missions and the investments and sacrifices they entail" (Le Breton-Miller & Miller, 2006).

Yet, if prioritized indiscriminately, desire for transgenerational continuity may shape governance in ways that undermine efficiency. Empirical evidence suggests that family

CEOs prioritizing dynastic succession are more likely to engage in international acquisitions, as a way of facilitating career opportunities for the family and/or amassing wealth for future generations (Strike, Berrone, Sapp, & Congiu, 2015). While establishing a wholly owned subsidiary through an acquisition may be the most efficient entry mode—for example, in host markets where required local assets are not easy to isolate and transact (Hennart, 2009)—it may be inferior to other governance modes, for example, contractual agreements, in situations where both the MNE's assets and capabilities and the host country's complementary ones are easy to transact (Grøgaard & Verbeke, 2012). On the other hand, family firms that prioritize transgenerational continuity may seek internationalization paths that are comparatively less risky (Gomez-Mejia et al., 2010)— for example, by consistently choosing lower commitment/non-equity operating modes such as exporting over foreign direct investment (FDI). De facto emphasis on dynastic succession may promote management entrenchment and conflict over succession (Berrone et al., 2012). Finally, *primo geniture* (succession to the first-born child), as the ultimate expression of dynastic succession, has been shown to result in substandard management practices (Bloom & Van Reenen, 2010) and, ultimately, to cause a negative effect on performance (Cucculelli & Micucci, 2008).

CONTINGENCIES FOR SEW CONTRIBUTION TO EFFICIENT INTERNATIONAL GOVERNANCE: BIFURCATION BIAS ECONOMIZING

Each dimension of SEW encompasses both functional and dysfunctional elements. The dual nature of FIBER is summarized in Table 11.2. Using SEW to their advantage requires family firms to engage in a continuous balancing act, whereby functional properties of SEW are separated from dysfunctional ones; and SEW-driven governance choices are evaluated against other, non-SEW-driven alternatives.

The dysfunctional impacts of SEW on international governance can be mitigated when family firms monitor for, and economize against, bifurcation bias. Bifurcation bias economizing constrains SEW pursuit, in that SEW in unbiased firms is assessed based on its compatibility with efficient governance. Specific socio-emotional preferences are promoted only if they have economizing and value-creating properties in host countries. For example, a family MNE may pursue internalization in a host country if sustained family control afforded by internalization reduces transaction costs through simplified decision-making, better intellectual property protection, or greater strategic flexibility. Conversely, if family control does not serve efficiency purposes (i.e. if the cost of market transactions is lower than the cost of organizing interdependencies inside the MNE), alternative operating modes are chosen.

Extant research has identified a number of practices employed in family firms to economize on bifurcation bias. These include the adoption of merit-based human

Table 11.2 Functional versus dysfunctional elements of SEW dimensions (FIBER)

SEW dimension	Functional elements (facilitate economizing on bounded rationality and bounded reliability in cross-border transactions; facilitate value creation)	Dysfunctional elements (trigger bounded rationality and bounded reliability in cross-border transactions; inhibit value creation)
F. Family control and influence	• Simplicity/speed of decision-making • Strategic flexibility	• Entrenchment • Autocracy
I. Identification with the firm	• Focus on reputation • Focus on quality	• Blurring boundaries between the family and the firm
B. Binding social ties	• Social capital • Relational competency	• Distrust of outsiders • Nepotism/asymmetric altruism
E. Emotional attachment	• Commitment to the firm • Commitment to innovation/continuous improvement	• Affect-based decision-making • Escalation of commitment
R. Renewal of family bonds to the firm through dynastic succession	• Long-term orientation	• *Primo geniture*/other entrenched succession practices • Conflict over succession

resource practices (Verbeke & Kano, 2012), targeted training of employees (Almodóvar, Verbeke, & Rodríguez-Ruiz, 2016), structured decision-making, performance benchmarking, exposure of the firm to objective outside scrutiny (Kano & Verbeke, 2018), participative practices (Eddleston et al., 2018; Eddleston et al., 2019), appointment of external managers in charge of internationalization (D'Angelo et al., 2016), and appointment of family managers with significant foreign experience (Majocchi et al., 2018). In the long term, family firms that employ such practices, or bundles of these practices, will make governance choices that tend toward efficiency even in the presence of SEW.

Economizing on bifurcation bias thus leaves room for family firms to pursue SEW-related objectives, provided that those do not interfere with efficiency of governance and are assessed on their economizing and value creation properties. Specific economizing strategies help family firms ensure that their international governance choices do not expose them to bounded rationality and reliability issues. For example, a number of family firms offer IB training and implement strict qualification requirements for family members who join the business—this means that the family can pursue its desire for family control and/or dynastic succession, while putting the most qualified individuals in charge of international operations. Forest E. Mars, Mars' second-generation family leader, established a rule that any family member who takes a high-level managerial position at Mars must have launched and run a successful autonomous venture abroad (Clark, 2008; Kaplan, 2013). Gruppo Lunelli, a third-generation family-owned producer of wines and beverages based in Italy, requires family members who wish to join the firm to have a Master's degree in either a technical field, such as oenology, or in business, as well as a minimum of three years of international experience in a firm not owned by the family (interview with Alessandro Lunelli, Head of Production and co-owner of Gruppo Lunelli[4]).

In their discussion of governance adaptation in response to cross-country differences and associated commitment failures, Verbeke and Fariborzi (2019) distinguish between different types of correction based on its timing and scale. The authors argue that the timing of governance adaptation can be swift (either anticipative or corrective) or delayed, while the scale can be narrow/localized (whereby only select economizing challenges are addressed in a targeted way) or large (whereby governance corrections target the organization as a whole). Applying this logic to bifurcation bias economizing, we argue that bifurcation bias-related corrections in family firms fall into different categories based on timing and scale.

Anticipative Bifurcation Bias Economizing

Anticipative bifurcation bias economizing occurs ex-ante, as part of the family's set of guiding principles and values. Anticipative economizing entails that the firm's behavior will purposefully and consistently align with efficiency-based principles. Since anticipative economizing targets the overall governance philosophy, it is typically large-scale and encompasses bundles of economizing practices at various levels and across geographies. Family MNEs that successfully practice anticipative bifurcation bias economizing may be able to achieve efficiency in international operations while capitalizing on unique advantages brought by SEW endowment. In their historical case study of six family-owned Spanish and Italian MNEs, Colli, García-Canal, and Guillén (2013) demonstrate that successful internationalization of family firms rests less on traditional FSAs such as technology and brands, and more on their binding social ties and unique ability "to organize, manage, execute and network." However, the most successful cases of such family MNEs are characterized by de facto constraints placed on family control and targeted strategies to eliminate bifurcation bias, for example, through delegation of crucial operational functions, such as CEO/CFO, to professional managers.

Corrective Bifurcation Bias Economizing

Corrective economizing represents an ex-post reaction to observed inefficiencies caused by unconstrained pursuit of SEW objectives, in situations where, for example, affect-based resource allocation decisions led to negative performance consequences. Corrective economizing can be localized or large scale. The former is a targeted inter-

---

[4] The interview was conducted in 2016 as part of data collection for a large-scale family firm governance research project.

vention to solve a particular observed efficiency challenge (Verbeke & Fariborzi, 2019): for example, replacing a non-performing family member managing a foreign subsidiary with a competent local manager. While this intervention may improve subsidiary performance, it does not solve the grand challenge of eliminating bifurcation bias from the firm's governance system. Large-scale corrective economizing, on the other hand, may be triggered by a particular challenge, but targets the organization as a whole, and represents a "wholesale" transition from affect-based to efficiency-based governance practices.

Large-scale corrective economizing can be illustrated by the abovementioned case of Peugeot. Prior to its brush with bankruptcy in 2012, the controlling family steered the company's international strategy toward maximizing family control and preserving the family's commitment to the home location. While Peugeot appointed non-family CEOs for decades, the family effectively overrode all management decisions that potentially led to SEW dissipation. Industry analysts claim that the family's fear of losing control of the firm is the reason why Peugeot failed to finalize alliances with partners such as BMW and Mitsubishi, which would have supported its international expansion (Seibt, 2014). However, after coming close to bankruptcy in 2012, the family appointed Carlos Tavares, a non-family CEO, hired from rival automotive producer Renault-Nissan, and retreated from direct influence in strategic decisions. Under Tavares, the firm changed course: Peugeot sealed a joint venture with the Chinese MNE Dongfeng, offshored production, and delegated strategic decisions to competent professional managers. As stated by Tavares: "I feel very free. I have a lot of autonomy. The shareholders know the detail of the plan, and they all ask for the same thing: please fix it. I meet the supervisory board every two months, but beyond that they're hands-off. It's a great way to work" (Cropley, 2014). Under Tavares, Peugeot not only recovered from its crisis, but dramatically improved its performance (Dupont-Calbo & Amiot, 2017).

Corrective economizing, while pushing the firm toward efficient international governance, may not be sufficient to offset the negative effects of previous inefficiencies, especially if it is adopted too late. In this case, NIT predicts that the underperforming family firm will be unable to sustain its present governance arrangements—that is, it may cease to exist, or cease to exist as an MNE or as a family firm (Verbeke & Kano, 2012). One such example is Firestone, a US-based tire producer, which by the 1950s had become one of the two leading companies in their industry at the global level, followed by Goodyear. Firestone's fate illustrates how unconstrained SEW priorities can threaten the survival of family firms. Specifically, when France's Michelin entered the US market with radial tires (i.e. a new, superior product), Goodyear promptly reacted by investing in new factories, closing old plants, and restructuring in order to invest in new products and processes. Firestone's controlling family, on the other hand, failed to respond. The impact of emotional attachment was particularly evident in the internal governance of the firm's international activities. The family's heritage practices, dubbed "Firestone loyalty," focused on generating and keeping jobs at home and abroad. In order to maintain "Firestone loyalty," the firm did not close any of its domestic or overseas factories producing the old type of tires, and instead invested in marketing aimed at convincing consumers not to switch to radial tires. Firestone also tried to reduce job losses by converting old factories at a higher cost than investing in new facilities (Sull, 1999). Then, after years of losses, the family brought in an external CEO. The new CEO attempted to enact a series of cost-cutting measures that the family previously refused to implement, such as introducing performance-driven remuneration and closing down loss-making operations in the US and abroad. However, even such strong measures could not rescue the firm from its financial troubles. Subsequently, the Japanese tire producer Bridgestone acquired Firestone in 1988, but it took the new owners several years to turn around Firestone's loss-making international operations (Schreffler, 2003).

SUMMARY AND CONCLUDING REMARKS

In this chapter, we link NIT with a discussion of affective decision drivers in family firms—SEW and bifurcation bias—to help explain the paradox of family enterprises, that is, the fact that some of the world's most successful, long-standing MNEs are family firms (Banalieva & Eddleston, 2011), whose international strategies are often impacted by non-efficiency considerations. We contend that the pursuit of SEW and propensity for bifurcation bias are inherent features of all family firms, yet they exhibit these features in different forms and combinations. Strategies to economize on bifurcation bias act as a constraint on dysfunctional SEW pursuit. Family firms that implement a concerted, "wholesale" and, preferably, anticipative effort to safeguard against bifurcation bias may effectively use their strong SEW priorities to achieve international success. These firms are able to evaluate their SEW preferences based on their functional properties (Table 11.2), and to successfully deploy their SEW-derived advantages—such as streamlined decision-making, focus on reputation and quality, strong social capital, and long-term orientation—to economize on bounded rationality and reliability in host markets.

Family firms driven by unconstrained SEW preferences may, in the short term, select and retain governance mechanisms that promote SEW at the expense of efficiency. NIT predicts that inefficient governance will be corrected in the long term. We explain that, indeed, some family firms are able to address these inefficiencies through corrective bifurcation bias economizing. However, such correction may not always occur: affective priorities may lead the firm to escalate its commitment to a suboptimal course of action until such time when correction is no longer possible, and the company either ceases to exist as a family firm or simply ceases to exist (Verbeke & Kano, 2012). This explains the untimely demise of the majority of family firms. We argue that the core thesis of NIT— that only efficient governance survives in the long run—holds for family firms *even* in the presence of strong SEW.

Our arguments have the potential to contribute to both IB strategy and family firm research. First, we augment NIT by introducing insights from family firm research— specifically, insights on unique, affect-based behavioral drivers of family firm managers such as SEW and bifurcation bias. Infused with additional micro-level assumptions "borrowed" from family firm research, NIT can account for theoretically misaligned governance choices of family firms, at least in the short term—in other words, the integrative NIT/SEW framework explains why managers in family-owned MNEs do not necessarily "behave the way theory suggests" (Buckley, Devinney, & Louviere, 2007). The combined perspective also explains how and when idiosyncratic features of family firms can contribute to efficient governance of international transactions.

Second, we contribute to the family firm internationalization literature, by linking SEW to predictive IB theory. SEW does not, on its own, explain family firm internationalization patterns, beyond suggesting that family firms internationalize "differently" than their non-family counterparts. Further, most extant studies treat SEW as an umbrella term to account for the affective endowment of family firms (Cruz & Arredondo, 2016; see Evert, Sears, Martin, & Payne, 2018 and Pongelli et al., 2019, for exceptions). In contrast, we unbundle SEW and analyze each dimension in terms of its efficiency properties as suggested in NIT: that is, impact on the firm's capacity to manage bounded rationality and bounded reliability, and to create a supportive context for novel value creation (Table 11.1). Such analysis underscores the idea that family firms are heterogeneous in their SEW preferences, meaning that both the extent of SEW emphasis and the weights attached to various FIBER dimensions differ across firms (Berrone et al., 2012; Chua, Chrisman, & Sharma, 1999). While we discussed the impact of each dimension of SEW individually, these impacts may exist in various combinations and are likely mutually reinforcing.

Our chapter also offers some practical implications. We suggest that economizing on bifurcation bias is a critical ingredient for international success of family firms and offer some real-life examples of such economizing observed in successful family MNEs. Further, we separate functional and dysfunctional elements of what constitutes SEW. We caution family MNE managers against indiscriminate prioritization of SEW and encourage them to proactively identify dysfunctional SEW practices and eliminate them from their governance systems. Finally, we offer an in-depth discussion of how functional SEW elements can enhance efficiency of governance, in the presence of bifurcation bias economizing. Non-family MNEs could benefit from emulating strategic advantages of family firms, by copying family firms' norms and value systems that promote functional elements of SEW.

Ultimately, the idea of the inherent tension between efficiency-based and affect-based decision-making is relevant beyond the realm of family firm internationalization research. In this chapter, we show how the explanatory power of NIT can be enhanced through an infusion of affective elements into micro-level assumptions. Future research can follow up by investigating more broadly the interaction of affect-based and efficiency-based decision-making in IB strategy choices.

References

Alessandri, T. M., Cerrato, D., & Eddleston, K. A. 2018. The mixed gamble of internationalization in family and nonfamily firms: The moderating role of organizational slack. *Global Strategy Journal*, 8(1): 46–72.

Almodóvar, P., Verbeke, A., & Rodríguez-Ruiz, Ó. 2016. The internationalization of small and medium-sized family enterprises: The role of human asset quality. *Journal of Leadership & Organizational Studies*, 23(2): 162–174.

Arregle, J. L., Duran, P., Hitt, M. A., & Essen, M. 2017. Why is family firms' internationalization unique? A meta-analysis. *Entrepreneurship Theory and Practice*, 41(5): 801–831.

Automotive World, 2011. Volkswagen and Suzuki: Irreconcilable differences. https://www.automotiveworld.com/uncategorised/89289-volkswagen-and-suzuki-irreconcilable-differences/. Accessed 31 May 2018.

Banalieva, E. R., & Eddleston, K. A. 2011. Home-region focus and performance of family firms: The role of family vs. non-family leaders. *Journal of International Business Studies*, 42(8): 1060–1072.

Bennedsen, M., & Fan, J. P. 2014. *The Family Business Map: Assets and Roadblocks in Long-Term Planning*. London: Macmillan.

Bennedsen, M., & Foss, N. 2015. Family assets and liabilities in the innovation process. *California Management Review*, 58(1): 65–81.

Berrone, P., Cruz, C., & Gomez-Mejia, L. R. 2012. Socioemotional wealth in family firms: Theoretical dimensions, assessment approaches, and agenda for future research. *Family Business Review*, 25(3): 258–279.

Berrone, P., Cruz, C., Gomez-Mejia, L. R., & Larraza-Kintana, M. 2010. Socioemotional wealth and corporate responses to institutional pressures: Do family-controlled firms pollute less? *Administrative Science Quarterly*, 55(1): 82–113.

Bloom, N., & Van Reenen, J. 2010. Why do management practices differ across firms and countries? *The Journal of Economic Perspectives*, 24(1): 203–224.

Boers, B. 2016. Go East! How family businesses choose markets and entry modes when internationalising. *International Journal of Globalisation and Small Business*, 8(4): 333–354.

Brenner, J. G. 1992. Life on Mars: The Mars family saga has all the classic elements. https://www.independent.co.uk/arts-entertainment/life-on-mars-the-mars-family-saga-has-all-the-classic-elements-1535722.html. Accessed 22 February 2018.

Buckley, P. J., & Casson, M. C. 1976. *The Future of the Multinational Enterprise*. London: Macmillan.

Buckley, P. J., Devinney, T. M., & Louviere, J. J. 2007. Do managers behave the way theory suggests? A choice-theoretic examination of foreign direct investment location decision-making. *Journal of International Business Studies*, 38(7): 1069–1094.

Calabrò, A., & Mussolino, D. 2011. How do boards of directors contribute to family SME export intensity? The role of formal and informal governance mechanisms. *Journal of Management and Governance*, 17(2): 363–403.

Calabrò, A., Torchia, M., Pukall, T., & Mussolino, D. 2013. The influence of ownership structure and board strategic involvement on international sales: The moderating effect of family involvement. *International Business Review*, 22(3): 509–523.

Carney, M. 2005. Corporate governance and competitive advantage in family-controlled firms. *Entrepreneurship Theory and Practice*, 29(3): 249–265.

Carr, C., & Bateman, S. 2009. International strategy configurations of the world's top family firms. *Management International Review*, 49(6): 733–758.

Casillas, J. C., & Pastor, F. 2015. *The top 250 multinational family firms*. Chair of Santander family business, Seville, Spain: University of Seville.

Chen, H. L., Hsu, W. T., & Chang, C. Y. 2014. Family ownership, institutional ownership, and internationalization of SMEs. *Journal of Small Business Management*, 52(4): 771–789.

Chrisman, J. J., Chua, J. H., De Massis, A., Frattini, F., & Wright, M. 2015. The ability and willingness paradox in family firm innovation. *Journal of Product Innovation Management*, 32(3): 310–318.

Chua, J. H., Chrisman, J. J., & Sharma, P. 1999. Defining the family business by behaviour. *Entrepreneurship Theory and Practice*, 23(4): 19–39.

Clark, A. 2008. Life in Mars: Reclusive dynasty behind one of world's most famous brands. https://www.theguardian.com/business/2008/may/02/mars.wrigley.secretive. Accessed 31 May 2018.

Colli, A., García-Canal, E., & Guillén, M. F. 2013. Family character and international entrepreneurship: A historical comparison of Italian and Spanish "new multinationals." *Business History*, 55(1): 119–138.

Corbetta, G., & Salvato, C. 2004. Self-serving or self-actualizing? Models of man and agency costs in different types of family firms: A commentary on "comparing the agency costs of family and non-family firms: Conceptual issues and exploratory evidence." *Entrepreneurship Theory and Practice*, 28(4): 355–362.

Cropley, S. 2014. *How Carlos Tavares plans to save PSA Peugeot Citroën*. https://www.autocar.co.uk/car-news/industry/how-carlos-tavares-plans-save-psa-peugeot-citroen. Accessed 4 June 2018.

Cruz, C., & Arredondo, H. 2016. Going back to the roots of socioemotional wealth. *Management Research: Journal of the Iberoamerican Academy of Management*, 14(3): 234–243.

Cucculelli, M., & Micucci, G. 2008. Family succession and firm performance: Evidence from Italian family firms. *Journal of Corporate Finance*, 14(1): 17–31.

D'Angelo, A., Majocchi, A., & Buck, T. 2016. External managers, family ownership and the scope of SME internationalization. *Journal of World Business*, 51(4): 534–547.

Davis, J., Allen, M., & Hayes, H. 2010. Is blood thicker than water? A study of stewardship perceptions in family business. *Entrepreneurship Theory and Practice*, 34(6): 339–358.

De Massis, A., Di Minin, A., & Frattini, F. 2015. Family-driven innovation: Resolving the paradox in family firms. *California Management Review*, 58(1): 5–19.

De Massis, A., Kotlar, J., Chua, J. H., & Chrisman, J. J. 2014. Ability and willingness as sufficiency conditions for family-oriented particularistic behavior: Implications for theory and empirical studies. *Journal of Small Business Management*, 52(2): 344–364.

De Massis, A., Kotlar, J., Mazzola, P., Minola, T., & Sciascia, S. 2018. Conflicting selves: Family owners' multiple goals and self-control agency problems in private firms. *Entrepreneurship Theory and Practice*, 42(3): 362–389.

Deephouse, D. L., & Jaskiewicz, P. 2013. Do family firms have better reputations than non-family firms? An integration of socioemotional wealth and social identity theories. *Journal of Management Studies*, 50(3): 337–360.

Dupont-Calbo, J. & Amiot, M. 2017. Tavares L'autre Carlos. https://www.lesechos.fr/05/05/2017/LesEchosWeekEnd/00075-008-ECWE_tavares-l-autre-carlos.htm. Accessed 10 July 2018.

Dutton, J. E., Dukerich, J. M., & Harquail, C. V. 1994. Organizational images and member identification. *Administrative Science Quarterly*, 39(2): 239–263.

Economic Times. 2017. Part 2: Who is Carlos Ghosn? His first stint with automotive industry at Michelin. https://auto.economictimes.indiatimes.com/news/industry/who-is-carlos-ghosn-his-first-stint-with-automotive-industry-at-michelin/56994358?redirect=1. Accessed 28 May 2018.

Eddleston, K. A., Kellermanns, F. W., & Kidwell, R. E. 2018. Managing family members: How monitoring and collaboration affect extra role behavior in family firms. *Human Resource Management*, 57(5): 957–977.

Eddleston, K. A., Sarathy, R., & Banalieva, E. R. 2019. When a high-quality niche strategy is not enough to spur family-firm internationalization: The role of external and internal contexts. *Journal of International Business Studies*, 50(5): 783–808.

Evert, R. E., Sears, J. B., Martin, J. A., & Payne, G. T. 2018. Family ownership and family involvement as antecedents of strategic action: A longitudinal study of initial international entry. *Journal of Business Research*, 84: 301–311.

Fainsilber, D. 2014. Les difficiles relations du patron de PSA avec la famille Peugeot. https://www.lesechos.fr/18/02/2014/lesechos.fr/0203324329502_les-difficiles-relations-du-patron-de-psa-avec-la-famille-peugeot.htm. Accessed 27 February 2018.

Family Firm Institute. 2017. *Global data points*. http://www.ffi.org page/globaldatapoints. Accessed 15 February 2018.

Fernandez, Z., & Nieto, M. 2006. Impact of ownership on the international involvement of SMEs. *Journal of International Business Studies*, 37(3): 340–351.

Firstpost, 2014. Retract claim by Sept-end, Suzuki tells Volkswagen. https://www.firstpost.com/business%20/retract-claim-by-sept-end-suzuki-tells-volkswagen-90134.html. Accessed 31 May 2018.

Gao, C., Zuzul, T., Jones, G., & Khanna, T. 2017. Overcoming institutional voids: A reputation-based view of long-run survival. *Strategic Management Journal*, 38(11): 2147–2167.

Gomez-Mejia, L. R., Makri, M., & Larraza-Kintana, M. L. 2010. Diversification decisions in family-controlled firms. *Journal of Management Studies*, 47(2): 223–252.

Graves, C., & Thomas, J. 2006. Internationalization of Australian family businesses: A managerial capabilities perspective. *Family Business Review*, 19(3): 207–224.

Grøgaard, B., & Verbeke, A. 2012. Twenty key hypotheses that make internalization theory the general theory of international strategic management. In A. Verbeke & H. Merchant (Eds.), *Handbook of Research on International Strategic Management*. Cheltenham: Edward Elgar.

Habbershon, T. G., Williams, M., & MacMillan, I. C. 2003. A unified systems perspective of family firm performance. *Journal of Business Venturing*, 18(4): 451–465.

Hennart, J. F. 1982. *A Theory of the Multinational Enterprise*. Ann Arbor, MI: University of Michigan Press.

Hennart, J. F. 2009. Down with MNE-centric theories! Market entry and expansion as the bundling of MNE and local assets. *Journal of International Business Studies*, 40(9): 1432–1454.

Hennart, J. F., Majocchi, A., & Forlani, E. 2019. The myth of the stay-at-home family firm: How family-managed SMEs can overcome their internationalization limitations. *Journal of International Business Studies*, 50(5): 758–782.

Hillemann, J., & Verbeke, A. 2015. Efficiency-driven, comparative institutional analysis in international business. *The Multinational Business Review*, 23(3): 189–199.

Inagaki, K. 2016. Suzuki Motor chief to step down over scandal. https://www.ft.com/content/58299976-2d68-11e6-bf8d-26294ad519fc. Accessed 16 February 2018.

Ivarsson, I., & Alvstam, C. G. 2010. Upgrading in global value-chains: A case study of technology-learning among IKEA-suppliers in China and Southeast Asia. *Journal of Economic Geography*, 11(4): 731–752.

James, H. S. 1999. Owner as manager, extended horizons and the family firm. *International Journal of the Economics of Business*, 6(1): 41–55.

Johanson, J., & Vahlne, J. E. 1977. The internationalization process of the firm—A model of knowledge development and increasing foreign market commitments. *Journal of International Business Studies*, 8(1): 23–32.

Johanson, J., & Vahlne, J. E. 2009. The Uppsala internationalization process model revisited: From liability of foreignness to liability of outsidership. *Journal of International Business Studies*, 40(9): 1411–1431.

Kano, L. 2018. Governance of global value chains: A relational perspective. *Journal of International Business Studies*, 49(6): 684–705.

Kano, L., & Verbeke, A. 2015. The three faces of bounded reliability: Alfred Chandler and the micro-foundations of management theory. *California Management Review*, 58(1): 97–122.

Kano, L., & Verbeke, A. 2018. Family firm internationalization: Heritage assets and the impact of Bifurcation bias. *Global Strategy Journal*, 8(1): 158–183.

Kaplan, D. A. 2013. Mars Incorporated: A pretty sweet place to work. http://fortune.com/2013/01/17/mars-incorporated-a-pretty-sweet-place-to-work/. Accessed 23 February 2018.

Kepner, E. 1983. The family and the firm: A coevolutionary perspective. *Organizational Dynamics*, 12(1): 57–70.

Kontinen, T., & Ojala, A. 2010. Internationalization pathways of family SMEs: Psychic distance as a focal point. *Journal of Small Business and Enterprise Development*, 17(3): 437–454.

Le Breton-Miller, I., & Miller, D. 2006. Why do some family businesses out-compete? Governance, long-term orientations, and sustainable capability. *Entrepreneurship Theory and Practice*, 30(6): 731–746.

Leleux, B. F., & Glemser, A. 2009. The Mercks of Darmstadt: What family can do (A). *IMD Case Studies: IMD-3-2136*.

Lien, Y. C., & Filatotchev, I. 2015. Ownership characteristics as determinants of FDI location decisions in emerging economies. *Journal of World Business*, 50(4): 637–650.

Majocchi, A., D'Angelo, A., Forlani, E., & Buck, T. 2018. Bifurcation bias and exporting: Can foreign work experience be an answer? Insight from European family SMEs. *Journal of World Business*, 53(2): 237–247.

Memili, E., Chrisman, J. J., & Chua, J. H. 2011. Transaction costs and outsourcing decisions in small- and medium-sized family firms. *Family Business Review*, 24(1): 47–61.

Memili, E., Misra, K., Chrisman, J. J., & Welsh, D. H. B. 2017. Internationalization of publicly traded family firms: A transaction cost theory perspective and longitudinal analysis. *International Journal of Management and Enterprise Development*, 16(1/2): 80–108.

Miller, D., & Le Breton-Miller, I. 2005. *Managing for the Long Run: Lessons in Competitive Advantage from Great Family Businesses*. Boston, MA: Harvard Business Press.

Miller, D., & Le Breton-Miller, I. 2014. Deconstructing socioemotional wealth. *Entrepreneurship Theory and Practice*, 38(4): 713–720.

Miller, D., Le Breton-Miller, I., Lester, R. H., & Cannella Jr, A. A. 2007. Are family firms really superior performers? *Journal of Corporate Finance*, 13(5): 829–858.

Miller, D., Wright, M., Le Breton-Miller, I., & Scholes, L. 2015. Resources and innovation in family Businesses: The Janus-face of socioemotional preferences. *California Management Review*, 58(1): 20–40.

Mitter, C., Duller, C., Feldbauer-Durstmüller, B., & Kraus, S. 2014. Internationalization of family firms: The effect of ownership and governance. *Review of Managerial Science*, 8(1), 1–28.

Pongelli, C., Calabrò, A., & Basco, R. 2019. Family firms' international make-or-buy decisions: Captive offshoring, offshore outsourcing, and the role of home region focus. *Journal of Business Research*, 103: 596–606.

Pukall, T. J., & Calabrò, A. 2014. The internationalization of family firms: A critical review and integrative model. *Family Business Review*, 27(2): 103–125.

PWC, 2016. 2016 Family Business Survey. https://www.pwc.com/gx/en/services/family-business/family-business-survey-2016.html. Accessed 12 November 2018.

Reuber, A. R. 2016. An assemblage-theoretic perspective on the internationalization processes of family firms. *Entrepreneurship Theory and Practice*, 40(6): 1269–1286.

Rugman, A. M. 1981. *Inside the Multinationals: The Economics of Internal Markets*. New York, NY: Columbia University Press.

Rugman, A. M. 1983. The comparative performance of US and European multinational enterprises, 1970–79. *Management International Review*, 23(2): 4–14.

Rugman, A. M., & Verbeke, A. 1992. A note on the transnational solution and transaction cost theory of multinational strategic management. *Journal of International Business Studies*, 23(4): 761–771.

Rugman, A. M., & Verbeke, A. 2004. A perspective on regional and global strategies of multinational enterprises. *Journal of International Business Studies*, 35(1): 3–19.

Sanderson, R. 2017. Ferrero's chocolate fortunes face consumer test. https://www.ft.com/content/b244b9a6-2040-11e7-a454-ab04428977f9. Accessed 28 November 2017.

Schmitz, H. 1999. From ascribed to earned trust in exporting clusters. *Journal of International Economics*, 48(1): 139–150.

Schreffler, R. 2003. Bridgestone took on world with Firestone acquisition. http://www.rubbernews.com/article/20130916/NEWS/130919964/bridgestone-took-on-world-with-firestone-acquisition. Accessed 23 February 2018.

Sciascia, S., Mazzola, P., Astrachan, J. H., & Pieper, T. M. 2012. The role of family ownership in international entrepreneurship: Exploring nonlinear effects. *Small Business Economics*, 38(1): 15–31.

Seibt, S. 2014. Comment la famille Peugeot a perdu le pouvoir absolu dans PSA. http://www.france24.com/fr/20140219-peugeot-famille-thierry-robert-accord-etat-dongfeng-histoire-automobile-psa. Accessed 4 June 2018.

Sestu, M. C., & Majocchi, A. 2020. Family firms and the choice between wholly owned subsidiaries and joint ventures: A transaction costs perspective. *Entrepreneurship Theory and Practice*, 44(2): 211–232.

Simon, H. A. 1961. *Administrative Behavior: A Study of Decision-Making Processes in Administrative Organization*. New York, NY: Macmillan.

Sirmon, D. G., & Hitt, M. A. 2003. Managing resources: Linking unique resources, management, and wealth creation in family firms. *Entrepreneurship Theory and Practice*, 27(4): 339–358.

Stadler, C., Mayer, M. C., Hautz, J., & Matzler, K. 2018. International and product diversification: Which strategy suits family managers? *Global Strategy Journal*, 8(1): 184–207.

Strike, V. M., Berrone, P., Sapp, S. G., & Congiu, L. 2015. A socioemotional wealth approach to CEO career horizons in family firms. *Journal of Management Studies*, 52(4): 555–583.

Sull, D. N. 1999. The dynamics of standing still: Firestone Tire & Rubber and the radial revolution. *Business History Review*, 73(3): 430–464.

Swinth, R. L., & Vinton, K. L. 1993. Do family-owned businesses have a strategic advantage in international joint ventures? *Family Business Review*, 6(1): 19–30.

Tabuchi, H. 2012. Suzuki, Small-Car Maker, Gives Up on U.S. Market. https://www.nytimes.com/2012/11/07/business/global/american-suzuki-files-for-bankruptcy-and-will-stop-selling-cars-in-us.html. Accessed 27 May 2018.

Tagliabue, J. 2003. Giovanni Agnelli, Fiat patriarch and a force in Italy dies at 81. http://www.nytimes.com/2003/01/25/business/giovanni-agnelli-fiat-patriarch-and-a-force-in-italy-dies-at-81.html. Accessed 25 March 2017.

The Economist. 2014. Business in the blood. https://www.economist.com/business/2014/11/01/business-in-the-blood. Accessed 23 May 2018.

Verbeke, A. 2013. *International Business Strategy*. Cambridge: Cambridge University Press.

Verbeke, A., & Fariborzi, H. 2019. Managerial governance adaptation in the multinational enterprise. *Journal of International Business Studies*, 50(8): 1213–1230.

Verbeke, A., & Kano, L. 2010. Transaction cost economics (TCE) and the family firm. *Entrepreneurship Theory and Practice*, 34(6): 1173–1182.

Verbeke, A., & Kano, L. 2012. The transaction cost economics theory of the family firm: Family-based human asset specificity and the bifurcation bias. *Entrepreneurship Theory and Practice*, 36(6): 1183–1205.

Verbeke, A., & Kenworthy, T. 2008. Multidivisional vs metanational governance of the multinational enterprise. *Journal of International Business Studies*, 39(2): 940–956.

Ward, J. L. 2004. *Perpetuating the Family Business: 50 Lessons Learned from Long-Lasting, Successful Families in Business*. Basingstoke: Palgrave Macmillan.

Williamson, O. E. 1996. *The Mechanisms of Governance*. New York: Oxford University Press.

Zahra, S. A. 2003. International expansion of US manufacturing family businesses: The effect of ownership and involvement. *Journal of Business Venturing*, 18(4): 495–512.

CHAPTER 12

INTERNATIONALIZATION OF EMERGING-MARKET MULTINATIONALS

The Role of the Underdevelopment of the Home Country

ALVARO CUERVO-CAZURRA, ALICIA RODRÍGUEZ, AND C. ANNIQUE UN

INTRODUCTION

THE internationalization of emerging-market firms is now a well-established reality. Their rapid international expansion in the 1990s and 2000s caught many by surprise. This led to a rush to explain the phenomenon and convince scholars that new models and theories of the multinational were needed to explain the behavior of emerging-market multinational enterprises (EMNEs) (Aulakh, 2007; Cuervo-Cazurra, 2011; Gammeltoft, Barnard, & Madhok, 2010; Guillen & Garcia-Canal, 2009; Luo & Tung, 2007; Mathews, 2006). By the late 2020s, the phenomenon is no longer new, and there are already well-established arguments and models explaining their international expansion (see entries in Cuervo-Cazurra & Ramamurti, 2014; Demirbag & Yaprak, 2015; Grosse & Meyer, 2019; Williamson, Ramamurti, Fleury, & Fleury, 2013). However, there are still lingering questions as to whether there is something genuinely new about MNEs originating from emerging markets, or a confusion concerning the drivers of their behavior (Cuervo-Cazurra, 2012; Hernandez & Guillen, 2018; Ramamurti, 2012; Ramamurti & Hillemann, 2018).

Hence, in this chapter, we take stock of our current understanding of EMNEs and the theoretical models that have been introduced to explain their internationalization. From our review of the EMNE literature and the theoretical models used to study these firms, we explain that, despite much fanfare about the novelty of EMNEs and the need for new models to explain their behavior, many of their apparent unusual internationalization patterns are driven by liberalization processes that support globalization, technological advances that facilitate global expansion, and challenges in the early stages of internationalization (Ramamurti, 2012). Such conditions apply both to firms from emerging markets as well as to those from advanced economies that have started their international expansion in recent years. We propose that a more fruitful avenue for both understanding EMNEs better and advancing models of the multinational is to pay more attention to the role of the conditions of the home-country context on internationalization (Cuervo-Cazurra, Luo, Ramamurti, & Ang, 2018). Specifically, we propose that the underdevelopment of the home country can help as well as hinder the international competitiveness of EMNEs and their subsequent internationalization decisions. We discuss four areas that can yield promising insights on the impact of underdeveloped home-country conditions on internationalization; these are frugal innovation, contractual innovation, upgrading escape, and institutional escape.

The remainder of the chapter is organized as follows. We review the phenomenon of EMNEs and the models that emerge in the 2000s to explain their internationalization and, in so doing, challenge previous models of the multinational. We then argue that what sets these firms apart from multinationals from advanced economies is the influence of the underdevelopment of their home markets. We then proceed to discuss in more detail how the economic and institutional underdevelopment of the home country may lead to four particular patterns of internationalization driven by either an innovation or an escape motive.

The Internationalization of Emnes: New Phenomenon, new Explanations, and new Concepts

New Phenomenon

The internationalization of EMNEs is not a recent phenomenon. EMNEs have engaged in international trade for centuries, not only importing advanced technologies but also manufacturing and exporting raw materials and, in some cases, semi-processed and processed goods. What is new is their internationalization using foreign direct investment (FDI), in which firms from emerging markets establish subsidiaries abroad to facilitate their international sales and the acquisition of inputs and factors of production.

Although we have examples of early EMNEs, like the Argentinean shoemaker Alpargatas, which was created in 1885 and established its first foreign subsidiary in Uruguay in 1890 and the second one in Brazil in 1907 (Alpargatas, 2019), these are an oddity rather than the norm. Very few emerging-market firms invested abroad until the 1980s. Their internationalization consisted mostly of importing advanced technology and machinery from developed countries and exporting low value-added products. The high level of government intervention in emerging countries around the world—not only in communist countries such as the Soviet Union or China but also in capitalistic countries under an import substitution model of development such as Brazil or India (see Yergin & Stanislaw, 2002)—protected domestic firms from the pressures of foreign competition and resulted in companies having limited international competitiveness.

The rapid expansion of multinationals from emerging markets started in the 1990s and accelerated in the 2000s and 2010s. A process of economic liberalization swept the emerging world starting in the 1980s, leading to the deregulation of industries, privatization of state-owned enterprises, and reduction of barriers to trade and investment. Communist countries became integrated in the world economy as they transitioned toward capitalism. Developing countries replaced import substitutions models of economic development with export-led approaches. At the same time, advances in transportation and communication technologies facilitated the coordination of activities across distances and new manufacturing technologies enabled the dispersion of supply chains around the world. These twin engines of globalization, namely economic liberalization and technological advances (Cuervo-Cazurra, Mudambi, & Pedersen, 2017), acted as catalysts for the global expansion of EMNEs. This meant that firms in emerging economies that had been sheltered from foreign competition and grew domestically by nurturing relationships with political actors (Ghemawat & Khanna, 1998) were forced to improve their competitiveness or be at risk of disappearing. Many did not survive the economic liberalization. However, those that did, as well as ventures newly created by entrepreneurs to take advantage of the opportunities afforded by the integration of their countries into the global economy, became efficient and sophisticated competitors. These firms joined the global supply chains of advanced-economy multinationals and some became multinationals themselves, expanding abroad to serve new customers and improve their efficiency and technological sophistication.

This recent improvement in competitiveness and foreign expansion is reflected in the rapid increase in outward FDI from emerging economies. Table 12.1 provides the evolution of the stocks of outward FDI, separating economies into advanced and emerging, as well as creating a third group of economies considered offshore financial centers and pass-through financial centers that tend to distort FDI statistics. The figures and their evolution reveal the rapid rise in outward FDI from emerging economies in the late 1990s. However, a similarly rapid rise happens in outward FDI from advanced economies, reflecting how firms in advanced economies also benefited from the implementation of pro-market reforms and advances in transportation and communication technologies. Despite this, there is a significant relative increase in multinationals from emerging markets since the 1990s, as the percentage of the total stock of FDI worldwide grows from 2 percent in 2000 to 12 percent in 2017 for emerging markets.

Table 12.1 Outward foreign direct investment stock by economic groups, selected years

	1980	1985	1990	1995	2000	2005	2010	2015	2017
Advanced economies, outward FDI stock, US$bn	502.4	835.7	2165.9	3845.7	7220.9	11355.2	19252.0	22293.5	26752.4
Emerging economies, outward FDI stock, US$bn	56.8	66.3	90.6	162.3	281.0	750.9	2204.6	4191.9	5210.5
Advanced economies, outward FDI stock, percentage of world	90	93	96	96	96	94	90	84	84
Emerging economies, outward FDI stock, percentage of world	10	7	4	4	4	6	10	16	16
Advanced economies, outward FDI stock excluding offshore financial centers, US$bn	502.4	835.7	2165.9	3845.6	7220.3	11351.6	19054.5	22094.1	26536.2
Emerging economies, outward FDI stock excluding offshore financial centers, US$bn	56.4	65.7	88.2	142.8	172.7	525.4	1630.2	3075.2	3945.0
Offshore financial centers, outward FDI stock, US$bn	0.4	0.6	2.4	19.6	108.9	229.1	771.9	1316.1	1481.7
Advanced economies, outward FDI stock excluding offshore financial centers, percentage of world	90	93	96	96	96	94	89	83	83
Emerging economies, outward FDI stock excluding offshore financial centers, percentage of world	10	7	4	4	2	4	8	12	12
Offshore financial centers, outward FDI stocks, percentage of world	0	0	0	0	1	2	4	5	5

(Continued)

Table 12.1 Outward foreign direct investment stock by economic groups, selected years (Continued)

	1980	1985	1990	1995	2000	2005	2010	2015	2017
Advanced economies, outward FDI stock excluding pass-through centers, US$bn	448.5	766.7	2021.3	3550.1	6451.4	9885.8	16346.7	17710.9	21361.0
Emerging economies, outward FDI stock excluding pass-through centers, US$bn	56.7	66.1	89.1	148.4	189.9	549.6	1736.2	3229.5	4094.7
Pass-through centers, outward FDI stock, US$bn	54.0	69.2	146.1	309.5	860.6	1670.8	3373.8	5545.0	6507.2
Advanced economies, outward FDI stock excluding pass-through centers, percentage of world	80	85	90	89	86	82	76	67	67
Emerging economies, outward FDI stock excluding pass-through centers, percentage of world	10	7	4	4	3	5	8	12	13
Pass-through centers, outward FDI stock percentage of world	0	0	0	0	1	2	4	5	5

Source: Created using data from UNCTAD (2018). Economies classified as advanced by the International Monetary Fund (IMF, 2018) are Australia, Austria, Belgium, Canada, Cyprus, Czech Republic, Denmark, Estonia, Finland, France, Germany, Greece, Hong Kong SAR, Iceland, Ireland, Israel, Italy, Japan, Korea, Latvia, Lithuania, Luxembourg, Macao SAR, Malta, Netherlands, New Zealand, Norway, Portugal, Puerto Rico, San Marino, Singapore, Slovak Republic, Slovenia, Spain, Sweden, Switzerland, Taiwan Province of China, UK, and, US. Among these economies, UNCTAD does not have FDI statistics for Puerto Rico and San Marino. Economies denominates as offshore financial centers by the International Monetary Fund (IMF, 2014) are Andorra, Anguilla, Aruba, Bahamas, Belize, Bermuda, British Virgin Islands, Cayman Islands, Cook Islands, Cyprus, Gibraltar, Guernsey, Isle of Man, Jersey, Liechtenstein, Macao, Malaysia, Monaco, Montserrat, Netherlands Antilles, Palau, Panama, Samoa, Seychelles, Turks and Caicos, and Vanuatu. Economies identified as the top pass-through centers by Damgaard, Elkjaer, & Johannesen (2018) are Bermuda, British Virgin Islands, Cayman Islands, Ireland, Hong Kong, Luxembourg, Netherlands, and Singapore.

The statistics also reveal insights that require a more nuanced discussion. The substantial increases in outward FDI from emerging economies are not as impressive when the destinations of such foreign investment are investigated. Taking the BRIC economies (Brazil, Russia, India, and China) (O'Neill, Wilson, Purushothaman, & Stupnytsk, 2005) as an example, the analysis of the main destinations and sources of FDI provides some indication of apparent round-tripping of FDI. Table 12.2 provides the top three destinations and sources of FDI stocks. Countries with supportive tax conditions and financial services industries appear among the top countries of destination and source of FDI. For instance, for Brazil, the Cayman Islands is the second leading destination, while the Netherlands is the third destination and the primary source of FDI stock. For China, Hong Kong and the British Virgin Islands are the first and second most important destinations and sources of FDI stock, while the Cayman Islands are the third top destination. In India, Mauritius appears as the second-largest destination and top source of FDI stock, and Singapore and the Netherlands are the first and third destinations. Finally, Cyprus, Netherlands, and the British Virgin Islands are the first, second, and third destinations and sources of FDI stock for Russia. Nevertheless, it should be noted that emerging-market firms are not the only ones taking advantage of low tax and transparency jurisdictions. The top advanced economies, namely France, Germany, Japan, the UK, and the US, have the Netherlands among the top three destinations and sources of FDI stock.

Country-level statistics mask much of the success that these firms have experienced. A number of EMNEs have not only become some of the largest publicly traded firms in the world but they have also become global leaders in their industries. A few examples of such remarkable EMNEs include the Thai seafood company Thai Union, the Mexican bakery goods company Bimbo, the Argentina seamless tubes producer Tenaris, the Chinese telecommunication equipment maker Huawei, or the Brazilian iron ore miner Vale. Other remarkable EMNEs have acquired top brands in advanced countries. Examples include the Turkish food conglomerate Yildiz Holding buying the US company

Table 12.2 Top three destinations and sources of FDI stocks in BRIC countries

	Destination (percentage of total)	Source (percentage of total)
Brazil	Austria (21), Cayman Islands (16.1), Netherlands (11.0)	Netherlands (28.5), US (15.2), Spain (10.9)
China	Hong Kong (57.6), British Virgin Islands (5.8), Cayman Islands (5.7)	Hong Kong (44.1), British Virgin Islands (9.6), US (6.6)
India	Singapore (26.9), Mauritius (15.5), Netherlands (13.9)	Mauritius (26.5), UK (16.3), US (14.9)
Russia	Cyprus (37.4), Netherlands (15.9), British Virgin Islands (11.5)	Cyprus (30.3), Netherlands (12.0), British Virgin Islands (9.9)

Source: Computed using data from UNCTAD (2019).

Godiva Chocolate; the Chinese automobile manufacturer Geely acquiring the Swedish carmaker Volvo; the Indian conglomerate Tata purchasing the British carmakers Jaguar and Land Rover as well as the renowned tea company Tetley; the Qatari Qatar Holdings purchasing the British retailer Harrods; or the Brazilian investment fund 3G Capital acquiring the US restaurant chain Burger King and food firms Heinz and Kraft and as well as the Canadian restaurant chain Tim Hortons.

Challenges to Traditional Models of Internationalization

This rapid and wide global expansion of EMNEs has somewhat taken academics by surprise because it did not fit well with the traditional models of the multinational. This is because some traditional models assume that for firms to be able to invest abroad, they have to reach levels of international competitiveness that are tightly associated with the development of the home country. For instance, the investment development path model (Dunning, 1981) argues that FDI evolves with the level of development of the country. It predicts that emerging economies are mostly recipients of FDI because they have growing markets and abundant and inexpensive factors of production that make them attractive to foreign investors from more advanced economies; at the same time, emerging-market firms are not sophisticated enough to be able to invest abroad. Only when countries reach a mid-level of development, are domestic firms able to upgrade their competitiveness and benefit from improvements in the innovation system and from the experience of serving wealthier and more demanding local consumers. This enables them to invest abroad and become multinationals. However, in recent times, many emerging-market firms do not seem to follow this pattern. Many are becoming multinationals even when their home countries are still underdeveloped, challenging the notion that firms have to learn to be internationally competitive from serving demanding customers at home before they are good enough to serve sophisticated customers abroad.

Other models expect firms to expand to countries similar to the home country, which enables them to transfer and use their sources of advantage more easily. For instance, the incremental internationalization model (Johanson & Vahlne, 1977) proposes that firms expand abroad sequentially. Managers select countries that are similar to the home country to be able to use most of the knowledge and experience gained in the home country. Firms are expected to start with small international investments to limit exposure to the host economy and risk of failure until they learn how to serve customers and operate effectively in the host country. As managers gain experience in a foreign country, they increase their level of investment and venture their firms into countries that are more different from the home country. However, this pattern of expansion does not seem to fit well with what firms from emerging markets were doing recently. Many are expanding into advanced countries, which are very different from their home countries and using high-commitment entry modes such as cross-border mergers and acquisitions (Cui & Aulakh, 2019). This has required the adaptation of the incremental internationalization process model to explain EMNEs (Meyer, 2014; Meyer & Thaijongrak, 2013; Santangelo, 2020). For example, Santangelo and Meyer (2017) extend the incremental internationalization process model to explain non-linear and discontinuous dynamics of internationalization processes by distinguishing between path-continuing and path-breaking resource commitment and relating them to a firm's exposure to risk, as well as the firm's embeddedness in the business ecosystem and the volatility of the home-country environment.

New Models of Internationalization

The conflict between the internationalization of EMNEs and the traditional theoretical models of the multinational resulted in the introduction of new models that aimed to provide more accurate theoretical explanations of the observed reality of these firms' strategies. For example, the Linkage, Leverage, and Learning (LLL) model discussed by Mathews (2006) proposes that emerging-market firms do not follow the Ownership, Location, and Internalization (OLI) model introduced by Dunning (1977). In the OLI model, a firm becomes a multinational when it has ownership advantages (controlling resources and capabilities than competitors lack), internalization advantages (being better at investing abroad and managing the cross-border transactions than by using contracts), and location advantages (benefiting from doing activities in other countries). The LLL model argues that emerging-market firms suffer from disadvantages from the underdevelopment of their home economies that lead them to use different sources of advantage in their internationalization. Specifically, they are expected to create "Linkages" to other firms to obtain external advantages, have an outward orientation, and sometimes expand abroad to obtain strategic assets. They "Leverage" their relationships with strategic partners and use their networks strategically to acquire resources. Finally, they "Learn" and create advantages from repetition and continuous improvement.

Another model explaining the internationalization of emerging-market firms is the Springboard model introduced by Luo and Tung (2007, 2018). This model uses the metaphor of jumping from a springboard as an explanation of how emerging-market firms use aggressive and high-risk modes of entry, such as acquisitions, to gain access to critical resources, generally those of advanced-economy firms, and compensate for the limited competitiveness of their home operations. EMNEs entering advanced economies using acquisitions runs counter to the incremental internationalization model (Johanson & Valhne, 1977); rather than markets, these firms are searching for resources that enable them to upgrade their home-country operations to become more credible global competitors.

A general framework termed the New Model of the Multinational discussed by Guillen and Garcia-Canal (2009) explains how, in contrast to the experience of firms from advanced economies discussed in the OLI and incremental internationalization models, EMNEs are internationalizing more quickly and widely. This is despite having significant constraints on their competitive advantage as a result of the underdevelopment of their home markets in the provision of sophisticated inputs, technologies, and skilled labor. EMNEs use alliances and acquisitions of firms from advanced economies to obtain more sophisticated capabilities. They also rely on organizational and political capabilities to achieve protection and support in their home economies that enable their internationalization.

Finally, the non-sequential internationalization model introduced by Cuervo-Cazurra (2011) argues that EMNEs do not have to follow the prediction of the incremental internationalization model in which firms invest first in countries similar to the home country and different countries later. Instead, they have two alternatives that reflect a dichotomy of benefits. On the one hand, EMNEs can choose countries that are similar to their home country, such as other emerging countries, in which they can use much of their knowledge and advantages, but many of these markets do not offer substantial market opportunities. On the other hand, firms from emerging markets can choose to invest in different countries, such as advanced ones, which offer better market opportunities, even if they may not be able to use much of their knowledge and sources of an advantage there.

New Concepts in Internationalization

The analysis of firms in emerging markets and their international competitiveness has resulted in the identification of novel ideas that have helped expand and refine our understanding of how firms operate across borders. Some propose new theoretical frameworks for analyzing firm strategy. For example, Khanna and Palepu (1997, 2010) introduce the concept of institutional voids to reflect how the underdevelopment of pro-market institutions in emerging economies result in firms that diversify to become business groups. Some of these firms are later restructured and become multinationals, with the affiliation to the business group supporting their international expansion (Guillen, 2002). Building on the importance of institutions, Peng (2002) and Meyer, Estrin, Bhaumik, & Peng (2009) propose the institution-based view as an explanation of how differences across countries influence the ability of firms to compete, complementing the resource-based explanation of competitive advantage that rests on the control of resources and capabilities discussed by Barney (1991) and the competition-based view that is based on the dominance of the industry explained by Porter (1985). Some companies can even develop an institution-based advantage (Martin, 2014) that enables them to outcompete other firms because they have a superior ability in their management of institutions and institutional differences.

Other scholars introduce concepts that are considered to explain better particular strategies of firms from emerging markets. For example, Cuervo-Cazurra and Genc (2008) discuss the idea that emerging-market firms convert institutional disadvantages into advantages. They propose that these firms suffer from operating in home countries with poor-quality institutions that limit their competitiveness. However, EMNEs can use their experience of operating in such conditions in other countries that also have weak institutions, gaining an advantage against advanced-economy multinationals, which are less accustomed to dealing with poor-quality institutions. Madhok and

Keyhani (2012) introduce the concept of the liability of emergingness to explain how firms from emerging economies suffer from an additional source of liability because the underdevelopment of their home country reduces their competitiveness and results in additional discrimination abroad. To remedy the liability of emergingness, EMNEs acquire firms from advanced economies and integrate their more sophisticated resources and capabilities with their home operations. Barnard (2014) proposes the concept of migrating multinationals to explain the movement of headquarters from emerging to advanced economies. Some firms aim to escape the negative association with originating in an emerging country by relocating headquarters to an advanced-economy and claiming that country as their domicile. Govindarajan and Ramamurti (2011) suggest the concept of reverse innovation. Some firms in emerging markets have created frugal innovations designed to meet the needs of the large segment of poorer consumers there (Asakawa, Cuervo-Cazurra, & Un, 2019). Some of these frugal innovations can be transferred and used in advanced economies, becoming reverse innovations.

The Underdevelopment of the Home Country and the Internationalization of Emerging-Market Firms

The analysis of the internationalization of firms from emerging markets has resulted in new models and concepts that have contributed to a better understanding of global strategy, but there are still many opportunities for deepening our understanding of these firms. These are driven by the analysis of what makes EMNEs different from multinationals from advanced economies traditionally studied in the literature: the underdevelopment of their home country and the role this plays in internationalization. The notion that the home country affects the internationalization of companies is a relatively recent focus of the literature (see articles in the special issue edited by Cuervo-Cazurra et al., 2018). Nevertheless, despite the continued focus on this relationship, there are still plenty of opportunities for contributing to a deeper understanding of EMNEs.

We outline four opportunities for further research based on a classification of themes illustrated in Table 12.3. The table separates topics based on two dimensions. One is the distinguishing characteristics used to classify economies as emerging: their lower level of economic development, which reflects the usual lower level of income and underdevelopment of the infrastructure; and the lower quality of their institutions, which points to the more challenging political, regulatory, and contract resolution conditions of many emerging economies. The other dimension is the influence of the country conditions on the drivers of internationalization: an innovation driver in which the underdevelopment of the country leads firms to create innovations that support their foreign expansion; or an escape driver in which the underdevelopment of the country induces firms to escape to other countries to remedy its negative impact on them.

Table 12.3 The impact of the underdeveloped economy and institutions on emerging-market firms' internationalization

		Internationalization driver	
		Innovation-based	Escape-based
Country characteristic	Underdeveloped economy	Frugal innovations	Upgrading escape
	Underdeveloped institutions	Contractual innovations	Institutional escape

Source: Adapted from Cuervo-Cazurra and Ramamurti (2017).

Frugal Innovations and the Internationalization of Emerging-Market Firms

Emerging-market firms can internationalize using frugal innovations created in response to the large segment of poor people that typifies emerging economies. Emerging markets tend to have a vast base of the pyramid, that is, the bottom of the income pyramid with individuals that earn less than US$1500 a year in power purchasing parity (Prahalad, 2004). Whereas some firms see this as a challenge for their growth because there are lots of consumers with very low income, others consider such segments as a source of profits once they innovate their products and services to make them affordable, that is, once they create frugal innovations. This frugality-based advantage (Asakawa et al., 2019) induces firms not just to modify and adapt existing products to minimize production costs so that consumers can afford them but rather to innovate business models and products that provide maximum value for a low price point. These frugal innovations can challenge the assumption that multinationals need to rely on a supportive national innovation system (Freeman, 1995) to become internationally competitive since some emerging-market firms create sophisticated innovation despite the unsupportive home-country environment. These innovations can then be the base for the internationalization of emerging-market firms in other emerging markets in which there is a large segment of the population with low income and considerable profit potential for the innovating firms. The frugal innovations could even be used to enter advanced economies because they offer higher value at a lower price, becoming reverse innovations (Govindarajan & Ramamurti, 2011).

Contractual Innovations and the Internationalization of Emerging-Market Firms

Managers in emerging economies create contractual innovations to address the challenge of operating in low-quality institutions and use these contractual innovations in the internationalization of their firms. Emerging-market firms have a lesser ability to rely on external contract dispute mechanisms because, in emerging economies, the judicial systems are overburdened and inefficient and, in some cases, politicized. Nevertheless, companies establish contracts with others. How emerging-market firms contract and enforce those contracts can provide useful insights into the internalization of cross-border transactions (Buckley & Casson, 1976; Hennart, 1982). Much of this literature focuses on the transaction rather than the firm (Hennart, 2009), but the study of EMNEs can help connect the home country to the transactions in the host country via the particular contractual mechanisms that emerging-market firms develop. The inability to rely on a supportive institutional environment induces managers to build social networks of reciprocity, such as *guanxi* (Luo, Huang, & Wang, 2012) that facilitate contractual relationships, and use such networks in their foreign expansion. EMNEs can also rely on social networks of migrants that facilitate the mutual understanding and exert social controls over potential misbehavior among contractual partners. The limitations in contracts also induce managers of emerging-market firms to have more control within the value chain to avoid hold-up situations with suppliers and distribution partners. This desire for control at home can be carried over in the internationalization of their firms, with the companies using full or majority control of foreign operations with more frequency than their advanced-economy counterparts.

Upgrading Escape and the Internationalization of Emerging-Market Firms

Emerging-market companies internationalize as part of their upgrading escape in search of more sophisticated technologies and marketing skills that can help them improve the competitiveness of their home-country operations. The underdevelopment of the innovation systems in emerging economies in comparison to those of advanced economies (Furman, Porter, & Stern, 2002) means that many firms suffer in their development of sophisticated technologies that hamper the global competitiveness of their products (Awate, Larsen, & Mudambi, 2012). Thus, these firms resort to escaping the home country and internationalizing in search of more sophisticated technologies that can help them improve their home-market operations. They can do this by acquiring firms in advanced economies not only to obtain the more advanced technologies (Madhok & Keyhani, 2012) but also to access the innovation systems of advanced economies and obtain tacit knowledge on the latest technological developments. This upgrading escape is not just a technological one. It can also take the form of marketing escape, in which emerging-market firms seek to avoid the connection with the home country and the usual discrimination that products generated in emerging markets suffer from due to the poor country image (Peterson & Jolibert, 1995). Thus, EMNEs purchase brands in advanced economies to reduce the association with the home country and upgrade their marketing capabilities, using the knowledge of the advanced-economy firms to improve the image of the emerging-market companies and their products.

Institutional Escape and the Internationalization of Emerging-Market Firms

Some firms in emerging markets escape their home countries as a solution to the low institutional quality they face at home. This idea of escape is usually associated with companies seeking to invest in countries to reduce the tax burden or to access a larger finance pool in nations with more developed capital markets (Coffee Jr, 2002; Witt & Lewin, 2007). However, such investments in search of reductions in the tax burden and access to abundant finance are a driver of the internationalization of firms from advanced countries as well as from emerging ones. Different from this idea, emerging-market firms follow an institutional escape to compensate for the low quality of the institutions in which they operate, and which tend to limit their international competitiveness. Thus, EMNEs invest in countries in which they can establish better contractual relationships with other companies, becoming bound by the superior institutional framework of those locations and helping reduce the perceptions of poor governance of firms originating from emerging economies (Siegel, 2009). They can also move headquarters to countries with better institutions to reduce the association with the country of origin and subsequent firm and product discrimination. This is the case of migrating multinationals (Barnard, 2014) that not only invest in countries with better quality institutions but actually move their headquarters there to dissociate their connection with their less reputable home countries.

CONCLUDING REMARKS

In this chapter, we reviewed the internationalization of emerging-market firms. This revealed how new theoretical models were introduced in contraposition to previous traditional theories, because the latter do not take into account the underdevelopment of the home country and its effect on the internationalization of firms. The traditional models of the multinational were based on the experience of European and US firms. Researchers analyzed and generalized from these experiences to explain the internationalization of all firms, implicitly assuming that the home country provided supportive conditions (macroeconomic stability, pro-market institutions, advanced capital markets, sophisticated national innovation systems, educated workforce and so on) that facilitated foreign expansion. The literature on emerging-market firms has questioned many of the assumptions associated with a supportive home country as EMNEs have expanded abroad—with some even becoming global leaders—despite originating from underdeveloped home countries. This has required a reconceptualization of the models explaining how firms internationalize when they do not have the supporting home conditions that characterize advanced economies.

In our discussion, we reflected on the future of the research on EMNEs and outlined potential topics of study that build on the influence of a multinational's home-country underdevelopment. The uniqueness of emerging-market firms is their home country.

There are many characteristics in their internationalization that are common to firms from advanced economies, such as the influence of the industry, the advances in technologies and integration of economies, and their early stage of internationalization (Ramamurti, 2012). It is the underdevelopment of the economic and institutional conditions of the home country that results in different drivers of internationalization of emerging-market firms: frugal innovation, contractual innovation, upgrading innovation, and institutional innovation. These ideas that we put forward respond to calls for contextualizing internationalization business research (see Delios, 2016; Teagarden, Von Glinow, & Mellahi, 2018), to be able to identify commonalities and differences in firms' behavior and decisions. Since international business theories are context-sensitive, research in emerging economies remains attractive for testing concepts and developing new models that can help us improve and refine our understanding of international business strategies.

ACKNOWLEDGEMENTS

We thank the editors and reviewers for useful suggestions for improvement on previous versions of the manuscript. We also thank the Ministry of Science and Innovation of Spain research grant PID2019-106874GB-I00/AEI/10.13039/501100011033.

REFERENCES

Alpargatas, 2019. *History*. http://www.alpargatas.com.ar/en.html#know-the-company/history. Accessed 13 September 2019.

Asakawa, K., Cuervo-Cazurra, A., & Un, C. A. 2019. Frugality-based advantage. *Long Range Planning*, 52(4): 101879.

Aulakh, P. S. 2007. Emerging multinationals from developing economies: Motivations, paths and performance. *Journal of International Management*, 3(13): 235–240.

Awate, S., Larsen, M. M., & Mudambi, R. 2012. EMNE catch-up strategies in the wind turbine industry: Is there a trade-off between output and innovation capabilities? *Global Strategy Journal*, 2(3): 205–223.

Barnard, H. 2014. Migrating EMNCs and the theory of the multinational. In A. Cuervo-Cazurra, & R. Ramamurti (Eds.), *Understanding Multinationals from Emerging Markets*. Cambridge: Cambridge University Press.

Barney, J. B. 1991. Firm resources and sustained competitive advantage. *Journal of Management*, 17(1): 99–120.

Buckley, P., & Casson, M. 1976. *The Future of the Multinational Enterprise*. London: Macmillan.

Coffee Jr, J. C. 2002. Racing towards the top: The impact of cross-listings and stock market competition on international corporate. *Columbia Law Review*, 102: 1757–1831.

Cuervo-Cazurra, A. 2012. How the analysis of developing country multinational companies helps advance theory: Solving the Goldilocks debate. *Global Strategy Journal*, 2(3): 153–167.

Cuervo-Cazurra, A. 2011. Selecting the country in which to start internationalization: The non-sequential internationalization argument. *Journal of World Business*, 46(4): 426–437.

Cuervo-Cazurra, A., & Genc, M. 2008. Transforming disadvantages into advantages: Developing country MNEs in the least developed countries. *Journal of International Business Studies*, 39(6): 957–979.

Cuervo-Cazurra, A., Luo, Y., Ramamurti, R., & Ang, S. H. 2018. The impact of the home country on internationalization. *Journal of World Business*, 53(5): 593–604.

Cuervo-Cazurra, A., Mudambi, R., & Pedersen, T. 2017. Globalization: Rising skepticism. *Global Strategy Journal*, 7(2): 155–158.

Cuervo-Cazurra, A., & Ramamurti, R. 2017. Home country underdevelopment and internationalization: Innovation-based and escape-based internationalization. *Competitiveness Review*, 27(3): 217–230.

Cuervo-Cazurra, A., & Ramamurti, R. 2014. *Understanding Multinationals from Emerging Markets*. Cambridge: Cambridge University Press.

Cui, L., & Aulakh, P. S. 2019. Emerging economy multinationals in advanced economies. In R. Grosse, & K. E. Meyer (Eds.), *Oxford Handbook of Management in Emerging Markets*. Oxford: Oxford University Press.

Damgaard, J., Elkjaer, T., & Johannesen, N. 2018. Piercing the veil. *Finance and Development*, 55(2): 50–53.

Delios, A. 2016. The death and rebirth (?) of international business research. *Journal of Management Studies*, 54(3): 391–397.

Demirbag, M., & Yaprak, A. 2015. Introduction: The rise of internationalizing firms from emerging markets. In: M. Demirbag, & A. Yaprak (Eds.), *Handbook of Emerging Market Multinational Corporations*. London: Edward Elgar Publishing.

Dunning, J. H. 1977. Trade, location of economic activity and the MNE: A search for an eclectic approach. In B. Ohlin, P. O. Hesselborn, & P. M. Wijkman (Eds.), *The International Allocation of Economic Activity*. London: Palgrave Macmillan.

Dunning, J. H. 1981. Explaining the international direct investment position of countries: towards a dynamic and development approach. *Weltwirtschaftliches Archiv*, 117(1): 30–64.

Freeman, C. 1995. The "national system of innovation" in historical perspective. *Cambridge Journal of Economics*, 19(1): 5–24.

Furman, J. L., Porter, M. E., & Stern, S. 2002. The determinants of national innovative capacity. *Research Policy*, 31(6): 899–933.

Gammeltoft, P., Barnard, H., & Madhok, A. 2010. Emerging multinationals, emerging theory: Macro-and micro-level perspectives. *Journal of International Management*, 16(2): 95–101.

Ghemawat, P., & Khanna, T. 1998. The nature of diversified business groups: A research design and two case studies. *Journal of Industrial Economics*, 46(1): 35–61.

Govindarajan, V., & Ramamurti, R. 2011. Reverse innovation, emerging markets, and global strategy. *Global Strategy Journal*, 1(3–4): 191–205.

Grosse, R., & Meyer, K. E. 2019. Conceptual approaches to managing in emerging markets. In R. Grosse, & K. E. Meyer (Eds.), *The Oxford Handbook of Management in Emerging Markets*. Oxford: Oxford University Press.

Guillen, M. F. 2002. Structural inertia, imitation, and foreign expansion: South Korean firms and business groups in China, 1987–1995. *Academy of Management Journal*, 45(3): 509–525.

Guillen, M. F., & García-Canal, E. 2009. The American model of the multinational firm and the "new" multinationals from emerging economies. *Academy of Management Perspectives*, 23(2): 23–35.

Hennart, J. F. 2009. Down with MNE-centric theories! Market entry and expansion as the bundling of MNE and local assets. *Journal of International Business Studies*, 40(9): 1432–1454.

Hennart, J. F. 1982. *A Theory of Multinational Enterprise*. Ann Arbor: University of Michigan Press.

Hernandez, E., & Guillen, M. F. 2018. What's theoretically novel about emerging-market multinationals? *Journal of International Business Studies*, 49(1), 24–33.

IMF, 2018. *Database—WEO groups and aggregates information*. https://www.imf.org/external/pubs/ft/weo/2018/02/weodata/groups.htm. Accessed 17 December 2018.

IMF, 2014. *Offshore financial centers (OFCs): IMF staff assessments*. https://www.imf.org/external/NP/ofca/OFCA.aspx. Accessed 13 September 2018.

Johanson, J., & Vahlne, J. E. 1977. The internationalization process of the firm: A model of knowledge development and increasing foreign market commitments. *Journal of International Business Studies*, 8(1): 23–32.

Khanna, T., & Palepu, K. G. 2010. *Winning in Emerging Markets: A Road Map for Strategy and Execution*. Boston, MA: Harvard University Press.

Khanna, T., & Palepu, K. G. 1997. Why focused strategies may be wrong for emerging markets. *Harvard Business Review*, 75(4): 41–51.

Luo, Y., Huang, Y., & Wang, S. L. 2012. Guanxi and organizational performance: A meta-analysis. *Management and Organization Review*, 8(1): 139–172.

Luo, Y., & Tung, R. L. 2018. A general theory of springboard MNEs. *Journal of International Business Studies*, 49(2): 129–152.

Luo, Y., & Tung, R. L. 2007. International expansion of emerging market enterprises: A springboard perspective. *Journal of International Business Studies*, 38(4): 481–498.

Madhok, A., & Keyhani, M. 2012. Acquisitions as entrepreneurship: Asymmetries, opportunities, and the internationalization of multinationals from emerging economies. *Global Strategy Journal*, 2(1): 26–40.

Martin, X. 2014. Institutional advantage. *Global Strategy Journal*, 4(1): 55–69.

Mathews, J. A. 2006. Dragon multinationals: New players in 21st century globalization. *Asia Pacific Journal of Management*, 23(1): 5–27.

Meyer, K. E. 2014. Process perspectives on the growth of merging economy multinationals. In A. Cuervo-Cazurra, & R. Ramamurti (Eds.), *Understanding Multinationals from Emerging Markets*. Cambridge: Cambridge University Press.

Meyer, K. E., Estrin, S., Bhaumik, S. K., & Peng, M. W. 2009. Institutions, resources, and entry strategies in emerging economies. *Strategic Management Journal*, 30(1): 61–80.

Meyer, K. E., & Thaijongrak, O. 2013. The dynamics of emerging economy MNEs: How the internationalization process model can guide future research. *Asia Pacific Journal of Management*, 30(4), 1125–1153.

O'Neill, J., Wilson, D., Purushothaman, R., & Stupnytska, A. 2005. How solid are the BRICs? *Goldman Sachs Global Economics Paper No. 134*.

Peng, M. W. 2002. Towards an institution-based view of business strategy. *Asia Pacific Journal of Management*, 19(2–3), 251–267.

Peterson, R. A., & Jolibert, A. J. P. 1995. A meta-analysis of country-of-origin effects. *Journal of International Business Studies*, 26(4): 883–900.

Porter, M. E. 1985. *Competitive Advantage: Creating and Sustaining Superior Performance*. New York: FreePress.

Prahalad, C. K. 2004. *The Fortune at the Bottom of the Pyramid: Eradicating Poverty through Profits*. Philadelphia, PA: Wharton Business School Press.

Ramamurti, R. 2012. What is really different about emerging market multinationals? *Global Strategy Journal*, 2(1): 41–47.

Ramamurti, R., & Hillemann, J. 2018. What is "Chinese" about Chinese multinationals? *Journal of International Business Studies*, 49(1): 34–48.

Santangelo, G. 2021. Internationalization process perspectives: Revisiting the link between market knowledge and market commitment. In K. Mellahi, K. Meyer, R. Narula, I. Surdu, & A. Verbeke (Eds.). *The Oxford Handbook of International Business Strategy*. Oxford: Oxford University Press.

Santangelo, G., & Meyer, K. E. 2017. Internationalization as an evolutionary process. *Journal of International Business Studies*, 48(9): 1114–1130.

Siegel, J. 2009. Is there a better commitment mechanism than cross-listings for emerging-economy firms? Evidence from Mexico. *Journal of International Business Studies*, 40(7): 1171–1191.

Teagarden, M. B., Von Glinow, M., & Mellahi, K. 2018. Contextualizing international business research: Enhancing rigor and relevance. *Journal of World Business*, 53(3): 303–306.

UNCTAD, 2019. *Bilateral FDI Statistics*. https://unctad.org/en/Pages/DIAE/FDI percent-20Statistics/FDI-Statistics-Bilateral.aspx. Accessed 13 September 2019.

UNCTAD, 2018. *UNCTADStat*. http://unctadstat.unctad.org/wds/ReportFolders/report-Folders.aspx. Accessed 17 December 2018.

Williamson, P., Ramamurti, R., Fleury, A., & Fleury, M. T. L. 2013. Introduction. In P. Williamson, R. Ramamurti, A. Fleury, & M. T. L. Fleury (Eds.), *The Competitive Advantage of Emerging Market Multinationals*. Cambridge: Cambridge University Press.

Witt, M. A., & Lewin, A. Y. 2007. Outward foreign direct investment as escape response to home country institutional constraints. *Journal of International Business Studies*, 38(4): 579–594.

Yergin, D., & Stanislaw, J. 2002. *The Commanding Heights: The Battle for the World Economy*. Simon and Schuster.

CHAPTER 13

STATE-OWNED MULTINATIONAL ENTERPRISES

Theory, Performance, and Impact

SAUL ESTRIN, JING LI, AND DANIEL M. SHAPIRO

INTRODUCTION

THERE is a growing body of literature on the emergence of the state-owned multinational enterprise (SOMNE) (Balbuena, 2016; Cuervo-Cazurra, 2018a, 2018b; Cuervo-Cazurra, Inkpen, Musacchio, & Ramaswamy, 2014; Lazzarini & Musacchio, 2018; Musacchio & Lazzarini, 2014). State-owned enterprises (SOEs) not only operate internationally, but their ownership has become more heterogeneous, with state ownership ranging from partial to full commitment in international markets as many SOEs list and trade on stock markets (Cuervo-Cazurra et al., 2014; UNCTAD, 2017). SOMNEs have been traditionally rare and found mostly in the extractive industries (Aharoni, 2018; Musacchio & Lazzarini, 2018), however, their recent growth and especially their increased internationalization has driven scholars to seek to understand the nature and significance of their international activities. As noted by Aharoni (2018), the rise of the SOMNE, and in particular those from emerging markets, is not straightforwardly consistent with international business (IB) theory, in which MNEs are characterized by the ownership of valuable intangible knowledge assets (Buckley & Casson, 2009). As such, SOEs are argued to suffer from a *liability of stateness* (Musacchio, Lazzarini, & Aguilera, 2015), whereby they find themselves at a competitive disadvantage relative to privately-owned firms (POEs). This would imply that SOEs do not possess the capabilities to expand abroad. Thus, any understanding of the SOMNE must begin with an understanding of what is meant by an SOE and whether there is, indeed, a liability of stateness. In examining this, the chapter concludes that the theory and evidence in support of a general liability of stateness is inconclusive and context dependent.

We consider and discuss the international strategies of SOMNEs. The IB literature proposes that any company operating abroad must overcome the *liability of foreignness*: the costs associated with operating in a different market (Zaheer, 1995); we explain that multinational enterprises (MNEs) often do this by bringing compensating advantages developed at home. We situate the SOMNE both within the theory of the MNE and the theory of the SOE. We conclude that theory must account for both the role and objectives of the home state in facilitating outbound investment and the role of domestic institutions in providing access to relevant resources. We emphasize the need to incorporate a clear understanding of the nature of "state capitalism" (Estrin, Liang, Shapiro, & Carney, 2019; Finchelstein, 2017; Mariotti & Marzano, 2019; Musacchio & Lazzarini, 2014; Musacchio et al., 2015). With specific reference to emerging markets, we point to the need to fully understand home country institutions, including the form of state ownership (Bruton et al., 2015; He, Chakrabarty, & Eden, 2016); the nature and quality of formal and informal institutions (Estrin, Meyer, Nielsen, & Nielsen, 2016; Hong, Wang, & Kafouros, 2015; Wang, Hong, Kafouros, & Wright, 2012); and the importance and impact of different home country diplomatic and political goals (Cuervo-Cazurra et al., 2014; Li, Newenham-Kahindi, Shapiro, & Chen, 2013; Li, Xia, Shapiro, & Lin, 2018b; Shapiro, Vecino, & Li, 2018b).

Through the introduction of state political goals into our assessment, we posit that SOMNEs may face an additional liability of foreignness arising from legitimacy concerns in the host market (Cuervo-Cazurra, 2018a; Cuervo-Cazurra et al., 2014; Cui & Jiang, 2012; Globerman & Shapiro, 2009; Meyer, Ding, Li, & Zhang, 2014). We refer to this as the *liability of legitimacy* and argue that it may result in additional regulatory and administrative costs being imposed on SOMNEs (Aharoni, 2018; Cuervo-Cazurra, 2018a; Shapiro & Globerman, 2012). Thus, we propose that SOMNEs potentially confront a double challenge abroad, requiring them to overcome both a liability of foreignness and a liability of legitimacy.

Overall, this rather daunting list of obstacles to the internationalization of SOMNEs suggests it is important to identify the factors that allow these firms to overcome them. We survey some of the recent empirical literature relating to why, how, and where SOEs invest abroad, and whether they are successful.

We find that, while on average SOEs are less likely to pursue international strategies (Li et al., 2018b; Tihanyi et al., 2019), outcomes are highly context specific: there is an emergence of SOMNEs when home country state and institutions are supportive, and when the ownership structure is appropriate. That is, there are conditions under which SOMNEs overcome the liability of stateness, albeit not always through the ownership of intangible knowledge assets. There is also evidence that SOMNE location and entry mode decisions are different from those of other MNEs, both because SOMNEs are less risk averse and because they confront a liability of legitimacy. We propose that future research may focus on identifying other mechanisms that support the international strategies of SOEs.

How Prevalent are Somnes?

Defining the SOE

An SOE is a corporate entity in which the state exercises control through its ownership (OECD, 2015); SOMNEs are SOEs that engage in international commercial activities (OECD, 2017). However, these simple definitions obscure a number of more finely grained specifics (Cuervo-Cazurra et al., 2014). First, there is the issue of whether the SOE is a legally separate entity, or simply a directly controlled arm of the state apparatus; the latter arrangements were common in the former Soviet Union and Western Europe prior to the 1980s (Estrin, Hanousek, Kočenda, & Svejnar, 2009). Even when the organization is a separate legal entity, there remain questions about who the owner is, and what ownership stake is required to yield "state ownership." The ownership can be direct by government agencies or indirect via shares held by state-owned banks, state-owned pension funds, other state-owned firms, or sovereign wealth funds (SWFs).

In practice, many SOEs have been partially privatized, so that the shareholding register may include both state and private shareholders. If the state is one shareholder amongst many, at what point does a firm become state owned? For example, minority state ownership concentrated in the hands of a single state agency may be sufficient to provide control if private ownership is dispersed, so that even with a minority stake the state may be able to enforce its objectives on the organization. For these reasons, SOEs are characterized as hybrid organizations with a variety of ownership structures (Bruton et al., 2015).[1] Fully incorporated entities represent some 92 percent of all SOEs, around half of which are listed on stock exchanges. Moreover, among SOMNEs, 63 percent are wholly or majority owned by the state (see Kalotay, 2018).

Furthermore, whole or majority state ownership may not fully capture the influence of the state. For example, Rodrigues and Dieleman (2018) highlighted the case of the Brazilian MNE Vale, where the government, although a minority owner, created a majority block to oust the CEO by joining forces with state pension funds and banks. Thus, Shapiro and Globerman (2012) proposed that *state-influenced enterprises* should be considered as a distinct category.

The Scale and Distribution of SOEs and SOMNEs

Although SOEs constitute a relatively small proportion of firms, even in "state capitalist" emerging economies (Estrin et al., 2019; Musacchio & Lazzarini, 2014), they are often

[1] The OECD (2017) proposes that firms with state shareholdings of more than 10 percent are SOEs. They identify four categories: majority-owned listed entities; minority-owned listed entities; majority-owned non-listed entities; and statutory corporations and quasi-corporations.

very large firms with significant international operations. Thus, UNCTAD (2017) identifies approximately 1,500 SOMNEs, which represents only 1.5 percent of the total number of MNEs. However, SOMNEs account for 15 percent of the top 100 non-financial MNEs (by assets) and they have almost 10 percent of the total affiliates (86,000). These larger SOMNEs are also disproportionately based in emerging markets; more than half (63 percent) are headquartered in emerging markets and 41 percent of the largest emerging economy MNEs (ranked by foreign assets) are state owned, notably based in China, Malaysia, South Africa, and Russia (Kalotay, 2018; Rygh, 2019).

OECD (2017) provides SOE information for forty countries, including some of the larger emerging markets such as China, India, and Brazil. SOEs and SOMNEs are particularly important in China; more specifically, China accounts for more than 51,000 of the total 54,000 SOEs. China is also home to some 17.5 percent of SOMNEs, which is about the same as the total of the five next largest home countries, all in developing or transition countries (Kalotay, 2018). The particular significance of China in the internationalization of SOEs is highlighted by the fact that thirteen of the top twenty SOMNEs (by assets) are from China (UNCTAD, 2017). There are no firms from developing economies except the five from China in the top thirty SOMNEs (UNCTAD, 2017), all either in the utilities or natural resources sectors.

This brief summary of the evidence has highlighted a few important issues that researchers interested in SOMNEs need to take into account. Perhaps most important is the ambiguity around the terminology used, and the need to more carefully define what SOMNEs are in both theoretical and empirical work. In particular, theoretical ideas concerning the liability of stateness may not be generally valid but may only apply to a subcategory of SOMNEs. For example, ambiguity in results concerning the impact of state ownership, which have until now been largely attributed to contextual factors (Estrin et al., 2016), may also be a result of insufficiently fine-grained definitions of the SOMNE. Finally, we note that any cross-country analysis of the effects of SOEs runs the danger of being disproportionately focused on China, which represents around 95 percent of SOEs in the OECD world sample. There are strong reasons to argue that China may be a special case with respect to the scale, role, and performance of SOEs, and it is important not to generalize inappropriately from evidence based only on a single home country market such as China.

Why are SOEs Different?

Scholars usually argue that POEs will outperform SOEs in terms of efficiency and productivity, a view captured in the IB strategy literature by the "liability of stateness" (Musacchio et al., 2015). If SOEs really perform worse than their private counterparts, it would be hard to explain the ownership advantages that they are able to exploit in international markets; the liability of stateness suggests that SOEs do not possess the resources and capabilities necessary for internationalization. In this section, we explore in more depth what the literature has found about the factors leading to a liability of stateness, and whether these are, indeed, limited by certain boundary conditions.

The Relative Performance of SOEs and POEs

There are two general issues underlying the proposed inefficiency of SOEs relative to POEs (Peng, Bruton, Stan, & Huang, 2016). The first and most widely discussed problem for SOEs concerns corporate governance; specifically, it is argued that SOEs tend to be unable to provide efficient monitoring and incentive arrangements (Vickers & Yarrow, 1991). These arguments are rooted in agency theory, and its particular application to SOEs, where it is proposed that managers of SOEs have more opportunity to engage in unproductive activities because monitoring is weak, and state ownership affords fewer opportunities to put in place mechanisms to constrain such behavior. In particular, it is argued that in the absence of traded shares, SOE managers are not subject to the discipline of stock markets, nor can they be motivated by high-powered incentives (Vickers & Yarrow, 1991).

A second set of arguments focuses on objectives. The primary objective of POEs is usually considered to be profit or value maximization, whereas when the state is an owner, it may also introduce non-commercial motives (Estrin & Perotin, 1991). In practice, governments can use SOEs to achieve a variety of desired policy outcomes, such as, for example, resolving market failure or promoting economic development (Musacchio et al., 2015). Both of these would normally result in a home economy focus. The state may also use their ownership of enterprises to promote non-economic objectives of a social or political nature. For example, the ruling group in a country may use its ownership of firms to create jobs in key political regions (Tihanyi et al., 2019). Moreover, the two problems—corporate governance and conflicting objectives—may be mutually reinforcing; that is, managers may exploit the conflicts in the firm's objectives to their private benefit via rent seeking (Poczter & Musacchio, 2018).

Thus, traditional theory suggests that, relative to POEs, SOEs are inherently poorly managed and commercially inefficient organizations that are likely to underperform across a variety of measures (Boycko, Shleifer, & Vishny, 1996; Megginson, 2017; Megginson & Netter, 2001). For developed economies where institutions are relatively strong, the empirical evidence for this view is quite robust but not unambiguous. For example, Boardman and Vining (1989) found performance advantages for POEs, whereas Caves & Christensen (1980) had not. The bulk of the empirical literature has considered the related issue of privatization, and there have been numerous studies regarding the effects of privatization summarized in surveys by Megginson and Netter (2001) and later by Estrin et al. (2009).

Most of this evidence supports the view that privatization has, indeed, led to improved corporate performance, but mostly in developed market economies. In turn, results are mixed with regards to privatization in emerging and transition economies (Cuervo-Cazurra et al., 2014; Estrin & Pelletier, 2018; Tihanyi et al., 2019). This leads us to consider the role of institutional and ownership contexts.

The Effects of Changing Ownership Arrangements and Institutions

The original arguments assigning superior performance to POEs applied to the context of developed economies. However, recent evidence is not as generally supportive. There are several reasons for this. First, the SOE of the traditional governance literature is not necessarily the same as the modern state-owned corporation. As we have noted, most SOEs are now incorporated according to company law, and almost all of the larger ones are either majority or minority owned listed companies. In this situation, standard governance problems may be alleviated, although corporate performance may, instead, be negatively affected by conflicts between different owners, that is, principal-principal issues (Young et al., 2008). Conflicting objectives between principals makes it harder for the owners to agree on targets and to monitor performance, and managers may be granted leeway to pursue private gain at the expense of owners. However, the fact that the firm is quoted on the stock exchange and subject to some if not all capital market disciplines may reduce the agency problems discussed above, especially in minority-owned SOEs when private shareholders hold the majority of shares (Inoue, Lazzarini, & Musacchio, 2013).

Furthermore, the outcome also depends on the objectives of the two principals: state and private actors (Bruton et al., 2015; Musacchio et al., 2015). In cases when they are aligned—for example, when the state as owner seeks profits in the same way as private owners—principal-principal problems may not be too significant. In fact, the state as owner may actually act to alleviate some of these tensions (Heugens, Sauerwald, Turturea, & van Essen, 2019). Alternatively, if the state pursues radically different objectives to private shareholders, there is the danger that the minority shareholders, whether state or private owners, are expropriated by the majority, with potentially deleterious effects on firm performance.

The second issue concerns assumptions about institutions. The agency argument assumed effective market-supporting institutions that would favor POEs. However, this may be an oversimplification. This is because, in some institutional environments, the agency problems that bedevil the performance of SOEs may also apply to private firms (Cuervo-Cazurra et al., 2014). Even in relatively developed economies, many individual shareholders often hold too small a stake in any of these firms to be able to, or have an incentive to, bear the cost of monitoring management themselves. Moreover, mixed commercial–social objectives are no longer uniquely an issue for SOEs because POEs now routinely develop and implement social objectives as well (Globerman, Hensyel, & Shapiro, 2020).

Further, the institutional arrangements in emerging markets may also not favor POEs because institutional voids, notably in capital markets (Khanna & Palepu, 2010), may limit external governance of POEs, particularly when other critical institutions such as the rule of law and the protection of private property rights are weak (Hoskisson, Wright, Filatotchev, & Peng, 2013). Recent IB literature has argued that home country institutions will influence the performance of SOEs as well as POEs (Estrin et al., 2016).

Thus, national institutions are argued to moderate the impact of state ownership on firm performance leading to the conclusion that the stronger the institutional controls over SOEs become, the more SOE internationalization will resemble that of POEs.

Therefore, there may be an argument that SOEs can perform as well as POEs if they are designed and governed to pursue economic (profit-maximizing) objectives and if the home country institutional and governance system is favorable (Cuervo-Cazurra et al., 2014; Musacchio et al., 2015). SOEs may even outperform POEs under specific institutional conditions that lead governments to channel resources in support of long-term SOE performance. In a recent study, Estrin et al. (2019) argue that such conditions might be provided under a set of interrelated institutional and policy arrangements that are often referred to as "state capitalism" (see also Mariotti & Marzano, 2019; Musacchio & Lazzarini, 2014). In an era of state capitalism, the objectives of SOEs may be to become commercially successful national champions and or to provide access to natural resources; this means that managers will be evaluated in accordance with these commercial objectives (Cuervo-Cazurra et al., 2014; Li et al., 2018c).

We conclude that the relative performance of SOEs is contingent on several factors, mostly associated with home country institutions and political economy factors. Despite the traditional literature which takes as axiomatic the relative inefficiency of SOEs as against POEs, more recent theory and evidence suggests that there should be no general assumption that SOEs always experience a liability of stateness. We identified some boundary conditions related to recent developments in SOE ownership, leading to improved external governance (Lazzarini & Musacchio, 2018); to a broader understanding of the objectives of SOEs and the resources the state provides to them (Shapiro et al., 2018b); and to a better understanding of the impact of institutional voids on the performance of both state and privately-owned firms (Estrin et al., 2016).

THEORY: WHY DO SOEs GO ABROAD?

Our discussion of key boundary conditions suggests that standard theoretical perspectives and models of the MNE such as the Ownership, Location, and Internalization (OLI) model and the country-specific advantages (CSA) and firm-specific advantage (FSA) perspective can be applied or modified to understand the nature of the SOMNE (Dunning, 1980; Rugman, 1981). In particular, the challenge is to use the theory to explain how SOMNEs overcome both the liability of stateness and the liability of foreignness, with the latter becoming magnified when firms suffer also from a liability of legitimacy. It is also known that these theories have been devised mainly based on the behavior and strategies of developed country firms, and as we have emphasized, the SOMNE is to a great extent an emerging market phenomenon. Thus, any discussion of ownership advantages or location choices must account for the specific context of emerging markets.

For example, the possibility that SOMNEs may achieve success abroad because of privileged access to state resources (including diplomatic channels) and nonmarket capabilities, suggests a different view of "O" (ownership) advantages (Cuervo-Cazurra et al., 2014; Cuervo-Cazurra & Ramamurti, 2014, 2017; Peng et al., 2016) to include relational networks and the ability to work with local governments. These same arguments further blur the distinction between FSAs and CSAs. For example, diplomatic channels can be viewed as CSAs when they are accessible to all firms from the home country or as FSAs when they are internalized as part of a firm's nonmarket network capabilities. The traditional theories also do not account for the possibility that SOEs expand abroad as an extension of home country national interests (Cuervo-Cazurra et al., 2014). Locational choices that include high-risk and fragile states are also difficult to explain without extending traditional theories and models to account for the political view of FDI.

In general, the emergence of SOMNEs suggests that theories need to put more emphasis on the role of home government and, more broadly, home institutions. The boundary conditions surrounding the liability of stateness point to the specific ways in which SOEs internationalize and overcome the liability of foreignness, while also pointing to the importance of context. We propose that theories explaining SOMNEs need to incorporate four interrelated perspectives/concepts: state goals; state support; country governance and firm governance; and the role of institutional challenges overseas.

State Goals and Support

The likelihood of the emergence of SOMNEs is contingent on state goals. As we have mentioned earlier, in some economies, SOEs exist mainly to solve domestic market failures. In other economies, however, SOEs may play a central role in the state's broader industrial strategy including the internationalization of national players. Thus, some SOMNEs are meant to be national champions (Liang, Ren, & Sun, 2015), and as such are encouraged to expand internationally (often to secure resources or technology but also to access new markets). Therefore, the first step in studying the emergence of SOMNEs is to understand their home country's objectives, which may include both economic and political interests and may range from domestic to international interests; home country objectives may also change over time.

Further, it is critical to understand the degree to which home governments actively support the internationalization of SOEs by providing access to state resources. The instruments that the state can employ include financial and administrative support, such as the provision of low-interest loans and subsidies and expedited administrative procedures to facilitate firm internationalization (Finchelstein, 2017). Home governments can also develop and strengthen their diplomatic networks to create good investment environments in specific foreign countries to help their SOEs develop business in those markets (Li et al., 2018a). For example, they can use loans, aid, or infrastructure projects to develop good relations with host governments, which reduces political risks and leads to investment opportunities for their firms (Li, Newenham-Kahindi, Shapiro, & Chen, 2013). They can actively engage foreign countries by developing bilateral investment treaties and proposing international economic cooperative initiatives (Ramamurti, 2001). SOEs can particularly benefit from good diplomatic relations (Duanmu, 2014; Shapiro et al., 2018b).

Country Governance and Firm Governance

As state objectives and state support play a critical role in explaining the motivation and resources of SOMNEs, cross-country differences in governance that affect state capacity and power are key to understanding variations in SOMNE strategic behavior. For example, SOEs from autocratic states may behave differently from those in democratic states because the former can consolidate resources to achieve goals more effectively (Clegg, Voss, & Tardios, 2018; Karolyi & Liao, 2017). The nature and quality of formal and informal institutions also affects the degree of convergence of SOEs and POEs in their internationalization activities; convergence is more likely to occur in places where minority shareholders can be better protected and SOE managers can be better monitored (Estrin et al., 2016; Hong et al., 2015). Governance arrangements at the firm level, including state ownership and state control, vary across SOEs, and these differences affect MNE strategy and performance (Bruton et al., 2015; He et al., 2016), including the decision to go abroad, and the state resources available to do so (Musacchio et al., 2015). Theories of SOMNEs should incorporate the interplay between country and firm governance quality and arrangements.

Institutional Challenges Overseas

SOMNEs may also suffer from legitimacy concerns in the host market (Aharoni, 2018; Cuervo-Cazurra et al., 2014; Cui & Jiang, 2012; Globerman & Shapiro, 2009). Some host countries are concerned about investment motivations and consequences of such investments for national security (Li, Xia, & Lin, 2017; Meyer et al., 2014; Shapiro & Globerman, 2012). This is particularly likely when SOMNEs are seen as serving primarily the national interests of the home country. Overcoming the liability of legitimacy may result in specific strategies. SOMNEs may choose locations and entry modes based on the degree to which the home country can help establish legitimacy. A complete theory of the SOMNE will therefore require a better specification of the nature of state capitalism across countries, the role of different ownership and governance structures adopted by SOMNEs, and the importance of international political economy and diplomacy. More attention is required to understand varieties of capitalism, dynamics of institutional change across countries, comparative corporate governance, and the extent of convergence across systems.

RECENT EVIDENCE ON SOMNES

We provide an overview of some of the recent evidence on SOMNEs, focusing on the last decade. On average, SOEs are less likely to internationalize (Li et al., 2018b; Tihanyi et al., 2019). As suggested by Li et al. (2018b), SOEs can be characterized by institutional compatibility at home but incompatibility overseas, thus leading to their low propensity to invest overseas. There is also evidence suggesting an "S" curve of SOEs' international expansion; this is the result of the balance between the "hindering hand" of state owner-ship and the "helping hand" of state ownership, arising from state support and resource advantages (Kalasin, Cuervo-Cazurra, & Ramamurti, 2019). We discuss specific evi-dence around the four conceptual perspectives suggested earlier as key to understand-ing SOMNE IB strategies.

First, there is evidence that internationalization of SOEs reflects state objectives. For example, SOMNEs from emerging markets often expand internationally as instruments of state policy to secure natural resources, a sector often characterized by significant conflict (Shapiro et al., 2018a). Moreover, SOEs owned by the central government are more inclined to be policy instruments in various economies including China, India, Indonesia, Malaysia, South Africa, and Vietnam (Li et al., 2014).

Second, there is evidence indicating that SOMNEs exhibit different international investment patterns related to the level of state support they receive. For example, SOEs from emerging markets are more likely to internationalize when the home country has an active state (Estrin et al., 2019). SOMNEs also tend to take on more risks because of soft budget constraints and diplomatic objectives, choosing riskier locations and entry strategies (Amighini, Rabellotti, & Sanfilippo, 2013; Buckley et al., 2018; Cannizzaro & Weiner, 2018; Knutsen, Rygh, & Hveem, 2011; Ramaswamy, Yeung, & Laforet, 2012). SOMNEs also pay higher acquisition premia in cross-border acquisitions reflecting benefits to the home country from access to technology (Bass & Chakrabarty, 2014; Karolyi & Liao, 2017). SOMNEs' international investments are sometimes accommo-dated by aid, loans, and infrastructure support provided by the home government to the host country, as has been documented in the case of Chinese investments in Africa and Latin America (Li et al., 2013; Shapiro et al., 2018b). SOMNEs are also better able to leverage diplomatic channels to benefit from them (Duanmu, 2014; Li et al., 2018a). Li et al. (2018a), for instance, find that Chinese SOEs are more likely to enter host countries that are friendly to their home country compared to private firms, and this effect is stronger when the SOEs are owned by the central government.

Third, research shows that home country governance institutions have a significant effect on SOEs' international strategies. Notably, Li et al. (2018b) explained that, while Chinese SOMNEs are less inclined to invest overseas than POEs, this is less true when they operate in regions with stronger market-supporting institutions. Li et al. (2017) had also shown that SOEs inherit different levels of institutional advantages that affect their overseas investments, depending on the market reforms experienced. This suggests that outcomes are context specific, dependent on home country institutions (Estrin et al., 2016).

Research also suggests that SOMNEs face legitimacy barriers set up by regulatory bodies in overseas markets. This means that it may take longer for SOMNEs to complete cross-border acquisitions deals in countries such as the U.S. (Chen et al., 2019; Li, Xia, & Lin, 2017), particularly in R&D intensive environments (Li et al., 2017). These results reflect regulatory concerns over foreign SOEs' acquisition behavior, especially when involving firms operating in knowledge-intensive industries. SOMNEs also take measures to overcome legitimacy problems abroad (Cui & Jiang, 2012; Meyer et al., 2014). They adjust their entry modes and control levels in response to institutional pressures and challenges to legitimacy in host countries (Meyer et al., 2014). In countries with legitimacy challenges, SOMNEs are less likely to enter by acquisition, and when they do, they enter with lower ownership stakes (Cui & Jiang, 2012; Meyer et al., 2014). They also address legitimacy challenges by avoiding countries that are hostile to the home country, and instead, choosing countries where state ownership is less prevalent or where the home country exerts sufficient influence to reduce such problems (Duanmu, 2014; Duanmu & Urdinez, 2018; Li et al., 2013; Li et al., 2018a; Shapiro et al, 2018b); this includes other emerging markets (Li & Shapiro, 2019). It is important to emphasize here that much of the evidence we have noted on the internationalization of SOMNEs is based on firms from China, and it is unclear whether Chinese SOMNEs represent a special type of MNE.

Future Research Directions

Our review of the literature leads us to conclude that a complete theory of the SOMNE will require a better specification of the nature of the state and its goals; the nature of state resources and how they are deployed in support of SOMNEs; the nature of home and host country institutions; and the role of different ownership and governance structures adopted by SOMNEs. In addition, a comprehensive theory should be both comparative and dynamic, fostering an understanding of varieties of capitalism and the dynamics of institutional change across countries. We summarize all these ideas in Figure 13.1. We have organized our discussion around the idea that, in order to explain the emergence of the SOMNE, we need to gain an understanding of how SOEs overcome the liability of stateness, a precondition for overcoming the combined liabilities of foreignness and legitimacy required to successfully operate abroad.

Home Country

We start our discussion with the role of the home country. The literature identifies a number of home country conditions that can facilitate the international operations of SOEs. We focus on three: state goals, state resources, and missing institutions. State goals include the extent to which the state considers SOMNEs as key to national

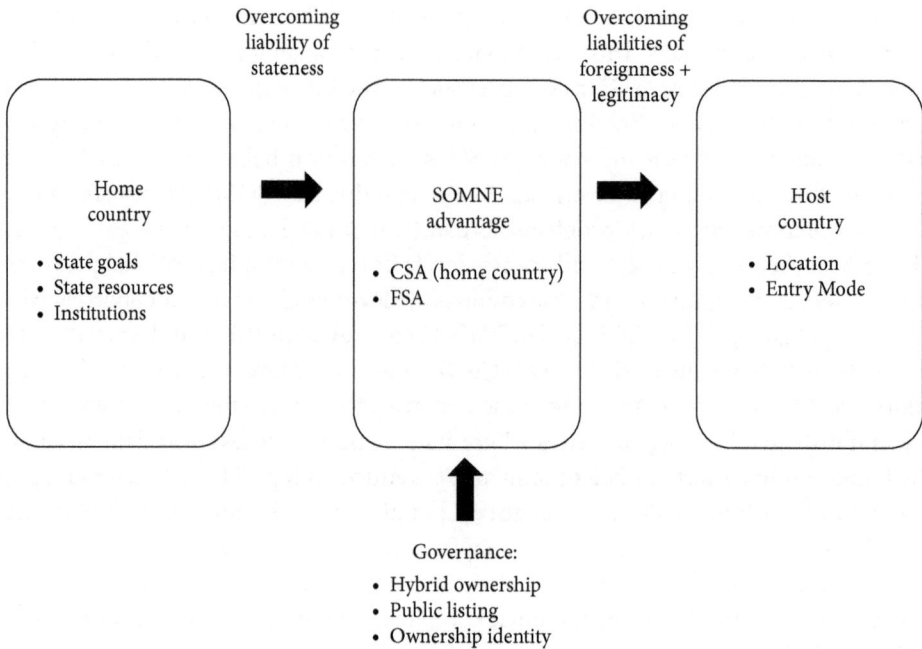

FIGURE 13.1 Internationalization of SOMNEs

development or national security goals, in which case it will deliberately encourage SOEs to internationalize. The goal may be to access technology, to access resources, and/ or to develop national champions that will subsequently contribute to home country development. These state goals are to be contrasted with goals that focus on the SOE as a domestic policy instrument, which is a purpose designed to alleviate market failures, including natural monopoly.

A second home country condition that can facilitate SOE international strategizing is state resources. State resources comprise the ways in which the state encourages internationalization. These include direct subsidies (e.g. low-interest loans from state banks); indirect subsidies in the form of privileged access to state-controlled and state-funded knowledge (research) as well as implicit or explicit protection against bankruptcy; and access to state diplomatic resources including foreign networks, as well as protection from expropriation abroad created by state-sponsored aid or loans (Benito, Rygh, & Lunnan, 2016).

Finally, other home country institutions may have an impact on the international operations of SOEs, in particular market-supporting institutions such as financial institutions, protection of minority shareholders, and an effective legal system. These are important because, in the presence of institutional voids, state-supported business groups may have an advantage over private firms because they are better placed to develop internal markets. We propose that there is still room to advance our understanding of the ways in which home country state policies and institutions affect the emergence and success of SOMNEs.

Specifically, one promising avenue for future research is to examine state goals through the lens of varieties of capitalism (Mariotti & Marzano, 2019), or institutional configurations (Estrin et al., 2019). While there is some evidence that the nature of state capitalism matters, that relies on existing classification schemes and it may be necessary to develop more fine-grained definitions, particularly in the case of emerging markets. For example, although configurations matter, home country-specific characteristics also matter and must be accounted for in assessing state goals (Lin & Milhaupt, 2013). In a relatively recent study, Bass and Chakrabarty (2014) point out that resource scarcity is another country-specific factor that might determine state policy with respect to SOMNEs.

Similarly, there is considerable room to advance our understanding of the specific resources the state brings to bear in support of SOMNEs' international activities. Although there is a generic list of possibilities, to our knowledge, no study brings them together. Thus, we do not know the degree to which different home countries rely on different bundles of support. For example, we have evidence in the form of single-country studies, such as those suggesting that Chinese diplomacy affects location and entry mode decisions (e.g., Duanmu, 2014; Duanmu & Urdinez, 2018; Li et al., 2018a). However, all of this evidence is focused on Chinese SOMNEs, and we do not know whether other countries employ similar strategies. In the same vein, we know very little about whether and how state-supported research activities or differences in national innovation systems can support SOMNEs (Melaas & Zhang, 2016; Tõnurist & Karo, 2016). There is some evidence (also primarily from China) that SOEs did not benefit significantly from state-supported research (Guan & Yam, 2015), and that even when SOEs do have access to state research resources, they tend to be less efficient at deploying them (Zhou, Gao, & Zhao, 2017). Nevertheless, there is more work to be done in understanding this aspect of the resources available to SOMNEs.

Although it is generally understood that home institutions are important in determining firm performance, much less is understood about the specific impact on SOEs and SOMNEs. In particular, the importance of institutional voids in emerging markets is widely acknowledged (Doh, Rodrigues, Saka-Helmhout, & Makhija, 2017), as is their role in fostering internalized benefits to business groups and their affiliates (Carney, Van Essen, Estrin, & Shapiro, 2018). What is less understood is whether institutional voids create advantages for SOEs relative to POEs, which in turn facilitate internationalization. Estrin et al. (2016) argue that stronger institutions make SOEs behave more like POEs in terms of internationalization. The implication is that in emerging markets, institutional voids may create advantages for SOEs, but these may not translate into increased international activity if they favor principally operations at home. This proposition has not been fully empirically tested, and so the impact of institutions (and which institutions) on the IB strategies of SOEs remains understudied.

Finally, we note that it is likely that these three home country conditions—state goals, state resources, and missing institutions—will interact, and therefore any discussion of home country effects of SOMNEs should, as much as possible, consider them jointly. In addition, future research may look further into the dynamics of change in the home country, including in the ways these home country conditions interact over time.

Do state goals change in ways that diminish the role of SOEs as market-supporting institutions strengthen and development proceeds? How do SOEs and home country institutions co-evolve, and in particular do SOEs become entrenched in ways that favor domestic over international operations?

SOE Advantage

Access to favorable home country policies, resources, and institutions may allow some SOMNEs to overcome the liability of stateness. Here we distinguish between CSAs and FSAs. We posit that the SOE advantage, if it exists, can involve any combination (bundle) of home country CSAs and FSAs. It is clear, for example, that when SOMNEs benefit from home country diplomacy and country to country aid and loans—that advantage classes as a CSA. The same may apply to privileged access to home country networks, in particular political networks and the resources that these networks may bring. Thus, the balance between CSAs and FSAs for any particular firm is likely to be context dependent, namely depending on the configuration of state policies, state resources, and institutional voids. The relevant bundle of advantages associated with a firm may explain whether, why, and how the international strategies of SOMNEs differ from those of other MNEs as well as how they differ across SOMNEs from different countries.

One important area for future research is therefore the nature of FSAs in SOEs, and in particular the determinants of innovation in SOEs, the translation into FSAs and the relationship to internationalization. There is some recent literature on SOE innovation (Belloc, 2014; Li et al., 2018c; Zhou et al., 2017), all indicating the potential for innovation by SOEs, but none that directly relate innovation activities to the FSAs that could lead an SOE to invest abroad. In addition, any understanding of FSAs must account for the governance characteristics of SOMNEs, including the nature of ownership (Aguilera & Crespi-Cladera, 2016; Milhaupt & Pargendler, 2017).

As we have discussed, the ownership of the SOMNE is often characterized by its hybrid nature, ranging from full to partial state ownership, and by widespread listing on public exchanges (Bruton et al., 2015; Musacchio et al., 2015). In cases where ownership is shared with private owners, the question is whether these owners exert sufficient influence on the SOE so that their strategies, in particular their international strategies, are consistent with those of POEs. Similarly, when the SOE is publicly listed, it must maintain certain governance standards. All of this limits the ability of the state to pursue non-commercial goals, to fully control the board, and to appoint politically approved managers. In short, sharing ownership and meeting global standards of governance limits the power of the state and makes the SOE more likely to behave similar to a POE. There is surprisingly little evidence on this point, and the comparative ownership and governance characteristics of SOMNEs and other MNEs, and the subsequent strategic implications of such findings, remains a fruitful area for future research.

Further to our earlier points, future research must carefully distinguish both the extent and nature of state ownership. For instance, we know that state ownership in developed country SOMNEs is often minority ownership. Yet, we lack a firm understanding of the nature and purpose of minority ownership, and whether and how it contributes to the development of FSAs for the focal firm. We also have little evidence regarding the nature and effects of ownership mixes, such as when the state has majority ownership. A notable exception is the study by Chen, Li, Shapiro, & Zhang (2014) who suggest that innovation in Chinese firms is higher with hybrid forms of ownership that include state, foreign, and domestic private owners, because each owner brings different sets of knowledge and capabilities. This contributes to the creation of FSAs, which could be leveraged internationally. When ownership is endogenous, chosen by the state, the analysis of ownership structure and its impact on the creation of FSAs that can be leveraged abroad becomes complex. These issues offer rich possibilities for future research.

Finally, there is limited research by international strategic management scholars on the different means by which state ownership and control is exercised. In particular we suggest that future research should devote more attention to the role of SWFs, with particular attention to their role in promoting internationalization strategies. Although the subject has attracted the interest of scholars from various disciplines (Fotak, Gao, & Megginson, 2017; Megginson & Fotak, 2015), it has received relatively little attention from international management scholars, perhaps because SWFs are seen as vehicles for portfolio investments. However, there is evidence that SWFs have diverse goals, which can include promoting national economic and security goals (Globerman et al., 2020). They are therefore not always simple passive investors, as much of their investments are abroad and often involve significant ownership stakes or partnerships with other state entities (Megginson & Fotak, 2015). Hence, an FSA attached to some SOMNEs may involve access to state financial resources housed in a related state organization.

Concerning the nature of SOE advantages, we conclude that the ability of an SOE to overcome the liability of stateness and develop the capabilities necessary to operate abroad depends significantly on both home country characteristics and firm-level governance and ownership characteristics. This suggests considerable heterogeneity in the ability of an SOE to generate FSAs, and in the degree to which foreign operations are built on FSAs, CSAs, or both. Future research should focus more on this heterogeneity.

Host Country

Much of the IB literature has focused on the host country, whether through locational choice, entry mode choice, or motivation for going abroad. One approach (Hennart, 2009) has been to match the FSAs of the MNE to the CSAs of the *host* country. The challenge is to understand how SOMNEs overcome the dual liabilities of foreignness and legitimacy when entering a host market, and the implications for key strategic decisions such as entry mode choices. One important research question is the extent to which these two factors are related, how they are related, and the degree of context specificity related to the host market. The literature surveyed in this chapter has, for the most part, discussed location and entry mode choices either through the lens of emerging markets firms (more likely to locate in other emerging markets with higher risk entry modes), or through the lens of legitimacy (more likely to enter markets with higher tolerance for SOEs through lower profile modes). It is not evident that these approaches are mutually consistent, suggesting the need for more research that clearly distinguishes them in order to determine the degree to which they have similar or different implications for location and entry mode choice.

In addition, future studies should consider the political economy issues surrounding the liability of legitimacy. In particular, it is now apparent that several countries have adopted foreign investment review provisions that are directly targeted at SOMNEs (Cuervo-Cazurra, 2018a; Wehrlé & Christiansen, 2017; Wehrlé & Pohl, 2016). Some recent trade agreements, notably the Comprehensive and Progressive Agreement for Trans-Pacific Partnership (CPTPP), devote an entire chapter to SOMNEs. These actions are clearly related to a liability of legitimacy and can raise the costs of entry for some of these SOMNEs. Their motivation and effects remain fruitful areas for future research, including the question of whether the effects, if any, largely affect Chinese SOMNEs.

A further legitimacy issue is the question of social responsibility and stakeholder relations. While there is evidence that stakeholder relations as well as corporate social responsibility (CSR) initiatives can confer legitimacy when entering a foreign host market (Henisz & Zelner, 2005; Rathert, 2016), there is, to our knowledge, no study that examines this question from the perspective of the SOMNE. There are now a number of studies that examine the CSR behavior of SOEs (Garde-Sanchez, López-Pérez, & López-Hernández, 2018; Inkpen & Ramaswamy, 2018), but from the perspective of the home economy, and not from the perspective of the liability of legitimacy. Thus, we do not know whether or how SOMNEs use CSR or stakeholder strategies to achieve legitimacy, and how their behavior compares with that of other types of MNEs. In an era when all companies are pressured to become involved in CSR and stakeholder engagement strategies, the gap between the goals of SOEs and POEs narrows in that both are concerned with broader social objectives (Globerman et al., 2020). It remains to be determined whether any prior experience with these broader objectives provides an advantage to SOMNEs that might overcome their liability of legitimacy.

Concluding Remarks

We conclude that the theory of the SOMNE will benefit from a better specification of the nature of state capitalism across countries, the role of different ownership and governance structures adopted by SOMNEs, and the importance of international political economy and diplomacy. More attention will be required to understanding the varieties of capitalism, the dynamics of institutional change across countries, comparative corporate governance, and the extent of convergence across systems. Extant evidence points both to factors that differentiate SOMNEs from MNEs and to factors indicating convergence. Differentiation often results from host country conditions characterized by an activist state and less developed market institutions. On the other hand, hybrid ownership and listing on stock exchanges can promote convergence of behavior. Extant research has identified elements of both, and it remains unclear how these elements interact. The nature of hybrid ownership remains underspecified, as is the evolutionary character of state capitalism and the impact of stronger market institutions on the extent and nature of SOMNEs. In addition, much of the evidence on the internationalization of SOMNEs comes from China, and it is unclear whether Chinese firms represent a special case or not. We believe that advancements of the SOMNE research agenda cannot be achieved without a strong overarching framework designed to better understand institutional dynamics and comparative corporate governance.

REFERENCES

Aguilera, R. V., & Crespi-Cladera, R. 2016. Global corporate governance: On the relevance of firms' ownership structure. *Journal of World Business*, 51(1): 50–57.

Aharoni, Y. 2018. The evolution of state-owned multinational enterprise theory. In A. Cuervo-Cazurra (Eds.), *State-Owned Multinationals: Governments in Global Business*. New York, NY: Palgrave Macmillan.

Amighini, A. A., Rabellotti, R., & Sanfilippo, M. 2013. Do Chinese state-owned and private enterprises differ in their internationalization strategies? *China Economic Review*, 27: 312–325.

Balbuena, S. S. 2016. Concerns related to the internationalisation of state-owned enterprises. *OECD Corporate Governance Working Papers*, 19.

Bass, A. E., & Chakrabarty, S. 2014. Resource security: Competition for global resources, strategic intent, and governments as owners. *Journal of International Business Studies*, 45(8): 961–979.

Belloc, F. 2014. Innovation in state-owned enterprises: Reconsidering the conventional wisdom. *Journal of Economic Issues*, 48(3): 821–848.

Benito, G. R. G., Rygh, A., & Lunnan, R. 2016. The benefits of internationalization for state-owned enterprises. *Global Strategy Journal*, 6(4): 269–288.

Boardman, A. E., & Vining, A. R. 1989. Ownership and performance in competitive environments: A comparison of the performance of private, mixed, and state-owned enterprises. *Journal of Law Economics*, 32(1): 1–33.

Boycko, M., Shleifer, A., & Vishny, R. W. 1996. A theory of privatisation. *Economic Journal*, 106(435): 309–319.

Bruton, G. D., Peng, M. W., Ahlstrom, D., Stan, C. V., & Xu, K. 2015. State-owned enterprises around the world as hybrid organizations. *Academy of Management Perspectives*, 29(1): 92–114.

Buckley, P. J., & Casson, M. 2009. The internalization theory of the multinational enterprise: A review of the progress of a research agenda after 30 years. *Journal of International Business Studies*, 40: 1563–1580.

Buckley, P. J., Clegg, L. J., Voss, H., Cross, A. R., Liu, X., & Zheng, P. 2018. A retrospective and agenda for future research on Chinese outward foreign direct investment. *Journal of International Business Studies*, 49(1): 4–23.

Cannizzaro, A. P., & Weiner, R. J. 2018. State ownership and transparency in foreign direct investment. *Journal of International Business Studies*, 49(2): 172–195.

Carney, M., Van Essen, M., Estrin, S., & Shapiro, D. 2018. Business groups reconsidered: Beyond paragons and parasites. *Academy of Management Perspectives*, 32(4): 493–516.

Caves, D. W., & Christensen, L. R. 1980. The relative efficiency of public and private firms in a competitive environment: The case of Canadian railroads. *Journal of Political Economy*, 88(5): 958–976.

Chen, V. Z., Li, J., Shapiro, D. M., & Zhang, X. 2014. Ownership structure and innovation: An emerging market perspective. *Asia Pacific Journal of Management*, 31(1): 1–24.

Chen, V. Z., Musacchio, A., & Li, S. 2019. A principals-principals perspective of hybrid leviathans: Cross-border acquisitions by state-owned MNEs. *Journal of Management*, 45(7): 2751–2778.

Clegg, L. J., Voss, H., & Tardios, J. A. 2018. The autocratic advantage: Internationalization of state-owned multinationals. *Journal of World Business*, 53(5): 668–681.

Cuervo-Cazurra, A. 2018a. Thanks but no thanks: State-owned multinationals from emerging markets and host-country policies. *Journal of International Business Policy*, 45:128–156.

Cuervo-Cazurra, A. 2018b. *State-Owned Multinationals: Governments in Global Business*. New York, NY: Palgrave Macmillan.

Cuervo-Cazurra, A., Inkpen, A., Musacchio, A., & Ramaswamy, K. 2014. Governments as owners: State-owned multinational companies. *Journal of International Business Studies*, 45: 919–942.

Cuervo-Cazurra, A., & Ramamurti, R. 2014. *Understanding Multinationals from Emerging Markets*. Cambridge: Cambridge University Press.

Cuervo-Cazurra, A., & Ramamurti, R. 2017. Home country underdevelopment and internationalization: Innovation-based and escape-based internationalization. *Competitiveness Review: An International Business Journal*, 27(3): 217–230.

Cui, L., & Jiang, F. 2012. State ownership effect on firms' FDI ownership decisions under institutional pressure: A study of Chinese outward-investing firms. *Journal of International Business Studies*, 43(3): 264–284.

Doh, J., Rodrigues, S., Saka-Helmhout, A., & Makhija, M. 2017. International business responses to institutional voids. *Journal of International Business Studies*, 48(3): 293–307.

Duanmu, J. L. 2014. State-owned MNCs and host country expropriation risk: The role of home state soft power and economic gunboat diplomacy. *Journal of International Business Studies*, 45(8): 1044–1060.

Duanmu, J. L., & Urdinez, F. 2018. The dissuasive effect of U.S. political influence on Chinese FDI during the going global policy era. *Business and Politics*, 20(1): 38–69.

Dunning, J. H. 1980. Toward an eclectic theory of international production. *Thunderbird International Business Review*, 22(3): 1–3.

Estrin, S., Hanousek, J., Kočenda, E., & Svejnar, J. 2009. The effects of privatization and ownership in transition economies. *Journal of Economic Literature*, 47(3): 699–728.

Estrin, S., Liang, Z., Shapiro, D., & Carney, M. 2019. State capitalism, economic systems and the performance of state-owned firms. *Acta Oeconomica*, 69(1): 175–193.

Estrin, S., Meyer, K. E., Nielsen, B. B., & Nielsen, S. 2016. Home country institutions and the internationalization of state-owned enterprises: A cross-country analysis. *Journal of World Business*, 51(2): 294–307.

Estrin, S., & Pelletier, A. 2018. Privatization in developing countries: What are the lessons of recent experience? *World Bank Research Observer*, 33(1): 65–102.

Estrin, S., & Perotin, V. 1991. Does Ownership Always Matter? *International Journal of Industrial Organization*, 9(1): 55–72.

Finchelstein, D. 2017. The role of the state in the internationalization of Latin American firms. *Journal of World Business*, 52(4): 578–590.

Fotak, V., Gao, X., & Megginson, W. L. 2017. A financial force to be reckoned with? An overview of sovereign wealth funds. In D. J. Cumming, G. Wood, I. Filatochev, & J. Reinecke (Eds.), *Oxford Handbook of Sovereign Wealth Funds*. Oxford: Oxford University Press.

Garde-Sanchez, R., López-Pérez, M. V., & López-Hernández, A. M. 2018. Current trends in research on social responsibility in state-owned enterprises: A review of the literature from 2000 to 2017. *Sustainability*, 10(7): 1–21.

Globerman, S., Hensyel, P., & Shapiro, D. 2020. State-owned enterprises and sovereign wealth funds: An economic assessment. In VanDuzer, A., & Leblond, P (Eds.), *Promoting and Managing International Investment: Towards an Integrated Policy Approach*. London: Routledge.

Globerman, S., & Shapiro, D. 2009. Economic and strategic considerations surrounding Chinese FDI in the United States. *Asia Pacific Journal of Management*, 26(1): 163–183.

Guan, J. C., & Yam, R. C. M. 2015. Effects of government financial incentives on firms' innovation performance in China: Evidences from Beijing in the 1990s. *Research Policy*, 44 (1): 273–282.

He, X., Chakrabarty, S., & Eden, L. 2016. The global emergence of Chinese multinationals: A resource-based view of ownership and performance. *Asian Business and Management*, 15(1): 1–31.

Henisz, W. J., & Zelner, B. A. 2005. Legitimacy, interest group pressures, and change in emergent institutions: The case of foreign investors and host country governments. *Academy of Management Review*, 30(2): 361–382.

Hennart, J. F. 2009. Down with MNE-centric theories! Market entry and expansion as the bundling of MNE and local assets. *Journal of International Business Studies*, 40(9): 1432–1454.

Heugens, P. P. M. A. R., Sauerwald, S., Turturea, R., & van Essen, M. 2019. Does state ownership hurt or help minority shareholders? International evidence from control block acquisitions. *Global Strategy Journal*, 1–29. doi.org/10.1002/qsj.1337

Hong, J., Wang, C., & Kafouros, M. 2015. The role of the state in explaining the internationalization of emerging market enterprises. *British Journal of Management*, 26(1): 45–62.

Hoskisson, R. E., Wright, M., Filatotchev, I., & Peng, M. W. 2013. Emerging multinationals from mid-range economies: The influence of institutions and factor markets. *Journal of Management Studies*, 50(7): 1295–1321.

Inkpen, A., & Ramaswamy, K. 2018. State-owned multinationals and drivers of sustainability practices: An exploratory study of national oil companies. In S. Dorobantu, R. V. Aguilera, J. Luo, & K, Ramaswamy (Eds.), *Sustainability, Stakeholder Governance, and Corporate Social Responsibility*. London: Emerald.

Inoue, C. F. K. V., Lazzarini, S. G., & Musacchio, A. 2013. Leviathan as a minority shareholder: Firm-level implications of state equity purchases. *Academy of Management Journal*, 56(6): 1775–1801.

Kalasin, K., Cuervo-Cazurra, A., & Ramamurti, R. 2019. State ownership and international expansion: The S-curve relationship. *Global Strategy Journal*, 1092): 368–418.

Kalotay, K. 2018. State Owned Multinationals: An Emerging Market Phenomenon? *The Journal of Comparative Economic Studies*, 13: 13–37.

Karolyi, G. A., & Liao, R. C., 2017. State capitalism's global reach: Evidence from foreign acquisitions by state-owned companies, *Journal of Corporate Finance*, 42: 367–391.

Khanna, T., & Palepu, K. G. 2010. *Winning in Emerging Markets: A Road Map for Strategy and Execution*. Boston, MA: Harvard Business Press.

Knutsen, C. H., Rygh, A., & Hveem, H. 2011. Does state ownership matter? Institutions' effect on foreign direct investment revisited. *Business and Politics*, 13(1): 1–31.

Lazzarini, S. G., & Musacchio, A. 2018. State ownership reinvented? Explaining performance differences between state-owned and private firms. *Corporate Governance: International Review*, 26(4): 255–272.

Li, J., Meyer, K. E., Zhang, H., & Ding, Y. 2018a. Diplomatic and corporate networks: Bridges to foreign locations. *Journal of International Business Studies,* 49(6): 743–752.

Li, J., Newenham-Kahindi, A., Shapiro, D. M., & Chen, V. Z. 2013. The two-tier bargaining model revisited: Theory and evidence from China's natural resource investments in Africa. *Global Strategy Journal*, 3(4): 300–321.

Li, J., & Shapiro, D. 2019. Investments by emerging economy multinationals in other emerging economies. In R. Grosse, & K. Meyer (Eds.), *Oxford Handbook of Management in Emerging Markets*. Oxford: Oxford University Press.

Li, J., Xia, J., & Lin, Z. 2017. Cross-border acquisitions by state-owned firms: How do legitimacy concerns affect the completion and duration of their acquisitions? *Strategic Management Journal*, 38(9): 1915–1934.

Li, J., Xia, J., Shapiro, D., & Lin, Z. 2018b. Institutional compatibility and the internationalization of Chinese SOEs: The moderating role of home subnational institutions. *Journal of World Business*, 53(5): 641–652.

Li, J., Xia, J., & Zajac, E. J. 2018c. On the duality of political and economic stakeholder influence on firm innovation performance: Theory and evidence from Chinese firms. *Strategic Management Journal*, 39(1): 193–216.

Li, M. H., Cui, L., & Lu, J. 2014. Varieties in state capitalism: Outward FDI strategies of central and local state-owned enterprises from emerging economy countries. *Journal of International Business Studies,* 45(8): 980–1004.

Li, M. H., Cui, L., & Lu, J. 2017. Marketized state ownership and foreign expansion of emerging market multinationals: Leveraging institutional competitive advantages. *Asia Pacific Journal of Management*, 34(1): 19–46.

Liang, H., Ren, B., & Sun, S. L. 2015. An anatomy of state control in the globalization of state-owned enterprises. *Journal of International Business Studies*, 46(2): 223–240.

Lin, L. W., & Milhaupt, C. J. 2013. We are the (national) champions: Understanding the mechanisms of state capitalism in China. *Stanford Law Review*, 65:697–760.

Mariotti, S., & Marzano, R. 2019. Varieties of capitalism and the internationalization of state-owned enterprises. *Journal of International Business Studies*, 50(5): 669–691.

Megginson, W., & Fotak, V. 2015. Rise of the fiduciary state: A survey of sovereign wealth fund research. *Journal of Economic Surveys*, 29(4): 733–778.

Megginson, W. L. 2017. Privatization, State Capitalism and State Ownership of Business in the 21st Century. *Foundations and Trends in Finance*, 11(1–2): 3–153.

Megginson, W. L., & Netter, J. 2001. From state to market: A survey of empirical studies on privatization. *Journal of Economic Literature*, 39(2): 321–389.

Melaas, A., & Zhang, F. 2016. National innovation systems in the United States and China: A brief review of the literature. *The Center for International Environment and Resource Policy*, 11: 1–30.

Meyer, K. E., Ding, Y., Li, J., & Zhang, H. 2014. Overcoming distrust: How state-owned enterprises adapt their foreign entries to institutional pressures abroad. *Journal of International Business Studies*, 45(8): 1005–1028.

Milhaupt, C. J., & Pargendler, M. 2017. Governance challenges of listed state-owned enterprises around the world: National experiences and a framework for reform. *Cornell International Law Journal*, 50(3): 473–542.

Musacchio, A., & Lazzarini, S. G. 2014. Reinventing state capitalism: Leviathan in business, Brazil and beyond. *Harvard University Press*, 1: 936–938.

Musacchio, A., & Lazzarini, S. G. 2018. State-owned enterprises as multinationals: Theory and research directions. In A. Cuervo-Cazurra (Eds.), *State-Owned Multinationals: Governments in Global Business*. New York, NY: Palgrave Macmillan.

Musacchio, A., Lazzarini, S. G., & Aguilera, R. V. 2015. New varieties of state capitalism: Strategic and governance implications. *Academy of Management Perspectives*, 29(1): 115–131.

OECD. 2015. *Guidelines on Corporate Governance of State-Owned Enterprises*. Paris: OECD.

OECD. 2017. *The Size and Sectoral Distribution of SOEs*. Paris: OECD.

Peng, M. W., Bruton, G. D., Stan, C. V., & Huang, Y. 2016. Theories of the (state-owned) firm. *Asia Pacific Journal of Management*, 33(2): 293–317.

Poczter, S., & Musacchio, A. 2018. Do state owned multinationals internationalize differently? Paper presented at the 6th Copenhagen Conference on Emerging Multinationals, Denmark.

Ramamurti, R. 2001. The obsolescing "bargaining model?" MNC-host developing country relations revisited. *Journal of International Business Studies*, 32(1): 23–39.

Ramaswamy, B., Yeung, M., & Laforet, S. 2012. China's outward foreign direct investment: Location choice and firm ownership. *Journal of World Business*, 47(1): 17–25.

Rathert, N. 2016. Strategies of legitimation: MNEs and the adoption of CSR in response to host-country institutions. *Journal of International Business Studies*, 47(7): 858–879.

Rodrigues, S. B., & Dieleman, M. 2018. The internationalization paradox: Untangling dependence in multinational state hybrids. *Journal of World Business*, 53(1): 39–51.

Rugman, A. M. 1981. *Inside the Multinationals: The Economics of International Markets*. Kent: Croom Helm Publishers.

Rygh, A. 2019. Bureaucrats in international business: A review of five decades of research on state-owned MNEs. In A. Chidlow, P. Ghauri, T. Buckley, E. Gardner, A. Qamar, & E. Pickering (Eds.), *The Changing Strategies of International Business*. The Academy of International Business. New York: Palgrave Macmillan.

Shapiro, D., Hobdari, B., & Oh, C. H. 2018a. Natural resources, multinational enterprises and sustainable development. *Journal of World Business*, 53(1): 1–14.

Shapiro, D. M., & Globerman, S. 2012. The international activities and impacts of state-owned enterprises. In K. P. Sauvant, L. Sachs, P. F. Wouter, & S. Jongbloed (Eds.), *Sovereign Investment: Concerns and Policy Reactions*. Oxford: Oxford University Press.

Shapiro, D. M., Vecino, C., & Li, J. 2018b. Exploring China's state-led FDI model: Evidence from the extractive sectors in Latin America. *Asia Pacific Journal of Management*, 35(1): 11–37.

Tihanyi, L., Aguilera, R., Heugens, P.M., van Essen, M., Duran, P., Sauerwald, S., & Turturea, R. 2019. State Ownership and Political Connections. *Journal of Management*, 45(6): 2293–2321.

Tõnurist, P., & Karo, E. 2016. State owned enterprises as instruments of innovation policy. *Annals of Public and Cooperative Economics*, 87(4): 623–648.

UNCTAD. 2017. *World Investment Report*. Geneva: United Nations.

Vickers, J., & Yarrow, G. 1991. Economic perspectives on privatization. *Journal of Economic Perspectives*, 5(2): 111–132.

Wang, C., Hong, J., Kafouros, M., & Wright, M. 2012. Exploring the role of government involvement in outward FDI from emerging economies. *Journal of International Business Studies*, 43(7): 655–676.

Wehrlé, F., & Christiansen, H. 2017. State-owned enterprises, international investment and national security: The way forward. *OECD Insights.* http://oecdinsights.org/2017/07/19/ state-owned-enterprises-international-investment-and-national-security-the-way-forward/, Accessed 03 August 2019.

Wehrlé, F., & Pohl, J. 2016. Investment policies related to national security: A survey of country practices. *OECD Working Papers on International Investment,* 2016/02.

Young, M., Peng, M., Ahlstrom, D., Bruton, G., & Jiang, Y. 2008. Corporate governance in emerging markets: A review of the principal-principal perspective. *Journal of Management Studies,* 45(1): 196–220.

Zaheer, S. 1995. Overcoming the liability of foreignness. *Academy of Management Journal,* 38: 341–363.

Zhou, K. Z., Gao, G. Y., & Zhao, H. 2017. State ownership and firm innovation in China: An integrated view of institutional and efficiency logics. *Administrative Science Quarterly,* 62(2): 375–404.

PART IV

···

DYNAMICS OF INTERNATIONAL BUSINESS STRATEGY

···

CHAPTER 14

....

DYNAMICS OF OPERATION MODES

Switches and Additions

....

GABRIEL R. G. BENITO, BENT PETERSEN, AND LAWRENCE S. WELCH

INTRODUCTION*

....

DESPITE the overwhelming focus on foreign entry mode choices, that is decisions on how to enter a foreign country to perform one or several value activities in that location, mode choices go beyond the initial entry commitment. Over time, many firms make mode switches in foreign markets, characteristically because their activities have grown in volume, and another operation mode offers a more efficient way of organizing those activities. Sometimes, companies also add new operation modes to existing ones, because they further activities in the host country, or because interacting with a more diverse set of actors requires different modes of organizing (Benito, Petersen, & Welch, 2009).

Entry mode research has primarily focused on the discrete choice made by a given company to enter a country (Brouthers & Hennart, 2007; see also Chapter 5). Such choices are important strategic decisions with long-term ramifications, and hence a static view has usually been seen as appropriate on such lasting decisions; once made, they are difficult to change (Anderson & Coughlan, 1987). However, to the extent that switches are made, or new modes are added to existing ones, more dynamic as well as more complex situations and choices emerge, which are not adequately described and

* **Acknowledgement:** We thank Keith Brouthers, Klaus Meyer, Øivind Revang, and Irina Surdu for very helpful comments. This chapter has evolved from previous versions presented at the 2019 ANZIBA conference (Perth), the 2018 AIB conference (Minneapolis), the 2018 EIBA conference (Poznan), and faculty seminars at BI Norwegian Business School and Molde University College. We are grateful for the many comments and suggestions provided by colleagues attending the presentations.

Lawrence S. Welch passed away just before this chapter was published. He will be truly missed by his co-authors and the entire International Business community.

explained by the usual static approaches to entry mode choice (Benito & Welch, 1994; Meyer & Gelbuda, 2006).

Over time, including in more recent years, research has exposed decisions involving mode dynamics, such as a switch from one mode to another, as well as the widespread use of multiple modes. Various studies report that mode switches are, in fact, commonplace (Benito, Pedersen, & Petersen, 2005; Calof, 1993; Chetty & Agndal, 2007; Fryges, 2007; Clark, Pugh, & Mallory, 1997; Putzhammer, Fainshmidt, Puck, & Slangen, 2018; Swoboda, Olejnik, & Morschett, 2011). Similarly, a "messier" reality of multiple modes has been noted in studies such as Benito, Petersen, & Welch (2011), Clark et al. (1997), Kedron & Bagchi-Sen (2011), Putzhammer et al. (2018), and Petersen & Welch (2002), which provide various examples of companies using several different modes simultaneously. Taken together, these studies suggest that companies take a dynamic approach to mode choice; modes can be, and are changed, and they can be used concurrently, either as interconnected parts of a mode package or alongside each other in a less connected manner. Either way, mode dynamics are key, as opposed to the traditional discrete and static view of foreign operation mode choices. Mode dynamics have been discussed previously (see e.g. Benito, Pedersen, & Petersen, 1999; Benito et al., 2009; Petersen, Welch, & Benito, 2010; Puck, Holtbrügge, & Mohr, 2009), but to move the research agenda beyond a mere description of such phenomena, we need a more comprehensive understanding of the drivers behind such mode dynamics, especially in terms of the tradeoffs involved.

In a concerted effort at moving international business (IB) strategy research and theory forward, this chapter first provides a systematic analysis of mode dynamics that covers around fifty years of research—stretching back to IB scholars' early recognition of mode dynamics as a topic deserving attention, but also covering more recent developments in the field. Then, we advance the understanding of the drivers of mode dynamics decisions. Our analysis demonstrates that scholars have, over time, developed considerable insight about mode switch drivers. In contrast, we still lack a basic understanding of the mode addition phenomenon and its underlying decision drivers. This is perhaps not surprising inasmuch as the study of mode switches appears as a natural extension of entry mode research; it maintains the singular mode as the unit of analysis and a discrete choice modeling approach. In contrast, the study of the mode addition phenomenon requires a different analytical approach to change, and because it involves more complex dependent variables, it is challenging to examine empirically. Drawing on earlier research on the disaggregation of local and global value chains into separate governance forms (e.g. Argyres & Liebeskind, 2002; Benito et al., 2011; Buckley, 2018; Contractor, Kumar, Kundu, & Pedersen, 2010; Hashai, Asmussen, Benito, & Petersen, 2010; Hernández & Pedersen, 2017; Petersen & Welch, 2002; Zenger & Hesterly, 1997), we suggest a powerful theoretical framework for understanding the mode addition phenomenon.

Against this background, the chapter proceeds as follows. In the next section, we outline the evolution of research on mode dynamics as a complement and corollary to the study of discrete choices of entry modes. This stream of research spans more than fifty years and has resulted in the establishment of several research templates of drivers of mode switch. In comparison, research on the drivers of mode addition is sparse. Next, we sketch the essential considerations involved in making decisions regarding the disaggregation of local value chains into separate governance forms and provide a theoretical basis (in the form of a set of assumptions) for analyzing the benefits and costs of mode additions. The analysis illustrates how the number of operation modes in a foreign market reflects an optimal balance of costs and benefits, which in turn are largely determined by exogenous factors. Lastly, we relax these restrictive assumptions and sketch how managerial intervention (in the form of changing the interdependence architecture between the operation modes through modularization) may shift the tradeoffs identified. The chapter concludes with some proposed avenues for further research.

THE EVOLUTION OF RESEARCH ON MODE DYNAMICS

Foreign operation modes have been a subject of IB strategy research from its early stages (Root, 1964), but especially after the mid-1980s as theoretical perspectives that had emerged throughout the preceding decade provided the basis for much empirical work. One prominent stream of research built on the economics-based approaches of internalization and transaction cost theories (Anderson & Gatignon, 1986; Buckley & Casson, 1976; Hennart, 1982; Brouthers, Brouthers, & Werner, 2003), which characteristically analyzed operation modes in terms of long-term strategic choices involving risk–control tradeoffs. Another stream of research was based on learning and decision behavior theories (Aharoni, 1966; Johanson & Vahlne, 1977), and considered foreign operation modes more as elements in evolving processes of internationalization than as independent focal choices in foreign market penetration (see also Dow, Liesch, & Welch, 2018). Evolutionary and resource-based approaches (Andersen, 1997; Kogut & Zander, 1993; Madhok, 1997; Verbeke, 2003) provided complementary perspectives on operation mode choices. Also, in the wake of the transformation of formerly communist countries into market-based economies (Buckley & Ghauri, 1994) and the rise of emerging markets, institutional approaches came into focus (Kostova & Zaheer, 1999; Meyer & Peng, 2005, Meyer, Estrin, Bhaumik, & Peng, 2009).

The Choice of (Entry) Mode

In the overwhelming bulk of research on foreign operation modes, the focus has been on entry modes, that is, the mode chosen by a company as it decided to go into a particular location to pursue some business activity there. Empirical studies proliferated as research templates emerged through the ground-breaking studies by Davidson and McFetridge (1985), Anderson and Coughlan (1987), Kogut and Singh (1988), and Hennart (1991). Several overview articles (Brouthers & Hennart, 2007; Canabal & White III, 2008) and meta-analyses (Morschett, Schramm-Klein, & Swoboda, 2010; Tihanyi, Griffiths, & Russell, 2005; Zhao, Luo, & Suh, 2004) have been published, which indicates that the choice of entry mode is a mature field of research.

Recognition of Mode Dynamics

Even if the research focus has been on entry modes, changing modes in foreign markets by internationalizing companies is commonplace. In fact, mode changes may be considered the norm for companies engaged in IB activities (Benito et al., 2009); particularly as many changes do not entail replacing one mode with another, but rather they involve one or more modes being added to the existing entry mode. As such, foreign operation mode dynamics represents an important aspect of mode development and internationalization in general, though receiving limited treatment in IB strategy (for exceptions see Benito, Dovgan, Petersen, & Welch, 2013; Petersen, Welch, & Welch, 2000; Putzhammer et al., 2018).

Indeed, mode dynamics, while recognized early in empirical foreign direct investment (FDI) research, was, in general, not pursued as a significant theoretical concern. Yet, Wilkins (1974), in her study of the US industry abroad, reflected on the need to develop a dynamic emphasis in such research:

> The present author's research brings her squarely in agreement with those theorists who look at the dynamics of direct foreign investments and view such investments as part of a process—a process developing over time out of the requirements of the innovative business enterprise.   (Wilkins, 1974: 414; see also Wilkins, 1970)

A similar concern was expressed by Horst (1972: 265) who argued that:

> If we are ever to unravel the complexity of the foreign investment decision process, a systematic study of the dynamic behavior of firms must be undertaken.

Of course, researchers who looked at firms' internationalization processes (IPs) inevitably observed frequent mode switches (Amdam, 2009; Johanson & Wiedersheim-Paul, 1975), but their focus was less on the switches themselves, and instead on the firms undergoing these changes (Welch & Luostarinen, 1988). Apart from notions of learning, experience, and (changes in) perceived uncertainty, process studies provided only limited impetus to theory development about mode dynamics. Various studies in the 1970s and 1980s indicated mode switches as companies progressed in their internationalization (e.g. Buckley, 1989), yet sometimes challenging the view that there was a general chain of events, as proposed by the concept of the "establishment chain." In fact, it was suggested that multinational enterprises (MNEs) leapfrogged stages (Björkman & Eklund, 1996; Hedlund & Kverneland, 1985; Millington & Bayliss, 1990), and that following the progression suggested by the "establishment chain" was inconsequential for performance.

Among the very first empirical studies to specifically focus on mode dynamics was that by Calof (1993), who investigated mode switches and the decision processes associated with them by interviewing managers in thirty-eight Canadian companies. In a subsequent article, Calof and Beamish (1995) identified 121 mode switches made by the thirty-eight companies, most of the switches being the move from exports to FDI. Somewhat later, Benito et al. (2005; see also Pedersen, Petersen, & Benito, 2002) combine transaction costs and resource-based theories with IP theory in their analysis of changes in international sales and distribution channels. They model switches in how exporters organize their activities in foreign markets as driven by factors that motivate switches as well as factors that work against making switches. Using data on 260 Danish exporters, following them over a five-year period, Benito et al. (2005) find evidence of both within-mode switches (e.g. substituting one intermediary with another) and between-mode switches (e.g. moving from a contractual arrangement with a distributor to an in-house operation), and the findings largely corroborate their model. Recently, Putzhammer et al. (2018) reported a study that tracked the operations of eighty Austrian MNEs in Central and Eastern Europe over twenty-four years (1990–2013). They combine institutional and learning (IP) theories to examine a total of 527 mode switches made by these companies. Switches were of two main types: (1) use of a mode that the company was already familiar with, and (2) use of a new (to the company) mode of entry. They find that using new modes is more likely when companies have substantial international experience. They also find that the type of change implemented depends on the institutional quality of the host country, thus supporting both theories.

Drivers of Mode Switch

Uncertainty, Learning, and Opportunities

A common baseline in IB is that firms are typically hesitant to commit resources to foreign operations in the early phases of their internationalization. Without appropriate experience and knowledge, decision makers will inevitably have a strong sense of risk and uncertainty, which is likely to constrain the range of operation modes that are considered. Conversely, the greater the depth of knowledge about and experience in foreign markets, the more confident a firm tends to be about making commitments, and about its judgment of the degree of exposure to risk. As an example, MNEs possessing technology and marketing skills may form joint ventures with local firms that have market knowledge, access to distributions channels, and close ties to regulatory bodies. As the joint venture partners exchange knowledge, the complementarity vanishes and the MNE may experience a growing desire to replace the joint venture with a sole venture (Nakamura, Shaver, & Yeung, 1996).

In their influential article on firm internationalization, Johanson and Vahlne (1977) argue that there is an interplay between accumulation of knowledge on the one hand, and firm actions on the other. Commitment decisions are based on the knowledge that firms already have. Knowledge is crucial in order to identify and assess problems and opportunities, which, in turn, drive the decisions that are made. In the decision-making process, the identification of appropriate alternative courses of action and their evaluation hinge on the knowledge that is available about relevant stakeholders in the market environment—including customers, competitors, and suppliers—and about the performance of the various activities undertaken by the firm. Much of the knowledge on hand is the so-called objective knowledge (or rather, information) of a fairly general kind, which can be treated more or less like a commodity and can be taught, or even bought. Nevertheless, the most important and relevant type of knowledge is the so-called experiential knowledge that is foremost learned through personal experience with actual operations in foreign markets, hence providing an important feedback loop in the process.

The IP model grew, in part, out of research showing a gradual approach to companies' foreign expansion and commitment (Johanson & Wiedersheim-Paul, 1975). In terms of foreign operation modes, the prediction typically generated by this perspective is that firms tend to increase their commitment step by step and over time.[†]

Despite the intuitive appeal of the basic ideas in the IP perspective, its empirical support has been far from conclusive and it has been challenged (Benito & Gripsrud, 1992; Dow et al., 2018; Petersen & Pedersen, 1997). In particular, studies have shown that firms may leapfrog stages in the establishment chain, for a variety of reasons including competitive motives (Hedlund & Kverneland, 1985), avoidance of costs involved in switching between modes of operation (Benito et al., 2005), and entrepreneurial action (Andersson, 2000). In this context, we propose that "within-mode" and mode addition changes provide a more nuanced side to incremental mode development. A richer conceptualization of modes allows a more comprehensive perspective on the nature of incrementalism in mode development (Benito et al., 2009).

Operating Cost Considerations

In a curiously overlooked article, Buckley and Casson (1981) provide a cost-based rationale for why companies switch modes. They distinguish between market, contract, and investment modes, and classify associated costs into fixed and variable costs. Investment modes imply relatively high fixed costs due to the setting up of a subsidiary and administering it, and such costs would, to a large extent, be independent of the volume of activity. However, once the administrative set-up (e.g. the hiring of personnel, the development of appropriate routines) is in place to handle an activity, the subsequent variable costs tend to be relatively low. In contrast, market modes usually incur low fixed costs, but transacting parties have to take on other costs each time a transaction is carried out—for example, costs associated with searching for relevant transaction parties, negotiating a deal, and ensuring that the elements of the deal are fulfilled— which leads to high variable costs. Setting up a contract will also incur costs, but because

---

[†] A common pattern regarding modes of operation being: (1) no regular export, (2) indirect engagement such as export via foreign intermediaries like agents or distributors), (3) establishment of a sales subsidiary, and (4) setting up a production subsidiary (Johanson & Wiedersheim-Paul, 1975).

contracts usually involve repeated transactions over an agreed period of time, there are likely to be some scale effects to contracting, and hence the ratio of variable-to-fixed costs typically lies between market transactions and in-house operations. As well as defining optimal choices in a static sense, cost differentials also help explain how changes in volume may lead to mode changes over time. Growing market size drives internalization because, while market-based (e.g. exporting) and contractual operation modes (e.g. licensing) tend to be cost efficient and more appropriate for small or medium-sized markets, large markets more readily support the use of investment modes.

Governance Cost Considerations

An important mechanism for mode switch was coined by Williamson (1985) as the "fundamental transformation," which describes the change from an initial competitive situation with many actors to a small numbers-bargaining situation, and eventually to a bilateral monopoly. The key issue is increasing asset specificity (Williamson, 1975, 1985), in which adaptation between transaction parties involves relation-specific investments. Even though each such investment can be relatively inconspicuous when examined in isolation, they add up and may result in a "lock-in" situation (Petersen et al., 2000). The costly negotiation about the quasi rents accruing from mutual adaptation may drive a move away from dealing with external parties—either at arms-length or, more inflexibly, in a contract—to investment modes, where ownership over specific assets replaces bargaining with decision-making authority.

Institutional Changes

Institutional contexts affect MNE operation mode choices because they reflect the "rules of the game" in the countries in which these firms operate. Because IB has become more global, in terms of a greater number and diversity of countries that companies are actively engaged in, the external environment of businesses has received increased research attention (Morschett et al., 2010). The increased involvement and significance of emerging countries for IB has been particularly pivotal in bringing attention to the growing role played by institutional factors (Hoskisson, Eden, Lau, & Wright, 2000).

According to North (1990), it is useful to distinguish between formal and informal institutions. Key formal institutions are government organs and the laws and regulations they impose, especially those that pertain to property rights, markets, and businesses. Informal institutions comprise of those institutional categories that Scott (1995) refers to as normative institutions (norms of behavior based on appropriateness and social obligation) and cognitive institutions (which guide behavior through habits, customs, and tradition, or otherwise referred to as culture). Both formal and informal institutional factors have been shown to influence the choice of foreign operation modes (notably, Meyer et al., 2009). Further, it is assumed that institutional factors tend to change slowly, although government changes may be accompanied by rapid institutional changes, such as those recently pertaining to Brexit in the UK. Typically, however, change occurs in a gradual manner as part of long-term processes of societal and cultural changes. As such, institutional factors will usually not be the direct trigger for a mode switch.

However, on occasions, institutions change markedly at particular points in time, which may then prompt corresponding adaptations in how companies operate in a country. This is especially the case for formal institutions like laws and regulations, which may lead to major changes in operation modes. Mode switches by European and UK companies were undertaken even before the Brexit process was completed. The transition from equity joint ventures to wholly owned subsidiaries as the dominant FDI form in China is another large-scale example of mode switches instigated by a regulatory shift; in the decade around the turn of the century wholly owned subsidiaries replaced equity joint ventures as the dominant FDI form in China (Branstetter & Feenstra, 2002). During these years, FDI regulations in various Chinese industries became relaxed, not least in relation to China's World Trade Organization accession in 2001, and many foreign investors, some of which having encountered problems in collaborating with local partners (Puck et al., 2009; Rosen, 1999), took advantage of these new options for full ownership.

EXPLAINING MODE ADDITIONS

The abovementioned research review suggests a broader understanding of the drivers of mode switch beyond the initial choice of entry mode. Researchers have, in particular, paid attention to the transition from low-commitment to high-commitment operation modes, seeing internalization as a process rather than a one-off operation. A strong motivator of this research has been the numerous empirical observations of mode switches (Benito et al. 2005; Calof, 1993; Fryges, 2007; Pedersen et al., 2002; Putzhammer et al., 2018), which suggest that it is common to engage in mode switches at some stage of MNE internalization. In contrast, there has been limited research on mode additions (or mode combinations)—the phenomenon of adding one or more modes to an entry mode instead of simply replacing the entry mode. The evidence of companies using several different modes simultaneously is largely anecdotal or case-based (Akbar et al., 2018; Benito et al., 2011; Kedron & Bagchi-Sen, 2011; Petersen & Welch, 2002). Moving beyond case evidence, Clark et al. (1997) undertook a systematic examination of twenty-five British MNEs' entry (679 entries in total) and development (203 changes in total) paths in foreign countries. They report that adopting mixed modes in a market was the second most frequent change observed in their sample (18 percent of changes); switching from exporting to FDI being the most common change (51 percent of changes). Additional evidence of concurrent mode usage is suggested in a relatively more recent large-scale European survey (N = 14,759), which revealed that the vast majority (76 percent) of companies with international operations were engaged in more than one internationalization mode (Altomonte, Aquilante, Békés, & Ottaviano, 2013). Twenty percent of companies with international activities used four or more modes. That said, this survey looked at modes across countries, not at multiple modes into a single host country.

From a theoretical perspective, mode addition cannot readily be seen as a natural extension of entry mode research or internalization theory—as is the case with mode switch research. On the contrary, the mode addition phenomenon appears more as an anomaly to internalization theory and entry mode research in general. One could argue that, from a standard transaction cost economics (TCE) perspective, the mode addition or mode combination phenomenon is explicable. After all, foreign operation modes usually comprise quite different types of transactions that basically call for different governance modes. So, from a TCE perspective, multiple governance modes in a foreign market may seem more obvious as the default governance structure than does a singular operation mode. Furthermore, economies of specialization could suggest more than one operator; though, the degree of specialization (i.e. division of labor) may be limited by the size of the market (Smith, 1776; Stigler, 1951), resulting in operators performing multiple activities in smaller markets. However, multiple modes are typically associated with higher coordination costs than singular modes, that is, one common governance structure (Asmussen, Benito, & Petersen, 2009). These considerations indicate that a first-step theorization of the mode addition phenomenon is to identify and describe its basic costs and benefits—as we seek to do in the following section. Our discussion is inspired by earlier research on the disaggregation of local and global value chains into separate governance forms (e.g. Argyres & Liebeskind, 2002; Benito et al., 2011; Benito, Petersen, & Welch, 2019; Buckley, 2018; Contractor et al., 2010; Hashai et al., 2010; Petersen & Welch, 2002; Zenger & Hesterly, 1997). We formulate a set of assumptions about the benefits and costs of mode addition.

Benefits of Mode Additions: Specialization

We focus on one particular benefit; namely that of economies of specialization. Hence, benefits are associated with gains in terms of production cost savings and/or product quality enhancements. In such a specialization perspective, mode additions may not seem sensible unless there are location advantages (e.g. Dunning, 1977) associated with more than one value chain activity to be carried out locally. While that may be true generally speaking, there are exceptions such as dual distribution (Dutta, Bergen, Heide, & John, 1995; Petersen & Welch, 2002); that is, a mix of local, independent distributors and outlets owned by the entrant firm itself, or a mix of franchised and company-owned outlets (Lafontaine & Kaufmann, 1994). Even in the case of a single value chain activity undertaken in the foreign market (such as franchising of independent operators), a few company-owned outlets among independent outlets can be beneficial as benchmarking instruments and credible threats of termination. Conversely, the entrant firm may hold a minority share of the local operators as a token of credible commitment (Welch, Benito, & Petersen, 2018). Furthermore, segmentation of local customers—for example, small, local buyers and large, multinational house accounts—may motivate the use of two simultaneous operation modes in a foreign market (Valla, 1986). It is, though, difficult to envision much mode diversity in a foreign market when only a single value chain activity is carried out. Thus, we assume:

Assumption #1:   The benefits of specialization through mode addition are associated with *localization* advantages across *multiple* value chain activities.

Another condition for mode addition is that internalization advantages are not so strong that all local activities should be carried out by a wholly owned subsidiary. Conversely, internalization advantages (Dunning, 1977) should not be completely absent—in which case the only operation mode in the foreign market would be a procurement office buying local goods and services at arm's length. An internalization advantage might lead to the outsourcing of local value chain activities, thereby making up a package of different contractual modes. A case in point is the Finnish elevator company Kone, which expanded the number of operation modes in Japan in cooperation with Toshiba from exporting in 1995, to exporting, licensing, a newly established equity joint venture, and a small equity position in Toshiba in 2001. By 2005, there had been additional elements of cooperation between the two companies—demonstrating the wide range of feasible mode changes over time, well beyond the concept of singular mode change (Benito et al., 2009). Other examples could involve outsourcing all the local value chain activities, such as when primary activities are split into contract manufacturing, warehousing and haulage agreements, as well as distributor and maintenance contracts; and support or back office activities divided into business process outsourcing contracts. In this latter example, the entrant firm would essentially only coordinate the outsourced value chain activities and constitute a nexus of external contracts (Reve, 1990). The outsourcing contracts would require close coordination over a period of time, but still not to the point where a "fundamental transformation" takes place (Williamson, 1985). In other words, the asset specificity, uncertainty, and transaction frequencies of these outsourced operations would not have reached sufficiently high levels to warrant a move to hierarchical governance. Conversely, value chain activities should not be standardized to the extent that price emerges as the obvious coordination mechanism; that is, a situation where the entrant firm just buys the needed goods and services at arm's length and/or on spot markets. Accordingly, we propose that:

Assumption #2:   The benefits of specialization through mode addition accrue in the presence of non-trivial internalization advantages across multiple local value chain activities.

Adam Smith's (1776) dictum, "the division of labor is limited by the extent of the market," also implies that the benefits of specialization increase with scale. The costs of organizing mode additions due to specialization—including contract and coordination costs—tend to be relatively fixed (i.e. invariant to scale), whereas the benefits of specialization in terms of cost savings and quality improvements tend to increase with the magnitude of the individual, specialized activity (e.g. a licensing agreement in a large market—see Welch et al., 2018). A pertinent question in this connection is the extent of the relevant market. If the foreign operations are motivated by market seeking goals

(Dunning, 1988), the relevant market is the local or regional market to which the entrant firm has access. However, if the foreign operations are driven by resource, efficiency, or strategic asset seeking goals (Dunning, 1988), the relevant market could well extend beyond the host country and adjacent countries to global markets, inasmuch as the sourcing unit may provide inputs to other corporate units scattered throughout the world. Thus, we argue the following:

Assumption #3:   The benefits of specialization through mode addition are scalable and increase with market size.

Taken individually, each of the three abovementioned assumptions indicates necessary, but not sufficient, conditions for obtaining the benefits of specialization through mode addition. However, the concurrent fulfillment of all three conditions is sufficient for amassing the specialization advantages associated with multiple operation modes. The next step in our theorization of mode addition is to focus on the optimal number of mode additions. In order to do so, we first make a basic assumption that the benefits of specialization vary across the local value chain activities. As an example, an entrant firm may choose to split production and marketing in the local market so that production is kept as an in-house activity whereas marketing is handed over to a specialized, independent distributor or vice versa (see Benito et al., 2009). The separation into two operation modes may result in a more effective marketing effort, utilizing the advantages (such as language) of a local marketing operation; whereas production does not change, remaining at the same level of efficiency as before the split. Next, we propose that coarse-grained specialization is generally more beneficial than fine-grained, so that at the margin a split into two operation modes has a better payoff than a split into numerous operation modes. Put differently, as the entrant firm adds more operation modes, the marginal benefit (MB) of specialization diminishes (see Figure 14.1).

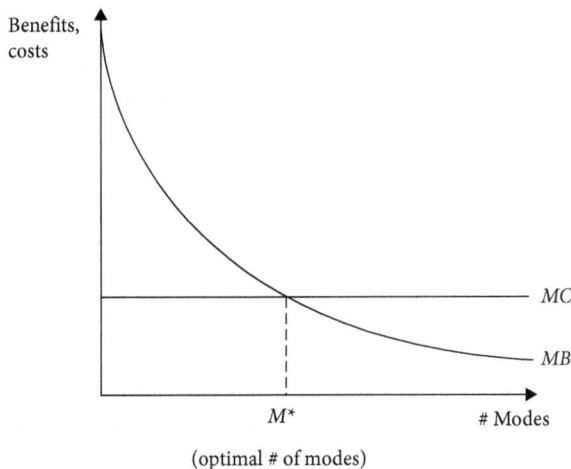

FIGURE 14.1 Marginal benefits and costs of mode additions

Given that *MB* is known, we can estimate the optimal number of mode additions if we also know their marginal cost (*MC*), since the optimal number M^* would be at the intersection where $MB = MC$. Hence, our final assumption regarding the benefits of mode addition is:

Assumption #4:   The benefits of specialization through mode addition are subject to diminishing returns to scale; the benefit of a mode addition is higher than (or equal to) that for the next addition.

Costs of Coordinating Mode Additions

We now turn to the cost side of mode addition. Costs arise in the form of extra transaction and governance costs. Although we recognize that there are many types of costs (e.g. communication, negotiation, contract, and control costs associated with governance arrangements) as well as transaction risks (e.g. free-riding and hold-up risks) associated with operation modes, we focus on coordination costs for reasons of simplification. This simplification seems appropriate insofar as extra coordination costs appear to be an inevitable and enduring effect of mode addition. As such, they are, most likely, a particularly burdensome type of cost associated with mode addition.

TCE revolves around the question of when technologically separable activities are most cost-efficiently carried out as intra-firm activities under common (hierarchical) governance, and when it is more economical to organize them as inter-firm activities through legally independent business units (Williamson, 1985). In the latter case, market transaction costs are traded off against the production cost advantages of specialization. Intuitively, we would expect multiple modes across firms to be associated with higher transaction costs than a singular operation mode under common governance. This expectation has to do with the abovementioned cost of negotiating, drafting, and enforcing contracts, but also—and not least—the costs of coordinating activities across independent firms. The notion of the superiority of hierarchical control over inter-firm task coordination has long been argued by organization design scholars (Barnard, 1938; Galbraith, 1977; Thompson, 1967). Equating a singular mode with hierarchical governance and multiple modes with inter-firm or contractual governance, we posit that:

Assumption #5:   All else being equal, the exercise of activities organized as multiple modes generate higher coordination costs than similar activities exercised as a singular mode.

Beyond establishing that inter-firm coordination in general is more costly than intra-firm coordination, we also need to recognize the interdependencies between activities carried out through various operation modes. After all, the level of coordination costs likely depends on these interdependencies (Galbraith, 1977; see also Asmussen et al., 2009). We adopt Thompson's classic distinction between three basic types of interdependencies (Thompson,

1967): pooled, sequential, and reciprocal. Pooled (or modular) interdependency is associated with the lowest coordination costs. The various organizational units (*in casu* operation modes) provide inputs to a central unit that coordinates and reallocates the pool of inputs. The coordination of inputs and related activities takes place on a bilateral basis between the central and affiliated units. Hence, the central unit administrating the resource pool guides the other units as to what to deliver to the central pool. Hence, our assumption is that:

Assumption #6:   All else being equal, coordination costs are at their lowest and increase monotonically with added modes when there is pooled interdependency between the multiple modes.

When the interdependency is sequential, the output of one unit (operation mode) is an input to another unit. Serial production is a prime example of sequential interdependency. Timing is essential since non-delivery delays the activity of the unit depending on the output. So, sequential interdependence describes the primary activities in the value chain consisting of a specific sequence of activities going from upstream to downstream. The value chain is time-sensitive and delivery-sensitive, so that the whole chain is at risk of disruption in the event of non-delivery on time by just one of the units. The key difference between pooled and sequential interdependence is that, in the latter case, the coordinating unit not only has to coordinate *what* the other units have to deliver but it also has to coordinate *when* each unit has to deliver inputs\resources and to whom. Needless to say, this implies extra coordination costs. The importance of timing of inter-firm delivery resonates with the TCE concepts of "temporal specificity" (Masten, Meehan Jr., & Snydner, 1991) or "time specificity" (Malone, Yates, & Benjamin, 1987), where an asset is time-specific if its value is highly dependent on reaching the user within a specified time period. From the above, we argue:

Assumption #7: All else being equal, coordination costs are higher when there is sequential instead of pooled interdependence between multiple modes. As with pooled interdependence the costs increase monotonically with added modes, but at a higher level due to the need for temporal coordination.

Reciprocal interdependence implies that each unit coordinates with all other units in the value chain. Moreover, coordination among the units is done in a simultaneous way given the time specificity. In other words, the units are integrated but with no central, coordinating unit in the foreign market. The units coordinate bilaterally. As we show in the next section, this type of interdependence is cost-sensitive to the number of units (*in casu* operation modes). Whereas pooled and sequential interdependencies "only" experience linearly and monotonically increasing coordination costs when new units are added, coordination costs increase exponentially. Hence:

Assumption #8:   All else being equal, coordination costs are at their highest and increase exponentially when there is reciprocal interdependence between multiple modes.

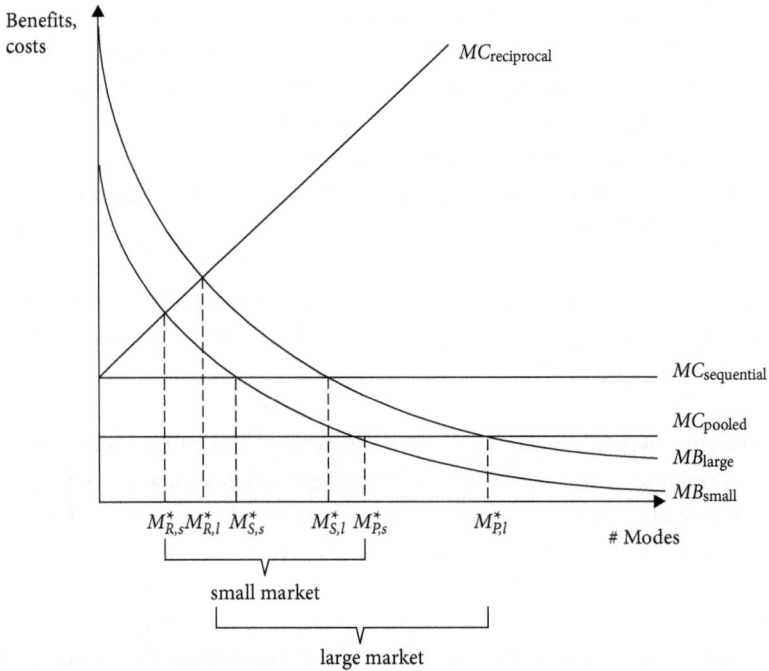

FIGURE 14.2 Marginal costs and benefits of mode additions for (i) small versus large market sizes, and (ii) type of interdependence between modes

The abovementioned reasoning is graphically summarized in Figure 14.2, which shows marginal cost curves for the three types of interdependence, with $MC_{Reciprocal} > MC_{Sequential} > MC_{Pooled}$. Generally, the simpler the interdependence, the easier it is to add modes without involving other activities and units in a company. Hence, as indicated in the figure, the optimal number of modes, M^* (given by $MB = MC$) is highest for pooled interdependent activities (M_P^*), and lowest for reciprocally interdependent activities (M_R^*). Also, the benefits of specialization depend on volume, and hence $MB_{large} > MB_{small}$, and given the type of interdependence, it follows that more modes are feasible in a larger than in a smaller market: $[M_{P,l}^* > M_{P,s}^*] > [M_{S,l}^* > M_{S,s}^*] > [M_{R,l}^* > M_{R,s}^*]$

Balancing Benefits of Specialization against Costs of Coordination

How many operation modes should a firm add to its entry mode? Following our theoretical treatment of mode addition, we can simplify this question and instead ask: How should an entrant firm balance the tradeoff between benefits of specialization and costs of coordination in terms of the number of added operation modes? The optimal balance can be expressed as the points of intersection between marginal costs and marginal benefits; as displayed in Figures 14.1 and 14.2. For MNEs whose business is based on reciprocal interdependence, the number of international operation modes is inevitably limited, especially for firms entering into small markets. However, as proposed in what follows, the situation may change if reciprocal interdependence is altered to sequential or pooled interdependence.

Lowering Coordination Costs through a Shift of Interdependence Architecture

As implied by assumptions 5–8, the magnitude of the coordination costs associated with multiple modes strongly depend on the interdependence architecture that applies to these modes. Modularization (Baldwin & Clark, 2000; Ethiraj, Levinthal, & Roy, 2008) is a mechanism that can potentially change the interdependence architecture from being reciprocal to being sequential, or even pooled.

One could obviously question to what extent organizational interdependence can be and/or is actually changed by managerial intent, for example, through the introduction of more modular designs of foreign operation modes. A modular design of foreign operation modes implies that one firm—*in casu* the entrant firm—would take on an architectural role, and hence above all: (1) specify which contractual partners will be part of the local value chain and conduct which activities; (2) describe how partners will fit together; and (3) define the standards for testing partner conformity to the overall value chain design rules. If feasible, the interfaces between the local partners would then be kept to a minimum whereas individual partners could be allocated a maximum of discretion as to how they perform their assigned activities as long as the activities are aligned with the value chain design rules laid out by the entrant firm. The aim of introducing a modular design is to fluidly integrate freestanding operational units, while simultaneously minimizing coordination costs. By design, the contrast to pooled interdependence is reciprocal interdependence, which is associated with higher coordination costs.

The literature suggests that modularity is, in fact, an outcome of organization design and thus subject to managerial intent. The computer industry (in which the term "modularity" originally emerged) provides classical examples of intended modularity, going back to the 1960s when IBM introduced its first modular computer, System 360. Another example is the introduction by Sun Microsystems of a workstation that relied on a simplified, non-proprietary architecture built with off-the-shelf hardware and software, including the widely available UNIX operating system (Baldwin & Clark, 2000). Today, modular designs of parallel programming/software development have become an industry standard.

The car manufacturing industry delivers other prominent examples of modularization. All major automotive manufacturers predominantly use modular systems, called scalable product architecture or just "platforms," which are proprietary to the individual corporations or groups (e.g. the Ford platforms, the Toyota platforms, the Volkswagen Group platforms) or, in some cases, jointly used in a strategic alliance (e.g. the Hyundai–Kia platforms). However, today's modular design in the car industry was preceded by organization designs that, instead of realizing pooled interdependency (but which nevertheless also included significant sequential interdependencies in the actual assembly phase of manufacturing), were dominantly based on sequential interdependency. The classic example is, of course, the Ford assembly line organization. However, before pioneers like Ford in the US and Citroën in Europe revolutionized car production, reciprocal interdependency (i.e. bespoke, hand-built cars) was the dominant approach, and interestingly still remains as a viable option for automotive products provided, of course, the customers have the means and willingness to pay for exceptional products.

Examples of modularization abound outside the computer and car industries (see Sanchez, 1999; Carlborg & Kindström, 2014), which supports our claim that modularization is a viable management tool for lowering coordination costs—even in the context of complexity that increases with mode addition—and, as such, should qualify as an important tradeoff-shifting mechanism.

Concluding Remarks

While foreign entry mode choices are key IB strategic decisions, and often intended for the long term, there is mounting evidence suggesting they are far from permanent. Over time, many MNEs make changes to their initial mode choices, by moving to other ways of operating in a foreign country, or by adding new modes to existing ones. Thus, the IB strategy literature would benefit from adopting a more dynamic view of entry modes—which we have generically termed "operation modes"—and develop and adapt theories and models accordingly.

In the preceding sections, we have presented a theoretical exposition of the scope for firms to deal with the motivation for and likelihood of mode changes as their IPs unfold. Such changes are typically driven by a range of potential internal and/or external developments.[‡] We emphasize that mode change is common, if not inevitable, as a by-product or even leading agent of internationalization (Benito et al., 2009). As such, it could be expected that theoretical treatment of mode dynamics would have

---

[‡] As firms move into disparate and different foreign markets it is difficult for them to maintain a "one size fits all" approach to foreign operation mode strategy. Different markets at the least mean different operating conditions, and different cultural, regulatory, market, and government contexts. Of course, over time such conditions change, prompting many firms to consider mode change as a way of responding to altered market circumstances. Internal perspectives also inevitably are adjusted as a result of learning, resource changes, strategy changes, and the like. A key factor is often the mix of increased foreign market sales and evolution in the relationship with e.g. foreign partners, such as intermediaries and master franchisees/licensees, or subcontractors, leading to a questioning of the mode being employed and its ability to contribute to market penetration and servicing goals, or to remain competitive in terms of costs, quality, and innovation.

developed strongly in that direction. Perhaps surprisingly, our discussion of the research background of mode dynamics has shown that this has not occurred and that the theoretical treatment of MNE mode dynamics could be considered to be still in its infancy. Our analysis explores the possibility of modifying key features of a company's business model, especially the nature of its operational interdependencies. Rather than merely making static tradeoffs, it may be possible to escape the tradeoff to some extent or, as we argue, to positively shift the tradeoff balance—increasing the benefit without incurring additional costs or reducing costs without reducing benefits. The altered position may involve additions of modes to an existing one. A key issue for the MNEs making these decisions relates to how many mode additions they can implement efficiently, that is, in ways that balance the benefits of specialization with the furthering of coordination costs.

We considered international decision-making in a world of mode dynamics. As such, our analysis contributes to a (re)orientation of theory toward the reality of change. While our theoretical exploration is undertaken in a restricted framework, it exposes many of the issues that today's MNE deals with.

REFERENCES

Aharoni, Y. 1966. *The Foreign Investment Decision Process.* Boston, MA: Harvard University Press.

Akbar, Y., Balboni, B., Bortoluzzi, G., Dikova, D., & Tracogna, A. 2018. Disentangling resource and mode escalation in the context of emerging markets. Evidence from a sample of manufacturing SMEs. *Journal of International Management*, 24(3): 257–270.

Altomonte, C., Aquilante, T., Békés, G., & Ottaviano, G. I. P. 2013. Internationalization and innovation of firms: Evidence and policy. *Economic Policy*, 28(76): 663–700.

Amdam, R. P. 2009. The internationalisation process theory and the internationalisation of Norwegian firms, 1945 to 1980. *Business History*, 51(3): 445–461.

Andersen, O. 1997. Internationalization and entry mode choice: A review of theories and conceptual frameworks. *Management International Review*, 37(2): 27–42.

Anderson, E., & Coughlan, A. 1987. International market entry and expansion via independent or integrated channels of distribution. *Journal of Marketing*, 51(1): 71–82.

Anderson, E., & Gatignon, H. A. 1986. Modes of foreign entry: A transaction cost analysis and propositions. *Journal of International Business Studies*, 17(3): 1–26.

Andersson, S. 2000. The internationalization of the firm from an entrepreneurial perspective. *International Studies of Management and Organization*, 30(1): 63–91.

Argyres, N. S., & Liebeskind, J. P. 2002. Governance inseparability and the evolution of US biotechnology. *Journal of Economic Behavior and Organization*, 47(2): 197–219.

Asmussen, C. G., Benito, G. R. G., & Petersen, B. 2009. Organizing foreign market activities: From entry mode choice to configuration decisions. *International Business Review*, 18(2): 145–155.

Baldwin, C. Y., & Clark, K. B. 2000. *Design Rules: The Power of Modularity.* Boston, MA: MIT Press.

Barnard, C. 1938. *The Functions of the Executive.* Boston, MA: Harvard University Press.

Benito, G. R. G., Dovgan, O., Petersen, B., & Welch, L. S. 2013. Offshore outsourcing: A dynamic operation mode perspective. *Industrial Marketing Management*, 42(2): 211–222.

Benito, G. R. G. & Gripsrud, G. 1992. The expansion of foreign direct investments: Discrete rational location choices or a cultural learning process? *Journal of International Business Studies*, 23(3): 461–476.

Benito, G. R. G., Pedersen, T., & Petersen, B. 1999. Foreign operation methods and switching costs: Conceptual issues and possible effects. *Scandinavian Journal of Management*, 15(2): 213–229.

Benito, G. R. G., Pedersen, T., & Petersen, B. 2005. Export channel dynamics: An empirical investigation. *Managerial and Decision Economics*, 26(3): 159–173.

Benito, G. R. G., Petersen, B., & Welch, L. S. 2009. Towards more realistic conceptualisations of foreign operation modes. *Journal of International Business Studies*, 40(9): 1455–1470.

Benito, G. R. G., Petersen, B., & Welch, L. S. 2011. Mode combinations and international operations: Theoretical issues and an empirical investigation. *Management International Review*, 51(6): 803–820.

Benito, G. R. G., Petersen, B., & Welch, L. S. 2019. The global value chain and internalization theory. *Journal of International Business Studies*, 50(8): 1414–1423.

Benito, G. R. G. & Welch, L. S. 1994. Foreign market servicing: Beyond choice of entry mode. *Journal of International Marketing*, 2(2): 7–27.

Björkman, I., & Eklund, M. 1996. The sequence of operational modes used by Finnish investors in Germany. *Journal of International Marketing*, 4(1): 33–55.

Branstetter, L. & Feenstra, R. 2002. Trade and FDI in China: A political economy approach. *Journal of International Economics*, 58(2): 335–358.

Brouthers, K. D., Brouthers, L. E., & Werner, S. 2003. Transaction cost-enhanced entry mode choices and firm performance. *Strategic Management Journal*, 24(12): 1239–1248.

Brouthers, K. D., & Hennart, J.-F. 2007. Boundaries of the firm: Insights from international entry mode research. *Journal of Management*, 33(3): 395–425.

Buckley, P. J. 1989. Foreign direct investment by small- and medium-sized enterprises: The theoretical background. *Small Business Economics*, 1(2): 89–100.

Buckley, P. J. 2018. *The Global Factory: Networked Multinational Enterprises in the Modern Global Economy*. Cheltenham: Edward Elgar.

Buckley, P. J., & Casson, M. C. 1976. *The Future of the Multinational Enterprise*. London: Macmillan.

Buckley, P. J., & Casson, M. C. 1981. The optimal timing of a foreign direct investment. *Economic Journal*, 91(361): 75–87.

Buckley, P. J. & Ghauri, P. N. (Eds.). 1994. *The Economics of Change in East and Central Europe: Its Impact on International Business*. London: Academic Press.

Calof, J. L. 1993. The mode choice and change decision process and its impact on international performance. *International Business Review*, 2(1): 97–120.

Calof, J. L., & Beamish, P. W. 1995. Adapting to foreign markets: Explaining internationalization. *International Business Review*, 4(2): 115–131.

Canabal, A. & White III, G. O. 2008. Entry mode research: Past and future. *International Business Review*, 17(3): 267–284.

Carlborg, P., & Kindström, D. 2014. Service process modularization and modular strategies. *Journal of Business and Industrial Marketing*, 29(4): 313–323.

Chetty, S., & Agndal, H. 2007. Social capital and its influence on changes in internationalization mode among small and medium-sized enterprises. *Journal of International Marketing*, 15(1): 1–29.

Clark, T., Pugh, D. S. & Mallory, G. 1997. The process of internationalization in the operating firm. *International Business Review*, 6(6): 605–623.

Contractor, F. J., Kumar, V., Kundu, S. K., & Pedersen, T. 2010. Reconceptualizing the firm in a world of outsourcing and offshoring: The organizational and geographical relocation of high-value company functions. *Journal of Management Studies*, 47(8): 1417–1433.

Davidson, W. H., & McFetridge, D. G. 1985. Key characteristics in the choice of the international technology transfer mode. *Journal of International Business Studies*, 16(2): 5–21.

Dow, D., Liesch, P., & Welch, L. S. 2018. Inertia and managerial intentionality: Extending the Uppsala model. *Management International Review*, 58(3): 465–493.

Dunning, J. H. 1977. Trade, location of economic activity and the MNE: A search for an eclectic approach. In B. Ohlin, P-O. Hesselborn & P. M. Wijkman, (Eds.). *The International Allocation of Economic Activity*. London: Macmillan.

Dunning J. H. 1988. The theory of international production. *International Trade Journal*, 3(1): 21–66.

Dutta, S., Bergen, M., Heide, J. B., & John, G. 1995. Understanding dual distribution: The case of reps and house accounts. *Journal of Law, Economics & Organization*, 11(1): 189–204.

Ethiraj, S. K., Levinthal, D., & Roy, R. R. 2008. The dual role of modularity: Innovation and imitation. *Management Science*, 54(5): 939–955.

Fryges, H. 2007. Change of sales mode in international markets: Empirical results for German and British high-tech firms. *Progress in International Business Research*, 1: 139–185.

Galbraith, J. R. 1977. *Organizational Design*. Massachusetts: Addison Wesley.

Hashai, N., Asmussen, C. G., Benito, G. R. G., & Petersen, B. 2010. Technological knowledge intensity and entry mode diversity. *Management International Review*, 50(6): 659–681.

Hedlund, G., & Kverneland, Å. 1985. Are strategies for foreign markets changing? The case of Swedish investment in Japan. *International Studies of Management and Organization*, 15(2): 41–59.

Hennart, J.-F. 1982. *A Theory of Multinational Enterprise*. Ann Arbor, MI: University of Michigan Press.

Hennart, J.-F. 1991. The transaction costs theory of joint ventures: An empirical study of Japanese subsidiaries in the United States. *Management Science*, 37(4): 483–497.

Hernández, V., & Pedersen, T. 2017. Global value chain configuration: A review and research agenda. *Business Research Quarterly*, 20(1): 137–150.

Horst, T. 1972. Firm and industry determinants of the decision to invest abroad: An empirical study. *Review of Economics and Statistics*, 54(3): 258–266.

Hoskisson, R. E., Eden, L., Lau, C. M., & Wright, M. 2000. Strategy in emerging economies. *Academy of Management Journal*, 43(3): 249–267.

Johanson, J., & Vahlne, J.-E. 1977. The internationalization process of the firm—A model of knowledge development and increasing foreign market commitments. *Journal of International Business Studies*, 8(1): 23–32.

Johanson, J., & Wiedersheim-Paul, F. 1975. The internationalization of the firm: Four Swedish cases. *Journal of Management Studies*, 12(3): 305–322.

Kedron, P., & Bagchi-Sen, S. 2011. US market entry processes of emerging multinationals, *Applied Geography*, 31(2): 721–730.

Kogut, B., & Singh, H. 1988. The effect of national culture on the choice of entry mode. *Journal of International Business Studies*, 19(3): 411–432.

Kogut, B., & Zander, U. 1993. Knowledge of the firm and the evolutionary theory of the multinational corporation. *Journal of International Business Studies*, 24(4): 625–645.

Kostova, T., & Zaheer, S. 1999. Organizational legitimacy under conditions of complexity. *Academy of Management Review*, 24(1): 64–81.

Lafontaine, F., & Kaufmann, P. J. 1994. The evolution of ownership patterns in franchise systems. *Journal of Retailing*, 70(2): 97–113.

Madhok, A. 1997. Cost, value and foreign market entry mode. *Strategic Management Journal*, 18(1): 39–61.

Malone, T. W., Yates J., & Benjamin, R. I. 1987. Electronic markets and electronic hierarchies. *Communications of the ACM*, 30(6): 484–497.

Masten, S. E., Meehan Jr., J. W., & Snydner, E. A. 1991. The costs of organization. *Journal of Law, Economics & Organization*, 7(1): 1–25.

Meyer, K. E., Estrin, S., Bhaumik, S. K., & Peng, M. 2009. Institutions, resources, and entry strategies in emerging markets. *Strategic Management Journal*, 30(1): 61–80.

Meyer, K. E., & Gelbuda, M. 2006. Process perspectives in international business research in CEE. *Management International Review*, 46 (2): 143–164.

Meyer, K. E., & Peng, M. 2005. Probing theoretically into Central and Eastern Europe. *Journal of International Business Studies*, 36(6): 600–621.

Millington, A. I., & Bayliss, B. T. 1990. The process of internationalisation: UK companies in the EC. *Management International Review*, 30(2): 151–161.

Morschett, D., Schramm-Klein, H., & Swoboda, B. 2010. Decades of research on market entry modes: What do we really know about external antecedents of entry mode choice? *Journal of International Management*, 16(1): 60–77.

Nakamura, M., Shaver, J. M., & Yeung, B. 1996. An empirical investigation of joint venture dynamics: Evidence from U.S.-Japan joint ventures. *International Journal of Industrial Organization*. 14(4): 521–541.

North, D. C. 1990. *Institutions, Institutional Change, and Economic Performance*. New York, NY: Norton.

Pedersen T., Petersen, B., & Benito, G. R. G. 2002. Change of foreign operation methods: Impetus and switching costs. *International Business Review*, 11(3): 325–345.

Petersen, B., & Pedersen, T. 1997. Twenty years after—Support and critique of the Uppsala internationalization model. In I. Björkman & M. Forsgren (Eds.), *The Nature of the International Firm*. Copenhagen: Copenhagen Business School Press.

Petersen, B., Welch, D. E., & Welch, L. S. 2000. Creating meaningful switching options in international operations. *Long Range Planning*, 33(5): 688–705.

Petersen, B., & Welch, L. S. 2002. Foreign operation mode combinations and internationalization. *Journal of Business Research*, 55(2): 157–162.

Petersen, B., Welch, L. S., & Benito, G. R. G. 2010. Managing the internalisation process. *Management International Review*, 50(2): 137–154.

Puck, J., Holtbrügge, D. & Mohr, A. 2009. Beyond entry mode choice: Explaining the conversion of joint ventures into wholly owned subsidiaries in the People's Republic of China. *Journal of International Business Studies*, 40(3): 388–404.

Putzhammer, M., Fainshmidt, S., Puck, J., & Slangen, A. 2018. To elevate or to duplicate? Experiential learning, host-country institutions, and MNE post-entry commitment increase. *Journal of World Business*, 53(4): 568–580.

Reve, T. 1990. The firm as a nexus of internal and external contracts. In M. Aoki., B. Gustafsson, & O.E. Williamson (Eds.), *The Firm as a Nexus of Treaties*. London: Sage.

Root, F.R. 1964. Strategic planning for export marketing. *The International Executive*, 6(4): 17.

Rosen, D. 1999. *Behind the Open Door: Foreign Enterprises in the Chinese Marketplace*. Washington, DC: Peterson Institute.

Sanchez, R. 1999. Modular architectures in the marketing process. *Journal of Marketing*, 63(4): 92–111.

Scott, R. W. 1995. *Institutions and Organizations—Ideas, Interests and Identities*. London: Sage.

Smith, A. 1776. *An Inquiry into the Nature and Causes of the Wealth of Nations*. London: George Routledge and Sons.

Stigler, G. J. 1951. The division of labor is limited by the extent of the market. *Journal of Political Economy*, 59(3): 185–193.

Swoboda, B., Olejnik, E., & Morschett, D. 2011. Changes in foreign operation modes. *International Business Review*, 20(5): 578–590.

Thompson, J. D. 1967. *Organizations in Action*. New York, NY: McGraw Hill.

Tihanyi, L., Griffiths, D. A., & Russell, C. J. 2005. The effect of cultural distance on entry mode choice, international diversification and MNE performance: A meta-analysis. *Journal of International Business Studies*, 36(3): 270–286.

Valla, J. P. 1986. The French approach to Europe. In P. W. Turnbull & J. P. Valla (Eds.), *Strategies for International Industrial Marketing*. London: Croom Helm.

Verbeke, A. 2003. The evolutionary view of the MNE and the future of internalization theory. *Journal of International Business Studies*, 34(6): 498–504.

Welch, L. S., Benito, G. R. G., & Petersen, B. 2018. *Foreign Operation Methods: Theory, Analysis, Strategy*, 2nd edition. London: Edward Elgar.

Welch, L. S., & Luostarinen, R. K. 1988. Internationalization: Evolution of a concept. *Journal of General Management*, 14(2): 34–55.

Wilkins, M. 1970. *The Emergence of Multinational Enterprise*. Boston, MA: Harvard University Press.

Wilkins, M. 1974. *The Maturing of Multinational Enterprise*. Boston, MA: Harvard University Press.

Williamson, O. E. 1975. *Markets and Hierarchies: Analysis and Antitrust Implications*. New York, NY: Free Press.

Williamson, O. E. 1985. *The Economic Institutions of Capitalism*. New York, NY: Free Press.

Zenger, T. R., & Hesterly, W. S. 1997. The disaggregation of corporations. *Organization Science*, 8(3): 257–274.

Zhao, H., Luo, Y., & Suh, T. 2004. Transaction cost determinants and ownership-based entry mode choice: A meta-analytical review. *Journal of International Business Studies*, 35(6): 524–544.

CHAPTER 15

SUBSIDIARIES AS SOURCES FOR LEARNING IN MULTINATIONAL ENTERPRISES

A Commentary on the Importance of External Embeddedness

ULF ANDERSSON, MATS FORSGREN, AND ULF HOLM

INTRODUCTION

ALTHOUGH the position of the subsidiary within the MNE had been highlighted in some of the earlier studies (e.g. Birkinshaw, 1998; Birkinshaw & Ridderstråle, 1999; Andersson & Forsgren, 2000; Holm & Pedersen, 2000), the two articles written by Andersson, Forsgren, and Holm in 2001 and later in 2002 represent some early attempts to explicitly discuss the causality between a subsidiary's embeddedness in its local business network and its role in the multinational enterprise (MNE). More specifically, the underlying idea was that close relationships with customers and suppliers have the potential to facilitate the possibility to pick up new knowledge from the subsidiary's external environment. This, in turn, has a positive impact on both the subsidiary's market performance and its ability to contribute to the competence development of sister units through transfer of new knowledge from the subsidiary to these units. Data on ninety-seven subsidiaries in twenty MNEs confirmed the proposed positive relationship between the subsidiaries' external embeddedness and market performance as well as their importance for the competence development of sister units (Andersson, Forsgren, & Holm, 2001, 2002). Figure 15.1 summarizes the analysis of the two articles.

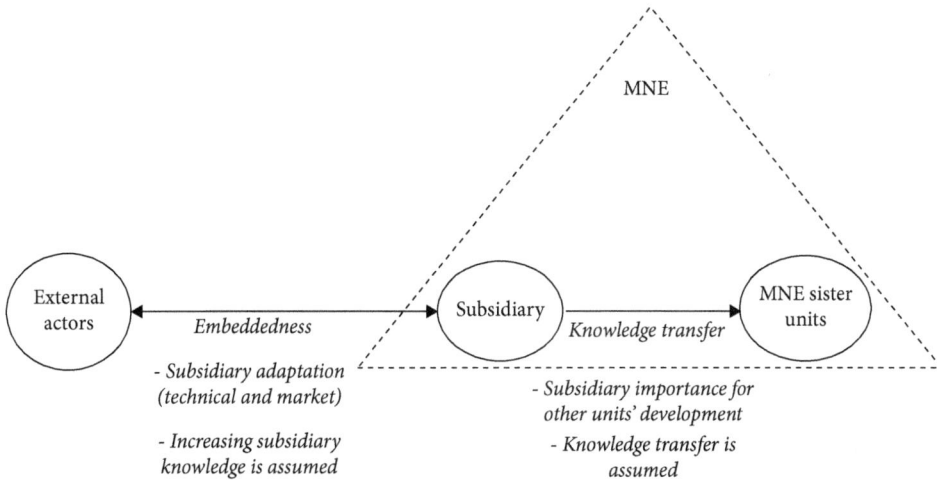

FIGURE 15.1 The relation between external embeddedness and knowledge transfer as in the 2001 and 2002 articles

As these two articles have since been consistently cited among international business (IB) strategy scholars, the present chapter analyzes the subsequent discussion of the relationship between embeddedness and subsidiary competence development, more or less inspired by these two articles. Then, we discuss how to conceptualize competence development and transfer in relation to subsidiary external embeddedness and propose some areas for future research for scholars interested in the roles of MNE subsidiaries.

KNOWLEDGE TRANSFER OR SPECIALIZATION IN CUSTOMER–SUPPLIER RELATIONSHIPS?

First, some comments on the two articles. Andersson et al. (2001, 2002) deal with learning in the sense of *transfer of knowledge*. The focus has been on understanding two interrelated aspects around knowledge transfer, namely (1) how a subsidiary can acquire new knowledge through its relationships with business partners; and (2) how this new knowledge will impact both its market performance and its position within the MNE as a "competence giver" to sister units. In retrospect, we argue that, although the impact of network embeddedness at the time was quite a new grip in an MNE context, our analysis was somewhat misleading when it comes to the knowledge transfer aspect. Our construct "network embeddedness" is defined as the depth of relationships with customers and suppliers, that is, what Richardson would have called *complementary* relationships (Richardson, 1972). Our rationale was that such relationships imply improved possibilities to learn, in that the closer the relationship, the greater the learning opportunities.

Although it is reasonable to argue that relationship embeddedness will facilitate exchange of fine-grained information,[1] this information concerns the subsidiary's knowledge about the partner's capability to carry out a certain activity, but not *learning about how to carry out the activity itself*. It is primarily not about transfer of competence but exchange of fine-grained information of how to best coordinate activities, to solve mutual problems, and adapt and develop each party's (different) knowledge areas to reach as good fit as possible between their respective products and processes. A complementary relationship is motivated primarily by the division of labor, specialization and consequently economizing on the transfer of knowledge, that is, *not* equalizing capabilities (Postrel, 2002). In retrospect, it is obvious that we overemphasized the "transfer of knowledge aspect" in our analysis of the consequences of network embeddedness in terms of the existence of complementary relationships.

The concept of *transfer* therefore is somewhat misleading in the customer–supplier case because rather than transferring a certain capability from one unit to another, *transfer* refers to the question of one unit's *understanding* of what its partner can do, without having any intentions of imitating it or doing the same thing itself. Such understanding is important in situations of problem-solving in the value chain. For instance, it seems obvious that communication across specialties is an important factor in making product development projects more successful (Hoopes & Postrel, 1999), and that close relationships between customers and suppliers are conducive to mutual problem-solving (von Hippel, 1988; Håkansson, 1989). However, it has also been convincingly argued that there is a tradeoff between specializing and understanding across the value chain, that is, *trans-specialist understanding*. The basic reason for this is that specialization and trans-specialist understanding are substitutes for one another, they are not complementary. In many cases, one specialist's capacity buffers the other from needing to understand its problems, in a similar way as having a stock of inventory between two stages of production allows each stage to optimize its own work cycle without synchronizing the units. In other cases, though, trans-specialist understanding can compensate for inferior specialization capability (Postrel, 2002).

An important conclusion from this reasoning is that trans-specialist understanding is not a prerequisite for the efficiency of a workflow system. On the contrary, based on the assumption that existent knowledge facilitates more learning in the same field rather than new fields, investing in specialized knowledge is often cheaper than investing in trans-specialist understanding. This implies that organizing an economy in which the "black-box principle" (of having a highly capable specialty that is opaque to others) is a common state of affairs, although interrupted by "islands" of understanding across specialties (Postrel, 2002). The fact that these "islands" play a vital role in certain situations, and also happen to be important features of management, should not mislead us into thinking that knowledge transfer in customer–supplier relationships is a dominant feature in MNE subsidiaries. It probably is not, and it should not be.

---

[1] As opposed to "simple" and explicit information regarding aspects such as price and quality, among others.

Hence, strong ties in the value chain do not automatically imply knowledge transfer, as illustrated in the study by Yli-Renko, Autio, and Sapienza (2001). In their study about the relationship between technology-based firms and their key customers, the authors found that relationship quality (in terms of trust) and knowledge acquisition as a consequence of customer relationships were *negatively* related. The authors suggest that one reason for this result would be that:

> [as] trust reaches a very high level, the expectation may exist that information will be provided when needed, so that the incentive to acquire external knowledge is reduced. In short, a high level of trust may allow a relationship to run smoothly and may reduce some of the transaction costs associated with managing the customer relationships but may not actually increase the knowledge acquisition.
>
> (Yli-Renko et al., 2001: 608)

One might add that knowledge transfer, because of a supplier–customer relationship, is dependent on the *relevance* of the knowledge in question (Yang, Mudambi, & Meyer, 2008). For such a relationship to be efficient, knowledge transfer in terms of investing in trans-specialist understanding is the exception rather than the rule. Expressed differently, a firm's possibility to be an efficient supplier is more contingent on developing its own capabilities than to learn about its customers' capabilities. However, as von Hippel (1988) shows, being able to understand what customers need and the motivations behind those needs, is imperative for the supplier's successful product and process development.

In the Andersson et al. (2001, 2002) articles, we assumed that there is a positive correlation between relational embeddedness and the transfer of specialized knowledge in these relationships; however, *we did not explicitly measure knowledge transfer or the "amount" of learning within the subsidiary* due to the specialized knowledge received from the external counterparts. Our main indicators of level of embeddedness in the relationships with suppliers and customers are the subsidiary's adaptation of different development activities. Hence a reasonable conclusion is that what we captured in our analysis is the degree of *efficiency in coordination and specialization* of the subsidiary's external business network, rather than actual *knowledge transfer* within this network. This reasoning would offer another explanation for a positive relationship between embeddedness and the subsidiary's expected market performance than the explanation using subsidiary knowledge as a mediating variable. Further, the impact of external embeddedness on subsidiary importance for other units' competence development potentially also gains a different meaning than we suggested in the two papers. Our theoretical reasoning in the two articles is more suitable for the opposite type of relationship in Richardson dichotomy, that is, *similar* relationships, for example, relationships with competitors or other counterparts that build their activities on similar technologies, which is what sister subsidiaries are frequently doing.

In the Andersson et al. (2002) article, relational embeddedness is measured in two different and distinct dimensions, namely business embeddedness and technical embeddedness. As the results show we find no direct relationship between *"Business*

Embeddedness" and "*Subsidiary Market Performance*" but we do so between "*Technical Embeddedness*" and "*Subsidiary Market Performance*." We also find that business embeddedness positively and significantly influenced technical embeddedness; this means that it is important for coordination of the different parties' business activities to be able to take advantage of the specialized knowledge residing in the different counterparts for development of specialized technology, in the subsidiary, to better fit the counterparts' needs regarding their technology.

In other words, what is "black-boxed" and therefore not directly measured in the two articles is the subsidiary learning and knowledge stock, that is, the subsidiary's increased knowledge of their counterpart's product and production process technologies, which helps in the development and adaptation process of its specialized technology. The knowledge developed in terms of how to develop their own technology to better adapt its products and processes to the (complementary) external counterparts' products and processes is the knowledge the subsidiary can transfer to its (similar) sister subsidiaries. What the subsidiary has to learn and the knowledge it has to develop in its own technology area is what it can transfer to its sister subsidiaries (within the same technology area), and it does not concern the specialized knowledge residing in their external counterparts (and their technological areas). Hence the concept of "sourcing knowledge" from the local network is not central to the 2001 and 2002 articles.

In the next section, we provide an overview of research conducted during the last fifteen years or so, which examines the relationship between embeddedness and subsidiary competence development. A common denominator of these contributions is that they have used the two articles as reference points in developing their contributions. The purpose of the review is to investigate to what extent IB strategy scholars have addressed some of the weaknesses of these two articles as revealed earlier:

- How have they conceptualized the transfer of knowledge in business relationships?
- What role does it play in different types of relationships?
- What impact will different types of relationships between MNE units have on the transfer of competence?
- What role does "context specificity" have on the relationship between network embeddedness and subsidiary competence development?

EXTERNAL EMBEDDEDNESS AND SUBSIDIARY KNOWLEDGE ACQUISITION IN LATER WORKS ON MNE SUBSIDIARIES

In a large number of articles, other scholars referred to Andersson et al. (2001, 2002) to examine network embeddedness and/or knowledge transfer in MNEs (notable studies include: Schmid & Schurig, 2003; Boehe, 2007; Yang et al., 2008; Phene & Almeida, 2008;

Garcia-Point, Canales, & Noboa, 2009; Fjeldstad & Sasson, 2010; Figueiredo, 2011; Meyer, Mudambi, & Narula, 2011; Tallman & Chacar, 2011; Nell, Ambos, & Schlegelmilch, 2011; Santangelo, 2012; Achcaoucaou, Miravitlles, & Leon-Barder, 2014; Asakawa, Park, Song, & Kim, 2018). The conceptualization of embeddedness and knowledge transfer in later contributions differ, though, both in relation to the two articles and across the different studies. Overall, none of the later contributions investigate specifically whether external embeddedness in terms of customer–supplier relationships has a positive impact on other subsidiaries' competence development. Although there are a few exceptions, the general impression is rather that a positive impact is more or less taken for granted rather than observed (e.g. Dhanaraj, Lyles, Steensma, & Tihanyi, 2004; Håkanson & Nobel, 2001; Karna, Täube, & Sonderegger, 2013; Mu, Gnyawali, & Hatfield, 2007; Yamao, Cieri, & Hutchings, 2009). Some of these articles focus specifically on external embeddedness, including customer–supplier relationships, but very few of them relate this more precisely to the ability of subsidiaries to absorb knowledge from its external network. One exception is the study by Schmid and Schurig (2003) who investigate the extent to which linkages to external suppliers and customers can explain the development of different types of capabilities among a large number of foreign subsidiaries. The general conclusion from this study is that the influence of "external partners for capability development is not considered to be high (below mean of a 7-point liker scale)," although it is found that relationships to external customers had a higher degree of influence than relationships with external suppliers. It should be noted that, in contrast to the 2001 and 2002 articles, external relationships with customers and suppliers are not measured independently of the assessment of a subsidiary's knowledge development (or transfer). Instead, what is measured is the subsidiary's own estimation of the extent to which a certain relationship has been important for a particular type of capability development. Consequently, the methodology differs significantly, which makes comparisons reasonably challenging. Even so, the study suffers from the same weaknesses as the 2001 and 2002 articles, namely that knowledge transfer is not directly measured, with the focus being on its assumed consequences.

In a study by Figueiredo (2011), the causal relationship between external embeddedness and subsidiary knowledge acquisition is also addressed. The quality of external embeddedness is assessed as a distinction between arm's-length relationships and collaborative relationships characterized by high degrees of trust. Subsidiary capabilities are defined as different levels of innovative and production performance, ranging from basic to world leading levels. These definitions are applied to a study of seven subsidiaries operating in the information and communication technologies industry. One basic finding from this study is that, regarding the impact of external embeddedness on subsidiary innovative performance, "counterparts like universities and research institutes proved more effective than suppliers, consulting firms and clients" (Figueiredo, 2011). At least among these seven firms, the relationships with "knowledge-producing" external organizations seem more important than the external customer–supplier relationships. As in the former study, knowledge transfer is not measured as such, only its assumed consequences.

In general, it is difficult to find any substantial evidence in studies after the 2001 and 2002 articles concerning the importance of external customer–supplier relationships for subsidiary knowledge transfer. To what extent customers and/or suppliers are included in the embeddedness concept is unclear and the findings are mixed. For instance, in the study by Santangelo (2012), who focuses on antecedents to subsidiary embeddedness, it is emphasized that subsidiaries having more pressures to innovate tend to create close relationships with local institutions rather than with local firms, like clients or suppliers.

Some contributions focus on external embeddedness including customers and suppliers but do not relate that to knowledge transfer. For instance, Nell et al. (2011) estimate the strength of external relationships in a large number of subsidiaries in Europe, but use the data to discuss to what extent and why headquarters (HQ) built up a similar network; in turn, they do not examine the impact of the network on the subsidiaries' knowledge acquisition. A relatively sophisticated measurement of external embeddedness is carried out by Boehe (2007) in a study of 146 foreign subsidiaries in Brazil. In this study a distinction is made between *cooperative* linkages aimed at developing new products jointly and *outsourcing* linkages, implying higher efficiency at the cost of less learning. This concept and measurement of embeddedness is then used to discuss the tradeoff between a subsidiary's local linkages and its involvement in a global workflow system; the author does not focus on investigating whether embeddedness has a positive impact on the subsidiary's ability to develop new knowledge.

Some contributions are more explicit when it comes to subsidiaries' competence-creating abilities, but instead, do not relate this to the subsidiary's external embeddedness (or do so in a rudimentary way). For instance, Yang et al. (2008) measure directly the extent of knowledge transfer between subsidiaries and HQs in 105 acquired subsidiaries. This knowledge transfer is then explained as a consequence of the characteristics of the knowledge in terms of relevance and the motives behind the acquisitions. External embeddedness does not play a major role in this analysis, apart from using customers and the market on both sides as the indicators of "overlapping knowledge," and therefore relevance. In a study by Phene and Almeida (2008) the scale and quality of subsidiary innovation is constructed by examining the patent portfolio at the subsidiary level and the citations received by the portfolio, while the knowledge assimilated by the subsidiary from host country firms is measured by identifying those cited patents that were assigned to a firm in the local country. One conclusion from this study is that knowledge assimilated from host country firms has a positive impact on both the scale and quality of subsidiary innovation. However, this study does not deal with the subsidiaries' external network embeddedness in general, or even less so with relationships with customers and suppliers, and therefore contributes less to the topic of the relationship between embeddedness and knowledge creation in subsidiaries and subsequent transfer to the MNE.

It can therefore be concluded that studies inspired by or based on the two articles show a very mixed picture, when it comes to both the concept of external embeddedness and the knowledge creation and transfer at the subsidiary level. Very few, if any, replicate these studies by looking precisely into the relationships between the subsidiary's external embeddedness and its ability to create and transfer new knowledge within the MNE. All the papers deal with more or less similar issues but in different ways, using different measurements, and with different purposes. One observation from these studies, though, is clear: there seems to be very limited empirical support for the conclusion that close relationships with external customers and suppliers also imply a high degree of knowledge transfer between the local environment and the subsidiary. As indicated earlier, knowledge transfer in conventional value chain relationships is rather a matter of information exchange than a matter of learning. In fact, Uzzi and Lancaster (2003) demonstrate that embedded ties (in terms of trust and reciprocity) are conducive to the transfer of private information. The context of this study is about the relationships between bank managers and clients, rather than conventional value chain relationships. This study also indicates that, in investigating the importance of external embeddedness on knowledge transfer, it is relevant to make a distinction between "information" and "learning." Close relationships with customers and suppliers will always facilitate information exchange. However, to what extent such relationships also imply *learning in terms of knowledge transfer* is a different matter, as there is always a tradeoff between acquiring knowledge about counterparts' capabilities and developing own capabilities. All knowledge transfer between units in a conventional value chain context is simply not relevant.

External Embeddedness and its Importance to Subsidiary Knowledge Transfer

One of the assumptions underlying the 2001 and 2002 articles was that a subsidiary's relationship embeddedness provides relational knowledge and enables adaptation in market and technical development activities vis-à-vis its specific counterparts. This embeddedness of the subsidiary varies across its external relationships, resulting in a multiplex set of relation specific knowledge and development activities, which, in consequence, provide a potential interest in the subsidiary's knowledge among other MNE units. In the articles, the importance for sister units' competence development is the dependent variable, which is assessed by divisional HQs, while the independent variable, the subsidiary's external embeddedness, is estimated by the subsidiary itself. As the knowledge transfer between the focal subsidiary and sister units is not measured directly, it is reasonable to discuss several possible explanations for the positive result between the subsidiary's external embeddedness and its importance for other units' competence development.

The intuitive conclusion is that knowledge transfer from the subsidiary to other MNE units *has* actually occurred and that it is related to the subsidiary's high degree of external embeddedness. This is the broad message of the two articles (Andersson et al., 2001, 2002). However, embeddedness in external relations to, for example, customers and suppliers, is probably not contributing with detailed technical knowledge in the actual technology class that the subsidiary is situated. These types of counterparts are complementary towards the subsidiary and they are therefore focused on competence developments that help them to perform better in what they do (in their specific part of the value chain). The knowledge and information that the subsidiary can better pick up in such relationships is rather about how their particular (technology class) product specifically is used by the counterpart, how it performs in their production process and what characteristics will make it perform even better in the specific counterpart's production process. Understanding this on a fine-grained level is imperative in developing the product. How to accomplish this technologically in the subsidiary's specific product is a question for the subsidiary itself as the specialist in this particular technology, that is, a deeper and better understanding of the subsidiary's own technology class, is a subsidiary internal issue. The outcome of technology improvements in terms of, for example, product developments can, in an embedded relationship, be tested and evaluated, not in terms of the product's technological advancements, but in terms of its performance. This is very much like Håkansson's (1989) understanding of the importance of customer requests or von Hippels' (1988) understanding of how customers, by formulating their needs and wants, are instrumental for a company's product developments and subsequent commercial success. Therefore, the knowledge gained from external (value chain) relationships is not necessarily of a technological nature for the product development but rather of a performance or outcome nature. Consequently, subsidiary "learning" from external customer–supplier relationships can be highly context specific and therefore more difficult to transfer to other units than it is usually assumed. This leads us to alternative explanations for the conclusion that highly externally embedded subsidiaries are deemed important for other units' competence development. We make an effort to explain the complex relationship between embeddedness and the competence development of other units in the following sections.

Network Embeddedness as a Benchmark for Other MNE Units

The first alternative explanation has to do with the development of a business network. There is ample evidence that establishing close relationships with customers and suppliers takes time (Forsgren, Holm, & Johanson, 2005). Therefore, a reasonable assumption is that MNE subsidiaries that are highly externally embedded in their local markets are also subsidiaries that, relatively speaking, are larger and more experienced, which the 2001 and 2002 articles did not control for. When a subsidiary becomes embedded in relationships with external actors through adapting its own capabilities, and learns about its counterparts' capabilities, needs, and requirements, it does not necessarily mean that it has created knowledge of importance to transfer to others. Hence a subsidiary's embeddedness through adaptation is a matter of development over time, reflecting increasing business experience and performance. In that sense, the subsidiary's evolvement into an integrated actor in its external network could simply be a benchmark for other units. The observed positive correlation between subsidiary external embeddedness and divisional HQs' evaluation of a subsidiary's importance for other units' competence development might therefore reflect that some subsidiaries are simply larger and/or more experienced, and a role model for other units.[2] The effective mechanism in this explanation is that some sister units would be informed about the consequences of the focal subsidiary's embeddedness vis-à-vis external counterparts. However, this does not imply that the sister units will use the same knowledge and behave in the exact same or similar manner as the focal subsidiary. The lessons learned may be simply that embeddedness in certain types of external relationships is often conducive for business development.

Network Embeddedness and Subsidiary Interdependence

Another possible explanation points to an alternative causal mechanism. In this case, a subsidiary's adaptation of business and technological activities can reflect its dependence on external business relationships. Unless the subsidiary adapts and develops its activities to fit the relationship requirements there is a risk of a negative business development, whereas doing so could mean a positive development. This is consistent with the findings in the 2001 and 2002 articles. However, the positive relationship between external technical embeddedness and the importance for other units may reflect a positive effect on the subsidiary's expected market performance (Andersson et al., 2001, 2002). In turn, the value of building embeddedness in the external network may affect corporate sister units' dependence on the subsidiary. Hence the dependence of the subsidiary on the external relationships may have indirect effects on the business development and importance for the subsidiary's corporate sister units as well. In other words, a subsidiary's dependence on another subsidiary's external customer–supplier relationships might be indirect, via internal business relationships with the latter subsidiary. The importance of the subsidiary for sister units therefore might reflect a case of a bridge-head function rather than a case of actual knowledge transfer.

---

[2] Subsidiary size and subsidiary external embeddedness were, however, included simultaneously in a model looking at subsidiaries being centers of excellence (Andersson & Forsgren, 2000). Here subsidiary importance for other units' competence development was part of the centers of excellence measure and size did not have a significant role in explaining subsidiary importance while external embeddedness did. Notably the empirical sample is the same as for the 2001 and 2002 articles. A similar result was observed in Forsgren et al. (2005).

Network Embeddedness and the Absorptive Capacity of MNE Units

A third possible explanation is related to who the knowledge receivers are within the MNE. While some research, for example, makes a distinction between vertical and lateral knowledge transfer (e.g. Michailova & Mustaffa, 2012), Andersson et al. (2001, 2002) are unclear on this issue and only discuss "other MNE units." One possible distinction, as mentioned earlier, can be made between the so-called similar and complementary relationships between MNE subsidiaries (Richardson, 1972). Firstly, we can assume that knowledge transfer to similar corporate units is relevant as they operate within the same business, meaning that they share similar market activities and market challenges. The absorptive capacity between such corporate units may be strong due to their relatively similar knowledge bases. There is reason to assume that, viewed from the divisional HQs' perspective, the sharing of knowledge between subsidiaries with similar technology and business is extremely important. However, the relations between subsidiaries with similar activities are also conditioned by them operating in geographically separated markets and often competing for internal resources and responsibilities. Consequently, one might expect a "political tension" between subsidiaries with similar technologies and business (Andersson, Forsgren, & Holm, 2007; Mudambi & Navarra, 2004; Andersson, Gaur, Mudambi, & Persson, 2015). This suggests that a subsidiary that has developed new knowledge of potential importance to similar corporate units may be unwilling to share this knowledge with those sister units.

The situation is different when it concerns relationships between complementary units, which are common in MNEs with extensive vertical integration between units. In these types of relationships, the subsidiary and corporate counterpart units are functionally interdependent. This implies that when changes of a certain product are made by the subsidiary unit, the corresponding change may be required by the corporate supplier of components. This has been described here as a situation of mutual interaction to solve problems rather than of transferring specific knowledge between units in the value chain. An interesting puzzle following from this distinction is that knowledge transfer between similar units may be more relevant but difficult due to less deep relationships and political tensions while knowledge transfer between units in complementary relationships is less difficult due to closer relationships, but at the same time of less relevance due to knowledge specialization. This should have bearing on the manner in which we define and study knowledge transfer between MNE subsidiaries.

To conclude, in retrospect, we find several possible reasons for the positive relationships between subsidiary external embeddedness and subsidiary importance for other units' competence development than the ones suggested in the Andersson et al. 2001 and 2002 articles. The main reason for this is that we do not measure *explicitly* to what extent and in what manner subsidiaries absorb knowledge from their external network, and even less so, what type of knowledge they acquire. We just measure their own degree of adaptation in technical and business-related functions. Furthermore, to what extent this knowledge is shared with other MNE units is also measured indirectly (again, see Figure 15.1), that is, as the divisional HQs' evaluation of subsidiary importance for other units' competence development. We can conclude that, to the best of our knowledge, subsequent research on network embeddedness and subsidiary competence development has, to date, made limited progress in addressing these weaknesses.

The Relationship between External Embeddedness and MNE Learning

Our analysis of past studies revealed that researchers have adopted a variety of approaches and methods to study and measure how subsidiaries' external embeddedness influences learning within the MNE. Particularly, we emphasize the need to distinguish between the impact of customer–supplier relationships on the subsidiary's own competence development on one hand, and on its role in transferring competences to other subsidiaries on the other hand. In the first case, it is probably a question of developing competences in complementary relationships through specialization and mutual problem-solving. In the second case, the question is whether this competence development is of relevance for sister units and to what extent it is transferrable to these units. Consequently, the usual conceptualization of the subsidiary's external embeddedness as a "knowledge source" and the subsidiary as an "internal knowledge giver" is problematic and needs to be updated and revisited. "Knowledge sourcing" in connection to customer–supplier relationships is primarily a question of information exchange in order to develop the subsidiary's role in the external network, rather than to attain completely new knowledge through this network. Even when there may be a rationale to assume new knowledge being acquired, the extent to which knowledge will be transferred to other units is unknown. Due to context specificity, the knowledge might be of less relevance or simply difficult to apply in other units or the focal subsidiary might be less interested in transferring the knowledge in the first place.

Let us assume that: (1) a subsidiary's relationships with customers and suppliers primarily have an impact on its ability to develop its specific role in the value chain; and (2) the subsidiary is likely to prioritize that development. In this case, one can argue that there is actually a tradeoff between the subsidiary's "own knowledge sourcing" in connection with its external network and the transfer of new knowledge to other subsidiaries. If this reasoning is correct, we may expect a negative relationship between a subsidiary's level of external embeddedness and its importance for other units' competence development.[3] To some extent, this has already been indicated in some relatively more recent studies (but not emphasized as central to this area of research). For instance, Najafi-Tavani, Giroud, and Sinkovics (2012) found that external embeddedness was negatively linked to subsidiary transfer of knowledge within the MNE. Likewise,

---

[3] This "negative" relationship was in fact hypothesized in the 2001 article but was found insignificant.

Holmström (2010) found that external embeddedness in terms of knowledge sourcing had a negative relation with other MNE units' use of subsidiary competence.

This reasoning should be equally applicable to the mechanism of how the subsidiary becomes important vis-à-vis other MNE units. In the same manner in which a subsidiary might develop its own competence in relation to its links with external counterparts, we can expect that the same development will also occur in customer–supplier relationships with internal counterparts. Through information exchange and mutual problem-solving in these relationships, competence development happens in terms of specialization and extended understanding of the counterparts needs. To a certain extent, we would also expect that competence development in the external network will drive the corresponding development in the internal network, and vice versa. In that sense we can analyze a focal subsidiary's importance for sister units' competence development. Again, we point out that this phenomenon is quite different from *the role of the subsidiary as a vehicle for new knowledge*, which is transferred from the external network to the sister unit(s). Subsidiaries might have such a role, but it is probably not a primary one, and, more important, *there is reason to doubt whether such a role is facilitated or becomes more important with higher levels of subsidiary external business network embeddedness.*

FUTURE RESEARCH DIRECTIONS ON EXTERNAL EMBEDDEDNESS AND LEARNING WITHIN MNES

Although Andersson et al. (2001, 2002) are highly cited and have inspired, we argue, many followers dealing with embeddedness and learning within MNEs, we now recognize that our previous findings raise more questions than they actually answer. Our reasoning in this chapter illuminates some serious problems in conceptualizing the subsidiary and its external network as a source of knowledge for other units' competence development. Consequently, research that can address this relationship in a more rigorous way is highly needed. In fact, we would like to see future research focusing on the following areas.

First, to the best of our knowledge, there is no research study that has replicated the analysis carried out in the 2001 and 2002 articles. This is somewhat surprising as our indicators for both the independent variable (closeness in a subsidiary's relationships with customers and suppliers) and the dependent variable (the subsidiary's importance for other units' competence development) are relatively straightforward and easy to measure. A crucial issue is whether similar data or data from another context in terms of, say, type of MNEs, will produce the same result. Or expressed differently, irrespective of the weaknesses in the conceptualization of knowledge transfer and competence development discussed here, the empirical result presented in the two articles is far from enough to make a general conclusion of a positive relationship between subsidiary network embeddedness and competence development in other MNE units. Hence, testing these ideas in different empirical contexts would be a starting point.

Second, future research on subsidiary embeddedness and MNE learning should try to elucidate what it actually means for a subsidiary's own competence development to have close relationships with external customers and suppliers. As we have indicated, close relationships will probably have a positive impact on the subsidiary's ability to develop its *own* technology to better adapt to the counterpart's technology, rather than to attain *new* technology from counterparts in the external network. A further question is whether such an increased ability is in any way relevant for and/or possible to transfer to other units, in other business contexts. Hence, future research must be more careful in assessing in depth the *nature* of the knowledge that the subsidiary develops as a consequence of its external embeddedness and what that implies for other units' competence development (if there are notable implications at all).

Third, in our early 2000s articles, the dependent variable—a subsidiary's importance for other unit's competence development—was measured by asking the divisional HQs to assess the level of importance; this makes it an indirect, subjective measure. It was then assumed that an increased importance reflects a knowledge transfer from the focal subsidiary to other sister units. In this chapter, we recognized that, measured in this way, an increased importance of competence development for other units might not reflect knowledge transfer. Consequently, future research needs to assess the extent of knowledge transfer from one subsidiary to other subsidiaries *directly*, that is, to what extent information exchange concerning new technologies actually occurs between units within an MNE. This is more challenging to address than how it was done in the two articles, but probably necessary in order to get a reliable picture of the causal relationship between subsidiary embeddedness and learning in MNEs.

Fourth, the operational relationships between the focal subsidiary and other units in the MNE are crucial for our understanding of knowledge transfer and learning in MNEs. In Andersson et al. (2001, 2002), no distinction was made between the subsidiary's complementary relationships and those with a competitive relationship with more or less similar technology. In future research on embeddedness and competence development in MNEs, such a distinction would be necessary, because the conditions for and meaning of knowledge transfer differ considerably between the two types of relationships. As has been indicated, transfer of knowledge in the sense of one unit learning about another unit's technology is, on the one hand, more relevant between similar units, but, on the other hand, more difficult to accomplish due to the tension between the units as (potential) competitors. The corresponding knowledge transfer might be easier to accomplish when the subsidiaries have a complementary relationship but will probably be less relevant as learning about the counterpart's technology is not the main motivation of that relationship. This paradox is a fascinating area for future research, further illustrated in Figure 15.2.

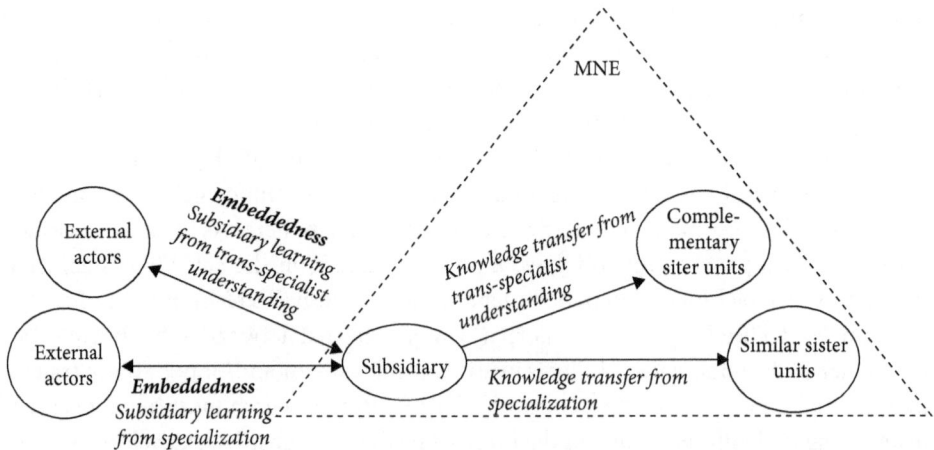

FIGURE 15.2 The relation between external embeddedness as specialization or trans-specialist understanding and knowledge transfer to complementary or similar sister units

Figure 15.2 points out that it is essential to identify the type and level of knowledge generated in the external relationship and to explicitly connect it to the transfer practices between the subsidiary and corporate counterparts. In a first scenario, a subsidiary's trans-specialist knowledge—about, for instance, the capabilities of an external supplier— can generate an understanding that can be transferred to an alternative corporate supplier (or even a corporate customer). This may concern needs for changes in product or production technologies that the focal subsidiary recognizes being of importance to the internal complementary counterparts. Hence this type of knowledge transfer can be essential to the subsidiary as well as its corporate counterparts, without actually influencing the subsidiary's own operational role as a business partner. Expressed differently, the subsidiary functions as a link to external knowledge of importance for complementary corporate counterparts. We may expect that the subsidiary and these corporate partners have developed as complementary business partners inside the MNE, which facilitates knowledge transfer. However, to the best of our knowledge, there is not much research done about the relevance and occurrence of this, which makes it a potential promising area for future research.

We also propose a second scenario with different implications. In this case, the subsidiary's development of its own specialist knowledge, stemming from the development of the demands and qualities of the external relationship, results in new competences. These competences may be of use to those corporate partners that have similar capabilities and business operations. However, while we expect that the relevance of this specialist subsidiary learning is high vis-à-vis similar corporate counterparts, the problem of knowledge transfer may be hampered due to internal motivational and managerial aspects within the MNE. Future research can investigate whether knowledge transfer is likely to occur if the subsidiary and its similar sister units have limited competition for internal resources and if their markets are separated. Hence knowledge transfer is likely when the benefit of knowledge transfer is greater than the risks associated with losing competitive advantage at the subsidiary level.

Finally, in some later studies, subsidiary embeddedness is viewed as a more multifaceted phenomenon, reflecting the fact that the subsidiary can concurrently be embedded in different contexts (e.g. Figueiredo, 2011; Meyer et al., 2011; Ciabuschi, Holm, & Martin, 2011; Ryan, Giblin, Andersson, & Clancey, 2018). This "multiple" embeddedness of the subsidiary is scarcely treated in the literature, but a very interesting topic. The idea of multiple subsidiary embeddedness opens up a complicated challenge to future research on how external embeddedness impacts the co-evolution of the relationship between the subsidiary and the rest of the MNE. This agenda is clearly fascinating but will further complicate an already complex set of relationships between subsidiaries learning in their external network and potential transfer of new knowledge internally to sister subsidiaries and the broader MNE.

References

Achcaoucaou, F., Miravitlles, P., & Leon-Barder, F. 2014. Knowledge sharing and subsidiary R&D mandate development: A matter of dual embeddedness, *International Business Review*, 23(1): 76–90.

Andersson, U. & Forsgren, M. 2000. In search of centre of excellence: network embeddedness and subsidiary roles in multinational corporations, *Management International Review*, 40(4): 329–350.

Andersson, U., Forsgren, M., & Holm, U. 2001. Subsidiary embeddedness and competence development in MNCs- a multi-level analysis, *Organization Studies*, 22(6): 1013–1034.

Andersson, U., Forsgren, M., & Holm, U. 2002. The strategic impact of external networks— subsidiary performance and competence development in the multinational corporation, *Strategic Management Journal*, 23: 979–996.

Andersson, U. Forsgren, M., & Holm, U. 2007. Balancing subsidiary influence in the federative MNC: a business network view. *Journal of International Business Studies*, 18: 802–818.

Andersson, U., Gaur, A., Mudambi, R., & Persson, M. 2015. Unpacking inter-unit knowledge transfer in multinational enterprises, *Global Strategy Journal*, 5(3): 241–255.

Asakawa, K., Park, Y., Song, J., & Kim, S. 2018. Internal embeddedness, geographic distance, and global knowledge sourcing by overseas subsidiaries, *Journal of International Business Studies*, 49(6): 743–752.

Birkinshaw, J. 1998. Foreign-owned subsidiaries and regional development: The case of Sweden. In J. Birkinshaw & N. Hood (Eds.), *Multinational Corporate Evolution and Subsidiary Development*. Basingstoke: Macmillan.

Birkinshaw, J., & Ridderstråle, J. 1999. Fighting the corporate immune system: a process study of subsidiary initiatives in multinational corporations. *International Business Review*, 8: 149–180.

Boehe, D. M. 2007. Product development in MNC subsidiaries: Local linkages and global interdependencies. *Journal of International Management*, 13(4): 488–512.

Ciabuschi, F., Holm, U. & Martin, O. 2011. Dual embeddedness, influence and performance of innovating subsidiaries in the multinational corporation. *International Business Review*, 23(5): 897–909.

Dhanaraj, C., Lyles, M. A., Steensma, H. K., & Tihanyi, L. 2004. Managing tacit and explicit knowledge transfer in IJVs: the role of relational embeddedness and the impact on performance. *Journal of International Business Studies*, 35(5): 428–442.

Figueiredo, P. 2011. The role of dual embeddedness in the innovative performance of MNE subsidiaries: Evidence from Brazil. *Journal of Management Studies*, 48(2): 417–440.

Fjeldstad, Ö. D., & Sasson, A. 2010. Membership matters: on the value of being embedded in customer networks. *Journal of Management Studies*, 47(6): 944–966.

Forsgren, M., Holm, U., & Johanson, J. 2005. *Managing the Embedded Multinational. A Business Network View*. Cheltenham: Edward Elgar.

Garcia-Point, C., Canales, J. I., & Noboa, F. 2009. Subsidiary strategy: the embeddedness component. *Journal of Management Studies*, 46(2): 182–214.

Håkanson, L. & Nobel, R. 2001. Organizational characteristics and reverse technology transfer. *Management International Review*, 41(4): 395–420.

Håkansson, H. 1989. *Corporate Technological Behaviour: Co-operation and Networks*. London: Routledge.

Holm, U., & Pedersen, T. 2000. *The Emergence and Impact of MNC Centres of Excellence. A Subsidiary Perspective*. New York, NY: MC Millan.

Holmström, C. 2010. Managing the transfer of externally embedded subsidiary knowledge: the role of headquarters' control mechanisms. In U. Andersson & U. Holm (Eds.), *Managing the Contemporary Multinational: The Role of Headquarters*. Cheltenham: Edward Elgar.

Hoopes, D., & Postrel, S. 1999. Shared knowledge, "glitches," and product development performance, *Strategic Management Journal*, 20(9): 837–865.

Karna, A., Täube, F., & Sonderegger, P. 2013. Evolution of innovation networks across geographical and organizational boundaries: A study of R&D subsidiaries in the Bangalore IT cluster. *European Management Review*, 10(4): 211–226.

Meyer, K. E., Mudambi, R., & Narula, R. 2011. Multinational enterprises and local contexts: The opportunities and challenges of multiple embeddedness. *Journal of Management Studies*, 48(2), 235–252.

Michailova, S., & Mustaffa, Z. 2012. Subsidiary knowledge flows in multinational corporations: Research accomplishments, gaps, and opportunities. *Journal of World Business*, 47(3): 383–396.

Mu, S., Gnyawali, D., & Hatfield, D. 2007. Foreign subsidiaries' learning from local environments: An empirical test. *Management International Review*, 47(1): 79–102.

Mudambi, R., & Navarra, P. 2004. Is knowledge power? Knowledge flows, subsidiary power and rent-seeking within MNCs. *Journal of International Business Studies*, 35(5): 385–406.

Najafi-Tavani, Z., Giroud, A., & Sinkovics, R. R. 2012. Mediating effects in reverse knowledge transfer processes. *Management International Review*, 52(3): 461–488.

Nell, P. C., Ambos, B., & Schlegelmilch, B. B. 2011. The MNC as an externally embedded organization: An investigation of embeddedness overlap in local subsidiary networks. *Journal of World Business*, 46(4): 497–505.

Phene, A., & Almeida, P. 2008. Innovation in multinational subsidiaries: The role of knowledge assimilation and subsidiary capabilities. *Journal of International Business Studies*, 39(5): 901–919.

Postrel, S. 2002. Islands of shared knowledge: Specialization and mutual understanding in problem-solving teams. *Organization Science*, 13: 303–320.

Richardson, G. B. 1972. The organization of industry. *Economic Journal*, 83: 883–896.

Ryan, P., Giblin, M., Andersson, U., & Clancey, J. 2018. Subsidiary Knowledge Creation in Co-evolving contexts. *International Business Review*, 27(5): 915–932.

Santangelo, G. D. 2012. The tension of information sharing: Effects on subsidiary embeddedness. *International Business Review*, 21: 180–195.

Schmid, S., & Schurig, A. 2003. The development of critical capabilities in foreign Subsidiaries: disentangling the role of the subsidiary's business network. *International Business Review*, 12(6): 755–782.

Tallman, S., & Chacar, A. 2011. Knowledge accumulation and dissemination in MNEs: A practice-based framework. *Journal of Management Studies*, 48(2): 278–304.

Uzzi, B., & Lancaster, R. 2003. Relational embeddedness and learning: The case of bank loan managers and their clients. *Management Science*, 49(4): 383–399.

von Hippel, E. 1988. *Sources of Innovation*. Oxford: Oxford University Press.

Yamao, S., Cieri, H., & Hutchings, K. 2009. Transferring subsidiary knowledge to global head-quarters: Subsidiary senior executives' perceptions of the role of HR configurations in the development of knowledge stocks. *Human Resource Management*, 48(4): 531–554.

Yang, Q., Mudambi, R., & Meyer, K. E. 2008. Conventional and reverse knowledge flows in multinational corporations. *Journal of Management*, 34(5): 882–902.

Yli-Renko, H, Autio, E., & Sapienza, H. J. 2001. Social capital, knowledge acquisition, and knowledge exploitation in young technology-based firms. *Strategic Management Journal*, 22: 587–613.

CHAPTER 16

POLITICAL STRATEGIES
OF SUBSIDIARIES OF
MULTINATIONAL
ENTERPRISES

MARIA A. DE VILLA

INTRODUCTION

RESEARCH on political strategies, organizational efforts to manage public policies in ways favorable to corporate interests, is receiving increasing attention in a variety of fields. Most studies focus on the domestic context (Hadani, Bonardi, & Dahan, 2017; Hillman, Keim, & Schuler, 2004; Rodriguez, Siegel, Hillman, & Eden, 2006). Yet, in the field of international business (IB) strategy, attention has focused on how multinationals manage public policies around the world (Boddewyn, 1988; Boddewyn & Brewer, 1994).

However, while a corporate level of analysis may be appropriate for studying headquarters, IB scholars argue that the subsidiary is the appropriate level of analysis when studying multinationals (Birkinshaw & Hood, 1998). Political strategies at the subsidiary level are important to multinational enterprises (MNEs) as a single multinational may often include various subsidiaries differently pursuing political strategies across host markets (De Villa, Rajwani, Lawton, & Mellahi, 2019; Meyer, Mudambi, & Narula, 2011). Political strategies are also important to subsidiaries as their operations may not be completely understood by the various external stakeholders in their host markets and there may be host country public policies that negatively affect subsidiaries' operations or are overly favorable to domestic firms (Wan & Hillman, 2006). Overall, as subsidiaries are the units of multinationals that are directly exposed to host country governments and public policies, research on political strategies from a subsidiary perspective is important for both the subsidiaries themselves and the MNEs they are part of.

Hence, in this chapter, I take stock of our current understanding of political strategies at the subsidiary level by review of literature at the crossroads of corporate political strategy and IB strategy. From the content analysis of 50 of the most relevant journal articles on the topic, I propose four relevant themes to political strategies of subsidiaries. These themes are as follows. First, the types of political strategies deployed by subsidiaries, that dichotomize into engaged and non-engaged, by their aim; and into legal and illegal, in accordance with their own nature or the institutional context of the host market. Second, the responses of subsidiaries to host political contexts, that are enabled through different types of political strategies and involve exercising either voice (by staying and shaping host country public policies); exit (by leaving); or loyalty (by staying while evading to shape host country public policies). Third, the determinants that explain the choice, approach (transactional or relational), level of participation (individual or collective), intensity, or dissimilarity of the political strategies of subsidiaries, which cluster into five levels: home country, host country, multinational, subsidiary, and managerial. Fourth, the outcomes of the political strategies of subsidiaries, in terms of legitimacy in the host country and performance.

Political Strategies

Political strategies are organizational efforts to manage public policies in ways favorable to corporate interests (Hillman et al., 2004; Shaffer, 1995). Other labels that have been used to refer to political strategies are non-market strategies (Baron, 1995; Mellahi, Frynas, Sun, & Siegel, 2016), non-market capabilities (Baron, 1995; Bonardi, Holburn, & Vanden Bergh, 2006), political capabilities (Holburn & Zelner, 2010) or lobbying capabilities (Lawton & Rajwani, 2011). This chapter will use the label of political strategies. Research on political strategies has largely drawn on institutional theory from the institutional economics and neo-institutional perspectives, as well as stakeholder theory, resource dependency theory, the resource-based view, and agency theory.

Table 16.1 shows that political strategies dichotomize into engaged and non-engaged (Puck, Lawton, & Mohr, 2018). On the one hand, engaged political strategies are efforts that aim to enable firms to exert influence over public policies by engaging with government (Baysinger, 1984; Hillman & Hitt, 1999). A large body of research discusses several taxonomies that list and describe engaged political strategies (e.g. Aplin & Hegarty, 1980; Baysinger, 1984; Boddewyn & Brewer, 1994; Bonardi, Hillman, & Keim, 2005; Getz, 1993; Hillman & Hitt, 1999; Hillman et al., 2004; Oberman, 1993; Oliver, 1991; Oliver & Holzinger, 2008). In particular, the taxonomy of three distinct engaged political strategies—information, financial incentive, and constituency-building—theoretically conceptualized by Hillman and Hitt (1999) drawing on exchange theory, has become the most cited.

On the other hand, through non-engaged political strategies firms choose to evade exerting influence over public policies. Rather, non-engaged political strategies are efforts that aim to enable firms to avoid, conform, actively adapt, or circumvent public

Table 16.1 Political strategies

	Engaged political strategies	Non-engaged political strategies
Aim	To enable firms to exert influence over public policies	To enable firms to avoid, conform, actively adapt, or circumvent public policies
Relation with government	Involves engaging with government	Involves evading engagement with government
Strategies	Information Financial incentive Constituency-building	Avoidance Acquiescence Low visibility Rapid compliance Reconfiguration Anticipation Circumvention
Approach to compliance	Involves complying with public policies while searching to shape or modify their contents in favorable ways to corporate interests	Involves complying with public policies without aiming to shape or modify their contents, except for the non-engaged political strategies of avoidance and circumvention, which do not involve complying with public policies
Other labels	Public policy shaping (Weidenbaum, 1980) Bargaining behavior (Boddewyn & Brewer, 1994) Political buffering (Blumentritt, 2003; Meznar & Nigh, 1995) Proactive corporate political activity (Hillman et al., 2004)	Passive reaction, positive anticipation (Weidenbaum, 1980) Non-bargaining behavior (Boddewyn & Brewer, 1994) Political bridging (Blumentritt, 2003; Meznar & Nigh, 1995) Reactive corporate political activity (Hillman et al., 2004)

Source: Adapted from De Villa et al. (2019).

policies by evading engagement with government (Boddewyn & Brewer, 1994; De Villa et al., 2019). In contrast to engaged political strategies, a paucity of research discusses several taxonomies that list and describe non-engaged political strategies (Boddewyn & Brewer, 1994; De Villa et al., 2019; Oliver, 1991; Oliver & Holzinger, 2008). This stream of research explains that first, avoiding public policies can be achieved by the non-engaged political strategy of avoidance (Boddewyn & Brewer, 1994; Oliver, 1991). Second, conforming to public policies can be enabled by the non-engaged political strategy of acquiescence (Oliver, 1991), also referred to as compliance (Boddewyn & Brewer, 1994) or reactive strategy (Oliver & Holzinger, 2008). Third, actively adapting to public policies can be achieved by any of the four non-engaged political strategies of low visibility, rapid compliance, reconfiguration, and anticipation (De Villa et al., 2019) or anticipatory strategy (Oliver & Holzinger, 2008). Fourth, circumventing public policies can be enabled by the non-engaged political strategy of circumvention (Boddewyn & Brewer, 1994). These non-engaged political strategies were conceptualized by the works of several scholars such as: Oliver (1991) building on institutional theory from a neo-institutional perspective and integrating it with resource dependence theory; Boddewyn and Brewer (1994) combining the business political behavior and IB strategy literatures; Oliver and Holzinger (2008) adopting a dynamic capabilities perspective; and more recently, De Villa and colleagues (2019) drawing on institutional theory from a neo-institutional perspective and political economy to provide empirical evidence.

It is important to note that engaged and non-engaged political strategies involve different approaches to compliance for firms. Through engaged political strategies, firms comply with public policies as they search to shape or modify their contents in ways favorable to their corporate interests. Through non-engaged political strategies to conform or actively adapt to public policies, firms comply with public policies without aiming to shape or modify their contents. However, through non-engaged political strategies to avoid or circumvent public policies, due to their nature, firms do not comply with public policies.

We also note that different labels are used to refer to engaged and non-engaged political strategies. For instance, engaged political strategies are often referred to as public policy shaping (Weidenbaum, 1980), bargaining behavior (Boddewyn & Brewer, 1994), political buffering (Blumentritt, 2003; Meznar & Nigh, 1995), and proactive corporate political activity (Hillman et al., 2004). Non-engaged political strategies are often referred to as passive reaction, positive anticipation (Weidenbaum, 1980), non-bargaining behavior (Boddewyn & Brewer, 1994), political bridging (Blumentritt, 2003; Meznar & Nigh, 1995), and reactive corporate political activity (Hillman et al., 2004).

With regards to the corporate political strategy literature, the work of Boddewyn (1988) and later Boddewyn and Brewer (1994) served as a catalyst for further research on political strategies to incorporate an international dimension. Nevertheless, subsequent studies often examine the multinational level of analysis rather than the subsidiary level of analysis (Blumentritt, 2003; Blumentritt & Nigh, 2002; Wan & Hillman, 2006). This is problematic because subsidiaries are the units of MNEs that are directly exposed to host country governments and public policies, meaning that *research on political strategies from a subsidiary perspective* is important for both subsidiaries and multinationals. Hence, the next section takes stock and discusses this body of research.

POLITICAL STRATEGIES FROM A SUBSIDIARY PERSPECTIVE

To identify articles informing political strategies from a subsidiary perspective, I used the ISI Web of Knowledge database. Emphasis was placed on articles published in management journals, such as *Academy of Management Journal (AMJ)*, *Academy of Management Review (AMR)*, *Journal of Management (JOM)*, *Journal of Management Studies (JMS)*, and *Strategic Management Journal (SMJ)*; articles published in IB journals, such as *International Business Review* (*IBR*), *Global Strategy Journal* (*GSJ*), *Journal of International Business Studies* (*JIBS*), *Journal of International Management* (*JIM*), *Journal of World Business* (*JWB*), and *Management International Review* (*MIR*); and those published in specialized journals, such as *Business & Politics* (*B&P*), *Business & Society* (*B&S*), *Journal of Politics* (*JOP*), and *Journal of Public Affairs* (*JPA*).[1]

Building on the content analysis of each article, I cross-checked all articles to identify relevant themes to our understanding of political strategies from a subsidiary perspective. The analysis revealed four relevant themes illustrated in Figure 16.1:

(1) the types of political strategies deployed by subsidiaries;
(2) the responses of subsidiaries to host political contexts;
(3) the determinants of the political strategies of subsidiaries; and
(4) the outcomes of the political strategies of subsidiaries.

I discuss each of these below.

Types of Political Strategies of Subsidiaries of MNEs

Subsidiaries of multinationals deploy political strategies that dichotomize into engaged and non-engaged, by their aim; and into legal and illegal, in accordance with their own nature or the institutional context of the host market. Table 16.2 summarizes the political strategies of subsidiaries and their tactics.

Engaged Political Strategies of Subsidiaries of MNEs

The engaged political strategies of subsidiaries are efforts that aim to enable these units to exert influence over host country public policies by engaging with the host government. The taxonomy of three distinct engaged political strategies—information, financial incentive, and constituency-building—conceptualized by Hillman and Hitt (1999) is used with prevalence to explain the engaged political strategies of subsidiaries. First, subsidiaries pursuing the information strategy affect the making of host country public policies by furnishing host country policymakers with specific information about public policy preferences, positions, or the costs and benefits of different outcomes. The information strategy includes tactics such as lobbying; commissioning research projects and reporting research results; testifying as expert witnesses in hearings or before other entities; and supplying decision makers with position papers or technical reports. Second, subsidiaries pursuing the financial incentive strategy use financial inducements to align the interests of host country policymakers with corporate interests. The financial incentive strategy includes tactics such as providing financial contributions to politicians

---

[1] Following Gaur and Kumar (2018), articles were content analyzed by coding, for instance, the year and journal, research question and design, variables, and findings. I included other relevant articles that were cited in the core articles reviewed.

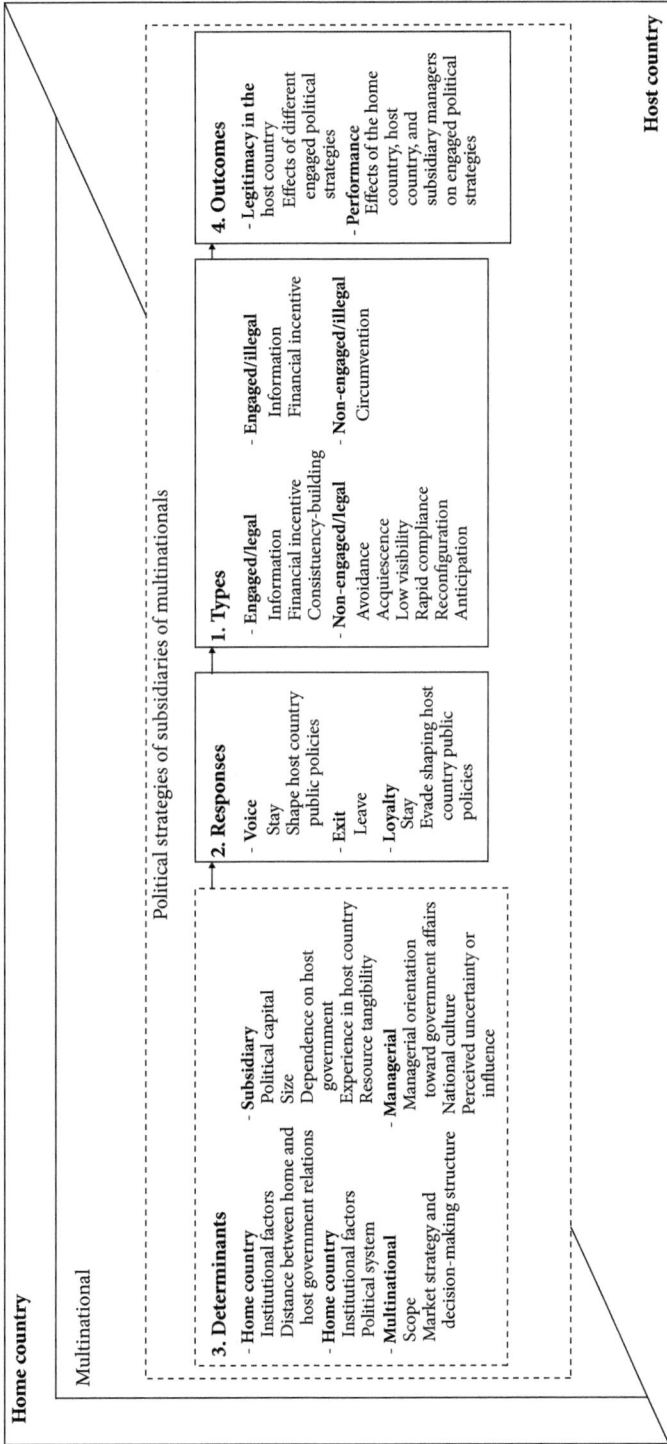

Home country

Multinational

Political strategies of subsidiaries of multinationals

3. Determinants

- **Home country**
  Institutional factors
  Distance between home and
  host government relations
- **Home country**
  Institutional factors
  Political system
- **Multinational**
  Scope
  Market strategy and
  decision-making structure

- **Subsidiary**
  Political capital
  Size
  Dependence on host
  government
  Experience in host country
  Resource tangibility
- **Managerial**
  Managerial orientation
  toward government affairs
  National culture
  Perceived uncertainty or
  influence

2. Responses

- **Voice**
  Stay
  Shape host country
  public policies
- **Exit**
  Leave
- **Loyalty**
  Stay
  Evade shaping host
  country public
  policies

1. Types

- **Engaged/legal**
  Information
  Financial incentive
  Consistency-building
- **Non-engaged/legal**
  Avoidance
  Acquiescence
  Low visibility
  Rapid compliance
  Reconfiguration
  Anticipation

- **Engaged/illegal**
  Information
  Financial incentive
- **Non-engaged/illegal**
  Circumvention

4. Outcomes

- **Legitimacy in the
  host country**
  Effects of different
  engaged political
  strategies
- **Performance**
  Effects of the home
  country, host
  country, and
  subsidiary managers
  on engaged political
  strategies

Host country

FIGURE 16.1 Four relevant themes to political strategies of subsidiaries of multinationals

Table 16.2 Political strategies of subsidiaries of multinationals

Type		Political strategies of subsidiaries	Tactics
Engaged	Legal/Illegal	Information strategy	- Lobbying - Commissioning research projects and reporting research results - Testifying as expert witnesses - Supplying position papers or technical reports
		Financial incentive strategy	- Contributions to politicians or their party - Honoraria for speaking - Paid travel, etc. - Personal service (hiring people with political experience or having a firm member run for office)
	Legal	Constituency-building strategy	- Grassroots mobilization of employees, suppliers, customers, etc. - Advocacy advertising - Public relations - Press conferences - Political education programs
Non-engaged	Legal	Avoidance strategy	- Avoiding operations
		Acquiescence strategy	- Complying with host country public policies without aiming to shape or modify their contents
		Low visibility strategy	- Evading influencing host governments - Pursuing a neutral political stance - Sustaining clear internal communications that center on operations rather than on political stances - Deploying locals to represent the subsidiary when interacting with the host government, other political actors, and customers - Adopting a low public profile and avoiding the media
		Rapid compliance strategy	- Not engaging in corruption - Developing tools to assure the subsidiary's operations rapidly comply with host country public policies and an adequate management of external inspections - Paying just prices to suppliers to comply with host country pricing policies - Ensuring the subsidiary's products rapidly comply with changing host country public policies - Modifying the subsidiary's structure or processes to rapidly comply with host country public policies

Reconfiguration strategy	- Modifying the subsidiary's structure or processes for competitiveness - Developing new ways to supply a restricted host market - Substituting imports for local production to appear as a local value-adding firm - Changing the country of origin in the legal structure of a subsidiary - Acquiring physical resources to overcome or manage challenging host country institutional conditions
Anticipation strategy	- Carefully evaluating future investments - Monitoring home and host government relations - Monitoring the host country's institutional context by using human capital with knowledge - Anticipating possibilities to comply with potential upcoming host country public policies - Investing in initiatives to sustain and improve the future competitive position of the subsidiary - Reducing operational costs to overcome increasing operational expenses related to host country public policies - Revising prices to maintain competitiveness and assure the best possible profit - Identifying products that can be profitably supplied in accordance with changing host country public policies - Mapping and analyzing the potential impact of key interest groups on the subsidiary's operations to design ways to manage these relations - Provisioning in financial statements the value of the investments that face potential expropriation - Creating plans to manage a potential expropriation
Illegal Circumvention strategy	- Trade smuggling

Source: Adapted from Hillman & Hitt (1999) and De Villa et al. (2019).

or their party; offering honoraria for speaking; paying travel expenses; and using personal service (hiring people with political experience or having a firm member run for office). Third, subsidiaries adopting the constituency-building strategy seek to gain the support of host country voters and citizens, who in turn, exert pressure on host country policymakers. The constituency-building strategy includes tactics such as grassroots mobilization of employees, suppliers, customers, retirees, and other individuals; advocacy advertising, wherein a particular policy position is advertised; public relations;

press conferences on public policy issues; and political education programs (Hillman & Hitt, 1999; Wan & Hillman, 2006).

The engaged political strategies of subsidiaries can be legal or illegal, in accordance with their own nature or the institutional context of the host market. For example, the engaged political strategy of constituency-building, that seeks to gain the support of host country voters and citizens, is legal in all host markets because of its own nature. However, the information strategy that involves lobbying, is legal in the UK and the US but illegal in India (*Fortune India*, 2018). Similarly, the financial incentive strategy that uses financial contributions to politicians or their party, is legal in countries such as Spain, Switzerland, the UK, and the US; whereas financial contributions are illegal in China (IDEA, 2012)—in fact, they are viewed as corruption or abuse of entrusted power for private gain (see Cuervo-Cazurra, 2016).

Non-Engaged Political Strategies of Subsidiaries of MNEs

The non-engaged political strategies of subsidiaries are efforts that aim to enable these units to avoid, conform, actively adapt, or circumvent host country public policies by evading engagement with the host government. The non-engaged political strategies that have been previously listed in this chapter are extensively used to explain the non-engaged political strategies of subsidiaries. In particular, to avoid host country public policies, subsidiaries pursue the avoidance strategy by avoiding operations in the host market. To conform to host country public policies, subsidiaries adopt the acquiescence strategy by complying with host country public policies without aiming to shape or modify their contents (Boddewyn & Brewer, 1994; Oliver, 1991). In contrast, when subsidiary managers perceive high host country political risk, to actively adapt to host country public policies, subsidiaries often use any of the following four non-engaged political strategies: low visibility, rapid compliance, reconfiguration, and anticipation.

The low visibility strategy ensures subsidiaries a minimal degree of attention from host country political and social actors, thereby reducing the likelihood of being the target of discriminatory policies or even expropriation. The low visibility strategy includes tactics such as evading influencing host governments; pursuing a neutral political stance; sustaining clear internal communications that center on operations rather than on political stances; deploying locals to represent the subsidiary when interacting with the host government, other political actors, and customers; as well as adopting a low public profile and avoiding the media.

The rapid compliance strategy leads subsidiaries to implement high-speed actions to obey the rules in host markets. This strategy resonates with the acquiescence strategy (Oliver, 1991). However, the main difference between these strategies is the speed of compliance. To actively adapt, particularly in host markets of high political risk, subsidiaries focus intensively on rapidly complying with fast-changing host country public policies because non-compliances are frequently used by host governments as rationales to disrupt operations or expropriate assets. The rapid compliance strategy includes tactics such as not engaging in corruption; developing tools to assure the subsidiary's operations rapidly comply with host country public policies and an adequate management of external inspections; paying just prices to suppliers to comply with host country pricing policies; ensuring that the subsidiary's products rapidly comply with changing host country public policies; and modifying the subsidiary's structure or processes to rapidly comply with host country public policies.

The reconfiguration strategy involves rearranging the structure or processes of subsidiaries to operate competitively in challenging host country institutional conditions. This strategy differs from the rapid compliance strategy in that subsidiaries modify their structure or processes not to rapidly comply with host country public policies but rather to efficiently sustain or start competitive operations. The reconfiguration strategy includes tactics such as modifying the subsidiary's structure or processes for competitiveness; developing new ways to supply a restricted host market; substituting imports for local production to appear as a local value-adding firm; changing the country of origin in the legal structure of a subsidiary to diminish the potential loss caused by an eventual expropriation; and acquiring physical resources (such as energy plants or back-up computer servers in another country) to overcome or manage challenging host country institutional conditions.

The anticipation strategy leads subsidiaries to predict host country public policies and analyze interest groups to anticipate responses. An anticipation strategy aims to gain subsidiaries a first-mover advantage by anticipating future public policy directions and ways to gain social support to enhance subsidiaries' legitimacy in the host country. The anticipation strategy, as a non-engaged political strategy, includes tactics such as: carefully evaluating future investments; monitoring home and host government relations; monitoring the host country's institutional context by using human capital with knowledge; anticipating possibilities to comply with potential upcoming host country public policies; investing in initiatives to sustain and improve the future competitive position of the subsidiary; reducing operational costs to overcome increasing operational expenses related to host country public policies; revising prices to maintain competitiveness and assure the best possible profit; identifying products that can be profitably supplied in accordance with changing host country public policies; mapping and analyzing the potential impact of key interest groups on the subsidiary's operations to design ways to manage these relations; provisioning in financial statements the value of the investments that face potential expropriation; and creating plans to manage a potential expropriation (De Villa et al., 2019).

Last, to circumvent host country public policies, subsidiaries pursue the circumvention strategy by incurring in trade smuggling activities (Boddewyn & Brewer, 1994).

The non-engaged political strategies of subsidiaries are legal or illegal, in accordance with their own nature. For example, the avoidance, acquiescence, low visibility, rapid compliance, reconfiguration, and anticipation strategies are legal in all host markets due to their own nature; whereas the circumvention strategy, that involves trade smuggling activities, is illegal in all countries.

Responses to Host Political Contexts and Types of Political Strategies of Subsidiaries of MNEs

Subsidiaries exercise Hirschman's (1970) responses of voice, exit, or loyalty toward host political contexts, through different types of political strategies. Figure 16.2 shows that the first response available to subsidiaries is *voice*, that implies staying in a host market while shaping host country public policies. To exercise voice, subsidiaries may deploy any combination of Hillman and Hitt's (1999) engaged political strategies with the aim of shaping host country public policies in ways favorable to corporate interests. It is important to note that despite the constituency-building strategy being legal in all countries, the information and financial incentive strategies can be legal or illegal in accordance with the institutional context of the host market.

The second response available to subsidiaries is *exit*, that implies leaving a host market (Meyer, Estrin, Bhaumik, & Peng, 2009; Rodriguez, Uhlenbruck, & Eden, 2005). To exercise exit, subsidiaries use the legal non-engaged political strategy of avoidance by avoiding operations in the host market. Thus, under exit, subsidiaries neglect their right to have voice as the result of being either unable or unwilling to invest in efforts to influence host country public policies (Boddewyn & Brewer, 1994).

Alternatively, a third response available to subsidiaries is *loyalty*. The response of loyalty involves no voice and no exit; it implies staying in a host market while evading to

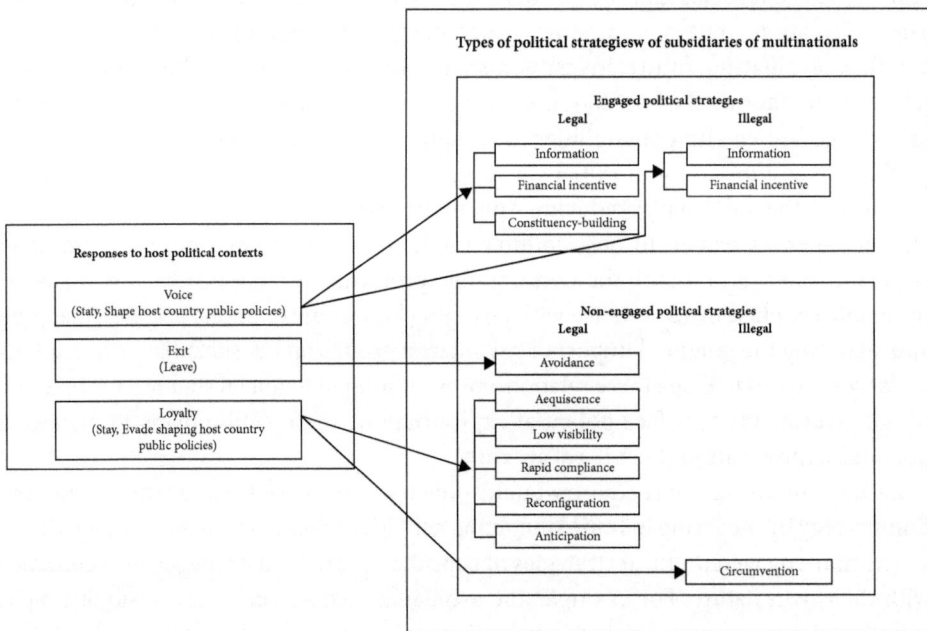

FIGURE 16.2 Responses to host political contexts and types of political strategies of subsidiaries of multinationals

Source: Adapted from De Villa et al. (2019).

shape host country public policies. To exercise loyalty, subsidiaries may choose legal non-engaged political strategies to conform (acquiescence) or actively adapt (low visibility, rapid compliance, reconfiguration, anticipation), or they may choose the illegal non-engaged political strategy of circumvention. A positive aspect of choosing legal non-engaged political strategies to exercise loyalty, is that subsidiaries can legally stay in host markets by minimizing the costs related to changes in host country public policies and host government interventions. Nevertheless, particularly in an era characterized by the growth of authoritarian regimes and the decline of liberal democracies, the response of loyalty suggests that subsidiaries can survive, and even be profitable, by flying under the radar of host governments and not being a force for the internationalization of the rule of law and international standards and norms (De Villa et al., 2019).

Determinants of Political Strategies of Subsidiaries of MNEs

Beyond the responses of subsidiaries to host political contexts, multiple determinants explain the choice, approach (transactional or relational), level of participation (individual or collective), intensity, or dissimilarity of their political strategies. These determinants cluster into five levels: home country, host country, multinational, subsidiary, and managerial.

Home Country-Level Determinants of Political Strategies of Subsidiaries

The determinants of political strategies of subsidiaries at the home country level include institutional factors as well as the distance between home and host government relations. Scholars draw on institutional theory from a neo-institutional perspective and resource dependence theory to explain how these determinants influence the choice or intensity of the political strategies of subsidiaries.

Institutional factors. The cultural-cognitive, normative, and regulative institutions of the home countries of subsidiaries can explain their willingness to choose engaged political strategies in host markets. Particularly, subsidiaries are more likely to choose engaged political strategies when they come from countries with high individualism, that value the abilities and responsibility of the individual within a society; low uncertainty avoidance, that is, when society feels low levels of threat by uncertain situations and does not avoid these situations; less corruption; high administrative distance, that involves important differences with the host country in colonial ties, language, religion, and legal systems (Brown, Yasar, & Rasheed, 2018); or high regulatory distance, that denotes important differences with the host country in regulatory quality and stringency resulting from the complexity of the regulatory environment (Luo & Zhao, 2013). Similarly, subsidiaries may find that political tie intensity (the extent to which senior managers provide time and resources in dealing with host government officials through engaged political strategies) can be influenced by their home country political institutions. In particular, when their home country offers political stability, subsidiaries' political tie intensity is likely to be greater (White, Fainshmidt, & Rajwani, 2018b).

Distance between home and host government relations. Two subsidiaries of two MNEs headquartered in different countries, similar in every other way, operating in a particular host market, may be treated differently by the host government. This differential treatment may be explained by the distance in relations between the host government and the governments of the countries where the two headquarters are located (Blumentritt, 2003; Blumentritt & Nigh, 2002). Host governments can give preferential treatment to subsidiaries from particular countries because of close relations or trade agreements between the subsidiaries' home and host governments. Otherwise, host governments can discriminate subsidiaries from particular countries because of distant or conflictive relations between the subsidiaries' home and host governments (see Cuervo-Cazurra, 2011). The lower the distance between home and host government relations, the more likely it is that subsidiaries find it fruitful to choose engaged political strategies (Frynas, Mellahi, & Pigman, 2006). In contrast, greater distance between home and host government relations, may signify that subsidiaries using engaged political strategies increase their visibility and risk exposure, thereby increasing the likelihood of being the targest of discriminatory policies or even expropriation. Under such conditions, subsidiaries may rather choose to deploy non-engaged political strategies (De Villa et al., 2019).

Host Country-Level Determinants of Political Strategies of Subsidiaries

The determinants of political strategies of subsidiaries at the host country level include institutional factors as well as the political system. Scholars draw on institutional theory from the institutional economics and neo-institutional perspectives, and the political science literature, to explain how these determinants influence the choice, approach (transactional or relational), level of participation (individual or collective), intensity, or dissimilarity of the political strategies of subsidiaries.

Institutional factors. The formal institutions of the host countries of subsidiaries determine control constraints, administrative constraints, and the degree of competition law effectiveness, that can influence their political strategies. Control constraints are the obstacles emanating from the host government's direct imposition of drastic measures to manage macroeconomic stability such as import/export restrictions, foreign exchange controls, or profit repatriation restrictions. Administrative constraints are the obstacles that arise from weak and fledgling administrative institutions or unclear and ill-enforced administrative principles such as corruption, bureaucracy, and discrimination. In particular, control constraints can strengthen political tie intensity, whereas administrative constraints may weaken political ties (Liedong & Frynas, 2018). The degree of competition law effectiveness is the extent to which a host country's competition laws encourage open/fair competition. Some host countries promote the entry of foreign firms by providing safeguards and opportunities, while others seek to limit foreign investment to protect their national industries. These differences affect the type of engaged political strategies which subsidiaries use. Thus, the heterogeneity of host countries' degree of competition law effectiveness is positively related to dissimilarity among the engaged political strategies of subsidiaries (Wan & Hillman, 2006).

An informal institution of the host countries of subsidiaries is culture, specifically cultural openness to foreign influence. As countries move toward a free market capitalist model, foreign firms are often welcome, while in other countries, cultural backlash brings hostility toward foreign firms. In host countries with a welcoming attitude, subsidiaries may choose to individually deploy engaged political strategies. In contrast, in hostile host countries, subsidiaries may be forced to join forces with domestic firms or associations or work through their home governments to deploy engaged political strategies at a collective level. Thus, heterogeneity among host countries' cultural openness to foreign influence is positively related to dissimilarity among the engaged political strategies of subsidiaries (Wan & Hillman, 2006).

Overall, the institutional pressures of host countries (from formal and informal institutions) often trigger subsidiaries to intensify their use of engaged political strategies (Nell, Puck, & Heidenreich, 2015). Yet, pressures from political institutions, interest groups, and the media often lead subsidiaries to deploy engaged political strategies through a relational approach; whereas pressures from regulatory and standards agencies can lead subsidiaries to use a transactional approach (Voinea & van Kranenburg, 2018).

Political system. A host country's political system, which can be corporatist or pluralist, can influence subsidiaries' political strategies. A corporatist political system, on the one hand, has institutionalized participation by certain interests in the public policy process. Corporatist countries emphasize cooperation and relations. A pluralist political system, on the other hand, has a wider variety of interest groups that can influence political decisions. Pluralist countries can lead firms to act selectively as competition among interest groups is constantly changing. Thus, subsidiaries may use the constituency-building strategy more in corporatist host countries, while they may pursue the information and financial incentive strategies more in pluralist host countries (Hillman, 2003; Hillman & Wan, 2005). Further, subsidiaries can be more likely to adopt a relational approach to collectively deploy engaged political strategies in corporatist host countries, while they may be more likely to adopt a transactional approach to individually deploy engaged political strategies in pluralist host countries (Hillman, 2003; Hillman & Hitt, 1999).

Multinational-Level Determinants of Political Strategies of Subsidiaries

The determinants of political strategies of subsidiaries at the multinational level include scope as well as market strategy and decision-making structure. Scholars draw primarily on the resource-based view, institutional theory from a neo-institutional perspective, and resource dependence theory, to explain how these determinants influence the choice, approach (transactional or relational), or dissimilarity of the political strategies of subsidiaries.

Scope. Corporate internationalization involves complex operations dispersed in multiple countries and demands substantial managerial information processing capacity.

Managing a myriad of host markets, with unique political contexts, poses an additional challenge for geographically dispersed multinationals. Therefore, highly internationalized multinationals may rely on subsidiaries in the formulation of political strategies because of subsidiaries' superior local knowledge. Differently, for multinationals with lower degrees of internationalization, the complexity of coordination among subsidiaries can be less demanding and headquarters most likely to coordinate the political strategies of subsidiaries. Thus, the degree of a multinational's scope of internationalization is positively related to dissimilarity among the political strategies of its subsidiaries (Wan & Hillman, 2006). Further, more internationalized multinationals may be more dependent on multiple sources of sovereignty, and thus, their subsidiaries may pursue the information, financial incentive, and constituency-building strategies (Hillman, 2003; Hillman & Wan, 2005).

Similarly, multinationals in a single business or with related-product diversification have a focused industry domain. Therefore, they are able to focus on a relatively smaller set of issues than more unrelated-product diversified multinationals. Thus, subsidiaries of highly related-product diversified multinationals are more likely to adopt a relational approach to engaged political strategies. In contrast, subsidiaries of more unrelated-product diversified multinationals may be more likely to pursue a transactional approach to engaged political strategies (Hillman & Hitt, 1999; Shirodkar & Mohr, 2015a).

Market strategy and decision-making structure. Market strategy indicates how a multinational competes in the marketplace and dictates the decision-making structure that guides the headquarter–subsidiary relationship. MNEs' market strategies are commonly conceptualized as multi-domestic or global. On the one hand, multinationals pursuing a multi-domestic market strategy give importance to responding to the demands of local environments and encourage their subsidiaries to gain legitimacy locally; their subsidiaries are under pressure to formulate political strategies that specifically cater to the host political context. Therefore, the decision-making structure of these multinationals is often dispersed throughout the organization, allowing subsidiary managers to customize political strategies to fit their idiosyncratic host markets. Thus, an MNE's multi-domestic market strategy and decentralized decision-making structure are positively related to dissimilarity among the political strategies of its subsidiaries (Wan & Hillman, 2006). On the other hand, multinationals pursuing a global market strategy focus on maximizing the operational efficiency of the global value chain often by sharing distinctive capabilities across subsidiaries. When multinationals follow a global market strategy, headquarters may want to maintain more coordinated political strategies to facilitate integration and maximize coordination benefits. Therefore, the decision-making structure of these MNEs is often more centralized. As a result, the political strategies of these multinationals are less likely to specifically cater the idiosyncrasies of host markets (Wan & Hillman, 2006). Further, when a multinational has a high level of global integration, this often implies cross-country intra-company transfers, that necessitate effective relationships with local government officials, industry associations, and labor unions across host markets. Thus, the higher the level of global integration of an MNE, the more its subsidiaries will use the constituency-building strategy (Hillman & Wan, 2005). Differently, some scholars argue that the higher the level of global integration of a multinational, the more likely this may reduce its subsidiaries' dependence on local resources, thus giving them room for a transactional approach to engaged political strategies. However, subsidiaries' dependence on local resources that are critical to their survival and ties to local businesses, can make subsidiaries less likely to use a transactional approach to engaged political strategies (Shidrokar & Mohr, 2015a).

Subsidiary-Level Determinants of Political Strategies of Subsidiaries

At the subsidiary level, the determinants of political strategies include political capital, size, dependence on host government, experience in host country, and resource tangibility. Scholars draw on resource dependence theory and institutional theory from a neo-institutional perspective, to explain how these determinants influence the choice, approach (transactional or relational), level of participation (individual or collective), or dissimilarity of the political strategies of subsidiaries.

Political capital. The ability to influence host country public policies is referred to as political capital (Shaffer & Hillman, 2000). This ability depends on a subsidiary's bargaining power resources that include its size, exporting, and technological and economic spillovers; this is because host governments are less likely to intervene large subsidiaries that export a large percentage of their sales and have high levels of technology. Further, political capital also depends on a subsidiary's allocation of resources to government affairs activities (Blumentritt & Rehbein, 2008). Overall, as subsidiaries often have different levels of political capital, this can explain the dissimilarity among their political strategies (Blumentritt & Rehbein, 2008).

Size. Firm size is an established proxy for resources and visibility and often determines the benefits of pursuing engaged political strategies (Schuler, Rehbein, & Cramer, 2002). In particular, subsidiaries with greater financial resources can be more likely to individually engage with the host government; while subsidiaries with fewer financial resources can be more likely to search for collective participation to engage (Hillman & Hitt, 1999). Further, the number of employees is directly related to a subsidiary's visibility and ability to generate constituency support. Thus, a high number of employees may increase the likelihood of a subsidiary choosing the constituency-building strategy, if the subsidiary has adopted a relational approach to political action (Hillman, 2003; Hillman & Hitt, 1999; Keim & Baysinger, 1988). Overall, the larger a subsidiary, the more likely the subsidiary will use the constituency-building and information strategies (Hillman, 2003; Hillman & Wan, 2005). This is because large subsidiaries have greater incentives to be politically active since they can receive greater benefits from changes in host country public policies than smaller subsidiaries. In addition, large subsidiaries are likely to choose their own political strategies with less accountability to headquarters. Thus, heterogeneity in the size of subsidiaries is positively related to dissimilarity among their political strategies (Wan & Hillman 2006).

Dependence on host government. The extent to which subsidiaries depend on the host government can influence their approach and choice of political strategies. Particularly, the higher the dependence of subsidiaries on the host government, the more likely they will choose a relational approach to deploy engaged political strategies (Hillman & Hitt, 1999). For example, nurturing political connections with the host government is important to access host government contracts (Sojli & Tham, 2017).

Experience in host country. The number of years of host country experience can influence the political strategies of subsidiaries. Reputation, credibility, and familiarity with the local context are all a function of the years of experience of a subsidiary in the host country (Hillman & Hitt, 1999; Luo, 2001; Woecke & Moodley, 2015). Subsidiaries that lack a local reputation may compromise their ability to influence host country public policies because credibility is often regarded as the most important factor for effective lobbying and constituency-building (see Keim & Baysinger, 1988). Thus, credible subsidiaries hold an advantage over less credible subsidiaries to exert political influence and are likely to adopt a relational approach to engaged political strategies (Hillman, 2003; Hillman & Hitt, 1999) and pursue the information strategy (Hillman & Wan, 2005). Similarly, subsidiaries that have developed ties to local businesses over the years spent in the host country, are also more likely to pursue a relational approach to engaged political strategies (Shirodkar & Mohr, 2015a).

Resource tangibility. Dependence on intangible or tangible resources can influence subsidiaries' choice of political strategies. Intangible resources include assets such as intellectual capital embedded within highly skilled employees, goodwill within business and political circles, reputation of brands and firm, and credibility in society. Tangible resources include assets such as land, machinery, raw materials, and natural resources; and are not socially constructed. Subsidiaries that depend on local intangible resources are more likely to use the information strategy, but less likely to provide direct financial incentives to host country policymakers; whereas subsidiaries that depend on local tangible resources are less likely to use the information strategy. Interestingly, subsidiaries that depend on both local intangible and tangible resources are more likely to use the constituency-building strategy (Shirodkar & Mohr, 2015b).

Managerial-Level Determinants of Political Strategies of Subsidiaries

The determinants of the political strategies of subsidiaries at the managerial level include managerial orientation toward government affairs, national culture, and perceived uncertainty or influence. Scholars draw on agency theory, resource dependence theory, institutional theory (from the institutional economics and neo-institutional perspectives), and stakeholder theory, to explain how these determinants influence the choice, level of participation (individual or collective), or intensity of the political strategies of subsidiaries.

Managerial orientation toward government affairs. Whether or not the managers of subsidiaries view government affairs as important can be a crucial determinant of subsidiaries' political strategies since managers have agency in shaping subsidiary choices (Blumentritt, 2003; White et al., 2018b). Prior research shows that managerial orientation toward government affairs may be even more important than the amount of bargaining power resources owned (Blumentritt, 2003). Among the factors that can make subsidiary managers disposed or indisposed toward government affairs are organizational, knowledge, and nationality factors. Organizational factors may include mandates from higher organizational levels or, less formally, through organizational norms. Thus, subsidiary managers may choose to either follow headquarters' established norms or abandon these norms and adapt to host country institutional norms, or they may employ ceremonial adaption without changing actual practices (Mellahi et al., 2016). Knowledge factors involve subsidiary managers' knowledge on how to exert influence over host country public policies. Subsidiary managers with greater knowledge of influencing host country public policies are more likely to deploy engaged political strategies, and to do so individually; while managers with less knowledge tend to pursue engaged political strategies collectively with other firms (Hillman & Hitt, 1999). Nationality factors can involve whether subsidiary managers are nationals of the host country or expatriates, and the extent of their contacts with local authorities (Blumentritt, 2003).

National culture. Subsidiary managers' national culture can explain their choice of political strategies; in that they may choose the information strategy because they have culturally grounded expectations that political decisions are taken by an elite of policy-makers who may be influenced. Subsidiary managers may choose the constituency-building strategy because their culture views the power to influence political decisions to be equally distributed across society. Further, subsidiary managers can pursue the financial incentive strategy when they have a cultural attachment to material possessions and money (Barron, 2011).

Perceived uncertainty or influence. Subsidiary managers' perceived uncertainty or influence can impact their choice and intensity of political strategies. Prior research explains that high levels of perceived political uncertainty in a host market may lead subsidiary managers to choose non-engaged political strategies, particularly the avoidance strategy to exit the host market (De Villa et al., 2019; Henisz & Delios, 2004; Oliver, 1991). In contrast, lower levels of perceived political uncertainty in a host market can lead subsidiary managers to choose engaged political strategies (De Villa et al., 2019; Oliver, 1991). However, high levels of perceived environmental uncertainty or perceived stakeholder influence in a host market may also lead subsidiary managers to intensify the use of engaged political strategies in an attempt to manage their perceived uncertainty or influence (Heidenreich, Mohr, & Puck, 2015; Holtbruegge, Berg, & Puck, 2007). Similarly, high levels of perceived regulator uncertainty or vulnerability to political pressures in a host market can lead subsidiary managers to intensify political ties (White, Boddewyn, Rajwani, & Hemphill, 2018a). Also, perceived legal system uncertainty in a host market, that involves ex-ante commercial law inadequacy and ex-post judicial arbitrariness, can affect subsidiary managers' political tie intensity. In particular, subsidiary managers' perceptions of ex-ante commercial law inadequacy and their intensification of political ties can grow stronger when a subsidiary is committed to organizational adaptation of capabilities to the local context; while subsidiary managers' perceptions of ex-post judicial arbitrariness and their intensification of political ties can grow stronger when a subsidiary is engaged in strategically positioning operations in an emerging market (White, Boddewyn, & Galang, 2015).

Outcomes of Political Strategies of Subsidiaries of MNEs

The outcomes of political strategies of subsidiaries have focused on engaged political strategies. From the neo-institutional perspective of institutional theory and stakeholder theory perspective, the outcomes of engaged political strategies of subsidiaries are explained in terms of legitimacy. From the institutional economics perspective of institutional theory, the outcomes of engaged political strategies of subsidiaries are explained in terms of their performance.

Legitimacy in the Host Country

Subsidiaries pursue engaged political strategies to negotiate and socially construct their legitimacy in the host country. Keeping with this view, prior research shows that internal pressures from headquarters and external pressures from the environment of the host country drive subsidiaries to increase political activism to ensure their legitimacy (Hillman & Wan, 2005). Thus, the deployment of engaged political strategies by subsidiaries is positively related to the goal achievement perceived by subsidiary managers (Nell et al., 2015). However, different engaged political strategies have different effects on subsidiaries' legitimacy. In particular, a relational approach can enable the financial incentive and constituency-building strategies to have a strong to moderate effect on subsidiaries' legitimacy. Differently, the information strategy has no effect on subsidiaries' legitimacy. Alternatively, mimetic isomorphism, that enables subsidiaries to model their behavior on local firms in host markets, has in fact, the strongest effect on achieving subsidiaries' legitimacy. Thus, a relatively easy way for subsidiaries to gain acceptance in the host market is to mimic the political strategies of already successful firms (Banerjee & Venaik 2018). Yet, in underdeveloped host markets, it is important to note that subsidiaries are increasingly expected by host governments to assist in the provision of collective goods to enhance their legitimacy (Boddewyn & Doh, 2011; Darendeli & Hill, 2016). A word of caution for subsidiary managers: overconfidence in that engaged political strategies can, on their own, bring legitimacy in the host country, may compromise a subsidiary's survival (Heidenreich et al., 2015).

Performance

As usual with performance studies, assessing the overall performance of engaged political strategies is difficult (Lawton, Mcguire, & Rajwani, 2013). Different attempts have been made by using measures such as greater market capitalization (Hillman, 2005), higher equity returns (Kim, 2008), higher firm value in stock markets (Goldman, Rocholl, & So, 2009), and improved financial performance (Shaffer, Quasney, & Grimm, 2000). However, these measures are often calculated at the multinational level, and less at the subsidiary level. Further, despite the measures used, extant research suggests that the engaged political strategies of subsidiaries and their effects on performance are influenced by a subsidiary's home country and host country, as well as by subsidiary managers. For instance, prior research shows that the fit between home country political stability and a subsidiary's political tie intensity in the host market can have a positive effect on performance. In particular, subsidiaries of MNEs from politically stable home countries may achieve better performance outcomes when they allocate greater managerial resources to intensifying a subsidiary's political ties in the host country (White et al., 2018b). In addition, low distance between home and host governments relations can enable subsidiaries to use engaged political strategies to positively impact performance; whereas high distance can reduce the value of engaged political strategies for subsidiaries (Blumentritt & Nigh, 2002; De Villa et al., 2019).

The context of the host country, on its own, can also influence the engaged political strategies of subsidiaries and their performance. For example, a relational approach to engaged political strategies can be more valuable for subsidiaries in emerging (vs. developed) countries, where relations may provide safeguards against transaction risks because social capital underlies political and economic exchange (Jean, Sinkovics, & Zagelmeyer, 2018; Rajwani & Liedong, 2015; White et al., 2014). Therefore, in emerging countries, subsidiaries using a relational approach to engaged political strategies may have a stronger positive influence on their performance by building a well-established reputation or a long trajectory of operations (Luo & Zhao, 2013). Differently, in developed countries, the information and financial incentive strategies are used more by subsidiaries to positively influence their performance, perhaps, because in these countries there are laws that regulate the policymaking process and political spending. Yet, unfortunately, corruption is often times the channel of superior performance for subsidiaries in developed countries, and even more in emerging countries (see Rajwani & Liedong, 2015).

Although the general view is that the engaged political strategies of subsidiaries improve performance, a stream of studies shows that the context of the host country can also lead subsidiaries' engaged political strategies to have negative effects on performance. For example, in emerging countries, the intensive use of engaged political strategies can be detrimental for the performance of subsidiaries when subsidiaries are highly visible (Puck Rogers, & Mohr, 2013). This is because in emerging countries, visibility may increase rather than reduce subsidiaries' risk exposure, thereby increasing the likelihood of subsidiaries being the target of discriminatory policies or expropriation (Henisz & Zelner, 2010). Even in a stable emerging country, political embeddedness can change over time from producing positive, to declining, to negative effects (Sun, Mellahi, & Thun, 2010; Sun, Mellahi, Wright, & Xu, 2015).

Last, subsidiary managers can also play an important role in the effects of engaged political strategies on performance. Subsidiary managers who are well connected with their colleagues in other units, have access to technical expertise, and develop valuable relationships with political actors may obtain favorable policies. Decentralized decision-making structures encourage the knowledge sharing that enables subsidiary managers to establish these internal and external connections. The end result of favorable policies can have a positive effect on subsidiaries' performance (Barron, Pereda, & Stacey, 2017).

FUTURE RESEARCH AND CONCLUDING REMARKS

The body of research on political strategies of subsidiaries of MNEs is growing. This reflects the increasingly important role of subsidiaries in managing multinationals' political contexts across different host markets. At the same time, multinationals continue to expand their operations, which in turn involves managing an increased diversity of host markets that bring in more host governments and varied public policies. As subsidiaries are the units of MNEs that are directly exposed to host country governments and public policies, the challenge for scholars is to keep in sight a subsidiary perspective to improve our understanding of political strategies in an international setting.

To advance research on political strategies at the subsidiary level, this chapter suggests promising opportunities for future research that, in my view, have the potential to make significant contributions to both theory and practice. For instance, to extend our understanding of the types of political strategies of subsidiaries, further research can direct more attention to empirical studies that offer context-specific contributions (Teagarden, Von Glinow, & Mellahi, 2018). For example, empirical studies can examine how subsidiary managers approach illegal political strategies to broaden our understanding of the differences in notions of illegality or corruption practices among subsidiary managers across various host markets. Extant research has focused on the legal political strategies of subsidiaries. Yet, we need to further explore illegal political strategies throughout host countries from a subsidiary perspective. Another avenue for empirical studies can analyze how subsidiary managers deploy non-engaged political strategies in different host markets. Advancing our understanding of non-engaged political strategies is important as not engaging with the host government remains an underexplored option that may be useful to some subsidiaries in some host countries. This is particularly the case in an era characterized by the growth of authoritarian regimes and the decline of liberal democracies in host markets.

Concerning the determinants of political strategies of subsidiaries, this chapter explains how internal (multinational, subsidiary, managerial) and external (home country, host country) factors exert influence on subsidiaries' political strategies. As a result, these organizational efforts are confronted with institutional duality, that refers to institutional pressures from within the multinational and institutional pressures stemming from the subsidiary's host and home countries (Kostova & Roth, 2002). However, prior research underscores that an MNE's market strategy is a crucial factor that dictates the decision-making structure that guides subsidiaries in their choice and deployment of political strategies. In particular, a multi-domestic market strategy directs subsidiaries to specifically cater their political strategies to the idiosyncrasies of their host market; whereas a global market strategy leads subsidiaries to prioritize integration and coordination benefits over customization (Wan & Hillman 2006). To this distinction, Baron (1995) and Kobrin (2015) propose that a multinational's market strategy can be global, but a global approach to non-market strategy (or political strategies) is unlikely to be successful. Thus, further research can extend our understanding of the relationship and tension between a multinational's market strategy and its subsidiaries' non-market (political) strategies. Particularly, future studies can contrast MNEs following a multi-domestic versus a global market strategy and examine how these multinationals' distinct decision-making structures shape the headquarter–subsidiary relationship, and subsequently, subsidiaries' choice and deployment of political strategies.

On the outcomes of political strategies of subsidiaries, future research can broaden our understanding of what relevant criteria and measures can be used at the subsidiary level of analysis. Particularly, to avoid relying on measures that are directly related to the multinational level of analysis and to capture longer term and intangible outcomes such as legitimacy in the host country. Further research can also reflect on the outcomes of *non-engaged* political strategies of subsidiaries to overcome the bias in extant research toward the outcomes of subsidiaries' *engaged* political strategies. Moreover, insights from practice can allow future research to explore the outcomes of illegal political strategies or corrupt practices, for both subsidiaries and society, to push for consensus and laws that discourage improper corporate behavior.

References

Aplin, J. C., & Hegarty, W. H. 1980. Political influence: Strategies employed by organizations to impact legislation in business and economic matters. *Academy of Management Journal*, 23(3): 438–450.

Banerjee, S., & Venaik, S. 2018. The effect of corporate political activity on MNC subsidiary legitimacy: An institutional perspective. *Management International Review*, 58(6): 813–844.

Baron, D. P. 1995. Integrated strategy: Market and nonmarket components. *California Management Review*, 37(2): 47–65.

Barron, A. 2011. Exploring national culture's consequences on international business lobbying. *Journal of World Business*, 46(3): 320–327.

Barron, A., Pereda, A., & Stacey, S. 2017. Exploring the performance of government affairs subsidiaries: A study of organisation design and the social capital of European government affairs managers at Toyota Motor Europe and Hyundai Motor Company in Brussels. *Journal of World Business*, 52(2): 184–196.

Baysinger, B. D. 1984. Domain maintenance as an objective of business political activity: An expanded typology. *Academy of Management Review*, 9(2): 248–258.

Birkinshaw, J., & Hood, N. 1998. Multinational subsidiary evolution: Capability and charter change in foreign-owned subsidiary companies. *Academy of Management Review*, 23(4): 773–795.

Blumentritt, T. P. 2003. Foreign subsidiaries' government affairs activities. *Business & Society*, 42(2): 202–233.

Blumentritt, T. P., & Nigh, D. 2002. The integration of subsidiary political activities in multi-national corporations. *Journal of International Business Studies*, 33(1): 57–77.

Blumentritt, T. P., & Rehbein, K. 2008. The political capital of foreign subsidiaries. *Business & Society*, 47(2): 242–263.

Boddewyn, J. J. 1988. Political aspects of MNE theory. *Journal of International Business Studies*, 19(3): 341–363.

Boddewyn, J. J., & Brewer, T. L. 1994. International-business political behavior: New theoretical directions. *Academy of Management Review*, 19(1): 119–143.

Boddewyn, J. J., & Doh, J. P. 2011. Global strategy and the collaboration of MNEs, NGOs, and governments for the provisioning of collective goods in emerging markets. *Global Strategy Journal*, 1(3–4): 345–361.

Bonardi, J. P., Hillman, A. J., & Keim, G. D. 2005. The attractiveness of political markets: Implications for firm strategy. *Academy of Management Review*, 30(2): 397–413.

Bonardi, J. P., Holburn, G. L. F., & Vanden Bergh, R. G. 2006. Nonmarket strategy performance: Evidence from U.S. electric utilities. *Academy of Management Journal*, 49(6): 1209–1228.

Brown, L. W., Yasar, M., & Rasheed, A. A. 2018. Predictors of foreign corporate political activities in United States politics. *Global Strategy Journal*, 8(3): 503–514.

Cuervo-Cazurra, A. 2011. Global strategy and global business environment: The direct and indirect influences of the home country on a firm's global strategy. *Global Strategy Journal*, 1(3–4): 382–386.

Cuervo-Cazurra, A. 2016. Corruption in international business. *Journal of World Business*, 51(1): 35–49.

Darendeli, I. S., & Hill, T. L. 2016. Uncovering the complex relationships between political risk and MNE firm legitimacy: Insights from Libya. *Journal of International Business Studies*, 47(1): 68–92.

De Villa, M. A., Rajwani, T., Lawton, T. C., & Mellahi, K. 2019. To engage or not to engage with host governments: Corporate political activity and host country political risk. *Global Strategy Journal*, 9(2): 208–242.

Fortune India. 2018. Lobbying: Legalize it, my lords!. https://www.fortuneindia.com/opinion/lobbying-legalise-it-my-lords/102079. Accessed 20 January 2019.

Frynas, J. G., Mellahi, K., & Pigman, G. A. 2006. First mover advantages in international business and firm-specific political resources. *Strategic Management Journal*, 27(4): 321–345.

Gaur, A., & Kumar, M. 2018. A systematic approach to conducting review studies: An assessment of content analysis in 25 years of IB research. *Journal of World Business*, 53(2): 280–289.

Getz, K. A. 1993. Selecting corporate political tactics. In B. M. Mitnick (Ed.), *Corporate Political Agency: The Construction of Competition in Public Affairs*. Newbury: SAGE Publications.

Goldman, E., Rocholl, J., & So, J. 2009. Do politically connected boards affect firm value? *The Review of Financial Studies*, 22(6): 2331–2360.

Hadani, M., Bonardi, J. P., & Dahan, N. M. 2017. Corporate political activity, public policy uncertainty, and firm outcomes: A meta-analysis. *Strategic Organization*, 15(3): 338–366.

Heidenreich, S., Mohr, A. T., & Puck, J. F. 2015. Political strategies, entrepreneurial overconfidence and foreign direct investment in developing countries. *Journal of World Business*, 50(4): 793–803.

Henisz, W. J., & Delios, A. 2004. Information or influence? The benefits of experience for managing political uncertainty. *Strategic Organization*, 2(4): 389–421.

Henisz, W. J., & Zelner, B. A. 2010. The hidden risks in emerging markets. *Harvard Business Review*, 88(4): 88–95.

Hillman, A. J. 2003. Determinants of political strategies in U.S. multinationals. *Business & Society*, 42(4): 455–484.

Hillman, A. J. 2005. Politicians on the board of directors: Do connections affect the bottom line? *Journal of Management*, 31(3): 464–481.

Hillman, A. J., & Hitt, M. A. 1999. Corporate political strategy formulation: A model of approach, participation, and strategy decisions. *Academy of Management Review*, 24(4): 825–842.

Hillman, A. J., Keim, G. D., & Schuler, D. 2004. Corporate political activity: A review and research agenda. *Journal of Management*, 30(6): 837–857.

Hillman, A. J., & Wan, W. P. 2005. The determinants of MNE subsidiaries' political strategies: Evidence of institutional duality. *Journal of International Business Studies*, 36(3): 322–340.

Hirschman, A. O. 1970. *Exit, Voice, and Loyalty: Responses to Decline in Firms, Organizations, and States*. Cambridge, MA: Harvard University Press.

Holburn, G. L. F., & Zelner, B. A. 2010. Political capabilities, policy risk, and international investment strategy: Evidence from the global electric power generation industry. *Strategic Management Journal*, 31(12): 1290–1315.

Holtbruegge, D., Berg, N., & Puck, J. F. 2007. To bribe or to convince? Political stakeholders and political activities in German multinational corporations. *International Business Review*, 16(1): 47–67.

IDEA. 2012. *Political finance regulations around the world*. https://www.idea.int/sites/default/files/publications/political-finance-regulations-around-the-world.pdf. Accessed 4 February 2019.

Jean, R. J. B., Sinkovics, R. R., & Zagelmeyer, S. 2018. Antecedents and innovation performance implications of MNC political ties in the Chinese automotive supply chain. *Management International Review*, 58(6): 995–1026.

Keim, G. D., & Baysinger, B. D. 1988. The efficacy of business political activity: Competitive considerations in a principal agent context. *Journal of Management*, 14(2): 163–180.

Kim, J. 2008. Corporate lobbying revisited. *Business & Politics*, 10(2): 1–23.

Kobrin, S. J. 2015. Is a global nonmarket strategy possible? Economic integration in a multi-polar world order. *Journal of World Business*, 50(2): 262–272.

Kostova, T, & Roth, K. 2002. Adoption of an organizational practice by subsidiaries of multi-national corporations: Institutional and relational effects. *Academy of Management Journal*, 45(1): 215–233.

Lawton, T. C., Mcguire, S., & Rajwani, T. 2013. Corporate political activity: A literature review and research agenda. *International Journal of Management Reviews*, 15(1): 86–105.

Lawton, T. C., & Rajwani, T. 2011. Designing lobbying capabilities: Managerial choices in unpredictable environments. *European Business Review*, 23(2): 167–189.

Liedong, T. A., & Frynas, J. G. 2018. Investment climate constraints as determinants of political tie intensity in emerging countries: Evidence from foreign firms in Ghana. *Management International Review*, 58(5): 675–703.

Luo, Y. 2001. Toward a cooperative view of MNC–host government relations: Building blocks and performance implications. *Journal of International Business Studies*, 32(3): 401–419.

Luo, Y., & Zhao, H. 2013. Doing business in a transitional society: Economic environment and relational political strategy for multinationals. *Business & Society*, 52(3): 515–549.

Mellahi, K., Frynas, J. G., Sun, P., & Siegel, D. 2016. A review of the nonmarket strategy literature: Toward a multi-theoretical integration. *Journal of Management*, 42(1): 143–173.

Meyer, K. E., Estrin, S., Bhaumik, S. K., & Peng, M. W. 2009. Institutions, resources, and entry strategies in emerging economies. *Strategic Management Journal*, 30(1): 61–80.

Meyer, K. E., Mudambi, R., & Narula, R. 2011. Multinational enterprises and local contexts: The opportunities and challenges of multiple embeddedness. *Journal of Management Studies*, 48(2): 235–252.

Meznar, M. B., & Nigh, D. 1995. Buffer or bridge? Environmental and organizational determinants of public affairs activities in American firms. *Academy of Management Journal*, 38(4): 975–996.

Nell, P. C., Puck, J. F., & Heidenreich, S. 2015. Strictly limited choice or agency? Institutional duality, legitimacy, and subsidiaries' political strategies. *Journal of World Business*, 50(2): 302–311.

Oberman, W. D. 1993. Strategy and tactic choice in an institutional resource context. In B. M. Mitnick (Ed.), *Corporate Political Agency: The Construction of Competition in Public Affairs*. Newbury: SAGE Publications.

Oliver, C. 1991. Strategic responses to institutional processes. *Academy of Management Review*, 16(1): 145–179.

Oliver, C., & Holzinger, I. 2008. The effectiveness of strategic political management: A dynamic capabilities framework. *Academy of Management Review*, 33(2): 496–520.

Puck, J. F., Lawton, T. C., & Mohr, A. T. 2018. The corporate political activity of MNCs: Taking stock and moving forward. *Management International Review*, 58(5): 663–673.

Puck, J. F., Rogers, H., & Mohr, A. T. 2013. Flying under the radar: Foreign firm visibility and the efficacy of political strategies in emerging economies. *International Business Review*, 22(6): 1021–1033.

Rajwani, T., & Liedong, T. A. 2015. Political activity and firm performance within nonmarket research: A review and international comparative assessment. *Journal of World Business*, 50(2): 273–283.

Rodriguez, P., Siegel, D. S., Hillman, A., & Eden, L. 2006. Three lenses on the multinational enterprise: Politics, corruption, and corporate social responsibility. *Journal of International Business Studies*, 37(6): 733–746.

Rodriguez, P., Uhlenbruck, K., & Eden, L. 2005. Government corruption and the entry strategies of multinationals. *Academy of Management Review*, 30(2): 383–396.

Schuler, D., Rehbein, K., & Cramer, R. 2002. Pursuing strategic advantage through political means: A multivariate approach. *Academy of Management Journal*, 45(4): 659–672.

Shaffer, B. 1995. Firm-level responses to government-regulation: Theoretical and research approaches. *Journal of Management*, 21(3): 495–514.

Shaffer, B., & Hillman, A. J. 2000. The development of business-government strategies by diversified firms. *Strategic Management Journal*, 21(2): 175–190.

Shaffer, B., Quasney, T. J., & Grimm, C. M. 2000. Firm level performance implications of nonmarket actions. *Business & Society*, 39(2): 126–143.

Shirodkar, V., & Mohr, A. T. 2015a. Explaining foreign firms' approaches to corporate political activity in emerging economies: The effects of resource criticality, product diversification, inter-subsidiary integration, and business ties. *International Business Review*, 24(4): 567–579.

Shirodkar, V., & Mohr, A. T. 2015b. Resource tangibility and foreign firms' corporate political strategies in emerging economies: Evidence from India. *Management International Review*, 55(6): 801–825.

Sojli, E., & Tham, W. 2017. Foreign political connections. *Journal of International Business Studies*, 48(2): 244–266.

Sun, P., Mellahi, K., & Thun, E. 2010. The dynamic value of MNE political embeddedness: The case of the Chinese automobile industry. *Journal of International Business Studies*, 41(7): 1161–1182.

Sun, P., Mellahi, K., Wright, M., & Xu, H. 2015. Political tie heterogeneity and the impact of adverse shocks on firm value. *Journal of Management Studies*, 52(8): 1036–1063.

Teagarden, M. B., Von Glinow, M. A., & Mellahi, K. 2018. Contextualizing international business research: Enhancing rigor and relevance. *Journal of World Business*, 53(3): 303–306.

Voinea, C. L., & van Kranenburg, H. 2018. Feeling the squeeze: Nonmarket institutional pressures and firm nonmarket strategies. *Management International Review*, 58(5): 705–741.

Wan, W. P., & Hillman, A. J. 2006. One of these things is not like the others: What contributes to dissimilarity among MNE subsidiaries' political strategy? *Management International Review*, 46(1): 85–107.

Weidenbaum, M. L. 1980. Public policy: No longer a spectator sport for business. *Journal of Business Strategy*, 1(1): 46–53.

White, G. O., Boddewyn, J. J., & Galang, R. M. N. 2015. Legal system contingencies as determinants of political tie intensity by wholly owned foreign subsidiaries: Insights from the Philippines. *Journal of World Business*, 50(2): 342–356.

White, G. O., Boddewyn, J. J., Rajwani, T., & Hemphill, T. 2018a. Regulator vulnerabilities to political pressures and political tie intensity: The moderating effects of regulatory and political distance. *Management International Review*, 58(5): 743–769.

White, G. O., Fainshmidt, S., & Rajwani, T. 2018b. Antecedents and outcomes of political tie intensity: Institutional and strategic fit perspectives. *Journal of International Management*, 24(1): 1–15.

White, G. O., Hemphill, T. A., Joplin, J. R. W., & Marsh, L. A. 2014. Wholly owned foreign subsidiary relation-based strategies in volatile environments. *International Business Review*, 23(1): 303–312.

Woecke, A., & Moodley, T. 2015. Corporate political strategy and liability of foreignness: Similarities and differences between local and foreign firms in the South African Health Sector. *International Business Review*, 24(4): 700–709.

CHAPTER 17

....

LOOKING BACK TO MOVE FORWARD

An Overview on Foreign Divestment Decisions

....

CARLOS M. P. SOUSA AND QUN TAN

INTRODUCTION

....

ALONGSIDE rapid economic globalization and intensified worldwide competition, multinational enterprises (MNEs) are experiencing important decisions concerning whether or not to divest from international markets. Foreign divestment, which involves the sale of international subsidiaries, closure of foreign plants, and exit from foreign markets, is increasingly, a part of international business (IB) strategizing (Soule, Swaminathan, & Tihanyi, 2014). Even so, foreign divestment decisions and the effective management of the exit process remain major challenges for MNE executives, most of whom may not know how to handle divestment efficiently and confidently (Arte & Larimo, 2019; Burgelman, 1996; Tan & Sousa, 2019). Indeed, it continues to be observed that managers do not conduct detailed analyses of the situations they are in, the events leading to market exit and the processes to be undertaken during and after divestment.

The literature reveals that we are yet to achieve a comprehensive understanding of why and how foreign divestment decisions are made, and what the consequences of these decisions are likely to be. Depending on the disciplines which they contribute to, studies have proposed various theoretical models on foreign divestment, with each focusing on a specific aspect of why and how MNEs divest their foreign businesses (Steenhuis & Bruijn, 2009). Empirical studies have examined the antecedents of foreign divestment from various perspectives such as resource-based view (RBV) theory, organizational learning-based theory, strategy-based theory, and relationship/network-based theory at the firm level, industry level, or country level (Tan & Sousa, 2019). Since the pioneering work of Boddewyn and his colleagues between 1973 and 1985, we have witnessed a growing body of research on foreign divestment; yet, there remain both research gaps and a series of contradictory findings.

In this chapter we propose that, notwithstanding the contributions of past studies to each level of analysis, insufficient efforts have been directed toward providing a comprehensive framework that can integrate research that has been approached from different perspectives, and thus guide future researchers toward some convergence in this field. Extant research has resulted generally in suggestions for more studies in different research contexts (e.g. emerging economies, service industries, see Burt, Dawson, & Sparks, 2008; McDermott, 2010), more studies testing new perspectives that may also possess explanatory power (see Brauer, 2006; Steenhuis & Bruijn, 2009), and/or those studies that include variables that have, so far, been largely ignored (c.f. Steenhuis & Bruijn, 2009). While, the addition of more perspectives and variables are important progressions in broadening our understanding of foreign divestment decisions, such suggestions may precipitate even more divergence in our already confusing and sometimes contradictory findings. This, in turn, may be detrimental to our understanding of the practical and managerial implications of MNEs exiting international markets (as such, also inhibiting the integration and development of both theory and applications). To advance the research agenda, Tan and Sousa (2015) have made a first step toward providing a comprehensive framework to understand the complexity of foreign divestment decisions; even so, their framework did not include important theoretical perspectives such as institutional theory and learning theory, nor did they take into account the managerial decision-making process.

We deem it important to better understand divestment decisions in terms of both their theoretical and practical implications. This chapter provides a process framework that theoretically integrates and coordinates the diverse body of extant knowledge on international divestment. In doing so, we also offer practical guidance to managers so that they acquire a better understanding of their decision-making processes, thereby improving the credibility and ultimate acceptance of the final divestment decision made. We continue this chapter with an overview of the existing (seemingly independent) research on foreign divestment. We present key theoretical lenses used in this literature and their main findings. This overview will be followed by a short discussion section, after which we introduce and explain our attribution theory-based process model to integrate the various perspectives currently employed in the literature and to make them practically relevant.

OVERVIEW OF RESEARCH ON FOREIGN DIVESTMENT

Foreign divestment has been studied in the IB and strategy literature for nearly half a century since the initial research in the 1970s. Overall, when compared with research on MNE international entry and expansion behavior, there is a general lack of research and relatively slow progress in international/foreign divestment behavior (Piepenbrink & Gaur, 2017; Tan & Sousa, 2015), mainly due to the great difficulty in persuading managers to share data associated with their market exits (Benito & Welch, 1997; McDermott, 2010; Paul & Benito, 2018). Despite this, extant research has examined the foreign divestment topic from a variety of theoretical perspectives, focusing on specific aspects and stages of this decision such as the antecedents, processes, and/or outcomes of foreign divestment (Tan & Sousa, 2019). Each of these aspects is now explored in detail.

Antecedents of Foreign Divestment Decisions

Antecedents of the foreign divestment decision have been the main focus of studies to date. Early research was mainly qualitative, and aimed to explain the phenomenon and drivers of foreign divestment through conceptualization and case studies (Boddewyn, 1979; Torneden, 1975). Nowadays, quantitative research using longitudinal data, panel data, and questionnaire survey data has become dominant in investigating the relationship between foreign divestment decisions and their antecedents (e.g. Berry, 2013; Tan & Sousa, 2019), with some studies further differentiating the antecedents for different types of foreign divestment strategies (Mata & Portugal, 2000). Our review also indicates that existing research has examined the antecedents of foreign divestment from as many as eight research perspectives (at the firm level and industry/country level), namely: RBV-based perspective, learning-based perspective, strategy-based perspective, relationship-based perspective, leadership-based perspective, evolution-based perspective, real options-based perspective, and institution-based perspective (see Table 17.1).

Firm-Level Antecedents

Firm-level antecedents account for the majority of the foreign divestment antecedents examined in the literature and include factors at both the subsidiary level and the parent company level.

One of the dominant research streams investigates the antecedents of foreign divestment from the RBV perspective. Generally, the RBV assumes that firms can be understood as heterogeneous bundles of resources and capabilities and that resource differences between firms persist over time (Eisenhardt & Martin, 2000). Therefore, the possession of valuable, rare, inimitable, and non-substitutable resources and capabilities becomes the key to gaining sustainable competitive advantage and superior performance (Barney, 1991; Teece, Pisano, & Shuen, 1997). Following RBV rationales, scholars have argued that the more resources and capabilities the subsidiaries and their parent firms have, the more likely the subsidiaries are to gain competitive advantage and survive internationally for longer. Specifically, empirical research based on RBV-related assumptions has found that subsidiaries' and/or parent firms' performance (Berry, 2013; Dai, Eden, & Beamish, 2013; Song, 2015), size (Belderbos & Zou, 2009), sunk costs (Dai et al., 2017), advantages in intangible assets such as marketing, R&D, and technological

Table 17.1 A perspective-level matrix: An overview of the antecedent factors of foreign divestment

Level Perspective	Firm level (including subsidiary level and parent company level)	Industry/country level
RBV-based perspective	Performance Firm size R&D/Technological capabilities Intangible assets Sunk cost	
Learning-based perspective	International experience Age Business relatedness	
Strategy-based perspective	Strategic fit Foreign ownership Entry strategy (e.g. entry mode, destination) Degree of diversification	
Relationship-based perspective	Business interdependence Subsidiary unit strength Subsidiary's degree of vertical integration with HQ	
Leadership-based perspective	Managers' resource commitment TMT involvement General managers' tenure Cultural difference in leadership	
Evolution-based perspective		Industrial foreign penetration Seller concentration Industrial technological level
Real options-based perspective		Environmental uncertainty Technological turbulence Country risk Industry growth Market attractiveness Economic development
Institution-based perspective		Geographic distance Economic distance Cultural distance Political distance Administrative distance Political openness

resources (Lee et al., 2012), and capabilities (Franco, Sarkar, Agarwal, & Echambadi, 2009; Giovannetti, Ricchiuti, & Velucchi, 2011) have the most significant impacts on the likelihood of foreign divestment.

The second dominant research stream examines the antecedents of foreign divestment from a learning-based perspective. Organizational learning theory holds that the ability to learn and adapt (as a key organizational capability) is critical to performance and the long-term success of organizations (Argote & Miron-Spektor, 2011). Scholars in this research stream usually emphasize the importance of knowledge and experience (Huber, 1991) as precursors to effective organizational learning. More specifically, organizational learning studies propose that the success of foreign subsidiaries relies primarily on the accumulation and utilization of relevant knowledge acquired through experience (Kang, Lee, & Ghauri, 2017; Paul & Benito, 2018) because knowledge and experience help to overcome the liability of foreignness and avoid the pitfalls associated with internationalization (Kim, Delios, & Xu, 2010). The critical role of relatedness between the company and its partners (Keil, Maula, Schildt, & Zahra, 2008; Xu & Lu, 2007) is also considered, because an increased level of relatedness among business units is expected to create greater value of learning (Tan & Sousa, 2018). Accordingly, empirical studies based on organizational learning theory have generally found foreign divestment to be negatively associated with subsidiaries' and/or the parent firms' age (Delios & Beamish, 2004), international experience (Mata & Portugal, 2002), failure experience in the same country (Yang, Li, & Delios, 2015), and business relatedness between a subsidiary and the parent company (Berry, 2013; Tan & Sousa, 2018), or between joint venture partners (Xu & Lu, 2007).

The third research stream examines the antecedents of foreign divestment from the strategy-based perspective. Strategic management scholars believe that strategic choices at entry and during the internationalization process are critical to the survival of foreign business units. The reason is that different strategies indicate different motivations (Mata & Portugal, 2000) and costs in initial investment and subsequent management in the foreign market (Li, 1995), which, in turn, influence the likelihood of a subsidiary's subsequent strategic choice to either divest a foreign business or remain in the market. Accordingly, empirical studies have found that the likelihood of foreign exit is significantly associated with strategic choices such as a subsidiary's entry mode and destination strategy (Koch, Koch, Menon, & Shenkar, 2016; Li, 1995), foreign ownership (Kim, Lu, & Rhee, 2012), the strategic fit between the subsidiary and the parent firm (Sousa & Tan, 2015), and the parent firm's degree of diversification/internationalization (Chung, Lee, & Lee, 2013).

The fourth research stream explains the antecedents of foreign divestment from the relationship-based perspective. Researchers in this stream emphasize the important role of subsidiary-headquarter (HQ) relationships in influencing the HQs' strategic decision on foreign divestment. They argue that, in the IB context, foreign subsidiaries' operations are heavily dependent on support from HQs (Song & Lee, 2017). A strong connection with its parent company and sister subsidiaries decreases the probability of a subsidiary's divestment from the foreign market, because such a connection not only enhances the parent firm's commitment to the subsidiary's business (Berry, 2013) but also makes the divestment of the foreign subsidiary detrimental to the parent firm's interest (Song & Lee, 2017). Accordingly, empirical studies have found that foreign subsidiaries are less likely to be divested when they are vertically integrated with the parent firm (Song & Lee, 2017), interdependent with sister subsidiaries (Duhaime & Grant, 1984) and when there is greater unit strength among subsidiaries (Tan & Sousa, 2019).

The fifth research stream, which explains the antecedents of foreign divestment mainly from the leadership-based perspective, has yet to attract significant scholarly attention (Cairns, Quinn, Alexander, & Doherty, 2010). Leadership theory generally holds that managers/leaders and the traits, attributes, and styles of leadership have a substantive effect on the overall performance of organizational strategies (Waldman, Ramirez, House, & Puranam, 2001), as strategic decisions in organizations are the reflections of the values and cognitive bases of organizational leaders (Finkelstein, Hambrick, & Cannella, 2009; Hambrick & Mason, 1984). Consistently, scholars in this research stream propose that managers and managerial leaders play a key role in the divestment decision, since changes in leadership can be a prior condition for, and also a consequence of, international divestment (Gilmour, 1973; Torneden, 1975). Accordingly, it is found that managers' resource commitment, TMT involvement, general managers' tenure, and cultural differences in leadership beliefs are significantly associated with foreign divestment (c.f. Koch et al., 2016).

Industry-Level and Country-Level Antecedents

Industry/country-level antecedents of foreign divestment have also gained some attention in the literature. We identified three broad research streams, namely the evolution-based perspective, the real options-based perspective, and institution-based perspectives. Evolutionary theory generally emphasizes Darwin's idea of survival of the fittest to argue that "individuals who managed to rise to the top of the hierarchy of domination and privilege did so because they were most fit" to cope with the environment (Hannan & Freeman, 1993). Population ecology is a theory that originates from evolutionary theory and discusses "Darwinian selection" in populations of organizations (Carroll & Hannan, 1995). At the industry level, scholars in this research stream argue that the survival chance of a firm is largely affected by the industrial condition of competition and population density (Demirbag, Apaydin, & Tatoglu, 2011; Silverman, Nickerson, & Freeman, 1997). The more intensive the foreign market competition, the more likely it is that a foreign subsidiary will be divested. Accordingly, it was found that the industrial technological level (Giovannetti, et al., 2011), seller concentration, and industrial foreign penetration (Mudambi & Zahra, 2007) are significantly associated with foreign divestment decisions.

In turn, real options theory holds that the real-life decisions made by firms regarding acquisition of resources, maintenance of international operations, or abandonment/ divestment can affect the value of other options available to the MNE and its subsidiaries (Trigeorgis & Reuer, 2017). Scholars in this research stream answer the question of whether and/or when MNEs should and should not divest a foreign subsidiary based on the real option value of such a decision. As the real option value of a decision is expected to rise with the uncertainty concerning the future gains and the irreversibility of the decision (Belderbos & Zou, 2009), studies focus on the role of environmental uncertainty and sunk cost[1] (indicating the irreversibility) in making divestment decisions (O'Brien & Folta, 2009). The main argument here is that, when the environment is highly uncertain, maintaining a subsidiary in the foreign market has great options value, because the initial entry cost (sunk cost) will re-occur if the company wants to re-enter the foreign market in the future (Dixit, 1989). Therefore, MNEs should keep the options open and not divest a poorly performing subsidiary until more information is gathered (Belderbos & Zou, 2009). Accordingly, empirical studies have found environmental uncertainty (Tan & Sousa, 2018), technological turbulence, and country risk (Efrat & Shoham, 2012) to be negatively associated with foreign exit. Meanwhile, some studies demonstrate the existence of the hysteresis effect in making foreign divestment decisions under uncertainty (e.g. Song, 2014). In addition, other variables that indicate the future value of the foreign business such as industry growth (Mudambi & Zahra, 2007), market attractiveness (Chung & Beamish, 2005), and economic development (Tan & Sousa, 2018) have also been found to be related to foreign divestment.

The final research stream, institution-based theory, holds that formal institutions (e.g. regulatory/legal, economic, and political institutions) and informal institutions (such as the culture of the home and host country) put pressure on IB strategizing, and therefore influence the performance of foreign subsidiaries (Marano et al., 2016). In this case, scholars aim to examine the impact of host country institutions, home country institutions, and the distance between home and host country on the survival of a foreign subsidiary. The influence of host country institutions is usually related to involuntary foreign divestment such as expropriation, nationalization, and confiscation (Sachdev, 1976), which happens less frequently in present times. The impact of home country institutions on foreign divestment is usually related to ethical divestment (e.g. foreign divestment from South Africa, Ennis & Parkhill, 1986; Nyuur, Amankwah-Amoah, & Osabutey, 2017) and the change of government preferential policy (Luo & Tung, 2007). The basic argument here is that, if the institutional distance in between the home country and the host country is significant, the liability of foreignness for MNEs' IB strategies will increase substantially (Barkema & Vermeulen, 1997; Sousa & Bradley, 2006; Xu & Shenkar, 2002). This subsequently increases the difficulty in performing well and the probability of a subsidiary's divestment from the foreign market (Barkema, Bell, & Pennings, 1996; Kang, et al., 2017).

Process of Foreign Divestment Decisions

In addition to examining the antecedents of foreign divestment, a small number of studies have attempted to conceptualize the foreign divestment decision-making process by, for instance, conducting in-depth interviews with relevant managers of

---

[1] Sunk costs have been used by scholars adopting real options theory and RBV.

the subsidiaries and or of MNE HQs. The idea here is to identify and discuss the typical stages/steps of the decision-making process associated with abandoning a foreign market after initial entry into that market. For example, Torneden (1975) detailed the decision-making process of foreign divestment using eight US MNEs; later, Ghertman (1988) described the decision-making process by focusing specifically on the stage of closing foreign subsidiaries. Based on in-depth interviews with current and ex-employees of a UK fashion retailer, Cairns, Doherty, Alexander, and Quinn (2008) presented a four-stage flowchart of the international retail divestment process; using seventeen case studies on the divestment of foreign manufacturing plants. Baquero-Rosas (2013) also reported a five-stage framework of the international divestment decision-making process. However, all the previous studies on the decision-making process have failed to emphasize and reflect the important role of mangers' underlying motivations, and therefore could not offer deeper insights into the foreign divestment phenomenon and the factors and actors underpinning each of these stages.

Outcomes of Foreign Divestment

There have also been considerably fewer studies focusing on the consequences of the foreign divestment decision. These few studies have tended to examine the relationship between the announcement of a specific divestment type (e.g. spin-off, sell-off, liquidation) and the stock price/abnormal returns. In most cases, the results showed that the announcement of a divestment decision, regardless of the divestment type, leads to an abnormal excessive return (e.g. Dittmar & Shivdasani, 2003). Generally, we need more research on the consequences of foreign divestment, and we need to also consider other possible long-term consequences of divestment such as negative reputational effects, damage to the MNE's brand image in the host market or broken business relationships and networks with key institutional actors.

DISCUSSION AND FUTURE
RESEARCH DIRECTIONS

We presented a summary of the key assumptions and findings associated with the decision to divest operations in foreign markets after initial entry into those markets. Based on our overview of the extant research on foreign divestment decisions, we discuss the major issues that prevent this body of research from progressing and that which, we propose, could be addressed in future studies.

Firstly, research thus far has drawn on different perspectives and, as such, remains extremely segmented. This is a valuable approach to theory development at the early research stage of examination because it allows for a deep understanding of the foreign divestment decision from each single and specific angle. However, as the research from each theoretical perspective/paradigm progresses, single perspective studies lead us to arrive at certain conclusions about divestment decisions on the basis of only a partial understanding of arguments that are often contradictory to each other. For instance, when a foreign subsidiary is divested, RBV proponents would argue that it is due to the lack of critical resources and capabilities; organization learning scholars would likely suggest that exit is primarily the result of a lack of experience; strategic management scholars may hold the view that it is because the wrong entry mode was chosen; relationship theory proponents may posit that the subsidiary had no close relationships with the parent company; whereas proponents of the institution-based view may argue that the cultural and other differences between the host country and the home country are too large, leading to international divestment. We therefore propose that a partial understanding of the divestment decision holds back theoretical and practical progress in this area, restricting the relevance of our findings for managerial decision makers. Our first message in this chapter is that we need to focus more on the overall divestment phenomenon and integrate insights from multiple theoretical perspectives. This is also consistent with the suggestion by Buckley, Doh, & Benischke (2017) on the future of IB strategy research more generally.

Secondly, current research on foreign divestment focuses on firm-level, industry-level, and country-level concerns and thereby largely ignores the important role played by MNE managers and managerial mindsets before, during, and after the decision-making process. This is problematic because in the "real world," when these foreign divestment decisions are made, managers are key players who have direct impact on the final decision. It is therefore important to investigate the role and characteristics of the manager, especially their underlying motivations, in order to gain a more in-depth understanding of foreign divestment decisions.

Thirdly, few studies focus on multiple aspects of the foreign divestment decision simultaneously. This is somewhat understandable as individual studies are constrained by time and cost and it is difficult to examine more than one aspect at a time. However, for a comprehensive understanding of foreign divestment decisions, it is essential to have a framework that incorporates the antecedents, processes, and outcome. We propose that these decisions are interdependent. For example, the longer the divestment process is and the more expensive the divestment becomes, the greater the impact on the firm, potentially also reducing the possibility of re-entry into the exited foreign market. Similarly, exit due to having chosen the wrong mode of operation may mean that the firm can exit and re-enter via a different mode (Surdu, Mellahi, & Glaister, 2019), whereas exit due to institutional changes may delay re-entry, thus leading to long-term, often negative outcomes associated with international divestment.

One approach to address some of the aforementioned limitations would be to develop a multi-theoretical framework as a means of establishing complementarities between the different theories and perspectives and thus, enhancing theory-construction efforts

(Gioia & Pitre, 1990). Although Tan & Sousa (2015) made a first step toward providing such a comprehensive framework, by linking the firm antecedents with key country-level and industry-level factors, they did not emphasize sufficiently the role of the manager. We address this point by proposing a manager-centered comprehensive framework, which can integrate and co-ordinate the various perspectives on the antecedents of international divestment and link them to the foreign divestment process and potential divestment outcomes. In doing so, we aim to provide the reader with a holistic picture of the foreign divestment decision.

A Holistic Framework Based on Attribution Theory

The decision to divest international operations is most likely considered as a negative outcome leading to the MNE not fulfilling its goals in the host market. As such, following market exit, organizations may seek to understand the reasons for their underperformance and learn from past mistakes in order to avoid behaviors that may lead to such unfavorable outcomes in the future.

Attribution theory is widely used by business researchers to enhance our understanding of individual and organizational behavior that focuses on important achievement-related goals (Cort, Griffith, & White, 2007; Weiner, 1985). An attribution is defined as a causal ascription for a positive or negative outcome (Martinko, Harvey, & Douglas, 2007). With the basic premise that people have an innate desire to seek to understand the causes of important outcomes in their lives (Heider, 1958; Martinko, Harvey, & Dasborough, 2011), attribution theory holds that individuals' attributions for successes and failures are very likely to influence their subsequent behavior. This means that, if a prior outcome was a positive one, individuals are likely to re-establish the prior cause to seek this outcome again; in turn, if the prior outcome was undesired, individuals are very likely to alter what they identify as the "cause," in order to produce a different, more positive outcome.

This process of identifying the cause of an event and forming perceptions about it which later may lead to behaviors is expected to take place in stages (see Weiner's model, 1985). The motivational sequence is initiated by an outcome that individuals perceive as positive or negative. A causal search is then conducted to discover why the outcome occurred, with a common bias toward a small number of causes. These causes generally have three dimensions, which carry psychological consequences relating to future behavior (Weiner, 1985), namely (1) locus, which refers to whether the cause of an event is perceived to be external (i.e. exit due to changes in the environment) or internal (exit due to firm inability to serve the market effectively); (2) stability, which refers to whether or not the cause of an event may change over time; and (3) controllability, which refers to whether the cause of an event can be controlled—in this case, radical political changes cannot be managed by the MNE, whereas changes in strategy could become implemented to serve the market better. How the causes for the exit are classified will most likely differ among MNEs and their decision makers.

We propose that attribution theory rationales are particularly pertinent to explain foreign divestment decisions. Firms' internationalization can be viewed as the achievement-orientation of firm management (Cort et al., 2007), whereby a subsidiary's performance achievement for a certain period of time is the important outcome. A foreign divestment decision is one of the behavioral consequences that management may invoke in response to the subsidiary's performance. We therefore propose a comprehensive research framework to reflect the whole picture of the foreign divestment phenomenon, and integrate the various theoretical perspectives taken by different research streams, while simultaneously addressing the broadly neglected role of the manager (see Figure 17.1).

The seven boxes on the top of Figure 17.1 refer to the seven stages of attributional theory, which has provided the foundation for our seven-stage framework of foreign divestment decision-making.

Stages 1–2: outcome and outcome-dependent affect. The starting point is the outcome, namely a foreign subsidiary's performance at a certain point in time. An outcome-dependent affect refers to the affect triggered by the positive (i.e. satisfied—above the aspiration level) or negative outcome (i.e. dissatisfied—below the aspiration level). If the performance is above the aspiration level (i.e. positive), managers are satisfied as they perceive the subsidiary business outcome as a success. If the performance is below the aspiration level (i.e. negative), managers are dissatisfied because they are likely to interpret the subsidiary business outcome as a failure. The lower the satisfaction of the managers, the more a search for the causes will be made (Cyert & March, 1963). Therefore, we propose that a dissatisfactory subsidiary performance is more likely to trigger managers' informational search for causes, whereas a satisfactory performance may not.

Stage 3: causal antecedents. A search for causal antecedents is undertaken at this stage to determine why a subsidiary has yielded satisfactory or dissatisfactory performance. In general, dissatisfactory performance is more likely to trigger the search for causes because the managers want to change the outcome via changing the causes. Managers with a satisfactory performance usually tend to have the same outcome by maintaining the input and are therefore less motivated to search for causes (depicted as a dashed line

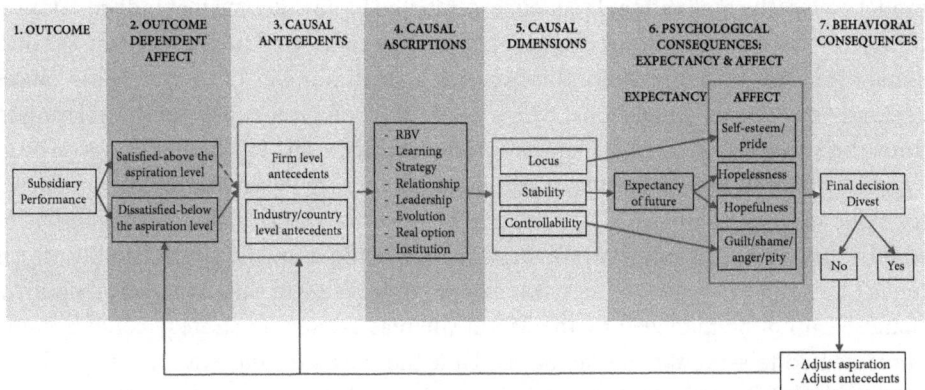

FIGURE 17.1 A framework of foreign divestment decision.

in Figure 17.1). The search for causes may involve internal, firm-level antecedents such as resources, capabilities, and strategies. It may cover external, industry-level and country-level antecedents such as environmental uncertainty and institution level factors.

Stage 4: causal ascriptions. Causal ascriptions, also called causal attributions, refer to the specific causal explanation and inference by the observer in order to predict and evaluate the observed behavior (Weiner, 1986; Weiner, Heckhausen, & Meyer, 1972). At this stage, managers try to explain why the dissatisfactory performance has occurred and decide which of the causes identified at stage 3 are present. The causal decision may be biased toward a small number of causes and certain types of antecedents. Furthermore, different managers are likely to hold different biases. Some managers may be biased toward factors associated with resources and capabilities, whereas other mangers may be biased toward factors linked to learning, strategy, relationship, leadership, real options, evolution, or institutions. Such biased ascriptions/attributions tend to correspond to the various perspectives explored within the different research streams, with some streams focused on or biased toward factors based on learning-based and strategy-based perspectives, and other research focused on or biased toward evolution-based and institution-based perspectives.

Stage 5: causal dimensions. Causal dimensions refer to the characteristics of causes that are used to describe and differentiate the causes. *Locus* refers to whether a cause is internal or external. In this case, firm-level and product-level antecedents such as resources, learning, and strategies are viewed as internal, whereas industry-level and country-level antecedents (generally associated with evolution, real options, and institution-based perspectives) are external (Cavusgil & Zou, 1994; Sousa, Martínez-López, & Coelho, 2008). Since *stability* depicts whether a cause is fluctuating or remains relatively constant—factors associated with resource-based and institutions-based perspectives are relatively stable, whereas factors discussed from an evolution and real options-based perspective tend to be less stable. Also, factors identified in the learning and strategy perspective are usually *controllable* by the firm, whereas (external) factors associated with research drawing on evolution, real options, and institution-based perspectives, are often not within MNE control.

Stage 6: psychological consequences. Each of the three dimensions has different psychological consequences, being related to *expectancy* of future success and *affect*, that is, the affective reaction to the three different dimensional causes. The stability of a cause influences the relative *expectancy* of future success. If the ascribed/perceived cause at stage 5 is stable, managers will expect a subsidiary reporting poor performance to continue to perform poorly in the future. This will lower their *expectancy* of future success, which in turn will precipitate feelings of hopelessness. In this case, managers are less likely to keep the subsidiary business in the foreign market. In contrast, if the ascribed/perceived cause at stage 5 is not stable, managers will expect a subsidiary with poor performance to improve in the future when there is more stability in the environment, and such belief will heighten their *expectancy* of future success. This greater expectancy of future success will lead to feelings of hopefulness, in which case, managers are more likely to keep the foreign subsidiary.

The locus of a cause also exerts an influence on managers' self-esteem and pride. Ascription to internal causes at stage 5 produces greater self-esteem when the subsidiary is successful, and less self-esteem when it is failing, than does ascription to external causes. In addition, controllability has an impact on social emotions such as guilt, shame, anger, and pity. If managers have participated in the business operations of the foreign subsidiary, their psychological consequences are self-directed affects (i.e. emotions that arise from responding to their own poor performance). In this case, when they perceive that the causes of poor performance are controllable, they are likely to feel guilt; when they perceive that the causes of poor performance are uncontrollable, they are likely to feel shame. Instead, if managers have not participated in the business operations of the foreign subsidiary, their psychological consequences are others-directed affects (i.e. emotions arise from responding to others' poor performance). In this case, when they perceive that the causes of poor performance are controllable, they are likely to feel anger; when they perceive that the causes of poor performance are uncontrollable, they are likely to feel pity toward the responsible decision maker(s).

Stage 7: behavioral consequences. The psychological consequences (i.e. *expectancy* and *affect*) are presumed to determine the behavioral consequences. If a subsidiary is perceived to be hopeful of gaining success in the future, managers are less likely to divest it from the foreign market. In contrast, if a subsidiary is considered to be hopeless and unable to achieve success in the future, it is very likely that managers will decide to divest it from the foreign market. In addition, the self-esteem, pride, and social emotions such as guilt, shame, anger, and pity are all likely to influence managers' final decision on whether to divest a subsidiary with dissatisfactory performance. For instance, managers with less self-esteem are more likely to divest the poorly performing foreign business, because they have lost self-confidence in managing the foreign business; whereas managers with feelings of guilt may want to keep the foreign business in the foreign market to correct their mistake. This is consistent with the view that individuals who experience guilt feel a sense of urgency about taking constructive action (Harder & Lewis, 1987) and are highly motivated to make amends, thereby expending great effort toward this goal (Baumeister, Stillwell, & Heatherton, 1995; Flynn & Schaumberg, 2012).

Following this attributions logic, if managers decide not to divest the foreign business, they may either need to adjust the aspiration level to reach a satisfactory performance in the future, or adjust the controllable antecedents so that the performance will be improved to a satisfactory level in the future.

CONCLUDING REMARKS

As the trend toward globalization has intensified worldwide competition, many firms experiencing difficulties in their foreign operations are forced to exit. Exit decisions are becoming a more regular occurrence, which have resulted in calls in the literature for a better understanding of this area of research. In this study, we provide an overview of what has been done and discuss the major issues that hinder advancement in the area. A framework is proposed based on Weiner (1985) through his attributional theory that integrates the various antecedents linked to the different research perspectives, and considers the decision-making process and outcomes of foreign divestment. While more work is required to understand the MNE's exit decision process, we hope this chapter takes a step forward toward a better understanding of the exit phenomenon and stimulates further research in this area.

References

Argote, L., & Miron-Spektor, E. 2011. Organizational learning: From experience to knowledge. *Organizational Science*, 22(5): 1123–1137.

Arte, P. & Larimo, J. 2019. Taking stock of foreign divestment: Insights and recommendations from three decades of contemporary literature, *International Business Review*, 28(6): 101599.

Baquero-Rosas, L. M. 2013. Foreign subsidiary divestment decision process: A descriptive model based on the multiple case studies of Puerto Rico pharmaceutical industry. *Journal of International Business Research and Practice*, 7: 86–103.

Barkema, H. G., Bell, J. H. J., & Pennings, J. M. 1996. Foreign entry, cultural barriers, and learning. *Strategic Management Journal*, 17(2): 151–66.

Barkema, H. G., & Vermeulen, F. 1997. What differences in the cultural backgrounds of partners are detrimental for international joint ventures? *Journal of International Business Studies*, 28(4): 845–64.

Barney, J. 1991. Firm resources and sustained competitive advantage. *Journal of Management*, 17(1): 99–120.

Baumeister, R. F., Stillwell, A. M., & Heatherton, T. F. 1995. Personal narratives about guilt: Role in action control and interpersonal relationships. *Basic and Applied Social Psychology*, 17(1–2): 173–98.

Belderbos, R., & Zou, J. 2009. Real options and foreign affiliate divestments: A portfolio perspective. *Journal of International Business Studies*, 40(4): 600–20.

Benito, G. R. G., & Welch, L. S. 1997. De-internationalization. *Management International Review*, 37(S2): 7–25.

Berry, H. 2013. When do firms divest foreign operations? *Organization Science*, 24(1): 246–61.

Boddewyn, J. J. 1979. Foreign divestment: Magnitude and factors. *Journal of International Business Studies*, 10(1): 21–27.

Brauer, M. 2006. What have we acquired and what should we acquire in divestiture research? A review and research agenda. *Journal of Management*, 32(6): 751–85.

Buckley, P., Doh, J., & Benischke, M. 2017. Towards a renaissance in international business research? Big questions, grand challenges, and the future of IB scholarship. *Journal of International Business Studies*, 48(9): 1045–1064.

Burgelman, R. A. 1996. A process model of strategic business exit: Implications for an evolutionary perspective on strategy. *Strategic Management Journal*, 17(S1): 193–214.

Burt, S., Dawson, J., & Sparks, L. 2008. International retail divestment: Review, case studies and (e) merging agenda. *European Retail Research*, 22: 29–49.

Cairns, P., Doherty, A. M., Alexander, N., & Quinn, B. 2008. Understanding the international retail divestment process. *Journal of Strategic Marketing*, 16(2): 111–128.

Cairns, P., Quinn, B., Alexander, N., & Doherty, A. M. 2010. The role of leadership in international retail divestment. *European Business Review*, 22(1): 25–42.

Carroll, G. R., & Hannan, M. T. 1995. *Organizations in Industry: Strategy, Structure, and Selection*. New York, NY: Oxford University Press.

Cavusgil, S. T., & Zou, S. 1994. Marketing strategy-performance relationship: An investigation of the empirical link in export market ventures. *Journal of Marketing*, 58(1): 1–21.

Chung, C. C., & Beamish, P. W. 2005. The impact of institutional reforms on characteristics and survival of foreign subsidiaries in emerging economies. *Journal of Management Studies*, 42(1): 35–62.

Chung, C. C., Lee, S. H., & Lee, J. Y. 2013. Dual-option subsidiaries and exit decisions during times of economic crisis. *Management International Review*, 53(4): 555–77.

Cort, K. T., Griffith, D. A., & White, D. S. 2007. An attribution theory approach for understanding the internationalization of professional service firms. *International Marketing Review*, 24(1): 9–25.

Cyert, R. M., & March, J. 1963. *A Behavioral Theory of the Firm*. Englewood Cliffs, NJ: Prentice-Hall.

Dai, L., Eden, L., & Beamish, P. W. 2013. Place, space, and geographical exposure: Foreign subsidiary survival in conflict zones. *Journal of International Business Studies*, 44(6): 554–578.

Dai, L., Eden, L., & Beamish, P. W. 2017. Caught in the crossfire: Dimensions of vulnerability and foreign multinationals' exit from war-afflicted countries. *Strategic Management Journal*, 38(7): 1478–1498.

Delios, A., & Beamish, P. W. 2004. Joint venture performance revisited: Japanese foreign subsidiaries worldwide. *Management International Review*, 44(1): 69–91.

Demirbag, M., Apaydin, M., & Tatoglu, E. 2011. Survival of Japanese subsidiaries in the Middle East and North Africa. *Journal of World Business*, 46(4): 411–425.

Dittmar, A., & Shivdasani, A. 2003. Divestitures and divisional investment policies. *Journal of Finance*, 58(6): 2711–2744.

Dixit, A. 1989. Entry and exit decisions under uncertainty. *Journal of Political Economy*, 97(3): 620–638.

Duhaime, I. M., & Grant, J. H. 1984. Factors influencing divestment decision-making: Evidence from a field study. *Strategic Management Journal*, 5(4): 301–318.

Efrat, K., & Shoham, A. 2012. Born global firms: The differences between their short-and long-term performance drivers. *Journal of World Business*, 47(4): 675–685.

Eisenhardt, K. M., & Martin, J. A. 2000. Dynamic capabilities: What are they? *Strategic Management Journal*, 21(10–11): 1105–1121.

Ennis, R. M., & Parkhill, R. L. 1986. South African divestment: Social responsibility or fiduciary folly? *Financial Analysts Journal*, 42(4): 30–38.

Finkelstein, S., Hambrick, D. C., & Cannella, A. A. J. 2009. *Strategic Leadership: Theory and Research on Executives, Top Management Teams, and Boards*. New York, NY: Oxford University Press.

Flynn, F. J., & Schaumberg, R. L. 2012. When feeling bad leads to feeling good: Guilt-proneness and affective organizational commitment. *Journal of Applied Psychology*, 97(1): 124–133.

Franco, A. M., Sarkar, M. B., Agarwal, R., & Echambadi, R. 2009. Swift and smart: The moderating effects of technological capabilities on the market pioneering—Firm survival relationship. *Management Science*, 55(11): 1842–1860.

Ghertman, M. 1988. Foreign subsidiary and parents' roles during strategic investment and divestment decisions. *Journal of International Business Studies*, 19(1): 47–67.

Gilmour, S. C. 1973. *The Divestment Decision Process*. Unpublished doctoral dissertation, Boston, MA: Harvard Business School.

Gioia, D. A., & Pitre, E. 1990. Multiparadigm perspectives on theory building. *Academy of Management Review*, 15(4): 584–602.

Giovannetti, G., Ricchiuti, G., & Velucchi, M. 2011. Size, innovation and internationalization: A survival analysis of Italian firms. *Applied Economics*, 43(12): 1511–1520.

Hambrick, D. C., & Mason, P. A. 1984. Upper echelons: The organization as a reflection of its top managers. *The Academy of Management Review*, 9(2): 193–206.

Hannan, M. T., & Freeman, J. 1993. *Organizational Ecology*. Cambridge, MA: Harvard University Press.

Harder, D. W., & Lewis, S. J. 1987. The assessment of shame and guilt. In J. N. Butcher, & C. D. Spielberger (Eds.), *Advances in Personality Assessment* (Volume 6). Hillsdale: Lawrence Erlbaum Associates.

Heider, F. 1958. *The Psychology of Interpersonal Relations*. New York, NY: Wiley.

Huber, G. P. 1991. Organizational learning: The contributing processes and the literatures. *Organization Science*, 2(1): 88–115.

Kang, J., Lee, J., & Ghauri, P. 2017. The interplay of Mahalanobis distance and firm capabilities on MNC subsidiary exits from host countries. *Management International Review*, 57(3): 379–409.

Keil, T., Maula, M., Schildt, H., & Zahra, S. A. 2008. The effect of governance modes and relatedness of external business development activities on innovative performance. *Strategic Management Journal*, 29(8): 895–907.

Kim, T. Y., Delios, A., & Xu, D. 2010. Organizational geography, experiential learning and subsidiary exit: Japanese foreign expansions in China, 1979–2001. *Journal of Economic Geography*, 10(4): 579–597.

Kim, Y. C., Lu, J. W., & Rhee, M. 2012. Learning from age difference: Interorganizational learning and survival in Japanese foreign subsidiaries. *Journal of International Business Studies*, 43(8): 719–745.

Koch, P. T., Koch, B., Menon, T., & Shenkar, O. 2016. Cultural friction in leadership beliefs and foreign-invested enterprise survival. *Journal of International Business Studies*, 47(4): 453–470.

Lee, H., Kelley, D., Lee, J., & Lee, S. 2012. SME survival: The impact of internationalization, technology resources, and alliances. *Journal of Small Business Management*, 50(1): 1–19.

Li, J. 1995. Foreign entry and survival: Effects of strategic choices on performance in international markets. *Strategic Management Journal*, 16(5): 333–351.

Luo, Y., & Tung, R. L. 2007. International expansion of emerging market enterprises: A springboard perspective. *Journal of International Business Studies*, 38(4): 481–498.

Marano, V., Arregle, J. L., Hitt, M. A., Spadafora, E., & van Essen, M. 2016. Home country institutions and the internationalization-performance relationship: A meta-analytic review. *Journal of Management*, 42(5): 1075–1110.

Martinko, M. J., Harvey, P., & Dasborough, M. T. 2011. Attribution theory in the organizational sciences: A case of unrealized potential. *Journal of Organizational Behavior*, 32(1): 144–149.

Martinko, M. J., Harvey, P., & Douglas, S. C. 2007. The role, function, and contribution of attribution theory to leadership: A review. *The Leadership Quarterly*, 18(6): 561–585.

Mata, J., & Portugal, P. 2000. Closure and divestiture by foreign entrants: The impact of entry and post-entry strategies. *Strategic Management Journal*, 21(5): 549–562.

Mata, J., & Portugal, P. 2002. The survival of new domestic and foreign-owned firms. *Strategic Management Journal*, 23(4): 323–343.

McDermott, M. C. 2010. Foreign divestment: The neglected area of international business? *International Studies of Management & Organization*, 40(4): 37–53.

Mudambi, R., & Zahra, S. A. 2007. The survival of international new ventures. *Journal of International Business Studies*, 38(2): 333–352.

Nyuur, R. B., Amankwah-Amoah, J., & Osabutey, E. L. 2017. An integrated perspective on foreign ethical divestment. *Thunderbird International Business Review*, 59(6): 725–737.

O'Brien, J., & Folta, T. 2009. Sunk costs, uncertainty and market exit: A real options perspective. *Industrial and Corporate Change*, 18(5): 807–833.

Paul, J., & Benito, G. R. G. 2018. A review of research on outward foreign direct investment from emerging countries, including China: What do we know, how do we know and where should we be heading? *Asia Pacific Business Review*, 24(1): 90–115.

Piepenbrink, A., & Gaur, A. S. 2017. Two decades of international business research: A review based on topic modeling. *Academy of Management Annual Meeting Proceedings*, 2017(1): 1–1.

Sachdev, J. C. 1976. Disinvestment: A new problem in multinational corporation host government interface. *Management International Review*, 16(3): 23–35.

Silverman, B. S., Nickerson, J. A., & Freeman, J. 1997. Profitability, transactional alignment, and organizational mortality in the U.S. trucking industry. *Strategic Management Journal*, 18(S1): 31–52.

Song, S. 2014. Entry mode irreversibility, host market uncertainty, and foreign subsidiary exits. *Asia Pacific Journal of Management*, 31(2): 455–471.

Song, S. 2015. Exchange rate challenges, flexible intra-firm adjustments, and subsidiary longevity. *Journal of World Business*, 50(1): 36–45.

Song, S., & Lee, J. Y. 2017. Relationship with headquarters and divestments of foreign subsidiaries: The hysteresis perspective. *Management International Review*, 57(4): 545–570.

Soule, S. A., Swaminathan, A., & Tihanyi, L. 2014. The diffusion of foreign divestment from Burma. *Strategic Management Journal*, 35(7): 1032–1052.

Sousa, C. M. P., & Bradley, F. 2006. Cultural distance and psychic distance: Two peas in a pod? *Journal of International Marketing*, 14(1): 49–70.

Sousa, C. M. P., Martínez-López, F. J., & Coelho, F. 2008. The determinants of export performance: A review of the research in the literature between 1998 and 2005. *International Journal of Management Reviews*, 10(4): 343–374.

Sousa, C. M. P., & Tan, Q. 2015. Exit from a foreign market: Do poor performance, strategic fit, cultural distance, and international experience matter? *Journal of International Marketing*, 23(4): 84–104.

Steenhuis, H. J., & Bruijn, E. J. D. 2009. International divestment: An overview and analysis. In 69th *Academy of Management Annual Meeting 2009: Green Management Matters*. Chicago, IL, 7–11 August 2009.

Surdu, I., Mellahi, K., & Glaister, K. W. P. Once bitten, not necessarily shy? Determinants of foreign market re-entry commitment strategies. *Journal of International Business Studies*, 50(3): 393–422.

Tan, Q., & Sousa, C. M. P. 2019. Why poor performance is not enough for a foreign exit: The importance of innovation capability and international experience. *Management International Review*, 59(3): 465–498.

Tan, Q., & Sousa, C. M. P. 2015. A framework for understanding firms' foreign exit behavior. *Advances in International Marketing*, 25(5): 223–238.

Tan, Q., & Sousa, C. M. P. 2018. Performance and business relatedness as drivers of exit decision: A study of MNCs from an emerging country. *Global Strategy Journal*, 8(4): 612–634.

Teece, D. J., Pisano, G., & Shuen, A. 1997. Dynamic capabilities and strategic management. *Strategic Management Journal*, 18(7): 509–533.

Torneden, R. L. 1975. *Foreign Disinvestment by U.S. Multinational Corporations: With Eight Case Studies*. New York, NY: Praeger.

Trigeorgis, L., & Reuer, J. J. 2017. Real options theory in strategic management. *Strategic Management Journal*, 38(1): 42–63.

Waldman, D. A., Ramirez, G. G., House, R. J., & Puranam, P. 2001. Does leadership matter? CEO leadership attributes and profitability under conditions of perceived environmental uncertainty. *Academy of Management Journal*, 44(1): 134–143.

Weiner, B. 1985. An attributional theory of achievement motivation and emotion. *Psychological Review*, 92(4): 548–573.

Weiner, B. 1986. *An Attributional Theory of Motivation and Emotion*. New York, NY: Springer-Verlag.

Weiner, B., Heckhausen, H., & Meyer, W. U. 1972. Causal ascriptions and achievement behavior: A conceptual analysis of effort and reanalysis of locus of control. *Journal of Personality and Social Psychology*, 21(2): 239–248.

Xu, D., & Lu, J. W. 2007. Technological knowledge, product relatedness, and parent control: the effect on IJV survival. *Journal of Business Research*, 60(11): 1166–1176.

Xu, D., & Shenkar, O. 2002. Institutional distance and the multinational enterprise. *The Academy of Management Review*, 27(4): 608–618.

Yang, J. Y., Li, J., & Delios, A. 2015. Will a second mouse get the cheese? Learning from early entrants' failures in a foreign market. *Organization Science*, 26(3): 908–922.

CHAPTER 18

FOREIGN MARKET RE-ENTRY STRATEGIES

The Role of Cognitive Biases in Decision-Making

IRINA SURDU

INTRODUCTION

THE international business (IB) strategies of firms do not follow a linear, sequential decision-making process. Firms enter foreign markets, but in some cases, divest their operations there and choose to re-enter. Foreign market re-entry (often referred to as re-internationalization) can be characterized by a process of initial market entry, whereby the multinational enterprise (MNE) accumulates market-specific knowledge and experience about operating in the host market, followed by a process of market exit,[1] and a subsequent period of time out, after which the firm renews its operations in the previously exited market (Javalgi, Deligonul, Dixit, & Cavusgil, 2011; Surdu, Mellahi, Glaister, & Nardella, 2018; Surdu, Mellahi, & Glaister, 2019; Yayla, Yeniyurt, Uslay, & Cavusgil, 2018; Welch & Welch, 2009). News of MNEs divesting their international businesses and re-entering previously exited markets after some time out is increasingly common and an integral part of business press reporting. Some noteworthy examples include the decision of Pepsi Co. (US), Carlsberg Group (Denmark), and Heineken International (Netherlands) to re-enter Myanmar (2013); fast food chains such as Dunkin' Brands (US) and Wendy's (US) returning to the Singapore market (2009); and Tata Motors (India) returning to multiple country markets including Russia (2014), Australia (2013), the Philippines (2012), the UK (2007), Egypt (2006), and Iraq (2004). Many other reported re-entries go unactualized, in part, due to managers' limited

---

[1] See Chapter 17, which provides an overview of market exit decisions and a detailed discussion of foreign market exit/international divestment antecedents and outcomes.

understanding of whether to re-enter and if so, what re-entry strategies to pursue in order to succeed in the host market the second time around.

Despite the prevalence of the re-entry phenomenon in business practice, we are yet to achieve a clear understanding of *how* and *why* firms choose to re-enter previously exited foreign markets (Surdu & Mellahi, 2016; Surdu & Narula, 2020). Extant literature has provided some initial evidence suggesting that larger firms with significant experience resources are not necessarily more likely to re-enter (Bernini, Du, & Love, 2016), and when they do, they do not necessarily re-enter faster than their less experienced counterparts (Surdu et al., 2018). Re-entrants with a higher degree of firm-specific, experiential knowledge were, in fact, found to commit less resources to the market upon re-entry (Surdu et al., 2019), potentially as a result of the inertia that characterizes large, highly experienced MNEs (Bernini et al., 2016). Previous sources of FSA (FSA)—such as knowledge acquired through experience—could have a negative effect on firms seeking to re-enter. Past experience may not be sufficiently applicable to changed market environments encountered upon re-entry (Surdu et al., 2018; see also Welch & Welch, 2009). Past knowledge may be partly forgotten, intentionally or unintentionally (Darr, Argote, & Epple, 1995; de Holan & Philips, 2004; see also Surdu & Narula, 2020) due to the failed initial entry, making past experience more difficult to access by decision makers.

Re-entry choices—and to some extent, I assume, most post-initial entry strategic choices—are driven by how decision makers remember, perceive, and interpret the value of past knowledge and experience in order to make subsequent decisions. Often, individuals are expected to construct their judgments based on the speed, ease, and frequency with which those memories can be retrieved, rather than objective, systematic calculations of the value or success of a past event (Gilovich, Griffin, & Kahneman, 2002). Understanding the process by which managerial perception and interpretation influences the strategic decisions of the MNE is important (Kano & Verbeke, 2015) because IB strategy theory has largely ignored the influence of managerial perception.

In particular, theory and evidence with regards to the role of cognitive biases in IB strategic choices of MNEs is sparse. In the context of entry–exit–re-entry, extant theorizations do not take into account that the applicability of experience and knowledge resources may, in fact, be revisited by firms in a similar context (i.e. *re*-entry). In some cases, exit may represent a form of "trauma" for the firm but also its decisions makers, previously charged with growing the company into international markets. When framed as an opportunity to mend the MNE's host market reputation, reduce home market dependency, address past mistakes and take advantage of host market opportunities, re-entry is likely to be preferred. In turn, the MNE's stakeholders, including other firms may interpret the exit as a significant failure, and further, a clear indication that the company does not have the necessary resources and capabilities to gain an advantage in the market; as such re-entry may be avoided, or if they decide to re-enter, firms would avoid committing significant resources there.

The remainder of the chapter is structured as follows. The chapter starts with an overview of the re-entry literature and key findings and theoretical contributions. Then, the discussion zooms in on the role of behavioral concepts, that is, cognitive biases, to explain what these biases are, as well as how and why they are important to understand managerial perceptions of re-entry. I develop a model that explains the interaction between learning from past knowledge and experience accumulated over time and the managerial framing of the exit experience itself. Since complex and dynamic MNE decisions such as re-entry are heterogeneous, we need more nuanced theoretical lenses to understand them.

OVERVIEW OF RESEARCH
ON RE-ENTRY DECISIONS

What constitutes market exit, withdrawal, and subsequent re-entry? In practice, some firms divest their foreign operations and exit the international market completely, while others (generally exporting firms) tend to engage in intermittent internationalization, whereby they are willing to fulfill international orders when these come up. In some instances, intermittent exporting leads to fully fledged international operations, while in others, contact with international customers and partners remains minimal (e.g. through a representative office) or even reduced to merely importing from international markets (in which case, one could consider this as a formal market exit). While inward international activities can, indeed, be used as a springboard for outward international-ization (Welch & Welch, 2009), this chapter focuses on firms partially or totally with-drawing from international sales and resuming these sales in the form of re-entry after a period of time out of the market.[2]

I provide a brief overview of studies that have examined the foreign market re-entry decisions of MNEs post initial entry and exit. Generally, studies have focused on under-standing why firms re-enter, how firms re-enter, that is, the modes of operation at re-entry, the process of re-entry, or the speed of re-entry, often measured as the period of time that had passed between a firm's exit and its re-entry. Some interesting findings emerge with regards to the effect of knowledge acquired through experience on the resource commitment and speed of re-entry.

---

[2] In order to be considered re-entrants, firms would have to have maintained their domestic oper-ations before engaging in re-entry. The international entrepreneurship literature discusses more exten-sively how entrepreneurs close down one business and start another that may have more chance of success in a given market, but this is beyond the scope of this chapter.

Foreign Market Re-Entry Motives

MNEs tend to reconsider previously exited markets for various reasons. MNEs usually exit foreign markets because of lack of firm-specific resources and capabilities needed to compete effectively in the foreign market and/or because of external social, political, and economic changes in the business environment that result in the host market becoming unattractive for the MNE (e.g. Benito, 2005; Bonaccorsi, 1992; Javalgi et al., 2011; Mellahi, 2003; Nummela, Saarenketo, & Sloane, 2016). Most MNEs have a limited number of resources to compete, thus choosing to re-allocate these resources to other country markets or refocusing resources and managerial attention on growth in the home market (Cairns, Doherty, Alexander, & Quinn, 2008). MNEs that have exited tend to return to previously exited foreign markets when more resources are available and/or when the host environment becomes more favorable (Surdu et al., 2019; see also Choquette, 2019; Welch & Welch, 2009). This means that firms, rather than self-selecting opportunities for growth, are often forced through intense competition to review markets in which they may have previously failed to exploit their firm-specific resources and capabilities.

In an indirect mention of the re-entry process, Loustarinen and Welch (1990) proposed a positive effect of organizational learning from prior knowledge and experience on the possibility of firms returning to previously exited market, although the authors do not discuss which lessons may have been more valuable for the MNE seeking to re-enter and what types of experiences matter most. Later, Welch and Welch (2009) explicitly discuss the importance of understanding re-entry decisions; the authors propose that the time-out period plays a significant role in whether or not firms decide to re-enter foreign markets. Changes in management as well as changes in the host institutional and economic environment are expected to be met with renewed interest in the market.

In the context of exporters more specifically, Crick (2004) found that firms that maintained an interest in re-entry were those who were highly confident in their exporting knowledge but required more market-specific knowledge. In a study on Turkish firms re-entering the Egyptian market during the Arab Spring (i.e. between 2010 and 2015), Yayla et al. (2018) found that a longer period of export inactivity, decreases the likelihood of re-entry. The authors explain re-entry as a function of market orientation and response to environmental changes, in that market-oriented firms, who are willing to learn and change their products and services to adapt to host market demand, are also more flexible in their exit/re-entry decisions, and thus tend to exit when market conditions are unfavorable and re-enter when market conditions are favorable. The role of context has also been emphasized in re-entry studies, with changes in the conditions of the host market and its institutions being expected to, at least in part, drive firms to re-enter irrespective of their size, age, and experiences-specific resources (Bernini et al., 2016; Javalgi et al., 2011; Surdu et al., 2018, 2019; Vissak & Francioni, 2013; Yayla et al., 2018; Welch & Welch, 2009).

Foreign Market Re-Entry Modes

The relationship between intangible resources such as past knowledge and experience and an MNE's mode of operation continues to be well-recognized in the IB strategy literature (e.g. Casillas and Moreno-Menendez, 2014; García-García, García-Canal, & Guillén, 2017). This research stream is underpinned by the idea that, with more knowledge acquired through experience, firms learn about international markets, overcome their liability of foreignness and increase their resource commitment to the foreign market. Following this rationale, re-entrants should escalate their commitment upon re-entry. Notwithstanding the relevance of these ideas to initial entry choices, I propose that the bias toward focusing on positive experiences and MNE learning may lead firms to be overconfident in the value of past experience accumulated over the years in which the firm has been an MNE. This may lead MNEs to miss out opportunities to learn from other, potentially negative experiences, such as the exit experience in the context of market re-entries. I argue that the options available to a re-entrant in terms of operation modes are more complex and should consider the effect of the exit experience on managerial perceptions of market attractiveness and their propensity to take high risks upon re-entry.

Specifically, upon re-entry a firm has a set of choices with regards to their mode of operation, all of which should relate back to the exit experience (Figure 18.1). To start with, MNEs may (1) choose not to change their market commitment, by re-entering via the same mode of operation in which they were operating prior to the exit (thus, manifesting path dependent behavior); or (2) they may alter their commitment by re-entering via a different mode of operation. For firms that decide to alter their commitment upon re-entry, they may either (1) escalate commitment, that is, MNEs that were previously operating via non-equity modes, re-enter via joint or wholly owned subsidiaries or (2) de-escalate commitment, that is, MNEs previously operating via wholly owned modes decide to lower resource investment and opt for a partner or merely export their products there (Surdu et al., 2019).

Some limited empirical evidence exists with regards to re-entry modes. For instance, Javalgi et al. (2011) discussed a number of anecdotal re-entry events that took place between 1920 and 2005 and found that some of re-entrants chose to escalate their market commitment while others were more risk averse and de-escalated commitment upon re-entry. The authors attributed re-entry commitment choices to the duration of the time-out period between exit and re-entry, that is, the longer the time passed, the more likely organizations are to forget, and thus place less value on past experience accumulated over time (see also Welch & Welch, 2009). In a recent study, Surdu et al. (2019) provided significant empirical evidence that many re-entrants tend to re-enter via the same mode of operation in which they were operating prior to exit (interestingly, irrespective of the time-out period); firms that do tend to change their commitment (escalate or de-escalate), do so mainly when the exit is specifically associated with a poor choice of operation mode during the initial market foray. This provides evidence of

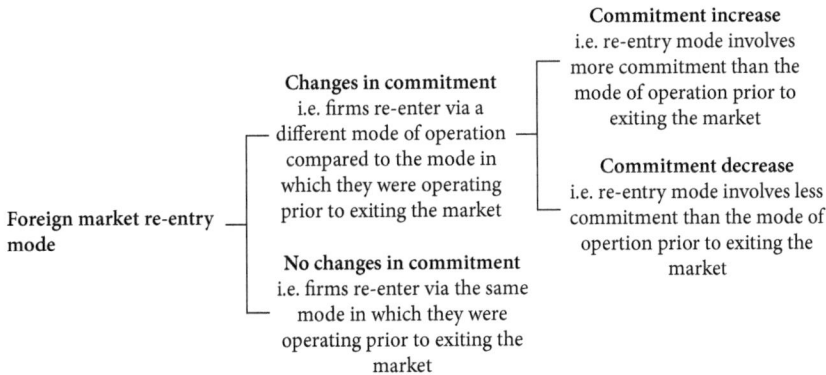

FIGURE 18.1 Foreign market re-entry commitment strategic options (Surdu et al., 2019)

organizational learning from the exit experience, irrespective of the experiential knowledge accumulated in the past. Exporters, licensors, and franchisors, which do not experience deep involvement in the market, and thus have fewer opportunities to learn from the exit, tend to be the ones most likely to re-enter via the same modes of operation (Bernini et al., 2016; Surdu et al., 2019).

Foreign Market Re-Entry Process

As suggested in Figure 18.1 also, the choices related to the modes of commitment in a re-entered market and the timing or speed of re-entry into that market are interrelated. Much of the IB strategy literature has assumed that decision makers are rational, that decisions are made to reduce transaction costs associated with operating in an international market, and that decision makers seek to accumulate as much knowledge as possible about that market, after which they can make more informed choices. For instance, the Uppsala model of internationalization[3]—often used to understand IB strategies—implicitly assumes that firms accumulate new knowledge from experiences accumulated over time, learn, and then make strategic decisions once they are at a stage when close to full market knowledge is acquired. In practice, market conditions change, making knowledge accumulated in the past less relevant. In fact, relying on the "outdated" knowledge and experience of managers may be detrimental. The empirical evidence that exists on re-entrants (Bernini et al., 2016; Surdu et al., 2018; Vissak & Francioni, 2013) appears to suggest that different types of firms value and learn from different types of experiences, which, in turn, influences their re-entry process.

---

[3] In Chapter 7, the author offers an overview of the Uppsala model perspective starting from its original formulation (Johanson & Vahlne, 1977) to its latest revision (Vahlne & Johanson, 2017), and in doing so providing a stimulating and open-ended debate on the relationship between market knowledge and experience and market resource commitment.

Vissak and Francioni (2013) used the context of a medium-sized construction MNE headquartered in Italy to explain that internationalization processes are not linear—that is, they are not a function of knowledge and market commitment, leading to increased and faster internationalization. In fact, some firms engage in multiple entries, exits, and re-entries depending on market demand, host institutional conditions, and managerial preferences. In turn, by focusing specifically on exporters, Bernini et al. (2016) explained that intermittent exporting is highly complex; the authors discuss how larger firms (despite being better resourced and more experienced) often suffer from inertia and fail to quickly recognize the need to change and exit the market when demand is low and re-enter when demand increases. Larger firms may be less likely to exit, but once they have exited, this size and experience does not help them re-enter faster (Bernini et al., 2016). Surdu et al. (2018) draw on organizational learning and institutional theory to explain what leads to more rapid re-entries; the authors find that firms re-enter faster when they have less experience and when the exit experience has been related to poor performance (see also Surdu et al., 2019); in order to address the causes for their past mistakes, firms need to re-enter before changes in their market strategy become outdated.

With regards to the effect of experiential learning on the re-entry process: firms may need time to distill the lessons learned from exit and overcome the potentially traumatic exit experience. Further, when significant time and managerial attention is invested in a market, re-entry may be delayed, allowing firms to recover from the initial failure to succeed internationally. Also interesting is that, while firm-specific factors matter soon after the exit happens, the more time that passes, the more firms use the external, institutional environment as a cue for re-entry (Surdu et al., 2018). Hence, there may be a benefit in understanding the role of perceptions as well as memory on re-entry choices.

Re-entrant MNEs must balance knowledge acquired through past experience of operating in the market with effective decision-making about how and when to *re*-enter. Although uncertainty and risk may be reduced by acquiring knowledge through experience of operating in foreign markets (Casillas & Moreno-Menendez, 2014) and controlling it through high investment operation modes, the exit may reduce the effectiveness of prior learning through market-specific (experiential) knowledge. Once the exit interrupts the linear cycle of acquiring knowledge and committing more to the market, MNEs and their managers must decide how they frame the exit (to themselves and the outside world) as well as how much of the past experience captured through learning over time can be used to re-enter the market.

New Lenses to Understand Re-Entry: The Role of Cognitive Biases

Managers do not and cannot always behave rationally (Aharoni, 2010; Aharoni, Tihanyi, & Connelly, 2011; Buckley et al., 2007; Elia, Larsen, & Piscitello, 2019; Schubert, Baier, & Rammer, 2018; Surdu et al., 2019). We have become increasingly aware that firms deal with complex environments where they lack complete information. The lack of information is further exacerbated when firms seek to make decisions based on future market and institutional changes. This is more so for MNEs which have to manage the uncertainties associated with information asymmetries both at home and abroad (Verbeke & Greidanus, 2009). The complexities of the international environment make it difficult not only to gain access to information about different markets, but also to process the information that the MNE gains access to. This chapter calls for the integration of ideas from behavioral economics into IB strategy research mainly to understand the challenges associated with making strategic choices in international contexts. Emerging from the behavioral perspectives, cognitive biases (Tversky & Kahneman, 1974) in particular represent a promising theoretical lens through which to explore foreign market re-entry choices.

The underlying rationale of behavioral concepts is that human judgment is rarely characterized by systematic reasoning. In turn, decisions are often the result of a reflexive process of cognition, which is biased by emotion and memory (Gigerenzer & Selten, 2001; Macleod & Campbell, 1992; Muramatsu & Hanoch, 2005). Heuristics—the mental shortcuts that speed up the process of decision-making by reducing the complexity and cognitive load associated with processing information about the environment— are influenced by cognitive biases (Cosmides & Tooby, 1994; Gigerenzer & Todd, 1999; Gigerenzer & Gaissmaier, 2011). Cognitive biases deviate from rationality in judgment and enable managers to focus on the information more easily retrievable at a given point in time, or which confirms their pre-existing values, beliefs, or ambitions (Tversky & Kahneman, 1974). Cognitive biases are the result of our memories being formed through subjective and often emotionally driven experiences and they become enacted particularly when complex choices (which are characterized by a certain level of uncertainty, and thus emotional loading) need to be made effectively (Huy & Zott, 2019; Macleod & Campbell, 1992). Thus, when making complex decisions, decision makers often have to prioritize certain categories of information over others, at the expense of systematic reasoning (Ardalan, 2018; Huy & Zott, 2019; Muradoglu & Harvey, 2012). We will explain some of these main categories of observed biases and how they may apply to foreign market re-entry decision-making.

Availability Heuristics

Availability heuristics (Tversky & Kahneman, 1974) offer a more nuanced understanding of how individuals estimate probability by prioritizing information that can be readily recalled from memory (Gilovich, Griffin, & Kahneman, 2002). Rather than individuals making additional cognitive efforts to search for, and retrieve, information that may be relevant to solving a problem, they seek to recall from memory similar events that might help them develop that solution effectively and efficiently. When individuals assume that their own memories are reflective of the external reality, the speed and ease with which past memories are recalled are used as a "surrogate" to estimate the probability of an event or outcome. Availability (of memory) thus becomes the lens through which decisions are made. Because "rare" events are often emotionally significant to the individual, they tend to weigh strongly in people's minds. Resultantly, rare events tend to be more memorable, and thus availability biases may skew perceptions of their frequency, making rare events "feel" more prevalent than they truly are.

I propose that availability heuristics may have significant implications concerning the speed with which firms re-enter previously exited markets. For instance, foreign market exit and re-entry, in practice, is much less common in the lifetime of most MNEs than initial market entry. At the same time, the extent to which a firm's decision to divest operations and exit an international market and the consequences of potential re-entry are much more frequently covered by the media, which, in turn, influences the relative importance of the re-entry decision (Surdu et al., 2019; Surdu & Narula, 2020). Media prominence makes exits and re-entries easier to recall than initial entries, because failure is fundamentally more appealing than success. Figure 18.2 shows how I view availability biases to be enacted with re-entry.

Based on the view that heuristics and biases are informed by two key dimensions—emotions and memory—I identified four approaches to re-entry that an MNE may experience. The influence of emotion on post-entry decisions such as re-entry is reflected in how managers frame the exit experience from neutral (or even positive) to negative experience. In turn, memory is reflected in whether the MNE is perceived to have incurred significant learning loses after exit compared to having captured significant learning from the time spent in the market before exit. Hence, there are four types of MNE re-entrants: *the once bitten, twice shy* (Q1: negative framing of exit experience and significant learning captured); *the traumatized* (Q2: negative framing of exit experience and significant learning lost); *the dragon slayers* (Q3: positive framing of exit experience and significant learning captured); and *the tabula rasa* (Q4: neutral/positive framing of exit experience and significant learning lost).

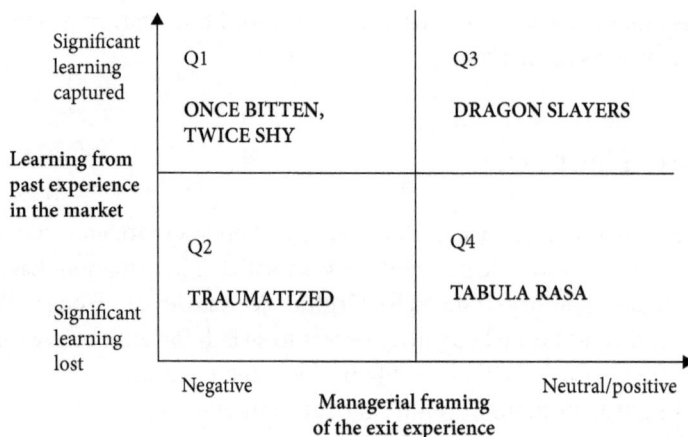

FIGURE 18.2 Availability biases at re-entry

From the MNE's perspective, the firm is likely to recollect the pre-exit experience in addition to the actual experiences and learning accumulated in the time spent in the foreign market. If the exit experience is a relatively mild one (or even positive), characterized by useful lessons about the motivations for the market failure, firms may re-enter early to address the causes of their failure and exploit the momentum that had been created by their exit decision. Firms that have accumulated significant experiential knowledge and have been able to learn from their experiences and embed these in organizational practices and routines—the dragon slayers (Q3)—may draw on their learning capabilities to understand what went wrong in the market the first time around and re-enter early with new strategies. Other MNEs may have learned less significant lessons in the market, or these lessons may be lost when managers leave the company (which is often the case when exits occur). Some firms—our tabula rasas (Q4)—have what we may refer to as a blank slate, and thus re-enter the market more like new entrants, particularly if the exit experience was a neutral one as it is often the case when exit is associated with host institutional changes, and not internalized as a firm-specific failure to perform.

In turn, if the exit experience is broadly negative, characterized by significant media attention, host market unemployment, loss of valuable assets and recalled by decision makers as well as other stakeholders such as customers, suppliers, and host country institutional actors, then re-entry is likely to be delayed. MNE re-entrants may therefore value more the exit experience than the experience associated with operating in the market for a longer period of time. This may lead to a positive bias if the perception around the exit experience is associated with learning about the market (Q1); and a negative bias if the exit experience prevents early re-entry, since early re-entry may mean that some of the intangible sources of advantage (business relationships, customer knowledge) are not necessarily lost (Q2). In the latter case, firms may be sufficiently traumatized to delay re-entry or avoid it altogether.

From a rationale perspective, what is the likelihood of a firm failing in a host market and having to divest? Event-specific information can influence subsequent international expansion choices; for example, decisions made based on the likelihood of them resembling past memorable events, rather than considering how rarely or often firms engage in exit. Hence, because it is linked to re-entry, exit requires less cognitive effort to use to evaluate re-entry options. Assigning probabilities of events happening based on availability biases may increase risk aversity associated with international growth. I propose this to be an important area for future research as very few studies (e.g. Buckley et al., 2007) capture, or even hint at, the difference between actual and perceived risks in their empirical designs.

Commitment Biases

The commitment bias arises when individuals support their ideas and past decisions even when they have been unsuccessful and when confronted by contradictory evidence (Staw, 1976). This does not mean that individuals consciously make decisions that are likely not to apply to new situational contexts. Instead, commitment biases result from human tendencies to look for confirmation that our extant knowledge is correct. In seeking to confirm existing beliefs, humans reduce the search for new information that may disconfirm past beliefs and actions. When we seek evidence to reinforce our prior knowledge and beliefs, future decisions become consistent with prior commitments. This is particularly the case when individuals feel the need to demonstrate to their peers that they have been correct in their beliefs and their associated behaviors all along. This chapter therefore explains that commitment biases may have significant implications concerning decisions such as re-entry mode choice and speed with which firms re-enter previously exited markets. The rationale is as follows.

IB strategy literature identifies the internationalization choices of MNEs to be largely path dependent (Hutzschenreuter, Pedersen, & Volberda, 2007). At the same time, within MNEs, managers are often rewarded for their international growth initiatives and compensated based on the size of the business that they run (Datta, Iskandar-Datta, & Raman, 2001). Thus, managerial decision makers are highly incentivized to expand rapidly into as many international markets as possible. In turn, when the MNE fails to perform in an international market, thus having to abandon that market, managers may also be found responsible for that failure—a reputational damage they seek to avoid. If individuals are less likely to recognize the negative outcomes associated with certain decisions, such as choosing the inappropriate mode of operation in the market, then they are likely to opt for the same mode of operation upon re-entry. In turn, the exit outcome can be blamed on other, often unforeseeable events (Kelley, 1973) in the market during the course of their operations there, such as changes in the institutional environment. This, again, means that the initial entry mode decision was the correct one all along.

Further, the more resources are invested to operate in an international market—time, physical effort, psychological effort, reputational risks—the greater the sunk costs accumulated. However, the costs in terms of time and psychological efforts associated with acquiring that market experience will be traded-off against the lack of success in the market, meaning perhaps that not all experiences turn into relevant firm learning. An MNE re-entrant endowed with market-specific experience may become less confident in the usefulness and applicability of these experiences acquired in the past, may become less flexible, and may not expose itself to higher degrees of other types of risks the second time around. Consequently, an experienced MNE requires a re-entry mode that provides this very flexibility to manage its overall level of host country risk exposure. Experiences associated with certain modes of operation are understood to become embedded in organizational practices and routines, meaning that changing from one mode to the other may take time and further effort; scholars have warned against assuming that the skills and resources required to set up a subsidiary are the same as those required to identify a joint venture partner or design and implement a franchise contract or integrate a newly acquired company (Nadolska & Barkema, 2007). Given the effort invested into a given type of operation mode, managers may drive re-entry via the same mode; this may be particularly the case when the MNE is incentivized to re-enter early.

Commitment biases can impede decision makers to make accurate assessments and choose the most appropriate operational mode of re-entry.

Another interesting application of commitment bias refers to the decision to exit itself. We know from the field of finance that investors tend to hold stocks for longer than they should effectively do so, because they have committed to a given investment. In the case of market exits, managers may stay in the market for longer than they should, to avoid feeling like the initial decision was wrong. Re-entrants may be unwilling to change because they are forced to reconsider the value of their existing FSAs. The international expansion trajectory of UK retailer Marks & Spencer reflects that commitment biases are often at play. In 2001, the company exited a number of European markets that it had entered a few years before in the hope of reducing their dependency on a declining home market. Despite their strategy proving unsuccessful early on, the manager at the time continued to grow the company; this was an attempt to deliver on its promise to shareholders and the public. Given the underperformance, Marks & Spencer eventually divested all international operations in order to focus on home market operations. Under new management, in 2011, the firm re-entered most of the previously exited markets, with blame for previous failure being largely attributed to the former leader's lack of international experience (BBC, 2011). Over time, this second venturing was also unsuccessful, following their second significant withdrawal from international operations. Similarly, British retailer Tesco PLC spent an unfruitful decade in the US market. Resources that could have been invested to combat increased competition and a looming financial recession at home, were not. Commitment to an investment and the desire "to be seen as being right" leads to irrational and underperforming choices. These types of biases can lead managers to overlook information that is pivotal in making a decision and miss out on new opportunities as a result of these biases.

Future research may benefit from looking at how commitment biases are likely to influence both individuals and organizations to better understand the context of emotion and memory (Green & Haidt, 2002). Behavioral concepts have been developed primarily to study how individuals behave in certain contexts. So, who is biased? The manager or the firm? Desires can be expressed at the individual level but also within a group. For instance, managers may be biased toward a certain decision and wish to maintain the approval of their top management team, either for status or financial benefits. These social pressures may often lead to a culture of groupthink in organizations. Indeed, the success of the group and the sharing of beliefs can create coherence, and thus more efficient decision-making. This, in turn, will also reduce the amount of time spent on debating choices made or reassessing previous decisions, which explains instances of path-dependent behavior sometimes observed with re-entrants (Bernini et al., 2016; Surdu et al., 2019).

Framing Effects

I discussed earlier that influence of emotion and memory on post-entry decisions such as re-entry is reflected in how managers frame experiences and allocate probabilities to certain events and outcomes. But how does framing exactly work?

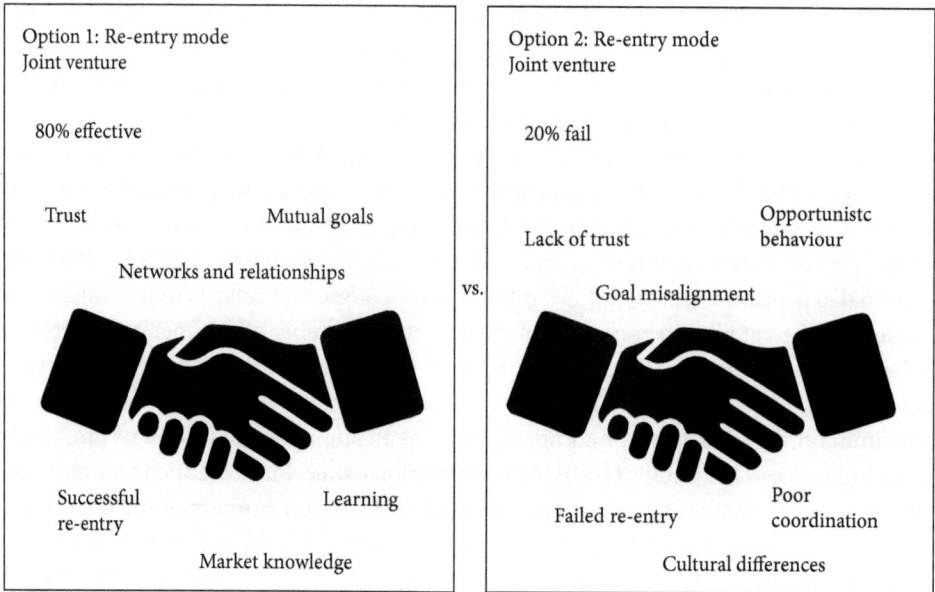

FIGURE 18.3 Framing biases: which re-entry option would you choose?

Take a quick look at Figure 18.3. Now, which of these strategic options would a re-entry manager most likely choose: an "80% effective" joint venture or a "20% failed" joint venture? Most individuals are likely to choose the first option, even though, rationally, these choices are identical, and thus have the same probability. This goes against the standard economic rationale, whereby individuals would always choose to maximize their expected utility when given the same outcomes. Kahneman and Tversky (1979) argued that humans make decisions depending on how the available choices are framed. This framing comes in the form of the expected gains (80 percent effective) versus the expected losses (20 percent failure). They go on to explain that these decisions are most likely unequal in their importance, namely a loss is perceived as more significant, and thus decision makers seek to avoid it (see Tversky, Slovic, & Kahneman, 1990). Individuals become risk seeking when a negative frame is presented to them.

In the case of re-entry speed, positive framing (early mover advantages) may result in firms focusing on the benefits associated with a strategic decision such as regaining access to the market and making use of the lessons learned. Negative framing (early mover risks) may result in firms focusing on making decisions that avoid taking high risks in the host market, such as re-entering after a "wait and see" period. Delayed re-entry may lower the perceived re-entry risk, when managers are fearful of a subsequent failure and less proactive in pursuing re-entry strategies.

In the case of re-entry mode, positive framing (high resource commitment—high benefits) may result in firms focusing on framing re-entry through the potential benefits associated with high commitment such as controlling operations in the host market to implement the lessons learned from the exit. In turn, negative framing (high resource commitment—high risk) may result in firms focusing on making decisions that avoid taking high risks in the host market such as opting for exporting or franchising re-entry modes. When negative framing is used, firms may therefore engage in low commitment modes, re-enter later, or decide to avoid the market altogether. Further, loss-aversive behavior also makes scaling back painful. For instance, firms commit to foreign markets through joint ventures based on the idea that they could always downsize if the relationship is unsuccessful. However, scaling back is emotionally taxing because it is considered a significant loss. Exercising the option to de-escalate commitment may make firms and their managers disheartened with the host market.

There are a number of avenues for future research in to order to understand the role of framing effects. First, MNE choices such as re-entry are likely to be ex-post justifications based on managerial and firm preferences. Most of the time framing may happen after the decision is made. My first question is: Are we more often than not capturing ex-post justifications of already made strategic choices?

Second, and relatedly, if decisions are made ex-post, what measurement challenges does this present IB strategy research?

Third, when considering the age of the firm, does framing induce greater breadth and depth of biases? When organizations mature, many activities that have become legitimized have become deeply embedded routines. These routines are often not submitted to stringent tests of relevance when situational contexts change. Organizational actors such as re-entrants might, in fact, pursue those activities that create resistance to change.

CONCLUDING REMARKS

Why are IB strategies such as re-entry after initial entry and market exit so important to examine and understand? Our choices are largely influenced by the way in which we frame them. Past studies have had a significant "success bias." The focus has been predominantly on how firms manage the liability of foreignness associated with being a new entrant into a foreign market, how firm-specific resources and capabilities constituted a source of international competitive advantage, and what factors drove some firms to become more successful than others. In many instances, performance is measured as the degree of international diversification, that is, how many international markets the firm entered; or intensity of international diversification, that is, amount of sales associated with international markets. Although we are familiar with the high rate of failures of international joint ventures and cross-border mergers and acquisitions and the intermittent nature of exporting behavior, failure is not something that is studied a lot in IB research. This is despite the fact that failure can be more easily recalled by decision makers compared to past international successes. In the case of complex strategic decisions such as re-entry, if sufficient time has passed after the exit, recall may be influenced by emotions, memory, and other subjective judgments. This, in turn, will affect the manner in which the lessons learned from the exit are embedded in organizational practices and routines. Firms without clear and objective processes to manage the formal planning of re-entry may—potentially—be influenced by the subjective and often outdated experience of managers.

This leads to biases in decision-making, which are enacted when complex, emotionally loaded decisions need to be made. IB strategy theory should focus more on the influence of managerial own emotions and memory in shaping managers' perceptions of events.

This chapter aims to start a conversation around how concepts from the behavioral sciences can help IB strategy scholars to advance the MNE research agenda toward studies with greater practical relevance. These ideas may prove to be applicable beyond re-entry decisions, to any cognitively loaded managerial choices made in conditions of high uncertainty and fear of subsequent international market failure.

References

Aharoni, Y. 2010. Behavioral elements in foreign direct investments. In T. Devinney, P. Torben, & T. Laszlo (Eds.), *The Past, Present and Future of International Business and Management*. Bingley: Emerald.

Aharoni, Y., Tihanyi, L., & Connelly, B. L. 2011. Managerial decision-making in international business: A forty-five-year retrospective. *Journal of World Business*, 46(2): 135–142.

Ardalan, K. 2018. Behavioral attitudes toward current economic events: A lesson from neuroeconomics. *Business Economics*, 53(4): 202–208.

BBC. 2011. Marks and Spencer to return to French retail market. Available at https://www.bbc.co.uk/news/business-12931495. Accessed 15 January 2020.

Benito, G. R. G. 2005. Divestment and international business strategy. *Journal of Economic Geography*, 59(2): 235–251.

Bernini, M., Du, J., & Love, J. H. 2016. Explaining intermittent exporting: Exit and conditional re-entry in export markets. *Journal of International Business Studies*, 47(1): 1058–1076.

Bonaccorsi, A. 1992. On the relationship between firm size and export intensity. *Journal of International Business Studies*, 23(4): 605–635.

Buckley, P. J., Devinney, T. M., & Louviere, J. T. 2007. Do managers behave the way theory suggests? A choice theoretic examination of foreign direct investment location decision making. *Journal of International Business Studies*, 38(7): 1069–1094.

Cairns, P., Doherty, A., Alexander, N., & Quinn, B. 2008. Understanding the international retail divestment process. *Journal of Strategic Marketing*, 16(2): 111–128.

Casillas, J. C., & Moreno-Menendez, A. M. 2014. Speed of the internationalisation process: The role of diversity and depth in experiential learning. *Journal of International Business Studies*, 45(1): 85–101.

Choquette, E. 2019. Import-based market experience and firms' exit from export markets. *Journal of International Business Studies*, 50(1): 423–449.

Cosmides L, & Tooby J. 1994. Better than rational: Evolutionary psychology and the invisible hand. *The American Economic Review*, 84(2): 327–332.

Crick, D. 2004. U.K. SMEs' decision to discontinue exporting: An exploratory investigation into practices within the clothing industry. *Journal of Business Venturing*, 19(4): 561–587.

Darr, E. D., Argote, L., & Epple, D. 1995. The acquisition, transfer, and depreciation of knowledge in service organizations: Productivity in Franchises. *Management Science*, 41(11): 1750–1762.

Datta, S., Iskandar-Datta, M., & Raman, K. 2001. Executive compensation and corporate acquisition decisions. *The Journal of Finance*, 6: 2299–2336.

de Holan, M. P., Phillips, N., & Lawrence, T. B. 2004. Managing organizational forgetting. *MIT Sloan Management Review*, 45(2): 45–51.

Elia, S., Larsen, M., & Piscitello, L. 2019. Entry mode deviation: A behavioural approach to internalization theory. *Journal of International Business Studies*, 50(8): 1359–1371.

García-García, R., García-Canal, E., & Guillén M. F. 2017. Rapid internationalization and long-term performance: The knowledge link. *Journal of World Business*, 52(1): 97–110.

Gigerenzer, G., & Gaissmaier, W. 2011. Heuristic decision making. *The Annual Review of Psychology* 62(Jan): 451–482.

Gigerenzer, G., & Selten, R. 2001. *Bounded Rationality*. Cambridge, MA: MIT Press.

Gigerenzer, G., & Todd, P. M. 1999. *Simple Heuristics That Make Us Smart*. New York, NY: Oxford University Press.

Gilovich, T., Griffin, D., & Kahneman, D. 2002. *Heuristics and Biases: The Psychology of Intuitive Judgment*. New York, NY: Cambridge University Press.

Green, J., & Haidt, J. 2002. How (and where) does moral judgement work? *Trends in Cognitive Sciences*, 6(12): 517–523.

Hutzschenreuter, T., Pedersen, T., & Volberda, H. W. 2007. The role of path dependency and managerial intention: Perspective on international business research. *Journal of International Business Studies*, 38(7): 1055–1068.

Huy, Q., & Zott, C. 2019. Exploring the affective underpinnings of dynamic managerial capabilities: How managers' emotion regulation behaviors mobilize resources for their firms. *Strategic Management Journal*, 40(1): 28–54.

Javalgi, R. R. G., Deligonul, S., Dixit, A., & Cavusgil, S. T. 2011. International market reentry: A review and research framework. *International Business Review*, 20(4): 377–393.

Johanson, J., & Vahlne, J.-E. 1977. The internationalization process of the firm—A model of knowledge development and increasing foreign market commitments. *Journal of International Business Studies*, 8(1): 25–34.

Kahneman, D., & Tversky, A. 1979. Prospect theory: An analysis of decision under risk. *Econometrica: Journal of Econometric Society*, 47(2): 263–292.

Kano, L., &Verbeke, A. 2015. The three faces of bounded reliability: Alfred Chandler and the micro-foundations of management theory. *California Management Review*, 58(1): 97–122.

Kelley, H. H. 1973. The process of causal attribution. *American Psychologist*, 28(2):107–128.

Loustarinen, R., & Welch, L. 1990. *International business operations*. Helsinki: Kyriri Oy.

Macleod, C., & Campbell, M. 1992. Memory accessibility and probability judgments: An experimental evaluation of the availability heuristic. *Journal of Personality and Social Psychology*, 63(6): 890–902.

Mellahi, K. 2003. The de-internationalization process: A case study of Marks and Spencer. In C. Wheeler, F. McDonald, & I. Greaves (Eds.), *Internationalization: Firm Strategies and Management*. Basingstoke: Palgrave Macmillan.

Muradoglu, G., & Harvey, N. 2012. Behavioural finance: The role of psychological factors in financial decisions. *Review of Behavioural Finance*, 4(2): 68–80.

Muramatsu, R., & Hanoch, Y. 2005. Emotions as a mechanism for boundedly rational agents: The fast and frugal way. *Journal of Economic Psychology*, 26(2): 201–221.

Nadolska, A., & Barkema, H. G. 2007. Learning to internationalise: The pace and success of foreign acquisitions. *Journal of International Business Studies*, 38(7): 1170–1186.

Nummela, N., Saarenketo, S., & Sloane, S. 2016. The dynamics of failure in international new ventures: A case study of Finnish and Irish software companies. *International Small Business Journal*, 34(1): 51–69.

Schubert, T., Baier, E., & Rammer, C. 2018. Firm capabilities, technological dynamism and the internationalisation of innovation: A behavioural approach. *Journal of International Business Studies*, 49(1): 70–95.

Staw, B. M. 1976. Knee-deep in the big muddy: a study of escalating commitment to a chosen course of action, *Organizational Behavior and Human Performance*, 16(1): 27–44.

Surdu, I. & Mellahi, K. 2016. "Theoretical foundations of equity based foreign market entry decisions: A review of the literature and recommendations for future research", *International Business Review*, 25, 5, 1169–1184.

Surdu, I., Mellahi, K., & Glaister, K. W. 2019. Once bitten not necessarily shy? Determinants of foreign market re-entry commitment decisions. *Journal of International Business Studies*, 50(3): 393–422.

Surdu, I., Mellahi, K., Glaister, K. W., & Nardella, G. 2018. Why wait? Organisational learning, institutional quality and the speed of foreign market re-entry after initial entry and exit. *Journal of World Business*, 53(6): 911–929.

Surdu, I., & Narula, R. 2020. Organizational learning, unlearning and re-internationalization timing: Differences between emerging-versus developed-market MNEs. *Journal of International Management* (forthcoming).

Tversky, A., & Kahneman, D. 1974. Judgment under uncertainty: Heuristics and biases. *Science*, 185: 1124–1131.

Tversky, A., Slovic, P., & Kahneman, D. 1990. The causes of preference reversal. *The American Economic Review*, 80(1): 204–217.

Vahlne, J-E., & Johanson, J. 2017. From internationalization to evolution: The Uppsala model at 40 years, *Journal of International Business Studies*, 48(9): 1087–1110.

Verbeke, A., & Greidanus, N. (2009). The end of the opportunism versus trust debate: Bounded reliability as a new envelope-concept in research on MNE governance. *Journal of International Business Studies*, 40(9): 1471–1495.

Vissak, T., & Francioni, B. 2013. Serial nonlinear internationalization in practice: A case study. *International Business Review*, 22(6): 951–962.

Welch, C. L., & Welch, L. S. 2009. Re-internationalisation: Exploration and conceptualisation. *International Business Review*, 18(6): 567–577.

Yayla, S., Yeniyurt, S., Uslay, C., & Cavusgil, E. 2018. The role of market orientation, relational capital, and internationalization speed in foreign market exit and re-entry decisions under turbulent conditions. *International Business Review*, 27(6): 1105–1115.

PART V

NEW DIMENSIONS OF INTERNATIONAL BUSINESS STRATEGY

CHAPTER 19

DIGITALIZATION AND ITS STRATEGIC IMPLICATIONS FOR THE MULTINATIONAL ENTERPRISE

The Changing Landscape of Competition and How to Cope with It

PINAR OZCAN AND BASAK YAKIS-DOUGLAS

INTRODUCTION

TECHNOLOGICAL and digital innovation has often been credited with having significant strategic implications for firms by shifting the competitive landscape and changing the market dynamics in an industry (Porter, 1985). Irrespective of whether they operate in international, domestic, or global market contexts, firms are confronted by digitally savvy customers with complex demands, while at the same time facing rising threats of digital disruptions from new entrants into their respective industries. This trend is evidenced by The International Data Corporation (IDC) report that firms are updating their business models by making significant investments in technologies that enable digital transformation amounting to an estimated $5.9 trillion over the years 2018 to 2021. The same report predicts that by 2020, at least 55 percent of organizations will be digitally defined, transforming markets and reimagining the future through new business models, products, and services.

Digitalization is likely to significantly alter the ways of doing business not only for start-ups but also established firms in a wide range of industries. Indeed, even large, multinational enterprises (MNEs) operating in traditional and/or heavy-manufacturing industries are not immune to these changes: Disney (US), for instance, issues wrist-bands donned with radio-frequency-identification technology, which customers can use as a substitute for credit cards, tickets, and keys. Similarly, McGraw-Hill (US) has evolved its digital technology to mold its printed materials into personalized learning experiences. At the risk of cannibalizing its own brand, Qantas Airways (Australia) established a lower-fare airline that employs intensive use of digital technology in book-ing, app-based loyalty programs, automated check-ins and baggage service. Intuit (US), fearing that fintech start-ups would start taking away some of its market share, acquired new digital assets to expand beyond its existing small business and tax products, in an effort to reach digitally adept consumers who preferred using apps to face-to-face or verbal exchanges while managing their financial assets. Telefónica (Spain) too sensed its own vulnerability and launched an independent start-up that involved online community-based digital forums to resolve customer queries. Last but not least, Nike (US) uses digital technologies to reach its customers all around the world and their exercise routines through integrated chip technology that it places in its products. All of these vignettes are indicative of a significant change in the way that businesses operate across different industries and markets.

For MNEs, digital disruption brings to the foreground particular issues such as the necessity for interorganizational collaboration and openness (Chesbrough, 2003; Whittington, Cailluet, & Yakis-Douglas, 2011; Hautz, Seidl, & Whittington, 2017); the emergence and diffusion of networks (Ghoshal & Bartlett, 1990; Zander, 2002); the increase in creation, exchange, and complexity of knowledge (Foss & Pedersen, 2004); the invention and adoption of new manufacturing technologies (Laplume, Petersen, & Pearce, 2016); as well as the advent of new business models leading to a "(digital) platform" or a "network economy" (Ozcan & Eisenhardt, 2009; Gawer & Cusumano, 2008; Kenney & Zysman, 2016).

While the majority of digitalization efforts bring the benefit of widening operations to involve new national contexts, MNEs will need to weigh these benefits with a set of challenges. On the one hand, many firms that participate in the digital economy have benefited from the absence of government regulation or hybrid governance structures (Van Tulder, Verbeke, & Piscitello, 2018). The "era of digital exceptionalism, in which online platforms have been inhabiting a parallel legal universe where they are not legally responsible, either for what their users do or for the harm that their services can cause in the real world" (*The Economist*, 2017 cited in Van Tulder et al., 2018). On the other hand, they are increasingly having to cope with new regulatory challenges, antitrust laws, and industrial and trade policies. Platform companies such as Airbnb are under pressure to adopt local safety regulations that often match those in traditional hotels; while Uber is compelled to implement minimum wage restrictions in some of the countries in which it operates. Google has recently been fined a record historical antitrust penalty of EUR 4.3 billion in July 2018 by the European Commission for abusing its dominant (network) position to discriminate against rivals. In the 2018 UK parliamentary committee report, social media companies such as Facebook and Twitter are accused of "undermining democracy" through systematic manipulation and use of public and private information for financial gain (Van Tulder et al., 2018; Hazlehurst & Brouthers, 2018). Digitalization, therefore, is fueling a new "breed" of MNEs (e.g., Brouthers, Geisser, & Rothlauf, 2016) and international business (IB) models (Baden-Fuller & Haefliger, 2013).

In this new world, firms entering markets with digital technologies are less likely to be dependent on mediators within value chains and will potentially have the freedom to exercise choice and control over delivery systems for their products and services (Bakos, 1998; Gellman, 1996; Katz & Gartner, 1988). Also, new entrants with digital technologies are likely to be able to employ advantages from platforms in the form of coordination, organization, and increased momentum (Nambisan, 2017; Thomas, Autio, & Gann, 2014; Yoo, Boland Jr, Lyytinen, & Majchrzak, 2012; Zittrain, 2006). As creators, complementors, or consumers, firms are increasingly finding themselves part of digital platforms such as Apple and its iOS system or its "app" ecosystem, Alphabet's Google Play or its Android ecosystem, or Amazon Marketplace.

New technologies can disrupt existing markets by causing vertical disintegration, as seen in the personal computer (PC) market at the turn of the second millennium (Baldwin & Clark, 2000; Gawer & Cusumano, 2002), and lead to the emergence of coopetitive ecosystems where the old and the new interact (Jacobides & Winter, 2005). Gawer & Phillips (2013) show how Intel became a platform leader when the market transitioned from a supply chain to a platform business model. More recently, research by Ozcan, Zachariadis, and Dinckol (2020) illustrates how the UK market entry of innovative financial technology (fintech) firms gave rise to challenger banks that provided customers with a digital marketplace where they could shop for financial services from various fintech complementors while domestic banks mostly struggled to leave their existing products behind to switch to a digital platform business model. In sum, digitalization is changing the competitive landscape in a plethora of industries and for a wide range of firms from local start-ups to global conglomerates. These changes have the potential to make what we know about business strategy and competition obsolete.

This chapter lays out how the classic principles of competitive strategy are transformed in today's markets due to digitalization and provides suggestions in terms of how MNEs can respond to these transformations. We build on some of the new research challenges proposed in Chapter 5, particularly with regards to the changing nature of competitive and cooperative relationships between firms. Thus, we start by outlining the key contextual changes associated with digitalization, namely increasing demand for internal and external connectivity, a need for improved understanding of consumer preferences and developing capability to address these, and increasing interdependence and convergence within and across industries. Following these contextual changes to the competitive landscape, we suggest that firms pursue strategies that are: (1) collaborative; (2) additive; and (3) open. In doing so, we draw on a diverse set of contemporary and historical examples from mobile gaming and fintech to Uber and Airbnb, focusing predominantly on the transformation of industries due to technology, and the implications of technology-related advancements on strategic thinking. Our chapter draws on a wide variety of studies conducted in various sectors, all of which emphasize the ever-increasing need for viewing industries in terms of platforms and networks, employing strategic maneuvers that are adaptive to this new competitive landscape, and going one step further by being proactive in shaping it.

Key Changes Associated with Digitalization

IDC predicts that by 2022, over 60 percent of global GDP will stem from digitized businesses arising in every industry from digitally enhanced offerings, operations, and relationships. Digitalization has already brought a significant impact on business activities ranging from distribution, services, access, and participation (Kulesz, 2017). Digital transformation might influence the evolution of institutions, and existing institutions might shape, in turn, how digital technologies diffuse and evolve (Lanzolla et al., 2018).

Above all, however, digital technologies are likely to dramatically alter organizational forms and firm strategy, causing disruption (Brynjolfsson, Malone, Gurbaxani, & Kambil, 1994; Sia, Soh, & Weill, 2016). These changes are likely to be quite pervasive among MNEs and global firms, as these are faced with fundamental and varying external uncertainties at the global scale (Mullner & Filatotchev, 2018) and need to adapt to immense changes due to the advent of new information and communication technologies (Hazlehurst & Brouthers, 2018). They will have to rethink strategic choices regarding locations, internationalization processes, and entry mode (Hazlehurst & Brouthers, 2018), undertake integrated approaches to various functional areas of management that are influenced by new stakeholders, and subsequently configure strategies to cope with these uncertainties (Mullner & Filatotchev, 2018). In particular, MNEs will have to integrate a plethora of new practices such as peer-to-peer (P2P) communication and crowd-based dynamics and technologies such as artificial intelligence (AI) and blockchain into their strategy and organization (Mullner & Filatotchev, 2018).

It is thus imperative for IB strategy scholars to understand these potentially dramatic consequences of digitalization, and relevant responses, for all firms, including MNEs, as they are expected to have great impact on the global economy (Van Tulder et al., 2018). To address these issues, we first introduce two key themes that have become relevant with regards to digitalization: (1) connectivity and advances in data analysis capability, and (2) interdependence and convergence.

Connectivity and Data Analysis Capability

The most evident theme to arise as a characteristic of new business models associated with digitalization is connectivity—both inside and outside the firm. Internally, systems that support mobile and disperse workforces are becoming imperative for businesses. Riedl and Woolley (2017) found that remote teams—characteristic in MNEs—communicate in bursts and that organizations that exchange messages quickly during periods of high activity perform much better than those whose conversations involve long lag times between responses. Similar observations exist for organizations with

---

Case 19.1: Disruption in banking

A striking real-life example of disruption in the face of *connectivity* and *data analysis* is from the banking sector. In their recent study on the UK and European banking sector, Ozcan, Zachariadis, et al. (2020) have studied how incumbent banks in these regions face major disruption due to a specific regulation that favors those players that can provide connectivity and superior data analysis.

The Open Banking regulation in the UK and the Revised Payment Systems Directive (PSD2) in the EU, which came into effect simultaneously in 2018, enable third party payment institutions to access consumer bank accounts. The purpose of enabling access to consumer accounts, which are mostly held by incumbent banks, is to allow analysis of relevant data and offer customers better and cheaper services. Since these regulations came into effect, banks such as Atom (UK), Monzo (UK), N26 (Germany), and Starling (UK) have entered the EU and UK markets. These new entrants, also called challenger or neo banks, competed with domestic banks along *connectivity* and *data analysis*. First, their offerings allowed customers to connect all their current, savings, mortgage, and other accounts from different banks, and even across countries in one platform. This connectivity across different products allowed the customers to have much better oversight over their finances and improve their decision making. Second, having access to customers' data across different banks meant that the data could be used for improved analysis, advice, and products offered in a more tailored manner to customers. Customers could, in turn, obtain benefits such as cheaper loans and higher savings based on these new players' superior data analysis capabilities.

As Ozcan, Zachariadis, et al. (2020) show in their recent analysis, incumbent banks' business model was significantly disrupted by these new entrants as incumbent banks did not have the technical capabilities and a platform/holistic mindset to compete in this new way. Despite operating in international markets themselves, many of the established market players even struggled to connect a customer's accounts with their own bank across different European markets. In fact, an independent PWC report also found that 30 percent of revenues of incumbent banks may be lost by 2020 due to the digital disruption trends illustrated above.

strong external connectivity. A study by Yankee Group found that 96 percent of customers prefer to shop at stores or companies that offer free Wi-Fi and 64 percent of people have chosen a restaurant based on free Wi-Fi availability.

The second characteristic of new business models associated with digitalization is an ever-increasing reliance on data analysis capabilities. Refined proficiency in data analysis allows organizations to understand customer behavior better, and as a result, construct better offers and responses. This is particularly relevant for some MNEs as they operate in a wide range of host country locations where better understanding of consumer behavior can lead to faster local adaptation strategies, or reduced dependence on a local partner. IDC predicts that by 2022, 30 percent of enterprises will be engaged in conversational speech technology for customer engagement and by 2024, AI-enabled user interfaces and process automation will replace one-third of today's screen-based apps, making the optimal analysis and management of data imperative for organizational success.

Interdependence and Convergence

Another key aspect of digitalization is the rise of *interdependence* and *convergence*. Interdependence relates to the dependence between two or more firms in order to make or sell their products or services; whereas convergence explains how traditionally separate businesses come together around new products and services. Interdependence, which denotes that individual innovations do not "stand alone" but are instead embedded in a network of interdependent technologies (Adner, 2017; Adner & Kapoor, 2010), has been the subject of many studies. For example, Adner and Kapoor (2016) studied the evolution of the semiconductor lithography industry as it evolved through ten technology generations in multiple national contexts and found that the introduction of new technologies was delayed when complements were lacking. Interdependence broadens the scope of technologies and changes that may affect a firm (Pierce, 2009; Hannah & Eisenhardt, 2018). Afuah (2000) studied twenty-three computer workstation manufacturers around the transition from complex instruction set computing (CISC) to reduced instruction set computing (RISC) chipset technology and found that manufacturers' performance suffered even when it was their suppliers that were disrupted. In line with these findings, Pierce (2009) observed that design changes made by upstream automobile manufacturers triggered subsequent shakeouts in downstream automobile lessors. Overall, this suggests that within interdependent industries, changes and technologies that transcend national contexts directly affect complementors and these may, in fact, be strategically material for an MNE.

An important type of interdependence that is critical, but often not easy to anticipate, is when products emerge at the intersection of previously separate industries. An IBM study published in 2016 revealed that two-thirds of global chief marketing officers (CMOs) saw industry convergence as their greatest business challenge, and 60 percent expected more competition to come from companies outside of their sector (IBM, 2016).

Digital transformation presents CMOs with unique organizational initiatives, but also poses pressures for understanding a much wider purview of industries, actors, and relationships. Well-known examples of convergence are autonomous vehicles—bringing together technology MNEs such as Apple (US) and Google (US) with multinational automobile and component manufacturers such as Honda (Japan), Bosch (Germany), and Delphi (UK)—or the marriage of consumer electronics and healthcare technologies in digital exercise-trackers to create portable health devices like Fitbit and Garmin. The Case 19.2 illustrates the hazards of failing to recognize the emergence of new markets between traditionally separate industries.

One of the ways in which firms experience convergence across industries and national contexts is through the emergence of platforms. In the last few decades, we have seen the emergence of platform business models that move away from the traditional vertical integration of the firm (also known as the pipeline business model) and introduce a flatter, more inclusive, and innovation-centric approach to value creation (Gawer, 2009). Central to this model is a platform that often "uses technology to connect people, organizations and resources in an interactive ecosystem in which amazing amounts of value can be created and exchanged" (Parker, Van Alstyne, & Jiang, 2016). This

---

Case 19.2: Emergence of mobile payments

Ozcan and Santos (2015) studied a case of convergence involving the financial industry and mobile communications that resulted in the emergence of mobile payment services. The authors found that the technology that enabled mobile payments, near-field communication (NFC), was available since the late 1990s, but this did not lead to commercialization. Their longitudinal study shows that the delay in commercialization was due to a lack of agreement around what the new market should look like. The authors observed that, despite their interdependence, multinationals (i.e. banks and telcos) that had dominant positions in their traditionally separate global industries were unable to agree on a market architecture. Due to their extant dominance in their respective industries, banks and telcos struggled in recognizing that this convergence between traditionally separate industries required a reshuffling of power dynamics and prior beliefs, that is, about who owned the customer and whose security standards should be adopted.

The authors also observed that once the market was blocked due to the lack of agreement between global banks and telcos, some local mobile payments solutions emerged, for example, in Kenya where the banks were not prominent, or in Japan where banks and telcos belonged to the same holding company, effectively solving the interdependence problem. However, these local solutions could not get adopted widely as global banks and telcos had "moved on," investing in alternative products in the rest of the world, such as contactless bank cards and smartphones without payment capability. In the end, it was not the banks or telcos, but Apple and other technology giants that jumpstarted the mobile payments service from 2014 onwards. Today, Apple, Google, Alibaba, and other technology firms still have the lion's share in mobile payments.

organizational formation can facilitate value-creating interactions among consumers (demand-side) and external producers (supply-side), and produce a multisided market to provide complementary services and cocreate value (Rochet & Tirole, 2006; Zhu & Iansiti, 2012).

Platforms are known to not only reduce transaction costs (Munger, 2015) but also foster innovation, as they combine the knowledge and the perspectives of various internal and external parties to create more innovative and personalized products (Baldwin & Clark, 2000; Baldwin & Woodard, 2009; Gawer, 2009, 2014). Due to these advantages, platforms have become central to many industries and markets such as e-commerce (e.g. Amazon and eBay), social media (e.g. Facebook and Twitter), video games (e.g. Xbox and PlayStation), PC and mobile operating systems (e.g. Google Android and Apple iOS), together with peer-to-peer sharing (e.g. Uber and Airbnb). Table 19.1 provides a simple comparison of new entrants versus incumbents across a number of industries to illustrate the prominence of platforms in our lives today and gives an indication of their ability to disrupt industries and compete with MNEs at a global scale.

The rise of digital platforms across different industries has significantly changed the nature of global competition. According to Teece (2018), in platform-based ecosystems, competition can take place in one of the following three forms. First, it may be between two platforms such as between Apple's iOS and Google's Android operating systems. Second, competition could take place between a platform and its partners, like in the case of Microsoft capturing value from browsers, streaming media, and instant messaging applications on its Windows operating system. Third, competition can be among complementors, each seeking a position within a platform-based ecosystem, as in the case of any two mobile apps, each targeting the same set of consumers. We will discuss the basic rules of platform management in more detail in the next section.

Table 19.1 Incumbents and new entrants

Firm	Year Founded	Employees	Market Cap (2016)
BMW	1916	116,000	$53B
UBER	2009	7,000	$60B
MARRIOT	1927	200,000	$17B
AIRBNB	2008	5,000	$21B
WALT DISNEY	1923	185,000	$165B
FACEBOOK	2004	12,691	$315B
KODAK	1888	145,000	$30B
INSTAGRAM	2010	13	$1B (acquisition in 2012)

Source: Parker and Van Alstyne (2016).

Thus far, we have shown that digital disruption has brought, and will continue to bring, significant changes to the ways in which firms operate. Organizations will experience increased pressure to not only invest in technologies that allow connectivity but also be ready to actively take part in two-way communications with their consumers. Furthermore, investment in ways to collect, analyze, and interpret vast quantities of data, as well as conceptualize their tasks and workforce in the context of AI and machine learning, will become imperative. Last but not least, firms will be dealing with shifting industry boundaries, the challenges of working with platforms, and increasing susceptibility to new entrants enabled by digital technologies. These changes may take varying forms and occur at different speeds depending also on the institutional environments in which MNE's operate, complicating the matter. In the next section, we outline three strategies for such firms facing digital disruption: (1) collaborative strategies, (2) additive strategies, and (3) open strategies.

Strategy in the Digital Age

Collaborative Strategies

We propose following collaborative strategies for MNEs as a means of dealing with increasing levels of interdependence and convergence due to digitalization. Interdependence emphasizes *collaboration* with other firms and is one of the most critical issues in today's competitive global environment. The most well-known type of interfirm collaborations is alliances, which can be defined as "arrangements between firms involving the exchange, sharing, or co-development of products, technologies or services" (Gulati, 1998). Alliances are known to improve a firm's strategic position in nascent markets in various ways. First, they can reduce supply uncertainty by enabling firms to share R&D and production costs in a nascent market (Adner & Kapoor, 2010; Miner, Amburgey, & Stearns, 1990; Ohmae, 1989; Powell, White, Koput, & Owen-Smith, 2005; Van de Ven & Polley, 1992). In addition, alliances can help firms reduce demand uncertainty by jointly create narratives and collective identities to help the adoption of the new products and services (Gurses & Ozcan, 2015). They can also reduce demand uncertainty by simply serving as signals for the legitimacy and size of the market entered (Eisenhardt & Schoonhoven, 1996; Ozcan & Eisenhardt, 2009).

The importance of alliances is amplified for firms operating in fast-changing technology markets where resource needs are in flux. However, collaborating does not just refer to formal alliances, it also means being aware and actively working with *complementors*. As Yoffie and Kwak (2006) point out, most companies benefit from complementors—other firms independently making products or services that increase the value of a firm's offering to mutual customers. For example, digital camera makers rely on manufacturers of affordable home photo printers to sell more cameras. Also, collaborating with complementors can lead to innovation. For example, Ansari and Munir (2008) found that incumbent telephone companies in the UK co-opted mobile challengers such as Virgin Mobile by licensing their complementary assets (e.g. access to spectrum) to the challengers. Similarly, Gomes-Casseres (1996) studied the early personal digital assistant (PDA) market and found that firms were able to use alliances as probes to experiment with different technologies and thus hedge against uncertainty. Finally, Gawer and Henderson (2007) traced Intel's history over fourteen years and observed that the firm was able to introduce novel technologies by integrating into the (related) markets of complementors in order to reduce the need to coordinate with them.

Case 19.3: Early collaborations in mobile gaming

In an empirical study, Ozcan and Eisenhardt (2009) illustrated that nascent markets are a great time to approach complementors. In fact, approaching potential partners early in the emergence of a market increases the likelihood of firms building a strong ecosystem. During this period, high market ambiguity and low competition work in favor of smaller firms. These favorable circumstances especially benefit entrepreneurial ventures, which would normally lose out to the competition in gaining valuable face time with prominent firms. Since most organizations lack a clear vision of what the new market will look like, start-up founders can take advantage of this by meeting with potential partners and then promoting and selling a vision of the future in which both parties play central roles. Then, through frequent inter-actions while working together, executives can strengthen these relationships before market competition intensifies.

The authors give the example of mobile gaming start-up Starclick and large telco Verizon Wireless. During the emergence of the wireless gaming industry, no one had a clear under-standing of the industry architecture. Starclick executives began by talking with several firms and promoting their own vision for the industry, terming it the "market ecosystem." Their vision relied on strong collaboration between carriers, platform developers, and publishers, not handset makers, to develop the industry. When Starclick approached Verizon Wireless (US) with this idea, Verizon was intrigued, because such a partnership would enable them to enhance their own position. Verizon needed good games to sell game-capable phones, because a gaming platform alone was not interesting; and Starclick could bring good games to the table. Starclick's blueprint defined the partners' subsequent interactions. Because of this strong, early tie between Starclick and Verizon, game-capable phones, embedded with a few starter games from Starclick, flooded the market in the Christmas of 2012, following Verizon's "buy one get one free" promotions. Starclick gained exceptional marketing and co-development opportunities from Verizon and consequently other telcos. It remained the number one US mobile games publisher until it was sold for a record amount to Electronic Arts in 2005. Verizon remained the market leader and received significant revenue from game-capable phones and mobile game downloads until the mobile content market was disrupted by Apple in 2008.

Thinking of interdependence and complementors is even more critical for start-ups with limited resources and no market recognition, as detailed in Case 19.3.

Beyond the evident challenges that alliance partners face associated with cultural and language barriers (discussed in detail in previous IB works), collaboration with other firms such as complementors can sometimes be tricky, even in the absence of such distances. We emphasize that firms in different market segments are unlikely to share the same incentives or views with respect to whether or how the new technology should be developed. For example, Casadesus-Masanell and Yoffie (2007) demonstrate that even in the case of perfect complementarity between Microsoft (US) and Intel (US), Microsoft always prefers to delay the implementation of new technologies relative to Intel, due to its ability to attain revenues from product updates. Similarly, studying the emergence and subsequent failure of the Symbian platform, Tee and Ozcan (2020) illustrated that despite their interdependence regarding R&D, handset manufacturers' divergent views of key characteristics of a smartphone (i.e. touchscreen, keyboard, or stylus pen) severely hampered their ability to jumpstart the smartphone market and, as a result, placed Apple in a significantly advantageous position. These findings show that understanding the economic incentives and cognitive priorities of complementors and partners is critical in reaching mutually beneficial outcomes in a timely manner.

A particular type of interdependence that deserves special attention and specific management skills is due to the advent of digital platforms. As we outlined in the previous section, digital platforms are associated with disruption across many industries and changes in ways that competition unfolds. Based on extant research, there are certain fundamental elements that aspiring or existing platform providers will need to consider. First, organizations need to think very carefully about how to populate the platform. Platform leaders must strive to establish a business model and set of relationships that are mutually beneficial for platform participants. In the platform literature, this is known as the "chicken-and-egg problem" where the platform leader needs to cultivate one side of the platform (i.e. consumers) in order to attract the other side (i.e. suppliers) (Gawer & Cusumano, 2014). If successful, this leads to a momentum and subsequently to network effects between the platform and its complementary products or services. This momentum, in turn, may erect barriers to entry for potential platform competitors and allow new markets to develop around only this platform—hence, the chicken-and-egg "problem." Researchers have suggested various solutions to this conundrum: Parker and Van Alstyne (2005) and Rochet and Tirole (2003, 2006) suggest that platform owners can resolve this problem by subsidizing or seeding complementors through adequate pricing or other financial incentives. In addition, Parker et al. (2016) discuss various "pull" and "push" strategies to kickstart the platform. They recommend that organizations can create a particular value proposition to a particular subset of potential users, and subsequently, transform the business by attracting a wider audience on both sides (see also Gawer & Cusumano, 2008). Another strategy is to "piggyback" onto another firm's existing user-base (or platform) and recruit third-party developers to populate the complementor side (see Parker et al., 2016).

The second most significant issue that firms operating in platforms need to take into consideration is ensuring effective integration and communication of players. Firms can maintain a central position in the ecosystem through investing in infrastructure and innovating their core functions. This also involves having the right modular architecture and providing easy to use APIs with detailed documentation, community, and access. Think of a physical platform like a shopping mall. The selling point is to create a "one-stop shop" for all customers' shopping needs. This includes being able to search through the products and services easily but also having comfortable access close to amenities such as food, parking, and entertainment. Therefore, in addition to the core product, the place needs to be able to house value-added services and make them easily accessible to consumers. In a similar fashion, the more accessible and integrated the services are on a platform, the easier it is to use. Maximizing interactions is what will bring competitive advantage and profitability to platforms in the medium to long term. Finally, platform owners need to establish clear rules and immediate resolutions. Uncertainty regarding liabilities can damage the reputation of a platform and discourage consumers from undertaking transactions (Zachariadis & Ozcan, 2017).

In sum, collaborative strategies offer organizations means for managing increasing levels of interdependence and convergence—a main outcome of digitalization. In the next section, we introduce additive strategies as a broader and complementary form of response to changes associated with digitalization.

Additive Strategies

In addition to thinking of formal and informal collaborations with partners and complementors, considering the larger sociopolitical ecosystem around the firm is critical in the age of digitalization, particularly for MNEs. Organizations operating internationally are now compelled to consider implementing organizational changes across countries they operate in; designing mechanisms that enable standardization; adopting intellectual property rights protection in multi-country contexts; and understanding the institutional conditions fostering individual and local creativity in potentially diverse national contexts (Mowery, 2009). For these MNEs, *additive strategies* offer a useful framework. Recently pioneered by Dorobantu, Kaul, and Zelner (2017), additive strategies involve complementing existing stakeholders in the environment, which may include competitors, consumers, legislators, and regulators all with potentially conflicting interests, characteristics, and requirements.

Additive strategies take the core idea of collaboration and amplify it to the larger ecosystem of stakeholders. For instance, in their study of the emergence of pay cable TV, Gurses and Ozcan (2015) found that when cable TV providers emerged in the 1940s, they emphasized providing cable services as an extension of regular TV channels to rural areas that could not receive over-the-air signals. This initial additive strategy allowed them to grow without resistance from incumbents or regulators for over a decade. As the authors illustrate, additive strategies can be particularly useful when a new technology is subject to regulation upon market entry. Providing positive externalities to the stakeholders in the larger ecosystem can help the firm in shaping a positive institutional environment that can lead to regulatory and sociopolitical legitimacy of its products and services.

Dorobantu et al. (2017) also point out that firms may pursue an additive approach by proactively sharing value with other stakeholders with the expectation of being rewarded for doing so in the future. Proactiveness can, in fact, be a critical component of additive strategies, as the relevant stakeholders may not even be aware of the firm's products and services or its relevance to them. A good example of this is comparing Airbnb and Uber in terms of their entry into the UK, as illustrated in Case 19.4.

Case 19.4: Airbnb versus Uber in the UK

Comparing Airbnb and Uber's market entry strategies across different countries, Uzunca, Rigtering, and Ozcan (2018) give the example of Airbnb's international strategy as a successful employment of additive strategy. For instance, Airbnb officially entered the UK market in early 2012. Interviews with the Airbnb UK community manager revealed how the platform prides itself on entering new markets through "collaboration and communication with local authorities and community." As part of its strategy, Airbnb created multiple community and public-related positions in its UK headquarters. Among these positions were global and country community managers, a public relations manager, and a head of policy. In London, Airbnb worked hand-in-hand with the municipality from the beginning by providing them information about the growth of tourism in London's outer boroughs to help spread the economic benefits across the city. It also worked with local fire departments to improve fire safety in homes and neighborhoods, particularly in poorer ones. The company framed these relational and additive strategies as "giving back to the community." Half a decade later, Airbnb's ecosystem-building strategy paid off. In 2015, Airbnb negotiated a more favorable deal with the City of London in comparison with Amsterdam, which allowed residents to rent their rooms or homes for up to 90 days per year and earn up to £7,500 without having to file taxes. This negotiation helped Airbnb grow exponentially from 1 million guests in 2015 to 8.4 million in 2018.

Uzunca et al. (2018) compared Airbnb's internationalization efforts to Uber and found that Uber has mostly followed an aggressive strategy in foreign market entry, focusing on populating its platform with drivers and users, but with virtually no attention to the larger ecosystem in the country. This strategy backfired with Transport for London announcing in 2017 that Uber's license would not be renewed. Following this decision, Uber embarked on a corporate overhaul and introduced free insurance for drivers in London and limited their operating hours. It opened a 24/7 customer helpline and promised to start reporting serious incidents to the police department. The changes, which were bolstered by a major public relations campaign and an apology from CEO Dara Khosrowshahi, earned Uber a fifteen-month extension of its license in London.

As apparent in the example in Case 19.4, an additive strategy is particularly important when MNEs' products and services are subject to different types and levels of regulation across countries. A country-by-country additive approach can play a key role in establishing a favorable institutional environment for new products and services that require regulatory approval.

Open Strategy

Digitalization is characterized by platforms, ecosystems, and open/user innovation (Altman & Tushman, 2017) made up of external individuals, organizations, and communities aimed at creating value through interactions (Gawer & Phillips, 2013). As we emphasized in our two former sections, due to digitalization, firms in general, and MNEs in particular, are increasingly moving to more distributed and networked forms (Benkler, 2007). In this new global context, we have explained why and how collaborative and additive strategies are becoming essential for (global) competition.

Our third suggestion for organizations is therefore a framework that embraces new forms of business that are associated with greater openness. These new business forms enable firms to interact with, and involve, internal and external constituents such as employees, customers, shareholders, and other stakeholders. Platforms and ecosystems, which are examples of innovative business forms enabled by digitalization, can lead firms to simultaneously manage closed and open ways of conducting business (Altman & Tushman, 2017). Business models enabled through digitalization "bring forth opportunities and challenges related to openness, engagement, interdependence and co-opetition as they revolve around interactions between firms and other parties outside their boundaries" (Altman & Tushman, 2017).

Openness has recently become a key feature in governance (Almirall, Lee, & Majchrzak, 2014; Tihanyi, Graffin, & George, 2014; Kube, Hilgers, Koch, & Füller, 2015; Dutt et al., 2016; Mergel, 2015) and innovation (Dahlander & Gann, 2010; Chesbrough & Bogers, 2014; Randhawa, Wilden, & Hohberger, 2016). Achieved through transparency and/or involvement (Whittington et al., 2011; Hautz et al., 2017), openness has recently become a recognizable theme in strategy literature (Matzler, et al, 2014; Alexy, West, Klapper, & Reitzig, 2018; Birkinshaw, 2017) and implemented by MNEs that are at the heart of digital transformation, varying from profit-based (i.e. IBM) to non-profit organizations (i.e. Wikimedia and Creative Commons).

The main reason for a need in increased openness is that platforms and similar business strategies involve a great deal of interactions between firms and their internal and external constituents and managing them effectively is key for performance (Boudreau & Jeppesen, 2015; Cennamo & Santalo, 2013; Gawer & Phillips, 2013). We suggest *open strategy* (Whittington et al., 2011; Hautz et al., 2017) as a framework that can assist firms in including and being transparent toward their potentially diverse and widespread sets of internal and external stakeholders. We posit that strategic openness as an organizational response to digital transformation can take two forms: (1) inclusion and (2) transparency. These two strategic responses to digital transformation are detailed below.

Regarding *inclusion*, open strategy can benefit firms not only in terms of integrating a diverse set of needs but also with regards to the pace of strategy (large MNEs are often considered to be particularly slow in implementing changes to their strategies). The breadth of digital means that strategizing today needs to move beyond chief strategy officers (CSOs), top management teams, and boards of directors. The pace of change driven by digitalization requires reflection on the frequency with which firms review their IB strategies and set new directions for the near future. Annual reviews of strategy can seldom keep pace with the demands introduced by digitalization. Strategic reviews are likely to take place in significantly shorter, more compressed timeframes. In parallel, there will probably be changes that require real-time refinements or more significant changes associated with strategy. Digitalization is also likely to introduce a plethora of issues stemming from complex competitive environments, invisible consumers, and diverse stakeholder environments. Through open strategy practices involving internal and external constituents, firms can address these issues by consulting with each other, identifying areas of improvement, and inclusion of stakeholders in strategic planning and implementation. For MNEs that operate in a large number of geographic locations, digitalization has made the implementation of an open strategy possible. In Case 19.5, we present IBM as an example for inclusion in open strategy.

The second aspect of open strategy—*transparency*—can help firms cope with the informational challenges associated with digitalization. The abundance of electronically available data, made possible through digitalization, often fails to translate into useful information in the absence of significant investment into understanding, analyzing, and interpreting data. Open strategy is not about making information available but rather

Case 19.5: IBM

Whittington (2019) gives examples of open strategy practices from past to present in *Opening Strategy*. A prominent example among MNEs is IBM, which not only introduced inclusion in open strategy but also still implements it. IBM has pioneered the implementation of inclusion in open strategy through WorldJam (or, commonly referred to as "jamming sessions"). Initiated in 2001, WorldJam was introduced by IBM's CEO as an event that would unfold over three consecutive days. Over three days, IBM employees from around the world used the company's intranet to post over 52,000 contributing comments about a select number of top-priority strategic issues within the company. Since then, IBM has carried out jamming sessions related to its strategic priorities (i.e. InnovationJam, ValueJam, etc.) with varying time intervals and increasing participation. These sessions are open to over 150,000 IBM employees located in more than 100 countries, business partners, and clients (from nearly eighty companies). One of these jamming sessions, InnovationJam—carried out in 2010—was recognized as the force behind creating ten new businesses within IBM, generating nearly US$700 million in revenues in less than five years.

about engaging with stakeholders in ways that will assist them in evaluating strategic moves. Open strategy enables transparency of strategy through, for instance, corporate disclosures. Targeted communications regarding strategy empower organizational constituents to overcome information asymmetries and hold decision makers responsible for the direction of and spending within the firm, thereby reducing mismanagement of resources and leading, ultimately, to superior performance (Cowen & Marcel, 2011; Shipilov, Greve, & Rowley, 2010; Zhang & Wiersema, 2009). While firms attempt to find ways to adapt to digital disruption, transparency through open strategy can lead to

---

Case 19.6: Uber's "closed" strategy

On 12 May 2019, Uber filed for an Initial Public Offering (IPO). Uber's listing was undeniably the year's highest profile and all eyes were on the taxi hailing app. However, not only was the market capitalization nearly 40 percent lower than estimated but Uber's stock fell 11 percent by the end of the second day, leaving the company's share price nearly 18 percent below its initial IPO price. Analysts following the company suggested that the cold reception from investors was due to the skepticism of public investors regarding the ride-hailing company's business model.

Uber's IPO experience, described as "catastrophic" by analysts, highlights the importance of opening strategy to investors and analysts, especially for organizations implementing what the *Financial Times* referred to as "untested business models." Indeed, uniqueness in strategy can be beneficial for competition, but not for market performance. Untested business models such as platforms can be associated with big unknowns for investors and this, in turn, can lead to significant disadvantages for listed companies implementing these novel strategies. For listed companies undertaking unique strategies or organizations dealing with circumstances characterized with information asymmetry, there is empirical evidence that opening strategy to investors, analysts, and specialist media can help share price reactions. For instance, Whittington et al. (2016) analyzed share price reactions to over 1500 strategy presentations and found that sharing long-term strategic plans with investors and analysts boosted share prices up by nearly 5 percent, especially when the circumstances of the companies were likely to drive shareholders to insecurity regarding the future direction of the firm (e.g. like the appointment of a new CEO).

Similarly, Yakis-Douglas et al. (2017) found that for firms that undertake unknown or novel strategies, the likelihood of successfully completing merger and acquisition deals was higher if they took the time and made the effort to carry out voluntary, public disclosures of their strategy. In Uber's case, the company may be suffering from a discount that markets apply to the unknown or it may be the case that investors are unconvinced about the future cash flow of the company. Either way, Uber would benefit from opening its strategy to investors and analysts through public disclosures and generating convincing narratives of their long-term strategy.

improvements in coordination (Mack & Szulanski, 2017), help external audiences make sense of organizational activities (Baptista, Wilson, Galliers, & Bynghall, 2017), and assist organizations in combating negative consequences tied to uncertainty and information asymmetry (Whittington et al., 2016; Yakis-Douglas, Angwin, Ahn, & Meadows, 2017). Case 19.6 highlights the potential consequences of lack of transparency in strategy practices.

Unlike marketing, strategy does not benefit naturally from the increase of digital data. And yet, changes in the form that data takes have raised expectations from internal and external stakeholders about pursuing similar benefits in strategy. Open strategy helps manage these expectations by increasing visibility in inputs and outputs of strategy such as the choice and details of strategic analyses (Matzler et al., 2014 Tackx & Verdin, 2014) or the way strategy is described in statements and why these statements are constructed the way they are (Tackx & Verdin, 2014). Open strategy can apply to different stages of the strategy process. Table 19.2 includes some examples of open strategy.

Table 19.2 Examples of open strategy

Examples of open strategy	Dimensions of transparency	Studies
Access to project results by outside constituents	External	Appleyard & Chesbrough (2017)
Widened access to content and information	External	Baptista, Wilson, Galliers & Bynghall (2017)
Making explicit the details underlying idea generation for future strategic direction	External	Dobusch & Muller-Seitz (2015)
Broadcasting (communicating relevant information)	External	Gegenhuber & Dobusch (2017)
Dialogue about strategy through wiki	External	Heracleous, Gößwein, Beaudette (2017)
Discussing strategic matters through shared mailing lists and open skype calls	Internal and External	Luedicke, Husemann, Furnari, Ladstaetter (2017)
Visibility of the strategy formulation process; combining participatory and inclusive practices	Internal	Mack & Szulanski (2017)
Increased visibility in inputs and outputs of strategy	Internal	Matzler, Füller, Hutter, Hautz, & Stieger (2014)
Making the strategy implementation process more explicit	Authors discuss the "inclusion scope" as internal versus external	Matzler, Füller, Koch, Hautz, & Hutter (2014)

(Continued)

Table 19.2 Examples of open strategy (Continued)

Examples of open strategy	Dimensions of transparency	Studies
Challenging organizational control over strategy process and related communication through social media	External	Plesner & Gulbrandsen (2015)
Sharing the results of open strategy initiative through letters written by top management	Internal	Stieger, Matzler, Chatterjee, Ladstaetter-Fussenegger (2012)
Details of strategic analyses; explanations of why strategy statements are constructed the way they are	Internal	Tackx & Verdin (2014)
Strategy presentations	External	Whittington, Yakis-Douglas, Ahn (2016)
Interim news events during M&A deals	External	Yakis-Douglas, Angwin, Ahn, Meadows (2017)

Source: Ohlson & Yakis-Douglas (2019).

Concluding Remarks

In this chapter, we have shown that while digital technologies can provide instantaneous, low-cost, and customized ways of connecting MNEs to their customers, this increased volume of connectivity implies managing these interactions, making sense of a large volume of data, and responding to the demands of customers—which are now set rather high thanks to enabling technologies. In addition to the increased levels of connectivity and the accompanying demand for improved ways of understanding the data that is generated, digitalization brings a great degree of interdependence and convergence in the form of platform technologies and ecosystems. Firms need to be astutely aware of the types of competition arising from other platforms, the platform itself, its partners, and complementors. While fighting off potential competition from these different fronts, in a variety of host locations, firms also need to better understand the ecosystem they operate in and be proactive in shaping it. For an MNE, this ecosystem includes home and host market institutional actors who will play a key role in the manner in which the effects of technological changes will unfold and who will most benefit from digitalization.

In order to address these challenges, we proposed that firms can implement *collaborative*, *additive*, and *open strategies* to adapt to more distributed and networked forms

Table 19.3 Strategic changes in the context of digitalization

Strategic changes in the context of digitalization	Future research agendas
Digitalization requires additive and collaborative strategies.	How can firms develop the capacity to act as aggregators? How can global or multinational firms develop the capability and knowledge to successfully coordinate, integrate, and align distinctive and potentially conflicting strategies while implementing additive and collaborative strategies?
Digitalization has given rise to platform businesses and other new business models.	How can platform businesses ensure smooth interactions among their users? Are there any "best practices" that strategy scholars can provide in terms of how platform companies can generate value? What defines competitive advantage of these platform business models from an international and/or global view and how is this different to what we already know about MNEs or conglomerates?
Digitalization and the new business models that it gives rise to are associated with geographically dispersed organizational structures and manufacturing systems.	What are the new kinds of organizational structures that are born out of necessity to respond to high dispersion? What unique strategic chances have materialized for organizations based in emerging markets due to expanding value chains? How can new technologies such as cloud computing and distributed work platforms shape global supply chains?
Digitalization brings with it an increased importance of ecosystem participation.	How can organizational leaders successfully orchestrate networks? What new forms of governance do organizations need to adopt in order to manage potential cross-border collaborations and partnerships? Is the success of an enterprise sustainable in the absence of the dominant firm that is at the heart of the network?
Digitalization is associated with changes, challenges, threats, and opportunities not only in competitive but also economic, technological, and social environments.	How can regulators, public institutions, and judicial bodies respond to the demands associated with these changes?
Digitalization brings about transformations in industry structures.	What role do digital technologies play in the transformation of traditional industries, emergence of new industries, or the convergence of the two? What do changes in industry structures imply for global start-ups and international ventures?

(Continued)

Table 19.3 Strategic changes in the context of digitalization (Continued)

Strategic changes in the context of digitalization	Future research agendas
Digitalization brings about non-linear change within organizations' institutional contexts that is difficult to plan for.	How can organizations undertake smooth transitions within and between different institutional and regulatory contexts?
Digitalization is associated with new and flexible production technologies that transcend beyond borders.	How can organizations build flexibilities associated with responses to changing political regulations or international treaties? How does digitalization influence national employment, domestic competition, or country-specific regulations regarding employment and production practices?
Digitalization is association with potential regulatory voids and loopholes from manufacturing to finance.	How can organizations cope with regulatory voids and loopholes? Does digitalization bring with it the need for new forms of national or regional regulations?

that involve a plethora of internal and external constituents. We suggested that firms can form alliances, investigate ways of complementing existing stakeholders in the environment such as their competitors, consumers, legislators, and regulators, as well as become more engaged in practices that enable inclusion of, and transparency toward, their internal and external stakeholders.

In addition, we invite future research to pay attention to a set of key strategic changes/challenges associated with digitalization, which we summarize in Table 19.3. This (non-exhaustive) list includes questions around how MNEs may be able to develop the capabilities and knowledge to successfully coordinate, integrate, and align distinctive and potentially conflicting strategies while implementing additive and collaborative strategies. This aligns with the ideas proposed in Chapter 21 on the pressure MNEs face to globally integrate their activities, while at the same time localizing their strategies and practices to the requirements of differing host markets. The ability to orchestrate external stakeholders and keep them satisfied is likely to provide MNEs with much needed regulatory and socio-political legitimacy. Regulators and other key institutional actors may respond differently to changes in digital technologies, which, in turn, will complicate MNEs' efforts to maintain institutional legitimacy in different host markets, and emphasize the benefits of adopting additive strategies upon market entry. Finally, and perhaps most importantly, future research should investigate the required changes in the organizational structure of MNEs for them to get the most out of their adoption of collaborative, additive, and open strategies to face the digital age.

References

Adner, R. 2017. Ecosystem as structure: an actionable construct for strategy. *Journal of Management*, 43(1): 39–58.

Adner, R., & Kapoor, R. 2010. Value creation in innovation ecosystems: How the structure of technological interdependence affects firm performance in new technology generations. *Strategic Management Journal*, 31(3): 306–333.

Adner, R., & Kapoor, R. 2016. Innovation ecosystems and the pace of substitution: Re-Examining technology S-curves. *Strategic Management Journal*, 37(4): 625–648.

Afuah, A. 2000. How much do your co-opetitors' capabilities matter in the face of technological change? *Strategic Management Journal*, 21(3): 397–404.

Alexy, O., West, J., Klapper, H., & Reitzig, M. 2018. Surrendering control to gain advantage: Reconciling openness and the resource-based view of the firm. *Strategic Management Journal*, 39(6), 1704–1727.

Almirall, E., Lee, M., & Majchrzak, A. 2014. Open innovation requires integrated competition-community ecosystems: Lessons learned from civic open innovation. *Business Horizons*, 57(3): 391–400.

Altman, E. J., & Tushman, M. L. 2017. Platforms, open/user innovation, and ecosystems: A strategic leadership perspective. In: J. Furman, A. Gawer, B. S. Silverman, & S. Stern (Eds.), *Entrepreneurship, Innovation, and Platforms*. London: Emerald Publishing.

Ansari, S., & Munir, K. 2008. How valuable is a piece of the spectrum? Determination of value in external resource acquisition. *Industrial and Corporate Change*, 17(2): 301–333.

Appleyard, M. M., & Chesbrough, H. W. 2017. The dynamics of open strategy: From adoption to reversion. *Long Range Planning*, 50(3): 310–321.

Baden-Fuller, C., & Haefliger, S. 2013. Business models and technological innovation. *Long Range Planning*, 46(6): 419–426.

Bakos, Y. 1998. The emerging role of electronic marketplaces on the internet. *Communications of the ACM*, 41(8): 35–42.

Baldwin, C. Y., & Clark, K. B. 2000. *Design Rules: The Power of Modularity (Vol. 1)*. Boston, MA: MIT press.

Baldwin, C. Y., & Woodard, C. J. 2009. The architecture of platforms: A unified view. In: A. Gawer (Ed.), *Platforms, Markets and Innovation*. London: Edward Elgar Publishing.

Baptista, J., Wilson, A. D., Galliers, R. D., & Bynghall, S. 2017. Social media and the emergence of reflexiveness as a new capability for open strategy. *Long Range Planning*, 50(3): 322–336.

Benkler, Y. 2007. *The Wealth of Networks: How Social Production Transforms Markets and Freedom*. New Haven, CT: Yale University Press.

Birkinshaw, J. 2017. Reflections on open strategy. *Long Range Planning*, 50(3): 423–426.

Bolwijn, R., Casella, B., & Zhan, J. 2018. International production and the digital economy. In: R. van Tulder, A. Verbeke, & L. Piscitello (Eds.), *International Business in the Information and Digital Age*. London: Emerald Publishing.

Boudreau, K. J., & Jeppesen, L. B. 2015. Unpaid crowd complementors: The platform network effect mirage. *Strategic Management Journal*, 36(12): 1761–1777.

Brouthers, K. D., Geisser, K. D., & Rothlauf, F. 2016. Explaining the internationalization of ibusiness firms. *Journal of International Business Studies*, 47(5): 513–534.

Brynjolfsson, E., Malone, T. W., Gurbaxani, V., & Kambil, A. 1994. Does information technology lead to smaller firms? *Management Science*, 40(12): 1628–1644.

Casadesus-Masanell, R., & Yoffie, D. B. 2007. Wintel: Cooperation and conflict. *Management Science*, 53(4): 584–598.

Cennamo, C., & Santalo, J. 2013. Platform competition: Strategic trade-offs in platform markets. *Strategic Management Journal*, 34(11): 1331–1350.

Chesbrough, H. 2003. The Era of Open Innovation. *MIT Sloan Management Review*, 44(3): 35–41.

Chesbrough, H., & Bogers, M. 2014. Explicating open innovation: Clarifying an emerging paradigm for understanding innovation. In: H. Chesbrough, W. Vanhaverbeke, & J. West (Eds.), *New Frontiers in Open Innovation*. Oxford: Oxford University Press.

Cowen, A. P., & Marcel, J. J. 2011. Damaged goods: Board decisions to dismiss reputationally compromised directors. *Academy of Management Journal*, 54(3): 509–527.

Dahlander, L., & Gann, D.M. 2010. How open is innovation? *Research Policy*, 39(6): 699–709.

Dobusch, L., & Müller-Seitz, G. 2015. Closing Open Strategy: Strategy as a Practice of Thousands in the Case of Wikimedia. Free University of Berlin working paper.

Dorobantu, S., Kaul, A., & Zelner, B. 2017. Nonmarket strategy research through the lens of new institutional economics: An integrative review and future directions. *Strategic Management Journal*, 38(1): 114–140.

Dutt, N., Hawn, O., Vidal, E., Chatterji, A., McGahan, A., & Mitchell, W. 2016. How open system intermediaries address institutional failures: The case of business incubators in emerging-market countries. *Academy of Management Journal*, 59(3): 818–840.

Eisenhardt, K. M., & Schoonhoven, C. B. 1996. Resource-based view of strategic alliance formation: Strategic and social effects in entrepreneurial firms. *Organization Science*, 7(2): 136–150.

Foss, N. J., & Pedersen, T. 2004. Organizing knowledge processes in the multinational corporation: an introduction. *Journal of International Business Studies*, 35(5): 340–349.

Gawer, A. 2009. Platform dynamics and strategies: from products to services. *Platforms, Markets and Innovation*, August: 45, 57.

Gawer, A. 2014. Bridging differing perspectives on technological platforms: Toward an integrative framework. *Research Policy*, 43(7): 1239–1249.

Gawer, A., & Cusumano, M. A. 2002. *Platform Leadership: How Intel, Microsoft and Cisco Drive Industry Innovation*. Boston, MA: Harvard Business Press.

Gawer, A., & Cusumano, M. A. 2008. How companies become platform leaders. *MIT Sloan Management Review*, 49(2): 28–35.

Gawer, A., & Cusumano, M. A. 2014. Industry platforms and ecosystem innovation. *Journal of Product Innovation Management*, 31(3): 417–433.

Gawer, A., & Henderson, R. 2007. Platform owner entry and innovation in complementary markets: Evidence from Intel. *Journal of Economics & Management Strategy*, 16(1): 1–34.

Gawer, A., & Phillips, N. 2013. Institutional work as logics shift: The case of Intel's transformation to platform leader. *Organization Studies*, 34(8): 1035–1071.

Gegenhuber, T., & Dobusch, L. 2017. Making an impression through openness: How open strategy-making practices change in the evolution of new ventures. *Long Range Planning*, 50(3): 337–354.

Gellman, R. 1996. Disintermediation and the internet. *Government Information Quarterly*, 13(1): 1–8.

Ghoshal, S., & Bartlett, C. A. 1990. The multinational corporation as an interorganizational network. *Academy of Management Review*, 15(4): 603–626.

Gomes-Casseres, B. 1996. *The Alliance Revolution: The New Shape of Business Rivalry*. Cambridge, MA: Harvard University Press.

Gulati, R. 1998. Alliances and networks. *Strategic Management Journal*, 19(4): 293–317.

Gurses, K., & Ozcan, P. 2015. Entrepreneurship in regulated markets: framing contests and collective action to introduce pay TV in the US. *Academy of Management Journal*, 58(6): 1709–1739.

Hannah, D. P., & Eisenhardt, K. M. 2018. How firms navigate cooperation and competition in nascent ecosystems. *Strategic Management Journal*, 39(12): 3163–3192.

Hautz, J., Seidl, D., & Whittington, R. 2017. Open strategy: Dimensions, dilemmas, dynamics. *Long Range Planning*, 50(3): 298–309.

Hazlehurst, C., & Brouthers, K. D. 2018. IB and strategy research on "new" information and communication technologies: Guidance for future research. In: R. Van Tulder, A, Verbeke & L. Piscitello (Eds.), *International business in the Information and Digital Age*. London: Emerald Publishing.

IBM, 2016. Redefining markets: Insights from the global C-Suite study—The CMO perspective. Available at: https://www.ibm.com/downloads/cas/P5MDVY0G. Accessed 20th June 2019.

Jacobides, M. G., & Winter, S. G. 2005. The co-evolution of capabilities and transaction costs: Explaining the institutional structure of production. *Strategic Management Journal*, 26(5): 395–413.

Katz, J., & Gartner, W. B. 1988. Properties of emerging organizations. *Academy of Management Review*, 13(3): 429–441.

Kenney, M., & Zysman, J. 2016. The rise of the platform economy. *Issues in Science and Technology*, 32(3): 61–69.

Kube, M., Hilgers, D., Koch, G., & Füller, J. 2015. Explaining voluntary citizen online participation using the concept of citizenship: an explanatory study on an open government platform. *Journal of Business Economics*, 85(8): 873–895.

Kulesz, O. 2017. *Culture in the Digital Environment*. Paris: UNESCO.

Lanzolla, G., Lorenz, A., Miron-Spektor, E., Schilling, M., Solinas, G., & Tucci, C. 2018. Digital transformation: What is new if anything? *Academy of Management Discoveries*, 4(3): 378–387.

Laplume, A. O., Petersen, B., & Pearce, J. M. 2016. Global value chains from a 3D printing perspective. *Journal of International Business Studies*, 47(5): 595–609.

Luedicke, M. K., Husemann, K. C., Furnari, S., & Ladstaetter, F. 2017. Radically open strategizing: How the premium cola collective takes open strategy to the extreme. *Long Range Planning*, 50(3): 371–384.

Mack, D. Z., & Szulanski, G. 2017. Opening up: how centralization affects participation and inclusion in strategy making. *Long Range Planning*, 50(3): 385–396.

Matzler, K., Füller, J., Koch, B., Hautz, J., & Hutter, K. 2014. Open strategy—A new strategy paradigm? In K. Matzler, H. Pechlaner, & B. Renzl (Eds.) *Strategie und Leadership*. Wiesbaden: Springer Gabler.

Mergel, I. 2015. Opening government: Designing open innovation processes to collaborate with external problem solvers. *Social Science Computer Review*, 33(5): 599–612.

Miner, A. S., Amburgey, T. L., & Stearns, T. M. 1990. Interorganizational linkages and population dynamics: Buffering and transformational shields. *Administrative Science Quarterly*, 35(4): 689–713.

Mowery, D. C. 2009. Plus ca change: Industrial R&D in the "third industrial revolution." *Industrial and Corporate Change*, 18(1): 1–50.

Müllner, J., & Filatotchev, I. 2018. The changing face of international business in the information age. In: R. van Tulder, A. Verbeke, & L. Piscitello (Eds.), *International Business in the Information and Digital Age*. London: Emerald Publishing.

Munger, M. C. 2015. *Public Choice Economics*. London: Elsevier.

Nambisan, S. 2017. Digital entrepreneurship: Toward a digital technology perspective of entrepreneurship. *Entrepreneurship Theory and Practice*, 41(6): 1029–1055.

Ohlson, T., & Yakis-Douglas, B. 2019. Practices of transparency in open strategy: Beyond the dichotomy of voluntary and mandatory disclosure. In D. Seidl, R. Whittington, & G. von Krogh (Eds.), *Cambridge Handbook of Open Strategy*. Cambridge: Cambridge University Press.

Ohmae, K. 1989. The global logic of strategic alliances. *Harvard Business Review*, 67(2): 143–154.

Ozcan, P., & Eisenhardt, K. M. 2009. Origin of alliance portfolios: Entrepreneurs, network strategies, and firm performance. *Academy of Management Journal*, 52(2): 246–279.

Ozcan, P., Gurses, K., & Mohlmann, M. 2020. Category kings and commoners: Within and cross-category spill-overs in the sharing economy. In I. Maurer, J. Mair, & A. Oberg (Eds.), *Theorizing the Sharing Economy: Variety and Trajectories of New Forms of* Organizing (Research in the Sociology of Organization, Vol. 66), London: Emerald Publishing.

Ozcan, P., & Santos, F. M. 2015. The market that never was: Turf wars and failed alliances in mobile payments. *Strategic Management Journal*, 36(10): 1486–1512.

Ozcan, P., Zachariadis, M., & Dinckol, D. 2020. "Platformication" of Banking: Strategy and challenges of challenger versus incumbent banks in response to regulatory change in the UK, Academy of Management Annual Meeting Proceedings. Available at: https://doi.org/10.5465/AMBPP.2019.17147abstract.

Parker, G., & Van Alstyne, M. W. 2005. Two-sided network effects: A theory of information product design. *Management Science*, 51(10): 1494–1504.

Parker, G., Van Alstyne, M. W., & Jiang, X. 2016. Platform ecosystems: How developers invert the firm. *Boston University Questrom School of Business Research Paper*, 2861574.

Pierce, L. 2009. Big losses in ecosystem niches: How core firm decisions drive complementary product shakeouts. *Strategic Management Journal*, 30(3): 323–347.

Plesner, U., & Gulbrandsen, I. T. 2015. Strategy and new media: A research agenda. *Strategic Organization*, 13(2), 153–162.

Porter, M. E. 1985. Technology and competitive advantage. *Journal of Business Strategy*, 5(3): 60–78.

Powell, W. W., White, D. R., Koput, K. W., & Owen-Smith, J. 2005. Network dynamics and field evolution: The growth of interorganizational collaboration in the life sciences. *American Journal of Sociology*, 110(4): 1132–1205.

Randhawa, K., Wilden, R., & Hohberger, J. 2016. A bibliometric review of open innovation: Setting a research agenda. *Journal of Product Innovation Management*, 33(6): 750–772.

Riedl, C., & Woolley, A. W. 2017. Teams vs. crowds: A field test of the relative contribution of incentives, member ability, and emergent collaboration to crowd-based problem solving performance. *Academy of Management Discoveries*, 3(4): 382–403.

Rochet, J. C., & Tirole, J. 2003. Platform competition in two-sided markets. *Journal of the European Economic Association*, 1(4): 990–1029.

Rochet, J. C., & Tirole, J. 2006. Two-sided markets: a progress report. *The RAND Journal of Economics*, 37(3): 645–667.

Schwab, K. 2017. *The Fourth Industrial Revolution*. London: Portfolio.

Shipilov, A. V., Greve, H. R., & Rowley, T. J. 2010. When do interlocks matter? Institutional logics and the diffusion of multiple corporate governance practices. *Academy of Management Journal*, 53(4): 846–864.

Sia, S. K., Soh, C., & Weill, P. 2016. How DBS bank pursued a digital business strategy. *MIS Quarterly Executive*, 15(2).

Strange, R., & Zucchella, A. 2017. Industry 4.0, global value chains and international business. *Multinational Business Review*, 25(3): 174–184.

Stieger, D., Matzler, K., Chatterjee, S., & Ladstaetter-Fussenegger, F. 2012. Democratizing strategy: How crowdsourcing can be used for strategy dialogues. *California Management Review*, 54(4), 44–68.

Tackx, K., & Verdin, P. 2014. Can co-creation lead to better strategy? An exploratory research. *CEB Working Paper*, 14/027.

Tee, R & Ozcan, P. 2020. Too early to separate? Collaborative ventures & product module boundaries in nascent markets. Manuscript under review.

Teece, D. J. 2018. Business models and dynamic capabilities. *Long Range Planning*, 51(1): 40–49.

Thomas, L. D., Autio, E., & Gann, D. M. 2014. Architectural leverage: putting platforms in context. *Academy of Management Perspectives*, 28(2): 198–219.

Tihanyi, L., Graffin, S., & George, G. 2014. Rethinking governance in management research. *Academy of Management Journal*, 57(6): 1535–1543.

UNCTAD. 2018. *World Investment Report: Investment and New Industrial Policies*. Geneva: United Nations.

Uzunca, B., Rigtering, J. C., & Ozcan, P. 2018. Sharing and shaping: A cross-country comparison of how sharing economy firms shape their institutional environment to gain legitimacy. *Academy of Management Discoveries*, 4(3): 248–272.

Van de Ven, A. H., & Polley, D. 1992. Learning while innovating. *Organization Science*, 3(1): 92–116.

Van Tulder, R., Verbeke, A., & Piscitello, L. 2018. Introduction: A challenging agenda. In: R. van Tulder, A. Verbeke, & L. Piscitello (Eds.), *International Business in the Information and Digital Age*. London: Emerald Publishing.

Whittington, R. 2019. *Opening Strategy: Professional Strategists and Practice Change, 1960 to Today*. Oxford: Oxford University Press.

Whittington, R., Cailluet, L., & Yakis-Douglas, B. 2011. Opening strategy: Evolution of a precarious profession. *British Journal of Management*, 22(3): 531–544.

Whittington, R., Yakis-Douglas, B., & Ahn, K. 2016. Cheap talk? Strategy presentations as a form of chief executive officer impression management. *Strategic Management Journal*, 37(12): 2413–2424.

Yakis-Douglas, B., Angwin, D., Ahn, K., & Meadows, M. 2017. Opening M&A strategy to investors: predictors and outcomes of transparency during organisational transition. *Long Range Planning*, 50(3): 411–422.

Yoffie, D. B., & Kwak, M. 2006. With friends like these: The art of managing complementors. *Harvard Business Review*, 84(9): 88–98.

Yoo, Y., Boland Jr, R. J., Lyytinen, K., & Majchrzak, A. 2012. Organizing for innovation in the digitized world. *Organization Science*, 23(5): 1398–1408.

Zachariadis, M. & P. Ozcan, 2017. *The API Economy and Digital Transformation in Financial Services: The Case of Open Banking*. SWIFT Institute Working Paper No. 2016-001.

Zander, I. 2002. The formation of international innovation networks in the multinational corporation: an evolutionary perspective. *Industrial and Corporate Change*, 11(2): 327–353.

Zhang, Y., & Wiersema, M. F. 2009. Stock market reaction to CEO certification: The signalling role of CEO background. *Strategic Management Journal*, 30(7): 693–710.

Zhu, F., & Iansiti, M. 2012. Entry into platform-based markets. *Strategic Management Journal*, 33(1): 88–106.

Zittrain, J. L. 2006. The generative internet. *Harvard Law Review*, 119(7): 1974–2040.

CHAPTER 20

....

CORPORATE SOCIAL RESPONSIBILITY, IRRESPONSIBILITY, AND THE MULTINATIONAL ENTERPRISE ENVIRONMENT

....

GIULIO NARDELLA AND STEPHEN BRAMMER

INTRODUCTION

....

SCHOLARS have studied the social responsibilities of businesses for many decades. In recent years, the discussion has become widespread as organizations face mounting pressure to attend to ever more profound social and environmental challenges, such as poverty, inequality, and climate change. This has led to scholars calling for more research on what is referred to as "grand challenges," that is, the different phenomena affecting societies all over the world, and implicitly, affecting the manner in which businesses conduct their operations, orchestrate their value chains, and adapt their products and services in order to develop effective competitive strategies (Wettstein, Giuliani, Santangelo, & Stahl, 2019). Accordingly, international business (IB) strategy research has begun to address matters of social responsibility and irresponsibility, primarily by conceptualizing the role of corporate social responsibility (CSR) (and to some extent, corporate social irresponsibility, or CSI) within the "non-market" strategies of multinational enterprises (MNEs) (e.g. Buckley, Doh, & Benischke, 2017: Doh, McGuire, & Ozaki, 2015; Mellahi, Frynas, Sun, & Siegel, 2016). Given their interest on the MNE and its performance across different international markets, IB strategy scholars have largely focused on the "social, political, legal and cultural arrangements that constrain or facilitate firm activity" (see Doh, Lawton, & Rajwani, 2012).

Overall, we find that the CSR/CSI agenda in IB strategy research remains focused on the influence of the environment on MNE strategy, thus providing limited explanation of the influence of MNE strategy on the broader social and ecological environment. In order to make progress in this area, we should start with some clearer definitions regarding the core constructs of CSR and CSI, and what they mean in the context of the MNE. This is important because "grand challenges" tend to be global phenomena; here, the traditional, large, and resource rich MNE, with its influence on global political and economic agendas, may play a significant part in addressing some of these challenges. Thus, our understanding would benefit from a more nuanced exploration of the MNE's impact on its environment.[1] We argue that it is critical to understand the impact of the MNE on its broader environment because the actual (or perceived) social and environmental harm caused by MNEs may expose them to considerable risks in international markets (Wang & Li, 2019) and may contribute to hostile non-market conditions, which could inhibit their strategic objectives.

To facilitate the development of a social responsibility agenda in IB strategy research, this chapter sets out to explore and clarify the concept of CSR by juxtaposing the related (yet often overlooked) literature on CSI. We start with a discussion of the CSR concept, enriched with insights regarding CSI because understanding the impact of the MNE on its environment requires a more nuanced and holistic consideration of both how the firm can "do good" while also "doing no harm" (Crilly, Ni, & Jiang, 2016). The chapter then goes on to develop an agenda for future research that reflects upon the roles played by location and institutions—both social and state—in shaping the formation, character, and management of MNE social (ir)responsibility. By discussing the challenges distinct to the MNE that have arisen from their disproportionate resourcefulness, mobility, and institutional complexity, our hope is that this chapter will form the basis of discussion, and stimulate debate, on the importance and increased relevance of CSR and CSI in the study of IB strategy.

CONCEPTUAL OVERVIEW OF CSR AND CSI

As stated earlier, in this chapter, we hope to convince the reader that the relationship between the MNE and corporate (ir)responsibility is important to understand. In order to build a foundation for our discussion concerning the relationship between CSR/CSI

---

[1] Since the term "grand challenges" has been used to understand a variety of societal and ecological problems, we do not focus specifically on one aspect of social responsibility/irresponsibility, but rather we explore the different definitions and meanings of these concepts with practical implications and examples. Chapter 22 furthers this argument by focusing specifically on key environmental challenges and MNE sustainability strategies.

and MNE strategic choices, we provide a review of the key CSR and CSI literatures, paying particular attention to the core lenses used to examine them.

CSR

CSR is a complex concept, and engagement in social responsibility may mean different things to different firms. As such, there are different "types" of CSR that are also reflected in highly cited definitions. In this way, CSR may broadly encompass the "actions that appear to further some social good, beyond the interests of the firm and that which is required by law" (McWilliams & Siegel, 2001). The EU Commission (2001) echoes this idea by articulating that CSR is "a concept whereby companies integrate social and environmental concerns in their business operations and in their interactions with their stakeholders on a voluntary basis." Other conceptualizations of CSR articulate motivations to engage in pro-social behavior. For example, the "enlightened shareholder value" approach (Jensen, 2001) suggests that CSR is important because "in order to maximize value, corporate managers must not only satisfy, but enlist the support of all corporate stakeholders." The differences in CSR definitions are relevant because they reflect that firms (including MNEs) differ in their commitment to CSR, as well as in their motivations concerning when and how to engage in socially responsible activities.

We summarize and categorize the main themes in the CSR literature in order to understand how CSR activities may be viewed by organizations (see Dahlsrud, 2008 for a full overview of the considerable landscape of CSR definitions). These themes are:

(1) CSR as arising from existential motivations (the *values-based perspectives*, which typically view CSR as being "the right thing to do");
(2) CSR as being concerned with responding to social and environmental pressures (the *institutional perspectives*, which consider CSR as "the expected thing to do"); and
(3) CSR as relating primarily to the self-interests of the firm (the *instrumental* or *economic perspective*, which consider CSR to be "the profitable thing to do") (see also Aguinis & Glavas, 2012).

As illustrated in Figure 20.1, perspectives on CSR can be represented on a conceptual spectrum between the values-based perspectives and instrumental or economic perspectives on CSR, with institutional perspectives sitting somewhere in the middle. We will discuss each of the three main perspectives from which to view social responsibility.

From a *values-based* perspective, there are virtuous reasons why organizations would engage in CSR. Some organizations espouse a deep concern for social and environmental issues. This is seen most strongly in organizations that take a particular stance on a matter of social contention, such as animal cruelty (e.g. The Body Shop), environmental sustainability (e.g. Unilever), or worker rights (e.g. Starbucks). From a values-based

| Values-based perspective | Institutional perspective | Instrumental perspective |

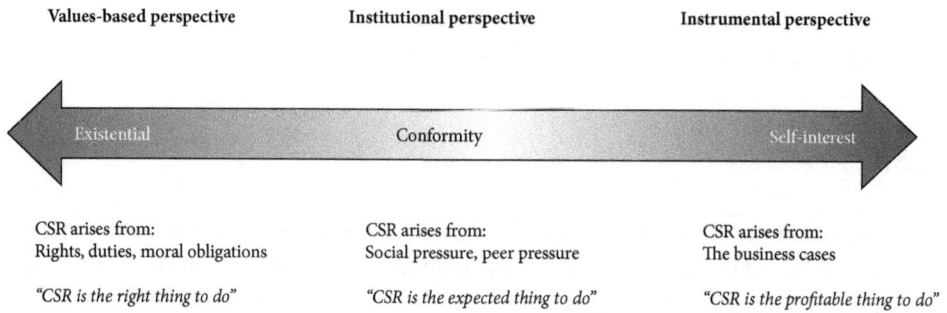

Existential   Conformity   Self-interest

CSR arises from: CSR arises from: CSR arises from:
Rights, duties, moral obligations   Social pressure, peer pressure   The business cases

"CSR is the right thing to do"   *"CSR is the expected thing to do"*   *"CSR is the profitable thing to do"*

FIGURE 20.1 The conceptual landscape of CSR

approach, MNEs are viewed as having moral obligations to engage in activities that positively impact society and the broader ecological environment. Because corporations are increasingly treated as citizens by law, with legal freedoms that are equivalent to or even exceed individuals' rights, such as those associated with limited liability law (Mintzberg, 2014), corporations have entered into an implicit social contract with society, which holds that corporations should contribute toward advancing social goals in return for extracting value from society's human, financial, and natural resources (see Donaldson & Dunfee, 1994). This is particularly the case for MNEs, as they have access to such resources in a variety of host international markets. Thus, the social contract between business and society mutually recognizes that without society's resources and continued support, the corporation would not have the tools to organize nor the social license to operate in the market (Buhmann, 2016). Breaches of this social contract are evident in cases of CSI, such as the privacy scandal at Facebook, the "Dieselgate" scandal at Volkswagen, or, indeed, the banking sector following the global financial crisis in 2008.

Another broad theme within the CSR literature emphasizes that organizations exist in an environment that is also made up of peers, competitors, and other stakeholder organizations that collectively produce norms around what constitutes legitimate and "expected" behavior. The *institutional* perspective underscores the importance of the environment, also referred to as a "field," and which is often defined by the type and size of the business in question (DiMaggio & Powell, 1983). Depending on the nature of the business, expectations are generated about what constitutes "normal" and acceptable or unacceptable business practice: this may refer to how much certain types of firms should financially compensate their employees, provide support to local communities, or impact the ecological environment. Depending on the size, type, and location of the firm (Ioannou & Serafeim, 2012), such social norms are subject to alteration. For example, norms around working conditions typically vary by location and are most evident when contrasting those of developed and non-developed countries. Therefore, social norms regarding CSR are context dependent. Prior expectations set the boundaries of acceptability for firm behavior.

Finally, a third theme within CSR research recognizes that the responsible treatment of stakeholders is important insofar as their support—or lack thereof—shapes an organization's success. *Instrumental* perspectives of CSR represent the most commonly applied view of the firm–society relationship (Brammer & Millington, 2008; McGuire, Sundgren, & Schneeweis, 1988; Young & Makhija, 2014). Proponents of this view present firms as being embedded in a wider social environment that consists of stakeholders with which companies have relationships. In this way, firms should develop good stakeholder relations in order to further organizational ends. Yet stakeholder groups yield varying degrees of *power, legitimacy,* and *urgency* over the organization (Mitchell, Agle, & Wood, 1997). Following an instrumental perspective on CSR, stakeholders yielding the most influence, most legitimately, and most frequently are considered imperative to the firm and should be managed most diligently. Depending on the location of the firm's operations, cultivating strong relationships with host governments may be critical to organizational success. As such, strong relationships with government may be relatively more critical in China than it is to develop the same strength of relationships in Italy.

CSI

We previously described that businesses are considered to have responsibilities and expected to act in ways that are deemed socially responsible. Implicit in these perspectives is that businesses also have responsibilities to *not* behave in ways that are socially irresponsible (Spiess, Mueller, & Lin-Hi, 2013). Thus, any considered understanding of the social responsibilities of business should also reflect the organization's capacity to do harm (Strike, Gao, & Bansal, 2006). Yet, this more balanced view of organizations, we argue, is seldom achieved. In this section, we explain that, in order to more accurately reflect the social responsibility of MNEs, we need to also understand the concept of CSI.

Though the genealogy of the CSR construct can be traced back to the 1950s (see Carroll, 1999), the study of corporate wrongdoing (Clews, 1906), misconduct (Hart & Prichard, 1939), scandals (Willis, 1934), and crime (Marx, 1859) significantly predates the study of CSR. Accordingly, a slew of related terminology has been developed to describe irresponsible conduct, yet the CSI concept itself is fairly nascent (Nardella, Brammer, & Surdu, 2020). Some early research broadly defines CSI as "unethical and morally distasteful behaviour" (Ferry, 1962) which may result in "a gain by one party at the expense of the total system" (Armstrong, 1977). However, CSI, like CSR, is considered morally ambiguous (Bitektine, 2011), and thus open to multiple conceptual definitions and interpretations.

Perceptions of what constitutes CSI may therefore be subject to interpretation. The motivations and proclivities of stakeholders may color their perceptions of corporate conduct, such as the degree to which the individual perceives irresponsible conduct and the harm caused as being severe or morally objectionable (Lange & Washburn, 2012). Individual perceptions of irresponsible conduct may be bounded by the norms and values associated with a given location where an MNE subsidiary conducts its operations. Other types of harm caused by CSI may transcend individual interpretation. Social norms or "hyper-norms" are a small set of "standards to which all societies can be held-negative injunctions" (Walzer, 1994). Events that are associated with the loss of human life are typically considered to transcend individual or cultural norms (Donaldson & Dunfee, 1999), thus influencing perceptions of MNE stakeholders as a whole. The Rana Plaza and Bhopal disasters are examples of circumstances where collective societal agreement of CSI can place significant stakeholder scrutiny on the MNE accused both in its home and host markets. While most instances of CSI are open to interpretive differences between stakeholders, in order to draw specific boundary conditions between right and wrong, as well as the severity of transgressions committed by organizations, legal perspectives on CSI assume that there is an objective basis for CSI so that any breach of extant legal statute or actions deemed to require alteration to the law can act to regulate and police CSI.

Yet, as mentioned earlier, the CSI literature is still nascent. In order to enrich our understanding of why certain MNEs engage in socially irresponsible behavior, we outline three core perspectives. To enable comparison, we label each perspective in line with our previous discussion of the CSR literature. The *values-based perspective* proposes that CSR and CSI are diametrically opposed. In this view, CSI is the nihilistic rejection of CSR's existential, moral foundations. Through this lens, MNEs are described as "psychopathic" (Bakan, 2005) and "depraved" (Chomsky, 2005) because they "pathologically" extract value from economic, social, and natural systems at the expense of the functional integrity of those systems. Furthermore, the values perspective argues that corporations are, in fact, adversarial to stakeholder interests (Heath, 2007), and more so, when possible, that they become proactive in obstructing progressive measures to develop regulation that protects stakeholder interests (Lessig, 2011). Critical perspectives assume broadly that CSI "does not matter" to the MNE, the perception of which may result in significant future challenges to market and non-market strategies, such as the breakdown of stakeholder–firm trust relations that may manifest in damage to MNE reputation advantages (Wang & Li, 2019). In this view, CSI becomes "something corporations are."

A second perspective emphasizes specifically the institutional context that MNEs inhabit. MNEs and their subsidiaries are driven to engage in irresponsible conduct as a result of attempts to conform with corrupt political customs and unethical industry norms (Spencer & Gomez, 2011). Thus, CSI may be necessary in order to effectively operate and succeed within certain market contexts (Brammer, Pavelin, & Porter, 2009). For example, operating in specific countries of concern such as Nigeria, India, and China may require activities that are considered morally or legally conflicting when compared to home market norms (e.g. Google's censorship in China). From an MNE perspective, failure to develop effective non-market strategies may translate into increased institutional risk (Liedong, Rajwani, & Mellahi, 2017). For instance, MNEs need to conform with questionable business practices in order to successfully compete in the fossil fuels, finance, or insurance industries because a lack of conformity with implicit industry norms places organizations at a competitive disadvantage. In this sense, CSI is understood as something organizations have to do in order to compete because CSI is "what everyone else does."

Values-based perspective	Institutional perspective	Instrumental perspective

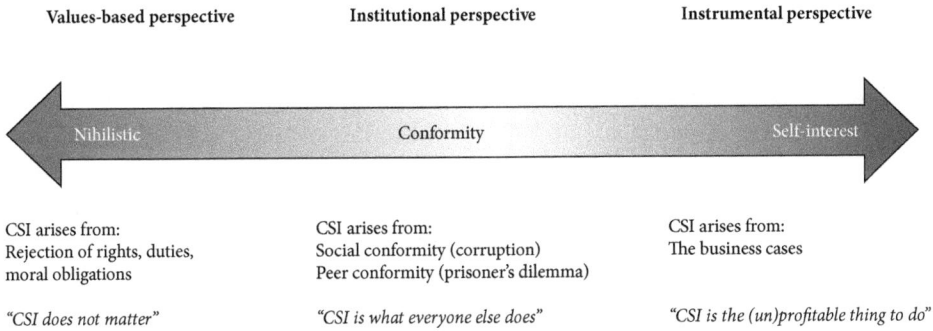

Nihilistic	Conformity	Self-interest

CSI arises from:	CSI arises from:	CSI arises from:
Rejection of rights, duties, moral obligations	Social conformity (corruption) Peer conformity (prisoner's dilemma)	The business cases
"CSI does not matter"	*"CSI is what everyone else does"*	*"CSI is the (un)profitable thing to do"*

FIGURE 20.2 The conceptual landscape of CSI

A third perspective views CSI through an economic lens. Instrumental viewpoints of CSI suggest that organizations primarily pursue their self-interests (Devinney, 2009). CSI therefore arises from the business case. Firms are motivated to engage in CSI because irresponsible activities represent a gain for the organization and its share-holders, potentially to the expense of other organizational stakeholders (Armstrong, 1977). However, it should be mentioned here that research from this perspective has focused on the risks and associated costs of CSI to the financial and operational stability of the firm (Alexander, 1999; Karpoff & Lott Jr., 1993) rather than the value extracting benefits of engaging in CSI. We attribute this bias to the relative difficulty in gaining access to data on irresponsible conduct. This is particularly the case for CSI data that has not entered into the public domain, where lack of stakeholder awareness serves as an important precondition to maximize the benefits and reduce the associated costs of CSI behavior. Overall, the instrumental perspective generally views CSI as a "(un)profitable thing to do," in that a considerable motivation to act irresponsibly is to advance the organization's self-interests. Yet, it may also carry substantial risks when revealed.

Reflecting on these core perspectives, a conceptual spectrum is presented in Figure 20.2 concerning the values-based, institutional, and instrumental approaches to CSI.

Themes in CSR/CSI: What we know and what we do not know about MNE Behavior

In this section, we outline some of the key themes that sit at the intersection between the CSR, CSI, and MNE literatures. These include the antecedents, moderators, and out-comes of responsible and irresponsible MNE behavior as well as decisions related to supply chains, the role of corruption, and the importance of managing stakeholder perceptions. In doing so, we are able to highlight important areas for future research that leave the relationship between CSR, CSI, and MNE strategy strategy incomplete.

Antecedents of CSR/CSI

The broad geographical diversification of the MNE may often enable it to seek out those locations with the lowest social standards, expectations, and norms. The degree of state power and the extent to which the state is involved in the economy may have distinct outcomes on the institutions that are responsible for capital allocation, education, labor systems, human rights, and environmental security (Buysse & Verbeke, 2003). By virtue of their size, MNEs may be permitted to avoid local regulations in some contexts, leading to a "race to the bottom" that brings about poor environmental and social outcomes (Mosley & Uno, 2007). So far, we have witnessed several globally significant instances of corporate irresponsibility connected with the capability of the MNE to leverage their size and influence with negative consequences to local communities. The Union Carbide disaster in Bhopal (India) is principally among those examples that represent a historical reminder of the inherent risks associated with MNE irresponsibility. At the same time, institutional voids also represent an opportunity for the MNE to have an influence on the betterment of social and environmental standards. One view is that coordinated market economies leave little space for firms to engage with social issues explicitly and visibly. While in contrast, the plentiful space in most liberal market economics allow firms in those contexts to make more explicit commitments to resolving social and environmental issues (see Walker, Zhang, & Ni, 2018). Overall, we find that extant research has yet to fully explicate the contextual circumstances that may motivate particular patterns of CSR and CSI behaviors, respectively.

We know that MNEs invest in foreign markets as part of resource-seeking as well as cost reduction strategies. In this way, MNEs may enter particular host countries because they offer advantages that would otherwise not be accessible in their home country environment. However, increasingly, countries previously presenting opportunities for MNEs to gain cost advantages (e.g. low-cost labor in China) are now also characterized by institutional development, placing added pressure on MNEs to make greater investments in CSR. This pattern may motivate MNEs focused on cost reduction, to move to other locations that have yet to (potentially) benefit from these socio-economic developments. Despite changes in MNE location patterns, our understanding of how market entry motivations will influence socially responsible MNE behavior in different host country locations, remains underdeveloped.

Several approaches have emerged regarding how MNEs adapt their practices abroad (Arthaud-Day, 2005). The predominant strategies to CSR embrace the local or *multi-domestic approach*, whereby firms adapt their CSR strategy to the conditions of the host country; and the *global approach*, whereby a consistent set of centralized CSR policies are implemented across international markets (Arthaud-Day, 2005). Multi-domestic approaches to CSR recognize that "no single, comprehensive, and universally applicable definition of [CSR] is possible" (see Epstein, 1989). In this way, MNEs are expected to adapt their social strategy to the host country context they find themselves in. Alternatively, a globalized approach toward CSR policy may be driven by a "universal or transcultural standard of corporate ethical behavior" (Frederick, 1991). In this way, strong MNE values may be expected to drive consistent behaviors in the different international markets entered. This means that, on the one hand, stakeholder and institutional diversity represent a risk to the MNE because non-conformity to institutional pressure may be penalized. On the other, conforming to the diverse moral, normative and legal contexts of host markets represent an increasing demand on the MNE's resources. What we propose as an important gap in our understanding is when and how MNEs recognize the need to adapt their CSR strategies versus deciding to mainly take advantage of host country institutional voids.

Moderators of CSR/CSI

In different international contexts, the firms' commitment to CSR may change (Gnyawali, 1996). This is the case irrespective of whether the motivations of MNEs are resource-seeking or market-seeking. In terms of the role that MNEs are capable of assuming, there are key differences in the scope for CSR between liberal market economies—that tend to be characterized by high levels of stock market capitalization, low levels of employment protection (flexible labor markets), a shareholder model of governance, and smaller government roles—and coordinated market economies, which in contrast, tend to be characterized by lower levels of stock market capitalization, a greater role for banks, greater employment protection, stronger unions and employee associations, stakeholder model of governance, and a dominant role of the government. Conformity with the moral, normative, and legal precedents of different institutional contexts can place considerable tensions between the established ethical orientation of the firm—which has been developed and informed by the conditions of its home (often developed) market—and those that are required to successfully operate in foreign markets. For example, Anglo-American MNEs have historically experienced challenges when operating in African host countries where bribery has long become an established political norm, and thus an expected type of non-market strategy. Moreover, the resource-seeking activities of an MNE may make it virtually inescapable to avoid engaging with corrupt institutions or institutions with divergent human rights practices, as has historically been the case with the extractive industries (O'Higgins, 2006). Similarly, market-seeking activities may also call into question the values of the firm, as has been and continues to be the case with Google's content censorship in China, which, in turn, influences the company's strategic choices such as their planned re-entry into the market.

MNEs operate in other types of contexts, which are not related to institutional environments, and thus less bounded by regulatory and legal pressures. Social or environmental activities not legislated or regulated then become referred to as business and industry self-regulation. Artifacts of business self-regulation range from mission statements and strategies, to operational plans and policies. Self-regulation may reflect how the firm, or groups of firms, establish standards of behavior, potentially as a means to exceed legal standards that may be considered too relaxed as per the MNE's home country standards. CSR, after all, encompasses voluntary behavior. Codes of conduct, business principles, or codes of ethics seek a concrete expression of the standards a company holds itself to (Baron, 1996). In theory, by documenting the MNE's principles and standards, these codes of conduct should act to moderate organizational behavior in different international markets by operating as a "yard-stick" by which to measure subsidiary performance against self-legislative criteria. More so, the criteria by which the MNE's actions are compared are also influenced and (potentially) scrutinized by its stakeholders. In order to pre-empt, and possibly avoid, legislative or regulatory solutions to problems felt by its stakeholders and promote a reputation or self-image as a socially responsible organization, codes of conduct may be expected to be deployed throughout the MNE, its subsidiaries, and its supply chains. Therefore, codes of conduct should serve to create an ethical corporate culture; although in practice, in the absence of regulation, MNEs have been associated with acting against their codes of conduct (Dunfee, 1996). We propose that artifacts of self-regulation represent a potential moderator of MNE and subsidiary behavior that has yet to be fully explored from an international strategy perspective.

In addition, MNE contexts change. Considerable socio-technological changes have occurred over the past decade, which means that MNE behavior is more widely observable and, potentially, objectionable than ever before (Wang, Reger, & Pfarrer, 2019). In other words, responsible as well as irresponsible MNE behavior displayed in a given host market may become familiar to stakeholders in the home market as well as other host locations in which the MNE operates. Resultantly, the management of diverging moral, normative, and legal precedent from the home country environment of MNEs presents ever increasing risk. CSR is often framed as a vehicle by which the firm attends to the social, economic, and environmental issues felt by various stakeholders in the host country context. By seeking to minimize the reputational risks associated with operating in markets that expose the firm to stakeholder criticality (Maggioni, Santangelo, & Koymen-Ozer, 2019), social performance is increasingly viewed as a priority for MNE managers (Alamgir & Banerjee, 2019; Maggioni et al., 2019; Porter & Kramer, 2006). By applying enhanced labor standards, fairer trade, and better environmental conditions than those typically experienced in host countries, MNEs are understood to balance the rewards of resource and market-seeking against the downside risks of reputation penalties (Wettstein et al., 2019). However, conceptually speaking, the lines of responsibility have become increasingly blurred between legal, ethical, governance, and policy frameworks (Mayer, 2009). This is, in part, due to the voluntary nature of CSR, as characterized by frameworks such as the UN Global Compact or ISO 26000 CSR standard. Here also, research has yet to unpack how management and stakeholder perceptions influence the CSR and CSI behaviors of the MNE, in an era of increased technological and social interconnectedness.

Outcomes of CSR/CSI

With over thirty years of encouragement to consider their broader social responsibilities, have MNEs been socially beneficial? Every year, the number of people regarded by the UN as being in abject poverty is lessening by 200,000 people (see Pinker, 2018).

Economic development has been understood to involve economic growth, increases in per capita income, and the possible attainment of a standard of living equivalent to that of industrialized countries. In this way, economic development becomes linked to social and technological progress typically indicated by improvements in literacy rates, life expectancy, and poverty rates. On all measures, globally, the picture looks rather positive (Pinker, 2018).

Since many of the world's largest economic entities are MNEs (Giuliani, 2018), there is the possibility for MNEs to make a further significant contribution, considering their role as employers, investors, and influencers in government policy development (Wettstein et al., 2019). MNEs occupy positions of considerable power in the global value chain, through which they can attempt to influence the practices and strategies within their industries. Practices such as responsible supply chain management is one example of CSR practices increasingly becoming more deeply embedded in MNE strategizing (Hoejmose, Brammer, & Millington, 2012). MNEs, on average, pay better than local companies in the developing world, offer improved and important employment opportunities to vulnerable workers, and represent an ever-growing role in the development of foreign countries (Giuliani & Macchi, 2014; Lipsey & Sjöholm, 2004; Mosley & Uno, 2007). Resultantly, from a policymaker's perspective, foreign direct investment activities of MNEs are mostly beneficial to the development of host countries.

However, the positive results of MNE behavior on social, environmental, and ethical outcomes may be largely overshadowed by public rhetoric, which claims the opposite. We believe that this imbalance may be fueling anti-globalization movements (Meyer, 2017), presenting opportunities for IB scholars to illustrate the effect of the MNE on the social and economic environments of different host markets. While studies tend to focus on economic development, it is questionable whether extant economic development research remains relevant (Narula & Pineli, 2019), particularly when considering the capacity of the MNE and local governments to use legal yet socially illegitimate methodologies such as tax havens to shift capital to offshore locations at the expense of fiscal redistribution and subsequent economic development (Jones & Temouri, 2016; Shaxson, 2007).

For MNEs, resolving global social issues may not always be compatible with the pursuit of strategic and economic objectives. In this way, the idea that businesses should chiefly concern themselves with "win–wins" for both themselves and society at large (Porter & Kramer, 2006) may be difficult to implement in practice. For instance, research on the "resource curse" suggests that, paradoxically, countries and regions with an abundance of non-renewable resources like minerals and fuels tend to have less economic growth and worse development outcomes than countries with fewer natural resources (Mehlum, Moene, & Torvik, 2006). The financial benefits associated with, often relatively short-term, resource exploitation by MNEs are seldom invested back into projects that deliver "real development" or increased gross domestic product (GDP). Often, the exploitation of natural resources leads to environmental problems that undermine a country/region's ability to sustain itself post-exploitation. Since most CSR may be instrumentally motivated by corporate interests, the likelihood that these coincide with developmental needs is contentious (Buckley, 2018; Mayer, 2018). We propose that research regarding the economic benefits of CSI is truly needed in order to build policies that better safeguard society and societal resources from socially irresponsible behavior.

Supply Chains

In strategic management, the prevailing wisdom holds that firms should primarily focus on their core businesses in order to develop effective products and services (Eisenhardt, 2002). This has led US MNEs such as Nike and Apple to famously outsource 100 percent of their manufacturing through global supply chains.[2] Conceptually speaking, the lines between one organization's responsibility and another organization's roles within the supply chain have become increasingly blurred. Lead-buy organizations (which are often MNEs) have introduced the prospect of "gaming" their responsibilities by outsourcing those areas of the business that are most closely or directly related with social and environmental risks. Pragmatically, the managerial problems associated with governing supplier relationships are increasingly complex because sensibly coordinating global supply chains involves close collaboration with the lead-buy organization. This has led to the development of supplier criteria that meet industry requirement standards, monitoring standards, and performance appraisal; these measures are designed to decrease the likelihood that problems arise, as well as introduce a process by which problems are identified and resolved, should they arise in the supply chain.

Even with these changes in monitoring global supply chains, research consistently recognizes a gap between policy and practice with regards to responsible supply chain management (see Bowen, Cousins, Lamming, & Faruk, 2002; Boström et al., 2015). This disparity may reflect the difficulties encountered by MNEs in implementing solutions to social problems, or it could represent "window dressing" (i.e. CSR used as a tool to enhance corporate image, but rarely embedded in organizational practices) rather than deeply embedded responses to social and environmental challenges. Broadly speaking, self-regulation has resulted in a range of approaches to supply chain management, with varying capacity to exhibit a real concern for those stakeholders most vulnerable to exploitative practices (Soundararajan & Brown, 2016). Nevertheless, research on the relationship between supply chain management and MNE CSR/CSI reveals that the formulation of CSR practices represents a shift toward explicit forms of self-regulation and away from the plausible deniability that lead-buy MNEs may have exploited in the past. Even so, our understanding of global supply chains and the considerable variation in MNE capacity for exploitation remains theoretically, but mostly empirically underdeveloped.

---

[2] A detailed discussion of global value chains is provided in Chapter 21.

Corruption

Corruption and irresponsible business practices represent two longstanding historical accounts of the MNE (Rodriguez, Siegel, Hillman, & Eden, 2006). Corruption is a multifaceted phenomenon. The pervasiveness of corruption reflects the number and frequency of transactions that involve illicit activities. These elicit activities can include, but are not limited to, bribery, embezzlement, and nepotism. Despite the complexities of these phenomena, most approaches to corruption attempt to capture corruption in a single indicator. Such measures typically capture perceptions about corruption, the experience of corruption, or the stringency of policies and institutions designed to tackle the problems associated with corruption. Countries with longstanding problems associated with corruption appear to be those where income (real GDP per capita) is low, education is limited, and media freedom is restricted (Svensson, 2005). At the micro-level, almost all research that evaluates the consequences of corruption on different stakeholders suggests that corruption is harmful (Olken, 2006; Mauro, 1997). To date, IB strategy research is limited by mostly focusing on the effects of corruption on the firm, as well as simplistic conceptualizations of core constructs (for a review, see Bahoo, Alon, & Paltrinieri, 2019). Therefore, our understanding of how and when corruption may carry inefficient and harmful effects versus more effective and potentially "beneficial" outcomes is largely undeveloped.

Perception of MNE Socially (Ir)responsible Behavior

MNE engagement in CSI, like corruption, has been proposed to represent considerable risks to the firm's reputation and organizational performance. Here, we propose that CSI may also represent a threat to the integrity of the host market context. In this way, CSI may appear to be a considerable burden for both business and society, particularly when brought to the attention of global audiences. As such, there may be organizational benefits that accrue as a result of CSI suppression from public knowledge. Hence, CSI may represent cost benefits, strategic advantages, or operational efficiencies to the firm as long as the downside risks of perceptual and financial penalties can be prevented.

What is more, relatively recent evidence suggests that "irresponsible" behavior may also be associated with some positive outcomes for the MNE. For example, in Bangladesh and many other areas of the world, informal labor economies rely on questionable organizational practices in order to support millions of workers who would otherwise not be able to take part in formal economic sectors (Narula, 2019). With little institutional support to gain access to such labor markets, compliance with more stringent MNE conduct may create negative unintended consequences for the labor market. Though counterintuitive, we caution approaching CSR and CSI research with a priori moral assumptions. The complexity of social systems necessitates a more holistic conceptualization of CSR and CSI before drawing conclusions regarding the fundamental nature of MNEs as either "psychopathic" or "virtuous." We highlight, as others have before us (Strike et al., 2006), that MNEs can simultaneously behave responsibly and irresponsibly. In practice, more meaningful social progress may require greater effort to compel socially responsible behavior and penalize irresponsible behavior, either by legal or social sanctions (Buckley, 2018; Devinney, Auger, Eckhardt, & Britchnell, 2006; Nardella et al., 2020). Research regarding social perception and perception management is generally understudied in IB strategy research and would therefore constitute a fruitful future research area.

Looking Forward

We highlighted a number of key themes regarding CSR and CSI research, paying particular attention to those areas of pertinence to future research. We argue that the field of IB strategy has yet to make a sustained contribution to the debate regarding the MNE's influence on its environment (Kolk, 2016) because it has largely focused on the non-market features of the business environment, which influence the non-market strategies of the MNE. Waning public support toward the MNE suggests that the influence that MNEs have had on their environment is not always perceived to be beneficial, thus exposing them to considerable social disapproval and, subsequently, reputation risks. Anti-globalization movements continue to emerge (Meyer, 2017) alongside some of the lowest levels of public trust in large corporations on record (see Gallup, 2019). Subsequently, policymakers are confronted by increasing pressure to mandate what was previously considered as voluntary CSR behavior. Recognizing this imbalance, other disciplines, such as the psychological sciences, have stepped in to outline the considerable economic, social, and environmental advancements achieved with the contribution of the MNE (see Pinker, 2018). Overall, it is our view that there remains substantial scope for the field of IB strategy to make valuable contributions to CSR/CSI research.

In order to enhance a CSR/CSI research agenda, a primary challenge for researchers is the development of a more nuanced conceptual logic that connects the CSR/CSI and IB strategy disciplines. To date, we lack an overarching theoretical framework to guide future research in the area. While some attempts have been made to draw scholars' attention to underlying theoretical issues (Rodriguez et al., 2006), social perspectives lack sufficient integration. Resultantly, we lack a coherent structure to support future research endeavors. In this sense, non-market strategy research, while offering a broad and largely instrumental conceptualization, focuses on "business" concerns, yet fails to address "social" concerns. It is our view that this reveals an opportunity for developing an overarching theoretical framework for IB and society.

A second area relates to the institutionally established normative standards by which the expectations and evaluations of CSR and CSI are made. Implications for firm-level adoption of CSR or CSI behavior are likely to be highly sensitive to the character of the wider institutional context within which the firm operates (Kobrin, 2015). Specifically, regulatory institutions define behaviors that are compliant and noncompliant with mandated standards and thereby establish the range of behaviors in particular domains. This means that institutions define (il)legitimate conduct and, through this, establish reference points against which organizations learn and acquire knowledge regarding socially acceptable and unacceptable behavior. Alongside established benchmarks for conduct, institutional contexts play an important role in shaping whether "ethical" behavior is adhered to, or "unethical" behavior emerges. However, research has yet to sufficiently explore the contextual circumstances in which "good" and "bad" conduct arises. That said, even when institutional contexts are characterized by substantial regulatory oversight, irresponsible behavior may still emerge. For example, the 2008 global financial crisis was not, as many commentators predicted, triggered by "overreaching" US hedge funds. Instead, it was the highly "regulated" US banking sector that provided the context in which serious financial misconduct was allowed to take place. In this sense, the presence of regulation (or lack thereof) may only represent one facet of a more complex process in which CSR and CSI behaviors emerge and develop as part of MNE international strategy in different host country markets.

A third and final area of research that, we believe, may offer productive opportunities for future work rests in understanding how companies use and manage CSR as a non-market strategy in different international market contexts. On the one hand, we have argued that the payoffs to particular social responsibility strategies are likely to be highly sensitive to the nature of the prevailing institutional norms in different countries. For example, the reputational harm associated with bribery might be particularly substantial within a liberal market setting, where there are comparatively strong institutional norms. However, our understanding of the costs associated with CSI in contexts characterized as having limited statehood is less well known. Exploring the benefits and costs associated with CSR and CSI in different institutional contexts, and how firms cope with the tensions associated with managing institutional variety, provides for a particularly interesting avenue for future research.

Concluding Remarks

We outlined the major perspectives on CSR and CSI. By identifying three distinct conceptualizations of CSR and CSI we explored the role played by the business context, particularly the influence of location and regulatory institutions in the character and management of CSR/CSI. Non-market strategy research has largely focused on the features of the social and regulatory environment that influences MNE strategy, rather than the features and behaviors of the MNE that influence the social, regulatory, and ecological environments in which the MNE operates. We assert that a more balanced and objective consideration of MNEs' social and environmental activities is needed. The field of IB strategy has yet to make a sustained contribution to the CSR/CSI debate in a context where public support of the MNE is waning, therefore exposing these firms to considerable risks. We hope to have convinced the reader that there is, indeed, significant scope for the field of IB strategy to make valuable contributions to the discussion regarding the socially responsible and irresponsible behavior of MNEs.

References

Aguinis, H., & Glavas, A. 2012. What we know and don't know about corporate social responsibility: A review and research agenda. *Journal of Management*, 38(4): 932–968.

Alamgir, F., & Banerjee, S. B. 2019. Contested compliance regimes in global production networks Insights from the Bangladesh garment industry. *Human Relations*, 72(2): 272–297.

Alexander, C. R. 1999. On the nature of the reputational penalty for corporate crime: Evidence. *Journal of Law and Economics*, 42(1): 489–526.

Armstrong, J. S. 1977. Social irresponsibility in management. *Journal of Business Research*, 5(3):185–213.

Arthaud-Day, M. 2005. Transnational corporate responsibility: A tri-dimensional approach to international CSR research. *Business Ethics Quarterly*, 15(1): 1–22.

Bahoo, S., Alon, I., & Paltrinieri, A. 2019. Corruption in international business: A review and research agenda. *International Business Review*. https://doi.org/10.1016/j.ibusrev.2019.101660

Bakan, J. 2005. *The Corporation: The Pathological Pursuit of Power*. Toronto, ON: Penguin.

Baron, J. 1996. Do no harm. In D. M. Messick, & A. E. Tenbrunsel (Eds.), *Codes of Conduct: Behavioral Research into Business Ethics*. New York, NY: Russell Sage Foundation.

Bitektine, A. 2011. Toward a theory of social judgments of organizations: The case of legitimacy, reputation, and status. *Academy of Management Review*, 36(1): 151–179.

Boström, M., Jönsson, A.M., Lockie, S., Mol, A., & Oosterveer, P. 2015. Sustainable and responsible supply chain governance: Challenges and opportunities. *Journal of Cleaner Production*, 107(16): 1–7.

Bowen, F., Cousins, P., Lamming, R., & Faruk, A. 2002. Horses for courses: Explaining the gap between the theory and practice of green supply. *Greener Management International*, 35: 41–60.

Brammer, S., & Millington, A. 2008. Does it pay to be different? An analysis of the relationship between corporate social and financial performance. *Strategic Management Journal*, 29(12): 1325–1343.

Brammer, S., Pavelin, S., & Porter, L. A. 2009. Corporate charitable giving, multinational companies and countries of concern. *Journal of Management Studies*, 46(4): 575–596.

Buckley, P. J. 2018. Can corporations contribute directly to society or only through regulated behaviour? *Journal of the British Academy*, 6(S1): 323–374.

Buckley, P. J., Doh, J. P., & Benischke, M. H. 2017. Towards a renaissance in international business research? Big questions, grand challenges, and the future of IB scholarship. *Journal of International Business Studies*, 48(9): 1045–1064.

Buhmann, K. 2016. Public regulators and CSR: The social licence to operate in recent united nations instruments on business and human rights and the justification of CSR. *Journal of Business Ethics*, 136(4): 699–714.

Buysse, K., & Verbeke, A. 2003. Proactive environmental strategies: A stakeholder management perspective. *Strategic Management Journal*, 24(5): 453–470.

Carroll, A. B. 1999. Corporate social responsibility: Evolution of a definitional construct. *Business & Society*, 38(3): 268–295.

Chomsky, N. 2005. *Chomsky on Anarchism*. Edinburgh: AK Press.

Clews, H. 1906. Publicity and reform in business. *The Annals of the American Academy of Political and Social Science*, 28(1): 143–154.

Crilly, D., Ni, N., & Jiang, Y. 2016. Do-no-harm versus do-good social responsibility: Attributional thinking and liability of foreignness. *Strategic Management Journal*, 37(7): 1316–1329.

Dahlsrud, A. 2008. How corporate social responsibility is defined: An analysis of 37 definitions. *Corporate Social Responsibility and Environmental Management*, 15(1): 1–13.

Devinney, T. 2009. Is the socially responsible corporation a myth? The good, the bad, and the ugly of corporate social responsibility. *Academy of Management Perspectives*, 23(2): 44–56.

Devinney, T. M., Auger, P., Eckhardt, G. M., & Britchnell, T. 2006. The other CSR: Consumer social responsibility. *Stanford Social Innovation Review*, 4(3): 30–37.

DiMaggio, P. J., & Powell, W. W. 1983. The iron cage revisited: Institutional isomorphism and collective rationality in organizational fields. *American Sociological Review*, 48(2): 147–160.

Doh, J. P., Lawton, T. C., & Rajwani, T. 2012. Advancing nonmarket strategy research: Institutional perspectives in a changing world. *Academy of Management Perspectives*, 26(3): 22–39.

Doh, J. P., McGuire, S., & Ozaki, T. 2015. Global governance and international nonmarket strategies. *Journal of World Business*, 50(2): 256–261.

Donaldson, T., & Dunfee, T. W. 1994. Towards a unified conception of business ethics: Integrative social contracts theory. *Academy of Management Review*, 19(2): 252–284.

Donaldson, T., & Dunfee, T. W. 1999. *Ties that Bind: A Social Contracts Approach to Business Ethics*. Boston, MA: Harvard University Press.

Dunfee, T. W. 1996. On the synergistic, interdependent relationship of business ethics and law. *American Business Law Journal*, 34(2): 317–325.

Eisenhardt, K. 2002. Has strategy changed? *Sloan Management Review*, 43(2): 88–91.

Epstein, E. M. 1989. Business ethics, corporate good citizenship and the corporate social policy process: A view from the United States. *Journal of Business Ethics*, 8(8): 583–595.

EU Commission, 2001. *Green Paper on Corporate Social Responsibility*. Brussels: EU Commission.

Ferry, W. H. 1962. Forms of irresponsibility. *The Annals of the American Academy of Political and Social Science*, 343(1), 65–74.

Frederick, W. C. 1991. The moral authority of transnational corporate codes. *Journal of Business Ethics*, 10(3): 165–177.

Gallup, 2019. Are businesses worldwide suffering from a trust crisis? https://www.gallup.com/workplace/246194/businesses-worldwide-suffering-trust-crisis.aspx. Accessed September 12, 2019.

Giuliani, E. 2018. Regulating global capitalism amid rampant corporate wrongdoing—Reply to "three frames of innovation policy." *Research Policy*, 47(9): 1577–1582.

Giuliani, E., & Macchi, C. 2014. Multinational corporations' economic and human rights impacts on developing countries: A review and research agenda. *Cambridge Journal of Economics*, 38(2): 479–517.

Gnyawali, D. R. 1996. Corporate social performance: An international perspective. *Advances in International Comparative Management*, 11: 251–273.

Hart, H. M., & Prichard, E. F. 1939. The Fansteel case: Employee misconduct and the remedial powers of the national labor relations board. *Harvard Law Review*, 52(8): 1275–1329.

Heath, J. 2007. An adversarial ethic for business: Or when Sun-Tzu met the stakeholder. *Journal of Business Ethics*, 72(4): 359–374.

Hoejmose, S., Brammer, S., & Millington, A. 2012. "Green" supply chain management: The role of trust and top management in B2B and B2C markets. *Industrial Marketing Management*, 41(4): 609–620.

Ioannou, I., & Serafeim, G. 2012. What drives corporate social performance: The role of nation-level institutions. *Journal of International Business Studies*, 43(9): 834–864.

Jensen, M. 2001. Value maximization, stakeholder theory and the corporate objective function. *Journal of Applied Corporate Finance*, 14(3): 8–21.

Jones, C., & Temouri, Y. 2016. The determinants of tax haven FDI. *Journal of World Business*, 51(2): 237–250.

Karpoff, J. M., & Lott Jr, J. R. 1993. The reputational penalty firms bear from committing criminal fraud. *The Journal of Law and Economics*, 36(2): 757–802.

Kobrin, S. J. 2015. Is a global nonmarket strategy possible? Economic integration in a multipolar world order. *Journal of World Business*, 50(2): 262–272.

Kolk, A. 2016. The social responsibility of international business: From ethics and the environment to CSR and sustainable development. *Journal of World Business*, 51(1): 23–34.

Lange, D., & Washburn, N. T. 2012. Understanding attributions of corporate social irresponsibility. *Academy of Management Review*, 37(2): 300–326.

Lessig, L. 2011. *Republic, Lost: How Money Corrupts Congress—and a Plan to Stop it*. New York, NY: Twelve.

Liedong, T. A., Rajwani, T., & Mellahi, K. 2017. Reality or illusion? The efficacy of non-market strategy in institutional risk reduction. *British Journal of Management*, 28(4), 609–628.

Lipsey, R. E., & Sjöholm, F. 2004. FDI and wage spillovers in Indonesian manufacturing. *Review of World Economics*, 140(2): 321–332.

Maggioni, D., Santangelo, G. D., & Koymen-Ozer, S. 2019. MNEs' location strategies and labor standards: The role of operating and reputational considerations across industries. *Journal of International Business Studies*, 50(6): 948–972.

Marx, K. 1859. *Crime and Capital Accumulation*. California City, CA: Mayfield.

Mauro, P. 1997. *Why Worry about Corruption?* Washington, DC: IMF Publications.

Mayer, A. E. 2009. Human rights as a dimension of CSR: The blurred lines between legal and non-legal categories. *Journal of Business Ethics*, 88(4): 561–577.

Mayer, C. 2018. The future of the corporation: Towards humane business. *Journal of the British Academy*, 6(S1): 1–16.

McGuire, J. B., Sundgren, A., & Schneeweis, T. 1988. Corporate social responsibility and firm financial performance. *Academy of Management Journal*, 31(4), 854–872.

McWilliams, A., & Siegel, D. 2001. Corporate social responsibility: A theory of the firm perspective. *Academy of Management Review*, 26(1): 117–127.

Mehlum, H., Moene, K., & Torvik, R. 2006. Institutions and the resource curse. *The Economic Journal*, 116(508): 1–20.

Mellahi, K., Frynas, J. G., Sun, P., & Siegel, D. 2016. A review of the nonmarket strategy literature: Toward a multi-theoretical integration. *Journal of Management*, 42(1): 143–173.

Meyer, K. E. 2017. International business in an era of anti- globalization. *Multinational Business Review*, 25(2): 78–90.

Mintzberg, H. 2014. *Rebalancing Society: Radical Renewal Beyond Left, Right, and Center*. Oakland, CA: Berret-Koehler Publishers.

Mitchell, R., Agle, B., & Wood, D. 1997. Toward a theory of stakeholder identification and salience: Defining the principle of who and what really counts. *Academy of Management Review*, 22(4): 853–886.

Mosley, L., & Uno, S. 2007. Racing to the bottom or climbing to the top? Economic globalization and collective labor rights. *Comparative Political Studies*, 40(8): 923–948.

Nardella, G., Brammer, S., & Surdu, I. 2020. Shame on who? The effects of corporate irresponsibility and social performance on organizational reputation. *British Journal of Management*, 31(1): 5–23.

Narula, R. 2019. Enforcing higher labour standards within developing country value chains: Consequences for MNEs and informal actors in a dual economy. *Journal of International Business Studies*, 50(9): 1622–1635.

Narula, R., & Pineli, A. 2019. Improving the developmental impact of multinational enterprises: Policy and research challenges. *Journal of Industrial and Business Economics*, 46(1): 1–24.

O'Higgins, E. R. E. 2006. Corruption, under-development and extractive resource industry: Addressing the vicious cycle. *Business Ethics Quarterly*, 16(2): 235–254.

Olken, B. A. 2006. Corruption and the costs of redistribution: Micro evidence from Indonesia. *Journal of Public Economics*, 90(4–5): 853–870.

Pinker, S. 2018. *Enlightenment Now: The Case for Reason, Science, Humanism, and Progress.* New York, NY: Viking.

Porter, M. E., & Kramer, M. R. 2006. The link between competitive advantage and corporate social responsibility. *Harvard Business Review*, 84(12): 78–92.

Rodriguez, P., Siegel, D. S., Hillman, A., & Eden, L. 2006. Three lenses on the multinational enterprise: Politics, corruption, and corporate social responsibility. *Journal of International Business Studies*, 37(6): 733–746.

Shaxson, N. 2007. Oil, corruption and the resource curse. *International Affairs*, 83(6): 1123–1140.

Soundararajan, V., & Brown, J. A. 2016. Voluntary governance mechanisms in global supply chains: Beyond CSR to a stakeholder utility perspective. *Journal of Business Ethics*, 134(1): 83–102.

Spencer, J., & Gomez, C. 2011. MNEs and corruption: The impact of national institutions and subsidiary strategy. *Strategic Management Journal*, 32(3): 280–300.

Spiess, S. O., Mueller, K., & Lin-Hi, N. 2013. Psychological foundations of corporate social responsibility: The importance of "avoiding bad." *Industrial and Organizational Psychology*, 6(4): 383–386.

Strike, V. M., Gao, J., & Bansal, P. 2006. Being good while being bad: Social responsibility and international diversification of US firms. *Journal of International Business Studies*, 37(6): 850–862.

Svensson, J. 2005. Eight questions about corruption. *Journal of Economic Perspectives*, 19(3): 19–42.

Walker, K., Zhang, Z., & Ni, N. 2018. The Mirror effect: Corporate social responsibility, corporate social irresponsibility and firm performance in coordinated market economies and Liberal market economies. *British Journal of Management*, 30(1): 151–168.

Walzer, M. 1994. *Thick and Thin: Moral Arguments at Home and Abroad.* Notre Dame: University of Notre Dame Press.

Wang, S. L., & Li, D. 2019. Responding to public disclosure of corporate social irresponsibility in host countries: Information control and ownership control. *Journal of International Business Studies*, 50(1): 1283–1309.

Wang, X., Reger, R. K., & Pfarrer, M. 2019. Faster, hotter, and more linked in: Managing social disapproval in the social media era. *Academy of Management Review*. https://doi.org/10.5465/amr.2017.0375.

Wettstein, F., Giuliani, E., Santangelo, G. D., & Stahl, G. K. 2019. International business and human rights: A research agenda. *Journal of World Business*, 54(1): 54–65.

Willis, H. P. 1934. Are the bankers to blame? *Current History*, 39(4): 385–393.

Young, S. L., & Makhija, M. V. 2014. Firms' corporate social responsibility behavior: An integration of institutional and profit maximization approaches. *Journal of International Business Studies*, 45(6): 670–698.

CHAPTER 21

GLOBAL VALUE CHAIN GOVERNANCE

A Multinational Enterprise Capabilities View

ANTHONY GOERZEN AND ARI VAN ASSCHE

INTRODUCTION

THE question of global value chain (GVC) governance has gained widespread attention in recent years (Gereffi & Lee, 2016; Laplume, Petersen, & Pearce, 2016; Magnani, Zucchella, & Strange, 2019; Taglioni & Winkler, 2016). The multinational enterprises (MNEs) that lead GVCs have come under significant pressure from key stakeholders such as governments, non-governmental organizations (NGOs), trade unions, and consumers to improve labor and environmental standards, particularly among their developing country supplier factories. Through both hierarchical and collaborative means, lead MNEs have taken various tentative steps to establish and maintain global standards along their GVC, including the participation in third-party certification arrangements, equity-oriented programs, and the promotion of internal corporate social responsibility (CSR) standards. Yet, to date, the evidence is mixed as to whether these measures have actually led to the envisioned economic and social upgrading that was intended (Locke, Amengual, & Mangla, 2009; Lund-Thomsen & Lindgreen, 2014; Ruwanpura & Wrigley, 2011).

The mixed success of a lead MNE in diffusing higher standards throughout its GVC highlights the need to develop a better theoretical understanding of the factors that influence that firm's ability to influence economic and social outcomes among its GVC partners. In this chapter, we tackle this question by discussing the key sources of disagreement between lead firms and other GVC members. Further, we explain why lead firms have been limited in their ability to address these disagreements with their GVC partners. We then build on both dynamic capabilities theory (Teece, Pisano, & Shuen, 1997; Teece, 2007) and convention theory (Diaz-Bone, Didry, & Salais, 2015; Gibbon,

Bair, & Ponte, 2008; Ponte & Gibbon, 2005; Thévenot, 2015) to discuss how lead MNEs can build routines that allow them to more effectively orchestrate social upgrading in GVCs. We explore this concept by focusing on the diffusion of CSR practices as one important way of understanding the nature of GVC governance.

GVC Governance and Supplier Upgrading: Current State of Knowledge

In the last forty years or so, international business strategy has shifted in profound ways. As a result of trade and investment liberalization, financial deregulation, and techno-logical advances in the movement of information, people, and products, the cost of transporting goods and information over long distances has declined dramatically. These reductions in spatial transaction costs have made it profitable for lead MNEs in developed countries to redesign their production processes, pushing them to abandon the practice of concentrating their value chain in a single location. Through outsourcing and offshoring, they have sliced up their production processes and dispersed their activities across multiple countries and suppliers to take advantage of various factors including preferential tax treatment, lower cost factors of production, and more accom-modating host country regulatory environments.

There is a growing recognition among academics and policymakers that GVCs pro-vide important development opportunities to suppliers in emerging markets. An important feature of GVCs is that they allow emerging market suppliers to become fully fledged participants in international production networks with direct links to MNEs in developed countries (Gereffi, 1999; Taglioni & Winkler, 2016). Under the right condi-tions, GVC participation can put suppliers on a dynamic learning curve that can help build up their technological capabilities (Gereffi, Humphrey, & Sturgeon, 2005; Morrison, Pietrobelli, & Rabellotti, 2008). This type of linkage-induced knowledge spillover can lead to economic upgrading if it leads suppliers to increase the value added that they create and appropriate (Sako & Zylberberg, 2019).

The literature on GVC governance and supplier upgrading continues to be updated, with scholars often revealing contradictory findings. We discuss some of the concepts introduced in this literature and key empirical findings concerning the evolution of GVC governance mechanisms and their links to MNE strategy. Humphrey and Schmitz (2002) identified four types of linkage-induced knowledge spillovers that can help sup-pliers to upgrade economically, namely:

(1) those that allow inputs to be more efficiently turned into output (*process upgrading*);
(2) those that permit the development of higher quality goods and services (*product upgrading*);

(3) those that allow suppliers to change the mix of value adding activities (*functional upgrading*); and

(4) those that let suppliers move into more skill-intensive industries (*industry upgrading*).

A range of empirical studies have used this upgrading typology to analyze how GVC participation may trigger economic development in different country contexts, including Bair and Gereffi's (2001) study of the apparel cluster in Torreon, Mexico, Guerrieri and Pietrobelli's (2004) analysis of the electronics industry in Taiwan, and Van Assche and Van Biesebroeck's (2018) study of the export processing regime in China.

In turn, some notable studies have highlighted that the relation between GVC participation and economic upgrading is far from linear as it critically depends on the structural constraints, that is, the governance structure, that are imposed by lead MNEs (Gereffi, 1999). Lead firms have the corporate power to define the terms and conditions of GVC membership and this, in turn, influences the type of knowledge and capabilities that suppliers can acquire (Schmitz & Knorringa, 2000). Lead MNEs are generally willing to tolerate or even support upgrading within production (along the dimensions of quality, flexibility, and productivity) since it helps strengthen the complementarities between the two value chain partners. At the same time, they may discourage and even hinder the acquisition of capabilities when it comes to functional upgrading (i.e. moving into higher value-added activities such as design, branding, manufacturing, and retailing) since this type of upgrading may encroach upon the lead MNE's core competence.

In this respect, the GVC literature has, indeed, paid attention to the different patterns of governance that lead MNEs adopt and how they may enhance or hinder different types of economic upgrading. Gereffi (1994), for example, pointed out that GVCs can be thought of as either "producer driven" or "buyer driven." In producer-driven GVCs, power is held by final product manufacturers and is characteristic of capital, technology-intensive, or skill-intensive industries. In contrast, in buyer-driven GVCs, retailers or marketers of final products to end users exert the most power through their ability to shape consumer expectations via strong brand names. Gereffi et al. (2005) proposes a more elaborate typology of five modes of governance that include (1) market, (2) modular, (3) relational, (4) captive, and (5) hierarchy. These modes are influenced, in turn, by three transactional characteristics such as the complexity of information exchanged, the codifiability of knowledge, and the supplier's capabilities.

More recent studies have expanded the GVC framework to study the role of GVC governance on social upgrading—the process of improvement in the rights and entitlements of workers (e.g. wages, job security) and the quality of their employment (e.g. safety and other aspects of working conditions) (Rossi, Luinstra, & Pickles, 2014). Their findings show that GVC participation of developing country suppliers does not necessarily lead to their social upgrading and, sometimes, it may have the opposite effect (Barrientos, Gereffi, & Rossi, 2011; Locke, Kochan, Romis, & Qin, 2007). Damodaran (2010), for example, documented that many jobs created within GVCs are poorly paid, insecure, and with difficult working conditions. Female workers in particular are often involved in the most insecure and lowest paid work (Mezzadri, 2014). In fact, this effect appears to be exacerbated by certain highly successful business models (like Zara's "fast fashion" approach) that emphasize speed-to-market, which cause peaks and valleys in demand and therefore encourage casual labor practices (Plank, Rossi, & Staritz, 2014). Barrientos et al. (2011) documented that an increasingly prevalent way that developing country suppliers in the food and apparel industries cope with short-term fluctuations in lead-firm demand is to engage third-party labor contractors as a channel for recruiting and employing irregular workers (often low-skill and migrant) on an as-needed basis. These labor practices, which often go unnoticed, can even enable bonded and forced labor at the heart of global production (Barrientos, 2013).

The accumulating evidence of vulnerable workers, child labor, and poor working conditions within many GVCs (Lund-Thomsen & Nadvi, 2010; Lund-Thomsen & Lindgreen, 2014; Lüthje, 2002) has led governments and NGOs to mount pressure on lead MNEs to improve governance practices that could be diffused throughout their GVC (c.f. Gereffi & Lee, 2016). This pressure includes well-coordinated campaigns by NGOs to force leading MNEs such as Nike and Starbucks to improve working conditions in their GVC and to participate in equity-oriented programs like "Fairtrade" (Mayer & Gereffi, 2010). It also includes pressure tactics on lead MNEs to develop CSR guidelines that outline the type of behavior to which suppliers should abide (Kolk & Van Tulder, 2005).

Overall, these insights on economic and social upgrading are significant because they highlight the central role that lead MNEs play within their respective GVC. What is particularly intriguing about GVCs is that the lead MNE typically has little or even no direct ownership of production (Bair, 2008; Dolan & Humphrey, 2000, 2004). Thus, GVC governance allows the lead MNE to exert control over the entire chain despite limited investment of their own resources through the shaping of business expectations, quality assessment, including even the guidelines that relate to local conditions such as factory conditions (De Marchi, DiMaria, & Ponte, 2014). In this sense, Ponte and Sturgeon (2014) suggest that lead MNEs have a "driving," "coordinating," and "normalizing" power over the GVC, where they can push member firms not only to adjust prices and product specifications but also to adopt certain practices to be compatible with a given internationally recognized standard or norm.

This view of GVCs comes with certain risks; in particular, scholars may overestimate the ability of lead MNEs to govern the GVC, and therefore immediately attribute fault to lead firms when certain goals are not attained. As Tokatli (2012) suggests in his study on economic upgrading:

> when manufacturing suppliers try and fail to enter into a high value-added activity, then we blame the discouragement and obstacles put up by the powerful buyers, and when they succeed, then we simply conclude that they must somehow have exploited the fragility of the power relationships despite the discouragement imposed by these relationships.

Similar arguments are often introduced in discussions about social upgrading. The reason why this is a concern is that there is growing evidence that a lead MNE's ability to dictate to the GVC is never guaranteed and, in fact, critically depends on its own distinctive capabilities and degree of economic power over GVC members (Soundararajan & Brown, 2016). Yet, this is an area that has been almost entirely neglected by the GVC literature, as illustrated by the absence of the concept of *lead MNE capability* in the seminal framework by Gereffi et al. (2005).

In sum, the GVC governance literature has uncovered the ability of lead MNEs to influence the economic and social behavior of its foreign value chain partners through its governance structure even if it does not have a direct ownership stake in them. This power, however, is in many cases incomplete, thus leading to the question of whether there are, indeed, certain lead MNE capabilities that may facilitate this ability to diffuse standards especially when an incentive misalignment problem exists with their idiosyncratic GVC. In the next section, we analyze this question by zooming in on the capabilities that lead firms need to develop to diffuse social upgrading throughout their GVCs.

Incentive Misalignment Problem

A lead MNE's ability to diffuse social standards to its suppliers through the implication of CSR policies is limited, and this is often expected to be the case despite good intentions (Lund-Thomsen & Lindgreen, 2014; Palpacuer, 2008; Soundararajan & Brown, 2016). A lead MNE's CSR policies are not naturally endorsed by its suppliers because both sides' interests are, in many cases, misaligned (Acquier, Valiorgue, & Daudigeos, 2017; Vogel, 2010). Even if the attempts by lead MNEs are genuine efforts to improve social conditions (which is not always the case: see Clarke & Boersma, 2015), suppliers do not necessarily have the information, motivation, or capabilities to comply with the lead MNE's demand for improved social conditions, and, in turn, lead firms do not have the capabilities to understand this problem.

Using the carrot–stick metaphor, an often-heard argument for supplier non-compliance is that lead MNEs either provide too small a carrot or threaten with too small a stick, or a combination of both. That is, it is often argued that lead firms heap the costs of compliance upon the suppliers without installing effective monitoring systems. In this case, the willingness of suppliers to comply to lead firms' demands is limited, the probability of non-compliance of a given supplier being discovered is remote and the penalties for non-compliance are small (Contractor & Kundu, 1998; Locke et al., 2009). This means that suppliers may choose to comply with a lead MNE's demands only when orders (or the entire supply relationship) are in jeopardy.

This argument, however, severely downplays the capabilities that lead MNEs need to develop in order to identify and implement the correct carrot–stick combination to its suppliers. In practice, suppliers in developing countries often do not have the same vision as the lead MNE as to what is socially or ethically acceptable, and lead firms are not necessarily aware of the source behind this misalignment with their suppliers, and even less so, how this can be resolved. The local socio-economic and cultural contexts of employment in which developing country suppliers are embedded often makes it difficult for them to understand the need to comply with social standards that have been imposed from overseas (Lund-Thomsen & Lindgreen, 2014). Recent research by Mueller, Hofstetter, Grimm, and Goerzen (2014), for example, sheds new light on the slow and faltering process to achieve even the minimum compliance with sustainability standards among developing country suppliers, which raises the question of why it is so difficult to reach these basic levels. Viewing such actions as a matter of lax morality or greed would be counterproductive and, most likely, not reflective of the actual reality; a more constructive view may be sensitive to the degree of economic desperation that sometimes underlies these behaviors (Roth, Tsay, Pullman, & Gray, 2008).

This lack of a common view between lead firms and suppliers is also evident in a recent poll of business executives in China that found that "an overwhelming proportion of them do not understand the benefits of responsible corporate behavior, such as environmental protection, or consider the requirements too burdensome" (Economy, 2007). Thus, the assumptions of conventional buyer-driven voluntary governance and the presence of shared value (Porter & Kramer, 2019) is time and again at odds with the realities of power, information asymmetry, and compliance–reward systems inherent in the framework of GVC management given a web of factors rooted in developing world suppliers' traditions, beliefs, local demands, and resource dependency that cause the cooperative paradigm to break down (Soundararajan & Brown, 2016). These misaligned incentives between lead MNEs and suppliers suggest that while CSR actions to improve economic and social conditions in GVCs are good in theory, they remain difficult to implement in practice (Lund-Thomsen & Lindgreen, 2014), particularly in scenarios with incomplete information.

The discrepancy between intention and outcome has led authors such as Simatupang, Wright, & Sridharan (2002) to call for a closer examination of the sources of GVC discontent. Soundararajan and Brown (2016) analyzes the perspective of suppliers in a global knitwear GVC that begins in India, finding that success in governing collaborative GVCs often falls short within the subcontracting stage, "where a stakeholder management mindset is elusive to most participants." In view of these interest misalignments among GVC actors, the question emerges of what can be done by lead MNEs to reduce this misalignment.

In Table 21.1, we outline the scope of the problem by examining a selection of MNE–GVC combinations, highlighting the variance in key issues as well as geographic dispersion within GVCs. Apple Inc., for example, was implicated in the Foxconn controversy, which has revolved around working conditions in offshore arm's length supplier factories as brought to the fore by the rash of worker suicides in China. If Apple were to take a leadership role in this matter, they would have to become knowledgeable, credible, and powerful sources of ideas around how to restructure assembly line work in a Chinese context—a task that is highly complex with a variety of important aspects that must be understood that are, most likely, beyond Apple's skill set.

A second example is BMW who has entered the smart car market and, as a result, requires cobalt resources to produce their electric car batteries. The majority of the world's cobalt, however, comes from the Democratic Republic of Congo—a country

Table 21.1 MNE–GVC configurations

Lead firm	Industry	Critical GVC issues	Critical issue epicenter
Apple	Mobile technology	Working conditions	China
Barrack Gold	Mining	Security, environmental degradation	Tanzania
BMW	Automotive	Fairtrade mining	DR of Congo
H&M	Fast fashion	Worker safety	Bangladesh
McDonalds	Fast food	Consumer waste, treatment of animals	US
Shell	Energy	Political stability, environmental degradation	Nigeria
TransCanada	Energy infrastructure	Indigenous people consent	Canada
Walmart	Retail	Worker freedom	Thailand

with many political, social, and regulatory problems. Nonetheless, BMW is pushed into this GVC that contains various weak institutions, fragile social conditions, and lax regulations; and it is surely a daunting task for a German automaker to even begin to know how to address these challenges.

A third relevant example can be derived from TransCanada, the Canadian energy infrastructure company; in their effort to build a natural gas pipeline, they have come into direct conflict with the Wet'suwet'en, a Canadian First Nations people who do not support TransCanada's project. To navigate this challenge, TransCanada requires deep knowledge of the aboriginal people they are addressing and, moreover, they need to have a significant asset embedded in local trust and credibility.

Taken together, this cursory examination suggests that lead firms need to possess nuanced capabilities to orchestrate the diffusion of social standards throughout their GVC. Thus, MNEs require wide ranging skills, knowledge, and experience, all of which are subject to time compression diseconomies (Dierickx & Cool, 1989) to enable them to connect to their idiosyncratic assembly of GVC members and unique business environments in which these members operate. This suggests that it may not be productive to search for generic resources and capabilities within an MNE that will enable them to gain influence and control over their GVC. Rather than attempting to establish a general GVC governance relationship, thereby making incorrect normative statements on optimal approaches, researchers should endeavor to penetrate the black box of MNE dynamic capabilities within the GVC context to discover the ways and means by which the unique challenges that face them can be addressed (Verbeke, Li, & Goerzen, 2009).

AN MNE CAPABILITIES VIEW

The dynamic capabilities framework developed by Teece and co-authors provides a useful perspective to reflect on the capabilities that MNEs need to develop in order to diffuse social standards throughout their GVC (Teece et al., 1997; Teece, 2007). Whereas traditional theories assume that markets exist and lead firms need to reduce transaction costs, the starting point in the dynamic capabilities theory is that lead MNEs must actively develop competences through the development of organizational routines that allow them to tackle such bottlenecks (Winter, 2003). Several researchers have elaborated on distinct types of routines that constitute a dynamic capability including sensing, learning, reconfiguration, and coordination (Helfat et al., 2007; O'Reilly III & Tushman, 2008; Zahra, Sapienza, & Davidsson, 2006).

In the context of the transmission of CSR policies to suppliers, *sensing* routines involve the assembly of information concerning supplier views through searching and exploration, *learning* routines relate to the conversion of information into knowledge and understanding, *transformation* routines pertain to the adjustment and reorganization of existing business logics, while *coordination* routines are those that allocate resources, assign tasks and synchronize activities. Collectively, these four categories of routines are understood to be key mechanisms by which organizations create and sustain competitive advantage (Schilke & Goerzen, 2010). Lead MNEs that develop these routines have a higher likelihood of successfully transmitting their social standards to suppliers, whereas those lacking these dynamic capabilities may not succeed despite their best intentions.

In line with this thinking, Pitelis and Teece (2018) recently developed a closely related concept of "orchestration theory" (see also Dhanaraj & Parkhe, 2006) that views the lead MNE as a force of integration along the GVC by creating and cocreating organizations, markets, and supporting business ecosystems within countries and across borders. Orchestration theory—which builds on the concept of dynamic capabilities—emphasizes the coordination role of the lead MNE to achieve a better fit with the unique challenges associated with international operations involving multiple tiers of suppliers and other partners (Gereffi, et al., 2005; UNCTAD, 2013). Thus, as appropriately summarized by Pitelis and Teece (2018), lead firms require capabilities aimed at the creation and cocreation of organizations, markets, and business ecosystems and to put in place strategies to develop, leverage, and manage the dynamic capabilities that allow them to capture sustainable cocreated value.

Building on this literature, we posit that GVC governance is a function of the lead MNE's dynamic capabilities, which allows them in a timely fashion to identify the sources of the incentive misalignment problem and to pinpoint the correct communication and coordination channels that are needed to develop the optimal carrot–stick combination (Goerzen, 2005; Kale, Dyer, & Singh, 2002; Schilke & Goerzen, 2010).

Furthermore, we extend this line of thought by introducing Convention Theory; in doing so, we propose that the expectations of suppliers are not endogenous, but rather can be influenced by lead firms' actions to improve alignment of expectations. Thus, as summarized in Figure 21.1, governance "misalignment" (i.e. poorer performance than required by GVC stakeholders) may be addressed by two main underlying factors:

(1) the scope for effective interfirm linkages to align incentives; and
(2) the ability of the lead MNE to influence conventions to align expectations.

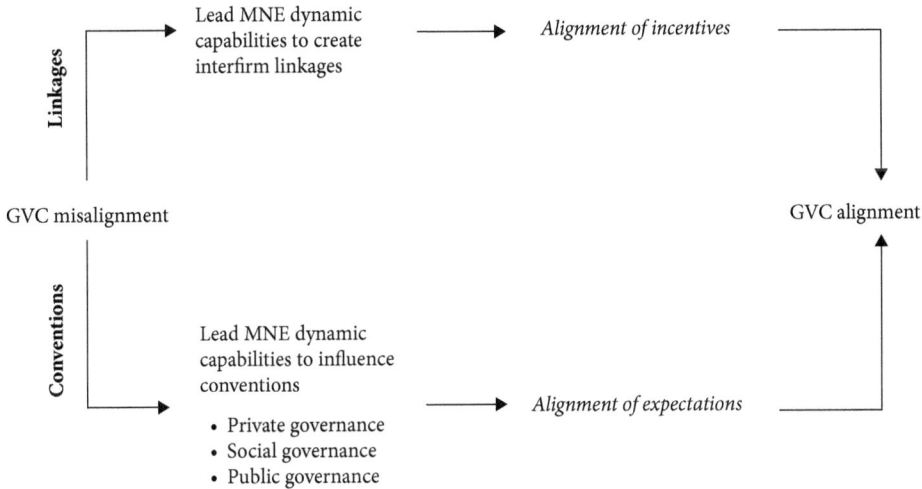

FIGURE 21.1 GVC governance mechanisms to create alignment

Incentive Alignment Capabilities: The Role of Coordination and Collaboration Routines

The ability of lead firms to address incentive misalignment problems critically depends on the routines it has developed to sense and learn from differences in visions and intentions with its suppliers, and especially those in idiosyncratic institutional environments. Shell, for example, needs to understand the political context in Nigeria and how it affects the lead MNE's ability to orchestrate social standards in that country; Walmart needs to comprehend the conditions under which slavery still exists in Thailand; and a retailer such as H&M needs to deal with regulations and practices of worker safety in countries like Bangladesh.

Understanding the incentive misalignment in CSR practices, however, is insufficient. Addressing it requires the lead firm to develop sophisticated *inter-organizational coordination* and *collaboration routines* that allow it to transmit its expectations to GVC partners and to appropriately monitor supplier actions. Simatupang et al. (2002) describe the need for GVC coordination, which includes the ability to synchronize interdependent processes, to integrate information systems, and to cope with distributed learning. Moreover, the authors propose that various modes of coordination including logistics synchronization, information sharing, incentive alignment, and collective learning, have a positive impact on GVC performance. Therefore, it is important to also recognize the need to reconcile the interests (economic and social) of the various parties involved through the establishment of inter-organizational linkages (i.e. coordination mechanisms) that either strengthen suppliers' incentives or fortify the monitoring of their actions. We posit that the ability of a lead MNE to establish effective interfirm linkages within its GVC is related to several key factors including MNE leadership, number and type of linkages, culture, and the presence of a dedicated GVC management function.

Expectation Alignment Capabilities: Using Convention Theory

Beyond the need for dynamic capabilities to create and maintain alignment of incentives, the lead MNE can also take action to alter the expectations of suppliers concerning CSR practices. Convention theory is a useful way to understand the power of such actions; we suggest that lead MNEs need to develop dynamic capabilities that address these differences in expectations as we discuss in detail in this section.

Convention theory defines a quality convention as a system of mutual expectations about the rules and standards that should be followed (Diaz-Bone et al., 2015; Gibbon et al., 2008; Ponte & Gibbon, 2005; Thévenot, 2015). These conventions can refer to product attributes (e.g., quality or type of ingredients), but they can also denote attributes related to production and process methods (e.g., labor and environmental standards). If there is a common agreement between the lead firm and its suppliers on a given convention and if there are monitoring mechanisms in place to verify adherence, conventions are more easily adopted and transmitted throughout the GVC. However, if GVC members do not share a common view of a specific attribute, or if the attribute is difficult to monitor and enforce, the uncertainty that emerges exacerbates the above-mentioned coordination problem (Ponte & Sturgeon, 2014).

A key point in Convention Theory is that quality conventions are not necessarily defined prior to the collaboration nor are they fixed in space and time or closed to challenge (Gibbon et al., 2008). Rather, they too are the result of a dynamic process that emerges as GVC members and their stakeholders attempt to solve interest misalignment problems (Ponte & Gibbon, 2005). From this perspective, conventions act in some cases not only as normative guides for action but also as collective systems that help legitimize those actions (Diaz-Bone et al., 2015). Conventions thus lead to a process of "normalizing" behaviors so that outcomes are compatible with expectations (Gibbon et al., 2008; Ponte & Gibbon, 2005; Thévenot, 2015).

A particularly potent factor that can generate an equivalence in views between GVC parties is a judgment that is drawn from a higher principle (Ponte & Sturgeon, 2014; Thévenot & Boltanski, 1991); a vibrant literature has built on this insight to study the influence of factors external to the GVC on the adoption of shared conventions between lead firms and suppliers. One group of studies has focused on the role of public governance, where government policies are put in place to not only regulate the activities of lead firms but also those of their suppliers (see e.g. Friedman, 1962; Shaffer, 1995). These studies suggest that government policies not only can improve monitoring but also help to align supplier expectations. A second group of studies has analyzed the role of social governance in which civil society (i.e. labor organizations and NGOs) puts pressure on firms to adopt and diffuse social standards throughout the value chain by monitoring and publicizing contentious issues (Gereffi & Lee, 2016). These studies, however, tend to downplay the ability of lead firms to help shape public and social governance, thus ignoring the importance of MNE capabilities in quality convention establishment.

Concluding Remarks

The increasingly global dispersion of GVCs has led to a renewed interest into how lead MNEs can develop and diffuse CSR standards to their suppliers, even if they do not own them. More recently, a vibrant literature has studied this issue by analyzing the role of governance structure and supplier capabilities. In this chapter, we have sought to provide complementary insights into this topic by focusing on another factor that has, to date, largely been neglected in the GVC literature: the role of lead MNE capabilities.

We have identified two reasons why lead MNE capabilities should be taken into account when studying economic and social upgrading. First, lead firms are often *less* potent in influencing their suppliers' behavior as it is generally portrayed and are endowed with widely varying capabilities of orchestrating their suppliers. Building on insights from the dynamic capabilities literature, we highlighted the routines that permit lead firms to better coordinate and collaborate the implementation and diffusion of their CSR practices with their suppliers, including their leadership skills, the number and type of linkages they govern, cultural proximity with the suppliers, and the presence of a dedicated GVC management function.

Second, lead firms may become *more* potent in shaping the institutions that influence their suppliers' behavior than is generally considered. MNEs often help form governmental regulations that guide their sustainable development activities and they collaborate with NGOs to develop and monitor private standards along the value chain. Building on the assumptions of convention theory, we have posited that lead MNEs can develop dynamic capabilities that allow them to better align lead firm–supplier expectations through collaborations with governments and NGOs. We consider this chapter as a first step in studying the role of lead firm capabilities in the diffusion of CSR throughout its GVC.

References

Acquier, A., Valiorgue, B., & Daudigeos, T. 2017. Sharing the shared value: A transaction cost perspective on strategic CSR policies in global value chains. *Journal of Business Ethics*, 144(1): 139–152.

Bair, J. 2008. Commodity chains: Genealogy and review. In J. Bair (Ed.), *Frontiers of Commodity Chain Research*. Palo Alto: Stanford University Press.

Bair, J., & Gereffi, G. 2001. Local clusters in global chains: The causes and consequences of export dynamism in Torreon's blue jeans industry. *World Development*, 29(11): 1885–1903.

Barrientos, S. 2013. 'Labour chains': Analysing the role of labour contractors in global production networks. *Journal of Development Studies*, 49(8): 1058–1071.

Barrientos, S., Gereffi, G., & Rossi, A. 2011. Economic and social upgrading in global production networks: A new paradigm for a changing world. *International Labour Review*, 150(3–4): 319–340.

Clarke, T., & Boersma, M. 2015. The governance of global value chains: Unresolved human rights, environmental and ethical dilemmas in the Apple supply chain. *Journal of Business Ethics*, 143(1): 111–131.

Contractor, F., & Kundu, S. 1998. Model choice in a world of alliances: Analyzing organizational forms in the international hotel sector. *Journal of International Business Studies*, 29(2): 325–356.

Damodaran, S. 2010. Upgradation or flexible casualization? Exploring the dynamics of global value chain incorporation in the Indian leather industry. In A. Posthuma, & D. Nathan (Eds.), *Labour in Global Production Networks in India*. New York, NY: Oxford University Press.

De Marchi, V., DiMaria, E., & Ponte, S. 2014. Multinational firms and the management of global networks: Insights from global value chain studies. In T. Pedersen, M. Venzin, T. M. Devinney, & L. Tihanyi (Eds.), *Orchestration of the Global Network Organization (Advances in International Management*, Vol. 27). Bingley: Emerald.

Dhanaraj, C., & Parkhe, A. 2006. Orchestrating innovation networks. *Academy of Management Review*, 31(3): 659–669.

Diaz-Bone, R., Didry, C., & Salais, R. 2015. Conventionalist's perspectives on the political economy of law. An introduction. *Historical Social Research*, 40(1): 7–22.

Dierickx, I., & Cool, K. 1989. Asset stock accumulation and sustainability of competitive advantage. *Management Science*, 35(12): 1504–1511.

Dolan, C., & Humphrey, J. 2000. Governance and trade in fresh vegetables: The impact of UK supermarkets on the African horticulture industry. *Journal of Development Studies*, 37(2): 147–176.

Dolan, C., & Humphrey, J. 2004. Changing governance patterns in the trade in fresh vegetables between Africa and the United Kingdom. *Environment and Planning*, 36(3): 491–509.

Economy, E. C. 2007. The great leap backward? The costs of China's environment crisis. *Foreign Affairs*, 86(5): 38–59.

Friedman, M. 1962. *Capitalism and Freedom*. Chicago, IL: University of Chicago Press.

Gereffi, G. 1994. The organisation of buyer-driven global commodity chains: How US retailers shape overseas production networks. In G. Gereffi, & M. Korzeniewicz (Eds.), *Commodity Chains and Global Capitalism*. Westport, CT: Praeger.

Gereffi, G. 1999. International trade and industrial upgrading in the apparel commodity chain. *Journal of International Economics*, 48(1): 37–70.

Gereffi, G., Humphrey, J., & Sturgeon, T. 2005. The governance of global value chains. *Review of International Political Economy*, 12(1): 78–104.

Gereffi, G., & Lee, J. 2016. Economic and social upgrading in global value chains and industrial clusters: Why governance matters. *Journal of Business Ethics*, 133(1): 25–38.

Gibbon, P., Bair, J., & Ponte, S. 2008. Governing global value chains: An introduction. *Economy and Society*, 37(3): 315–338.

Goerzen, A. 2005. Managing alliance networks: Emerging practices of multinational corporations. *Academy of Management Executive*, 19(2): 94–107.

Guerrieri, P., & Pietrobelli, C. 2004. Industrial districts' evolution and technological regimes: Italy and Taiwan. *Technovation*, 24(11): 899–914.

Helfat, C. E., Finkelstein, S., Mitchell, W., Peteraf, M. A., Singh, H., Teece, D. J., & Winter, S. G. 2007. *Dynamic Capabilities: Understanding Strategic Change in Organizations*. Malden: Blackwell Publishing.

Humphrey, J., & Schmitz, H. 2002. How does insertion in global value chains affect upgrading in industrial clusters? *Regional Studies*, 36(9): 1017–1027.

Kale, P., Dyer, J., & Singh, H. 2002. Alliance capability, stock market response, and long-term alliance success: The role of the alliance function. *Strategic Management Journal*, 23(8): 747–767.

Kolk, A., & Van Tulder, R. 2005. Setting new global rules? *Transnational Corporations*, 14(3): 1–17.

Laplume, A. O., Petersen, B., & Pearce, J. M. 2016. Global value chains from a 3D printing perspective. *Journal of International Business Studies*, 47(5): 595–609.

Locke, R., Amengual, M., & Mangla, A. 2009. Virtue out of necessity? Compliance, commitment, and the improvement of labor conditions in global supply chains. *Politics and Society*, 37(3): 319–351.

Locke, R., Kochan, T., Romis, M., & Qin, F. 2007. Beyond corporate codes of conduct: Work organization and labour standards at Nike's suppliers. *International Labour Review*, 146(1–2): 21–40.

Lund-Thomsen, P., & Lindgreen, A. 2014. Corporate social responsibility in global value chains: Where are we now and where are we going? *Journal of Business Ethics*, 123(1): 11–22.

Lund-Thomsen, P., & Nadvi, K. 2010. Global value chains, local collective action and corporate social responsibility: A review of empirical evidence. *Business Strategy and the Environment*, 19(1): 1–13.

Lüthje, B. 2002. Electronics contract manufacturing: Global production and the international division of labor in the age of the internet. *Industry and Innovation*, 9(3): 227–247.

Magnani, G., Zucchella, A., & Strange, R. 2019. The dynamics of outsourcing relationships in global value chains: Perspectives from MNEs and their suppliers. *Journal of Business Research*, 103: 581–595.

Mayer, F., & Gereffi, G. 2010. Regulation and economic globalization: Prospects and limits of private governance. *Business and Politics*, 12(3): 1–25.

Mezzadri, A. 2014. Indian garment clusters and CSR norms: Incompatible agendas at the bottom of the garment commodity chain. *Oxford Development Studies*, 42(2): 238–258.

Morrison, A., Pietrobelli, C., & Rabellotti, R. 2008. Global value chains and technological capabilities: A framework to study learning and innovation in developing countries. *Oxford Development Studies*, 36(1): 39–58.

Mueller, M., Hofstetter, J., Grimm, J., & Goerzen, A. 2014. The role of voluntary sustainability initiatives as means to improve supplier compliance: Evidence from the Business Social Compliance Initiative in Bangladesh and India, *GRONEN Research Conference*. Helsinki, Finland.

O'Reilly III, C. A., & Tushman, M. L. 2008. Ambidexterity as a dynamic capability: Resolving the innovator's dilemma. *Research in Organizational Behavior*, 28: 185–206.

Palpacuer, F. 2008. Bringing the social context back in: Governance and wealth distribution in global commodity chains. *Economy and Society*, 37(3): 393–419.

Pitelis, C., & Teece, D. 2018. The new MNE: "Orchestration" theory as envelope of "Internalisation" theory. *Management International Review*, 58(4): 523–539.

Plank, L., Rossi, A., & Staritz, C. 2014. What does "fast fashion" mean for workers? Apparel production in Morocco and Romania. In A. Rossi, A. Luinstra, & J. Pickles (Eds.), *Towards Better Work: Understanding Labour in Apparel Global Value Chains*. London: Palgrave Macmillan.

Ponte, S., & Gibbon, P. 2005. Quality standards, conventions and the governance of global value chains. *Economy and Society*, 34(1): 1–31.

Ponte, S., & Sturgeon, T. 2014. Explaining governance in global value chains: A modular theory-building effort. *Review of International Political Economy*, 21(1): 195–223.

Porter, M. E., & Kramer, M. R. 2019. Creating shared value. In G. G. Lenssen, & N. C. Smith (Eds.), *Managing Sustainable Business: An Executive Education Case and Textbook*. Dordrecht: Springer.

Rossi, A., Luinstra, A., & Pickles, J. 2014. Introduction. In A. Rossi, A. Luinstra, & J. Pickles (Eds.), *Towards Better Work: Understanding Labour in Apparel Global Value Chains*. London: Palgrave Macmillan.

Roth, A. V., Tsay, A. A., Pullman, M. E., & Gray, J. V. 2008. Unraveling the food supply chain: Strategic insights from China and the 2007 recalls. *Journal of Supply Chain Management*, 44(1): 22–39.

Ruwanpura, K. N., & Wrigley, N. 2011. The costs of compliance? Views of Sri Lankan apparel manufacturers in times of global economic crisis. *Journal of Economic Geography*, 11(6): 1031–1049.

Sako, M., & Zylberberg, E. 2019. Supplier strategy in global value chains: Shaping governance and profiting from upgrading. *Socio-Economic Review*, 17(3): 687–707.

Schilke, O., & Goerzen, A. 2010. Alliance management capability and alliance portfolio performance: Conceptualization and measurement. *Journal of Management*, 36(5): 1192–1219.

Schmitz, H., & Knorringa, P. 2000. Learning from global buyers. *Journal of Development Studies*, 37(2): 177–205.

Shaffer, B. 1995. Firm-level responses to government regulation: Theoretical and research approaches. *Journal of Management*, 21(3): 495–514.

Simatupang, T. M., Wright, A. C., & Sridharan, R. 2002. The knowledge of coordination for supply chain integration. *Business Process Management Journal*, 8(3): 289–308.

Soundararajan, V., & Brown, J. A. 2016. Voluntary governance mechanisms in global supply chains: Beyond CSR to a stakeholder utility perspective. *Journal of Business Ethics*, 134(1): 83–102.

Taglioni, D., & Winkler, D. 2016. *Making Global Value Chains Work for Development*. Washington, DC: World Bank.

Teece, D. J. 2007. Explicating dynamic capabilities: The nature and microfoundations of (sustainable) enterprise performance. *Strategic Management Journal*, 28(13): 1319–1350.

Teece, D. J., Pisano, G., & Shuen, A. 1997. Dynamic capabilities and strategic management. *Strategic Management Journal*, 18(7): 509–533.

Thévenot, L. 2015. Certifying the world: Power infrastructures and practices in economies of conventional forms. In P. Aspers, & N. Dodd (Eds.), *Re-Imagining Economic Sociology*. Oxford: Oxford University Press.

Thévenot, L., & Boltanski, L. 1991. *De la justification: Les économies de la grandeur*. Paris: Gallimard.

Tokatli, N. 2012. Toward a better understanding of the apparel industry: A critique of the upgrading literature. *Journal of Economic Geography*, 13(6): 993–1011.

UNCTAD. 2013. *Global Value Chains and Development: Investment and Value Added Trade in the Global Economy*. Geneva: United Nations.

Van Assche, A., & Van Biesebroeck, J. 2018. Functional upgrading in China's export processing sector. *China Economic Review*, 47: 245–262.

Verbeke, A., Li, L., & Goerzen, A. 2009. Toward more effective research on the multinationality-performance relationship. *Management International Review*, 49(2): 149–161.

Vogel, D. 2010. The private regulation of global corporate conduct: Achievements and limitations. *Business and Society*, 49(1): 68–87.

Winter, S. G. 2003. Understanding dynamic capabilities. *Strategic Management Journal*, 24(10): 991–995.

Zahra, S. A., Sapienza, H. J., & Davidsson, P. 2006. Entrepreneurship and dynamic capabilities: A review, model and research agenda. *Journal of Management Studies*, 43(4): 917–955.

CHAPTER 22

SUSTAINABILITY STRATEGIES

Research and Practice in International Business

RENATO J. ORSATO, SIMONE R. BARAKAT, AND JOSÉ GUILHERME F. DE CAMPOS

INTRODUCTION

IF firm-specific advantage (FSA) is achieved by doing better by being different, what is the scope of sustainability strategies? What is sufficiently different about sustainability that deserves a special treatment in international business (IB) strategy research and practice? Previous research has shown that both subtle similarities and differences exist in the way sustainability strategies relate to the strategy of the firm (Orsato, 2009; Orsato, 2006; Orsato, Barakat, & de Campos, 2017; Orsato, de Campos, & Barakat, 2019). Identifying such differences therefore not only serves academic purposes but also contributes to the practice of management and policy, including informing the research field of IB strategy and MNE activities and operations.

The interface between sustainability strategies and IB is relatively scarce in mainstream journals (Hitt, Li, & Xu, 2016). From the few papers published in IB journals, a fair share were, in fact, published in special issues (Kolk & Van Tulder, 2010; Kolk, 2016) such as those on "Sustainable Business" in the *Journal of World Business* (Mort, 2010), "Climate Change Strategy" in the *Thunderbird International Business Review* (Schotter & Goodsite, 2013), and "Building Sustainable Organizations in China" in the *Management and Organization Review* (Marquis, Jackson, & Li, 2015). This trend remains conspicuous as suggested by recent special issues, such as "Companies in the circular economy" in the *Thunderbird International Business Review* (Shapiro, Hobdari, & Oh, 2018), and the call for papers ongoing in the special issue "Strategic Agility for International Business Sustainability" in the *Journal of International Management*. This is perhaps surprising, given that the primary interest of IB scholars in the IB arena equip them to study the so-called *grand challenges*—very complex problems not confined by national, economic, and societal borders (Buckley Doh, & Benischke, 2017). Considering that climate change and poverty alleviation are examples of such grand challenges, the growing relevance of sustainability for IB research and practice is now becoming evident.

By building on the interface between firm strategy and sustainability, Orsato (2006, 2009) developed a typology of sustainability strategies that companies may pursue, which can become a source of competitive advantage or a manner to enter new market spaces. This chapter is anchored in his work to update the research surrounding the topic of sustainability strategies—from 2009 until 2018, with special attention on the interface between strategy and sustainability choices in an international context. Using our typology for the characterization of sustainability strategies allows us to provide the reader with a basic mapping of a broad and diverse field of inquiry and suggest future research directions associated with strategizing for sustainability.

Specific to the IB strategy context, this investigation is important since there may be some idiosyncrasies associated with MNEs implementing such strategies, given the need to act in highly distant markets and cope with distinct regulatory and societal expectations. Hence, in order to investigate the more recent developments in sustainability strategy research in the context of MNE strategies, we performed a review of this body of literature in the mainstream IB and management journals. We complemented the systematic review with selected publications in other top tier journals that addressed firm sustainability strategies. Such complementary work, rather than representing an exhaustive literature review, was intended to help with the updating of research.

The rest of the chapter is structured as follows. In the next section, we present the framework of sustainability strategies as research areas and discuss the evolution of research and practice within each strategy. This section also indicates potential areas where future IB research might engage with sustainability issues, bringing both theoretical and practical contribution. Then we continue our analysis by identifying relevant challenges and opportunities faced by MNEs that relate to sustainability strategies, as well as broader trends and research opportunities in the field.

SUSTAINABILITY STRATEGIES AND RESEARCH

The sustainability strategies framework developed by Orsato (2006, 2009) clarifies the relationship between sustainability-oriented investments and firm strategy. Researchers

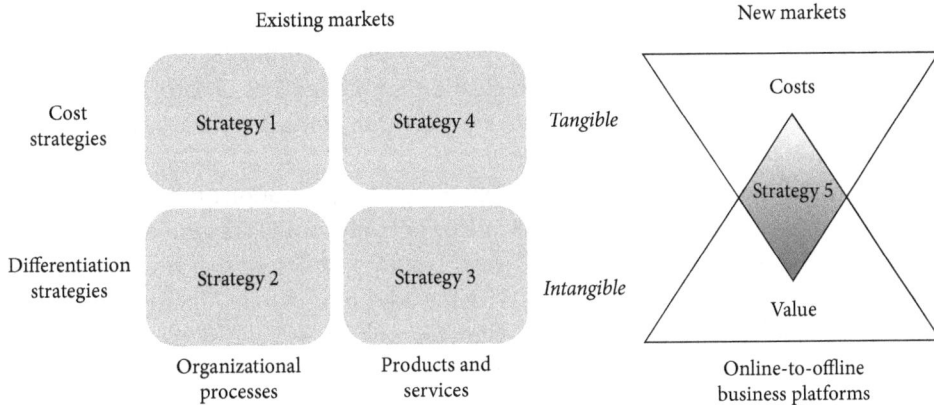

FIGURE 22.1 Sustainability strategies.

Source: Adapted from Orsato (2009).

in the field of IB strategy, aiming at identifying *when, why,* and *how* eco-investments may generate tangible or intangible value, can use this framework to design research and to evaluate their outcomes. Figure 22.1 presents the framework, which depicts five sustainability strategies, all of which may become potential research areas in IB strategy.

Broad Categories of Sustainability Strategies

We start by explaining these five sustainability strategies and then proceed with their applications to IB strategy research. Cost-oriented sustainability strategies (Quadrants 1 and 4) can be used to reduce costs of processes and products as well as to pursue extra revenues via the sales of by-products (Orsato, 2009). As depicted in Figure 22.1, cost-oriented sustainability strategies may relate to organizational processes (Strategy 1) that lead to a more efficient employment of resources and reduction of waste, or to products or services that present both lower cost as well as reduced environmental impacts (Strategy 4). On the other hand, differentiation strategies (Quadrants 2 and 3) refer to the creation of uniquely desirable products or services that allows the company to differentiate from its competitors. They can be divided according to process-oriented differentiation (Strategy 2), and product-oriented differentiation (Strategy 3).

Upstream and *downstream* activity systems can also be essential components of sustainability strategies. Depending on how these activity systems are managed, they facilitate or hinder the efficacy of sustainability strategies. This is not to say, however, that they are strategies per se. *Upstream* activity systems constitute extensions—beyond the physical borders of a company—of sustainability strategies that have their focus of processes, products/services, or platforms. In the same way that sustainability strategies need to be aligned with the strategy of the firm, greener practices from suppliers have to be aligned with the low-cost focus of a wholesaler (Strategies 1 and 4) or the endorsement of principles of voluntary environmental standards, which normally increase the cost of upstream practices for firms (Strategies 2 and 3).[1] In turn, eco-investments in *downstream* can eventually facilitate a close-loop recycling system, minimizing the risks of being taken by surprise, in case a take-back regulation is imposed (see Orsato, Den Hond, & Clegg, 2002). Such practices may create synergies for product recovery and recycling and may affect firm reputation positively.

Notwithstanding, research about the greening of organizations has also identified innovative business models as crucial elements not only for the creation of competitive advantage but also for the ecological sustainability of systems of production and consumption (Wells & Orsato, 2005). With the advent of mobile (phone) computing, including cloud storage and improved data processing speed and statistics (known as big data) digital business platforms could emerge and grow exponentially, reducing the need of physical assets and the consumption of resources. We argue that, compared to the traditional MNEs, which would take decades to grow, network effects allow business platforms to become multinationals in a fraction of that time.

Sustainability Strategies in IB Strategy Research

We performed a review of the literature about the interface between IB strategy and sustainability. The findings were characterized according to strategies presented in Figure 22.1, emphasizing the IB perspective in each quadrant. The selection of journals was based on four criteria. First, we chose journals with focus on IB from the more recent *Financial Times* list of top fifty journals (2016) in management (n = 1). Second, the IB journals listed in the Journal Quality List (2018) (Harzing, 2019) (n = 16). Third, IB journals in the Association of Business Schools (ABS) list (2018) with rating 3 or 4 (out of 4*) (n = 9). Finally, we selected the IB journals from the SCImago/SJR top 100 ranking on Business, Management and Accounting (2017) (n = 15). This resulted in a final selection of sixteen top tier journals. We searched for papers published in the last decade in each of the sixteen journals using the following keywords (Montiel & Delgado-Ceballos, 2014): sustainability, sustainable, environmental, and ecological. As result, we identified ninety-six papers. After a more thorough reading of the papers, thirty-one articles were removed from the sample (e.g. they focused on very specific functional areas; focused entirely on CSR; books reviews or editorials; articles targeting practitioners only). The final sample consists of sixty-five papers reviewed.

Following our analysis of these papers, we observed a growth in publications on the relationship between IB strategy and sustainability issues from 2012 onwards (see Figure 22.2), with some peaks in the years 2010, 2013, and 2018. Almost a third of the papers were published in special issues (twenty papers), meaning that less than ten papers per year were published in regular issues. Broadly, we confirm previous findings

---

[1] In Chapter 21, the authors provide an overview of the causes of misalignment between lead firms and their global supply chain partners, which makes it difficult to ensure that suppliers and wholesalers are focused on the same goals.

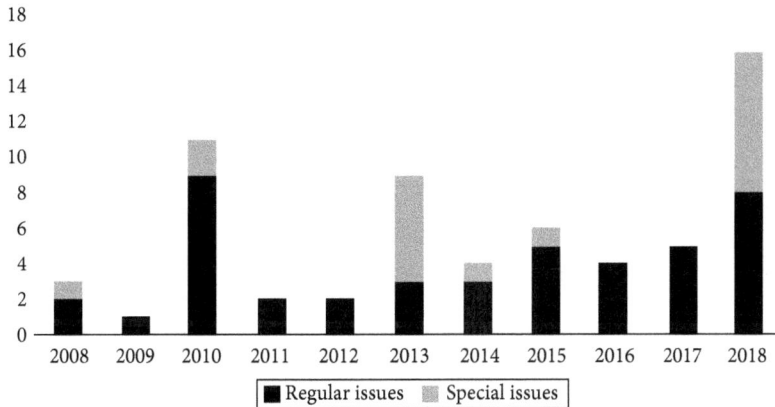

FIGURE 22.2 Publishing year of reviewed papers.

that the issue of sustainability remains a marginally addressed subject in the IB strategy literature (see also Kolk & Van Tulder, 2010; Kolk, 2016).

Figure 22.3 shows the main concepts and theories used as theoretical background. Overall, there was a prevalence in using institutional theory (n = 23) as the lens of analysis. The resource-based view (RBV) of the firm (n = 8) was often used in conjunction with institutional theory. As expected, corporate sustainability (n = 24) was the most adopted concept in these studies. Finally, theories and concepts traditionally associated with the IB field—namely country-specific advantage (CSA) and FSA (n = 6), FDI (n = 3) and internationalization (n = 3)—were also present. More recent sustainability-related concepts emerged in 2016 within these journals, such as: cradle-to-cradle, closed-loop supply chain, reverse logistics, reverse marketing (n = 3), and circular economy (n = 6). Meanwhile, climate change (n = 6) lost its momentum around 2013.

In terms of research design, there is a slight predominance of quantitative approaches, which is specific to IB research in general. Most papers with quantitative design are based on survey data (n = 16) and secondary databases (n = 14). Such predominance resulted in a great number of countries as empirical settings: 108 countries were represented in at least one study. Papers with qualitative design are based on case studies (n = 10) and document analysis (n = 1). Literature review and theoretical papers (n = 15) also represented an important share of the reviewed papers. China (thirteen studies) and the US (twelve studies) were the most commonly studied countries. European countries are the second major group, followed by some countries from Oceania (Australia and New Zealand) and Asia (India, Malaysia, Japan). The most underrepresented group is formed by countries from Africa, Latin America, and Eastern Europe (again, similar to other strategic decisions studied in IB). This is coherent with recent papers calling for more empirical research on emerging economies (e.g. Garcia, Mendes-Da-Silva, Orsato, 2017; Ben Brik, Mellahi, & Rettab, 2013; Tatoglu et al., 2014) or in developing countries (e.g. Barkemeyer, Preuss, & Lee, 2015; Goyal, Esposito, & Kapoor, 2018).

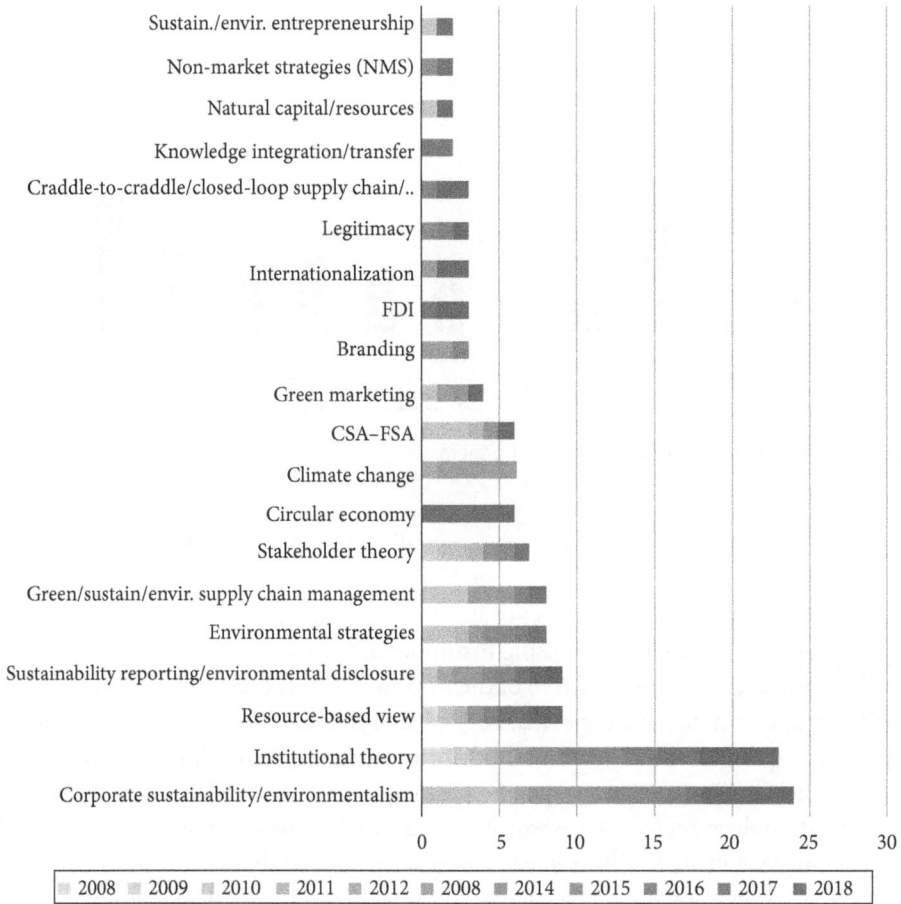

FIGURE 22.3 Main theoretical background and concepts in the reviewed papers.

Finally, considering the five sustainability strategies described in Figure 22.1, the most discussed in our review is Strategy 2—beyond compliance leadership (n = 45). This strategy is based on building legitimacy, which is coherent with the strong use of institutional theory and the study of specific organizational practices such as sustainability reporting (see Figure 22.3). Strategy 1—Eco-efficiency (n = 22)—and Strategy 3—Eco-Branding (n = 21)—were relatively well represented also. The use of RBV and related theories is very common in discussing those two strategies, along with the theoretical background of specific areas, for instance, supply chain management for Strategy 1 and green marketing for Strategy 3 (see Figure 22.3). Finally, there is a relative lack of studies on Strategy 4—e-cost leadership (n = 4)—and Strategy 5—sustainable value innovation (SVI) (n = 7)—which are based on more cutting-edge technologies and/or business models. However, this scenario may change, since in the last few years, new approaches such as circular economy (see Figure 22.3) and emergent industries such as electric vehicles (Andersen & Rask, 2014) and clean tech (De Lange, 2016) have gained momentum.

Now, let us delve deeper into the most relevant findings of the literature review on IB and sustainability strategies.[2]

Strategy 1: Eco-Efficiency

In broad conceptual terms, eco-efficiency represents the relationship between environmental and economic performance within a specific system, which might be a country, an industry, a company, a product, or a service. Eco-efficiency embraces actions such as waste reduction, pollution prevention, lifecycle management, and industrial symbiosis. Hence, eco-efficiency may be pursued in almost every stage of the supply chain—from the extraction of raw materials, to distribution, production, logistics, retailing, and the use and disposal of the product.

For companies with global value chains (GVCs), which therefore engage in offshoring activities and depend on subcontractors, the need to coordinate an international supply chain might be addressed by an effective eco-efficiency approach. For instance, within an international buyer–supplier relationship, coordination is needed to make use of integrated marketing and logistics for the recovery of recyclable products. In this respect, more research is needed to understand the buyer–supplier relationship in the integration of international sustainable supply chains (Gupta, 2016). Regarding the relationship between parent and subsidiary firms and the adoption of productive cleaner technologies, Cerdeira Bento and Moreira (2018) identified an important shift: firms seem not to be adopting cleaner technologies only in their home countries, where environmental legislation is usually more stringent, but also transferring those technologies to their subsidiaries. According to the authors, the well-known "Pollution Haven Hypothesis" (PHH) may not apply as often as it used to in the past.

The ultimate approach of eco-efficiency outside national borders, involved the MNE integrating its supply chain, and can be referred to as *industrial symbiosis*. By developing an industrial symbiotic system, two or more companies become interdependent by exchanging materials, processes, and energy, in which the waste of a company becomes the raw material for another, leading therefore to the formation of closed-loop systems. Usually, the industrial symbiosis occurs through a physical arrangement called Eco-Industrial Parks (EIPs), which means that it also depends on the physical location of the firms involved. Coordinating motivations and interests of diverse organizations into a clear, broader, long-term vision is certainly a challenge, and it is also one of the reasons EIPs depend mostly on top-down government incentives in the form of subsidies and taxes (Susur, Hidalgo, & Chiaroni, 2019). IB strategies may, indeed, be a deterrent for the formation of EIPs. Unless plans of expansion are coordinated with symbiotic partners, moving operation overseas may limit the formation of EIPs. Further empirical research is needed to understand the conditions under which geographically distant industrial

---

[2] Some of our recommendations relate to the ideas raised by Chapter 21 in relation to the capabilities that MNEs require in order to manage social issues within their global value chains more successfully.

symbiotic systems might be more or less successful, including the kind of waste, the constellation of actors involved in the relationship, and whether the presence of an external third part coordinator could make such a system perform better (Prosman, Wæhrens, & Liotta, 2017).

It is also possible to create a whole business model around the management of resource flows across the value chain. Circular economy (CE) and other related concepts such as closed-supply chain and reverse logistics (Geisendorf & Pietrulla, 2018) are generating new breed of business models based on logistics, design innovation, and collaborative ecosystems. Goyal et al. (2018) show how start-ups in developing economies are playing a significant role in the adoption of the circular economy on large scales and the importance of the government in providing business support for those business in their inception phase.

We emphasize here that, an eco-efficiency strategy may pay-off not only by reducing operational costs but also via some extra sources of revenue. The *carbon credit trading scheme* has been the most prominent example of such extra revenues acquired through eco-efficiency. However, the efforts required to implement an international trade-scheme on a global scale are too significant (Pinkse & Kolk, 2012). The main problem relates to the presence of multiple regulatory environments, differing climate policies, carbon targets, prices and methodologies, and varying national and regional priorities, all of which generate uncertain outcomes (Green, 2017; Tuerk, Mehling, Flachsland, & Sterk, 2009; Boyce, 2018). As result, MNEs may find it difficult to adopt coordinated global actions in their different subsidiaries (Pinkse & Kolk, 2012). A global carbon market appears only as a long-term alternative, contingent on the creation of an international regulatory organization (Tuerk et al., 2009; Boyce, 2018), such as a global carbon bank (Green, 2017).

Strategy 2: Beyond Compliance Leadership

The main rationale behind the *beyond compliance leadership* strategy is reputational risk and value. By reducing the impact of organizational processes and improving social benefits of their activities, firms indicate the intention to behave responsibly. The implementation is made via environmental certifications or voluntary environmental initiatives (VEIs) (Prakash, 2001). MNEs voluntarily choose to comply with predefined processes or objectives established by these certification services or clubs in order to enhance their reputations in host markets and reduce the risks associated with future regulation. Much of the research about this strategy sought to understand the motivations MNEs have to engage in sustainability policies and practices that are not mandatory by law, as well as the conditions that favor such initiatives and their outcomes (e.g. Prakash, 2001; Orsato et al. 2015, Garcia et al., 2017).

Previous studies have identified several external and internal factors that may influence an MNE's willingness to go beyond compliance. Some of the external factors relate to institutional and stakeholder pressures associated with: (1) a stricter set of laws, which increases the cost of compliance and expands managers' and corporate liability; (2) stakeholder activism against MNEs considered social and/or environmentally irresponsible; and (3) competitive pressures to operate in ways that enable MNEs to maintain profitability while minimizing negative social and environmental impacts (Dechant & Altman, 1994). Some examples of internal factors are size, degree of internationalization, position in the value chain, and managerial attitude and motivations (González-Benito & González-Benito, 2006; MacLennan & Barakat, 2017). Notably, Orsato et al. (2015) analyzed why companies that present low levels of (direct) carbon emissions participate in carbon clubs, which have the goal of managing and reducing greenhouse gas emissions. They found reputational value as the key internal driver, along with greater access to knowledge, possibility to influence the regulatory environment, pioneering, and innovation opportunities as well as risk mitigation. In reality, the success of green clubs addressing climate change depends on specific circumstances. For instance, Potoski (2017) added that green clubs are more likely to be effective if they help participants achieve private benefits that are aligned with the environmental benefits generated in the club. Overall, the levels of economic benefits of investments in sustainability depend on a wide array of variables, ranging from internal capabilities to the structure of the local industry in which the MNE operates (Orsato, 2006).

Indeed, research has shown that MNEs often hold a superior social and environmental performance (Christmann & Taylor, 2001; Buysse & Verbeke, 2003). This may be due to their size and scope (Etzion, 2007; MacLennan & Barakat, 2017) since large companies usually (1) have more resources to invest in environmental practices; (2) are more exposed to pressures from stakeholders; and (3) have sufficient scale to offset investments in technology and certification (González-Benito & González-Benito, 2006). MNEs adopt proactive social and environmental practices because they benefit from knowledge transfer (Yang, Mudambi, & Meyer, 2008) and generally define their policies based on the stricter requirements of the home country (Christmann & Taylor, 2001; Buysse & Verbeke, 2003; González-Benito & González-Benito, 2006).

Within the IB strategy literature, scholars have mainly studied VEIs in the scope of disclosure initiatives (e.g. Kolk, 2010; Barkemeyer et al., 2015; Cuadrado-Ballesteros, Martínez-Ferrero, & García-Sánchez, 2017; Martínez-Ferrero & García-Sánchez, 2017) and environmental management systems, namely, ISO 14001 (e.g. Darnall, Jolley, & Handfield, 2008; Kang & He, 2018; Orcos, Pérez-Aradros, & Blind, 2018). Those standards may serve as "one-size-fits-all" strategy for MNEs. However, in a review of Global Reporting Initiative reports of more than 1000 companies across several countries and industries, Barkemeyer et al. (2015) identified an overall lack of diversity in the content, suggesting that they may not be very effective in giving stakeholders meaningful information. They found that firms in non-developed countries have more comprehensive reporting practices, which challenges the PHH.

A similar counterintuitive finding refers to the internationalization of MNCs, which seems to be strongly associated with less environmental disclosure, with the exception of highly sensitive industries and high-standard countries. Due to the limitations of such studies, however, more research is needed to confirm and better explain such findings

(Kolk & Fortanier, 2013). The credibility and associated assurance mechanisms of the environmental information published by MNEs is one area requiring further research (Martínez-Ferrero & García-Sánchez, 2017). Finally, further research may also investigate how MNEs develop VEI in emerging economies, in response to challenging institutional environments (Ben Brik et al., 2013; Tatoglu et al., 2014).

Strategy 3: Eco-Branding

The *eco-branding* sustainability strategy is achieved through the provision of unique eco-friendly features that customers value. Sustainability strategies based on product differentiation rely on the assumption that the eco-friendly qualities of products or services have the potential to generate competitive advantage. To differentiate from competitors, MNEs may develop products and services with lower environmental impacts while satisfying other usual requirements, such as quality, convenience, and aesthetics. Satisfying such demands, however, is not an easy task; it requires an understanding of consumer behavior across various countries and cultures.

We are experiencing a growing consumer awareness and preference for environmentally friendly products and services. According to the 2014 *Greendex* (a collaborative analysis by the *National Geographic* and *GlobeScan*, a global research consultancy), sustainable consumer behavior has increased, albeit slowly, in nearly every country tracked since the release of the survey in 2008. The survey found that environmentally friendly behavior has improved in nine of the seventeen countries that were surveyed in 2012 and has decreased in five other countries. Such data is important for MNCs, since it suggests that green behavior is not only shaped by individuals' inherent values but also depends on the cultural context in which they are embedded, requiring different national, regional, and even local strategies to effectively communicate the ecological attributes of a product or service (Wang & Kuah, 2018). In a study on the subsidiaries of an international new venture, Andersen and Rask (2014) showed that international firms need to adapt their discourse, which emphasizes one or more given attribute of the "sustainable product," accordingly to the institutional context. Such a contingent approach resonates with the need for considering global versus regional strategies that MNEs might adopt according to local cultural, social, and institutional contexts (e.g. Gifford & Kestler, 2008; Grinstein & Riefler, 2015; De Lange, 2016). For instance, extending the CSA–FSA framework (Rugman & Verbeke, 1998), Aguilera-Caracuel, Aragón-Correa, and Esther Hurtado-Torres (2011) propose that the environmental institutional distance between home and host countries is instrumental in choosing between a standard environmental strategy or a country-specific one.

Even within a given country, one may find consumers with varying degrees of awareness and commitment toward the environmental attributes of a product or service (e.g. Grinstein & Riefler, 2015; De Lange, 2016). Marketing and psychology scholars studied the effect of culture on pro-environmental consumption behavior (e.g. Cordano et al., 2011; Soyez, 2012). Consumers willing to buy green products and services still face the challenge of finding credible and non-controversial information about pro-environmental features. Ecolabels have been designed with such a purpose, by assuring that environmental claims presented in the products are reliable (Dechant & Altman, 1994). The Fair-Trade ecolabel is an example. The label guarantees that no forced labor or child slavery has been used in the production of the coffee, and that a minimum price is paid to farmers (often above market prices). Such third-party certifications also have the important role of reducing transaction costs and risks associated with liabilities across the supply chain (Chkanikova & Lehner, 2015). In this respect, IB scholars may find the ecolabels as an appropriate object for studying the role of business in alleviating poverty and inequality (Kolk, 2016; Shapiro et al., 2018; Wettestein, Giuliani, Santangelo, & Stahl, 2019). In cases such as the Fair-Trade ecolabel, poverty alleviation and local development are addressed via the integration of underprivileged workers into the supply chain, actions that are also expected to yield reputational gains for the MNE (Gold, Hahn, & Seuring, 2013; Rosca & Bendul, 2019).

Although strategic tools such as ecolabels are important means for eco-branding strategies, they may not be sufficient to generate competitive advantage, as they can also be easily adopted by competitors. The development of a private eco-brand allows MNEs to proactively address sustainability issues, helping them to communicate the image of their environmental responsibility and differentiate products from competitors. Änglamark, for instance, was the first eco-brand developed by Coop, a large Swedish supermarket chain. Sales of Änglamark products increased from EUR3 million in 1991 to a yearly average of EUR55 million between 2004 and 2008, conferring the leadership of the eco-brand in the Swedish market in that period. More recently, other global retailers in Sweden (ICA, for instance) and abroad developed their own eco-brands, intensifying global competition. In turn, the successful deployment of eco-branding strategies requires MNC to consider the availability of reliable and non-controversial information provided by ecolabels, the willingness of consumers to pay price premiums for products or services, and the inimitability by competitors, normally granted by private eco(brands).

Strategy 4: Environmental Cost Leadership

While eco-efficiency is desirable and might help companies to be more competitive, when competing in price sensitive markets, customers buy products and services because of their lowest prices, rather than their eco-attributes (Orsato, 2006). Nonetheless, in certain circumstances, the search for lowering the environmental impact of the product may actually help companies reach the lowest costs. Incorporating eco-attributes in existing or new products that lead to consistent lower costs is not a simple task, though; it may demand radical technological innovation, investment in product redevelopment, eco-design, and even new forms of commercialization.

An exemplary source of reducing economic and environmental costs is *eco-design*. Its scope encompasses the concept of Life Cycle Analysis (LCA) and, more recently, the Life Cycle Cost Analysis (LCCA), which extended the LCA logic with the proposition that environmental attributes of products could also help companies reduce their total costs (Kumaran, Ong, Tan, & Nee, 2001). An iconic example is Space X. After fifteen years of massive investments in R&D, in 2017 the company managed to launch a rocket carrying a communications satellite and land the rocket for reuse in another mission. This represented a breakthrough in the aerospace industry, as each launch is less costly than using disposable rockets and less resource-intense, since rockets can be used several times. Eco-design has also benefited from technological innovations in bioengineering, nanotechnology, and material science, which allowed the development of more radical approaches. Blue Planet, a Californian company founded in 2013, epitomizes such principles by sequestering carbon dioxide to produce carbonate rocks, the main component of cement. The technology (bio) mimics the mineralization process deployed in the growth process of coral reefs. Once the production scales-up and the price of carbon raises, the company may gain a global competitive advantage. NotCo, is a Chilean start-up founded in 2015 that uses a machine learning-based digital platform to analyze the molecular structure of foods derived from animals (e.g. meat and milk) in order to identify the best plant-based alternative. The products are more nutritious and can be retailed with the same price as non-vegan versions. In 2019, it raised 30 million dollars from venture capitalists (among them, Jeff Bezos from Amazon) to expand their portfolio and international markets.

Availability of supply is a key motivation for a more efficient use of resources. While the demand for goods from emerging markets has grown steadily, expanding the supply of some commodities has proven to be extremely difficult. This is the case of the so-called rare earth elements (neodymium, europium, terbium) used as raw materials in electronic products, electric cars, and renewable energy generation and storage. The market domination of these rare minerals by China increases the availability risks (Golev et al., 2014; Valero, Valero, Calvo, & Ortego, 2018). Suppliers from conflict areas (Kolk, 2016) also pose major challenges for MNEs not only for the risk of reduced availability of resources, but also for the risk of price volatility and geopolitical instability.

Finally, an e-cost strategy can be developed by focusing on the deployment of a product–service system (PSS). By moving from ownership to usership and selling the functions that the products are supposed to deliver, the same service level can be reached with less use of resources (Orsato, 2009). Typical examples of PSS include car, bike, or scooter-sharing and the pay-per-wash system of Electrolux. In the business-to-business (B2B) market, there are also several examples. Safechem, a German chemical cleaning company, provides solvents and services of training, taking-back, waste analysis, and so on (called Complease) at a fixed monthly rate. These examples indicate some challenges that MNEs would face to move from selling to renting, leasing, or sharing. They would need to reframe the reasoning of customer involvement and education, companies' competences, and data processing and valuation (Orsato, 2009; Tukker, 2015).

Considering the central role of technology and innovation for this strategy, some IB scholars have analyzed how technology transfer and knowledge integration among MNCs, suppliers, and subsidiaries affect corporate sustainability. In a study about Malaysian MNCs subsidiaries, Fazal, Al Mamun, Wahab, and Mohiuddin (2017) found that knowledge transfer from parent companies is associated with the improvement of corporate sustainability in subsidiaries and that government policies are essential to foster this transfer. Likewise, Li, Zhou, and Wu (2017) uncovered that knowledge integration between international customers (B2B) and Chinese exporting suppliers may help companies to improve their environmental performance. Both studies were conducted in contexts where the main recipient of the knowledge is located in a non-developed country. Therefore, future research may investigate the knowledge integration or transfer the other way around, that is, when the subsidiary or supplier located in a non-developed country is the main source of information or knowledge.

Strategy 5: Sustainable Value Innovation

The fifth sustainability strategy, SVI, focuses on the deployment of innovative business models for the creation of new market spaces, in alignment with the demands for corporate environmental and social responsibility (Orsato, 2009). The point of departure for the creation of SVI is the identification of the ultimate service a product is supposed to deliver. Individual motorized mobility, for instance, can be done not only via the private ownership of cars but also via carsharing systems provided by companies such as Car2Go and ZipCar. Compared with private car ownership, such businesses show that it is possible to satisfy the demands for individual motorization more efficiently at both lower costs and environmental impacts. As the growth of carsharing membership suggests—from negligible in 2005 to around 2 million in 2018—these new businesses can create *new markets*. Nonetheless, the growth of the carsharing market was dwarfed by the remarkable growth of car-riding, constructed on business platforms: Uber, for instance, since its launch in 2009, grew to 75 million monthly users in 2019. This was possible because of a key difference between the two business models: carsharing is based on the provision of cars to be shared among users, assisted by mobile computing and geo-localization technology. This means that the growth of carsharing requires investments for the expansion of the car fleet, characterizing a *one-sided market*, a one-directional market, from providers of cars to users. The growth of the car-riding business, on the other hand, does not require investment in cars. Instead, these business platforms motivate car owners to join the platform to become providers of mobility and optimize the investments of their own assets. Since car owners can be both providers and users of car-riding services, the business platform enables a *two-sided market*. In the logic of SVI strategy, the system inefficiencies tapped by companies like Uber and Lift indicate latent, untapped market spaces. As explained in more detail in Chapter 19, such business platforms were possible mainly because the advent of mobile computing, geo-localization, and the decrease of costs of data processing and communication, which facilitated the interaction between producers and consumers, who otherwise would not transact with each other (Gawer, 2014). Thus, business platforms are designed as networks to mediate exchanges between groups of users and create *two or multi-sided markets* in which buyers and sellers may swap positions at any time (Landsman & Stremersch, 2011;

Rysman, 2009). The value a new user adds to existing members generates positive *network effects*, in which growth in the number of platform users will motivate others to adopt it.

Compared to digital-only platforms, such as Spotify (music) and Dropbox (digital files), there is a physical component involved in businesses such as Uber (cars) and Airbnb (houses/apartments), which characterizes them as online-to-offline (O2O) business platforms. The physical component embeds (positive or negative) social and environmental impacts. After all, the majority of successful business platforms were not conceived with the aim of reducing environmental impacts but rather generating profits for owners and shareholders. Nonetheless, the *sharing* characteristic of these platforms may reduce environmental impacts, for it would eventually lead to the *servicization* of the economy and, consequently, a reduced material and energy intensity of societies (Müller et al., 2017; Valero et al., 2018). In this respect, SVI strategy relates to the so-called *sharing economy*. Since sharing, in principle, reduces the resource intensity of the economy and increases the accessibility of goods and services to lower income classes, it has the potential to assist a radical shift toward sustainability (Cohen & Kietzmann, 2014). The scale of impact of this strategy tends to be significant because it often implies a global business model from inception: scaling-up fast and prioritizing large-scale international expansion. With this rapid internationalization orientation, we require further research to understand how MNEs can build local legitimacy in host countries and deal with associated social impacts (e.g. precarious working conditions, especially in emerging economies) (Parente Geleilate, & Rong, 2018).

Although the sharing economy may generate environmental benefits, financial attractiveness is the primary motivator for participation in business platforms (Engel-Yan & Passmore, 2013; Hamari, Sjöklint, & Ukkonen, 2015). Embedding a value proposition into what we could call a *business platform for sustainability* confronts the underutilization and waste of resources associated with the unequal distribution of wealth, reducing the cost of accessing goods and services and enabling greater operational efficiency of resources according to demand (Botsman & Rogers, 2010). While the sustainability of industries and societies remains to be further studied before it is fully understood, the use of business platforms for the deployment of SVI strategies has the potential to increase the chances of MNEs creating truly sustainable businesses.

SUSTAINABILITY STRATEGIES AND IB: A SUMMARY

This chapter presented sustainability strategies that go beyond regulatory requirements, focusing on cost reduction, differentiation, and new value propositions through O2O business platforms. We brought an updated perspective of sustainability strategies from both theory and practice, with special attention to their relevance to the MNE. We explored how of the ways in which sustainability strategies may help MNEs to become more competitive in international markets.

Reducing costs can be achieved through the implementation of *lean principles*, seeking to minimize waste and promote radical improvements in resource productivity within the MNE. Further gains can be obtained by extending lean principles beyond the borders of the organization via *industrial symbiosis* systems. Finally, companies can also profit from the eco-efficiency strategy by trading waste and environmental off-sets, such as *carbon credits*. Furthermore, we explained that proactive companies can also aim at achieving *beyond compliance leadership* by subscribing to several VEIs. In doing so, MNEs can enhance their reputations, while having access to knowledge and innovation opportunities for participating in the initiative. In the last decade, various VEI have emerged, some focused on specific issues such as climate change and others embracing multiple issues. Research on VEI and green clubs are mainly focused on understanding the drivers and outcomes associated with MNE involvement in these initiatives.

In order to differentiate products and services with eco-friendly prerogatives, firms need to observe three requirements. First, products need to present credible and non-controversial information about the pro-environmental features; we explained why third-party certified ecolabels are normally used for this purpose. Second, the eco-differentiation should not be easy to be imitate, which can be done via *eco-branding*. The development of a brand based on eco-attributes should hinder imitation. Finally, consumers have to be willing to pay a price premium for the eco-differentiation. This type of sustainability strategy deserves, in our view, further research. Among personal preferences, cultural differences play a major role and they must be understood by MNEs choosing to differentiate using eco-friendly prerogatives. In turn, when competing in markets where price premium is not possible, MNEs may choose to invest in sustainability-driven innovation to reach *environmental cost leadership*. To do so, firms often need to deploy eco-design, biotechnology, and product–service systems. Such innovations require massive investments in cutting-edge technologies and new value propositions for products and services, which certainly bear uncertainties (as discussed in Chapter 21, misalignment with GVC partners may hinder these types of developments)—but may results in market leadership.

Finally, since the publication of the *Sustainability Strategies* (Orsato, 2009), technological breakthroughs allowed the development of SVI in a more compelling manner. Developments in mobile computing allowed the emergence of two interlinked phenomena: O2O business platforms and business models based on the so-called sharing economy. Besides enabling SVI strategies, there is a concealed hope that business models based on digital platforms will eventually make the world more sustainable. Although only time and research will bring us the answer, we do hope that it will be the case.

RESEARCH OPPORTUNITIES AND CONCLUDING REMARKS

This chapter explains the sustainability strategies that MNEs have available to them and the importance in considering sustainability goals when designing IB strategies. Yet, there are other aspects of IB strategy that future studies could link with sustainability goals. Concerning the interface between sustainability strategies and IB strategies, future research may seek to understand the following key questions:

- How do MNEs migrate from global product-based to global platform-based businesses?
- How do macro-level institutions affect the international diffusion of certified environmental standards?
- How do new business models influence stakeholders' perceptions about MNE legitimacy?

Some performance-related issues also bring questions to be investigated in the context of sustainability strategies, such as:

- What is the influence of green attributes of products and services on the overall performance of the brand at the regional and global levels?
- What is the performance in foreign markets of MNEs that hold CSAs derived from natural resources?

Regarding FSAs, future research on sustainability strategies may investigate the following:

- How does the degree of internationalization influence business practices related to emergent issues, such as human rights?
- What is the strategic importance of subsidiaries on MNE sustainability strategies?
- What are the differences in equity and non-equity entry modes in foreign markets and their impacts on the environment for certain types of MNEs?

Few studies discuss the role of MNEs in tackling poverty and other issues related to national development in emerging host countries (see Kolk, 2016; Narula, 2018; Shapiro et al., 2018); social and environmental impacts of new business platforms and the sharing economy (Parente et al., 2018); the interplay between new production technologies and social and environmental issues (Wettstein et al., 2019); and impacts of new models of production–consumption respective to developing versus developed countries (Goyal et al., 2018). In this respect, the following questions can be investigated:

- What is the importance of cross-sector partnerships in determining the success of entry strategies in Base of Pyramid (BoP) markets?
- How can MNEs improve the integration of people from the BoP into the supply chain?

Finally, IB research may also focus on the timing of sustainability strategies adoption. Longitudinal studies may investigate the period for building local legitimacy (Gifford &

Kestler, 2008; De Lange, 2016) and local-bonded knowledge (Poisson-de Haro & Bitektine, 2015); the stage development of entry markets (Chen, Newburry, & Park, 2009); the changes in issue salience and stakeholders' perceptions over time (Poisson-de Haro & Bitektine, 2015; Eiadat, Kelly, Roche, & Eyadat, 2008); and the aspiration of a first-mover advantage (Pinkse & Kolk, 2012).

While these suggestions are not exhaustive, we hope that they provide insights to researchers and managers interested in understanding how and why sustainability strategies should become part of the IB strategy agenda.

References

Aguilera-Caracuel, J., Aragón-Correa, J. A., & Esther Hurtado-Torres, N. 2011. Extending the literature on the environmental strategy of MNEs. *Multinational Business Review*, 19(4): 299–310.

Andersen, P. H., & Rask, M. 2014. Creating legitimacy across international contexts: The role of storytelling for international new ventures. *Journal of International Entrepreneurship*, 12(4): 365–388.

Barkemeyer, R., Preuss, L., & Lee, L. 2015. On the effectiveness of private transnational governance regimes—Evaluating corporate sustainability reporting according to the global reporting initiative. *Journal of World Business*, 50(2): 312–325.

Ben Brik, A., Mellahi, K., & Rettab, B. 2013. Drivers of green supply chain in emerging economies. *Thunderbird International Business Review*, 55(2): 123–136.

Botsman, R., & Rogers, R. 2010. *What's Mine is Yours: The Rise of Collaborative Consumption*. New York, NY: HarperCollins.

Boyce, J. K. 2018. Carbon pricing: Effectiveness and equity. *Ecological Economics*, 150: 52–61.

Buckley, P. J., Doh, J. P., & Benischke, M. H. 2017. Towards a renaissance in international business research? Big questions, grand challenges, and the future of IB scholarship. *Journal of International Business Studies*, 48(9): 1045–1064.

Buysse, K., & Verbeke, A. 2003. Proactive environmental strategies: A stakeholder management perspective. *Strategic Management Journal*, 24(5): 453–470.

Cerdeira Bento, J. P., & Moreira, A. 2018. Environmental impact of FDI—The case of US subsidiaries. *Multinational Business Review*, 27(3): 226–246.

Chen, D., Newburry, W., & Park, S. H. 2009. Improving sustainability: An international evolutionary framework. *Journal of International Management*, 15(3): 317–327.

Chkanikova, O., & Lehner, M. 2015. Private eco-brands and green market development: Towards new forms of sustainability governance in the food retailing. *Journal of Cleaner Production*, 107: 74–84.

Christmann, P., & Taylor, G. 2001. Globalization and the environment: Determinants of firm self-regulation in China. *Journal of International Business Studies*, 32(3): 439–458.

Cohen, B., & Kietzmann, J. 2014. Ride on! Mobility business models for the sharing economy. *Organization & Environment*, 27(3): 279–296.

Cordano, M., Welcomer, S., Scherer, R. F., Pradenas, L., & Parada, V. 2011. A cross-cultural assessment of three theories of pro-environmental behavior: A comparison between business students of Chile and the United States. *Environment and Behavior*, 43(5): 634–657.

Cuadrado-Ballesteros, B., Martínez-Ferrero, J., & García-Sánchez, I. M. 2017. Mitigating information asymmetry through sustainability assurance: The role of accountants and levels of assurance. *International Business Review*, 26(6): 1141–1156.

Darnall, N., Jolley, G. J., & Handfield, R. 2008. Environmental management systems and green supply chain management: Complements for sustainability? *Business Strategy and the Environment*, 17(1): 30–45.

De Lange, D. E. 2016. Legitimation strategies for clean technology entrepreneurs facing institutional voids in emerging economies. *Journal of International Management*, 22(4): 403–415.

Dechant, K., & Altman, B. 1994. Environmental leadership: From compliance to competitive advantage. *Academy of Management Perspectives*, 8(3): 7–20.

Eiadat, Y., Kelly, A., Roche, F., & Eyadat, H. 2008. Green and competitive? An empirical test of the mediating role of environmental innovation strategy. *Journal of World Business*, 43(2): 131–145.

Engel-Yan, J., & Passmore, D. 2013. Carsharing and car ownership at the building scale: Examining the potential for flexible parking requirements. *Journal of the American Planning Association*, 79(1): 82–91.

Etzion, D. 2007. Research on organizations and the natural environment, 1992-present: A review. *Journal of Management*, 33(4): 637–664.

Fazal, S. A., Al Mamun, A., Wahab, S. A., & Mohiuddin, M. 2017. Host-country characteristics, corporate sustainability, and the mediating effect of improved knowledge: A study among foreign MNCs in Malaysia. *Multinational Business Review*, 25(4): 328–349.

Garcia, A. S., Mendes-Da-Silva, W., & Orsato, R. J. 2017. Sensitive industries produce better ESG performance: Evidence from emerging markets. *Journal of Cleaner Production*, 150: 135–147.

Gawer, A. 2014. Bridging differing perspectives on technological platforms: Toward an integrative framework. *Research Policy*, 43(7): 1239–1249.

Geisendorf, S., & Pietrulla, F. 2018. The circular economy and circular economic concepts—A literature analysis and redefinition. *Thunderbird International Business Review*, 60(5): 771–782.

Gifford, B., & Kestler, A. 2008. Toward a theory of local legitimacy by MNEs in developing nations: Newmont mining and health sustainable development in Peru. *Journal of International Management*, 14(4): 340–352.

Gold, S., Hahn, R., & Seuring, S. 2013. Sustainable supply chain management in "Base of the Pyramid" food projects—A path to triple bottom line approaches for multinationals? *International Business Review*, 22(5): 784–799.

Golev, A., Scott, M., Erskine, P. D., Ali, S. H., & Ballantyne, G. R. 2014. Rare earths supply chains: Current status, constraints and opportunities. *Resources Policy*, 41: 52–59.

González-Benito, J., & González-Benito, Ó. 2006. A review of determinant factors of environmental proactivity. *Business Strategy and the Environment*, 15(2): 87–102.

Goyal, S., Esposito, M., & Kapoor, A. 2018. Circular economy business models in developing economies: Lessons from India on reduce, recycle, and reuse paradigms. *Thunderbird International Business Review*, 60(5): 729–740.

Green, J. F. 2017. Don't link carbon markets. *Nature News*, 543(7646): 484–486.

Grinstein, A., & Riefler, P. 2015. Citizens of the (green) world? Cosmopolitan orientation and sustainability. *Journal of International Business Studies*, 46(6): 694–714.

Gupta, S. 2016. Enhancing brand equity through sustainability: Waste recycling. *Thunderbird International Business Review*, 58(3): 213–223.

Hamari, J., Sjöklint, M., & Ukkonen, A. 2015. The sharing economy: Why people participate in collaborative consumption. *Journal of the Association for Information Science and Technology*, 67(9): 2047–2059.

Harzing, A. W. 2019. Journal Quality List (64th ed.). https://harzing.com/resources/journal-quality-list. Accessed 15 February 2019.

Hitt, M. A., Li, D., & Xu, K. 2016. International strategy: From local to global and beyond. *Journal of World Business*, 51(1): 58–73.

Kang, Y., & He, X. 2018. Institutional forces and environmental management strategy: Moderating effects of environmental orientation and innovation capability. *Management and Organization Review*, 14(3): 577–605.

Kolk, A. 2010. Social and sustainability dimensions of regionalization and (semi) globalization. *Multinational Business Review*, 18(1): 51–72.

Kolk, A. 2016. The social responsibility of international business: From ethics and the environment to CSR and sustainable development. *Journal of World Business*, 51(1): 23–34.

Kolk, A., & Fortanier, F. 2013. Internationalization and environmental disclosure: The role of home and host institutions. *Multinational Business Review*, 21(1): 87–114.

Kolk, A., & Van Tulder, R. 2010. International business, corporate social responsibility and sustainable development. *International Business Review*, 19(2): 119–125.

Kumaran, D. S., Ong, S. K., Tan, R. B., & Nee, A. Y. C. 2001. Environmental life cycle cost analysis of products. *Environmental Management and Health*, 12(3): 260–276.

Landsman, V., & Stremersch, S. 2011. Multihoming in two-sided markets: An empirical inquiry in the video game console industry. *Journal of Marketing*, 75(6): 39–54.

Li, E. L., Zhou, L., & Wu, A. 2017. The supply-side of environmental sustainability and export performance: The role of knowledge integration and international buyer involvement. *International Business Review*, 26(4): 724–735.

MacLennan, M. L. F., & Barakat, S. R. 2017. Environmental strategies in emerging markets as a source of competitive advantage. *International Journal of Business and Emerging Markets*, 9(4): 332–353.

Marquis, C., Jackson, S. E., & Li, Y. 2015. Building sustainable organizations in China. *Management and Organization Review*, 11(3): 427–440.

Martínez-Ferrero, J., & García-Sánchez, I. M. 2017. Coercive, normative and mimetic isomorphism as determinants of the voluntary assurance of sustainability reports. *International Business Review*, 26(1): 102–118.

Montiel, I., & Delgado-Ceballos, J. 2014. Defining and measuring corporate sustainability: Are we there yet? *Organization & Environment*, 27(2): 113–139.

Mort, G. S. 2010. Sustainable Business. *Journal of World Business*, 45(4): 323–325.

Müller, F., Kosmol, J., Keßler, H., Angrick, M., & Rechenberg, B. 2017. Dematerialization—A disputable strategy for resource conservation put under scrutiny. *Resources*, 6(4): 1–32.

Narula, R. 2018. Multinational firms and the extractive sectors in the 21st century: Can they drive development? *Journal of World Business*, 53(1): 85–91.

Orcos, R., Pérez-Aradros, B., & Blind, K. 2018. Why does the diffusion of environmental management standards differ across countries? The role of formal and informal institutions in the adoption of ISO 14001. *Journal of World Business*, 53(6): 850–861.

Orsato, R. J. 2006. Competitive environmental strategies: When does it pay to be green? *California Management Review*, 48(2): 127–143.

Orsato, R. J. 2009. *Sustainability Strategies: When Does it Pay to be Green?* London: Palgrave Macmillan.

Orsato, R. J., Barakat, S. R., & de Campos, J. G. F. 2017. Organizational adaptation to climate change: Learning to anticipate energy disruptions. *International Journal of Climate Change Strategies and Management*, 9(5): 645–665.

Orsato, R. J., de Campos, J. G. F., & Barakat, S. R. 2019. Social learning for anticipatory adaptation to climate change: Evidence from a community of practice. *Organization & Environment*, 32(4): 416–440.

Orsato, R. J., de Campos, J. G. F., Barakat, S. R., Nicolletti, M., & Monzoni, M. 2015. Why join a carbon club? A study of the banks participating in the Brazilian "Business for Climate Platform." *Journal of Cleaner Production*, 96: 387–396.

Orsato, R. J., Den Hond, F., & Clegg, S. R. 2002. The political ecology of automobile recycling in Europe. *Organization Studies*, 23(4): 639–665.

Parente, R. C., Geleilate, J. M. G., & Rong, K. 2018. The sharing economy globalization phenomenon: A research agenda. *Journal of International Management*, 24(1): 52–64.

Pinkse, J., & Kolk, A. 2012. Multinational enterprises and climate change: Exploring institutional failures and embeddedness. *Journal of International Business Studies*, 43(3): 332–341.

Poisson-de Haro, S., & Bitektine, A. 2015. Global sustainability pressures and strategic choice: The role of firms' structures and non-market capabilities in selection and implementation of sustainability initiatives. *Journal of World Business*, 50(2): 326–341.

Potoski, M. 2017. Green clubs in building block climate change regimes. *Climatic Change*, 144(1): 53–63.

Prakash, A. 2001. Why do firms adopt "beyond-compliance" environmental policies? *Business Strategy and the Environment*, 10(5): 286–299.

Prosman, E. J., Wæhrens, B. V., & Liotta, G. 2017. Closing global material loops: Initial insights into firm-level challenges. *Journal of Industrial Ecology*, 21(3): 641–650.

Rosca, E., & Bendul, J. C. 2019. Value chain integration of base of the pyramid consumers: An empirical study of drivers and performance outcomes. *International Business Review*, 28(1): 162–176.

Rugman, A. M., & Verbeke, A. 1998. Corporate strategies and environmental regulations: An organizing framework. *Strategic Management Journal*, 19(4): 363–375.

Rysman, M. 2009. The economics of two-sided markets. *Journal of Economic Perspectives*, 23(3): 125–143.

Schotter, A., & Goodsite, M. E. (2013). Interdisciplinary perspectives on competitive climate strategy in multinational corporations. *Thunderbird International Business Review*, 55(6): 629–632.

Shapiro, D., Hobdari, B., & Oh, C. H. 2018. Natural resources, multinational enterprises and sustainable development. *Journal of World Business*, 53(1): 1–14.

Soyez, K. 2012. How national cultural values affect pro-environmental consumer behavior. *International Marketing Review*, 29(6): 623–646.

Susur, E., Hidalgo, A., & Chiaroni, D. 2019. A strategic niche management perspective on transitions to eco-industrial park development: A systematic review of case studies. *Resources, Conservation and Recycling*, 140, 338–359.

Tatoglu, E., Bayraktar, E., Sahadev, S., Demirbag, M., & Glaister, K. W. 2014. Determinants of voluntary environmental management practices by MNE subsidiaries. *Journal of World Business*, 49(4): 536–548.

Tuerk, A., Mehling, M., Flachsland, C., & Sterk, W. 2009. Linking carbon markets: Concepts, case studies and pathways. *Climate Policy*, 9(4): 341–357.

Tukker, A. 2015. Product services for a resource-efficient and circular economy—A review. *Journal of Cleaner Production*, 97: 76–91.

Valero, A., Valero, A., Calvo, G., & Ortego, A. 2018. Material bottlenecks in the future development of green technologies. *Renewable and Sustainable Energy Reviews*, 93: 178–200.

Wang, P., & Kuah, A. T. 2018. Green marketing cradle-to-cradle: Remanufactured products in Asian markets. *Thunderbird International Business Review*, 60(5): 783–795.

Wells, P., & Orsato, R. J. 2005. Redesigning the industrial ecology of the automobile. *Journal of Industrial Ecology*, 9(3): 15–30.

Wettstein, F., Giuliani, E., Santangelo, G. D., & Stahl, G. K. 2019. International business and human rights: A research agenda. *Journal of World Business*, 54(1): 54–65.

Yang, Q., Mudambi, R., & Meyer, K. 2008. Conventional and reverse knowledge flows in multinational corporations. *Journal of Management*, 34(5): 882–902.

CHAPTER 23

NEW INTERNATIONAL HUMAN RESOURCE MANAGEMENT APPROACHES AND MULTINATIONAL ENTERPRISE STRATEGIES

KIERAN M. CONROY AND DANA MINBAEVA

INTRODUCTION

IN the context of what is often now referred to as strategic international human resource management (SIHRM), scholars have drawn from two parallel but largely distinct strands of research; international HRM (IHRM) and international strategy (IS). Despite both streams considering broadly similar issues on the behaviors and actions of multinational enterprises (MNEs), they have largely failed to engage in a mutually reinforcing dialog (Andersson et al., 2019). In parallel, scholars and practitioners call for a broader, more strategic view of IHRM, in order to better understand how the human resources (HR) function contributes to the challenges of implementing IS (Schuler, Jackson, & Tarique, 2011). Given the explicit lack of integration between the two perspectives, there is a need to start a more intense conversation on how the field of SIHRM can move forward by integrating knowledge from these two areas of research.

Most of the work in the SIHRM field was largely developed in the context of a relatively stable and predictable global environment, assuming a relatively homogeneous workforce (culture aside); therefore, the implementation of strategy for MNEs from an HR perspective was far less complicated. A contemporary problem that needs greater recognition is that MNEs continuously change strategies and expand into new markets without fully accounting for the pressures that these decisions create for their HR function (Andersson et al., 2019). We argue that there is a need to move the conversation forward to account for the complexity that contemporary MNEs with increasingly diverse workforces are confronted with in implementing their ISs. Specifically, the aim of this chapter is to conceptualize the changing nature of HR's role in the implementation of strategy across the MNE. In doing so, we explore more broadly how IS and IHRM scholars can more effectively learn from each other in order to move the field of SIHRM forward.

Is and IHRM: Common Themes

There are a number of important themes that are common across the two streams of literature in IS and IHRM. First, scholars from both domains consider the problem of how MNEs balance the inconsistencies and tensions between global and local contexts, generally considered through the home–host country perspective. For example, one of the key issues for IHRM scholars is understanding how MNEs achieve an effective balance between internal consistency and local adaptation of their HR policies and practices (Rosenzweig & Nohria, 1994; Pudelko & Harzing, 2007). Tensions exist between standardizing HR practices so that they may be exploited as firm-specific advantages, and adapting these HR practices to the varying cultural and institutional demands of local environments (Al Ariss & Sidani, 2016). Equally, IS scholars have focused on the importance of developing strategies that achieve a delicate balance between global integration and local responsiveness (Ghoshal & Bartlett, 1990). Work here considers how this dilemma is balanced through the headquarters (HQ)–subsidiary relationship, with traditional approaches emphasizing HQ control and coordination activities, whereas more recent work illuminates on the importance of subsidiary autonomy and influence (notably, Kostova, Marano, & Tallman, 2016). Therefore, both IS and IHRM consider how global and local tensions, dualities, or dilemmas are managed in the context of the HQ–subsidiary relationship.

A second dominant theme common across both streams is the importance of knowledge transfer within the MNE. Studies argue that the HR function is important for overcoming barriers to knowledge exchange as it provides the means and mechanisms through which knowledge is assimilated and shared. For instance, IHRM work has shown that HR practices can facilitate increased flows of tacit and complex knowledge exchange internally and enhance the absorptive capacity of knowledge carriers and the MNE as a whole (Minbaeva et al., 2014). IHRM studies emphasize the importance of international assignments for mobilizing and disseminating knowledge, and hence, enhanced learning between HQ and subsidiaries (Harzing, Pudelko, & Reiche, 2016). Equally, IS studies have considered the MNE as a differentiated network where relevant and valuable local knowledge should be transferred and exploited globally (Gupta & Govindarajan, 2000).[1] Much of the literature here considers the direction of knowledge flows, with previous work focusing on intra-organizational flows from HQ to subsidiaries, while more recent studies highlight the importance of reverse knowledge transfer from subsidiaries to HQ (Yang et al., 2008). Other studies focus predominantly on the importance of inter-organizational knowledge flows to generate learning (Monteiro & Birkinshaw, 2017) and solve problems within the MNE (Tippmann, Scott, & Mangematin, 2012). However, there has been very little effort over the years to integrate what we have learned about knowledge transfer from IHRM studies with work done on the importance of knowledge transfer for international business (IB) strategies.

Third, in reflecting on the above two commonalities, scholars in both domains have largely built their work on two seminal frameworks that share mutual insights. In particular, the foundations of IHRM are built on Perlmutter's (1969) EPRG framework on staffing orientations of MNEs, with IS research drawing on Bartlett and Ghoshal's (1989) seminal typology of ISs. There are four broad types of staffing orientations that determine how an MNE mobilizes its human resources across borders (ethnocentric, polycentric, regiocentric, and geocentric), and each of these align to the four types of ISs (global, multidomestic, regional, and transnational). For example, an ethnocentric orientation likely leads to a global strategy with a focus on hierarchical top down strategy development, ensuring global integration of HR systems and policies through parent country nationals. A polycentric orientation focuses more exclusively on a multidomestic strategy developed from the bottom up and driven through the adaptation and subsequent sharing of HR policies and practices from host country nationals in subsidiaries with increased autonomy. Multinationals pursuing a transnational strategy will look to balance global integration with local responsiveness through a geocentric staffing orientation, mobilizing a cadre of highly talented individuals, tapping into and sharing knowledge within and across the MNE. More recently, we have witnessed a rise in regional strategies of MNEs, invoking a regiocentric orientation (Heenan & Perlmutter, 1979), where firms will staff their operations with individuals from given regions and adapt their HR policies and practices to regional idiosyncrasies rather than global parameters or local adjustments. Ultimately, these seminal works provide us with common knowledge on how MNEs utilize their HR function in implementing strategies in an IB context and how these two decisions are often interrelated.

An important avenue for linking seminal work on IHRM with the strategic needs of the MNE is through the field of SIHRM. Schuler, Dowling, and De Cieri (1993) were the first to consider SIHRM as a distinct theoretical domain and defined SIHRM as "HRM issues, functions and policies and practices that result from the strategic activities of multinational enterprises and that impact the international concerns and goals of those enterprises" (Schuler et al., 1993). Others have built on these insights in response to the growing external challenges faced by MNEs, such as aging workforce, skill

[1] See Chapter 15 for a discussion on network embeddedness and the transfer of knowledge between MNE subsidiaries.

shortages, industrial disputes, natural disasters, economic recessions, and political changes (De Cieri & Dowling, 2012). These revised conceptualizations have emphasized that reciprocal relationships exist between external and organizational factors that impact the corporate HR function and ultimately the MNE's strategic performance (Minbaeva & De Cieri, 2014). Studies have further emphasized the importance of an HR architecture that allows for a more integrative strategy across the MNE, balancing centralized HR policies and practices with decentralized autonomous initiative taking at the subsidiary level (see Morris, Snell, & Bjorkman, 2016).

However, as has already been suggested, a significant challenge that the field of strategic IHRM faces is the increasingly dynamic and complex nature of the global environment. This complexity forces many MNEs to persistently re-evaluate their approaches to developing IS (Andersson et al., 2019), which challenges the strategic role of HR in this context (Caligiuri, 2014). This complexity is compelling HR functions to be more formally integrated and aligned with the development and implementation of strategy (Reiche, Lee, & Allen, 2019). We maintain that, although the way in which an MNE reflects on, and responds to, these growing changes is largely through its SIHRM structure, there is a need to design more flexible and innovative policies and practices (Becker & Huselid, 2006). While the pervasive breadth of this global complexity means that a thorough investigation is beyond the scope of this chapter, we introduce what we see as three significant ways in which this complexity is manifested, and how we foresee it impacting the role of HR in the implementation of IS. Next, we discuss these challenges, after which we outline some directions for future research.

Contemporary Challenges for Sihrm

Although the strategic role of HR remains an imperative to MNE strategy implementation, the specific ways in which it executes this mandate have become more challenging due to a variety of disruptions. These challenges include the growing digitization of global work, the changing face of global mobility, and the shifting role of the corporate HR function in line with a more networked MNE structure. We zoom in on those changes in the external environment of the firm that are most likely to impact how the MNE transforms its HR function.

Digitization of Global Work

The digitization of work is a growing concern for HR and involves a myriad of factors, such as big data, analytics, and artificial intelligence (AI), robotics, and automation (Meijerink, Boons, Keegan, & Marler, 2018). The HR field has yet to fully appreciate the impact of digitization on HRM practices and policies or the broader positive, as well as potentially negative impacts that they may have on the strategic role of HRM within the MNE (Angrave et al., 2016).

One way to consider the scale of impact of digitization on HR is to distinguish between "being digital" from "doing digital." Many organizations invested enormous amounts of resources to transform their traditional (analog) business processes into digital formats. It applies to all business functions, including HR, and it is usually initiated at the HQ. Corporate HR functions digitalize their recruitment systems, upgrade performance management processes, and establish app-based strategic workforce planning. In the literature, this digital "face-lifting" of HR is termed as e-HR/electronic-HR. Bondarouk and Ruel (2009) define e-HR as "an umbrella terms covering all possible integration mechanisms and contents between HRM and Information Technology aiming at creating value within and across organizations for targeted employees and management" (p. 507). But simply transforming HR processes from analog to digital is not enough. How different then is "being digital" for HR?

As it is argued, digitization is driven by the user experience. For HR, the starting point of digital transformation should then be recentering on the employee experience and revamping their own processes through continuous innovation and experimentation. For example, IBM, a US company with over 400,000 employees worldwide, used a variety of experiments to transform to digital HR (Kiron & Spindel, 2019). After employee hackathon, performance management was reinvented to include a new feedback process that dramatically increased engagement and strategic alignment (Zillman, 2016). In response to employees' feedback, IBM shut down its global learning management system and replaced it with a new digital learning platform enabling employees to publish any content they deemed important and recommend external learning they found useful. Cognitive Human Interface Personality (CHIP) replaced the HR services hotline: an AI-based cognitive assistant can handle a wide range of HR-related questions, in various contexts and in different languages.

However, we argue that there remain a number of challenges associated with rewriting the rules of the game for IHRM in the digital age. Exponential rate of technological change is one such challenge. The use of automation, robotics, and AI for global value creation is yet to be understood by all parties: academics, practitioners, and consultants; as such, the full benefits (and drawbacks) of technological advancements are yet to be discovered. Another example of a related, but distinctive, challenge is the changing nature of work as a result of greater digitization in what has become known as the "gig economy" and the rise of gig workers (McDonnell, Burgess, Carbery, & Sherman, 2018). The debate in this context has focused on whether gig workers are similar to traditional employees or more akin to independent contractors with legal challenges impacting and affecting the nature of global work in this unique context (Fabo, Karanovic, & Dukova, 2017). Ethical implications of digitization of global work are of serious concern not just for businesses but also for civil society and governments. Deloitte's 2017 Global Human Capital Trends report accurately identified HR's opportunity to help close the gaps created by the rate of change among technology, individuals, businesses, society, and governments. The report states that: "HR has a unique role to play: It can help leaders and organizations adapt to technology, help people adapt to new models of work and careers, and help the company as a whole adapt to and encourage changes in society, regulation, and public policy" (Deloitte, 2017). Such opportunity remains yet to be explored for the vast majority of MNEs.

With an increased recognition that the structure of the MNE is becoming more complex and matrixed in its design, digitization should become a tool that allows for the creation of a more flexible global workforce (Schotter, Buchel, & Vashchilko, 2018). IS scholars are beginning to recognize the importance of the HR function in building greater agility, particularly in the design of global virtual work and its influence on knowledge exchanges across the MNE (Nurmi & Hinds, 2016). Ongoing digitization may impact how the HQ adds value to its global network of subsidiaries in that it may provide timelier and better access to information (Schmitt, Decreton, & Nell, 2019). In order to take full advantage of this, HR organizations in HQs need to become more platform-based, ensuring they have the required digital talent at all levels in the organization. For example, HR teams require fewer generalists and more senior HR consultants. As one chief HR officer (CHRO) mentioned: "To manage my global organization, I will need mini-CHROs like me to push strategy implementation at frontlines and a solid back up at the corporate HR function, consisting of centers of excellence in various HR disciplines and run as digital platform." Other studies in IS are increasingly recognizing the importance of digitization for ISs in the context of platform-based business models that connect buyers and sellers (Stallkamp & Schotter, 2019) as well as how this challenges traditional IB frameworks. Based on the aforementioned arguments, it is clear that the digitization of work is an increasingly important issue that will impact HR's role in the implementation of strategy across the MNE.

Changing Face of Global Mobility

One of the most widely considered issues in the context of IHRM is the global mobility of the MNE's workforce (Bonache, Brewster, Suutari, & Cerdin, 2017). Global staffing is a central part of the mobility process and considers the importance of sending individual managers on international assignments. Much of the literature in this area has focused on the importance of traditional expatriation, which involves deploying HQ employees to foreign subsidiaries, usually on a long-term assignment between one and three years (Collings & Isichei, 2018). As outlined earlier in Perlmutter's EPRG model, much of the extant research on expatriates is considered from an ethnocentric perspective, in that parent country expatriates ensure greater HQ control and coordination of their strategies (Harzing, 2001). More recently, due to the costs of expatriation and the need for more flexible ways of implementing strategy in globally dynamic environments, MNEs have begun to design alternative forms of mobility (Caligiuri & Bonache, 2016). We have witnessed an emergence of various types of mobility, such as short term (one–twelve months), virtual, frequent flyers, and self-initiated assignments (Shaffer, Kraimer, Chen, & Bolino, 2012). These assignees are increasingly deployed for strategic purposes such as tapping into valuable knowledge in unknown markets and sharing this with relevant actors in the MNE (Duvivier, Peeters, & Harzing, 2019). In adapting to growing demands to become more flexible over the next five years, KPMG's global mobility survey found that 72 percent of firms expect to rely on short-term assignments, such as extended business trips (three months), with a 28 percent reduction in use of expatriates (KPMG, 2018).

This is problematic because, recent work on IB travelers—individuals that regularly travel across borders, often staying in a location for up to four weeks, without fully relocating (Meyskens, Von Glinow, Werther, Jr, & Clarke, 2009)—demonstrates that these individuals face unique challenges related to health and family stability (Welch, Welch, & Worm, 2007). These unique challenges may subsequently impact on their effectiveness to build the relevant social capital needed to share knowledge back to HQ (Bozkurt & Mohr, 2011). Others have detailed how these alternative assignees are often not formally controlled through the HR function (Makela & Kinnunen, 2018), instead being managed in an informal capacity through their line managers with very little training and support provided in comparison to traditional expatriates (Conroy, McDonnell, & Holzleitner, 2018). It is clear that these more temporary forms of mobility are crucial channels through which knowledge is being mobilized and transferred across the MNE (Bathelt & Henn, 2014); however, there is a risk that the potential strategic value expected to be gained is not fully captured due to their lack of integration with the HR function. This shift creates contemporary challenges for current IHRM policies and practices that have been preserved to accommodate expatriates, compelling the HR function to be more innovative. The development of these alternative assignments has implications for how knowledge is shared, and more broadly how strategy is implemented in a dynamic environment (Harzing et al. 2016).

Another significant challenge for IHRM in the context of global mobility comes in the form of global talent management, which involves attracting and retaining high-performing employees that are critical to the MNE's strategic success (Stahl et al. 2012). Global talent management work focuses on the management of employees with high levels of human capital and considers the importance of HR practices for those talented individuals being aligned with the MNE's strategy intent (Collings, 2014). More recently, scholars have argued that, in implementing strategy, MNEs should focus less on recognizing talented individuals for leadership succession at the HQ and more on identifying central strategic positions across the MNE (Collings, Mellahi, & Cascio, 2019). As the complexity and dynamism increases, MNEs may need to widen their search in order to fill these positions, ensuring that subsidiary employees are provided with more opportunities. Collings and Mellahi (2009) argue that MNEs need to develop strategic talent management agendas with differentiated architectures that maximize the potential for exploiting talent pools to fill such pivotal positions.

Further to the importance of integrating HR practices with dynamic MNE strategies, Morris et al. (2016) identified how different configurations of talent portfolios tend to be emphasized and integrated depending on the IS of the MNE. Their work presents an architecture for global talent management, moving beyond aligning HR practices with strategy and demonstrating how staffing can become a dynamic capability when decisions are based on the human capital profile of the individual, rather than their nationality or location. For example, MNEs with a transnational strategy will likely build a talent portfolio that integrates subsidiary and corporate human capital, where learning is driven from the bottom up. Employees in this context are, therefore, expected to develop human capital that reflects a balance between global and local experiences. Others have noted how matrixed MNE structures have talent systems that are increasingly based on project work, placing more emphasis on the importance of global teams. For example, Cisco (US) uses app-based technology to enhance performance of individuals within teams as well as knowledge sharing with peers and feedback to supervisors (Cappelli & Tavis, 2018). Collings et al. (2019) developed a multilevel perspective arguing that individual level human capital can impact subsidiary and corporate level strategies, but there needs to be alignment between the global talent system and the MNE's IS. Notwithstanding the abovementioned insights, the field of global talent management is very much in its infancy and very little work has been done to explicitly integrate these insights with IS research studies.

Corporate HR Transformation

Although research has considered the role of the corporate HR function, and how this has changed over time regarding its IHRM structures, its link to IS is less evident (Novicevic & Harvey, 2001). Scullion and Starkey (2000) found that it is likely that MNEs with global strategies will have more centralized corporate HR functions, with a variety of practices and policies being developed and shared from the center. The seminal work of Farndale, Scullion, and Sparrow (2010) considers various typologies of the corporate HR function that determine the primary IHRM structure of the MNE. This work details that the corporate HR function is rarely static but often dynamic and emergent as its relationship with subsidiaries evolves.

We identify two major changes in IS and IHRM literatures that complicate the role of the corporate HR function in implementing strategy. First, recent work in IS has detailed how MNEs are becoming less hierarchical and more networked in their design, with an emphasis on the role of subsidiary strategy in enhancing local learning. These studies demonstrate how the role of the HQ is changing through the increased disaggregation of parenting responsibilities to regional HQs or subsidiaries with COE mandates (Nell, Kappen, & Laamanen, 2017). Much of this transformation is due to managing a more complex MNE structure that is spatially dispersed, creating bounded rationality challenges for MNE executives (Kunisch, Menz, & Birkinshaw, 2019). Research has largely failed to consider how the creation of these "intermediary structures" complicates the implementation of strategy and the relationship between the HQ and foreign subsidiaries

(Conroy, Collings, & Clancy, 2017). This represents a significant shift in power and has important implications for the location of IHRM structures as well as the flow of knowledge in the MNE. Despite these observations, research in IS focuses on global and local as two extremes, but the reality is that we need to "highlight the middle" and develop a more nuanced analysis of hybrid strategies in nested MNE structures (Andersson et al., 2019).

Second, we have witnessed a similar change in IHRM studies, with an increase in strategic HR capabilities being devolved to local subsidiaries, along with more outsourcing and offshoring of HR activities. Annual surveys from Deloitte (2017) have detailed the growing importance of shared services with MNEs like Siemens and DHL announcing cost savings of nearly 50 percent (Richter & Bruehl, 2017). Although, the increase in outsourcing of HR to external service providers is largely efficiency based, other work has shown how it may lead to a more strategic role for HR (Ulrich, Younger, & Brockbank, 2008). The creation of a shared services center may be a factor of corporate strategy, as it involves "insourcing" of corporate HR administrative tasks to a new business unit, usually to create greater integration within a region or business division (Reichel & Lazarova, 2013). IKEA, for example, provide global HR services through such centers in order to enhance strategic control and coordination of HR practice sharing (Farndale et al., 2010). Therefore, the use of an HR shared services model has become a popular way for the corporate HR function to focus on the development of strategic level issues (Farndale, Paauwe, & Hoeksema, 2009). An important implication of this may be the move away from global HR policies and practices, orchestrated through a centralized strategy, and the passage toward more of a localized IHRM structure (Farndale et al., 2010). Studies have found that higher levels of subsidiary HR autonomy have the potential to enhance subsidiary performance, but this may be impacted by the existence of intermediary structures such as HR shared service centers (Belizon et al., 2013). This shift will create significant challenges for how the corporate HR function is managed, as well as where and how global talent is sourced and managed (Farndale et al., 2010). These studies suggest that the significant changes around the temporal and spatial structure of the corporate HR function creates greater levels of complexity for HR's role in implementing strategy.

Some studies have pointed to the need to develop an integrative strategy process as the MNE expands and becomes a more complex structure (Taylor, Beechler, & Napier, 1996). Notably, Minbaeva and De Cieri (2014) suggest that a global–regional–local HR model would allow for the implementation of subsidiary initiatives locally while freeing up the corporate HR function to focus on strategy. This regionalized HR function would ensure that the HR role in a nested structure aligns to a philosophy of centralized inspiration–regionalized development–local implementation. This integrative approach allows us to view HR's role at the "middle" or intermediary level in terms of implementing IS. Notwithstanding these arguments, we still have a limited understanding of how changes in the design of the corporate HR function impact the implementation of IB strategy.

FUTURE RESEARCH DIRECTIONS

Although the MNE continues to serve as an important context in which to study SIHRM, there remains much room for shared dialog between scholars in IS and IHRM domains. To advance greater sharing of ideas between these two mutually reinforcing pathways, we believe that it is imperative for future research to:

(1) acknowledge a shift in the SIHRM mandate from strategy implementation to enabler of IB strategy;

(2) consider the increasingly diversified workforce, its origins, and consequences for strategy implementation; and

(3) theorize about the effects of context in order to understand what triggers the variations in strategy implementation in various international contexts.

Changing SIHRM Mandate

For many years, the SIHRM function has been generally regarded as "a tool for the implementation of the strategy-structure changes" (Welch, 1994) with the main role being that of implementer of a top-driven strategy. This formal planning approach is useful in stable environments, as it clearly defines the firm's general strategic direction that is used by the HR function to identify long-term priorities in managing the global workforce. But as we pointed out earlier, the global business environment for most MNEs is not stable. Hypercompetitive and turbulent market conditions with frequent changes and unknown effects create a need for responsive initiatives by local employees. Yet, SIHRM lacks the mechanisms to help employees respond to unexpected changes and quickly adapt to new business realities.

We therefore argue that the view of SIHRM's mandate as strategy implementer is limited and outdated. It fitted well with a traditional centralized strategy-making approach and the "value chain" model, where HR was marked as one of the "support activities." The new reality of strategy making is described by such concepts like "customer-centricity," "digital first," "platforms," and "eco-systems." We ask:

- What is the mandate of SIHRM in this new reality?
- How can global HR processes sensitize managers on all levels to the complexity of the strategic challenge facing MNEs globally?
- What can be done to instill a general awareness for adaptive strategic responses in the diverse global competitive environment?
- What can we do to recruit, develop, and retain talents who are "big picture conscious" as well as "detail conscious" (Hodgkinson & Clarke, 2007) regardless of where they are located?

These are questions that must be addressed in the future research concerning the SIHRM mandate.

Increasingly Diversified Global Workforce

Scholars in IS have continuously called for greater focus on unpacking the behaviors, experiences, and activities of individuals in implementing strategy (Contractor, Foss, Kundu, & Lahiri, 2019). There have been calls for intentionally introducing individual heterogeneity into the research models used in international management as opposed to acknowledging it as an empirical limitation (Minbaeva, 2016). IHRM provides us with the theoretical foundations to illuminate how micro-level factors of an increasingly diversified workforce may impact broader strategic outcomes (Minbaeva, Makela, & Rabbiosi, 2012). Borrowing from its focus on the psychological aspects of HR (Andersson et al., 2019) may allow for a greater understanding of the cognitive schema that corporate executives enact in making strategic decisions or when choosing to transfer HR practices. Equally, work on expatriates and their challenge of adjusting to new contexts (Shaffer et al. 2012) could be useful for exploring how subsidiary managers adapt to changing demands from HQ, and how this impacts the development of strategy in a dynamic local context. This would be particularly important to unpack the cognitive schema that subsidiary individuals use to interpret the value of HR practices that are transferred from HQ and how this impacts the overall transferability process.

Moreover, in the context of global mobility, more individuals across the MNE are increasingly enacting boundary spanning activities, and confronting challenges across various spatial, temporal and cultural boundaries (Pedersen, Soda, & Stea, 2019). Increased multinationality proliferates the geographical breadth and hierarchical depth of the MNE, increasing the variability of boundaries that individuals are confronted with. As such, the complexity of these boundary spanning roles and activities are significant and these individuals may oscillate between the HQ and the frontier of unknown markets the MNE has recently entered (Makela, Barner-Rasmussen, Ehrnrooth, & Koveshnikov, 2019; Minbaeva & Santangelo, 2018). Despite some studies considering the importance of expatriates and inpatriates as boundary spanners (Au & Fukuda, 2002; Reiche, 2011), we still have a limited view on how alternative forms of assignees, such as frequent flyers or virtual assignees, impact the overall flow of knowledge and the strategic linkages between HQ and foreign subsidiaries. As such, more studies should consider the micro-level experiences and activities of individuals in central knowledge sharing positions that drift between the boundaries of global, regional, and local contexts (Schotter, Stallkamp, & Pinkham, 2017). This perspective could be neatly complemented with emerging insights on the micro foundations of IB strategy to emphasize the important role of talented individuals in central positions contributing to the implementation of "integrative" ISs in MNEs.

The Role of Context

There is a growing need to better understand and utilize context heterogeneity in SIHRM research (Minbaeva, 2016). Context has an influence on the effectiveness of the SIHRM function and impacts how the corporate HR function transfer practices to subsidiaries as well as the mobility of individual assignees when sharing knowledge across the MNE. Many studies in the SIHRM field remain, however, "context blind" (Michailova, 2011), failing to fully understand the underlying reasons for variation in the implementation of HR practices across the MNE. As an example, work on global talent management (GTM) has been heavily criticized for its assumption that internal talent systems in MNEs are globally coordinated and talent is effectively mobile (Minbaeva & Collings, 2013). However, recent work on macro talent management has begun to acknowledge these limitations and theorize how GTM is impacted by the wider context as well as accounting for different levels of analysis (Khilji et al., 2015). In this sense, context often exists at a different level of analysis, and one way to account for its importance is to develop more multilevel theorizing that unpacks contextual influence on the phenomenon under investigation (Collings et al., 2019).[2] A major problem for most SIHRM research is that the context lacks heterogeneity and is confined to an Anglo-North American lens, which has led to a homogenization of theories and methodological approaches (see Tsui, 2007).

However, work on emerging-market MNEs (EMNEs) is somewhat beginning to recognize the importance of context. Firms from emerging markets enact novel strategies and organizational forms that challenge our current understanding (Luo & Tung, 2007). These firms tend to be smaller in size with considerably less resources and, therefore, limited ability to strategize through the transfer of knowledge internally (Gullien & Garcia-Canal, 2009). EMNEs, in turn, rely on accessing new resources through "linkages" with external partners, "leveraging" the resources of these partners, and "learning" through repeated and ongoing interactions (Mathews, 2006). As these EMNEs generally come from contexts with less developed institutional environments, knowledge sharing tends to manifest itself through reverse diffusion from subsidiaries in more established contexts (Govindarajan & Ramamurti, 2011). This new knowledge may then be exploited in other emerging markets. From an SIHRM perspective, EMNEs may apply different HR practices in developed and emerging country subsidiaries (Khavul, Benson, & Datta, 2010). Although some Indian firms have a desire to localize their management teams globally, they typically find it difficult to attract top talent in developed markets, due to perception of their brand and, instead, rely on expatriates in these markets (Thite, Wilkinson, & Shah, 2012). Others have found that Indian firms have developed specific HR practices for their "Yopatriates" (Gen Y expatriates) who are highly qualified and mobile knowledge workers seeking shorter-term assignments so

---

[2] Chapter 8 provides a detailed overview of how to use multitheoretical frameworks appropriately in our research.

that they can travel and learn simultaneously (Pereira et al., 2017). Chinese MNEs deploy HR practices that leverage country of origin effects such as low-cost labor and company loyalty so that resource-based advantages are exploited abroad, particularly in other emerging markets (Luo & Zhang, 2016). This is particularly evident for companies such as Huawei and ZTE when initially entering emerging markets in Africa (Cooke, 2012). Research carried out on South African MNEs such as SABMiller revealed that they develop HR strategies with a low level of alignment to their ISs (Horwitz, 2017).

Notwithstanding these studies, the majority of studies do not account for context heterogeneity and adopts western-based theories and frameworks of SIHRM (Cooke, 2009). Further studies need to consider how IS and IHRM scholars use this unique context to enhance our understanding of the complexity of HR for strategy implementation and more broadly the field of SIHRM (Meyer & Xin, 2018). Each of the three challenges detailed in this section could be considered in the context of EMNEs, considering, for example, how their SIHRM approaches may differ from those of advanced economy MNEs. This may be an opportunity for learning from the best practices of each type of MNE.

Concluding Remarks

SIHRM has gained prevalence as an area of research over the last few decades. However, to address the significant challenges that the field faces, scholars need to do more to promote the cross fertilization of ideas between IS and IHRM streams and develop a more mutually reinforcing dialog. By identifying three major challenges to the field of SIHRM, our chapter argues that, although in many instances the strategic role of HR remains an imperative to strategy implementation in the MNE, the specific ways in which it executes this mandate have changed. Specifically, these challenges consist of the growing digitization of global work, the changing face of global mobility, and the transformation of the corporate HR function. Our intention is to illuminate these emerging challenges and identify key trends for future research in terms of a changing SIHRM mandate, an increasingly diversified global workforce, and the need to focus more of our empirical efforts on the effects on context on SIHRM. Growing complexity and unpredictability ultimately require that IS and IHRM scholars converse more frequently and share ideas more effectively in order to move the field of SIHRM forward.

References

Al Ariss, A., & Sidani, Y. 2016. Divergence, convergence, or crossvergence in international human resource management. *Human Resource Management Review*, 26(4): 283–284.
Andersson, U. R., Brewster, C. J., Minbaeva, D. B., Narula, R., & Wood, G. T. 2019. The IB/IHRM interface: Exploring the potential of intersectional theorizing. *Journal of World Business*, 54(5): 100998.

Angrave, D., Charlwood, A., Kirkpatrick, I., Lawrence, M., & Stuart, M. 2016. HR and analytics: Why HR is set to fail the big data challenge. *Human Resource Management Journal*, 26(1): 1–11.

Au, K. Y., & Fukuda, J. 2002. Boundary spanning behaviors of expatriates. *Journal of World Business*, 37(4): 285–296.

Bartlett, C. A., & Ghoshal, S. 1989. *Managing Across Borders: The Transnational Solution*. Boston, MA: Harvard Business School Press.

Bathelt, H., & Henn, S. 2014. The geographies of knowledge transfers over distance: toward a typology. *Environment and Planning A*, 46(6): 1403–1424.

Becker, B. E., & Huselid, M. A. 2006. Strategic human resources management: Where do we go from here? *Journal of Management*, 32(6): 898–925.

Belizon, M. J., Gunnigle, P., & Morley, M. 2013. Determinants of central control and subsidiary autonomy in HRM: The case of foreign-owned multinational companies in Spain. *Human Resource Management Journal*, 23(3): 262–278.

Bonache, J., Brewster, C., Suutari, V., & Cerdin, J. L. 2017. The changing nature of expatriation. *Thunderbird International Business Review*, 60(6): 815–821.

Bondarouk, T. V., & Ruel, H. J. 2009. Electronic Human Resource Management: challenges in the digital era. *The International Journal of Human Resource Management*, 20(3): 505–514.

Bozkurt, O. & Mohr, A. T. 2011. Forms of cross-border mobility and social capital in multi-national enterprises. *Human Resource Management Journal*, 21(2): 138–155.

Caligiuri, P. 2014. Many moving parts: Factors influencing the effectiveness of HRM practices designed to improve knowledge transfer within MNCs. *Journal of International Business Studies*, 45(1): 63–72.

Caligiuri, P., & Bonache, J. 2016. Evolving and enduring challenges in global mobility. *Journal of World Business*, 51(1): 127–141.

Cappelli, P., & Tavis A. 2018. HR goes agile. *Harvard Business Review*, 96(2): 46–52.

Collings, D. G. 2014. Integrating global mobility and global talent management: Exploring the challenges and strategic opportunities. *Journal of World Business*, 49(2): 253–261.

Collings, D. G., & Isichei, M. 2018. The shifting boundaries of global staffing: Integrating global talent management, alternative forms of international assignments and non-employees into the discussion. *The International Journal of Human Resource Management*, 29(1): 165–187.

Collings, D. G., & Mellahi, K. 2009. Strategic talent management: A review and research agenda. *Human Resource Management Review*, 19(4): 304–313.

Collings, D. G., Mellahi, K., & Cascio, W. F. 2019. Global talent management and performance in multinational enterprises: A multilevel perspective. *Journal of Management*, 45(2): 540–566.

Conroy, K. M., Collings, D. G., & Clancy, J. 2017. Regional headquarter's dual agency role: Micro-political strategies of alignment and self-interest. *British Journal of Management*, 28(3): 390–406.

Conroy, K. M., McDonnell, A., & Holzleitner, K. 2018. A race against time: Training and support for short-term international assignments. *Journal of Global Mobility: The Home of Expatriate Management Research*, 6(3/4): 299–315.

Contractor, F., Foss, N. J., Kundu, S., & Lahiri, S. 2019. Viewing global strategy through a microfoundations lens. *Global Strategy Journal*, 9(1): 3–18.

Cooke, F. L. 2009. A decade of transformation of HRM in China: A review of literature and suggestions for future studies. *Asia Pacific Journal of Human Resources*, 47(1): 6–40.

Cooke, F. L. 2012. The globalization of Chinese telecom corporations: Strategy, challenges and HR implications for the MNCs and host countries. *The International Journal of Human Resource Management*, 23(9): 1832–1852.

De Cieri, H., & Dowling, P. J. 2012. Strategic international human resource management in multinational enterprises: Developments and directions. In G. Stahl, I. Bjorkman, & S. Morris (Eds.), *Handbook of International HRM Research*. Cheltenham: Edward Elgar.

Deloitte. 2017. Rewriting the rules for the digital age. Global Human Capital Trends https://www2.deloitte.com/content/dam/Deloitte/global/Documents/About-Deloitte/central-europe/ce-global-human-capital-trends.pdf Accessed on 25 August 2019.

Duvivier, F., Peeters, C., & Harzing, A. W. 2019. Not all international assignments are created equal: HQ-subsidiary knowledge transfer patterns across types of assignments and types of knowledge. *Journal of World Business*, 54(3): 181–190.

Fabo, B., Karanovic, J., & Dukova, K. 2017. In search of an adequate European policy response to the platform economy. *Transfer: European Review of Labour and Research*, 23(2): 163–175.

Farndale, E., Paauwe, J., & Hoeksema, L. 2009. In-sourcing HR: shared service centres in the Netherlands. *The International Journal of Human Resource Management*, 20(3): 544–556.

Farndale, E., Scullion, H., & Sparrow, P. 2010. The role of the corporate HR function in global talent management. *Journal of World Business*, 45(2): 161–168.

Ghoshal, S. & Bartlett, C. A. 1990. The multinational corporation as an interorganizational network. *Academy of Management Review*, 15(4): 603–626.

Govindarajan, V., & Ramamurti, R. 2011. Reverse innovation, emerging markets, and global strategy. *Global Strategy Journal*, 1(3–4): 191–205.

Gupta, A. K., & Govindarajan, V. 2000. Knowledge flows within multinational corporations. *Strategic Management Journal*, 21(4): 473–496.

Harzing, A. W., 2001. Of bears, bumble-bees, and spiders: The role of expatriates in controlling foreign subsidiaries. *Journal of World Business*, 36(4): 366–379.

Harzing, A. W., Pudelko, M., & Reiche, B. S. 2016. The bridging role of expatriates and inpatriates in knowledge transfer in multinational corporations. *Human Resource Management*, 55(4): 679–695.

Heenan, D., & Perlmutter, H. 1979. *Multinational Organizational Development: A Social Architecture Perspective*. Reading: Addison-Wesley.

Hodgkinson, G. P. & Clarke, I. 2007. Conceptual note: Exploring the cognitive significance of organizational strategizing: A dual-process framework and research agenda. *Human Relations*, 60(1): 243–255.

Horwitz, F. 2017. International HRM in South African multinational companies. *Journal of International Management*, 23(2): 208–222.

Khavul, S., Benson, G. S., & Datta, D. K. 2010. Is internationalization associated with investments in HRM? A study of entrepreneurial firms in emerging markets. *Human Resource Management*, 49(4): 693–713.

Khilji, S. E., Tarique, I., & Schuler, R. S. 2015. Incorporating the macro view in global talent management. *Human Resource Management Review*, 25(3): 236–248.

Kiron, D. & Spindel, B., 2019. Rebooting Work for a Digital Era. *MIT Sloan Management Review*, 6(3): 1–10.

Kostova, T., Marano, V., & Tallman, S. 2016. Headquarters–subsidiary relationships in MNCs: Fifty years of evolving research. *Journal of World Business*, 51(1): 176–184.

KPMG. 2018. Global assignment policies and practices survey: Global Mobility Services. https://assets.kpmg/content/dam/kpmg/xx/pdf/2018/10/2018-gapp-survey-final.pdf. Accessed on 6 September 2019.

Kunisch, S., Menz, M., & Birkinshaw, J. 2019. Spatially dispersed corporate headquarters: a historical analysis of their prevalence, antecedents, and consequences. *International Business Review*, 28(1): 148–161.

Luo, Y., & Tung, R. L., 2007. International expansion of emerging market enterprises: A springboard perspective. *Journal of International Business Studies*. 38(4): 481–498.

Luo, Y., & Zhang, H. 2016. Emerging market MNEs: Qualitative review and theoretical directions. *Journal of International Management*, 22(4): 333–350.

Makela, K., Barner-Rasmussen, W., Ehrnrooth, M., & Koveshnikov, A. 2019. Potential and recognized boundary spanners in multinational corporations. *Journal of World Business*, 54(4): 335–349.

Makela, L., & Kinnunen, U. 2018. International business travellers' psychological well-being: the role of supportive HR practices. *The International Journal of Human Resource Management*, 29(7): 1285–1306.

Mathews, J. A. 2006. Dragon multinationals: New players in 21st century globalization. *Asia Pacific Journal of Management*, 23(1): 5–27.

McDonnell, A., Burgess, J., Carbery, R., & Sherman, U. 2018. Special issue Gig Work: Implications for the Employment Relationship and Human Resource Management. *International Journal of Human Resource Management*. https://doi.org/10.1080/09585192.2018.1495410

Meijerink, J., Boons, M., Keegan, A., & Marler, J. 2018. Digitization and the transformation of human resource management. *International Journal of Human Resource Management*. https://doi.org/10.1080/09585192.2018.1503845

Meyer, K. E., & Xin, K. R. 2018. Managing talent in emerging economy multinationals: Integrating strategic management and human resource management. *The International Journal of Human Resource Management*, 29(11): 1827–1855.

Meyskens, M., Von Glinow, M. A., Werther, Jr, W. B., & Clarke, L. 2009. The paradox of international talent: Alternative forms of international assignments. *The International Journal of Human Resource Management*, 20(6): 1439–1450.

Michailova, S. 2011. The "tortuous evolution" of international management research: Critical issues on the way to maturity. *Thunderbird International Business Review*, 53(3): 299–310.

Minbaeva, D. 2016. Contextualizing the individual in international management research: Black boxes, comfort zones and A future research agenda. *European Journal of International Management*, 10(1): 95–104.

Minbaeva, D., & Collings, D. 2013. Seven myths of global talent management, *International Journal of Human Resource Management*, 24(9): 1762–1776.

Minbaeva, D., & De Cieri, H. 2014. Strategic HRM. In D. G. Collings, G. G. Wood & P. Caligiuri (Eds.) *The Routledge Companion to International Human Resource Management*. Abingdon: Routledge.

Minbaeva, D., Makela, K., & Rabbiosi, L. 2012. Linking HRM and Knowledge Transfer via Individual-level Mechanisms. *Human Resource Management*, 51(3): 387–405.

Minbaeva, D., Pedersen, T., Bjorkman, I., Fey, C.F. & Park, H.J., 2014. MNC knowledge transfer, subsidiary absorptive capacity and HRM. *Journal of International Business Studies*, 45(1): 38–51.

Minbaeva, D., & Santangelo, G. 2018. Boundary spanners and intra-MNC knowledge sharing: The role of controlled motivation and immediate organizational context. *Global Strategy Journal*, 8(2): 220–241.

Monteiro, F., & Birkinshaw, J. 2017. The external knowledge sourcing process in multinational corporations. *Strategic Management Journal*, 38(2): 342–362.

Morris, S., Snell, S., & Bjorkman, I. 2016. An architectural framework for global talent management. *Journal of International Business Studies,* 47(6): 723–747.

Nell, P. C., Kappen, P., & Laamanen, T. 2017. Reconceptualising hierarchies: The disaggregation and dispersion of headquarters in multinational corporations. *Journal of Management Studies,* 54(8): 1121–1143.

Novicevic, M. M. & Harvey, M. 2001. The changing role of the corporate HR function in global organizations of the twenty-first century. *International Journal of Human Resource Management,* 12(8): 1251–1268.

Nurmi, N., & Hinds, P. J. 2016. Job complexity and learning opportunities: A silver lining in the design of global virtual work. *Journal of International Business Studies,* 47(6): 631–654.

Pedersen, T., Soda, G., & Stea, D. 2019. Globally networked: Intraorganizational boundary spanning in the global organization. *Journal of World Business,* 54(3): 169–180.

Pereira, V., Malik, A., Howe-Walsh, L., Munjal, S., & Hirekhan, M. 2017. Managing Yopatriates: A longitudinal study of generation Y expatriates in an Indian multi-national corporation. *Journal of International Management,* 23(2): 151–165.

Perlmutter, H. 1969. The tortuous evolution of the multinational corporation. *Columbia Journal of World Business,* 4: 9–18.

Pudelko, M., & Harzing, A. W. 2007. Country-of-origin, localization, or dominance effect? An empirical investigation of HRM practices in foreign subsidiaries. *Human Resource Management,* 46(4): 535–559.

Reiche, B. S. 2011. Knowledge transfer in multinationals: The role of inpatriates' boundary spanning. *Human Resource Management,* 50(3): 365–389.

Reiche, B. S., Lee, Y. T., & Allen, D. G. 2019. Actors, Structure, and Processes: A Review and Conceptualization of Global Work Integrating IB and HRM Research. *Journal of Management,* 45(2): 359–383.

Reichel, A., & Lazarova, M. 2013. The effects of outsourcing and devolvement on the strategic position of HR departments, *Human Resource Management,* 52(6): 923–946.

Richter, P. C., & Bruehl, R. 2017. Shared service center research: A review of the past, present, and future. *European Management Journal,* 35(1): 26–38.

Rosenzweig, P. M., & Nohria, N. 1994. Influences on human resource management practices in multinational corporations. *Journal of International Business Studies,* 25(2): 229–251.

Schmitt, J., Decreton, B. & Nell, P. C. 2019. How corporate headquarters add value in the digital age. *Journal of Organization Design,* 8(1): 1–10.

Schotter, A.P., Buchel, O., & Vashchilko, T. 2018. Interactive visualization for research contextualization in international business. *Journal of World Business,* 53(3): 356–372.

Schotter, A. P., Stallkamp, M., & Pinkham, B. C. 2017. MNE headquarters disaggregation: The formation antecedents of regional management centers. *Journal of Management Studies,* 54(8): 1144–1169.

Schuler, R. S., Dowling, P. J., & De Cieri, H. 1993. An integrative framework of strategic international human resource management. *Journal of Management,* 19(2): 419–459.

Schuler, R. S., Jackson, S. E., & Tarique, I. 2011. Global talent management and global talent challenges: Strategic opportunities for IHRM. *Journal of World Business,* 46(4): 506–516.

Scullion, H., & Starkey, K. 2000. In search of the changing role of the corporate human resource function in the international firm. *International Journal of Human Resource Management,* 11(6): 1061–1081.

Shaffer, M. A., Kraimer, M. L., Chen, Y. P., & Bolino, M. C., 2012. Choices, challenges, and career consequences of global work experiences: A review and future agenda. *Journal of Management,* 38(4): 1282–1327.

Stahl, G., Björkman, I., Farndale, E., Morris, S. S., Paauwe, J., Stiles, P., Trevor, J., & Wright, P. 2012. Six principles of effective global talent management. *Sloan Management Review*, 53(2): 25–42.

Stallkamp, M. & Schotter, A. P. 2019. Platforms without borders? The international strategies of digital platform firms. *Global Strategy Journal*. https://doi.org/10.1002/gsj.1336

Taylor, S., Beechler, S., & Napier, N. 1996. Toward an integrative model of strategic international human resource management. *Academy of Management Review*, 21(4): 959–985.

Thite, M., Wilkinson, A., & Shah, D. 2012. Internationalization and HRM strategies across subsidiaries in multinational corporations from emerging economies—A conceptual framework. *Journal of World Business*, 47(2): 251–258.

Tippmann, E., Scott, P. S., & Mangematin, V. 2012. Problem solving in MNCs: How local and global solutions are (and are not) created. *Journal of International Business Studies*, 43(8): 746–771.

Tsui, A. S. 2007. From homogenization to pluralism: International management research in the academy and beyond. *Academy of Management Journal*, 50 (6): 1353–1364.

Ulrich, D., Younger, J., & Brockbank, W. 2008. The twenty-first-century HR organization, *Human Resource Management*, 47(4): 829–850.

Welch, D. 1994. Determinants of international human resource management approaches and activities: a suggested framework. *Journal of Management Studies*, 31(2): 139–164.

Welch, D. E., Welch, L. S., & Worm, V. 2007. The international business traveller: A neglected but strategic human resource. *The International Journal of Human Resource Management*, 18(2): 173–183.

Yang, Q., Mudambi, R., & Meyer, K. E. 2008. Conventional and reverse knowledge flows in multinational corporations. *Journal of Management*, 34(5): 882–902.

Zillman, C. 2016. IBM is blowing up its annual performance review. *Fortune*. https://fortune.com/2016/02/01/ibm-employee-performance-reviews/ Accessed on 30 August 2019.

Index

CONTENTS

CONTENTS

Audio Shakespeare

Shakespeare Performances in England, 2024

The Year's Contribution to Shakespeare Studies

ILLUSTRATIONS

(GRASS)ROOT AND (TREE)BRANCH: BUILDING COMMUNITY IN THE EARLY MODERN ENSEMBLE TRAINING MODEL

PETER KIRWAN WITH TREEHOUSE SHAKESPEARE ENSEMBLE[1]

Between May 2022 and April 2023, a theatre company called Treehouse Shakespeare Ensemble operated in the small town of Staunton, Virginia. Made up of the nine-teen students in that year's Master of Fine Arts (MFA) cohort of the Mary Baldwin University (MBU) Shakespeare & Performance programme, Treehouse produced an eclectic season of early modern plays staged in venues around Staunton and the wider Shenandoah Valley area, with a particular mission to create work with and for the community. And then the company dis-banded, its members graduating with their MFA degrees, its life even briefer than that of the arboreal edifice for which it was named.

The legacy of university theatre is notoriously ephemeral, as the contributors to Andrew James Hartley's *Shakespeare on the University Stage* repeatedly point out.[2] Productions which are designed to serve an immediate pedagogical purpose (for some, simply to fill a course requirement) are mounted, burn brightly and then are quickly forgotten, often leaving no archival traces. Students themselves move on, the production line of the education industry rarely slowing its pace enough to reflect on the lasting impact of student work on the immediate university community and the larger communities within which it is contextualized.

For these reasons, the relationship between university theatre and community theatre is deeply vexed. The uni-versity community is structurally transient, with even its most enduring traditions and practices complicated by the constant turnover of students and the consequent necessity of re-forming the community each year. Community theatre, on the other hand, is usually understood as meeting the needs of a community – whether of location or of interest, in the terms usefully introduced by Caoimhe McAvinchey – which has relative stability and longevity.[3] The oft-overstated, but still deeply felt, traditional division

of 'town' and 'gown' is regularly framed in ways that inadvertently sustain typological division between 'the university' and 'the community', with the short-term needs of students and the long-term needs of others in the locality often even constructed as diametrically opposed. Further, university theatre in the neoliberal insti-tution usually serves predominantly the needs of its (pay-ing) participants for course credit, professional training and artistic expression; *can* university theatre serve the trad-itional purposes of a community theatre understood as a theatre serving a broader political, social and identity-forming function within a non-instrumental context?

We believe it can.

Treehouse Shakespeare Ensemble chose a name which aligned with the mission it established during its formation, which we share here to contextualize the work described in this article:

Treehouse Shakespeare Ensemble is a Staunton-based theatre group reaching out with the plays of Shakespeare and his contemporaries to audiences new and familiar, near and far. We create supportive environments for education and per-formance where we dare to illuminate lesser-known texts and reinvent familiar titles. We engage with audiences through resident and touring shows, workshops and supplemental

---

[1] Treehouse Shakespeare Ensemble were: Andrew Steven Knight, Ariel Tatum, Beth Harris, Beth Somerville, Cameron Taylor, Chase Fowler, Cole Metz, Dylan Mabe, George Durfee, Jordan Willis, Kailey Potter, Kara Hankard, Katelyn Spurgin, Keith Taylor, Kelsey Harrison, Madison Mattfield, Madison Rudolph, Rachel Louis and Rosemary Richards.

[2] Andrew James Hartley, 'Introduction: tragedians of the city, little eyeases, or rude mechanicals?' in *Shakespeare on the University Stage*, ed. Andrew James Hartley (Cambridge, 2015), 1–9; p. 1.

[3] Caoimhe McAvinchey, 'Introduction: right here, right now', in *Performance and Community: Commentary and Case Studies*, ed. Caoimhe McAvinchey (London, 2014), 1–20; pp. 1–3.

digital resources to give voice to stories of female agency, sexual identity and communities in peril.

Built on a stable foundation, a treehouse is a safe place for personal development through imagination and exploration. Like building a treehouse in the supportive branches of an old tree, we believe that theatre can build on existing cultural conversations to help inspire creative solutions for communities while encouraging creativity in our audiences. Through our commitment to unifying performance and education, we hope that the seeds of conversation and creativity will continue to flourish within and beyond our found community long after our season.

Treehouse Shakespeare Ensemble is branching out and building up. Come grow with us.

In this article, we seek to explain how the unique ensemble-based MFA training model practised at MBU encouraged and enabled the company to become a full community partner in Staunton. By combining the frugality and flexibility of grassroots theatre practice with the fresh perspectives and joy of discovery characteristic of the student experience, Treehouse was able to build meaningful relationships and take advantage of serendipitous opportunities. We do not claim that the company enacted radical transformation on the community – indeed, such claims for transformation would risk implying change forced *upon* a community by guests within it. Rather, we argue in this article that the necessary work of community-building which university involves can be intentionally and respectfully inclusive and responsive to the larger ecosystem.

We begin by explaining the grassroots company model practised at MBU and its distinctiveness within normal understandings of university and community theatre, before then going on to discuss the key ways in which Treehouse's community mission was realized. The first of these was through the dramaturgical work done within the company's season to 'give voice to stories of female agency, sexual identity and communities in peril', in which the personal identities and priorities of company members worked to consolidate a *community of interest* around core questions and values. Then, we shift to the company's collaborations and partnerships within Staunton and the wider locality, showing how the grassroots model enabled even temporary residents to become part of a *community of location*. Our hope is that this article will not only contribute to the neglected archive of university theatre, but also inspire further creative thought about how university theatre can be structurally reimagined to serve both its existing and its aspirational stakeholders.

THE MFA COMPANY MODEL

The three-year graduate programme in Shakespeare & Performance at MBU, in partnership with the American Shakespeare Center (ASC), is structured as a two-year MLitt degree followed by a one-year MFA degree. The MLitt takes a traditional form, with discrete courses covering academic and practical training. The MFA, on the other hand, operates within an innovative holistic 'company model', overseen by programme co-director Doreen Bechtol. Beginning with a three-week May Term intensive before the summer break, MFA students are invited to found a theatre company. Under the guidance of faculty members Bechtol and Molly Seremet, they name the company, devise its mission and principles, select a season of plays, and allocate cast and production roles. In August, the company reconvene to create and perform a devised show directed by Bechtol and Seremet, and then go directly into rehearsals for the first of their company-selected productions.

The company model is designed as a pre-professional training programme that privileges entrepreneurship, community-forming and, most importantly, collaboration. As opposed to competitive programmes in which the focus is on the individual's personal achievements as measured against an elite metric of a particular kind of vocational practice, the company model instead trains students to build work around the skills, priorities and ideologies of the members of a group, and to create their own opportunities for work. Students choose a concentration in either acting, directing, dramaturgy or education, but work collaboratively to create work according to community-oriented and pedagogic briefs which encourage them to think flexibly within a series of constraints. Each year, the company is required to create an education production designed for touring to local middle and high schools; a number of small-scale productions on the model of Actors From The London Stage, in which a company of around five to six actors, along with a director and dramaturg, perform all of the roles; a large-scale production directed by a guest professional artist in the ASC's Blackfriars Playhouse; and a 'Renaissance-style' director-less show using cue-scripts following the conventions of the ASC's 'Actors' Renaissance Season'. At the end of the academic year, the company remount the majority of these productions in a festival, placing high demands on the company to pivot quickly between several different roles and responsibilities.

In addition, throughout the course of the year, the students learn how to run a company. Through committee work, they manage a modest budget, pursue fundraising opportunities, organize touring engagements, oversee publicity and marketing, manage the company's costume/prop stock and more. More significantly for the purposes of this article, they also take on a number of community responsibilities. These range from taking responsibility for the upkeep of The Wharf – a downtown building owned by the university which is shared by a number of users, and which becomes the MFA company's home for the year – to mentoring MLitt students working on their thesis projects, to organizing fundraising events and staged readings, to building partnerships with local businesses. We will discuss Treehouse's approach to this in more detail below.

Treehouse's season began with a devised show, *CQD*, directed by Bechtol and Seremet. The Fall education show was an hour-long cut of *Macbeth*, directed by Treehouse members Andrew Steven Knight and Katelyn Spurgin. For the small-scale season later in Fall 2022, the company split into three groups, performing *The Two Gentlemen of Verona* (directed by Kelsey Harrison and Beth Somerville), *Galatea* (directed by Cole Metz) and *The Duchess of Malfi* (directed by Chase Fowler). Following the winter break, visiting artist Michael Manocchio directed the full company in *Edward II* at the Blackfriars Playhouse, before the company went into their final week-long self-directed 'Renaissance-style' rehearsal period for *The Birth of Merlin*. All of the shows (apart from *CQD*) were then performed in repertory during the festival week. Alongside this, the company produced staged readings of Sor Juana Inés de la Cruz's *House of Desires* (directed by Beth Harris and Madison Mattfield), *The Roaring Girl* (directed by Kara Hankard), Ellen McLaughlin's *Lysistrata* (directed by Somerville), James Goldman's *The Lion in Winter* (directed by Visiting Professor Kelley McKinnon) and Knight's self-written adaptation of Sophocles' Theban plays, *The Fall of Thebes* (directed by Fowler).

This MFA is an academic programme, in which the students are assessed holistically on their work across their primary concentration, production roles, collaborative contribution to company success, and their individually written thesis projects. But it is also an exercise in creating a supported context for a group of theatre-makers to establish their own grassroots theatre company. Grassroots theatre, as defined by Robert E. Gard and developed in relation to Shakespeare by William Floyd Wolfgang, is intensely local, amateur, low-budget, and allows a company 'to shape the work to fit their specific regional perspective, molding it to suit any

number of desires'.[4] This is theatre which is 'not designed for audiences outside local communities', and which is thus to some extent *necessarily* a form of community theatre.[5] Indeed, it is our argument that the MFA company model offers a bridge between traditional conceptions of university theatre and community theatre.

TREEHOUSE AS COMMUNITY THEATRE

Community theatre, as Katherine Steele Brokaw sets out, is an umbrella term describing a wide range of practices and ethos, from middle- or working-class amateur groups providing entertainment to their peers, to forum theatre geared towards direct political action, to theatre designed to serve the needs of specific marginalized groups, to applied theatre directed towards social change.[6] The aspirations of Treehouse Shakespeare Ensemble, as expressed in a mission statement which makes three explicit references to community/ies, are both local and expansive, concerned with both 'communities of location' in the Staunton area and 'communities of interest' of activism in relation to gender, LGBTQA+ rights and more, to return to McAvinchey's terms. But implicit in the mission statement is the sense that the company will discover and form 'our found community' through the act of existing and working.

Student theatre created in the context of a degree sits awkwardly within the traditional paradigms of community theatre. As Andrew James Hartley notes:

Student groups may work close to community theatre/amateur dramatics models in terms of shoestring budgets and a non-profit esprit de corps, but they also may have access to grants from specific departments, awards taken from student activity fees, and access to buildings, playing spaces, and other resources lent to them gratis by the school or subsections thereof because their host institutions see such activity as essentially a Good Thing.[7]

---

4 William Floyd Wolfgang, 'Grassroots Shakespeare: "I love Shakespeare, and I live here" – amateur Shakespeare performance in American communities', *Shakespeare Bulletin* 39 (2021), 355–73; p. 358.
5 Wolfgang, 'Grassroots Shakespeare', p. 355.
6 Katherine Steele Brokaw, *Shakespeare and Community Performance* (Basingstoke, 2023), pp. 6–31.
7 Hartley, 'Introduction: tragedians of the city', p. 2.

This is even without considering the facilities and contexts of Theatre departments, which, depending on a university's size and scale, may be comparable to large-scale professional theatres. Within the context of MBU's MFA programme, the work has an instrumental educational function, forming the basis of assessment for students who are mostly training to be professional theatremakers. Participation in the theatre is by default confined to fee-paying students, most of whom have usually already completed two degrees and are completing a third terminal one. And the default audience is 'demographically quite different from that of the average professional or community theatre model', incorporating as it does a large proportion of fellow students and theatre specialists.[8] As such, as community theatre, it does not meet the criteria of 'efficacy' and 'agency' set out so cogently by Emine Fişek, in which the primary themes of community performance concern political effectiveness and the collaboration of community members in the creation of the art.[9] The claim of this article is *not* that Treehouse's work models a community theatre practice of enabling mass participation in theatre by/for those who would otherwise not have that access. Nor is it a claim of the company that Treehouse's work models applied theatre – again, a major focus of current scholarship on community theatre.

However, grassroots theatre models a different kind of community-forming experience. As Brokaw puts it, 'Grassroots and amateur theatre-makers tend to be brought together because they live in the same geographical community and because they share a desire to create, in [Raymond] Williams's term, "an alternative set of relationships" through their shared love of theatre'.[10] Indeed, to take another aspect of Fişek's definitional work, for many, 'community indicates a social grouping organized around a particular identity or locality; for others, it can encapsulate a desire for a grouping yet to come'.[11] Fişek's description applies equally well to university theatre-making, created by people brought together by locality and required to form community with one another. The idea of 'found community' is perhaps *best* epitomized by the transient and temporary nature of university theatre. The community-forming which happens within university, and which is so explicitly integral to Bechtol's training method of ensemble-building, can generate the 'activist potential' which Fişek identifies in community theatre: 'two themes tend to underline activist potential: first, the political effectiveness or efficacy of community formation in promoting progressive causes, and second, the importance of self-expression and agency for the community in question, as well as the individuals that form its parts'.[12]

It is within this framing, we argue, that Treehouse Shakespeare Ensemble's work was best understood as community theatre. The student experience is one of developing self-expression and agency; the MFA company model requires the students to form that identity collectively, however, seeing themselves as individuals who are already in community at the point of formation. But the process of community formation with a specific mission in mind led Treehouse to identify its temporary existence as one which would promote progressive causes within its larger community. Thus, Treehouse enacted – or aimed to enact – a progressive community ideal in (and as) the process of discovering who it was itself.

The other key aspect of Treehouse's grassroots identity was its frugality. As the contributors to Hartley's volume note, much university theatre is characterized by its large-scale budgets and professional-quality technical resources, which can result in impressive theatre but also necessarily subsumes the identity of any particular cohort of students to that of the institution. Paul Menzer argues that much university theatre – especially that in well-funded Theatre departments – is characterized by surplus in design, technical aspects and, crucially, bodies, while also depending upon free labour.

Campus Shakespeare inculcates the future producers and consumers of Shakespeare to the terms of its rationale and evaluation: the language of labour and capital, surplus and deficit. Above all, Campus Shakespeare ends up offering our students the unsentimental education that capital inheres in institutions and material, but that labour is infinitely fungible.[13]

The MBU MFA model, however, makes a virtue both of economy and of shared (rather than compartmentalized) labour. Part of Brokaw's definition of grassroots community theatre is that such theatres 'have only minimal financial imperative, freeing them to direct their energy toward social causes and allowing their art to be unburdened by worries about donor

---

[8] Hartley, 'Introduction: tragedians of the city', p. 2.

[9] Emine Fişek, *Theatre & Community* (London, 2019), p. 16.

[10] Brokaw, *Shakespeare and Community*, p. 13.

[11] Fişek, *Theatre & Community*, p. 5.

[12] Fişek, *Theatre & Community*, p. 61.

[13] Paul Menzer, 'The laws of Athens: Shakespeare and the campus economy', in *Shakespeare on the University Stage*, ed. Hartley, 201–15; pp. 203–4.

sensibilities'.[14] Wolfgang pinpoints the dependence on ingenuity: 'An ambitious organization of resourceful actors can secure rent-free performance spaces and low-cost costuming to mount a production with no external funding.'[15] As opposed to the large budgets and resources of the dedicated Theatre departments Hartley alludes to, the MFA company runs on a shoestring budget.[16] Productions employ minimal scenery, and props and costumes are sourced through a combination of loans, recycling and thrift shop purchases. Company members are obviously not paid (indeed, they pay fees to study); tickets to all productions are free, and any donations are used to offset production costs or disbursed to charitable partners. As such, without a financial imperative, the company is freed to pursue its collectively agreed artistic and social mission without the compromises of ensuring income or longevity; more importantly, its aesthetic and ideological identity is entirely defined by the company's labour and ingenuity. Indeed, the MFA company rarely even performs on campus; the company's stages are created ad hoc for each new performance, whether at The Wharf downtown or touring to local community venues.

It is important, however, to note that this grassroots model does not constitute an anti-capitalist theatre (although many company members might share principles in that direction). A small grassroots company does not have the luxury or the financial security to attempt to abolish capitalism, and training theatremakers who wish to make a living from their art will need to engage with the financial imperative. What the model instead trains students to do is to create art that is financially sustainable, cost-effective and tailored to the needs of its local community. Rather than eschewing the needs of commerce, Treehouse instead embraced the opportunity to create partnerships with local businesses that would provide an economic boost within the community; a tourist town is reliant on commerce, and thus cross-promotion and shared advertising opportunities become key to building community *within* a fundamentally capitalist framework. The model gives students a scaffolded structure for founding and building their own community grassroots theatres, and alumni of the programme have gone on to do precisely that, founding companies such as the Flagstaff Shakespeare Festival (Arizona), Starling Shakespeare Company (touring), Pigeon Creek Shakespeare (Michigan) and Silk Moth Stage (Virginia), to name a few. Where Menzer notes that much university theatre trains students for professional disappointment by offering a surplus that few professional theatres can match, the MBU MFA training model actually

trains students to create from-scratch work in a sustainable way.[17]

While the MFA company in any given year, therefore, should not necessarily be considered as a community theatre company in its own right (and, indeed, MFA companies in different years may have a greater or lesser interest in pursuing a social mission), part of what distinguishes the programme from other educational theatre models is its structuring around grassroots principles: small-scale, microbudget theatre, generated without financial imperative, with an artistic agenda determined by collective and non-hierarchized agreement between company members. Treehouse's response to this brief, as articulated in its mission statement, was to orient its work around the 'found community' that is the necessary experience of being at a university. Students may come from a diverse range of backgrounds but are united by a common geographical location and contextual situation, and thus necessarily reconstitute themselves as a new community which Treehouse sought to identify with the wider Staunton community and with the communities of identity represented within the ensemble.

In the remainder of this article, we will expand upon the ways in which Treehouse realized its community mission in two major ways. First, we will explore the directorial and dramaturgical choices within the company's season which aimed to uplift the stories of communities in peril; within this work, Treehouse aimed to expand its own 'communities of interest'. Then, we will move to the company's more diffuse work and relationships within the wider 'community of location', arguing that the agility and flexibility enabled by the grassroots training enabled the company to take advantage of serendipity and reciprocity, becoming a full-fledged member of the Staunton and wider Shenandoah Valley community.

COMMUNITIES OF INTEREST: THE SEASON

Kailey remembers that 'when we arrived in Staunton [in Fall 2020], we were labeled the "pandemic cohort" and out of necessity kept isolated from the rest of the

---

[14] Brokaw, *Shakespeare and Community*, p. 9.
[15] Wolfgang, 'Grassroots Shakespeare', p. 358.
[16] Treehouse's production budget (not covering professors' salaries) was $3,800 for all seven shows in the season.
[17] Menzer, 'The laws of Athens', p. 206.

Shakespeare & Performance program, the rest of the MBU campus, and the rest of Staunton. Our entire first year was spent masked, distanced and mostly online.' The experience of beginning a graduate programme during the early stage of the COVID-19 pandemic shaped the company's self-formation of its identity:

I think the marks that our first two years of S&P left on our cohort became really apparent in our MFA season selection. We were drawn to stories about communities in peril, of groups of people gathered together to face seemingly insurmountable odds. While we didn't shy away from tragic titles, Treehouse was invested from the start in stories about people banding together – to work for a better future, to witness the end of an era, to tell a story that needed to be told. Even our name, Treehouse Shakespeare Ensemble, was fueled by our desire to create a physical space where we could play together and invite in as many collaborators as we could.

While the idea of 'communities in peril' and 'people banding together' was not an overdetermined thematic rationale in Treehouse's season selection, it was everywhere one cared to look. Treehouse's season particularly stressed stories in which states and communities were jeopardized by acts of self-interest, and in which the resolution often involved communities needing to reconstitute themselves in order to resolve the situation. This was perhaps most obvious in *Macbeth* (especially with the replacement of Menteith with Donalbain, allowing for a scene in which Jordan Willis's Malcolm and George Durfee's Donalbain reunited in order to take down the tyrant), but recurred at the political level in the tense interpersonal conflicts over the English throne in *Edward II* and *The Birth of Merlin* and over the state in *The Duchess of Malfi*. The staged reading series twice returned to questions of civic duty in the ancient world at the individual and collective level, to comedic effect in *Lysistrata* and tragic in *The Fall of Thebes*. And the choice of Lyly's *Galatea* was in part driven by that play's inciting crisis of a community in existential peril, and the choice of two parents (mothers in this production, both played by Harris) to privilege individual survival over collective sacrifice.

The company was particularly, and more specifically, invested in stories that would enable it to uplift LGBTQA + stories and to speak to challenges faced by the queer community, building on what Chad Allen Thomas points to as the shared 'critical, pedagogical, and perhaps even political agenda' of campus Shakespeare and queer Shakespeare.[18] This most obviously underpinned the choice of *Galatea* – a rare play which stages two young women falling in love with one another, leading the gods

to transform the gender of one of them at the play's end – and *Edward II*, a play which generations of theatremakers have found productive as a vehicle for interrogating attitudes towards same-sex relationships.

But a choice of a play alone is not sufficient statement in itself, especially with plays that are inevitably rooted in sixteenth- and seventeenth-century values and which rarely align neatly with the progressive values of the present moment. Brokaw, reviewing the community impact of the Public Works (National Theatre of Great Britain) and Public Acts (New York Public Theater) projects, argues that:

Applying the Public Works and Public Acts values to Shakespearian drama means being intentional and radical in adapting the text, de-emphasizing textual and directorial authority, and considering how the archaic words and often violent or offensive plotlines of these plays are conveyed (or not) to audiences. It means being self-aware and being Shakespeare-aware, and putting one's community – the cast and team, audience, and surrounded [*sic*] population – at the very center.[19]

Working in line with these principles, Treehouse staged dramaturgical interventions to take responsibility for and ownership of the details and impacts of the stories it wished to share. The most visible of these occurred in *Edward II*, during which the company confronted the question of how to stage the murder of Edward without participating in the perpetuation of images of violence against queer persons. Eventually, the company decided not to stage the murder at all, but instead to replace it with the company's rejection of the mimetic reproduction of queer violence entirely.

At the point of the murder, the scene between Metz's Edward and Willis's Lightborn paused, with the two of them sitting upon the ground (Figure 1). One by one, the rest of the acting company emerged, and spoke a new text compiled and written by Knight, Fowler, and Keith Taylor. The ensemble members neutrally narrated the build-up to the murder as a series of spoken stage directions, interspersed with Metz and Willis delivering lines imported from *Richard II* 3.1: 'For God's sake, let us sit upon the ground ... '. At the point of the murder, ensemble members merely said 'They bind the king, and kill him in a manner / Which only rumours have brought down to us'. They continued with the lines:

---

[18] Chad Allen Thomas, 'Queering Shakespeare in the American South', in *Shakespeare on the University Stage*, ed. Hartley, p. 216.
[19] Brokaw, *Shakespeare and Community*, p. 106.

1 The cast of *Edward II* break from the play to collectively refuse the staging of Edward's murder.
Photo: Miscellaneous Media.

All that we know is that King Edward died.
And where he went from thence we cannot say.
To heaven or to hell, perhaps to Hades,
Or not a place at all but into death.

The new moment aimed to create critical distance between the company and received history, acknowledging that history itself is freighted with homophobia, and that the 'truth' of a story is far more ambiguous. Knight, who helped create the structural frame of the intervention, shares that:

the idea was to present the lens through which our company was viewing the scene, both as a grotesque act of homophobia and as an important part of a play that would influence Shakespeare's writing. The result was a piece written by several voices, including Shakespeare, to be performed by the ensemble. Rather than just my perspective, the final piece came together as the work of a group, in accordance with TSE's community-oriented approach to theater.

For Fowler,

Edward II is a very personal play to me as a queer person and as someone who comes from a really random groupings of religion in my life. There has always been a slight undercurrent of

religion involved in things I've written . . . I wrote a prayer of sorts when Lightborn (a bastardized version of Lucifer) was brought into the text. But I wasn't interested in giving the image of Edward going to Hell – his life in the play was enough of that. Instead, I was interested in the reunion of faith and queerness.

The act of collaborative writing led to a powerful stage moment in which almost all of the Treehouse company members stood together onstage outside of the diegesis of the text, taking responsibility for commenting on the play it was performing, and in doing so epitomizing the company's desire to intervene radically and intentionally in classical texts.[20] As Fowler says, 'it didn't take too long for us to find a through-line and mix . . . into a moment that existed outside of time, that

---

[20] The only Treehouse members who didn't appear onstage were those in non-acting roles for this production; conversely, while the production featured two guest actors from outside the company, Genevieve K. Henderson and Margaret Levin, those two actors were not included in this moment – it was visibly a commentary by Treehouse themselves.

could be felt by not just the queer folks in the room but by anyone who has felt love and pain in their life'.

Fowler's phrasing here is a salient reminder that Treehouse's mission was one of community-forming; the privileging of LGBTQA+ stories was designed not to segregate the company and its audiences into separate communities of identity, but to bring the community together around the issues which the company prioritized. In contrast to the austere pathos of *Edward II*, the small-scale production of *Galatea* directed by Metz achieved a similar impact through joy. This production featured a cast of five (Kara Hankard, Beth Harris, Rosemary Richards, Ariel Tatum, and guest 'journeyman' actor Mikaela Hanrahan), all female-identifying or non-binary. A framing device established the five actors as Girl Scouts on a camp, first discovered playing hide-and-seek and singing the Osborne Brothers' 'Rocky Top', before beginning to tell the story of the monstrous Agar's threat to drown the village as a ghost story, lit by torches (Figure 2).

Throughout the production, the actors played their Girl Scout characters, who created the characters of *Galatea* using their camp equipment: zips on backpacks served as the mouths of puppeteered gods; conversations between the three brothers Rafe, Robin and Dick were performed by Richards speaking to socks on her hands; and the sashes of the Scouts became the bows wielded by Venus' nymphs. But in telling this story, the Scouts playing Galatea and Phyllida (Tatum and Hankard) themselves became closer. Tatum's Scout was initially an outsider, perhaps new to the group and unsure of their place. *Galatea* served as a vehicle through which the young women could, in the safety of this community, discover who they and who the others were. The production concluded with the Scouts sitting in a circle within the thrust stage space as if around a campfire, belting out a cover of Taylor Swift's 'Mine' as they celebrated the queer love found within their group *and* their collective solidarity.

Other dramaturgical interventions kept queer stories front and centre even when not the primary focus. Fowler created a framing device for *The Duchess of Malfi* based on stone-tape theory, in which, as Fowler puts it, 'ghosts, at least as we think of them, are created by an event or trauma so impactful that it leaves a lasting impression on the physical space around the occurrence'. Five urban explorers broke into a disused theatre, finding costumes and objects, before one of them began reading from a book that turned out to contain the outlines of Webster's play. As she read, an ancient radio suddenly began playing music, and the young explorers were drawn to pieces of clothing that would

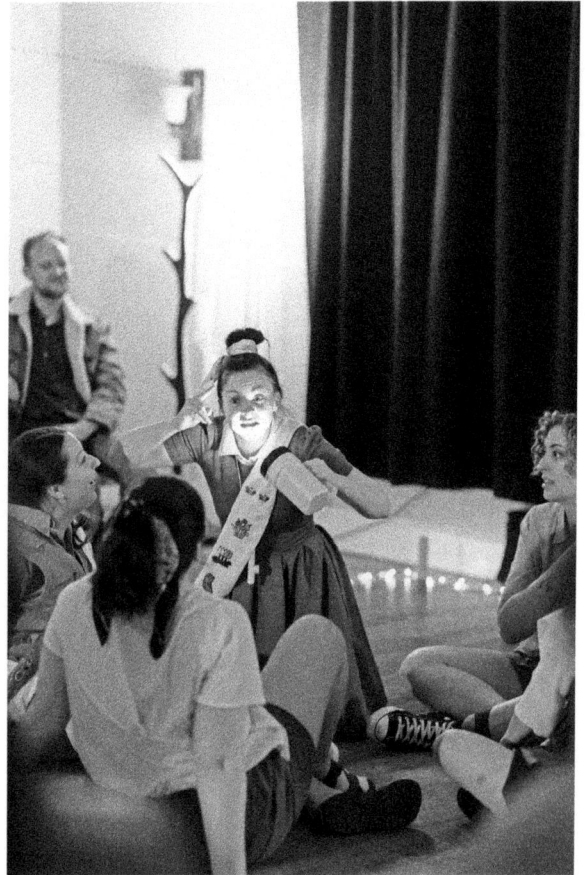

2 The senior scout (Rosemary Richards) begins telling the story of Galatea. Photo: Miscellaneous Media.

temporarily cause them to embody the characters of *Malfi*. As Rachel, who played the Duchess, points out:

the framing device allowed us to draw a parallel between the trauma experienced by the Duchess and Antonio – persecution for who they chose to love – and the same kind of trauma often experienced by modern queer people. The majority of Treehouse identifies as some form of queer, and so naturally telling queer stories was a vital part of our mission statement: 'We engage with audiences . . . to give voice to stories of female agency, sexual identity and communities in peril'. The queer representation the urban explorers set up was perhaps the most purposeful and personal use of our framing device.

In Knight's *The Fall of Thebes*, meanwhile, the company added to the Theban plays a relationship between Antigone and Creon's niece Hermione, and a redemptive epilogue in which Antigone and her sister Ismene were spared from death and left Thebes to travel the world and 'speak out against the monstrous force / That leads both kings and people into madness'. Dramaturgical choices such as this were aligned by proximity with more 'traditional' cross-gendered casting typical of university productions. *Macbeth*, for instance, toured schools in the western Virginia area with female-identifying actors (Potter and Richards) as both Macbeth and Lady Macbeth. Such casting choices are typical of professional practice in the region, most notably at the ASC (where cross-gendered casting is a standard practice, though not usually the re-gendering of characters), but cannot necessarily be assumed to be uncontroversial, especially in a state which has in recent times pursued aggressive culture war policies in the education sector.[21]

The company's work to interweave stories of queer love and advocacy against homophobia into its classical repertoire resulted in MBU awarding the company that year's Lavender Award. Lavender Graduations in the US have, since 1995, served to honour the contributions and achievements of LGBTQA+ students and allies on university campuses.[22] The award of the 2023 prize to all nineteen members of the ensemble respected the company's commitment to the idea of shared responsibility and shared agency in the service of its mission. Perhaps most important to the mission of advancing a community of interest, though, was the visibility of the storytelling mechanics being used within the productions. The plays themselves were not sufficient to advance Treehouse's mission, and the company's integration of what Nora Williams calls 'paratheatrical additions' to 'complete' the dramaturgy of the story it wanted to tell also made clear that agency and responsibility for advancing the community's shared interest lie with the community, not with the text.[23]

COMMUNITIES OF LOCATION: PUTTING DOWN ROOTS IN STAUNTON

Fişek argues that 'community theatre's objectives can range from securing recognition for a community's particular experience to demanding public intervention on a topic of social or political concern to revitalizing the cultural life of a given locality'.[24] While the company's onstage storytelling was probably the most prominent arena in which it pursued its community mission in relation to its communities of interest, perhaps more important – because far more *optional* in relation to the curriculum of the programme, and thus requiring more self-generated labour from company members – was its contribution to the cultural life of Staunton and the wider region. As already noted, university theatre can struggle to bridge the town/gown divide, especially given the short periods for which students are present in a locality; Treehouse, however, made a conscious effort to look outwards.

Some aspects of engagement with the culture of the region did appear onstage. Notably, in the director-less 'Renaissance-style' production of *The Birth of Merlin*, the Devil – played by Dylan Mabe, an Appalachian native – was imagined as a regional folk devil in trilby and patterned jacket, who duetted with Joan Go To't (Hankard) on 'Didn't Leave Nobody but the Baby' (Figure 3). But, rather than co-opting regional culture as an aesthetic within productions, the company instead contributed most to the region's cultural life both through its commitment to participating in mass community events and in its curation of bespoke relationships with local businesses and community partners.

At the mass participation end of the scale, Treehouse set aside a weekend in late September 2022 to be one of nearly 200 organizations taking part in the October Queen City Mischief & Magic Festival. This annual festival welcomes some 20,000 visitors each year to a one-horse town for a two-day celebration of witchcraft and wizardry which, the organizers are at pain to stress, is absolutely in no way affiliated with Warner Bros, J. K. Rowling or Bloomsbury Publishing. During the festival, the roads are closed and local businesses pour onto the streets to share displays and shows, magic-themed versions of their usual produce, and activities for kids. Jumping on the convenient opportunity to cross-promote the company's then-in-rehearsal production of *Macbeth*, members of Treehouse volunteered to be semi-official costumed actors (with an entirely coincidental resemblance to certain *Harry Potter* characters), mounted stage combat demonstrations on the festival stage, and ran a stall boasting magical tricks, face-painting, trivia games and other magic-themed entertainments for the tourist audience. But what was perhaps

[21] See, for instance, American Civil Liberties Union (ACLU) Virginia, 'Virginia Department of Education ignores public opposition and greenlights anti-LGBTQ student policies', ACLU Virginia, 19 July 2023, www.acluva.org/en/press-releases/virginia-department-education-ignores-public-opposition-and-greenlights-anti-lgbtq.

[22] 'Lavender Graduation', Human Rights Campaign, n.d., www.hrc.org/resources/lavender-graduation.

[23] Nora Williams, 'Incomplete dramaturgies', *Shakespeare Bulletin* 40 (2022), 1–22; pp. 17–18.

[24] Fişek, *Theatre & Community*, p. 14.

3 The Devil (Dylan Mabe). Photo: Miscellaneous Media.

interesting was the longevity of the impact of Treehouse's commitment to this major public event. In the responsibilities and profile that the company took on, they found themselves playing the role of a local community institution, on a par with longstanding businesses and activist groups, and the company committed to continuing to play this role – in line with its mission – for the rest of the year.

The magic theme provided a focal point for much of Treehouse's Staunton-facing community engagement. One company member, Rachel, found that the local interest in tarot reading was sufficient to enable her to begin a business at the end of the company's year, continuing to provide readings for people in the Staunton area. The company partnered with candle store Redwood & Co. to sell bespoke season-themed candles alongside the shows. And the company's final show, *The Birth of Merlin*, resulted in cross-promotional partnership with Staunton's Medieval Fantasies Company (home of the Dragon Preservation Society of Staunton (DPSS) VA). This idiosyncratic gyfte shoppe and educational organization, run by Sir Blackwolf and Lady Dawn, has

a twenty-year history of community partnerships within Staunton, curating the town's collection of dragons for the enjoyment and edification of locals and visitors alike. The DPSS liaised with the company to donate the spectacular dragon masks used in the production and give a Welsh blessing to the company on the stage of the Blackfriars Playhouse, all captured in a charming six-minute video put together by the DPSS in order to promote Treehouse's decision to stage a play with dragons in it.[25] Connections of this kind are invaluable, we argue, precisely because of their lack of value within any traditional framework. They do not generate revenue (entrance to all Treehouse productions was free to the public); they do not contribute to a definable activist agenda; they do not appear as a line on a CV – Treehouse disbanded only six weeks later at the close of the academic year. But even if the student theatre company

---

[25] Dragon Preservation Society of Staunton VA, 'Visiting the dragons at the Treehouse Shakespeare Ensemble performance', YouTube, posted 22 March 2023: www.youtube.com/watch?v=QzuUzlxJLzo.

itself is transient, its after-effects linger on in the community partners whose own identities evolved in relation to the company's work.

The mutual benefits of a student theatre ensemble working not within the confines of a university campus, but within the surrounding town, could be felt in various other ways. Positive cross-promotional partnerships enabled the company to call on additional favours, such as Redwood hosting the company's wrap party at the end of its year, for instance. As another example, Kailey recalls that:

Treehouse members had been enjoying eating at Accordia [a wine bar and bistro one block from the Wharf] for months before we connected with them as a cohort, which happened when they posted our *Edward II* poster on their business FB page with a positive review of the show. I noticed the post, commented and shared it on TSE's FB page, and from there the cohort members who had more of a relationship with the business reached out to chat about partnerships, which is how we organized Accordia hosting us for our final night of Festival week.

The company worked to establish a model in which serendipity was answered by reciprocity; community partners were recognized for their donations of labour, goods, even attention, and that recognition led to more opportunities for exchange of resource and goodwill. The company then channelled that into its charitable giving; donations were taken at all three of the company's Fall small-scale shows, and were donated to charities associated with that production's particular areas of interest (*Galatea* to the Girl Scouts Association, *The Duchess of Malfi* to the Shenandoah LGBTQ Center, and *Two Gentlemen of Verona* to Shenandoah Valley Animal Services).

One of the more visible community partnerships came, again, towards the end of the company's existence, when *The Duchess of Malfi* – first performed at the Wharf in Fall – was restaged in the Arcadia in downtown Staunton. The Arcadia Project is a major non-profit initiative that is transforming and repurposing the derelict historic Dixie Theater (originally built in 1913) into a multipurpose community venue. As of 2023, the main room was a grand, cavernous, damp, and somewhat eerie space, in which Treehouse negotiated permission to stage *Malfi*. As Cameron Taylor (who played Ferdinand) explains:

Firstly, there was already a crystal clear connection between the theater itself and [director] Chase [Fowler]'s overall framing device of the urban explorers in an abandoned theatre. Theatres, of course, are houses for storytelling, containing the

ghosts and echoes of hundreds of different films and plays that have come before. The Arcadia Project is no different: an 'enchanting old ruin' (in the words of *The Grand Budapest Hotel*) that time has not been kind to. Being able to shed some light on the power of theatre spaces through Malfi became so much more powerful within Arcadia. It felt like we were able to, for a few hours, help breathe some life into that beautiful old building.

While the production was not designed with the Arcadia as its intended venue, the production took on new life as a rediscovery of a found space in line with the Arcadia Project's own mission of restoration, 'honoring its past and broadening its uses', while serving as a proof-of-concept of the Project's larger aims to be a space for the wider community, even before fundraising was complete for the renovation.[26] A similar partnership set up with Hazy Mountain Vineyards & Brewery – which provided a mountainside venue 25 miles outside town, with spectacular panoramic views, for Treehouse's production of *The Two Gentlemen of Verona* – opened up a touring relationship that subsequent MFA companies have been able to take advantage of.

Lastly, the company did not neglect its own university community, and the company's work within Mary Baldwin is part of its lasting legacy. With faculty encouragement, the company inaugurated the tradition of MFA company members (most of whom had completed their MLitt the previous year) chairing the presentations of the current second-year MLitt students at the annual Thesis Festival, taking on a role previously held by faculty members. The mentoring of the next generation of students was of particular importance, as George argues, in the post-2020 environment: 'Treehouse set out to reforge many of the usual connections students across S&P enjoy . . . we craved that camaraderie that so many of our predecessors upheld'. This craving resulted in Treehouse members holding thesis workshops to help MLitt students prepare for their public presentations of their work-in-progress, developing community across the different year groups of the Shakespeare & Performance programme; Katelyn, one of the company's production managers, notes that the company worked to break down what had sometimes been experienced as the 'MFA exclusivity' of the Wharf space to 'let it be a place where people could just hang out, relax, have a conversation, do homework, or just

---

[26] 'Our mission', The Arcadia Project, n.d.: https://thearcadiaproject.org/our-mission.

take a break'. The company also worked hard to bridge the gap with the undergraduate Theatre programme; company member Kelsey Harrison directed the undergraduate production of Emily C. A. Snyder's *Cupid and Psyche*, and undergraduate and MLitt students were invited to participate in Treehouse's season as journeymen actors in staged readings and main stage productions, and as understudies and stage managers.

Looking back on the year of Treehouse's existence, we would argue that the company fulfilled its mission to its community predominantly through its responsiveness. The dangers of a university-based theatre company which forms for only a short period are that it develops the product which it wants to create, then creates a rationale for why it feels its prospective audiences need it. This is understandable within a compressed framework in which students rarely have the lead-in time to fully research the community which they have only just joined. But Treehouse's successes in building relationships with its local partners came about through listening and responding to what businesses and audiences brought to the table, to their missions and principles, and then working with those partners to align our values.

LEGACY AND CONCLUSIONS

As Fişek notes, in her summary of Raymond Williams's definitions of community, 'community is an *existing* but also a *yearned for* grouping, and references to community almost always mix the factual and the ideal'.[27] Treehouse began with an aspiration that 'the seeds of conversation and creativity will continue to flourish within and beyond our found community long after our season', and as we write, a year after the company graduated, what was planted does indeed continue to grow. Indeed, many Treehouse graduates are still in town, tending the branches that the company extended to its community partners: teaching MBU undergraduates, working in local businesses, performing at the ASC, building community in administrative roles. A tree remains even if a treehouse is dismantled; and for many, the found community they found while members of the company has turned into a lasting attachment.

A theatre training model built on grassroots, ensemble principles can, we argue, lead to a student company becoming a meaningful community actor, partly by modelling the values of reciprocal care which underpin the best ensemble ethos. Company member Beth Somerville says that 'above all else we looked out for each other, took care of our mental and physical well-being, and worked through disagreements with respect and compassion. By fostering a healthy internal community, we were better able to serve the larger S&P, MBU and Staunton communities.' Key to Beth's comment here is the word 'serve'; Treehouse did not necessarily know what it was going to do for and with the communities it found, but the collaborative training model prepared the students to listen and respond to the needs of others. The frugality and flexibility of a grassroots ethos which privileges student ingenuity, collaboration and entrepreneurship, moreover, enabled the company to meet those needs as they emerged.

As McAvinchey argues:

The multiplicity of meanings of, and desires for, 'community' reveal it as a term and social process that is fluid and complex ... The word can have connotations of unity, consensus and sameness. But community is also a highly charged word and idea: as a form of social organization, it simultaneously prompts a sense of belonging and exclusion. You are either one of us or one of them.[28]

Our hope is that we have laid out here some of the ways in which the grassroots company-building model allows for a simultaneous set of paired processes – becoming a community, and becoming part *of* a community – in which responsive and collaborative partnerships allow for the lines between 'one of us' and 'one of them' to be blurred, if not entirely broken down. The metaphor of the treehouse imagines a temporary structure interwoven both with the tree in which it is built and with the larger canopy that defines the ecosystem. We hope that preserving some of our work in this format inspires future models for finding points of connection between university theatre and communities of interest and location, which will look very different from those that we found, but which will be similarly reciprocal and collaboratively built.

---

[27] Fişek, *Theatre & Community*, p. 7.
[28] McAvinchey, 'Introduction: right here', pp. 18–19.

FAT HAM AND THE PROBLEM OF COMMUNITY

SHARON O'DAIR[1]

In this article, I aim to complicate Shakespearians' understanding of community, contributing to the minority position of scholars who think community is too often invoked as if community were transparent, with a clear and obvious meaning, or in ways that assume communities are easy to create and maintain. King Lear knows better. After setting in motion the collapse of his kingdom, his court, his knights and his family, he imagines a community of two, with his daughter Cordelia, in prison:

> and so we'll live
> And pray, and sing, and tell old tales, and laugh
> at gilded butterflies, and hear poor rogues
> Talk of court news, and we'll talk with them too –
> Who loses and who wins, who's in, who's out – .[2]

I begin by dipping a toe into the sea of literature on community by social scientists. Then I dip another toe a bit deeper into the pond of literature on community by Shakespearians to consider disciplinarity and research methods. Finally, I offer a reading of a recent winner of the Pulitzer Prize in the United States, James Ijames's adaptation of *Hamlet*, *Fat Ham*. All this will, I hope, tease out the problem of community as it is commonly used by Shakespearians.

Social scientists have long fretted over the definition of community. In 1955, rural sociologist George A. Hillery Jr, observed that it 'is characteristic of any discipline that its members are not always able to agree on the nature of the phenomena they examine'.[3] Hillery Jr proceeded to (try to) make sense of ninety-four definitions of community, a number he admitted was partial. His attempt failed and, seventy years later, debate about definition continues: writes one scholar, '*One of the continuing theoretical debates in community studies is about the definition of community, especially whether the concept of community includes groups of people who share common interests and interaction but who do not share common geographical locality.*'[4] Ecologists are equally contentious – as James T. Stroud et al. observe. Contentiousness leads to confusion, so much so that some ecologists have called for a Convention of Ecology Nomenclature for their young science.[5]

Turning to the historians[6] and the early modern, in 2002 Peter Burke gave the Wiles Lectures at Queen's University in Belfast. Published two years later as *Languages and Communities in Early Modern Europe*, Burke

---

[1] This article originated in Julie Sanders and Isabel Kerremann's seminar for the International Shakespeare Congress, 2024, 'Community and mobility on the Shakespearean stage'. Many thanks to the organizers, the members of the seminar, and especially Susan Anderson, Sonya Freeman and Ari Friedlander, who responded to my work.

[2] *King Lear*, ed. R. A. Foakes (London, 2006), 5.2.11–15.

[3] George A. Hillery Jr, 'Definitions of community: areas of agreement', *Rural Sociology* 20 (1955), 111–23; p. 111.

[4] Ted K. Bradshaw, 'The post-place community: contributions to the debate about the definition of community', *Community Development: Journal of the Community Development Society* 39 (2008), 5–16; p. 5; italics in original.

[5] James T. Stroud, Michael R. Bush, Mark C. Ladd, Robert J. Nowicki, Andrew A. Shantz and Jennifer Sweatman, 'Is a community still a community? Reviewing definitions of key terms in community ecology', *Ecology and Evolution* 5 (2015), 4757–65; p. 4757.

[6] I avoid Benedict Anderson's *Imagined Communities: Reflections on the Origin and Spread of Nationalism* because few of the articles I examined by colleagues invoke Anderson, because addressing its legacy is beyond the scope of this article, and because doing so would add to the conceptual confusion. Gemma Blok, Vincent Kuitenbrouwer, and Claire Weeda observe that Anderson's ideas have been applied to a 'bewildering variety of communities: in the past, present and future, and on a local, national and transnational level'. A testament to the 'intellectual vitality' of imagined communities, this variety can 'obfuscate the concept's analytical power', as it has been deployed around the world by almost anyone for anything – for example, by both 'regimes and insurgents . . . to mobilize support for their political goals' (Gemma Blok, Vincent Kuitenbrouwer and Claire Weeda, 'Introduction', in *Imagining Communities: Historical Reflection on the Process of Community Formation*, ed. Gemma Blok, Vincent Kuitenbrouwer and Claire Weeda (Amsterdam, 2018), 7–20; p. 7).

begins by observing that community is a problem: 'Community is at once an indispensable term and a dangerous one, whether we are practising history or sociology or simply living our everyday lives. In this respect, it is rather like the term "identity", or indeed the word "culture".' The danger of these terms 'is that they seem to imply a homogeneity, a boundary and a consensus that are simply not to be found when one engages in research at the ground level, whether this "fieldwork" is historical, sociological or anthropological'.[7] A few years later, historians Karen Spierling and Michael Halvorson and the contributors to their edited collection *Defining Community in Early Modern Europe* share Burke's concern about the term. It is indispensable because 'understanding the way that particular groups in European society – political, religious, economic, familial, and others – defined their membership, organized themselves, and interacted with other groups is vital to a full comprehension of the dynamics of change and continuity in early modern Europe'. Yet, like Burke, Spierling and Halvorson see danger. It 'lies not in trying to analyze community dynamics but in attempting to impose too great a clarity, simplicity, or transparency on the operations of any particular community'.[8]

The social scientists fret over definitions and the historians over a tendency to simplify the definition – to assume 'clarity, simplicity, or transparency'. What the historians suggest is that communities are messy, fluid, and they certainly can be conflictual, even when boundaries and insider–outsider statuses are clearly established in official or unofficial rhetoric, rules or laws. Establishing and maintaining a community requires nearly continuous negotiation between insiders and outsiders, and between insiders themselves. Communities can be large or small. People sometimes form a community willingly; people sometimes compromise to form one. Other times, people need nudging or persuading or even the force of law to do so, though the latter may beg the question of community altogether. Some people in communities have strong bonds, others weak ones. People can belong to overlapping communities, or to several that do not overlap at all. Communities usually are local, rooted in a place, but can be widely dispersed, communicating through the written word – whether on paper or, nowadays, in cyberspace. A classroom or a theatre company can be inclusive and not a community of any lasting sort or effect. Communities take work, and sometimes too much work, whether in a town, in a theatre company or on a college or university campus.

Turning to Shakespearians,[9] only rarely do colleagues provide a definition of community when they invoke the term. Sometimes colleagues do get in the weeds about 'community dynamics' of the sort just described – such as Matt Kosusko in 'Bard in a barn: iconography, appropriation, and Shakespeare at Winedale', Hardy Cook in 'SHAKSPER: an academic discussion list' or Su Mei Kok in 'Malaysian Moors: ethnicity, speech, and identity in *Jarum Halus* (2008)'. Kosusko describes how a student community forms at the University of Texas's 'Shakespeare at Winedale' summer programme; the students are 'sequestered' and develop their own 'private language, both of camaraderie and conflict'. This language, rooted in Shakespeare, 'is constitutive and exclusive: it builds and binds its members in solidarity'.[10] In 2006, Cook details tensions between academic members of his listserv and more recent and numerous members he describes as 'enthusiasts', tensions leading to his decision to moderate the listserv in order 'to regain the academic focus of the early days of the list', which he knew would not please everyone.[11] *Jarus Halus*, a film adaptation of *Othello* set in contemporary Kuala Lampur, 'can hardly be termed a commercial success' but it did attract the attention of Mark Thornton Burnett who analysed its interethnic tensions but without, as Su Mei Kok argues, fully addressing 'the complexities of ethnic identification in Malaysia' among the Malay, Malay-Chinese and Malay-Indian, which, because identities are set in official discourse, vary widely in practice and

---

7   Peter Burke, *Languages and Communities in Early Modern Europe* (Cambridge, 2004), p. 5.
8   Karen Spierling and Michael Halvorson, 'Introduction: definitions of community in early modern Europe', in *Defining Community in Early Modern Europe*, ed. Karen Spierling and Michael Halvorson (Aldershot, 2008), 1–23; p. 1.
9   Like Hillery Jr, I cannot claim to have examined all the articles citing 'community' in *Shakespeare Quarterly*, *Shakespeare Studies*, *Shakespeare Bulletin* or *Borrowers and Lenders: The Journal of Shakespeare and Appropriation*. But I did examine over 200 examples. *Shakespeare Bulletin* and *Borrowers and Lenders* by far offer the most examples, no doubt because of the journals' emphasis on performance and adaptation; use of the term has grown in recent years.
10 Matt Kosusko, 'Bard in a barn: iconography, appropriation, and Shakespeare at Winedale', *Borrowers and Lenders: The Journal of Shakespeare and Appropriation* 1 (2005), 1–13; p. 6, https://borrowers-ojs-azsu.tdl.org/borrowers/article/view/6/12.
11 Hardy Cook, 'SHAKSPER: an academic discussion list', *Borrowers and Lenders: The Journal of Shakespeare and Appropriation* 2 (2006), 1–13; pp. 8, 9, https://borrowers-ojs-azsu.tdl.org/borrowers/article/view/42/83.

on the street, especially as Malaysia modernizes and hosts more immigration.[12]

Even so, while documenting tension or conflict, Kosusko, Cook and Kok slip into the kind of 'clarity, simplicity, or transparency' Spierling and Halvorson warn against. Kosusko speaks of 'the local community' in Round Top, Texas,[13] the town closest to Winedale; Cook of 'the world-wide Shakespearean academic community';[14] and Kok – because she uses official designations – of 'the culture and political dominance of the Malay community' or the 'difficulties in identity formation among the Malaysian-Chinese community'.[15] Indeed this is the typical usage: we write about 'the X community'. Shakespearians explain, for example, that 'racial conflict ... involves the South Asian and Black communities';[16] that 'the past decades do, in fact, reveal an increased public engagement with Shakespeare from the queer community';[17] that 'The result was a sense of (company) community within the (regional) community, a sense of shared ownership';[18] that 'to be a minority included in any theatre production still makes me feel valued in the wider theatre community';[19] that a commitment to accessibility 'sent an important message to the Deaf community';[20] that 'the questions this play raises about community are also relevant to the theatrical community of players and audience';[21] and that 'Free Shakespeare in the park or other public sites establishes Shakespeare as a gift returned to the neighborhood for the benefit of the community.'[22]

Like Shakespeare in these examples, community is all over the map. What do these groups have in common, other than sharing the same designation? And how would one know? When I hear or read about 'community' in our field, I register a feeling or an aspiration, but mainly a feeling. Community makes us feel good, or at least better than some of its synonyms, including group, city, company, family, clique, brotherhood, gang or nation. But where does that feeling lead? This is exactly what cultural theorist Miranda Joseph asked over twenty years ago in *Against the Romance of Community*. Joseph writes that what she hopes 'to assist in wearing away' is

[t]he self-evidence [of] community. I hope that this book will give pause, will insert a hesitation into the next sentence you utter that seems inevitably to require *community*. I hope that hesitation will open a space for creative thinking about the constitution of collective action, where the term *community* would operate so effectively to shut down such thought. Community is almost always invoked as an unequivocal good, an indicator of a high quality of life, a life of human understanding, caring, selflessness, belonging.[23]

As with Hillery Jr, seventy years ago, Joseph seems to have failed in her aim since the term continues to be invoked often in academia, in scholarship, in the popular press and – well, everywhere. And, generally speaking, the term is invoked as 'an indicator of a high quality of life, a life of human understanding, caring, selflessness, belonging'.

And yet everything gets more complicated – the problems expand – when one adds community-based theatre, community engagement and applied theatre or community performance to the mix, all increasingly common avenues of professional activity by Shakespearians in 'what some are calling the "amateur turn"'.[24] These forms of professional activity are closely related when, as Katherine Steele Brokaw observes, 'Shakespearean production ... allies itself with, involves, and addresses the concerns of a particular

---

[12] Su Mei Kok, 'Malaysian Moors: ethnicity, speech, and identity in *Jarum Halus* (2008)', *Shakespeare Bulletin* 6 (2018), 225–50; pp. 226, 227.

[13] Kosusko, 'Shakespeare', p. 9. [14] Cook, 'SHAKSPER', p. 9.

[15] Kok, 'Malaysian', pp. 240, 227.

[16] J. Katherine Burton, 'Performing race: interrogating Gareth Hinds' graphic novel adaptation of Shakespeare's *Romeo & Juliet*', *Borrowers and Lenders: The Journal of Shakespeare and Appropriation* 15 (2024), 27–49; p. 45.

[17] Trevor Buffone, 'Yassified Shakespeare', *Borrowers and Lenders: The Journal of Shakespeare and Appropriation* 15 (2023), 111–18; p. 115.

[18] Andrew James Hartley, 'Ended revels: the absence left by Georgia Shakespeare', *Shakespeare Bulletin* 39 (2021), 469–85; p. 474. Parentheses here demonstrate a small part of the problem. Hartley tries to distinguish one community from another. One might call it a 'nesting' problem.

[19] Kristen Perkins, 'Taking the kissing path: making the homoerotic modern in *Fixing Troilus and Cressida*', *Borrowers and Lenders: The Journal of Shakespeare and Appropriation* 12 (2019), 1–12; p. 9, https://borrowers-ojs-azsu.tdl.org/borrowers/article/view/226/450. Here, with Perkins, is another example of a 'nesting' problem.

[20] Jim Amberg, '"Teach him how to tell my story": access at the Oregon Shakespeare Festival', *Borrowers and Lenders: The Journal of Shakespeare and Appropriation* 8 (2013), 1–12; pp. 2–3, https://borrowers-ojs-azsu.tdl.org/borrowers/article/view/131/260.

[21] Charles Whitney, 'Appropriate this', *Borrowers and Lenders: The Journal of Shakespeare and Appropriation* 3 (2008), 1–23; p. 17, https://borrowers-ojs-azsu.tdl.org/borrowers/article/view/73.

[22] Vanessa I. Corredera and Louise Geddes, '"A Fair House built on another man's ground": public Shakespeare at Seneca Village', *Shakespeare Bulletin* 41 (2023), 579–600; p. 582.

[23] Miranda Joseph, *Against the Romance of Community* (Minneapolis and London, 2002), p. vii. One of the essays I examined, by Alessandro Simari, alerted me to Joseph's work. See his 'Volunteer labor and theatrical community in Emma Rice's *A Midsummer Night's Dream*', *Shakespeare Bulletin* 38 (2020), 77–95.

[24] Katherine Steele Brokaw, 'Shakespeare as community practice', *Shakespeare Bulletin* 35 (2017), 445–61; p. 446.

community.' Brokaw advocates ethnography and collaboration with theatre practitioners, while initiating 'projects that are interventionist, that involve and impact local communities not directly or usually involved with theater'. Such engagements crucially purport to allow laypeople to be co-creators or co-investigators of knowledge and research.[25] Such engagements make everything more complicated because Shakespearians are moving into fields different from those in which they are trained: performance studies, social work, therapy, and politics, especially social justice activism. Doubtless a continuation of longstanding efforts in the field – Shakespearians doing history, for example, or theory – these moves also continue what John Guillory would call the dissolution of the disciplinary object: literature, or, in our case, Shakespeare. These moves also continue the equally longstanding efforts by Shakespearians to achieve political efficacy in society, efforts that themselves respond to the diminished place of literature in democratized and media-saturated societies.[26] Such efforts, Guillory argues, suffer from 'an overestimation of aim' – an overestimation of what criticism or scholarship can achieve.[27] Overestimating the effects of scholarship is not new – it gives Guillory 'the working hypothesis for an analysis of literary scholarship with the emergence in the nineteenth century of "professional society"'.[28] Still, as *Professing Criticism* makes clear, this overestimation enters hyperdrive from the 1960s:

The profession of literary criticism is committed to its scholarship and teaching as instruments for realizing larger social and political aims, far beyond the interpretation of literary texts. Criticism, as many understand it, is an Archimedean lever for moving the world ... In the event, however, ... criticism, as a discourse intended to leap the gap between specialized scholarship and a larger public sphere, is undermined by the rumor that the professoriate is for some reason attacking its object of study, literature itself.[29]

These moves into other fields amplify what sociologist Michèle Lamont identified in her 2009 ethnographic examination of five elite grant-making foundations, which documents English's 'legitimation crisis' – one 'experienced by its own practitioners' and the result of a collapse of 'disciplinary consensus regarding the pursuit of knowledge and the associated question of how to define and evaluate excellence'.[30] As a result, when competing for prestigious grants, 'literary scholars [are] in a vulnerable position when competing on theoretical or historical grounds with scholars whose disciplines [such as philosophy or history] "own" such terrains'.[31] One hesitates to suggest 'we follow the money', but when external funding

becomes more difficult, if not impossible, to obtain, scholars naturally look to other sources to fund their projects, mainly to their institutions. And these institutions face strong pressures to increase enrolments, reduce costs and engage with their immediate surroundings – or communities. Shakespeare's plays, of course, reside in the public domain, out of copyright, making them attractive financially and as objects of appropriation and adaptation. As community outreach, then, Shakespearian performance projects make a lot of sense/cents.[32] Legitimately, then, one might question what drives this 'amateur turn' or 'service turn'[33] – the needs of these communities, these *people*, or the needs of individual scholars and institutions? Of course, the answer might be 'both'. Still, as Michael P. Jensen asks, 'Shakespeare is the literary 900 pound gorilla but how important is the "Shakespeare" [to these efforts]?

25 Brokaw, 'Shakespeare', pp. 445, 446, 445.
26 See John Guillory, *Professing Criticism: Essays on the Organization of Literary Study* (Chicago, 2022). Notably, Guillory mentions the word 'discipline' twenty-two times in 1993's *Cultural Capital: The Problem of Literary Canon Formation* (Chicago, 1993). In 2022's *Professing Criticism*, Guillory mentions the word eighty-eight times, a fourfold increase.
27 Guillory, *Professing Criticism*, pp. x, xii, xiii, 9.
28 Guillory, *Professing Criticism*, p. x.
29 Guillory, *Professing Criticism*, pp. 44, 69.
30 Michèle Lamont, *How Professors Think: Inside the Curious World of Academic Judgment* (Cambridge, 2009), pp. 59, 4. Literary study is, as one English professor (and a member of the grant-making committee) put it to Lamont, a 'sort of no-man's land or an open field where everybody can be kind of a media expert', p. 74. Now, apparently, everybody can be a theatre professional, a social worker, a therapist or a political activist.
31 Lamont, *Professors*, p. 73. Promoting laypeople as co-creators or co-investigators of knowledge can only add to one of the problems identified by Guillory and Lamont, that of deprofessionalization. On this, see Sharon O'Dair, '"Pretty much how the internet works"; or, aiding and abetting the deprofessionalization of Shakespeare studies', in *Shakespeare Survey 64* (Cambridge, 2011), 83–96.
32 This is true of professional theatre as well. Amberg's essay about the Oregon Shakespeare Festival (OSF) indicates that creating access for 'the Deaf community' is also a marketing strategy for OSF: 'Instead of providing access because it was required by law, it became part of the way OSF did business, and we started looking actively for ways to expand our access programs' ('Teach', p. 1). And although I am loath to suggest this, these moves may make sense in a higher education system, such as that in the United States, where students will not – and, in too many cases, cannot – read, a situation unlikely to improve as artificial intelligence sweeps into education.
33 'Service Shakespeare' is Michael P. Jensen's term for these moves. See Michael P. Jensen, '"What service is here?" exploring service Shakespeare', *Borrowers and Lenders: The Journal of Shakespeare and Appropriation* 8 (2013), 1–6; p. 1, https://borrowers-ojs-azsu.tdl.org/borrowers/article/view/136/270.

Can some other writer do? When can some other writer do? Is Shakespeare and his prestige ever needed, and if it is, when?'[34]

Further, unlike history or theory, which can be seen to illuminate the literary works they address, even if we do not '"own" such terrains', these new moves into other disciplines have little relationship to Shakespeare, or literature more generally. Indeed, the object of study shifts from Shakespeare to those being addressed by the Shakespearian experience: students, prisoners, marginalized peoples, diasporic groups and so on. The object of study is – or should be – the responses of those so addressed. We need to know whether these projects work: 'Surely there must be programs that attempt to, but fail to serve different populations. We should ask why they failed – was Shakespeare inappropriate, or did the problem lie in the execution or the concept of the program?'[35] As such, Shakespearians would seem to need significant training in the research methods of social science – research design, data collection, qualitative analysis, and quantitative analysis.[36] To her credit, Brokaw advocates an 'incorporative methodology that combines tools and values drawn from a number of scholarly practices more closely allied with performance studies than traditional Shakespearean scholarship', including a form of ethnography derived from anthropology, practice as research, and applied theatre / community performance.[37] But it is unclear still how easily or effectively, and with what consequences, Shakespearians can incorporate the tools of social science. Valerie Fazel dissects part of the problem in her piece on YouTube Shakespeare, which 'is a rich resource for Shakespeare performance and reception studies, [but] also opens a Pandora's Box of ethical issues that have yet to be addressed within Shakespeare studies'.[38] Inside the 'Box' are serious questions: the status of online communications – whether they are public or private; the research object – whether it is the posted YouTube Shakespeare or the people who created the post or responded to it; the propriety of Shakespearians' normal research methods for texts that are highly mutable and indeed may in fact be a living human person, a living human person who is 'not dead, literally or figuratively, and through the medium of YouTube, very likely contactable';[39] and finally, the propriety of research on human subjects *tout court*. For Fazel, the question is this: 'What should we borrow from the social sciences, and of that, what should we alter? Clearly the paradigms that have governed our own literary theories will necessarily undergo reshaping – what

can we afford to discard on the wayside . . . and to what must we hold fast . . . ?'[40] Or, as I might put the question: what is being lost, what will be lost in this amateur or service turn, this switch from literary object, whether text or performance, to human object as the locus of scholarly work?

Guillory argues that 'in the absence of a means to assess literary study's real effects in the world, the discipline has been forced into the position of *justification by faith*'.[41] And much work remains to be done on the effects of service interventions, both conceptually and, especially, empirically. In addition to the problems identified by Fazel, David W. Hartwig relates his experience as an 'embedded researcher with New World Shakespeare Company (NWSC) in Salt Lake City', which 'reshapes Shakespeare's works for a local community'.[42] Trying to discover the effectiveness of NWSC's efforts to do so, Hartwig constructed a survey available to audiences, which received a low response rate of 20 per cent; rightly, he is cautious about drawing conclusions. Three-quarters of respondents cited 'family' and 'friends' as the two most important parts of their community, and many of those family or friends were associated with the NWSC. As Hartwig concedes, 'The audience survey thus suggests that there is a certain amount of "preaching to the choir" when it comes to NWSC's [civic] interventions'.[43] I hope I am not too cynical in suggesting that 'preaching to the choir' may characterize most documentations of service or community-based Shakespeare. In another register, Jensen observes that his own work bringing Shakespeare to Alzheimer's patients aims to achieve the 'therapeutic effects

---

[34] Jensen, 'What?', p. 5. [35] Jensen, 'What?', p. 5.

[36] The status of any of these fields – perhaps especially Performance Studies – as social sciences is subject to debate. Nevertheless, regardless of internal division or interdisciplinary moves, what we continue to call the social sciences do require facility in such research methods. Further, some ability to assess the effectiveness of these interventions may be required of principal investigators by their funders, which also requires facility in these methods.

[37] Brokaw, 'Shakespeare', p. 445.

[38] Valerie Fazel, 'Researching YouTube Shakespeare: literary scholars and the ethical challenges of social media', *Borrowers and Lenders: The Journal of Shakespeare and Appropriation* 10 (2016), 1–28; p. 2, https://borrowers-ojs-azsu.tdl.org/borrowers/article/view/281/560.

[39] Fazel, 'Researching', p. 18. [40] Fazel, 'Researching', p. 13.

[41] Guillory, *Professing Criticism*, p. xiii.

[42] David W. Hartwig, 'Local interventions: civic engagement through Shakespearean performance', *Shakespeare Bulletin* 39 (2021), 375–92; p. 376.

[43] Hartwig, 'Local', p. 389.

of music, art, photography, and similar activities … formally studied by Alzheimer's researchers [with] the benefits documented in medical journals'. But he knows that 'Medical journals have no interest in an anecdotal story such as mine; they want the data of a proper research study, and correctly so.'[44]

'Shakespeare is the literary 900 pound gorilla but how important is the "Shakespeare"?' For the plot of *Fat Ham*, the 'Shakespeare' is important. From *Hamlet*, the playwright gives us 'a kind of' Hamlet (Juicy), Horatio (Tio), Ghost (Pap), Claudius (Rev), Gertrude (Tedra), Polonius (Rabby), Ophelia (Opal), Laertes (Larry), and even Yorick.[45] Even a 'kind of' Yorick shows up. From *Hamlet*, Ijames takes two famous speeches by Hamlet ('I have heard / that guilty creatures sitting at a play . . .', and 'What a piece of work is a man! . . .'); he plays with some of Shakespeare's lines, riffing to wonderful comic effect. And, of course, the playwright lifts the scaffolding of the plot and its driver, the command to revenge. Juicy is a 'pensive, thicc, and gay' (5) young Black man whose father, Pap, owned a bar-b-que joint, until he killed one of his workers with a prized, handed-down-through-the-generations butcher's knife. ('This is what I was raised in', Juicy explains, 'pig guts and bad choices' (24)). With Pap in prison, Juicy's mother, Tedra, has taken up with Rev, Pap's brother, who is a 'pig farmer' and fellow 'pit master' (5). Pap's ghost returns to his home on the day Rev celebrates his wedding to Tedra. The Ghost tells Juicy his uncle ordered his killing in prison; he demands vengeance. Juicy is reluctant – very reluctant. He ponders; he thinks; he talks about killing, about murder, about suicide in duets with, variously, Tio, Opal and Larry.

Violence simmers throughout the play, erupting twice. Rev and Juicy provoke each other repeatedly, while Tedra tries unsuccessfully to mediate, eventually prompting Rev to say to Juicy, 'Your mouth is real smart. / How smart are them hands?' Juicy is forced to fight, throwing a few listless punches into Rev's hands; Rev retaliates with a strong punch to Juicy's stomach. Tedra objects, but Rev makes Juicy tell her, 'I'm good' (46, 47). Larry, the Marine home from war who is 'trying to recover from PTSD' (5), reveals to Juicy his attraction to him, an opening to vulnerability, but becomes enraged when Juicy outs him to his mother and refuses to apologize. In a tense scene, one that seemingly ends tenderly between the two young men, Larry 'slams Juicy's face into the table two times', not wanting to kill him, but to hurt him (131, 133). When Rabby tells Juicy, 'He should have broken your neck', he acknowledges her point:

'You're probably right' (135). But Ijames rejects tragedy: 'I think I had a hunger for a play depicting Black people that didn't require tragedy for the story to be fulfilling.'[46] Despite the characters' faults, they are not tragic, and *Fat Ham* mutates into a comedy. Rev dies, but decidedly not by Juicy's refusal of violence or murder, the cycle of toxic masculinity. This I must emphasize, since some reviewers insist he does so choose:[47] Rev dies by accident and his own homophobia. Watching Rev choke on a pork rib, first Rabby and then a distraught Tedra tell Juicy to do 'the heimlich' on him, and Juicy offers, but Rev refuses his help (145, 146, 147). As the stage directions say, 'Rev, in a kind of choking-man's charade, indicates to everyone that he "don't want Juicy touching him … Cause that nigga gay"' (146, 147). Rev dies, and the play ends when Larry emerges from offstage having become an 'utterly divine masterpiece' of 'Drag, fashion, camp' (154). To bright club music, the actors, even Pap/Rev, raised from the dead, open up to a fabulous 'celebration of the feminine' (154).

The play celebrates the ability of these very young adults to mature within the family and community.[48] Tedra knows how difficult life is for her son, 'being someone like you … in a place like this' (119). Juicy, Opal and Larry each come out (to someone) during the

---

44 Jensen, 'What?', p. 4.

45 James Ijames, *Fat Ham* (New York, 2023), p. 5. Subsequent citations are in the text.

46 Victor Fiorillo, 'Q&A: south Philly's Pulitzer-winning playwright James Ijames on his big Broadway debut', *Philadelphia* (3 March 2023), www.phillymag.com/news/2023/03/21/james-ijames-fat-ham-broadway.

47 Kevin Byrne writes, 'In the end, Juicy chose not to follow the story, not to continue the cycle of violence, and didn't kill his uncle' ('Review of *Fat Ham*, by James Ijames, and *White Girl in Danger* by Michael R. Jackson', *Theatre Journal* 76 (2024), 93–6; p. 94). Tim Teeman writes, 'The strength of Juicy is not that he backs down from confrontation, and not that he isn't capable of violence; he is … He just ultimately chooses to turn away from both' ('Review: "Fat Ham" on broadway is pretty delicious', *Daily Beast*, 12 April 2023, www.thedailybeast.com/review-fat-ham-on-broadway-is-pretty-delicious).

48 I define this community in terms of Juicy's family, Rabby's family, the church, and the bar-b-que joint. One can imagine other crucial institutions in this community, such as other Black businesses, the schools and sports teams. As I discuss below, Ijames models this community on the one where he grew up – Bessemer City, North Carolina. In 2022, Bessemer City had a population of 5,470 people, 10 per cent of whom were Black or African-American (non-Hispanic), which is about 550 people: https://datausa.io/profile/geo/bessemer-city-nc#:~:text=The%205%20largest%20ethnic%20groups,(Hispanic)%20(2.92%25).

play, but each is a fragile work in progress. Opal has had sex with other young women, an experience of delight for her because 'we open. We get to be each other's escape hatch. Whole galaxy on the other side' (77). An embarrassed Juicy, in contrast, tells his mother that he likes men '[i]n theory' (62), and Larry's stint in the Marines has only just made him realize his attraction to Juicy. For all of them, alienation is palpable. Within the play's first minute, Juicy tells Tio, 'I hate it here' (9). Much later, Opal counsels Juicy to 'leave. Just run away.' But Juicy cannot: 'I don't wanna leave my mama' (94). (Opal, too: she does not want to be what her mother wants her to be, a young woman in a pretty dress who will be 'doing the debutante' (79). Still, she says, 'I don't be wanting to want to hurt her feelings' (75)). This deep connection holds even between Juicy and his father, despite Pap's brutality. In a poignant soliloquy, Juicy recalls his childhood:

When I was just about seven years old
I asked my mother for a doll.
A Black Barbie dressed in pink.
She bought the doll and wrapped it up in gold . . .
I ripped into it and found the brown perfection.
Adornments, ornaments, and crisp brown skin.
The doll was mine and taught me beauty.
Softness. Tenderness. Realness.
Pap took the doll I loved so much and threw it in the smoker.
He laughed. He said he did it for my own good.
Just be a man, just be more like the boys.
And man I cried, I cried all night it seemed.
I cried so much I thought I could not breathe.
'Screw all this', I said and had the thought
To drown myself in one of the old ponds.
But . . .

(pp. 58–9)

Juicy asks Pap's ghost, 'In life, what made you . . . so mean?', and the Ghost responds, 'I ain't mean' (17–18). Nervously trying to handle this encounter, Juicy uses his inhaler and then unwraps a candy bar, starting a stand-off with Pap about it, almost taunting him with it. Pap commands Juicy not to eat it: 'Put that down. Eat some raisins or something . . . We got suga in our family' (21, 20). When Juicy brings the candy bar closer to his mouth, saying he is an adult and hungry, Pap shouts, demonstrating that, yes, he is mean:

PAP Put. That. Away.
JUICY You gonna stop me?
PAP You talking to me like you lost yo mind. Huh?! I'm your
    father. You do what the hell I say.

JUICY You dead. Ain't been dead for a week and you
    already haunting me. So I know I got something you
    need. Cause one thing about my daddy that I know for
    sure is that that negro only darkens your door when he
    want something. So. What. Do. You. Want?
PAP Ooooohoohoohoo . . . You finally gonna stand up to your
    pap. Over a candy bar. You pansy. You girlie-ass puddle
    of shit. You put that in your mouth and I'll end you.
JUICY This is not the way to get me to listen to you.
PAP Can't stand you.
JUICY And there it is.

(pp. 21–2)

Nevertheless, Juicy tells his mother, 'He was awful but he wasn't nothing' (32), and later, 'I miss him.' Tedra asks 'why?' and Juicy says, 'I don't know . . . I feel like I'm supposed to' (64–5), which Tedra sanctions because 'missing him don't cost nothing so . . . carry on' (65).

Struggling with familial history and social expectations, the young counsel each other. Tio, who has been in therapy, tells Juicy, 'cycles of violence are like deep . . . But you don't got to let it define you' (35). Juicy tells Opal, 'You don't have to be what your mama wants you to be' (76). Larry tells Juicy, 'People decide what they want you to be. It's hard to fight against that'; Juicy tells him that fighting against it is 'worth it though' (109). But fight against it how? And to what end? Juicy knows love and social expectations compel him to miss his father. And Juicy loves his mother, knows his mother needs him, and wants her to need him, even if she mocks his ambition and 'doesn't really look at me. She talks at me' (76). Does one fight against love or the parental bond? Does one fight against the church? (Being weird 'ain't Christian', Rabby judges – nor is homosexuality (129)). Fighting against it, for Juicy, appears to be taking it in the gut, literally and figuratively. From childhood, Juicy has had no choice but to take it in the gut again and again. Undercutting the comic resolution, then, for Juicy, for all of them, is awareness that the self is fragile and that adulthood and the truth about one's sexuality do not solve the problem of self and family or community. Their hopes for their futures are neither grand nor certain. Juicy does not want to work in the 'family business', cutting up pigs and getting 'all that smoke in my clothes' (71); he likes 'paperwork', so he is working on a degree in Human Relations, even though it does not pay well – and even though, as Opal says, 'You not good with people!' (72). Larry, newly open to his sexuality, wants to be a performer; Tio wants to marry his preferred personal state – being high – to a business, a marijuana dispensary. Opal wants to join the Marines or open a shooting range or a '[s]hooting-range-themed buffet restaurant', since 'all people do 'round here is shoot at each other and eat' (105). Juicy asks his friends, 'Is this what grown feels like? Sort of lonely and confused . . . ghetto as hell' (125).

'Shakespeare is the literary 900 pound gorilla but how important is the "Shakespeare"?' For James Ijames, the 'Shakespeare' in *Fat Ham* has been very important. *Fat Ham* has brightened an already promising career. Think television, perhaps Hollywood.[49] For audiences, the 'Shakespeare' is very important too, as an inducement not only to attend but to think: *Fat Ham* is metatheatrical, breaks the fourth wall multiple times, and much of the poignancy, comedy and artistic pleasure of the play circulates during these moments of allusion and collision between *Fat Ham* and *Hamlet*, playwright and audience, and onstage characters and audience. Unsurprisingly, therefore, reviews of *Fat Ham* by Shakespearians and theatre critics have been almost universally glowing, highlighting the comedic and metatheatrical deconstruction of Shakespeare's tragedy. Indeed, '*Fat Ham* imagines a world of possibilities beyond the limitations of both' Shakespeare and tragedy, a world that 'treats Black and queer bodies with tenderness'.[50] *Fat Ham* 'dances on the bones of Hamlet', using 'the silhouette of Shakespeare's masterwork to birth something new, a vicious critique of masculinity and violence infused with a much-needed hilarity'.[51] This 'raucous domestic comedy'[52] becomes a play about queer love, about 'pride, safety, and community – and right at the end, joy and dancing'.[53] For Shakespearians, for theatre critics, this adaptation is catnip. Juicy's asthma, his sensitivity, his softness, his empathy, his sexual orientation, his philosophical inclinations, his appreciation of Shakespeare and his loyalty to his mother, all combine to vanquish the brutality of Black men, his father and uncle, the patriarchs, to our ideological delight.

To this celebratory chorus of laughter, joy and dancing, one that validates femininity and 'specifically Black queer joy',[54] several critics offer quieter, more serious notes. After all, Ijames and we have to survive the violence to find that joyful end. The play is 'frank and funny in its depiction of a family in the throes of transition', writes one reviewer.[55] Another judges that Juicy, Opal and Larry struggle with 'being who they truly are amidst a family that hasn't quite evolved into acceptance'.[56] 'Evolved', like 'transition', is bandied about in contemporary discourse, and it is, I would wager, a subtext of many of the reviews cited here – the family and the community need to evolve – but its

use is surely inaccurate, for evolution is not teleological. Evolution may have a direction, but it does not have a goal, even one of accepting queer love or soft masculinity. Further, Juicy's family and community are not solely to blame for what is problematic in his relationships with them. Juicy himself is 'not perfect'; he sulks and he 'can be cruel' (133), outing Larry to his mother and refusing to apologize, as I have already noted. Rev complains that Juicy throws attitude 'like he better than me and his mama' (55), and Ijames offers support for Rev's judgement. When Juicy suggests a party game, charades, which will be his version of the 'Mousetrap', Tedra happily instructs 'everyone to write down a movie or a TV show or a book'. A bit under his breath, Juicy says, 'like they read'. Tedra asks, 'what you say, Juicy?', who says in reply, 'A good book indeed' (93). When Juicy asks Opal what he should do, she suggests, 'You could stand to be more honest?' (95)

Ijames may shatter *Hamlet* but, writes Maya Phillips, 'he builds it back up into something that's more – more tragic but also more joyous, more comedic, more political, more

---

49 Fiorillo, 'Q&A', www.phillymag.com/news/2023/03/21/james-ijames-fat-ham-broadway.

50 Shanelle E. Kim, 'Review of *Fat Ham*', *Shakespeare Bulletin* 40 (2022), 545–8; pp. 545, 548. Kim argues that Shakespeare's inability to so imagine Black and queer bodies means Shakespeare should 'go' – out of the canon and out of our lives. '*Fat Ham* is not Shakespeare', she writes, 'nor is it a tragedy. How wonderful that it is neither of those things' (p. 548). Kim seems to have forgotten that *Fat Ham* would not exist without this unimaginative Shakespeare. In her disdain for Shakespeare, Kim illustrates Guillory's 'rumor', noted above, 'that the professoriate is for some reason attacking its object of study, literature itself'. And, weirdly, her disdain for Shakespeare resembles that of Juicy's uneducated parents.

51 Gloria Oladipo, 'Fat Ham review – Pulitzer-winning Hamlet revision hits Broadway', *The Guardian*, 13 April 2023, www.theguardian.com/stage/2023/apr/13/fat-ham-review-broadway-hamlet-pulitzer.

52 Jesse Green, 'Review: skewering masculinity, in a hot and sizzling "Fat Ham"', *New York Times*, 12 April 2023, www.nytimes.com/2023/04/12/theater/fat-ham-review.html.

53 Teeman, 'Review'. 54 Teeman, 'Review'.

55 Charles Isherwood, '"Fat Ham review: to bbq or not to bbq', *Wall Street Journal*, 13 April 2023, www.wsj.com/articles/fat-ham-james-iljames-pulitzer-prize-hamlet-william-shakespeare-marcel-spears-billy-eugene-jones-nikki-crawford-adrianna-mitchell-caivin-leon-smith-benja-kay-thomas-11653599511.

56 Kevin Taft, 'Theater review: "Fat Ham" cooks up family drama southern American Shakespeare style', *We Live Entertainment*, 9 April 2024, https://weliveentertainment.com/we-live-entertainment/theater-review-fat-ham-cooks-family-drama-american-southern-shakespearean-style.

contemporary'.[57] Phillips's judgement is germane. Her assertion that *Fat Ham* is 'more tragic' than *Hamlet* rests, I think, on her awareness – she herself is Black – that 'toxic masculinity and homophobia ... plague the Black community'.[58] A plague in a community is not arrested by a comic ending to a play, even one that 'has been on a whirlwind quest for theatrical domination across the United States'.[59] More importantly, Ijames may want Juicy to be able to live his queerness with his family and in his community; reviewers tend to think this is the point. Ijames may want that community to be different, to learn from its past, but does he want it erased or 'evolved' out of existence? Apparently not: *Fat Ham* is, Ijames says, a 'love letter to this place' – his small, rural town of origin, this 'particular expression of Black Southern identity'.[60] That expression flowers, finds its musicality, in language and speech, from the Black church in which he was raised – 'the Black church with all of the history, all of the style, all of the cultural idiosyncrasies of that institution has had a big impact on how I think about what theatricality can do'[61] – and from everyday life where people live in a 'tradition of storytelling, embodying the story'. He aimed for an 'overlapping speech' among his characters, the kind of 'Black Southern electric conversation that happens in summer at barbecues'.[62] Southerners 'are constantly using language to identify themselves'. Southerners embody the story: 'it's like the things that I say are who I am, the things that I think are who I am.'[63]

'Shakespeare is the literary 900 pound gorilla but how important is the "Shakespeare"?' To the fictional community in *Fat Ham*, the 'Shakespeare' is not important, nor is college. Compellingly, I think, college is like other social expectations here, a somewhat vague and potentially fraught possibility, like joining the military, getting married or owning a business. Something, perhaps, to try or consider. Juicy has been enrolled at the University of Phoenix for some time, studying Human Resources and, though mildly supportive of his educational ambitions, both his parents – one dead and one alive – tell him college is a 'scam' (19, 49). Like his brother, Rev, the ghost of Pap thinks Juicy 'got a smart mouth'. He asks his son,

PAP You still going to that little
    online school.
JUICY It's called the University of Phoenix.
PAP 'It's called the University of Phoenix'. Let me tell you something. It's a bubble. Themthemthemthem for-profit colleges. Just taking poor people's money ... you get skills, sure but like ... it's not sustainable. They started all those little colleges all over the place ... taking people's money. For what? A digital degree? What you majoring in?

JUICY Human resources.
PAP What. Is. You. Gonna do with that?
JUICY Get-a-job-in-human-resources?
PAP Scam. Who goes to college online to learn how to manage human beings. Them things don't go.

(p. 19)

Juicy tries a different tack: 'You always said go to college', to which Pap retorts, 'Howard, Morehouse, hell, Caldwell Community College ... ', but not go 'to school on a laptop' (19–20).[64] 'Them things don't go': when Juicy expresses doubt about his father's murder in prison, Pap says to him,

I ain't trying to be out here hypothesizing with yo ass. The inmate that stabbed me said ... 'Rev said what's up'. Like he was in one of them HBO shows with the dragons and whatnot. I don't need no human resources degree to figure that dark shit out.

(p. 28)

Still, Rabby wants her daughter to go to college and she wants her to major in Human Resources – 'something useful' – but Opal will have nothing of it: 'I don't like dealing with people' (105). Human Resources is the major *du jour*: what the parents offer their children is vague support for the idea of college, but they are incapable of offering specific guidance, while they wonder whether college is worth the cost or time. If something comes up – remarriage or remodelling, as is the case for Tedra – college

57 Maya Phillips, '"Fat Ham" review: dismantling Shakespeare to liberate a gay Black Hamlet', *New York Times*, 26 May 2022, www .nytimes.com/2022/05/26/theater/fat-ham-review.html.

58 Maya Phillips, '"Fat Ham" review'.

59 Danielle Rosvally, 'Review of *Fat Ham* dir. by Stevie Walker-Webb', *Shakespeare Bulletin* 41 (2023), 629–33; p. 629.

60 Amy Levinson, 'Finding and sharing inspiration: an interview with playwright James Ijames', *Playbill Geffen Playhouse* (2024), 28–30; p. 29. Ijames is very specific about speech: he grew up with a 'very distinct mix of Tidewater accent with this sort of coastal accent coming from one direction, and an Appalachian thing coming from another' (Levinson, 'Finding', p. 29).

61 Ijames enrolled at Morehouse College intending to major in music, specifically choral music conducting, only later moving into theatre. The profound influence of the Black church on American – and world – popular music since the 1950s is indisputable, from Little Richard to Beyoncé.

62 Teeman, 'Review'.

63 Jessica Bedford, 'James Ijames on "Fat Ham", the South, and embodying the story', *Southern Review of Books*, 4 May 2021, southernreviewof books.com/2021/05/04/fat-ham-james-ijames-interview.

64 Juicy replies, 'a desktop' (20). Rabby, too, mocks him for going to school 'on his cell phone' (128).

becomes expendable. In this, the parents resemble many Americans, increasingly doubtful about college.[65]

What Rabby does know is the potential, even the likelihood, for deracination that attends college, particularly at an integrated or elite college. She is a bit late to the wedding celebration because she 'had to go to this thing up at the church ... Preacher's daughter's baby shower' (65–6). Rabby is appalled that the girl married outside their race, resisted the community:

RABBY She met some boy from Norway in college. He so pale you can see his veins through his skin. That baby gonna look like a ghost.
TEDRA Not a ghost!!
RABBY She used to like Larry. Larry! Didn't that Patterson girl use to like you? She thought the world of Larry. They would have made some pretty babies. Thought I was gonna get me some cute grandbabies.
TEDRA AWWWW what happened Larry?
LARRY She went off to –
RABBY He had that girl running in behind him all through high school and she went off to college and got hooked up with that translucent boy.

(66–7)

College is not an unalloyed good, and not just because of its expense. Many working-class, ethnic and rural families fear or suspect, as Rabby apparently does, that college and its attendant effects – secularization, ideological change, upward mobility – will alienate them from their children, deracinate them, encourage them to 'hook ... up with [some] translucent boy'.[66]

But Ijames's funniest barbs about higher education – or, at least, the most pertinent to this discussion – are those directed at Shakespeare. Attempting to mediate between her son and his uncle, Tedra says,

TEDRA I uh ... I wanna talk to you.
JUICY About what?
TEDRA Your daddy.
JUICY My daddy is dead.
TEDRA You know what I'm talking about.
JUICY The king, my queen, is dead.
TEDRA Huh?
JUICY It's Shakespeare. Kind of.
TEDRA You watch too much PBS.
JUICY How can one watch too much PBS?
TEDRA You don't need to know all that.
JUICY It's harmless.
TEDRA Whatever.

(pp. 114–15)

Tedra implores Juicy to stop upsetting Rev and asks her son to:

TEDRA Just be nice!
JUICY How nice the quarrel was ...
TEDRA What?
JUICY Shakespeare.
TEDRA If you bring up that dead old white man one mo time. Don't nobody wanna talk about his ass. You act like he got all the answers. You look crazy out here quoting Shakespeare and shit.
JUICY It seems appropriate.
(Pap appears and stands beside Tedra.)
TEDRA Appropriate my ass.

(p. 116)

At this point in *Fat Ham*, 'quoting Shakespeare and shit' does seem appropriate in both senses of the word, for Pap's ghost's reappearance prompts another moment when Ijames breaks the fourth wall. These metatheatrical moments do much of the work in turning the play from tragedy to comedy. In a review, Cristina León Alfar argues that 'breaking of the fourth wall ... implicates the audience in racism and sexism',[67] but my reading suggests, instead, that Juicy stands as an intermediary between the audience and his friends and family onstage and, crucially, breaking the fourth wall allows the other characters to swerve from tragedy to comedy, to reject the *Hamlet* imperative. They, not Juicy, reject the *Hamlet* imperative. After Rev dies, Juicy looks to the audience but tells everyone on stage, 'You know what [the audience] think bout to happen, right? ... I mean ... All of us are supposed to die' (149). Everyone objects:

TIO Well ... technically Horatio ...
RABBY They gonna be waiting a long time for me to die. My mama lived to be a hundred and thirty.
OPAL I ain't dying for nobody.
TEDRA Who says we gotta die?

(p. 149)

Juicy, still looking at the audience and still ambivalent, is bound to genre and story: 'It's how these kinds of

---

65 For a recent exploration, one more dismal than most, see Erik Baker, 'What are you going to do with that?' *Harper's Magazine* (2024), https://harpers.org/archive/2024/09/what-are-you-going-to-do-with-that-erik-baker-college-education. Baker teaches, although not on the tenure track, at Harvard University.

66 On this problem, see Jennifer M. Morton, *Moving Up without Losing Your Way: The Ethical Costs of Upward Mobility* (Princeton, 2019). I addressed the fears of working-class parents about their upwardly mobile children in Sharon O'Dair, *Class, Critics, and Shakespeare: Bottom Lines on the Culture Wars* (Michigan, 2000).

67 Cristina León Alfar, 'Abandoning tragedy in James Ijames's *Fat Ham*', *Borrowers and Lenders: The Journal of Shakespeare and Appropriation* 15 (2023), 97–101; p. 99.

things end . . . Cause this a tragedy. We tragic' (149, 151). The stage direction instructs: 'They all tense up a bit. As if they don't know for sure if violence is about to erupt' [149]; and only Opal 'appears ready and capable to fight' (150). The rest offer comic flailing, half-hearted attempts to kill one another with, perhaps, plastic forks and pork ribs, or a purse. Mostly, they scream at each other, which is, according to the stage direction, 'ridiculous. But ultimately charming and cathartic' (150). Still Juicy persists, 'We just gotta . . . uh . . . commit' because 'stories have plot, structure . . . '. The others object again: Opal asks, '[do] they?' And Tio adds, 'Nope'. Rabby confesses, 'It did feel good to just scream. I should scream more often', and she does (151).

Significantly, Pap's ghost and Tedra, especially, intervene in two of Juicy's addresses to the audience, and each one asks, 'What you tell them?' (24, 58).[68] But, unlike Pap's ghost, Tedra pleads with Juicy to 'be factual', to tell 'the truth' to the audience; he rather snidely asks, 'What's that mean, huh?' (61), which is a good question for Juicy, too. She knows 'they think I'm trashy. Cause I married my late-husband's brother' (59). A weird metatheatrical moment this, since she does not know *Hamlet*. But she does know 'They did it in the Bible all the time' (59). Who is the audience for her? Who does she think is judging her? Perhaps her own community: when Tedra and Rev are arguing loudly inside the house, Rabby says to her children, 'See what happens . . . When you don't live right' (104)). Juicy must tell them 'how much of a son of a bitch your daddy was' (60), and his mother reveals some of his offences even Juicy did not know. To her son, she rather heatedly insists:

TEDRA I ain't trying to be talking all deep with you. Them people judging your mama. They done already made up they minds about what I'm worth. What I get to feel. What I get to do . . . But you make it plain up in here bout the facts. I don't want them saying nothing about my life choices and why I did what I did.

JUICY You got some feeling about all this, don't you?

TEDRA I just want it to be factual.

JUICY Duly noted.

TEDRA You tell em.

JUICY I'll do that.

(pp. 61–2)

'Truth-telling' is what the characters have done or tried to do in the heat of very tense, potentially violent moments (134). But the 'truth-telling' is undercut wonderfully, I think, by some of the funniest lines in the play, when Tio and Juicy dip out of the language of their community and into the language of another community, that of therapy:

TIO Well we all just learned some things about each other and uh . . . I just wanna say I think this new level of transparency and vulnerability is just so refreshing.

JUICY Would it be helpful . . . to process
You know. If anyone wanted to share.

(p. 136)

What to make of this play? What does this play reveal about a community and Shakespearians' approaches to understanding, analysing or serving it? As I suggested above, *Fat Ham* is catnip for Shakespearians, for upper-middle-class audiences. But also, as I suggested above, the young people do not want to leave the family, the community, not even therefore the church that helps define their community, their musicality, their language. The conflict in this play's community may be between generations, but the young still love their parents and do try to follow what, in Rabby's words, 'you SUPPOSED-TA-DO'. Juicy may not want to carve pigs, rub 'em, and 'que them, but this community, I suspect, agrees with Rev – who 'knew his way 'round that pig' – about not selling the family's bar-b-que joint to 'that chain barbeque place . . . them sweet-and-sour-barbeque-sauce-peddling motherfuckers' (148, 152, 43), a chain that will homogenize the specificities of the community's barbeque.

One reviewer, as I have noted, says this family, and by extension this community, is 'in transition',[69] but to what? Is this family and community to become, or even resemble, that, say, of the playwright and the audience, of people who say 'queer' (not 'gay'),[70] who like Shakespeare (not Rick James (97)), and who, for solace, turn to therapy (not Christianity)? Is the upper-middle-class audience – are Shakespearians – supposed to enjoy this comic portrait – even for some, I suspect, a takedown – of lower-middle-class Black American culture, of 'country' (83) Black American culture? If so, towards what end? Assimilation,

---

[68] Opal accidentally witnesses Juicy addressing the audience with Hamlet's 'I have heard . . .' speech. Her response: 'You weird Juicy' (94).

[69] Isherwood, 'Fat', www.wsj.com/articles/fat-ham-james-iljames-pulitzer-prize-hamlet-william-shakespeare-marcel-spears-billy-eugene-jones-nikki-crawford-adrianna-mitchell-caivin-leon-smith-benja-kay-thomas-11653599511.

[70] The word 'queer' does not appear in the play. The word 'gay' does not appear in the academic reviews and rarely in those in the popular press.

secularization or atomization? Perhaps, but with what cost? According to the *New York Times*, the cost may be high. Miraculously, if I may say, and as I put final touches to this article, the *New York Times* reported on the precarious state of the Black Church in the United States. Churchgoing is in decline everywhere in the United States and in Europe, but 'the singular standing of the Black church means that its declining numbers have far-reaching consequences for social cohesion and Black political power writ large. For centuries, the church has been not only the spiritual and social center of Black life but also a political force.'[71] Putting aside the potentially negative consequences for liberal politics in the United States – organizing, getting out the vote, fracturing a large and reliable block of the Democratic Party, and so on – one must focus on 'social cohesion', too: how Black or 'country' would such an assimilated, secularized or atomized family and community be?[72] Therefore – and I follow the lead of the social scientists with whose work I began this article – I suggest that the Black and 'country' community in *Fat Ham* – if not in Black communities offstage, in real life – is negotiating its mores and its boundaries in a messy and conflictual

process that will, I hope, persist. Like a good Shakespearian comedy, *Fat Ham* ends happily, with two scapegoats bearing the sins of the community. But this fictional Black and 'country' community abides: not homogeneous, always negotiating and learning from its mistakes, it is rooted in a place, and, I hope, going nowhere. Like tolerance, this, too, is part of *Fat Ham*'s meaning.

---

[71] Clyde McGrady, 'The Black church has a Gen-Z issue: "they don't come into the building anymore"', *New York Times*, 29 September 2024, www.nytimes.com/2024/09/29/us/politics/black-church-gen-z-attendance.html.

[72] See Olivier Roy, *The Crisis of Culture: Identity Politics and the Empire of Norms*, trans. Cynthia Schoch and Trista Selous (Oxford 2023). Roy would argue that such a community would not be very Black or very 'country'. And he would argue that the process of 'transition' reviewers identify in *Fat Ham* exemplifies a contemporary global society engaged in the 'deculturation of cultures', including the 'content of the cultural canon' – Kim's notion that Shakespeare and tragedy must go – and the 'obliteration of anthropological cultures', such as that in *Fat Ham*. Replacing cultures are autonomous subcultures 'reduced to codes of communication' (p. 32) – 'queer', not 'gay'; or the lingo of therapy, not of Christianity.

SHAKESPEARE UNDER THE HOOD: TEACHING, RESEARCHING AND LEARNING SHAKESPEARE FROM WITHIN

DAVID STERLING BROWN[1]

What's under the hood? Not the hood of your car, if you have one, but what's under the metaphorical hood of your being, your *self*? What's going on inside of you that no one can see right now? Or what was going on around you – in whatever environment you were in – on the worst, most difficult day of your life to date? How did that day impact you? How did it change who you are? How did it cause you to evolve in some way, shape or form in response to the trauma you experienced? Did you metabolize and eventually transform the trauma into something useful for you or perhaps useful for others?[2] In other words, did you find a way to 'use the negative to your advantage?'[3]

I begin with this set of key questions because, retrospectively, I discovered those important inquiries were unconsciously plaguing me, and guiding me, as I drafted *Shakespeare's White Others*.[4] Those questions led me to conclude my first book with a personal, experiential anecdote that reflects, in part, how I developed an interest in, and commitment to, activism and social justice: because of racist trauma created for me by police officers in my own 'hood, on the street where I grew up. I sometimes wonder if that's how we consciously or unconsciously locate our intellectual passions, extracting them from deep within ourselves because they are inextricably linked to some memory, some experience, that gets treated, managed or resolved through our life's work, through our vocation of choice or, perhaps, through the vocation that chooses us. My book *Shakespeare's White Others* was born out of intersecting traumatic experiences that, once metabolized over the course of nearly twenty years, allowed me to use the negative to my advantage. In between the lines of the book, I recall hauntings of the past in order to deal and attempt to heal.

When I, as a grad student, encountered in Ayanna Thompson's *Colorblind Shakespeare* volume Margo

Hendricks's essay 'Gestures of performance: rethinking race in contemporary Shakespeare', I was triggered. I was stunned, even. Not because Hendricks made an astute argument about Shakespeare, performance and race, the scholarly combination of which was new to me back then, but because one of Hendricks's analytical examples examined the 2000 film *Romeo Must Die*, which starred Jet Li and the late singer-actor-model Aaliyah, who tragically died in a 2001 plane crash at the height of her short-lived but impactful career. Hendricks's insightful essay, which arrives at a beautiful conclusion about interracial couple Romeo (Li) and Juliet (Aaliyah) 'beget[ting] a new racial model',[5] triggered me because it unexpectedly brought me back to the day Aaliyah died. I remember vividly that day and the many days thereafter because my teenage self entered a state of shock as my world seemingly froze and thawed and froze again while I processed the devastating news. And then I plunged into a prolonged state of deep grief, as if I had lost the thing I loved most in the world – maybe, that day, I did.

You see, Aaliyah was, and still is, my diva, in the same way Beyoncé, Mariah Carey, Celine Dion, Whitney Houston, Gladys Knight and others fill that role for

---

[1] I thank William Germano, author of *Getting it Published* and *From Dissertation to Book,* for discussing my title with me and offering suggestions.
[2] See Resmaa Menakem, *My Grandmother's Hands: Racialized Trauma and the Pathway to Mending Our Hearts and Bodies* (Las Vegas, 2017), p. 25.
[3] I thank Milla Cozart Riggio for instilling this philosophy in me.
[4] David Sterling Brown, *Shakespeare's White Others* (Cambridge, 2023).
[5] Margo Hendricks, 'Gestures of performance: rethinking race in contemporary Shakespeare', in *Colorblind Shakespeare: New Perspectives on Race and Performance*, ed. Ayanna Thompson (New York: Routledge, 2006), 187–203; p. 200.

their most devoted fans.[6] I did not expect to encounter *my* diva in a critical essay on Shakespeare, performance and race, hence my shock. And thus, I did not expect, while conducting my research back then, to return to a place in my past that allowed love, heartbreak and trauma to merge in my present in such a beautiful way that would eventually inform my own approaches to being a Shakespeare literary critic and pedagogue. Beyond walking away from Hendricks's essay with new critical insights that informed my thinking as a grad student, I walked away beginning to understand how the critical, personal and experiential can and should matter to me in my life's work, for *Romeo Must Die* solidified my diva, Aaliyah, as part of the Shakespeare on film and Shakespeare and race legacies.[7] Until I read Hendricks's essay, I had no idea that was possible.

What I am suggesting here is that by drawing on the work of a beloved music icon, Hendricks made space for me, and for others, to connect with her scholarship in a generative way that mattered on a level that seemingly had little to do with my developing scholarly self. And yet I could not have been more wrong. I understand that now, retrospectively. As I waded deeper into the profession, I discovered that scholars, especially the Black scholars whose work I encountered,[8] were wont to be anecdotal in their scholarship in ways that triangulated the critical, personal and experiential. In hindsight, then, I realized as I began to produce my own scholarship how deeply I had been influenced by many critics whose work I sat with as I tried to find my scholarly voice – as I tried to make sense of how those scholars were doing what they did so that I, too, could participate in the production of scholarship that had practical applicability in my life and, perhaps, in the lives of my readers.

The influence of such scholars is partly the subject of this article, which aims to highlight the possibilities for, and value of, operating with a critical–personal–experiential style. In short, when executed deliberately and with care, this style is a way to draw people in from the margins. It is even a way to draw in marginalized people who get to discover some part of themselves in the work, in the same way I often discover parts of myself in Shakespeare's dramatic literature and in the lives of his 'great vast gallery of people', as James Baldwin labels them in his essay 'Why I stopped hating Shakespeare'.[9] As I have discovered over the years, having synergy among the critical, personal and experiential in one's scholarship and teaching can enhance the impact on readers and students, in many ways, especially as it

pertains to broader utility and rhetorical accessibility. Moreover, I imagine such synergy is also relevant to theatrical practice.

In her official endorsement of *Shakespeare's White Others*, poet, playwright and author Claudia Rankine writes from a place of knowing a little about the personal struggles and challenges I faced as I wrote my first book and saw it through to publication. Rankine writes:

With *Shakespeare's White Others*, David Sterling Brown engages racial whiteness and provokes interdisciplinary dialogue through his rhetorically accessible 'critical-personal-experiential' style. The book's unexpected final words, documenting Brown's own racial profiling experience, anticipate the depths of this brilliantly bold Shakespearean discourse that seamlessly blends genres while reimagining the scholarly monograph mode.[10]

Rankine's words call attention to her knowledge of *some* of my personal history when she asserts that my book blends genres, as it is indeed memoir-esque overtly and most certainly in between the lines. Specifically, Rankine highlights the 'critical–personal–experiential' style of *Shakespeare's White Others*, a style that is indeed a throughline representing for me the metabolization of trauma of all kinds – and not just my own. Additionally, that critical–personal–experiential style is at the heart of my pedagogical methodology, anchored by what I call 'productive discomfort':[11] a teaching 'practice [that] leans into difficult discourses on a variety of contentious topics and fearlessly engages students' personal backgrounds, identities, and experiences [by using] the learning process to expand the boundaries of students'

---

[6] I must thank my dear friend – the one and only Jericho Brown – for helping me realize that Aaliyah was, and still is, my diva. Thus, in this article, I identify her as such to honour her lasting legacy and her impact on my life.

[7] Hendricks, 'Gestures', pp. 198–9.

[8] Many of those scholars, and their work, are mentioned in a previously published article of mine. See endnote 5 in David Sterling Brown, 'Things of darkness: the blueprint of a methodology', *The Hare: An Online Journal of Untimely Reviews in Early Modern Theater* 5, Special Issue: Critical Race Studies (September 2020).

[9] James Baldwin, 'Why I stopped hating Shakespeare', in *The Cross of Redemption: Uncollected Writings*, ed. Randall Kenan (New York, 1964), 65–9.

[10] See *Shakespeare's White Others*.

[11] See David Sterling Brown, 'Discomfort is the point: why "safe spaces" do a disservice to students', *Liberal Education* (American Association of Colleges and Universities), March 2024, www .aacu.org/liberaleducation/articles/discomfort-is-the-point.

comfort zones [and] challenge their existing assumptions and biases'.[12]

When I engage with students in this way – and I always have since I became a professor in 2015 – I am conscientiously encouraging them to leave no parts of themselves out of our discourse. I want everyone – to whatever extent they feel comfortable – raising their metaphorical hoods in my classroom. I want them to use our literature and the critical theories we study to make sense of what is under the hood, so to speak. I want them to apply the critical–personal–experiential pedagogical practice not only to how they learn but also to how they teach – themselves, me, their peers and other people whose paths they may cross outside of our academic space at Trinity College in Hartford, Connecticut.

This approach to scholarship and teaching relates to what science education professor Christopher Emdin would refer to as being 'ratchetdemic'.[13] Ratchetdemic as a concept or academic philosophy is not easy to summarize, so I extract here what is for me one of the most salient aspects of how Emdin outlines the term in *Ratchetdemic: Reimagining Academic Success*. Emdin explains:

To be ratchetdemic is to have no role in starving part of the self in pursuit of 'academic' knowledge. It is a recognition that any education that is disconnected from helping students understand themselves and the power structures that influence their worlds and how these structures operate to stifle or obfuscate young people's purpose is not education at all.[14]

Being ratchetdemic requires integration of the critical, personal and experiential in one's pedagogical approach. It requires seeing, valuing and honoring the uniqueness of the learners in each distinctive classroom. And being ratchetdemic requires the acceptance, or at least tolerance, of productive discomfort, which in my classroom experience is where the real growth opportunities are for anyone who engages with the kind of work, assignments or conversations that produce such discomfort.

Those uncomfortable feelings and moments are necessary for the learning process; and that necessity becomes most apparent almost always in hindsight when one processes and reflects on the uncomfortable moments and feelings. Ultimately, 'discomfort is the point', as I contend. To be ratchetdemic is to make students aware that acknowledging what's under the hood – and doing regular maintenance on what is under the hood, so to speak – is essential for the educational process. It is essential to the learning and the *un*learning students will have to do throughout their lives – and certainly in all my courses. Anything that is *not* prompting self-examination and broader reflection on the sociopolitical power systems that shape our world and that need interrogating, as Emdin forcefully and rightly asserts, is not education at all. I wholeheartedly believe that, too.

While attending the 2024 ISC in Stratford-upon-Avon, England, I had the privilege of hearing director Brendan O'Hea discuss his RSC *As You Like It* production.[15] During his lively, enlightening conversation with Michael Dobson, O'Hea said something that triggered me, something that maybe even touched other people who were present for this candid conversation. Brendan mentioned that one of the actors, a friend of his, 'is in recovery'. Furthermore, O'Hea added – with a level of sensitivity I appreciated – that the actor had been to 'dark places' that aided in useful ways his acting ability, his theatre practitioner process. The dark places rhetoric was triggering for and resonated with me because I, too, know people who have been to dark places. I am, in fact, one of those people. Thus, I appreciated that O'Hea chose to be frank and *go there*. In so doing, he normalized for me a particular reality that people, notably scholars in this case, do not always discuss as much as we should: that people struggle with and manage daily all kinds of challenges in life, from addiction to (mental) health issues to financial problems to racist abuse to food insecurity and more. Having real conversations about such subjects can indeed be uncomfortable and make people feel uncomfortable for a variety of reasons. Yet, to engage – in my humble opinion – is to feed, rather than starve, part of the self that seeks scholastic development.[16] We humans all need nourishment – intellectually, emotionally and, of course, physically.

With a gentle tone laced with compassion and care, O'Hea promoted awareness about managing, and *overcoming*, one's personal struggles. And, as a friend to the actor in question, O'Hea offered direct and indirect

---

12   Sterling Brown, 'Discomfort'.
13   Christopher Emdin, *Ratchetdemic: Reimagining Academic Success* (Boston, 2021), p. ix.
14   Emdin, *Ratchetdemic*, p. 2.
15   The brief quoted language from the conversation is verbatim.
16   Since O'Hea's friend was not present for this conference conversation, I decided not to include his name out of respect for his recovery process and his privacy.

support that suggests he did not shame or look down upon his friend for having struggled or for owning that he has struggled – that is quite admirable on both their parts. For me, O'Hea's disclosure was an unexpected and important moment during the conference because it was, and is, very much relevant to Shakespeare's work and to the work we all do in our field, broadly speaking. And when I say broadly, I am thinking about many people, including professors, theatre practitioners and, of course, the students many of us teach.

As I develop as a scholar and as I look back at my work since officially joining the profession, and even as I revisit the scholarship of the many brilliant colleagues whose work I have had the privilege of sitting with or citing over the years, I find that I have become more and more honest as a writer. But, to date, it is only *retrospectively* that my awareness of that honesty, my authorial honesty, registers for me. And for me, that is a bit of a problem. As such, lately I have been wondering if that is true for other colleagues. Is that true for you, the honesty matter I just mentioned? Have you ever spent time thinking deeply about your contributions to Shakespeare Studies and how the scholarship you produce represents *you* and who you are? *You*. Have you ever reflected deeply on how your contributions to the field develop distinctly from the uniqueness of what you have experienced in your life?

Or do you steamroll through it all? Do you produce your scholarship, thinking and believing it is all just that – merely *intellectual* contributions devoid of anything remotely personal? Or anything remotely experiential? Please know when I ask those questions that I do so without judgement. Rather, I am hoping I am not alone in the retrospective realizations I had only after writing my first book. And so, I will bring it right on home with some necessary rephrasing: if you have ever engaged with my scholarship, have you looked at it and thought that it is all just the result of time spent studying the pages of books and journal articles and listening to talks, completely separate from the life I live as a Black, gay man, as someone's son, as someone's brother, as someone, as *me* – as David Sterling Brown, who was *only* that before I was doctor or professor or scholar or literary critic or Shakespearian? I am, at my core, just David Sterling Brown.

How honest are you in your writing and with yourself *when* you write? That is to say, how do your life experiences, all of them, inform what your intellectual interests are? Regardless of whether you write for academics only or for the general public or for both, how honest are you with your audience? How much do they get to know you through your writing? And do they know how you are being honest and when you are being honest? Do they know *how* you are disclosing personal, experiential anecdotes about yourself in your critical work in ways meant, consciously or unconsciously, to remind people of your raw humanity?

As Hamlet reminds us in act 4, scene 3 of Shakespeare's great tragedy, 'Your fat king and your lean beggar is but / variable service – two dishes, but to one table. That's the end' (4.2.23–5).[17] Hamlet makes a fascinating point rooted in a raw reality: that *is* the end. Regardless of race, gender, socio-economic status, physical abilities, geographic origins, we are all *human* – king, queen or not. And when I say 'human', I do not mean that in the clichéd universalist kind of way. It's quite the contrary for me. When I say we are all human, I mean that with acute recognition of the distinct, minute aspects of our individuality that make us all different in some way. Hypothetically speaking, even if we all were to have the same race, the same gender, the same sexuality, and were born in the exact same place in the exact same year, we would still be quite different because of the individual life experiences that would have shaped us.

This mindset, one of acute attention to difference, which I then like to alchemize into something productive, describes what I defined a few years ago in Diana E. Henderson and Kyle Sebastian Vitale's *Shakespeare and Digital Pedagogy* volume, and more recently in *Shakespeare's White Others*, as my critical–personal–experiential pedagogical style. And that is where I want to return our attention right now. My pedagogical methodology depends on the people in my classroom bringing all aspects of themselves into the space, whatever they are willing to bring – I don't force them. I need and welcome as much of them into the room as possible because it challenges me and keeps my pedagogy current and of the moment, a subject I had the pleasure of discussing with Peter Holland during the 2024 ISC.[18] Additionally, having my students bring all of themselves into the room requires me to *make* my pedagogy relevant to their world, to our world. No student is the same today as they were last week. Quiet as it's kept, no

---

[17] William Shakespeare, *Hamlet*, in *The Complete Works of William Shakespeare*, ed. David Bevington (New York, 2014).

[18] I thank Peter Holland for taking time to speak with me about his pedagogical practice.

professor is the same today as they were last week, either. Therefore, in my classroom, I aim to adjust to the evolution of my learners and to my own evolution.

As the world turns, things change. Life changes. We as individuals change. We adapt, we progress, we grow – or maybe sometimes we don't. Yet even that, the lack of growth, is still part of the progress. And through my life experience, I have discovered on a personal level that those changes, the progress or the stagnation, impact *everything* about who I am and how I operate and how I interact with the people around me, from students to colleagues to family to the strangers I engage with in passing. Because my own personal trauma in life has trained me to be hypervigilant about so many things, including who surrounds me or who I am around, I have become sensitive to being aware of who is around me or who I am around and how that impacts me at any given moment. It's all a part of personal healing because, as the succinct title of Bessel van der Kolk's book reveals, 'the body keeps score'. That is to say, trauma generated by incredibly challenging experiences remains within us at all times and can impact our responses to anything at any given moment, unless that trauma is carefully processed and metabolized as I have suggested previously.[19]

And yes, it's about to get really critical–personal–experiential in this article, so brace yourself. Grip your chair, or grab a tissue, or check out mentally if you must, though I hope the latter won't be your go-to. Stay with me, please. I want you to stay present with me and my words because I believe it is through conscientious personal–experiential vulnerability that we can continue to move our field forwards and push it in new directions that just might benefit the growth of our individual selves *and* the people we encounter through our life's work, especially students. For Emdin reminds us, 'The ratchetdemic educator understands that true knowledge is not given; it is discovered. By designing learning environments and curricula to awaken curiosity, hard work, and determination, the ratchetdemic educator creates conditions that allow young people to make their own discoveries.'[20] The educational conditions are what condition the extent to which one engages, or not, the personal and experiential in relation to the critical.

Whether it's critical race studies, feminist studies, ecocriticism, disability studies, media studies, queer theory, domesticity studies, sexuality studies, or any other field or subfield you can imagine, I am becoming more and more convinced that the personal and experiential are there, informing the critical thoughts and generating

synergy that helps us all create new knowledge, knowledge that comes from within. I am convinced that if we each took time to look under the hood, metaphorically speaking, we could identify all the essential components within ourselves that keep us going – the engines that enable it all to work. Examining what is under the hood is vital, then, because it allows for a deeper appreciation for what drives our intellectual interests, our passions. It also can allow for a deeper understanding of other people that then facilitates the implementation of a pedagogy of compassion and care. I am not suggesting such a teaching approach is everyone's goal. Like Emdin, however, I argue that it should be.

When teaching undergraduates, I begin each class with a question, which is: How are you doing today? And that's not a rhetorical question. I tell my students at the start of the term I will ask that question at the beginning of each class session; and they are to respond by raising a hand in the air, if they are able,[21] and indicating with their fingers, on a scale of one to five, how they are doing. I also participate in this empirical survey at the top of each class session so my students have a sense of how *I* am doing. Over the years, I have occasionally been treated by students as if I am some kind of scholarly automaton that appears for 75 minutes of their lives twice a week and then disappears once my office hours end, until the next week's teaching cycle begins. To mitigate this issue that unintentionally denies me my full humanity, I often find subtle ways to signal to my students: 'Hey, I am human, too.' That is a truth worth articulating – one that can easily get taken for granted and impact the teacher–student dynamic in ways that have potential to create stress for the instructor.

My 'how are you doing?' inquiry, which helps me establish trust with my students, is quite simple and permits me to do instant data analysis about their individual and collective states: one digit means they are not doing well at all; five digits mean they are feeling great. And two, three or four digits puts them somewhere in the middle, closer to feeling great or not so great. Essentially, what I am asking them when I take this informal poll at the start of each class is: what's under the hood today? Is there something they are bringing into the classroom space that I cannot see but may need

---

[19] Menakem, *My Grandmother's Hands*, p. 7.
[20] Emdin, *Ratchetdemic,* p. 2.
[21] I recognize that some of the learners in my classroom might be disabled. In such cases, I adjust this practice.

to know so I can proceed accordingly, adapting my lesson if necessary, because if all my students raise one or two digits in the air instead of four or five, then that tells me something about their mental, physical or emotional states. If my classroom audience, as I like to think of them, is so collectively distracted or checked out for whatever reasons, then it instantly becomes my responsibility to improvise ways to draw them in and ensure they take away something useful from a given class session.

And I have been in that situation before, with almost everyone in my class raising only one or two digits in the air – or sometimes just a fist, which represents zero. Without getting too much into the weeds, I will say this: in the rare moments when that has happened, I instantly become aware that I will likely have to do more heavy lifting to get us through a class session. If you, dear reader, will humour me right now, I'd like to ask that you pause for a few seconds and think about how you are doing, how you are feeling right now on a scale of one to five, with one being not so great and five being great. You are even welcome to ball up your fist if zero is where you are at. That's real and that's OK. You don't have to raise your digit(s) in the air, of course. I just want you to get present with yourself in this very moment, wherever you are. Pause. I want you to give yourself space to acknowledge how you truly feel on a scale of one to five right now. Pause. I want you to take a moment, however long you need, to understand what's happening under the hood for you and pause.

The title of this article borrows from the main concept of my second book that, in various ways, will consider what's under the hood.[22] This second book project of mine builds on *Shakespeare's White Others*, especially its conclusion.[23] In that book I am working through my retrospective awareness of the personal–experiential matter, or life content, that I consciously and unconsciously embedded in between the lines while writing. Having had some distance now from the writing process, I can see how I have a direct or indirect personal–experiential attachment to each of the subjects I critically engage in the monograph. Personal and experiential connections are things I have noticed in the work of other scholars, too (or through my conversations with them about their work). Thus, to say the personal and experiential are always there is not necessarily all that new, but I think exploring *how* they are always there, and bringing that to the forefront, could be an incredibly useful ongoing practice that, to reiterate, can enhance what and how one learns. I say that with the

utmost conviction because my classroom environment depends on my students bringing the personal and experiential into the room, a process I guide them into;[24] and I am always fascinated by how *who* they are and *what* they have experienced shapes their engagement with Shakespeare's texts and our critical theories. Each academic term, I learn something new. And so do the students, particularly those who choose to fully embrace my teaching philosophy.

If you have ever read Arthur L. Little Jr's *Shakespeare Jungle Fever* or if you have had the opportunity to hear him speak, then you know he does not shy away from acknowledging how the scholarly work we do is always personal – he suggests as much in that first book of his and in a *Public Books* article.[25] Furthermore, as his 2017 Shakespeare Association of America plenary panel titled 'The color of membership' demonstrated – with engaging papers by Dennis Austin Britton, Jean E. Howard, Arthur Little himself, Joyce Green MacDonald and Jyotsna Singh – Little is not the only one who draws connections between the critical, personal and experiential, which are, to put it plainly, inseparable.[26]

In fact, post-2017, we saw Ayanna Thompson begin her 2021 book *Blackface* with a personal-experiential anecdote about a visit to her son Dash's private school when he was in third grade. Thompson recounts her shocking experience with being subjected to, as she describes it, 'several little white children in full-on blackface makeup' who were dressed up as a famous person they each had researched – all to Thompson's 'horror

22 'Shakespeare Under the Hood' is the tentative title of my second book, which is under contract with Cambridge University Press.

23 See *Shakespeare's White Others*, pp. 182–7.

24 See David Sterling Brown, '(Early) modern literature: crossing the color-line', *Radical Teacher* 105 (Summer 2016), 69–77. Also see Brown, '(Early) modern literature: crossing the "*Sonic* color line"', in *Shakespeare and Digital Pedagogy*, ed. Diana E. Henderson and Kyle S. Vitale (London, 2021), 51–62.

25 Arthur L. Little Jr, *Shakespeare Jungle Fever: National-Imperial Re-visions of Race, Rape, and Sacrifice* (Stanford, 2000). Also see David Sterling Brown and Arthur L. Little Jr, 'To teach Shakespeare for survival: talking with David Sterling Brown and Arthur L. Little', *Public Books*, November 2021. That article stemmed from a September 2020 recorded University of Maryland anti-racism series conversation: www.youtube.com/watch?v=OHTaNbkXrEk.

26 See 'The color of membership', Shakespeare Association of America plenary panel (7 April 2017), www.youtube.com/watch?v=4f8_sOAucWw&t=387s.

and dismay', as she writes.[27] And in *Shakespeare and the Cultivation of Difference: Race and Conduct in the Early Modern World*, Patricia Akhimie concludes with a coda titled 'Pedestrian check' that touches on the personal and experiential as she thinks about her brother and the relationship between the Black person's body and policing in the United States.[28] And in his groundbreaking *Shakespeare Quarterly* article 'Othello's black handkerchief', Ian Smith ultimately reveals, partly through the personal and experiential, how a textual moment that gave him pause and, perhaps, produced intellectual discomfort for him (specifically the handkerchief being defined as 'dyed in mummy') allowed him to develop a deeper awareness of how reading practices shape what scholars know and what we *think* we know.[29]

In addition to those examples, I want to highlight Marianne Novy's 2005 enlightening book, *Reading Adoption: Family and Difference in Fiction and Drama*. In that text, Novy reflects on how her relationship with her adoptive parents, as well as her birth mother, influenced how she reads texts. As the content of Novy's book makes clear, she is literary critic *and* adoptee, and those positionalities matter, as did her being a daughter, woman, mother and wife in her writing process.[30] I first read Novy's book when I was working on my dissertation in grad school at New York University. I was fascinated by her personal disclosure about being an adoptee in part because of what I understood years ago as a negative stigma around adoption – which has waned, thankfully. The personal information I gleaned from Novy's text drew me in. The information served as an early example of how the critical, personal and experiential can and do often merge, thus informing our scholarship and our pedagogical agendas in productive ways. For, as Virginia Mason Vaughan asserts in the Preface to *Performing Blackness on English Stages, 1500–1800*, 'Scholarship is not crafted by nameless, faceless people: every work of literary criticism issues from individuals with histories that influence their work.'[31] *We*, all of us, are those people who have names and faces and histories that influence the decisions we make about the work we do and the work we choose not to do.

Vaughan adds that her larger critical inquiries were motivated by her desire to understand 'racism in the society in which [she] live[s] and work[s]', particularly as a white woman from a middle-class background, a white woman who grew up in the southern United States under the parental authority of a mother who did not want her associating with 'those people' – and by that, her mother meant the Others.[32] Not the 'white others',[33] as I have termed them, but Other with the capital 'O', as in someone who looks like me – racially different, ethnically different. That's one motivating factor for Vaughan's writing that she discloses in her book, but I imagine there are others. And I know from speaking with other white scholars – such as Thomas Dabbs, who also grew up in the Jim Crow South – that it was relatively commonplace for white parents to admonish their children for hanging out with the others – as in other white folks who were deemed less-than-ideal or not good enough, perhaps because of their social standing – and the Others, as in people who existed on the other side of the DuBoisian interracial colour-line.[34]

Those anecdotes from Vaughan and Dabbs lead me to ask: Where are *you* in your scholarship? Where do you find yourself? Where is your queerness? Your straightness? Your womanhood? Your manhood? Where is your first-generation background? Your social class? Your racial identity? Your childhood trauma? Your adulthood trauma? Where is your joy? Your heartbreak? Your love? I can almost hear some of your thoughts already, along the lines of 'I don't want to think about that right now.' And that is totally fine; I absolutely respect that. But, as I asserted on the 'In plain sight: whiteness in Shakespeare Studies' panel at the 2024 Shakespeare Association of America conference, and as I will repeat now, I have become more and more

[27] Ayanna Thompson, *Blackface* (New York, 2021), pp. 1–2.

[28] Patricia Akhimie, 'Coda', in *Shakespeare and the Cultivation of Difference: Race and Conduct in the Early Modern World* (New York, 2018).

[29] Smith speaks about this topic moment in a recorded conversation with Ato Quayson and David Sterling Brown. See '*Shakespeare's White Others* and *Black Shakespeare*', Contours: The Cambridge Literary Studies Hour Webinar with Ato Quayson, September 2024, www.youtube.com/watch?v=d9vuvypxcrs. Also see Ian Smith, 'Othello's black handkerchief', *Shakespeare Quarterly* 64 (2013), 1–25.

[30] Marianne Novy, *Reading Adoption: Family and Difference in Fiction and Drama* (Ann Arbor, 2005), pp. 1–4.

[31] Virginia Mason Vaughan, *Performing Blackness on English Stages, 1500–1800* (Cambridge, 2005), p. xi.

[32] Vaughan, *Performing*, p. xi.

[33] Brown, *Shakespeare's White Others*, pp. xi–xiv.

[34] W. E. B. Du Bois, *The Souls of Black Folk* (United States, 2011), p. 2. See Matthew W. Hughey, 'The (dis)similarities of white racial identities: the conceptual framework of "hegemonic whiteness"', *Ethnic and Racial Studies* 33 (September 2010), 1289–1309; p. 1290. Also see 'Speaking of Shakespeare' episode #56, hosted by Thomas Dabbs: www.youtube.com/watch?v=xWM1SCIX55E. In this episode, Dabbs speaks of his southern United States upbringing and his personal understanding of white othering.

interested in generating what I call 'productive discomfort', not just for my students but for you, too.[35] Productive discomfort is an essential part of my critical–personal–experiential pedagogical methodology, so much so that if I could create a course evaluation that includes just one key question, it would be this: At any given point during the term, did the instructor succeed in generating productive discomfort within you and, if so, how? I believe the answers to that single question will tell me if my students have, in fact, learned – if I have, in fact, succeeded in my quest to teach them about what it means to nourish themselves intellectually.

Returning to where this article started, I will note that *Shakespeare's White Others* is in some ways an exploration of trauma, and not necessarily my own trauma – but certainly some of that is there because, in hindsight, I discovered I was really focused on discovering what is under the hood for me and my prospective readers. When I wrote the book, I really only saw my conclusion as being relevant to my personal trauma because I end with a letter I wrote when I was eighteen years old, a letter that I sent in 2002 to the mayor, police chief and police commissioner of my hometown of Norwalk, Connecticut, because I was being racially profiled by the police in my own neighbourhood on my own street. But beyond that, primarily because of personal healing work I am trying to do, I have discovered that so much more is there in my scholarship. And I have Shakespeare and Shakespeare Studies to thank for inspiring me to intertwine the personal and experiential with the critical work. As highlighted previously through the various scholarly examples, I am not alone in triangulating the critical, personal and experiential.

Before concluding this article, I want to turn to Arthur L. Little Jr's robust edited volume – *White People in Shakespeare* – because, notably, it ends with a turn to such triangulation via the two final chapters authored by pioneering Shakespearians Jean E. Howard and Peter Erickson. In one of her introductory paragraphs, Howard explains, 'I am a white female Shakespearean at an Ivy League institution. While the woman part has brought difficulties through the decades, the white part has brought many privileges.'[36] Later in the essay, Howard adds critical–personal–experiential details related to an experience she had in a 2018 Shakespeare Association of America workshop that required her to consider how critical race studies could and should become a throughline in her teaching.[37] She also gestures towards the value of productive discomfort when she

asserts that white people can and should 'learn strategies for overcoming the "white fragility" that can make white people hang back from fully engaging with their own race or the race of others. This is hard work . . . '.[38] Howard's reflective insights offer a useful transition into Erickson's essay, which is about as vulnerable and honest as I have seen a white male Shakespearian be thus far in my career. I thank Erickson for his honesty and for consistently being uniquely bold in the scholarship he has produced as a white Shakespearian. The field needs more of that honesty, still.

Advocating for 'the urgent work of critical whiteness', a phrase that doubles as his chapter's title, Erickson wastes no time articulating in his opening paragraph the positionality his essay interrogates. He begins provocatively with what reads as a confession: 'I am a white person in Shakespeare. That is, I am a white scholar in the field of Shakespeare Studies. I have not always thought of myself as white. Consciousness of my white identity, and the unearned white privilege that goes with it, has been a gradual development over the course of my life.'[39]

For white people, and white people in Shakespeare studies, naming (one's) whiteness does not always feel comfortable.[40] This is, in part, because white people are not necessarily socialized to think of themselves as white in the same way that we Black people, for example, are socialized to think of ourselves as Black, as being Other. Thus, when I encountered Erickson's chapter, I was struck by his third sentence in the quotation above that, as a stand-alone idea, reflects his awareness of how the personal and experiential inform the arguments he makes and the conclusions he comes to in a chapter devoted to helping readers realize that critiquing racial whiteness is their ongoing, lifelong responsibility. He notes, 'We have an obligation to interrogate and to interrupt systemic racism in our field. The academy is called the ivory tower for a reason – it is white. If we are

---

[35] Access to a recording of my 2024 Shakespeare Association of America presentation is available on my website in the Audio section: www.davidsterlingbrown.com/audio. The title of my talk was '(Un)healed: treating white invisibility'.

[36] Jean E. Howard, 'The white Shakespearean and daily practice', in *White People in Shakespeare: Essays on Race, Culture and the Elite*, ed. Arthur L. Little Jr (London, 2023), p. 265.

[37] Howard, 'The white Shakespearean', p. 268.

[38] Howard, 'The white Shakespearean', p. 270.

[39] Peter Erickson, 'No exeunt: the urgent work of critical whiteness', in *White People in Shakespeare*, ed. Little Jr, p. 277.

[40] See Brown, *Shakespeare's White Others*, p. 1.

not to be a slave to our whiteness, we must start with an acknowledgement of how it shaped Shakespeare and how it shapes us.'[41]

Acknowledging his own racial whiteness through the usage of 'we', as opposed to distancing himself from whiteness by using the phrase 'white people', as some folks do, Erickson leans into the productive discomfort that implicates him, and all white people, in the global perpetuation of anti-Black racism. His attention to the 'ivory tower' signals how white dominance and racism are large-scale *institutional* problems that get reproduced regularly and impact us all daily. They are problems that have existed for centuries. The shaping Erickson speaks of is real, shaping that occurs due to the generational transfer of toxic knowledge and pervasive apathy that continue to outpace anti-racist actions.[42] Yet, things don't have to remain that way forever. There is hope. That hope is in healing.

In his book titled *My Grandmother's Hands: Racialized Trauma and the Pathway to Mending Our Hearts and Bodies*, Resmaa Menakem writes, 'Contrary to what many people believe, trauma is not primarily an emotional response. Trauma always happens *in the body*. It is a spontaneous protective mechanism used by the body to stop or thwart further (or future) potential damage.'[43] Menakem adds that 'an embedded trauma response can manifest as flight, flee, or freeze – or as a combination of constriction, pain, fear, dread, anxiety, unpleasant (and/ or sometimes pleasant) thoughts, reactive behaviors, or other sensations and experiences. This trauma then gets stuck in the body – and stays stuck there until it is addressed.'[44] I greatly appreciate that articulation because, as I have argued in this article, especially with my allusions to the criticism of other scholars, what is happening under the hood, *within* us all, is incredibly relevant to the critical–personal–experiential work we create.

---

[41] Erickson, 'No exeunt', p. 285.

[42] See David Sterling Brown, 'Don't hurt yourself: (anti)racism and white self-harm', *Los Angeles Review of Books* (Anti-racism mini-series), July 2021.
https://lareviewofbooks.org/article/antiracism-in-the-contemporary-university/#_ftn2.

[43] Menakem, *My Grandmother's Hands*, p. 7.

[44] Menakem, *My Grandmother's Hands*, p. 7.

MIND'S EYE: AUDIO-DESCRIBED SHAKESPEARE

ROBERT SHAUGHNESSY[1]

HAMLET My father, I think I see my father.
HORATIO Where, my lord?
HAMLET In my mind's eye, Horatio.

(Hamlet 1.2.183–4)

This article addresses an artistic practice that is geared towards the needs of a community that sooner or later any of us may inhabit. The community is that of the blind, partially sighted and visually impaired – or BPS – and the practice is that of Audio description, or AD. I start with *Hamlet*, Shakespeare's most searching meditation on inner vision (and also a play organized around, as David Sterling Brown cogently puts it, 'white people watching other white people, surveilling, judging, and critiquing'[2]), and specifically with Hamlet's words to Horatio, and a phrase that not only has long served as a metaphor for the visual imagination (though, as the Arden Third Series editors point out, the phrase is not Shakespeare's coinage and had long been a commonplace[3]), but also succinctly defines the aim of AD for theatre performance. AD is a means of enabling BPS persons to see the unseen in their mind's eye, to engage with experiences from which they might otherwise be excluded. It does so by providing important visual information (which can include settings, effects, appearances and facial expressions, to name but a few) in spoken narrative form, relayed in screen media through an add-on audio track, and in live settings, usually, through portable media technology. AD is used in a range of exhibition settings, including museums and galleries, and in film and television, where it has been a feature since the 1980s. In 1996, in the United Kingdom, AD became a legal obligation for terrestrial broadcasters, who are currently required to audio-describe 10 per cent of their output, and it is often discussed in predominantly screen-centric terms (the UK's Royal National Institute

for the Blind's website, for example, defines AD as 'additional commentary that explains what's happening on screen ... [it] describes body language, expressions and movements, making the programme clear through sound'[4]). AD in the theatre is a more recent, more occasional and still less ubiquitous practice. The first theatre AD system was developed in the United States in 1981 by Margaret Pfanstiehl and Cody Pfanstiehl, who also codified some influential AD 'rules', which included their much-cited dictum that the audio describer should 'not evaluate or interpret, but rather be like the faithful lens of a camera';[5] a contentious proposition we shall return to below. The first examples of theatre AD in the UK and US also date from the 1980s, but it is only in the past decade that it has been established as an element of most professional performances.

This article will focus on two aspects of AD in the theatre. The first part considers its workings and practicalities, and in particular the significance of memory in its composition, delivery and reception. The second part addresses some of the critical challenges – and opportunities – that contemporary Shakespeare

[1] My thanks to Josefa MacKinnon, the Royal Shakespeare Company's Access Co-ordinator, for invaluable help with the research for this article, which included access to Audio description (AD) materials and introductions to key practitioners. Thanks also to Jenny Stewart-Cosgrove, Carolyn Smith and Ellie Packer for sharing their scripts and for providing invaluable insights into AD practices.
[2] David Sterling Brown, *Shakespeare's White Others* (Cambridge, 2023), p. 61.
[3] *Hamlet*, ed. Ann Thompson and Neil Taylor (London, 2006), p. 159.
[4] www.rnib.org.uk/living-with-sight-loss/assistive-aids-and-technol ogy/tv-audio-and-gaming/audio-description-ad.
[5] Quoted in 'The play's the thing: audio description in the theatre – Margaret and Cody Pfanstiehl', *British Journal of Visual Impairment* 3 (1985), 91–2; p. 91.

performance offers both to existing AD practices and to newer forms of AD that are experimental, creative and motivated by an understanding of inclusivity that sets the needs of the BPS community in a wider context of diversity and access. It does so by highlighting what, for Shakespeare practitioners and audio describers alike, has been the especially contentious question of the representation of race, using the Royal Shakespeare Company's widely praised 2016 production of *Hamlet*, in which this question was posed with unusual sharpness. Built around Paapa Essiedu, the first actor of colour to play the title role on the RSC's main stage, the production had a majority Black cast, directly confronting the whiteness of the *Hamlet* performance tradition by transposing the play into a world where this was both logical, and amenable to the RSC's largely white audiences. In this production, Elsinore had the generalized ambience of the contemporary sub-Saharan African continent: a brightly lit stage backed by a cyclorama which ranged between scorching yellow and cool blue suggested a militarized state, bristling with khaki-clad sentries touting submachine guns and a Claudius (Clarence Smith) presiding in a splendidly medalled and braided dress uniform; the Ghost (Ewart James Walter) appeared 'wrapped in Kente (traditional Ghanaian) cloth',[6] and the Players entered, chanting, singing, clapping and dancing, in 'a riot of tie-dye colours.'[7] Thunderous drumbeats accompanied the interpolated scene of Hamlet's father's funeral, the entrance of the Ghost, the arrival of the Players, and the duel between Hamlet and Laertes (Marcus Griffiths), which was staged as a bout of Nguni stick fighting, with thick staves taking the place of rapiers. Reviewers were quick to meld the familiar signifiers of the exotic-despotic into the generic composite of a postcolonial African state; and if this enabled the long overdue RSC debut of a Black actor in the title role, the risk of cliché was considered a price worth paying. Curiously, though, by naturalizing and (imprecisely) localizing what in Stratford-upon-Avon looks like racial difference, the production invited its viewers both to see race and unsee it, and this was reflected in the reviews: once mentioned, the fact of Blackness – especially Essiedu's – could effectively be disregarded. 'All the build-up to this production has concentrated on the fact that Paapa Essiedu is – rather shockingly – the first black Hamlet in the 55-year history of the RSC', as one critic put it, 'But all the post-show reaction will celebrate the fact that he is simply a terrific Hamlet.'[8] To an extent, this is symptomatic of the ongoing sensitivities of well-intentioned white commentators caught

between the need to acknowledge race and the desire to indicate that, at least to them, it doesn't matter. Renni Eddo-Lodge has called this 'the fallacy of meritocracy': 'this claim to not see race is tantamount to compulsory assimilation. My blackness has been politicised against my will, but I don't want it wilfully ignored in an effort to instil some sort of precarious, false harmony.'[9] Ayanna Thompson has likewise argued, in relation to the ostensibly meritocratic practice of 'colour-blind' Shakespeare (a now-discredited term that seems even more problematic in the current context), that 'Practitioners, theorists, reviewers and audiences can no longer function as if race is an illusion that need not be addressed'; and, she asserts, 'Race informs the way I experience the world in so many complex ways that I do not want it whited out or e-raced by others.'[10] In a similar way, the art of audio description has also confronted questions of the extent to which it sees, or doesn't see, race.

AD in the theatre shares the core principles of AD for screen but has a number of unique additional practical elements. First and foremost, theatre AD is, of necessity, almost always live and not, as in its screen media form, pre-recorded. The AD for a film or TV programme is an optional feature, an item on the accessibility menu that also includes subtitles and, sometimes, signing, and available every time the user chooses to experience the programme. For the simple logistical reason that theatre AD is delivered live by a team of (usually) two specialist audio describers, audio-described performances are infrequent. With the exception of *A Midsummer Night's Dream*, which took a more experimental approach to AD, the 2024 RSC Stratford-upon-Avon season scheduled at most two AD performances for each of its eleven productions: one near the beginning of the run, one towards its end; one a matinee, and one an evening performance. On occasions, AD is combined with other forms of access provision, as part of a performance that is also captioned, signed, chilled or

---

[6] Anne Treneman, *The Times*, 23 March 2016.

[7] Dominic Cavendish, *Daily Telegraph*, 23 March 2016.

[8] Sarah Crompton, *Sunday Times*, 27 March 2016.

[9] Renni Eddo-Lodge, *Why I'm No Longer Talking to White People about Race* (London, 2018), pp. 81–2.

[10] Ayanna Thompson, '"Ay, there's the rub": race and performance studies', in *New Directions in Renaissance Drama and Performance Studies*, ed. Sarah Werner (Basingstoke, 2010), 178–94; p. 191; Ayanna Thompson, 'Practicing a theory / theorizing a practice: an introduction to Shakespearean colorblind casting', in *Colorblind Shakespeare: New Perspectives on Race and Performance*, ed. Ayanna Thompson (London and New York, 2006), 1–24; p. 22.

a combination of one or more of these.[11] Transmitted through in-house radio technology, received on a portable device borrowed from the box office, and listened to through headphones, the consumption of AD is a solitary, private experience; its production is the work of the describing team, who develop their script from observing the show in the final stages of rehearsal (they may also have access to a video recording). For *Hamlet*, the describer for the first half was Ellie Packer, and for the second, Carolyn Smith.[12] Act 1, scene 3 opens thus (AD marked in square brackets):

[At Polonius's house, a table and two matching chairs are brought in. Ophelia sits at the table, idly going through the contents of a cardboard box. Laertes comes in, ready for travel, his suitcase and hold-all packed and his fighting sticks in a canvas bag.]

LAERTES

My necessaries are embarked; [- Laertes]
farewell. [- he picks her up and spins her round]
And sister, as the winds give benefit
And convoy is assistant, do not sleep
But let me hear from you.

In her guide to the craft of audio-description writing, Louis Fryer points out that its narrative generally follows a set sequence: 'the spatio-temporal setting is noticed first (the *When/Where*) followed by *Who* is in the scene, *What* they are doing and *How* they are doing it'.[13] Here, the *where* is the house of Polonius (Cyril Nri), the *who* Ophelia (Natalie Simpson) and Laertes (identified as such when he first speaks), and the *what* and the *how* are Ophelia's and Laertes's movements, actions and gestures ('going through the box' is the what, 'idly' is the how). It is a simple instance, but AD presents technical challenges in terms of both its delivery and its reception. It is an AD rule that it should not overlap with or distract from actors speaking, which means that it must be delivered in whatever pauses, gaps and silences there may be within and between speeches, bits of action or scenes. The transition from the Court to the Polonius residence affords a relatively leisurely 20 seconds, just long enough for fewer than 50 words of scene-setting designed to convey the physical set-up, the position of the characters in it, and the relationship between them.[14] This was a relatively straightforward scene to describe; elsewhere the play's action and production's staging presented more significant challenges. The duel scene (5.2) was a complex action sequence that was also verbally dense and rapid, requiring the AD to communicate the duel's ceremonial framing, the complex choreography of a bout that involved an exchange of weapons, the actions and reactions of participants and onlookers, the fatal wounding of Hamlet and

Laertes, and the simultaneous poisoning and death of Gertrude. Claudius's order, 'Come begin' (5.2.225), cues a passage of AD with more than 100 words (around a minute to speak) that commences as 'Hamlet and Laertes face the thrones, raise their sticks in the air and strike them on the ground as they bow' and concludes on 'They engage, clashing their sticks together – Laertes rushes at Hamlet, who side-steps and counter-attacks.' A few minutes and 30 lines later:

LAERTES

Have at you now! [Horatio rushes to Hamlet. Hamlet leaps up and charges at Laertes – knees him in the stomach – Laertes falls head over heels. In the confusion, they have exchanged weapons. Laertes struggles up.]

If keeping up is a challenge for the audio describer, it is also one for their auditors; the constant stream of rich new information generated by a performance 'needs to be processed while, at the same time, information it has superseded must be held in working memory ... long enough that connections between the two information states may be made'.[15] As Diana Calderazzo cautions, 'Too much information during a production will likely result in Working Memory overload, considering that consumers are attending not only to the audio description, but also to the actors and sound effects coming from

---

[11] The terms refer to the different varieties of access that the RSC, in common with most major UK theatres, currently offers. Signed Performances have a British Sign Language (BSL) interpreter at the side of the stage, providing a BSL translation of the spoken text. As with live AD, this is labour-intensive, demanding and not without cost, and the RSC also offers to meet the needs of d/Deaf and hard-of-hearing audience members via Captioned Performances, wherein the text is relayed either as surtitles through onstage screens or on individual handheld devices (this can be of benefit to other users, such as those for whom English is not a first language). Chilled Performances are the RSC's variant on the practice of Relaxed Performances, where the auditorium environment and protocols of audience behaviour are adapted to make shows more accommodating of neurodiverse members.

[12] Ellie Packer wrote and delivered the AD for the production's act 1 up to 3.3.74: 'Now might I do it pat', with Hamlet standing behind the kneeling Claudius, cocked pistol to his head, about to fire – blackout, interval, cliffhanger; act 2, with AD by Carolyn Smith, began where act 1 left off: '[Claudius is still at prayer – Hamlet, behind, still aims a gun at him] And now I'll do it.'

[13] Louise Fryer, *An Introduction to Audio Description: A Practical Guide* (Abingdon, 2016), p. 58.

[14] I derive my timings from the RSC's commercial video recording of the production, released on DVD in 2016 and also available on the educational streaming platform Digital Theatre+ (DT+).

[15] Fryer, *Introduction*, p. 30.

the stage.'[16] In consequence, AD is characterized by brevity and concision, and by the use of strategic details that immediately communicate the essentials of character, situation and narrative. In Laertes, Polonius and Ophelia's 135-line, 7-minute, scene, there are 14 further AD interventions, most of which are short phrases rather than full sentences: 'To his unmastered importunity [– her head in her hands]' (1.3.31); 'Marry well bethought [Polonius sits] ... 'Tis told me he hath very oft of late / Given private time to you ... [removes his shoes] ... and you yourself / Have of your audience been most free and bounteous ... [she brings his slippers]' (1.3.89–92). In a way, the term 'description' is potentially misleading: the objective is not to replicate for the BPS member what the non-blind audience member sees, but to deliver enough clues for them to construct in their mind's eye a version of it; with salience as the priority, AD is an art of narrative rather than illustration (Joel Snyder likens its individual utterances to 'a type of poetry – a haiku'[17]). The business with Polonius's footwear is reported not for the purposes of decorative embellishment, but for what it tells us about the relationship between father and daughter.

Adding to the challenge, the visual information conveyed by AD is delivered solely auditorily, which is in contrast to the sighted theatregoer's multi-modal combination of the visual and the auditory; and perception studies research has shown that while 'our memory of images is robust' and 'complex scenes can be understood very rapidly', 'when dealing with auditory materials less information is recalled and it takes longer to be remembered'.[18] In Shakespeare performance, the demands of listening to the AD are intensified by those of attending to a dense, verbally intricate and archaic spoken text that for many, or perhaps most, listeners (sighted or not) is challenging to follow and often difficult to comprehend. 'Shakespeare does not see a thing', Simon Palfrey declares, 'without seeing around it, before it, and beyond it, seeing at the same time that thing's forebears, shadows, likenesses, opposites and potential consequences.'[19] Shakespeare's all-seeing eye overlooks a multi-perspectival dramaturgy in which vision and visuality are recurrent, even obsessive, preoccupations – where what's not seen is as often of the essence as what is. Ever proleptic, though, Shakespeare's optics also include several varieties of audio description. Sometimes this is in the form of a speaker announcing the actions or appearance of another character (Rosalind's 'Here comes my sister, reading' (*As You Like It* 3.2.121)), and sometimes it is to the ends of a non-illusionistic

stagecraft: Horatio's 'morn in russet mantle clad' (1.1.147), Banquo's 'temple-haunting martlet' (*Macbeth* 1.6.3–9), the horses 'Printing their proud hoofs' in *Henry V* (Chorus 27). Elsewhere, it can be for the darker purposes of deception, fantasy and hallucination: the 'bay windows transparent as barricadoes' of Malvolio's dark house (*Twelfth Night* 4.2.37–8), Edgar and Gloucester's cliff (*King Lear* 4.5.11–27). Audio-described performances of Shakespeare involve a further aural (and extra-metrical) layering of an already multivocal, auto-descriptive score.

Unlike most AD for screen, theatre AD is supplemented by materials and activities that support, enhance and prepare for the live commentary, but also further add to the listener's cognitive load. Calderazzo notes:

an audience member who is a consumer of AD is not only encoding new information (schemas) into LTM, but also is recalling conceptual information (previous schemas) received and encoded in Long Term Memory during the pre-show description and applying it in Working Memory within the context of newly perceived information while experiencing the live theatre event.[20]

As is the case elsewhere, the RSC's audience members can take an advance touch tour of the theatre and set (and sometimes meet members of the cast), enabling them to integrate tactile memory into their reception of the show. In addition, describers provide Audio Introductions, available on request from the box office and posted online on the show pages. Partly the aural equivalent of the production programme, providing details of cast and creatives, plot synopsis, running times and the like, the Audio Introduction (AI) also includes detailed descriptions of settings, costumes and the actors' physical appearances. The AI to the 2016 *Hamlet* is just over 3,000 words in length, around 22 minutes of listening time. The first section details the show's settings in order: the University of Wittenberg,

---

[16] Diana Calderazzo, 'The "stage in the head": a cognitive approach to understanding audio description in the theatre', *Theatre Topics* 20 (2010), 171–80; p. 174.

[17] Joel Snyder, 'Audio description: the visual made verbal', *International Congress Series* 1282 (1985), 935–9; p. 936.

[18] Nazaret Fresno, 'Is a picture worth a thousand words? The role of memory in audio description', *Across Languages and Cultures* 15 (2014), 111–29; p. 118. This is balanced by the consideration that many blind persons find that their heightened auditory awareness compensates for the loss of vision.

[19] Simon Palfrey, *Doing Shakespeare* (London, 2005), p. 27.

[20] Calderazzo, '"Stage in the head"', p. 173.

a guard post, the great hall at Elsinore, Polonius's residence, the palace lobby that serves both as Hamlet's art studio and as performance area for the Players, and Gertrude's closet.

Perhaps in order to create a sense both of Hamlet's backstory as a student at Wittenberg (imagined as a university in the United States), and of the burden of the memory of his father's recent death, the play was prefaced with two short interpolated sequences. The second of these was the funeral of Hamlet's father, rendered thus in the AD:

'DRUMS' – At Elsinore, three black-suited courtiers and a drummer escort a glass coffin, containing the body of Hamlet's father wrapped in traditional, tribal robes. Young Hamlet, the only mourner, follows the cortège. Above, the new King Claudius and his new wife, Hamlet's mother, Gertrude, wave and smile at their people.

This was preceded by Hamlet's graduation – as per the AI:

This production is set in contemporary sub-Saharan Africa, except for the first scene, when Hamlet receives his degree at Wittenberg, a modern American university ... In the centre at the back is a low platform reached by three shallow steps, upon which is a lectern. Behind this is a navy-blue banner hanging from ceiling level to the floor, which bears the university crest, gold and cream circles enclosing a red torch flame ... Eight dark grey, moulded plastic and tubular steel chairs are placed at intervals facing the lectern, suggesting rows of seats ... The wooden floor, platform and wall remain throughout, other scenery being brought on to represent different locations. When the action moves to Hamlet's palace in Elsinore, we see a windowed security hut containing an orange plastic chair and an old-fashioned TV monitor, a tower of grey metal bars rising behind it, with two loudspeakers attached.

With more room for manoeuvre than the dynamic AD, the AI accesses a range of schemas to facilitate play-world building while keeping the theatrical environment in mind – Africa, the university, palaces, Elsinore – toggling between the theatrical means and their effects, the material stage and the fictional play-world. On the one hand, the wooden floor and platform; on the other, plastic chairs that suggest the 'rows of seats' of Wittenberg's graduation hall – what is described as visible points also towards what is not seen but inferred. We note the small, telling detail: the 'old-fashioned' TV indicates the rundown state of Denmark; elsewhere, the 'childhood pictures of Ophelia and Laertes' in Polonius's house touchingly suggest the family's closeness.

Whether they listened to the AI (perhaps more than once) in advance of the show or as it played during the half, the AD auditor had the opportunity to embed at least some of this information in their long-term memory. Transitioning from AI to AD, this is what the audience heard in the opening minutes:

[In a sleek, modern, featureless hall at the University of Wittenberg, a group of eight students, wearing gowns and mortarboards, sit with their backs to us. They face a podium where the Chancellor of the University stands at a lectern, ready to address them.]

CHANCELLOR Hamlet, Prince of Denmark.

[Hamlet makes his way, between the seated students, towards the podium. Before reaching it he embraces Horatio and kisses Guildenstern. He joins the Chancellor on the platform, they shake hands and a flash photograph captures the moment. The university disappears.]

The scene-setting refers back to, but modifies – indeed, animates and activates – that of the AI; AD becomes dynamic. The 'modern American University' is particularized as 'a sleek, modern, featureless hall'; the 'windowed security hut' brought to life as a 'narrow, glass-walled Guard Post, lit by a bare bulb'. We hear that Hamlet, on his way to collect his degree certificate, 'embraces Horatio and kisses Guildenstern'. It's a Chekhov's gun moment, setting up the friendship between university pals that will pay off when they are reunited later in the play, and what about that kiss? A kiss can take many forms and mean many things, but in the generally heteronormative world of *Hamlet* performance, it sounds like a bold move.

Those familiar with the AI knew that this *Hamlet* would not break new interpretive ground by positing a bromance between the prince and the rookie investigator, as Guildenstern in this production was a woman, played in the production's first run by Bethan Cullinane. For what it is worth, no one whom I have spoken with who saw the production noticed this moment, and it is impossible to make out in the DT+ video recording of the production. Strictly speaking, this identification of Rosencrantz and Guildenstern violates the AD 'rule' that its users, in order to have an experience of the show as close as possible to that of sighted audience members, should not be privy to information that the latter do not have; here, if they noticed it at all, non-blind spectators might at this stage have registered Hamlet encountering two fellow students, one male, one female, both white. This principle of equivalence sits within a larger framework of rules and protocols that is strongly informed by the idea (initiated, as noted earlier, by the Pfanstiehls in the 1980s) that AD should describe but not interpret. It should be obvious by now that the notion that an unpositioned, unaligned audio describer can adopt a stance of photographic neutrality and objectivity is, to put it mildly, quaint: questionable whenever any person watches any other person or group of persons (and so surveills, judges, critiques), unthinkable when the observed, the observer – or both – are anything other than white, male and able-bodied. As I hope to have shown, the AD for *Hamlet*, a creative writing practice as much as it is an access provision, is anything but neutral, and does not pretend to be. The AI describes Cullinane as 'an attractive young woman, her long brown hair tied back in a loose ponytail, wearing a short blue dress and espadrilles'. 'Later, having taken of Elsinore's shopping opportunities', she 'appears in a succession of knee-length, African-print frocks, worn with flat, leather sandals'. This is both physical description and thumbnail character sketch, and it is echoed by reviewer Grace Godwin's comment that the 'inept' spies' visit to Elsinore was an 'espionage-laced gap year, with Guildenstern dabbling in African garments and hair wraps, Rosencrantz experimenting with djembe drums, and both expressing visible disappointment when ordered back to England with shopping bags on each arm'.[21] Cullinane was also – and the AI explicitly identifies her as such – one of three white actors in a company of eighteen – the others being James Cooney, who played Rosencrantz, and Byron Mondahl, who doubled the Wittenberg Chancellor with the English Ambassador and various uncredited appearances as an Elsinore functionary (as Stephen Purcell noted, 'the figures associated with Hamlet's education' were all white[22]).

In the context of this production's casting, this identification was necessary, and just as that casting interrogated majority whiteness as performance's default setting, so too did its AD and AI. While the discourse of 'colour-blind' Shakespeare, devised to combat the racist and exclusionist practices of previous generations, has been superseded by colour-*conscious* casting, talking about race in inappropriate or offensive ways has sometimes given way to not talking about, not seeing, race at all. These concerns have been felt in the AD community, and efforts have been made to address them. In 2020, the leading AD provider VocalEyes and a group of AD researchers at Royal Holloway, University of London, produced the report *Describing Diversity*,

which was frank about the nature of the challenges involved.[23] As a practice of inclusion, AD must address 'when and how we should describe the personal characteristics of the diverse range of characters that appear on stage, and in particular, the visible physical markers of race, gender, impairment/disability, age and body shape'.[24] Surveying the VocalEyes archive of AD scripts, the report's authors found numerous 'unconscious biases, imbalances and avoidance of describing physical characteristics':

In plays with no non-white characters, skin colour was not mentioned either as a general overview or in reference to individual characters. This contrasts with references to a play with 'an all-Black cast'. Whiteness thus appears to have been presented as the default ... Where Whiteness was evoked, it was mainly done implicitly, through references to colouring: blonde, ginger hair, ivory skin, blue eyes. Blackness was either unambiguously stated, or suggested by description of usually both skin colour and hair colour and style.[25]

The AI for *Hamlet* is acutely sensitive to what is at stake in its individual physical descriptions, which it prefaces with the statement that 'Apart from three exceptions, the whole company is black', thus inverting the whiteness default of which the report speaks by inviting auditors to assume that a performer is Black unless it is specifically stated otherwise, and it chooses its words with care. References to skin tone and colour are eschewed, and ethnicity is indicated largely through costume details; thus, Polonius is an 'affable bustling man in his fifties' who has 'receding hair, a neat beard just starting to grey, a benign expression and a ready laugh' – the giveaway detail being the 'Nehru collar' of his 'perfectly cut grey suit'. Ewart James Walters doubled the Ghost and First Gravedigger, with the first wearing 'the clothes he was buried in, the traditional robe of a tribal chieftain', the second, 'a tall, loose-limbed, lanky figure in an ancient, stained, cotton jacket and shorts, faded

---

[21] Grace Godwin, 'Basquiat cases: *Hamlet, Doctor Faustus*, and *The Alchemist* at the Royal Shakespeare Company', *Shakespeare Bulletin* 35 (2017), 675–86; p. 677.

[22] Stephen Purcell, 'Shakespeare performances in England, 2016', in *Shakespeare Survey 70* (2017), 287–325; p. 302.

[23] Rachel Hutchinson, Hannah Thompson and Matthew Cock, *Describing Diversity: An Exploration of the Description of Human Characteristics and Appearance within the Practice of Theatre Audio Description* (London, 2020).

[24] Hutchinson, Thompson and Cock, *Describing Diversity*, p. 3.

[25] Hutchinson, Thompson and Cock, *Describing Diversity*, p. 13.

turquoise T-shirt and a battered felt hat'; the heavily accented patois Walters adopted in this role contributed to a vocal soundscape which was described by Nour el Gazzaz as 'a mix of distinct English Received Pronunciation and vague African accents'.[26] Nonetheless, the very nature of AD, as a discourse that demands above all brevity, concision and clarity, means that it is sometimes almost impossible not to utilize descriptors that can seem reductive, or skirt the borders of stereotyping. The *Describing Diversity* report mentions hair colour, texture and style as commonly used racial markers: here, Guildenstern/Cullinane's 'long brown hair' and Rosencrantz/Cooney's 'light brown hair' are signs of whiteness (and Cullinane's 'attractive' looks are value-laden), whereas the cornrows of both Gertrude (Tanya Moodie) and the Second Gravedigger (Marième Diouf) are a style particular to the Afro-Caribbean community. Possibly because it is such a strong feature of the bare-chested duel scene, the physicality of both Hamlet and Laertes is emphasized: Essiedu is 'lean, muscular and energetic', with 'large, glowing, almond-shaped eyes which eloquently express the intensity of his rapidly-changing emotions', and Griffiths is 'a tall, confident, muscular youth' with 'a large eyed, handsome face'. The muscularity of both actors is, of course, a simple fact, one that the staging wanted us to notice, and one that the AI has to take into account, but the fetishizing spectacle of powerful Black bodies in close combat was one of the more problematic aspects of the production's racial imaginary.

AD creates images of white or Black actor-characters in its auditors' mind's eye by activating schemata that are coloured and shaded by their perceptions, predispositions and, sometimes, prejudices; its task is to summarize the human complexity of an individual in a couple of memorable sentences (possibly just one for lesser parts), maybe heard only once. In a way, this is a distillation of the process whereby, as Amy Cook has shown, the mechanisms of casting manage spectatorial expectations through compression, working 'to reduce the possibilities of a character', consolidating 'what is complicated and diffuse into what is focused and essential in order to decrease cognitive load, increase associations, and facilitate memory'.[27] The *Hamlet* AI, of necessity, typecasts its performers, and at the same time, like the production, resists and challenges such typecasting, in the sense offered by Cook: 'Casting can also increase complexity, in a pleasurable way, when the actor does not fit the text and we must reimagine the story – and our politics – to make sense of the scene before us.'[28]

How might AD contribute to that reimagining? The *Describing Diversity* report make a series of recommendations for better practice, some of which are aimed at AD practitioners themselves: to 'Name Whiteness, not just Blackness'; to 'Avoid judgments and micro-aggressions, e.g. contrasting or comparing features with an "acceptable" norm'; and to 'Use privileged information to name the actor's ethnicity, disability, gender or other identity if you can, and with their input.'[29] The last recommendation is particularly important, in that it signals a shift in the understanding of what AD is, and who has ownership of it: it should not be supplementary to the creative process but integral to it. This shift is reflected in experiments with adventurous versions of AD as a mode of writing and performance. Confronting the fallacy of neutral, non-interpretative AD directly, and arguing that the conventional format sells its users short because 'it focuses on the description of what is seen ... rather than on what is meant to be seen in the director's vision', John Patrick Udo and Deborah I. Fels have examined the 2006 production of *Hamlet* at the University of Toronto's Hart House Theatre as an example of how AD can be made into 'one of many creative components of an entertainment experience'.[30] Andrea Wasserman, the production's director, worked with audio describer Paul Leishman on an AD text that was composed in part as more-or-less regular blank verse and, taking its cue from Hamlet's dying injunction to his companion to 'report me and my cause aright' (5.2.324), had Horatio as its narrator. The play opened with a brief prologue:

> At first, I tell of shadows from the grave
> who come and go with sounds of knocking wood
> atop the narrow of the tower bridge
> high above the castle of Denmark's King
> before the sun does rise they will appear

26 Nour el Gazzaz, 'Review of Shakespeare's Hamlet (directed by Simon Godwin for the Royal Shakespeare Company) at the Royal Shakespeare Theatre, Stratford-upon-Avon, 8 June 2016. Shown as part of "Culture in quarantine" on BBC iPlayer, 23 April to 22 August 2020', *Shakespeare* 17 (2021), 69–73; p. 69.

27 Amy Cook, *Building Character: The Art and Science of Casting* (Ann Arbor, MI: 2018), pp. 35, 38.

28 Amy Cook, *Shakespearean Futures: Casting the Bodies of Tomorrow on Shakespeare's Stages Today* (Cambridge, 2020), p. 23.

29 Hutchinson, Thompson and Cock, *Describing Diversity*, p. 61.

30 John Patrick Udo and Deborah I. Fels, '"Suit the action to the word, the word to the action": an unconventional approach to describing Shakespeare's Hamlet', *Journal of Visual Impairment and Blindness* 103 (2009), 178–83; pp. 179, 180.

now soldiers armed 'gainst fear do try to keep
the peace against the cold and warring friends.[31]

The dynamic AD varied between the 'haiku' style (Polonius's 'Who in her duty and obedience, mark / Hath given me this' [A letter] (2.2.109)) and pentameter lines: 'Alone and bold he stands before the Ghost' (1.5.1). There were also more expansive descriptive passages designed to convey not the setting and 'exact layout of the stage', but 'the metaphorical meaning that the set was constructed to support ... the director's vision of the set, rather than the set itself'.[32] At the end of act 3, scene 3, following the aborted assassination of Claudius:

> A home is now transformed into a maze
> as Hamlet passes through the castle halls,
> up stairs to landings leading to more stairs
> thru secret chambers into hidden rooms.

Compiling post-show evaluations by partially and non-sighted audience members, Udo, Fels and co-researcher Beatrice Avecedo found that the production was in general favourably received (though one respondent, when asked how the experience could be improved, wrote 'no Shakespeare'), with commendations in particular for the blended and integrated nature of the AD, leading the researchers to conclude: 'participants would prefer using AD that allows them to become lost in the entertainment experience rather than AD that consistently distinguishes itself as an access strategy'.[33]

Udo, Avecedo and Fels's preferred term for this approach is 'alternative', an indication that it is meant to complement rather than replace the conventional form. A more radical experiment in what was publicized as 'creative audio description' was conducted for the RSC's 2024 production of *A Midsummer Night's Dream* (directed by Eleanor Rhode). For this, the company worked with Benjamin Wilson and Vicky Ackroyd to create an AD script that was delivered by multiple cast members, primarily the Fairies and Mechanicals. The Fairies were conceived as 'orbs of energy' ('alive with light and colour', as the AI has it), of whom some assumed human form – Oberon, Titania, Puck – and others – Peaseblossom, Cobweb, Moth and Mustardseed – did not; their voice actors delivered both their lines and the AD from a soundproof booth backstage. For the AI, the cast not only self-described, but also did so in character:

[BALLY GILL] My name is Theseus, Duke of Athens. I'm British Indian, six foot tall, black, slicked-down hair, quite skinny, and I'm wearing a pinstripe dark blue suit, cowboy string necktie, and it's all very sensible and serious.

[NICHOLAS ARMFIELD] Hi, my name's Demetrius. Um, I'm a stocky white man, about five foot ten ... I wish I was six foot but that didn't happen to me.

[BOADICEA RICKETTS] I am Helena, and have light brown skin, bright purple and pink makeup, and a curly eighties brown hair power bob.[34]

The self-portraits displayed varying degrees of vanity, self-regard, self-deprecation and self-awareness, according to character; but it was Matthew Baynton's Bottom that stole the AI show:

My name is Nick Bottom. I'm a tall, thin, elegant fellow: white man; beautiful Paul Weller-esque moptop. I wear a double-breasted suit, pinstriped, with a puff of colour from a yellow and orange striped shirt and tie and *lemon socks*. I'm the best-dressed person I know. In Rita Quince's masterpiece *Pyramus and Thisbe* my costume is a Pierrot-like white, all white like a French mime, white tights, and a flowing white blouse with beautiful puffy sleeves.

This is classic Bottom: pretentious, delusional but nonetheless good-natured and likeable.[35] Making use of a convention I would never have thought possible for audio description, it is the speech of an unreliable narrator; one that, Feste-like, lies to us in the dark – but without knowing that he is doing so.

This indeterminacy was also manifested in the dynamic AD, delivered by its speakers in 'their own inimitable and characterful ways', as the RSC's web copy had it – which meant that it was subjective, occasionally opinionated, and sometimes a little uncertain of

---

31 I quote from the unpublished AD script (kindly provided by Deborah I. Fels), which does not capitalize the first letter of verse lines.

32 Udo and Fels, '"Suit the action"', p. 181.

33 J. P. Udo, B. Avecedo and D. I. Fels, 'Horatio audio-describes *Hamlet*: blind and low-vision theatre-goers evaluate an unconventional audio description strategy', *British Journal of Visual Impairment* 28 (2010), 139–56; pp. 151–2.

34 For the transfer to London's Barbican Theatre in December 2024, there were some cast changes: notably Andrew Richardson replaced Bally Gill as Theseus/Oberon, and Katherine Pearce took over from Rosie Sheehy as Puck. The AI was re-recorded to reflect this.

35 As is increasingly common, Quince (Helen Monks) was cross-cast. The citation of Paul Weller as a role model was odd, though: as the frontman of Mod-influenced New Wavers The Jam in the 1970s and funk-popsters The Style Council in the 1980s, and then as a singer-songwriter solo artist since then, the 66-year-old's heyday of cool was, by 2024, long past. Unless, of course, that was the joke.

itself. 'By the way', said Moth (Michael Olatunji), as he related the sorting of the lovers into their proper pairings (4.1.100), 'you're listening to Moth, Titania's favourite fairy and number one fixer'. Seeing Demetrius and Helena arrive in the forest (2.1.187), Philostrate (Adrian Richards) sighed 'And here's the ever-so-interesting Demetrius, followed by Helena', and embellished his 'The women embrace' on 'To seek new friends and strange companions' (1.1.219) with an 'Aah'. Observing Hippolyta's guarded response to Oberon's opening overture (1.1.7–11), Cobweb (Esme Hough) fancied her body-language reading skills:

> Four nights will quickly dream away the time . . . [They
> stand side by side, a bit
> awkward, like two
> teenagers at a school
> disco.]
> And then the moon, like to a silver bow
> New bent in heaven, shall behold the night
> Of our solemnities.   [O god, it's somehow
> getting even more
> awkward.
> Who's this?]

At the close of act 4 (4.1.184–5):

> We'll hold a feast in great solemnity [Uh-oh, this could be awkward (pause).
> Come Hippolyta.He's offered her his hand . . . but, er . . .
> hmmm . . . Oh,
> she's taken it. But I think there might be trouble ahead.]

Snug (Laurie Jamieson) was less sure of himself, following the highly aroused Titania's advance on Bottom (3.2.130) with goggle-eyed disbelief: 'She wants him. What? She wants *him*? [short gasp] Bottom's ears just got . . . ooh . . . taller.' Finally, faced with the melee of entrances, exits, slapstick stunts and pratfalls that followed Puck's gleeful promise to 'lead them up and down' (3.2.300), he just gave up: 'this is crazy . . . Ah, everyone's to-ing and fro-ing, disappearing, coming from all sorts of angles.' The larky, bantering tone also allowed for a couple of gags about inclusion and diversity: Helena's 'And therefore is winged Cupid painted blind' (1.1.235) earned the admonition 'Nothing wrong with being blind, Helena'; Thisbe's death-throes (5.1.342), the remark 'Thisbe collapses on the floor – and pulls his wig off. Ahem, his, hers – Athens is quite progressive.'

Inventive as all this was, it was uniquely geared to this production, and to this play: what works for the ludic, spirit-haunted and metatheatrical comic world of *Dream* would probably not for, say, *King Lear* (though that play's thematics of sight and blindness surely call for an equally creative response). I found it engaging enough, but as a non-blind audience member it is not for me to say how effective it was as AD – that is for the RSC's non-sighted or partially sighted patrons to judge. Playfulness and creativity have their place, but not at the expense of the primary purpose of AD, which is to meet the needs of that constituency. Whether it was a one-off or a prototype for future practice, only time will tell; at the RSC at least, the established forms of AD continue. Although the integrated nature of *Dream*'s AD meant that it was live for every performance, it was still offered as optional, an individual audio stream accessed via headphones by those who choose to do so; and was probably regarded by most sighted audience members (if they considered it at all) as an access tool rather than a creative component in its own right. As the *Describing Diversity* report notes, 'non-blind people rarely listen to AD, though when they do, they often state how interesting they found the experience'.[36] My own exposure to AD confirms this, and I vividly recall two stand-out moments during a performance of the RSC's 2022 version of *Henry VI, Part 2* (retitled *Henry VI: Rebellion*), which respectively demonstrated the cogency of non-neutral, interpretative description and the performative power of AD as spoken text. The first half of the play was described by Julia Grundy, the second by Gethyn Edwards, a gender shift that seemed somehow in tune with the escalating terror, mayhem and violence of the play's second half. The two especially memorable moments were: Mariah Gale's tremendous Margaret, confronting Mark Quartley's cowering Henry with 'Why do you rate my lord of Suffolk thus?' (3.2.56), 'bends over and speaks to him as if to a child'; and the percussive marking of the Lieutenant's hideous just-out-of-sight execution of Suffolk (4.1.140): 'blow after blow after blow, he cuts off Suffolk's head'.

This performance was not only audio-described but also captioned and chilled, and this conjunction of multiple forms of access provision prompts a final thought about its place within the wider diversity, accessibility and inclusivity agenda.[37] Unlike AD,

---

36 Hutchinson, Thompson and Cock, *Describing Diversity*, p. 15.
37 See Robert Shaughnessy, 'Shakespeare, performance and neurodiversity: Bottom's Dream', in *Shakespeare, Education and Pedagogy: Representations, Interactions and Adaptations*, ed. Pamela Bickley and Jenny Stevens (London, 2023), 120–8.

captioning, signing and the protocols of Relaxed and Chilled Performances are conducted in plain sight, and they invite hearing, neurotypical and otherwise able-bodied spectators to at least tolerate and at best share that provision, and to welcome into our theatregoing communities those who are far too often excluded from them. Following this logic, a more radically inclusive AD, as advocated by *Describing Diversity*, would mean, at some performances at least, 'blind or not, you will hear the audio description'.[38] Whether this is delivered over the sound system, from the stage by the actors themselves, or by some other means yet to be imagined is for creatives and users – sighted, partially sighted and non-sighted – to determine. It is with this in mind that we might return, on rather less ominous terms, to this article's opening suggestion that we all might one day become part of the BPS community; the opportunity is there to transform the individualized experience of access into a collective one. In the theatres of tomorrow, no one will be forced to sit alone in the dark.

---

[38] Hutchinson, Thompson and Cock, *Describing Diversity*, p. 15.

'THE NEW MAP WITH THE AUGMENTATION OF THE INDIES': GEOGRAPHICAL KNOWLEDGE COMMUNITIES AT THE INNS OF COURT AND SHAKESPEARE'S *TWELFTH NIGHT*

GAVIN HOLLIS

'THE WORLD'S PROPORTION DISFIGURED IS'[1]

For intellectual communities in sixteenth- and early seventeenth-century Europe, the world seemed to be coming to an end. As Mary Thomas Crane has characterized, this was a 'period of ferment, confusion, and angst ... when the settled Aristotelian, Galenic, and Ptolemaic accounts of how the universe worked began to fall apart and the new ideas that would replace them were still inchoate and in flux'.[2] The resulting epistemic and ontological crises were founded not so much on there being less known about the world than before, but rather on there being, to quote Ann Blair, 'too much to know' – the result of the emergence of the new science but also, significantly, of an expanded geographical view of the world.[3] The so-called 'voyages of discovery' rapidly and dramatically expanded the contours of the known world for Europeans from the fifteenth century onwards, opening up what Peter Sloterdijk has called 'the two abysses, cosmological and ethnological'.[4] The influx of new information, propelled by the 'shattering' moment when 'the human location, the planet Terra, took on increasingly explicit contours', resulted, in Sloterdijk's account, in humans confronting the fact that 'The final boundaries are no longer what they once were' – a realization he calls 'the dysangelium of the Modern Age'.[5] A better-known world – in physical and metaphysical terms – was a world barely known at all.

As literary critics including Katherine Eggert and Debapriya Sarkar have claimed, the response to the crises in knowledge in English cultural circles varied, from what Eggert calls 'disknowledge' – a conscious embrace of wrongheadedness – to the formal and poetic innovations and habits of thought emphasized by Sarkar, figured on the 'possible' rather than the categorically known.[6] Here I want to focus on the collective response of a specific community to new knowledge – the Inns of Court. My questions, though, are not about how communal knowledge was generated and circulated, per se – already traced in the work of, among others, Deborah Harkness in her fascinating reconstruction of the sixteenth-century community of natural scientists in London and northern Europe.[7] Rather, they are about how a community might generate and circulate knowledge for self-interested reasons – not so much to generate new world-views in place of collapsing ones, but rather to erect, maintain and even police the boundaries of what we might call 'knowledge communities'. Aggregating individual responses to 'the crisis of the abyss' is one way of coming to an understanding of the intellectual responses to new knowledge. I am interested here in the social quality of the responses. After all, if, as Arjun Appadurai

---

[1] 'An anatomy of the world: the first anniversary', in *John Donne: The Major Works*, ed. John Carey (Oxford, 1990, revised 2000/2008), p. 214.

[2] Mary Thomas Crane, *Losing Touch with Nature: Literature and the New Science in Sixteenth-Century England* (Baltimore, 2014), p. 2.

[3] Ann M. Blair, *Too Much to Know: Managing Scholarly Information before the Modern Age* (New Haven, 2010).

[4] Peter Sloterdijk, *In the World Interior of Capital*, trans. Wieland Hoban (Malden, 2013), p. 29.

[5] Sloterdijk, *In the World Interior of Capital*, pp. 5–6, 29.

[6] Katherine Eggert, *Disknowledge: Literature, Alchemy, and the End of Humanism in Renaissance England* (Philadelphia, 2015); Debapriya Sarkar, *Possible Knowledge: The Literary Forms of Early Modern Science* (Philadelphia, 2023).

[7] Deborah Harkness, *The Jewel House: Elizabethan London and the Scientific Revolution* (New Haven, 2007).

famously argued, things have a social life, so too, we might infer, does knowledge.[8]

As such, my analysis adapts Pierre Bourdieu's notion of cultural capital set out in *Distinction*, made up of those intangible factors that are nevertheless contingencies for social mobility – factors that might include skillsets, experiences and knowledge – around which groups cultivate competencies that distinguish themselves from other classes of people.[9] Here I stress that knowledge competency (defined as the capacity to sift, accumulate and perform knowledge within social settings) determines members of a community in contrast to those who do not possess that knowledge and are not, as it were, in the know. I am interested in how knowledge competency was operative in a period of 'ferment, confusion, and angst' – that is, how a community expresses knowledge competency when so much that was known about the world was in flux. What then does competency look like, and how might the performance of competency be a form of social capital (and the failure to perform, a source of opprobrium), when the grounds for that competency were shifting? Even more broadly, I follow Martin Heidegger's characterization of modernity as 'the Age of the World Picture', in which moderns are those who are 'in the picture', 'being well informed, being equipped and prepared'. If, for Heidegger, a 'modern' subject had to 'fight for the position in which he can be that being who gives to every being the measure and draws up the guidelines', what might that 'fight' look like across communities – even those consisting of people who, ostensibly, are like-minded in terms of their 'world view'?[10]

The knowledge in question here is geographical – as it were, what constituted the 'measure' informing 'the guidelines' of the emerging modern 'world view'. More specifically, by geographical knowledge I mean information about the world, ranging from superficial (identifying a place on a map) to deep forms of knowledge of anything ranging from climate to trade routes, social mores and internal politics (in all of which cases, a map would need to be supplemented by other sources of information), which could then be relayed for practical purposes (ranging from safe navigation to engendering hospitality in a foreign land to acting effectively in a diplomatic capacity). The knowledge might be accrued through travel, but also – given the rise of travel writing in the late sixteenth century, and the concurrent boom in the London map trade – might be assembled from reports of the travels of others.

The community in question, the Inns of Court, was characterized by the poet (and one-time member of Inner Temple) Thomas Churchyard as a place where 'wit & knowledge floes'.[11] Geographical knowledge formed a significant part of what Jessica Winston calls (in her brilliant study of the cultural life of the Inns) its 'intellectual topography'.[12] John Donne became a member of Lincoln's Inn in 1591; his interest in geography and cosmography has long been marked, as has his disquiet with 'the new philosophy call[ing] all in doubt'.[13] Churchyard himself published works drawing on his knowledge and experience of foreign policy and exploration, including a prose account, *A Prayse and Report of Maister Martyne Frobishers Voyage to Meta Incognita* (1578).[14] Across the hyper-competitive environments of the various Inns, knowing and not knowing the world could mark out one's place in the social hierarchy. To quote Winston, 'Common lawyers could wield their knowledge to intimidate others.'[15] How then, in a world about which knowledge was expanding and constantly changing with every new map, with every new report, with every new 'discovery' and interaction (and with every filtering of that knowledge across various written, oral and graphic media), did this knowledge community express knowledge competency; and what was the cost of failing to perform this knowledge?

In the next three sections of this article, I sketch the ways in which geographical knowledge was important within the context of the Inns, so as to argue that such knowledge was an important component in the

---

8 Arjun Appadurai, 'Introduction: commodities and the politics of value', in *The Social Life of Things: Commodities in Cultural Perspective*, ed. Arjun Appadurai (Cambridge, 1986), pp. 3–63.

9 Pierre Bourdieu, *Distinction: A Social Critique of the Judgement of Taste*, trans. Richard Nice (Cambridge, 1984).

10 Martin Heidegger, 'The age of the world picture', in *Off the Beaten Track*, trans. and ed. Julian Young and Kenneth Haynes (Cambridge, 2002), 57–85; pp. 67, 71.

11 Thomas Churchyard, *A Light Bondell of Livly Discourses Called Churcheyards Charge* (London, 1580), STC 5240, D4r. Quoted in Jessica Winston, *Lawyers at Play: Literature, Law and Politics at the Early Modern Inns of Court, 1558–1581* (Oxford, 2016), p. 42.

12 Winston, *Lawyers at Play*, p. 23.

13 Donne, 'Anatomy', p. 212. See also Katherine Rundell, *Super-Infinite: The Transformations of John Donne* (New York, 2022).

14 Winston dates Churchyard's date of admission to Inner Temple at 1577 – surprisingly late in his life (his birth is around 1520), but one year prior to the publication of his account of Frobisher's voyage: Winston, *Lawyers at Play*, p. 231.

15 Winston, *Lawyers at Play*, p. 34.

performance of social competency and that its affectation (if made apparent) could mark one out for derision. The latter half of this article turns to *Twelfth Night* and thinks through how some characters (notably Viola and Sebastian) perform geographical knowledge competently, and how others (notably Sir Andrew and Malvolio) do not. It places these observations in the context of Middle Temple during the first known performance of Shakespeare's *Twelfth Night* on 2 February 1602. In the final section, it turns to a reference to a 'new map with the augmentation of the Indies', a phrase used to describe Malvolio's contorted grin, which is uttered within earshot of Sir Andrew Aguecheek (3.2.74–5).[16] Long associated with Edward Wright's world map (or the Wright–Molyneux map), the allusion might have been one that lawyers at the Inns would have been expected to get – and anyone who didn't may have fleetingly felt less in the know. Wright's map, then, is afforded social capital, around which two communities form: those who know it, and those who do not; or, to put it differently, those who could perform knowledge competency and those who could not. At the same time, however, the map reference is something of a conundrum. While it may recall Wright's map, it is not named as Wright's map. Indeed, this 'new map' sounds like it has a real-world corollary, as do many of the play's allusions to places and peoples – all of which, it turns out, are fictional. The 'new map' evocation seems designed not only to highlight the limited geographical knowledge of certain characters (Malvolio and Sir Andrew, in particular) but also to play on anxieties within the ever evolving knowledge communities of early modern London – places like the Inns of Court. If it is a real map, those who can identify it can demonstrate knowledge competency. But what if it is not?

'FAIRE GEOGRAPHY': GEOGRAPHICAL KNOWLEDGE AT THE INNS OF COURT

In the prefatory matter to his translation of Mercator's *Historia mundi* (1635), Wye Saltonstall offered a dedication to the gentlemen of the Inns of Court.

To you that are the *Ornament* of the Temples,
And by your actions give such faire Examples
Vnto the Vulgar, that their *Iudgements* can
Discerne that Vertue makes a *Gentleman*:
To you *Mercator* offers by my hand
The *Worlds Potraicture*, wherein Sea and Land

Which make one *Globe*, are drawn forth in each Part
In *Plano*, with such Iudgement, *Truth*, and *Art*,
That *Pictures* of all mortall beauties are
Weake shaddowes of fraile dust, nor can compare
With these sweete *Pieces*; for who would not be
A Lover? when he sees *Geographie*
Drawne forth in such fresh colours, that invite
The *eye* to gaze with wonder and delight?
And while it gazes doth such pleasure finde
That it convayes loves flame into the minde.
I know your *Iudgements,* let none henceforth be
Your Mistresses but faire Geographie.[17]

In Saltonstall's wry verse, the gentlemen of the Inns are worthy dedicatees, as the epitome of 'Lovers . . . [of] *Geographie*'. But in his dedication Saltonstall also alerts us to the connection between members of the Inns and geographical knowledge. As Lesley Cormack has argued, Oxford and Cambridge fostered and promulgated geographical knowledge in the early modern period and served to spur the imperial imaginings of generations.[18] But the Inns were not far behind in influence. Saltonstall gestures in his dedication to the Inns' history of accumulating and practising geographical knowledge.[19] This seems to have been a feature of his own Inn, Gray's.[20] Early Virginia colonists included Gray's Inn members Sir Thomas Gates (admitted 1598), Gabriel Archer (admitted 1602), William Strachey (admitted 1605) and Sir Francis Wyatt (Virginia's first royal governor; admitted 1640). Early Virginia Company administrators included Thomas Wriothesley, Earl of Southampton (and patron to William Shakespeare; admitted 1588), and Nathaniel Rich (1610). Sir Francis Bacon, whose essay 'Of Travel' puts forward the idea that 'Travel, in the younger sort, is a part of education', was also a Graysian (1576).[21] A payment for 'A mapp of the

---

16 All references to Shakespeare are from *William Shakespeare: The Complete Works*, 2nd ed., ed. Stanley Wells, Gary Taylor, John Jowett and William Montgomery (Oxford, 2005).
17 Wye Saltonstall, 'To the vertuous and learned Gentlemen of Innes of Court', in *Historia mundi, or Mercators Atlas* (London, 1635).
18 Lesley B. Cormack, *Charting an Empire: Geography at the English Universities 1580–1620* (Chicago, 1997).
19 On practical 'geographical' knowledge, specifically that which aided in matters of estate management and beyond (which is less my concern in this article), see Henry S. Turner, *The English Renaissance Stage: Geometry, Poetics and the Practical Spatial Arts 1580–1630* (Oxford, 2006).
20 The following paragraph is indebted to *The Pension Book of Gray's Inn, Volume I: 1569–1669*, ed. Reginald J. Fletcher (London, 1901).
21 'Of Travel', in *Francis Bacon: The Major Works*, ed. Brian Vickers (Oxford, 1996), 374–6; p. 374.

whole world & for the frame' in 1580 (two months following Drake's return from the circumnavigation) indicates that a large world map was on display prominently in the halls.[22]

Many Middle Templars showed interest in geography, cosmography and cartography.[23] It was, after all, at the Middle Temple chambers of his cousin that the schoolboy Richard Hakluyt first saw 'certain books of Cosmography, with a Universal Map', which inspired his career.[24] Sir Robert Cotton, whose extensive collection of books and manuscripts included a number of manuscript and printed maps, studied law at Middle Temple from 1589. Robert Ashley, admitted in 1588, called to the Bar in 1595, and an inhabitant on and off for most of his life, left his personal library of around 4,000 books to Middle Temple when he died in 1641. In addition to hundreds of law books in a range of languages, he also owned several atlases, travel accounts, books on geometry and on navigation (including a copy of his brother's translation of Lucas Janszoon Waghenaer's *The Mariners Mirror* (1588)), celestial and terrestrial globes by Isaac Habrecht of Strasbourg, and a French translation of Hues's *Tractatus de globis et eorum usu* (1594; French edition 1618).[25] John Savile (admitted 2 May 1600) was the nephew of Sir Henry Savile, who endowed the chairs of Astronomy and Geometry at Oxford University (his older brother, also Henry, was admitted in 1593). William Crashaw, preacher to Inner Temple, also attempted to bequeath his collection of books to Middle Temple in an undated letter, a collection which included books on cosmography and 'one of the fairest paire of globes in Englande'.[26]

Crashaw was also one of many Middle Templars whose interest in geography extended beyond bookish theoric. A Virginia Company member, he delivered a sermon prior to the departure of its governor, Lord De La Warre, in February 1610. John Ofley (admitted 19 January 1602) was the grandson of Sir Thomas Ofley, one of the founder members of The Muscovy Company. Humphrey Weld and Humphrey Slaney (both admitted 11 August 1601) invested in a range of overseas enterprises, including the Virginia Company. Middle Templar John Doddridge (admitted 1577) was instrumental in writing the first three Virginia Company charters (1606, 1609, 1612), and George Sandys (admitted 1594) served as treasurer of the Virginia Company. Martin's Hundred Plantation in Virginia was named for Richard Martin, MP for Barnstaple in Devonshire, who had been elected the Prince D'Amour for the 1597–8 holiday festivities at Middle Temple. Martin also helped mount *The Memorable Masque* of 1613, which promoted the Virginia colony in a part-court-masque, part-urban-procession, to mark the wedding of Princess Elizabeth to Frederick V of the Palatinate.

Not just investors and boosters, Middle Templars were actively involved in transoceanic trade, travel and early colonization. Sir Thomas Roe, who was ambassador to the Mughal Empire in the 1610s, entered Middle Temple in 1597 (he also ventured up the Amazon in 1610). Other notable Middle Templars include Philip Amadas (co-captain of the first Roanoke voyage of 1584; admitted 15 March 1582); Ralph Lane was the first governor of Virginia (1585–6; admitted 3 December 1554); while George Percy (admitted 12 May 1597) and George Thorpe (admitted 20 February 1598) were early Virginia settlers after the founding of Jamestown. Middle Temple also allied itself with explorers and traders. Sir Walter Raleigh, John Hawkins and Martin Frobisher were honorary members, while Sir Francis Drake was welcomed triumphantly upon his return from Santo Domingo, Cartagena and St Augustine in 1586. Timbers from the *Golden Hind*, the ship used for Drake's earlier circumnavigation, were used to create an oak table in Middle Temple Hall. One assumes that the table was either present in the room at the first known performance of *Twelfth Night* or was moved to let the action commence.

PERFORMING GEOGRAPHICAL KNOWLEDGE COMPETENCY

A reference to a new map would likely have struck a chord at Middle Temple. This was a knowledgeable audience, with many interested (intellectually, financially)

---

[22] *The Pension Book*, Appendix I, p. 488. The map cost 28 shillings and 3 pence, expensive for a map of the day – which suggests that the map was large.

[23] The following survey is indebted to *The Register of Admissions to the Honourable Society of the Middle Temple, Volume I: From the Fifteenth Century to 1781* (London, 1949).

[24] Richard Hakluyt, *The Principal Navigations, Voyages, Traffiques and Discoverie of the English Nation* (London, 1589), 'Dedication to the Right Honorable Sir Francis Walsingham Knight'.

[25] Bartholomew Shower, *Bibliotheca illustris Medii Templii Societatis* (London, 1700). On Ashley's interests, see Virgil Heltzel, 'Robert Ashley: Elizabethan man of letters', *Huntington Library Quarterly* 10 (1947), 349–63.

[26] See R. M. Fisher, 'William Crashawe and the Middle Temple globes 1605–15', *Geographical Journal* 140 (Feb. 1974), 105–12; and R. M. Fisher, 'William Crashawe's library at the Temple 1605–1615', *Library* 30 (1975), 116–228.

in 'farre distant countries', and with many owning maps and knowledgeable about their production. For all that the Inns of Court were associated with the legal profession, few admitted were called to the bar – Philip J. Finkelpearl calculates only 15 per cent of members were called between 1570 and 1600.[27] Rather, the Inns were seen as a stepping stone or finishing school where (to quote Jessica Winston) 'sons of the aristocracy and the gentry who did not intend a common law career came to acquire some legal knowledge and to develop the urbanity and social connections that would help them thrive at court and in other elite social and political circles'.[28] For these students, geography was an important form of knowledge to cultivate, as part of what Frank Whigham has described as the emerging market for a 'repertoire of rules' whereby a place in the ruling elite could be acquired (rather than being solely the result of one's birth).[29] As Cormack writes, 'The study of geography ... provided polish for courtly conversations and information for investment and adventurous exploits.'[30]

Take the commonplace book of Edward Hoby. Hoby, of Middle Temple (1584) and a member of an elite family (his mother was Elizabeth Russell, Countess of Bedford, and his uncle was William Cecil), recorded adages that were useful for political life.[31] Hoby was in some sense typical, as this was a practice common among members of the gentry as a display of what András Kiséry calls 'political competence ... a familiarity with – and a facility in discussing – the business of politics that is put on display in sociable exchange as a marker of distinction'.[32] As one might expect of the son of the first English translator of *Il Cortegiano*, Sir Thomas Hoby, Edward was attentive to the importance of conversation. And it is clear from the commonplace book that Hoby prized geographical knowledge as part of his repertoire. Alongside the phrases is transcribed a copy of a tract by George Popham (nephew of noted Middle Templar Sir John Popham) promoting colonization and detailing the kinds of people and professions needed for such a task. Repeatedly, Popham (and in recording him, Hoby too) stresses the importance of measurement and mapping as a means to comprehend and apprehend the territory encountered. Hoby also copied 'Instructions to be Observed by Thomas Bavin' – a surveyor on Humphrey Gilbert's 1582 voyage to Newfoundland – in which Bavin is instructed to 'never go att any tyme w[th]out a payer of writing tables'.[33] Whether or not Hoby intended this knowledge to be applied is unclear, as he himself does not seem to have travelled far, although he did serve as an ambassador-of-sorts to the court of James

VI of Scotland (future James I of England) in the 1580s and sailed with Essex to Cadiz in 1596. Acquiring this knowledge seems to have been important for Hoby nonetheless. Indeed, that he seemed intent on incorporating geographical knowledge in his repertoire – and recorded not just the knowledge itself but also the best ways to acquire and then regurgitate it – alongside other forms of political knowledge (whether that be the gossip of the day or axioms that could be deployed in conversation) indicates that he thought it useful in the assemblage of political competence.[34]

It is in this context of performing political competence that we might understand the revels for which the Inns of Court were famous. A way for members to blow off steam (much of their reputation for disreputable behaviour stems from them), the entertainments also served as extensions of the communal learning exercises of the Inns (moots, readings, even dining) to aid them in their post-Inns lives. The *Gesta Grayorum* of 1594, the first night of which famously devolved into 'The Night of Errors', staged conflabs between The Prince of Purpoole and ambassadors from 'The State of Templaria' (Inner Temple) and from Faman Bega, 'an Ambassador from the mighty Emperor of Russia and Moscovy, that had some Matters of Weight to make known to His Highness'. These interactions serve as comedic dress rehearsals elaborating on the correct forms of embassy with foreign dignitaries.[35] The Middle Temple Revels of the Christmas season 1597–8 cast its lord of misrule, or in this case 'Prince of Love', as 'Great Commander of all the Seas from the Streights of *Genua* to the Bay of *Porto desiderato*; and chief General of all *Venus* forces, from *Iapan* to *Quevera* by the West; and from *Rio des*

---

[27] Philip J. Finkelpearl, *John Marston of the Middle Temple: An Elizabethan Dramatist in His Social Setting* (Cambridge, 1969), p. 10.

[28] Winston, *Lawyers at Play*, p. 27.

[29] Frank Whigham, *Ambition and Privilege: The Social Tropes of Elizabethan Courtesy Theory* (Berkeley, 1984), p. 5.

[30] Cormack, *Charting*, pp. 160–1. According to Cormack, of the sixty-eight students of descriptive geography at the universities, 'A full 30 percent ... attended the Inns of Court' (160).

[31] Sir Edward Hoby's Commonplace Book, British Library MS Add. 38323.

[32] András Kiséry, *Hamlet's Moment: Drama and Political Knowledge in Early Modern England* (Oxford, 2016), p. 9.

[33] Hoby's Commonplace Book, fol. 3v.

[34] See Lauren Workings, 'Locating colonization at the Jacobean Inns of Court', *Historical Journal* 61 (2018), 29–51; on Hoby, see pp. 29–31.

[35] *Records of Early English Drama: The Inns of Court*, ed. Alan H. Nelson and John R. Eliot Jr, vol. 1 (Cambridge, 2010), p. 414.

Amazones to *Lapland* by the North.'[36] As this title suggests, the Revels revelled in thinly veiled innuendo, which is frequently evoked in geographical terms. The 'Prince of Love' lays claim to a number of fictional places, such as '*Hartsbroken*, an ancient, but now decayed Castle in *Gelderland*' and '*Florida* and *Exultantia*, in which counties he served young under *Cupid*'; he appoints a High Admiral to 'be sure so to keep the Winde of any ship he meeteth that he may safely (discharging his Ordnance) come off and on at his pleasure'.[37] But, coupled with this sexual humour, the Revels repeatedly return to ideas of the Prince's education, in which geographical knowledge seems to be prized. On Candlemass, the concluding night of the festivities, the Prince asked his councillors to what career he should turn, and two out of the four suggestions involve travel: 'One advised him to follow the Sea; another to Land travel.'[38] *The Comedy of Errors*, performed as part of the *Gesta Grayorum,* the Gray's Inn celebrations of 1594 (its first known performance), features the famous geographical blazon of Nell: 'She is spherical, like a globe. I could find out countries in her' (3.2.116–17). Akin to the celebrations at Middle Temple a few years later, Shakespeare's play maps far-off places onto a female body for the purposes of bawdy humour. However, in contrast to the Prince of Love, who is imagined as a sexually confident 'conqueror', Dromio is, of course, terrified by his encounter with the globe.

PERFORMING GEOGRAPHICAL KNOWLEDGE INCOMPETENCY

Of course, performing geographical knowledge poorly could index one's political incompetence. As Inns members would have known, in a period of ever-changing informational currency, it was all too easy to possess and peddle inaccurate or out-of-date knowledge. Maps in particular were questioned and distrusted. Sir Dudley Digges (bencher at Gray's Inn from 1631 and from a long line of Graysians) wrote in objection to 'all our moderne Globes and Mappes', preferring instead Ptolemy, however outdated. Digges reasoned that such objects were not to be trusted because 'Trauellours be seldome *Mathematicians*.'[39] Specifically, Digges rejected globes and maps because they did not show the Northeast Passage – that is, because they were 'out of date' and one might just as well use Ptolemy. James Rosier, who accompanied Bartholomew Gosnold (admitted to Middle Temple, 9 February 1593) on his 1602 voyage down the eastern seaboard from modern-day Maine to Cape Cod, Massachusetts, wrote disparagingly of the maps available for sea-voyaging, stating that 'our sea charts [are] very false, putting land where none is'.[40] It wasn't as if mapmakers themselves were ill attuned to the limitations of their craft. The impetus for Edward Wright to draw his map was that 'ordinary charts are in many places much like an inextricable labyrinth of error, out of which it will be very hard for a man easily to unwinde himself'.[41] Anthony Ashley (brother of the aforementioned Robert) acknowledged that 'diverse mouthes & entries or rivers … are moveable, & have not always their being in one self place, as in these Tables or Chartes, rightly, fitly & faithfully they are set down'. This was something that 'all Masters and Pilots do understand', but an awareness that maps were not entirely reliable and could mislead was something that marked out learned map-users from superficial ones.[42]

In addition, there was wariness among some Inns members that map readers were allured by the object without fully understanding what they were looking at. In his translation of Mercator, Saltonstall flirts with this idea in his dedication to the gentlemen of the Inns, emphasizing the 'wonder and delight' elicited by staring at '*Geographie* / Drawne forth in such fresh colours', which in turn 'convayes loves flames into the mind'. Saltonstall characterizes the Inns' encounters with 'faire Geographie' as pleasurable and almost titillating, in contrast to how he characterizes the universities' geographical knowledge in the more staid Latin verse dedications to them in the front matter of *Historia mundi*. The access that maps and atlases gave their readers was frequently

---

[36] Benjamin Rudyerd, *Le Prince d'Amour or the Prince of Love. With a Collection of Several Ingenious Poems and Songs by the Wits of the Age* (London, 1660), p. 1.

[37] Rudyerd, *Le Prince*, pp. 3–4, p. 28.

[38] Rudyerd, *Le Prince*, p. 89. The Prince eschewed these options, along with 'marry[ing] a rich widow', and instead selected a fourth option, 'to study the Common Law'.

[39] Sir Dudley Digges, *Of the Circumference of the Earth, or, A Treatise of the Northeast Passage* (London, 1612), pp. 2, 9.

[40] James Rosier, *A True Relation of the Most Prosperous Voyage Made This Present Yeere 1605, by Captaine George Waymouth, in the Discouery of the Land of Virginia* (London, 1605), fol. A4v.

[41] Edward Wright, *Certaine Errors in Navigation* (London, 1599), ¶¶. Neither Wright nor his collaborator Henry Briggs were members of the Inns, but both of them had a number of connections with the Inns. See Cormack, *Charting*, p. 125.

[42] Lucas Janszoon Waghenaer, *The Mariners Mirror*, trans. Anthony Ashley (London, 1588), ¶¶.

trumpeted: Saltonstall extolled the virtues of 'eye-travell' in *Historia mundi*, for example.[43] Others condemned the easy pleasures afforded by the map. Thomas Blundeville (a member of Gray's Inn in the 1560s) was spurred into writing *A Briefe Description of Vniversal Mappes and Cardes* (dedicated to Sir Francis Windham of Lincoln's Inn) by the 'many that delight to looke on Mappes ... but yet for want of skill in Geography, they knowe not with what maner of lines they are traced, nor what those lines do signifie, nor yet the true use of Mappes in deed'.[44] In his *Epistolae Ho-Elianae*, the Welsh writer James Howell mocked 'the sedentary *Traveller* ... [who was] penn'd up between Wals, ... poring all day upon a Map', and was like those 'who thought to bee a good Fencer, by looking on *Agrippa*'s book-postures only'. Howell, while not a member of the Inns, was familiar with them (many of the addressees of his letters resided at Gray's Inn), and his choice of fencing – a courtly pursuit – as an analogous activity to travel is telling: one can as soon learn about the world from a map as one can learn fencing from a book.[45]

As Howell's sneer indicates, there was a general leeriness regarding the ways in which geographical knowledge could be abused by wannabes – those who deployed geographical knowledge for social advancement in craven and suspect ways. The 'sedentary traveller', about whom Blundeville and Howell were critical, became the focus of satire – a genre that dominated the literary output of the Inns of Court in the 1590s.[46] In 'The New Cry', Ben Jonson (who did not attend the Inns but had a long, sometimes complicated association with them) ridicules 'Ripe statesmen', who claim to 'know the states of Christendom' but in effect do not know 'the places', because they 'have seen the maps, and bought them too / And understand 'em, as most chapmen do'.[47] Another Jonson satire, 'To Captain Hungry', depicts its title character as a man who claims that he has geographical knowledge from 'Ireland, Holland, Sweden ... Hungary and Poland, Turkey too', but this knowledge has been acquired from a 'punk' who has lain with a 'young statesman', since after all even 'a flea [can] at twice skip in the Map'.[48] Perhaps the most famous example of this type in Jonson's work is Sir Politic Would-Be from *Volpone* who seems to have garnered his (wayward) knowledge of Venice from geography books. Everard Guilpin's (Gray's Inn, 1591) first satire ridicules the 'foisting traveller' whose claims of travel are extravagant: 'Mandevile, Candish, sea experienst Drake / Came never neere him'.[49] Middle Templar John Marston's Second Satire berates 'Bruto the

Travailer' for his pompous attitude and pretentious clothing, and claims that all he has picked up from his travels ('some countries have I seen') are venereal diseases.[50] In the 'fondling motley humorist' and his acquaintances of 'Satyre I', who huff tobacco (and 'excel / Th'Indians') and affect 'French and Italian', John Donne finds an analogous figure to Marston's Bruto – albeit, unlike Bruto, Donne's target does not seem to have travelled anywhere and merely affects a sophisticated, well-travelled demeanour.[51]

'STRANGERS UNGUIDED': GEOGRAPHICAL (IN)COMPETENCY IN ILLYRIA

For men who hoped for advancement – like Malvolio and Sir Andrew Aguecheek in *Twelfth Night* – geographical knowledge was increasingly significant currency. Performing competence in this knowledge – even if one had not travelled and hence had to assemble it – might lead to career advancement (for example, as a diplomat) or social advancement (for example, as someone who could be a diplomat). This class of men made up some of the audience of the first known performance of Shakespeare's play. I do not claim that *Twelfth Night* was written for the Inns, although there are site-specific details in the play that recall the architectural peculiarities of Middle Temple and possibly even some of its more prominent inhabitants and frequenters.[52] Yet, for

---

43 Saltonstall, 'Preface', in *Historia mundi*.

44 Thomas Blundeville, *A Briefe Description of Vniversal Mappes and Cardes* (London, 1589), 'To the Reader'.

45 See James Howell, *Epistolae Ho-Elianae: The Familiar Letters of James Howell*, vol. 1 (1645; reprinted Boston and New York, 1907), pp. 69, 73. For the mixed reception of maps in England within the religious atmosphere of the period, see Gavin Hollis, 'The end of all: worldliness, piety, and the social life of maps in post-Reformation England', in *Making Worlds: Global Invention in the Early Modern Period*, ed. Angela Vanhaelen and Bronwen Wilson (Toronto, 2022), 332–64.

46 See Michelle O'Callaghan, *The English Wits: Literature and Sociability in Early Modern England* (Cambridge, 2007).

47 Ben Jonson, *The Complete Poems*, ed. George Parfitt (London, 1975), pp. 64–5

48 Jonson, *Poems*, pp. 73–4.

49 Everard Guiplin, *Skialethia or The Shadowe of Truth in Certaine Epigrams and Satyres* (London, 1598), p. 32.

50 *The Works of John Marston*, ed. J. O. Halliwell, vol. 3 (London, 1856), p. 221.

51 'Satire I', in *John Donne: The Major Works*, ed. Carey, 6–8; p. 8.

52 See Anthony Arlidge, *Shakespeare and the Prince of Love: The Feast of Misrule in Middle Temple* (London, 2000).

members of Middle Temple, especially those who viewed the Inns of Court as an entry-point to London society or as a means for advancement at the royal court, *Twelfth Night*'s trafficking in geographical knowledge, and its frequent obfuscation of that knowledge, would have resonated.

Twelfth Night repeatedly dramatizes how travelling without knowledge is a dangerous thing. Sebastian proclaims his own 'determinate voyage' to be 'mere extravagancy' (2.1.9–10) – that is, aimless wandering. Antonio, however, recognizes the danger of being a foreigner in Illyria, since Sebastian is 'skilless in these parts, which to a stranger, / Unguided and unfriended, often prove / Rough and inhospitable' (3.3.9–11). Sebastian heeds Antonio's advice, agreeing to stay in the 'south suburbs' (presumably a quieter spot, in stark contrast to London's own) (39), and deciding to use his time in Illyria to see 'the relics . . . the memorials and the things of fame / That do renown this city' (19, 23–4). Antonio approves, saying that this will 'feed your knowledge' (41). This information-gathering will allow Sebastian to ingratiate himself in Illyrian society, giving him the requisite 'skill' to ward off 'rough and inhospitable' treatment. Knowing Illyria's monumental history – that is, acquiring geographical knowledge about Illyria through observant wandering (rather than 'mere extravagancy') will mitigate his strangeness. Sebastian, it seems, already knows that this is an apt method for adapting to and surviving in a foreign land.

Viola cultivates this 'skill' as well. Like Sebastian, she is reliant on a trustworthy guide with whom she cultivates a careful relationship. The Captain 'was bred and born/Not three hours' travel from this very place' (1.2.20–1). She already has some geographical knowledge competence regarding Illyria: she is already aware of Orsino, having 'heard my father name him' (24). She is able to fill in the gaps by asking questions about the sociopolitical climate of Illyria: 'Who governs here?'; 'What is his name?'; 'What's she?' (of Olivia) (22, 23, 31). Having elicited significant information from her set of questions, she devises a plan to ensure her hospitable treatment through courtly skills that seem to have constituted her pre-shipwreck education. As Valentine notes two scenes later, Orsino 'hath known you but three days, and already you are no stranger' (1.4.2–4). Through (among other things) geographical knowledge competence, born partly of education (from her father) and partly from knowing what questions to ask, she moves from the position of outsider to insider within a short space of time.

While the twins navigate their way to harbour by gathering Illyrian knowledge (about its history and its current politics), other 'stranger' characters present cautionary tales. This is particularly true of Sir Andrew Aguecheek and Malvolio. Andrew is not local, and unlike the twins he fails to cultivate Illyrian habits. His robotic (or 'manikin'-like (3.2.51)) copying of Sir Toby, the Antonio to his 'unguided' Sebastian, repeatedly falls short. He cannot master courtship, linguistic bravado, intellectual endeavour, martial valour – in part because Sir Toby, unlike Antonio, is uninterested in helping Andrew 'feed [his] knowledge'. His failings are cast in terms of geography and travel. He fails to 'front [Maria], board her, . . . assail her' (terms associated with ships; 1.3.53–4), while Fabian warns him that Olivia's disfavour is akin to having 'sailed into the north of my lady's opinion' (3.2.25). Moreover, he fails because he lacks the geographical knowledge that can form part of the 'politic talk' that will engender hospitable welcome (rather than have him under the constant threat of being thrown out). In the drinking scene, Andrew recalls Feste's talk 'of the Vapians passing the equinoctial of Queubus' (2.3.22–3). The reference is unclear – editors have offered not wholly convincing readings (many of which fall back on this being a compositor's error). Feste could be referring to the movement of peoples or of a constellation (or to neither of these things). 'Vapian' might be a mistake for 'Pavian', which could refer to Pavia, Lombardy, or the 'pavene', a dance (Sir Andrew has earlier been associated with dancing). The coinage 'Vapian' implies movement – its etymological breakdown from the Italian *va* ('go') and *piano* ('slowly').[53] The word 'equinoctial' refers to either the celestial or the terrestrial equator, and hence could be used in relation to geography or astrology. Andrew's unthinking repetition (and possible misremembering) of Feste underscores his being out of place – that is, he performs geographical knowledge poorly, because he unquestioningly parrots questionable information that someone (such as Viola and Sebastian) might know to query. Indeed, we might suspect that Feste lays knowledge traps for Andrew. In response to Feste's follow-up – which contains another obscure geographical reference ('The Myrmidons' (27)) – and eager to fit in, Andrew replies 'Excellent!' (28). By so doing, Andrew both hopes to demonstrate that he understands this 'fooling' and indexes that he has

---

[53] On Vapia/Pavia, see Steve Sohmer, *Reading Shakespeare's Mind* (Manchester, 2017), p. 91.

not understood it at all (primarily because, given its quality of nonsense, there is nothing to understand).

Malvolio, by contrast, is no stranger to Illyria. However, his desire to ascend from steward to Olivia's husband leads to his ostracism. Even before he finds Maria's letter, he is described as one who 'cons state without book and utters it by great swathes' (2.3.143) – that is, someone who curates political talk to advance their social standing. Maria's letter itself could be said to be a book of state – that is, an instructional manual for how Malvolio should comport himself in the position to which he imagines himself best suited (both as Olivia's husband and as 'sitting ... in my state' rather than serving as steward (2.5.42)). Yet this preparation for 'greatness' is marked as affected, here synonymous with foreignness. He is 'Monsieur Malvolio' (2.3.129). His yellow stockings are not only ill favoured by Olivia but had a raft of cultural associations in early modern England that he seems to unwittingly put on, which again marks him out as ill suited for the place to which he aspires. Yellow stockings connoted bachelordom; women wore them in protest against philandering husbands; more generally, yellow had a range of connotations in early modern fashion, including effeminacy and profaneness.[54] Encouraged to adopt the yellow stockings once more (failing to note Olivia's distaste), Malvolio becomes the walking sign of his own inability to fit in, as he adopts attire that at every turn is inapt for someone trying to assert and display their competence. Although at home, Malvolio becomes an outcast.

Malvolio also sifts information poorly, in a manner that is characterized as that of an outsider. In the same scene that features Maria's comparison of Malvolio's face to 'the new map' (more of which anon), Maria states that 'Yon gull Malvolio is turned heathen, a very renegado, for there is no Christian that means to be saved by believing rightly can ever believe such impossible passages of grossness' (3.2.65–8).

Maria's description of Malvolio as heathen is presumably in part because of his 'very strange manner' (3.4.8) – his physical appearance and comportment – but is also specifically related to how he has interpreted the letter. Malvolio has read Maria's letter, with its 'impossible passages of grossness' (i.e., with its declarations of love), and taken them as true, in the same way that a heathen or a renegade (a convert to Islam) fails to 'believe rightly' and follows 'gross passages' of their own doctrines.[55] Malvolio starts the play as an insider, albeit one who is reminded of their lower social standing by his superiors (and taunted for it by Sir Toby). His aspirations revolve around accumulating knowledge so that he can perform

the role of the courtier – by regurgitating what he learns from 'politic authors' (2.5.156). However, he fails to vet the information: despite clues (in particular 'M.A.O.I.', and there being 'no consonancy in the sequel' (135, 126–7)), Malvolio chooses to 'crush this a little' (136) and make the letters conform to his name rather than dismiss the letter's provenance. That is, he fails to show the requisite skills, and hence outs himself as a foreigner, akin to one who is 'skill-less in these parts ... a stranger / Unguided and unfriended', and lacks the competence to sort, assemble and perform the geographical knowledge that might enable him to travel safely.

'THE NEW MAP'

According to John Manningham (the only person who recorded any details about the first known performance of *Twelfth Night* at Middle Temple), the play had 'a good practice in it to make the steward beleeue his lady widow was in loue with him'.[56] Manningham, then, seems to have viewed the play as exemplary in the way that it corrects Malvolio's errancy.[57] Yet, while the play follows Manningham's logic, it also casts this corrective glare outwards to its own audience. *Twelfth Night*'s forays into nonsense and uncertainty, then, as Stephen Booth and Adam Zucker have claimed, seem designed to catch out not only characters in the play, but members of the audience too.[58] *Twelfth Night* is stocked with

[54] See Loreen L. Giese, 'Malvolio's yellow stockings: coding illicit sexuality in early modern England', *Medieval and Renaissance Drama in England* 19 (2006), 235–46; and Anne Rosalind Jones and Peter Stallybrass, *Renaissance Clothing and the Materials of Memory* (Cambridge, 2000), esp. chapter 3, 'Yellow starch: fabrications of the Jacobean court', 59–85.

[55] On the way in which 'the play figures [Malvolio] as a renegade to explain his class aspirations', see Su Fang Ng, 'The frontiers of *Twelfth Night*', in *Early Modern England and Islamic Worlds*, ed. Bernadette Andrea and Linda McJannet (Basingstoke, 2011), 173–96; p. 182.

[56] *The Diary of John Manningham of the Middle Temple, 1602–1603*, ed. Robert Parker Sorlien (Hanover, 1976), p. 48.

[57] Manningham may well have taken Malvolio's treatment as a warning sign – less of what might happen to the over-reaching upstart (a likely motive for Manningham's membership of the Inns, after all), and more of what might happen to the over-reaching upstart who fails to accumulate the requisite political knowledge and social capital or perform that knowledge adequately. See Kiséry, *Hamlet's Moment*, esp. pp. 9–11.

[58] Stephen Booth, *Precious Nonsense: The Gettysburg Address, Ben Jonson's Epitaphs on His Children, and Twelfth Night* (Berkeley, 1998); Adam Zucker, '*Twelfth Night* and the philology of nonsense', *Renaissance Studies* 30 (2016), 88–101.

invocations to fake authorities – 'Quinapulus' (1.5.32), 'Pigrogromitus' (2.2.22) and 'the old hermit of Prague' (4.2.13–14) – who may well have caused furrowed brows amongst the Middle Temple audience, as they have among editors of the play when attempting to provide adequate glosses. We can extend this nonsensicality to the geography of *Twelfth Night*. Possibly only *The Tempest* in the Shakespeare canon is as vague in its geographical coordinates. Illyria's location on the Dalmatian coast was at a crossing-point between the Islamic world and Christian Europe, but the Illyria of the play (while undoubtedly drawing on these Mediterranean associations) seems to be a hodgepodge of Italy and England, and a nation, a city or town, and two aristocratic houses as well.[59] While not necessarily a no-place – Illyria seems, if anything, to suffer from surfeit of places – the very name also sounds lyrical, as if to remind us of the play's preoccupation with poetics. Illyria may sound like a real place that one might find on a map – indeed, it is a real place one might find on a map – but the play repeatedly confounds expectations, presenting opportunities to those who can navigate its strange geographies while confounding others who have not acquired either sufficient geographical knowledge or the requisite skill to put that knowledge into practice.

Another point of seeming geographical certainty in the play is, of course, Maria's map:

[Malvolio] does obey every point of the letter that I dropped to betray him. He does smile his face into more lines than is in the new map with the augmentation of the Indies: you have not seen such a thing as 'tis.

(3.2.74–6)

On 14 June 1878, in a paper delivered to the New Shakespere Society at University College London, Charles Henry (C. H.) Coote of the British Museum claimed that the Wright–Molyneux map fitted all of the criteria laid out in Maria's description. A map of the world, it had only recently been made (in manuscript around 1595; engraved and inserted in two different states into the second edition of Richard Hakluyt's *The Principal Navigations* (1598–1600); updated and included in a variant form in the second edition of Wright's *Certaine Errors in Navigation* – a version of which is reprinted here as Figure 4). Drawing mostly on the geographical knowledge present on Emery Molyneux's terrestrial globe (1592), the map was constructed using a new projection, calculated by Wright (following Mercator). It was also heavily lined with intersecting rhumb- and meridian lines, and hence could be said to

resemble a wrinkled face, with laugh lines around the mouth or, given the way that rhumb-lines radiate from compass points, around the eyes. Coote concluded, 'the most reasonable and natural explanation of the matter [given its striking appearance] is, that it was suggested to the mind of Shakespere by a glance at our "new map" with many lines'.[60] Two years later, Coote himself described how: 'It is a source of pleasure to add that the arguments in its favours have, thus far, been accepted by competent critics as sound and conclusive.'[61] And he was not wrong: his findings were almost immediately adopted by subsequent editions of the play, which concluded (to quote one editor) that the map 'answers to Maria's description in every respect'.[62] Coote's claim continues to have an enduring afterlife in the late twentieth and twenty-first centuries. 'We know', writes Steve Mentz, 'that Shakespeare saw Wright's map', and thanks to Coote this conclusion does seem feasible.[63]

However, the four things that we know about Maria's map – its lines, its newness, its 'augmentations', and that it is of the Indies – are worth a second look. Its lines, the things that (according to Coote) struck Shakespeare the most, were not a novelty in and of themselves. They are common on manuscript portolans, and also increasingly on print maps towards the end of the sixteenth

---

[59] On debates about the importance of Illyria as a location, see Elizabeth Pentland, 'Beyond the "lyric" in Illyricum: some early modern backgrounds to *Twelfth Night*', in *Twelfth Night: New Critical Essays*, ed. James Schiffer (London, 2011), 149–66.

[60] C. H. Coote, 'On Shakespere's new map in *Twelfth Night*', in *Transactions of the Shakespere Society* (London, 1878), 88–100; p. 94.

[61] Coote, 'New map', p. 99; Coote, 'Note on the "new map"', in *The Works of John Davis, the Navigator*, ed. Arthur Hastings Markham (London, 1880), lxxxvi–xcv; esp. lxxxvii.

[62] See, for example, the notes in *Twelfth Night or What You Will*, ed. W. A. Wright (Oxford, 1885), pp. 143n, 73; *Twelfth Night or What You Will*, ed. Henry Morley (London, 1890), pp. 5–7; *Twelfth Night; or What You Will*, ed. A. W. Verity (Cambridge, 1894), p. 124, n. 75; *Twelfe Night, or What You Will: New Variorum Edition*, ed. Horace Howard Furness (Philadelphia, 1901), pp. 209–10; *Shakespeare's Comedy of Twelfth Night or What You Will*, ed. William J. Rolfe (New York, 1904), pp. 193–4; *Twelfth Night*, ed. Arthur D. Innes, rev. Frederick E. Pierce (London, 1916), p. vi; *Twelfth Night: The Cambridge Dover Wilson Shakespeare*, ed. John Dover Wilson (Cambridge, 1930, repr. 2009), pp. 148n, 77–8. The quotation comes from A.W. Verity's edition for Cambridge University Press.

[63] Steve Mentz, 'Mapping uncertainty: marine cartography, the Wright–Molyneux map, and *Twelfth Night*', *English Language Notes* 52 (2014), 53–9; p. 55.

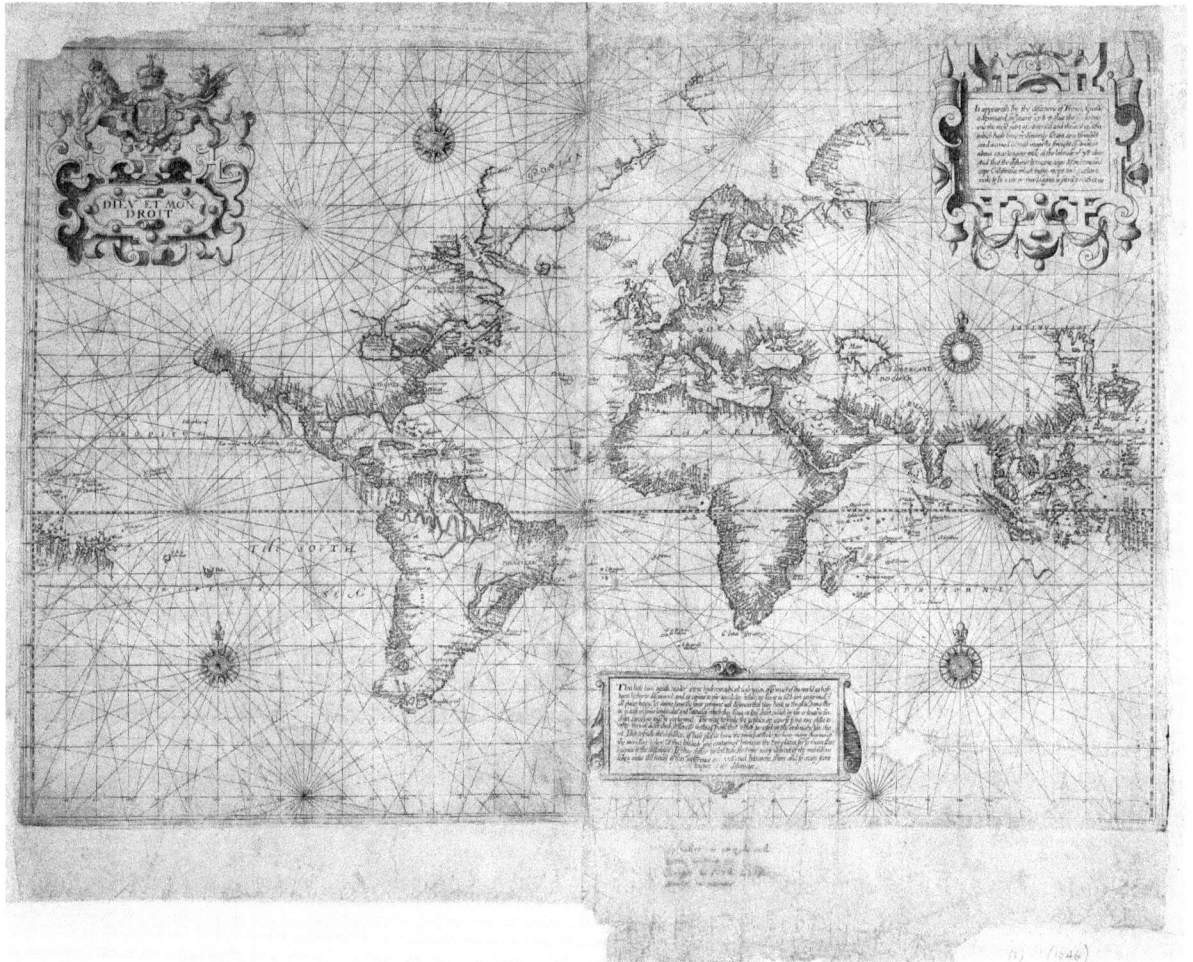

4 The Wright–Molyneux map, from Richard Hakluyt, *The Principal Navigations*, 2nd ed., 1599. Reprinted with permission from the Bodleian Library, Oxford University.

century.[64] Just as the map was not novel in appearance, nor was it in terms of its projection. Of course, Mercator's maps had used the projection beforehand: the importance of Wright's discovery was not that it was new, per se, but that he managed to unravel the mystery of Mercator's mathematics. While cartographic historians have heralded Wright's projection, the Wright–Molyneux map in *The Principal Navigations* may not have been viewed as revolutionary at the time. As Sarah Tyacke points out, despite Wright's vaunted position – first as Professor of Mathematics at Gonville and Caius, Cambridge, then as tutor to Prince Henry, and then as hydrographer to the East India Company – 'his work does not seem to have influenced the emerging chartmaking trade as much as he, and indeed the East India Company, would have liked'.

Tyacke counts only one map in her study that bears witness to Wright's influence before 1660.[65]

And what of the 'Indian augmentation'? Coote claimed that this referred to Japan, which 'began to

---

[64] For example, Mercator's famous 21-sheet wall-chart, *Nova et aucta orbis terra descriptio ad usum navigantium emendate accommodate* (1569) – the first to use the projection which Wright would then recreate – used them.

[65] Sarah Tyacke, 'Chartmaking in England and its contexts, 1500–1660', in *The History of Cartography*, vol. 3: *Part 2*, ed. David Woodford (Chicago, 2007), 1722–53, esp. p. 1744. Even later maps which acknowledged their indebtedness to Wright's projection seem oddly uninfluenced by him. John Thornton's *A New Mapp of the World According to Mr. Edward Wright Commonly Called Mercator's Projection* (1685) and *A New and Correct Mapp of the World According to Mr Edward Wright Commonly*

assume its modern shape', and to 'traces of the first appearance of the Dutch under [Cornelis de] Houtman at Bantam'.[66] Yet it is not clear to which Indies Maria's map refers. John Dover Wilson, for example, concluded that '"The Indies", i.e. America, are to be found in all maps of the world at this period, but in "the new map", ... take a much larger place than in any before.'[67] Philip Armstrong claims that Wright's map featured 'additions to the western coastline of the Americas, made during Drake's circumnavigation of 1577'.[68] However, if anything, there is less of America than on earlier or contemporaneous maps. In the bottom left-hand corner of the map (in its second state), a cartouche tells us that, after Drake's voyage in 1577, 'the southwest coast of America called Chili was found not to trend to the northwestwards as it hath been described but to the eastwards of the north as it is here set downe'. On the top right-hand corner, the map states that the distance between Cape Mendocino and Cape California (Baja peninsula) had been overestimated 'on sea charts ... to be 1200 or 1300 leagues [but] is scarce so much as 600'. Rather than augment, therefore, the Wright–Molyneux decreases its 'western' 'Indies', scaling back the west coasts of the north and south continents. Arguably, the map's eastern augmentations (the basis of Coote's argument) are even more negligible than their western ones. As Ronald Shirley states, while 'The chart is supposedly the "new map"', 'the phrase "the augmentation of the Indies" is a little puzzling', because while 'The Wright-Molyneux map certainly delineates the East Indies and Japan fully', it does so 'in no greater detail than maps by others such as Plancius, Ortelius or Mercator in circulation during the previous decade'.[69] To quote John Gillies, 'Coote appears to have overstated the degree to which Wright's map does in fact show '"an augmentation of the Indies"'.[70]

My point here is not that Coote was wrong about the identity of Maria's map – Shakespeare may well have been inspired, at least in part, by the Wright–Molyneux map. In part, my point is that we should doubt that Maria is specifically referring to this map and no other. But, more importantly, it is that we should not assume that there is a map to be identified. The map sounds like a real map – the phrase 'the new map with the augmentation of the Indies' sounds like a map title – but to peg Maria's map to a real map in the real world is to limit how the map reference functions in *Twelfth Night*, a play that dramatizes knowledge competency, within both the communities in Illyria and those watching the play.

How might we interpret 'the new map with the augmentation of the Indies' as 'map-effect' rather than map? And how might have Middle Templars?

These questions seem significant when we consider the person to whom this map reference is attached: Malvolio, an outsider to the Illyrian community which knows more than he does; and one of the auditors of Maria's description – Sir Andrew Aguecheek, an outsider to the Illyrian community which knows a whole lot more than he does. Figures of derision, to be sure, Malvolio and Andrew may also have been recognized by the audience as distorted mirrors of themselves. It is conceivable, after all, that Middle Templars were similarly unsure of the veracity of Pigrogromitus and the Vapians. It is conceivable too that the audience saw Malvolio's heathenish 'strange manner' as something that they might all too readily adopt themselves in a bid to perform competency. Commentators and editors have fallen down the hermeneutic rabbit hole in other regards when it comes to this play, as Adam Zucker has demonstrated.[71] Why not also with Maria's map? Importantly, the map functions not only as an allusion to a (possibly real) material object outside the bounds of the play, but also as an example of what Henry S. Turner calls 'the map conceit', a poetic trope that 'evoked a visual image that encapsulated, in condensed form, emotional states, abstract qualities, or metaphysical ideas'.[72] As an example of the map conceit, it indexes Malvolio's strangeness, with its Indian augmentations stressing just how extreme, even profane, his courtly performance has become. Moreover, the map seems to be evoked to lead astray any audiences that try to locate it in the real world. It tempts audience members to see

Called Mercator's Projection (dated between 1733 and 1748) pare down Wright's extensive rhumb-lines to just two sets of compass and rhumb-lines in the eastern and western hemispheres.

[66] Coote, 'New map', p. 95.
[67] *Twelfth Night: The Cambridge Dover Wilson Shakespeare*, 148n, pp. 77–8.
[68] Philip Armstrong, 'Spheres of influence: cartography and the gaze in Shakespearean tragedy and history', *Shakespeare Studies* 23 (1995), 39–70; p. 43.
[69] Ronald W. Shirley, *The Mapping of the World: Early Printed World Maps 1472–1700* (London, 1993), p. 239.
[70] John Gillies, *Shakespeare and the Geography of Difference* (Cambridge, 1994), p. 41.
[71] Zucker, '*Twelfth Night* and the philology of nonsense'.
[72] Henry S. Turner, 'Literature and Mapping in early Modern England, 1520–1688', in *The History of Cartography*, vol. 3: *Part 1*, ed. David Woodford (Chicago, 2007), 412–26; p. 412.

themselves in Malvolio – subject to ridicule (and hence 'Unguided and unfriended') if they adhere to suspect knowledge as a means by which to gain social credibility. It tempts them to be like Andrew, wordlessly (in this instance) nodding along to a piece of geographical knowledge about which he almost certainly (given his ignorance elsewhere in the play in such matters) has no knowledge.

★

That the Wright–Molyneux was Shakespeare's map reference has been taken to be a Shakes-fact. That said, to criticize repetition of C. H. Coote's claims would suggest a certainty that the Wright–Molyneux map is *not* the map that Shakespeare glanced at. It could be: some of the play's first known audience at Middle Temple, knowledgeable about developments in descriptive and mathematical geography for intellectual, financial, professional, and personal reasons, would likely have recognized it as such. But it might not be: this appeal to fake authority is consistent with the play, and consistent too with the atmosphere of Middle Temple, where geographical knowledge was a constitutive part of the performance of one's social competency, but its affectation a cause for derision and exclusion. The repetition of Coote's claim as quasi-fact not only makes Shakespeare conform to that ideal of knowledgeable, cosmopolitan, mathematically inclined, and map-minded that many of us would like to imagine him to have been – it also downplays the ways in which this play thinks through knowledge less as something to be possessed and more as something that defines community, in terms of both those 'in the picture' and those who are not. This tension would have been readily apparent to the play's first known audience, who lived, worked, and competed within a community where knowledge could be weaponized, even as that knowledge itself was uncertain and ever changing in an age where orthodoxies about the world were coming undone.

MUSIC AND DRAMA AT THE EARLY MODERN INNS OF COURT: *TWELFTH NIGHT* AND *HYDE PARK*

SIMON SMITH

Item to Mr Hamerton for the musicions and Actors dinner
the Maskeing daie   [3] 4 li.[1]

The Lincoln's Inn 'Black Book' includes amongst its many financial records a reckoning of the costs borne by the Inn when they staged the 1613 *Memorable Masque* in collaboration with Middle Temple. Among their enormous outlay of well over £1,000, we find the above item: dinner for the musicians and actors on the day of the masque (15 February).[2] Presumably eaten before the performers processed from the Master of the Rolls' house to the Whitehall performance space, the meal glimpsed in this archival record evokes a compelling image of interaction and even intimacy between professional musical performers (including such eminent figures as John Dowland and Philip Rosseter) and theatrical performers (seemingly Innsmen rather than hired professionals) within the cultural milieu of the Inns of Court.[3] Indeed, to envisage Inns of Court performances as occasions where 'musicions and Actors' might sit and converse together before the show is to emphasize the spirit of creative collaboration and exchange that theatrical performance entails.

What is more, these creative exchanges cross many boundaries. Some of these would undoubtedly have felt significant to those concerned, while others may have more to do with later critical and disciplinary frameworks. A law student from an especially privileged background choosing to perform in a masque might work closely with a professional musician of more humble social origins to perfect his dance steps, for instance; or an aspirant poet might collaborate with an established and experienced composer to produce music and text for a performance. The status boundaries being crossed could work both ways around, too: an Innsman from a more modest family seeking social advancement through a court career may

only dream of the kind of familiarity and ease with royal household culture that a long-standing court musician might have, for example.[4] It is also worth noting that these exchanges were not always a matter of amateur Innsmen hiring in musical expertise to fill the gaps in their own competencies, either: the 1634 *Triumph of Peace* masque instead saw the recruitment of James Shirley, probably the most prominent professional dramatist then working, to supply text, while some of the music for the masque was composed by Middle Templar and amateur musician Bulstrode Whitelocke, by 1634 an established and high-flying lawyer holding the post of Recorder of Abingdon.[5] When performances were mounted at the early modern Inns of Court, rigid separations along lines of status, occupation and even aspiration soon break down. Neither are musical and theatrical culture readily disentangled from one another within this community, as this article will explore.

The early modern Inns of Court have long been recognized by musicologists as significant environments

---

[1] LI Arch: A1a6, fols. 526r–7v, transcribed in *Records of Early English Drama: Inns of Court*, ed. Alan H. Nelson and John R. Elliott, 3 vols. (Cambridge, 2010) [hereafter cited as '*REED*'], vol. 1, pp. 156–7.

[2] For the full accounts, see *REED*, vol. 1, pp. 156–7.

[3] For an account of the procession, see the published description: George Chapman, *The Memorable Maske of the two Honorable Houses or Inns of Court the Middle Temple, and Lyncolns Inne* (London, [1613]), A1r–A4v. On the personnel involved, see Martin Wiggins with Catherine Richardson, *British Drama 1553–1642: A Catalogue*, 11 vols. (Oxford, 2012–), vol. 6: #1699.

[4] On socially aspirant courtiers at the Inns, see Jackie Watson, 'Sense and community: *Twelfth Night* and early modern playgoing', in *Shakespeare/Sense: Contemporary Readings in Sensory Culture*, ed. Simon Smith (London, 2020), 224–44; pp. 224–7.

[5] See Ira Clark, 'Shirley, James', and Ruth Spalding, 'Whitelocke, Bulstrode', in *Oxford Dictionary of National Biography* (Oxford, 2004–) (hereafter *ODNB*), www.oxforddnb.com.

for music – for both the professional employment opportunities they provided and the widespread culture of recreational performance they fostered.[6] Likewise, theatre historians have been attentive to the Inns' rich theatrical culture that encompassed regular amateur performance and, by the seventeenth century, habitual professional performance, not to mention the various Innsmen – such as John Marston – who would go on to write for the commercial stage.[7] Certain occasions have received particularly extensive critical attention, such as the Candlemas 1602 *Twelfth Night* performance at Middle Temple recorded in John Manningham's diary, or the 1634 *Triumph of Peace* masque, the music for which is especially well documented in terms both of surviving notation, and of information about personnel, cost and practical arrangements.[8] Yet the parliament books, stewards' accounts, miscellaneous loose receipts in unsorted archive boxes, and other similarly unglamorous records offer many further glimpses of musical and theatrical culture at the Inns, all now readily available thanks to Alan H. Nelson and John R. Elliott's *Records of Early English Drama* Inns of Court volume. Full attention to these records not only allows a clearer picture of the wider musical and theatrical culture in which events like the 1602 *Twelfth Night* performance sat: the evidence also suggests close links between the professional musicians and the acting companies who were both engaged regularly at Middle Temple and Inner Temple in the seventeenth century. Focusing primarily on the performance of commercial drama at the Inns by professional playing companies, rather than the better-documented masques and entertainments that have been well studied by previous critics, this article proposes a new account of how musical culture and dramatic culture intersected at the Inns. In doing so, it suggests why this intersection is significant for our understanding of commercial drama, taking as its case studies the two extant plays with known Inns performances in the first half of the seventeenth century: *Twelfth Night*, and James Shirley's *Hyde Park*.

DRAMATIC RECORDS

Records of plays being performed at the Inns reach back into the fifteenth century at the Inns of Chancery, indicating a long-standing association between drama and feast days or holidays by the time professional playing companies were establishing a firm foothold in London in the mid-Elizabethan period.[9] This appears to have been a hybrid culture, combining some performances 'played by the Gentlemen of the same house, the

ground, and matter whereof, is devised by some of the Gentlemen of the house', as Henry VIII's royal commission on the Inns noted, and others by visiting players.[10] The Children of the Chapel visited Lincoln's Inn on Candlemas (2 February) in 1565 and 1566, for example, as did Lord Rich's players for the same feast day in 1570. Familiar – and extant – 'in-house' plays such as *Gorboduc* (Inner Temple, 1562) and *Supposes* (Gray's, 1567) punctuate the records until *The Misfortunes of Arthur* (Gray's) in 1578, after which visiting playing companies seem to have been preferred exclusively for plays, and in-house energies seem to have focused instead on revels such as *Le Prince d'Amour* and the *Gesta Grayorum*.[11]

---

[6] See Robert W. Wienpahl, *Music at the Inns of Court during the Reigns of Elizabeth, James, and Charles* (Ann Arbor, 1979); John R. Elliott Jr, 'Invisible evidence: finding musicians in the archives of the Inns of Court, 1446–1642', *Royal Musical Association Research Chronicle* 26 (1993), 45–57.

[7] See chapters by Lorna Hutson, Bradin Cormack, Richard C. McCoy and Alan H. Nelson in *The Intellectual and Cultural Worlds of the Early Modern Inns of Court*, ed. Jayne Elisabeth Archer, Elizabeth Goldring and Sarah Knight (Manchester, 2011), 245–314; Jackie Watson, 'Satirical expectations: Shakespeare's Inns of Court audiences', *Actes des Congrès de La Société Française Shakespeare* 33 (2015), https://doi.org/10.4000/shakespeare.3352.

[8] Manningham's diary entry is transcribed in *REED*, vol. 2, p. 685. For recent work on the *Twelfth Night* performance, see Watson, 'Sense and community'. For the records relating to *The Triumph of Peace*, see *REED*, vol. 1, pp. 234–341; vol. 2, pp. 591–612. The extensive scholarship on the masque includes Andrew Ashbee, 'James Shirley's The Triumph of Peace revisited', *The Consort: The Journal of The Dolmetsch Foundation* 72 (2016), 31–48; Martin Butler, 'Politics and the masque: "The Triumph of Peace"', *Seventeenth Century* 2 (1987), 117–41; Brent Whitted, 'Street politics: Charles I and the Inns of Court's Triumph of Peace', *Seventeenth Century* 24 (2009), 1–25; Stephen Tabor, 'James Shirley's Triumph of Peace: analyzing Greg's nightmare', *Studies in Bibliography: Papers of the Bibliographical Society of the University of Virginia* 60 (2018), 107–211; John R. Elliott Jr, 'The Folger manuscript of The Triumph of Peace procession', *English Manuscript Studies 1100–1700* 3 (1992), 193–215; Andrew J. Sabol, 'New documents on Shirley's masque "The Triumph of Peace"', *Music & Letters* 47 (1966), 10–26, https://doi.org/10.1093/ml/47.1.10; Murray Lefkowitz, 'New light on Shirley's "Triumph of Peace"', *Journal of the American Musicological Society* 18 (1965), 42–66.

[9] *REED*, vol. 2, p. 758.

[10] Edward Waterhouse, *Fortescus illustratus* (London, 1663), Wing W1046, p. 546, transcribed in *REED*, vol. 1, p. 62.

[11] *REED*, vol. 2, pp. 758–9. However, see Tom Harrison and James Loxley's recent argument that annotations in a copy of the 1640 Ben Jonson folio may indicate a return to amateur performance at Gray's Inn later in the seventeenth century: 'Amateur theatre at the early modern Inns of Court? The implications of a performance copy of Jonson's 1640 Folio', *Early Theatre* 26 (2023), 93–132.

The surviving account of the 1594–1595 Gray's Inn *Gesta Grayorum* Christmas festivities records a performance of *The Comedy of Errors* by visiting players on 28 December alongside in-house activities, but there is not sufficient evidence from the 1590s to indicate that such Christmas performances were customary at this time.[12] What is clear from the records, however, as Elliott and Nelson's aforementioned *REED* volume has established, is that feast day performances on 1 November (All Saints') and 2 February (Candlemas) by professional playing companies had become a convention by the early seventeenth century. These feast days – often referred to as the 'revels' – involved a meal, followed by dancing. The records even suggest standing arrangements with particular companies by the end of the Caroline period, with the King's Men the only company to appear in the Inner Temple records after 1630, and Queen Henrietta Maria's Men and Beeston's Boys both used extensively by Middle Temple in the late 1630s and early 1640s.[13]

The Inner Temple accounts survive from 1605–1606 onwards and preserve a clear pattern of payments in accordance with the convention of All Saints' and Candlemas plays.[14] Moreover, the fact that the pattern is already in place at the point from which the records happen to have survived suggests this is the first archival trace of a longer-standing custom, rather than an innovation of 1605–1606. The convention is even acknowledged explicitly in the Inner Temple 'Parliament Book' for 1611–1612, following a suppression of the custom in 1610–1611:

Where[of] of late yeares vpon the two festivall dayes of All Saintes and Candlemasse playes haue beene vsed after dinner for recreacion which haue lately beene layd downe by order in Parliament It is now ordered that the same order shall henceforth stand repealed.[15]

The ban appears still to have been in place in November 1611, since the All Saints' revels saw no play, albeit the lifting was complete in time for a theatrical performance the following Candlemas.[16] Where scholars had previously wondered whether the 2 February 1602 *Twelfth Night* production at Middle Temple Hall was a special arrangement (or even a specific commission), then, *REED* paints a clear documentary picture of regular Inns of Court performance on Candlemas and All Saints' Day by professional playing companies. This suggests the plays would have been drawn from the companies' standing repertories – just as they seem to have been for the court Christmas season each year – rather than being the kind of special commissions associated with masques at the Inns.[17]

Whilst the Inns' records are patchy, and far more likely to record the fact of a play's performance than its identity, we do know of five named plays performed professionally on feast days at the Inns in the seventeenth century through to the civil war, as well as *The Comedy of Errors* performed in 1594 at Gray's. To the familiar 1602 *Twelfth Night* performance, we can add a record of James Shirley's comedy *Hyde Park*, performed at Middle Temple on 1 November 1632, as well as three plays now presumed lost: an 'Oxford Tragedy' (Inner Temple; Candlemas 1608); 'The Bridegroom and the Madman' (Middle Temple, Candlemas *c.*1619); and 'City Shuffler' (Middle Temple, All Saints' Day 1633).[18] These playtexts and titles are tantalizingly suggestive about the parts of a company's repertory that may have been most popular for Inns' performances, although of course they represent only a tiny sample of the dozens that came to the Inns across the decades, records of these particular performances only surviving by chance.

Whilst it is difficult to establish genre from a title alone, 'The Bridegroom and the Madman' is described as a 'Comody' on the payment receipt, while the tricks of a 'city shuffler' would be very much at home in a comedy in the tradition of *Beggars' Bush* and other plays that bring roguery onstage as a central attraction of a play.[19] If so, all

---

12 *Gesta Grayorum, or the Prince of Purpoole* (London, 1688), Wing C444, pp. 1–68, transcribed in *REED*, vol. 3, pp. 380–435.

13 See 'Appendix 8' in *REED* for a full summary and analysis of all documented performances (vol. 2, pp. 757–61).

14 See *REED*, vol. 1, p. 137 onwards.

15 IT Arch: PAR/1/2, fol. 105v, transcribed in *REED*, vol. 1, pp. 146–7.

16 In the November 1611 accounts, the regular payment of £5 or £6 for a feast-day play found in the Inner Temple records for this period is replaced by a total outlay of £4 10s for alternative All Saints' revels entertainment. Candlemas then records a £6 payment 'for a play' – IT Arch: FIN/1/1, fols. 64r–v, transcribed in *REED*, vol. 1, p. 147.

17 Anthony Arlidge has made the most extensive claims in this regard, even suggesting that the small roles of Curio and Fabian may have been written for Innsmen joining in with the professional players, in *Shakespeare and the Prince of Love: The Feast of Misrule in the Middle Temple* (London, 2000).

18 *REED*, vol. 2, pp. 757–61. The payment receipt for 'The Bridegroom and the Madman' simply states 'Candlemas Day last' (MT Arch: MT.7/GDE/10, transcribed in *REED*, vol. 1, pp. 204–5), but has been categorically dated by Tucker Orbison to 1612–1619, with 1619 the most likely date. See Tucker Orbison, 'Traces of two Jacobean dramatic performances at the Middle Temple', *Yearbook of English Studies* 1 (1971), 55–62.

19 In 1633, 'shuffler' was a relatively new term for 'One who acts in a shifty or evasive manner; a slippery, shifty person'. See *OED*, 'shuffler, n. 2'.

four named plays performed at Middle Temple would be comedies, with Inner Temple represented exclusively by the 'Oxford Tragedy'. A preference for comedy might, among other things, imply a taste for song-rich plays. Likewise, the stage tradition of performing madness through music, from Ophelia to the Passionate Lord in Fletcher's *The Nice Valour*, makes the loss of 'The Bridegroom and the Madman' particularly frustrating with music in mind.[20]

As we have seen, the evidence suggests that professional playing companies would have drawn on their current repertories for these occasions, rather than producing special commissions. Yet, if a company's standing annual commitments include feast day Inns performances, as well as court performances, it seems reasonable to imagine playwrights and company members considering the practicalities and possibilities of transferring a play to those spaces in addition to thinking about the commercial venues that would see the great majority of a play's performances.[21] Perhaps playwrights might even write in such a way as to take advantage of the resources of each performance context, too.

MUSICAL RECORDS

Professional musicians are even more prominent in the Inns' records than visiting players: they occur repeatedly in account books across the period, being retained and remunerated for their duties on 1 November and 2 February, these entries often immediately alongside payments to playing companies for their contribution to those same evenings. The Inns appear to have retained 'house' musician servants from as early as the fifteenth century, with Robert Jugleger and John Brayne, alias Drayne, the first named individuals to appear in the record, in the Lincoln's Inn accounts for 1546–1547.[22] Middle Temple's records are especially patchy until the 1630s, but nonetheless identify Nicholas Killingsworth as a 'minstrell of this temple' in 1551–1552, and in 1572–1573 discuss a payment structure combining an annual salary with a one-off payment for revels duties.[23] This payment structure recurs at other Inns through the period, and may well represent the visible portion of a remuneration regime that also included ad hoc collection for the musicians on revels evenings, as Nelson has speculated.[24]

The distinction between salary and payments for the revels might give the impression that the latter represent additional recompense for irregular contributions, but in fact the full records indicate that this was simply a convention for rewarding a regular and expected commitment. Besides the fact that, where multi-year account books survive, such entries are typically as regular as those for salary payments, the repeated honouring of these fees even when the revels were cancelled suggest that they were essentially treated as a standing commitment on both sides. Entries survive from as early as 1578 and 1582 for payments honoured when revelling at Inner Temple was thwarted by plague (and, in the latter case, all of Michaelmas term cancelled), while at Gray's in 1604, 'Mr Michell & the musicions' received a standard 40 shillings (£2) 'for their attendance' – which is to say committing their availability for Candlemas evening, despite the fact that 'the late infection' meant 'they then did not performe their service'.[25] Perhaps equally telling is the indignation of the Inner Temple musicians who, in February 1590, 'greatly complaine[d]' that 'they receive great damage for that during the tyme of Christmas they neither be reteyned in service here as before they have ben nor yet have convenient notice given unto them from the fellowshipped

---

[20] 'The Bridegroom and the Madman' is included in a King's Men repertory list of 1641, preventing its printing without their consent, and also appears to be referenced in a damaged manuscript in Sir George Buc's hand, perhaps indicating that it was under consideration for court performance in the 1610s. See *The Lost Plays Database*, https://lostplays.folger.edu/Bridegroom_and_the_Madman,_The. E. K. Chambers speculated that the play may in fact be *The Nice Valour*, since the latter appears to have ended up in the King's Men's repertory in order to be printed in the 1647 Beaumont and Fletcher folio, but this seems unlikely: *The Nice Valour* does not feature a bridegroom, and is now generally dated to 1622. See Chambers, 'Review of Frank Marcham, The King's Office of the Revels, 1610–1622 (London: Frank Marcham, 1925)', *Review of English Studies* 1 (1925), 479–84 (p. 482); Gary Taylor, 'Thomas Middleton, *The Nice Valour* and the Court of James 1', *Court Historian* 6 (2001), 1–27; Wiggins with Richardson, *British Drama*, vol. 7, #2023.

[21] Tracey Hill has shown, too, that a company's commitments might also include performances in a livery company's hall during a feast, and at a city inn like the Bull, the latter practice persisting well into the era of purpose-built playhouses: Tracey Hill, 'Drama beyond the playhouses', in *The Arden Handbook of Shakespeare and Early Modern Drama: Perspectives on Culture, Performance and Identity*, ed. Michelle M. Dowd and Tom Rutter (London, 2023), 147–62.

[22] LI Arch: A1a4, fols. 195v, 209v, 222r, transcribed in *REED*, vol. 1, pp. 72–3.

[23] MT Arch: MT.1/MPA/No. 3, fols. 6v, 105v, transcribed in *REED*, vol. 1, pp. 75, 97.

[24] Alan H. Nelson and John R. Elliott, 'Drama, entertainment, and music', in *REED*, vol. 1, p. xxxi.

[25] IT Arch: PAR/1/1, fols. 204v, 220v, transcribed in *REED*, vol. 1, pp. 101, 106; GI Arch: PEN/1/1, fol. 261v, transcribed in *REED*, vol. 1, p. 136.

of this howse of their determynacion so as they maye provide for themselves elsewhere'.[26]

Parliament resolved to give them at least three weeks' notice of Christmas plans in future, the absence of which would free the musicians 'to provide for themselves elsewhere during all the saide tyme of Christmas', as well as granting a rather generous fee for Candlemas duties that year that may have served as unspoken recompense for the lost income.[27]

Early modern professional musicians often held multiple appointments alongside ad hoc engagements, from Robert Johnson seemingly working as a composer for the King's Men whilst a court lutenist in the 1610s, to William Saunder working concurrently as a city wait and a theatre musician in 1641.[28] It is no surprise, then, that in later years, musicians known to have roles in commercial theatre bands appear regularly among those receiving payment from the Inns, including Geoffrey Collins whom we find collecting and distributing the Middle Temple musicians' yearly fee in the 1630s.[29] Collins is listed among the King's Men's 'musicians and other necessary attendants' from Henry Herbert's famous protection list of 1624 (this was a document to protect from arrest the personnel required by the King's Men for their court performances that Christmas season; it is the principal source of information about the company's musical personnel in the post-Shakespearian period), and by 1634 he appears as a musician of the Cockpit theatre in documents relating to the *Triumph of Peace* masque.[30] Nelson and Elliott also note multiple musicians engaged at Inner Temple towards the end of the period – including John Adson and the aforementioned William Saunder – who are known to have been employed by the King's Men, too.[31] Cognate interpersonal relationships between musicians who might have played for the revels on Candlemas 1602 and those members of the Lord Chamberlain's Men who presented *Twelfth Night* are a little harder to track in the absence of equivalent documentary evidence from earlier years. But early modern London was a small world, and never more so than in the professional circles of performers with regular court and Inns commitments.

Of course, the principal duties of the musicians at the revels were dance-related, just as the dancing was the heart of the festivities: Bulstrode Whitelocke's extensive account of his time as Master of the Revels for Middle Temple in 1628–9 has much to say about dancing (as well as financial matters and disputes over apt governance structures), but makes no mention at all of any plays presented as part of those revels, for instance. This is despite the fact that he was an avid playgoer, his account book for the same period recording numerous visits to 'ye blackfryars playhouse' (presumably to the strains of 'Whitelock's coranto'), at a cost 1s 6d a time.[32] Yet with musicians potentially on site, perhaps with nothing to do but refresh themselves in anticipation of dancing to follow (the 1628–1629 Inner Temple Christmas Accounts includes 11s 8d spent on 'wine for the musick' [i.e. musicians], on top of their substantial fee), the opportunity to draw upon an available human resource seems a significant one.[33]

That the musicians are likely to have been around during the revels for much more of the evening than the dancing alone is confirmed by a number of glimpses of their presence in the records. In addition to sporadic payments for spending an extra evening in rehearsals to allow the Innsmen to practise their dancing, a bread-related dispute at Lincoln's Inn in 1602 indicates that the musicians were given supper before the revels that concluded the evening:

> Wheras at this Counsell it was informed by Mr Hughes and Mr Ley
> two of the Masters of the benche
> ... that the musicions claime to have after their supper & the revells two loaffes of bredd a pece to carye home with them
> ... which Claymes, Challenges & demaundes are vtterly misliked
> therefore it is ordered that from henceforth not any suche allowances or Claymes be permitted but altogether abolished[.][34]

26 IT Arch: PAR/1/2, fol. 11r, transcribed in *REED*, vol. 1, p. 115.

27 IT Arch: PAR/1/2, fol. 11r, transcribed in *REED*, vol. 1, p. 115.

28 See Matthew Spring, 'Johnson, Robert (c. 1583–1633)', in *ODNB*; Nelson and Elliott, 'Drama, Entertainment, and Music', p. xxx.

29 MT Arch: MT.2/TRB/1, fol. 59r, transcribed in *REED*, vol. 1, p. 355; MT.2/TRB/2, fol. 15r, transcribed in *REED*, vol. 1, p. 357; MT.2/TRB/4, fol. 17, transcribed in *REED*, vol. 1, p. 362.

30 See British Library Add. MS 19256, transcribed in G. E. Bentley, *The Jacobean and Caroline Stage*, 7 vols. (Oxford, 1941–68) vol. 1, pp. 15–16; Longleat House: Longleat MSS Parcel 2, Number 9, item 13A, transcribed in *REED*, vol. 1, pp. 305–6.

31 Nelson and Elliott, 'Drama, entertainment, and music', pp. xxix–xxx.

32 *REED*, vol. 2, pp. 806–7. Whitelocke boasts extensively about his Coranto and its apparent popularity at Blackfriars in his autobiographical 'Annals', transcribed in *REED*, vol. 1, p. 279. For traces of other playgoing Innsmen, see the diaries of John Greene (LI) and Edward Heath (IT), also in *REED*, Appendix 14.

33 IT Arch: COM/9/1, fol. 55v, transcribed in *REED*, vol. 1, p. 218.

34 LI Arch: A1a6, fol. 105Br, transcribed in *REED*, vol. 1, p. 135.

Besides providing an unusually explicit example of lawyers keeping bread from the mouths of working people's families, the reference to the musicians' customary supper – and with it the implication that their subsistence whilst engaged by the Inn is already covered – gives a clear impression of their presence onsite throughout the festivities, rather than their simply dropping in to fulfil their obligations.

A playing company's opportunistic use of available resources would by no means be unprecedented in the period, either: *The Winter's Tale*'s apparent incorporation of choreography and satyr costumes acquired from the King's Men's participation in a recent court masque is one comparable instance.[35] Such revels-night contributions over and above the musicians' primary duty of playing for the dancing would presumably entail further remuneration, though, and this is indeed documented, albeit somewhat patchily. The payment receipt for 'The Bridegroom and the Madman' confirms that the performance entailed specific musical costs, on top of the players' £12 fee: '[the actors] being at charges for extreordynary mvsikve, for the better Content of thowse reverent persons [i.e. the judges and the benchers,] toward that Charg [the actors have] recevd more xis'.[36]

There are a number of ambiguities here, including whether the playing company subcontracted this 'extreordynary mvsikve' from the revels musicians or from another group. There is precedent for hiring multiple groups of musicians for feast evenings: the 1611–1612 Inner Temple records preserve separate payments for the revels musicians and for a 'Consort of Musicke the same day', the latter part of the substitute entertainment in the absence of a stage-play on All Saints' 1611 – alongside 'Antickes or puppittes'.[37] Moreover, the fact that Prince Charles's Men say they have borne the musicians' 'charges' themselves before seeking to claim some of the cost back from the Inn, rather than Under-Treasurer Richard Baldwin simply paying the musicians directly, may suggest that these are not 'house' musicians whom Baldwin would be paying anyway, but perhaps others associated with the company rather than with Middle Temple directly.[38]

Another suggestive record appears in the 1628–1629 Inner Temple accounts, when 'by direction of M*aster* T*reasourer* att the Bench Table', the musicians received an additional £1 'in regard of theire extraordinarie Musicke on Candlemas night and some other nights'. This was on top of the standard 4 marks which had been their conventional remuneration in the previous three years' accounts, seemingly covering standard revels duties

at All Saints', 5 November and Candlemas.[39] There was indeed 'a playe on Candlemas day' that year, for which Inner Temple's then-standard fee of £7 was paid. Might 'extraordinarie Musicke' once again indicate musical augmentations to the unnamed company's performance,[40] this time explicitly supplied by the same musicians tasked with accompanying the revels?

A final possible example appears on a loose sheet in the Middle Temple records. During the same 1618–1619 season that apparently saw 'The Bridegroom and the Madman' performed with its 'extreordynary mvsikve' on 2 February, Baldwin records a 40s payment to Andrew Tye 'for the vse of my selfe and the reste of the mvsicions of this howse ... in full discharge of the mvsicke for this yeare'. Yet despite this 'full discharge' to the 'howse' musicians, Baldwin also records an additional 4s payment to 'henery feld for all holland daye for playing vppon the treble viallyn'.[41] Whilst the phrase 'extraordinary music' does not appear this time, it is just possible that this small fee to a musician not otherwise connected to Middle Temple in the documentary record[42] might reflect some musical additions upon the 'treble viallyn' to the now forgotten play that was presumably given at the Inn for All Saints' Day

35 See Melissa D. Aaron, *Global Economics: A History of the Theater Business, the Chamberlain's/King's Men, and Their Plays, 1599–1642* (Newark, 2005), p. 94.

36 MT Arch: MT.7/GDE/10, transcribed in *REED*, vol. 1, pp. 204–5.

37 IT Arch: FIN/1/1, fols. 64r–v, transcribed in *REED*, vol. 1, p. 147.

38 Elliott notes that in the last two decades of the Elizabethan period, Lincoln's Inn paid their 'Revels Musicians' by means of the Steward directly collecting contributions from Innsmen, rather than by Treasurer's disbursement from the central account (itself ultimately funded by member contributions). It would not be unprecedented, then, for contributions to have been raised in this manner in 1628–1629, nor indeed for similar collections to have taken place in other years without leaving a trace in the accounts if they were then paid directly. See 'Invisible Evidence', pp. 49–50.

39 IT Arch: FIN/1/1, fols. 178v, 184v, 192r, 198v, transcribed in *REED*, vol. 1, pp. 214, 215, 217, 221.

40 The company was possibly the King's Men, who worked regularly with Inner Temple in the 1620s and 1630s, though Queen Henrietta Maria's Men had given the 1628 Candlemas performance the year before.

41 MT Arch: MT.7/GDE/9, transcribed in *REED*, vol. 1, p. 205.

42 Some years later, Field re-emerges as a performer in *The Triumph of Peace* (1633–1634), member of the Blackfriars theatre band, and leader of the Inner Temple consort (1636–1637). See Longleat House: Longleat MSS Parcel 2, Number 9, items 13, fol. 1r, and 13A, transcribed in *REED*, vol. 1, pp. 302, 305–6; IT Arch: PAR/1/2, fol. 247v, transcribed in *REED*, vol. 1, p. 344.

1618, in the very same year that Middle Temple appear to have embraced the practice of adding 'extreordynary mvsikve' to their Candlemas feast play – and paying for the privilege.

HYDE PARK

If professional musicians were present on revels nights, and potentially willing to supply the players with 'extra-ordinary music' for the right fee, then what might this have meant for the plays presented in the course of the festivities at a space like Middle Temple Hall? Strikingly, both *Twelfth Night* and *Hyde Park* offer intriguing opportunities to make use of such musicians during their performance, and there is even scope for some metatheatrical play with their presence in both cases. *Hyde Park* was allowed by the Master of the Revels on 20 April 1632 and was subsequently played at the Cockpit by Queen Henrietta Maria's Men, reaching Middle Temple on All Saints' Day the same year.[43] There is no evidence to suggest that Shirley conceptualized the play as Inns-specific, unlike *The Triumph of Peace* on which he would work the year after *Hyde Park* was performed at Middle Temple, and by which time he had been admitted as an associated member of Gray's Inn himself.[44] Nonetheless, *Hyde Park*'s Inns-flexible – and indeed Inns-resonant – moments are striking, perhaps indicating why it was selected. Scholarship interested in the play's early performance history has tended to focus on its public-stage context – Eleanor Collins in relation to Queen Henrietta Maria's Men's repertory and the Cockpit audience, and Eugene Giddens in relation to the Cockpit's physical theatre space – with the Inns performance largely overlooked.[45] The generative recent Revels edition of the play does not mention this performance at all in its stage history, for instance, although it usefully notes that *Hyde Park* is 'particularly adaptable to different venues and touring', thanks to its exclusive use of hand-props.[46] Shirley Bell has also recently demonstrated how fundamental music is to this play, as part of a wider study of Caroline theatre music.[47]

The play dates from a far better-documented period in the Middle Temple records than does *Twelfth Night*: as well as the payment receipt confirming the play's performance on 1 November 1632, further loose-sheet receipts survive. One reveals that Prince Charles's Men were the company engaged for 2 February 1633 but that the performance was 'put off' despite the company's attendance that evening. Another records that Geoffrey Collins collected an annual musicians' fee of 53s 4d (i.e. 4

marks) for 1632–1633, as well as a further 10s 'for our paines in the hall with the Revellers one night*es* practise'.[48] The larger payment to Collins may be relevant to *Hyde Park*, since it includes an extra mark on top of the £2 conventionally paid for musicians' salaries through the period. This may reflect further duties at the 5 November feast (at Inner Temple at least, this occasion was often remunerated separately at this rate),[49] or perhaps simply indicates the negotiation skills of the Middle Temple musicians. It is by no means out of the question, though, that the musicians – including at least one member, in Collins, who by the early 1630s appears to have been employed as a theatre musician at the Cockpit, where *Hyde Park* had recently premiered – were by this period contributing additional music to revels plays including *Hyde Park*, as part of the justification for a higher salary.[50]

Fittingly for a revels evening, *Hyde Park* is a play about dancing, in substantial part. One of the three main plotlines revolves around a supposed widow's remarriage, and her still-living husband, Bonavent, who is presumed long drowned yet has returned to London disguised (or perhaps merely unrecognizably bearded).[51] His enforced and incompetent dancing after gatecrashing her second wedding is a catalyst for the plot, and indeed for another of the play's dominant interests: threats of

43 Wiggins with Richardson, *British Drama*, vol. 9, #2367.

44 See Clark, 'Shirley, James'.

45 Eleanor Collins, 'Queen Henrietta Maria's Men and the Cockpit repertory, 1625–1637', unpublished doctoral thesis (University of Birmingham, 2008), pp. 262–3; Eugene Giddens, 'Introduction', in James Shirley, *Hyde Park*, ed. Eugene Giddens (Manchester, 2022), 16–23.

46 *Hyde Park*, ed. Giddens, pp. 16–17.

47 Shirley Bell, 'Music in Caroline drama: Richard Brome, James Shirley and Ben Jonson', unpublished doctoral thesis (Sheffield Hallam University, 2022), pp. 156–78.

48 MT Arch: MT.7/GCE/16, transcribed in *REED*, vol. 1, pp. 233–4. Another loose MT receipt for 1629–1630 indicates the same annual musician rate, this time with an additional 20s for two nights' dancing practice: MT Arch: MT.7/GDE/14, transcribed in *REED*, vol. 1, p. 228.

49 See, for instance, the 5 November payment in the 1633–1634 records – IT Arch: FIN/1/1, fol. 235r, transcribed in *REED*, vol. 1, p. 243.

50 See Longleat House: Longleat MSS Parcel 2, Number 9, item 13A, transcribed in *REED*, vol. 1, pp. 305–6.

51 Whilst it is clear that Bonavent's beard makes him unrecognizable to his wife and others, Eugene Giddens points out that he never claims to have disguised himself deliberately by growing it. Whether he is 'in disguise' or not, then, is a matter of interpretation: *Hyde Park*, ed. Giddens, 2.1.0SD.

honour-based violence. To this end, the second act opens with offstage music and dancing. Bonavent's immediate comment, 'Musicke and revelles? They are very merry',[52] may well have resonated metatheatrically with the Innsmen merrily awaiting their own musical revelling later that evening, just as Feste's refrain at the end of *Twelfth Night*, 'the raine it raineth euery day' (TLN 2563), never fails to amuse playgoers at the reconstructed Globe theatre and other open-air venues when weather conditions oblige. Bonavent learns from a servant that this is not, in fact, a dancing school; his opprobrious response that 'yet some voyces sound like women' (C3v) may too have resonated in the usually all-male space of Middle Temple Hall, in which mixed company and female dancing was a particularly charged issue: the previous year, Middle Temple parliament dissolved the Commons over Christmas, ordered 'the hall dores lockt vp', and stipulated 'that certayne Officers and others be appointed to attend and guard the house', after at a previous revels 'the yonger gent*lemen*' used 'the Gallery over the Skreene to bring in there Ladies and Gentlewomen to looke on', even daring to 'bring downe [the] Ladies and Gentlewomen and daunce with them in the Hall when the Benche [i.e. the senior lawyers] are gonne', all in breach of the claimed custom that no 'forraine men or women spectators' be allowed to attend the revels.[53]

After Bonavent establishes that this is in fact a nuptial celebration, the following scene opens with a spectacular entry of the wedding party 'dancing', as Bonavent stands aside and 'peepes' at them (C4r). If ever there was a theatrical use to which musicians hired to play for festive dancing might be put, then surely it is playing for festive dancing within the dramatic world. Quite what an audience would make, moreover, of the sound of music and dancing coming from outside of the hall in the middle of a feast is a compelling question – as is the carefully choreographed entry of the dancers into the performance space a few lines later (C4r). The dancing continues through the scene before the revellers dance offstage once again at the end. This theatrically framed dancing may thus have echoed the hall space's use as part of the evening's 'real life' revels to follow later, the play reflecting an aural and visual self-image back to the attendant revellers as they await their own turn on the floor. Possible responses – from a competitive desire to outdo the performances of the Queen's Men when given their turn, to more neutral excitement and anticipation at what is to follow, or even apprehension at their own imminent public display – would undoubtedly have made this portion of the play of particular interest to watching Innsmen and their guests, and especially so if Geoffrey Collins and his colleagues supplied the dancing music both within and without the play-world that evening.

The scene is not just about the display of skilled dancing, however; its main contribution to the play's narrative is through failed attempts to dance skilfully. When Lacy, Mistress Bonavent's new husband, spies Bonavent 'peep[ing]' at the festivities, he insists that he 'shall dance', despite Bonavent's repeated insistence that he 'cannot' and that it is unseemly for Lacy to force him to do so while 'circled with your friends' (C4r–v). The ensuing social embarrassment of his clumsy dancing – 'something like' a 'hobby horse', according to Mistress Carol (C4v) – prompts a convoluted revenge plot culminating in Bonavent forcing Lacy to dance to the bagpipes at swordpoint in Hyde Park (H1r). Apprehension about one's dancing abilities would surely have been on the mind of at least some revellers watching the play and acutely aware that their own skill would be on display in turn later that evening. Anxieties about social accomplishments, from sight-singing to language skills, are widely articulated in texts of the period;[54] that dance is the lightning rod for such feelings in Shirley's play may even have been one of the reasons it was chosen for performance at a revels evening.

Other aspects of the play beyond its musical elements would have resonated with an Inns audience too, from Mistress Bonavent's complaint that 'suits in love, should not / Like suits in Law, be rack'd from tearme to tearme' (C3r) to the duel that breaks out in act 3, scene 2 (F1v). For certain of the benchers, perhaps the latter recalled

---

52 James Shirley, *Hide Parke, a comedie* (London, 1637), fol. C3v. Hereafter cited in the text.

53 MT Arch: MT.1/MPA.No. 5, pp. 102–3, transcribed in *REED*, vol. 1, fols. 232–3. The customary absence of outside guests seems to have been a fiction maintained for the sake of parliament, since their presence is often remarked upon. See, for instance, Whitelocke's account of the November 1628 revels: 'Att Allhallowtide they began their Revells, which grew so much noted for excellent order, hansome gentlemen & good dauncers, that the Hall was crowded with Company[,] both gentlemen & Ladyes[,] to see them every Revells night, the Courtiers themselves[,] Lords & Ladyes[,] would vouchsafe to be present att them, & the Master was often sent for to bring some of his Revellers to the Court, to daunce with the great Ladyes there ...': Bulstrode Whitelocke, '1628–9', in *The Diary of Bulstrode Whitelocke, 1605–1675*, ed. Ruth Spalding (Oxford, 1989), p. 57.

54 See the respective embarrassment of Philomathes and Sir Andrew Aguecheek in Thomas Morley, *A Plaine and Easie Introduction to Practicall Musicke* (London, 1597), fol. B2r; and *Twelfth Night*, TLN 205–8.

a notorious incident in the very same hall a generation earlier, when, on 9 February 1598, John Davies broke a 'bastinado' stick over Richard Martin's head before fleeing to a boat waiting on the Thames whilst brandishing a sword over his head.[55] Yet it is the play's fascination with music and dance that resonates most with the Inns context, and that provides an obvious opportunity for musical collaboration as part of a revels evening. In this light, Mistress Carol's declaration that 'We must have a time to dine, and dance to bed' (I4v) may well have met with widespread approval from this particular audience.

TWELFTH NIGHT

The other extant play with a known Inns performance in the seventeenth century, *Twelfth Night*, is often rightly described as one of Shakespeare's musical plays, but it is less often noted for its similarly extensive musical flexibility. The text of *Twelfth Night* that survives in the 1623 folio does, of course, post-date the Middle Temple performance on Candlemas 1602 by some two decades. Since Manningham makes no explicit comment on what music was included, it is, then, worth keeping in mind the possibility that the folio text reflects later revisions including musical changes. Perhaps Cesario sang in an earlier version, as act 1, scene 2 appears to anticipate, for instance.[56] Yet – with that caveat – as the text stands, the range of musical possibilities are striking. This is true from the very start: Orsino's opening call for music to 'play on' (TLN 5), and then abruptly stop when its sweetness wears off, could be minimally fulfilled by a single actor onstage as one of Orsino's servants as part of this household scene. We know from actor-sharer Augustine Phillips's 1604 bequest of a lute and other string instruments to his current and former apprentices, for example, that the skill and resources to fulfil this role were probably available from amongst the actors themselves in the early 1600s.[57] Yet if a band of professional musicians were to hand, then their integration into the scene – the music cues clearly embedded in the dialogue via Orsino's authoritative instructions (TLN 5, 8, 11) – would scarcely require extensive rehearsal.

This is equally true of another musical moment in act 2, scene 4, in which the absent Feste, at large in Orsino's household for no clear reason, is sought out in order to sing 'Come away, come away death' (TLN 884–952). Leaving aside questions of possible revision in this scene,[58] the text as it stands once again offers flexibility through Orsino's instruction to 'play the tune the while' (TLN 897): minimally, a company member with sufficient musical competence and a lute to hand might fulfil this role as an onstage servant in Orsino's household, who make up the 'others' populating the scene (TLN 883). Yet, with musicians to hand and a bossily clear cue from Orsino (TLN 897), little more than a 'top and tail' would be required to incorporate their skills: the musicians would need no more than a rough sense of when in the play this moment might be coming, for, provided they are in the room, the text embeds their cues and fictionalizes their effective co-option into the drama.

As in *Hyde Park*, non-musical aspects of the play would surely have resonated with an Inns audience too, from the cod-duelling plot to Malvolio's social ambition; indeed, many of these aspects of *Twelfth Night*'s early reception history have already been explored productively by critics, most recently by Jackie Watson in an important account of Middle Templars and social precarity.[59] Perhaps it is worth returning to Sir Andrew Aguecheek's dancing in the context of *Hyde Park*, though. It is not entirely clear from the text whether his 'caper' (TLN 229) and 'backe-tricke' (TLN 231) are truly impressive – evidence of time wasted on less prestigious pursuits than the language-learning he is repeatedly exposed as having neglected, for instance – or whether this is yet another accomplishment of the courtly gentleman that he is lacking, along with verbal wit, courageous swordplay and a good singing voice. It is striking, though, that the two extant plays known to have been performed professionally at Middle Temple share an emphasis on dancing as an embodied skill to be judged by onlookers, as well as sharing dramaturgies that put music at the centre of their stagecraft.

One final point of comparison that appears significant in the context of Middle Temple Hall is the use of music in both plays to defy or even humiliate another, as part of homosocial male conflict over status and honour. As noted above, Bonavent's social embarrassment at his lack of dancing skill stimulates a revenge plot culminating

---

[55] *Middle Temple Records*, ed. Charles Henry Hopwood, 4 vols. (London, 1904–1905), vol. 1, pp. 379–80. See Charles Cathcart's account of this incident in '*Poetaster* and the Prince of Love', *Ben Jonson Journal* 14 (2007), 206–17.

[56] On potential revision, see Tiffany Stern, *Documents of Performance in Early Modern England* (Cambridge, 2009), pp. 147–8.

[57] *Playhouse Wills, 1558–1642: An Edition of Wills by Shakespeare and his Contemporaries in the London Theatre*, ed. E. A. J. Honigmann and Susan Brock (Manchester, 1993), p. 73.

[58] Stern, *Documents*, pp. 147–8.

[59] Watson, 'Sense and community'.

in him cornering Lacy in Hyde Park, demanding 'shake your heeles', to the tune of a 'galliard' on the bagpipes. The commencement of the music even appears to be choreographed to coincide with Bonavent drawing his sword (H1r). That the enforced dancing is a form of displaced physical conflict and a challenge to Lacy's honour is clarified by Bonavent's remark that 'now we are on even tearmes, and if / You like it not, Ile use my tother instrument' (H1v), a further bout of duelling almost breaking out afterwards until Bonville intervenes.

No one is made to dance to the bagpipes at swordpoint in *Twelfth Night* (although Cesario and Andrew's unwilling duel in Olivia's orchard shares some similarities), but Toby does turn to music in order to challenge what he perceives as Malvolio's impertinence in attempting to pull rank on him in act 2, scene 3. Following Malvolio's reprimand and his suggestion that Toby might wish to leave Olivia's household, Toby sings at Malvolio in defiance of his demand that he, Andrew, and Feste be quiet. He reworks a contemporary song, Robert Jones's love complaint 'Farewell, Dear Love', into a dialogue with Feste about whether he 'dare' cross Malvolio and 'bid him go' (TLN 798–808). Toby concludes he 'dare not' do so – but like the bagpipe dance that stands in for physical violence, here Toby's song itself provides the riposte that he does not voice directly. He does not in the end 'bid' Malvolio 'go' – that is, tell him to 'go to', the modern equivalent of which would involve somewhat colourful language. Yet, nonetheless, his singing, having just been told to be quiet, functions equally subversively, and serves as a yet more targeted destabilization of Malvolio's authority. The precise social conventions of respect, honour and social hierarchy in play in both cases would have been acutely visible to Innsmen shaping emergent and aspirant careers in the hyper-competitive homosocial space of Middle Temple. If similar conflicts between Middle Templars ever involved bagpipes or sung insults, these details have not made their way into the historical record – but even assuming that they did not, these hyper-theatrical moments would surely have resonated with the concerns of young men in the intellectual and social environment of the Inns of Court.

INNS-FLEXIBLE DRAMATIC COMPOSITION

This article has traced the potential in both *Hyde Park* and *Twelfth Night* for a richer musical dramaturgy when performed at the Inns, if extra musical resources were indeed available. It has explored, too, how both plays might resonate metatheatrically with the revels evenings in different ways if performed in that context. The archival documents and payment records explored may not seem like the most illuminating – or indeed the most exciting – traces left by early modern musicians and actors, yet when put in conversation with extant play-texts and other materials, new suggestions begin to emerge about the relationship between music and drama at the early modern Inns of Court. The two plays share many aspects apt for Inns performance, and were certainly well chosen from the repertories of the Lord Chamberlain's Men and Queen Henrietta Maria's Men respectively.

To look outward from performance history records in one very specific context to the bigger picture of early modern drama, we can consider how the Inns of Court performance culture sketched in this article might help us think about the wider practice of commercial dramatists such as Shakespeare. We know that *Twelfth Night* was a flexible play, meeting with approval from Innsmen such as John Manningham in 1602, returning for court performances in 1618 and 1623, and likely seeing numerous commercial performances at the Globe and Blackfriars as well.[60] The flexibility of the play, and its aptness for performance with a strikingly wide range of musical resources – from a sole company member who can do enough to get by on the lute, right up to a full professional consort – perhaps offer us another way of thinking about Shakespeare's dramaturgy. It is long recognized that Shakespeare makes extensive use of music in his plays (particularly post-1609). Perhaps we can add the further suggestion that Shakespeare is characteristically *flexible* in his writing, anticipating the Inns of Court as one of several performance contexts in which a play might need to succeed, as part of the company's annual obligations at the Globe, at court, at the Inns, and perhaps elsewhere in London and beyond – in this case by being ready to make the most of musical opportunities when they arose.

---

[60] See Wiggins with Richardson, *British Drama*, vol. 4, #1297.

REIMAGINING THE COMMUNITY:
A TRANSATLANTIC TALE OF TWO SCHOLARS

RUI CARVALHO HOMEM[1]

This article discusses the extraordinary cases of two public intellectuals, based respectively in Portugal and Brazil, who in the late nineteenth century co-opted Shakespeare into discussions with broader implications than the scholarly and theatrical concerns that ordinarily prevail in his reception. Such discussions involved the reimagining and remaking of the communities in question at a crucial point in their social, political and constitutional histories.

In its phrasing, the title above plainly echoes Benedict Anderson's *Imagined Communities*, a now classic study of 'the Origin and Spread of Nationalism' (1983, 1991, 2006), which defined nations as 'political communities' that are 'imagined' in the sense that its members will never get to know most of their fellow members, and 'yet in the minds of each lives the image of their communion'. Anderson added that 'communities are to be distinguished, not by their falsity/genuineness, but by *the style* in which they are imagined'.[2] The discussion below will bring out that in the 1880s, on either side of the Atlantic, Shakespeare was invoked, cited and translated into Portuguese with a regularity that reflected a steadfast belief in the rhetorical effectiveness of his drama for verbalizing the contents and the 'style' of momentous political change. Exploring such uses of Shakespeare requires some historicizing – so as to bring out the distinctiveness that textual transactions from a century and a half ago derived from the respective conditions of a colonial power (Portugal) and one of its former colonies (Brazil), situated in opposite hemispheres, at a time when imperial designs were being fundamentally transformed. Against the binarism of these specificities, one also has to balance the more general and complex patterns (including homologies) that emerge from the 'reimaginings' set off by the Shakespearian text when it meets the expressive needs of variously positioned communities.

Late nineteenth-century Portugal and Brazil shared not just the language, but much of their institutional and public cultures.[3] This reflected the continuities that had marked Brazilian independence, declared in 1822 by the heir to the Portuguese throne, who was promptly acclaimed as Peter I, 'emperor' of the former colony. This conversion of a colony into a new (tropical) monarchy led by the crown prince of the colonizing power was unusual in a Latin American context that had seen other former colonies reach their independence (in their case, from Spain) as republics, but it was supported by segments of the colonial elites that translated overnight into the sociopolitical apparatus of the new South Atlantic empire.[4] The persistence of strong transatlantic links, made evident by dynastic continuity, was consolidated by the habit of having those elites educated in Portugal, at the University of Coimbra – a habit that ensured a to-ing and fro-ing of politicians, administrators, professionals and scholars.[5] However, in the final quarter of the century both Portugal and Brazil were moving, though at different speeds, towards constitutional change, from monarchies to republics; but the

[1] Research for this article was funded by FCT – Fundação para a Ciência e Tecnologia, I.P., under project no. UID/04097/2025.

[2] Benedict Anderson, *Imagined Communities: Reflections on the Origin and Spread of Nationalism*, revised ed. (London and New York, 2006) p. 6 (italics mine).

[3] As noted by Anderson, in the Americas 'it was precisely the sharing with the metropole of a common language (and common religion and common culture) that had made the first national imaginings possible' (Anderson, *Imagined*, p. 197).

[4] Much has been written on the singularity and intricacies of this political process. For a recent overview and reappraisal, see Lilia M. Schwarcz and Heloisa M. M. Starling, *Brazil: A Biography* (Milton Keynes, 2019 [2015]), esp. pp. 215–66.

[5] José Murilo de Carvalho, 'Political elites and state building: the case of nineteenth-century Brazil', *Comparative Studies in Society and History* 24 (1982), 378–99; pp. 383–4.

similarities stop at this factual level, since the contents and consequences of such changes were to be markedly different – and even opposite in some fundamental respects (as noted below).

This is the general framework in which the two authors in question, José António de Freitas (1849–1931) and Joaquim Nabuco (1849–1910), engaged with Shakespeare's work, and did so in ways that show writing and circumstance reflecting each other. Both were Brazilians, and born in the same year – but they had markedly different careers. Of the two, only José António de Freitas could describe himself as a Shakespeare scholar.

ON SHAKESPEARE, SCIENCE – AND SOCIAL CONSERVATISM

Having moved to Lisbon for his education early in life, José António de Freitas trained in artillery and letters, and is described as a teacher of a range of subjects – from physics and chemistry to Latin – who obtained sufficient recognition to be made a member of the 'Academia Real das Sciencias'.[6] His profile as a polymath did not occlude the prominence of Shakespeare among his endeavours, which included versions of *Othello* (1882) and *Hamlet* (1887). These translations, noted for being among the first done directly from English source texts, rather than from French intermediate versions,[7] were framed by (for the time) unusually sizeable introductions and notes. Such scholarly distinction was matched by theatrical success, since both were staged to great acclaim in Lisbon at the National Theatre.[8]

Like most of Freitas's known publications, those two Shakespeare translations date from the 1880s. As the decade began, he was barely in his thirties, having resisted a family command to return to Brazil and decided to make a living in Lisbon from his scholarly talents and social graces.[9] A string of references in the contemporary press provides a useful gauge of his integration in the intellectual elites of the host country, thorough enough to warrant the perception (sustained also by Brazilian scholars) that the Portuguese literary and cultural scene, rather than that of his personal origins, proves the adequate context for reading the work of this Brazilian expatriate.[10]

Understanding his success story, with Shakespeare at its centre, requires noting how momentous the 1880s were in Portugal, the febrile politics of the period favouring perceptions of the mutuality of national character and imaginative production. The decade started off with massive commemorations of the third centenary of Luís de Camões, author of the national epic. Opposition

groups, consisting mostly of republicans (whose ultimate aspirations were to be realized only thirty years later, with the end of the Portuguese monarchy), made the 1880 Camões centennial a choice occasion for national-(ist) feeling.[11] As a prominent strand in their discourse of identity and uniqueness, with a comparative bent, they often drew on a repertoire of national stereotypes to invoke national poets as both factors and indices of the import and distinctiveness of their cultures.

A case in point was Teófilo Braga – a distinguished politician but also a literary scholar, and a positivist (indeed, the renowned author of a *General Outline of Positive Philosophy – verified by modern scientific discoveries* (1877)).[12] In a contribution to a periodical (aptly entitled *Positivism*) in 1880, he expanded at some length on centennial celebrations as catalysts of civic virtues:

the *Centenaries* of great men are the festivals of national consecration. Each people chooses the genius that synthesizes its national character … the figure of Cervantes will symbolize Spain for all times, as Voltaire represents the French genius in all its manifestations; Dante, Petrarch and Michelangelo for

---

[6] Such achievements were noted in detail and with pride by his contemporaries in Brazil, judging from the effusive tone of an entry under his name in a bibliographic dictionary published just a few years after what appears to have been the heyday of his fame in Lisbon: A. V. A. Sacramento Blake, *Diccionario Bibliographico Brazileiro*, vol. 4 (Rio de Janeiro, 1898), pp. 294–5.

[7] See Carlos de Moura Cabral, 'Livros e Theatros', *Jornal do Domingo – Revista Universal* 42 (10 December 1882), 334–5.

[8] Gabriela Terenas, '"The great universal genius": the reception of Shakespeare in Portuguese periodicals of the second half of the 19th century', *Anglo Saxonica* 22 (2024), 1–29; esp. p. 13.

[9] Cabral, 'Livros e Theatros'.

[10] Marcia do Amaral Peixoto Martins, 'A instrumentalidade do modelo descritivo para a análise de traduções: o caso dos *Hamlets* brasileiros', unpublished doctoral thesis (São Paulo University, 1999), p. 142; Marcia A. P. Martins, 'Shakespeare no Brasil: fontes de referência e primeiras traduções', *Tradução em Revista* 5 (2008), 1–11; p. 10.

[11] Amadeu Carvalho Homem, 'O avanço do republicanismo e a crise da monarquia constitucional', in *História de Portugal*, vol. 5: *O liberalismo (1807–1890)*, gen. ed. José Mattoso (n.p., 1993), 131–45; pp. 138–40; Maria Manuela Lucas, 'Organização do império', in *História de Portugal*, vol. 5, ed. Mattoso, 285–311; pp. 308–11; José M. Tengarrinha, '1870–1890: Charneira entre o velho e o novo Portugal', in *História contemporânea de Portugal*, ed. João Medina, vol. 1 (Lisbon, n.d.), 177–96; pp. 186–7.

[12] Teófilo Braga, *Traços Geraes de Philosophia Positiva – comprovados pelas descobertas scientíficas modernas* (Lisbon, 1877). Throughout this article, translations of sources (including titles) from Portuguese, and occasionally French, are my own.

Italy, Shakespeare or Newton for England, Luther and Goethe for Germany, Spinoza for Holland.[13]

The Newton inclusion is telling, as regards the element of scientism in such elevations of the new secular saints of communities in the process of being reimagined.

For Freitas, as a Shakespeare scholar who was notably also a teacher of physics and chemistry, the positivistic ideological underpinnings of such paeans for bardic value had an evident appeal. A commitment to generating fresh knowledge is announced from the opening page of the 'Critical Study' with which Freitas prefaced his version of *Hamlet*. It promises a 'new interpretation' of the character, a critical breakthrough played up as a reflection of the author's 'temerity', but formulated after pondering 'English, French and German' critics.[14] Such international credentials, reassuring in a Portuguese cultural context that was all too aware of its peripherality, are thus balanced against the novelty element claimed for the author-translator's scholarship. Indeed, the argument for his originality is consolidated with a long second paragraph lining up views of Hamlet that Freitas, with self-proclaimed boldness, is prompt to dismiss: 'the prototype of a noble temper, . . . of immaculate virtue', 'driven to pessimism by a noble sentiment'. But all of this proves a build-up for the single statement that (with calculated shock) takes up his third paragraph: 'In our opinion, Hamlet is a hysteric.'[15]

The rest of Freitas's 110-page-long introduction substantiates this diagnosis with much close reading and a vast array of sources – from the worlds of letters, academia and science. Cited authorities range from Lessing (on 'mirror[ing] nature') and Goethe (on Shakespeare as 'an oak tree' made to grow in a 'plant pot') to contemporaries of Freitas's such as the experimental psychologist Théodule-Armand Ribot (on the 'complexities' of human 'motivation'), the physiologist and anatomical artist Paul Richer, and the Parisian neurologist and pioneering psychiatrist Jean-Martin Charcot (specifically on hysteria).[16] What is especially striking about this roll-call is how Freitas commits to blending a discourse of genius with a set of scientist claims. On the one hand, he pre-empts objections of anachronism by granting that Shakespeare would, of course, have no conception of '*neurosis*, the fashionable disease of our times'.[17] On the other, he pointedly notes that it was the prerogative of a genius to anticipate perceptions yet to be theorized and named: for example, '[Shakespeare] also ignored the modern doctrines of ethnography, and yet [featured] . . . characters of all the races that peopled Europe', at all levels forerunning 'the scientific rigour of our days'.[18]

Freitas regularly contributed articles on 'Popularized Science' for a Lisbon Sunday magazine.[19] His interest in using insights from new knowledge to try to extend our understanding of past creations prompts him to argue, in his 'Critical Study', that Shakespeare 'drew the character [of Hamlet] as he would *logically* be' – since any person with the prince's 'individual circumstances . . . could hardly fail to prove hysterical'.[20] Rather pointedly and with undisguised pride, as a basis for the 'scientific' authority he claims for his learned discussion, Freitas's fascination with hysteria breathes 'l'air du temps': his *Hamlet* was exactly coeval with the best-known representation of Charcot's (in)famous public demonstrations of women's hysteria, André Brouillet's painting *La leçon clinique de Charcot à La Salpêtrière* ('Charcot's Clinical Lesson at the Salpêtrière Hospital', 1887). And Freitas would have been working on his version around 1885–1886, when Sigmund Freud spent five months researching under Charcot – years before the passages on Hamlet in *The Interpretation of Dreams* (1900) and in 'Psychopathic characters on the stage' (1905–1906).[21] For Freitas, who refers to Hamlet as 'our patient',[22] the prince was a clear-cut case of psychopathology successfully rendered into drama. (Intriguingly, Freud himself was to prove a lot more reticent with regard to the dramatic persuasiveness of pathological profiles, when

---

[13] Teófilo Braga, 'O Centenario de Camões em 1880', *O Positivismo* 2 (1880), 1–9; p. 2.

[14] José Antonio de Freitas, trans., *William Shakspeare, Hamlet – Estudo Crítico e Versão Portugueza* (Lisbon, 1887), p. 5. As suggested by the late João de Almeida Flor, the psychological focus would have been encouraged by actor Eduardo Brazão, who had in fact commissioned the translation – and was intent (prior to playing Hamlet) on immersing himself in the character's mental profile: João de Almeida Flor, 'Hamlet (1887): tradução portuguesa de um caso patológico', in *Shakespeare entre nós*, ed. Maria Helena Serôdio et al. (Lisbon, 2009), 184–201; p. 185.

[15] Freitas, *William Shakspeare, Hamlet*, pp. 5–6.

[16] Freitas, *William Shakspeare, Hamlet*, pp. 11 (on Lessing), 15–16 (on Goethe), 31–2 (on Ribot), 67, 93–4 (on Richer), 85 and *passim* (on Charcot).

[17] Freitas, *William Shakspeare, Hamlet*, p. 7.

[18] Freitas, *William Shakspeare, Hamlet*, p. 8.

[19] See Fernando de Mello Moser, 'O lugar de José António de Freitas na moderna crítica Shakespeariana', *Memórias da Academia das Ciências de Lisboa. Classe de Letras XXII* (1981–1982), 299–302; p. 301.

[20] Freitas, *William Shakspeare, Hamlet*, p. 11 (italics mine).

[21] On Freud with Charcot, see https://dergipark.org.tr/en/download/article-file/1637991.

[22] Freitas, *William Shakspeare, Hamlet*, p. 35.

he noted that 'psychopathic characters [tend to] become as useless for the stage as they are for life itself'.)[23]

Reading *Hamlet* in the light of modern science, Freitas surely saw himself addressing an imagined community defined by a love of cutting-edge knowledge. In the actual, historical community of his readers, however, many responded with derision to his 'hysterical' Hamlet. A well-known man of letters of the era, Pinheiro Chagas, launched a public controversy with a review in which he thoroughly ridiculed Freitas's essay, noting (among other boutades) how unfortunate it was for Claudius that the plot were not unfolding 'in the age of Charcot', since the king would merely have to commit Hamlet to some 'infirmary'.[24] Another reviewer, contributing under an alias to a satirical magazine, claimed, with irony and casual misogyny, that Freitas had thoroughly convinced him: he now had no doubt that Hamlet was as hysterical as any young lady on Fanqueiros Street (a bourgeois commercial and residential area in Lisbon).[25]

Five years earlier, Freitas had been a lot more successful in seeing his reading of *Othello* acclaimed. Both the translation and its introduction appear to have tuned in to prevalent expectations in an era of neo-imperial ambitions. A renewed expansionary drive was a common element to key public events that bracketed the 1880s in Portugal and had a major impact on the national sociopolitical mood. The decade opened in excitement over the Camões tricentenary, a celebration of a national bard renowned for having given the country an epic of maritime expansion; and it closed with a major national humiliation – the British Ultimatum of 1890. The latter event saw the country's partner in the oldest extant political agreement in Europe (the Anglo-Portuguese alliance) impose a diktat for withdrawal from disputed central African territories. The Ultimatum culminated years of Anglo-Portuguese squabbling as part of the scramble for Africa, with its midpoint in the Berlin Conference of 1884–1885 – in which the various European colonial powers presented and attempted to substantiate their rival territorial claims.[26] In this context, there was evident topicality in translating into Portuguese an English play about the fascination and disruption embodied in a larger-than-life African warrior. If Freitas's *Hamlet* vindicated Shakespeare's genius by welcoming him into a community of knowledge, his *Othello* had therefore a backdrop of clashing constituencies and incompatible imperial designs – to which one has to add a set of patriarchal preconceptions (as shown below).

Freitas's published version and its stage success insinuate that both the translator and his audiences were responding promptly to the ample opportunities for racism and misogyny afforded by the tale of *Othello*. His long 'Preface' repeatedly encourages this perception, besides offering glimpses into the complexities of its author's intellectual and ethical make-up. It starts off from a celebration of 'Man' (*sic*) as 'the most beautiful and most perfect manifestation of life on earth', with a 'starting point in the material atom' (a reflection of his scientism) and its 'apogee, its sublimity in the human spirit'.[27] This balancing of 'spirit' against the 'material atom' is quickly followed by hailing 'the Creator' as the source, and Shakespeare as the superlative instance of 'genius'.[28] In sum, God very much rules Freitas's universe – and, indeed, his *Othello* came out in the same year as his translation of Johannes Alzog's *History of the Church*, 'with the approval and under the auspices of the Portuguese and Brazilian episcopate'.[29]

Freitas's discussion and translation of *Othello* suggest that his conservative Catholicism trumped his positivistic scientism, leading to an engagement with Shakespeare's tragedy of the 'extravagant and wheeling stranger' and the young Venetian patrician that could hardly contemplate an inclusive understanding of humankind as defined by its diversities. His introduction is sustained by serious research – but its scholarly qualities do not make it less (potentially) mortifying for a 21st-century readership, largely due to two sets of issues. The first concerns Freitas's penchant for lacing his scholarship with biographical fantasizing: whole paragraphs are dedicated to extolling Shakespeare's qualities of body and mind, and hence also his mundane and amorous successes – as the scholar-translator imagines the young Stratfordian 'gallantly' triumphing in 'duels of beer and wine' with his contemporaries, and ('bodily handsome',

[23] Sigmund Freud, 'Psychopathic characters on the stage' [1905–1906], trans. Henry Alden Bunker, *Tulane Drama Review* 4 (March 1960), 144–8; p. 147.

[24] Pinheiro Chagas, 'O Hysterismo de Hamlet', *Pacotilha – Jornal da Tarde* 164 (Maranhão, 6 July 1887), n.p.

[25] Pan-Tarantula, 'Livros Novos', *Pontos nos ii* (28 April 1887), 130–1.

[26] Nuno Severiano Teixeira, *The Portuguese at War: From the Nineteenth Century to the Present Day* (Eastbourne, 2019), pp. 26–35.

[27] José Antonio de Freitas, trans., *William Shakspeare, Othello, ou o Mouro de Veneza* (Lisbon, 1882), p. i.

[28] Freitas, *William Shakspeare, Othello*, pp. iii–iv.

[29] João Alzog, *Historia Universal da Egreja, posta em linguagem por José Antonio de Freitas* (Porto, 1882); the episcopal endorsement features on the book's title page.

with a 'frank countenance' and 'charming in conversation') not missing opportunities in love and conquering 'many hearts'.[30] The second (and most striking) involves Freitas's discussion, punctuated by jokes, of the challenges posed by the plot and text of *Othello* on matters of ethnicity and gender.

Freitas's attempt to confront – and settle – such issues finds a focal point in a passage from his introduction in which, lightheartedly, he refers to the 'animated controversy' that, with regard to the 'physical qualities' of the 'redoubtable Moor', engaged 'writers of the Old and New World' in trying to ascertain 'whether Othello was black ... or tanned, like an Arab'.[31] He quickly chooses the latter, an option for which he cites Coleridge as a precedent, but also François-Victor Hugo – as indeed he should, since Hugo's introduction to his own 1868 translation of the play into French is recognizably the source on which Freitas rather freely draws for his speculative musings on Othello's ethnic profile. Passages that are a blend of summary and literal borrowing from Hugo (whose discussion is considerably more detailed and balanced than Freitas's) include considerations on the 'union of Othello and Desdemona' as a 'congenial merger of two primordial types of human beauty, the Semitic and the Caucasian'.[32] This line of argument (apparently framed by then recent notions from racial anthropology – but unreferenced both in Freitas and in Hugo, his transparent source) sees the two scholars pondering the perceived probability of interracial attraction in specific sociohistorical contexts. While sustaining his strenuous argument for a Levantine or Arabic Othello, Hugo appears a lot more alert to the pitfalls of casual racism in such an exercise, as indicated by his vehement denunciation of 'monstrous preconceptions that – alas – still persist', denying Africans 'intelligence, soul and will', and indeed their 'title to the human'.[33] Such concerns are not relayed into Freitas's reasoning, which also omits Hugo's more nuanced consideration of the implications of his argument on race for Desdemona's characterization: in Freitas's version of that argument, attributing a lighter complexion to the Moor is blatantly presented as necessary for exculpating Desdemona from what otherwise would be 'a depraved taste'.[34]

This racialized and misogynous indictment in Freitas's introduction is matched in his translation by the zest with which he manages, through either amplification or euphemism, racial and sexual slurs in the text of *Othello*. In some occurrences, the translator opts for a lexical unfolding that spells out or maximizes

the offensive implications in the source – as when, in Brabantio's line on the Moor's 'sooty bosom' (1.2.71), the single adjective is rendered into the equivalents to 'swarthy and repellent';[35] or, in translating Roderigo's epithet for Othello as 'the thick-lips' (1.1.66), he picks a phrase that gives the denoted trait a risible ring in Portuguese, boosting the slur's appeal and the possible gusto with which it was to be spoken on stage.[36] A related but somewhat distinct approach can be found with regard to sex, involving the particular economy of innuendo and invective in this translation – and how it relates to its source. Freitas deploys with transparent pleasure the full lexical range of the target language for the transgressive woman, but this amounts to often blunting the incisiveness of 'strumpet' (4.2.84), 'lewd minx' (3.3.478) and 'cunning whore' (4.2.93), rendered into phrasings that indict the woman while, through laughter, making the language of misogyny socially palatable.[37] And this is even more evident in a protection of patriarchal pride that eventuates in 'that cuckold' (3.3.171) and 'a hornèd man' (4.1.60) always becoming (the equivalent to) a 'deceived husband'.[38] Throughout, Freitas's version of a play that proved to touch sensitive political and ethical nerves in Portugal in the 1880s repeatedly confirms how densely the translator's outlook and discourse were fashioned by what our era would describe as a toxic politics of race and gender.

ON SHAKESPEARE, ENSLAVEMENT AND FREEDOM

A striking contrast is provided by Freitas's countryman and contemporary, Joaquim Nabuco, a major name in late nineteenth-century Brazilian political – but also intellectual – history. In his context, as in Freitas's, Africa and Africans could hardly be out of sight or out of mind, but the reasons for this, in the case of Brazil, were even more pressing and poignant. In Portugal's

---

30 Freitas, *William Shakspeare, Othello*, pp. xiii–xv.
31 Freitas, *William Shakspeare, Othello*, pp. xxxvii–xxxviii.
32 François-Victor Hugo, trans., *Oeuvres Complètes de Shakespeare, Tome V – Les Jaloux, II, Cymbeline, Othello*, 2nd ed. (Paris, 1868), p. 60; Freitas, *William Shakspeare, Othello*, p. xxxviii.
33 Hugo, *Oeuvres Complètes de Shakespeare, Tome V*, pp. 58–9.
34 Freitas, *William Shakspeare, Othello*, p. xxxix.
35 Freitas, *William Shakspeare, Othello*, p. 18.
36 Freitas, *William Shakspeare, Othello*, p. 6.
37 Freitas, *William Shakspeare, Othello*, pp. 113, 120, 157.
38 Freitas, *William Shakspeare, Othello*, pp. 101, 139.

most valuable (and treasured) former colonial territory, the impetus for political freedom that one inevitably associates with a colony's process of independence had not been matched by a libertarian design on one crucial front: slavery. Notoriously, the decades following 1822 had seen a continued and massive use of enslaved labour, reflecting a political make-up in which plantation owners, running a labour-intensive agriculture of great importance for their and the country's wealth, enjoyed much influence in government.[39] The scale to which the new country's socio-economic make-up depended on enslavement had a huge impact on how the community imagined itself – as also on how it was seen from abroad. The contentious conditions that this delineated grew and grew with the abolitionist campaign that was to triumph in 1888. Within it, Joaquim Nabuco was a major player, as an inspired and inspiring public figure, writer and orator – who regularly cited Shakespeare. An appealing symmetry frames the two authors discussed in these pages: if Freitas, who displaced himself from his native Brazil to achieve a measure of fame in the former colonial capital, was primarily a scholar involved in literary transactions that were culturally and politically topical, then Nabuco, whose discernible goals always seemed to be centred on Brazilian public life, was primarily a politician and statesman whose fame was compounded by scholarly achievements.

The process by which Nabuco's talents as a man of letters came to bear on his public reputation seems to extend that symmetry further, also in its contents and chronology, since it finds a focal point in the Camões commemorations of 1880. These took some specific forms in Brazil, the former colony that proudly claimed co-ownership over Portuguese as a literary language, but also accommodated traits that recurred in commemorative practices in Europe – prominently including opportunities for exploring comparisons with other national poets, among which Shakespeare inevitably featured. There were important antecedents (both scholarly and political) to the 1880 events in which Nabuco was to feature. In 1872, aged only twenty-three, Nabuco had published a monograph on Camões and the Lusiads to mark the third centenary of the poem, proving his ability to use a humanistic competence to make himself central to a celebration that was both literary and civic.[40] Over the following years, he acquired a reputation for brilliant public oratory; the admiration he garnered had a generous political latitude, but, tellingly for his positioning, the venues of his public lectures included the 'Grande Oriente Unido', then Brazil's most prominent

masonic lodge.[41] By 1880 Nabuco had travelled extensively, and had occupied diplomatic positions in London and Washington, developing all along a network of contacts that included major advocates of abolition in the English-speaking world; and, at the end of that year, in Lisbon, '[he] was received in the Chamber of Deputies as the leader of the abolitionist "party" in the Brazilian legislature'.[42]

Months earlier, his public profile had led to an invitation to give the keynote lecture at the most prominent Brazilian event honouring Camões – held at a theatre in Rio, with the emperor and empress in attendance. The solemnities were promoted by the Gabinete Português de Leitura (a library that represented Portuguese culture at its highest), but their preparations became enmeshed in controversy when some in the local Portuguese community objected to the choice of a Brazilian (rather than Portuguese) scholar-politician as guest speaker.[43] In his lecture – published shortly after the event, as a slim monograph – Nabuco courteously rose to the occasion by hailing the two countries' shared language and connecting his contribution to other commemorative highlights, such as laying the first stone of the new Portuguese Library and issuing a commemorative edition of The Lusiads.[44] He exalted patriotism as a lay 'religion, an ardent mysticism'[45] – possibly an echo of the 'religion of humanity' vibrantly propounded by Auguste Comte (whose positivistic motto, 'Order and Progress', was to be inscribed in the Brazilian flag, just nine years later, as one of the decisions made to mark the inception of the country's First Republic).[46] And it is precisely at this point that, preparing to launch with due elevation the final stage of his speech, Nabuco equates great protagonisms (in letters as in other nation-making endeavours) with a mystical quest – and prominently quotes Shakespeare: 'This evening I have traversed the whole territory of art with you. "A true-devoted pilgrim

[39] Schwarcz and Starling, Brazil, pp. 243ff.

[40] Joaquim Nabuco, Camões e Os Lusiadas (Rio de Janeiro, 1872).

[41] Blake, Diccionario Bibliographico Brazileiro, vol. 4, p. 99.

[42] Leslie Bethell, Brazil: Essays on History and Politics (London, 2018), esp. pp. 125–6.

[43] Figueiredo Magalhães, Camões e os Portuguezes no Brasil; reparos críticos (Rio de Janeiro, 1880), esp. pp. 10–11; Maximiano de Carvalho e Silva, 'Joaquim Nabuco e as comemorações camonianas de 1880', in Joaquim Nabuco, Camões: discurso pronunciado a 10 de junho de 1880 por parte do Gabinete Português de Leitura, facsimile ed. (Rio de Janeiro, 1980 [1880]), 14–18.

[44] Nabuco, Camões, pp. 8–10.   [45] Nabuco, Camões, p. 17.

[46] Schwarcz and Starling, Brazil, pp. 355–6.

is not weary", says a character in Shakespeare, "To measure kingdoms with his feeble steps".'[47]

Nabuco's choice of this passage from *The Two Gentlemen of Verona* (2.7.9–10) – a play that, in a non-Anglophone context, could hardly count on a prompt recognition, even from a sophisticated audience – insinuates that his use of Shakespeare as a rhetorical trophy in his paean to Camões rested on more than incidental knowledge (and appreciation) of his work. This is confirmed when, just four paragraphs down, Nabuco offers his own version of the bardic gallery as a topos in positivistic celebrations of national identity/ies. In this version, Shakespeare is given pride of place in a distribution, among great poets, of 'essential' qualities that, for Nabuco, make up 'modern man' at his best: 'To the ideal statue of modern man has Shakespeare given the life, Milton the grandeur, Schiller the liberty, Goethe the art, Shelley the ideal, Byron the rebelliousness, and you [Camões] have given it the fatherland.'[48] Though rhetorically framed to culminate with Camões, this anticipated monumentalization of 'modern man' credits Shakespeare with (Pygmalion-like) providing the 'life', or 'lifelike' qualities, of a statue imagined as the proverbial living monument. Through this trope, Nabuco binds his commemorative praise of great poets to one of the forms that the civic cultures of his day and age influentially developed for ennobling public causes through invocations of hallowed precedents.

Nabuco's own public causes, centring on abolition (as the major goal of his political career), made it clear and explicit that his 'modern man' – whom he found animated in Shakespeare's drama and saw as compounding 'grandeur', 'liberty', 'art', 'ideal', 'rebelliousness' and 'fatherland' – was inclusive and libertarian, envisioning a common humanity across geographies and ethnicities. A theatre in Rio[49] hosted his Camões paean in 1880; *another* theatre in Rio[50] was four years later the setting for one more acclaimed lecture, on that occasion supporting 'An Abolitionist Confederation'. Nabuco's fiery speech then closed by saluting the inception of a modernity in which 'human dignity' would be the birthright of 'a new generation, the future citizens of a free Brazil'.[51]

The terminology and values that overlap in those two speeches recur in other writings that consolidate Nabuco's political arguments by explicitly enlisting Shakespeare – whom he declares (again, apropos of Camões) unique, resisting any comparisons, indeed 'a world apart' in global letters.[52] In an account of his formative experience, Nabuco admits to an early admiration, encouraged by a mentor he had in his youth, for

English cultural self-confidence, construed as the quality that 'allowed England to give a Shakespeare to the world'.[53] Emulating that self-confidence, without compromising the cultural cosmopolitanism that allows him to cite great authors writing in foreign languages, is part of the mental and discursive apparatus with which Nabuco imagines his own national community, as he draws on Shakespeare for troping the perplexities of late nineteenth-century Brazil. Other examples of this practice include comparing the Brazilian Liberal Party, at a difficult juncture in 1886, to Hamlet 'at the point of reciting his *To be or not to be* monologue, able neither to commit suicide nor to carry out his mission'.[54]

Hamlet also provides Nabuco with an image through which he insists on the importance of matters of principle in public life, even when they may appear mere details, since 'rightly to be great' may require 'greatly to find quarrel in a straw / When honour's at the stake' (4.4.53–6).[55] He makes this point in *Why I Remain a Monarchist*, a pamphlet published after some of the most momentous events Nabuco witnessed in his public career. The so-called 'Golden Law', which ended slavery in Brazil, had finally been passed in 1888 – a culmination, for someone who had for years and years been the acknowledged leader, in Brazilian politics, of the campaign for abolition. But this was swiftly followed by the coup that toppled the monarchy in 1889 and ushered in a republic. Paradoxically, and bitterly for those who would associate republicanism with libertarian values, that epoch-making constitutional change had been prompted in part by the resentment of segments of the Brazilian elites (especially plantation owners) over the imperial family's endorsement of abolition.[56] And Nabuco, in the pamphlet that signalled his loyal gratitude

---

[47] Nabuco, *Camões*, p. 28. [48] Nabuco, *Camões*, p. 29.

[49] Specifically, the Imperial Teatro Dom Pedro II – named in Nabuco, *Camões*, p. 5.

[50] Theatro Polytheama – named on the title page of the published lecture.

[51] Joaquim Nabuco, *Confederação Abolicionista – Conferencia a 22 de Junho de 1884 no Theatro Polytheama* (Rio de Janeiro, 1884), p. 50.

[52] Joaquim Nabuco, *Pensamentos Soltos: Camões e Assuntos Americanos. Obras Completas de Joaquim Nabuco*, vol. 10 (São Paulo, 1949), p. 382.

[53] Joaquim Nabuco, *Minha Formação. Obras Completas de Joaquim Nabuco*, vol. 1 (São Paulo, 1949), p. 246.

[54] Joaquim Nabuco, *Campanhas de Imprensa, 1884–1887. Obras Completas de Joaquim Nabuco*, vol. 12 (São Paulo, 1949), p. 213.

[55] Joaquim Nabuco, *Porque Continuo a Ser Monarchista. Carta ao Diario do Commercio* (London, 1890), p. 17.

[56] Bethell, *Brazil*, pp. 142–3.

to a monarchy that had proved more enlightened and humane than some republicans, found in *Hamlet* lines that allowed him to ventriloquize his view of 'great[ness]' and 'honour' in politics and affairs of state.

Unsurprisingly, Shakespeare often provides this ardent abolitionist with images of bondage and release. Such images occasionally bear, rather abstractly, on the remit of literature and the arts, as when they assist Nabuco's plea for construing creation as imaginative freedom. This is an argument we find him pursuing when he weighs into authorship controversies to dismiss Bacon for his supposed inability to release his imagination sufficiently from the 'fetters' of rationality.[57] In other occurrences, however, tropes of subjection and liberation acquire a vivid literalness, when Nabuco employs them to co-opt Shakespeare directly into his advocacy of abolition. Such is the case when (in a footnote, curiously) he alludes to *The Merchant of Venice* to argue that 'slavery is the worst kind of usury', and then extends his rhetorical use of Shylock's bond from a general (fairly abstract) monetary metaphor to physical, somatic imagery of flesh and blood, claiming that the iniquities of slavery could only be adequately punished and cleansed with a (verbal) 'redhot poker' wielded by 'a Shakespeare'.[58]

The passionate rawness of such passages is absent, however, from Nabuco's engagement with *Othello* – a play that one might expect to find resonating intensely with the cause that he so passionately championed. His discussion of the play dates from 1886, a period that saw him writing some of his most fiery tracts, but it features among his 'literary writings and speeches'. Specifically, it is part of the script for a memorial lecture honouring actor and director João Caetano, a founding father of Brazilian theatre who excelled in Shakespearian roles.[59] Possibly wary of the obvious, Nabuco refuses to make race the argumentative core of his remarks on Othello, whom he acknowledges as 'the most popular role in [Shakespeare's] vast repertoire of the human'[60] – and this concern with 'the human' indeed provides the focus and tone for his lecture. Instead of reading into *Othello* the *agon* of ethnicity that his long campaigning might inspire, Nabuco celebrates the character rather as an embodiment of human complexity, and of a tragic pathos for which he claims universal significance. Bypassing the expectation that he might racialize the character as a strategy for encouraging prompt sympathy, he hints rather that taking the easy path of sentiment, served by his discursive talents as a tribune and amplified by the context of his campaigning, would be tantamount

to denying both the actor and the character their full dignity of talent and humanity – honouring (were he to yield to that temptation) neither the great cause of his life nor the 'force and scope' of Shakespeare's creation.[61]

KNOWLEDGE, COMMUNITY, HUMANITY (A CLOSING NOTE)

My reading of the Shakespearian transactions in which these two scholars engaged, nearly a century and a half ago, was driven by the heuristic gains of balancing the traits they had in common against the diverging elements in their experience and pronouncements. Both dimensions emerge with sharp definition from the reading above. The almost uncanny parallel development of their public lives is clear, as exactly contemporary Brazilians enjoying public prominence and deploying their knowledge of (and passion for) Shakespeare in a turbulent era for the communities that framed their lives and careers. Both José Antonio de Freitas and Joaquim Nabuco responded to the turbulence around them through Shakespeare, and did so with great zest – but also very differently.

Indeed, the contrasts between them are glaring: Freitas, the fully acculturated all-round scholar, came to captivate readers and theatregoers in Lisbon, the former colonial capital, with Shakespeare criticism and translation that shuttled between applied Enlightenment values and a conservatism that accommodated casual racism and misogyny, easily found to shine through his writing. Very much against this, Nabuco was the eloquent statesman in a colony turned empire who repeatedly found in

---

[57] Nabuco, *Pensamentos Soltos*, p. 301.

[58] Joaquim Nabuco, *O Abolicionismo: Conferências e Discursos Abolicionistas. Obras Completas de Joaquim Nabuco*, vol. 7 (São Paulo, 1949), pp. 32–3. Reflecting the cosmopolitanism of his training and career, these remarks were part of 'a major work of political propaganda for which Nabuco had researched for more than a year in the late Richard Cobden's library in Brighton and in the British Museum' (Bethell, *Brazil*, p. 130). His international network of contacts and allegiances is also in evidence in his correspondence with British abolitionists, compiled in Leslie Bethell and José Murilo de Carvalho, eds., *Joaquim Nabuco e os Abolicionistas Britânicos – correspondência, 1880–1905* (Rio de Janeiro, 2008).

[59] See José Roberto O'Shea, 'Early Shakespearean stars performing in Brazilian skies: João Caetano and national theater', in *Latin American Shakespeares*, ed. Bernice W. Kliman and Rick J. Santos (Madison, 2005), 25–36.

[60] Joaquim Nabuco, *Escritos e Discursos Literários. Obras Completas de Joaquim Nabuco*, vol. 9 (São Paulo, 1949), p. 28.

[61] Nabuco, *Escritos*, p. 29.

Shakespeare expressive footholds for viewpoints that were both broadly existential, and specifically political – relating, often forcefully, to his impassioned abolitionism. This cause, for which he became (fairly early in his life) an uncontested leader, helping propel his country into a distinct stage in its social history, has necessarily made Nabuco a secular saint of political modernity (even if he was not immune to partisanship in his day and age).[62]

Both men clearly saw themselves as agents of innovation, striving to enlighten their respective constituencies. In one case (Freitas's), this involved bringing 'the scientific rigour of our days' to be acknowledged as bearing on all forms of knowledge, including one's ability to read Shakespeare anew by recognizing (in the light of a new science of the mind) the continued cogency of his dramatic replications of the human. In the other instance (Nabuco's), it required enlisting a unique literary and theatrical talent from the past on behalf of what he saw as an equally unique force for justice, in the attempt to bring about a momentous historical (rather than just constitutional) change of such scope that it equalled the dawn of a new era. The latter venture singles Nabuco out as indeed a prime example of a libertarian who proved alert to how vital the theme of freedom is in Shakespeare – and who, from a cognitive standpoint defined by his militancy, derived a strong sense of congeniality from realizing that 'freedom in Shakespeare is always a struggle for freedom',[63]

and that an awareness of this 'struggle' has proved a 'central' strand in the historical processing of his work. His passion for freedom appears to be co-extensive in Nabuco's work with an understanding that the future should belong to an unfettered humanity – and for this he recurrently finds support in Shakespeare. Perhaps the most notable manifestation of this comes when Nabuco's advocacy of the singularity of *Othello* appears predicated on extricating that play (of all plays) from the contingencies proper to Nabuco's own cause, preferring to read it rather as a memorable (and timeless) representation of the challenges of the human.

Distinct as those two public intellectuals were in their make-up and action, and in spite of their glaringly different potential for cultural congeniality in our era, their legacies reflect the resilience and continuity, across the contexts in which they rose to public prominence, of an intense sense of mutuality between imaginative production and the imagining of the communities in which they were active. That this mutuality was powered by Shakespeare intriguingly confirms the persistent and ubiquitous cultural operativity of his text.

---

[62] See Bethell, *Brazil*, esp. pp. 134–5.
[63] Ewan Fernie, *Shakespeare for Freedom: Why the Plays Matter* (Cambridge, 2017), esp. p. 7.

'TO BE OR NOT TO BE IN UKRAINE': RUINING SHAKESPEARE AND REBUILDING COMMUNITIES IN *H-EFFECT* AND *THE HAMLET SYNDROME*

CHRISTINA WALD

On 8 March 2022, as columnist Maureen Dowd wrote in the *New York Times* soon thereafter, 'an actor not known for classical performance spoke the opening of Hamlet's soliloquy with more dramatic weight than Gielgud, Burton, Olivier or Cumberbatch'. Addressing the UK Parliament in a video call, the Ukrainian President Volodymyr Zelensky had declared: 'The question for us now is to be or not to be. This is the Shakespearean question. For 13 days, this question could have been asked. But now I can give you a definitive answer. It's definitely yes, to be.'[1] Zelensky's speech juxtaposed the rhetoric of determination and mobilization with the tragedy of hesitation, invoking quotes from *Hamlet* to appeal to shared values. As Dowd's article shows, Zelensky's appeal resonated beyond Europe; in championing Ukraine as a nation united in its defence against the Russian invasion, Dowd presented the country as an ideal to which a polarized American society could aspire:

They are united as a democracy in a way America has not been for a long time, as we have become more and more riven over politics … Ukraine is showing a collective will, an inspiring community of people working together. Their heroic efforts against a gobbling tyrant set on empire recall America's own beginning.[2]

The multiple communities evoked in Zelensky's *Hamlet* speech and its international interpretations show that when contemporary public figures invoke the notion of community, it often is both 'an ideal and … real; … both an experience and an interpretation':[3] it often involves a return to an imagined past, and often the projection of a future community. Shakespeare's *Hamlet* has become an integral part of this interpretation and experience, as it has been employed repeatedly in order to explore the question of what strengthens a sense of Ukrainian community, what divisions and destructions need to be overcome, and how transnational communities respond to the Ukrainian situation.

This article focuses on a transmedial *Hamlet* project that has become an important strand of this larger adaptational network. In 2020, Ukrainian theatre director Roza Sarkisian devised a postdocumentary performance titled *H-Effect* that was inspired by Shakespeare's tragedy, its postdramatic rewriting in the German playwright Heiner Müller's *Hamletmachine*, and the life stories of Ukrainian performers. The performance was first shown online during the height of the COVID-19 pandemic in 2020 and then premiered in September 2021 during the festival Close Strangers: East at the Teatr Polski in Poznań; it was also shown in Lviv.[4] From the outset, *H-Effect* was intertwined with a documentary film project by the Berlin-based Polish filmmakers Elwira Niewiera and Piotr Rosołowski, jointly produced by the European French–German TV station arte and the German TV station SWR. *The Hamlet Syndrome* was completed shortly before the escalated

[1] Maureen Dowd, 'Zelensky answers Hamlet', *New York Times*, 12 March 2022, www.nytimes.com/2022/03/12/opinion/zelensky-ukraine-russia-biden.html; see also Amy Lidster and Sonia Massai, 'Introduction: a material history', in *Shakespeare at War: A Material History*, ed. Amy Lidster and Sonia Massai (Cambridge, 2023), 1–5; p. 3, for a contextualization of this quote in its long history of war mobilizations.
[2] Dowd, 'Zelensky answers Hamlet'.
[3] Gerard Delanty, *Community*, 3rd ed. (London, 2018), p. 5.
[4] This article works with the filmed 2020 version in Russian and Ukrainian, which has English subtitles. My thanks go to the director Roza Sarkisian, who provided the Vimeo link to this video and access to the file, which is currently private. See Feniks Film, *H-Effect*, Vimeo, 26 October 2020, https://vimeo.com/472119699.

Russian invasion of Ukraine in February 2022, released in summer 2022 at film festivals before being shown in cinemas from autumn 2022 onwards, and won a number of awards.[5] The film interweaves the process of conceiving and rehearsing *H-Effect* with scenes from the performers' lives outside the theatre. After meeting some eighty potential collaborators, the directors eventually worked with five performers – Katya Kotliarova, Sławik Gavianets, Roman Kryvdyk, Rodion Shuygin-Grekalov and Oksana Cherkashyna – who were deliberately cast because they represent several diversities of what is often called the Maidan generation, the first generation born in independent Ukraine: a conservative Eastern Ukrainian prisoner of war, a patriotic female soldier, a feminist actor concerned about the remasculinization of war-torn Ukraine, an LGBTQIA+ activist who grew up with homophobic violence in Donbas, and an actor who volunteered as a paramedic but found himself unprepared for the challenges of the battlefield. They were all involved in the Maidan revolution of 2013–2014, when protesters on Kiev's Independence Square, the Maidan Nezalezhnosti, opposed President Yanukovych's decision to strengthen Ukraine's ties with Putin's Russia rather than intensifying its rapprochement with the European Union. The considerable success of the protests was accompanied by police violence and over a hundred deaths. Yet the events were followed by the Russian annexation of Crimea and the invasion of Eastern Ukraine. For the Maidan generation, the dream of national liberation and its hopeful outlook to a future of new possibilities clashed with the experience of wartime destruction and a foreclosing of futures.

With *Hamlet* as a 'key', as the film directors put it,[6] the performers reflect on their traumatic experiences, their troubled relationship with the national(ist) community, and the question of what future communities are worth fighting for. Both the film and the theatre performance explore, in different ways, the stark divisions in Ukrainian society and their potential reconciliation through theatre-making, thus raising the question of whether and how divisions that pre-empt a sense of community can be transformed into an imagined community, in Benedict Anderson's sense, that tolerates or even values diversity. Such a community-to-come will nonetheless be characterized by frictions and tensions, as the conflicts between the performers show; it will not accomplish the ideal state of a nonconflictual community of 'deep, horizontal comradeship'[7] and will instead be closer to the 'inoperative community' envisioned by Jean-Luc Nancy as 'what happens to us – question,

waiting, event, imperative – in the wake of society';[8] it will be 'a potentiality that is always on the horizon, but never fully actualised'.[9]

While the film's title *The Hamlet Syndrome* refers to a condition of hesitation and overthinking in the face of difficult decisions, thus continuing a long Eastern European tradition of using 'Hamlet as a symbol for the modern intellectual's prevarications, hesitations, and rationalizations in the face of tyranny and terror',[10] it was released at a moment when the performers were given little time to ponder life-changing decisions, such as fighting against the Russian army or fleeing Ukraine. As Zelensky's speech indicates, the political discourse on *Hamlet* by then had clearly shifted towards a question of survival and the focus on Hamlet's willingness 'to take arms against a sea of troubles' (*Hamlet* 3.1.61).[11] As I will argue in the latter part of this article, this new situation not only transformed the marketing and reception of the film, which was advertised with the subtitle 'To be or

---

[5] Among them were the Grand prix de la Semaine de la critique at the Locarno Film Festival 2022; the Best Documentary at Adelaide Film Festival 2022, Krakow Film Festival, and Opole Lamy Film Festival; as well as the Roman Brodmann Award 2022.

[6] They used this metaphor during the film discussion at Zurich's Kosmos cinema in November 2022, during the conversation with Rosołowski on 8 July 2023 at the European Shakespeare Research Association (ESRA) conference as well as in printed interviews. See 'Hamlet-Syndrom: Ein Dokumentarfilm porträtiert die "Generation Maidan"; Regisseurin Elwira Niewiera und Kameramann Piotr Rosołowski im Gespräch mit den MDR KULTUR-Filmexpert*innen Anna Wollner und Lars Meyer', MDR KULTUR – Das Radio, 21 October 2022, www.mdr.de/kultur/kino-und-film/audio-dok-leipzig-hamlet-syndrom-100.html; Elisa Reznicek, 'Das Hamlet-Syndrom in Locarno ausgezeichnet', Dokumentarfilm. Info, 15 August 2022, https://dokumentarfilm.info/index.php/dok-aktuelles/1333-das-hamlet-syndrom-in-locarno-ausgezeichnet.html.

[7] Benedict Anderson, *Imagined Communities*, rev. ed. (London, 2006), p. 7.

[8] Jean-Luc Nancy, *The Inoperative Community*, trans. Peter Connor, Lisa Garbus, Michael Holland and Simona Sawhney (Minneapolis, 1991), p. 11.

[9] Anderson, *Imagined Communities*; Martin Middeke, 'The inoperative community in twenty-first-century British theatre', *Journal of Contemporary Drama in English* 12 (2024), 34–57; p. 34, https://doi.org/10.1515/jcde-2024-2002.

[10] Jonathan Kalb, *The Theater of Heiner Müller* (Cambridge, 1998), p. 109.

[11] All *Hamlet* quotations are taken from *William Shakespeare: The Complete Works*, ed. Stanley Wells, Gary Taylor, John Jowett and William Montgomery (Oxford, 2005).

not to be in Ukraine', but also turned the screenings and panel discussions of the film into activist interventions.

The transmedial, two-part *Hamlet* adaptation is part of a larger and growing adaptational network that employs *Hamlet* to reflect on the current Ukrainian situation. Kiev's Left Bank Theatre, for instance, completed its planned *Hamlet* production directed by Tamara Trunova, after its rehearsals were prevented by the Russian invasion, at Berlin's Deutsches Theater in March 2023, in a new, fragmented, rewritten form entitled *Ha*l*t* – that is, '*Hamlet*, from which "me" was torn out as a person' – a situation of deprivation and loss similar to Hamlet's.[12] Its opening premise is that the performers believe that they are still in Kiev and have just performed their *Hamlet* production, but slowly begin to realize their new political and artistic circumstances. At the end of the performance, Fortinbras takes part virtually in a film projection recorded at the front line. Or, to give another example: at the Schaubühne Berlin, a documentary performance entitled *To Take Arms against a Sea of Troubles* by Stas Zhyrkov and Pavlo Arie premiered in September 2022. By invoking fragmentary lines of Shakespeare's *Hamlet*, it reflects on the difficult situation of Ukrainian theatremakers who had to decide whether they were willing and capable of fighting against the Russian invaders.

These current Ukrainian versions of *Hamlet* can be situated in a theatrical tradition of using the tragedy for political reflection, and as a catalyst for change in Ukraine. Indeed, the very first Ukrainian translation of the play was part of a growing national self-confidence in the late nineteenth century, when Ukraine slowly liberated itself from the Tsar's ban on theatre performances in Ukrainian and proved its cultural legitimacy by developing a literary language; among the words invented for this first translation is the Ukrainian term for 'indifference'.[13] World War II was another important time for *Hamlet*'s linguistic, theatrical and political role in Ukraine, as the play was staged at a decisive moment: it was in Lviv under Nazi occupation in 1943, shortly before Russian forces recaptured the city, that the first Ukrainian *Hamlet* was produced in a new translation by Mykhailo Rudnytsky, an author with Jewish roots, who had to flee the city on the night of the premiere to escape deportation.[14] In this performance, Hamlet's dilemma was presented as that of 'Ukraine and its destiny: to be swallowed up by either the Nazis or the Soviets'.[15] The very existence of the community was at stake, and the Ukrainian language an important tool for national self-assertion. This prehistory is part of the current perception of *Hamlet* in Ukraine, where once again Russia – in its old role as imperial power and dominant force within the Soviet Union – is aiming to enlarge its territory and power, while reactivating anti-Nazi discourse to justify its war. And in this constellation, many in Germany, because of its own Nazi history in Ukraine of invasion and war crimes, perceive the country as bearing a special responsibility to support Ukraine. *H-Effect* and *The Hamlet Syndrome* thus continue a tradition of political Ukrainian *Hamlet*s, drawing on both Shakespeare's plays and its later adaptations, chiefly Müller's *Hamletmachine*.

TESTING COMMUNITIES, RUINING *HAMLET* IN *H-EFFECT*

Heiner Müller's view of Shakespeare as a playwright speaking from the ruins left by war and failed revolution is an apt starting point for the *H-Effect* project. As Müller argued, 'out of every heap of rubble of history sings speaks cries Shakespeare', to call for a different world.[16] *Hamletmachine* is also an apt intertext here because Müller directed it himself in combination with Shakespeare's *Hamlet* as *Hamlet / Maschine* in March 1990 at the Deutsches Theater in East Berlin, where it was rehearsed and staged against the backdrop of the fall of the Wall. The production thus turned *Hamlet* into a play about 'a man trapped between the end of a state and the

12 European Theatre Convention, 'Ha*l*t, Left Bank Theatre, 8 March 2023', www.europeantheatre.eu/news/halt.
13 Andriy Zayarnyuk and Ostap Sereda, *The Intellectual Foundations of Modern Ukraine: The Nineteenth Century* (London, 2023), p. 96. To this day, language plays an important and ambivalent role in national community-building realized through *Hamlet*: after the Russian invasion, the rejection of Russian and the privileging of Ukrainian as a language with the potential to foster national unity and patriotic ideology have been strengthened. However, in *H-Effect* and *The Hamlet Syndrome*, the performers speak both Russian and Ukrainian, as is typical of Ukrainian society; Rodion, for instance, only began to learn Ukrainian in reaction to the war.
14 Ola Hnatiuk, *Courage and Fear* (Boston, 2019), pp. 301–97; Irena R. Makaryk, 'Wartime Hamlet', in *Shakespeare in the Worlds of Communism and Socialism*, ed. Irena R. Makaryk and Joseph G. Price (Toronto, 2006), 119–35.
15 Makaryk, 'Wartime Hamlet', p. 127.
16 Kulturstiftung der Länder, Heiner-Müller-Archiv, *Patrimonia 152* (Berlin, 1998), p. 3812; see also Alexander Karschnia, 'William Shakespeare', in *Heiner Müller Handbuch: Leben – Werk – Wirkung*, ed. Hans-Thiel Lehmann and Patrick Primavesi (Stuttgart, 2003), 164–71; p. 165.

beginning of another'.[17] Thirty years later, the repercussions of the Soviet Union's dissolution – that is, Putin's attempt to return to the grandeur of an empire – constitutes the backdrop for *H-Effect*'s exploration of the Ukrainian revolution and its defence against the Russian invasion. Many commentators argue that Europe again has reached a historical turning point, but it is still unclear what the future will be and how the transnational European community will be impacted by the war. To come to terms with this situation of indeterminacy, *H-Effect* and *The Hamlet Syndrome* repurpose *Hamlet* and *Hamletmachine* as plays about political, historical and psychological crisis, about a 'time out of joint' (1.5.186) and a 'distracted globe' (1.5.97).

For Müller, Shakespeare's plays were to be overcome in order to free the present and future from the past; famously, he stated in his speech 'Shakespeare a Difference' that 'The horror that emanates from Shakespeare's mirror images is the recurrence of the same.'[18] In Müller's view, merely reactivating *Hamlet*'s plot in contemporary circumstances would mean continuing its vengeful violence. Instead, Müller argued, authors should transcend *Hamlet* and find a relation to the past that goes beyond repetition: 'Our task ... is the work at this difference. Hamlet, the failure, didn't accomplish it, this is his crime.'[19] Establishing such a difference, Müller continues, would mean creating a future that no longer reflects Shakespeare's tragic cycle of retaliation – that develops radically new plots, characters and topics: 'Shakespeare is a mirror through the ages, our hope a world he does not reflect any more. We haven't arrived at ourselves as long as Shakespeare is writing our plays.'[20] After Müller had translated *Hamlet*, he wrote *Hamletmachine* in 1977 – with a destructive impulse, as he noted himself – in order to overcome his own decades-long obsession with the *Hamlet* material and create a new kind of play.[21] Critics such as Eric Mallin have likewise argued that what the present moment needs is not reproductions of *Hamlet*, but interventions that undo and question the play's 'strangely worshipful patriarchal ideology ... valorizing the male assumption of violent privilege';[22] and James Ijames's recent adaptation *Fat Ham* makes the same point from an African American and queer perspective, effectively turning *Hamlet* into a tragicomic romance with a happy ending. *H-Effect* takes up this task by critically asking about the meanings that *Hamlet* might have today and for the future. For *H-Effect*'s artistic team, Shakespeare functions not only as a mirror image of destruction, but also as a warning against such

devastation; potentially, at least, they see the tragedy as a source of catharsis. *H-Effect* and *The Hamlet Syndrome* navigate between these opposed notions of Shakespeare as an icon of a destructive past and as a resource for a better future and more inclusive community to come.

Hamletmachine was performed in Ukrainian for the first time in 2016, after the Maidan revolution, and director Vitalij Golzov's commentary indicates the appeal that this radical *Hamlet* deconstruction might have held for the *H-Effect* team: 'It is a performance about the time of catastrophe; a ruin that has become everyday life. On the other hand, every ruination is an attempt at revival.'[23] Müller's own production signalled this idea of destruction and reanimation by starting the performance with all Shakespearian characters dead on the floor, who then wake up to perform the tragedy once more.[24] As Alfred Jarry articulated the dilemma of such deconstructivist approaches to intertexts: 'We shall not have succeeded in demolishing everything unless we demolish the ruins as well. But the only way I can see of doing that is to use them to put up a lot of fine, well-designed buildings.'[25] Paradoxically, radical destruction in this logic is only possible through careful reconstruction; and vice versa, reconstruction requires prior fragmentation, a production principle that aptly describes the adaptation work of *H-Effect*, which ruins its intertexts, turns them into a quarry, reassembles parts of them, and thus helps them to gain relevance in a new form. This is already evident in the title, which retains only the 'H' from *Hamlet* and *Hamletmachine*, while the political

---

[17] Miguel Ramalhete Gomes, *Texts Waiting for History: William Shakespeare Re-imagined by Heiner Müller* (Amsterdam, 2014), p. 172; see also Arlene Akiko Teraoka, *The Silence of Entropy or Universal Discourse: The Postmodernist Poetics of Heiner Müller* (New York, 1985), p. 100; David Barnett, 'Resisting the revolution: Heiner Müller's *Hamlet/Machine* at the Deutsches Theater, Berlin, March 1990', *Theatre Research International* 31 (2006), 188–200.

[18] Heiner Müller, 'Shakespeare a difference: text of an address', in *A Heiner Müller Reader: Plays, Poetry and Prose*, ed. Carl Weber (Baltimore, 2001), 118–21; p. 121.

[19] Müller, 'Shakespeare a difference', p. 121.

[20] Müller, 'Shakespeare a difference', p. 119.

[21] Heiner Müller, *Rotwelsch* (Berlin, 1982), p. 43.

[22] Eric Mallin, *Reading Shakespeare in the Movies: Non-adaptations and Their Meaning* (Basingstoke, 2019), p. 238.

[23] Goethe-Institut Ukraine, 'Aufführung: Die Hamletmaschine, 19.10.2016', www.goethe.de/ins/ua/de/ver.cfm?event_id=20847021.

[24] Gomes, *Texts Waiting for History*, p. 169.

[25] Cited from Kalb, *The Theater of Heiner Müller*, p. 110.

and psychological 'effect' of this fragmenting and reconstructive work becomes central.

H-Effect's artistic team called the piece a postdocumentary performance. After the Maidan revolution, documentary theatre in Ukraine gained new popularity as a form for engaging with the paradoxical individual and collective experience of renewal and damage. The revolution also led to a new understanding of the dramatist's political role: 'With the Maidan as a prototype for collective civic action, many post-Soviet playwrights re-conceptualized their own position as influencers, or even activists, within a national public discourse.'[26] *H-Effect* adheres to the characteristics of this 'new drama' for a new community; its use of 'verbatim or documentary texts to give voice to ordinary citizens', is 'associated with human rights activism' and enables 'certain therapeutic functions for the theatre'. Aesthetically, it employs 'a stripped-down range of staging practices'; displays 'unabashed frankness in using the vernacular language of everyday speech, including obscenities and many non-standard usages'; and shows 'a remarkable fearlessness in tackling taboo themes such as homosexuality and gender identity issues, youth disaffection ... police brutality ... political corruption and violence'.[27] In other respects, however, the performance departs from the documentary method, as it includes dance and music, and, of chief concern for this article, employs dramatic intertexts. The performance also goes beyond documentary theatre in attempting to explore the impact of trauma, which cannot be documented in a straightforward way. *H-Effect* does not offer a linear plot, but juxtaposes unrelated and sometimes enigmatic scenes, which the performance often repeats in variations and fragments, letting them compete with, interrupt, and supersede each other. As the director explains on her website, she deliberately created a theatrical form to capture the distortion of causality and linearity typical of traumatization: trauma 'breaks through into consciousness in the form of shattered fragments. It does not give in to logic and chronology, escapes from linearity. The construction of the performance is therefore a mosaic: a mosaic of stories, events, quotations from reality, memories and images'.[28] Sarkisian's metaphor of shattered fragments presents traumatization as a kind of mental explosion or ruination that is best represented in disjointed theatrical form.

In this fragmented, associative form, references to *Hamlet* become nodal points that bind together the performers' confessions and introspections and test their sense of community. For the postdocumentary performance, the self-examination of Shakespeare's protagonist, his political role, and the metatheatrical distance from role-play in Müller's postdramatic adaptation thus take on equal importance. As Sarkisian explains in one of the filmed rehearsals: 'I want to understand through *Hamlet* and your stories what it is that we fight for today when we ask to be or not to be? To do or not to do? To find a compromise or not? To be radical or not?'[29] Taking its cue from Hamlet's difficulties in adopting the role assigned to him by the genre of the revenge tragedy, *H-Effect* explores various dilemmas experienced by the performers in making private and political decisions impacted by revolution and war. By drawing attention to little-known stories from and perspectives on Ukrainian society, *H-Effect* 'is also a manifesto', as reviewer Monika Krawczak notes, 'of disagreement with war's appropriation and monopolization of history, censoring and belittling private experience in the name of heroic abstraction'.[30] This approach, another critic noted, 'sparked a debate among the audience, who found it difficult to come to terms with the fact that there are more fronts to fight on than the one with Russia';[31] in the new circumstances after the Russian invasion of February 2022, *H-Effect* might presumably be even more challenging for Ukrainian audiences.

Citing fragments from both *Hamlet* and *Hamletmachine*, *H-Effect* formally keeps little of Shakespeare's dramaturgy as developed across five acts and of Heiner Müller's five scenes. Instead, the play is structured around the confessions and interactions of five performers, collated in non-linear fashion to convey the impact of traumatization.[32] The performance expands on Müller's attempt to multiply the piece's perspectives beyond the protagonist's excessive introspection and to see the monologues as

26 Julie A. E. Curtis, 'Introduction: recent developments in Russian, Ukrainian and Belarusian drama', in *New Drama in Russian: Performance, Politics and Protest in Russia, Ukraine and Belarus*, ed. Julie A. E. Curtis (London, 2021), 1–21; p. 3.

27 Curtis, 'Introduction', p. 3.

28 Roza Sarkisian, '*H-Effect*', https://rozasarkisiann.blogspot.com/2022/10/h-effect-international-project-created.html.

29 Feniks Film, *H-Effect*, min. 7.

30 Monika Krawczak, '*H-Effect*', Byłam Widziałam, 15 October 2021, https://bylamwidzialam.pl/2021/10/15/h-effect.

31 Ola Salwa, 'Elwira Niewiera and Piotr Rosołowski, directors of *The Hamlet Syndrome*', Cineuropa, 11 August 2022, https://cineuropa.org/en/interview/428755.

32 As Barnett recounts, Müller initially planned to cast five different actors as Hamlet in his staging of *Hamlet/Machine*, one for each act: 'Resisting the revolution', p. 191.

crystallization of different and conflicting collective experiences,[33] guided by the topics of revolution, the devastation of war, and an interest in multiple perspectives. *H-Effect* thus adapts Shakespeare and Müller by reassembling the ruins of the *Hamlet* material in fragmented and innovative forms that intensify Müller's 'thematic explosion' of Shakespeare: 'The impressions are even more splintered and the wide associative trenches hardly lead to generally binding destinations', Klaus Peter Steiger wrote, yet 'nowhere in *Hamletmachine* does one actually escape the pressure waves of Shakespearean drama'.[34] Even the title of the Ukrainian performance, *H-Effect*, signals both a departure from and continuing impact of Shakespeare's tragedy and Müller's adaptation: it is an allusion to Brecht's notion of the V-effect as a form of alienation (*Verfremdung*) that invites the audience to critically reflect on the action and probe the characters, their motivation, and the sociopolitical contexts shaping their choices. For Brecht, Shakespeare's plays offered a model of a prebourgeoisie, prerealistic theatre saturated with V-effects,[35] and *H-Effect*, via *Hamletmachine*, advances this estrangement of *Hamlet*. At least some of the performers disagreed with Brecht's political view of *Hamlet*, however, which saw the hesitation of Shakespeare's protagonist as reasonable and his eventual revenge as a regression to the logic of perpetual war and destruction.[36] Their approach accordingly rejects Brecht's fairly clear-cut parables, drawing instead from the forms of aesthetic ambiguity and openness in Müller's piece that require the audience's active meaning-making.[37]

In *Hamlet*'s opening, for instance, external threats to the community and internal divisions coincide, calling for complex crisis management. *H-Effect* starts with lines adapted from the opening of Müller's play. One of the performers, Sławik, says: 'I was Hamlet. I stood over the sea and talked to the surf. Blah blah blah. The ruins of Donetsk airport stood behind me' – a reference that now replaces Müller's 'ruins of Europe'.[38] The opening thus literalizes the idea of a ruined Europe and directly links it to the Ukrainian situation. Audiences will later learn that Sławik belonged to the soldiers who defended Donetsk airport during the early phase of the Russian invasion and that he was held captive by Russian forces after the airport was blown up. The brave defenders of the airport are referred to as 'cyborgs' in Ukraine, a moniker conveying a notion of invincibility and emotional coldness which both the performance and the documentary film deconstruct in focusing on Sławik's doubts, fears and traumas. Later in the performance, the scene is repeated

with variation, and Sławik explains that when he was about to be executed by Russian soldiers, he felt freedom: 'My brain is no longer a scar. I am Hamlet. A cyborg. A machine',[39] thus directly referencing and newly contextualizing Müller's notion of the Hamletmachine.[40] After his opening statement, Sławik puts on a sniper's camouflage, which looks in the theatrical context like a monstrous, half-animalistic disguise and which, importantly for the context of war, is not legible as the uniform of a particular nation. His 'questionable shape' is then interrogated, just as in the opening of *Hamlet* (1.4.44), by the others who defend the country's borders: is he a defender of Ukraine? Does he know the password that would prove his identity? Faced with his silence, the four performers declare their own paroles instead, launching the performance with a mosaic of political visions: was the revolution and is the war about national liberation? About feminist emancipation? About queer rights? About nationalist glory? From the beginning, it becomes clear that the imagined community of the Ukrainian nation differs from each perspective.

Each imagined community requires a different hero or heroine. Accordingly, the performers compete in their claims to play the part of the protagonist in

---

33 Jean Jourdheuil, 'Die Hamletmaschine', in *Heiner Müller Handbuch*, ed. Lehmann and Primavesi, 221–7; p. 224.

34 Klaus Peter Steiger, *Moderne Shakespeare-Bearbeitungen: Ein Rezeptionstypus in der Gegenwartsliteratur* (Stuttgart, 1990), p. 49.

35 Bertolt Brecht, *Werke*, vol. 22: *Große kommentierte Berliner und Frankfurter Ausgabe, Schriften 2, 1933–1942* (Frankfurt am Main, 1993), p. 737.

36 Brecht, *Werke*, vol. 22, p. 611.

37 For Müller, Shakespeare served as an 'antidote' to Brecht's simplifications; Karschnia, 'William Shakespeare', p. 167. See also Barnett's discussion of Müller's distaste for theatrical allegories: 'Resisting the revolution', p. 189. As Brian Walsh has put it, 'Müller challenges the notion that defamiliarization and alienation render "moral" lessons legible. *Hamletmachine* is an alienated performance of *Hamlet*, and this alienation foregrounds, contrary to Brecht's impulses, the *lack* of moral in Shakespeare's play'; 'The rest is violence: Müller contra Shakespeare', *PAJ: A Journal of Performance and Art* 23 (2001), 24–35; pp. 29–30.

38 Feniks Film, *H-Effect*, min. 0; Heiner Müller, *Hamletmachine and Other Texts for the Stage*, trans. and ed. Carl Weber (New York, 1984), p. 53.

39 Feniks Film, *H-Effect*, min. 21.

40 See Heiner Müller, 'Die Hamletmaschine' in *Die Stücke 2* (Frankfurt am Main, 2001), 545–54; p. 553. Müller's lines 'Meine Gedanken sind Wunden in meinem Gehirn. Mein Gehirn ist eine Narbe. Ich will eine Maschine sein' (553) have been translated as: 'My thoughts are lesions in my brain. My brain is a scar. I want to be a machine' (Müller, *Hamletmachine*, 57).

a series of what Douglas Lanier has called 'idiosyncratic identifications'.[41] Oksana addresses the monster/sniper creature who identified as Hamlet with Müller's line in *Hamletmachine*: 'I know that you are an actor, I am also an actress and I'm playing Hamlet.'[42] Holding him at gunpoint, she recites Hamlet's 'To be or not to be' monologue in Ukrainian. In turn, she is threatened with the same gun by a third performer, Roman, who claims that 'maybe I'm Hamlet', a 'Hamlet 3.0, I'm a humanoid, I can do anything.'[43] A fourth actor, Katya, subdues him, making clear that 'I'm not Hamlet. He is a coward and he cannot make any decisions.'[44] In increasingly fast switches between positions of power and submission, the characters vie with each other to assume the privileged (not-)Hamlet position, thereby also multiplying the central questions that are at stake: 'to live or not to live, to shoot or not to shoot, to go to the front line or not, to go to the right or to go to the left, to speak or not to speak, to choose or not to choose'.[45] From its very beginning, then, the performance fuses the Shakespearian template with Müller's deconstructive rewriting and its own documentary material, distilled from improvisations and conversations during the rehearsal process to determine which hero ought to take what kind of action for what kind of community.

In what follows, the performers further develop their contradictory attitudes towards Hamlet and towards the community for which they are ready to fight. As in earlier 'deconstructive adaptations, Hamlet is not a psychological subject but a semantic figure, charged with complex and often contradictory meanings'.[46] Oksana, for instance, a well-known feminist Ukrainian actress who started the #MeToo debate in Ukrainian theatre, asks: 'Why does a woman play a male part? To reaffirm that a great tragedy is for men and a little drama is for women?'[47] She rejects the part, as does Katya, who fought at the front and despises Hamlet's cowardice. Roman, who worked as a paramedic, declares himself a 'proud Hamlet'[48] because he sees himself as a successor to his 'dead comrades'[49] in the fourteenth division of Hitler's Waffen-SS, called the Galicia Division, which was comprised of Ukrainians who fought the Soviet Red Army in World War II. He is confronted by Rodion, who grew up as a queer person in Donetsk and sees their experiences as akin to war: 'I am a Hamlet by right, by birth and by choice. My war began in 95 [when they were born] and no one knows what I and the likes of me lived through.'[50] Rodion will later report the violence they suffered in their family, at school, and on the streets because of their non-normative gender identity. Given

the multiple claims to the Hamlet position, the title's abbreviation 'H' offers a gender-neutral marker, a cipher that can be appropriated for different identities and ideologies.

The opening of the play thus indicates that *H-Effect* creates a collision between various traumas and dilemmas, where they sometimes compete to be acknowledged as tragic suffering. It makes clear that Hamlet has become choric, a touchstone for the creation and undoing of communities; what is performed here is not synchronous speech by a homogeneous body politic, but a polyphony of conflicting voices. When Rodion directly addresses Sławik, 'do you think I wasn't in this terminal?',[51] they question the notion of heroism, presenting it as a privilege of soldiers in an emergency situation, and highlight the constant, daily fight by the queer community that has often been left unacknowledged rather than nationally celebrated and remembered. Oksana similarly draws attention to the cause of feminism and sexualized violence, while Katya reports that the army was initially clueless about how to respond to a female volunteer, committed as they were to a notion of male soldierly comradery. As in *Hamletmachine*, in both *H-Effect* and *The Hamlet Syndrome* conflicted gender constellations become a forum to negotiate political conflict and belonging to communities. Struggling for a community-to-come, the performance also includes one scene in which each vision becomes a dystopian notion of totalitarian control. Katya, for instance, announces a fight against 'this pressure of pluralism', whereas Rodion declares: 'Heterosexual society has fallen, it has not survived the race of evolution. Finally,

---

[41] Douglas M. Lanier, '*The Hamlet Syndrome*: Shakespearean reparativity and experimental performance in wartime Ukraine', talk on panel 3, '*Hamlet*s today: retooling *Hamlet* for the new century', ESRA conference, Budapest, 8 July 2023, https://esra2023.btk.ppke.hu/panels/panel-3-hamlets-today-retooling-hamlet-for-the-new-century.

[42] Feniks Film, *H-Effect*, min. 1; Müller 'Hamletmaschine', p. 546.

[43] Feniks Film, *H-Effect*, min. 2.

[44] Feniks Film, *H-Effect*, min. 2.

[45] Feniks Film, *H-Effect*, mins. 2–3.

[46] Aneta Mancecwicz, *Hamlet after Deconstruction* (Basingstoke, 2022), p. 15.

[47] Feniks Film, *H-Effect*, min. 3.

[48] Feniks Film, *H-Effect*, min. 4.

[49] Feniks Film, *H-Effect*, min. 4.

[50] Feniks Film, *H-Effect*, min. 7. Since Rodion identifies as queer and the theatre performance and film give no clear gender indications, I use the pronoun 'they'.

[51] Feniks Film, *H-Effect*, min. 24.

our society can spit proudly into the face of heterosexuals' and intern them in prisons.[52] Thus, the performance explores not only the reconciliation and inclusiveness of communities, but also their potential for exclusion, suppression and uniformity.

THERAPEUTIC THEATRE AND GENDERED COMMUNITIES IN *H-EFFECT* AND *THE HAMLET SYNDROME*

Compared to the traumatized aesthetics of *H-Effect* and its adaptational principle of ruination, the documentary film follows a more ordered structure and is interested in the therapeutic affordances of theatre and tragedy. While the theatre performance uses stark imagery to explore the ambivalences of traumatic experiences, thereby involving audiences in a potentially disruptive acting out of unresolved pain, the film documentary approach relies largely on the verbal working through of past experiences via narrativization. It nonetheless offers a 'deeply immersive experience', as the jury of the Roman Brodmann Award put it, through close-ups and interactions that are highly charged, emotionally and politically.[53] The film also unfolds the performers' backgrounds in more detail and thus clarifies the differences between their stage personae and their actual biographies. For instance, Roman is not the right-wing nationalist whose part he takes over in the performance's exposition. Instead, audiences witness how he meets his therapist to come to terms with his trauma of having served as an untrained paramedic in the war, and being forced to swiftly make critical decisions about how to treat wounded soldiers and how to take care of their corpses.

The documentary approach of the film highlights *Hamlet* and plays down *Hamletmachine*, as immediately signalled in the title, which clearly refers to Shakespeare as opposed to the ambiguous, fragmented 'H' in the title of the theatrical performance. Accordingly, the film starts with a voice-over by Sławik, in which he cites parts of Hamlet's 'To be, or not to be' monologue in Ukrainian, alongside archival videos of police violence during the Maidan protests,[54] and then asks audiences to 'imagine you are Hamlet who made difficult decisions'.[55] The film's opening thus invites audiences to identify with the young Ukrainian generation via *Hamlet*, which not only serves to highlight the universal aspects of this particular sociohistorical constellation but also offers a model of audience reception inherent to tragedy, in which

feelings of fear and pity foster identification as part of a transnational community of witnessing.

Sławik's story also exemplifies particularly well the therapeutic aspect of the Ukrainian theatre project.[56] The film includes stark archival material in which his capture by Russian forces is shown: blindfolded, he is pushed into a car and then forced to address his parents in a video message. These videos were filmed on mobile phones by the Russian forces and uploaded on YouTube – visual salvos meant to demoralize the Ukrainian defenders. Hence Sławik's trauma becomes particularly palpable for audiences. As the film directors recounted in interviews, Sławik intended to reiterate and re-enact his experiences for *H-Effect* until he felt like a mere performer of his own story. The theatrical stage offered him a forum to work through his trauma, underscoring the healing, reconstructive effect of the project. The film shows how difficult this process is and how Sławik is deeply affected by particular scenes. Whenever he tries to re-enact a phone call with his father, for instance, he gets 'sucked back into the drama', as he puts it in one filmed rehearsal.[57] The film also shows Sławik meeting his father and asking for forgiveness for having gone to war and causing his parents such intense pain and anxiety. *The Hamlet Syndrome* unfolds the whole spectrum of therapeutic and retraumatizing aspects of the theatre project, of community-building and the difficulties of communicating in a group representing the nation's division. At a critical point in the rehearsal process, the director asks: 'How can we talk about our country if we cannot agree in the space of these 20 square meters?'[58] Shortly afterwards, Roman declares, 'I am sick of all the theatre' and 'I have nothing left to say.'[59]

---

52 Feniks Film, *H-Effect*, min. 46.

53 'Gewinner des Roman Brodmann Preises: "Das Hamlet Syndrom"', Dokumentarfilm.Info, 28 April 2022, www.dokumentarfilm.info/wp-content/uploads/2023/04/Laudatio-Roman-Brodmann-Preis-2022.pdf.

54 This material was contributed by the Ukrainian film collective Babylon 13.

55 Feniks Film, *H-Effect*, min. 5.

56 As the filmmakers have pointed out in interviews, all participants had to undergo psychotherapy before working on *H-Effect*; see Salwa, 'Elwira Niewiera'.

57 Elwira Niewiera and Piotr Rosolowski, dir., *The Hamlet Syndrome* (Berlin, 2022), min. 1:05, https://german-documentaries.de/en_EN/films/the-hamlet-syndrome.20896.

58 *The Hamlet Syndrome*, min. 1:15.

59 *The Hamlet Syndrome*, min. 1:16–1:17.

The film thus shows both the divisions within the heterogeneous group and the unlikely alliances and friendships that grow from its members' – sometimes hostile – encounters. Sławik's conservative socialization initially hinders any appreciation of Rodion's life as a queer activist, for instance, but the two performers develop an intense friendship. Sławik even asks Rodion to become godparent to his daughter, depicted in the film in a rehearsal scene not included in the final performance: in it, Sławik carefully hands over a little bundle to Rodion, whom we see thoroughly delighted by this gesture. For a moment, the three of them constitute a non-heteronormative family unit. The film juxtaposes this scene with images taken at the daughter's baptism, where Rodion pensively sits alone amidst a party celebrating heteronormative reproduction. Yet Rodion's very presence in Sławik's conservative family, in this celebration together with a priest, signals that a new, more inclusive Ukrainian society is possible, giving both the performance and the film a hopeful stance. As theatre director Sarkisian ironically put it in the rehearsals, their work has aspects of community-(re)building or even nation-(re)building: '*Hamlet* unites Ukraine.'[60] This moment and the overall concern of the project underline that 'community is not simply a social ideal that theatre represents or addresses; it is also something theatre enacts in its practices',[61] as Emine Fişek points out in her study *Theatre & Community*. This notion of community entails a practice that involves performers and audiences alike, who not only come together in witnessing the destruction of communities, but might also create 'moments in which audiences feel themselves allied with each other, and with a broader, more capacious sense of a public, in which social discourse articulates the possible'.[62] As Jill Dolan argues, this kind of theatre can create 'Utopian performatives', if only fleetingly, moments that 'make palpable an affective vision of how the world might be better'.[63]

In their multiplication of perspectives, both *H-Effect* and *The Hamlet Syndrome* are particularly interested in questions of gender and sexuality. Müller's *Hamletmachine*, while itself still being caught in the reproduction of some gender stereotypes, sought to empower the Ophelia figure and turn her into a representative of European women who suffer violence. The performance and the film expand and sharpen this focus on female suffering, raising troubling questions about war crimes. Repeatedly, Katya and Oksana stage a scene in which Oksana is interviewed about her experience of sexualized violence in the war. As the interview makes clear, Oksana here stands in for a different woman who experienced and reported this violence; partly for this reason, the performer cannot give the detailed answers demanded by Katya. The interviewer wants to determine whether Oksana was raped by Ukrainian or Russian soldiers, but the victim is unable to differentiate between their nationalities and asks whether and how this changes the violence done to her. In a powerful pantomime towards the end of the performance – a scene with which the documentary film also ends – Oksana re-enacts the rape, using the Ukrainian flag as an instrument of violation and torture and thus raising questions about the harmful impact of nationalism. The documentary film shows that those performers who fought for Ukraine, and especially Katya here, find this irreverent treatment of the flag as a stage prop to be almost unbearable, as it was often ceremonies involving the Ukrainian flag, such as for the funeral of fallen comrades, that helped them deal with their own traumatic war experiences.

Such scenes allow both the performance and the film to directly tackle the question of whose voice has a right to be heard in wartime: are the words of soldiers more trustworthy, more valuable, than those of civilians who have experienced violence? At one point in the film, during the rehearsals, Oksana desperately laments the fact that her stories cannot equal those of the 'group of soldiers whose memories are sacred'.[64] The performance transforms this uneasiness into a scene in which Oksana, upon being forbidden to speak, asks the others to teach her how to be silent about the war: 'Where to be silent about the war, with whom and how to be silent about the war. The main question is how long? How long should I be silent about the war? Five years, seven, 10, 20 . . . how long?'[65] She receives no reply: no one offers to help her learn how to speak correctly about the war, how to devise properly patriotic performances, or how to be silent. In response, she covers her mouth with a strip of black tape and uses more tape to write 'No Art, No War' onto the back wall of the stage, which is showing the ruins of the Ukrainian airport.

[60] *The Hamlet Syndrome*, min. 1:01.
[61] Emine Fişek, *Theatre & Community* (London, 2019), p. 19.
[62] Jill Dolan, *Utopia in Performance: Finding Hope at the Theatre* (Ann Arbor, 2005), p. 2.
[63] Dolan, *Utopia in Performance*, p. 6.
[64] Feniks Film, *H-Effect*, min. 33.
[65] Feniks Film, *H-Effect*, mins. 42–43. Ellipses in the original.

Another way of resurrecting Ophelia from the ruins of war is to question the clear division between the genders in the character of Rodion, who grew up in Donbas in a context where, as they put it at one point in the performance, 'no one … knows what nonbinary is'.[66] In the performance, they interact, dressed in a white bridal dress, with a male mannequin wearing a black suit; the same mannequin in the opening scene represented a war casualty and the ghost of Hamlet's father. In their white dress, wearing a black beard and long, dyed hair, and smoking a cigarette, Rodion is eerily calm in recounting the abuses they have suffered since kindergarten, from teachers, attackers on the street, the police and their own mother. They end with a combative provocation: 'What else can you do that hasn't been done to me yet?'[67]

H-Effect and *The Hamlet Syndrome* thus not only portray the Ophelia performers as victims, but also emphasize their readiness to fight and their actual service in the army. After Sławik, the former cyborg, refused the part of the nationalist hero and admitted that this Hamlet is 'foreign' to him,[68] Oksana takes his weapon and delivers a variation of Müller's Ophelia monologue:

This is Electra speaking. These bodies laid in an open pit for two weeks.… Pieces of charred meat. And worms have already started eating them.… I knew them until recently.… Where are their heads? … I take back the peace that I gave rise to. The joy of obedience – get out. Long live war, rebellion, and death. And the quote: The truth is to be revealed to you when it breaks into your bedrooms with butcher knives.[69]

As in Müller's ending, Ophelia here is turned into a reckless revenger, respecting no division between the political and the private, or between war zones and civilian life. Directly after this announcement, *H-Effect* ends with the re-enactment of Sławik's experience as a prisoner of war. Taking over the role of the Russian soldier, he demands that Oksana kill her fellow Ukrainian soldier to save herself. When she eventually pulls the trigger after a long moment of hesitation, it turns out that the weapon is not loaded. This re-enactment demonstrates the dehumanizing escalation of violence at wartime, which also subverts the division between fellow soldier and enemy – the difficult decoding of questionable shapes with which the performance began. While *Hamletmachine* has been interpreted as 'a powerful intervention into the *Hamlet* story in its careful attention to gender and violence against women as a potential point of resistance',[70] *H-Effect*'s final image of two female soldiers implicated in the escalation of

violence in war no longer sees such gendered possibilities of resistance. When Oksana, in the filmed premiere, slowly raises the weapon and aims into the empty auditorium, the piece ultimately involves the audience in this gruesome test of loyalties, distorting the sense of a harmonious theatrical community of performers and audiences. While *The Hamlet Syndrome* uses the mock execution it stages for its promotional poster, it ends with Oksana's aggressive re-enactment of her rape, a scene that likewise focuses on the nexus of victimization and revenge, persecution and protest, ruination and resurrection. Both the theatre production and the film thus make palpable the pain of a country under attack, which is caught in a spiral of violence and ruination but keeps hoping for the reconstruction of a more just, and liberated, postwar community.

GHOSTLY AFTERLIVES

In the summer of 2022, after the escalation of the Russian invasion, *The Hamlet Syndrome* was released in a profoundly changed situation, with several of the performers having returned to the frontline or having fled their homeland. As reviewer Marta Bałaga notes, 'the demons these people have been trying to exorcise returned in February, stronger than ever'.[71] While the film directors initially created the film to draw attention to the largely neglected situation of Ukraine under attack, in the changed situation their comments also emphasized the hopeful aspects of their film. They reported that Ukrainian audiences in this midst of crisis perceived the film to have an optimistic outlook, as it suggests that trauma might be overcome and a new, more inclusive national community established after the war. The filmmakers also turned their various appearances at festivals and cinema events into political performances. They staged one such protest against the Russian invasion on the red carpet of the Locarno Film Festival, where *The Hamlet Syndrome* was awarded the Grand prix de la Semaine de la critique in summer 2022, where they appeared carrying posters and with the

---

66 Feniks Film, *H-Effect*, min. 24.
67 Feniks Film, *H-Effect*, min. 25.
68 Feniks Film, *H-Effect*, min. 46
69 Feniks Film, *H-Effect*, mins. 48–9; see also Müller, 'Hamletmaschine', p. 554.
70 Walsh, 'The rest is violence', p. 32.
71 Marta Bałaga, 'Review: *The Hamlet Syndrome*', Cineuropa, 22 August 2022, https://cineuropa.org/en/newsdetail/429047.

names of the cities in which Russian soldiers had committed war crimes written in red letters on their white clothes. At cinema events such as the one at the Kosmos cinema in Zurich in November 2022, which I attended, Elwira Niewiera again wore a white blouse with red letters reminding audiences of the atrocities in Mariupol and Irpin; she wore the same blouse for TV interviews when the film was released in German cinemas. As though taking up the demand for remembrance and retribution made by Shakespeare's ghost, the filmmakers appealed to a European responsibility to support the Ukrainian forces, and in particular to the German obligation to atone for Germany's war crimes during World War II. At the film screening during the 2023 ESRA conference in Budapest, a mobile phone video was shown after the credits. In it, Roman reports from the front on the horrors that he faced during the liberation of Russian-occupied cities, and appeals to the solidarity of the audience. These film screenings, supplementary film material, audience discussions and protest performances extend and adapt *Hamlet*'s network to each respective context.

In contrast to more limited adaptations, then, this particular *Hamlet* project takes shape expansively, through a prolonged casting process, forty days of rehearsals, digital and live performances, the filming and cutting of the film, and the film's marketing and academic reception. All of this has become part of a performative project that unfolds over years and employs *Hamlet* to create temporary communities of remembrance, compassion and debate to grapple with the ruinous violence in Ukraine and imagine the country's possible reconstruction. It is an invitation to work towards the dissolution of this tragic cycle, even if such a rebuilding can only be deferred to an imagined future, and to a different stage.

RED *KABUKI* ACTORS PERFORM SHAKESPEARE IN OCCUPIED JAPAN (1945–1952): ZENSHINZA'S 'THEATRE FOR YOUNG PEOPLE'

REIKO OYA[1]

Japanese theatre faced unprecedented difficulties after the country's defeat in World War II. The economy was in ruins; theatre buildings, stage sets and costumes were destroyed during the air raids; and many theatre practitioners had died or had yet to return from the battlefields overseas. Stage productions, which had been severely censored by Japan's wartime government since 1937, were now subject to a completely different set of restrictions imposed by the General Headquarters (GHQ) of the US-led occupying force. Amidst these troubles, a theatre company called Zenshinza (literally, 'Progressive Theatre Company') started the *seinen gekijo undo* ('Theatre for Young People'), bringing live theatre to secondary school students and factory workers throughout Japan. Zenshinza is primarily a *kabuki* troupe that is active to this day, but between 1947 and 1950, it staged four Shakespearian plays, around a thousand times in total, for young audiences: *The Merchant of Venice*, *Much Ado About Nothing*, *A Midsummer Night's Dream* and *Romeo and Juliet*.[2] The course of the company's ambitious Shakespeare project never did run smooth. The GHQ first promoted the demilitarization and democratization of Japan, but then, with the rise of Cold War tensions, it reversed many of the initial policies to pursue the country's economic reconstruction and remilitarization. This so-called 'Reverse Course' would directly affect Zenshinza's Shakespearian performances.

Zenshinza's Theatre for Young People has been almost totally overlooked in the Shakespearian literature, probably because the company is best known for its *kabuki* repertory and its activities can easily escape the attention of Shakespeare researchers.[3] In addition, the troupe's performances outside Tokyo were not covered by major media outlets and were neglected by contemporary reviewers. The following article will focus on the Shakespeare performances that Zenshinza put on in the immediate aftermath of the war and examine how the *kabuki* actors interpreted and staged the early modern English plays at unconventional venues such as school auditoriums, gymnasiums and playgrounds, as well as factory canteens across Japan. This exploration aims to clarify how Zenshinza's interpretations of the four plays first supported and then contradicted the changing cultural policies of occupied Japan.

'PROGRESSIVE' *KABUKI* ACTORS

In May 1931, dissatisfied with the nepotistic hierarchy of the *kabuki* world, socially aware young actors led by Chojuro Kawarasaki and Kan'emon Nakamura broke away from the entertainment company Shochiku, which

[1] I am most grateful to Ann Thompson, Yuji Kaneko and Matthew Hanley for their incisive comments on an earlier version of this article. I would also like to thank Masayo Kikuchi of Zenshinza's public relations team for helping me explore the materials in the company's extensive archive, and the staff members of the Tsubouchi Memorial Theatre Museum Library, Waseda University and the Miyagi Prefectural Archives for their invaluable guidance and help. The research for this paper has been supported by Keio University's grant-in-aid assistance for researchers engaged in sabbatical research.

Unless otherwise indicated, translations from the Japanese are mine.

[2] Performance records (the duration of the run; the number of performances; the total number of spectators) of the four plays are as follows: *The Merchant of Venice* (October 1947 – April 1949; 612; 1 million), *Much Ado About Nothing* (May–July 1948; 108; NA), *A Midsummer Night's Dream* (May–December 1949; NA; NA) and *Romeo and Juliet* (February 1950 – December 1950; 225+; 0.2 million). See Masaharu Miyagawa et al., eds., *Gurafu Zenshinza: soritsu 45 shunen kinen* ('Zenshinza: 45th Anniversary Photo Album') (Tokyo, 1975), pp. 27–31.

[3] Early forays into this topic include Yoshio Arai, *Sheikusupia-geki joen-ron* ('Shakespearian Stage Productions') (Tokyo, 1972), pp. 284–8; Kazuo Hayakawa, 'Zenshinza-to Sheikusupia' ('Zenshinza and Shakespeare'), in *Sheikusupia-no shiki* ('The Four Seasons in Shakespeare') (Tokyo, 1984), pp. 568–78.

then managed all *kabuki* actors, and formed an independent theatre troupe, Zenshinza, aiming to 'ensure the livelihood of the company members while also meeting the progressive artistic demands of a broad audience'.[4] Initially comprising thirty-one male and female actors from both *kabuki* and modern theatre, Zenshinza not only performed a wide variety of classical and contemporary plays but also appeared on radio and in films such as Sadao Yamanaka's masterpiece *Ninjo kamifusen* ('Humanity and Paper Balloons') (1937). Zenshinza was managed in an exceptionally democratic manner for its time: all its plans and rules, including pay policies, were decided at its members' general meetings. In 1935, they built a communal housing complex complete with an office block and rehearsal rooms in Kichijoji, Tokyo, where all the members and their families began living together. When the war intensified, Zenshinza toured the countryside with war-supportive performances, under the pressure of the military government. As soon as the war ended, they wholeheartedly embraced the GHQ's policies of demilitarization and democratization of Japan and performed such translated plays as Jean-Richard Bloch's *Toulon*, a story of the Free French forces battling against Nazi Germany, and John Drinkwater's *Abraham Lincoln*, alongside a small number of *kabuki* pieces that are clear of feudalistic, militaristic or nationalistic values and sentiments. As the company's long-serving producer Masaharu Miyagawa explained, 'truly democratic plays had yet to be written in Japan' at that time and had to be imported from abroad. Moreover, Japanese theatre 'had been severed from the outside world during the war and now needed to start learning from and incorporating in its repertory first-rate works by overseas dramatists'.[5]

In war-torn Tokyo, Zenshinza suffered from slow ticket sales and theatre shortages. Theatre tickets were too expensive for most citizens: to help make up for budget shortfalls, the Japanese government imposed a 200 per cent entertainment tax on theatre tickets as of 1946.[6] Performance venues were in short supply – many theatres in metropolitan areas had been destroyed by air raids – and the few remaining buildings were in the hands of harsh capitalists.[7] To address these problems, Zenshinza launched the Theatre for Young People. The company separated into three to five travelling troupes, of which one or two gave school performances by setting up makeshift theatres. Other groups also toured the nation, mainly performing *kabuki* plays. The target audience of the Theatre for Young People was secondary school students, but they also performed for factory workers and farmers who were hungry for culture and

entertainment after the dark wartime years. Ticket prices were kept very low: the company did not have to pay for the venues, and theatre tickets were exempt from taxation when the performance was hosted by an educational institution. The actors cut costs even further by not only playing multiple roles on stage but also doubling as stagehands (Figure 5). The ticket price was 50 yen in 1949, and to make ends meet, the company needed to give two performances a day to at least 1,250 spectators each time. The proceeds, of roughly 125,000 yen a day, would go to the host of the show, who would pay Zenshinza 66,000 yen, inclusive of travel expenses.[8]

The company's daily routine was arduous. They would start work at 6 a.m., bringing in stage equipment, props and costumes to the venue and arranging classroom desks in an empty hall to form a thrust stage like that of a Shakespearian playhouse (Figure 6). After giving two performances (starting at 9 a.m. and 12 noon respectively, with each running 2 to 2½ hours), cast members would take questions from the students (Figure 7), pack everything back up again and load the truck, before riding on another truck to the next destination (Figure 8). They repeated this procedure every day of the week, sometimes without having a single day off in a month.

The first programme, Victor Hugo's *Les Misérables*, was popular with students and was performed 634 times between November 1946 and August 1949.[9] From the next production, however, the company decided to focus on Shakespeare. As Chojuro Kawarasaki explained, *Les Misérables* was adapted for stage by novelist and minor playwright Masao Kume, and there was nothing remarkable about its dramatic construction. Zenshinza 'should rather work on theatrical masterpieces and decided to tackle a series of plays by Shakespeare'.[10] Shakespeare's

---

4   Miyagawa, *Zenshinza*, p. 6. For the company's early history, see also Kan'emon Nakamura, *Gekidan gojunen* ('Zenshinza: The First Fifty Years') (Tokyo, 1980).

5   Masaharu Miyagawa, 'Repatori-ni tsuite' ('On Zenshinza's repertory'), *Zenshinza* new series 4 (1947), 4.

6   'Nyujozei-o teppai seyo' ('Abolish the admission tax'), *Nihon News*, Nihon Eiga Shinsha, 1946, online video recording, NHK Archives, www2.nhk.or.jp/archives/movies/?id=D0009181345_00000.

7   Chojouro Kawarasaki, 'Za-no seinen engeki undo' ('Our company's Theatre for Young People'), *Zenshinza*, 19 November 1946.

8   Akira Nakamura, *Fuan to hanko* ('Anxiety and Revolt') (Tokyo, 1954), p. 183.

9   A sequel to *Les Misérables* was also staged from April to July 1947.

10 Taizo Sasamura, 'Zenshinza-no shinbunya: Kawarasaki Chojuro-to kataru' ('A new direction for Zenshinza: a conversation with Chojuro Kawarasaki'), *Maru* 1 (1948), 64.

5 Zenshinza actors doubling as stagehands (© Zenshinza).

6 Zenshinza's *Much Ado About Nothing* performed on a makeshift thrust stage (© Zenshinza).

7 Zenshinza actors responding to students' questions (© Zenshinza).

8 Zenshinza actors travelling to the next destination (© Zenshinza).

plays were originally staged without elaborate sets or lighting, so they would also be suitable for the troupe's performance at venues with inadequate facilities.[11]

The first Shakespearian play for the youth project was *The Merchant of Venice*, which would prove to be the company's signature piece: it would be staged 618 times, attracting a total audience of 1 million people. The story of the Jewish moneylender had been well known in Japan since the Meiji era (1868–1912) as Mary Lamb's prose retelling in *Tales from Shakespeare* was widely available in translations and adaptations, and excerpts from Lamb's and other writers' narrative versions often appeared in English school readers for secondary school students. The play, however, had rarely been performed in its entirety: most early productions staged the trial scene alone.[12] Zenshinza performed the entire play. According to Kawarasaki, who played Shylock, efforts were made to reduce the overall running time 'by streamlining the dialogue, speeding up the actors' entrances and exits and eliminating blackouts between scenes'.[13] The actors tried to understand Shakespearian dramaturgy by rehearsing and performing the play. Zenshinza normally staged a *kabuki* play after just a week's preparation, but they rehearsed *The Merchant of Venice* day and night for three weeks before the first performance and made it a rule to take a week off after each month-long tour to review and fine-tune their acting and staging styles. The rehearsals were 'suffocatingly intense':

We thought long and hard to unravel the complex relationships among the numerous dramatic characters. Sometimes, things got so stressful that it gave me heart-wrenching anxiety. The interactions of the exquisitely portrayed characters and the torrents of words rushing out of their mouths convey the story vividly and interestingly. If actors misunderstand them and act and deliver the lines incorrectly, a Shakespearian performance would be plunged into sheer chaos.[14]

The company's goal was not 'to interpret Shakespeare in a new way', but 'to truly understand him' by performing his plays: 'To rehearse and stage a play, to fail and rise again and study the piece further – these practical approaches have been lacking in Shakespeare studies in Japan.'[15] Zenshinza started touring *The Merchant of Venice* nationwide in October 1947. Shingoro Nakamura, as Launcelot, opened the show by humorously explaining the play's background, and the first half of the performance flew by at a frenzied pace, with Jessica's tryst with Lorenzo, the casket scenes and the exchanges between Shylock and Tubal among the highlights. The curtain fell at Bassanio's departure for Venice, and, after a fifteen-minute interval, thespians showcased their acting prowess in the courtroom scene before the happy denouement in Belmont. Students were entranced by the company's energetic performance. Actress Shizue Kawarasaki, who played Portia, vividly recalls the complete silence that fell during the trial scene. The auditorium would normally be packed with around 1,500 students and be oppressively hot in the summer, but the young spectators would hold their breath and focus on the stage.[16] A secondary school student (signed 'H. T.') recorded his/her excited reaction soon after a performance in Kawasaki City, Kanagawa Prefecture. The student was on the organizing committee for the Zenshinza event and had seen the company's performance beforehand in Tokyo. When the show started at the local school, 'I wanted my friends to see all the wonderful scenes as soon as possible and I wanted to explain all their beauties to them':

Portia's innocence and her pleasant, lovely demeanour, the way in which she loses herself in the heat of passion as she tries to save her husband and her husband's friend, and how happy and fulfilled she becomes in the final scenes … all of these are deeply engraved in my memory … Meanwhile, I could also clearly see that even though Shylock is a Jew, he loves his daughter deeply. How shocking that his heart should uncontrollably harden towards Jessica when his riches are lost.

The actors' single-minded devotion to the performance and their harmonious teamwork also impressed the student deeply:

Zenshinza seemed to embody the spirit of unity, freedom and responsibility to perfection. I noticed how the older members

---

[11] Chojuro Kawarasaki, 'Sheikusupia-to kurasu ichinenkan' ('Living with Shakespeare for an entire year'), in *Sheikusupia kenkyu* ('Studies in Shakespeare'), ed. Yoshio Nakano (Tokyo, 1949), 227–310; pp. 299–300.

[12] I discussed the reception of *The Merchant of Venice* in the Meiji era, in Oya, '"And which the Jew?": representations of Shylock in Meiji Japan (1868–1912)', in *Shakespeare Survey 76* (Cambridge, 2023), 102–11. See also Kohei Uchimura, 'Sheikusupia-to eigo-kyoiku: Chugakko-yo eigokyokasho-ni okeru' ('A bibliographical approach to Shakespeare incorporated into locally produced EFL school readers authorized for use in Japanese secondary schools between 1886 and 2016'), *Nihon kyoikushi kenkyu* 33 (2018), 29–58.

[13] C. Kawarasaki, 'Living with Shakespeare', pp. 290–1. A promptbook of Zenshinza's *The Merchant of Venice* is in the archival collection of the Tsubouchi Memorial Theatre Museum Library.

[14] C. Kawarasaki, 'Living with Shakespeare', p. 292.

[15] C. Kawarasaki, 'Living with Shakespeare', pp. 292–3.

[16] Shizue Kawarasaki, 'Machi-kara mura-e' ('Travelling from town to village'), *Nihon engeki* 6 (1948), 18–19; p. 19.

of the company support the younger ones, who respect the veteran actors in return. The relations between them, however, are not hierarchical. Your organization sets a wonderful, valuable example for all of us to follow.[17]

Zenshinza's Shakespeare tour did not simply inspire the teenagers of the war-torn country. It was an enlightening learning process for the actors who delved deep into the dynamics of Shakespeare's dramaturgy by staging *The Merchant of Venice* hundreds of times and observing the audience's reaction to their performance. Before the tour started, the actors reacted against the expressions 'Jew' and 'the Jew' that Christian characters use when they call and refer to Shylock. Kan'emon Nakamura even suggested amending these politically incorrect expressions. However, 'we soon came to see that Shakespeare's dramatic instinct was unerring'. Shylock 'must first be despised and humiliated' to become as defiant and antagonistic as he is to Christian characters, and the tension and conflict thus created are essential to the play.[18] The actors were also uncomfortable with the exchange between Launcelot and Gobbo, as it felt 'disrespectful' and therefore 'unpleasant and educationally undesirable' for a son to poke fun at his elderly, visually impaired father. Once the performance started, the actors immediately conceded that Shakespeare was absolutely right yet again. The two characters representing the lowest social class in the play were loveable, cheeky and full of folksy humour onstage. The audience loved them and always laughed delightedly when the pair appeared on stage.[19]

Zenshinza actors came to believe that, by portraying all the characters vividly and compellingly, Shakespeare was 'striving to achieve the ideals of humanism'. In the brochure for the performance, they asked the students to stop being judgemental about the drama's characters and instead to embrace all of them wholeheartedly, avoiding the binary opposition of 'good' and 'evil'.[20] By interpreting and performing *The Merchant of Venice* in this way, Zenshinza was giving expression to the ideas of humanism and individualism not yet realized in the hierarchical and group-oriented Japanese society.

SHAKESPEARE AND THE GHQ'S REFORM AGENDA

The Theatre for Young People had a far-reaching impact on Japan's post-war culture and education, and Zenshinza was seen as a torchbearer of the ongoing democratic and humanistic revolution. 'You probably think that you are just performing a play', journalist Kan Niizuma wrote to the company members, 'but your performance in Kamakura yesterday was in fact helping reconstruct Japan in a way that might look remote but is indeed most effective':

Why? It is because *The Merchant of Venice*, which you perform with the same earnestness and dedication as you would in front of theatre connoisseurs, is being shown to young generations who are the hope for the country's future. They are like fields of virgin soil, and you are planting seeds that will flower and bear fruits in time to come.[21]

Zenshinza's Shakespeare broadened the cultural horizons of the young audience, exposing them to new ideas and points of view.

On 9 and 16 November 1947, Zenshinza gave a special performance of *The Merchant of Venice* using the outdoor stage of the Tsubouchi Memorial Theatre Museum, Waseda University, which was modelled after Edward Alleyn's Fortune Theatre (1600–1621) (Figure 9).[22] It was a momentous occasion attended by numerous dignitaries from the worlds of politics and culture, including families of GHQ officials and British diplomats. Prime Minister Tetsu Katayama enjoyed the performance in a private capacity. When asked to give a speech, he addressed the 1,000-strong audience at the top of his voice, 'This remarkable event signals the start of the building of a *bunka kokka* ['cultural state'] here in Japan.'[23] Ikuo Oyama, political scientist and member of the House of Councillors, also gave a speech: 'Japan's defeat in the war meant the defeat of the military government and the liberation of the people. Militarists are gone but the nation's arts and culture are here to stay.'[24] At this point, Zenshinza's Shakespeare project was perfectly aligned with the cultural policies of the GHQ and the Japanese government.

---

[17] 'H. T.', 'Venisu-no shonin-o mite' ('Some remarks on Zenshinza's *The Merchant of Venice*'), *Zenshinza* new series 6 (1948), 14.

[18] C. Kawarasaki, 'Living with Shakespeare', pp. 284–5.

[19] C. Kawarasaki, 'Living with Shakespeare', p. 285.

[20] See the brochure for a school performance in Toyama Prefecture (5 and 6 July 1948), in The Zenshinza Archive, Tokyo.

[21] Kan Niizuma, 'Zenshinza-no min'na-ni' ('To all the members of Zenshinza'), *Zenshinza* new series 6 (1948), 13.

[22] For a video of part of the performance on 16 September, see '*Venisu-no shonin*' ('*The Merchant of Venice*'), *Nihon News*, Nihon Eiga Shinsha, [1947], online video recording, NHK Archives, www2.nhk.or.jp/archives/movies/?id=D0009182042_00000.

[23] 'Katayama shusho-mo kazoku-to kenbutsu' ('PM Katayama and his family in the audience'), *Tokyo Shimbun*, 10 November 1947.

[24] Quoted in K. Nakamura, 'Zenshinza', p. 300.

9 Zenshinza's *The Merchant of Venice* at the Theatre Museum, Waseda University, 1947 (© Zenshinza).

Zenshinza went on to receive the prestigious Asahi Prize for 1947, in recognition not just of their 'enlightening school performances', but also of the company's 'democratic management style'. As the citation for the prize put it, Zenshinza 'organized school tours and worked towards enlightenment of people through theatre' while overcoming 'economic hardships by implementing a democratic joint management system, which sets the direction of theatre troupe management in post-war Japan'. Zenshinza's school tour was called 'democracy in action' and 'a significant contribution to theatre culture'.[25] Indeed, Zenshinza's artistic and organizational principles perfectly agreed with the GHQ policy to eradicate the militarism and ultra-nationalism that had overshadowed Japanese society and education in the

---

[25] *Asahi Shimbun* (Osaka ed.), 12 January 1948.

preceding decade. Zenshinza was deemed so exemplary and reliable by the Allied Occupation that it was allowed to perform whatever play it wanted without going through the censorship process.[26] When *The Merchant of Venice* was performed for the second time at the Theatre Museum on 14 October 1948, Chojuro Kawarasaki underlined the company's worthy mission:

We are tirelessly travelling across the nation with just a back-pack on our shoulders, to bring culture to the young students around the country, and the young men and women working in factories, mines and farms. With your kind support and help, we are hoping to continue serving our country.[27]

Firmly convinced that their youth project was in the service of the newly democratized country, Kawarasaki and his colleagues staged a second Shakespeare play, *Much Ado About Nothing*, from May to July 1948. Kan'emon Nakamura, who played Benedick, believed that the comedy would uplift the spirit of, and bring joy to, young students who had endured challenging times in their entire childhoods:

In these gloomy days, people are always knitting their brows and making wry grimaces. A significant element of Shakespearian comedy is its lively and exuberant portrayal of human liberation, which also characterizes the spirit of the Renaissance. By performing *Much Ado About Nothing* and realizing the play's energy, wholesomeness and cheerfulness onstage, we hope to rouse the hearts of the students and brighten the dark, overcast sky spreading all over Japan.[28]

It was a very happy time for Zenshinza, when performing Shakespeare was believed, both by themselves and by society, to be instrumental to the well-being of Japanese people. However, this was due to change completely when the members of the company and their families joined the Japanese Communist Party (JCP) the following year.

ZENSHINZA 'WORKERS' IN JAPAN'S CHANGING POLITICAL LANDSCAPE

Zenshinza members had always been socially oriented and had left-wing sympathies ever since they revolted against the hierarchical *kabuki* world to form an egalitarian, consensus-based collective. After touring the country performing Shakespeare, the company leaned even further to the left. Chojuro Kawarasaki reminisced: 'I learned a great deal by performing for the ingenuous young students and people of the proletariat. By escaping

commercialism, we connected directly with the general public. The experience changed our outlook on art.' *Kabuki* actors such as Kawarasaki were taught to practise art for art's sake, but while waiting in the wings for the next entrance cue for Shylock, he was overwhelmed by just how much those students and workers were relishing every moment of the Zenshinza show:

I seriously questioned the creed of 'art for art's sake'. I wanted to stage Shakespeare in a way that was interesting, enjoyable and understandable to all these wonderful people. It is actors' and theatre companies' social responsibility to perform a play handsomely and entertainingly so that every single one in the audience can clearly hear, understand and enjoy it.[29]

The members of Zenshinza decided to discard their 'petit-bourgeois values and artistic temperaments' and reinvent themselves as 'theatre workers':

Shakespeare taught me to truly love the public. His dramaturgy is perfect technically and his genius and demonic energy that shaped those beautifully crafted plays never fail to astound me profoundly. Even more important, however, is the fact that Shakespeare had the public in mind as he wrote plays ... He always loved the public. He always tried to speak and appeal to the public, to entertain them, please them and teach them. That is why Shakespeare is immortal.[30]

In testimony of their commitment to the workers' cause, all but a couple of the Zenshinza members and their families joined the JCP in March 1949.

Meanwhile, the GHQ's Occupation policies were shifting drastically, reflecting the volatile political and economic landscape in Japan and abroad. From the end of the war in 1945 and into 1947, the Allied Powers demilitarized Japan and promoted democracy by down-grading the emperor's status from that of the 'sovereign' to the 'symbol' of the state, and granting more rights to the parliament. They also democratized the economic system by carrying out land reform and breaking up (if imperfectly) the *zaibatsu* ('large business conglomerates'). The new Constitution of Japan, enacted in 1947

---

[26] K. Nakamura, 'Zenshinza', p. 292. Normally, theatre companies were required to submit a copy of their playscripts to both the Civil Censorship Detachment (CCD) and the Civil Information and Education Section (CIE) of the GHQ.

[27] Audio recording, in the Tsubouchi Memorial Theatre Museum Library (CT1-000145).

[28] Kan'emon Nakamura, *Engi jiden* ('My Life in Acting') (Tokyo, 1973), p. 274.

[29] C. Kawarasaki, 'Living with Shakespeare', p. 317.

[30] C. Kawarasaki, 'Living with Shakespeare', p. 318.

under the GHQ's guidance, renounced the nation's right to engage in war or use military force to resolve disputes. It also empowered previously marginalized groups, legalizing the Communist and Socialist parties and giving rights and privileges to workers and to women. In late 1947 or early 1948, however, an economic crisis in Japan and the spread of Communism in Asia sparked a reversal of the Occupation policies. Economic rehabilitation of Japan was prioritized over democratization and demilitarization. In accordance with the GHQ's 'Reverse Course', the Japanese government began to suppress labour union activities and left-wing movements, purging Communists from various public and private offices between 1950 and 1952.

The GHQ's and the Japanese government's swing to the right dealt a serious blow to Zenshinza's Theatre for Young People. When the company members joined the JCP, the Ministry of Education and the Tokyo Metropolitan Board of Education immediately withdrew their sponsorship of the company's Shakespeare tours, stating that 'it is against the Fundamental Law of Education to host a performance of a theatre troupe most of whose actors are members of a particular political party'.[31] The GHQ also sent a missive to the educational boards of various cities and towns to stop them providing performance venues to Zenshinza.[32] The company could no longer use school auditoriums and other public halls.

All these difficulties notwithstanding, Zenshinza would stage two more Shakespeare plays, *A Midsummer Night's Dream* and *Romeo and Juliet*. According to their interpretation, the two plays are about young people staying true to their love in a feudalistic society, in defiance of their parents' opposition. In the course of the last two Shakespeare tours, the company encountered various interferences from the police, the tax office and local governments. Their bookings of venues were cancelled on account of their connection with the JCP, and arrests were made of Zenshinza actors and local event organizers on the pretext of tax evasion and criminal trespass on the premises of theatres.[33] For instance, Zenshinza was set to perform *A Midsummer Night's Dream* at Osaka Gakugei University (now Osaka Kyoiku University) on 6 August 1949, but the university cancelled the booking of the venue just a week before the performance day, even though 4,000 tickets had already been sold. The police blocked the company members who tried to ferry in stage properties on 5 August. On the performance day, a 200-strong riot

police squad was deployed to guard the premises.[34] The actors were unflappable: using the athletics grounds near the original venue, they staged the show later the same day, which more than 4,000 people attended. Interference by the police and the tax office was repeated at other venues, but Zenshinza carried on performing Shakespeare. When they were denied access to the hall they had booked, they would immediately move to an alternative location such as 'the grounds of a temple, an empty lot where discarded oil drums served as our stage, and the playground of a primary school'. Attendance at their outdoor performances 'tripled or even quadrupled' thanks to 'the publicity generated by the undue interference' and to the fact that 'outdoor spaces can accommodate larger numbers of spectators than indoor halls'.[35] Chojuro Kawarasaki, who played Bottom in *A Midsummer Night's Dream*, protested against the gross interference by the government and the police, stating that 'to suppress a Shakespeare play in this manner is an act of folly unprecedented in history'.[36] Shingoro Nakamura, who played Egeus, made the same point when he wrote: 'Officers in Japan won't let us perform Shakespeare's world-famous masterpiece even when people are waiting to see it outside the theatre. This is unheard of anywhere else in the world.'[37]

RED SHAKESPEARE

Zenshinza insisted that they would stay away from Communist 'agitprop' (or agitational propaganda) and that their Shakespeare shows had nothing to do with their political beliefs.[38] As a matter of fact, Zenshinza's JCP membership changed the way in which Shakespeare was staged and shown to the public. Their performances

---

[31] *Yomiuri Shimbun*, 24 March 1949; quoted in K. Nakamura, 'Zenshinza', p. 307.

[32] K. Nakamura, 'Zenshinza', p. 307.

[33] The Miyagi Prefectural Archives hold full records (S25-2035) of a case where eleven event organizers of Zenshinza's *A Midsummer Night's Dream* (at Tohoku Theatre in Sendai City, 24 and 25 October 1949) were interrogated by the police on suspicion of tax evasion related to ticket sales revenue. No arrests were made in the end.

[34] *Shin-Osaka Shimbun* (evening ed.), 6 August 1949.

[35] Shingoro Nakamura, 'Jun'en hokoku' ('A report on our recent tour'), *Zenshinza* 3rd series, 1 (1950), 2.

[36] *Akahata*, 5 September 1949.

[37] S. Nakamura, 'A report', p. 2.

[38] Koji Toita, 'Zenshinza-no Kyosan-to iri' ('Zenshinza joined the JCP'), *Jiji Tsushin* 1015 (1949), 7–8.

were now hosted by JCP's regional bureaux and related cultural clubs, often with an endorsement from various labour unions. JCP members would hand out flyers for the shows and put up posters that read 'Let's go and see Zenshinza'. The performances were open to the public and remained popular with students, but the company's primary target was now unionized workers. Introducing *A Midsummer Night's Dream*, Chojuro Kawarasaki addressed the *hataraku taishu* ('working masses') by saying that 'Shakespeare, we actors, and the masses in the audience ... these three parties become united and create a new theatre for the workers'.[39] The front page of a leaflet for *Romeo and Juliet* prominently featured the slogan: 'For Workers'.[40] The company's commitment to the proletariat was more than obvious.

Communism also changed Zenshinza's acting style. When they performed their first Shakespearian play, *The Merchant of Venice*, the actors took advantage of their backgrounds in *kabuki* theatre. Critic Shunji Yoshida saw several similarities between Shakespeare and *kabuki*, which is thought to have originated in the early seventeenth century. The early *kabuki* stage protruded out into the audience in a way similar to the public playhouses of Shakespeare's time. Female roles were played by male actors and a play's action can take place in any number of locations.[41] For Chojuro Kawarasaki, *kabuki*'s 'exaggerated elocution' came in handy when the company performed 'to a large audience in a factory without a stage or in a dock facing the sea in the suburb of Hiroshima Prefecture'.[42] Most spectators appreciated the company's acting style, thinking that the *kabuki* techniques were 'a great asset' when performing a Shakespeare play.[43] Theatre practitioners and critics with left-wing sympathies, however, championed Socialist Realism and attacked Zenshinza's *kabuki*-flavoured delivery and gestures, saying that the company's style was archaic and lacking in 'realism'.[44] The most astute among the critics was Yoshi Hijikata, a former aristocrat turned Communist theatre director who had worked as assistant to Aleksey Popov at the Moscow Revolution Theatre from 1933 to 1937. Back in Japan, he emerged as an exponent of the Stanislavski System, giving Shakespeare acting classes at a left-wing drama school, Butai Geijutsu Gakuin, in Tokyo.[45] To Hijikata, Shakespeare is 'a realist' and the formalistic *kabuki* acting is therefore 'totally useless, whether the performance takes place outdoors or indoors'. After seeing Zenshinza's *The Merchant of Venice*, he wrote: 'If the company performs Shakespeare again in the future, the actors should discard their *kabuki* mannerisms and

start from scratch by learning realistic acting and direction.'[46] Zenshinza took Hijikata's suggestion to heart and tried to adopt the Stanislavski System. In April 1949, they invited Hijikata to be the company's advisor and director of *A Midsummer Night's Dream* (jointly with Masaharu Miyagawa) and *Romeo and Juliet*.[47] In 1951, the company members started a 'systematic study' of Iosif Matveevich Rapoport's *The Work of the Actor* (1936), then a standard textbook about the Realist style of performance for actors.[48]

Sometimes, the company's Communist faith and sympathy with the working-class audience affected, or even distorted, their interpretation of Shakespeare. In the leaflet for Zenshinza's *A Midsummer Night's Dream* tour, Hijikata underlined how Shakespeare empathized with the working class and resented that Quince, Bottom and other mechanics, who have 'youthful, healthy energy and down-to-earth wisdom (or at least wit)', should end up making fools of themselves by staging *Pyramus and Thisbe*. Shakespeare gave verse to

---

[39] C. Kawarasaki, 'Manatsu-no goaisatsu' ('Introducing *A Midsummer Night's Dream*'), in the brochure for the matinee and evening performances on 22 and 23 July 1949, at Himeji Kokaido, Hyogo Prefecture: The Zenshinza Archive.

[40] See the brochure for the matinee and evening performances on 7 August 1950, at Yamagata City Elementary School IV, Yamagata Prefecture: The Zenshinza Archive.

[41] Shunji Yoshida, 'Zenshinza-to iu gekidan' ('The theatre troupe named Zenshinza'), *Jikei* 25 (1953), 108–11; p. 110.

[42] A. Nakamura, 'Anxiety and revolt', pp. 181–2.

[43] Kazumitsu Miyoshi, 'Shibai-no tanoshisa' ('The pleasure of theatre'), *Zenshinza* new series 6 (1948), 12. For a similar view, see also Shiko Tsubouchi, 'Kabuki-no engi-to Sheikusupia geki' ('*Kabuki* acting and Shakespearian drama'), *Zenshinza* new series 6 (1948), 8; Yonezo Hamamura, 'Zenshinza-no Saou geki' ('Zenshinza's Shakespeare performance'), *Zenshinza* new series 6 (1948), 8.

[44] Katsuichi Wada, 'Mondai-o haramu yagaigeki' ('A problematic outdoor performance'), *Zenshinza* new series 6 (1948), 10. See also Tomoyoshi Murayama, '*Venisu-no shonin*-o miru' ('Looking at *The Merchant of Venice*'), *Zenshinza* new series 6 (1948), 12; and 'Hihan-to jikohihan' ('Criticism and self-criticism'), *Teatro* 12 (1950), 16–17.

[45] Yoji Yamada, 'Kantoku shugyo: Hijikata Yoshi-ni mananda engeki' ('A director prepares: studying theatre with Yoshi Hijikata'), *Asahi Shimbun*, 8 April 2023.

[46] Yoshi Hijikata, 'Oku-no shisa' ('Many new possibilities'), *Zenshinza* new series 6 (1948), 11.

[47] Hijikata was probably responsible for the choice of plays for Zenshinza's last two Shakespeare tours, as he had directed *A Midsummer Night's Dream* and *Romeo and Juliet* in 1946 and 1948, respectively.

[48] Kan'emon Nakamura, 'Engi-ron' ('On acting'), *Teatro* 14 (1952), 6–41; pp. 21, 28–35.

the aristocratic characters and prose to the lower-class ones so that the latter's lines should be delivered in a 'positive, real and powerful' way to the audience.[49] The actors took the director's interpretation to its logical limit. While touring the play, they constantly received complaints from audience members that Shakespeare was 'remote' from their everyday concerns. The workers would say: 'Why should Zenshinza perform *A Midsummer Night's Dream*? . . . Why not choose a play that directly reflects the struggle we are engaged in today?' To address this issue, the actors modified the performance without consulting Hijikata. The play was now about 'the confrontation between the social class represented by the mechanics and the feudal and bourgeois upper classes that also encompass Oberon and Titania'. The new ending portrayed the triumph of the workers: the aristocratic spectators were 'so moved by the tragedy of "Pyramus and Thisbe" that they burst into tears uncontrollably'. Playwright and theatre director Masami Uryu, who was an assistant to Hijikata at that time, caught the show halfway through the tour and was shocked at the 'distortion' that the actors had created. According to Uryu, even though theatre must address the exigencies of the time and 'support people's struggle to protect peace and freedom against the warmongers and international imperialists', the mission 'cannot be achieved by simply discarding Shakespeare':

We are building a national anti-war front in the face of the war hawks who would quash love between man and woman, freedom and peace. Now is the time to learn from the Revolutionary Romanticism of *A Midsummer Night's Dream*, which powerfully promotes humanism and holds romantic love in high regard.[50]

Being fervent believers in Marxism–Leninism–Stalinism, Zenshinza actors listened to Uryu and subjected themselves to serious 'self-criticism'. They abandoned their 'workers vs non-workers' schematism when they tackled their fourth, and final, Shakespeare play, *Romeo and Juliet*. Now their 'struggle' was 'to portray each dramatic character as a living, breathing human being, and thereby maximize the Revolutionary Romanticism' of Shakespearian drama.[51]

REPERCUSSIONS

For all their 'struggles', it appears that the company's Shakespeare failed to convince the working-class audiences. Students still wanted 'more Shakespeare', but workers kept saying 'We want to see Zenshinza's *kabuki*,

why don't you play *kabuki*?' and 'You certainly play Shakespeare well, but I should also like to see a Japanese play.'[52] To satisfy the expectations of both groups, the company's final Shakespeare tour was a double bill of *Romeo and Juliet* and a *kabuki* play, *Kochiyama Soshun*. The tour wrapped in December 1950, and Zenshinza stopped performing Shakespeare until 1997, when *The Merchant of Venice* was revived to commemorate the fiftieth anniversary of the Theatre for Young People.

Zenshinza only produced four Shakespeare plays but the scale of their undertaking was monumental: they visited all the regions of the war-torn country, giving some 1,000 performances in total and attracting around 1.4 million audience members. The Shakespeare shows left a lasting impression on the schoolchildren and workers in remote areas, many of whom saw a live performance for the first time. Takako Miyanaga, then ten years old, attended *The Merchant of Venice* in November 1947 in a small town, Sahara, in Chiba Prefecture. She was totally mesmerized by the beauty and graciousness of Shizue Kawarasaki's Portia as she confronted her husband Chojuro Kawarasaki's forceful Shylock. This experience prompted her to become involved in various cultural activities in the town. In 2007, her long-cherished dream came true. The Katori-shi Sahara bunka kyokai ('Katori-city Sahara Association for Cultural Promotion'), of which she is chair, hosted a Zenshinza performance for local people just sixty years after the memorable Shakespeare show.[53] Kazuo Inui, from Okayama Prefecture, saw *The Merchant of Venice* at a shabby hall ('a cinema or a theatre, I wasn't sure which') as a high school student. The substandard theatre facilities did nothing to detract from the amazing experience: 'I was stunned beyond words at the sight of flesh-and-blood humans living in and acting out the world of literature. My whole body was tingling with

---

49 Yoshi Hijikata, '*Manatsu-no yo-no yume*-ni tsuite' ('On *A Midsummer Night's Dream*'), in *Enshutsusha-no michi* ('A Director's Footsteps') (Tokyo, 1969), 282–4; pp. 283–4.

50 Masami Uryu, 'Zenshinza-no sozo-hoho' ('Zenshinza's creative methods'), *Teatro* 12 (1950), 59–66; pp. 61–3.

51 Uryu, 'Zenshinza', pp. 62–4.

52 Chojuro Kawarasaki, 'Atarashii repatori-ni tsuite' ('About our new repertory'), in the brochure for a *Romeo and Juliet* and *Kochiyama Sochun* show: The Zenshinza Archive.

53 A personal phone interview with Takako Miyanaga, 12 April 2024. About the 2007 Zenshinza performance in Sahara, see also Keisuke Yagyu, 'Venisu-no kuzuya-san?' ('The rubbish collector of Venice?'), http://koendayori.blog111.fc2.com/blog-entry-115.html.

excitement.' He would go on to establish the Okayama engeki kansho kyokai ('Theatre Appreciation Association of Okayama') in 1955 and served as its secretary for over thirty years.[54]

Zenshinza's Shakespeare performance helped not only to provide *joso kyoiku* ('aesthetic education') to young students, but also to 'enhance regional theatre activities'.[55] Amateur theatre gained significant traction and popularity in Occupied Japan thanks to the GHQ's and the Japanese government's promotion of cultural policy. People themselves were also yearning for entertainment and arts that had been suppressed during the war. Zenshinza's Shakespeare tours had 'a far-reaching influence' on the activities of the school and workplace drama clubs across the country, and the company's acting and staging techniques, and even their mannerisms, were avidly copied by amateur actors.[56] Nishiki Miura was a member of the drama club of her high school when Zenshinza visited Aomori Prefecture: 'I was ashamed to realize how naive and childish our performance was compared to Zenshinza's *The Merchant of Venice*. I wanted to deliver as impassioned a performance as that, once in my life.' After graduation, she got a job with a regional bank and immediately joined the drama society for its workers.[57] Meanwhile, Kotaro Tomita was a high school teacher in Kumamoto Prefecture when he saw *The Merchant of Venice* in January or February 1949. The performance inspired him to first create a student theatre company at his school, and then to leave the school to become a professional actor himself.[58] Akiyoshi Ikeda's career traced a reverse trajectory. He was a Zenshinza actor when *The Merchant of Venice* toured Okayama in 1948. He left the company soon after and, in 1952, helped launch an amateur troupe, Okayama Shingekijo, in the prefecture.[59]

Zenshinza's Theatre for Young People also prompted other professional companies to stage plays specifically for young audiences. In 1948, Haiyuza (meaning 'Actors' Theatre'), Bungakuza ('Literary Theatre'), left-wing Shinkyo Gekidan ('New Cooperative Theatre Company'), Baraza ('Rose Theatre') and Tokyo Seinen Gekidan ('Tokyo Youth Theatre Company') all started projects for (mainly) primary school children. The plays featured in their programmes, however, were the likes of *Jack and the Beanstalk* and Maurice Maeterlinck's *The Blue Bird* and were considerably less challenging to stage than, say, Zenshinza's *Much Ado About Nothing*. Most of the companies discontinued their youth projects after one or two plays.[60] This only shows the enormity of the scope and ambition of Zenshinza's Theatre for Young People. The 'Progressive' actors were out on the road performing Shakespeare twice a day, day after day, for four years, battling against not just the elements but also the GHQ, national and local governments, the police and the tax office. By bringing Shakespeare's vividly conceived characters to life, Zenshinza introduced the novel concepts of humanism and individualism to students and workers in Occupied Japan, inspiring them to enjoy theatre and sometimes to participate in it actively throughout their lives.

---

54 Kazuo Inui, *Butai-ni yume yosete* ('Chasing a Dream in Theatre') (Okayama, 1990), pp. 17–25.

55 The Social Education Office, Okayama Prefecture, ed., *Shakai kyoiku hoshin* ('Social Education Policy') (Okayama, 1948), p. 116.

56 *Niigata-ken nenkan* ('Niigata Prefecture Yearbook') (Niigata, 1949), p. 161; Sotaro Miura, *Iwate-ken-ni okeru tenkeiki-no gunzo* ('People of Iwate Prefecture at a Time of Transition') (Iwate, 1962), p. 111.

57 Nishiki Miura, 'Watashi-no ayumi' ('The footsteps of my life'), in *Aogin juso junen-shi* ('The Aomori Bank Trade Union: The First Ten Years'), ed. the Aomori Bank Trade Union ([Aomori], 1959), 127–32; p. 128.

58 The Kumamoto Nichinichi Shimbun, ed., *Kyushu jinkokuki* ('The Eminent People of Kyushu') (Kumamoto, 1966), pp. 233–4.

59 Itaro Yamamoto, *Okayama-no engeki* ('Theatre in Okayama Prefecture') (Okayama, 1984), p. 149.

60 *Nihon jidogeki zenshu* ('A Complete Collection of Japanese Children's Plays'), 4 vols. (Tokyo, 1961), vol. 3, p. 457. Haiyuza continued its youth programme until around 1960, staging 23 plays (629 performances) for primary school students. It only staged 3 plays (34 performances) for older students and workers. See Koreya Senda, 'Haiyuza-no ayumi' ('A history of Haiyuza'), https://haiyuza.net/haiyuza-history/step.

'UNRESPECTIVE BOYS': THE FORMATION AND BETRAYAL OF CHILD PEER COMMUNITIES IN *RICHARD III*

BENJAMIN S. REED

In 2012, an archaeological project was undertaken by the Richard III Society to verify claims made by Audrey Strange (1975)[1] and David Baldwin (1986)[2] that the king's remains had been buried underneath a car park in Leicester where Greyfriars Church once stood. The dig, costing over £35,000, revealed a skeleton. Based on DNA and dental records, the University of Leicester confirmed in February 2013 that the bones belonged to the deposed monarch. While this long-unsolved mystery of Richard III had reached a conclusion, scholars and history buffs alike remain concerned with a different set of remains buried in Westminster Abbey: those allegedly belonging to the king's nephews Edward V, king of England, and Richard, Duke of York. Until recently, these two boys, often named the 'princes in the Tower', were exclusively read as martyrs, murdered by their power-hungry uncle, and remain a frequent talking point in documentaries such as BBC Select's *Who Killed the Princes in the Tower?* (2022). Historians and literary critics argue that Shakespeare's play *The Tragedie of Richard the Third* (hereafter *Richard III*)[3] helped propagate this popular myth as a means of legitimizing Henry VII's usurpation.[4] While the princes are historically embedded within an adult-constructed narrative that portrays them as voiceless victims, Shakespeare's play also humanizes the young royals by portraying them as individuals with their own desires, wants and awareness of experiences. Furthermore, the princes are not the only children with speaking parts in *Richard III*; there are three others of noble and servant backgrounds whom scholars have largely ignored when reading the play. This article argues that all five children take on the role of agents within spheres of influence identified by childhood studies scholars Miller and Yavneh, such as the home, family and peer groups.[5] Furthermore, agency among children is a double-edged sword: it creates protective peer communities, but the alliances formed are undermined by moments of self-preservation and self-policing.

Despite *Richard III*'s multiple moments of children forming peer communities, current and past scholarship has seemed predisposed to forward the mythologizing of the 'princes in the Tower'. Historian Matthew Lewis astutely observes that Shakespeare's play 'for centuries became accepted as the true history of King Richard III so that an overwhelming majority believes that they know Richard was an evil monster who murdered ... his nephews'.[6] Conversely, the historian John Ashdown-Hill curtly tells readers that

---

[1] See Audrey Strange, 'The Grey Friars, Leicester', *The Ricardian* 3 (September 1975), 3–7.

[2] See David Baldwin, 'King Richard's grave in Leicester', *Transactions of the Leicestershire Archaeological and Historical Society* (London, 1986), p. 60.

[3] All quotations from this play will come from *William Shakespeare: The Complete Works*, ed. Stanley Wells, Gary Taylor, John Jowett and William Montgomery (Oxford, 2005).

[4] For a historical overview of the princes and how their myth developed in early modern and modern culture, see John Ashdown-Hill, *The Mythology of the 'Princes in the Tower'* (Stroud, 2018); and Matthew Lewis, *The Survival of the Princes in the Tower: Murder, Mystery, and Myth* (Stroud, 2018). The term 'myth' also shows up frequently in recent literary critiques on *Richard III*, see Elizabeth Harper, '"And men ne'er spend their fury on a child": killing children in Shakespeare's early histories', *Shakespeare* 13 (2017), 193–209; Katie Knowles, 'Shakespeare's "terrible infants?": children in *Richard III, King John*, and *Macbeth*', in *The Child in British Literature: Literary Constructions of Childhood, Medieval to Contemporary*, ed. Adrienne E. Gavin (New York, 2012), 38–53; and Joseph Campana, 'Killing Shakespeare's children: the case of *Richard III* and *King John*', *Shakespeare* 3 (2007), 18–39.

[5] Naomi J. Miller and Naomi Yavneh, 'Introduction: early modern children as subjects – gender matters', in *Gender and Early Modern Constructions of Childhood*, ed. Naomi J. Miller and Naomi Yavneh (Farnham and Burlington, 2011), 1–14; p. 7.

[6] Lewis, *The Survival*, p. 8.

Shakespeare 'was a playwright, not a historian ... known to have invented a number of features of what he presented on stage as part of his dramatization of the story',[7] while also suggesting the entire 'princes in the Tower' myth was promulgated by Henry VII's government as an excuse for the execution of three 'pretenders' to the throne.[8] Both scholars' works, while providing important contributions to demystifying the role of Shakespeare in the perception of *Richard III*, nevertheless also assign the princes a passive role. I argue that the play remains important to both early modern and childhood studies because it provides child actors the opportunity to play children as agents with nuanced emotions and desires.

Although recent readings of the play do consider its portrayal of childhood, they remain focused on only the princes and their role in the murder 'myth'. For example, Elizabeth Harper posits that 'The fates of children in the early history plays thus reveal the tragic precariousness of mortal existence precisely because they are the mystified objects of future promise.'[9] Katie Knowles arrives at a similar conclusion that 'In death, the [princes] are immortalized and idealized: the image of the murdered princes ... is a lasting one which enshrines the boys as unassailable paragons of beauty and innocence and turns characters and audience against the tyrannous king'.[10] Joseph Campana decries such descriptors as 'predictable' and 'sentimental' concepts of childhood, but even his promising claim that Shakespeare's children 'constitute uncanny signifiers whose threatening overload of sexual, affective and temporal meaning requires minimization or elimination' largely focuses on what others say about the children instead of what they actually do in the play.[11] All three of these critics' conclusions, while seeking to empower the princes as fully developed characters, paradoxically revert to reducing the boys into mythical objects which are acted upon, rather than considering how they interact with each other. By broadening the scope of analysis and bringing all five children together, the princes can finally step down from the lonely pedestal of myth to engage with their peers. In so doing, the children in *Richard III* transform into navigators of complex societal systems alongside an adult world that attempts to protect and manipulate them, prompting diverse actions and reactions.

A key way these interactions play out is through the construction of peer communities among the children, which include social rituals of inclusion and exclusion. The formation of child peer groups is a point of interest in current childhood studies. Sidsel Boldermo from The Arctic University of Norway identifies that children as young as two years old have demonstrated 'fleeting moments of caring and sharing, shared joint experiences and ongoing negotiations of mutual bonds, hierarchies and group boundaries' that play pivotal roles in the establishment of belonging among peers.[12] Also inherent to the formation of these groups was their interaction with adults. In Boldermo's case study, a multicultural kindergarten in Norway, the adult teachers and researchers remained in the role of instructors and observers and were subjected to moments of exclusion. For example, children would declare the teacher could not participate in nap time with the other children[13] and also exhibit verbal and visual signs of discomfort based on the researchers' proximity, prompting withdrawals from observation for certain students.[14] Daily negotiations of membership in communal groups and performance of inclusive and exclusive rituals were also observed among the children, leading to positive moments such as a child helping his peer with a spilled drink before the adults could react,[15] and confrontational ones such as excluding a child from activities since they were 'too small' and a 'baby'.[16] I posit that these rituals and behaviours are also observable in the behaviours of all five child characters present in *Richard III*, especially when considering whether adults are included within the community's membership.

---

[7] Ashdown-Hill, *The Mythology*, p. 15.

[8] Ashdown-Hill, *The Mythology*, p. 161.

[9] Harper, '"And men"', p. 205.

[10] Katie Knowles, *Shakespeare's Boys: A Cultural History* (Basingstoke, 2014), p. 30.

[11] Campana, 'Killing', pp. 20–2.

[12] Sidsel Boldermo, 'Fleeting moments: young children's negotiations of belonging and togetherness', *International Journal of Early Years Education* 28 (2020), 136–50; p. 136. For further scholarship on belonging and togetherness in childhood studies, see Merja Koivula and Maritta Hännikäinen, 'Building children's sense of community in a day care centre through small groups in play', *Early Years* 37 (2017), 126–42; Cathy Nutbrown and Peter Clough, 'Citizenship and inclusion in the early years: understanding and responding to children's perspectives on "belonging"', *International Journal of Early Years Education* 17 (2009), 191–206; Tina Stratigos, Ben Bradley and Jennifer Sumison, 'Infants, family day care and the politics of belonging', *International Journal of Early Childhood* 46 (2014), 171–86; and Selma Jo Wastell and Sheila Degotardi, '"I belong here; I been coming a big time": an exploration of belonging that includes the voice of children', *Australasian Journal of Early Childhood* 42 (2017), 38–46.

[13] Boldermo, 'Fleeting', p. 136.

[14] Boldermo, 'Fleeting', p. 139.

[15] Boldermo, 'Fleeting', p. 145.

[16] Boldermo, 'Fleeting', p. 143.

This article rethinks and expands the conversation regarding all five children within *Richard III* through reading them as part of a peer community. The first section examines the two pairs of royal children in the play and how they establish community with their siblings to push back against adult control. Conversely, the second section argues that King Richard's pageboy, largely ignored in the scholarship, undermines these communities via his betrayal of fellow children in what I argue is an effort to protect himself from punishment. Furthermore, such self-preserving behaviours parallel attitudes towards the administration of corporal punishment in early modern grammar schools as documented in student accounts, manuals on teaching, and Thomas Ingelend's sixteenth-century morality play *The Disobedient Child*. While extant accounts of school life written by a child's hand are limited from the period, these portrayals are crucial in understanding what young schoolboys experienced growing up, and how they simultaneously viewed their peers as allies and enemies. These combined perspectives not only push forward our understanding of the play and its conceptions of childhood communities, but also place it within a history of children responding to threats of violence that carries into our modern era.

COMMUNITY BUILDING THROUGH SOCIAL RITUAL: THE FOUR ROYAL SIBLINGS

The political stage of *Richard III* is undeniably volatile and dangerous for its many players, particularly the young heirs bereft of their biological fathers through sickness and murder. As the adults lament and scheme in response to the deaths of King Edward IV and his brother, the Duke of Clarence, the surviving children also make sense of their loss and new circumstances through a combination of observation and action. The four royal children of *Richard III*: Edward and Margaret Plantagenet, Prince Edward V and Richard, Duke of York, all cope similarly by distancing themselves from relying on adult support networks and finding comfort among their siblings. However, they achieve this via differing sets of social rituals, such as prayer, mourning and play. Such actions do not go unnoticed by the adults, who seek to either dissuade or integrate themselves into these communities, bestowing on children a gatekeeper status that allows them to permit or deny inclusion as they see fit.

It is easy to overlook Edward and Margaret Plantagenet, our first pair of children appearing in the play, given King Richard's general disinterest in their future (4.2.53–5) and the frequent editorial choice to cut them from productions.[17] However, such a lack of consideration ignores that both children actively seek to comprehend their loss and receive justice for wrongs committed against them. Act 2, Scene 2 opens with the recently fatherless children seeking answers from their grandmother:

> BOY Good grannam, tell us, is our father dead?
> DUCHESS No, boy.
> DAUGHTER Why do you weep so oft, and beat your breast?
> And cry, 'O Clarence, my unhappy son?'
> BOY Why do you look on us, and shake your head,
> And call us orphans, wretches, castaways,
> If that our noble father were alive?
>
> (*Richard III* 2.2.1–7)

Even though the Duchess of York attempts to recant her words, her grandchildren still, as observed by Charlotte Scott, 'interpret her actions as gestures of distress and markers of grief'.[18] I argue, however, that, instead of the children 'search[ing] for the right words to represent their situation', they understand it clearly.[19] Repeating the list of 'orphans, wretches, castaways', is a rhetorical move voicing a sense of loss not only within their family structure, but also in their social position. Such a change in status presents immediate and future dangers for the heirs. Not only are they robbed of key protections in the patriarchal early modern system, they are also now, through association by blood, a surviving legacy of the alleged traitor Clarence. Therefore, the Plantagenet children must simultaneously experience grief, seek protection in their vulnerable state, and demand justice for the wrongs committed against them.

We can read an example of Edward seeking justice in a conversation with his grandmother, the Duchess of

---

[17] James R. Siemon, 'Introduction', in *The Arden Third Series Edition of King Richard III*, ed. James R. Siemon (London, 2017), 1–123. Siemon's introduction traces a long history of cutting the Plantagenet children from productions, starting with Colly Cibber's 1700 edition that would remain the go-to text for 150 years. Siemon also notes that, despite the return of characters such as Margaret into modern productions, 'Clarence's children, the Citizens and Queen Elizabeth's extended family still frequently go missing' – see pp. 87–9.

[18] Charlotte Scott, '"Incapable and shallow innocents": mourning Shakespeare's children in *Richard III* and *The Winter's Tale*', in *Childhood, Education and the Stage in Early Modern England*, ed. Richard Preiss and Deanne Williams (Cambridge, 2017), 58–78; p. 69.

[19] Scott, '"Incapable"', p. 69.

York. After the Duchess fails to conceal the fate of her son, the young heir responds:

BOY Then you conclude, my grannam, he [his father] is dead.
The King [Edward IV] mine uncle is to blame for it.
God will revenge it – whom I will importune
With earnest prayers, all to that effect.
DAUGHTER And so will I.
DUCHESS Peace, children, peace! The King doth love you well.
Incapable and shallow innocents,
You cannot guess who caused your father's death.

(*Richard III* 2.2.12–19)

While Edward and Margaret exhibit a reliance on God to enact their call for divine retribution against the uncle who wronged them, they also understand that God must hear their spoken prayers first in order for them to achieve their desired 'effect'. The Duchess of York's response exhibits fear and discomfort as she realizes that the pair may not be as 'incapable' as originally thought, potentially resulting in either an answer from God or accusations of treason.[20] While she attempts to reinstate the children to a lower position by calling them both 'innocents' and 'incapable', the fact that she argues with them in the first place concedes control. Such moments mirror those described by Allison James in which children are 'not just engaging in activities as individual[s] that promote changes in cognition' (their new status as orphans), but becoming 'involved in social relations and activities of different kinds and [are] thus positioned, foremost, as social actor[s]'.[21] Edward's and Margaret's new roles as social actors are validated when their need for vengeance is promptly answered by the arrival of Queen Elizabeth announcing the death of King Edward IV (2.2.34–8), thereby overruling the Duchess of York's insistence on her son's innocence in favour of her grandchildren's needs and placing them in a privileged position over their elder.

Both children continue exercising their powers as social actors in the subsequent lines via their unsympathetic responses to the older women's mourning and subsequently voicing their own grievances at losing a parent:

BOY Ah, aunt! You wept not for our father's death.
How can we aid you with our kindred tears?
DAUGHTER Our fatherless distress was left unmoaned;
Your widow-dolour likewise be unwept.
QUEEN ELIZABETH Give me no help in lamentation,
I am not barren to bring forth complaints:
. . .
Ah, for my husband, for my dear lord Edward!
CHILDREN Ah, for our father, for our dear lord Clarence!

DUCHESS Alas for both, both mine, Edward and Clarence.
QUEEN ELIZABETH What stay had I but Edward? And he's gone.
CHILDREN What stay had we but Clarence? And he's gone.
DUCHESS What stays had I but they, and they are gone?
QUEEN ELIZABETH Was never widow had so dear a loss!
CHILDREN Were never orphans had so dear a loss!

(*Richard III* 2.2.62–7; 71–8)

Edward and Margaret's interjections should not be interpreted as a simple miming or parroting of the adults in the room. Rather, the children utilize the rhetorical strategies of pathos and ethos to voice their own griefs and loss (why should we spare time to mourn your loss when the same respect was not afforded to us?). Furthermore, they appropriate the status of 'orphan' into their argument by continually speaking the name of their departed father, reminding those present that they are currently lacking patriarchal support. This strategy clearly has an impact, as the Duchess herself adopts their strategies to gain sympathy from anyone who will provide it, be it the queen or audience members providing continued patronage to the company and its productions.

This reading of Edward and Margaret establishes their value in the play as young children who lament and seek vengeance on behalf of a parent, rather than the typical tragic heroes seen in Shakespeare. While they may not have the same lengthy soliloquies as Titus Andronicus or King Lear to voice their grief, the Plantagenets nevertheless are a presence onstage that other characters acknowledge and respond to with underlying senses of unease. The fact that they use their own versions of rhetoric and inquiry alongside communal rituals of mourning and prayer sets them apart as a unified pair which cannot fully be controlled by the adults, warranting their continued reinstatement in future productions alongside our other pair of royal siblings: Prince Edward V and Richard, Duke of York.

Despite their frequent appearance both onstage and in the play's scholarship, the surviving children of King

---

[20] Perhaps some of this discomfort and helplessness comes from the involvement of her son Richard, who has spoken words of deceit to Clarence's surviving heirs. As she sorrowfully admits, 'He [Richard] is my son, ay, and therein my shame, / Yet from my dugs he drew not this deceit', referencing Richard's childhood while attempting to deny her own involvement in how he grew up (*Richard III* 2.2.29–30).

[21] Allison James, 'Agency', in *The Palgrave Handbook of Childhood Studies*, ed. Jens Qvortrup, William A. Corsaro and Michael-Sebastian Honig (Basingstoke, 2009), 34–45; p. 38.

Edward IV are frequently read as adults' 'most prized possessions' and as tools of propaganda within England's political struggles.[22] They too, however, exhibit moments of childhood agency and community-building which adults seek to comprehend and navigate with varying degrees of success. When Prince Edward V first arrives onstage, Richard notes his morose disposition and assumes that 'The weary way hath made [him] melancholy' (3.1.3). Edward corrects him by stating 'No, uncle, but our crosses on the way / Have made it tedious, wearisome and heavy. / I want more uncles here to welcome me' (3.1.4–6). Much like the Plantagenets, Edward feels a distinct lack of familial support following the recent deaths and arrests and attempts to comprehend his situation from a religious perspective. Rather than turning to prayer, however, Edward V associates his status as victim with imagery of the cross and Christ's famous lament to God: 'why hast thou forsaken me?'[23] This rhetorical move not only demonstrates awareness of the divine nature associated to royalty in Edward's time, but also emphasizes the feelings of separation and loneliness experienced by the young heir.

Edward confirms this sense of separation through inquiring after the presence of his mother and brother and insulting Lord Hastings as being a 'slug' for his slow delivery of news concerning their arrival (3.1.22). While Edward initially asks for his mother, his interest quickly shifts towards seeing his brother, who has been taken into 'sanctuary' by their fearing parent (3.1.28). According to Hastings, however, the younger brother 'Would fain have come with me to meet your grace' and shortly after the siblings are together (3.1.29). This shared desire between Edward and his brother Richard to reunite demonstrates a prioritized sense of community not merely defined by ties of blood, but also age. Given the elder prince's previous complaints of tediousness on his journey, the apparent remedy is games and play.

The act of play within young communities is another example of social ritual whereby children establish rules, boundaries and meaning. Ann-Carita Evaldsson argues that, when we shift our focus from *what* games children play to *how* they play them, 'participation in play [becomes] a central part of childhood and children's meaning making, emotional sharing, language use, and creativity in their everyday lives', while also providing agentive opportunities through rule making and establishing 'social identities' in terms of 'gender, age, ethnicity, etc.'.[24] Early modern writers and artists, as demonstrated by Katherine R. Larson, were also concerned with the 'moral spectrum' of games and how they could define and gender characteristics of childhood, especially when it did not 'take place under the watchful eye of tutors and parents'.[25] Thus it is through play that the two princes in *Richard III* seek to strengthen their sense of community, while also unknowingly providing King Richard the opportunity to insert himself into a position of manipulative power that undermines their communal efforts.

Although King Richard's ability to manipulate is well documented by scholars, he is able to gain further favour with the boys due to his similarly marginalized status.[26] The play's famous opening soliloquy frequently emphasizes his 'unfinished' (1.1.20) state, which parallels the Duchess's description of her grandchildren as 'shallow' and 'incapable' (2.2.18). Early modern audiences may have also been more willing to accept this moment if the role of the king was played by a young actor. While Burbage is often documented for performing the role, Siemon also finds evidence in Thomas Heywood's Red Bull 'Prologue and Epilogue' (published 1637) which 'are spoken by "*A young witty Lad playing the part of* Richard *the third: at the Red Bull*"' who apologizes for being a '*Richard* the third . . . shrunke up like his arm'.[27]

Once Edward's brother arrives, the three begin their play in earnest. This is particularly evident during the following exchange regarding the gifting of a dagger:

YORK I pray you, uncle, render me this dagger.
RICHARD My dagger, little cousin? With all my heart.
EDWARD A beggar, brother?
YORK Of my kind uncle that I know will give,
And being but a toy which is no grief to give.
RICHARD A greater gift than that I'll give my cousin.
YORK A greater gift? O, that's the sword to it.
RICHARD Ay, gentle cousin, were it light enough.
YORK O, then I see you will part but with light gifts;
In weightier things you'll say a beggar nay.
RICHARD It is too heavy for your grace to wear.
YORK I'd weigh it lightly, were it heavier.
RICHARD What, would you have my weapon, little lord?
YORK I would, that I might thank you as you call me.
RICHARD How?
YORK Little.

---

22 Knowles, *Shakespeare's Boys*, p. 20.
23 Matthew 27.46, King James Version.
24 Ann-Carita Evaldsson, 'Play and games', in *The Palgrave Handbook of Childhood Studies*, ed. Qvortrup, Corsaro and Honig, 326–31; pp. 319–20.
25 Katherine R. Larson, '"Certein childeplayes remembred by the fayre ladies": girls and their games', in *Gender and Early Modern Constructions of Childhood*, ed. Miller and Yavneh, 67–86; pp. 70–1.
26 See Knowles, *Shakespeare's Boys*, esp. pp. 29–30.
27 Siemon, 'Introduction', p. 86.

EDWARD My lord of York will still be cross in talk. –
Uncle, your grace knows how to bear with him.
YORK You mean to bear me, not to bear with me. –
Uncle, my brother mocks both you and me.
Because that I am little, like an ape,
He thinks that you should bear me on your shoulders.

(*Richard III* 3.1.110–31)

While the footnotes in the Arden Shakespeare third series largely focus on the insults spoken by the Duke of York to his uncle,[28] the scene also shows a family at play. Even the morose Edward coyly participates in the fun, which lends further credence to Richard III's earlier observation of 'So wise, so young' (3.1.79).[29] By including King Richard into their play activities, the young princes complicate the long-held view that children are always the miniature adult attempting to insert themselves into the grown-up sphere. While the Duke of York pursues items associated with manhood (the phallic sword and dagger), he nevertheless continues to acknowledge his diminutive size and behaviour. Furthermore, because King Richard willingly plays along, he performs a similar act of mimesis to the Duchess of York, where the adult places themselves within the language and attitudes of the child's sphere. This moment in the play creates a miniature community in which the children are the model and also the gatekeepers of who participates in their games. Unfortunately, it is this gatekeeping which enables the social chameleon and fellow outcast King Richard to infiltrate their community and betray the boys' trust as he arranges for their imprisonment in the Tower and their subsequent murders.

Following this violent schism with their uncle, the princes' communal bonds are strengthened in the afterlife. On the night before the Battle of Bosworth Field, both Richard III and Henry VII receive visions. Richard III's wife, Lady Anne, hints earlier that he is plagued by 'timorous dreams' (4.1.84) that keep her awake at night. Scholarship by Carole Levin traces how historical chronicles by More, Holinshed and Richard Baker all agree that Richard himself had sleepless nights.[30] However, while these accounts make obfuscated references to tormenting demons and devils, 5.3 of *Richard III* offers insight into what truly terrifies the king. One by one, the various victims of his rise to power arrive and curse him, the two princes participating and stating in unison:

GHOSTS [OF PRINCES] *(to Richard)* Dream on thy cousins
    smothered in the Tower.
Let us be lead within thy bosom, Richard,
And weigh thee down to ruin, shame, and death.

Thy nephews' souls bid thee despair and die.
(to Richmond) Sleep, Richmond, sleep in peace and wake in joy;
Good angels guard thee from boar's annoy.
Live, and beget a happy race of kings;
Edward's unhappy sons do bid thee flourish.

(*Richard III* 5.5.100–7)

While Knowles claims that the princes have taken on the role of 'gentle lambs' with their murder in the Tower,[31] here the analogy of ferocious lions or impish tricksters[32] appears more apt given they clearly seek to torment Richard III, their previous confidant and betrayer of their children's community. Compared to the prayers of Edward and Margaret Plantagenet for God to support their call for justice, the princes demonstrate an even greater shift from victims into the roles of social actors. Indeed, it is the very act of *speaking* and punishing that gives the princes this power, an act which should be impossible now that they are dead. Furthermore, with their entreaty of Henry VII to 'beget a happy race of kings' (not to mention the queen who would be the patron of many of Shakespeare's works), the princes reappropriate one of their key forms of power that caused great unease in king and court alike: the power to continue a royal line.

So far, I have analysed four historically confirmed extant children hailing from royal lines. While Shakespeare imbues these young people with their own cognizance, desires, emotions and building of peer communities through various social acts, some might still argue that, because of their royal upbringing, these sons and daughters would be afforded special privileges that children of common status would not possess. Although the political assassinations of all four royals, speculative or otherwise, allow me to push back against this claim, there is also a child of lower social standing who is the most troubling and liminal of them all: King Richard's pageboy. The pageboy remains a surprising gap in *Richard III*'s scholarship, given that he actively and knowingly betrays his fellow children by helping orchestrate the murder of the princes in the Tower, making him the antithesis to these budding peer

---

28   See Siemon's footnotes for *Richard III* 3.1.110–31 and 3.1.130–1.
29   Of course, the conclusion of this line is 'do never live long', indicating that to demonstrate such wit is a danger for children (*Richard III* 3.1.79).
30   See Carole Levin, *Dreaming in the Renaissance: Politics and Desire in Court and Culture* (New York and London, 2008), pp. 103–5.
31   Knowles, 'Shakespeare's "terrible infants"', p. 42.
32   For scholarship on how children simultaneously inhabited the term 'imp' as mischievous trickster and imperial successor, see chapter 1 of Knowles, *Shakespeare's Boys*.

communities. However, I argue these actions do not make the pageboy himself an antithesis to childhood, but rather are demonstrative of how children protected themselves by appealing to adult systems of power at the expense of undermining efforts to form protective communal groups.

UNMAKING COMMUNITY AND SELF-PRESERVATION: KING RICHARD'S PAGEBOY

Once Richard is crowned king, he grows increasingly paranoid about threats to his power, especially from his two young wards. Upon speaking his desire to see 'the bastards dead, / And [having] it immediately performed' (4.2.18–19), he grows angry when his adult allies get cold feet, and vows: 'I will converse with iron-witted fools / And unrespective boys. None are for me / That look into me with considerate eyes' (4.2.28–30). He then turns his attention away from all of his advisors towards his young pageboy:

KING RICHARD Know'st thou not any whom corrupting gold
Will tempt unto a close exploit of death?
PAGE I know a discontented gentleman
Whose humble means match not his haughty spirit.
Gold were as good as twenty orators,
And will, no doubt, tempt him to anything.
KING RICHARD What is his name?
PAGE His name, my lord, is Tyrrel.
KING RICHARD I partly know the man. Go, call him hither, boy.

(*Richard III* 4.2.35–42)

Such a character might seem an invention of Shakespeare to help move along the plot by providing a convenient accomplice, but the page does have a place within the chronicled history of Richard III's life. Edward Hall's *Chronicle*, written from 1547 to 1548,[33] explains that Richard III immediately begins plotting the murder after his coronation and first sends John Greene with letters of execution to where the princes are held.[34] When the order is not carried out, Richard confides to 'a secret page' that he needs someone else to fulfil his decree, since 'they that I sent woulde haue moost surely serued me, euen those fayle me and at my commaundemente will do nothynge for me'.[35] Here the page replies that 'there lieth one in the palet chamber with out that I dare wel say, to do your grace pleasure the thing that were right hard that he would refuse'.[36]

Thus far, few scholars and historians have said anything regarding the role of the pageboy. Horatio (Horace) Walpole (1717–1797), the fourth Earl of Orford and an 'uncompromising Ricardian',[37] questions the boy's very existence in *Historic Doubts on the Life and Reign of King Richard the Third* (1768). He argues that, in a trial determining Richard's guilt in the princes' murder, the pageboy would have provided important witness testimony and asks 'why was no inquiry made after Greene and the page?'[38] Mark Lawhorn finds in the boy a 'vexing question of what structurally, thematically or culturally significant purpose the boy figure might be serving',[39] which Gemma Miller responds to in her recent book *Childhood in Contemporary Performance of Shakespeare*. Miller's analysis focuses on Sean Holmes's 2003 production of *Richard III* and its portrayal of the pageboy as Richard's doppelgänger, dressed in similar clothing and sporting a limp like his master.[40] When the King dies at the production's end, the pageboy emerges to take the sword from Richard's corpse and deliver it to Richmond, which Miller reads as him fulfilling the role of a 'future killing anti-child'.[41] Miller's reading of the pageboy is long overdue and I wish to build upon her observations with a counterpoint that the king's servant is not strictly an 'anti-child'. Rather, the pageboy provides important historical context for how early modern children might not only coexist within self-formed communities, but compete with and undermine them.

Richard III's pageboy occupies a unique role in Shakespeare's works as a child complicit in the murder

---

[33] While other chronicles such as those written by More and Holinshed were published at earlier dates, sources such as the Oxford Dictionary of National Biography Online establish *Hall's chronicle* as influential material for the historic works of Shakespeare; see Peter C. Herman, 'Hall, Edward (1497–1547)', ODNB Online, para. 9, www.oxforddnb.com/display/10.1093/ref:odnb/9780198614128.001.0001/odnb-9780198614128-e-11954?rskey=4fkS3C&result=5.

[34] Edward Hall, *Hall's chronicle; containing the history of England, during the reign of Henry the Fourth, and the succeeding monarchs, to the end of the reign of Henry the Eighth, in which are particularly described the manners and customs of those periods. Carefully collated with the editions of 1548 and 1550* (London, 1809); p. 377.

[35] Hall, *Hall's chronicle*, p. 377.

[36] Hall, *Hall's chronicle*, p. 377.

[37] Paul Langford, 'Walpole, Horatio [Horace], fourth earl of Orford (1717–1797)', ODNB Online, para. 46.

[38] Horace Walpole, *Historic Doubts on the Life and Reign of King Richard the Third* (London, 1768), p. 57.

[39] Mark Lawhorn, 'Appendix 1: "Children in Shakespeare's plays: an annotated checklist"', in *Shakespeare and Childhood*, ed. Kate Chedgzoy, Suzanne Greenhalgh and Robert Shaughnessy (Cambridge, 2007), 233–49; p. 239.

[40] Gemma Miller, *Childhood in Contemporary Performance of Shakespeare* (London, 2021), pp. 36–7.

[41] Miller, *Childhood*, p. 26.

of his fellow children. If the stage directions are to be believed and the page accompanies his lord to the meeting with his advisors,[42] he would also have been privy to King Richard's desires. Where adult consul fails, a child readily provides it and sets this crucial plot point into motion with the speed that Richard hopes for. Rather than take Richard at his word that the boy is only a useful ally because he is 'unrespective'[43] and therefore an ignorant pawn, examining the pageboy's behaviour reveals it mirrors practices in the early modern classroom where children would be pitted against one another to earn the schoolmaster's favour while simultaneously avoiding his ire.

The administration of corporal punishment to students was a divisive topic among early modern educators. Roger Ascham's *The Scholemaster* (1570), despite reprimanding 'crooked' teachers who 'when they meete with a hard witted scholer, they rather breake him, than bowe him, rather marre him, then mend him',[44] nevertheless advises that children be 'kept vp in Gods feare, and preserued by his grace, finding paine in ill doing, and pleasure in well studyng'.[45] Richard Mulcaster's *Positions Concerning the Training Vp of Children* (1581) similarly advises 'that in any multitude the rod must needs rule; and in the least paucitie it must be seene, howsoeuer it found. Neither needeth a good boye to be afraid, seeing his fellow offender beaten, any more than an honest man, though he stand by the gallows, at the execution.'[46] While these educators perform lip service towards the child's well-being, the decision regarding how to administer discipline is entirely in the hands of the instructor and, of course, is incredibly subjective.

Conversely, Erasmus is wholly against the application of physical punishment to students. In his treatise *A Declamation on the Subject of Early Liberal Education for Children*, he decried the practice as being detrimental to the physical, mental and emotional development of these young scholars via personal account:

My teacher had more affection for me than for any other pupil, and on the pretext that he had conceived the greatest hopes for me, he kept a closer watch on me than on anyone else. Finally, wishing to ascertain for himself how well I could stand up to the rod, he charged me with an offence I had never even dreamed of committing and then flogged me. This incident destroyed all love of study within me and flung my young mind into such a deep depression that I nearly wasted away with heart-break.[47]

The examples Erasmus provides of schoolroom punishments to boys are brutal and vile, including how 'human excrement was squeezed into [the student's] mouth, and with such force, that he could not spit it out but had to swallow most of it'.[48] It is clear to Erasmus that any necessity for establishing obedience from a large group of students is not worth the risk of irreparable trauma. Whether or not Erasmus embellished or intentionally picked the worst cases of punishment to cite in his treatise is up for debate, but more importantly it exposes a system of child abuse perpetrated in public education. And while beatings that, as Erasmus puts it, turned schools into 'torture-chambers' were a tool in the hands of adults, they also served as a catalyst for the formation and breaking of child communities in an effort to avoid physical pain.[49]

We see another example of a child's attitude towards corporal punishment in Thomas Ingelend's morality play *The Disobedient Child*. Little is known about the playwright other than that the title page marks him as a 'late student in Cambridge', and the play is estimated to have been written sometime during the 1560s. Scholarship on *The Disobedient Child* largely focuses on how it subverts the prodigal son narrative and its attempts to blend morality play with comedy.[50] Ursula Ann Potter, however, performs an extensive and thought-provoking reading of the play in terms of

---

[42] The Arden third series lists the pageboy as entering with Richard at the beginning of 4.2. While the First Folio does not mention the Boy by name in these opening directions, it does say that Richard arrives 'in pompe', which implies that his royal retinue was onstage. Furthermore, the pageboy has no individual entrance mentioned at line 33, but does have an exit when told to summon Tyrell at line 41. Such conclusions are similarly arrived at in Miller's analysis, or, at the very least, they see nothing preventing the boy from being present and that it increases his dramatic significance; see Miller, *Childhood*, p. 30.

[43] 'Defined in the *Oxford English Dictionary* as "inattentive" or "heedless"' (*Richard III* 4.2.29n).

[44] Roger Ascham, *The Scholemaster, or plaine and perfite way of tea-chying children, to vnderstand, write, and speake, the Latin tong . . .*, transcribed by Judy Boss, Project Guttenberg (Aug. 1999), p. 188.

[45] Ascham, *The Scholemaster*, p. 203.

[46] Richard Mulcaster, *Positions vvherin those primitiue circumstances be examined, which are necessarie for the training vp of children, either for skill in their booke, or health in their bodie . . .*, EEBO (London, 1581), p. 283.

[47] Desiderius Erasmus, *A Declamation on the Subject of Early Liberal Education for Children*, in *Collected Works of Erasmus*, ed. J. K. Sowards, vol. 26 (Toronto, 1985), 292–346; p. 326.

[48] Erasmus, *A Declamation*, p. 329.

[49] Erasmus, *A Declamation*, p. 325.

[50] See John Doebler, 'Beaumont's *The Knight of the Burning Pestle* and the prodigal son plays', *Studies in English Literature 1500–1900* 5 (1965), 333–44; and Ervin Beck, 'Terence improved: the paradigm of the prodigal son in English Renaissance comedy', *Renaissance Drama* 6 (1973), 107–22.

the grammar school and how it applies to Erasmus's earlier attitudes towards corporal punishment.[51] To briefly summarize the play, a rich man and his son are at odds concerning the child's future. While the father wishes for further education, the child has no interest in receiving beatings and would rather be married. The outcome not only results in his disinheritance but, ironically, makes him the recipient of beatings and abuse from his new wife. When asking his father for forgiveness, he is offered the adage 'as he had brewed, that so he should bake' and returns to his marriage.[52] Interspersed among this domestic drama is also the appearance of the Devil, who delights in sending the son along the path of disobedience (pp. 45–9).[53] The prodigal son returns to his marriage and an Epilogue is spoken on the importance of obedience, followed by a song honouring Queen Elizabeth.

A considerable portion of the play's beginning involves the son speaking his reasons against pursuing education to his father – namely, a fear of receiving beatings:

THE SONNE At other boyes hands, I haue it learned,
And that of those turelye most of all other
Which for a certen tyme haue remained
In the house and pryson of a Scholemayster

. . .

Their [the students'] tender bodyes both nyght and daye
Are whipped and scourged, and beate lyke a stone
That from toppe to toe, the skyn is awaye.

. . .

THE FATHER: But I am sure that this kynde of facion
Is not shewed to children of honest condicion.
THE SONNE: Of trouth, with these maisters is no difference,
For alike towards all is their wrathe and violence.
(*The Interlude of the Disobedient Child*, p. 8)

While Potter treats the line regarding 'other boyes hands' as 'following a policy of consciously using hearsay and hyperbole to manipulate his own father', I read this instead as an instance where child communities are engaged in the act of protecting one of their own.[54] Another example appears in an anecdote regarding Richard Mulcaster turning a moment of beating into what Lynn Enerline's *Shakespeare's Schoolroom: Rhetoric, Discipline, Emotion* claims is a 'theatrical' spectacle[55] by stating 'I aske the banes of matrimony between this boy his buttockes, of such a parish, on the one side, and Lady Burch, of this parish on the other side.' A fellow boy observing the punishment, however, speaks up that 'all partyes are not agreed' – in other words, 'I object!' – and his classmate's body is spared the whipping.[56] In this moment a rallying of a childhood community is successful in protecting one of its own, using their collective wit as a form of defence.

While communal acts from children could sway an instructor from administering punishment, these young people also dealt with the knowledge that beatings could come at any time and for any reason. The son's claim in *The Disobedient Child* that being of 'honest condicion' is not enough to escape the 'violence' of a schoolmaster supports this. Such a statement coincides with Erasmus's earlier anecdote concerning his unjust punishment and further contests Mulcaster's claim that well-behaved students had nothing to fear from their schoolmasters. Nor, it turned out, could boys always rely on their classmates to deliver them. The same boy forced to eat human excrement, as well as being 'stripped and raised aloft by ropes slung underneath his arms . . . and savagely beaten until he nearly died' was only in that position because he was accused of pranks performed by 'the mad teacher's nephew on his sister's side' who brought in 'a lucrative fee'.[57] Given the risks of such conditions, no wonder the son in *The Disobedient Child* has reservations about pursuing an education in a place where honesty and obedience, virtues lauded by his father, do not guarantee safety. Furthermore, as we will now observe, budding childhood communities in the early modern grammar school faced significant internal and external pressures that tempted its members into betrayal in exchange for protection and other benefits.

Alongside the risk of a schoolmaster's sadistic nephew making someone his scapegoat, there existed other social hierarchies in the early modern grammar school that threatened the stability of childhood communities. Enterline describes the importance of grammar-school boys being able to imitate their lessons. Schoolmasters

---

[51] Ursula Ann Potter, 'The spectre of the shrew and the lash of the rod. Gendering pedagogy in *The Disobedient Child*', in *Early Modern Academic Drama*, ed. Jonathan Walker and Paul D. Streufert (Farnham, 2008), 65–86.

[52] Thomas Ingeland, *The Interlude of the Disobedient Child*, ed. James Orchard Halliwell (London, 1848); p. 30. All references for *The Disobedient Child* are page numbers. There are no act, scene or line divisions in Halliwell's edition.

[53] For more on Ingeland's portrayal of the Devil, see John D. Cox, 'Stage devils in English Reformation plays', *Comparative Drama* 32 (1998), 85–116.

[54] Potter, 'The spectre', p. 75.

[55] Lynn Enterline, *Shakespeare's Schoolroom: Rhetoric, Discipline, Emotion* (Philadelphia, 2012), p. 49.

[56] As quoted in Enterline, which takes the anecdote both from Alan Stewart, *Close Readers: Humanism and Sodomy in Early Modern England* (Princeton, 1997), pp. 98–9, and from Foster Watson, *Richard Mulcaster and his 'Elementarie'* (London, 1893), p. 5.

[57] Erasmus, *A Declamation*, pp. 329–30.

'habitually compared acting to declaiming as an important means for disciplining the young bodies and "babbling mouths" of students', and sought to turn 'early modern schoolboys into self-monitoring, rhetorically facile subjects who modulated their performances of acceptable speech, bodily deportment, facial movement, vocal modulation, and affective expression by taking the institutional scene of judgment inside, as their own'.[58] While children were expected to self-govern their behaviours, there was also an insidious force at work among their community, known as the 'monitors':

These Monitors kept them strictly to speaking of Latine in theyr several commands; and withal they presented their complaints or accusations (as we called them) everie Friday morn: when the punishments were often redeemed by exercises or favours shewed to Boyes of extraordinarie merite, who had the honor (by the *Monitor monitorum*) manie times to begge and prevaile for such remissions. And so (at other times) other faultes were often punished.[59]

At first the monitor sounds like a Foucauldian Panopticon for its capability to maintain inmates' incarceration by disciplining one another. However, the model described in the 'Consuetudinarium' contains an additional form of hierarchy which schoolboys attempted to negotiate, bargain and 'begge' their way through in order to not be on the receiving end of the schoolmaster's cane.

When these aspects of the grammar schools and their administration of corporal punishment are taken into consideration alongside *The Disobedient Child*, the relationship between the princes and Richard's pageboy takes on a new dimension. The games and performance enacted by the two young royals is akin to a grammar-school rhetoric exercise, one which does not please the 'schoolmaster' King Richard. The pageboy, meanwhile, understands his role and therefore inhabits the role of disciplinary 'monitor' for his fellow children. While the adult advisors fail the horrific exercise Richard places before them and discipline is swift (death in Lord Buckingham's case), the pageboy is able to provide the answer which helps to keep his lord's anger in check and saves him from punishment.

The pageboy's act of obedience to Richard III further builds upon what Enterline refers to as the 'unresolved moral landscape' of a play like *The Disobedient Child*.[60] While the son might blame the Devil for his behaviour, what happens when God's appointed king demands something as horrific as infanticide? Certainly, Richard III's adult advisors pay for their disobedience with their lives, but the king himself receives divine punishment

from the souls of his victims. Furthermore, as Enterline argues, the reasons and fears voiced by the son are 'legitimate' ones that anyone with a background in grammar-school education, such as Shakespeare, would have been aware of.[61] I agree with Enterline on this point and argue that more attention should be placed on the legitimacy of these claims as they are one of the few means we have for hearing early modern children speaking out against the adult power systems they were subject to. If one subscribes unthinkingly to a 'spare the rod, spoil the child' mentality promoted by writers such as Ascham, Mulcaster and Ingelend, one ignores the plight of the boy in Erasmus's account who, 'the more he protested that he was in fact innocent, the more fiercely the torture was intensified'.[62]

Although readers might find discomfort in condoning the actions of the pageboy, they nevertheless serve as a means of self-preservation. While children such as the princes attract too much attention and are subsequently murdered, the pageboy is able to quietly depart from the play after successfully completing his task. He does not die like Falstaff's 'boy' in *Henry V*, nor does he become embroiled in the ensuing fallout if we take Walpole's earlier inquiry to heart. Instead, his preservation in texts such as Shakespeare's play and Hall's *Chronicle* portray him as an obedient subject, whilst those texts decry King Richard's monstrous acts through moments such as Henry VII's battlefield speech.[63] In a time when history sought to create distinct heroes and villains, the pageboy appears to be spared any sort of lasting judgement despite his affiliations.

The pageboy's desire for self-preservation complicates our considerations of childhood community when compared to the play's other children. The characters' status is important here because the pageboy is in a clearly defined role of subservience to a king prone to punishing those who cross him. Considerations of status and class were also important when it came to a play such as *The Disobedient*

---

[58] Enterline, *Shakespeare's Schoolroom*, p. 44.

[59] 'Consuetudinarium', quoted in Enterline, *Shakespeare's Schoolroom*, p. 36. Enterline describes the 'Consuetudinarium' (*c.*1610) as 'an account of daily life – one of the few extant accounts of its kind written by a student rather than a school authority … [giving] a pupil's perspective of how imitation operated in the school's daily economy of reward and punishment': p. 34.

[60] Enterline, *Shakespeare's Schoolroom*, p. 104.

[61] Enterline, *Shakespeare's Schoolroom*, p. 105.

[62] Erasmus, *A Declamation*, p. 329.

[63] See *Richard III* 5.6.191–224, and Hall, *Hall's chronicle*, p. 417.

Child. Potter explains that 'Grammar schools in early Elizabethan England had few problems filling their classes with boys from the lower ranks and the middling sort, but they were less successful in attracting boys from wealthier and gentle families', and that Ingelend's play can be read as a means of promoting this educational mode to wealthier patrons.[64] This struggle is mirrored in the situation of the rich man, and his son where the path of education is not pursued thus leading to an heirless father and an emasculated husband. In this case, *Richard III*'s four royal children represent these social elites. However, unlike the father in *The Disobedient Child*, whose lack of a stern hand is part of what he blames for his child seeking 'wantonnes' (p. 15), the royal children are robbed of this paternal guidance via their orphaning. Consequently, they must look for a protection within their peer communities, resulting in ritual making and decisions on how they will interact with outside authorities such as God, and adults like King Richard. The pageboy's status, meanwhile, is closer to that of the grammar school and its curriculum of adherence to the will of the master. However, his unassuming status and quick compliance come with great reward through the preservation of his life and continued future.

The actions of the pageboy in *Richard III*, though deceptively brief, mark a shift in privilege and power that places the young servant above others in the court. Such a rise in esteem, however, comes with a choice regarding what the pageboy considers his place among his peers. Indeed, King Richard initially demands from the boy nothing like he does with Lord Buckingham, but rather inquires into his social network. The pageboy therefore must decide whether to share his knowledge,

fabricate it or outright deny it. Only after the pageboy confirms his connection with Tyrell does Richard give the order to fetch him and therefore fully brings the young servant into their complicit pact. This interaction demonstrates that a child's choice to share what they know to those outside their peer culture group, while demonstrating agency, risks exposing them to further adult control. The inherent lack of a peer culture also isolates the page from the other children in the play. While the royal siblings have peers they can ally with through language and common desire, the page is notably alone in an adult court and therefore can neither be pressured nor supported in promoting his marginalized group. This form of separation ultimately underlies the ideals behind the grammar school monitor: to disband disruptive childhood communities and return authority back to the adults. Despite saying only a handful of lines in the play, *Richard III*'s pageboy serves as a bridge between scholars such as Enterline and Miller who are interested in how childhood was perceived in the early modern era. Texts such as the 'Consuetudinarium', *A Declamation on the Subject of Early Liberal Education for Children* and *The Disobedient Child*, when read alongside *Richard III*, demonstrate that communal relationships among children were both nuanced and complex, with competing structures of power, therefore further complicating questions of childhood agency and offering new insight into Shakespeare's most popular historical play.

---

[64] Potter, 'The spectre', p. 65.

'HERE'S COMPANY': FRACTURED ENGLISHNESS AND CONFLICTED COMMUNITIES IN *THE MERRY WIVES OF WINDSOR* AND *HENRY V*

CHLOE FAIRBANKS

There is surprisingly little that is merry about the opening scene of Shakespeare's *The Merry Wives of Windsor*. The titular wives appear only briefly towards the end – and, in the Folio text, as non-speaking roles, and the scene as a whole is characterized less by 'pleasaunt and excellent conceited comedie' than by local conflicts between the Windsorians and Falstaff's party.[1] Responding to the (entirely accurate) accusation that he has picked Master Slender's pocket, Falstaff's disreputable associate Pistol lives up to his bellicose name. Denouncing Slender as a liar, Pistol announces his 'craue[ing]' for 'combat'.[2] The Folio edition of the play makes a striking addition to the speech; where in the quarto Pistol begins by addressing Falstaff ('Sir *Iohn,* and Maister mine'), the Folio line is addressed to the Welsh parson Sir Hugh Evans, who has added his voice in support of Slender's accusation.[3] Pistol's reply is prefaced with an additional outburst: 'Ha, thou mountain-foreigner!' (*Merry Wives* 1.1.147). At first glance, the insult seems to confirm the xenophobia critics have historically associated with the play – a reading in which difference from particular cultural 'others' becomes a foundational aspect of English national identity. In Pistol's case, however, this is far from straightforward. The residential and legal statuses of both men transform the apparent Anglo-Welsh conflict into one of the play's many – and frequently unresolved – intranational conflicts between Englishmen.

'Foreign' could mean very different things to early moderns. In addition to encompassing those entering England from overseas – for whom the preferred term was 'alien' or 'stranger' – 'foreigner' referred primarily to internal migrants, although the terms could be used interchangeably.[4] A 1606 Act prohibited 'diuers and sundry strangers borne, *and likewise* Forreiners from the liberties of the saide Cittie' from keeping shops in London, while John Cowell's dictionary defines

'*Forein* mater' as 'mater triable in another countie'.[5] Shakespeare himself was one such 'foreigner', having migrated to London from Warwickshire. Pistol himself appears to be another; in *Henry IV* he is associated with a distinctly London crowd, and *Merry Wives* presents him as a visitor to Windsor. In contrast, Hugh Evans is clearly a Windsor resident of some duration, with long-standing relationships in the area. Evans's Welshness compounds this definitional duality, particularly given the temporal uncertainty of the play. On the strength of repeated references to Fenton's friendship with Prince Hal, critics

---

[1] William Shakespeare, *A most pleasaunt and excellent conceited comedie, of Syr Iohn Falstaffe, and the merrie wiues of Windsor Entermixed with sundrie variable and pleasing humors, of Syr Hugh the Welch knight, Iustice Shallow, and his wise cousin M. Slender. With the swaggering vaine of Auncient Pistoll, and Corporall Nim. By William Shakespeare. As it hath bene diuers times acted by the right Honorable my Lord Camberlaines seruants. Both before her Maiestie, and else-where* (London, 1602), title page.

[2] Shakespeare, *Merrie wiues*, sig. A4r.

[3] Shakespeare, *Merrie wiues*, sig. A4r. The relationship between the quarto and Folio editions of *Merry Wives* has been the subject of considerable debate. To enumerate at length upon these debates is beyond the remit of this article, but they are comprehensively summarized – and deftly extended – in Laurie Maguire and Emma Smith, 'Theater, revision, and *The Merry Wives of Windsor*', *Shakespeare Quarterly* 72 (2022), 177–202.

[4] *OED Online*, 'foreigner, n. 1', www.oed.com; see also James A. Picton, ed., *City of Liverpool: Selections from the Municipal Archives and Records, From the 13th to the 17th Century Inclusive*, 2 vols. (Liverpool, 1870), vol. 1, p. 75.

[5] 'By the Mayor. An act of Common Councell, prohibiting all strangers borne, and forrainers, to vse any trades, or keepe any maner of shops in any sort within this citty, liberties and freedome thereof' (London, 1606) (italics mine); and *The interpreter: or Booke containing the signification of vvords wherein is set foorth the true meaning of all, or the most part of such words and termes, as are mentioned in the lawe vvriters, or statutes of this victorious and renowned kingdome, requiring any exposition or interpretation* (London, 1607), sig. 2G1v.

have typically set *Merry Wives* during the reign of Henry IV and/or V, at which point Wales had not yet been legally incorporated into England, thereby making Evans an 'alien'.[6] This is complicated, however, by the two Folio references to Queen Elizabeth (*Merry Wives* 5.5.45, 59), which would seem to place the play in Shakespeare's own time, qualifying Evans's alien status. Even after Wales had been incorporated, however, the national status of its people remained somewhat ambiguous. Evans, then, can be understood as foreign in both senses of the word. He is at once English and non-English, and, as such, Pistol's insult speaks to a broader undercurrent of intranational tension within English counties which this article will argue is endemic to Shakespeare's treatment of national identity in both *The Merry Wives of Windsor* and *Henry V*.

Both plays have long been read as deeply invested in the idea of a shared 'construct of essential Englishness' which is defined in opposition to and conflict with other nations.[7] *The Merry Wives of Windsor* is often described as 'Shakespeare's English comedy', or his 'most "English"' of staged Englands', while *Henry V* is widely understood 'as orchestrating a relation between opposed terms, between a core and its periphery, or English and non-English'.[8] Indeed, despite critical recognition that 'the percentage of strangers in the city was always dwarfed by the number of residents from elsewhere in the realm', studies of difference in early modern London have tended to frame difference in terms of core and periphery, or English and non-English.[9] This article challenges that perception, arguing that the oppositional dynamics of *Henry V* and *Merry Wives* are not limited to England's archipelagic or continental neighbours, but in fact encompass a wide variety of tensions within England as well. A more recent body of work has begun to challenge the idea that these plays are exclusively English, demonstrating the ways in which their multilingual, multicultural elements disrupt the idea of English hegemony.[10] Vital as this work has been, it nevertheless presupposes that Englishness itself is a coherent or even stable concept. Matthew Greenfield has rightly observed the problematic depiction of 'English culture as a homogeneous entity with clear boundaries, uncomplicated by the British question'.[11] This article applies that thinking more locally, demonstrating that, in addition to being complicated by 'the British question', the nation is complicated by what might be termed 'the English question'. While it is certainly true that England has historically elided its archipelagic neighbours, the assumption that England itself was a homogeneous entity warrants closer scrutiny.

Tracing moments of internal conflict in these plays, this article proposes that we should rethink Shakespeare's treatment of Englishness as far more provisional and divergent than has traditionally been understood. Amy Lidster and others have drawn attention to the extent to which our overreliance upon the Folio's generic divisions has elided or otherwise sidelined those early modern plays which take non-English pasts as their subjects.[12] In expanding our definition of a history

---

6 This happened in 1536, during the reign of Henry VIII. See 'An act gyuyng the kynges hignes auctoritie newely to allotte the towneshyppes in the fhyres and marches of Wales, at any tyme within. Iii. Yeres nest enfuing', in *Actes made in the parlyament bego[n]ne and holden at Westm[inster] the. VIII. daye of Iune, in the. XXVIII. yere of the reygne of our most drad soueraigne lorde kynge Henry the. VIII* (London, 1536), sig. A3v.

7 Peter Erickson, 'The Order of the Garter, the cult of Elizabeth, and class–gender tension in *The Merry Wives of Windsor*', in *Shakespeare Reproduced: The Text in History and Ideology*, ed. Jean E. Howard and Marion F. O'Connor (Abingdon, 2005), 116–42; p. 128.

8 Jean E. Feerick, 'The imperial graft: horticulture, hybridity, and the art of mingling races in *Henry V* and *Cymbeline*', in *The Oxford Handbook of Shakespeare and Embodiment: Gender, Sexuality, and Race*, ed. Valerie Traub (Oxford, 2016), 211–27; p. 218. See also, for example, Stephen Greenblatt, 'Invisible bullets: Renaissance authority and its subversion, *Henry IV* and *Henry V*', in *New Historicism and Renaissance Drama*, ed. Richard Dutton and Richard Wilson (London, 1992), 83–108; Richard Helgerson, *Adulterous Alliances: Home, State, and History in Early Modern European Drama and Painting* (Chicago, 2000); Cathy Shrank, 'Formation of nationhood', in *The Oxford Handbook of Shakespeare*, ed. Arthur F. Kinney (Oxford, 2011), 571–86; and Cora Fox, 'Merriness, affect, and community in Shakespeare's *Merry Wives of Windsor*', in *Positive Emotions in Early Modern Literature and Culture*, ed. Cora Fox, Bradley J. Irish, and Cassie M. Miura (Manchester, 2021), 136–50.

9 Jacob Selwood, *Diversity and Difference in Early Modern London* (Farnham, 2010), p. 23.

10 See, for example, Andrew S. Keener, 'Windsor's world of words: multilingualism in *The Merry Wives of Windsor*', *ELR* 51 (2021), 409–11; Marjorie Rubright, 'Incorporating Kate: the myth of monolingualism in Shakespeare's *Henry the Fifth*', in *The Oxford Handbook of Shakespeare and Embodiment*, ed. Traub, 468–90; Margaret Tudeau-Clayton, *Shakespeare's Englishes: Against Englishness* (Cambridge, 2019).

11 Matthew Greenfield, '*1 Henry IV*: metatheatrical Britain', in *British Identities and English Renaissance Literature*, ed. David J. Baker and Willy Maley (Cambridge, 2002), 71–80; p. 71.

12 See, for example, Daniel Woolf, *Reading History in Early Modern England* (Cambridge, 2001); Michael Hattaway, 'The Shakespearean history play', in *The Cambridge Companion to Shakespeare's History Plays* (Cambridge, 2002), 3–24; Paulina Kewes, 'The Elizabethan history play: a true genre?', in *A Companion to Shakespeare's Works*, ed. Richard Dutton and Jean E. Howard, vol. 3 (Malden, 2003), 170–93; Teresa Grant and Barbara Ravelhofer, ed., *English Historical Drama, 1500–1660: Forms outside the Canon* (Basingstoke, 2008); Amy Lidster,

play, however, such studies fall short of interrogating the stability – or, indeed, accuracy – of the vision of Englishness Shakespeare's plays present. The genre of history has become more capacious, but our definition of Shakespeare's English histories remains one defined as the biographies of historic English kings. By situating *Henry V* alongside *The Merry Wives of Windsor*, a different picture emerges – one in which English history is equally defined by the lower and middle classes. Instead of a Henriad focused on Prince Hal's trajectory towards becoming Henry V, we find a duology focused on the interactions of a group of lower- and middle-class characters (e.g. Pistol, Nim, Bardolph, Shallow, Slender).[13] I will begin locally, highlighting the centrality of inter-English conflict (domestic, gendered and regional) to the plot of *The Merry Wives of Windsor*.[14] I'll then show how the presence of internal tensions amidst the national unity purportedly inspired by *Henry V*'s war in France shifts focus from duck/rabbit debates over Henry's character to the experiences and concerns of ordinary Englishmen.

'MOCK[ING] HIM HOME TO WINDSOR'[15]

As markers of English domestic instability, the inter-linked conflicts between Falstaff and the Fords/Pages and within the Page family implicate Shakespeare's comedy within broader societal divisions. As Ian Archer has noted, 'the prevailing rhetoric of community' propounded by Elizabethan government elites '[assumes] a cohesive society united in the pursuit of the same goals', but 'elites show a tendency to insist upon such a rhetoric precisely as a means of concealing real divisions in the society'.[16] The domestic conflicts which dominate *The Merry Wives of Windsor* insist that we take seriously the existence of these divisions. In doing so, they suggest that in his 'most "English" of staged Englands', Shakespeare presents a vision of community which not only directly challenges the state-sponsored vision of a stable English identity often associated with Shakespeare's plays, but does so through an emphasis on the experiences and concerns of a much broader cross-section of society.

From the title page – which may well have served as an advertisement for the play – of the first quarto edition in 1602, *The Merry Wives of Windsor* highlights the variety which characterizes Shakespeare's Windsor. The urban unity of Windsor, already differentiated from Falstaff's London milieu, is quickly complicated by the promise of 'sundrie variable and pleasing humors' that have been acted 'diuers times … Both before her Maiestie, and elsewhere'.[17] Not only is the play advertised as containing various humours, but the reference to its performance history removes Windsor from its geographical location by implying its re-enactment at various theatrical and courtly locales. This locational unfixity is compounded by the not insubstantial differences between the text of the 1602 quarto and the 1623 Folio. Leah Marcus's work on the quarto edition of the play has demonstrated that text 'systematically avoids references to Windsor' – such as Datchet Mead – which later appear in the Folio edition.[18] Not only that, but the quarto edition is saturated with references to specific London locations and practices. Announcing his intended seduction of Mistresses Ford and Page, Falstaff proclaims, 'I must cheat, I must conycatch'.[19] Cony catching was particularly associated with London at the time of *The Merry Wives of Windsor*'s first performance, having been popularized by Robert Greene's 1591 pamphlets. Falstaff's classification of his courtship as 'cony catching' thus associates his plotline with London's criminal community. In what might be considered an ironic reference to his criminal activities in *Henry IV*, Falstaff tells Mistress Ford that he 'loue[s] to walke by the Counter gate', a prison located on Poultry St and Wood St in London, and in Southwark, not too far from where the Globe was located.[20] Nor is Falstaff the only English 'foreigner' resident in Windsor. The title page establishes Windsor as a town peopled not only by local householders and their servants, but also by Londoners such as Falstaff, Pistol and Nim, as well as Justice Shallow and his cousin Slender, whom audiences might remember as Gloucestershire men from earlier performances of *2*

Publishing the History Play in the Time of Shakespeare: Stationers Shaping a Genre (Cambridge, 2022).

13 The characters appear in *1* and *2 Henry IV* as well, but the present study focuses on *Henry V* and *Merry Wives* given their shared reputation as representing something quintessentially English.

14 I use the term 'inter-English' primarily to refer to conflicts between the English characters; however, the temporal ambiguity of the play means that the term at times encompasses Evans's involvement in these conflicts – although primarily as a would-be mediator.

15 *Merry Wives* 4.4.64.

16 Ian W. Archer, *The Pursuit of Stability: Social Relations in Elizabethan London* (Cambridge, 1991), p. 59.

17 Shakespeare, *Merrie wiues*, title page.

18 Scott Oldenburg, *Alien Albion: Literature and Immigration in Early Modern England* (Toronto, 2014), p. 151.

19 Shakespeare, *Merrie wiues*, sig. A3v.

20 Shakespeare, *Merrie wiues*, sig. D4v.

Henry IV. This is made explicit in the Folio, where their opening lines assert their Gloucestershire background:

SHALLOW I will make a Star
Chamber matter of it. If he were twenty Sir John
Falstaffs, he shall not abuse Robert Shallow, Esquire.
SLENDER In the County of Gloucestershire, Justice of Peace and
Coram.

(*Merry Wives* 1.1.1–5)

Shallow's line sets up two key elements of the plot. Firstly, it introduces the undercurrent of inter-English conflict upon which much of the comedy is founded, and secondly, it establishes Falstaff, a fellow Englishman, as the primary antagonist of the play. Falstaff's courtship, which provides both the main comic plot and the main source of conflict, is founded upon the knight's inability to correctly interpret the behaviour of Englishwomen. Speaking of Mistress Ford, Falstaff believes he 'sp-[ies] entertainment in her. She discourses, she / carves, she gives the leer of invitation' (*Merry Wives* 1.3.39–40). The knight has interpreted – or, rather, *mis*interpreted – Mistress Ford's hospitality as sexual availability. Similarly, he claims that Mistress Page 'even now / gave me good eyes too, examined my parts with most / judicious oeillades' (*Merry Wives* 1.3.52–4). Pistol heightens the sense of England's internal incoherence by figuring Falstaff as a translator – 'He hath studied her well, and translated her will: / out of honesty, into English' (*Merry Wives* 1.3.44–5). Although Pistol may simply be alluding to the language of courtship, that translation should be necessary nonetheless implies some degree of linguistic difference between Windsor and London. The play's primary conflict is thus initiated by one Englishman's inability to understand another.

Falstaff's comic misreading of the situation could, however, have very serious implications. Upon receipt of Falstaff's love letter, Mistress Ford laments: 'O that my husband saw this letter! It would give eternal food to his jealousy' (*Merry Wives*, 2.1.95–6). Although Ford's bark proves worse than his bite, Mistress Ford's anxiety introduces darker undertones to an otherwise comic scene in a period when men were legally entitled to beat their wives, and male fears over cuckoldry were profound.[21] Although Ford directs substantial ire towards Falstaff, denouncing him as 'a damned epicurean rascal' and 'one that does me ... wrong', he is similarly vitriolic towards his wife (*Merry Wives* 2.2.276, 284). Indeed, in a play often read as a celebration of Englishness over outsiders, it is striking that Ford professes that he 'will rather trust a Fleming with my butter, Parson Hugh the Welshman with my cheese, an Irishman with my aqua-vitae bottle, or a thief to walk my ambling gelding, than my wife with herself' (*Merry Wives* 2.2.290–3).

Ford's invocation of national culinary stereotypes conveys the magnitude of his distrust. The Flemings' overfondness for butter was commonly accepted during the period – Andrew Boorde's *Dietary* notes that 'douche men doth eate it [butter] at all tymes in the day' – and the same was true for stereotypes regarding the Welsh and cheese, or the Irish and liquor.[22] That Ford regards his wife as less trustworthy than the Flemings (who made up a sizeable chunk of London's immigrant population, and could provoke economic conflict) and the Irish (with whom the English were at war between 1593 and 1603) suggests that spousal conflict is a more serious consideration than national rivalries.[23] It is perhaps this more than anything else which underscores the severity of inter-English conflict within the play. In a period where the well-ordered home functioned as a microcosm for the state, discord between a husband and wife becomes a matter of national significance.[24] Wendy Wall has argued persuasively that 'the household harboured supposedly indigenous rituals, languages, and practices that bound the *natio*'.[25] English womanhood thus becomes crucial to conceptions of national identity, rendering the gendered

---

[21] Lucy Wooding, *Tudor England: A History* (New Haven, 2022), p. 138. The common citation for legal precedent here is William Blackstone, *Commentaries on the Laws of England*, 4 vols. (London, 1768), vol. 1, p. 432.

[22] Andrew Boorde, *A compendyous regyment or a dyetary of healthe made in Mountpyllyer, by Andrewe Boorde of physycke doctour, newly corrected and imprynted with dyuers addycyons dedycated to the armypotent Prynce and valyent Lorde Thomas Duke of Northfolke* (London, 1547), sig. G3r.

[23] Andrew Pettegree, *Foreign Protestant Communities in Sixteenth-Century London* (Oxford, 1986), p. 291, and Marjorie Rubright, *Doppelgänger Dilemmas: Anglo-Dutch Relations in Early Modern English Literature and Culture* (Philadelphia, 2014), p. 4.

[24] In *Of domesticall duties* (London, 1622), William Gouge referred to the family as 'a little commonwealth' (sig. C1v), and the phrase occurs across domestic literature of the period; see, for example, Thomas Smith, *De republica Anglorum* (London, 1585), sig. C3r; Josias Nichols, *An order of household instruction* (London, 1595), sig. B6v; Robert Cleaver, *A godlie forme of householde gouernment for the ordering of priuate families, according to the direction of Gods word* (London, 1598), sig. A7r; and William Perkins, *Christian oeconomie: or, A short survey of the right manner of erecting and ordering a familie according to the scriptures* (London, 1609), sig. ¶3r.

[25] Wendy Wall, *Staging Domesticity: Household Work and English Identity in Early Modern Drama* (Cambridge, 2002), pp. 5–6.

conflict between the Pages a threat to both local and national concord.

Nor is this discord resolved once the wives' plot to 'be revenged on' Falstaff is revealed (*Merry Wives* 2.1.89). Although Ford begs his wife's pardon, and the two couples are momentarily reconciled in their determination to punish Falstaff's presumption '[a]nd mock him home to Windsor', their newfound amity remains unstable (*Merry Wives* 4.4.64). For one thing, that amity is established by agreeing to displace their conflict onto Falstaff. Conflict is not resolved, but simply reassigned, and to one of Shakespeare's best-known Englishmen. As the target of the couples' wrath, Falstaff's punishment has a distinctively local and English flavour, drawn from 'an old tale' about 'a keeper here in Windsor Forest' (*Merry Wives* 4.4.27, 28). The location is significant. Jeffrey Theis has traced the way early modern England 'continually sustained and defined itself in terms of the woods', within which the oak functioned 'as a symbol of the monarch'.[26] Not only does this local landmark drive home Falstaff's status as an outsider, but the choice of an oak tree – symbolic of the nation – underscores the extent to which the spousal conflict he inspired risked damaging Englishness itself. At the same time, the phallic imagery associated with horns and trees reinforces the very specific threat Falstaff poses to English womanhood. Falstaff's attempt to defile a symbol of English nationhood thus points towards anxieties about women's subversive potential to disrupt the patriarchal order – and, by extension, national identity. Even when those women are presented as victims – for example, Lucrece, Lavinia – the association between women and extramarital sex remains a profoundly disruptive force.

Even after deciding on Falstaff's 'disgrace', the English household unit remains in the state of conflict introduced in act 3, scene 2 regarding Anne Page's marriage (*Merry Wives* 4.4.15). After Falstaff's punishment, Page suggests a union of the two men against his wife, telling the former, 'I will desire you to laugh at my wife that now laughs at thee. Tell her Master Slender hath married her daughter' (*Merry Wives* 5.5.169–71). Mistress Page retorts in an aside that 'Doctors doubt that! If Anne Page be my daughter, she is, by this, Doctor Caius's wife' (*Merry Wives* 5.5.172–3). The exchange implies that the punishment of a courtly outsider takes a backseat to the Windsorians' efforts to outwit each other. Although the conflict between Anne's suitors is, on the face of it, between an Englishman and a Frenchman, it primarily functions as displacement for conflict between Master Page, who favours Master Slender, and Mistress Page, who prefers

Doctor Caius. The competition between the two suitors is figured in largely comedic terms, with Slender seeming at best only mildly interested, and at worst coerced into it by Shallow and Evans. When the matter of 'marrying' is first broached, it is not by Slender himself, but by his cousin Shallow, while it is Evans who first broaches the idea of 'Anne Page' and her 'pretty virginity' (*Merry Wives* 1.1.22, 41, 42). Although Slender registers slight interest, enquiring if 'her grandsire le[ft] her seven hundred pound', the remainder of the conversation is entirely between Shallow and Evans (*Merry Wives* 1.1.53–4). Slender himself seems far more interested in discussing the recent failure of Master Page's 'fallow greyhound' in a hunting competition than his proposed future bride (*Merry Wives* 1.1.82). When approached directly about the matter, he figures his courtship as the result of his cousin's wishes rather than his own interest in Anne ('I will do as my cousin Shallow says'; 'if it be so, I will marry her upon any reasonable demands'; 'upon your request, cousin') and, when pressed by Anne herself, admits that 'for mine own part, I would little or nothing with you. Your father and my uncle hath made motions' (*Merry Wives* 1.1.200, 208–9, 222–3, 3.4.59–61). The overall picture is hardly one in which Slender appears as an eager wooer. His pursuit of Anne may therefore be read as a vehicle for conflict between her parents, designed to enable their dispute and her disobedience.

Anne herself offers another striking example of inter-English conflict. Not only is she in love with the courtier Fenton, but her efforts to wed him put her in direct conflict with her parents, and her ultimate success destabilizes their authority. Anne's father is particularly opposed to the match, telling the Host that 'He is of too high a region; he knows too / much' (*Merry Wives* 3.2.67–8). Although Master Page clearly disapproves of Fenton's conduct when he 'kept company with the wild Prince / and Poins' – and, he implies, his debts – it is significant that amongst his complaints he makes reference to the gentleman's social status (*Merry Wives* 3.2.66–7). Page, although well off, is of a lower social class than his daughter's suitor. His citation of this difference as a reason against the match, combined with his determination to match his daughter with her social equal, Slender, invokes an undercurrent of class tension which undermines any sense of English hegemony. At the same time, the tension between husband, wife and

---

[26] Jeffrey Theis, *Writing the Forest in Early Modern England: A Sylvan Pastoral Nation* (Pittsburgh, 2009), p. 10.

daughter strikes at the heart of the household as a stable unit of Englishness. Conduct books were clear about the 'interest, power, and authoritie, that parents haue in bestowing their children' in marriage and stipulated that children ought to 'cheerefully doe their [parents'] commandements, will and pleasure'.[27] Anne directly flouts such expectations, misleading both of her parents; upon learning that

> Her father hath commanded her to slip
> Away with Slender, and with him at Eton
> Immediately to marry . . . [and]
> Her mother – ever strong against that match
> And firm for Doctor Caius – hath appointed
> That he shall likewise shuffle her away

she makes 'seemingly obedient' promises to both parents, but when the Host asks 'Which means she to deceive, father or mother?', Fenton reveals that she intends to deceive them both (*Merry Wives*, 4.6.23–8, 32, 45). Anne's filial disobedience further undermines the stability of the English home and, by extension, that of the English nation itself. The latter is particularly significant in a play whose conclusion features multiple references to the monarchy and which, it has been suggested, was performed as part of the Garter ceremonies. At the same time, Anne's subplot also works alongside the other inter-English conflicts which characterize the play to foreground the concerns of an emerging middle class. The long critical history which attempts to associate the play with royalty, then, begins to look, as Emma Smith has suggested, 'like attempts to pimp the play towards a more socially elevated status as a kind of overcompensation for the fact that it is so resolutely middle class'.[28] We may want this play, like the histories, to focus on the social elite, but its subplots routinely pull us back into the concerns of the lower and middle classes.

'MATTER IN MY HEAD AGAINST YOU'[29]

Although the Pages' marital conflict remains a key focal point of the plot, much of the conflict in the play takes place between Falstaff's company and the Windsorians. This is evident from the play's opening lines, in which Falstaff's fellow Englishman Justice Shallow insists that he 'will make a Star Chamber matter of it [i.e. his grievance against Falstaff]' (*Merry Wives* 1.1.1–2). It transpires that Falstaff (who, if *Merry Wives* is taken to follow *Henry IV* chronologically, already owes Shallow 1,000 pounds)

has apparently 'beaten [Shallow's] men, killed [his] deer, and broke open [his] lodge' (*Merry Wives* 1.1.104–5). Two things are worth noting here. The first is that, as Shallow's first words indicate, it is the 'mountain-foreigner' Evans who seeks to make amends between the two Englishmen; and the second, that Shallow's proposal for extracting redress goes to the heart of English government. Located in Westminster Palace, the Star Chamber was intimately linked to the monarch, drawing its judges 'primarily from the royal council'.[30] Shallow's threat to take the matter to this particular court, then, immediately associates his local grievance with the nation's capital. Internal tensions are thus a key feature of Englishness from the outset. Despite Evans's repeated attempts 'to make / atonements and compremises between' the Englishmen, the matter is never settled, leaving the spectre of Shallow's discontent to haunt the play even after Falstaff's sexual transgressions have been addressed (*Merry Wives* 1.1.30).

Nor is Falstaff the only visitor to provoke conflict in this 'most "English" of staged Englands'. Anne's reluctant suitor, Shallow's cousin Slender, complains in the same scene of 'matter in [his] head against [Falstaff], and against [his] cony-catching rascals, Bardolph, Nim, and Pistol', whom he accuses of having 'carried [him] to the Tauerne and made [him] drunke, and afterward picked [his] pocket' (*Merry Wives* 1.1.16–18).[31] The conflict escalates quickly following the accusation – Nim appears to threaten Slender with a weapon ('Slice, I say *pauca, pauca*. Slice, that's my humour'), while Pistol explicitly calls for a trial by combat to decide the matter: 'I combat challenge of this latten bilbo' (*Merry Wives* 1.1.123, 148). The moment is, of course, comedic; Slender is amusingly resistant to physical combat, and the scene often elicits laughs in performance. Yet it is worth noting that what is comic to an audience is not necessarily so to a character; to quote Henri Bergson, 'a comic character is generally comic in proportion to his ignorance of himself. The comic person is unconscious.'[32] In addition

---

27 Cleaver, *Householde gouernment*, sigs. I4v and Y4r.
28 Emma Smith, '*The Merry Wives of Windsor*', Approaching Shakespeare, 2017, https://podcasts.ox.ac.uk/merry-wives-windsor.
29 *Merry Wives* 1.1.116.
30 K. J. Kesselring and Natalie Mears, *Star Chamber Matters: An Early Modern Court and Its Records* (London, 2021), p. 1.
31 Shakespeare, *Merrie wiues*, sig. A3r.
32 Henri Bergson, *Laughter: An Essay on the Meaning of the Comic*, trans. Cloudesley Brereton and Fred Rothwell (New York, 2005), p. 18.

to the inherent comedy, then, the scene also contains what is, for Slender, a very real grievance against the thieves, and a very real fear that they might cause him bodily harm should he pursue the matter. The social classes of these three characters are significant here: Slender, unlike his would-be assailants, is a gentleman. The late sixteenth and early seventeenth centuries saw significant tensions between the English government and its citizens regarding issues of food scarcity, military conscription and increased taxation (issues which Shakespeare explores to great effect throughout his oeuvre) and the lower classes were typically disproportionately affected by these crises. The conflict instigated by the theft – and the potential for that conflict to break into violence – thus highlights the undertones of class conflict running through both *Merry Wives* and early modern society. To present such scenes as merely comedic without also attending to their political implications, then, risks missing a vital aspect of the context against which they were written and performed, and of how such scenes might have been received in the political climate of the late sixteenth and early seventeenth centuries. As with the Pages' domestic conflicts, the scene with Slender shows us a narrative of Englishness characterized not by court entertainments, but by internal tensions between ordinary Englishmen of varying social classes.

The conflict associated with Pistol and Nim is evident even within Falstaff's party. The unified front the three characters present in 1.1 has collapsed by the close of 1.3, in which Nim and Pistol first refuse to assist with Falstaff's wooing scheme and then begin plotting revenge for the 'wrongs' he has done them. As soon as the latter has left the stage, Pistol exclaims 'Let vultures gripe thy guts!', and Nim announces that he has 'operations which be humours of revenge' (*Merry Wives* 1.3.79, 84). The scene concludes with the pair deciding to reveal Falstaff's schemes to Masters Page and Ford: 'I will incense Ford to deal with poison', Nim proclaims, 'I will possess him with yellowness; for this revolt of mine is dangerous' (*Merry Wives* 1.3.92–4). Nim's use of 'poison' and 'revolt' may have recalled recent events such as Essex's rebellion or Roderigo Lopes's alleged plot to poison Elizabeth I, lending a particularly charged air to the conflict between employer and employee(s). Falstaff appears similarly displeased with his attendants, complaining to Pistol in 2.2 that the latter has 'la[id] my countenance to pawn', and that Falstaff is 'damned in hell for swearing to gentlemen my friends you were good soldiers and tall fellows' (*Merry Wives* 2.2.6–7, 10–12).

Crucially, these conflicts, like that between Falstaff and Shallow, are never actually resolved. The closest Slender comes to resolution is his assertion 'I'll ne'er be drunk, whilst I live, again, but in honest, civil, godly company, for this trick. If I be drunk, I'll be drunk with those that have the fear of God, and not with drunken knaves' (*Merry Wives* 1.1.165–8). Falstaff retorts that his companions deny the allegations, but the scene then shifts to discussion of the proposed marriage between Shallow and Anne Page before any resolution can be reached. Pistol, meanwhile, keeps company with Falstaff despite revealing his scheme to Ford, while Nim disappears from the play entirely after doing the same to Page. Nim's final lines reiterate that 'He [Falstaff] hath wronged me in some humours. I should have borne the humoured letter to her; but I have a sword, and it shall bite upon my necessity', leaving his discontent (and his sword) hanging over the play (*Merry Wives* 2.1.123–5). Scholars who assume that the play's conclusion 'recuperates' the discord between Falstaff's party and the Windsorians, then, fail to realize that the promised reconciliation between the parties in 1.1 and 1.3 is never achieved.[33] Even if the final scene is taken to resolve any lingering discord, to dismiss these moments of conflict on account of their eventual resolution is to overlook the significance of their presence there in the first place. Once again, the social classes of the characters are relevant here. Any reconciliation that takes place in the final scene is between the middle-class and courtly characters, while the conflict between the lower-class characters and their social superiors remains unresolved. Both Pistol and Nim disappear from the play before its conclusion, only to reappear in conflict with each other in *Henry V*.

'A QUARREL BETWEEN US'[34]

Scholarship on *Henry V* has tended to focus primarily on its title character, following a Rabkinian model in which Henry's military prowess renders him an ideal monarch, a Machiavellian strategist, or both at the same time. I would like to suggest an alternate avenue into the play by shifting focus to its more minor named characters: Bardolph, Nim and Pistol. Rather than view the play solely as the culmination of the Henriad, I position it within what might be called the 'Bardolphiad', in

33 Erickson, 'Order of the Garter', p. 124.
34 *Henry V* 4.1.204.

which Henry's alehouse companions repeatedly feature. The three men are not particularly prepossessing characters, so it is perhaps unsurprising that they have been often overlooked in both criticism and performances of *Henry V*. They appear only briefly in the play, and under circumstances which lack the grandiosity of Henry's battlefield speeches. Yet focusing on these minor, lower-class characters offers a very different perspective on Shakespeare's dramatization of English history.

The primary conflict of *Henry V*, unlike that of *Merry Wives*, is explicitly between the English and an overseas other – in this case, the French – and its monarch takes pains to stress the unity of his 'band of brothers'. Although scholarship on internal conflict within the play does exist, it has typically focused on the archipelagic tensions between the four captains in 3.2. Yet *Henry V* is a play equally invested in local and particular tensions, from the petty squabbles of an Eastcheap tavern, to the ideological differences between king and commoner, to acts of full-blown treason by the nobility. The act 2 Chorus certainly casts the idea of national unity into doubt. Although it opens by proclaiming that 'honour's thought / Reigns solely in the breast of every man', within twenty lines those honourable breasts have been replaced by the 'hollow bosoms' of 'three corrupted men' (*Henry V* 2.0.3–4, 21–2) . This rapid slippage from 'every man' to 'three corrupted men' raises questions as to the constancy not only of Henry's army, but of the English population more broadly. Yet when the scene changes, it is not, as the Chorus promises, 'unto Southampton [that] we shift our scene', but rather to Eastcheap (*Henry V* 2.0.42). Instead of the traitors Cambridge, Scroop and Grey, we are confronted with a familiar figure: *Merry Wives*' disgruntled Corporal Nim, who this time has lost both his fiancée and 8 shillings to his erstwhile friend Pistol. On the face of it, the two scenes could not be more dissimilar. Yet their juxtaposition encourages us to read them concomitantly, and a closer examination reveals striking parallels between the two.

For one thing, five of the six men in question have at one point had a personal connection to Henry. Cambridge, Scroop and Grey were all favoured by the king, while both Bardolph and Pistol formed part of Henry's tavern circle in *Henry IV*. Nim's betrayal by Pistol and Nell Quickly may not have the national ramifications of Scroop's attempted regicide, but reduced to their simplest form both represent personal betrayal by a close companion. Despite his assertion that 'touching our person seek we no revenge', Henry appears deeply affected by his betrayal by Scroop, whom he describes as one who 'knew'st the very bottom of [his] soul' (*Henry V* 2.2.171, 94). National treachery here becomes fraternal treachery writ large, thereby allowing us to read 2.1 as a synecdoche for both 2.2 and broader inter-English tensions within both *Henry V* and the Henriad. The distinction between the two scenes is further blurred by timing of their respective exits and entrances in the Folio. In 2.2, Bedford, Exeter and Westmorland enter before the traitors, while there is no explicit direction for the exit of Pistol, Nim, Bardolph and Quickly. Depending on the staging, the soldiers could still be onstage when the noblemen enter, casting the referent of Bedford's opening line – "Fore God, his grace is bold to trust these traitors' – into possible doubt (*Henry V* 2.2.1). Certainly, none of the three soldiers will prove particularly trustworthy once in France. Bardolph and Nim are hanged for looting, while the circumstances of Pistol's return to England place him in company with the vagrant soldiers warned against in the 1589 'Proclamation against vagarant Souldiers and others' and again in the 1598 'Proclamation for suppressing of the multitudes of idle Vagabonds'.[35] The punishment for these outrages was hanging, suggesting that Pistol will meet the same end as his erstwhile companions. From start to finish, Henry's 'band of brothers' is plagued by treachery from within. Attending more closely to these often-overlooked moments in the play, then, reveals a narrative of Englishness defined as much by internal discord as it is by overseas warfare.

Fraternal divisions lie at the heart of much of *Henry V*'s internal and external conflict. The play as a whole insists on ideals of friendship and brotherhood while at the same time challenging and interrogating our assumptions regarding the unity they imply.[36] The first reference to friendship appears in 2.1 – encountering Nim, Bardolph asks 'what, are Ensign Pistol and you friends / yet?' – and reappears with subtle but persistent emphasis throughout the scene (*Henry V* 2.1.3). The interrogative 'yet?' sets the tone for the rest of the play, in which the bonds of friendship and brotherhood are repeatedly cast into doubt. Bardolph himself invokes the term a further

---

35 Humfrey Dyson, ed. *A booke containing all svch proclamations, as were pvblished dvring the Raigne of the late Queene Elizabeth* (London, 1618), p. 276, 356. See also Joel Altman, '"Vile participation": the amplification of violence in the theater of *Henry V*, *Shakespeare* 42 (1991), 1–32; p. 32; and Jonathan Dollimore and Alan Sinfield, 'History and ideology: the instance of *Henry V*, in *Alternative Shakespeares*, ed. John Drakakis (London, 2002), 210–31; p. 226.

36 Variants of the word 'friend' appear twenty-eight times in the text, and 'brother(s)' and 'brotherhood' twenty-seven times.

four times in the scene, each time as either a question or a plea. This insistence on the interlinked concepts of friendship, brotherhood and fraternity undermines their power, particularly as the terms frequently appear at moments in which their validity is called into question. Christopher Dowd has argued that brotherhood offers a potent metaphor for 'the notion that unity can be forged from divisive conflict' because it 'implies an undeniable unity but not necessarily equality or closeness'.[37] Shakespeare's use of the term may therefore indicate a desire to legitimate the otherwise problematic tensions within the emerging nation state. Yet its presence within the play feels uneasily conditional, as all too often the fraternal obligations invoked – be they of kinship or friendship – are revealed to be ephemeral ones.

Perhaps the most explicit instance of this occurs in the final act, wherein both the English and French monarchs repeatedly profess fraternal or otherwise familial bonds. Greeting each other as 'brother' and 'sister', Henry and the French royal couple agree to be further united in marriage, 'that never may ill office or fell jealousy ... make divorce of their incorporate league' (*Henry V* 5.2.2, 10, 358–61). Within twenty lines, this display of familial unity has been firmly dashed. The Chorus informs us that the offspring of this 'blessed marriage' will in fact not only lose France, but 'ma[ke] his England bleed' (*Henry V* Epilogue 12). The consequence of these professions of fraternity, then, is not unity, but rather the violent rending asunder of both Anglo-French and local English relationships alike. The epilogue may sound the harshest death knell for fraternal obligations, but the preceding scene itself prefigures their demise. Although she moves swiftly past it to wish that this not be the case, the French queen recognizes that 'ill office [and] fell jealousy ... [trouble] oft the bed of blessed marriage' (*Henry V* 5.2.358–9). From its outset, the brotherhood espoused by the two monarchs is shadowed by the possibility of its division.

But how is all this related to Corporal Nim and the lower classes? Bardolph's increasingly desperate attempts to foster amity between the recalcitrant Nim and Ensign Pistol are, after all, marginally more effective than the oaths sworn by Henry and the French king. As previously noted, however, the scene's position is significant. Not only does it displace the treason from its announced appearance, but it – and its partner in 2.3 – offer the only glimpse of non-noble English interactions prior to the army's arrival in France. And they are not particularly inspiring ones. The Chorus's assurance that 'honour's thought / Reigns solely in the breast of every man' – already cast into doubt by its mention of the traitors – is further eroded by the scene in Eastcheap (*Henry V* 2.0.3–4). The quarrel revolves around two distinctly dishonourable actions: Pistol's theft of Nim's fiancée, and his failure to pay his debts. Although the scene implies that both issues have been settled, it is by no means clear that this is the case. Pistol promises 'present pay', but the sum is less than that owed, and we do not witness the money change hands (*Henry V* 2.1.102). Nor does Nim seem entirely reconciled to the loss of Nell Quickly; resentfully grumbling that he 'cannot kiss' her as the trio departs for France (*Henry V* 2.3.56). Pistol and Nim may be ordinary soldiers, but they are at the same time representatives of a national military entity. As such, their unresolved dissent points towards underlying fractures in the unity of the 'happy few' Henry casts in opposition to the French. In this, Nim and his companions are representative of a broader lack of enthusiasm for the war which runs throughout the scenes with common soldiers, and even shadows Henry's interactions with his fellow noblemen. By studying these moments of inter-English conflict, then, we gain a better understanding of the popular opposition to the late Elizabethan government's military endeavours which challenges Britain's history of invoking *Henry V* to inspire unity in the face of international conflict.[38]

When Westmorland wishes for 'but one ten thousand of those men in England', his words highlight both the uncertainty of the English army and a crucial piece of information regarding wider popular sentiment towards the war (*Henry V* 4.2.17). The implication is that, despite the protestations of King and Chorus, a substantial

---

[37] Christopher Dowd, 'Polysemic brotherhoods in *Henry V*', *Studies in English Literature, 1500–1900* 50 (2010), 337–53; pp. 339, 350.

[38] See, for example, the broadside 'Shakespeare's ghost! our immortal bard, – who was as good an Englishman as a poet; whose breast glowed as much with enthusiastic love of his country, as his fancy with poetic fire, – addresses his countrymen in the following animated strain' (c. 1803), produced at the outset of the Napoleonic Wars; Frank Benson's performances during World War I; the 1942 BBC broadcast of *Henry V* featuring Laurence Olivier; Olivier's film of the same in 1944; Kenneth Branagh's film as the Cold War was coming to an end; and the 2012 production of *The Hollow Crown* as London hosted the 2012 Olympics. Amy Lidster has recently shown how the wartime Council for the Encouragement of Music and the Arts (CEMA) used *Merry Wives* to similar effect – see *Wartime Shakespeare: Performing Narratives of Conflict* (Cambridge, 2023), pp. 212–13.

section of the population has elected not to join the war effort. At the time of *Henry V*'s composition there was significant popular resentment regarding both conscription and the fees levied to fund the war in Ireland. This resentment is played out not only in the more disreputable characters of Bardolph, Pistol and Nim, but in the sentiments of those soldiers depicted as conventionally honourable, such as John Bates and Michael Williams. When the disguised Henry proclaims that 'the King's . . . cause' is 'just and his quarrel honourable', Williams merely replies, 'that's more than we know', and the soldiers evidently do not believe that Henry refuses to be ransomed (*Henry V* 4.1.126–8). Their challenge to the dominant narrative provokes a division imposed by Henry between himself and the soldiers – one which Henry later attempts to displace onto Fluellen, thereby shifting the quarrel to a more conventionally acceptable Anglo-Welsh conflict. Williams remains firm in his beliefs when the deception is revealed. He refuses to accept blame for the challenge, and it is unclear to whom his 'I will none of your money' is addressed, as he has not spoken in between Henry's offer of financial compensation and that of Fluellen (*Henry V* 4.8.68). These glimpses into popular sentiment undermine Henry's claims that 'We carry not a heart with us from hence / That grows not in a fair consent with ours' (*Henry V* 2.2.20–1). As Dollimore and Sinfield remind us, 'the hegemonic class . . . needed, urgently, to deny divisions and insist that everyone's purpose was the same', yet in *Henry V* those divisions continue to bubble to the surface.[39] This too had its analogue in Elizabethan London. Francis Bacon's 1593 testimony to Parliament reveals resentment among the lower orders for the increased taxation that resulted from foreign wars, and Falstaff's taking bribes from mustered men keen to ignore military service in *Henry IV* was likewise rooted in popular practice.[40] The overall effect is to cast the purported national unity inspired by war into significant doubt, suggesting that the internal discord of *The Merry Wives of Windsor* is merely displaced, rather than replaced, in *Henry V*.

Redirecting our gaze to these moments of inter-English tension therefore allows us to challenge the idea that England as a whole was a homogeneous entity, and to consider how its varied and often conflicted identities were understood by its inhabitants. In early modern London, for example, playgoers were in the midst of a substantial immigrant community composed of both strangers (those coming from overseas) and 'Englishmen forren' such as Shakespeare, who had migrated to London from more rural areas. Yet even London was not necessarily representative of the nation as a whole; its (im)migrant communities were often a source of conflict, as *Sir Thomas More* demonstrates, and class disputes – particularly complaints about the city's apprentices – were not uncommon. For a play seemingly obsessed with national victory and fraternal communities, *Henry V* remains riddled with internal tensions, and its epilogue reminds us that the victory in question dies with Henry – as, in many ways, does the brotherhood associated with it. Yet that is not to say that some degree of division is incompatible with Shakespeare's portrayal of English nationhood. Instead, this article argues that reading these moments of inter-English conflict and resistance to the whims of the nobility alongside *Merry Wives* reveals an alternative perspective on Englishness, one defined as much by the concerns of the lower and middle classes as by the military exploits of Lancastrian monarchs. In doing so, it asks us to reconsider Shakespeare's England as a composite of parts rather than a cohesive whole, offering an alternative perspective on the problematic boundaries of the early modern nation.

---

[39] Dollimore and Sinfield, 'History and ideology', p. 218.
[40] J. E. Neale, *Elizabeth I and Her Parliaments* (London, 1957), pp. 309–10.

'NECESSITY HAS NO LAW': JUSTICE AND AFFECTIVE COMMUNITIES IN *2 HENRY VI*

LUKAS ARNOLD

The aim of this article is to bring scholarship on early modern communal justice into a productive conversation with recent insights generated by affect theory.[1] Over the course of the last two decades, several literary critics – including Lorna Hutson, Marissa Greenberg, Virginia Lee Strain and, more recently, Penelope Geng – have investigated the theatrical representations of commoner judicial participation in the dramatic works of Shakespeare and his contemporaries.[2] As these critics highlight, commoners shaped legal proceedings in a number of ways, such as raising the 'hue and cry', aiding in evidence collection, giving witness testimony, and even serving as jurors in common law trials.[3] Playwrights, they argue, incorporated these facets of everyday legal experience into their dramas and, by doing so, could shape collective ideas about the nature of law and justice.[4] These approaches belong to a broader trend in the field of early modern law and literature: a move away from the long-established 'tradition of attending to the law's thematic resonances . . . in order to extrapolate ahistorical ethical questions' and towards 'meticulously contextualis[ing] the literary texts in relation to early modern legal culture'.[5] Holger Schott Syme exemplifies this new direction when he observes that 'there is a striking mismatch between the ways justice was done in early modern England and the judicial processes depicted on stage'.[6] For instance, one of the hallmarks of sixteenth- and seventeenth-century common law proceedings – 'the process of twelve jurors assessing the credibility of a particular set of charges'[7] – was not staged by 'a single play written between the opening of the first commercial theatres in the 1570s and their closure in 1642'.[8] However, this absence should not be regarded as a mimetic deficiency of the period's drama. Rather, it should alert us to the fact that popular theatre engaged with justice in an 'extra-legal

capacity',[9] and that this engagement involved cognitive judgement as well as affective responses.

Both the courtroom and the playhouse offered its practitioners different cognitive and affective affordances through which notions of justice could be articulated.[10]

---

[1] Affect has become a prolific theoretical framework for the study of early modern literature in the last few years. For some recent examples, see the two essay collections by Amanda Bailey and Mario DiGangi, eds., *Affect Theory and Early Modern Texts: Politics, Ecologies, and Form* (New York, 2017), and Jonathan Baldo and Isabel Karremann, eds., *Memory and Affect in Shakespeare's England* (Cambridge, 2023).

[2] Lorna Hutson, *The Invention of Suspicion: Law and Mimesis in Shakespeare and Renaissance Drama* (Oxford, 2007); Hutson, 'Noises off: participatory justice in *2 Henry VI*', in *The Law in Shakespeare*, ed. Jordan Constance and Karen Cunningham (Basingstoke, 2007), 143–66; Marissa Greenberg, *Metropolitan Tragedy: Genre, Justice, and the City in Early Modern England* (Toronto, 2015); Virginia Lee Strain, 'Shakespeare's living law: theatrical, lyrical, and legal practice', *Literature Compass* 12 (2015), 249–61; Penelope Hui Geng, *Communal Justice in Shakespeare's England: Drama, Law, and Emotion* (Toronto, 2021).

[3] Geng, *Communal Justice*, especially pp. 3 and 8.

[4] Geng, *Communal Justice*, p. 8.

[5] Strain, 'Shakespeare's living law', p. 249.

[6] Holger Schott Syme, '(Mis)representing justice on the early modern stage', *Studies in Philology* 109 (2012), 63–85; p. 63. Also see Syme, *Theatre and Testimony in Shakespeare's England: A Culture of Mediation* (Cambridge, 2012).

[7] Syme, '(Mis)representing', p. 68.

[8] Syme, '(Mis)representing', p. 65.

[9] Syme, '(Mis)representing', p. 85.

[10] Ecological psychologist James J. Gibson defines affordances as possibilities for and constrictions of certain modes of action that arise from the relationality between an animal and its environment: Gibson, *The Ecological Approach to Visual Perception* (New York, 1986), p. 127. This concept has also been productive in early modern studies. Evelyn Tribble and John Sutton, for example, argue that an affordance-based approach enables scholars to consider the complex cognitive ecology of theatrical performance:

In comparison to the courtroom, where the evidentiary basis of a given case was assessed and judged in relation to legal precedent,[11] theatre enabled its audience to consider questions about justice through the emotional affects of performance. In a ground-breaking essay, Steven Mullaney has conceptualized the early modern theatre as a type of 'inhabited affective technology', writing that the playhouses offered their practitioners 'a way of thinking *through* virtual and (yet) real bodies – those of the actors on stage, and those of the audience, too – in order to think *about* the larger social body . . . in a collective sense and by means of a collective experiential process'.[12] Gail Kern Paster builds on this understanding, arguing that the collective emotional experience of theatre enabled spectators to become part of an affective community 'for the duration of a performance'.[13] Drama, she explains, enacted scenes that topically resonated with the lives of its spectators, which presented them with an opportunity to respond collectively on the basis of their emotional experience.[14] While the actual emotional responses of Shakespeare's historical spectators are lost, it is possible to reconstruct a field of potential responses based on the affective affordances of the playtext.[15]

Engaging with these affordances in William Shakespeare's *The Second Part of King Henry VI* reveals how the play utilizes the entwined problems of dearth and enclosure to enable its audience to think about the nature of justice through what Mullaney terms 'the emotional logic of theatre'.[16] Both of these issues were central to commoner subsistence politics in the late 1580s and 1590s. When Shakespeare wrote *2 Henry VI*, England had just emerged from the most severe harvest failure of the sixteenth century up to that point. In 1586, wheat prices rose to nearly 36 shillings per quarter, a record high that would only be surpassed during the four consecutive harvest failures between 1594 and 1597.[17] Adding to this hardship, land prices had also increased exponentially over the sixteenth century. On average, the copyhold rent for an acre of farmland was around 8d per annum in 1500.[18] By comparison, the same acre possessed a market value of 86½d by the time *2 Henry VI* was first performed.[19] This development made a significant portion of the population dependent on wages, which were unable to keep up with the rapidly rising cost of living.[20] As a result, there were roughly seventeen 'instances of disorder' between 1586 and 1597: 'three, possibly four, in 1586; five in 1595; two in 1596; [and] five in 1597'.[21] Fearing that these riots could eventually become large enough to threaten the established social order, Queen Elizabeth's government responded by issuing the Book of Orders in 1586, an instructive set of legal ordinances that were designed to alleviate the suffering of the poor.[22] Performed in this context, the commoner politics of Shakespeare's history play presented emotionally provocative material. Particularly, by adapting the Jack Cade rebellion of 1450 for the stage, Shakespeare's play utilized the nation's past

---

Tribble and Sutton, 'Cognitive ecology as a framework for Shakespearean Studies', *Shakespeare Studies* 39 (2011), 94–103. Also see Tribble, *Cognition in the Globe: Attention and Memory in Shakespeare's Theatre* (New York, 2011).

[11] In common law, this precedent conceptually consisted not just of prior cases but also of 'the collected, uncodified practices of the English people and the wisdom of generations of lawyers and judges': Stephanie Elsky, *Custom, Common Law, and the Constitution of English Renaissance Literature* (Oxford, 2020), p. 4.

[12] Steven Mullaney, 'Affective technologies: toward an emotional logic of the Elizabethan stage', in *Environment and Embodiment in Early Modern England*, ed. Mary Floyd-Wilson and Garrett A. Sullivan (Basingstoke, 2007), 71–83; p. 73.

[13] Gail Kern Paster, 'Communities: *Julius Caesar*', in *Shakespeare and Emotion*, ed. Katharine A. Craik (Cambridge, 2020), 94–108; p. 94. I further follow Paster in using the terms 'affect' and 'emotion' as mostly interchangeable (p. 94). Whereas earlier affect scholars more rigidly distinguished between affects and emotions, Benedict S. Robinson views this distinction as the product of, rather than an alternative to, the Cartesian mind/body dualism. Tracing the history of these concepts, he finds that 'they are versions of the same break with an earlier theory of the passions as the simultaneously cognitive and embodied responses of a soul' (p. 123). In 'Thinking feeling', in *Affect Theory and Early Modern Texts*, ed. Bailey and DiGangi, 109–28.

[14] Paster, 'Communities', pp. 94–5.

[15] Isabel Karremann, 'Introduction', in *Shakespeare/Space: Contemporary Readings in Spatiality, Culture and Drama*, ed. Isabel Karremann (London, 2024), 1–21; p. 9.

[16] Mullaney, 'Affective technologies', p. 71.

[17] William G. Hoskins, 'Harvest fluctuations and English economic history, 1480–1619', *Agricultural History Review* 12 (1964), 28–64; pp. 28–9.

[18] Jane Whittle, 'Land and people', in *A Social History of England, 1500–1750*, ed. Keith Wrightson (Cambridge, 2017), 152–73; p. 160.

[19] Whittle, 'Land', p. 160.

[20] On the growing demographic of wage-dependent labourers in early modern England, see Keith Wrightson, *Earthly Necessities: Economic Lives in Early Modern Britain* (New Haven, 2002); and Steve Hindle, *On the Parish? The Micro-Politics of Poor Relief in Rural England, c. 1550–1750* (Oxford, 2004).

[21] John Walter, *Crowds and Popular Politics in Early Modern England* (Manchester, 2006), p. 68.

[22] For in-depth discussions of the Book of Orders, see Paul Slack, *Poverty and Policy in Tudor and Stuart England* (New York, 1988); and Slack, 'Dearth and social policy in early modern England', *Social History of Medicine* 5 (1992), 1–17.

to explore one of its possible futures: a vision of England in which the corruption and economic malfeasance of the nobility results in a violent uprising.

Whereas an earlier generation of scholars, including Stephen Greenblatt and Richard Helgerson, had viewed *2 Henry VI* as ridiculing commoner politics,[23] since the mid-1990s there has been a shift in critical perspective towards taking the play's enactment of subsistence issues seriously. The pendulum first began to swing in the opposite direction with the publication of Thomas Cartelli's seminal chapter 'Jack Cade in the garden', which traces the underlying class consciousness of the play's commoner politics.[24] Chris Fitter, who presents the 1591 William Hacket rising as another important context for *2 Henry VI*,[25] makes a similar argument, writing that Shakespeare had a 'surprising degree of sympathy with plebian suffering' and that 'Cade embodied a radical class anger.'[26] Along similar lines, Anne-Marie Schuler interprets Shakespeare's depiction of the Cade rebellion as 'a type of plebian counsel' that 'critiques the ability of paternalist ideals to serve the needs of all members of the commonwealth'.[27] Each of these scholars identifies the garden scene as a key moment for considering the play's commoner politics, arguing to various extents that Cade's death at the hands of Alexander Iden, a Kentish esquire and proprietor of the garden, does not retroactively erase the concerns raised by the play's rebellion.

Although this work has led to valuable insights for our understanding of the play in its context, their approaches are at risk of reducing the emotional complexity with which Shakespeare depicts the commoners' politics, especially in the garden scene. Hillary Eklund, for instance, locates something different in the topicality of Cade's hunger: an '"anticipatory consciousness" – a consciousness of that which has yet to happen – of political alternatives still in the offing'.[28] Hence, rather than collapsing the play's subsistence politics into a particular position, she urges us to instead 'explore the rich possibilities of precisely the chaotic polyvocality with which critics have struggled'.[29] Jeffrey Doty makes a similar observation, writing that 'Shakespeare's theatre contributed to a popular political culture less from taking positions on issues than by publicly exploring political controversies with a rationality unusual to the period's more typical political discourses.'[30] This article builds on these insights by tracing the affective affordances that centrally inform the audience's understanding of the garden scene over the course of the play. By doing so, it will demonstrate that *2 Henry VI* does not necessarily lead its spectators towards a specific conclusion on the

issues of dearth and enclosure but enables them instead to consider what constitutes justice through their collective emotional experience as an affective community.

I

There are three main thematic strings that eventually tie together to shape the affective affordances of the garden scene: the play's engagement with subsistence issues, its metaphorical expressions of political positions through images of human and non-human bodies, and its depiction of the English judicial system as corrupt. In many instances, several of these themes overlap, as is the case in 1.3. Here, three petitioners enter the stage and attempt to present their grievances to Duke

---

[23] In Greenblatt's reading, 'Shakespeare depicts Cade's rebellion as a grotesque and sinister farce, the archetypal lower class revolt both in its motives and in its ludicrousness': 'Murdering peasants: status, genre, and the representation of rebellion', *Representations* 1 (1983), 1–29; p. 23. While Richard Helgerson admits that 'one cannot represent rebellion, however negatively, without permitting it to speak its discontent', he nevertheless concludes that '*The Contention* constitutes an attack as well as representing one. It not only makes fun of Cade and his fellow rebels, it exposes popular rule as inimical to the very existence of the institution by which it and other plays like it were produced': *Forms of Nationhood: The Elizabethan Writing of England* (Chicago, 1992), p. 213.

[24] Thomas Cartelli, 'Jack Cade in the garden: class consciousness and class conflict in *2 Henry VI*', in *Enclosure Acts: Sexuality, Property, and Culture in Early Modern England*, ed. Richard Burt and John Michael Archer (Ithaca, 1994), 48–67.

[25] See Chris Fitter, '"Your captain is brave and vows reformation": Jack Cade, the Hacket rising, and Shakespeare's vision of popular rebellion in *2 Henry VI*', *Shakespeare Studies* 32 (2004), 173–219; Fitter, 'Emergent Shakespeare and the politics of protest: *2 Henry VI* in historical contexts', *English Literary History* 72 (2005), 129–58; and Fitter, *Radical Shakespeare: Politics and Stagecraft in the Early Career* (New York, 2012), ch. 3.

[26] Fitter, 'Shakespeare, Jack Cade, and "Kentish men": England's earliest working-class rebel-heroes?', *Journal for Early Modern Cultural Studies* 20 (2020), 89–111; p. 89.

[27] Anne-Marie E. Schuler, 'Shakespeare's mad, unruly mob: petition, popular revolt, and political participation in *King Henry VI, Part 2*', *Selected Papers of the Ohio Valley Shakespeare Conference* 7 (2016), 156–71; p. 157.

[28] Hillary Eklund, 'Revolting diets: Jack Cade's "sallet" and the politics of hunger in *2 Henry VI*', *Shakespeare Studies* 42 (2014), 51–62; p. 53. Eklund borrows the term 'anticipatory consciousness' from Ernst Bloch, *The Principle of Hope*, trans. Neville Plaice, Stephen Plaice and Paul Knight, 3 vols. (Cambridge, 1986), vol. 2, pp. 74–5 and 113.

[29] Eklund, 'Revolting diets', p. 56.

[30] Jeffrey S. Doty, 'Shakespeare and popular politics', *Literature Compass* 10 (2013), 162–74; pp. 170–1.

Gloucester, the Lord Protector, but mistakenly deliver them to Queen Margaret and Duke Suffolk. Two of these supplications address the topic of land dispossession on different scales. The First Petitioner recounts how John Goodman, a servant of Cardinal Beaufort, has taken his 'house and lands and wife and all from [him]' (1.3.19).[31] Suffolk mocks the supplicant's predicament: 'Thy wife too? That's some wrong indeed' (1.3.20). Similarly, when the second suit accuses Suffolk of 'enclosing the commons of Melford' (1.3.23), he insults the Second Petitioner by replying 'How now, sir knave?' (1.3.24). These petitions both highlight the commoners' nuanced understanding of England's social hierarchy and signal their awareness of the nobility's corruption to the audience. Indeed, the petitioners' only option for recourse, Craig Bernthal points out, is 'to get an impartial hearing from [Gloucester]' because 'Suffolk controls the administration of justice in his own dukedom.'[32] Furthermore, according to In-Hwan Doh, depicting Suffolk as an encloser was a creative liberty by Shakespeare. 'Hall's chronicle', she writes, documents 'Suffolk's oppression of the poor' but makes 'no mention of enclosure'.[33] While I concur with Doty that this scene 'cast[s] Suffolk as an enemy of the people', it is not necessarily 'the politics of enclosure' that accomplishes this affective positioning but Suffolk's callousness towards the victims of enclosure.[34] His mistreatment of the petitioners might have evoked a negative set of emotions, such as anger, frustration or disdain, in the play's spectators, which afforded them the possibility to feel the injustice of enclosure suffered by the supplicants.

The play further fosters these potential feelings of animosity through performance. Both the 1594 Quarto and 1623 Folio editions of the text contain stage directions indicating that the commoners' petitions are destroyed onstage. In the Quarto, Suffolk tears the Second Petitioner's supplication to pieces. By contrast, the Folio is more ambiguous as to who performs this action, as the instruction changes from 'He teares the papers' (Q 1.3.40–1)[35] to 'tear the supplication' (F 1.3.38–9)[36] and occurs during Margaret's dialogue.[37] While both versions display a disdain for the commoners' customary means towards political redress, having Margaret destroy the petitions also underlines her conception of politics as *arcana imperii*. Indeed, right after dismissing the petitioners, Margaret turns to Suffolk and mocks the idea that commoners could be part of the political sphere:

MARGARET My Lord of Suffolk, say, is this the guise,
Is this the fashions in the court of England?
Is this the government of Britain's isle,
And this the royalty of Albion's king?

(F 1.3.41–4)

In these lines, Margaret utilizes the connotations of 'guise' and 'fashion' to connect the visual signifiers of power with the, in her opinion, exclusive privilege of the elite to shape the polity of the nation. The word 'guise' can mean both '[s]tyle or fashion of attire' and 'custom, habit, [and] practice'.[38] Similarly, 'fashion' could also refer to attire or '[a] prevailing custom ... characteristic of a particular place or period of time'.[39] To Margaret, the place of politics is clear: 'the court of England' (F 1.3.42). Moreover, those who are allowed to partake in this practice ultimately derive their power to do so from King Henry. Accordingly, by questioning petitioning as part of 'the royalty of Albion's king' (F 1.3.44), Margaret mocks the idea that commoners, who lack both title and rank, could participate in politics.

These affective affordances of 1.3 certainly appear to facilitate the class-conscious readings that have dominated academic attention in recent years. In *Radical Shakespeare*, for example, Fitter dedicates a considerable amount of time to imagining how groundlings might have reacted to *2 Henry VI*'s enactment of subsistence politics.[40] My point here is not that Fitter's argument presents a misreading of the play. On the contrary, in

[31] Unless indicated otherwise, references to the play are from William Shakespeare, 'The first part of the Contention', in *William Shakespeare: The Complete Works*, 2nd ed., ed. Stanley Wells et al. (Oxford, 2005), 55–124.

[32] Craig A. Bernthal, 'Jack Cade's legal carnival', *SEL: Studies in English Literature 1500–1900* 42 (2002), 259–74; p. 261.

[33] In-Hwan Doh, 'Popular politics in *2 Henry VI*: everyday forms of resistance and hidden transcripts', *Cahiers Élisabéthains: A Journal of English Renaissance Studies* 89 (2016), 27–44; p. 32.

[34] Doty, 'Shakespeare', p. 166.

[35] Citations of the Quarto are to William Shakespeare, *The First Part of the Contention. The First Quarto, 1594: A Facsimile, by Photolithography* (London, 1889).

[36] References to the Folio version of the play are from William Shakespeare, 'The second part of King Henry the Sixth', in *The Norton Shakespeare*, 3rd ed., ed. Stephen Greenblatt et al., 2 vols. (London, 2016), vol. 1, 181–264.

[37] Roger Warren, 'Introduction', in William Shakespeare, *Henry VI, Part Two*, ed. Roger Warren (Oxford, 2003), 51.

[38] "Guise, 4.a and 2," in *OED Online*, www.oed.com/dictionary/guise_n?tab=meaning_and_use#2322792.

[39] "Fashion, 3.b and 8.a," in *OED Online*, www.oed.com/dictionary/fashion_n?tab=meaning_and_use#4793522.

[40] Fitter, *Radical*, pp. 39–45.

imagining possible audience responses, he does not go far enough. While Greenblatt was overly concerned with how the Elizabethan authorities might have viewed Shakespeare's play,[41] we should be careful not to make a similar mistake by only thinking about the groundlings. After all, theatre audiences were diverse, consisting of people from across the social scale. Therefore, rather than reading the play as appealing either to commoners or to their social superiors, I want to suggest that the affective affordances of Shakespeare's petitioning scene might have had the potential to unite its audience. This becomes particularly apparent in the scene's final supplication, when the apprentice armourer Peter Thump accuses his master, Thomas Horner, of 'saying that the Duke of York was rightful heir to the / crown' (1.3.28–9). Although this petition is successful, at least insofar as the matter is brought before Henry, Suffolk and Margaret do so not out of concern for their monarch's safety but because it provides them valuable political ammunition against York's faction:

SUFFOLK As for the Duke of York, this late complaint
Will make but little for his benefit.
So, one by one, we'll weed them all at last,
And you yourself shall steer the happy helm.

(1.3.100–3)

In combination, the three petitions highlight a breakdown of paternalistic relations. In early modern England, the starkly unequal power dynamics of the social hierarchy were justified through the twin concepts of paternalism and deference, which were ideologically modelled on the familial relationship between a parent and their children.[42] Those in a position of power were conceptualized as having a duty of care towards their subjects; and subordinates, in turn, were expected to be obedient to their superiors.[43] Seeing how Suffolk and Margaret neglect their paternalistic duties, spectators belonging to the middling and upper sorts might have shared in the commoners' potential aversion to these characters.[44] In other words, the affective affordances of this scene could have transformed Shakespeare's spectators into an affective community through their shared emotional experience of injustice from above.

If the play attempts to evoke these emotions in its spectators, then it also allows for their eventual cathartic release. In 4.1, shortly after Suffolk has been banished for his involvement in the murder of Gloucester, he is captured by a crew of pirates. This is another scene with substantial differences between the Quarto and Folio.

Whereas the Quarto ties Suffolk's execution to his affair with Margaret as well as his role in Gloucester's death (Q 4.1.46–9), the Lieutenant's indictment is nearly thirty lines longer in the Folio and presents a far more comprehensive list of Suffolk's crimes. In addition to the two accusations above, the Folio's Lieutenant also condemns Suffolk '[f]or swallowing up the treasure of the realm' (F 4.1.74); '[f]or daring to affy a mighty lord / Unto the daughter of a worthless king' (F 4.1.80–1); for the loss of Anjou and Maine, which were exchanged for Margaret's hand in marriage (F 4.1.86); as well as for indirectly causing an uprising in Picardy:

LIEUTENANT The false revolting Normans thorough thee
Disdain to call us lord, and Picardy
Hath slain their governors, surprised our forts,
And sent the ragged soldiers wounded home.

(F 4.1.87–90)

While several of these charges are borrowed directly from Hall's *Chronicle*,[45] the last crime is again an invention by Shakespeare, possibly made with a view to inciting an emotional response in the audience.[46] In recounting Suffolk's misdeeds, Cartelli suggests, the Lieutenant appears to assume 'the voice of the

---

[41] Greenblatt, 'Murdering peasants', pp. 23–5.

[42] James Stuart, for example, famously wrote that 'the king towards his people is rightly compared to a father of children': in *The True Law of Free Monarchies: Or the Reciprock and Mutuall Dutie Betwixt a Free King, and His Natural Subjectes* (Edinburgh, 1598), B–E3; p. D3.

[43] Commoners could also utilize this rhetoric to legitimize their political interventions. According to Andy Wood, 'Paternalism maintained a dominant set of interests; and yet it gave subordinates room for manoeuvre, handing to them a tool which, if used carefully, could win important concessions': 'Deference, paternalism and popular memory in early modern England', in *Remaking English Society: Social Relations and Social Change in Early Modern England*, ed. Steve Hindle, Alexandra Shepard and John Walter (Woodbridge, 2013), 233–53; p. 238. For how commoners historically mobilized the concept of paternalism during times of dearth, see Hillary Taylor, 'Paternalism and the politics of "toll corn" in early modern England', *Social History* 48 (2023), 214–31.

[44] Peter Lake similarly locates 'the roots' of commoner politics in Shakespeare's play 'in the dereliction of duty of their social superiors and natural rulers, and thus in the machinations of court politics': *How Shakespeare Put Politics on the Stage: Power and Succession in the History Plays* (New Haven, 2017), p. 96.

[45] Thomas Cartelli, 'Suffolk and the pirates: disordered relations in Shakespeare's *2 Henry VI*', in *A Companion to Shakespeare's Works, Volume II: The Histories*, ed. Richard Dutton and Jean E. Howard (Malden, 2003), 325–43; p. 330.

[46] Warren, *Henry VI, Part Two*, p. 232.

commonweal itself rising up in righteous indignation'.[47] Consequently, his speech 'is "calling for" audience approval'.[48] And, indeed, it is not difficult to imagine that an audience who has witnessed Suffolk commit a number of these crimes on stage would cheer at his demise.

II

In a similar manner, the Jack Cade rebellion also builds on the affective affordances set up in 1.3. In 4.2, for example, the play returns to Margaret's metaphorical use of attire as a way of describing the rebels' desire for political reform:

FIRST REBEL Jack Cade the clothier means to dress the commonwealth, and turn it, and set a new nap upon it.
SECOND REBEL So he had need, for 'tis threadbare. Well, I say it was never merry world in England since gentlemen came up.

(4.2.5–10)

Whereas Margaret expressed her views on politics through a hierarchical code of attire, the rebels' metaphor utilizes an artisanal vocabulary that emphasizes the material production of clothes. Drawing on the metaphor of the body politic, here the commonwealth is envisioned as dressed in threadbare fabrics. The phrase 'came up', as Roger Warren points out, is a synonym for having become *fashionable*.[49] Consequently, in saying that 'it was never merry world in England' (9) since the rise of the gentlemen, the rebels link the worn-out state of the commonwealth's clothes to the corruption among the nobility that the play's audience has witnessed over the course of the preceding three acts. Furthermore, the identification of Cade as a clothier is also significant in relation to the play's historical context.[50] Warren notes that Cade 'is not given a trade in the chronicles'.[51] In fact, according to historian Alexander Kaufman, 'we have no firm knowledge regarding Jack Cade's true identity' at all.[52] Regardless of whether Shakespeare invented this detail or not, associating Cade with the cloth trade links him to one of the dominant groups involved in two grain-related incidents in 1586. In the West Country, as a result of grain shortages, 'crowds, 500–600 strong, in which clothworkers almost certainly predominated, twice attacked barges moving grain down the Severn'.[53] These historical instances of unrest resonate in the passage above, as the rebels express the political reform of the commonwealth through the process of improving a piece of cloth.

In a turn of events more reminiscent of the 1381 Peasant Revolt than the 1450 Jack Cade rebellion,[54] Shakespeare's rebels soon identify the law as the site of their systemic oppression. Still in 4.2, Dick the Butcher, another prominent figure among the rebels, proclaims that they should 'kill all the lawyers' (4.2.78). Cade goes one step further, expressing how the material production of the law in itself presents an act of violence, one that thematically links the slaughter of innocent animals with the suffering of the poor:

CADE Is not this a lamentable thing, that of the skin of an innocent lamb should be made parchment? That parchment, being scribbled o'er, should undo a man? Some say the bee stings, but I say, 'tis the beeswax; for I did but seal once to a thing, and I was never mine own man since.

(4.2.79–84)

The figure of the 'innocent lamb' evokes the Christian liturgical tradition of the 'Agnus Dei', a short prayer that was spoken during holy communion: 'Lamb of God, Son of the Father, that takest away the sins of the world, have mercy upon us.'[55] However, rather than absolving the world of sin, the innocent lamb in Cade's speech is butchered and skinned to materially enable a legal system that propagates the suffering of the indigent. Put differently, in the parchment, Cade glimpses a part of the law's material ecology and realizes the violence inherent in its written form.[56] As the law

---

[47] Cartelli, 'Suffolk', p. 330. [48] Cartelli, 'Suffolk', p. 340.

[49] Warren, *Henry VI, Part Two*, p. 236.

[50] Although Cade is referred to as 'the Diar of Ashford' (Q 4.2.6) in the Quarto, this profession still associates him with the clothworkers. Furthermore, when Sir Humphrey Stafford enters the stage to quell the commoner uprising, the Folio version of the play reiterates Cade's professional experience in the cloth trade. As Cade insists that he is 'rightful heir unto the crown' (F 4.2.120), Stafford retorts: 'Villain, thy father was a plasterer, / And thou thyself a shearman, art thou not?' (121–2). While Stafford similarly questions the legitimacy of Cade's claim in the Quarto by highlighting that his 'father was but a Brick-laier' (Q 4.2.85), the reference to Cade's own occupation is absent.

[51] Warren, 'Introduction', p. 51.

[52] Alexander L. Kaufman, *The Historical Literature of the Jack Cade Rebellion* (Farnham, 2009), p. 152.

[53] Walter, *Crowds*, p. 68. [54] Bernthal, 'Jack Cade', p. 262.

[55] James Cornford, ed., *The Book of Common Prayer, with Historical Notes* (London, 1880), p. 167.

[56] Julian Yates makes a similar observation, as he first describes Cade in this moment as 'discern[ing] the constellation of animal, vegetable, and mineral matter that funds the legal forms of writing of Renaissance England' (149), and later as 'see[ing] some of the network of human and non-human actors that constitute a parchment'

undoes both the lamb and the poor, Cade finds a kind of kinship between the two that stands in stark contrast to much of the period's anti-enclosure writing, which often presented sheep as emblematic of the practice.[57] Satirist Thomas Bastard, for example, portrays sheep as having become monstrous, capable of consuming 'whole villages and towns' (2).[58] Likewise, courtier John Harington describes them as 'a cruel beast' (9) that 'spares not house nor village, Church nor Steeple, / And makes poor widows mourn, orphans lament' (11–12).[59] In the Folio, Cade's comparison also recalls an earlier moment in the play. During act 2, when York discusses his plans to become king with Salisbury and Warwick, he cautions that they should not yet make their move. Instead, deposing Henry will be easier once Suffolk, Beaufort and Buckingham 'have snared the shepherd of the flock, / That virtuous prince, the good Duke Humphrey' (F 2.2.73–4).[60] Consequently, after Gloucester's death in act 3, there is no avenue of recourse left for the commoners to address their grievances within the playworld's legal system. Thus, they turn their ire against the system itself.

The rebellion's 'antilegal impetus' also builds on the affective affordances created by the petitioners' failed supplications. The Butcher's proposed course of action quickly escalates into the wholesale prosecution of anyone who is literate. Thus, when the clerk Emmanuel is brought onstage, he is tried and subsequently sentenced to death solely for his ability to 'write and read and / cast account' (4.2.86–7).[61] The name 'Emmanuel', as Roger Chartier reminds us, 'means "God with us", a formula frequently used as heading for legal documents' in the early modern period.[62] For Bernthal, this animosity towards literacy presents a form of 'revenge tragedy'.[63] Katharine Eisaman Maus notes that one of the defining characteristics of heroes in revenge tragedies is that they '[take] matters into [their] own hands because the institutions by which criminals are made to pay for their offences are either systematically defective or unable to cope with some particularly difficult situation'.[64] Building on this observation, Bernthal argues that audience members, who had previously witnessed the petitioners' failed attempts to redress their issues through writing, could have interpreted the rebels' hatred towards literacy as a kind of retribution.[65] Moreover, if the petitioning scene enables playgoers to potentially feel anger, frustration or disdain at Suffolk's and Margaret's dereliction of paternalistic duties, then the play may have utilized these affective affordances as a way to emotionally justify the rebellion's ensuing violence. Indeed,

according to Michael Hattaway, spectators might have felt a sense of 'glee as the privileged get their come uppance'.[66]

These opportunities for gleeful response are present throughout the rebellion and centrally shape its performance of commoner politics. For instance, as the rebels seize London, the Butcher petitions Cade, requesting that, henceforth, 'the laws of England may come out of your mouth' (4.7.5–6). Although building on the rebellion's previously established aversion towards the written law, this alternative form of legislature is turned into an opportunity for laughter in the playhouse. John, another rebel, quips that ''twill be sore law then, for he was thrust in the mouth with a spear, and 'tis not whole yet' (4.7.7–9). Similarly, the Weaver adds, 'Nay, John, it will be

---

(153). In 'Skin merchants: Jack Cade's futures and the figural politics of *Henry VI, Part II*', in *Go Figure: Energies, Forms, and Institutions in the Early Modern World*, ed. Judith H. Anderson and Joan Pong Linton (Fordham, 2011), 149–69. On law as an ecology in Shakespeare's plays, see Kevin Curran, *Shakespeare's Legal Ecologies: Law and Distributed Selfhood* (Evanston, 2017).

[57] Similarly, Yates argues that the innocent lamb becomes, in Donna Haraway's term, a 'companion species' to Cade: 'Skin merchants', pp. 152–3. Also see Donna Jeanne Haraway, *The Companion Species Manifesto: Dogs, People, and Significant Otherness* (Chicago, 2003).

[58] Thomas Bastard, 'Sheep have eat up our meadows and our downs (1598)', in *Literature and Nature in the English Renaissance: An Ecocritical Anthology*, ed. Todd Andrew Borlik (Cambridge, 2019), 405; p. 405.

[59] John Harington, 'Of sheep turned wolves (c. 1600)', in *Literature and Nature in the English Renaissance*, ed. Borlik, 405–6; p. 405.

[60] While these lines are absent from the Quarto, Gloucester refers to himself as a shepherd in both versions when he is arrested by Beaufort's men. In the Quarto, Gloucester laments that Henry 'puts his watchfull sheapeard from his side, / Whilst wolves stand snaring who shall bite him first' (Q 3.1.100–1). The Folio's lines are only slightly different: 'Thus is the shepherd beaten from thy [Henry's] side, / And wolves are gnarling who shall gnaw thee first' (F 3.1.191–2).

[61] Bernthal further notes that the rebellion's series of mock-trials moves up the judicial ladder, 'starting with the lowliest legal operative, a clerk, and ending with a judge and counselor, Lord Say': 'Jack Cade', p. 261.

[62] Roger Chartier, 'Jack Cade, the skin of a dead lamb, and the hatred for writing', *Shakespeare Studies* 34 (2006), 77–89; p. 81.

[63] Bernthal, 'Jack Cade', p. 263.

[64] Katharine Eisaman Maus, 'Introduction', in *Four Revenge Tragedies* (Oxford, 1995), ix–xxxi; p. ix. For a more extensive discussion of justice in revenge tragedies, see Derek Dunne, *Shakespeare, Revenge Tragedy and Early Modern Law: Vindictive Justice* (London, 2016).

[65] Bernthal, 'Jack Cade', p. 264.

[66] Michael Hattaway, 'Introduction', in William Shakespeare, *The Second Part of King Henry VI*, ed. Michael Hattaway (Cambridge, 1991), 1–69; p. 31.

stinking law, for his breath stinks with eating toasted cheese' (4.710–11). Jokes of this kind are the rule of, rather than the exception to, the rebellion's affective tone. Hence, when Cade speaks to the subsistence politics of the 1590s, he engages with the issues of dearth and enclosure by presenting a hyperbolic, utopian vision of what England would be like under his rule:

CADE There shall be in England seven halfpenny loaves sold for a penny, the three hooped pot shall have ten hoops, and I will make it felony to drink small beer. All the realm shall be in common, and in Cheapside shall my palfrey go to grass.

(4.2.67–71)

By imagining Cheapside, 'the chief market area of Elizabethan London',[67] as a pasture for his horse, Cade articulates not only an alternative societal model in which 'there shall be no money' (4.2.74), but also one in which England's land becomes *un*enclosed. Recent critical approaches to the play have argued, as Schuler does, that 'Shakespeare's depiction of Cade as a Lord of Misrule does not undermine the populace's social and economic condition. Rather, clowning sets up Cade as a critic of the aristocracy's abuses of the people.'[68] Fitter concurs with this perspective and postulates that the rebellion's comedic tone enabled Shakespeare to stage the uprising in the first place: 'An authentic populist rebel leader, persuasive to the commons like the historical Cade, could not, of course, have been objectively presented under the gaze of Elizabethan censorship.'[69] Following these arguments, it seems that Shakespeare's use of comedy might not have been an artistic choice but a theatrical necessity to enact the rebels' subsistence politics.

While I concur that the carnivalesque mode of the rebellion might have allayed the fears of Elizabethan censors, the play's comedy also functioned as more than just social licence. Early moderns were aware that laughter, perhaps more so than other affects, has a potential to unite spectators in their emotional experience.[70] In *Playes Confuted* (1582), anti-theatrical writer Stephen Gosson was concerned about the ability of plays to produce laughter precisely because of its potential to transform audiences into affective communities: 'in the Theaters they [the lower sorts] generally take up a wonderful laughter, and shout altogether with one voice, when they see some notable cosenedge practised'.[71] This 'wonderful laughter' might have been, as Stephen Longstaffe suggests, 'the loudest thing an early modern person would ever hear off a battlefield';[72] and to Gosson, it was a portent of social upheaval. 'The rudest of the people', he writes, 'are sometimes ravished with every gewgawe … that they runne

together by heapes, they know not whither; and lay about with theire clubbes, they see not why.'[73] Consequently, Gosson views the emotional affects of theatre as antithetical to reason and impartial judgement. 'Blinded with affection', audiences would become 'a monster with many heads', a violent and irrational mob that threatened the established social order.[74]

Throughout his argument, Gosson makes it clear that only the lower sorts of people are affected by their emotions in this way, only 'they are caried away with every rumour, and so easily corrupted'.[75] Yet it is unlikely that laughter operated along class lines in the Elizabethan playhouses. Instead, I argue that the humour of the Jack Cade rebellion is an affective affordance that has the potential to bring spectators of diverse backgrounds together through laughter. In her monograph on the cultural history of laughter, Indira Ghose summarizes Shakespeare's humour as generally 'inclusionary and playful', adding that the playwright primarily used laughter as a tool 'to create a sense of community'.[76] In *2 Henry VI*, one such moment of community construction could have occurred during Cade's self-introduction:

---

[67] Warren, 'Footnotes', p. 239, fn. 63–4.

[68] Schuler, 'Shakespeare's mad', p. 158. On Cade's function as a Lord of Misrule, see François Laroque, *Shakespeare's Festive World: Elizabethan Seasonal Entertainment and the Professional Stage* (Cambridge, 1991), ch. 8.

[69] Fitter, *Radical*, p. 67.

[70] In her own reading of this passage, Sabina Z. Amanbayeva similarly points out that 'Gosson singles out loud laughter and imagines the audience as one organism': Amanbayeva, 'Laughter in *Twelfth Night* and beyond: affect and genre in early modern comedy', *Early Modern Literary Studies: A Journal of Sixteenth- and Seventeenth-Century English Literature* 17 (2014), 1–21; p. 9.

[71] Stephen Gosson, 'Plays confuted in five actions', in *The English Drama and Stage Under the Tudor and Stuart Princes 1543–1664*, by William Carew Hazlitt (London, 1869), 157–217; pp. 183–4.

[72] Stephen Longstaffe, 'The plebeians revise the uprising: what the actors made of Shakespeare's Jack Cade – or, laughing with the English radical tradition', in *Shakespeare and the Politics of Commoners: Digesting the New Social History*, ed. Chris Fitter (Oxford, 2017), 124–45; pp. 141–2.

[73] Gosson, 'Playes', p. 184. [74] Gosson, 'Playes', p. 184.

[75] Gosson, 'Playes', p. 183.

[76] Indira Ghose, *Shakespeare and Laughter: A Cultural History* (Manchester, 2008), p. 4. Additionally, Matthew Steggle describes laughter in the early modern playhouses as a 'communally generated, auditory effect': *Laughing and Weeping in Early Modern Theatres* (London, 2007), p. 107. Accordingly, to Shakespeare as well as the actors onstage, laughter might have comprised a phenomenological measure of their performance's success.

CADE We, John Cade, so termed of our supposed father –
DICK Or rather of stealing a cade of herrings.

...

CADE My father was a Mortimer –
DICK He was an honest man and a good bricklayer.
CADE My mother a Plantagenet –
DICK I knew her well; she was a midwife.
CADE My wife descended of the Lacys.
DICK She was indeed a peddler's daughter, and sold many laces.

...

CADE Therefore am I of an honorable house.
DICK Ay by my faith, the field is honorable; and there was
  he born, under a hedge, for his father had never a house but
  the cage.

(4.2.33–53)

Here, the Butcher's interjections communicate to the audience that the rebels are well aware that Cade's supposed noble lineage is fake. Even so, the excerpt's humour might not have been at Cade's expense. Until the early 2000s, editors traditionally marked the Butcher's lines as asides,[77] which creates a close connection between the rebels and the audience. However, if the lines are spoken for all to hear, then there is the possibility that Cade might have been 'in' on the joke, making fun of his own made-up genealogy.[78] The laughter that might have been produced as a result could function as an 'emotional contagion'. According to Pascale Aebischer, this term describes how 'the affective impact of "feeling-technologies"' was 'communicated and shared' between spectators and actors.[79] As an emotional contagion, laughter had the potential of 'turn[ing] parts or the whole of the audience into a coherent and responsible/response-able group of co-performers fully involved, along with the actors, in the communal process of playing'.[80] By inviting its audience to laugh alongside each other as well as the rebels on stage, Shakespeare's play may have generated an awareness among its spectators that their emotional experience was not only individual but also collective – that they have become an affective community through their shared responses to theatrical performance.

III

The themes and affective affordances discussed in the preceding pages eventually culminate in the final scene of act 4. Although there are differences between the Quarto and Folio versions of the garden scene, both render Cade's trespass in the politically charged vocabulary of enclosure. The Folio, for example, opens with the following soliloquy:

CADE Fie on ambitions! Fie on myself, that have a sword and yet am ready to famish! These five days have I hid me in these woods and durst not peep out, for all the country is laid for me. But now am I so hungry that if I might have a lease of my life for a thousand years, I could stay no longer. Wherefore o'er a brick wall have I climbed into this garden to see if I can eat grass or pick a salad another while.

(F 4.10.1–7)

Here, hunger quite literally overwrites the law. Even if Cade had 'a lease of [his] life for a thousand years' (F 4.10.4–5), his lack of sustenance renders this hypothetical legal prerogative moot. Therefore, he justifies his illicit entry by arguing that his corporeal needs supersede the property rights of the garden's owner. To Elizabethan audiences, this might have functioned as a legitimate legal defence. According to social historian Peter Lawson, there is a causal link between economic hardship and an increase in prosecution for property-related crimes in the later Tudor period, with spikes generally occurring either in or immediately after dearth periods.[81] Yet Lawson's data should not be interpreted as evidence that the English judicial system was unsympathetic towards the suffering of the poor. As Steve Hindle points out, 'the theft of food-stuffs was generally dealt with mercifully'.[82] Circuit judges even recommended 'pardons for those offenders who had been convicted of thefts of "small value" on the grounds that these were "crimes of opportunity, weakness, or need"'.[83] Although the concept of equity as well as its place in early modern legal proceedings cannot be adequately surmised here,[84] there was a widespread belief

---

77 Warren, 'Introduction', p. 52.
78 Warren, 'Introduction', p. 52.
79 Pascale Aebischer, *Shakespeare, Spectatorship and the Technologies of Performance* (Cambridge, 2020), p. 12.
80 Aebischer, *Shakespeare*, p. 12.
81 Peter Lawson, 'Property crime and hard times in England, 1559–1624', *Law and History Review* 4 (1986), 95–125; pp. 102–3. Steven Hindle adds that 'casual theft by the disorderly poor was undoubtedly widespread, and is probably under-represented in the archives of criminal justice since the goods stolen frequently did not justify the expenses of prosecution': *On the Parish?*, p. 82.
82 Hindle, *On the Parish?*, p. 84.
83 Hindle, *On the Parish?*, p. 88.
84 The academic literature on early modern equity is vast. For an overview of the concept and its various contexts, see Mark Fortier, *The Culture of Equity in Early Modern England* (Aldershot, 2005). Additionally, on the early modern equity courts, see John Baker, *Introduction to English Legal History*, 5th ed. (Oxford, 2019), especially ch. 6 on 'The court of Chancery and equity', 105–25; Dennis R. Klinck, *Conscience, Equity and the Court of Chancery in Early*

that the letter of the law should be attenuated by the unique circumstances of a crime, a sentiment that was epitomized in the popular proverb 'Necessity has no law.'[85]

While the Quarto strikes many of the same notes, it does so in a more dispersed fashion throughout the garden scene. In the Quarto, Cade's line 'I have eate no meate this five days' (Q 4.10.15) occurs much later in the scene, shortly before his altercation with Iden turns physical. Although it is possible that spectators could have inferred Cade's hunger from the actor's performance – the Quarto's stage directions at the beginning of the scene read: 'Jacke Cade lies downe picking of hearbes and eating them' (Q 4.10.1) – its severity might not be immediately apparent. Anna Ullmann argues that, by presenting this information sooner, 'the Folio makes us sympathize with Cade from the moment the scene opens'.[86] Another difference between the two texts lies in the fact that the Quarto more explicitly presents Iden's garden as an enclosure. Whereas Folio Cade climbs over a brick wall, in the Quarto, Iden complains that Cade 'broke my hedges, / And entered into my ground' (F 4.10.11–12). According to historian Nicholas Blomley, hedges transformed communal pastures into private property by 'prevent[ing] the forms of physical movement associated with the commoning economy'.[87] It is unsurprising, then, that popular movements against enclosure, such as the Midland Rising of 1607, often destroyed these boundaries in an effort to restore the customary rights of affected communities.[88] Despite these differences, both versions of the play may have evoked pity in their respective playgoers. Although Cade differs from historical criminals of necessity in that his need is the result of him being a wanted insurrectionist, the image of a starving vagrant forced to commit petty larceny to ensure his own survival may nevertheless have resonated with many Elizabethan spectators.

The Folio further builds on the notion that crimes can be permissible on the grounds of necessity. As Cade threatens to 'make [Iden] eat iron like an ostrich and swallow [his] / sword like a great pin' (F 4.10.25–6), Iden retorts by enumerating Cade's legal infractions:

IDEN Is't not enough to break into my garden,
And like a thief to come to rob my grounds,
Climbing my walls in spite of me the owner.
But thou wilt brave me with these saucy terms?

(F 4.10.30–3)

Cade had anticipated this legal rhetoric in an earlier aside to the audience: 'Here's the *lord of the soil* come to *seize* me for a stray for entering his *fee-simple* without leave' (F 4.10.22–3; italics mine).[89] However, it is not necessarily Cade's criminal conduct that infuriates Iden – although it certainly contributes towards his anger – but rather Cade's refusal to adhere to the social scripts pertaining to the relationship between lord and subject. There is an implication in these lines that Cade, whose identity is still unknown to Iden at this point in the scene, could have become another member of the allegedly countless poor that Iden sends 'well pleasèd from [his] gate' (F 4.10.21). In opposition to Suffolk and Margaret, Iden is willing to perform the paternalistic duties that are socially expected of him. However, he makes his charitable deeds contingent on the indigent's display of deference. Thus, when Cade refuses to perform the 'traditional gesture[s] of deference',[90] their encounter escalates into a physical altercation and eventually culminates in Cade's death.

Modern England (Abingdon, 2016); and Lorenzo Maniscalco, *Equity in Early Modern Legal Scholarship* (Leiden, 2020). Finally, on equity's cultural currency in the period's literary works, see Andrew J. Majeske, *Equity in English Renaissance Literature: Thomas More and Edmund Spenser* (London, 2006); Randall Martin, *Women, Murder, and Equity in Early Modern England* (London, 2008); and Mark Fortier, 'Literature and equity in early modern England', in *Law and Literature*, ed. Kieran Dolin (Cambridge, 2017), 109–23.

[85] Robert W. Dent, *Proverbial Language in English Drama Exclusive of Shakespeare, 1495–1616: An Index* (Berkeley, 1984), p. 547. This proverb is also echoed in the play's second act. During a hunting expedition, Henry, Margaret, Gloucester, Beaufort and Suffolk receive news that 'a blind man at Saint Alban's shrine / Within this half-hour hath received his sight' (F 2.1.61–2). Gloucester soon exposes this claim by Simpcox and his wife as attempted fraud. Simpcox's wife then tries to justify their actions, imploring that they 'did it for pure need' (155). Yet her plea falls on deaf ears, and the couple is sentenced to 'be whipped through every market-town / Till they come to Berwick, from whence they came' (156–7). For an in-depth discussion of this scene, see William Leahy, '"For pure need": violence, terror and the common people in *Henry VI, Part 2*', *Shakespeare Jahrbuch* 143 (2007), 71–83.

[86] Anna N. Ullmann, 'Making commotion: riot and protest in the texts of 2 Henry VI', *Studies in Philology* 121 (2024), 253–72; p. 270.

[87] Nicholas Blomley, 'Making private property: enclosure, common right and the work of hedges', *Rural History* 18 (2007), 1–21; p. 5.

[88] Briony McDonagh and Joshua Rodda, 'Landscape, memory and protest in the Midlands Rising of 1607', in *Remembering Protest in Britain since 1500: Memory, Materiality and the Landscape*, ed. Carl J. Griffin and Briony McDonagh (London, 2018), 53–79; p. 56.

[89] According to Warren, the term 'fee-simple' describes a type of property on which the 'landowner had the freehold right to *seize* any *stray* animal': 'Footnotes', p. 265, fn. 24–5.

[90] Emily Gruber Keck, '"Famine and no other hath slain me": Jack Cade in the garden of Iden', *Early Modern Culture* 11 (2016), 1–26; p. 17.

Their ensuing fight then renders the unjust distribution of resources that results from enclosure physically visible through the bodies of the two combatants. Whereas Iden's appearance in the Quarto can only be gleaned from Cade's brief description of 'this burly-bond churle' (Q 4.10.23), Folio Iden articulates a comparative blason that contrasts his own well-fed body with Cade's emaciated frame:

IDEN See if thou canst outface me with thy looks.
Set limb to limb, and thou art far the lesser:
Thy hand is but a finger to my fist,
Thy leg a stick comparèd with this truncheon.
My foot shall fight with all the strength thou hast,
And if my arm be heavèd in the air,
Thy grave is digged already in the earth.

(F 4.10.43–9)

Ronda Arab suggests that the effect of this excerpt might have been bolstered in performance through the actors' actual bodies: 'I imagine a beefy, brawny man greatly out-weighing a muscular but sinewy (as well as hunger-weakened) Cade.'[91] Even if the characters were cast differently, by insisting that 'famine and no other hath slain me' (F. 4.10.56), Cade makes it clear that his defeat is not the result of a lack in combat skill. Rather, he is 'undone' by the 'systematic failures of justice' that have been articulated over the course of act 4:[92] 'Let ten thousand devils come against me', he curses, 'and give me but the ten meals I have lost, and I'd defy them all' (F 4.10.56–8). In comparison, Iden frames his victory in the language of medieval chivalry. His sword 'shall wear [Cade's blood] as a herald's coat / To emblaze the honor that [its] master got' (F 4.10.65–6). Moreover, Iden plans to hang his sword over his tomb (F 4.10.63), where it will preserve the memory of his deed in posterity.

These two competing perspectives have been at the heart of the scene's criticism over the last forty years. With the rise of New Historicism, and especially in the wake of Greenblatt's influential model of subversion and containment,[93] a number of critics have viewed Cade's death as the moment in which the play re-establishes and affirms the hegemony of the early modern social order. For instance, in *Stages of History*, Phyllis Rackin traces how 'Shakespeare's representation of Iden's act and his character rationalizes a new source of status, the ownership of private property, in the emblems of an older world.'[94] In the process, Cade is 'reduced to a mechanism for ideological containment'.[95] Richard Wilson broadens this argument by emphasizing that 'Shakespeare's commercial playhouse ... must be

viewed as part of the apparatus of the English nation-state: as an institution, in fact, of separation and enclosure, where bourgeois "order" was legitimated by the exclusion of the "anarchy" and "sedition" of the mob'.[96] These positions have since been challenged in subsequent criticism. Doty, for example, contends that interpretations emphasizing the ideological containment of Shakespeare's rebels overly totalize the theatrical experience of the audience. Spectators did not experience 'plays in terms of a wholeness with particular weight to act five'.[97] Instead, they 'frequently plucked wise, "commonplace" quotations out of their literary or dramatic contexts for future use or reflection'.[98] Both Schuler and Fitter share Doty's perspective, maintaining that Cade's demise does not erase the commoner politics that preceded it.[99] Generally, these newer approaches follow the logic of Jonathan Dollimore, as they effectively argue that closure was often 'perfunctory rather than a profound reassertion of order' and would therefore not 'retroactively guarantee [the] ideological erasure of what, for a while, existed prior to and independently of it'.[100] In short, the dominant academic perspective of the garden scene has shifted from Iden's to Cade's account of events.

However, the hermeneutic possibilities the garden scene offered to spectators were more complex than these positions suggest, especially in the Folio version of the play. After Cade's death, Iden drags his corpse 'headlong by the heels / Unto a dunghill, which shall be [his] grave' (F 4.10.75–6). There, he will 'cut off [Cade's] most ungracious head, / Which [he] will bear in triumph to the King' (F 4.10.77–8). These lines reverse the relationship between Cade and the garden established at

---

91 Ronda Arab, 'Ruthless power and ambivalent glory: the rebel-labourer in *2 Henry VI*', *Journal for Early Modern Cultural Studies* 5 (2005), 5–36; p. 21.

92 Eklund, 'Revolting diets', p. 60.

93 Stephen Greenblatt, *Shakespearean Negotiations: The Circulation of Social Energy in Renaissance England* (Berkeley, 1988), pp. 29–31.

94 Phyllis Rackin, *Stages of History: Shakespeare's English Chronicles* (Ithaca, 1990), p. 216.

95 Rackin, *Stages*, p. 216.

96 Richard Wilson, '"A mingled yarn": Shakespeare and the cloth workers', *Literature & History* 12 (1986), 164–80; p. 169.

97 Doty, 'Shakespeare', p. 171.

98 Doty, 'Shakespeare', p. 171.

99 See Fitter, *Radical*, pp. 79–80; and Schuler, 'Shakespeare's mad', pp. 166–7.

100 Jonathan Dollimore, *Radical Tragedy: Religion, Ideology and Power in the Drama of Shakespeare and His Contemporaries* (Brighton, 1984), pp. 60–1.

the scene's outset. Whereas Cade initially enters Iden's property in a desperate attempt to subsist on its plants, his headless body now decomposes on a dunghill, 'where', as William Carroll writes, 'it will presumably help one day to fertilize the gardens and enclosed fields of Kent'.[101] Furthermore, this scene also recalls Cade's earlier speech on the innocent lamb, as his body is now quite literally being 'undone' to maintain the enclosed space of Iden's garden. It is difficult to say what Shakespeare's audience would have made of Cade's demise. Some spectators may have interpreted his death as a theatrical embodiment of how enclosure creates a system of economic hardship that exploits the poor. Others might have seen it as the just consequences for leading a rebellion against Henry. It is also feasible that these perspectives were not mutually exclusive, as audience members might have simultaneously felt pity for the starving Cade and thought that his death was deserved.

Where does this leave the question of justice? While the garden scene does not emotionally legitimize any specific perspective on Cade's death, the play's affective affordances nevertheless enable a particular mode of cognition for its audience. As enclosure grew more widespread over the course of the sixteenth century, communities became increasingly stratified. According to social historian Malcolm Gaskill, 'Parish elites retreated from the lower orders, encouraged by enclosure and capitalist investment in land', which led to 'absentee landlords exploit[ing] people they never met'.[102] Theatre had the potential to counteract this widening social rift, even if only temporarily. The affective experience of performance comprises, in the words of Benedict Robinson, a type of 'thinking feeling' — a form of cognition that depends on a degree of emotional identification between the audience and the play's dramatic characters.[103] Plays like Shakespeare's *2 Henry VI* invited its spectators to feel not only alongside its characters but also alongside their fellow playgoers. The emotional experience of injustice at the mistreatment of the petitioners in 1.3, the comedy of the play's rebels during act 4, and Cade's hunger in 4.10 had a potentially levelling effect, as these scenes could create affective bonds between audience members of vastly different social standings. Subsequently, as an affective community, playgoers could respond collectively to the action on stage based on what they felt to be just; and it is by this emotional process of community formation that the playhouse becomes a unique forum in which collective notions of justice could be articulated.

As the preceding paragraphs have shown, Shakespeare's play utilizes the affective affordances of theatre to enable its audience to consider questions about justice. It does so not necessarily to lead its spectators towards a particular position on the issue of enclosure but in an effort to facilitate a type of collective emotional cognition. This affective engagement with justice differs fundamentally from the period's courtrooms. Although trials were (and still are) by no means emotionless affairs,[104] judges, lawyers and jurors assess the evidence and circumstances of a case and, if the actions of the accused constitute a crime, pass a verdict that is in line with the law and legal precedent. In comparison, theatre is not bound by the same framework. Instead, it can refract and reimagine justice through the prism of affective judgement. Accordingly, it is paramount that literary critics in the field of communal justice not only 'meticulously contextualis[e]' their interpretations but also consider how any given scene may have functioned in performance.[105] While it might appear speculative, especially to New Historicist sensibilities, to imagine what spectators could have felt or how they might have responded, elucidating these potentialities lets us glimpse how theatre could explore and articulate collective ideas about justice.

---

[101] William C. Carroll, '"The nursery of beggary": enclosure, vagrancy, and sedition in the Tudor–Stuart period', in *Enclosure Acts*, ed. Burt and Archer, 34–47; p. 43.

[102] Malcolm Gaskill, 'Little commonwealths II: communities', in *A Social History of England, 1500–1750*, ed. Wrightson, 84–104; p. 97.

[103] Robinson, 'Thinking', p. 110.

[104] See Merridee L. Bailey and Kimberley-Joy Knight, 'Writing histories of law and emotion', *Journal of Legal History* 38 (2017), 117–29.

[105] Strain, 'Shakespeare's living law', p. 249.

THE BBC'S TELEVISION ADAPTATIONS OF *HENRY VI* AND BRITAIN'S NATIONAL IDENTITY CRISES

BENJAMIN BROADRIBB

On 27 July 2012, Kenneth Branagh stepped onto a stage in London and performed lines written by William Shakespeare. On the surface, this statement appears unremarkable. However, Branagh was not performing as a Shakespearian character, but as nineteenth-century civil engineer Isambard Kingdom Brunel. The stage was not in London's theatre district, but in the centre of the Olympic Stadium in Stratford. And neither the in-person audience, nor those watching at home on television, were there to see a Shakespeare production, but the opening ceremony of the 2012 Summer Olympics directed by Danny Boyle. Branagh as Brunel appeared as one of what L. Monique Pittman describes as an 'abundance of heart-thumping metonyms for Britain'.[1] He recited Caliban's full 'Be not afeard' speech (*The Tempest* 3.2.138–46) near the start of the ceremony at the base of a replica of the Glastonbury Tor, whilst Elgar's 'Nimrod' variation played behind him. 'Standing in as a metonym for the Great Poet', argues Pittman, 'Branagh in many ways replicated the manner in which Shakespeare serves as a metonym for Great Britain.'[2] Erin Sullivan goes further, arguing that, during Branagh's performance of Caliban's speech in particular, 'Shakespeare was working overtime, standing in as a symbol of British cultural prestige, social inclusion, national achievement, creative potential and citizen empowerment all at once.'[3] Indeed, rather than being a lone reference, Shakespeare permeated the whole ceremony, entitled 'Isles of Wonder', which took *The Tempest* as its inspiration. The ceremony's writer, Frank Cottrell Boyce, states that 'Shakespeare was ambient . . . it's not like we were trying to get Shakespeare in, he's just there, part of the cultural air that we breathe.'[4]

Widening her focus to both the Olympic and Paralympic ceremonies of 2012, Sullivan notes how 'Shakespeare became a repeated point of focus in the desire to celebrate British creativity and the influence it has subsequently had on the rest of the world.'[5] It is undeniable that Shakespeare is now a global phenomenon, with his plays performed, translated and studied around the world. However, the prominent presence of Shakespeare's work as a symbol of Britishness in the 2012 ceremonies offers a compelling example of Shakespeare's continuing status as a symbol of British cultural and national identity in the twenty-first century. Boyle's opening ceremony may have offered a celebratory fusion of Shakespeare and Britishness, but it also occurred in the same year that the word 'Brexit' – the commonly used term for the British public vote to leave the European Union (EU) – was first coined.[6] Whilst not the only contributing factor, Brexit, including both the years leading up to the EU membership referendum in 2016 and its ongoing aftermath, was central to the shaping of British national identity in the 2010s. Richard T. Ashcroft and Mark Bevir identify 'a consistent discursive connection between Brexit and British national identity', and describe Brexit as 'the latest stage in a debate over national identity that has been ongoing since 1945, when

---

[1] L. Monique Pittman, 'Shakespeare and the cultural Olympiad: contesting gender and the British nation in the BBC's *The Hollow Crown*', *Borrowers and Lenders: The Journal of Shakespeare and Appropriation* 9 (2015), https://borrowers-ojs-azsu.tdl.org/borrowers/article/view/294/585.

[2] Pittman, 'Shakespeare and the cultural Olympiad'.

[3] Erin Sullivan, 'Olympic performance in the year of Shakespeare', in *A Year of Shakespeare: Re-living the World Shakespeare Festival*, ed. Paul Edmondson, Paul Prescott and Erin Sullivan (London, 2013), 3–11; p. 5.

[4] Frank Cottrell Boyce, quoted in Paul Prescott and Erin Sullivan, 'Performing Shakespeare in the Olympic year: interviews with three practitioners', in *A Year of Shakespeare*, ed. Edmondson, Prescott and Sullivan, 43–77; pp. 45–6.

[5] Sullivan, 'Olympic performance in the year of Shakespeare', p. 7.

[6] Lise Fontaine, 'The early semantics of the neologism BREXIT: a lexicogrammatical approach', *Functional Linguistics* 4 (2017), https://doi.org/10.1186/s40554-017-0040-x.

decolonization led to a series of changes that radically altered Britain'.[7] With Brexit's roots going all the way back to the end of World War II, it is in many ways unsurprising that the Shakespeare plays that ultimately became most intertwined with the cultural sensibility of Brexit Britain were three which had seen the greatest resurgence in popularity during the post-war era: the *Henry VI* plays.

Stuart Hampton-Reeves and Carol Chillington Rutter describe the three parts of *Henry VI* as 'plays that put England at the edge of chaos and contemplate questions of national identity from the marginal position of imminent disaster', linking their revival since the mid twentieth century to 'a wider anxiety about the nature and authenticity of Englishness itself, which . . . has been in crisis since the *de facto* end of Empire after the Second World War'.[8] Similarly, Roger Warren argues that the *Henry VI* plays 'have come fully into their own since the end of the Second World War' due to their 'uncompromising violence . . . from which earlier generations had shrunk', and that they 'dramatize contemporary as much as Elizabethan issues: the struggle for power, the manoeuvres of politicians [and] social unrest'.[9] During the second half of the twentieth century, the *Henry VI* plays, along with *Richard III* – the first tetralogy – became the dark counterpoint to the second tetralogy – *Richard II*, the two parts of *Henry IV* and *Henry V* – for which 'mid-twentieth-century orthodoxy was to see an arc . . . toward the making of the nation, with *Henry V* a brief apogee'.[10] In contrast, the *Henry VI* plays have been imbued with their own orthodoxy during the same time period. If the second tetralogy is about the making of the nation, with *Henry V* as the zenith of this story, then the first three plays of the first tetralogy focus upon the breaking of the nation, with *Richard III* the brutal nadir.

Whilst *Richard III* received two major big-screen adaptations in the twentieth century – Laurence Olivier's 1955 film, in which he also played the title role; and Richard Loncraine's 1995 film with Ian McKellen as Richard – none of the *Henry VI* plays have yet been adapted into feature films, most likely due to their relative obscurity for mainstream audiences (although both Olivier and Loncraine include lines and events from *3 Henry VI* in their films). It is notable therefore that the BBC has televised adaptations of the first tetralogy on four separate occasions. The broadcaster's relationship with the cycle began with *An Age of Kings* (directed by Hayes, 1960), a fifteen-part serialization of both the first and second tetralogies, with the closing seven episodes based upon

the three parts of *Henry VI* and *Richard III*. Five years later, the BBC broadcast *The Wars of the Roses* (dirs. Midgley and Hayes, 1965), John Barton and Peter Hall's conflation of the four plays into a trilogy, originally performed in 1963 by the Royal Shakespeare Company (RSC) onstage in Stratford-upon-Avon. The first tetralogy was next adapted as part of the *BBC Television Shakespeare* series, broadcast between 1978 and 1985, through a sequence of productions directed by Jane Howell transmitted over four Sundays in January 1983. The most recent BBC adaptation of the first tetralogy is *The Hollow Crown: The Wars of the Roses*, directed by Dominic Cooke from an adapted screenplay by Cooke and Ben Power. The series was central to the BBC's 2016 'Shakespeare Festival', a month-long season of programming to mark 400 years since Shakespeare's death. With Sam Mendes as executive producer, *The Hollow Crown: The Wars of the Roses* features a cast of high-profile actors from film, television and stage, including Judi Dench, Hugh Bonneville and Sally Hawkins, and led by Benedict Cumberbatch as Richard. The series offers a continuation from the 2012 series *The Hollow Crown*,[11] which is based on the second tetralogy and features a cast of similarly recognizable names, including Patrick Stewart, Ben Whishaw and Tom Hiddleston.

Whilst the BBC's Shakespeare Festival was broadcast as part of Shakespeare's quatercentenary, this milestone was overshadowed by the unfolding political events of the first half of 2016 concerning Brexit. Political debates, current affairs programmes, news reports and referendum broadcasts from 'Vote Leave' and 'Britain Stronger in Europe' – the official 'Leave' and 'Remain' campaigns respectively – were a near-constant presence in television schedules alongside *Hollow Crown* Series Two when it was first broadcast over three Saturday evenings in May 2016. The broadcast scheduling ties the BBC's Shakespeare Festival to the cultural moment of the

[7] Richard T. Ashcroft and Mark Bevir, 'Brexit and the myth of British national identity', *British Politics* 16 (2021), 117–32; p. 121.

[8] Stuart Hampton-Reeves and Carol Chillington Rutter, *Shakespeare in Performance: The* Henry VI *Plays* (Manchester, 2006), p. 1.

[9] Roger Warren, 'Introduction', in *Henry VI Part Two*, ed. Roger Warren (Oxford, 2008), 1–74; p. 1.

[10] Ruth Morse, '*The Hollow Crown*: Shakespeare, the BBC, and the 2012 London Olympics', *Linguaculture* 5 (2014), 7–20; p. 16.

[11] Hereafter in this article, *The Hollow Crown* and *The Hollow Crown: The Wars of the Roses* will be referred to as 'Series One' and 'Series Two' respectively, in order to clearly distinguish the two series from each other – and to distinguish the second series from other adaptations of the first tetralogy which have used 'Wars of the Roses' in their titles.

Brexit campaign by temporal proximity at the very least. However, as Kinga Földváry suggests, with regard to *Hollow Crown* Series Two in particular:

with the advantage of historical hindsight, one can hardly fail to wonder how the broadcast of the second cycle, dominated by a haunting sense of an internally divided kingdom, ruled by manipulative and monstrous monarchs, just preceded the Brexit referendum, when British identity and the country's relationship to Europe was at its most uncertain.[12]

Whilst the political machinations of the fifteenth century's ruling classes, and the battles and bloodshed that occurred as a result, cannot be considered to correlate directly with Britain's 21st-century vote to leave the EU, the echoes of a divided country and fractured national identity noted by Földváry cannot be denied. Reading Russell Foster's description of 'Brexit Britain', written three years after the vote to leave, the parallels with the contention between the houses of York and Lancaster in his characterization of 'Leavers' and 'Remainers' – those who voted for and against Brexit respectively – are potent:

In the new, poisonous political atmosphere of Brexit Britain, two nations inhabit the same space ... Both of these nations exhibit the traditional tropes of nationalism – an imagined community, a whitewashed and selective version of history, a belief in a collective destiny, and a visible intolerance to outsiders. In Brexit Britain, the 'outsider' is not merely the EU ... but the opposing nation of Leavers or Remainers, each of which is imagined to be incompatible with, and anathema to, the other, and thereby unwelcome in the same nation. The result is an intolerant climate in which two nationalisms ... struggle to neutralise the other, and as the contest is based not in the quantifiable realm of economics or policy but in the vague, fluid and amorphous realm of identity, the Manichean struggle between Leavers and Remainers cannot be won by either side.[13]

Hollow Crown Series Two is not alone in being linked to a particular moment in British history: each of the twentieth-century BBC adaptations of the first tetralogy identifiably reflect the contemporary social and political landscape – and by extension the national identity – of Britain at the respective times in which they were made. Patricia Lennox describes *An Age of Kings* as 'a post-World War II celebration of national idealism moderated by knowledge of the human cost of war';[14] whereas Susanne Greenhalgh considers it to be 'a narratively gripping power play rather than a conservative pageant, presenting a vision of politics in tune with current international events'.[15] Whilst these interpretations differ, the influence of

post-war politics and national identity upon the series is clear. *The Wars of the Roses*, broadcast only five years after *An Age of Kings*, reflects the shifting politics of contemporary Britain and beyond. Hall describes how he 'became more and more fascinated by the contortions of politicians, and by the corrupting seductions experienced by anybody who wields power', and 'became convinced that a presentation of one of the bloodiest and most hypocritical periods in history would teach many lessons about the present'.[16] Translated to the screen by the BBC, the recorded production offers 'a sense of arrogant, self-centred swagger in a senseless political maelstrom' in which 'There seems little attempt by the characters to understand the meaning of what is going on – politically or morally.'[17] Similarly, Howell's quartet of adaptations for the *BBC Television Shakespeare* series were 'filmed from September 1981 to April 1982 ... turbulent months which saw, on both the national and world stage, political assassinations, war, violent protests and jubilant street parties – all potent cultural material for any production of *Henry VI*, creating adaptations which 'took Shakespeare's exploration of political factions and their impact on society and made out of them a contemporary parable that continues to strike a chord'.[18] Despite these 'turbulent' times, Michael Manheim suggests that Howell 'seems rooted in an outlook, identifiable most recently with the immediate post-Vietnam War period, that has not given up on the human spirit'.[19]

[12] Kinga Földváry, '"Sad stories of the death of kings": *The Hollow Crown* and the Shakespearean history play on screen', in *The Cambridge Companion to Shakespeare on Screen*, ed. Russell Jackson (Cambridge, 2020), 105–18; p. 108.

[13] Russell Foster, '"Cry God for Harry, England, and Saint George": Europe and the limits of integrating identity', *Global Discourse* 9 (2019), 67–87; p. 69.

[14] Patricia Lennox, '*Henry VI*: a television history in four parts', in *Henry VI: Critical Essays*, ed. Thomas A. Pendleton (London, 2001), 235–52; p. 237.

[15] Susanne Greenhalgh, 'Sticky or spreadable? Shakespeare and global television', in *The Shakespearean World*, ed. Jill L. Levenson and Robert Ormsby (London, 2017), 418–43; p. 425.

[16] John Barton and Peter Hall, *The Wars of the Roses* (London, 1970), p. x.

[17] Michael Manheim, 'The English history play on screen', in *Shakespeare and the Moving Image: The Plays on Film and Television*, ed. Anthony Davies and Stanley Wells (Cambridge, 1994), 121–45; pp. 131, 132.

[18] Hampton-Reeves and Rutter, *Shakespeare in Performance: The Henry VI Plays*, pp. 124, 118.

[19] Manheim, 'The English history play on screen', p. 132.

Just as the BBC's twentieth-century adaptations of the first tetralogy reflect the changing British national identity through the influence of the months and years leading up to their broadcast, *Hollow Crown* Series Two can similarly be considered to be influenced by the sociopolitical shifts during the years in which it was filmed and televised to become a cultural artefact of early 21st-century Britain. Whilst Britain voted 'Leave' in 2016, 'Brexit is the expression of conflicts which have been building in the electorate for decades, not their cause.'[20] The victory of the UK Independence Party (UKIP) in the European Parliament election of May 2014 – the first win in a national election for the forthrightly Eurosceptic party, and the first time neither the Labour nor Conservative parties had won such an election since 1910 – demonstrated the growing appetite amongst the British public for Brexit.[21] The casting of Cumberbatch in *Hollow Crown* Series Two was announced a month before UKIP's victory,[22] and by October 2014 principal photography on the series had begun.[23] The production period for the series therefore overlapped with the years leading up to Brexit, providing Cooke's serialization of the first tetralogy with its own 'turbulent months' of 'potent cultural material' in a manner which powerfully echoes the filming of Howell's adaptations in particular during the early 1980s. Whether consciously or subconsciously, the political developments which formed a backdrop to *Hollow Crown* Series Two's production likely impacted on Cooke and Power's adaptation of the first tetralogy.

With the *Henry VI* plays having been linked since at least the mid twentieth century to ideas of a crisis of national identity, it is impossible to deny the timeliness of the BBC's latest adaptation of this cycle of plays in reflecting the social and cultural character of Britain at a time of significant political upheaval when the nation's identity was being reshaped once again. This article presents an exploration of the adaptation of the *Henry VI* plays within *Hollow Crown* Series Two through the lens of Brexit as a tipping point in Britain's national identity, and makes the argument for *Hollow Crown* Series Two to be seen as a cultural successor to *An Age of Kings*, *The Wars of the Roses* and Howell's first tetralogy adaptations, offering close analysis of how specific scenes from the *Henry VI* plays are adapted – or omitted – in all four productions. In doing so, this article positions the adaptation of the *Henry VI* plays within *Hollow Crown* Series Two as the most recent point in a line of screen adaptations of the plays to capture the tensions and crises simmering within Britishness, articulating how the small-screen history of the *Henry VI* plays offers insight into the changing national identity of Britain.

The funeral of Henry V as presented in act 1, scene 1 of *1 Henry VI* appears in all four BBC adaptations – not only providing a logical point of comparison, but also offering insight into how the plays have been shaped for the small screen. The adaptation of the funeral by the respective directors and screenwriters of the successive BBC productions is essential in giving immediate insight into the nature of their adaptation of the plays as a whole. Edward Burns notes that, in the play, 'It is not completely clear whether we see the delayed and disrupted beginning of the funeral … or the end of the funeral as the coffin leaves Westminster Abbey', but argues that 'It is an important irony in the scene that the very concerns raised by the death of Henry prevent a properly respectful completion of the ritual of his funeral.'[24] It is not only each director's creation of the funeral itself that is important, therefore, but also to what extent the ceremony is disrupted and in what manner this disruption takes place.

The adaptation of act 1, scene 1 of *1 Henry VI* appears at the start of *An Age of Kings*'s ninth episode 'The Red Rose and the White'. The synopsis of the episode in the published screenplay states that 'The dissension that is to dominate the reign of this youthful Henry [VI] is evident even before his father has been laid to rest in Westminster Abbey', suggesting an adaptation in line with Burns's reading of the funeral scene.[25] This is initially evident in Michael Hayes's choice to begin the episode *in medias res* with Henry V's funeral already

---

[20] Maria Sobolewska and Robert Ford, *Brexitland: Identity, Diversity and the Reshaping of British Politics* (Cambridge, 2020), p. 2.

[21] Patrick Wintour and Nicholas Watt, 'Ukip wins European elections with ease to set off political earthquake', *Guardian*, 26 May 2014, www.theguardian.com/politics/2014/may/26/ukip-european-elections-political-earthquake.

[22] Leo Barraclough, 'Benedict Cumberbatch to play Richard III in Neal Street's film for BBC', *Variety*, 6 April 2014, https://variety.com/2014/tv/global/benedict-cumberbatch-to-play-richard-iii-in-neal-streets-film-for-bbc-1201153203.

[23] 'Principal photography begins on *The Hollow Crown: The Wars of the Roses*', BBC Media Centre, 1 October 2014, www.bbc.co.uk/mediacentre/latestnews/2014/hollow-crown-roses.

[24] Edward Burns, in *King Henry VI Part 1*, ed. Edward Burns (London, 2000), footnote p. 115.

[25] Nathan Keats and An Keats, '9. The Red Rose and the White', in *An Age of Kings: The Historical Plays of William Shakespeare as Presented on the British Broadcasting Corporation Television Series 'An Age of Kings'*, ed. Nathan Keats and An Keats (New York, 1961), 310–11; p. 310.

under way as Bedford (Patrick Garland) begins his opening speech. The director places Henry's coffin at the centre of the set, allowing Gloucester (John Ringham) and Winchester (Robert Lang) to bicker across the dead king's body. However, Hayes's adaptation proves to be the least chaotic of the funeral scenes across the four BBC adaptations of the play, imbued as it is with clear reverence towards Henry V as monarch and dignified solemnity at his passing. The original broadcast of *An Age of Kings* in 1960 temporally places it midway between the BBC televising the coronation of Elizabeth II in 1953, and the state funeral of Winston Churchill twelve years later in 1965; both aesthetically and politically, Hayes's adaptation of *1 Henry VI* act 1, scene 1, and the *Henry VI* plays more widely, sits between these two events. The adaptational choices by both Hayes and screenwriter Eric Crozier demonstrate a more measured approach to the funeral scene, capturing the restrained optimism and nostalgia of British national identity during the post-war period.

In the play, Bedford's prayer to the ghost of Henry V (*1 Henry VI* 1.1.44–56) is interrupted by the entrance of the first messenger, breaking off mid-sentence – 'A far more glorious star thy soul will make / Than Julius Caesar, or bright –' (1.1.55–6) – his incomplete speech emphasizing the disruption of the funeral. By cutting short Bedford's line as he begins to eulogize Henry V through comparison to great leaders of the past, Shakespeare also suggests the abrupt end of an era of such leadership through the king's premature death, as well as foreshadowing the troubled reigns of both Henry VI and those who will follow him until Richmond claims the throne at the end of *Richard III*. Adapting the scene for *An Age of Kings*, Crozier removes not only Bedford's final incomplete line but every line other than his first, reducing both the sense of disruption and the suggestion of the turmoil to come. As a result, Bedford simply urges his fellow nobles to 'Cease, cease these jars and rest your minds in peace' (1.1.44), bringing his hands together in prayer as he speaks. Gloucester and Winchester then follow his reverent example by crossing themselves at Henry's coffin as if in apology to the dead king for their argument. Whilst the director has an ominous drumbeat sound as the first messenger enters following this, the messenger then stands respectfully at the head of Henry's coffin and also crosses himself before speaking – an action repeated by the second and third messengers. This not only emulates the reverential actions of Bedford, Gloucester and Winchester, but also adds a pause of several seconds between Bedford's

line and the first messenger's speech, reducing further still the sense of disruption to Henry's funeral.

The Wars of the Roses represents a significant shift away from the post-war nostalgia and nationalism which underpinned *An Age of Kings*, and towards a postmodern cynicism stemming from a collective national consciousness disenchanted by the political world. This is translated into the dark, oppressive and claustrophobic shooting style of Hayes and Robin Midgley, which foreshadows the Jan Kott-influenced nihilism of Peter Brook's *King Lear* (1971) – another screen adaptation with its roots in an RSC production from the same period. Similarly, the funeral of Henry V in the first episode of *The Wars of the Roses*, simply titled 'Henry VI', feels considerably more chaotic than it did in *An Age of Kings*. The opening image offers a long shot of the empty throne silhouetted against an iron lattice and shot through the bars of a similar grille in the foreground. This immediately highlights the sense of Hayes and Midgley's adaptation being encased in a prison cell, foreshadowing Henry VI's feelings of being trapped upon the throne: 'Was never subject long'd to be a king / As I do long and wish to be a subject' (*2 Henry VI* 4.9.5–6).

The choices made by Hall and Barton in adapting Shakespeare's play result in the scene being considerably truncated – for example, through reducing the number of messengers interrupting the funeral from three to one – and increase the sense of urgency in the nobles' abandonment of the funeral. More notable in the funeral scene in 'Henry VI' are the elements not taken directly from the play, and the ways in which they ironically anticipate the events set to unfold over the first tetralogy. Just as in the stage version of *The Wars of the Roses*, Barton opens his adaptation with the prologue-like 'latest will and testament' of Henry V (taken from Edward Hall's *Chronicle*, one of Shakespeare's sources for the *Henry VI* plays) and spoken by 'the voice of King Henry V' as a voiceover.[26] From beyond the grave, Henry instructs his noblemen 'to love and join together in one league and one unfeigned amity', making the rapid descent of his funeral into arguments between the same nobles all the more poignant in their betrayal of the late king's wishes. As Henry speaks, the camera pans across the faces of the nobles kneeling around the king's body lying in state, the use of close-up – verging on extreme close-up in the case of some of the characters, their faces barely fitting the screen – emphasizing the egocentricity of each

---

[26] Barton and Hall, *The Wars of the Roses*, p. 3.

man. Hayes and Midgley introduce these men to the audience as separate individuals, complete with identities and ambitions that the camera can barely contain, rather than the unified group Henry wills them to be.

Howell's sequence of four adaptations reflects not only a significant shift in British national identity during the 1980s, but also the BBC's need to redefine its identity at the time of their broadcasting, especially as the *BBC Television Shakespeare* series had gained a poor reputation since its inception in 1978. Martin Banham argues that 'The opportunity in this television series was to astonish and delight "the layman", not to confirm his prejudices that Shakespeare is wordy and dull or to seduce him with a scenic tour of Europe' – an opportunity he believes the series unequivocally missed.[27] Howell's first tetralogy was in part a direct reaction to this, creating productions which 'launche[d] an all-out assault on the assumption that televised Shakespeare must use "realistic" film techniques and naturalistic production designs'.[28] The four episodes were originally transmitted on BBC Two only two months after the launch of Channel 4 in November 1982. The new commercial channel had been 'Charged by Parliament ... "to be innovative and experimental in content and form", and "to disseminate education and educational programmes"'.[29] The broadcast of *An Age of Kings* in 1960 had been commissioned partly to win the BBC the rights to launch BBC Two in 1964 as the UK's third television channel.[30] Howell's radical approach to televising Shakespeare's histories can similarly be seen as a reaction to new competition, as the initial remit of Channel 4 was similar in many ways to that which had defined BBC Two at its inception nearly two decades earlier.

Where *The Wars of the Roses* reflects the politically numbed national identity of the mid 1960s, Howell's productions tap into the active contempt for politics and authority which characterized British counterculture during the late 1970s and early 1980s. The clearest example of Howell's progressive approach to staging the first tetralogy is what she describes as the 'adventure playground set' – an edifice of wooden ramps, rope ladders, and swinging doors upon which all four plays are enacted.[31] The set is brightly painted in blocks of colour at the beginning of the cycle, but gradually becomes ravaged and blackened by the events of the plays. Howell sees the nobility in the *Henry VI* plays as being 'like ... prep-school children', whom she costumes in dressing-up-box style attire which similarly begins brightly coloured but grows increasingly dull and worn out across the tetralogy.[32]

Howell's adaptation of the funeral scene at the start of 'The First Part of Henry the Sixth' offers arguably the greatest sense of ceremony of all the BBC adaptations. As the scene begins, a lone soldier sings a lament accompanied by occasional chants and drumbeats from a cortège of black-robed figures, as Henry V's crown and coffin are ceremonially carried onto the set. However, the sincerity of the funeral procession and soldier's song are soon undermined as the lighting gradually brightens to reveal the multi-coloured adventure-playground set, with the crudely painted structure causing the solemnity of the actors to appear absurd. The pageantry of the scene is also contrasted by Henry's coffin: an uncovered wooden box with a simple painted skeleton adorning the lid – childlike and primitive in contrast to the pageantry surrounding it. Echoing Hall and Barton's adaptation of the scene at the beginning of *The Wars of the Roses*, Howell opens her version of the funeral with lines that historically predate Shakespeare's play. The lyrics of the soldier's lament are closely adapted from a fifteenth-century prayer originally composed not for the historical Henry V, but in honour of Henry VI in the years following the later king's death.[33] Moreover, the soldier is portrayed by Peter Benson, the actor who plays Henry VI across Howell's four adaptations. This choice of doubling lends the opening song an additional haunting nature: the adult Henry VI paradoxically mourns his father whilst also singing an elegy for himself, foreshadowing his own troubled reign and bloody end. The director also shrewdly doubles actors in the roles of the three messengers who interrupt the funeral. Howell's messengers are played by Brian Protheroe, Paul Jesson and Ron Cook, who also play, respectively, Edward IV, George, Duke of Clarence, and Richard III in subsequent episodes – as if the disorder yet to come has uncannily managed to intrude upon the funeral of Henry V.

---

[27] Martin Banham, 'BBC Television's dull Shakespeares', *Critical Quarterly* 22 (1980), 31–40; p. 34.

[28] Hardy M. Cook, 'Jane Howell's BBC first tetralogy: theatrical and televisual manipulation', *Literature/Film Quarterly* 20 (1992), 326–31; p. 330.

[29] Dorothy Hobson, *Channel 4: The Early Years and the Jeremy Isaacs Legacy* (London, 2004), p. vii.

[30] John Wyver, *Adapting the Histories: An Age of Kings on Screen* (booklet accompanying DVD release) (London, 2013), p. 20.

[31] Jane Howell quoted in Henry Fenwick, 'The production', in *The BBC Television Shakespeare: Henry VI Part 1*, ed. Peter Alexander (London, 1983), 21–31; p. 23.

[32] Howell quoted in Fenwick, 'The production', p. 23.

[33] David Grummit, *Henry VI* (Abingdon, 2015), p. 240.

In a parallel to Hayes and Midgley's ominous shot of the throne at the beginning of *The Wars of the Roses*, establishing the tone and approach of Hall and Barton's bleak version of the first tetralogy straight away, Cooke and Power make a similar choice for the opening moments of *Hollow Crown* Series Two, which immediately ties their adaptation to contemporary British national identity. Episode One[34] begins with a sweeping aerial shot of the sea, soon revealed to be the English Channel as the white cliffs of Dover come into view. Graham Holderness contends that the cliffs 'occupy a peculiar and privileged place in the iconography and mythology of British nationalism' as they are 'regarded by tradition as the source of [the] nation's genesis'.[35] However, he also highlights the paradoxical nature of the cliffs, suggesting that they 'provide us with our most characteristic national image of vulnerability, exposure, openness to the peril of foreign invasion' so that 'The point where the nation's identity begins is also the point where it could most easily be violated or re-conquered.'[36]

Melanie Küng notes that 'In the build-up to the vote on the EU referendum, the white cliffs were far from symbolising togetherness and openness, standing instead overwhelmingly for divisiveness and inhospitality', but nonetheless argues that 'it is useful to think of the coastal landscape around Dover as a cultural palimpsest where meanings are multi-layered and overlapping'.[37] This palimpsestic status has been literalized in the way in which messages have been projected directly onto the cliffs by both 'Leave' and 'Remain' supporters to promote and further their own ideologies. For example, on 29 March 2017, the date on which Prime Minister Theresa May formally triggered the Brexit process by invoking Article 50 of the Treaty of the European Union, the 'Leave'-supporting *Sun* newspaper projected its celebratory tabloid headline – 'Dover & Out' – onto the cliffs, sending 'a direct message to people on the Continent' as the cliffs 'can be seen by the naked eye from the equivalent French cliffs, Cap Blanc Nez, just west of Calais'.[38] Similarly, on the morning of 31 January 2020, the final day of Britain's EU membership, anti-Brexit campaign group Led By Donkeys projected a filmed message to the EU onto the cliffs, featuring interviews with veterans of World War II, who expressed their sadness over Brexit and hope for greater unity in the future.[39] Initially, therefore, Cooke's use of the white cliffs of Dover might appear to present an idealized and straightforward image of Britishness. But, due to the complexities within the location's symbolism, and the contradictory ways in which the cliffs

have featured in the nation's popular imagination in the months and years both before and since the EU referendum, Cooke's opening shot in fact reflects the fractious nature of British national identity both within the first tetralogy and in Brexit Britain.

As the camera travels over the English Channel, opening narration is spoken by Judi Dench as a voiceover. Dench's Received Pronunciation accent, and her association as a highly regarded and recognizable Shakespearian actress, lend the voiceover a sense of British authority. This is complicated, however, by Dench's role in Episode Three as the Duchess of York, taking over from Lucy Robinson who plays the character in Episodes One and Two. Dench's voiceover therefore provides a sense of foreshadowing at the opening of Episode One that echoes Benson's lamenting soldier in Howell's 'The First Part of Henry Sixth', as if the elderly Duchess of York is looking back on the events leading up to her son Richard's bloody reign. In a further parallel to both Howell's adaptation and the opening moments of *The Wars of the Roses*, Dench's lines are not taken from any part of the first tetralogy. However, rather than drawing on historical sources, Cooke and Power draw from elsewhere in the Shakespearian canon, closely adapting a passage originally spoken by Ulysses in *Troilus and Cressida*:

> The heavens themselves, the planets and this [earth]
> Observe degree, priority and place,

---

34 The three episodes of *Hollow Crown* Series Two are entitled 'Henry VI, Part 1', 'Henry VI, Part 2' and 'Richard III'. However, the first episode is in fact mostly adapted from *1 Henry VI* and *2 Henry VI*, whilst the second almost entirely presents an adaptation of *3 Henry VI*; only the third episode is named consistently with its source play. Therefore, to avoid confusion between the titling of the episodes and the names of Shakespeare's plays, I will refer throughout this article to the three episodes of *Hollow Crown* Series Two as 'Episode One', 'Episode Two' and 'Episode Three'.

35 Graham Holderness, '"What ish my nation?": Shakespeare and national identities', *Textual Practice* 5 (1991), 74–93; pp. 79–80.

36 Holderness, '"What ish my nation?"', p. 81.

37 Melanie Küng, 'Guards of Brexit? Revisiting the cultural significance of the white cliffs of Dover', in *The Road to Brexit: A Cultural Perspective on British Attitudes to Europe*, ed. Ina Habermann (Manchester, 2020), 199–214; pp. 200, 201.

38 Sam Lennon, 'The Sun newspaper uses the White Cliffs of Dover signal the start of the Brexit process', Kent Online, 29 March 2017, www.kentonline.co.uk/dover/news/writings-on-the-wall-or-123105.

39 Sarah Turnnidge, 'Led By Donkeys' farewell message to Europe has people in tears', HuffPost, 31 January 2020, www.huffingtonpost.co.uk/entry/led-by-donkeys-brexit-white-cliffs-dover_uk_5e33f63ec5b69a19a4ad4d03.

. . .

Office and custom, in all line of order.

. . .

Take but degree away, untune that string,
And hark what discord follows.

(1.3.85–6, 88, 109–10)

On a literal level, the lines provide a fitting precursor to the events at the beginning of *1 Henry VI*: the death of Henry V is the trigger to 'take but degree away', with 'discord' following almost immediately. More significantly, however, the use of lines from *Troilus and Cressida* also has implications for *Hollow Crown* Series Two's relationship to national identity. Pittman argues that 'Stripped of their context in [*Troilus and Cressida*] and presented in conjunction with the powerful symbolism of [the white cliffs] . . . this transplanted speech fuses claims of right order with British national identity – a nation bounded by the seas, protected by its terrain, and ordered by nature itself.'[40] Moreover, by replacing Ulysses's original phrase 'this centre' (1.3.85) with 'this earth', Pittman suggests that Cooke and Power bring to the audience's mind John of Gaunt's deathbed speech from act 2, scene 1 of *Richard II*, which uses the phrase twice. 'Both the explicitly quoted passage from *Troilus and Cressida* and the ghosted lines from *Richard II*', Pittman argues, 'appear in dramatic contexts that undermine the sureness of those virtues and the assertion that a Providential natural order guides and protects the British nation.'[41] Comparing *Troilus and Cressida*'s relationship with national identity to that of Shakespeare's histories, Matthew Greenfield argues that 'Shakespeare's tetralogies and the other English history plays move toward closures in which the nation heals and the dream of community reasserts its claim', whereas '*Troilus and Cressida* explores a more pessimistic political argument. If Shakespeare's histories maintain an investment in some idea of national community, *Troilus and Cressida* works programmatically to reveal the nation as a collection of fictions.'[42] In a parallel to the renewed fortunes of the *Henry VI* plays in the second half of the twentieth century, Efterpi Mitsi notes that 'Shakespeare's cynical and irreverent treatment of the Trojan legend' gained popularity after World War II: 'In one of the most violent centuries in the history of humanity, the staging of *Troilus and Cressida* provided theatre practitioners and theatregoers with the opportunity to reflect on the absurdity of war.'[43] As a result, when combined with the complex national symbolism evoked by the white cliffs, Cooke and Power's choice to draw the first lines of Shakespeare heard in *Hollow Crown* Series Two from *Troilus and Cressida* further drives the series' conceptualization of national identity towards cynicism, crisis and destruction.

The opening scene at the white cliffs directly leads into Cooke's adaptation of the funeral of Henry V, as Sir William Lucy (Tom Beard) – who performs the function of the first (and here, only) messenger who interrupts the nobles – is seen riding along the cliffs on his journey to Westminster Abbey. In a further departure from both the play and previous BBC adaptations, an intertitle preceding Cooke's version of act 1, scene 1 informs the audience that the action takes place 'Just after the funeral of Henry V'. The reason for this may simply be one of continuity: Thea Sharrock included extratextual scenes from the king's funeral in her adaptation of *Henry V* for *Hollow Crown* Series One, so Cooke's choice to move the action to immediately after the funeral allows Series Two to pick up moments after Series One ended. However, in making this change, Cooke allows the funeral to go uninterrupted, going against Burns's idea that the prevention of the king's burial is an important irony at the start of the play. As a result, *Hollow Crown* Series Two's version of act 1, scene 1 takes on a notably different character from earlier BBC adaptations.

With the ceremony over, Gloucester (Bonneville) removes the crown from Henry's coffin and carries it to an area at the side of the cathedral. A door is closed behind him, and the dialogue begins. The play calls for Bedford, Gloucester, Exeter, Warwick, Winchester and Somerset to be present at the start of the scene – as well as 'the funeral' (1.1.0.1), which Burns notes potentially adds a further six extras – with the three messengers entering and exiting at points throughout.[44] In contrast to this, Cooke makes the opening scene a distinctly intimate discussion between Gloucester, Winchester (Samuel West), Exeter (Anton Lesser) and Lucy. This becomes an even more conspicuous choice when considering the continuity implied from Sharrock's *Henry V*, in which the funeral is well attended, with people also seen lining the streets outside the church. By setting the

---

[40] L. Monique Pittman, *Shakespeare's Contested Nations: Race, Gender, and Multicultural Britain in Performances of the History Plays* (London, 2022), p. 134.

[41] Pittman, *Shakespeare's Contested Nations*, p. 135.

[42] Matthew A. Greenfield, 'Fragments of nationalism in Troilus and Cressida', *Shakespeare Quarterly* 51 (2000), 181–200; p. 181.

[43] Efterpi Mitsi, 'Introduction', in *Troilus and Cressida: A Critical Reader*, ed. Efterpi Mitsi (London, 2019), 1–12; pp. 7, 3.

[44] Burns, in *King Henry VI Part 1*, footnote p. 115.

scene after the funeral rather than during it, and having the dialogue happen in an enclosed room between just three nobles and Lucy, Cooke makes the events of the scene notably more private, even clandestine in nature. The adaptation of the funeral scene also sets out the director's overall approach to adapting the first tetralogy: the separation of public and private, of the lower classes and nobility, is a theme which permeates *Hollow Crown* Series Two.

The division of public and private continues during Cooke and Power's adaptation of *1 Henry VI* throughout the first half of Episode One. This is evidenced in their version of the dispute between Gloucester and Winchester in act 3, scene 1. In the play, the argument is augmented by violence between the servingmen of the two nobles: first in the city streets, as reported by the Mayor of London; and then in the Parliament itself, where the action is set, through the intrusion of three brawling servingmen. In Episode One, however, Cooke and Power remove both the three servingmen from the scene and any reference to violence taking place outside the Parliament, confining the disagreement to the argument between members of the nobility. This approach continues in the next scene, which offers Cooke and Power's version of the coronation of Henry VI (Tom Sturridge) in Paris, adapted from act 4, scene 1. The scene initially depicts a lavish ceremony attended by crowds of people, but swiftly cuts to a private area within the cathedral after Henry is crowned; much like the earlier funeral of Henry V, the majority of the scene is moved to take place after the ceremony. This contrasts with the two previous BBC versions of act 4, scene 1 in *The Wars of the Roses* and *BBC Television Shakespeare*,[45] in which the entirety of the scene occurs during Henry's coronation ceremony as in the play. By once again shifting the action so that it no longer takes place in public view, Cooke and Power shift the political nature of their adaptation. The ceremony gives the false impression to the commoners that all is well, whilst the disorder that follows is kept behind closed doors. The dispute between the servants Vernon and Basset is also revised considerably: the lower-class characters are removed from the scene entirely in Cooke and Power's version, and it is Henry who initiates the discussion with York and Somerset about the wearing of roses, making the rift between the two houses confined solely to the nobility.

Cooke and Power's excision of the lower-class characters becomes more noticeable still during the second half of Episode One, which offers a considerably truncated adaptation of *2 Henry VI* – a play well known for being populated by many lower-class characters. Maya Mathur argues that, whilst lower-class characters and scenes were a source of comedy in Elizabethan drama, 'Rather than enforcing the boundaries between "high" and "low" characters, comic situations could be used to blur the border between them.'[46] Prominent scenes in the play featuring these characters include the miracle at St Albans, which forms much of act 2, scene 1; the petition and combat of an armourer, Thomas Horner, and his apprentice, Peter Thump, introduced in act 1, scene 3 and concluded in act 2, scene 3; and, most notably, the rebellion led by Jack Cade, which unfolds throughout act 4. Cade and the rebels are regularly singled out as the foremost example of the comedic social commentary offered by the play. Ronda Arab, for example, suggests that 'through their self-referential, sometimes self-parodic humour [the rebels] control a great deal of the political rhetoric of the play'.[47] That Shakespeare put the Cade rebellion on the Elizabethan stage during a period of social turmoil is also noteworthy. According to Knowles, 'The earlier, mid-Tudor depiction of Cade in *The Mirror for Magistrates* (1559) is moral and theological', but 'By the 1590s Cade's rebellion was generally seen in more political than theological terms.'[48] Arab argues that the Cade rebellion scenes demonstrated to Elizabethan audiences 'the well-known, and to many minds justified, discontent of contemporary food and enclosure rioters in England', and that *2 Henry VI* therefore 'articulates the potential power, as well as the motives, of late sixteenth-century labourers to wreak bloody havoc on the social body'.[49]

Shakespeare's depiction of the Cade rebellion in act 4 of the play can therefore be considered both inherently political and knowingly satirical, a status which is perpetuated in the BBC's twentieth-century screen adaptations of *2 Henry VI*. As the emblematic character of act 4, Jack Cade himself becomes a pivotal figure in

---

45 The scene is not included in *An Age of Kings*.

46 Maya Mathur, 'An attack of the clowns: comedy, vagrancy, and the Elizabethan history play', *Journal for Early Modern Cultural Studies* 7 (2007), 33–54; p. 36.

47 Ronda Arab, 'Ruthless power and ambivalent glory: the rebel-labourer in *2 Henry VI*', *Journal for Early Modern Cultural Studies* 5 (2005), 5–36; p. 6.

48 Ronald Knowles, 'The farce of history: miracle, combat, and rebellion in *2 Henry VI*', *Yearbook of English Studies* 21 (1991), 168–86; p. 176.

49 Arab, 'Ruthless power', p. 5.

how the rebellion in each adaptation specifically reflects British national identity at the time it was made. The earliest BBC version of the rebellion occurs in *An Age of Kings*'s eleventh episode, 'The Rabble from Kent', which offers the most comedic screen version of Cade. Esmond Knight's performance choices as Cade recall those of Frank Pettingell, who plays Falstaff earlier in the series. Knight's first entrance is accompanied by a jaunty fanfare, immediately making it clear that Hayes's version of Cade is primarily a clown. Combined with Knight's Falstaffian performance, Cade's costume and appearance in *An Age of Kings* – a cowl over his shoulders, feathers protruding from his cap, standing with arms akimbo in most of his scenes – also brings to mind popular depictions of Robin Hood. As a result, Cade is characterized as both a heroic outlaw working for the common people and a music-hall-style source of comic relief within the series' aesthetic of post-war nostalgia.

Cade appears at the start of the second episode of *The Wars of the Roses* trilogy, 'Edward IV', played by Roy Dotrice. In contrast to Knight's jaunty figure, Dotrice's Cade wears a military-style armoured costume, marked out by his scarred cheek and disfigured scalp as a soldier who has experienced the savagery of war. Dotrice also makes Cade much more menacing and aggressive than Knight does, as evidenced in his uncomfortable intimidation of the Clerk of Chartham in the sequence adapted from act 4, scene 2. Hall and Barton also make clever use of doubling by casting Dotrice both as Cade and as Edward Plantagenet, later King Edward IV. The actor 'played both Cade and Edward IV with a cocky exuberance that seduced the audience even as they shuddered at his deeds' – the rebellion of the former being echoed by the reign of the latter, with both presaging the enigmatic tyranny of Richard III.[50] This is demonstrated in Hayes and Midgley's filming of Cade's final speech from act 4, scene 8, after his followers abandon him. Dotrice looks straight into the camera, which zooms in on his face, transforming his aside into a one-way conversation with the viewer that foreshadows the soliloquies of Ian Holm's Richard yet to come.

Offering a significantly different Cade once again, Howell describes the character as played by Trevor Peacock in 'The Second Part of Henry the Sixth' as a 'Lord of Misrule', who offers 'some sort of devilishness that is in all of us'.[51] Peacock sees this version of Cade as being linked to the sociopolitical moment of the early 1980s:

I think Cade is a bit of a lunatic but the people did respond to him ... That still happens: look at the riots in this country now [late 1981]. The National Front is a very Cade-like thing ... Someone says, 'March with us and bash people' – Pakistanis, or, in Cade's case, the nobility – and they do. Though the plays are historical they are about continual processes in human beings.[52]

The anarchic madness Peacock's Cade brings to the production reaches its zenith in a sequence that occurs between Howell's adaptations of the sixth and seventh scenes of act 4. Following Cade's final lines of scene 6, in which he commands his followers to 'set London Bridge on fire' and 'burn down the Tower too' (4.6.14–15), Howell depicts the rebels carrying out a carnivalesque book-burning. The director superimposes over this sequence a close-up of Peacock's maniacally laughing face. Cade's opening lines of scene 7 are delivered in the same fashion: Peacock's head fills the screen as he orders the rebels to 'pull down the Savoy' and 'th'Inns of court' (4.7.1–2), presenting Cade as the colossal puppet-master of the rebellion. Peacock's face appears again over a close-up of the blazing pages in the final book-burning scene. With wide eyes and bared teeth, the actor's face dissolves into the flames, shifting Cade from a dictatorial to a diabolical presence and ending the scene on an apocalyptic note. Howell further suggests the demonic nature of Cade by slowing down both the audio and video of Peacock's closing laughter, transforming it into a monstrous roar which continues as the audience sees the rebels gather in the centre of the now blackened and scorched set.

Two further screen adaptations of Cade, found in productions not commissioned by the BBC, are noteworthy. The first appears in the English Shakespeare Company's (ESC's) *The Wars of the Roses*, an adaptation of both the first and second tetralogies into a heptalogy by Michael Bogdanov and Michael Pennington. After touring the production during the second half of the 1980s, all seven plays were recorded for television and broadcast in 1991. In an adaptive choice that echoes Peacock's observations about Cade, the ESC gives the rebellion a 'hooligan, National Front theme'. Bogdanov describes the rebels in the sixth of the seven

50 Annalisa Castaldo, 'Introduction to the Focus Edition', in *King Henry VI: Parts I, II and III*, ed. Annalisa Castaldo (Indianapolis, 2015), ix–xviii; p. xvii.

51 Jane Howell quoted in Henry Fenwick, 'The production', in *The BBC Television Shakespeare: Henry VI Part 2*, ed. Peter Alexander (London, 1983), 18–29; p. 27.

52 Trevor Peacock, quoted in Fenwick, 'The production', in *The BBC Television Shakespeare: Henry VI Part 2*, ed. Alexander, p. 27.

plays – televised as 'Henry VI: The House of York' (directed by Bogdanov, 1991) – as a 'drink-sodden, totem-twirling, Union Jack brigade of Doc Martened bovver boys' led by Pennington's Cade, 'a machete-twirling tornado, with spiky red hair and a Union Jack vest'.[53] The appearance of Pennington's Cade is most obviously based upon Johnny Rotten, frontman for punk rock band the Sex Pistols, who were formative in establishing British punk counterculture. Ruth Adams suggests that 'Punk could be argued to be a reframing of national identity in the image of (certain elements of) the working classes, rather than that of the ruling classes', offering a logical connection between the rebels and punk counterculture across the centuries.[54]

The second notable screen Cade outside the BBC's adaptations appeared as part of *The Complete Walk*, Shakespeare's Globe's series of thirty-seven short films created to commemorate the quatercentenary of Shakespeare's death. The films were originally screened along the South Bank of the Thames over the weekend of 23 and 24 April 2016 (only weeks before the first episode of *Hollow Crown* Series Two was broadcast) and subsequently made available for one month on the BBC's iPlayer streaming service, as well as being shown in other UK cities, and internationally in Shanghai and Beijing. Alongside footage from recorded Shakespeare's Globe performances and clips taken from the British Film Institute archive, each short film also incorporates new adaptations of scenes filmed on location around the world. The newly filmed sections of *The Complete Walk: Henry VI Part 2*, directed by Nick Bagnall, relocate the action of the Cade rebellion to modern-day Spitalfields Market. Bagnall also highlights the contemporary political parallels of the rebellion by including footage of the riots which began in London and spread to other locations across England in August 2011. As Cade, Neil Maskell presents the most naturalistic screen version of the character yet seen, offering none of the humour or theatricality of those that came before him. Maskell's modern costume is a simple overcoat and scarf of muted greys and blues, and his performance is driven by revolutionary anger.[55]

The decision by Cooke and Power to remove not only all scenes involving Jack Cade and the rebels from *Hollow Crown* Series Two, but also any references whatsoever to either Cade or the uprising, sets it apart from all major screen versions of the first tetralogy which have preceded it. Considering the increasingly politicized depictions of the Cade rebellion in adaptations of the *Henry VI* plays, its absence from *Hollow Crown* Series

Two is, at the very least, highly conspicuous. Földváry suggests that the removal of the Cade rebellion and other subplots allows 'The remaining narrative [to] find its focus much earlier on the rise of Richard III to power', allowing Cumberbatch – 'the long-awaited sight for sore eyes for a significant portion of the viewing public' – to make his appearance as early in the series as possible.[56] Similarly, Cooke has described his vision for the series as a 'trilogy [which] poses the question, "How many bad decisions does it take to put a psychopath [Richard] in power?"', cutting 'Any elements which didn't fit that central story'.[57]

The complete removal of the Cade rebellion from *Hollow Crown* Series Two means that comparison with past screen adaptations of the characters is not possible. However, there is equal value in considering not only the impact of removing these characters upon Cooke and Power's version of the first tetralogy, but also the potential reasons for their removal in the context of Brexit Britain. Eleanor Rycroft argues that the removal of the lower-class characters and scenes 'mean[s] that the version of Britain presented almost entirely belongs to a white, male ruling class', and that 'the production enacts a series of intersectional erasures … that deliberately suppress elements of difference in favour of a monolithic "Englishness"', and suggests that 'Through its blanket use of RP for the courtly elite, [*Hollow Crown* Series Two] seems at pains to eschew any class dialectic from its adaptation of the source texts.'[58] The homogeneity of the British accents in the series is likely to have been at least in part a practical decision to allow the series to translate easily to the US market. However, whilst also potentially intended to de-politicize the *Henry VI* plays in particular, the excision not only of the

53 Michael Bogdanov and Michael Pennington, *The English Shakespeare Company: The Story of the Wars of the Roses, 1986–1989* (London, 1990), p. 111.
54 Ruth Adams, 'The Englishness of English Punk: Sex Pistols, Subcultures, and Nostalgia', *Popular Music and Society* 31 (4) (2008), 469-488; p. 476.
55 At the time of writing, *The Complete Walk* short films have not been publicly available since 2017. However, a one-minute clip of Maskell as Cade is available on the BBC's *Shakespeare Lives* website: www.bbc.co.uk/programmes/p03wowps.
56 Földváry, '"Sad stories of the death of kings"', p. 110.
57 Dominic Cooke quoted in BBC Media Centre (2016), *The Hollow Crown: The Wars of the Roses, Henry VI Part I, Henry VI Part II and Richard III*, 3 May 2016, http://downloads.bbc.co.uk/mediacentre/hollow-crown-RIII.pdf.
58 Eleanor Rycroft, 'Hair in the BBC's *The Hollow Crown: The Wars of the Roses*: class, nation, gender, race, and difference', *Shakespeare* 17 (2021), 29–48; p. 32.

lower-class characters, but also of almost all British accents other than RP across the series, has the opposite effect. The contention between the houses of York and Lancaster, and the ruptures it wrought across Britain, is framed by *Hollow Crown* Series Two as a political conflict which concerned the ruling classes only. Against the backdrop of Brexit, the series seems to suggest that the division between 'Leave' and 'Remain' can be seen in the same manner: the common people become insignificant, with any meaningful consequences and impact lying with those in power.

Whilst the warring houses of York and Lancaster, and the infighting and bickering between the nobles who inhabit them, give directors ample opportunities to reflect the political machinations of their time, Cade and the rebels have provided potent material to reflect the anti-establishment sentiment of their cultural moment as has been demonstrated throughout the screen adaptations of *2 Henry VI* by the BBC and others. It is therefore pertinent when considering the absence of the Cade rebellion in *Hollow Crown* Series Two to take into account that, during the months leading up to Brexit, the strongest anti-establishment sentiment purported to come from members of the establishment itself. The official 'Vote Leave' campaign positioned itself as anti-establishment most clearly through undercutting the messages of Remainers as the establishment attempting to maintain the status quo for their own benefit:

> The Remain campaign mobilized a whole panoply of experts and apparently authoritative sources to warn of the risks and dangers of leaving the EU. Characterizing the Remain campaign as 'Project Fear', the Leave movement drew a sharp distinction between the 'threats' issuing from the 'establishment' and the simple desires of 'ordinary people' to 'take back control' of their society and their country.[59]

This anti-establishment self-styling by the 'Leave' campaign was epitomized in a statement by Conservative politician Michael Gove who, when asked in a live television interview to name economic experts who supported Brexit, answered: 'I think people in this country have had enough of experts.' In the same interview, Gove – and the 'Leave' campaign more widely – was also accused of employing 'the "post-truth" politics of Donald Trump', specifically in their repeated citation of the disproved statistic that Britain sends £350 million to the EU every week and would therefore be better off by this amount after Brexit.[60]

The figure of Cade in many ways appears to fit comfortably within the context of post-truth politics, in which the lines between establishment and anti-establishment,

fact and opinion, have become blurred or insignificant. The 'Leave' campaign rhetoric of mistrusting experts echoes the status of the rebels as 'the enemies of . . . all learning and of the learned professions'.[61] Dick the Butcher's famous suggestion – 'The first thing we do, let's kill all the lawyers' (4.2.71) – with which Cade agrees, provides the earliest indication of the rebels' animosity towards the educated members of the establishment. This is further evidenced through the treatment of the Clerk of Chartham – declared 'a villain and a traitor' (4.2.98–9) by the rebels for being able to write his name, and ordered by Cade to be hanged 'with his pen and inkhorn about his neck' (4.2.100–1) – as well as the execution of Lord Saye by Cade because he 'hast most traitorously corrupted the youth of the realm in erecting a grammar school' (4.7.29–30).

Hampton-Reeves suggests that, to Cade and his followers, 'Truth, identity, history, and authority rest on self-determination rather than the determination of historical record' – a viewpoint which closely parallels the post-truth politics of the twenty-first century.[62] This can be seen when Stafford's brother outrightly describes Cade's right to the throne as 'false' (4.2.130), to which Cade replies: 'Ay, there's the question; but I say 'tis true' (4.2.131). Stafford's brother then declares: 'Jack Cade, the Duke of York hath taught you this' (4.2.144); Cade responds in an aside, 'He lies, for I invented it myself' (4.2.145). Cade's retort is included for comic effect, but it also demonstrates him admitting freely that his claim is based on falsehoods – or 'alternative facts'. In contrast, Stafford's accusation is based in fact: York earlier states in a soliloquy that he has

> seduced a headstrong Kentishman,
> John Cade of Ashford
> To make commotion, as full well he can,
> Under the title of John Mortimer.
>
> (3.1.355–8)

59 John Clarke and Janet Newman, '"People in this country have had enough of experts": Brexit and the paradoxes of populism', *Critical Policy Studies* 11 (2017), 101–16; p. 110.

60 Henry Mance, 'Britain has had enough of experts, says Gove', *Financial Times*, 3 June 2016, www.ft.com/content/3be49734-29cb-11e6-83e4-abc22d5d108c.

61 Peter Lake, *How Shakespeare Put Politics on the Stage: Power and Succession in the History Plays* (New Haven, 2016), p. 98.

62 Stuart Hampton-Reeves, 'Kent's best man: radical chorographic consciousness and the identity politics of local history in Shakespeare's *2 Henry VI*', *Journal for Early Modern Cultural Studies* 14 (2014), 63–87; p. 70.

This positions Cade not as a true anti-establishment figure as he claims to be, and as he has been characterized in screen adaptations of *2 Henry VI*, but at least in part as a puppet of the nobility. In this sense, Cade offers a parallel to 'Leave' campaigners such as Gove who positioned themselves as anti-establishment, but in truth were very much part of the ruling class. Moreover, when Stafford asks Cade's supporters 'And will you credit this base drudge's words, / That speaks he knows not what?' (4.2.141–2), they reply: 'Ay, marry, will we; therefore get ye gone' (4.2.143). Again, the rebels' response is comic, but more importantly reveals they are willing to follow Cade even though they know what he says is not true. This offers a further parallel to 21st-century post-truth politics, with personal beliefs being more important than factual accuracy.

If the Cade rebellion has the potential to fit so well into the sociopolitical moment of 2016, then its complete removal from *Hollow Crown* Series Two can be considered even more striking. Alongside their stated reason for cutting any plotlines which did not directly relate to Richard's path to power, Cooke and Power may have wanted their adaptation to come across as apolitical and stand apart from the current affairs which surrounded its production and broadcast, with Episode One, in particular, attempting to establish a version of the first tetralogy separate from the cycle's links to British national identity in crisis. Cade may therefore have been excised completely to avoid any parallels, intentional or otherwise, with the contemporary events that formed a backdrop to the series. This is a generous reading, however, and arguably lets both the director and writer off the hook too easily. The inherently political nature of the *Henry VI* plays, and their renewed resonance, critical attention and presence on stage and screen since the mid twentieth century, arguably make adapting the first tetralogy in an entirely politically neutral manner an impossible task.

Hampton-Reeves and Rutter describe *2 Henry VI* as 'arguably the only one of the histories that gives a substantial voice to the presence of ordinary people in history and their ability to mobilise themselves in sufficient numbers . . . to disrupt the conventional notion of history as the story of kings and nobles'.[63] By removing these characters, *Hollow Crown* Series Two reverses this notion, re-establishing the idea of history and national identity as being shaped not by 'ordinary people', but solely through political manoeuvring by those in power. Whether intentional or not, this too reflects the political landscape and national identity of Brexit Britain. The idea of Brexit being 'the will of the people' – and those who oppose it being 'the enemies of the people' – have become standard in the political lexis in Brexit Britain.[64] In truth, however, David Cameron's decision in 2013 to call a referendum on Britain's membership of the EU was not driven by a desire to know 'the will of the people'. The Conservative party had been deeply divided on Britain's economic and political relationship with Europe since at least the late 1980s, and since being elected as prime minister in 2010 Cameron had had to contend with the increased support for UKIP's populist anti-European platform.[65] The EU referendum was his attempt to resolve both the deep-seated rifts within his own political party and fend off threats from outside it. Much as the nobles in the *Henry VI* plays only value the opinions of the British people insofar as they allow them to further their own ambitions, Cameron gambled on 'the will of the people' being to remain in Europe in order to achieve his own goals. By removing Cade and the other lower-class characters from *Hollow Crown* Series Two, Cooke and Power offer a parallel to Brexit Britain by bringing this reality into sharp focus. 'The will of the people' is just another fabrication: the common people are not needed, because the story – whether that of the first tetralogy or of Brexit Britain – is ultimately not about them.

---

[63] Hampton-Reeves and Rutter, *Shakespeare in Performance: The Henry VI Plays*, p. 21.

[64] Alex Powell, '"The will of the people": the UK constitution, (parliamentary) sovereignty, and Brexit', in *On Brexit: Law, Justices and Injustices*, ed. Tawhida Ahmad and Elaine Fahey (Northampton, 2019), 81–95; p. 91.

[65] Oliver Daddow, 'Strategising European policy: David Cameron's referendum gamble', *RUSI Journal* 160 (2015), 4–10; p. 4.

A LION, AN ASS, A DOG AND A WALL: *A MIDSUMMER NIGHT'S DREAM*'S ECOLOGICAL THEATRICALITY

GILLIAN WOODS

Trying to convince Hermia that marriage to a man she has rejected would be preferable to celibacy as a nun, Theseus reaches for a botanical analogy:

> But earthlier happy is the rose distilled
> Than that which, withering on the virgin thorn,
> Grows, lives, and dies in single blessedness
> (*A Midsummer Night's Dream* 1.1.76–8)[1]

Critics often focus on the patriarchal tenor of this metaphor, whereby Theseus – himself shortly to marry a woman he has won doing 'injuries' with his 'sword' (1.1.16–17) – insists that Hermia will be happier if she only bends her will to that of her father. But the metaphor's vehicle also connects Theseus's patriarchal logic to a firmly anthropocentric vision, in which plants feel 'happy' to be 'distilled' in human usage.[2] To Theseus, the minotaur-slaying representative of 'civilization', roses reach a fuller potential in human processing than in a natural cycle of growing, dying and fertilizing the soil. His axiom takes for granted nature's role in servicing any needs or desires humans might invent; just as Hermia is 'but as a form in wax' (1.1.49), subject to whatever imprint her father might choose, so too is nature pliant to an improving human agency.

However, the larger play challenges Theseus's assumptions. Rhetorically fecund in flora and fauna, *A Midsummer Night's Dream* is one of Shakespeare's most environmentally explicit dramas. The action crosses boundaries between human structures and natural spaces, situated as it is in Athens, the birthplace of Western civilization, and the adjacent wood. But the wood's vegetation is detailed far more extensively than Athens's civic features. Characters plot their movements via botanical and arboreal coordinates, meeting, for example, in the wood with 'primrose beds' (1.1.215), at 'the Duke's oak' (1.2.102) or at a bank of 'wild thyme', 'oxlips', 'violet', 'woodbine',

'musk-roses' and 'eglantine' (2.1.249–52). Cross-species transformations breed throughout the play's metaphors and malapropisms, spilling into a plot where a human weaver is famously 'translated' (3.2.112) into an ass. And while various humans (and fairies) seek to assert their will through and on nature, nature proves to be not so easily 'distilled'. This article explores how *A Midsummer Night's Dream* stages the relationship between humans and the natural environment, focusing in particular on how its pointedly flawed attempts to represent nature work to unsettle any sense of human dominion over the wild.

EARLY MODERN CLIMATE CHANGE

Early in the play's supernatural action, Shakespeare flags an environmental reality for his early modern audiences. Titania tells Oberon that their marital spat is wreaking colossal climatic damage: 'winds' are dumping 'Contagious fogs' on the land and causing rivers to burst their banks, ruining the crop of 'corn' and leaving crows to glut themselves on 'the murrain flock' of infected sheep (2.1.88–97). The disaster's scale is detailed in a 37-line speech, which describes how even the seasons themselves are altered: 'The spring, the summer, / The childing autumn, angry winter change / Their wonted liveries' so that the 'mazèd world ... knows not which is which' (2.1.111–14). As editors and scholars have long noted,

---

[1] William Shakespeare, *A Midsummer Night's Dream*, in *William Shakespeare: The Complete Works*, ed. Stanley Wells, Gary Taylor, John Jowett and William Montgomery (Oxford, 2005); unless otherwise stated, all references are to this edition.

[2] Information about the uses to which distillations of early modern roses were put is found in John Gerard, *The Herball or Generall Historie of Plantes* (London, 1597), p. 1082.

Titania's account speaks of the 1590s audiences' immediate experience of nature.[3] This decade, falling within a period subsequently known as the 'Little Ice Age', was the coldest of the sixteenth century.[4] The era saw 'increased variability of the climate', which in Europe made conditions generally 'cooler and stormier'.[5] The years 1593–1597, in particular, saw a succession of much commented-upon wet, cold summers. Simon Forman wrote that May, June and July in 1594 were 'wonderfull cold like winter', while William Camden reported 'continuall raine in Summer' in 1595. John Stowe likewise described 'continuall raines euery day or night' flooding 'high wayes' in 1596.[6] In reality, as in Titania's speech, natural 'distemperature' (2.1.106) ruined the work of the 'ploughman' (2.1.94), producing a 'series of four very bad years' of harvest failures and widespread hunger.[7]

At such times, human dependence on nature and vulnerability to its vagaries were grimly evident in agricultural, economic and social terms. Bad weather produced 'economic depression, widespread poverty and high mortality from plague and starvation', so that, for example, the death rate in London in 1597 was double the average for the decade.[8] Bad harvests meant 'In England corn prices doubled or trebled between 1590 and 1596–7.'[9] Market practices were interrogated as royal authorities brought in new regulation and preachers railed against 'wretched cornemongers' and the 'rich' who 'hoord vp their corn'.[10] But the scale of human suffering raised much larger questions across society about why the populace was being subjected to these natural disasters. Edward Topsell reported (blasphemous) cries of 'Shall this indure alwaie? ... Is this the fruit of the Gospell?'[11] 'Witchcraft accusations soared', as people felt a supernatural intensity in their plight and blamed their neighbours.[12] The most standard explanation, though, was provided by religious commentators who recognized a broader human culpability, identifying the 'distemperature' as God's 'vengeance' for sin. There was, after all, ample biblical precedence for God expressing his displeasure with human behaviour via natural means.[13] This theological reading implicated humans in the malfunctioning of the ecological systems on which they depend. Such environmental ethics might appeal in the climate emergency of the twenty-first century and the catastrophic fires and floods of man-made climate change. But, ironically, this early modern anthropogenetic understanding also informs an anthropocentric attitude which

became increasingly destructive: nature is reduced to a tool for rewarding or punishing human behaviour.[14]

By providing a less theologically orthodox account of environmental upheaval, Shakespeare loosens anthropocentric logic. Titania's speech removes the neat link between human misdeeds and the weather. In sermons responding to the Swiss dearth of the 1570s and translated by William Barlow for the English dearth of the

---

[3] Editions since William Shakespeare, *A Midsummer Night's Dream*, ed. Arthur Quiller-Couch and John Dover Wilson (Cambridge, 1924) have identified the topical allusion in Titania's speech.

[4] Brian Fagan, *The Little Ice Age: How Climate Made History 1300–1850* (New York, 2000), p. 94.

[5] Michael E. Mann, 'The Little Ice Age', in *The Earth System: Physical and Chemical Dimensions of Global Environmental Change*, ed. Michael McCracken and John Perry (Chichester, 2002), p. 504; Fagan, *Little*, p. 90.

[6] Simon Forman, MS Ashm. 384, as quoted in 'Introduction: *A Midsummer Night's Dream*', in *The Works of William Shakespeare*, James Orchard Halliwell, 16 vols. (London, 1853), vol. 5, p. 3; William Camden, *Annales* (London, 1635), p. 450; John Stow, *A Summarie of the Chronicles of England* (London, 1598), sig. Ee5r; see also discussion in Sidney Thomas, 'The bad weather in *A Midsummer Night's Dream*', *Modern Language Notes* 64 (1949), 319–22; Peter Clark, 'A crisis contained? The condition of English Towns in the 1590's', in *The European Crisis of the 1590s*, ed. Peter Clark (London, 1985), p. 45; and Sophie Chiari, *Shakespeare's Representation of Weather, Climate and Environment* (Edinburgh, 2017), pp. 31–56.

[7] W. G. Hoskins, 'Harvest fluctuations and English economic history, 1480–1619', *Agricultural History Review* 12 (1964), 28–46; p. 32. John Walter qualifies Hoskins's conclusions about 'famine', but does not dispute the fact of the bad harvests or that they caused serious financial and social pressures: 'The social economy of dearth in early modern England', in *Famine, Disease and the Social Order in Early Modern Society* (Cambridge, 1989), 75–128.

[8] Peter Clark, 'Introduction', in *European Crisis*, p. 6; Clark, 'Crisis', p. 47.

[9] Clark, 'Introduction', p. 8; R. B. Outhwaite, 'Dearth, the English Crown and the "Crisis of the 1590s"', in *European Crisis*, ed. Clark, pp. 28–9.

[10] *A proclamation for the dearth of corne* (London, 1596); William Burton, *God wooing his church* (London, 1596), pp. 147–8. See also Outhwaite, 'Dearth', p. 32; and Clark, 'Crisis', p. 57.

[11] Edward Topsell, *The Reward of religion* (London, 1596), p. 25.

[12] Fagan, *Little*, p. 91; see also Clark, 'Introduction', p. 13.

[13] John Fotherby, *The Couenant betweene God and Man* (London, 1596), p. 40. See also Henry Bull, *Christian Praiers and holie Meditations* (London, 1596), p. 423; John Norden, *A Christian familiar comfort* (London, 1596), p. 16.

[14] A study of the ideological causes of our current ecological crisis falls outside the scope of this article; they are complex and include historical developments in science and philosophy. In noting how certain impulses in Christianity were a contributing factor, I am not suggesting they were pre-eminent, nor that Christianity did not in other ways encourage environmental respect.

1590s, Ludwig Lavater fulminated that it was 'a question often discussed and much debated, both by learned men and Idiottes: *Whether Sorserers or Witches, Faires or Spirits'* could 'raise anie tempests, or bring downe such Hayle as wee oft see?' For Lavater, to blame fairies was to deny God's 'righteous iudgement' and, crucially, human guilt.[15] Shakespeare's fiction thus avoids an explanation that involves humans having natural responsibility or agency. Of course, Titania's account retains a degree of anthropocentrism in her belief that the 'dissension' between her and Oberon makes them the 'parents and original' of the 'progeny of evils' (2.1.115–17). It might be fairy rather than human misconduct standing behind the environmental shifts, but the cause-and-effect account centres behaviour that feels humanly familiar: a quarrel between husband and wife. (Indeed, when detailing sins that provoked God's environmental vengeance Lavater specified that 'Man and wife agree like Dogges and Cats, continually iarring and snarling'.)[16] But the play disrupts such thinking. Henry Turner argues that the speech shakes off Titania's attempts to map an 'identifiable cause' onto natural 'forces that operate randomly with no regard for human interests', because the scale of the disorder is so demonstrably out of kilter with her account of its origins.[17]

It is also striking that the play raises this real-life crisis only to drop it. The young lovers struggle through a supernatural fog in the wood (3.2.358), but there is no discussion of unseasonal weather giving them trouble. The conditions of the dearth are kept ambiguously present through the cast of 'handicraft' men (4.2.10), who 'work for bread upon Athenian stalls' (3.2.10). Artisans, whom Puck abusively labels 'rude mechanicals' (3.2.9), were especially vulnerable to food inflation because many would be paid a simple wage, unlike farm labourers and household servants who were routinely given meals as part of their employment.[18] Proclamations and books of orders designed to mitigate the dearth repeatedly made special provisions for 'Poor Artificers' and 'poore handicrafts men' to whom corn could be sold directly rather than in the open market because their working hours might make travel difficult.[19] That an artisanal character should be named 'Starveling' would have been obviously appropriate in the 1590s. But the play features these characters without directly discussing the specifics of their situation. Shakespeare tethers the play's openly fantastical plot – with its fairies and metamorphoses – to a real environmental circumstance, but does so explicitly only by the thread of Titania's speech. Audiences are reminded of their very urgent dependence on natural order. But rather than probe further at the causes of a particular moment of climate change, the play pulls back and instead explores a deeper environmental epistemology, about how humans try to know and engage with the natural world of which they are a part. The comedy's theatrical playfulness as it endeavours to stage a diverse ecology is integral to this investigation.

A LION AND AN ASS

The challenge of representing nature is made explicit when Bottom and his artisanal friends produce a performance of *Pyramus and Thisbe* for the courtly nuptials. Snout, slated to play the lion, worries about the verbal complexity of the role: 'Have you the lion's part written? Pray you, if it be, give it me; for I am slow of study' (1.2.62–3). But his companions consider the animal dangerously easy to perform. Snout's comically anthropomorphic assumption that a lion's part would be scripted is dismissed by Quince: 'You may do it extempore; for it is nothing but roaring' (1.2.64–5); the lion's nonverbal 'roaring' is easily imitable by a human performer, requiring no preparation. Bottom's characteristic readiness to play this part in addition to his own similarly shrinks the lion's representation to a matter of noises: 'Let me play the lion too. I will roar that I will do any man's heart good to hear me. I will roar that I will make the Duke say "Let him roar again, let him roar again!"' (1.2.66–9). Bottom promises a performance that will thrill human spectators in its wildness, though his grandiose presumption is undercut as his repeated cue ('roar again . . . roar again') directs Quince to speak over him (perhaps further increasing the volume of Bottom's roars). Quince worries that Bottom would be rather too effective: 'you should do it too terribly, you would fright the Duchess and the ladies that they would shriek, and that were enough to hang us all' (1.2.70–2). These amateur performers see the problem of representing a lion not as nature's challenge to their mimetic capacity (how

[15] Ludwig Lavater, *Three Christian sermons*, trans. William Barlow (London, 1596), pp. 22–3.

[16] Lavater, *Christian*, p. [79]. Resonantly for *A Midsummer Night's Dream*, he also complains that '*Artizans* [are] idle in their trade'.

[17] Henry S. Turner, *Shakespeare's Double Helix* (London, 2008), p. 36.

[18] Outhwaite, 'Dearth', p. 38.

[19] See, for example, *A New Charge given by the Queenes commandement* [. . .] *of sundry order published the last yeere for staie of dearth of Graine* (London, 1595), pp. 5, 7.

to be good enough to capture the part's liony essence), but rather as a need to rein in their human skilfulness (how to avoid being too good). Their comical over-confidence speaks to the play's interrogation of both theatricality and social rank, as these craftsmen tangle themselves in various confusions over how performance should work.[20] But what it means to bring nature within the compass of representation is also at issue here.

The artisans' belief both that lions entertain humans and that they might be too wild for a courtly setting is also found in another theatrical 1590s performance which, as Malone first suggested, may have inspired Shakespeare's lion material in *A Midsummer Night's Dream* (though the analogue is ideologically illuminating even if there was no direct line of influence).[21] The description of a Scottish masque performed for the celebrations for Prince Henry's baptism in 1594 details a plan to have a chariot 'drawn in by a *Lyon*' that was abandoned 'because his presence might have brought some feare, to the neerest, or that the sight of the lights and torches might haue commoued his tamenes'.[22] A lion-driven chariot would celebrate royal power as human dominion over nature – but the reality of nature isn't so easily co-opted into the anthropocentric theatrical vision. Indeed, other natural symbolism in the masque was also undermined by environmental reality. The masquers staged '*Ceres*, with a sickle in her right hand, and a handful of Corne in the other' bearing the sentence '*Fundent vberes omnia Campi*, which is to say, the plenteous Fields shall affoord all things'; the unseasonal weather of the next three years instead brought dearth.[23] The lion's omission speaks to a relationship between humans and nature that the masque itself attempts to contradict. If theatrical representation is a means for humans to tell themselves stories about how things are, the reality of nature is too unpredictable to be subsumed into it. The lion cannot play a lion because it is too much of a lion. Human representation of a lion, by contrast, is only ever partial.

It is the very 'wildness' of the lion which seems to spark human desire to distil it into cultural symbolism and appropriate its value for human use. The traditional status of the lion as the 'king of beasts' was well established.[24] Lions were represented widely in early modern iconography. For example, Kathryn Will reports that 'The lion appears on more European arms than any other animal', outnumbering appearances of 'the next most common creature' by well over three times in the designs of English, Scottish and Irish family arms.[25] Indeed, the heraldist John Bossewell told his

readers 'As of beastes, the Lion is to be commended & preferred before all others'.[26] The lion was a beast of 'national symbolic importance':[27] they featured on the first English royal coat of arms (used by Richard I or the 'Lionheart'), and continued to appear on those of both Elizabeth I and James VI and I.[28] Yet the qualities that made the lion such an appealing symbolic proposition were also what made full representational purchase difficult. Henry Peacham placed lions at the top of a list of animals that were 'more hard to be drawn for their shape and action'.[29] Edward Topsell's devotion of the longest section of his *Historie of Foure-footed Beastes* to the lion, whose 'dignitie' required a 'large and copious tractate', also speaks to the challenge of being able to 'expresse the whole nature' of a beast, associated with fully wild rage and noble courage.[30] Symbolism discursively tames the lion whose lack of tameness is the symbolic appeal.

Of course, the iconographic exploitation of non-human animals in the early modern period did not produce the same human/animal binarism that post-dates Descartes. Laurie Shannon describes the 'representational archive [as] *zootopian* – not a utopia for animals, but a domain constituted by a more pervasive cognizance of them than our own' and points out that 'Early modern idioms are also more broadly zoographic than

---

[20] For an alternative discussion of the artisan players that recognizes their need to emphasize, in the disorderly 1590s, that they pose no real threat to the aristocrats, see Ronda Arab, *Manly Mechanicals on the Early Modern English Stage* (Selinsgrove, 2011), p. 108.

[21] Edmund Malone, *Plays and Poems*, 10 vols. (London, 1790), vol. 10, pp. 578–9.

[22] William Fowler, *A True Reportarie of the Most Triumphant, and Royal Accomplishment of the Baptisme of the most Excellent, right High, and mightie Prince, Frederick Henry* (Edinburgh, 1594), sig. [C]4r. In the event, the lion was replaced by a '*Black-Moore*', highlighting the connection between anthropocentrism and racism also discussed below. For further discussion, see Kim F. Hall, *Things of Darkness* (Ithaca, 1995), pp. 23–4; and Sujata Iyengar, *Shades of Difference* (Philadelphia, 2005), p. 83.

[23] Fowler, *True Reportarie*, sig. [C]3v.

[24] Edward Topsell, *The Historie of Foure-footed Beastes* (London, 1607), p. 456.

[25] Kathryn Will, 'When is a panther not a panther? Representing animals in early modern English heraldry', *Early Modern Culture* 11 (2016), 78–98; pp. 81–2.

[26] John Bossewell, *Workes of Armorie* (London, 1572), p. 21.

[27] Will, 'Panther', p. 89.

[28] Margaret Haist, 'The lion, bloodline, and kingship', in *The Mark of the Beast: The Medieval Bestiary in Art, Life, and Literature*, ed. Debra Hassig (New York, 1999), p. 9.

[29] Henry Peacham, *The Art of Drawing with the Pen* (London, 1606), p. 40.

[30] Topsell, *Beastes*, p. 456.

ours.'[31] The symbolic currency of lions in the period did not amount to a fixed or reliable discursive hierarchy in which humans absolutely controlled the meaning of animals to whom they were superior. After all, returning to the example of heraldry, animalistic associations of 'courage, furie and rage' are used to bolster the status of the human, whose own courage, fury and rage needs supplementing.[32] Yet there are anthropocentric impulses in heraldry, and early modern discourse more broadly, that create the conditions for the damaging segregations of humans and animals that follow. The appropriation of 'beasts' for representational use can (though did not necessarily always) presume that humans, exceptionally, have the ability to 'distil' other animals into various symbols to tell stories about themselves. The anthropocentric arrogance of the plans to chain a lion to a chariot in the 1594 baptism masque is an extension of such logic. Paying attention to the mechanics of representation, and not just its content, helps illuminate assumptions about the power dynamics of the relationship between humans and nature.

Shakespeare's Athenian craftsmen presume the exceptionalism of human agency in believing that their performance of a lion will be so convincing as to terrify courtly ladies. Certainly, it is the *lion* that is expected to be frightening, but lying behind that conviction is an anticipation of a highly effective representation in which the human can speak for the animal. However, through this material's comedy, Shakespeare makes the opposite point. After all, this play, saturated as it is in references to some sixty-five different species of fauna, goes to great lengths to avoid representing an animal on its own terms. Bottom's solution for managing the performance's likely terror is to unpick its representational illusion: Quince 'must name [the actor Snug's] name, and half his face must be seen through the lion's neck' and Snug must deny he is a lion and announce himself 'a man, as other men are' (3.1.33–40). These precautions will prevent the lion from being misleadingly realistic, but they also avoid Shakespeare's players having to attempt animalistic illusion. This strategy keeps the performers of *A Midsummer Night's Dream* in control of the comedy, even as the performers of *Pyramus and Thisbe* are not.

But Shakespeare's representational games with nature are not limited to the challenges of staging a lion. Meeting in the wood for rehearsal, Quince declares 'This green plot shall be our stage, this hawthorn brake our tiring-house' (3.1.2–3). As Tiffany Stern has observed, at this point, Quince is stood on an actual stage in front of a real tiring-house.[33] The irony of the moment further underlines Quince's theatrical ineptitude: he wouldn't recognize a playhouse when stood in one. But it is another moment of theatrical irony that avoids directly representing nature. The 'hawthorn brake' does not have to look entirely like a hawthorn brake because the joke is that it is a tiring-house. Of course, early modern theatre did not consistently (or perhaps even ever) aim for naturalistic illusion. And the point here is not really about how Shakespeare cannily worked around tricky staging problems, but rather that *A Midsummer Night's Dream* flags various elements of nature in metatheatrical terms that acknowledge the imperfection of human representation.

In this same rehearsal scene at the 'hawthorn brake', Bottom suggests the ludicrous strategy of performing the lion with a man's face. But moments after encouraging audiences to laugh at such a ridiculous spectacle as theatrically clumsy, the play stages, as a 'reality' within its fictional world, an equivalently silly image when Bottom is 'translated' by Puck (3.1.112). As in the plan for Snug's performance of the lion, Bottom is not fully transformed into an ass but remains identifiable as himself: Snout cries, 'O Bottom, thou art changed' (3.1.109). The amateur players are comically terrified by the very representational strategy they had designed to dispel fear: the performance of a beast that still looks like a man. Significantly, the maladroit representation of nature is couched in multiple levels of theatricality. The Folio stage direction reads '*Enter Piramus with the Asse head*' (TLN 927), emphasizing that at this moment the audience does not simply see an actor pretending to be (part) ass, but an actor playing Bottom, playing Pyramus, transformed into a man with an ass's head. For Jonathan Bate, the situation of this 'metamorphosis in the middle of a play-rehearsal' is Shakespeare going 'out of his way' to remind us that the 'ass's head is nothing more than a stage prop'. The metatheatricality keeps the translation comically fictional, diffusing what would be 'unpleasant' in 'A man becoming an ass and a woman making sexual advances to the creature.'[34] But the moment also

---

[31] Laurie Shannon, 'The eight animals in Shakespeare; or, before the human', *PMLA* 124 (2009), 472–9; p. 472.

[32] John Ferne, *The Blazon of Gentrie* (London, 1586), p. 236; also cited in Will, 'Panther', p. 78.

[33] Tiffany Stern, '"This wide and universal theatre": the theatre as prop in Shakespeare's metadrama', in *Shakespeare's Theatres and the Effects of Performance*, ed. Farah Karim-Cooper and Tiffany Stern (London, 2013), 11–32.

[34] Jonathan Bate, *Shakespeare and Ovid* (Oxford, 1998), p. 144.

oscillates between theatrical humility and theatrical audacity. The representation of the ass in *A Midsummer Night's Dream* is only as sophisticated as the amateur representation of the lion in *Pyramus and Thisbe*. At the same time, Shakespeare hardly rejects the power of representation. Where Bottom had earlier shown off his ability to 'roar' like a lion, not to mention a lion as a 'sucking dove' and a 'nightingale' (1.2.77–8), the actor playing Bottom now plays the ass, even as Bottom himself is comically unaware of his asinine transformation, believing instead that his friends have played a trick on him. The 'nay' (3.1.126) at which he breaks off his self-soothing song affords the actor an obvious opportunity to bray like an ass.[35] Only now, this is the braying of a professional actor, rather than of a professional-playing-an-amateur-playing-an-animal. And there is a certain dramaturgical swagger in inviting audiences to accept a spectacle so close to the one they have just been invited to mock (man wearing animal-head prop). The play celebrates the fun to be had in suspending disbelief. Nevertheless, the kind of anthropocentric chauvinism that underpins, say, the (attempted) display of a lion pulling a golden chariot is unsettled in this comically awkward representation of an animal. At an immediately visual level, the spectacle of a man with an ass's head insists on humanity's connection with what Topsell referred to as 'creatures without reason'.[36] Moreover, Shakespeare seems to acknowledge that humans cannot effectively pin down animals with representation. Even as he shows humans to be a part of the natural world, he reveals human representations of it to be partial, denying the possibility of theatrical dominion over nature.

Later in the play, when Bottom wakes without the ass's head, representational humility remains key. His speech continues to trouble distinctions between the animal and the human. Once again, Bottom is the unwitting butt of his own asinine rhetoric. Declaring 'Man is but an ass if he go about to expound' the 'rare vision' he has experienced, he immediately attempts an exposition (4.1.202–4). And he is not just a metaphorical ass: his 'Heigh ho!' (4.1.199) allows the actor to vocalize an animalistic 'hee haw', as if the transformation were not yet complete. The liminality of Bottom's condition is framed in theatrical terms, since he awakens remembering the moment he was transformed in rehearsal: 'When my cue comes, call me, and I will answer' (4.1.198). 'Bottom' hovers somewhere between representational layers that include a tradesman, an Ovidian lover, and an ass. Indeed, he also points metatheatrically out of the play as well as theatrically into the plot when

he announces himself a 'patched fool' (4.1.207) if he offers to describe the experience: the actor playing this part is, after all, a professional clown. The speech affords opportunities for a display of his comedic skill:

Methought I was – there is no man can tell what. Methought I was – and methought I had – but man is but a patched fool if he will offer to say what methought I had. The eye of man hath not heard, the ear of man hath not seen, man's hand is not able to taste, his tongue to conceive, nor his heart to report what my dream was! I will get Peter Quince to write a ballad of this dream

(4.1.205–12)

The lacunae enable varied physical and bawdy humour, as actors might gesture to missing ears, tails, and phallic appendages. Bottom's self-implicating reversals and confusion invite laughter.

But while he is still ass-like, his inability to speak for the ass he once was renders him human. In this way, Bottom implicitly endorses Montaigne's sceptical arguments about humanity's epistemological limitations when it comes to understanding what animals do or do not know, feel or understand: 'The defect which hindereth communication betweene them and vs, why may it not as well be in vs, as in them? It is a matter of divination to guesse in whom the fault is, that we vnderstand not one another.'[37] What Bottom sensed with his ass's head is now beyond his and any other human's ken: 'no man can tell what'. The biblical verse Bottom reconfigures speaks to humanity's spiritual limitations relative to God's grace: 'Eye hath not seen, nor ear heard, / Neither have entered into the heart of man, / The things which God hath prepared for them that love him' (1 Corinthians 2. 9). As Shannon contends, Bottom 'not only gets the point of Corinthians right but even develops the theme by means of the garbled synesthesia of his report'.[38] So Bottom demonstrates the verse's point about human limitation by failing to quote it accurately. We might also note how Bottom's speech associates grace and matters of the spirit (the content of the biblical verse) with a fully sensate experience, introducing extra senses to the biblical line and drawing

---

35 Trevor Griffiths, ed., *A Midsummer Night's Dream: Shakespeare in Production* (Cambridge, 1996), 3.1.111n.

36 Topsell, *Beastes*, p. 460.

37 Michel de Montaigne, *The Essayes*, trans. John Florio (London, 1603), p. 260. For further discussion of Montaigne's scepticism, see Laurie Shannon, *The Accommodated Animal: Cosmopolity in Shakespearean Locales* (Chicago, 2013), pp. 184–98.

38 Shannon, *Accommodated*, p. 212.

attention to them through the muddle. Human exceptionalism was founded on an Aristotelian concept of the tripartite soul, made up of a nutritive soul (common to plants, animals and humans), the sensitive soul (common to human and non-human animals) and the rational soul (possessed exclusively by humans). In this model, only humans function metaphysically, while also possessing all the faculties available to plants and other animals.[39] But Bottom's reworking of the Corinthian verse collapses the spiritual and the sensate in a way that grants the animal something sensually ineffable that humans cannot access. Bottom's deficiency is not particular to his character and his social station, but is more fully human. As a performer, Bottom's irrepressible self-confidence might be underpinned by implicit faith in human exceptionalism, but his translation into an ass qualifies this presumption. The wisdom of his humble acknowledgement of his limitation is thrown into relief when set against the play's aristocratic characters and their persistently anthropocentric attitudes.

THE ARISTOCRATIC ANIMAL

Bottom's association with non-human animals is the most theatrically striking of the comedy, but the courtly characters are also conspicuously zoological in their conversations, as they trade in animal metaphors to describe themselves and each other. Where Bottom's metamorphosis takes place during a theatrical rehearsal, the courtiers' animalistic rhetoric is tied to a plot about young love. The artisans seek to understand how to represent something other (ancient lovers, a lion, moonshine), but the lovers try to work out who they are and what they want. As Robert Watson argues, 'Our acts of sexual selection are at once the apex of personal choice and the epitome of our servitude to biological systems beyond our comprehension.'[40] This tension is explored in scenes depicting the courtiers' frantically shifting desires. Their zoological rhetoric situates their efforts at sexual maturity on discursive boundaries between animals and humans. Interspersed between scenes in which Bottom is transformed into an ass, the courtiers' love tangle works as a counterpoint. Rebecca Ann Bach argues: '*Midsummer* takes what are clearly intended to be amusing pains to indicate just how significant the distinctions are between its aristocrats and its workers, and at the same time that it emphasizes those distinctions, the play often aligns its workers with nonhuman animals.'[41] Bach's article brilliantly illuminates the emphatic animal presence in *A Midsummer Night's Dream* and reveals

unfamiliar early modern configurations of humans and beasts. My article is influenced by Bach's pioneering work but my interpretations are different. I suggest the play's dizzying rhetorical, theatrical and metatheatrical games with species and status unsettle social hierarchies, as well as the anthropocentrism to which they are tethered. While there are significant differences between groups of characters, the distinctions do not straightforwardly elevate the aristocrats. Instead, the assumptions underpinning the courtiers' rhetoric are disrupted by the conditions of the play.

When the lovers first enter the wood, some of their creaturely metaphors seem to speak to human–animal affinity. Helena pleads:

> I am your spaniel, and, Demetrius,
> The more you beat me I will fawn on you.
> Use me but as your spaniel: spurn me, strike me,
> Neglect me, lose me; only give me leave,
> Unworthy as I am, to follow you.
> What worser place can I beg in your love –
> And yet a place of high respect with me –
> Than to be usèd as you use your dog?
>
> (2.1.203–10)

Helena is emphatically doggy in her devotion. Her infatuation can be played as comically exaggerated or as bleakly submissive. Alternatively, Melissa Sanchez suggests compellingly that 'Instead of upholding patriarchal power, Helena's relentless devotion demonstrates how, taken to a masochistic extreme, fantasies of female submission and obedience can pervert and threaten men's privileged access to sexual initiative and agency ... Helena upsets clear distinctions between domination and submission.'[42] But, however it is interpreted, Helena's metaphor buys into a notion that to be a dog is to be abased (something to 'use' and 'beat'). The force of the image derives from the disjunction between Helena-as-human and Helena-as-spaniel. Helena's masochistic empowerment stems not from being a dog but from rhetorically *playing* the dog to gain human

---

[39] Erica Fudge, *Brutal Reasoning: Animals, Rationality, and Humanity in Early Modern England* (Ithaca, 2006), p. 8.

[40] Robert N. Watson, 'The ecology of self in *A Midsummer Night's Dream*', in *Ecocritical Shakespeare*, ed. Lynne Bruckner and Dan Brayton (Farnham, 2011), p. 35.

[41] Rebecca Ann Bach, 'The animal continuum in *A Midsummer Night's Dream*', *Textual Practice* 24 (2010), 123–47; p. 124.

[42] Melissa E. Sanchez, '"Use me but as your spaniel": feminism, queer theory, and early modern sexualities', *PMLA* 127 (2012), 493–511; p. 505.

agency. A spaniel does not choose to be a spaniel as Helena does here. This is not to say that dogs in the sixteenth or twenty-first centuries are inherently debased because they are dogs, but rather that the logic of Helena's metaphor presumes this to be the case. Her imagery depends upon human difference even as it seems to express cross-species kinship. Something similar happens when Helena declares herself 'as ugly as a bear' (2.2.100). The simile's emotional pull derives from an understanding that the human woman should not be like a bear, which has been deemed definitively 'ugly' by human standards. Karl Steel points out that in familiar rhetorical devices, such as the 'ravenous wolf', the 'animal metaphor sloughs off nearly the whole of animal life'.[43] Laurie Shannon describes such discourse as putting animals in the 'yoke of human symbolic service'.[44] Helena's imagery is in this anthropocentric mode, albeit at an end emotionally sympathetic to animals. For all that her metaphors seem to draw her closer to spaniels and bears, they nevertheless depend upon a distinction between the species. She appropriates animal identities in a demonstration of rhetorical agency that guarantees her human exceptionalism. Her linguistic strategies connect her more immediately with Bottom and his confident promises to roar like a lion than they do to actual animals.

Other aristocratic uses of animal metaphors become more obviously anthropocentric, but this attitude is challenged by the play's action. Bewitched by Puck's botanical magic, Lysander switches his affection from Hermia to Helena and exclaims 'Who will not change a raven for a dove?' (2.2.120). His rhetorical question presumes a commonsense preference for fair women over dark women. Behind this statement is another ideological commonplace: animals distil conveniently into metaphors for human discourse. But the comedy's action challenges the obviousness of this observation, since not all animals remain passively rhetorical in language controlled by humans. Instead, the varying stability of different characters' metaphors playfully tests differences between humans and between species. Lysander's stylistic control is more secure than that of the artisans, whose metaphors prove unreliable. Having unwittingly gained an ass's head, poor Bottom rails at his friends, thinking they are playing a joke on him: 'You see an ass head of your own, do you' (3.1.111–112); 'This is to make an ass of me' (3.1.114). Bottom quite reasonably uses metaphors without knowing that something implausibly literal has happened – and the action mocks him for it. The transformation underlines the weaver's

lack of linguistic control and manifests his animality. Bach regards the metamorphosis as making a comically literal lesson out of a tradesman with ideas above his station: 'Bottom is only and always an ass.'[45] Certainly, the ass's associations with labour as a 'burthen-bearing' and 'cart-drawing' beast fit with Bottom's social status. And aspects of the weaver's character, who frequently misspeaks and misapprehends, are proverbially asinine, since asses were known for their 'stupidity' and for being 'blockish'.[46] By contrast, the play does not subject the young courtiers to such apparent theatrical indignity: their metaphors remain rhetorical and their bodies remain human.

However, if Bottom is mocked for being ass-like, the courtiers are mocked more subversively for their humanity. After confidently expressing his love for fair women / doves over dark women / ravens, Lysander explains to Helena:

> The will of man is by his reason swayed,
> And reason says you are the worthier maid.
> Things growing are not ripe until their season,
> So I, being young, till now ripe not to reason.
> And, touching now the point of human skill,
> Reason becomes the marshal to my will
>
> (2.2.121–6)

Reason, the faculty Lysander references four times in these six lines, was understood to be the defining distinction between humans and animals (Lysander calls it 'human skill'), and what made humans superior.[47] But, of course, Lysander's enthusiastic self-confidence in his reason is undermined by what he has just reasoned: that he now suddenly loves Helena instead of Hermia. Erica Fudge explains that free will was a 'crucial' condition for human reason: 'an animal does not make choices; instead it merely exists in a predisposed way, whereas a human uses reason, makes judgments, and acts on the basis of those judgments'.[48] Since Lysander's free will has been removed by Puck's drug, he cannot exercise reason here. His inability to identify reason, while claiming it, devalues reason's status as a distinguishing and elevating

43 Karl Steel, 'Beasts, animals, and animal metaphors in Shakespeare and his fellow dramatists', in *The Routledge Handbook of Shakespeare and Animals*, ed. Karen Raber and Holly Dugan (London, 2021), p. 62.

44 Shannon, *Accommodated*, p. 5. 45 Bach, 'Animal', p. 139.

46 Topsell, *Beastes*, pp. 20–1, 25.

47 This point is also made by Watson, though he misidentifies Lysander as Demetrius (itself a reasonable mistake given the interchangeability of these characters): 'Ecology', p. 35.

48 Fudge, *Brutal*, p. 29.

human characteristic. Bottom provides a neat counterpoint to and commentary on this moment when, in the very next scene, he warns Titania that 'reason and love keep little company together nowadays' (3.1.136–7). Speaking through his ass's head, the craftsman has a better understanding of reason than the courtier, even if Lysander's metaphors are more stable. And Bottom's clearer understanding is framed in negative terms: reason is elusively elsewhere; this human skill turns out not to be so reliable. Indeed, the comedy of Bottom's characterization may centre on his human insufficiencies (such as his inability to speak well), but the comedy of Lysander's declaration centres on the misplaced vanity of humanity. And other human attributes that might elevate the courtiers are also shown to be questionable. Bach is likely right that audiences would hear the 'musical contrast' between the aristocrats' 'musical use of rhyme and rhythm and the workmen's pedestrian poetry' in their performance of *Pyramus and Thisbe*.[49] But, however melodic the courtly lovers' language, the harmony of their rhymes does not secure clear thinking. In this scene, Lysander forges an aurally persuasive link between his 'will' and 'skill', suggesting that his 'reason' is in 'season', but the theatrical situation renders these connections specious. The comedy is firmly sceptical about human attributes – eloquence, reason – that supposedly lift humans above beasts (and some humans above other humans).

As the young lovers' distance from reason grows, so too does the anthropocentrism of their rhetoric, as their animal metaphors take the form of insults. Fearing that Demetrius has killed Lysander while he slept, Hermia exclaims:

> Out, dog! Out, cur! . . .
> Could not a worm, an adder do so much? –
> An adder did it, for with doubler tongue
> Than thine, thou serpent, never adder stung
>
> (3.2.65–73)

The metamorphic accusations reveal Hermia's fear of the wild space into which she has fled: Demetrius embodies a terrifying lack of civility best captured for her in animalistic terms. When Lysander appears alive and unmurdered, though, and all the lovers encounter one another, frantic with unrequited passion and confusion, the name-calling only intensifies and ranges across an ideologically revealing variety of categories. Nature-based insults make clear the courtiers' anthropocentric attitudes as they label one another: 'cat' (3.2.261), 'serpent' (3.2.262), 'vixen' (3.2.325), 'burr' (3.2.261),

'canker-blossom' (3.2.283), 'knot-grass' (3.2.330) and 'acorn' (3.2.331). These names are mixed in with other dehumanizing terms such as 'puppet' (3.2.289), 'painted maypole' (3.2.297) and 'bead' (3.2.331), as well as assertions of immorality such as 'juggler' (3.2.283) and 'counterfeit' (3.2.289). The list also includes racist and ableist slurs: 'Ethiop' (3.2.257), 'tawny Tartar' (3.2.264) and 'dwarf' (3.2.329), indicating the way anthropocentrism also devalues a majority of humans, since it does not merely prioritize humans above and against nature, but does so in order to define certain attributes as more ideally human.[50] On the one hand, the play punctures these attitudes by undermining the speakers' pretensions of superiority. Their childish tantrums are framed by a still larger sense of human insufficiency. Shannon astutely argues that '*Midsummer*'s Athenians make a case study of human sensory and cognitive weakness' since the nighttime setting of the scenes in the wood 'exposes man's vaunted competencies as intermittent and qualifies his claimed sovereignty as merely episodic'.[51] Stumbling in the dark, the young Athenians are demonstrably less competent than nocturnal beasts that can see, move and hunt after nightfall. The courtiers, who are 'Bedabbled with the dew, and torn with briars' (3.3.31), conclude the night collapsed asleep on the 'dank and dirty ground' (2.2.81). But, on the other hand, the play frames their racist and ableist insults as comedic. Even if part of the joke is on the speakers as their impassioned confusion strips them of their civility, the premise of the slurs casually excludes as 'other' people who are reduced to undesirable types. As Patricia Akhimie explains, 'Racist humor produces social difference by teaching audiences how to hold themselves as a group apart and position themselves above another group.'[52] Where the comedy's theatrical games pull an ass's head out of a metaphor and give the handicraft men recuperative performance time, the 'Ethiop', 'tawny Tartar' and 'dwarf' are pinioned in and as mere rhetoric (though there are opportunities for productions to intervene here). *A Midsummer Night's Dream* disrupts without dismantling hierarchies, and some participants in its

[49] Bach, 'Animal', p. 134.

[50] See also Hall, *Darkness*, pp. 1–24. Bach comments that the scene 'shows us how culturally pervasive the association was between racialized others and nonhuman animals'; 'Animal', p. 130.

[51] Shannon, *Accommodated*, pp. 215, 174.

[52] Patricia Akhimie, 'Racist humor and Shakespearean comedy', in *The Cambridge Companion to Shakespeare and Race*, ed. Ayanna Thompson (Cambridge, 2021), p. 50.

ecology remain cast as outsiders. One plot line, after all, pivots around possession of an 'Indian boy' who has no stage time.[53]

If the night in the wood exposes belief in human exceptionalism as folly, the morning brings with it a renewed articulation of human pre-eminence. Heralded by hunting horns (4.1.99 SD.2), Theseus and Hippolyta arrive in the wood, with Theseus determined to impress his bride with 'the music of my hounds' (4.1.105). He asserts:

> We will, fair Queen, up to the mountain's top,
> And mark the musical confusion
> Of hounds and echo in conjunction
>
> (4.1.108–10)

As Jeffrey Theis points out, these dogs 'embody a link between nature and culture; they manifest Theseus's implied belief that he controls nature'.[54] Theseus frames the hounds' barking – echoing around the mountain and wood – as 'musical'. He has had them

> bred out of the Spartan kind,
> So flewed, so sanded; and their heads are hung
> With ears that sweep away the morning dew;
> Crook-kneed, and dewlapped like Thessalian bulls;
> Slow in pursuit, but matched in mouth like bells,
> Each under each.
>
> (4.1.118–23)

Managing nature through breeding, Theseus has cultivated the appearance and sound of his hounds at the expense of their ability to run (they are 'Slow in pursuit'). The young lovers spent the night as metaphorical spaniels, bears, doves, cats and vixens, but Theseus's dogs behave 'like bells'. Hippolyta teases or taunts (depending on how this relationship is interpreted) that Hercules's and Cadmus's hounds produced the most 'gallant chiding' she has ever encountered: 'I never heard / So musical a discord, such sweet thunder' (4.1.116–17). Theseus's lengthy counter-description clarifies the hounds' function in his self-identification: 'A cry more tuneable / Was never halloo'd to nor cheered with horn / In Crete, in Sparta, nor in Thessaly' (4.1.123–5). These animals are firmly co-opted in a human script about Theseus's competitive status and wealth. The conversation seems to return the play to a daylight order in which hierarchies are restored: weavers reclaim their human forms, courtiers return to court, and the Duke asserts his dominion over nature (and other men). However, the play's theatrical games continue to undermine such order with a rather different ecological vision.

THE MOON, A DOG AND A WALL

The return to the Athenian court offers a structural promise of putting everything and everyone back in their 'proper' place. The humans leave the wood and rejoin a social hierarchy headed by Theseus, with men and women paired off in heterosexual marriages and the craftsmen performing as supplicants to the court. The apparent ineptitude of the artisans' performance might seem to consolidate these traditional hierarchies by demonstrating their lack of sophistication in the face of their social betters. However, the scene's theatrical dynamics resist this order.

During the artisans' performance, the aristocrats use the same language of animal insults that they spoke in the wood but now direct them at the craftsmen rather than each other. Lysander sneers that Quince 'hath rid his prologue like a rough colt' (5.1.119), so that the uneducated speaker who fails to observe punctuation is rendered equivalent to an untrained horse – bestial and yet to satisfy human requirements properly. When Theseus asks incredulously if the lion will speak, Demetrius quips 'one lion may, when many asses do' (5.1.152). The artisans had worried their performance would be too effectively animalistic, but the courtiers see them as ineffectively human.[55] The callback to Bottom's asinine transformation might suggest that the courtiers' reading of the performers is encouraged by the larger play – except that this aristocratic behaviour is problematic even by its own explicitly voiced standards. Before the artisan performance began, Hippolyta had objected to the prospect of seeing 'wretchedness o'ercharged, / And duty in his service perishing' (5.1.85–6), only for Theseus to assure her that they would be 'kinder' in giving them 'thanks for nothing' (5.1.89). But there is little kindness in the onstage audience's ongoing critique of the workmen's production, which is heard by the performers themselves, as is clear when Moonshine goes off-script because of the courtiers' interruptions (5.1.252), and Bottom directly answers them (5.1.182–5). When Hippolyta complains that she is 'aweary' of Starveling's Moon, punning that he should 'change' (5.1.246), Theseus joins in the joke only to catch himself: 'in courtesy, in all reason, we must

---

[53] See Margo Hendricks, '"Obscured by dreams": race, empire, and Shakespeare's *A Midsummer Night's Dream*', *Shakespeare Quarterly* 47 (1996), 37–60.

[54] Jeffrey S. Theis, *Writing the Forest in Early Modern England: A Sylvan Pastoral Nation* (Pittsburgh, 2009), p. 99.

[55] See Bach, 'Animal', pp. 124–8.

stay the time' (5.1.249–50). Flagging – without showing – 'courtesy', the line might be straightforwardly patronizing or an awkwardly superficial attempt to behave better, but either way, aristocratic 'reason' is again rendered questionable by the context in which it is raised. Castiglione castigated those nobles who 'taunted' individuals of significantly lower status, insisting 'it prouoketh no laughter to mocke & scorne a sillie soule in miserie and calamitie'.[56] In the 1590s dearth, when the environmental crisis provoked calls for 'fellow-feeling' and proclamations enjoined the wealthy to 'keepe hospitalitie', the spectacle of aristocrats ridiculing a tradesman called 'Starveling' might have seemed especially ignoble.[57] Their jokes do not necessarily encourage the offstage audience to buy into the social and anthropocentric order they are designed to consolidate. Flaunting their verbal agility, the aristocrats attempt to assert their own superiority over less eloquent men whom they are categorizing as less than men:

LYSANDER This lion is a very fox for his valour.
THESEUS True; and a goose for his discretion.
DEMETRIUS Not so, my lord, for his valour cannot carry his discretion; and the fox carries the goose.
THESEUS His discretion, I am sure, cannot carry his valour; for the goose carries not the fox. It is well: leave it to his discretion

(5.1.228–34)

The aristocrats respond to Snug's untheatrical declaration that he is 'Snug the joiner' (5.1.221) and a man rather than a beast by reading him as multiple animals. Their wordplay depends upon a proverbial (and thus anthropocentric) understanding of animals, and renders Snug somehow less than each animal with which he is identified: lions are famed for their valour, so Snug is a fox; foxes are known for their discretion or cunning, so Snug is a goose (reputedly stupid). But the long-winded joke runs out of steam, with Theseus awkwardly concluding, 'It is well: leave it to his discretion'. The aristocrats' anthropocentric wordplay – and the attitudes underpinning it – seem especially flat in relation to the *Pyramus and Thisbe* comic set-piece.

If the earlier rehearsal scenes promised that the production would be ludicrous, the staging in the final scene more than delivers. The artisans repeatedly spoil theatrical illusion by announcing their real identities (5.1.155, 221), confuse classical allusion (Helen is cited as a type of fidelity (5.1.196)), mispronounce names ('Limander' for Leander (5.1.195), 'Shafalus' for Cephalus (5.1.197–8), 'Ninny' for Ninus (5.1.201)), shuffle senses ('I see a voice . . . I can hear my Thisbe's

face' (5.1.191–2)), and speak thuddingly clumsy poetry (5.1.271–82, 290–300, 319–42). Centrally ridiculous are their attempts to perform inappropriately ambitious or unnecessary roles, including animals, inanimate objects and even the moon. If Snug's hybrid performance of a lion has already been anticipated by Bottom's incomplete transformation into an ass, the comedy nevertheless pushes into new representational territory in the performance of the moon: 'All that I have to say is to tell you that the lanthorn is the moon, I the man i'th'moon, this thorn bush my thorn bush, and this dog my dog' (5.1.252–6). This is the most fully and yet simultaneously most fractured anthropocentric representation of the play. The moon is played as a 'man i'th'moon', but also by a prop ('the lanthorn') held by the other sign for the same thing. *A Midsummer Night's Dream* has elsewhere avoided direct representations of nature: its copious flora and fauna are largely linguistic; the hawthorn brake is a tiring house and Bottom's ass is still Bottom. (Oberon makes magical use of 'love in idleness' – a pansy – so that the prop may be represented 'naturally' or 'supernaturally'.) But here Starveling points directly to two items that are, as he states, tautologically themselves: 'this thorn bush my thorn bush, and this dog my dog'. Except that, as themselves, they are symbols for the moon. The artisans' deferential fear of alarming the court has seen them repeatedly clarify how their theatrical signs work: the lion (signified) is really a man (signifier). The thorn bush and especially the dog disrupt this order because now signifieds ('this dog my dog') seem to be playing signifiers (part of a sign for the moon). The folly of anthropocentric representation is pushed to its limit with the staging of a real animal.[58] Of course, a live dog creates further opportunity for theatrical chaos

---

[56] Baldassare Castiglione, *The Courtier*, trans. Thomas Hobby (London, 1588), sig. [O7r].

[57] Topsell, *Reward*, p. 202; *The Queenes Maiesties Proclamation [. . .] and a Prohibition to Men of Hospitalitie* (London, 1596); see also *Orders for the Redresse of Abuse in Diet* (London, 1595).

[58] That a live dog is not an excessively challenging staging demand is evident in the number of other early modern plays which feature dogs: *Sir Clyomon and Clamydes*, *Magnificence*, *Old Wives Tale*, *Every Man Out of His Humour*, *Every Woman in Her Humour*, *The Staple of News*, *Histriomastix*, *The Roaring Girl*, *The Merry Devil of Edmonton*, *The Distracted Emperor*, *The Late Lancashire Witches*, and Shakespeare's own *Two Gentlemen of Verona*. See Louis B. Wright, 'Animal actors on the English stage before 1642', *PMLA* 42 (1927), 656–69; and Michael Dobson, 'A dog at all things: the transformation of the onstage canine, 1550–1850', *Performance Research* 5 (2000), 116–24.

during the artisans' performance.[59] But simply the dog's presence extends the play's experiments with what it means to stage nature. Where lions and asses have been performed by humans with comic awkwardness, an actual animal now plays a non-animal. Bottom's ass's ears are all too clearly a theatrical prop, but 'this dog' is too animal for its part as part-moon. In entirely opposite ways, both pieces of stagecraft demonstrate that nature is not easily reducible to human representation.

The raucous comedy of artisans' performance obviously frames their strategies as ridiculous, with their production's ecological inclusivity being a key part of the humour. For example, the decision to make Wall a speaking part rather than a prop is a risible category error. At the same time, though, this inset play makes a similar point to that of the larger comedy: that humans are not as separate from their environment as 'civilized' sensibilities might suggest. Having a man perform a Wall enables sexual innuendo and physical humour as Thisbe reports having 'often kissed thy stones' (5.1.189), and later bemoans that she kisses 'the wall's hole' (5.1.200) rather than Pyramus's lips.[60] These brilliantly silly moments also literalize an idea of human connectedness with the environment. It may be foolish for the artisans to animate the non-human elements of the *Pyramus and Thisbe* story, but the comedy seems to acknowledge and embrace such foolishness as a better vision. The aristocrats' attempts to skewer the craftsmen with witticisms that put them in their place do not have the same comedic appeal as the performance which is the central focus of the scene. *Pyramus and Thisbe* requires on the part of the actors playing the artisans a highly skilled performance of a lack of skill. This skilled foolishness is key to what I am terming the play's ecological theatricality: a consummate performance that is nevertheless humble in its terms, acknowledging that humans might not be exceptional and central even whilst, being the work of humans, it inevitably focuses on their stories.[61]

At the end of the performance, theatrical as well as social power is explicitly given to the Duke, who has the privilege of choosing a bergomask rather than an epilogue to close the entertainment. But such power is fleeting. Following that dance, Theseus's last speech could conventionally end the larger play. He shepherds the courtiers offstage 'to bed' (5.1.357, 361) and speaks in conclusive rhyming couplets promising future festivity: 'A fortnight hold we this solemnity / In nightly revels and new jollity' (5.2.362–3). The further theatrical framing that continues the play past this point decentres Theseus's Athenian authority. At the end of the *Pyramus and Thisbe* performance, he and Demetrius had scoffed at the surplus of non-human characters:

THESEUS Moonshine and Lion are left to bury the dead.
DEMETRIUS Ay, and Wall, too.

(5.1.344–5)

But *A Midsummer Night's Dream* similarly features non-human roles with its cast of fairies, and it is they rather than Theseus who close the play. Of course, with their greater literary precedence and human likeness, the fairies are less inherently ridiculous than Wall and Moonshine, but their supernatural presence nevertheless demonstrates that Theseus's environment is fuller than he understands and that powers other than his own are at work. After Theseus attempts to clear the stage and end the play, Puck re-enters and returns attention to ecological diversity: 'Now the hungry lion roars, / And the wolf behowls the moon' (5.2.1–2). His speech insists upon the night-rule of beasts and fairies who are active while the human 'snores' (5.2.3) or 'lies in woe' (5.1.7) worrying about death.[62] And instead of ending the play in a strictly courtly setting with a human speaker, Shakespeare provides multiple supernatural frames that promise, but then resist, closure. Puck's speech works like an epilogue, but is followed by the entrance of Oberon and Titania and their train of fairies, who provide varied moments of potential conclusion as they sing, dance and give a blessing, only for Puck to remain and give another, really final, epilogue.[63] The shifting theatrical frames flout the neat order of Theseus's Athenian court. It matters too that the fairies have the final word, since throughout the play they have served as an ambiguous bridge between humans and other parts of

---

[59] Griffiths reports that 'Ray Llewellyn's real dog at Birmingham Town Hall in 1973 caused havoc among the members of the City of Birmingham Symphony Orchestra on stage to play Mendelssohn's music': *Dream*, 5.1.244n. This unpredictability is presumably why the dog is, as Michael Dobson notes, 'usually represented by a puppet in modern productions': 'Dog', p. 124, n.1.

[60] Gordon Williams defines 'stone' as 'testicle' and 'hole' as 'anus': *A Dictionary of Sexual Language and Imagery in Shakespearean and Stuart Literature* (London, 2000), pp. 1320, 671.

[61] I am influenced here by Matthew Kendrick's related argument about 'skilled rudeness', which concentrates on labour and social rank rather than broader ecological structures: *At Work in Early Modern English Theater: Valuing Labor* (Madison, 2015), p. 143.

[62] For an excellent discussion of the significance of 'night-rule' in *A Midsummer Night's Dream*, see Shannon, *Accommodated*, pp. 174–217.

[63] See Michael Mangan, *A Preface to Shakespeare's Comedies: 1594–1608* (London, 1996), pp. 174–8.

the natural world. Like humans, the fairies have a sometimes exploitative and confrontational relationship with nature. For example, Oberon uses the 'juice' of the flower 'love-in-idleness' (2.1.168–70) as a love drug (recalling Theseus's metaphorically distilled rose), and Titania's fairies 'kill cankers' or caterpillars, and 'war with reremice [i.e. bats] for their leathern wings / To make [her] small elves coats' (2.2.3–5). But they are also more comfortably connected with the natural environment than are humans. Unlike both the courtiers and the craftsmen, the fairies move confidently through the wood and beyond, and have names such as Cobweb, Peaseblossom and Mustardseed.[64] The play does not resolve finally into a narrowly Athenian order with carefully policed social and species hierarchies. Instead, it stages a broader ecology, in which other forces are simultaneously at work.[65]

A Midsummer Night's Dream engages audiences with nature's wildness while pointedly failing to contain it. At a moment of ecological crisis in the 1590s, and in a play fertile in natural references, Shakespeare decentres, and acknowledges the imperfection of, human agency both through a plot in which 'reason and love keep little company', and through a theatrical form which is joyously foolish in its clunky attempts to represent nature. But, for all its frivolity, *A Midsummer Night's Dream* is not simply a light distraction from its age's climatic upheaval and economic challenges – after all, the play explicitly draws attention to the contextual 'distemperature'

(2.1.106), and social tensions are kept in the drama's peripheral vision with the presence of artisans desperate to be 'made men' (4.2.17). Comedy instead here offers a particular environmental epistemology, situating characters in an unruly ecosystem and drawing attention to the limits of human knowledge. The recreative aspects of the genre – the laughs it draws showing 'what fools these mortals be' (3.2.115) – recreate the human as a demonstrably flawed participant in the natural world, not its master. A play about fairies and a man-turned-ass does not offer any solutions to the environmental crises of the past or the present. But understanding its ecological theatricality shows how comedy can nudge audiences away from humanity's deep-rooted and damaging assumptions about its pre-eminence. It is more than time to 'restore amends' (5.2.16).

---

[64] Discussing the insectoid form of the play's fairies, Todd Andrew Borlik makes a point related to this article about how the comedy qualifies human agency: 'In representing the unrepresentable agency of insects, *A Midsummer Night's Dream* dramatizes the epistemological limitations of human sight, revealing that it is not coextensive with the environment': 'Shakespeare's insect theater: fairy lore as Elizabethan folk entomology', in *Performing Animals: History, Agency, Theater*, ed. Karen Raber and Monica Mattfeld (University Park, 2017), p. 138.

[65] Watson, 'Ecology', makes a similar point, focusing on the supernatural interventions in the love plot rather than the play's theatrical mechanisms.

HITCHCOCK'S HAMLET

MISHA TERAMURA

In August 1945, during the final days of World War II, newspapers across North America announced strange news from Hollywood: the celebrated director Alfred Hitchcock was planning to produce the first English-language film adaptation of *Hamlet*, starring Cary Grant in the title role. By 1945, Hitchcock was well known to audiences on both sides of the Atlantic. After a string of early films produced in England, including *The Man Who Knew Too Much* (1934), *The 39 Steps* (1935) and *The Lady Vanishes* (1938), Hitchcock moved to America, where he would direct such films as *Rebecca* (1940), *Suspicion* (1941) and *Shadow of a Doubt* (1943). If film industry observers may have suspected Hitchcock of trying to emulate the recent success of Laurence Olivier's *Henry V* (1944), press reports of Hitchcock's project made it clear that his would be no ordinary Shakespeare adaptation. 'Hamlet will be shown as a modern man with problems', Cary Grant told an Associated Press reporter. 'I won't attempt to portray the role in the traditional Shakespearean manner.'[1] In fact, the text would not be Shakespearian at all, but a thorough translation into modern English, set in the contemporary world. 'The plot, situations, psychology and characters will be retained', Hitchcock added, 'but the action and sets will be modern.' Over the coming months, Hitchcock teased more details about what this modernization might look like, floating the possibility of Hamlet's father as an industrial magnate rather than a king, and a setting in England or Detroit instead of Denmark. 'The soliloquies might be recited on a psychoanalyst's couch and the ghost might end up a ouija board.'[2] Indeed, Hitchcock's version would not be a tragedy but a 'psychological thriller'.

While filming had originally been planned for early 1946, the start date was repeatedly delayed. 'Hitchcock "Hamlet" stalled', read a headline in *Variety*.[3] Grant reportedly wanted Vivien Leigh to play Ophelia, but no further casting announcements were made, although one journalist speculated that Hitchcock, already famous for his walk-on cameos, would appear in the film as one of the gravediggers.[4] In June 1946, a reporter asked when the production would begin. '"Just as soon," growled Hitchcock good-naturedly, "as we get the ham out of this Hamlet."'[5] While Hitchcock's apparent irreverence in undertaking an abbreviated and modernized *Hamlet* had already perturbed some Shakespearian purists, the more significant threat to the project came in the form of a lawsuit. Within days of their initial press announcement, Hitchcock received telegrams from multiple people claiming prior ownership to the idea of a modernized *Hamlet*.[6] By January 1946, the press was reporting that the number had grown to thirty-seven.[7] The most litigious of these, claiming that his own *Hamlet* 'rendered into modern American colloquial English' had been copyrighted in 1941, sued for damages totalling $1.25 million.[8] However, by that time, Hitchcock's

---

1   Rosalind Shaffer, 'Modernized version of Hamlet Hollywood's latest project', *Windsor Daily Star*, 23 August 1945, 9.
2   Bob Thomas, 'Hollywood: Hitchcock and Grant plan modern "Hamlet"', *Lansing State Journal*, 16 January 1946, 10.
3   'Hitchcock 'Hamlet' stalled', *Variety*, 5 December 1945, 11.
4   Sheilah Graham, 'Hollywood gossip', *Evening Citizen* (Ottawa), 29 September 1945, 15; Earl Wilson, 'Hitchcock hates eggs and fat men', *Courier-Post* (Camden, NJ), 13 September 1945, 24.
5   Earl Wilson, 'Author-farmer has chicken herd', *Miami Daily News*, 2 June 1946, 7-A.
6   Margaret Herrick Library, Academy of Motion Picture Arts and Sciences, Alfred Hitchcock Papers (AHP), files 1124–5.
7   Bob Thomas, 'Plans go on to produce film Hamlet', *Austin Statesman*, 16 January 1946, 2.
8   'Unproduced modern "Hamlet" pic basis of fancy Fed'l C't claim', *Variety*, 28 May 1947, 8. The materials of the lawsuit are in AHP, file 1125.

Hamlet had already seemed doomed: by the end of 1946, Grant had pulled out, leaving the film without its star.[9] As the lawsuit dragged on, Laurence Olivier released his lavish *Hamlet* in 1948, a commercial and critical success, winning the Academy Award for Best Picture. Meanwhile, Hitchcock's 'psychological thriller' adaptation of *Hamlet* would never be made, becoming an all-but-forgotten footnote in movie history.[10]

If Shakespearian cinematic adaptation is nearly as old as the medium itself, extending from incunabular silent films to the global cinematic industries of the twenty-first century, the episode of Hitchcock's unfilmed *Hamlet* can be placed in a kind of shadow history of this tradition, joining the ranks of such unrealized projects as Laurence Olivier's *Macbeth* and Orson Welles's *King Lear*.[11] Unlike Olivier and Welles, however, Hitchcock, who never attempted another Shakespearian adaptation, is a director almost always excluded from scholarly accounts of Shakespeare on film. And yet, Shakespeare – and *Hamlet* specifically – haunts Hitchcock's filmography. As Mark Thornton Burnett has recently shown, *Hamlet* has proven exceptionally amenable to cinematic reinterpretations across time and space.[12] Hitchcock's engagements with the play, if not formally adaptations as such, provide a different perspective on *Hamlet*'s cinematic malleability, involving a broad range of intertextual strategies addressed in recent work on the politics and poetics of Shakespearian citations, allusions and appropriations in screen media.[13] Attending to Hitchcock's uses of *Hamlet* both sheds light on Shakespeare's status in early twentieth-century popular entertainment and provides a complex case study of how one influential filmmaker found in Shakespeare a kind of problem: in fact, the reason why Hitchcock never made a Shakespeare adaptation arguably constitutes an important piece of evidence for our understanding of Shakespeare's cinematic afterlife.

What was *Hamlet* to Hitchcock, and Hitchcock to *Hamlet*? While most critical attention to this question has been spent debating whether or not the cryptic title *North by Northwest* (1959) alludes to Hamlet's 'I am but mad north-north-west',[14] this article will argue that Hitchcock's earlier encounters with *Hamlet* tell a more consequential story. In a series of films throughout the first two decades of his career – *Elstree Calling* (1930), *Murder!* (1930), *The Man Who Knew Too Much* (1934), *Secret Agent* (1936) and *Spellbound* (1945) – Hitchcock's shifting engagements with *Hamlet* trace an evolving consideration of how Shakespearian cultural capital could be both an asset and a liability for filmmakers. For Hitchcock, this question involved not just the critics and the box office but, more

importantly, an urgent set of concerns about filmmaking as a form of authorship. Indeed, one of the most notorious parts of Hitchcock's reputation – along with voyeurism, sadism and misogyny – is his preoccupation with establishing his identity as a directorial *auteur* in the fundamentally collaborative milieu of cinema, an industry dependent on the contributions of screenwriters, actors, composers, costume and set designers, cinematographers, editors, producers, camera technicians, studio employees and more. As Emma Smith has shown, Hitchcock's self-fashioning as an authorial personality within his films can be compared to Ben Jonson, whose cameo-like self-interpolations into his plays and manipulation of implicit contracts with his audience mirror Hitchcock's strategies to foreground the primacy of his own directorial role.[15] As this article argues,

9   Sheilah Graham, 'Maxie Rosenbloom's wife looms as champion editor', *Miami Daily News*, 12 August 1946, 10-A .

10 Some brief discussion of the project can be found in Caroline Moorehead, *Sidney Bernstein: A Biography* (London, 1984), pp. 173–4; Leonard J. Leff, *Hitchcock and Selznick: The Rich and Strange Collaboration of Alfred Hitchcock and David O. Selznick* (New York, 1987), pp. 256–8; Patrick McGilligan, *Alfred Hitchcock: A Life in Darkness and Light* (New York, 2003), pp. 387, 399, 575; Sidney Gottlieb, 'Unknown Hitchcock: the unrealized projects', in *Hitchcock: Past and Future*, ed. Richard Allen and Sam Ishii-Gonzáles (London, 2004), 97; Stephen Whitty, *The Alfred Hitchcock Encyclopedia* (Lanham, MD, 2016), s.v. '*Hamlet*.' The most extensive compilation of information can be found in The Alfred Hitchcock Wiki, s.v. '*Hamlet*', https://the.hitchcock.zone/wiki/Hamlet.

11 Anthony Guneratne, 'The greatest Shakespeare film never made: textualities, authorship, and archives', *Shakespeare Bulletin* 34 (2016): 391–412.

12 Mark Thornton Burnett, *'Hamlet' and World Cinema* (Cambridge, 2019).

13 See, for example, Douglas Lanier, *Shakespeare and Modern Popular Culture* (Oxford, 2002), 50–81; Richard Burt, ed., *Shakespeares after Shakespeare: An Encyclopedia of the Bard in Mass Media and Popular Culture*, 2 vols. (Westport, CT, 2007); Eric S. Mallin, *Reading Shakespeare in the Movies: Non-adaptations and Their Meaning* (Cham, 2019); Elisabeth Bronfen, *Serial Shakespeare: An Infinite Variety of Appropriations in American TV Drama* (Manchester, 2020); Alexa Alice Joubin and Victoria Bladen, eds., *Onscreen Allusions to Shakespeare: International Films, Television, and Theatre* (Cham, 2022).

14 The best-known discussion appears in Stanley Cavell, '*North by Northwest*', *Critical Inquiry* 7 (1981), 761–76, although other critics are cited in Christopher D. Morris, 'The Direction of *North by Northwest*', *Cinema Journal* 36 (1997), 43–56; p. 55, n.9. An innovative and thought-provoking exception is Marjorie Garber's reading of *Hamlet* through the Hitchcockian concept of the McGuffin in *Profiling Shakespeare* (New York, 2008), pp. 228–52.

15 Emma Smith, 'Performing relevance / relevant performances: Shakespeare, Jonson, Hitchcock', in *New Directions in Renaissance Drama and Performance Studies*, ed. Sarah Werner (Basingstoke, 2010), 147–61.

Hitchcock himself looked to the early modern world and found in *Hamlet* a versatile tool for negotiating his role as a filmmaker. While *Hamlet* could, at times, be emblematic of Shakespearian canonicity, actorly virtuosity and psychological complexity, it was the *Mousetrap* scene in particular – the critical moment of dramatic rewriting and spectatorship – that most inflects Hitchcock's engagements with the play. As Shoshana Felman famously observes in her analysis of the interpretative controversies surrounding *The Turn of the Screw*, 'The scene of the critical debate is thus a *repetition* of the scene dramatized in the text', a symptom of the 'uncanny trapping power of Henry James's text'.[16] In Hitchcock's career, the scene of repetition in *Hamlet* (of repeating in performance the crime that has happened in reality in order to trap a spectator) finds its own repetitions, both onscreen and behind the scenes, although it is sometimes unclear who has been trapped.

I

Should Shakespeare's plays be adapted into films? That was the question that occasioned a public dispute between Hitchcock and Harley Granville-Barker in 1937 in the pages of the BBC's weekly magazine *The Listener*. Granville-Barker, a stage actor and director, was in the midst of publishing his *Prefaces to Shakespeare*, a series of studies taking a theatre-focused approach to the plays. In the same year that he published his volume on *Hamlet*, Granville-Barker wrote an opinion piece in *The Listener* vociferously arguing against adaptations of Shakespeare on both film and radio. While Granville-Barker had only seen two such films – Max Reinhardt and William Dieterle's *A Midsummer Night's Dream* (1935) and George Cukor's *Romeo and Juliet* (1936) – he was convinced that cinematic adaptations of Shakespeare were an impossibility. The crux of Granville-Barker's accusation was that filmmakers are necessarily directed by visual priorities rather than fidelity to the text, and this instinct to show rather than tell evacuates Shakespeare's language of its power. For Granville-Barker, Shakespeare's 'medium and the cinema's have so little that really matters in common; their chief qualities, in fact, are so definitely opposed to each other, that I do not see how the two are ever to be reconciled'.[17]

Hitchcock, by now an established filmmaker and defensive about the cultural status of cinema, bristled at Granville-Barker's insinuation that film itself was inherently inferior to drama. In a response published the following week, Hitchcock inverts Granville-Barker's hierarchy: 'Shakespeare was an imaginative playwright – he wrote his scenes as taking place in forests and ships at sea. He had

almost the scenario writer's gift for keeping the story moving from setting to setting. But, for all his flow of imagination, sixteenth-century stagecraft let him down.... The cinema has come to Shakespeare's rescue.'[18] For Hitchcock, the visual language of filmmaking, rather than undermining the power of Shakespeare's poetry, in fact fulfils the promise of Shakespeare's imagination: in a teleological evolution of the arts, cinema represents an 'improvement' on the inherent limitations of literature and theatre.

However, in a surprising swerve in his argument, Hitchcock agrees with Granville-Barker about the incompatibility of Shakespeare and film, although on very different grounds. While Hitchcock knew that filmmakers since Méliès had found subjects in Shakespeare, this was specifically a calculated risk by a new film industry, 'for to the majority of the public anything connected with Shakespeare is as dull as ditchwater', 'too pregnant with classroom memories to smack of entertainment'. Hitchcock, who had been required to memorize Shakespeare as a student at St Ignatius College, knew exactly how much these 'classroom memories' could make for box office poison.[19] 'What is poetry to the busy housewife but a lot of nonsense and something they teach her kid at school? ... In other words, Shakespeare spells considerable gloom to the average mind of today.'

For Hitchcock, Shakespeare's soporific reputation was not a new theme. Seven years before his exchange with Harley Granville-Barker, Hitchcock had already satirized the idea of Shakespeare as popular entertainment in *Elstree Calling* (1930), a revue of musical hall numbers and comedy sketches. While Hitchcock's involvement in the production was limited, he was responsible for a thread that runs throughout the film in which an actor, played by Donald Calthrop, haplessly tries to prime the audience for his big Shakespeare performance.[20] Entering in an Elizabethan costume,

---

[16] Shoshana Felman, 'Turning the screw of interpretation', *Yale French Studies* 55/56 (1977), 94–201; pp. 101–2.

[17] Harley Granville-Barker, 'Alas, poor Will!', *The Listener* 17 (1937), 387–9, 425–6; p. 389.

[18] Alfred Hitchcock and Val Gielgud, 'Much ado about nothing?' *The Listener* 17 (1937), 448–50 (Hitchcock) and 450 (Gielgud). The essay is reprinted in Sidney Gottlieb, ed., *Hitchcock on Hitchcock: Selected Writings and Interviews* (Berkeley, 1995), 179–82.

[19] McGilligan, *Alfred Hitchcock*, p. 19.

[20] In Alain Kerzoncuf and Charles Barr's assessment, based on the Adrian Brunel scripts at the British Film Institute (BFI), Hitchcock, brought in after December 1929, simplified the Calthrop scenes

10 Shakespeare gets a pie in the face. Anna May Wong and Gordon Begg in *Elstree Calling* (directed by Adrian Brunel and Alfred Hitchcock, 1930).

Calthrop announces his intention to 'present to you Shakespeare in a manner befitting his great gen – ' but a closing curtain silences him. Undeterred, he pokes out again, and each time, another curtain closes, as he complains: 'They don't want to do my Shakespeare even though I told them that you can make Shakespeare just as entertaining as Lily Morris, who's coming on next, and I'm going to show them whether they like it or not, and I'm going to show *you* whether you like it or not!' Later in the show, Calthrop reappears, sneaking on screen dressed as a magician to address the audience secretly. 'As you know, Shakespeare is usually presented in a rather dull and uninteresting manner', he says before loudly declaiming Hamlet's 'To be or not to be' soliloquy while attempting to keep up his ruse by ineptly performing magic tricks involving a rabbit, a chicken and a butterfly net. Ironically, one of the first instances of 'To be or not to be' ever filmed[21] is delivered as a satire of the 'dull and uninteresting' performances that Hitchcock knew made Shakespeare 'dull as ditchwater' to the average filmgoer.[22] Fittingly, when Calthrop's big scene does arrive, his attempts to transform Shakespeare into '100% entertainment' result in a slapstick burlesque version of *The Taming of the Shrew*, culminating in Anna May Wong as Katherine throwing a custard pie at William Shakespeare himself, a symbolic act of *lèse-majesté* that underscores Shakespeare's status as an emblem of stuffy pretensions to be mocked (Figure 10).

The distance between popular cinema and Shakespeare's high-culture associations – conveniently emblematized by Hamlet's 'To be or not to be' soliloquy – not only was a subject for comedy, but could take on more sinister dimensions. In *The Man Who Knew Too Much*, the villainous Abbott (Peter Lorre) sends a thinly veiled threat to Jill Laurence that he will kill her husband and daughter if she does not comply with his demands: 'Tell Mrs Laurence that little Betty and her husband are very well. Tell her they may soon be leaving us. Leaving us for a long, long journey … How is it that Shakespeare says? "From which no traveler returns." Great poet.' Anticipating the dangerous cultured villains in later Hitchcock films (John Dall in *Rope*, James Mason in *North by Northwest*), Abbott's quotation from *Hamlet* and praise of Shakespeare signals his sadism, taking pleasure in a Shakespearian turn of phrase at the very moment he threatens to kill a father and daughter. Reading this moment in light of the cultural politics of Shakespearian quotation discussed by Douglas Lanier – whether or not we notice Abbott's misquotation – in the popular culture medium of film, the kind of character who would construct his high-culture credentials by quoting *Hamlet* and praising Shakespeare is marked as nefarious, as though the very cultural elitism that upholds Shakespearian cultural superiority is itself similarly suspect.[23]

In his 1937 essay in *The Listener*, then, Hitchcock remained unchanged in his wariness about the cultural distance between Shakespeare and cinema. And yet, despite their differences, Hitchcock and Granville-Barker implicitly agreed about the future of Shakespearian adaptation. While Granville-Barker thought the visual

---

and re-shot the *Taming of the Shrew* parody. See *Hitchcock Lost and Found: The Forgotten Films* (Lexington, 2015), pp. 90–7. See also Anthony R. Guneratne, *Shakespeare, Film Studies, and the Visual Cultures of Modernity* (New York, 2008), pp. 17–19.

21 For *Elstree Calling* in the context of other early examples, see Luke McKernan and Olwen Terris, *Walking Shadows: Shakespeare in the National Film and Television Archive* (London, 1994), p. 49.

22 Shakespeare plays a similar role in the early American sound showcase, MGM's *Hollywood Revue of 1929*, in which studio executives demand updated dialogue for *Romeo and Juliet* (Lanier, *Shakespeare and Modern*, p. 63).

23 On the rise of the Shakespeare-quoting villain, see Lanier, *Shakespeare and Modern*, pp. 66–7.

priorities of cinema will always betray Shakespeare's actual language, he offered the possibility that filmmakers might yet create Shakespearian adaptations by 'follow-[ing] Shakespeare's example': 'He stole the stories for his plays. Let the cinema steal the stories *of* his plays.... He drastically changed the stories to suit his dramatic purpose, without respect to their authors. Let the cinema boldly do the same to suit its pictorial purpose, without respect to him.'[24] Granville-Barker, then, strikes a paradoxical position. The author of *On Poetry in Drama* clearly found the essence of Shakespeare in the language spoken on stage and yet recognized the adaptive freedoms of filmmakers to use Shakespeare as a departure point for their own idiosyncratic visions: 'I reach then, after all, the satisfactory conclusion that Shakespeare in the cinema will do – with Shakespeare left out.'

This freer adaptive method was in fact one with which Hitchcock himself had already experimented: in the same year that *Elstree Calling* used Hamlet's 'To be or not to be' soliloquy to satirize the dullness of Shakespeare, another Hitchcock film explicitly cites *Hamlet* in its own story about a troupe of travelling actors and a secret murderer found out through an ingenious process of detection. Adapted from the novel *Enter Sir John*, by Clemence Dane and Helen Simpson, by Hitchcock, his wife Alma Reville and Walter C. Mycroft, *Murder!* (1930) involves the famous stage actor Sir John Menier (Herbert Marshall), who serves on the jury in the murder trial that finds the actress Diana Baring (Norah Baring) accused of killing her fellow actress Edna Druce. During deliberations, Sir John is the last member of the jury to entertain the possibility of Baring's innocence, but he is browbeaten into unanimity and she is found guilty and sentenced to death. Realizing that he was wrong, Sir John turns detective and, aided by another actor named Ted Markham, tries to discover the true murderer before Baring is hanged. As the investigation develops, clues point towards Handel Fane (Esme Percy), another performer in Baring's troupe. Watching Fane perform in a circus act, Sir John has an epiphany:

SIR JOHN Markham, I've an idea. Do you know your *Hamlet*?
MARKHAM Every line of it, sir.
SIR JOHN Then let me suggest for your consideration, the series of events embodied in act 3, scene 2.
MARKHAM That's the play scene, isn't it?
SIR JOHN Yes. The play scene. Do you remember the title, *The Mousetrap*?

When Markham asks what the 'cheese' in their mousetrap will be, Sir John informs him that he will offer Fane a juicy role in a new play to get him into his office, and once there, they will prepare a *Hamlet*-like mousetrap to test Fane's guilt. Even before the device itself, however, Sir John's epiphany while watching Fane's circus act has already re-enacted the moment of Hamlet's own revelation after witnessing the First Player's Hecuba speech:

> I have heard
> That guilty creatures sitting at a play
> Have, by the very cunning of the scene,
> Been struck so to the soul that presently
> They have proclaimed their malefactions

Whereas Hamlet's epiphany may have reminded early modern London audiences of the Norfolk woman who confessed to murder during a performance of 'Friar Francis',[25] Sir John explicitly cites *Hamlet* as the source for his idea. But his plan goes further: he will not simply add 'a speech of some dozen or sixteen lines', but write a scene from scratch, one that does not depend on inferred parallels between the dramatic action and the hidden crime as in *Hamlet*, but explicitly dramatizes the crime itself. When Fane arrives, Sir John asks him to read out a part of act 3 of a play about 'the inner history of the Baring case', having Fane act out the moment of the script right before the murder. As the scene develops, Fane becomes increasingly distraught as he is forced to re-enact his crime, until the script breaks off and Fane is left in agonized silence as the assembled onlookers behold his stricken, sweating face. This climactic scene not only repeats *Hamlet*'s play-within-the-play by forcing the murderer to confront the details of his own crime, but, in another turn of the screw, has the actor-murderer himself re-enact it in front of an audience, listening to the same words that motivated the killing in the first place. The layers of repetition and re-enactment in this scene are tightly nested: Fane's re-enactment of his crime is itself a re-enactment of *Hamlet*, a re-enactment just as true of the film itself.

If the use of *Hamlet* in *Murder!* then shows one variation on Shakespeare 'with Shakespeare left out' – Shakespearian situations stripped of Shakespearian language – another is suggested by *Secret Agent*, Hitchcock's 1936 spy thriller starring John Gielgud, Madeleine Carroll and Peter Lorre. While the film was

---

[24] Granville-Barker, 'Alas, poor Will!', p. 425.
[25] 'Friar Francis', Lost Plays Database, ed. Roslyn L. Knutson, David McInnis, Matthew Steggle and Misha Teramura, https://lostplays.folger.edu/Friar_Francis.

adapted from two stories in W. Somerset Maugham's *Ashenden: Or the British Agent* (1927), Gielgud recalled years later that 'Hitchcock seduced me into doing *The Secret Agent* by telling me it was *Hamlet* by other means.'[26] The appeal to Gielgud would have been clear. Throughout the early 1930s, Gielgud had established himself as one of the pre-eminent interpreters of the role. His first *Hamlet*, which opened in April 1930 at the Old Vic before transferring to the West End, was immediately hailed as 'the high-water mark of English Shakespearean acting in our time'.[27] Four years later, his West End revival ran to 155 performances in London before touring for a further five weeks. Triumphant onstage, Gielgud nevertheless rebuffed the offers from directors to produce film adaptations: keenly aware of the different approach that the new medium required, Gielgud had 'no wish to risk [his] stage Shakespeare reputation by appearing in what might be very unsatisfactory film versions of the same plays'.[28] Not only did the idea of trying to translate his celebrated Hamlet to the screen seem to him 'impossible' and 'ridiculous', but he failed to see 'how anybody would ever manage to make a totally satisfactory film of *Hamlet*'.[29] Hitchcock's description of *Secret Agent* as '*Hamlet* by other means' then offered an opportunity: by presenting a character *like* Hamlet but in the context of a spy thriller, Gielgud could break into the world of the cinema by drawing on his celebrated strengths without the risk of compromising his theatrical reputation.

The parallel between *Secret Agent* and *Hamlet* would have been obvious even from a description of the plot. Set during World War I, the film centres around the novelist and spy Edgar Brodie, who is sent to Switzerland under the assumed name of Richard Ashenden to kill a German agent. However, when the agent is identified and a plan is hatched to eliminate the target, Ashenden falters. 'We aren't hunting a fox, we're hunting a man', he says. 'Oh, I know it's war and it's our job to do it. But that doesn't prevent it being murder, does it? Simple murder.' When the opportunity presents itself during a mountain hike, Ashenden cannot bring himself to act. However, this Hamlet-like predicament – the inability to commit a murder to which he is bound – ultimately proves superficial, and, despite Hitchcock's claim that the film would be '*Hamlet* by other means', as Gielgud would grudgingly discover, *Secret Agent* was 'nothing of the kind'.[30] Unlike Hamlet's tortured inability to comprehend the reason for his delay, Ashenden's reasons for inaction are obvious, torn as he is between duty and conscience, and, as the film goes on, this Hamlet-like reluctance to murder is primarily experienced by Elsa (Madeleine Carroll). In retrospect, as Gielgud's use of the word 'seduction' suggests, Hitchcock's description of *Secret Agent* as a reimagined *Hamlet* was chiefly a ruse to hook Gielgud. What happened behind the scenes then inverted the *Mousetrap* scenario of repetition and re-enactment in *Murder!* The actor *wants* to re-enact a veiled version of his celebrated Hamlet, repeating on screen what he had already acted onstage. And yet the result is 'nothing of the kind': his shock comes in how *little* it resembles the original act. The 'crime' is not anterior to the play, it *is* the play, and the 'cheese' in Hitchcock's mousetrap was the cultural prestige of *Hamlet* itself.

However, just as Gielgud wanted to avoid the risk of compromising his reputation by attempting a Shakespearian performance on film, Hitchcock may have had similar reasons of his own, left unspoken in his 1937 *Listener* essay, for avoiding a Shakespearian adaptation. Despite his claims of disinterest ('The cinema can do without Shakespeare'), perhaps a more compelling reason had to do with what Elsie Walker has discussed as the complex dynamics of authorship at stake in all Shakespearian cinematic adaptations.[31] If filmmakers like Méliès might adapt Shakespeare precisely to align the new medium of cinema with high cultural prestige and to consolidate their own claims of authorship, Hitchcock was also aware that literary adaptations could in fact compromise a director's status as an auteur. In his famous 1962 interviews with Hitchcock, François Truffaut noted the director's 'reluctance to adapt great literary works to the screen', asking whether he would 'undertake the screen version of such a major classic as Dostoyevsky's *Crime and Punishment*, for instance'.[32] Hitchcock: 'Well, I shall never do that, precisely because *Crime and Punishment* is somebody else's achievement.' On the one hand, as Hitchcock went on to clarify, any novelistic masterpiece has already found the 'definitive form' of its material and any attempt to adapt it would compromise that

---

26 Quoted in Peter Conrad, 'From a vigorous Prospero, a farewell without tears', *New York Times*, 17 November 1991, Section 2, p. 18.

27 James Agate, quoted in Sheridan Morley, *John G: The Authorised Biography of John Gielgud* (London, 2001), p. 70.

28 Quoted in Morley, *John G*, p. 129.

29 Jonathan Croall, *John Gielgud: Matinee Idol to Movie Star* (London, 2011), p. 191.

30 Conrad, 'From a vigorous', p. 18.

31 Elsie Walker, 'Authorship: getting back to Shakespeare: whose film is it anyway?', in *A Concise Companion to Shakespeare on Screen*, ed. Diana E. Henderson (Malden, MA, 2006), 8–30.

32 François Truffaut, with the collaboration of Helen G. Scott, *Hitchcock*, revised ed. (New York, 1984), pp. 69, 71.

form. However, as Truffaut observed, the auteurist Hitchcock also preferred starting with less prestigious literary sources precisely so that 'they ultimately become a Hitchcock creation'. While actors such as Gielgud could be celebrated for their realizations of Shakespeare's plays onstage, Hitchcock's ideal of the filmmaker not as an interpreter but as an auteur made Shakespeare a risky choice – an author function so conspicuous that it would threaten to usurp his own. In this respect, Hitchcock's attitude gestures towards a parallel history of Shakespeare on film, one centred not on the adaptations that did get made, but on the reasons why filmmakers may have avoided Shakespeare in the first place. And yet it was arguably this very problem that shaped Hitchcock's vision for a modernized *Hamlet*.

II

The year 1945 was a pivotal moment in Hitchcock's career.[33] Since 1938, he had been under contract with David O. Selznick, the producer who persuaded him to move from London to Hollywood. Despite the success of the films Hitchcock directed during these years (for which he earned two Academy Award nominations), the collaboration with Selznick was often marked by tensions, as Hitchcock resented the amount of creative control that Selznick would exert throughout the filmmaking process. As the Selznick contract neared its end, Hitchcock began a partnership with Sidney Bernstein to start their own independent production company, Transatlantic Pictures, which would allow Hitchcock unprecedented creative control over his own films. One initial problem came with finding material to serve as the basis of new projects, since the fledgling Transatlantic Pictures found itself competing with bigger, richer studios, who had extensive staff for locating stories, and deeper pockets to pay for film rights.[34] It was under these conditions that Hitchcock sent a telegram to Bernstein:

493 BEVERLY HILLS CALIF 405 1/52 10
NLT SIDNEY BERNSTEIN CX 545
ARLINGTON HOUSE PICCADILLY LONDON
WOULD LIKE TO GET YOUR REACTION ON THE FOLLOWING IDEA FOR OUR ENGLISH PRODUCTION THIS IDEA WOULD ILLUSTRATE ITSELF CLEARER TO YOU IF I INDICATED THE BILLING WHICH WOULD BE QUOTE SYDNEY BERNSTEIN PRESENTS CARY GRANT AS ALFRED HITCHCOCKS HAMLET A MODERN THRILLER BY WILLIAM SHAKESPEARE UNQUOTE STOP AS YOU WILL SEE THE IDEA IS TO TAKE THE SHAKESPEARE TEXT AND TRANSCRIBE IT INTO MODERN ENGLISH THE PLAY WOULD HAVE AN ENGLISH SETTING AND WOULD BE

PRESENTED AS A PSYCHOLOGICAL MELODRAMA I WAS OVER TO SEE CARY GRANT YESTERDAY AT WARNERS STUDIO AND HE EXPRESSED GREAT ENTHUSIASM FOR THE IDEA I TOLD DAN OSHEA ABOUT IT AND HIS REACTION WAS THAT IT WOULD BE A TERRIFIC PIECE OF SHOWMANSHIP THE MOST ESSENTIAL THING WOULD BE TO MAKE CERTAIN THE PUBLIC REALIZED THAT THEY WOULD BE SEEING A MODERN STORY THE PROCESSES REQUIRED TO GET A SCRIPT OF THIS WOULD BE AS FOLLOWS FIRST OF ALL TO GET A PROFESSOR OF ENGLISH TO TAKE THE ORIGINAL PLAY AND DO A MODERN LANGUAGE VERSION OF IT THEN TO TURN THIS INTO A FILM TREATMENT AND TO REINTERPRET THE SITUATIONS INTO MODERN IDIOM AFTER THIS PROCESS HAS BEEN COMPLETED THE THE [*sic*] NEXT STEP WOULD BE TO TAKE THIS TREATMENT WITH ITS STRAIGHTFORWARD ENGLISH DIALOGUE AND HAVE IT GONE OVER BY A TOP PLAYWRIGHT FOR THE FINAL VERSION NATURALLY I AM CONCERNED ABOUT MAINTAINING SECRECY ON THIS BECAUSE THE IDEA IS IN PUBLIC DOMAIN AND COULD EASILY BE STOLEN IF IT LEAKED OUT BECAUSE IT IS A VERY HARD THING TO REGISTER FOR PRIORITY DO YOU THINK A SIMULTANEOUS ANNOUNCEMENT BOTH HERE AND IN LONDON WOULD BE THE BEST MEANS OF SAFE GUARDING THE PROPERTY ASSUMING YOU LIKE THE IDEA DO YOU THINK IT POSSIBLE FOR YOU TO FIND SOMEBODY TO DO THE FIRST DIALOGUE TRANSCRIPTION IN DIALOGUE FORM PREFERABLY A PROFESSOR OF ENGLISH BUT DEFINITELY NO ONE IN SHOW BUSINESS AFTER THIS IS COMPLETED THEN I WOULD LIKE TO HAVE SOME STOOGE WRITER CUT HERE SUCH AS JOCK ORTON WHO WOULD BE INEXPENSIVE BUT WHO WOULD CARRY OUT MY IDEA FOR THE PICTORIAL AND INCIDENTAL TREATMENT OF THE ACTION I THINK HE COULD BE GOTTEN FOR AROUND FIVE HUNDRED DOLLARS A WEEK WITH A SIX MONTHS GUARANTEE THE FINAL PHASE WE COULD DISCUSS TOGETHER WHEN YOU GET OUT. HERE PLEASE TELEPHONE ME IF YOU NEED ANY CLARIFICATION LOVE HITCH =

ALFRED HITCHCOCK[35]

In context, Hitchcock's decision to light on *Hamlet* as material for a film may have been in part conditioned by financial circumstances, since a play in the public

---

33 For context, see Moorehead, *Sidney Bernstein*; Leff, *Hitchcock and Selznick*; David Sterritt, 'From Transatlantic to Warner Bros.', in *A Companion to Alfred Hitchcock*, ed. Thomas Leitch and Leland Poague (Malden, MA, 2011), 309–28; McGilligan, *Alfred Hitchcock*, pp. 350–96.

34 McGilligan, *Alfred Hitchcock*, pp. 382–7.

35 Reproduced in Dan Auiler, *Hitchcock's Notebooks* (New York, 1999), p. 553. Dan O'Shea was an executive at Selznick

domain could be adapted without a bidding war. But the very idea of modernizing a Shakespearian play was itself something that could be scooped if another studio got wind of it, thus the urgently conspiratorial tone of the telegram with its insistence on 'maintaining secrecy'. Perhaps deliberately, this process of secretive adaptation – of rewriting an older text to reflect present circumstances – evokes events in *Hamlet* itself that Hitchcock had already reimagined on film: to adjust Felman's formulation, the scene of *adaptation* is a repetition of the scene dramatized in the text. And yet the telegram, the first document of the project's inception, shows Hitchcock already grappling with the problem of contested authorship that he would later acknowledge in his interviews with Truffaut. If his preference for a 'stooge writer' and a 'professor of English' safely removed from the entertainment industry to 'carry out my idea' serves as one way of consolidating his authorial control among the film's collaborators, the desired billing 'ALFRED HITCHCOCKS HAMLET A MODERN THRILLER BY WILLIAM SHAKESPEARE' purposely plays with authorship and temporality. Billing himself before Shakespeare, Hitchcock is given the primary possessive relation – this *Hamlet* will be *his*. And yet Shakespeare too is jarringly resurrected as the author of a 'modern thriller', marking the present in both time and genre. *The time is out of joint.*

Clearly, part of the purpose of this incongruous defamiliarization of Shakespeare was Hitchcock's insistence that audiences understand this would not be a 'dull as dishwater' Shakespeare adaptation, but rather Shakespeare 'with Shakespeare left out'. Predictably, Hitchcock took pains in press interviews to emphasize popular accessibility: the script would be 'as faithful as possible to Shakespeare's text, yet modern enough to appeal to the widest possible audience'. The idea of modernizing Shakespeare's language raised some eyebrows: one commentator in Australia was reminded of the satirist A. E. Wilson's 'Americanese' translation, 'To quit or not to quit; that's what I'm up against.'[36] However, when Cary Grant gave the press his own speculations about what the script might sound like, it was even further removed from Shakespeare's original: '"To be or not to be" will probably read "What the hell do I do now?"'[37] Beyond language, Hitchcock strategically made clear that neither would he be constrained by any reverence for Shakespearian dramaturgy: as he mused with calculated insouciance, 'The main trouble is that there are too many deaths at the end. We would

have to kill some of them off-screen, because we couldn't have so many corpses cluttering up the place.'[38]

Even the casting of Cary Grant was in itself part of this unsettling of Shakespearian expectations. Far from the prestigious training and stage experience of Gielgud, Grant had begun in vaudeville and became famous for his performances in light screwball comedies such as *Bringing Up Baby* (1938), *His Girl Friday* (1940) and *Arsenic and Old Lace* (1944). When Robert Helpmann, who had just performed Hamlet in 1944 at the Old Vic under the direction of Tyrone Guthrie, heard about Hitchcock's casting choice, he was appalled by the incongruity between Grant's on-screen personality and the role, with not a little jealousy. 'Hamlet was an introvert – that's me', Helpmann complained. 'I *am* Hamlet.'[39] Even Grant himself publicly commented on the oddity that he should take on the role: 'Isn't it funny? ... I'm the only actor in the world who never had any ambition to play Hamlet, and I'm liable to end up doing it.'[40] Of course, this was all part of Hitchcock's plan: casting against type was not only a financially prudent way of assuring his audiences that this would not be dull schoolroom Shakespeare, but also a way of signalling that this at once was and was not Shakespeare's play.

Beyond the specifics of language and setting, the most salient aspect of Hitchcock's modernized *Hamlet* project was its generic melodrama, another signal of both authorial and temporal appropriation – at once a savvy strategy for marketing the story to a wide audience while also implicitly signalling the ways Hitchcock planned to approach the film. In a 1950 interview with the *New York Times*, as he elaborated on his idea that most films' plots are fundamentally constructed as a chase, Hitchcock was asked whether *Hamlet* met the same criteria. 'I'd say there's certainly a chase in *Hamlet*', Hitchcock responded, 'because Hamlet is a detective.'[41] In billing the project as a 'modern thriller', Hitchcock presumably implied that

---

International Pictures and J. O. C. Orton had co-written Hitchcock's 1944 propaganda film *Bon Voyage*.
36 'Uncle Samlet', *Mail* (Adelaide, Australia), 1 September 1945, p. 4. Cf. A. E. Wilson, *Theatre Guyed: The Baedeker of Thespia* (London, 1935), p. 80.
37 Earl Wilson, 'Grant's in town', *Times Recorder* (Zanesville, OH), 25 February 1946, p. 4.
38 Thomas, 'Hollywood', p. 10.
39 Mary Elsom, 'Report for weeks ended 22 & 29th Sept [1945]', in AHP, file 1410.
40 Thomas, 'Hollywood', p. 10.
41 Alfred Hitchcock, 'Core of the movie – the chase', *New York Times Magazine*, 29 October 1950, 22.

Hamlet's pursuit of Claudius, as Sir John in *Murder!* had already foreshadowed, could be generically reimagined in the context of a murder mystery. And yet, as the second generic distinction makes clear, Hitchcock also recognized the second level of mystery was internal to Hamlet himself. As Margreta de Grazia has discussed, the famous problem of Hamlet's delay had long attracted the attention of psychologists as early as the field's nascency in the late eighteenth century, who found in Hamlet's contradictions and opacity a character who fundamentally does not understand himself or his motivations ('I do not know / Why yet I live to say "This thing's to do," / Sith I have cause, and will, and strength, and means / To do 't').[42] While books such as W. Dyson Wood's *Hamlet; From a Psychological Point of View* (1870) attempted to bring medical understanding to unlock Hamlet's mysteries, it was of course Freud's discussion of the play in *The Interpretation of Dreams* (1899) that would prove the most influential, especially as it was expanded upon by his disciple Ernest Jones, who published 'The Œdipus-Complex as an explanation of Hamlet's mystery: a study in motive' in 1910.[43] By the 1930s, Jones's Freudian interpretation of the play had begun to influence performers, convincing Laurence Olivier in 1937 that 'Hamlet was a prime sufferer from the Oedipus complex.'[44]

Whether or not Hitchcock intended to make the Freudian approach itself central to his own *Hamlet*, his suggestion that Hamlet's 'soliloquies might be recited on a psychoanalyst's couch' clearly intended to incorporate the psychoanalytical critical approaches into the world of the narrative itself.[45] This was another commercially shrewd move: Hitchcock's own *Spellbound* (1945) was among the earliest films to capitalize on the rise of psychoanalysis in American culture, boosted by an influx of European therapists displaced by World War II and the anticipation of traumatized soldiers returning from the battlefield, and throughout the later 1940s the 'psychological melodrama' as a cinematic genre would continue to draw on the increasing familiarity with Freudian psychology.[46] *Hamlet*, then, was a ready-made, royalty-free way to reimagine a well-known cultural object in trendy contemporary terms, and the immense commercial success of *Spellbound* after its fall release would have only confirmed Hitchcock's instincts.

Seen in the light of Hitchcock's career, his proposed 'modern thriller' version of *Hamlet* would have clearly avoided the pitfalls he identified in his debate with Harley Granville-Barker, underscoring that this would indeed be Shakespeare 'with Shakespeare left out'. In fact, although Hitchcock would avoid the risk of adapting classic works of literature, there may have been a special appeal of inaugurating the phase of his career after Selznick with a project that could stake a claim for his directorial authorship by taking a classic and showing how *un*-faithful he could be – or, rather, how much he could apply his own distinctive directorial style in making 'ALFRED HITCHCOCKS HAMLET'. Even after Cary Grant pulled out and Transatlantic Pictures was dissolved, Hitchcock did not give up on the idea. In a 1955 interview for *Cahiers du Cinéma*, once the lawsuit had been finally dismissed, Hitchcock was asked for an update: 'for the moment I've abandoned the project, but I may take it up again. A modern Hamlet but with exactly the same problems.'[47]

According to Stanley Cavell, Hitchcock *did* attempt a modern *Hamlet* in *North by Northwest* (1959): in Cavell's reading, the title's suggestive allusion cues the viewer to notice a series of *Hamlet* echoes in that film's narrative of mistaken identity and subterfuge. Other critics have found similar resonances in *Vertigo* (Kim Novak's

---

[42] Margreta de Grazia, *Hamlet without 'Hamlet'* (Cambridge, 2007), pp. 160–5.

[43] Jones would later expand his argument to nearly 100 pages as 'A psycho-analytic study of Hamlet', the first chapter in his *Essays in Applied Psycho-analysis* (London, 1923), and eventually his influential 1949 monograph *Hamlet and Oedipus* (London).

[44] Laurence Olivier, *Confessions of an Actor* (London, 1982), p. 102; quoted in Peter Donaldson, 'Olivier, Hamlet, and Freud', *Cinema Journal* 26 (1987), 22–48; p. 23.

[45] Hitchcock's suggestion that 'the ghost might end up a ouija board' at once reflects the director's general avoidance of the supernatural and also implies a level of ambiguity in the film about whether Hamlet's father genuinely communicates from beyond the grave or whether the message is some version of Hamlet's own unacknowledged desires, an idea later implied in the 1948 film by Olivier, who played both Hamlet and the Ghost.

[46] Maureen Turim, 'Fictive psyches: the psychological melodrama in 40s films', *boundary 2* 12/13 (1983), 321–31; Jonathan Freedman, 'From *Spellbound* to *Vertigo*: Alfred Hitchcock and therapeutic culture in America', in *Hitchcock's America,* ed. Jonathan Freedman and Richard Millington (New York, 1999), 77–98; Nicholas Haeffer, *Alfred Hitchcock* (New York, 2014), p. 85.

[47] François Truffaut and Claude Chabrol, 'Entretien avec Alfred Hitchcock', *Cahiers du Cinéma* 8 (February 1955), 19–31; p. 27; translated by James M. Vest in Sidney Gottlieb, ed., *Hitchcock on Hitchcock: Selected Writings and Interviews*, vol. 2 (Oakland, 2015), 191–200; p. 197. On Chabrol's own cinematic reimagining of *Hamlet*, see Karen Newman, *Essaying Shakespeare* (Minneapolis, 2009), pp. 77–84.

11 A Shakespearian epigraph. *Spellbound* (directed by Alfred Hitchcock, 1945).

Ophelia-like plunge into San Francisco Bay), *Psycho* (Oedipal mother–son dynamic), *Shadow of a Doubt* (murderous uncle) and even *The Birds* ('our little hamlet').[48] But arguably the film that bears the most complex and significant intertextual relationship with *Hamlet* is the very film that Hitchcock was completing when the idea for the modernized adaptation occurred to him – namely, *Spellbound* (1945), a film about memory and forgetting, madness and sanity, concealed murder, fratricide, organized around a double mystery (criminal and psychological), and the most explicitly psychoanalytical of all Hitchcock films. While the absence of direct allusions to *Hamlet* might categorize this film among what Eric S. Mallin has called 'non-adaptations' – or, 'movies that do not know they are Shakespeare plays'[49] – the film's insistent foregrounding of psychoanalysis as a method of interpretation provides a method by which to seek out its submerged Shakespearian intertext, and, with it, cunningly constructs Hitchcock's status as an auteur.

III

Spellbound begins with a Shakespearian epigraph, as the words 'The fault ... is not in our stars, / But in ourselves ... ' appear on screen imposed above a wide shot showing the grounds of the Green Manors psychiatric hospital (Figure 11). In the next shot, we move closer to Green Manors, and a longer text moves across the screen:

Our story deals with psychoanalysis, the method by which modern science treats the emotional problems of the sane. The analyst seeks only to induce the patient to talk about his hidden problems, to open the locked doors of his mind. Once

---

[48] James M. Vest, 'Reflections of Ophelia (and of *Hamlet*) in Alfred Hitchcock's *Vertigo*', *Journal of the Midwest Modern Language Association* 22 (1989), 1–9; Tony Howard, 'Mr. Hitchcock's Shakespeare', *Around the Globe: The Magazine of Shakespeare's Globe* (Winter 1999), 33; Tom Cohen, *Hitchcock's Cryptonymies*, vol. 2: *War Machines* (Minneapolis, 2005), p. 59.

[49] Mallin, *Reading Shakespeare*, p. 1.

the complexes that have been disturbing the patient are uncovered and interpreted, the illness and confusion disappear ... and the devils of unreason are driven from the human soul.

This will be the central narrative problem of *Spellbound*, as Ingrid Bergman, playing the psychoanalyst Dr Constance Petersen, labours to unlock the doors of Gregory Peck's troubled mind. An amnesiac who cannot remember his name, Peck's character believes that he has committed a murder and Constance's quest is both to save him from his psychological complexes and, thereby, to prove his innocence. As Jonathan Freedman observes, this was an innovation for American films, in which psychoanalysis was often associated with charlatanry or even criminality: 'it was in *Spellbound* that psychoanalysis first became, for the Hollywood cinema, the means of solving a crime, not a means of committing one', exploiting the now-familiar homology between psychoanalytic interpretation and crime detection.[50] Indeed, these are intimately connected in *Spellbound*, a story that juxtaposes two mysteries in need of solution – the true perpetrator of a murder, and the psychological cause of a man's amnesia. The relationship between the film's two prefatory texts then is apparently straightforward: the clinical definition of psychoanalysis provides a medicalizing gloss on the Shakespearian 'fault ... in ourselves' as psychological complexes awaiting discovery. However, the juxtaposed texts invite another reading, whereby the relationship between the two might work inversely. If the psychoanalytic quest depicted in the film invites the audience to watch the film itself psychoanalytically, enfolding cinematic interpretation into the homology of psychoanalysis and crime detection, could it be that the 'story' presents its own locked doors behind which is a Shakespearian 'complex', eclipsed by narrative amnesia, waiting to be uncovered?

When the film opens, Green Manors is undergoing a transition of leadership.[51] The ageing Dr Murchison (Leo G. Carroll) has been unwillingly replaced as head of the hospital by the celebrated Dr Anthony Edwardes (Gregory Peck), whom none of the hospital's staff has yet met, but whose psychoanalytical writings are well known to Dr Constance Petersen (Ingrid Bergman). When he arrives, the new doctor is handsome, charismatic and surprisingly young, but Constance soon notices him exhibiting erratic behaviour, becoming distressed whenever he sees 'dark lines' on white backgrounds, such as fork marks on a white tablecloth or

the stitching on Constance's robe. His most extreme outburst comes when the doctors observe the surgery of a patient named Mr Garmes, who, racked with guilt believing that he has killed his father, has cut his own throat. During the surgery, Edwardes becomes agitated again, shouting, 'He did it. He told me. He killed his father. Put the lights on!', before he faints. When he regains consciousness, he confesses to Constance: 'I remember now: Edwardes is dead. I killed him and took his place.' As the sequence of disclosures unfolds, the resonances with *Hamlet* come into focus: the new head of Green Manors is a fraud who has taken the rightful place of the man he has murdered, and the moment that precipitates this revelation is one that mirrors his crime back to him – although not a literal performance, it is in an operating *theatre* that he encounters another man guilty of the same crime of murder that he himself has concealed.[52] Being forced to confront the semblance of his own crime, combined with the gaze of those beholding the agitated guilt of their new leader, becomes too much to bear. 'Put the lights on!', he shouts. (Claudius: 'Give me some light. Away!')

This question of the impostor's guilt becomes the central problem that the psychoanalyst-detective Constance tries to solve by probing his interior. However, the nature of this investigation is inverted: she is convinced that he is actually innocent and that his memories of murder are purely delusional. Ironically, the real Anthony Edwardes had written about this phenomenon in his book *Labyrinth of the Guilt Complex*, which describes the very condition that Constance believes Peck's character experiences: a traumatic event has caused him to forget his identity and to feel guilt for a murder he did not commit. Peck's character, whose initials are discovered to be J. B., is convinced that his amnesia is a psychological reaction to his crime: 'You remain sane by forgetting something too horrible to remember. You put the horrible thing behind a closed door.' As Constance insists: 'We have to open that

---

50   Freedman, 'From *Spellbound*', pp. 82–3. Freedman's splendid reading goes on to show how the film subverts the very legitimization of psychoanalysis it seems to establish.

51   *Spellbound* was written by Hitchcock and Ben Hecht, very loosely adapted from Hilary Saint George Saunders and John Palmer's 1927 novel *The House of Dr. Edwardes*.

52   In an earlier treatment for the film, developed by Hitchcock and Angus MacPhail in 1944, this confession occurs after 'Dr Edwardes' becomes distressed rehearsing a scene from Congreve's *The Way of the World* with a group of patients, a more explicitly theatrical analogy with Hamlet's *The Mousetrap* (AHP, file 646).

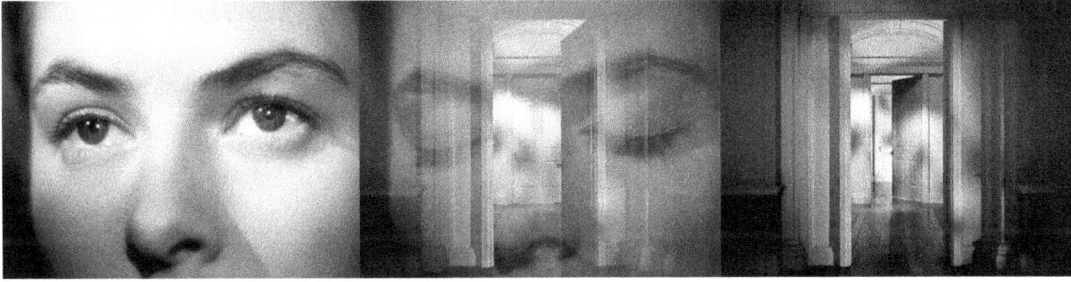

12 Opening the locked doors of the mind. Ingrid Bergman in *Spellbound* (directed by Alfred Hitchcock, 1945).

door.' However, while J. B.'s case of amnesia represents the central psychological problem of the film, the same issues of incomplete self-knowledge are universal. Soon after 'Dr Edwardes' arrives, Constance finds his book in the library and enters his room before she has her own moment of revelation: 'I thought I wanted to discuss your book with you. I'm amazed at the subterfuge. I don't want to discuss it at all. . . . It's quite remarkable to discover that one isn't what one thought one was.' Earlier that day, during a lunchtime stroll, Constance had been cynically discussing the discrepancy between the actual experience of love and the expectations set by artistic representations. Poets, she says, make people expect love to be like a 'flight of angels', 'embraces to be like Shakespearean dramas'. But that night, when the two lovers finally do embrace, a close-up of Constance's face fades to a series of doors, slowly opening in sequence, creating a corridor that grows deeper and deeper (Figure 12). The visual symbolic language of the moment underscores Constance's self-revelation: that, in truth, she did not want to discuss a book, but rather her love. But these opening doors, aligned as they are with the cinematic screen, also invite the viewer to wonder what remains sealed off behind the closed doors of the film's narrative: perhaps if the film puts *love* on the surface, what lies behind this surface is a *book* after all, and a Shakespearian drama specifically.

The growing love between Constance and J. B., and her quest to exonerate him, is always haunted by the spectre of an unnamed story that he can never quite remember and the possibility that his fragile sanity may give way to violence. Often, when triggered by some stimulus that evokes this buried memory, J. B. lashes out against Constance with abusive, often misogynistic, outbursts ('If there's anything I hate, it's a smug woman'). Throughout the film, the recurring trigger is the sight of dark lines on a white backdrop, and when they arrive at the Rochester home of Constance's mentor Dr Alexander Brulov, the lines of shadow on the white bedspread

immediately provoke a violent reaction from J. B.: 'Don't stand there with your wiseacre look. I'm sick of your double-talk.' Constance, the consummate analyst, urges him: 'The night you kissed me, you pushed me away because of my robe. It was white; it had dark lines on it. Try to think. Why does the color white frighten you? Why do lines frighten you?' Within the narrative of the film, we come to discover what the origin of this aversion is: the dark ski tracks made on white snow the day that the real Edwardes was killed. And yet, lurking behind the closed door of the film, we might suspect a deeper visual analogy: that of lines of words on a white page, implying that the repressed narrative is not simply a life experience but specifically a *text*. Indeed, it is at these moments, when J. B. confronts the visual reminders of the story he suppresses, that he most resembles the 'mad' Hamlet in his misogynistic abuse of Ophelia ('God hath given you one face, and you make yourselves another.... Go to, I'll no more on 't. It hath made me mad').

However, the most consequential reimagining of *Hamlet* occurs during the film's most famous episode, the surrealist dream sequence designed by Salvador Dalí. Despite J. B.'s initial reluctance to recount his dreams to Constance and Alex ('I don't believe in dreams; that Freud stuff's a lot of hooey'), he eventually submits to their analysis. Throughout the sequence, Peck's narration is visually illustrated as a surrealist film-within-a-film: gambling tables with women's legs, curtains painted with giant eyes, a chimney with tree roots, a veiled figure holding a melting wheel, the shadow of wings moving across the face of a pyramid. What we see in this opaquely symbolic imagery is a refracted version of a murder that transpired before the film began – indeed, setting in motion the events of the film's main narrative: a kind of *Mousetrap*, as stylistically distinct from the rest of Hitchcock's film as the mannered rhetoric of *The Mousetrap* is from the rest of *Hamlet*. As in *Hamlet*, the nature of the relationship between re-presentation and reality must be discovered: it is at once a question of *whether* this film-within-the-film reflects a murder (did J. B. kill the real Edwardes?) and *how* it does so (what do the cryptic symbols of the dream mean?). As the unconscious deviser of the dream and the one who stages it for himself, J. B. is at once author, actor and audience – Hamlet, Player and Claudius. Ironically, the clues from this dream, as correctly interpreted by Constance, while confirming J. B.'s innocence of killing Edwardes, will ultimately result in two real murders being discovered. At the end of the film, the *Mousetrap* scene replays yet again when Constance describes J. B.'s dream to the real killer, who, Claudius-like, correctly recognizes that this stylized representation of reality incriminates him. More disturbing, however, is the revelation, unanticipated by anyone, that J. B. as a child had accidentally killed his brother. 'That's what has haunted you all your life', Constance confirms: the ghost of fratricide has caused J. B.'s madness.

Perhaps more important than the dream itself is the idea of what dreams represent. As the Freud-like Alex explains to J. B.: 'They tell you what you are trying to hide. But they tell it to you all mixed up, like pieces of a puzzle that don't fit. The problem of the analyst is to examine this puzzle and put the pieces together in the right place.' If *Spellbound* invites the audience to turn an analyst's eye to the film itself, the narrative that it depicts – of discovering the repressed origin story that J. B. cannot acknowledge, one critically evoked by dark lines on a white background – arguably dangles the possibility that there is a textual origin story that the film itself has been repressing, and that if the audience is to reassemble the mixed-up puzzle pieces of that story, perhaps that story is *Hamlet*, the text that Hitchcock would soon propose to film as a 'psychological thriller' just like *Spellbound* itself.

Did Hitchcock *intend* for these parallels with *Hamlet* throughout *Spellbound*? Did Hitchcock hope that these scattered echoes would trigger the audience's sense that they had experienced this before, like Claudius watching *The Mousetrap* – what James Newlin has discussed as the 'uncanny' recognition of a Shakespearian intertext?[53] Or does the relationship work the opposite way? Hitchcock at one point wanted to name the film *Hidden Impulse*,[54] a title that at once describes the psychological problem depicted in the narrative while also suggestively implying that the film itself is the product of creative instincts not fully understood. If *Spellbound* invites the audience to read its surface psychoanalytically, might the fractured echoes of *Hamlet* throughout the film imply

a singular mind that has repressed and re-presented this narrative?

In August 1945, after filming on *Spellbound* had been completed (and the day after Hitchcock announced his plans for *Hamlet*), Paul MacNamara at Vanguard Films proposed an idea for a trailer, in which Hitchcock himself would address the audience about the dark layers of the human mind, the possibility that anyone could be a murderer.[55] The script for this proposed trailer survives among the Hitchcock papers at the Academy of Motion Picture Arts and Sciences.[56] In it, Hitchcock sits in an empty projection room. As he speaks, the image on a projecting screen shows footage from *Spellbound*: 'That screen up there is like a mind', Hitchcock would say to the viewer, 'we here in Hollywood can make anything happen there.' In the conceit of the trailer, the screen 'like a mind' at first might be understood to be the captive mind of the audience, controlled by the director. But the physical arrangement seems to cast the screen as a visualization of the *director's* mind, the expression of his innermost thoughts. This is how the trailer begins:

```
FADE IN
  INT. PROJECTION ROOM SEMI-LONG SHOT
(FROM REAR OF ROOM)
  A man is sitting in the middle of the pro
jection room, his back to the camera. The
room is lighted, and there is nothing on
the square patch of screen in the back-
ground. The man sits quietly looking up at
the empty screen; after a moment, he begins
to speak, without turning.

          MAN
There are stranger things in heaven and
earth, Horatio, than are dreamed of in our
philosophy .... Shakespeare said that ....

(pause; then the man turns casually, look-
ing fully into the camera and into the audi-
ence's face as he places one arm lesiurely
[sic] over the back of the seat)
```

53 James Newlin, *Uncanny Fidelity: Recognizing Shakespeare in Twenty-First-Century Film and Television* (Tuscaloosa, 2024).
54 Leff, *Hitchcock and Selznick*, p. 160.
55 Paul MacNamara to Alfred Hitchcock, 24 August 1945, in AHP, file 651.
56 Mel Dinelli, 'Suggested Trailer Material for "Spellbound"', 3 September 1945, in AHP, file 650. The complete text is reproduced in Auiler, *Hitchcock's Notebooks*, pp. 556–9.

THE CAMERA MOVES IN TO

CLOSE SHOT THE MAN

> MAN
>
> I'm Alfred Hitchcock .... and I've just fin-
> ished directing a picture which deals with
> some of those strange things Mr.
> Shakespeare spoke of .... it's called
> 'Spellbound', and it stars Miss Ingrid
> Bergman and Mr. Gregory Peck ....

In this paratext to the film, the (mis)quotation from *Hamlet* does complex work in conditioning the audience's expectations. At the most literal level, 'Hitchcock' seems to say that the story of *Spellbound* will depict strange events that exceed the bounds of everyday thought. But the phrasing also implies that what the film 'deals with' is, in fact, 'some of those strange things Mr. Shakespeare spoke of" – namely, the strange events of *Hamlet*. A smoking gun? Perhaps. But what exactly has happened? Is this disclosure inten-tional, a calculated clue to the audience, an act of misquotation showing the text of *Hamlet* already undergoing a Hitchcockian transformation? Or has 'Hitchcock' made a Freudian slip, unwittingly reveal-ing the repressed intertext that haunts the film? The ambiguity is in turn glossed by the quotation itself: the inadequacy of 'our philosophy' implies not only that rational thinking cannot fully comprehend the realities of the world, but also the fallibility of the mind to comprehend even itself. The trailer not only cues the audience (intentionally or not) to detect the puzzle pieces of *Hamlet* in the film, but positions Hitchcock as the thinking subject whose film – like a dream that plays upon the screen of the mind – exceeds the bounds of even his complete comprehension. It is a film, moreover, in which the depiction of psycho-analysis encourages the viewer to take on the role of analyst, to unlock the closed doors. And yet, as potentially vulnerable as this analytical scrutiny would seem to make the director, in one final turn of the screw, we can recognize this in fact to be the ruse of the auteur: to frame the film as the product of one singular directorial mind eclipses the labour and creativity of all those who collaborate in the filmmak-ing process. By assuming the ostensibly privileged position of the analyst, the audience implicitly ratifies Hitchcock's claims of authorship: the very attempt to put together the mixed-up puzzle pieces of *Hamlet* throughout *Spellbound* is to find oneself unwittingly caught in Hitchcock's mousetrap.

GERMAN HERMENEUTICS OF RACECRAFT IN THOMAS OSTERMEIER'S *OTHELLO* (2010)

NORA GALLAND

The idea of this article initially stemmed from the apparent gap between Anglo-American theatre and Continental Europe in regard to racial representation. Speaking about Laurence Olivier's blackface performance as Othello at the Chichester Festival Theatre in 1964, Steven Berkoff argued he was lucky 'to witness this great event before the fiends of political correctness in all their self-righteousness had struck a no-go zone for white actors on that particular role.... Great drama is colourblind.'[1] In Anglo-American theatre, Berkoff deplored the fact that over the past decades most of the actors playing Othello have been Black, while a consensus gradually developed to condemn blacked-up white actors as offensive and racist. Analogously, in 2015, Stanley Wells urged the theatre industry to 'grow up' and to allow white actors to play the part of Othello.[2]

There is a significant contrast in the way theatrical embodiment is conceived on stage in the UK and the US, on the one hand, and in Continental Europe on the other hand – a contrast which is directly related to the understanding of race in both geographical areas. Even though Critical Race Theory (CRT) has been developed in the 1990s as a theoretical framework used to address the intricacies of American race relations, it is possible – and necessary – to resort to CRT to address the issue of race in Continental Europe without projecting the American realities onto the European continent and falling into the traps of 'dehistoricization', 'derealization' and 'false universalization'. Fatima El-Tayeb points out that Continental Europe does have a specific way of perceiving and constructing race, which should not be regarded as a cultural and social monopoly of the UK or the US. She argues that Europe perceives itself as a continent 'free of race (and by implication racism)' and that addressing race in a Continental European context implies 'violat[ing] the powerful narrative of Europe as

a colorblind continent'.[3] Over the past few years, Continental Europe has thus been struggling to face its inherent systemic racism, mainly because of the myth of a 'colour-blind' society. Conceptual tools are therefore crucial to deconstruct both white supremacy and the fantasy of 'colour-blindness' in Europe, and CRT is a valuable framework as it engages with race critically and may shed a new light on theatrical practices such as casting.

Thomas Ostermeier's temporary experimentation with blackface is a striking example of rethinking the representation of race on stage. In his 2010 production of *Othello*, the German stage-director raised this question by casting a white actor, Sebastian Nakajew, to play the eponymous Black character. Ostermeier's tradaptation – an adaptation relying on a translation of the dramatic text – premiered during the Hellenic Festival Epidaurus in Greece (August 2010) before opening in Berlin (October 2010). The archival film was shot in the teething phase of this production while Ostermeier was still experimenting to come up with a relevant way to deal with race on stage. Blackface was not used after the shooting of this archival video; it was clearly ruled out by Ostermeier in the following performances. Indeed, Nakajew appears without face or body make-up in photos and videos from Epidaurus, and in all photos on the Schaubühne website and from a touring appearance in

[1] Georgia Snow, 'Steven Berkoff attacks "no-go zone" for white actors', *The Stage*, 17 June 2015, www.thestage.co.uk/news/steven-berkoff-attacks-no-go-zone-for-white-actors.

[2] Georgia Snow, 'Stanley Wells: "White actors should be allowed to play 'Othello'"', *The Stage*, 8 May 2015, www.thestage.co.uk/news/stanley-wells-white-actors-should-be-allowed-to-play-othello.

[3] Fatima El-Tayeb, *European Others: Queering Ethnicity in Postnational Europe* (Minneapolis, 2011), p. 81.

Paris in 2011. What does it mean to represent Othello's race onstage? Is the visual presence of his Blackness essential? The director and actors evidently struggled with these questions long after the production had premiered.

Before devoting a thorough analysis to Ostermeier's production, a brief state of the field regarding the existing studies on the history of blackface, *Othello* and theatre in Germany is necessary to comprehend the dynamics at stake in Ostermeier's case. From the 2010s onward, blackface in Germany has particularly drawn the attention of critics; a series of articles was published on the online platform 'Textures' set up by the International Research Center for Advanced Studies on Interweaving Performance Cultures of the Freie Universität Berlin: Joy Kristin Kalu's 'On the myth of authentic representation: Blackface as reenactment'; '"Ich bin kein Nazi!" – the blackface debate in the German mainstream media' by Julia Lemmle; Daniela Daude's 'Racialization in contemporary German theater'; Sharon Dodua Otoo's '(Ab)using Fadoul and Elisio: unmasking representations of whiteness in German theatre'; and Sandrine Micossé-Aikins's 'Not just a Blackened face'.[4] These publications came in the wake of a major scholarly symposium entitled 'Blackface, Whiteness, and the Power of Definition in German Contemporary Theatre' and funded by the Freie Universität Berlin in October 2012. Jonathan Wipplinger also contributed to the scholarship on German blackface with his article 'The racial ruse: on Blackness and Blackface comedy in "fin-de-siècle" Germany'.[5] Somehow, all this research on blackface and race in Germany is always connected to the power – more or less obvious – of white supremacy and its way of influencing our understanding of race and representation.

The issue of Othello's Blackness and the possibility of resorting to blackface on the German stage has been the focus of many articles published over the past few years as well. In his emblematic chapter 'How Black must Othello be? Polemical reflections on the representation of cultural foreignness in theatre', Christopher Balme points out that German theatre prefers a metaphorical aesthetic of representation to deal with race, arguing that it is not uncommon to have a white actor playing a Black character on the German contemporary stage.[6] Likewise, in 'Who is Othello? On the construction of identity and foreignness in contemporary productions of Shakespeare's Othello' (my translation), Miriam Dreysse explores the representation of Othello's racial identity on the German stage

with a focus on Stefan Pucher's 2004 production of the play with a white Othello in blackface.[7] She claims that, in this performance, blackface is a masquerade, the artificiality of which denounces the racist dimension of the theatrical practice. In 2015, with 'Race, guilt and "innocence": facing blackfacing in contemporary German theater', Katrin Sieg intends to assert that blackface is part of the German cultural tradition in theatre but also that it is not an offensive practice.[8]

In this article, I will build my argument on this scholarship, arguing that blackfacing is an artificial metaphor to represent race on stage and that the impact (offensive and abusive) can sometimes be different from the intention (a critique of racism). More recently, Alessandra Bassey published 'Brown, never Black: Othello on the Nazi stage', in which she explores the denial of Othello's dark skin in the Nazi era; and Bettina Boecker addressed the racial difference of Othello in her chapter 'A tragedy? *Othello* and *The Merchant of Venice* in Germany during the 2015–16 refugee crisis'.[9] In 2022,

---

4   Joy Kristin Kalu, 'On the myth of authentic representation: Blackface as reenactment' Textures, 2012, www.textures-archiv.geisteswissenschaften.fu-berlin.de/index.html%3Fp=2616.html; Julia Lemmle, '"Ich bin kein Nazi!" – the Blackface debate in the German mainstream media', Textures, 2014, www.textures-archiv.geisteswissenschaften.fu-berlin.de/index.html%3Fp=3142.html; Daniele Daude, 'Racialization in contemporary German theater', Textures, 12 May 2014, www.textures-archiv.geisteswissenschaften.fu-berlin.de/index.html%3Fp=3467.html; Sharon Dodua Otoo, '(Ab)using Fadoul and Elisio: unmasking representations of whiteness in German theatre', 27 May 2014, www.textures-archiv.geisteswissenschaften.fu-berlin.de/index.html%3Fp=3216.html; Sandrine Micossé-Aikins, 'Not just a Blackened face', Textures, 2013, www.textures-archiv.geisteswissenschaften.fu-berlin.de/wp-content/uploads/2013/12/micosse-aikins_not_just_a_blackened_face_2013_12.pdf.

5   Jonathan Wipplinger, 'The racial ruse: on Blackness and Blackface comedy in "fin-de-siècle" Germany', *German Quarterly* 84 (2011), 457–76.

6   Christopher Balme, 'Wie schwarz muss Othello sein? Polemische Überlegungen zur Repräsentation kultureller Fremdheit in Theater', in *Inszenierungen. Theorie, Ästhetik, Medialität. Ausgewählte Beiträge des Kongresses 'Ästhetik der Inszenierung'*, ed. Christopher Balme and Jürgen Schläder (Stuttgart, 2002), 105–16.

7   Miriam Dreysse, 'Wer ist Othello? Zur Konstruktion von Identität und Fremdheit in zeitgenössischen Inszenierungen von Shakespeares Othello', in *Theater und Subjektkonstitution: Theatrale Praktiken zwischen Affirmation und Subversion*, ed. Nadine Peschke and Nikola Schellmann (Berlin, 2012), 587–601.

8   Katrin Sieg, 'Race, guilt and "innocence": facing Blackfacing in contemporary German theater', *German Studies Review* 37 (2015), 117–34.

9   Alessandra Bassey, 'Brown, never Black: Othello on the Nazi stage', *Multicultural Shakespeare: Translation, Appropriation and Performance* 22

Lawrence Guntner offered a critical overview of the representation of the Moor of Venice on the German stage, from a performance in Dresden in 1661 to *Othello, nach Shakespeare* ('Othello, After / According to Shakespeare') in 2016.[10] As Guntner argues, Othello's visible Blackness as a racial marker was avoided until the late twentieth century, which marks a turning point in the representation of race on the German stage. Towards the end of the twentieth century, race and racism had become the main issues of *Othello*, which influenced translations and performances of the play.

The theoretical framework of this article draws from two concepts which emphasize the constructedness of race and the scope of playing in/with the race of the other, and from materialist critical race studies. In the Ostermeier performance of *Othello* under consideration, blackface involves both cross-racial casting and racial prosthetics, *i.e.* the production of 'racecraft' which refers to the illusion of race produced by racism – which is related to 'mental terrain and to pervasive belief'.[11] This article aims to investigate racecraft, or the way Blackness was constructed and designed in Ostermeier's production, and to examine how it is theatrically invested with the cultural power of white supremacy through the experimental blackface carried out onstage. I will first present blackface as playing in/with the race of the other, having thus a ludic dimension for the white actor in blackface onstage. I argue that blackface is a traumatic, harmful theatrical practice related to play as torture for the BIPOC audience.[12] Play can be pleasant but also heinous, for it all depends on perspective. As a result, what is pleasant, harmless play for whiteness may be experienced as torture play for BIPOC people. Aaron Trammel advocates for a rethinking of the phenomenology of play to study 'the most insidious ways that play has functioned as a tool of subjugation. A tool that hurts as much as it heals and has been complicit in the systemic erasure of BIPOC people from the domain of leisure.'[13] Indeed, as a practice that 'divide[s] and exclude[s]', blackface 'only exacerbate[s] the problem of racist exclusion'.[14] Blackface will thus be analysed through the prism of play as torture to emphasize its material effects on the bodies and minds of the BIPOC audience.

I will then examine the theatrical practice of blackface by adopting a materialist approach, thus not limiting myself to theoretical principles but taking into account the material consequences of blackface on both the white body of the actor on stage and the Black body being conjured up by blackface, thereby engaging in a critique of the performative approach to blackface

inherited from the linguistic turn. For instance, Susan Gubar argues that blackface is a case in point of 'race-change', defined as a way 'to suggest the traversing of race boundaries, racial imitation or impersonation, cross racial mimicry or mutability, white posing as black or black passing as white, pan racial mutability'.[15] Racechange involves 'test[ing] the boundaries between racially defined identities' and enhances the power clashes at stake in the representation of race.[16] Her performative approach to blackface suggests focusing on the discursive rather than on the material. Talking of racechange is problematic insofar as it denies the authenticity of trans lives experienced by real bodies. By arguing in favour of racial transubstantiation on stage, Gubar ignores the specificities of transness and the materiality of trans bodies through the parallelism she makes between the symbolic, racial 'transformation' of the white body in blackface onstage and the real transformation of bodies such as trans ones, thus marked as 'transitive' and 'transversal' to use Snorton's concepts.[17] Indeed, trans lives cannot be reduced to performances and used symbolically to refer to theatrical practices, for it denies the very authenticity of their bodies by stigmatizing their materiality.

I will explore the ways in which Blackness was represented onstage with a special focus on the black make-up used on Nakajew in the archive performance of the production recorded by the Schaubühne am Lehniner Platz in Berlin. I will put an emphasis on a performance of the play temporarily experimenting with blackface, arguing that it follows the German casting tradition of

(2020), 51–66; Bettina Boecker, 'A tragedy? *Othello* and *The Merchant of Venice* in Germany during the 2015–16 refugee crisis', in *Shakespeare's Others in 21st-Century European Performance: The Merchant of Venice and Othello*, ed. Boika Sokolova and Janice Valls-Russell (London, 2021), 209–27.

[10] Lawrence Guntner, 'Othello on the German stage: from "The Moor of Venice" to "Chocco", from Schlegel-Tieck to "Kanak Sprak"', in *Othello in European Culture*, ed. Elena Bandin, Francesca Rayner and Laura Campillo Arnaiz (Amsterdam and Philadelphia, 2022), 81–96.

[11] Karen E. Fields and Barbara J. Fields, *Racecraft: The Soul of Inequality in American Life* (London and New York, 2012), p. 18.

[12] Travis Trammel, *Repairing Play: Black Phenomenology* (Cambridge, 2023), p. 3.

[13] Trammel, *Repairing Play*, p. 4.

[14] Trammel, *Repairing Play*, p. 4.

[15] Susan Gubar, *Racechanges: White Skin, Black Face in American Culture* (Oxford, 1997), p. 5.

[16] Gubar, *Racechanges*, pp. 5, 10.

[17] Riley C. Snorton, *Black on Both Sides: A Racial History of Trans Identity* (Minneapolis and London, 2017).

cross-racial casting, with white actors regularly playing Black characters with or without blackface, but also on the practice of blackface which is deeply rooted in German cultural history. I will discuss the scope of black-up in Ostermeier's tradaptation of *Othello* while taking into account the fact that it was a temporary experimentation carried out in a context of theatrical instability. I will also argue that the perspective of white supremacy orients the German perception and conception of race. Blackness is closely linked to whiteness, which means that when one examines blackface – which is a representation of Blackness – whiteness must also be taken into consideration.

In order to fully understand Ostermeier's view of Othello, one must first gain an understanding of the context in which the play was produced: Germany's self-perception as a white country and the banality of blackface in German cultural history have had an influence on the depiction of the protagonist. The following pages will offer insights into pre-Ostermeier German productions of *Othello* with a focus on the representation of the eponymous character's racial difference, while taking into account the wider theatrical context of the post-Ostermeier German stage to emphasize Germany's complicated historiography of race in the contemporary theatre. Then, a close analysis of the metatheatrical prologue of the production and its postmodern racial prosthetics will enable me to address the theatrical strategies developed by Ostermeier in this experimental performance of *Othello*. Eventually, I will discuss the conceptual chiaroscuro of critical whiteness and cosmetic Blackness onstage to spotlight the tensions between the director's and the creative crew's intentions, as well as the impact of the performance on the audience.

IMMIGRATION OR THE GREAT GERMAN DENIAL: SELF-PERCEPTION AND WHITE SUPREMACY

When he refers to casting politics on the German contemporary stage, the German theatre critic Christopher Balme presents Germany as a country which perceives itself as white and without a significant racial diversity. For him, casting a white actor in a Black role is due to the composition of German theatre companies, thus suggesting that Germany is a country without POC minorities.[18] Such directorial decisions were always justified, 'but nevertheless masked racist operations in

German theatre at the institutional level'.[19] There seems to be a conflict between policies implemented regarding immigration and the mainstream discourse on national identity, and the German self-perception as white, symptomatic of the myth of Europe being homogeneously white.[20]

In the post-war era, the western German 'economic miracle' increased the need for labour, which became even more urgent with the building of the Berlin Wall in 1961.[21] The Federal Republic of Germany started a recruitment plan to hire 'guest workers'. The first agreement was made with Italy in 1955, and between 1960 and 1968 others followed suit – Greece, Spain, Turkey, Morocco, Portugal, Tunisia and Yugoslavia. After the 1973 oil crisis, the recruitment of workers from outside the European Economic Community stopped, but 4 million foreigners were already living in Germany at this point. It amounted to about 5 million in 1989. The German Democratic Republic also had a similar recruitment plan from the mid-1960s, but to a much lesser extent.[22] Foreign nationals mostly came from the European member states of the Council for Mutual Economic Assistance, and later from Algeria, Cuba, Mozambique, Viet Nam, Mongolia, China and Angola. Until the 1980s, asylum immigration was quantitatively low, and mostly from countries of the former Eastern Bloc. It rose to 438,000 people in 1992, but in 2004, it amounted to about 36,000 individuals. During the 1990s, Germany also granted protection to 345,000 refugees from Bosnia-Herzegovina, and, from 1999, 195,000 refugees from Kosovo. However, most of them returned to their native countries afterwards. In the 1990s, the number of Jewish immigrants coming from the states of the former Soviet Union started to increase – in 2004, it amounted to 219,000 applications sent to the Federal Republic of Germany. This meant Germany had the third-largest Jewish community in Europe after France and the UK.[23] The 2000 Reform of the Nationality Law

[18] Balme, 'Wie schwarz'.
[19] Priscilla Layne and Lizzie Stewart, 'Racialisation and contemporary German theatre', in *The Palgrave Handbook of Theatre and Race* (New York, 2021), 66–97; p. 66.
[20] Gloria Wekker, *White Innocence: Paradoxes of Colonialism and Race* (Durham and London, 2016), p. 3.
[21] Mark E. Spicka, *Selling the Economic Miracle: Economic Reconstruction and Politics in West Germany, 1949–1957* (New York and Oxford, 2007).
[22] Rita Chin, *The Guest Worker Question in Postwar Germany* (Cambridge, 2007).
[23] Mary Fullbrook, 'Germany for the Germans? Citizenship and nationality in a divided nation', in *Citizenship, Nationality and Migration in*

changed everything by granting German nationality to foreign children born in Germany. It also introduced new regulations for adult foreigners – reducing, for instance, the time required for naturalization. Moreover, the Green Card Initiative of the Federal Chancellor Gerhard Schröder encouraged IT-skilled workers to immigrate. New institutions were also created, such as the independent commission 'Immigration' by the Federal Minister of the Interior Otto Schily in 2000, and the Federal Office for the Recognition of Foreign Refugees was centralized in 2004.[24]

However, Dietrich Thränhardt points out that Germany is an 'undeclared immigration country'.[25] Christian Joppke insists that, according to official declarations, Germany is 'not a country of immigration', even though the guilt of the Nazi era made it the world's first major country to grant asylum: 'The discrepancy between *de facto* immigration and its political denial is the single most enduring puzzle in the German immigration debate.'[26] Germany is not alone in not defining itself as a country of immigrants, but it is the only one 'that has not become tired of repeating it, elevating the no-immigration maxim to a first principle of public policy [adopted by the federal government in 1977] and national self-definition'.[27] Joppke argues that immigration was opposed to the 'ethnocultural mode of German nationhood ... in principle delegitimized by its racist aberrations under the Nazi regime'.[28] This nationhood was actually reinforced and maintained by both the division of Germany and the 'scattering of huge German diasporas in communist Eastern Europe and the Soviet Union'.[29] Germany introduced itself as 'the homeland of all Germans, and it prioritized the immigration of co-ethnics'.[30] However, Joppke contends that, with the reunification, 'the grounding of the compulsively reiterated no-immigration maxim in incomplete nationhood is no more'.[31] The 2005 Immigration Act changed German legislation as regards the integration of foreign nationals. It paved the way for the 2007 Residence Act, which put an emphasis on long-term permanent residency for legal immigrants. The opposition from the Christian Democratic Union was clear since they started a cultural debate, or 'Leitkulturdebatte', about 'Ausländerpolitik' (policy dealing with 'foreigners', or immigration policy), integrationism and the jeopardized 'German national identity'.[32] This controversial debate focused on the criminalization of immigrants, and particularly the large Turkish community living in Germany. It was followed by a rise of racism and xenophobia, symbolized by Thilo Sarrazin's *Deutschland schafft sich*

ab – wie wir unser Land aufs Spiel setzen ('Germany Abolishes Itself: How We're Putting Our Country in Jeopardy'), published in 2010.

The denial of structural racism in Germany is also encapsulated by the limits of the *Erinnerungskultur* – that is, the German culture of remembrance. After the reunification, it became one of the most important elements of German nation-building – 'A highly curious but nevertheless surprisingly successful case of national reprofiling'.[33] *Erinnerungskultur* was used to foster 'a new national pride' through a collective acceptance of shame and guilt as regards German previous crimes. The aim of *Erinnerungskultur* is to remember the past, but above all to shape national identity by 'internalizing elements of history'.[34] It is based on a paradox, for it is not about creating a sense of national pride thanks to glorious events of the past, but precisely through the commemoration of past crimes:

This act of accepting almost unacceptable shame and admitting almost inadmissible guilt quite ingeniously recycles shame and guilt into a form of post heroic grandeur. Guilt is converted into guilt-pride. It is a moral pride that claims ethical exceptionality for having the strength to remember and thereby to take on responsibility for one of the greatest sins ever committed. This is the narrative of *Erinnerungskultur*.[35]

If the German government did not skimp on measures to remember the victims of the Holocaust – they enacted state-funded monuments such as the 2005

Europe, ed. David Cesarani and Mary Fullbrook (New York and London, 1996), 88–105; Karin Weiss, 'Zwischen Integration und Ausgrenzung. Jüdische Zuwanderer aus der ehemaligen Sowjetunion in Deutschland', *Jahrbuch für Antisemitismusforschung* 11 (2002), 249–70.

[24] Rogers Brubaker, *Citizenship and Nationhood in France and Germany* (Cambridge, MA, 1992); Amélie Constant, Olga Nottmeyer and Klaus Zimmermann, 'Cultural integration in Germany' in *Cultural Integration of Immigrants in Europe*, ed. Yann Algan, Alberto Bisin, Alan Manning and Thierry Verdier (Oxford, 2012), 69–124.

[25] D. Thränhardt, 'Germany: an undeclared immigration country', *Journal of Ethnic and Migration Studies* 21 (1995), 19–35.

[26] Christian Joppke, *Immigration and the Nation-State: The United States, Germany, and Great Britain* (Oxford, 1999).

[27] Joppke, *Immigration*, p. 62.   [28] Joppke, *Immigration*, p. 63.

[29] Joppke, *Immigration*, p. 63.   [30] Joppke, *Immigration*, p. 63.

[31] Joppke, *Immigration*, p. 63.

[32] Hartwig Pautz, 'The politics of identity in Germany: the Leitkultur debate', *Race & Class* 46 (2005), 39–52.

[33] Hans-Georg Moeller and Paul J. D'Ambrosio, *You and Your Profile: Identity after Authenticity* (New York, 2021), p. 98.

[34] Moeller and D'Ambrosio, *You and Your*, p. 98.

[35] Moeller and D'Ambrosio, *You and Your*, p. 100.

Holocaust Memorial in the centre of Berlin – other German war crimes have not received the same attention. The remembrance of German colonization results rather from the efforts of activists than from the state itself: many colonial monuments were redefined as anticolonial monuments to fight against 'colonial amnesia'.[36] Indeed, remembering colonialism is not part of the official commemoration policy, or 'at most a marginal one, just as colonialism has not found its way into Germany's foundational national myths'.[37] Sieg points out that the Herero genocide in German South-West Africa 'demands the same labor of mourning' as the Holocaust.[38] As Zeller explains, the critical discourse on German colonization is only developed by an academic minority and activists who 'face a widespread lack of interest among the broader public, if not an enduring nostalgia that goes hand in hand with mechanisms of suppression'.[39] What is more, these mechanisms operate insidiously within society through the fantasy of a white German national identity, which results in the maintenance of white privileges.

Although race seems to have been erased from the post-war public discourse, it has been part of the construction of white German identity, which contrasts with the country's traditional immigration history. Discussing race in Germany is complicated because of this contradiction, but also because of a linguistic deficiency: the very word 'rasse' has been expunged from the vocabulary during the denazification process of the post-war period. As a result, the notion of race was not addressed at all in Germany, which is also confirmed by the fact that the 'vocabulary to have the conversation is often missing', with a view to avoid resorting to the typical national socialist language from the Nazi era.[40] In an attempt to fill this critical gap, Sieg studied the tradition of racial impersonation in twentieth-century Germany, and she coined the phrase 'Ethnomaskerade' ('ethnic drag') to refer to the theatrical practice of blackface, for instance through racial prosthetics and cross-racial casting.[41] In her article 'Far away so close: race, whiteness, and German identity', Ulrike Anne Müller focuses on the role of whiteness in the racialization process – which results in a fantasy of German national identity – and shows how institutional racism is deeply rooted in German politics.[42] Racism is indeed far from being merely 'a concept expressed by right-wing extremists' as the mainstream German opinion too often believes.[43] For instance, it appears through the cultural practice of blackface and, above all, its banality in German cultural history.

THE BANALITY OF BLACKFACE IN GERMAN CULTURAL HISTORY

The way we eat, we laugh, we celebrate and we entertain ourselves may, at first, be considered as non-racial issues, but they are definitely racial in Germany. Blackface pastries, carnival disguise, figures used as shooting targets, and comedy are cultural traditions regarded as harmless, ordinary and socially accepted by the white majority of Germans.[44] They are part and parcel of what Philomena Essed calls 'everyday racism' (*Alltagsrassismus*) that she describes as being 'infused with familiar practices' and involving consistently 'socialized attitudes and behavior'.[45] Everyday racism is indeed 'transmitted in routine practices that seem "normal," at least for the dominant group'.[46] However, it is 'not recognized, not acknowledged – let alone problematized – by the dominant group.... To expose racism in the system, we must analyze ambiguous meanings, expose hidden currents, and generally question what seems normal or acceptable.'[47] All this contributes to normalizing blackface as a commonplace cultural practice, the banality of which makes it a non-issue. Indeed, Tiffany Florvil argues that 'both overt and subtle forms of anti-Black racism were not purged in post-war West Germany, as evinced by the prevalence of blackface, colonial stereotypes, and the (hyper)sexualization of nonwhite bodies in popular images'.[48] In order to grasp the

---

[36] Joachim Zeller, 'Decolonization of the public space? (Post)Colonial culture of remembrance in Germany', in *Hybrid Cultures – Nervous States: Britain and Germany in a (Post)Colonial World*, ed. Ulrike Lindner, Maren Möhring, Mark Stein and Silke Stroh (Amsterdam and New York, 2010), 65–88.

[37] Zeller, 'Decolonization', p. 77.

[38] Sieg, 'Race, guilt and "innocence"', p. 122.

[39] Zeller, 'Decolonization', p. 78.

[40] Layne and Stewart, 'Racialisation', p. 69.

[41] Sieg, 'Race, guilt and "innocence"'.

[42] Ulrike Anne Müller, 'Far away so close: race, whiteness, and German identity', *Identities: Global Studies in Culture and Power* 18 (2012), 620–45.

[43] Mark Terkessidis, 'Discriminating minds: three perspectives on racism, part I', *German Times*, July 2020, www.german-times .com/discriminating-minds-three-perspectives-on-racism-part-i.

[44] A parallel can be drawn with the cultural tradition of Zwarte Piet ('Black Pete') in the Netherlands, mainly considered as 'an innocent and thoroughly pleasant children's traditional festivity' (Wekker, 28).

[45] Philomena Essed, *Understanding Everyday Racism: An Interdisciplinary Theory* (Newbury Park, 1991), p. 3.

[46] Essed, *Understanding Everyday Racism*, p. 10.

[47] Essed, *Understanding Everyday Racism*, p. 10.

[48] Tiffany Florvil, *Mobilizing Black Germany: Afro-German Women and the Making of a Transnational Movement* (Urbana, Chicago and Springfield, 2020), p. 8.

scope of this phenomenon, we will now see a few examples of 'practices that may seem mundane and trivial' that turn out to be 'instantiations of everyday racism' in contemporary German cultural history.[49]

On 14 February 2020, the German author and columnist Jasmina Kuhnke – a.k.a. '@quattromilf' on Twitter – posted a tweet to denounce blackface pastries sold at the bakery Café Konfiserie Fromme, in Cologne. A friend of hers had sent her a picture of dark chocolate treats featuring thick, red lips and googly eyes. She tweeted the following post (originally in German): 'I just got a photo from a good friend from a traditional café in Cologne (no, the white ones [white pastries] are not supposed to represent a balance, they represent North Africans): Dear Café Konfiserie Fromme, I dislike your baked goods!' The bakery called them 'Funny Carnival Heads' in its display, but changed the name to 'Mohrenkopf' ('Moor's Head') or 'Othello' after the carnival. In Germany, the pastry was officially formerly known as 'Mohrenkopf' ('Moor's Head'), but it has recently officially been renamed 'Schokoküss' ('Chocolate Kiss'). In an interview given to Kendra Stenzel for the newspaper Kölner Stadt-Anzeiger, the owner of the bakery stated: 'We decorate it for carnival in the same way as many carnival costumes were designed in the past.... We have no racist thoughts behind it.' It is worth noticing the difference between the innocent intent and its racist impact. Kyla Wazana Thompkins argues that the image of the Black body 'as an edible object is a strong and consistent trope ... that carries the weight of many centuries of forced labor, of coercive and violent sexual desire, and of ongoing political struggle'.[50] She shows that eating articulates 'the dialectical struggles between pleasure and disgust, affect and aesthetics, dominance and resistance, and the interpenetrations of all of the above', in particular through this trope of the edible Black body.[51] Thus, the consumption of blackface pastries by white people reveals the cultural power of German white supremacy through the paradox of a 'racial indigestion': the Black body is eaten but not fully digested by whiteness – hence the dialectics of fascination and repulsion towards the Black body itself.[52]

On 4 October 2014, Bernd Kastner wrote an article for the newspaper Süddeutsche Zeitung, exposing the use of blackface figures in a historic shooting range at the Oide Wiesn during the Oktoberfest folk festival in Munich. The 130-year-old blackface figure heads have clay pipes attached to them, and are moving up and down. Florian Pointner, the employee handing out air rifles to the shooters, declared: 'We also shoot white people here.... Most understand that there are no racist ulterior motives.' In his article, Kastner opened with a symbolic question: 'Is that tradition or racism?' ('Ist das Tradition oder Rassismus?'). Tradition and racism were opposed as if they were mutually exclusive – as if a cultural tradition could not be racist. This would imply that a cultural heritage cannot be denounced as unethical and offensive because of its longevity.

The same issue is at stake with the 'Sternsinger' tradition that refers to young star singers, or Epiphany singers, who dress up as the biblical Three Wise Men visiting the infant Jesus. Some of those carol singers dress up as stereotypical Africans in blackface. The children walk from house to house to collect money for charities. The use of blackface to dress up as an African is not uncommon in Germany, particularly during the 'Rosemontag' ('Rose Monday') carnival parade. On 7 January 2015, Tom Barfield wrote an article for The Local.de about the apparition of Christian Lindner, the Free Democratic Party leader, on national TV, next to a blacked-up 'Sternsinger'. Vicky German, a spokesperson for 'Initiative Schwarze Menschen in Deutschland' ('Initiative for Black People in Germany'), told Barfield: 'It objectifies black people in a very racist way with the assumption that blackness is something that can be assumed.'[53] Asked about the tacit support of Lindner for the charity collectors in blackface, the Free Democratic Party declared on Twitter that they were not 'responsible for the way they're dressed or made-up'.[54] The party implied that Lindner could not be held accountable for this decision to appear next to a blacked-up 'Sternsinger', even though his presence normalized and legitimized blackface.

In April 2021, the cabaret artist Helmut Schleich performed in blackface to play the role of Maxwell Strauss, a fictional character introduced as the head of the fictitious state of Mbongalo. It was intended to be a parody of Franz Josef Strauss, a former member of the Christian Social Union, who was well known for his coarse

---

[49] Essed, Understanding Everyday Racism, p. 10.

[50] Kyla Wazana Thompkins, Racial Indigestion: Eating Bodies in the 19th Century (New York and London, 2012), p. 8.

[51] Thompkins, Racial Indigestion, p. 8.

[52] Thompkins, Racial Indigestion.

[53] Tom Barfield, 'Blackface king at FDP summit angers activists', The Local.de, 8 January 2015, www.thelocal.de/20150107/blackface-king-fdp-angers-activists.

[54] Barfield, 'Blackface king'.

pronunciation. Schleich gave advice to the German people on how to cope with the current pandemic and stated that he would be an excellent chancellor, the first Black chancellor of Germany, as he was waving a stuffed animal. The TV show *SchleichFernsehen* was aired by a public service broadcaster, Bayerischer Rundfunk, which defended Schleich's use of blackface and, consequently, his stigmatization of African people, on Twitter: 'The character of "Maxwell Strauss" which has been created by Helmut Schleich is explicitly a caricature of Franz Josef Strauss and in no way aimed at POCs.' Again, the discrepancy between the innocent intent and the racist impact is striking.

With all these examples, it becomes obvious that the practice of blackface is well rooted in the German cultural tradition, without it being seen as racist or unethical, except by a 'woke' minority. It is necessary to acknowledge blackface as a stereotypical representation of Blackness and to redraw 'the linkages between the historical development of imagery, colonialism and our contemporary moment – linkages that belie the idea that Blackface could exist in total isolation and neutrality on a German stage'.[55] We must therefore bear in mind that this cultural practice does conjure up offensive and humiliating images and representations of Blackness with a political dimension, regardless of intent, for 'all cultural statements occur in a political and social situation and therefore have a political dimension'.[56] Those who think that blackface is just an aesthetic fact of life need to realize that 'nowadays in Germany it is a politically used instrument to deny white responsibility'.[57] One might argue that there is a difference between a naive critical inquiry into the nature of systemic racism and an active praise of white supremacy. However, this claim downplays the insidious power of white supremacy in the delineation of Blackness as a prescriptive racialized identity. Blackface is part of what Mark Terkessidis calls 'racist knowledge', which he defines as follows: 'A form of societal knowledge generally widespread and often reinforced across politics and the media. Whether consciously or unconsciously, this racist knowledge legitimizes the differences and inequalities between "us" and "them" even though democratic principles forbid discrimination of this kind.'[58] Thus, resorting to blackface in Germany – or elsewhere – contributes to the normalization of a racist practice that legitimizes a certain representation of Blackness through an offensive stereotype. In this, I strongly disagree with Julia Lemmle: even if she acknowledges that blackface is 'a racist practice with the capacity to offend', she also argues that it is a cultural practice which should not be avoided, for 'its repetition enables the production of new and entirely different meanings'.[59] Theatrical aesthetics is always political and always contextual. If the intent may differ and suggests a wide variety of justifications, it seems to be that the impact – or part of the reception – always comes down to the same conclusion: that is, the dissemination and maintaining of the cultural power of white supremacy to control the representation of race through the imposition of prescriptive racialized identities, and yet another experience of racial violence, terror and torture for a BIPOC audience.

GERMANY'S COMPLICATED HISTORIOGRAPHY OF RACE ON THE CONTEMPORARY STAGE

From the mid twentieth century onwards, East and West German directors built a reputation of developing a politically and aesthetically radical body of work, in particular through *Verfremdung*, used in the representation of race onstage. This theatrical anti-naturalistic practice (*Verfremdung*), emerging from Bertolt Brecht's work on theatre, has been 'a valuable tool for many theatre practitioners in the Federal Republic of Germany and beyond who are interested in exposing race as a construct'.[60] This deconstruction of race through the *V-effekt* onstage is, however, not the way Brecht himself used it. It is worth noticing how Brechtian stagecraft inspired German directors to develop a characteristic racecraft to construct blackface onstage. According to the Brechtian theory of acting, the actor must not make the audience believe that they are their character – the point is to debunk the dramatic illusion fooling spectators. Precisely, the actor has the responsibility to break this illusion to emphasize the discrepancy between the actor and the character. Sieg argues that the rationale behind this is that '[a] "naturalistic" mimetic style of representation ... always reproduces the operations of racial ideology, whereas cross-racial masquerade contests or even transforms

---

55 Micossé-Aikins, 'Not Just a Blackened Face'.
56 Lemmle, 'Ich bin kein Nazi'.
57 Lemmle, 'Ich bin kein Nazi'.
58 Terkessidis, 'Discriminating minds'.
59 Lemmle, 'Ich bin kein Nazi'.
60 Layne and Stewart, 'Racialisation', p. 67.

social relations organized around race'.[61] Cross-racial acting and blackface have thus been two ways to engage with race critically on the German contemporary stage when it comes to defining race as a social and cultural construct.

The most significant German production of *Othello* in the post-war period is undoubtedly that of Peter Zadek, who staged the play in 1976 at the Deutsches Schauspielhaus in Hamburg. He decided to have Ulrich Wildgruber – a white actor in blackface – impersonate Othello to create 'a cartoon caricature of a cannibal'.[62] Zadek also resorted to paralinguistic features to convey a caricatural racist imagery – Wildgruber mimicked 'a King Kong figure, scratching for lice'.[63] Throughout the performance, Othello's black make-up came off on Desdemona, which highlighted the artificiality of blackface and made it look like 'a postmodern parody'.[64] Zadek emphasized the racism of the play in the embodiment of Othello on stage, but also in his body language, which polarized both the audience and critics. Resorting to blackface was a way to prevent the audience from suspending their disbelief: racial prosthetics was here introduced onstage as a tool to achieve the *V-effekt* in order to define race as an external projection of stereotypes. The audience was therefore encouraged to see the constructedness of race through Othello's blackface, instead of passively looking at a mimetic cosmetic Blackness.

In 2003, Feridun Zaimoglu and Günter Spenkel translated and adapted Shakespeare's *Othello* to produce a new playtext staged by Luk Perceval at the Munich Kammerspiele. In this production, Othello was played by Thomas Thieme, a white actor. Commenting on this production, Gad Kaynar argues that Othello's whiteness 'is but a histrionic mask for the part that he acts on . . . stage', and he adds that Othello is incapable 'of internalizing the "white" mask that he himself has grafted onto his face'.[65] Kaynar introduced whiteness as a theatrical mask that Othello uses to play 'white' in the play. In addition, Christian M. Billing underlined the 'unashamedly overt expressions of intolerance' and the 'succession of commonplace jibes and taunts' employed to echo 'the prejudicial vocabularies of the Nazi era'.[66] Billing insisted on the stigmatization of the white Othello through verbal violence with racist undertones. Othello was also played by a white actor, Alexander Scheer, in Stefan Pucher's 2005 *Othello* at the Deutsches Schauspielhaus (Hamburg). Pucher had his lead white actor play in blackface, with disproportionately huge red lips. In Jette Steckel's 2009 *Othello* at Deutsches Theater in Berlin, the eponymous character

was performed by a white actress, Susanne Wolff. She repeatedly changed her appearance throughout the performance: having long, then short, hair; appearing in a gorilla costume, and later a red dress. Steckel addressed both racism and sexism in a production that played with racial and gender stereotypes. The Brechtian *Verfremdung* has thus been used to represent race with critical distance through blackface and cross-racial casting in pre-Ostermeier productions of the play: 'The near-standard practice of casting white Othellos in German productions even throughout the 1990s and early 2000s often seems to have entailed minimal efforts to avoid racial caricature.'[67] It seems relevant to point out that this influenced the audience's expectations as regards the representation of Othello's race onstage: 'The present experience is always ghosted by previous experiences and associations while these ghosts are simultaneously shifted and modified by the process of recycling and recollection.'[68] It was therefore not uncommon for the German audience to face a blacked-up white Othello onstage when Ostermeier started to work on the play, and it does not seem unreasonable to think that Ostermeier was aware of it and took it into account in his experimental performance. The issue at stake is to examine Othello's blackface to see whether the racecraft used produces a 'racial caricature' that recycles and recollects the cosmetic Blackness of previous German *Othello* productions.

61 Sieg, 'Race, guilt and "innocence"', p. 5.
62 Ron Engle, 'The Shakespeare of Peter Zadek', in *Foreign Shakespeare*, ed. Dennis Kennedy (Cambridge, 1998), 93–105; p. 100.
63 Julie Hankey, 'Introduction', in *Shakespeare in Production: Othello*, ed. Julie Hankey (Cambridge, 1987), 1–111; p. 85.
64 Philip C. Kolin, 'Blackness made visible: a survey of Othello in criticism, on stage and on screen', in *Othello: New Critical Essays*, ed. Philip C. Kolin (New York, 2013), 1–88; p. 5.
65 Gad Kaynar, 'Textual dramaturgy and dramaturg-as-text: traditional versus new dramaturgy in the era of German post-dramatic theatre', in *Performance Studies in Motion: International Perspectives and Practices in the Twenty-First Century*, ed. Atay Citron, Sharon Aronson-Lehavi and David Serbib (London, 2014), 86–104; p. 98.
66 Christian Billing, '"Othello was a white man': review of Othello (directed by Luk Perceval for Münchner Kammerspiele) at the Royal Shakespeare Theatre, April 2006', *Shakespeare* 3 (2007), 189–99; p. 189.
67 Chris Thurman, 'Multilingual Shakespeare: a South African reflects on translation and performance in Germany', in *Translation Studies beyond the Postcolony*, ed. Kobus Marais and Isle Feinauer (Cambridge, 2017), 94–129; p. 104.
68 Marvin Carlson, *The Haunted Stage: The Theatre as Memory Machine* (Ann Arbor, 2003), p. 2.

A CLOSE ANALYSIS OF THE METATHEATRICAL PROLOGUE AND POSTMODERN RACIAL PROSTHETICS IN OSTERMEIER'S *OTHELLO*

Ostermeier's experimental performance began with an extradiegetic, metatheatrical sequence showing the intimacy of the couple of Othello and Desdemona, standing in front of what was probably the nuptial bed. While Desdemona was heading towards Othello, he got naked. It was not a love scene, but an erotic moment. Othello was a white man, and he was being painted black by Desdemona, who used a black, mud-like substance. She stroked Othello's body with a light, sensual touch as she smeared the dark make-up all over his body and face – a rather strong theatrical gesture thus emphasizing the artificiality of the racialization process which benefits from the metaphorical potential of theatre.[69] Blacking-up Othello's body seemed to be a source of erotic desire for her. It was a scene of fetishization of Blackness that turned the blacked-up body into an erotic commodity. One might observe that Desdemona experienced some kind of transgressive pleasure from this blackface, while she was preparing Nakajew to impersonate Othello as a Black man. Using her own fingers instead of a brush, Desdemona was dominating him while pleasuring herself, asserting her white privilege through the monopoly of racial definition. In this iconic scene, Ostermeier was constructing Blackness from his white perspective, and, by doing so, was universalizing whiteness impacting the process of reception. The audience may therefore adopt the white gaze on Blackness or adopt an 'oppositional gaze' rejecting this universalization of whiteness through the very act of racial marking.[70] Ostermeier argued that, in this prologue, he intended to show Othello's body as a canvas on which to project one's perception of the other, 'the projection of what I see in the other, what the others see in him others' (my translation).[71] Moreover, he points out that it is a way to show that Othello's 'soul is much more white' for he is 'a very assimilated Black man in white society' (my translation).[72] Here, he reflects on what it means to play this part in a play by a white playwright who wrote a Black role for a white actor.

This scene showed the complexity of blackface that interweaves 'abomination and adoration'.[73] On the one hand, Desdemona defiled Othello's body with the black mud that threatened his whiteness – she was creating an 'abomination' by turning white into Black. On the other hand, she also adored it, brushing against it voluptuously. She denigrated Othello's body by sullying him with dark paint, but she was also mesmerized by this body that became, through her gaze, a fetishized commodity. Precisely, Trammel explains that that play – here, theatrical play – may include and provide pleasure, or exclude and cause torture.[74] Drawing on Trammel's Black phenomenology of play, I argue that blackface, in this archival version, is 'a form of play that focuses on exploring the deep, painful, and . . . traumatic depths' of BIPOC lives also 'contributing to the cultural erasure of BIPOC today'.[75] Desdemona's white gesture of blacking-up Othello's body is a 'coercive' technique through which she subjugates him and denies him agency.[76] As Desdemona painted him black, Othello stood perfectly still, looking ahead. He was turned into a racial stereotype, an image that relies on 'a kind of "living death," the zombie-like condition of the borderline between the animate and the inanimate'.[77] This in-between state characterized Othello's body onstage, for the inanimate black paint came to life when being put on Nakajew's animated body. Othello's cosmetic Blackness was simultaneously both a material object – a racial prosthesis – and a living embodiment through the actor's corporeal presence. Throughout the production, Ostermeier gave in to interracial temptation by blacking-up his lead actor, which went beyond mimesis. As the performance unfolded, the black make-up of Othello started to fade out and smudge because of the contact with the water onstage and with the other characters. Gradually, Othello thus became whiter and whiter; he was undergoing a *Mohrenwäsche* – that is, being washed white.[78]

---

[69] Balme, 'Wie schwarz'.

[70] Nyong'o cited in Ayanna Thompson, 'The Blackfaced bard: returning to Shakespeare or leaving him?', *Shakespeare Bulletin* 27 (2009), 437–56; p. 449.

[71] Susanne Burkhardt, 'Thema ist eine subtil rassistische Welt', *Deutschlandfunk Kultur*, 6 August 2010, www.deutschlandfunkkultur.de/thema-ist-eine-subtil-rassistische-welt-100.html.

[72] Burkhardt, 'Thema ist'.

[73] W. J. T. Mitchell, *What Do Pictures Want? The Lives and Loves of Images* (Chicago, 2005), p. 33.

[74] Trammel, *Repairing Play*, p. 14.

[75] Trammel, *Repairing Play*, p. 14.

[76] Trammel, *Repairing Play*, p. 12.

[77] Mitchell, *What Do Pictures?*, p. 296.

[78] Micossé-Aikins, 'Not Just a Blackened Face': The "Mohrenwäsche" (washing of the moor) is also a figure of speech that has traditionally been used to describe the futile attempt to clear someone's culpability by using false evidence.' This whitewashing has thus an ironic

Nonetheless, in the end, he remained in a racial in-between whiteness and a cosmetic Blackness. Neither white nor Black, this experimental Othello appears as of mixed race.

Ostermeier's racecraft in this performance does not seem to be part of an agenda to deconstruct race. Rather, it aims to reconstruct race through the representation of fetishized, gendered, cosmetic Blackness onstage. This directorial choice is reminiscent of Ostermeier's own words when he shared his theatrical aesthetics with Gerhard Jörder:

I am, if you will, the little brother of the Deconstructionists – when the big brothers have torn everything apart, someone has to collect the pieces and put them together again. And that's what I do. But always in the hope that the joins between the pieces are visible. In Japanese culture they have an expression for it – *Kintsugi*. A ceramic object is only truly beautiful after it has been broken and put back together again. Making the joins visible is the goal of the aesthetic. I don't deconstruct, I reconstruct.[79]

Thus, in this experimental performance, we may infer that Ostermeier's goal is not to avoid racial caricature, but precisely to engage with it critically, head on. However, Ostermeier does not define his work as post-dramatic as most of the contemporary German directors do, but as a 'politically engaged, realistic theatre' – to quote Jörder's words that Ostermeier approved in the interview.[80] One may therefore wonder how blackface and cross-racial casting contribute to a realistic theatrical aesthetics. To be exact, he does not define his realist perspective as naturalistic:

He unites . . . [the] essentially political core values of his theatre work in the notion of 'realism' that underpins his work, which he understands as something very different from any theatrical 'kitchen-sink realism' or plain naturalism[,] distinct from representations of face-value, literal realities which in their recognisability affirm the world as we believe we know it.[81]

Ostermeier's definition of his directorial choices as 'realist' implies that his theatre will challenge clichéd human behaviour through a process of research with the creative crew, as he did for the experimental performance we are focusing on:

The director's and the actors' shared search in rehearsal manifests itself in the exploration of different possibilities for a scenic solution, and to try out, in an extreme and radical way, even the most far-fetched, and most contradictory responses that go against the clichés of human behaviour as a part of this search for different possibilities. Eventually, we will settle together on the one solution, which, in the

context of the ensemble's world view, appears to be the most exciting and the least expected. This is how realist theatre distinguishes itself from a simple movie or television realism.[82]

Paradoxically, it is by resorting to blackface that Ostermeier seems to intend to make a critique of this stereotypical cosmetic Blackness, and thus to construct a 'realist' blackface onstage for his white actor, Sebastian Nakajew. Ostermeier's iconoclastic aesthetics, intended to challenge clichés and stereotypes, seems to be intrinsically postmodern in the sense that it questions the doxa's representations, or fantasies: 'Those metanarratives or "grand" narratives are, broadly speaking, the supposedly transcendent and universal truths that underpin western civilization and that function to give that civilization objective legitimization.'[83] The postmodern racial prosthetics utilized onstage to create the necessary racecraft in order to make Nakajew blacked-up onstage appear to conjure up a theatrical practice to (paradoxically) challenge it. In this experimental performance with blackface, Ostermeier's Othello is embodying a stereotyped representation of race while challenging its very legitimacy. However, if Ostermeier's intent was to resort to Brechtian, postmodern racial prosthetics to create a 'realist' representation of Blackness onstage, its impact seems rather different. Conjuring up a tradition in order to challenge its very existence is always risky for it may confirm this tradition's validity instead of discrediting it. If Ostermeier's intent is to reconstruct blackface onstage to engage critically with race, the impact may not be received by everyone as an antiracist critique, but rather as a new repetition onstage of a theatrical practice recapitulating racialization and structural violence – a practice which maintains, and gives even more visibility to, a German cultural practice whose banality defuses it and contributes to getting rid of its offensive, racist and humiliating dimension. Joy Kristin Kalu rightfully argues that:

From its inception, . . . blackface was a racist practice of entertainment. Its political dimension, *i.e.* legitimizing the white

dimension in the performance, for it starts to be visible from act 3, scene 3, in which Iago convinces Othello to give in to revenge.
79 Gerhard Jörder, *Ostermeier Backstage* (Berlin, 2014), pp. 2–3.
80 Jörder, *Ostermeier Backstage*, p. 7.
81 Peter M. Boenisch, *The Theatre of Thomas Ostermeier* (New York, 2012), pp. 2–3.
82 Boenisch, *The Theatre*, p. 24.
83 Hans Bertens, *The Idea of the Postmodern: A History* (London and New York, 1995), p. 124.

majority's preservation of power, was always part of its concept. It is for this reason that blackface simply cannot be understood as a neutral theatrical sign for marking difference – even today, and even in Germany.[84]

The neutrality of blackface, or its being completely defused and deprived of its racist content, seems to be a fantasy which overlooks the cultural power of whiteness and the way it controls the racial narrative onstage – through the blackface of Nakajew, to have him perform Othello.

THE CONCEPTUAL CHIAROSCURO OF WHITE SUPREMACY AND COSMETIC BLACKNESS

In the rest of the performance, the audience may connect the Chechen-sounding name of Nakajew and his working-class East German accent as a way to represent Othello's otherness onstage through an invisible cultural marker of difference. This intersection of class and race suggests a complex process of marginalization to construct Othello's otherness with an allusion to the hierarchy of the German cultural and class system related to the specificity and complexity of German whiteness.

In an interview given to Jikta Pelechová, Ostermeier explained that the use of racial prosthetics in the metatheatrical prologue was not a scene that was part of the first performances of the play: 'And even now, I am not entirely convinced by the solution we found. It might still evolve. We play this version only for the sixth time; before, it was different.'[85] The German director went on to justify the choice of cross-racial casting by arguing that it was due to the lack of racial diversity in Germany: 'It is true that today, it [Othello's Blackness] raises an entirely different issue; not only on the racism of our society, but also on the fact that there aren't many black actors in German theatre. This debate is very topical in Germany' (my translation).[86] With this statement, Ostermeier somehow denied any ethical responsibility in his casting choice, virtually blaming Black Germans for being invisible on the German stage, instead of blaming white supremacy for keeping Black Germans – particularly Black German actors – invisible. Other German directors followed suit, resorting to the same excuse to justify the blackface.

By contributing to the invisibility of Black German bodies on the contemporary stage, Ostermeier admits his ignorance of the historical presence of Black people in Germany, and to a lesser extent the very existence of Black Europe.[87] In *Mobilizing Black Germany* (2020), Tiffany N. Florvil successfully manages to uncover the overlooked history of the modern Black German movement of the 1980s to the 2000s with a focus on the two main Black German organizations: Initiative Schwarze Deutsche ('Initiative for Black Germans', ISD) founded in 1985, and Afrodeutsche Frauen ('Afro-German Women', ADEFRA) founded in 1986. Florvil shows that both organizations made 'Black Germanness visible in a majority-white nation that failed to acknowledge its colonial past and its afterlife, its long-standing multiracial and multicultural populations, and the persistence of racism and racial violence after the fall of the Third Reich'.[88] They also enabled the emergence of Black German Studies[89] (BGS) which also took part in the destabilization of white supremacy, the debunking of the myth of a 'colour-blind', anti-racist Germany, as well as in the normalization of Black German identity in order to redefine Germanness and fight the 'epistemology of ignorance' which also impacts Ostermeier.[90] Notwithstanding, the time of 'white ignorance' has long passed and cannot remain a relevant excuse to deny the unethical dimension of blackface on the German contemporary stage.[91]

Barely two years later, in an interview given to the German website The Local.de, Tahar Della, a spokesperson for Initiative Schwarze Menschen in Deutschland said such a justification was 'idiotic', for 'There are more than enough black actors in Germany,

---

84 Kalu, 'On the myth'.

85 Jitka Pelechová, 'Le théâtre de Thomas Ostermeier: phénomène culturel ou démarche artistique? Suivi d'un entretien avec Thomas Ostermeier', *Cahiers d'Études Germaniques* 64 (2013), 335–50, https://journals.openedition.org/ceg/9110 (my translation).

86 Pelechová, 'Le théâtre de Thomas Ostermeier'.

87 Sara Lennox, ed., *Remapping Germany: New Perspectives on Afro-German History, Politics and Culture* (Amherst and Boston, 2016), p. 2.

88 Florvil, *Mobilizing Black Germany*, p. 3.

89 See the seminal work of Peggy Piesche, '"Black and German?" East German adolescents before 1989 – a retrospective view of a "nonexistent issue" in the GDR', in *The Cultural After-Life of East Germany: New Transnational Perspectives*, ed. Leslie Adelson (Washington, 2002), 37–59.

90 Charles W. Mills, 'White ignorance', in *Race and Epistemologies of Ignorance*, ed. Shannon Sullivan and Nancy Tuana (Albany, 2007), 11–38.

91 Mills, 'White ignorance'. See The Black German Heritage Research Association (BGHRA) website to find out more about the scholarship on the historic and contemporary presence of Black people in Germany: http://bghra.org.

especially in Berlin.'[92] Della made this statement while talking about Thomas Schendel's 2012 production of *Ich bin nicht Rappaport* ('I am not Rappaport') at the Schlosspark Theater in Berlin in which the white actor Joachim Bliese performed in blackface to play Midge. In this play by the American playwright Herb Gardner (1985), Midge Carter, an old Black man from Harlem, meets Nat Moyer, an old Communist Jew, on a Central Park bench in New York. Since 1987, the play had been performed over forty times on the German stage, but the role of Midge was only played twice by a Black actor. In the productions, the performance of Blackness had mainly been the domain of white German actors. A few days after the production started, thousands of comments about the offensive character of blackface surged on the Facebook page of the Schlosspark Theater. In an interview given to Jessica Ware, Schendel explained that 'Many older black actors come from the music industry, and that wasn't a fit for the play as it isn't a musical. When we couldn't find an elderly black actor who fit the role and could speak with a perfect German accent, we opted for blackface make-up.'[93] He added that, in Germany, 'blackface is part of a theater tradition that was never intended to be racist', and he confessed not to understand the anti-racist pushback against blackface; as he pointed out, 'I tried to make a play about racism and ended up being called a racist.'[94] Apparently, both Schendel and Ostermeier have used blackfacing onstage in order to challenge its very validity, to act as a racial theatrical marker, but they overlooked the risk that racial prosthetics and cross-racial casting may instead maintain the cultural power of white supremacy in German theatre. Contrary to their justifications based on the lack of racial diversity in German contemporary theatre, Black German actors do exist. Two years after Ostermeier's *Othello*, they started to fight more openly against their being confined to invisibility.

In the 2012 John von Düffel's production of *Unschuld* ('Innocence') at the Deutsches Theater in Berlin, white actors Andreas Dönler and Peter Moltzen performed in blackface. Written by the German playwright Dea Loher (2003), the play tells the story of two illegal, Black asylum-seekers, Elisis and Fadoul. Onstage, Dönler's and Moltzen's faces were painted black with disproportionately big lips drawn with strawberry-red make-up. At the same time, German anti-racist activists joined forces and founded Bündis Bühnenwatch ('Alliance Stage Watch') to deal with the blackface tradition in German theatre (Bruce-Jones 54).[95] During one of the first performances of *Unschuld*, forty-two activists left the auditorium at the

same time, as the two actors in blackface entered the stage. Members of Bündis Bühnenwatch waited at the entrance of the Deutsches Theater to hand out flyers retracing the performance history of blackface, and explained why it was offensive, with a view to exposing systemic racism in German theatre. After a discussion with the Deutsches Theater, the play was performed with Dönler and Moltzen in whiteface instead of blackface for the rest of the season. Düffel seemed to have become sufficiently aware of the problem raised by Bündis Bühnenwatch, as he agreed to stop having blacked-up actors onstage for this play. However, the actors in blackface still appeared in the photos and promotional videos of the production on the theatre's website.

Sieg explained that members of Bündis Bühnenwatch 'forcefully asserted that the meanings and effects of racialized symbolic practices cannot be determined by (white) artistic intent alone, but must take the context of reception and the responses of audiences of color into account as well', while defenders of blackfacing invoked innocent pragmatism by arguing that there were 'neither enough qualified actors of color, nor enough roles to warrant their permanent employment in stable ensembles'.[96] The issue of the representation of race on the German contemporary stage as a symptom of white supremacy was addressed at a panel discussion called 'Facing Black People' hosted in May 2012 by the Ballhaus Naunynstrasse, a theatre in Berlin-Kreuzberg. This conversation between Black German writers and performers as well as anti-racist activists led to raising the question of theatrical embodiment and blackface, as well as 'the larger problem with the roles assigned to people of color in German theatre, and with the institution's reluctance to address colonialism and race relations as part of its larger project of historical remembering, reckoning, and democratization'.[97] This panel discussion witnesses how institutional racism deeply affects German contemporary theatre, which turns a blind eye – apart from a few exceptions such as the Ballhaus Naunynstrasse – to the consequences of having a white actor in blackface for actors of colour.

As Kalu puts it, in blackface performances, 'The hierarchy, not merely represented but created [...] extends

[92] Jessica Ware, 'Blackface in Berlin play just "tradition"', *The Local. de*, 6 January 2012, www.thelocal.de/20120106/39967.

[93] Ware, 'Blackface in Berlin'. [94] Ware, 'Blackface in Berlin'.

[95] Eddie Bruce-Jones, *Race in the Shadow of Law: State Violence in Contemporary Europe* (New York, 2017), p. 54.

[96] Sieg, 'Race, guilt and "innocence"', pp. 120, 121.

[97] Sieg, 'Race, guilt and "innocence"', p. 131.

beyond the stage and unfolds its offensive potential there.'[98] She explained that the use of blackface onstage defines power relationships in favour of whiteness, and that the white supremacy onstage is closely linked to the white supremacy offstage. In the experimental *Othello* performance under consideration, racial hierarchy was first *re-presented* through the use of racial prosthetics in the prologue, and then *re-produced* onstage through cross-racial casting, with the white Sebastian Nakajew playing the Black Othello. If the intent of German contemporary directors using Brechtian, postmodern racecraft is to highlight the constructedness of race and to promote anti-racism, one must also take into account the impact, or 'the paradoxical effect its usage can have on propagating structures of exclusion and racialised ways of viewing within the theatre in Germany'.[99] Through the use of such racecraft on the contemporary stage, German actors of colour are excluded 'both from unmarked roles and from those where the character to be played is a person of Colour'.[100] They are too Black to play white characters or racially 'unmarked' roles, and too Black to play Black characters for directors not interested in a naturalistic, mimetic representation of race onstage. In the end, 'inevitably the preference for whiteness and Germany's understanding of itself as white is what often excludes People of Colour from the theatre, whether or not they are fluent in German'.[101] The development of racecraft that involves the white actor in blackface on the grounds that the German theatre is lacking racial diversity seems to be an epitome of what Ayanna Thompson calls 'the inherent white supremacist logic of white innocence'.[102] Indeed, the very presence of white bodies performing Black characters reflects the cultural weight of white supremacy by acting as an instrument of established hegemonic power. Through blackface, whiteness appears as the racial, invisible norm imposing itself with a universal, infinite potential of representation, and 'minoritized people are made to act as "killjoys" when they describe their play experiences as torturous'.[103] Denouncing the unethical dimension of blackface thus means to kill the white joy of playing in/with the race of the other by asserting the agency of

BIPOC people and the material consequences of such theatrical practices on their own bodies.

To conclude, the cross-racial casting and racial prosthetics used in this experimental performance of *Othello* reflect Germany's self-perception as white and the cultural power of white supremacy on the German contemporary stage. Indeed, blacking-up a white actor to play a Black character is a commonplace theatrical practice which is part of German cultural history. Set in the context of Germany's complicated historiography of race on the contemporary stage, Ostermeier's experimental performance of *Othello* explores the theatrical phenomenon of blackface through the use of postmodern racial prosthetics as it is staged in the metatheatrical prologue. Even if Ostermeier's use of cosmetic Blackness may have aimed to emphasize race as a cultural and social construct, and to denounce blackface as a racist practice, it nevertheless has a different impact and promotes white supremacy under the cover of white innocence. This article attempted to show the extent to which the racecraft developed by Ostermeier onstage contributes – consciously or unconsciously – to give white actors the monopoly on the performance of Blackness, thereby confining actors of colour to invisibility by choosing cosmetic Blackness over the material bodies of actors of colour. In this performance, blackface suggests the power dynamics at stake in systemic racism which favours whiteness over Blackness. Even though the very corporeality of Black actors onstage may run the risk of reinforcing racist stereotypes, it also decolonizes the stage by offering both visibility and agency to actors of colour, which would show that Black bodies – and lives – *do* matter.[104]

---

[98] Kalu, 'On the myth'.

[99] Layne and Stewart, 'Racialisation', p. 90.

[100] Layne and Stewart, 'Racialisation', p. 81.

[101] Layne and Stewart, 'Racialisation', p. 83.

[102] Ayanna Thompson, *Blackface* (London, 2021), p. 12.

[103] Trammel, *Repairing Play*, pp. 13–14.

[104] Hugh Quarshie, *Second Thoughts about Othello* (Chipping Camden, 1999), p. 5.

'BLOODY CREDITOR[S]' AND THE BLOOD-MONEY METAPHOR IN *THE MERCHANT OF VENICE*

HARVEY WILTSHIRE

In *The Merchant of Venice* (1598), following Bassanio's successful negotiation of the casket test, Shakespeare presents a fleeting moment of perfectly equitable exchange that pushes back against the otherwise usurious impulses of the play: as instructed by the leaden casket's scroll, Bassanio moves to 'claim' his prize – Portia – by paying out 'a loving kiss' and receiving one in return, declaring, 'I come by note, to give and to receive' (3.2.138–40).[1] As an echo of Antonio's insistence that he 'neither lend nor borrow, / By *taking* nor by *giving* of excess' (1.3.61–2, emphasis added), this vision of equal gift-giving and receipt presents a powerful counterpoint to the financial hustling of Venice. Quarantined in Belmont from the problematic financial dealings of the city, Bassanio and Portia's romantic reciprocation represents the potential for absolute equity that appears to stand in stark contrast to – and promises a remedying of – the deeply troubling bond between Shylock and Antonio.[2] Within the limits of the play, however, this kiss is never explicitly exchanged. Instead, Portia presents Bassanio with a ring – a material, metallic token of their union – effectively converting their love into transactable gold and drawing their romantic subplot back into the commercial economy of Venice.[3] Rather than standing apart from the commercial clamour of the city, Bassanio's desire 'to give and to receive' demonstrates how pervasively the capitalist mindset infiltrates the culture of Belmont.

Shakespeare's Venice is a place where economic fungibility exists in the extreme, where kisses are construed as marketable and profitable, and the relentless pursuit of extractable value puts social cohesion under strain. Under these extremes, *The Merchant of Venice* insists on working through forms of exchange, conversion, reciprocity and circulation that have meaning far beyond the mercantile, and which instead figure relationships and obligations between individuals and institutions. In this article, I argue that the unsettling nexus of this

relationship between market and community is played out through the figurative, and eventually literal, association of blood and money, as Shakespeare presents blood exemplifying conceptions of intrinsic value – or rather, the fiction of intrinsic value. In *Merchant*, blood is both assumed to represent something inherent – the essential substance of common humanity – and also drawn into the commercial exchanges of the city, unsettling the play's presentation of a radical form of commensurability between bodies and commodities. To the Venetian merchants and usurers, this commensurability – which describes their ability to value different commodities against each other – is a constituent part of their venture capitalism, but Shakespeare forces this way of thinking to a point of crisis that – in laying bare not only the inherent

---

[1] William Shakespeare, *The Merchant of Venice*, in *The Norton Shakespeare*, 3rd ed., gen. eds. Stephen Greenblatt et al. (London and New York, 2016); all references to the play are to this edition.

[2] For more on Belmont as an extension of Venice's mercantile economy, see Karoline Szatek, '*The Merchant of Venice* and the politics of commerce', in *The Merchant of Venice: Critical Essays*, ed. John W. Mahon and Ellen Macleod Mahon (New York and London, 2002), 325–52; Nancy E. Hodge describes Belmont as 'an aristocratic retreat from a mercantile centre' – see 'Making places at Belmont: "You are welcome notwithstanding"', *Shakespeare Studies* 21 (1993), 155–74; p. 155.

[3] Throughout, I refer to *economy* in its common post-nineteenth-century sense, as 'the organisation or condition of a community or nation with respect to economic factors, esp. the production and consumption of goods and services and the supply of money … a particular economic system' (*OED Online*, n. 11). During the early modern period, *Oeconomie* more directly relates to the management of the household, even if this meaning does begin to be applied to the 'universall government of the State, or particular regiment of the Cittie' – see Thomas Wright, *The Passions of the Minde in Generall* (London, 1604), n.p. – and the management of the body through therapy and diet, both of which draw on the general sense of management or governance: Richard Huleot's *Dictionary Newelye Corrected* (London, 1572) defines '*Oeconomia*' as 'Houshold ordering, or governaunce' (sig. Zijv).

difference between 'person' and 'purse', but also Venice's powerlessness to escape the discourses of financial evaluation – is itself representative of something quite radical. Indeed, Eric Spenser proposes that the 'relentless thematizing of value … suggests that the play consciously stages this impasse'.[4]

In this play, blood is embroiled in the complex workings of economic and social circulation, resonating with early modern efforts to conceptualize the distribution of coin and power in relation to the movement of blood around the body. In *The Customers Alphabet* (1608), for example, English customs official Thomas Milles contends that 'Money in a Kingdome [is] the same that Blood is in the Body.'[5] Indeed, having established the analogous relationship between money and blood, Milles goes on to observe that, like blood in the body, monetary exchange represents the 'cyment' and 'glewe' that holds society together: 'Exchange of Goodnes by Gold & Silver, the Body & Blood of Kings and Kingdoms (represented to us in currant Coyne,) be the Spirit of Trafficke, and mysticall Cyment that glewes so fast together the mutuall conjunction betweene Soveraignes & Subjects.'[6]

In Milles's conception, blood and 'currant Coyne' are analogous precisely because their distribution binds bodies – corporate and corporeal – together like 'glewe', but also because of their role as a mediator of 'exchange' that holds individuals together in 'mutuall conjunction'. What Milles articulates here is what Marxists subsequently call the 'Cash Nexus', the name given to the reduction of human relationships, within a capitalist system, to forms of monetary exchange.[7] Indeed, the image that Milles creates is at once static and dynamic, as the reciprocal 'Trafficke' of exchange – of taking and giving – is understood as something that fixes 'fast together'.

During the early modern period, blood and money are, therefore, consistently and conceptually linked: in his sermon *A Caveat for the Covetous*, William Whately declares that a 'peece of money goes from him as a drop of bloud from his heart', with the fellow Puritan, John Dod, likewise preaching that conscience should be 'more deare unto us, then eyther money, or our heart blood'.[8] Underlying these theological associations, the *locus classicus* of the collocation of blood and money during this period is Judas' betrayal of Christ, with Miles Coverdale's English translation of the Bible providing the earliest instance of 'bloudmoney'. When Judas returns the thirty silver coins that he was paid for betraying Christ, the Temple priests refuse to accept it back into the Temple coffers: they 'toke the sylver pens, and sayde: It is not laufull to put them in to

the Gods chest, for it is bloudmoney'.[9] Even when, in plays such as *1 Henry IV*, Shakespeare draws on the association between money and blood in a political and martial context, the Christological connotations reverberate. Evoking Christ's wounds, Hotspur declares 'Yea, on his part I'll empty all these veins / And shed my dear blood drop by drop in the dust' (1.3.133–4), before rebuking Henry IV as 'this proud king … who studies day and night / To answer all the *debt* he owes to you / Even with the *blood payment* of your deaths' (183–6, emphasis added).

By reading *Merchant* through the lens of developments in monetary and mercantile knowledge, we can gauge the ways in which this play imbricates the depiction and significance of blood and money, showing how and why Shakespeare thinks about blood in economic and peculiarly circulatory terms. Shakespeare's depictions of circulating and reciprocating bodies and blood animate contemporary and commonplace metaphors and correspondences that imagined the body through emergent economic structures, and vice versa.

CIRCLES OF COMMERCE IN EARLY MODERN ENGLAND

As Michael J. Neuss has shown, William Harvey's landmark publication on the movement of the heart and blood, *De motu cordis et sanguinis* (1628), and the experimentalism that it represents are in large measure 'an exercise in accounting' and in a number of places exhibit the 'precise language of accountancy'.[10] Moreover, and as Charles Webster points out, Harvey's 'family and social situation of necessity familiarized him with the broader commercial and economic context' of his time.[11] All of

4 Eric Spenser, 'Taking excess, exceeding account: Aristotle meets *The Merchant of Venice*', in *Money and the Age of Shakespeare*, ed. Linda Woodbridge (Basingstoke, 2003), 143–58; p. 147.

5 Thomas Milles, *The Customers Alphabet* ([London?], 1608), sig. G2r.

6 Milles, *The Customers Alphabet*, sig. K2v.

7 On the cash nexus in Shakespeare, see Kenneth Muir, '*Timon of Athens* and the cash nexus', in *The Singularity of Shakespeare, and Other Essays* (Liverpool, 1977), 56–75.

8 William Whately, *A Caveat for the Covetous* (London, 1609), p. 16; John Dod, *A Plain and Familiar Exposition* (London, 1610), p. 144.

9 Miles Coverdale, *Byblia the Byble … Faithfully Translated in to Englyshe* (London, 1535), sig. CC2V, Matthew 27.

10 Michael J. Neuss, 'Blood money: Harvey's *De motu cordis* (1628) as an exercise in accounting', *British Journal for the History of Science* 51 (2018), 181–203; p. 181.

11 Charles Webster, 'William Harvey and the crisis of medicine in Jacobean England', in *William Harvey and His Age: The Professional*

Harvey's five brothers – Daniel, Eliab, John, Matthew and Michael – were directly involved in the emerging world of early modern transnational trade and commerce, each being associated with either the East India, Grocer's or Levant companies. As the seventeenth-century merchant and proto-economist Thomas Mun makes clear in *England's Benefit and Advantage*, of all the 'Qualities which are required in a perfect Merchant', arithmetic and 'accompt[ing]' – the now obsolete word for accounting – are the most important.[12] Similarly, Sir Lewes Roberts, a Levant Company captain, writes in his *Merchants Map of Commerce* – an extensive guide to mercantilism that was dedicated to William Harvey and his brothers – that 'It is required, that he [the merchant] be well skild in the *art* of Arithmetique and numbering, which indeed is the principall steppe to this art of accounting.'[13] Unlike his brothers, Harvey was not a merchant; as will be shown, however, Harvey employs the rhetoric of account-keeping in *De motu*, demonstrating his familiarity with early modern bookkeeping practices. Moreover, Harvey's work illustrates the underlying similarities between dynamic principles that emerged in the largely unrelated fields of physiology and early economic theory, at the beginning of the seventeenth century. For Harvey's early readers, as Neuss suggests, 'accounting for blood as though it were money required little inference, given the importance of the blood–money metaphor in the tracts of the merchants who advised the royal court'.[14]

Comparably, Shakespeare's plays and poems demonstrate considerable familiarity with the language of contemporary accounting; as Linda Woodbridge observes, in *Othello* Iago's naming of Cassio as a 'debitor and creditor' and a 'counter-caster' (1.1.30) suggests that Shakespeare understood the rudiments of bookkeeping.[15] Likewise, in *1 Henry IV* the prodigal Prince Hal employs the language of accounting when he claims he will 'redeem' his past wrongs 'When I will wear a garment all of blood, / And stain my favours in a bloody mask' (3.2.135–6). In Hal's estimation, future martial honour will compensate past dishonour, calculating how Hotspur's downfall will convert his own 'indignities' to 'glorious deeds' (3.2.146): 'I will call him to so strict *account* / That he shall render every glory up, ... | Or I will tear the *reckoning* from his heart' (*1 Henry IV* 3.2.149–52, emphasis added). Not only does Hal's intention to 'redeem' himself harbour commercial connotations, from the Latin *redemptiō* as an act of buying or the purchasing of a contract, but his plan to 'tear the reckoning from [Henry Percy's] heart' employs the meaning of 'reckoning' as the act of calculating and the provision of a financial account (*OED Online*, n. 2, 3.

a). In 1588, John Mellis – who established a school of arithmetic and accounting in Southwark not far from where the Globe Theatre was built in 1599 – issued a reprint of Hugh Oldcastle's now lost 1543 translation of Luca Pacioli's *Summa de arithmetica, geometria, proportioni et proportionalita* (1494), the earliest printed treatise on double-entry bookkeeping.[16] Whether Shakespeare ever came into contact with Mellis or any pupils from his accounting school is impossible to determine, but his plays frequently employ technical accounting terms to which Elizabethan tradesmen, merchants and bookkeepers would have been well accustomed.

In response to the economic rhetoric of Michel de Montaigne's *Essais* (but equally appropriate to Shakespeare's works), Philippe Desan explains that the ubiquity of economic discourse in early modern literature illustrates how widespread economic thinking became during this period:

It appears that ways of apprehending social relationships, as well as all forms of human activity – including the arts and literature – have straddled the economic mode of organization ever since the end of the sixteenth century. The literary text from then on was approached and organized as a commercial object and thought of itself strictly as merchandize. It is thus normal that not only the content of a literary work but also its structure would be tightly linked to the economic sphere.[17]

During the early modern era, emergent economic knowledge offered new ways of thinking through forms of distribution, balance and reciprocity that can be seen to impact on Shakespeare's depiction of blood and its significance to social and political relationships.

---

and Social Context of the Discovery of the Circulation, ed. Jerome J. Bylebyl (Baltimore and London, 1979), 1–27; p. 21.

[12] Thomas Mun, *England's Benefit and Advantage* (London, 1698), p. 4.

[13] Lewes Roberts, *The Merchants Map of Commerce: Wherein the Universal Manner and Matter of Trade is Compendiously Handled* (London, 1638), p. 37; for Roberts's dedication to the six Harvey brothers, see sig. A3r.

[14] Neuss, 'Blood money', p. 201.

[15] Linda Woodbridge, 'Introduction', in *Money and the Age of Shakespeare*, ed. Woodbridge, 1–18; p. 2.

[16] See Woodbridge, 'Introduction', pp. 1–2.

[17] Philippe Desan, 'Quand le discours social passe pas le discours économique: les Essais de Montaigne', *Sociocriticism* 4 (1988), 59–86; p. 84, here translated by Nancy P. Epstein and quoted in 'Montaigne's Essais: metaphors of capital and exchange', in *The New Economic Criticism: Studies at the Intersection of Literature and Economics*, ed. Mark Osteen and Martha Woodmansee (London and New York, 1999), 210–20; p. 210.

During the early modern period, both blood and money are drawn into a broad range of questions relating to individual identity, social and economic relationships, and the nature and distribution of social power.[18] In *Merchant*, Shakespeare explores these themes through various economies of blood, or rather through a range of mercantile, romantic and social economies – structures and interpersonal associations and obligations, as well as systems of financial or commercial exchange – that exploit the material and symbolic value of blood and the heart's role in its distribution. At this time, blood and money are, conceptually, shown and understood to have a lot in common: their shared material and symbolic function in nourishing the body and the state; their currency and portability, between palms and purses in the case of coins, or within and between bodies in the case of blood; and the ways in which both blood and money can cross boundaries – somatic or social. At the same time, just as coins were beginning to be understood as a medium for different and increasingly competing forms of value – both intrinsic (the value of the gold or silver from which they were made) and extrinsic (the financial and symbolic value ascribed to them by the monarch or by individuals and communities) – blood was routinely invested with symbolic values that adhered to, but also unsettled, its physiological function.

Since the coining of the term 'The New Economic Criticism' in 1991, the relationship between literature and economic theory has received a great deal of critical attention. Responding to and building on the first wave of economic criticism, which appeared during the late 1970s, and which is epitomized by Marc Shell's *The Economy of Literature* (1978), 'The New Economic Criticism' has continued to interrogate historical trends in economic decision-making, the economic conditions of artistic production, individual and collective economic behaviour, and the resemblances between economic and linguistic systems.[19] In *The Economy of Literature*, Shell persuasively argues that all literary texts are 'composed of small tropic exchanges or metaphors, some of which can be analysed in terms of signified economic content and all of which can be analysed in terms of economic form'.[20] In more recent years, widespread interest in early modern economics has led to a significant number of studies that examine the place and purpose of money, coins, debt and commerce in early modern English literature, as illustrated by the publication of *Money and the Age of Shakespeare: Essays in New Economic Criticism* in 2003.[21] Furthermore, Stephen Deng and David Landreth have examined

how, in early modern England, the wildly fluctuating difference between the intrinsic and extrinsic value of coins fostered a wide variety of social relationships – political, charitable, artistic – that were not always directly associated with forms of commercial exchange. As Jean-Christophe Agnew suggests:

In the century preceding the English Civil War, Britons could be described as feeling their way round a problematic of exchange; that is to say, they were putting forward a coherent and repeated pattern of problems or questions about the nature of social identity, intentionality, accountability, transparency, and reciprocity in commodity transactions – the who, what, when, where, and why of exchange.[22]

Put simply, in addition to fulfilling its role as commercial currency and a medium of exchange value, during the early modern period money functions as what Huey-Ling Lee calls 'a form of social currency'; accordingly, money can be seen to simultaneously satisfy both the financial and the social needs of early modern communities, enabling individuals and groups to manage the shifting needs and dynamics of 'both inter-group as well as intra-group relations'.[23] As Landreth explains, 'it is money's particular job to be ubiquitous: that's what it means to be currency, to be current, that money flows across otherwise uncrossable distances, and over such otherwise insuperable divides'.[24] In other words, it is

---

[18] See Craig Muldrew, *The Economy of Obligation: The Culture of Credit and Social Relations in Early Modern England* (New York, 1998).

[19] For a thorough digest of the evolution of The New Economic Criticism, see Mark Osteen and Martha Woodmansee, 'Taking account of The New Economic Criticism: an historical introduction', in *The New Economic Criticism: Studies at the Intersection of Literature and Economics*, ed. Mark Osteen and Martha Woodmansee (London and New York, 1999), 3–50.

[20] Marc Shell, *The Economy of Literature* (Baltimore and London, 1978), p. 7.

[21] For more on early modern coinage, see Linda Woodbridge, ed., *Money and the Age of Shakespeare: Essays in the New Economic Criticism* (New York, 2003); David Hawkes, *Idols of the Market Place: Idolatry and Commodity Fetishism in English Literature, 1580–1680* (New York, 2001); Stephen Deng, *Coinage and State Formation in Early Modern English Literature* (New York, 2011); David Landreth, *The Face of Mammon: The Matter of Money in English Renaissance Literature* (Oxford, 2012); Craig Muldrew, '"Hard food for Midas": cash and its social value in early modern England', *Past and Present* 170 (2001), 78–120.

[22] Jean-Christophe Agnew, *Worlds Apart: The Market and the Theatre in Anglo-American Thought, 1550–1750* (Cambridge, 1986), p. 9.

[23] Huey-Ling Lee, 'The social meaning of money in Dekker's *The Shoemaker's Holiday* and Shakespeare's *The Merchant of Venice*', *Comparative Drama* 49 (2015), 335–66; p. 335.

[24] Landreth, *The Face of Mammon*, p. 5.

the materiality of money that contributes directly to its efficacy as a medium of financial, commercial and social exchange; as Eric Spenser puts it, money performs 'a necessary mechanism of community'.[25]

As a result of a widespread economic recession in England during the second decade of the seventeenth century, the final years of Shakespeare's life are marked by a phase of intense debate among the period's more prominent mercantilists, notably between Edward Misselden and Gerard Malynes.[26] However, although this period of debate was precipitated by the immediate experience of economic decline, it reflects a number of broad and long-standing approaches to fiscal intervention that stretch back into the preceding century. In brief, this period of dispute began in 1622 with Misselden publishing *Free Trade, Or the Means to Make Trade Flourish*, in response to a treatise by Malynes in which the latter argued in favour of a fixed exchange rate between English and foreign coin. In response, Misselden, whilst acknowledging that English coin was undervalued, counters Malynes by asserting that the value of specie is and should be determined by the continual flux of market demand and international trade. Conversely, in *The Maintenance of Free Trade*, the next treatise to be published, Malynes again lobbies in favour of a fixed exchange rate between domestic and foreign coin, arguing that '*overballancing* doth expell our moneys out of the Realme'.[27] In Malynes's eyes, it was the difficulty faced by merchants and tradesmen in accurately determining and converting the cash value of their wares, and also the dishonesty of foreign merchants, that was causing economic recession. In reply, a consortium of English merchants wrote to the Privy Council, arguing that a fixed rate of exchange would inhibit their practical experience and knowledge of commercial evaluation.[28] Claiming almost the exact opposite of Malynes, Misselden and his fellow merchants, including Thomas Mun, believed that it was trade that set the value of coins, rather than the value of coins that stimulated trade. Ultimately, Mun and Misselden held that even a relatively small quantity of continuously and vigorously circulating coin could sustain a healthy balance of import and export, and that any effort to fix the value of English coins would counterproductively inhibit transnational trade. In contrast to Malynes, who feared the effects of English specie leaving the domestic economy, Misselden and Mun saw this outpouring of English money as a crucial mechanism in the balancing of the economy. Underlying this dispute, Misselden and Mun held close affiliations with the chartered trading companies of London, whose international trade they wanted to see expand, whereas Malynes, who had no such affiliations, can be seen to lobby for greater intervention by the crown in economic affairs, investing his efforts in systems of aristocratic patronage and monopolism. Consequently, Malynes's writing empowers the system of court patronage which fundamentally relied on the buoyancy and balance of royal power at its centre; were the crown to fix the value of English coin in relation to foreign currencies, Malynes believed that other European powers would no longer capitalize by undervaluing English money, which drew it out and away from the domestic economy.

Throughout these exchanges, the physiology of the body and the diagnosis and treatment of disease can be seen to offer a framework within which late Elizabethan and Jacobean mercantilists expressed their economic philosophies, as the title of Gerard Malynes's earliest mercantilist treatise – which, for its self-association with medical discourse, is worth giving in full – illustrates:

A Treatise of the Canker of Englands Common Wealth Devided into Three Parts: Wherein the Author Imitating the Rule of Good Phisitions, First, Declareth the Disease. Secondarily, Sheweth the Efficient Cause Thereof. Lastly, a Remedy for the Same.

Here and throughout, Malynes describes England's economic woes as a 'canker', the name given to chronic, gangrenous and cancerous sores. As Malynes's title suggests, *The Canker of England's Common Wealth* takes the form of a medical treatise, '*Imitating the Rule of Good Physicians*', by describing, clarifying and remedying the monetary maladies of the realm. As Malynes explains, the disease affecting the English body politic is 'an overballancing of forreine commodities with his home commodities, or in buying more then he selleth', which spells disaster for England as 'the wealth of the realme doth decrease, and as it were his expences become greater, or do surmount his incomes or revenues'.[29] As in all of

25 Spenser, 'Taking excess', p. 143.
26 For a thorough account of this period of mercantilist debate, see Lars Magnussen, 'The 1620s debates', in *The Political Economy of Mercantilism* (London and New York, 2015), 133–72.
27 Gerard Malynes, *The Maintenance of Free Trade* (London, 1622), p. 22; for a more thorough discussion of the 1622–3 Pamphlet War between Malynes and Misselden, see Jonathan Gil Harris, *Sick Economies: Drama, Mercantilism, and Disease in Shakespeare's England* (Philadelphia, 2004), pp. 138–41.
28 See 'Several treatises and notes relating to foreign exchanges, and to the balance of trade; 1622–23', British Library Add. MS 34324 ('Collection of Political and Other Papers by Sir Julius Caesar'), fols. 153–78.
29 Gerard Malynes, *A Treatise of the Canker of Englands Common Wealth* (London, 1601), pp. 2–3.

Malynes' fiscal treatises, the problem is one that only the crown's direct intervention in establishing a fixed exchange rate for coin can remedy; accordingly, Malynes offers a corporeal, top-down system of economic governance wherein the 'head . . . may commaund and direct all the other parts and members of the body'.[30] Throughout, Malynes leans heavily on a medical framework and bodily language in order to formulate his remedy to England's economic troubles; like so many works of this period, his treatise is firmly rooted in a system of correspondences that solidify the perceived relationships between the macrocosm and the microcosm, giving his fiscal policies broader appeal and legitimacy through their association with the workings of the body.

Throughout Misselden's and Malynes's treatises from the early 1620s, the humoral body thus offers a way of thinking about commerce and economic distribution through widely understood medical images; as Jonathan Gil Harris points out, 'the physiology of blood is also at the heart . . . [of] the pamphlet war of 1622–23'.[31] In *The Center of the Circle of Commerce* (1623) – Malynes's response to Misselden's *The Circle of Commerce*, published earlier in the same year – Malynes employs an extended physiological metaphor of the economy as a sick body in order to explain how 'States-men or Politicians (which are the Phisitians of Common-weales)' have considered the 'internal parts' of the economy.[32] Here, he argues, they have

found the liver (*Money*) obstructed, and the condinct pipes of *Bullion* and *Moneys* for importation stopt, whereby the *Hepaties* could not minister good bloud, with spirits sufficient to comfort the heart of (*our native commodities*) by a naturall heate: for the gaule of *Customes and impositions* is overflown also, depriving the stomacke of his appetie: hence the braine (*Exchange,* wanting sleepe) is distempered, whereby the body is overtaken with a *Trepidation* or shaking, shewing the very *Symptomes* of death.[33]

Here, in his description of money and bullion being 'obstructed' as an issue with the body's '*Hepaties*', Malynes can be seen responding to and redeploying Misselden's earlier evocation of money pouring out of England to the Continental markets as a hepatic condition: 'the Hepatites, or Liver veine of this Great body of ours being opened, & such profusio[n]s of the Life bloud let out'.[34] Evoking the English domestic economy as a wounded and bleeding body, Misselden similarly explains that he 'beheld this former flourishing Trade of ours, to be threatened by many as eminent as imminent dangers, and the very life thereof to lie a bleeding'.[35]

Over a decade earlier, Thomas Milles – the English customs official who evokes blood and the exchange of money as 'cyment' and 'glewe' – had described the minting and movement of money through the image of chyle – the substance produced from food, which the body turned into blood – and blood coursing through the body, from the liver to the heart and then through the veins, to the benefit of all men:

let the hart by the lyver, receive his tinctured Chylus, by his owne mouth and stomacke, and the blood with the Spirits shall fill all the vaines. And if Nature have taught all men to affect the generall Good by particular Trades, and appoynted each Trade his proper Materialls by the helpe and use of Money, leave Bullion for Princes, and the World can want no Coyne; the easie course and recourse of whose Exchange, shall set all things in tune, and serve all Mens turnes.[36]

Here, Milles's image of a nourishing economy follows the pattern of a Galenic conception of healthy bloodflow in which a steady supply of blood/money works its way to all men, who understand their 'appoynted . . . Trade'. Certainly, Milles's account of the 'easie course and recourse' of exchange evokes the ebbing and flowing – 'the carrying and recarryinge' as Helkiah Crooke describes it – of blood in the pre-Harveian body.[37] Just as the uninhibited movement of blood nourishes the body, the 'easie course' of money keeps everything as it should be, alive and 'proper'; as Scipion de Gramont, a cabinet secretary to Louis XIII, writes 'L'argent . . . est le sang & l'ame des hommes, & celuy qui n'en a point chemine mort entre les vivans' ('money . . . is the blood and soul of men, and he who has none wanders dead among the living').[38]

In *The Circle of Commerce*, Misselden explains that 'All the rivers of Trade spring out of this source, and empt[y] themselves againe into this Ocean. All the waight of Trade falle's to this Center, & comes within the circuit of this *Circle*.'[39] By evoking the natural cycle

---

[30] Malynes, *A Treatise of the Canker*, p. 31.

[31] Gil Harris, *Sick Economies*, p. 137.

[32] Gerard Malynes, *The Center of The Circle of Commerce* (London, 1623), pp. 128–9.

[33] Malynes, *The Center*, p. 129.

[34] Edward Misselden, *The Circle of Commerce. Or The Ballance of Trade in Defence of Free Trade* (London, 1623), p. 10.

[35] Misselden, *Free Trade*, p. 2.

[36] Milles, *The Customers Alphabet,* sig. f2r.

[37] Helikiah Crooke, *Mikrokosmographia: A Description of the Body of Man* (London, 1615), p. 656.

[38] Scipion de Gramont, *Le Denier royale* (Paris, 1620), p. 9.

[39] Misselden, *The Circle of Commerce*, p. 143.

of water, coursing through rivers, from and back into the ocean, Misselden employs a characteristically Aristotelian image. However, in Misselden's *The Circle of Commerce*, his conception of autonomous economic recirculation is, crucially, defined by its lack of a governing centre. In contrast, it is Malynes, in *The Center of the Circle of Commerce*, who suggests that the balance of trade could be secured by establishing a heart-like centre to the circle, by fixing the value of coins. Drawing economic, political and corporeal language together, in a direct address to James I, Malynes asserts 'Your Highnes therefore may be pleased to advance the establishing of this Center in the course of Trade, whereby his Majesties Kingdomes and Dominions will flow with Bullion and Moneys, and infuse life thereunto, which will be felt by the *Pulces*, the Hammers of the Mint.'[40]

By imagining the 'pulc[ing]' hammers of the Royal Mint, Malynes establishes a corporeal hierarchy of the monarch as the brain and the falling hammers of the coineries as the economic heart of the realm. Later, Malynes returns to this image of coin production as the 'pulce' of the commercial circuit:

the obstruction of the Liver ... must be opened by the meanes of the Braine, (*Exchange*) to minister good Bloud and Spirits to the Heart of our native *Commodities*, to make a lively Trade, whereby *Bullion* brought to the Mint, will cause the hammers (as the pulses of the Body of Trade) to beate with temperate strokes, by meanes whereof the distemperature of the Braine (*Exchange*) will be qualified.[41]

By drawing on physiological structures to frame their ideas, both Malynes and Misselden illustrate and contribute to a set of underlying conceptual similarities between competing dynamic principles of monetary circulation. However, whilst the treatises of Malynes and Misselden are initially rooted in corporeal and pathological metaphors, as their dispute developed Misselden increasingly adopted, as Gil Harris points out, a 'disembodied discourse based on quantitative analysis'.[42]

'THIS BOND DOTH GIVE THEE HERE NO JOT OF BLOOD': CONVERTING BLOOD IN *THE MERCHANT OF VENICE*

In *The Merchant of Venice*, money is everything. Each of the play's central protagonists – Antonio, Bassanio, Portia and Shylock – insists that they are not interested in money, and yet in expressing what does motivate them cannot escape the language of profit, exchange and conversion. Money is on their minds and on their lips nearly all of the time, and yet, as Landreth observes, they seem to talk about money 'in order to claim that what they are really talking about is something incommensurable to money'.[43] The Venetian society that Shakespeare depicts is so invested in the structures and language of commercial exchange that – despite the play's engagement with questions of friendship, family, love, religious identity, mercy and justice – it is unable to raise itself above the all-encompassing matter of money. Both the bond that Shylock strikes with Antonio and the nuptial bonds struck in Belmont enmesh flesh and gold, and, as Robert N. Watson suggests, money 'permeates the play at a micro-level ... shaping its diction and imagery, and lending a kind of queasy flavour to all of its gestures towards romantic comedy'.[44] However, even as these figures try and fail to talk about something other than capital, their interactions demonstrate the ubiquity of commercial evaluation in such a way as to reveal the fiscal nature of community and social bonds. Just as money offers a medium for exchange, the relationships that are presented and understood through the exchange value of money are shown to be fashioned from and strengthened by forms of reciprocation, conversion and evaluation.

Fittingly, then, the play circles around a complex of words prefixed by 'co-', 'con-' and 'com-' that simultaneously convey ideas of exchange and intimacy, such as 'conversion', 'convenience', 'commonality', 'commodity' and 'commendation'.[45] In 'convert' (3.5.32) and 'converse' (3.4.12) especially – two words linked by the Latin root *convertere*, meaning 'to turn together' – there is a shared sense of cohesion, as in conversing with someone or converting them to a shared outlook. Similarly, during Antonio and Bassanio's goodbye, Antonio is reported to have told Bassanio that 'love ... shall *conveniently* become you' (2.8.45, emphasis added), which draws out the

---

40 Malynes, *The Center*, sig. A4r–A4v, emphasis added.
41 Malynes, *The Center*, pp. 130–1.
42 Gil Harris, *Sick Economies*, p. 141.
43 Landreth, *The Face of Mammon*, p. 150.
44 Robert N. Watson, *Back to Nature: The Green and the Real in the Late Renaissance* (Philadelphia, 2006), pp. 266–7.
45 Surprisingly, Shakespeare does not use the word 'commerce' in *Merchant*, but does elsewhere: in *Troilus and Cressida*, for example, Ulysses remarks on 'All the *commerce* that you have had with Troy' (3.3.205).

connotations of union as well as that of ease and agreement. At the same time, however, these conversions camouflage the opposing suggestion of inherent separation, by structurally bringing together what is otherwise set apart; consequently, the play grapples with the idea of concurrent togetherness and separation through the conversions, conversations and commercial exchanges that pass between and bind together the central protagonists.

In market terms, money enables the merchants of Venice to compare and exchange unlike commodities, to trade in 'spices' and 'silk' (1.1.33–4), and to make all things commensurable and thereby fungible. Indeed, as Misselden's and Malynes's commercial treatises make clear, the balancing of trade – import and export – assumed a fundamental fungibility between goods and money: especially for Misselden, coin and bullion could leave the country, so long as an equal or greater value of commodities came back in return. In *Merchant*, this balancing of import and export, and the merchants' ability 'to give and to receive', offers a framework through which social and erotic obligations and relationships are established, solidified and understood. Just as ducats can be seen to enable and mobilize commercial networks, in *Merchant* friendships and familiarities are fundamentally a matter of money.

Alongside this economic framework, however, there exists a current of blood images that become steadily embroiled in the play's commercial discourse. Registering the play's engagement with ideas relating to the conversions and commensurations of the marketplace, moments of familial recognition – such as in Old Gobbo's claim 'thou art mine own flesh and blood' (2.2.88) – are set against rejections of familial unity and similitude, such as Jessica's declaration 'though I am a daughter to his blood / I am not to his manners' (2.4.18–19), which introduce competing valuations of social connectedness. Blood is assumed to offer a tangible and intrinsic assurance of association, but the play demonstrates that these values are capricious and mutable. When Shylock echoes Jessica's claim to their blood bond – 'My daughter is my flesh and blood' (3.1.33) – even when she has rejected their similarity in 'manners', Salanio's subsequent report of Shylock wailing in the street, 'My daughter! O my ducats! O my daughter ... o my Christian ducats ... my ducats, and my daughter!' (2.8.15–17), illustrates how the value of gold is allowed to override the value of consanguinity, or at least bring the bonds of blood into a kind of market and linguistic competition with

coins. Shylock's later claim to absolute physiological and ontological 'resembl[ance]' (3.1.61) with his Christian neighbours in his questioning 'if you prick us do we not bleed?' (3.1.58) thus exemplifies the opposing impulse to the otherwise outright desire to economically evaluate 'person' as 'purse'. At the moment when Shylock's desire and motivations for revenge take form, he cites the Christians' rejection of a shared recourse to the base matter of blood as his grounds for requital. As such, Shylock's rhetorical claim to a common humanity borne in physiological and sanguineous similarity with his Christian brethren is absolutely ensnared in the pursuit of Antonio's forfeit to the bond between them. Put another way, just as Antonio desires to impose his 'person' on Bassanio's borrowing, Shylock highlights and literalizes Antonio's refusal to commit his 'person' to the similarly economic association between a Christian and a Jew.

Rather than borrowing from a friend, on first approaching Shylock as a potential creditor Antonio seeks an arrangement of negative reciprocity secured by the harshest of terms: 'lend it rather to thine enemy, / Who if he break, thou may'st with better face / Exact the penalty' (1.3.130–2). Nevertheless, by setting a portion of Antonio's flesh – which Shylock regards as valueless since it is 'not so estimable, profitable neither' (1.3.162) – as the collateral for his loan, Shylock speaks a version of equitable, non-profiteering and Christian exchange that Antonio understands. Indeed, it is Antonio's desire to solidify his friendship with Bassanio, rather than to profit financially from him, that leads him to 'unlock' his 'purse', his 'person' and his 'extremest means' (1.1.138–9), and to allow Bassanio to 'try' his 'credit' (180). In turn, Shylock seeks to lend to Antonio 'to buy [his] favour' and to 'extend ... friendship' (1.3.164) – to profit by him not in financial but in social terms: 'I would be friends with you, and have your love, / Forget the shames ... | Supply your present wants' (134–6). This can, of course, be read as Shylock duping Antonio through the performance of false friendship. But, taken at face value, how different are Shylock's motives in lending Antonio money from what Antonio seeks to gain from Bassanio? Just as Antonio makes his credit available to Bassanio in order to strengthen their love and friendship, Shylock makes his credit available to Antonio – for Shylock has actually borrowed the money from Tubal – to make Antonio his friend and have his love, to show Antonio that variety of 'kindness' (1.3.139) that has more to do with similarity and kinship (*OED Online*, 'kind, *adj.* [†]5') than with benevolence.[46]

Unlike the Christians of Venice, figureheaded by Antonio, who profess to use money to make friends and to solidify social relationships, Shylock and his Jewish brethren are known to use money for profit by lending it out at interest. Yet Shylock's bond with Antonio subverts this expectation and, at least before Antonio defaults on the loan, demonstrates that, even across religious and community divides, the movement of money works to underwrite the formation of social relationships. In these early exchanges of the play, the commercial value of money is, therefore, subtended by its function as 'social currency'.[47] In a similar fashion to Antonio's transnational ventures – to Tripolis, the Indies, Mexico and England – in which the boundary-crossing efficacy of money is conditioned by the huge geographical distances that it mediates as it shrinks the conceptual size of the navigable world to tallies of import and export, the financial bond between Shylock and Antonio draws them closer together by subtly converting the commercial value of money into something sociably redeemable.[48]

From the outset, however, these exchanges harbour clues to the inevitable costs of imbricating financial and social currency. During the earliest movements of the play, when Salerio and Salanio metaphorically convert Antonio's passions into 'the tossing ocean' (1.1.8) and 'the wind' (18) on which his commercial investments are imagined to pitch and roll, and which 'blows' him 'to an ague' (23) Shakespeare can be seen testing out the possibilities of imagining the passionate body as part of the processes of commercial exchange. Nevertheless, Antonio quickly rejects the idea that his disposition is tied to his investments – 'my merchandise makes me not sad' (45). Presently, however, Antonio directs Bassanio to conflate purse and person by 'try[ing]' his credit in the city. Here, Antonio's direction to 'try' simultaneously suggests both the idea of testing and attempting, in the sense that Bassanio should see how much money Antonio's credit and reputation can raise, but it also carries the idea of material separation and distinction, in that to 'try' can also mean 'to separate (one thing) from another' (*OED Online*, v.1a). When Aragon later selects the silver casket in Belmont, the scroll's message states that 'The fire seven times tried this; / Seven times tried that judgement' (2.9.62–3), playing on the sense of metallurgical *trying* as the refinement of metal (*OED Online*, v.3) – separating metal from ore – and to *try* in the sense of a legal trial (*OED Online*, v.6a). Thus, even when Antonio suggests that Bassanio 'try' his 'credit', conflating 'person' and 'purse', this process of 'try[ing]'

already conceals the sense of separating out and extricating different forms of value – financial, somatic and social. That is, the money that Bassanio borrows from Antonio simultaneously brings them together in friendship, even as it separates them from one another, enabling Bassanio to travel to Belmont and eventually gaoling Antonio in Venice. Understood in this sense, *Merchant* is fundamentally about forcing this mindset, of the absolute fungibility of flesh and cash, to a point of crisis, during which the metaphoric association of blood and money, of person and purse, is split wide open. If financial dealings initially promise the potential of reaching out across social divides and of bringing Shylock and Antonio together in friendship, the play ends with Shylock being forced to convert to Christianity. Shylock's bond, at least in outward show, is offered in good faith and in hope of kindness, but it ends with Shylock being un-kinned from his Jewish neighbours, as the Venetian Christians force him to become exactly like them, to fix him and the value he represents through conversion.

From the very beginning, the play's protagonists desire to make and treat money as something other than itself: when money most straightforwardly resembles itself – gold, silver, 'three thousand ducats' (1.3.1) – the Venetians want it to be anything but specie; when cash is converted into something other than coin, they desperately attempt to exchange it back into gold, by evaluating it in cash terms. As Landreth suggests, at the beginning of the play 'Antonio wants the money that Bassanio demands of him not to be money, and he accomplishes this by imposing his "person" upon it.'[49] There is, then, a profound irony in that, having willingly imposed his

---

[46] This follows Bassanio and Shylock's neat exchange of 'kindness':

> SHYLOCK This is kind I offer.
> BASSANIO This were kindness.
> SHYLOCK This kindness will I show. (1.3.135–6)

David Hawkes offers a slightly more sinister reading of Shylock's proposed 'kindness', by suggesting that 'Antonio is under the impression that the word "kind" here means "kin" ... but Shylock's grim vow gives it the sense of "according to kind," or "according to my nature"', tacitly reminding us that Shylock cannot easily be separated from the anti-Semitism expressed in the play, or the Semitic stereotypes that Shakespeare and his contemporaries played on – see Hawkes, *Idols of the Market Place*, p. 112.

[47] Lee, 'The social meaning', p. 359.

[48] Shylock does also reject community – 'I will not eat with you, drink with you, nor pray with you' (1.3.36–8) – but this does not contradict the social value of money, as he categorically denies his own pursuit of financial profit.

[49] Landreth, *The Face of Mammon*, p. 155.

'person' on Bassanio's borrowing, first figuratively and then literally, by accepting the terms of Shylock's loan, Antonio then struggles to extricate – to 'try' – his person from the cash sum he has attached it to. The sheer force of this irony is likely to be one that would not have been lost on the play's early audiences, as it speaks directly to how, in a late Elizabethan domestic economy that suffered from a profound shortage of coin, everyday financial transactions depended heavily on the quality of a person's character, as a guarantee of financial liquidity. As Amanda Bailey has shown, during this period, even when the reputation of a debtor faltered, the actual body of the borrower performed the role of an 'animated gage', essentially underwriting the debt with flesh and blood.[50] Whether for financial or familial profit, the borrowings and lendings of the play establish and unsettle networks of reciprocation, in which the movement of money exposes the circulation of social value.

Here, Marshall Sahlin's three categories of reciprocity – generalized, balanced and negative – provide a useful structure to understand these forms of exchange.[51] Whereas balanced reciprocity 'supposes some fairly direct one-for-one exchange ... or a near approximation of balance' and does little to establish or affect social relationships, generalized reciprocity refers to forms of gift-giving in which the expectation of the original gift being requited is delayed.[52] Consequently, generalized reciprocity fosters social relationships by establishing reciprocal interactions between individuals over time. Finally, negative reciprocity, in which the terms of the exchange are either intentionally punitive or intended to benefit one individual at the expense of another, essentially establishes a potentially adverse relationship of indebtedness. By refusing to 'lend n[or] borrow / Upon avantage' (1.3.64–5), Antonio precludes the possibility of negative reciprocity; however, as becomes clear, this is not the kind of reciprocation that Shylock expects or demands, since Shylock is happy to loan Antonio his 3,000 ducats simply on the expectation that they are repaid in 'three months' (1.3.61). Shylock attaches Antonio's 'pound of flesh' to the bond but at a time when no one reasonably believes that the merchant's investment can fail. As the only profit from this generalized exchange, Shylock – at least outwardly – intends to gain social acceptance from Antonio. To be clear, Shylock's bond is not reciprocation in the sense of gift-exchange, because it is a financial arrangement with fixed and forfeitable terms, but Antonio and Shylock's transaction does bear similarities to Sahlin's categorization.

What happens when Antonio's investments are lost and he is forced to default on his bond with Shylock is

that their arrangement of generalized, friendship-building reciprocation rapidly becomes one of negative reciprocity. As William O. Scott observes, by demanding the pound of flesh now owed to him, 'Shylock effectively converts a loan transaction into a purchase'; the attempted use of money as social currency between Shylock and Antonio collapses, and, through Shylock's seemingly callous reconversion of the social value of money back into its commercial value – its pure purchasing power – the punitive cost of their deal threatens to cut deep.[53] At the beginning of the play, however, money is presented as both commercially and socially current: Antonio seems assured of his foreign investments and, although he is unable to produce the money needed by Bassanio, he is able to borrow from Shylock, who in turn has borrowed the money from his friend Tubal; through our earliest interactions with Shakespeare's Venice, money is clearly seen to solidify existing relationships and to facilitate the formation of new ones. As Jonathan Parry and Maurice Bloch observe, 'what money means is not only situationally defined but also constantly re-negotiated', and this is what we see in Venice as the social and commercial currency of money is repeatedly recalibrated.[54]

As the centre point of the play, Bassanio's journey to Belmont initially appears to leave the reality of financial dealing behind in Venice, carrying him instead towards the moment of mystified 'giv[ing]' and 'receiv[ing]' that the gold casket calls for. However, as we know, Bassanio harbours the secret of his own financial obligations from Portia – having borrowed heavily from Antonio to fund his trip, having been 'too prodigal' (1.1.129) with his own wealth – hoping, in vain, to extricate the economies of

---

[50] Amanda Bailey, '*Timon of Athens*, forms of payback, and the genre of debt', *ELR* 41 (2011), 375–400; p. 378.

[51] See Marshall Sahlins, *Stone Age Economics* (New York, 1972). Sahlin's theory is influenced by Claude Lévi-Strauss's discussion of reciprocity in *Elementary Structures of Kinship* (1949), which in turn made use of Marcel Mauss's *Essai sur le don* ('The Gift') (1925), which is the foundational text for later social theories of reciprocity and gift-exchange. For an application of Lévi-Strauss's theory of gift-exchange to *The Merchant of Venice*, see Karen Newman, 'Portia's ring: unruly women and structures of exchange in *The Merchant of Venice*', *Shakespeare Quarterly* 38 (1987), 19–33.

[52] Sahlins, *Stone Age Economics*, p. 223.

[53] William O. Scott, 'Conditional bonds, forfeitures, and vows in *The Merchant of Venice*', *English Literary Renaissance* 34 (2004), 286–305; p. 301.

[54] Jonathan Parry and Maurice Bloch, 'Introduction: money and the morality of exchange', in *Money and the Morality of Exchange*, ed. Jonathan Parry and Maurice Bloch (Cambridge, 1989), 1–32; p. 23.

finance and love. In the world of the play, such extrication is impossible, and even before news of Antonio's imprisonment and the forfeiting of his bond with Shylock reaches Belmont and swiftly lays bare Bassanio's finances – as a measure of value that is presumed to underwrite his social and romantic capital – to Portia, the couple's language of love is already ominously infused with the logic of commercial and monetary venture. Waiting, then, for his love to be 'confirm'd, sign'd, ratified' (3.2.148) with a kiss, Bassanio's bond-language recalls not only Antonio's 'seal[ing]' (1.3.152) of his bond with Shylock, but also Lorenzo's efforts to 'seal love's bonds' (2.6.6) during his elopement with Jessica, and it further foreshadows Shylock's 'sign[ing]' (4.1.397) of the order for his own legal, financial and religious dispossession. Instead, however, of 'confirm[ing]' and 'ratify[ing]' their love-bond, Portia first looks to express her own feelings of social insufficiency, adopting the language of usury. First, reckoning herself 'alone' (3.2.150) – 'You see me . . . where I stand / Such as I am' (3.2.149–50) – Portia offers an inflationary account of her desire to be 'much better' (3.2.152) than she is:

> I would be trebled twenty times myself,
> A thousand times more fair, ten thousand times more rich,
> That only to stand high in your account,
> I might in virtues, beauties, livings, friends,
> Exceed account.
>
> (3.2.153–7)

Here, Portia's litotic speech – which extorts 'ten thousand' from one – abounds with verbal echoes that draw the language of finance and usury into the amorous economy of Belmont, such as between the close attention that Shylock pays to 'such sum or sums as are / Express'd' (1.3.147–8) in Antonio's bond, and Portia's equally sibilant self-accounting of 'the full sum of me | Is the sum of something' (3.2.157–8).[55] This also recalls the themes of currency and inflation in *Venus and Adonis*, in which Venus' 'kiss-money metaphor', as Anthony Mortimer describes it, presents a 'buy[ing] and pay[ing]' of love and the pecuniary excess of 'a thousand kisses buy [ing her] heart'.[56] Venus initially advises Adonis that 'one sweet kiss shall pay this countless debt' (84), but it does not take long for the penalty for defaulting to become far greater:

> What is ten hundred touches unto thee?
> Are they not quickly told and quickly gone?
> Say, for non-payment that the debt should double,
> Is twenty hundred kisses such a trouble?
>
> (*Venus* 519–22)

In *Venus*, Shakespeare employs various associations between kisses, wounds, lips and blood to unsettle gendered conceptions of desire in the early modern period. In *Merchant*, these associations are not as clear-cut; nevertheless, Portia's image of multiplication reveals the degree to which the play's money metaphors infiltrate Belmont and the discourses of love.[57] As Karoline Szatek observes, 'Belmont embraces the commercialism Venice introduced to it, and Belmont exploits the merchandizing to such a degree that its own capitalist ethos and commercial practices far outmeasure those of the large place nearby.'[58]

When Portia substitutes Bassanio's confirmatory and ratifying kiss for 'this ring' (3.2.171), abstracting all that she is and all that she owns – 'Myself, and what is mine, to you and yours / Is now converted' (3.2.166–7) – into a small, gold token, her cautionary note to Bassanio – that if he should 'part from, lose, or give [it] away' (3.2.172) it will 'presage the ruin of [his] love' (3.2.173) – conveys the critically overdetermined value of the ring. As Watson suggests, *Merchant* is 'obsessed with how to attach financial values to human ones, how to weigh precious metal against living bodies', and here, although in less explicit terms, Portia and Bassanio's negotiation closely mirrors that of Antonio and Shylock, in crediting what are essentially financial transactions with an excess of social significance.[59] By reversing the multiplication of Portia's singular 'I' to 'trebled twenty times myself' back down to the discrete article of gold, the balance of the ring's intrinsic and extrinsic value, its limited material worth and its immense emblematic significance, becomes wildly unstable. In turn, Bassanio's reaction to Portia's volatile accounting is to wed the value of the ring to his own flesh and blood: 'when this ring / Parts from this finger, then parts life from hence; / O then be bold to say Bassanio's dead' (3.2.183–5).

In contrast to Portia's inflationary account, Bassanio's ledger is distinctly lacking; lost for words, Bassanio reverts

---

[55] See, also, Shakespeare's Sonnet 4: 'Profitless usurer, why dost thou use / So great a sum of sums, yet canst not live?' (7–8).

[56] Anthony Mortimer, *Variable Passions: A Reading of Shakespeare's Venus and Adonis* (New York, 2000), p. 96.

[57] The female body is, of course, heavily implicated in the male-dominated exchanges in the play, and Portia's gifting of her ring undoubtedly plays on the common early modern ring/vulva pun. For more on Portia's part in the play's networks of exchange, see Harry Berger Jr, 'Marriage and mercifixion in *The Merchant of Venice*: the casket scene revisited', *SQ* 32 (1981), 155–62.

[58] Szatek, '*The Merchant of Venice* and the politics of commerce', p. 326.

[59] Watson, *Back to Nature*, p. 267.

to an expression of self-valuation grounded in the somatic and social economy of blood-based worth: 'Madam, you have bereft me of all words, / Only my blood speaks to you in my veins' (3.2.175–6). Recalling the Prince of Morocco's earlier instruction to 'make incision for [Portia's] love, / To prove whose blood is reddest' (2.1.6–7), Bassanio's assertion rests on the assumption of intrinsic worth, but also plays directly into the play's examination of the conversion of words into blood. Morocco imagines bleeding as a way of overcoming prejudices against his 'complexion' (2.1.1) – an idea that itself anticipates Shylock's cutting consideration of the consanguinity and common humanity between Christian and Jew, 'If you prick us, do we not bleed?' – by externalizing an internal and intrinsic truth about himself. In *King Lear*, Edmund's self-wounding – 'Some blood drawn on me would beget opinion [*Wounds his arm*] / Of my more fierce endeavour' (2.1.32–3) – manipulates this trope by exploiting the assumed capacity of blood to prove an individual's nobility and humoral temperament. Lacking adequate words to express his feelings, then, Bassanio fumbles to convert the 'confusion' (3.2.177) in his blood to something 'express[ible]' (3.2.183), resolving that his 'blood speaks' when he cannot: blood becomes articulate.

Compounding the promise of imminent festive release, Lorenzo and Jessica's betrothal then introduces the prospect of a double nuptial; however, as the play springs towards comic resolution – with the plans for feasting and extravagant gift-giving already under way – news of Antonio's imprisonment and the forfeiting of his bond brings the scene of celebration crashing back to reality:

> O sweet Portia,
> Here are a few of the unpleasant'st words
> That ever blotted paper! Gentle lady,
> When I did first impart my love to you,
> I freely told you all the wealth I had
> Ran in my veins
> . . .
> Here is a letter, lady;
> The paper as the body of my friend,
> And every word in it a gaping wound,
> Issuing life-blood.   (3.2.250–66)

The arrival of the letter alerts Bassanio and the inhabitants of Belmont to Antonio's plight, and forces Bassanio to apprise Portia of his true 'rate' (3.2.256), by admitting that he has 'engag'd [him]self to a dear friend, / To feed [his] means' (3.2.261–2). Prefiguring *King Lear*, written around five years later, Bassanio admits 'My state was nothing . . . I was worse than nothing' (3.2.258–9), offering an analogue

to Lear's 'Nothing can come of nothing' (1.1.90) in a play that pivots on the failed conversion of filial gratitude into material inheritance. Bassanio claims to have 'freely told' his wealth, as being no more than the noble blood running in his 'veins', but even here, in his claim to honesty and openness, the infiltration of economic language surfaces through the financial connotation of *telling* – as in counting or reckoning. Hence, Bassanio's 'freely told', rather than suggesting honesty, harbours the sense of counting and valuing his worth too liberally. Nevertheless, Bassanio quickly moves to reinvest in the notion of blood-based worth as a system of value that stands separate from the ownership and circulation of money. Confessing his indebtedness to Antonio, Bassanio alternatively seeks shelter in an economy of social value, in which his credit is deemed better: 'I was a gentleman, – / And then I told you true' (3.2.254–5). Having recently converted his blood into words – 'my blood speaks to you in my veins' – Bassanio now attempts the reverse conversion and, in much the same way that Shylock forces the immateriality of a financial bond to convert gold into flesh, he attempts to transfer 'word[s]' into '[i]ssuing life blood'. Indeed, as Patricia Parker observes, *Merchant* is 'pervaded by cuts and incisions of multiple kinds', and 'At the same time, it is traversed by the sense of writing (or *graphein*) as a grafting or cutting.'[60] In effect, Bassanio's figuring of Antonio's 'word[s]' as '[i]ssuing life-blood' closes the circle by providing a material replication of Shylock's 'merry bond' (1.3.169); just as the bond between Antonio and Shylock prescribes the potential for a gaping wound, the letter passed between Antonio and Bassanio evokes, through Bassanio's reaction, the reality of Antonio's imminent wounding and the spilling of his blood. Bassanio attempts to offer Portia a true reckoning of his worth – 'Only my blood speaks to you in my veins' – but ends up losing all track of the distinction between wealth and blood; consequently, at precisely the point at which Bassanio is able to be valued for nothing more than his body's blood, Antonio's letter unavoidably reconflates money and 'lifeblood', thwarting the fulfilment of nuptial rites.

Mirroring her self-effacing multiplication of 'trebled twenty times myself', Portia quickly moves to ward off tragedy with a seemingly illimitable injection of cash: 'Pay him six thousand, and deface the bond: / Double six

---

[60] Patricia Parker, 'Cutting both ways: bloodletting, castration/circumcision, and the "Lancelet" of *The Merchant of Venice*', in *Alternative Shakespeares 3*, ed. Diana E. Henderson (London and New York, 2008), 95–118; p. 96.

thousand and then treble that' (3.2.298–9). But, in a play in which, according to Eric Langley, 'language is shown to operate as a verbal currency of fluctuating tokens of negotiable price', all of the central protagonists continue to pour money into a system that – by endlessly converting cash into bonds, social and moral value into financial liquidity, and words into blood – has lost all sense of value.[61] As Salerio observes, 'in a word, but even now worth this, / And now worth nothing' (1.1.35–6) – that is, commercial value is as mutable and capricious as the exchanging of words. Indeed, more so than any other of Shakespeare's other plays, *Merchant* lays bare the hazards of mistaking one's 'person' for one's 'purse'; Antonio's profligate (if well-intentioned) gifting of money to Bassanio – 'My purse, my person, my extremest means, / Lie all unlock'd to your occasions' (1.1.138–9) – offers a blunt premonition of the financial recklessness of *Timon of Athens*, in which Timon foolishly confuses financial liquidity and social worth. Tied, throughout, to the global, mercantile circulation of commodities, in which investments are put out to 'venture forth' (1.1.15) in 'expect[ation of] return' (1.3.158), *Merchant* considers the complexity of converting and confusing different forms of value, and, in doing so, plots the abject failure of mingling somatic, social and financial economies on the presumption of absolute fungibility and substitutable worth. Consequently, the attempted conversion of 3,000 ducats to an 'equal pound / Of ... fair flesh' (1.2.149–50), but also the practical impossibility of extricating flesh from blood, first leads Antonio and then Shylock into perilously deep water. However, instead of pursuing a desire to get to a form of value, or means of communication, that is more concretely *real* than simply the words that are written or gold that is circulated – to get, in a sense, to a bedrock of intrinsic value, be that moral 'sufficien[cy]' or unquestionable humoral integrity – the play's incessant pursuit of monetary worth sets up a situation in which Shylock is able to take Venice's Christian merchants at their words, by demanding his 'pound of man's flesh' (1.3.161).

When, during the court scene, Shylock rejects Bassanio's financial restitution, declaring 'If every ducat in six thousand ducats / Were in six parts, and every part a ducat, / I would not draw them, I would have my bond' (4.1.85–7), his image of exponential financial multiplication works, through the sheer scale of its imagined increase, to negate the value of the very thing it describes: by talking so much about money, it becomes clear that Shylock – and the play in general – is not interested in, or talking about, money at all. Instead,

what Shylock pursues is his bond, as an artefact of an obligation between himself and Antonio, which is now utterly divorced from the monetary agreement with which it started. Nevertheless, with opposing desires for revenge and survival, both Shylock and Antonio want their respective claims to be judged in purely financial terms: Antonio to be able to settle his forfeit in cash, and Shylock to extract the flesh owed as if it were money. As such, both men desire that the terms of their bond be understood as something other than what they are. Subsequently, Bassanio's offer to pay Antonio's debt 'ten times o'er, / On forfeit of my hands, my head, my heart' (4.1.206–7) further inflates the play's increasingly absurd commensuration of flesh and money, by equating 'ten times' the original value of the bond with the value of his 'hands', 'head' and 'heart'. In attempting to rescind the imminently violent terms of Shylock's 'merry bond', and in the hyper-inflationary economy of Venice, Bassanio offers more money but also presents the potential for more dismemberment.

Three scenes earlier, Antonio miserably declares that 'These griefs and losses have so bated me, / That I shall hardly spare a pound of flesh | Tomorrow, to my bloody creditor' (3.3.32–4). Here, Antonio's claim that he has been 'bated' animates a number of associations that efficiently elaborate his predicament, between the terms of his bond with Shylock and his inevitable forfeiture. Echoing Sempronius's obstinate rejection in *Timon of Athens* of Timon's appeal for cash – 'Who *bates* mine honour shall not know my coin' (3.3.26, emphasis added), as Sempronius schemingly feigns irritation for not having been approached for money ahead of Timon's other 'friends' – Antonio's declaration draws on the commercial themes of the play: being 'bated' in the sense that his 'losses' have reduced or deflated his value (*OED Online*, v[2].4), literally wasting the flesh on his body and lowering his weight. Additionally, Antonio's 'bate[d]' body figuratively anticipates the excising of flesh from his breast, by evoking Shylock's sharp blade through the connotation of 'bating' as beating or blunting a blade's edge (*OED Online*, v[2] 3).[62] Two scenes later, the sharp reality of Shylock's blade is materialized, as he begins to hone its edge:

[61] Eric Langley, *Shakespeare's Contagious Sympathies: Ill Communications* (Oxford, 2018), p. 77.

[62] In the opening speech of *Love's Labour's Lost*, Ferdinand pits 'devouring time' against enduring 'honour', suggesting that social distinction will 'bate [time's] scythe's keene edge' (1.1.6), that long-lasting 'honour' will blunt Death's scythe.

BASSANIO Why does thou whet thy knife so earnestly?

SHYLOCK To cut the forfeiture from that bankrupt there.

GRATIANO Not on thy sole: but on thy soul, harsh Jew, Thou
 mak'st thy knife keen; but no metal can, No, not the
 hangman's axe, bear half the keenness Of thy sharp envy.
 Can no prayers pierce thee?

(4.1.121–6)

Whereas Antonio's 'bated' body conjures both his flesh and the knife associated with his forfeiting of the bond, Shylock's literal blade is converted, by Gratiano, into a metonym for his 'sharp envy'. Shakespeare keeps Shylock's incising blade in sharp focus, even as Gratiano attempts to rhetorically turn its point towards Shylock, and as Antonio tries to find solace in 'Fortune' charitably 'cut [ing him] off' (4.1.264–8) from his miserable condition. What Shakespeare subsequently presents is a ramping up of the play's conflation of words and wounds, blood and money, into a near frenzy of commensurability. When Antonio imagines his 'tale is told' (4.1.272), and figures his death as the final settling of Bassanio's debt, 'For if the Jew do cut but deep enough, / I'll pay it presently with all my heart' (4.1.276–7), the evocation of tale-telling figures a form of final reckoning as Antonio's story is 'told' (*OED Online*, v.II 17.a), but also as a kind of 'count[ing] out in payment' (*OED Online*, v.II 18.b), which primes the monetary connotations of 'pay[ing]' Bassanio's debts with his own 'heart'. Recalling Bassanio's 'every word in it a gaping wound, | Issuing life-blood', Antonio is envisioning his death as a 'pay[ing]' out of all that his 'heart' contains. Portia has, after all, already begun the preparations for bloodshed, by instructing Shylock to 'Have some surgeon ... to stop his wounds, lest he do bleed to death' (4.1.253–4).

Despite the inkling that Portia has been orchestrating this scene from the beginning, supressing her awareness of the loop-hole in Shylock's bond in order to hoist Shylock by his own petard, Shylock's rejection of Portia's instruction to ensure that Antonio's wounds are 'stop[ped]' – ''tis not in the bond' (4.1.258) – explicitly positions the exact letter of his bond as the crux of this scene:

> Tarry a little, there is something else, –
> This bond doth give thee here no jot of blood,
> The words expressly are 'a pound of flesh':
> Take then thy bond, take thou thy pound of flesh,
> But in the cutting it, if thou dost shed
> One drop of Christian blood, thy lands and goods
> Are (by the laws of Venice) confiscate
> Unto the state of Venice.

(4.1.301–8)

The trial scene turns on Portia's tactic of twisting Shylock's insistence on the letter of his bond against him, utilizing, as Clayton Koelb asserts, the 'contradictory possibilities in the rhetoric of flesh-and-blood'.[63] Primed by Shylock's determination that she 'pursue sentence' (4.1.294) and follow 'the very words' (250) of the bond, Portia's declaration that the bond does not permit Shylock to draw a single 'jot of blood' marks the point at which the attempted conversion of word to flesh fails. In essence, Portia's defence rests on a semantic quibble, and numerous critics – including Koelb – have pointed out the legal insufficiency of her argument, insofar as it is impossible to separate flesh and blood, and therefore necessary bloodshed is implicit in the bond. Nevertheless, the play has consistently trained us to conceive of blood as something demonstrably and significantly distinct from both flesh and metallic wealth. In semantically extricating flesh from blood, and the terms of the bond and the reality of the forfeit, Portia's dispute homes in on the smallest writerly mark, drawing on the typographic connotations of the 'jot', as 'the least letter or written part of any writing' (*OED Online*, n.1), figuratively equating it to the smallest quantity of blood. In paying such close attention to the words of Shylock's bond, and refuting the possibility of converting words to flesh and blood, Portia's 'jot' evokes Protestant arguments against Catholic transubstantiation, as in the Swiss reformer Heinrich Bullinger's critique of the mass:

> They say ... by the power of God, and of the words of consecration, the substance of bread and wine is turned, yea transubstantiated in to [th]e substance of the body and blood of Christe, no one *jot* of the substance of the bread and wine remaining.[64]

In addition to evoking the materiality of Shylock's written bond, Portia's 'jot' focuses attention onto the smallest of details: a single drop of blood, in the context of the play's depiction of both inflationary economics and the unlimited fungibility of bodies and money, marks the moment at which commensurability is rejected.

In what remains of the play, the overturning of Shylock's bond leads to his forced conversion to

---

63 Clayton Koelb, 'The bonds of flesh and blood: having it both ways in *The Merchant of Venice*', *Cardozo Studies in Law and Literature* 5 (1993), 107–13; p. 110.

64 Heinrich Bullinger, *Of the End of the World and Judgement of our Lord Jesus Christe to Come*, trans. Thomas Potter (London, 1580), sig. B4v, emphasis added.

Christianity and the confiscation of his worldly possessions. The thwarted nuptials of act 3 are remedied by Shylock's sentence, Antonio's foreign investments are miraculously realized, order is restored, and the commercial and social structures of Venice are seemingly secured. However, key moments during the final scene suggest that the merchants of Venice will quickly and easily back-slide and continue to commensurate blood and money. When Portia challenges Bassanio for giving away the matrimonial ring that she gave to him, Antonio's deeply unsettling declaration that 'I once did lend my *body* for his wealth . . . I dare be bound again, / My *soul* upon the forfeit' (5.1.252–5, emphasis added), suggests that, rather than learning from his experience, he is ever willing to up the stakes of his financial and social speculations. Having narrowly avoided losing his life under the terms of his bond with Shylock, Antonio now appears ready to forfeit his soul: even if only rhetorically, the potential price for failed payment is set at permanent perdition. Although the quick succession of comic revelation and bawdy innuendo works hard to override the ease with which Antonio reinvests in the commercial and somatic commensurability that nearly saw him dead, the play ends with a lingering sense that the events and misjudgements will be repeated.

In *The Merchant of Venice*, Shakespeare depicts the dynamics of economic, romantic and social circulation through the materiality and movement of individual bodies and the interactions between individuals. As such, Shakespeare can be seen to exploit the unifying and fungible qualities of blood and money in order to register and depict the complex circulations of bodies, as well as economic, romantic and social obligations and relationships.

'AND NOW LET ME ALONE TO END THE TRAGEDY': *OTHELLO*, COMEDY AND CANDLELIGHT IN JOHN FLETCHER'S *WOMEN PLEASED*

DOMENICO LOVASCIO

John Fletcher's extensive, career-long, imaginative and often irreverent engagement with the works in the Shakespeare canon ranks as one of the most distinctive traits of his dramatic craft and art.[1] Fletcher and his collaborators repeatedly echo the verbal and structural texture of Shakespeare's plays and, more importantly, typically redeploy dramatic sequences and bits of stage business, character types and relationships, themes and motifs that they find in the drama of their predecessor. They do so with a playful attitude, to capitalize on previous box-office hits, to achieve a surprise theatrical effect or to provide playgoers with a self-conscious dramatic re-enactment seeking to tickle the sophisticated palates of the better-off and better-educated section of the audience, and to stimulate, to some extent, reflections on the relationship between plays across the repertory of the King's Men. And yet, even though the fact that many of the plays in the canon of Fletcher and his collaborators are in some kind of conversation with those of Shakespeare is now old news, that canon is so large (totalling around fifty plays) and still so comparatively neglected that some instances of Fletcher's engagement with Shakespeare's plays remain either undiscovered or underexplored. A discussion of a previously unacknowledged early response to Shakespeare's tragedy *Othello* (1603–1604) in Fletcher's lively tragicomedy *Women Pleased* (1620) is precisely the subject of this article.

Scholarship has already identified a few Shakespearian presences in *Women Pleased*. First, the names Soto and Petruccio link Fletcher's play to *The Taming of the Shrew*, as does the redeployment of the trope of the husband's starvation of his wife (which occurs in the subplot of *Women Pleased*).[2] Second, *The Merry Wives of Windsor* seems to have exerted a structural influence on *Women Pleased*, act 4, scene 3: Daniel Morley McKeithan

argues that Fletcher combines what he found in the eighth tale of the eighth day in Giovanni Boccaccio's *Decameron* with the sequence of Falstaff's being surprised in Ford's house, to which he had come to woo the latter's wife, in *The Merry Wives of Windsor*, act 4, scene 2, especially by borrowing 'the idea of having the lustful old wooer hide up the chimney', which is not to be found in Boccaccio's novella.[3] Third, Martin Wiggins suggests that *Women Pleased* may be indebted to Fletcher and Shakespeare's lost 'Cardenio'; the influence would pertain to 'the sequence in which Silvio, in the country, is pursued by an off-stage singer, as Dorotea does Cardenio (and Violante does Julio

---

[1] See, among others, Daniel Morley McKeithan, *The Debt to Shakespeare in the Beaumont-and-Fletcher Plays* (Austin, TX, 1938); Clifford Leech, *The John Fletcher Plays* (Cambridge, MA, 1962), p. 162; David L. Frost, *The School of Shakespeare: The Influence of Shakespeare on English Drama 1600–42* (Cambridge, 1968), pp. 209–45; Gordon McMullan, 'Introduction', to William Shakespeare and John Fletcher, *King Henry VIII (All Is True)* (London, 2000), 1–199; pp. 114–15; Clare McManus, 'Introduction' to John Fletcher, *The Island Princess* (London, 2012), 1–95; p. 11; Misha Teramura, 'The anxiety of *auctoritas*: Chaucer and *The Two Noble Kinsmen*', *Shakespeare Quarterly* 63 (2012), 544–76; p. 576; Domenico Lovascio, *John Fletcher's Rome: Questioning the Classics* (Manchester, 2022), pp. 134–5.

[2] On the (complicated) relationship between *The Taming of the Shrew* and *Women Pleased*, see James J. Marino, 'The anachronistic shrews', *Shakespeare Quarterly* 60 (2009), 25–46; Barbara Hodgdon, 'Introduction', to William Shakespeare, *The Taming of the Shrew* (London, 2010), 1–131; pp. 29–35; Martin Wiggins with Catherine Richardson, *British Drama 1533–1642: A Catalogue*, 9 vols. (Oxford, 2012–2018), #1965; Gary Taylor and Rory Loughnane, 'The canon and chronology of Shakespeare's works', in *The New Oxford Shakespeare: Authorship Companion*, ed. Gary Taylor and Gabriel Egan (Oxford, 2017), 417–602; pp. 501–2.

[3] McKeithan, *Debt*, p. 123.

in *Double Falsehood*)'.[4] Finally, a couple of analogies between *Othello* and *Women Pleased* have indeed been traced in passing by Celia Caputi, who mentions how Lopez 'soliloquiz[es] Othello-like over his sleeping wife' in an article that, however, focuses on female doubling and dyads in Fletcher's *The Chances* and *Women Pleased* within a larger argument about Fletcher's proto-feminist attitude, and in which no extensive discussion of the relationship between *Othello* and *Women Pleased* would have been either possible or pertinent.[5]

The present article examines Fletcher's dissection of *Othello* in *Women Pleased* in terms of dramatic structure, staging, setting, genre, characterization and thematic concerns, in order to argue that *Women Pleased* features an early, complex, overlooked and thought-provoking response to *Othello* that calls attention to some crucial theatrical and literary aspects of Shakespeare's play in such a way as to make Fletcher emerge, to a certain extent, as one of the first critics of Shakespearian drama, enacting his criticism onstage in a dramatic riposte to one of the most successful and popular plays of his former collaborator, with whom he wrote 'Cardenio', *All Is True; or, King Henry VIII* and *The Two Noble Kinsmen*.

WOMEN PLEASED AND OTHELLO: CONNECTIONS

Although *Women Pleased* cannot be numbered among Fletcher's best-known plays, the fact that its links to Shakespeare are found exclusively in act 3, scene 4 makes it unnecessary to provide a synopsis of the whole play here. For the readers' convenience, it will suffice to say that the play is set in Florence, with a main plot centring around the love between the gentleman Silvio and Belvedere, the daughter of the Duchess of Florence, and the several obstacles that the young lovers need to face before they can finally get married. Unlike *Othello*, then, this is a double-plot play. Although the two plots only actually intersect in the final scene, they are thematically in dialogue with each other for the whole time, in that they both grapple, in different ways, with issues of female power, gender hierarchy and gender expectations in relation to marriage.[6] The main characters of the subplot are the miserly jeweller Lopez and his wife Isabella. Lopez has been mistreating Isabella by keeping her in penury for some time, which has disposed her to cheat on him with the merchant Ruggio (who is the gentleman Claudio in

disguise). After an unsuccessful encounter thwarted by the unexpected arrival of Lopez in act 2, scene 6, Isabella devises a new strategy to sneak out of the house unbeknownst to Lopez and spend some time with Ruggio.

This second cheating attempt is dramatized in act 3, scene 4, in which Isabella gets ready for a nightly meeting with Claudio, tying a string around her finger that she expects him to pull when he gets to her house so that no one will notice. She falls asleep, and Lopez finds her in bed. He discovers the string and exits to try to catch Isabella's lover. She wakes up and, in a variation of the traditional bed-trick plot device, she persuades her maid Jaquenet to take her place in bed. Before leaving, Isabella puts out the candle in the room. Lopez returns and beats up Jaquenet in the dark, thinking that she is Isabella, and then goes to fetch Isabella's friends and kinsfolk with a view to humiliating her. His plan, however, backfires: Isabella is found unhurt, reading quietly in her room, and the visitors harshly criticize Lopez's violent and irrationally jealous behaviour. They force him to apologize to her, and she claims that she was trying to trap Bartello, the captain of the citadel of Florence (and the character who eventually connects the main plot with the subplot), who has been annoying her for some time out of a foolish infatuation with her.[7] While this short description of the scene does not make any connections between Fletcher's and Shakespeare's play particularly evident, *Women Pleased*, act 3, scene 4, in fact exhibits several points of contact with *Othello*, especially act 5, scene 2.

For one thing, Lopez is a jealous husband like Othello, and, like Othello, he is an outsider living in an Italian Renaissance city state (Venice in *Othello*; Florence in *Women Pleased*), who has married a beautiful, gentlewomanly Italian wife (Desdemona in *Othello*; Isabella in *Women Pleased*). Unlike Othello, however, Lopez is apparently not Black and, even though his name, coupled with his miserliness, may have awakened oblique associations

---

[4] Wiggins with Richardson, *British Drama*, #1965. I follow the convention of the Lost Plays Database (https://lostplays.folger.edu) in indicating titles of lost plays by using quotation marks.

[5] Celia Caputi, '"A whore you are, madam", or the binary that wasn't: female dyads and doubling in John Fletcher's *The Chances* and *Women Pleased*', *Early Modern Literary Studies* Special Issue 27: European Women in Early Modern Drama (2017), 1–15; p. 10, https://extra.shu.ac.uk/emls/journal/index.php/emls/article/view/407/290.

[6] For a discussion of the correspondences between the main plot and the subplot in *Women Pleased*, see Caputi, 'Female dyads and doubling', pp. 8–14.

[7] Wiggins with Richardson, *British Drama*, #1965.

with stereotypes about Jews – and, in particular, with Roderigo Lopez (*c.*1517 – 7 June 1594), the Portuguese-born New Christian of Jewish ancestry who served as a physician-in-chief to Queen Elizabeth I from 1581 until his death by execution – the text never openly presents Lopez as a Jew, so that similarities between the condition of Othello and Lopez on the ground of racial difference ought not to be overstated; what is more, Roderigo Lopez had been dead for over twenty-five years when *Women Pleased* was first staged, and the association would not have been as immediate to playgoers in the early 1620s as it would have been in the late 1590s or the early 1600s.[8] Incidentally, the choice of Florence itself might be viewed as a submerged response to *Othello*, as Cassio, Desdemona's supposed lover, is a Florentine. Second, in both *Women Pleased*, act 3, scene 4, and *Othello*, act 5, scene 2, a jealous husband violently assaults his wife (or whom he *thinks* is his wife in Lopez's case) on a bed, and the wife is reduced to silence during the struggle: in Shakespeare because *Othello* chokes Desdemona to death; in Fletcher because the maid Jaquenet has promised to Isabella that she will remain silent throughout. Third, in both scenes the husband delivers a monologue and kisses his wife while she is asleep, and the wife awakes after her husband has spoken. The similarity is in this case reinforced by means of verbal parallels: Lopez's words 'Now will I steal a kiss, a dear kiss from her, / And suck the rosy breath of this bright beauty' (*Women Pleased* 3.4.61–2), uttered right before noticing the string tied to Isabella's finger, recall Othello's 'When I have plucked thy rose ... I'll smell thee on the tree – / O balmy breath, that doth almost persuade / Justice to break her sword' (*Othello* 5.2.13, 15–17); Lopez also describes the song he sings for Isabella as a 'sacrifice' (*Women Pleased* 3.4.59) to her beauty, which obliquely alerts memories of Othello's own twisted notion of Desdemona's murder as 'sacrifice' (*Othello* 5.2.70).[9] Fourth, after the violence, someone knocks *within* (Emilia in *Othello*; Lopez himself in *Women Pleased*), and an onstage audience (Montano, Graziano, Iago and Emilia in *Othello*; Bartello, a Gentleman and two Gentlewomen in *Women Pleased*), including one relative of the wife (the Gentlewoman in *Women Pleased*; Graziano in *Othello*), appear as witnesses and criticize the violently jealous husband. Yet the most evident connection – and the one that playgoers would have probably picked up in real time – is that the main sequence in both scenes revolves around a candle being put out in a bedchamber, thereby (supposedly) making the room completely dark. Lopez's ravings to Jaquenet (whom he assumes to be his wife) as he re-enters the bedroom after unsuccessfully

chasing Isabella's lover – 'Have you put your light out? I shall stumble to ye, / You whore, you cunning whore!' (*WP* 3.4.92–3) – unmistakably echo Othello's ominous and much more famous line 'Put out the light, and then put out the light' (*Othello* 5.2.7), as well as his earlier nastily sarcastic answer to Desdemona: 'I took you for that cunning whore of Venice / That married with Othello' (*Othello* 4.2.93–4).

Such a complex interplay between character and audience memories would have had an even stronger impact if the actor playing Lopez had also recently played Othello and if the same boy actor had played the roles of both Isabella and Desdemona; in this way, the company would have taken advantage of the ghostly echoes of prior and current performances embodied by both the individual roles and the actors who performed them.[10] Yet, even if the King's Men did not avail themselves of the possibility to reinforce the link between *Othello* and *Women Pleased* through casting choices, the connection would still have been apparent enough for spectators.

That Fletcher wanted playgoers to think of *Othello* as they watched *Women Pleased*, act 3, scene 4, unfold becomes indisputable when the Fletcher–Shakespeare connections are triangulated with the main narrative source upon which Fletcher drew for this scene. Most of the subplot of *Women Pleased* is based on three different *novelle* in Boccaccio's *Decameron*: act 2, scene 6, on the sixth tale of the seventh day (the name of Isabella coming directly from this novella); act 3, scene 4, on the

---

[8] On the interplay between racial construction, humour and theatrical form and genre, see, among others, M. Lindsay Kaplan, 'Jessica's mother: medieval constructions of race and gender in *The Merchant of Venice*', *Shakespeare Quarterly* 58 (2007), 4–10; Patricia Akhimie, 'Racist humor and Shakespearean comedy', in *The Cambridge Companion to Shakespeare and Race*, ed. Ayanna Thompson (Cambridge, 2021), 47–61; Dennis Austin Britton, 'Flesh and blood: race and religion in *The Merchant of Venice*', in *The Cambridge Companion to Shakespeare and Race*, ed. Thompson, 108–22.

[9] All parenthetical references to Fletcher's play are to John Fletcher, *Women Pleased* (henceforth abbreviated to *WP*), ed. Hans Walter Gabler, in *The Dramatic Works in the Beaumont and Fletcher Canon*, gen. ed. Fredson Bowers, 10 vols. (Cambridge, 1982), vol. 5, 441–538. All parenthetical references to Shakespeare's play are to *William Shakespeare: The Complete Works*, ed. Stanley Wells, Gary Taylor, John Jowett and William Montgomery (Oxford, 2005). Quotations from all early modern English texts are modernized in spelling and punctuation or are taken from modernized editions.

[10] On the idea of the use of the 'recycled body of an actor' on the stage, see Marvin Carlson, *The Haunted Stage: The Theatre as Memory Machine* (Ann Arbor, MI, 2002), p. 8.

eighth tale of the seventh day; and act 4, scene 3, as mentioned above, on the eighth tale of the eighth day (though loosely so). As it happens, a new English translation of Boccaccio's collection by John Florio had just been published in London.[11] This is already doubly interesting in itself. First, because Fletcher was relying on the Italian novella tradition for narrative source material just as Shakespeare had done for *Othello*, the plot of which is based on the seventh tale of the third day in Giovan Battista Giraldi Cinzio's *Gli Ecatommiti* – although it is true that drawing upon Italian *novelle* had been common practice among early modern English playwrights since the Elizabethan age. Second, because Fletcher's use of Florio's translation fits into the typical Fletcherian pattern of pouncing on recent books, whether printed in England or on the Continent, for writing his plays.[12] Even more important for the purpose of the present article, however, is the fact that a comparison of some key passages of *Women Pleased*, *Othello* and the *Decameron* proves to be crucial to appreciate the extent to which Fletcher deviates from the eighth tale of the seventh day in Boccaccio's *Decameron* in ways that make his dramatization thereof closer to *Othello*. It would be of little use here to present a full comparison between Fletcher's scene and Boccaccio's novella; hence, I will only remark upon and discuss those passages that are relevant in connection with *Othello*.

First, the husband's name in Boccaccio's tale is Arriguccio Berlinghieri; given that Berlinghieri was a typically Florentine surname, there is no reason to surmise that he is an outsider in Florence, unlike Lopez and Othello. Second, in the *Decameron* husband and wife are in bed together when the husband notices the string, while Fletcher follows Shakespeare in only having the woman sleeping in bed as the husband enters the room and approaches her. Finally, when writing Lopez's speech to Jaquenet in bed, Fletcher had in Florio's translation of *Decameron* a ready-made series of three sentences that he could have easily borrowed and adapted, all the more so given the conveniently iambic rhythm of the first two: 'Where is this lewd and wicked woman? Hast thou put out the light because I should not find thee? That shall not avail thee, for I can well enough find a drab in the dark!' (*Decameron*, sig. M3v). On the contrary, as mentioned above, Lopez uses a phrasing that includes two distinct verbal echoes from *Othello*: '*Have you put your light out?* I shall stumble to ye, / *You whore, you cunning whore!*' (*WP* 3.4.92–3, italics mine).

The triangular comparison between Fletcher, Shakespeare and Boccaccio leaves little room for

doubt: Fletcher purposely created a dramatic sequence that would readily arouse memories of *Othello* in the audience. Why would he want to do that, though, apart from having fun writing it and seeing it acted? The answer to this question, I would like to argue, is at least twofold: on the one hand, Fletcher possibly wished to bring to the fore the comedic roots of *Othello* and experiment with them by dramatizing a similar story that would, however, end in comedy rather than tragedy; on the other hand, he may have been reflecting – either ironically or retrospectively, or both – on (unrecorded) recent performances of *Othello* held in the indoor theatrical space of the Blackfriars.

WHAT IF *OTHELLO* DID END IN COMEDY?

At least since Douglas J. Stewart first argued that '*Othello* reproduces great chunks of plot enginery and many of the techniques of role portraiture that are native to ... comedy', the play's roots in both Roman comedy and the Italian *commedia dell'arte* have been variously discussed by scholars.[13] *Othello*'s structural debt to comedy is perceptively summed up by Susan Snyder as follows:

Courtship and ratified marriage, the whole story of comedy, appear in *Othello* as a preliminary to tragedy. The play's action up until the reunion of Othello and Desdemona in Cyprus (2.1) is a perfect comic structure in miniature. The wooing that the two of them describe in the Venetian council scene (1.3) has succeeded in spite of barriers of age, color, and condition of life; the machinations of villain and doltish rival have come to nothing; the blocking father has been overruled by the good

[11] Giovanni Boccaccio, *The Decameron, Containing a Hundred Pleasant Novels, Wittily Discoursed between Seven Honourable Ladies and Three Noble Gentlemen*, trans. John Florio (London, 1620).

[12] Wiggins with Richardson, *British Drama*, #1911, #1998; Lovascio, *Fletcher's Rome*, pp. 36–9, 43–5, 50–1, 126–7.

[13] Douglas J. Stewart, '*Othello*: Roman comedy as nightmare', *Emory University Quarterly* 22 (1967), 252–76; p. 252. See also Robert A. Watts, 'The comic scenes in *Othello*', *Shakespeare Quarterly* 19 (1968), 349–54; Barbara Heliodora C. de Mendonça, '*Othello*: a tragedy built on a comic structure', in *Shakespeare Survey 21* (Cambridge, 1969), 31–8; Ann Blake, 'The comedy of *Othello*', *Critical Review* 15 (1972), 46–51; Stephen Rogers, '*Othello*: comedy in reverse', *Shakespeare Quarterly* 24 (1973), 210–20; Susan Snyder, *The Comic Matrix of Shakespeare's Tragedies* (Princeton, 1979), pp. 73–90; Frances Teague, '*Othello* and new comedy', *Comparative Drama* 20 (1986), 54–64; Colin Burrow, *Shakespeare and Classical Antiquity* (Oxford, 2013), pp. 158–61; Akhimie, 'Racist humor and Shakespearean comedy', pp. 47–50.

duke; and nature has cooperated in the general movement with a storm that disperses the last external threat, the Turks, while preserving the favored lovers.[14]

As for character types, Othello has been discussed in connection with the *miles gloriosus*; Iago has been viewed as a tragic version of the *callidus servus* or as a *zanni* who deceives his master; Brabantio has been seen as the *senex* or a Pantalone figure whose daughter marries someone he dislikes; and Roderigo has been described as the *adulescens* or gulled gentleman.[15] *Othello* also features a number of theatregrams, as well as dramatic techniques and devices, that are traditionally the province of comedy.[16] The most glaring examples are the particular scenic disposition (typical of Italian Renaissance comedy) of the first scene in the street, in front of a house with a window above and a door below; the servant of the main character's awakening an old father to inform him of his daughter's inappropriate marriage; and the eavesdropping scene, in which the comic effect that should arise from the fact that the conversation between Iago and Cassio about Bianca is played so that Othello should think that the topic of discussion is in fact Desdemona becomes one of the mainsprings of tragedy.

Fond as Fletcher was of questioning and experimenting with generic boundaries and generic uncertainty, he must have instantly realized the extent to which *Othello* is peculiar among Shakespeare's tragedies in its ample comedy-like reliance on plot construction for its development, and he must have perceived that the comic aspects mostly inform the first three acts of the play rather than the last two.[17] Starting from this awareness, Fletcher seems to have approached the penning of the sequence between Lopez and Isabella (and Jaquenet) with an underlying question in mind: 'What if *Othello* did end in comedy?' As a matter of fact, Fletcher sends an unequivocal signal roughly mid-scene that the Lopez–Isabella plot will not end in tragedy, when Isabella twice reassures Jaquenet that, if she takes her place in the bed and faces the furious jealousy of Lopez, 'It can bring but a beating' (*WP* 3.4.85) and 'The worst will be but beating' (*WP* 3.4.89); put differently, Isabella is informing both her maid and the audience that Lopez – despite his raging threats to Jaquenet as he beats her: 'I will kill thee' (*WP* 3.4.96) – unlike Othello, will *not* kill her: no-one will die, because the subplot unfolds in the realm of comedy and not of tragedy. About fifteen lines later, as Isabella sets out to dupe her husband after he has beaten Jaquenet, the line she delivers to ask her maid to leave her alone is crucial to the whole scene: 'And now let me

alone to end the tragedy' (*WP* 3.4.113). This is a bold metaliterary and metatheatrical announcement on her part in terms of where the subplot of the play is now headed, which self-consciously exposes the foundations on which Fletcher built the analogy between *Women Pleased* and *Othello*, and also primes playgoers both to observe the implications of the generic contraposition that they are about to see and to enjoy how the tragic potential bound in a comic intrigue, which was so central to *Othello*, will be annihilated by a crafty, comical ruse of the wife.[18]

It is not coincidental, I believe, that Fletcher's toying with generic conventions and boundaries enables *Women Pleased* to draw attention to some of the most important thematic issues that are raised in the concluding segment of *Othello*, which would be widely discussed by literary critics in the ensuing centuries, such as Othello's obsession with the notion of the 'ocular proof' and the disintegration of his identity at the end of the play. *Othello* makes much of its title character's thirst for an 'ocular proof' that could incontrovertibly prove Desdemona's unfaithfulness,

---

[14] Snyder, *Comic Matrix*, pp. 73–4.

[15] Stewart, '*Othello*: Roman comedy as nightmare', pp. 252, 261; Heliodora C. de Mendonça, '*Othello*: a tragedy built on a comic structure', p. 34; Rogers, '*Othello*: comedy in reverse', p. 210; Teague, '*Othello* and new comedy', pp. 55–60; E. A. J. Honigmann, 'Introduction', to William Shakespeare, *Othello* (Walton-on-Thames, 1997), 1–111; pp. 75–7.

[16] 'Theatergram' is a term coined by Louise George Clubb, *Italian Drama in Shakespeare's Time* (New Haven, 1989), p. 8, to designate well-established units of repertoire, prominent action and character clusters, or compelling bits of stage business that dramatists use through 'permutation and declension by recombination with compatible units, whether of person, association, action or design'. On theatregrams in *Othello*, see also Clare McManus, '"Sing it like poor Barbary": *Othello* and early modern women's performance', *Shakespeare Bulletin* 33 (2015), 99–120.

[17] On Fletcher's habitual 'experiments with generic uncertainty', see José A. Pérez Díez, 'Introduction', to John Fletcher and Philip Massinger, *Love's Cure, or The Martial Maid* (Manchester, 2022), 1–61; pp. 5, 37; Gordon McMullan, *The Politics of Unease in the Plays of John Fletcher* (Amherst, MA, 1994), pp. 257–62; McManus, 'Introduction', pp. 58–62.

[18] Fletcher's dramaturgical self-consciousness is discussed by Russ McDonald, 'Fashion: Shakespeare and Beaumont and Fletcher', in *A Companion to Shakespeare's Works*, vol. 4: *The Poems, Problem Comedies, Late Plays*, ed. Richard Dutton and Jean E. Howard (Malden, MA, 2003), 150–74; p. 165; and Lee Bliss, 'Tragicomic romance for the King's Men, 1609–1611: Shakespeare, Beaumont, and Fletcher', in *Comedy from Shakespeare to Sheridan: Change and Continuity in the English and European Dramatic Tradition*, ed. Albert R. Braunmuller and James C. Bulman (Newark, DE, 1986), 148–64; p. 160.

and it highlights how Iago's subtleness and Othello's gullibility eventually make the handkerchief convincing enough for Othello as the smoking-gun evidence of Desdemona's affair with Cassio – even though it is clearly *not* the 'ocular proof' on which one could rely to certify her guilt.[19] Fletcher cleverly reverses this situation, and he does so twice. Whereas what Othello believes is the 'ocular proof' of his wife's infidelity is in fact fabricated evidence coupled with clever plotting and excellent skills of persuasion, which eventually lead Othello to accept slander as hard evidence, Lopez, who is already jealous of his wife, does find what Othello would have wanted more than anything in the world, that is, a real 'ocular proof' of his wife's planned tryst with another man (i.e., the string tied to Isabella's finger as she sleeps), but he is eventually defeated by his wife's superior plotting abilities, so that the evidence he has found ultimately amounts to nothing.

Moreover, there is a second type of 'ocular proof' that is unpredictably dismissed in *Women Pleased*, act 3, scene 4, and that more strikingly brings to the fore an idea that is absolutely central to *Othello* – namely, that seeing is *not* knowing; yet in *Women Pleased* this gives rise to comedy rather than plunging the husband into the abyss of tragic desperation. After Lopez has assaulted Jaquenet, beating and scratching her repeatedly, he runs outside to rouse some of his neighbours and bring them to his house in order for them to see first-hand Isabella's 'whorish villainies' (*WP* 3.4.98): 'I'll fetch your kindred and your friends, whore, / And such a justice I will act upon thee' (*WP* 3.4.104–5). Lopez leaves the house, Isabella takes Jaquenet's place again, and then Lopez comes back with Bartello, a Gentleman and two Gentlewomen. Lopez knocks *within* and, as he waits to be admitted into the bedchamber, insultingly yelling at his wife, he triumphantly announces to the bystanders: 'Here's the blood, gentlemen: / *Ecce signum!*' (*WP* 3.4.122–3), alluding to the blood that the beating and scratching of the woman whom he thought was his wife has left on his hands. The door opens, however, and the appearance of Isabella without a scratch instantly belies the story Lopez has related to them and ridicules the supposed solemnity of his Latin exclamation.

Lopez is in total disbelief and confusedly asks: 'Is not this blood?' (*WP* 3.4.138), as he examines his hands up and down, palms and backs. Lopez has done what Othello had sworn not to – 'Yet I'll not shed her blood' (*Othello* 5.2.3) – and has an 'ocular proof' of the beating in the form of physical traces of the assault on his own body, but even such a theoretically strong piece of evidence

becomes nothing in the face of Isabella's plotting, and it only causes Lopez to be unanimously reproached for his 'jealous itch' (*WP* 3.4.147), with Bartello even graphically prefiguring that 'every boy i'th' town will piss upon thee' (*WP* 3.4.177). Lopez and Othello both succumb to the superior scheming of another character: Iago convinces Othello that he has found an ocular proof where in fact there is none; Isabella manages to persuade the onstage spectators not to take into account Lopez's *actual* ocular proof. As in *Othello*, in *Women Pleased* seeing is *not* knowing, but here the implications are firmly located in the realm of comedy: Isabella even asks for a divorce, and Lopez needs humbly to kneel and beg for forgiveness (while Bartello even tries to arrange an encounter with Isabella in a series of asides while Lopez is *right there*).

In *Othello*, the experience of not being able to trust one's own senses stands at the origin of tragedy, in that it brings a man's identity to disintegration, and *Women Pleased* does reckon with that, offering some potential openings in that direction. Lopez cannot believe what is happening to him as he watches Isabella unscathed despite the blood that he can see and feel and smell on his own hands; 'I *think* I am alive still, / And in my wits' (*WP* 3.4.164–5, italics mine), he says, then adding: 'I *think* I am here too, / And once I would have sworn I had taken her napping. / I *think* my name is Lopez' (*WP* 3.4.167–9, italics mine). Lopez's perception of reality has been called into question: he repeats the phrasing 'I think' three times in a mere five lines: absolute certainty has temporarily vanished for him. He *thinks* he is still alive and sane; he *thinks* he is actually in that place with those people; he *thinks* he knows his own name, but he definitely can no longer swear that he has beaten his wife. In tragedy, this would have been an excellent prelude to a devastating identity crisis; Lopez might have ended dissociated – cf. 'That's he that was Othello: here I am' (*Othello* 5.2.290) – his identity split into two different personalities, as occurs to Othello, who in his final speech commits suicide by smiting that part of himself that he now sees as 'a malignant and a turbaned Turk', as a 'circumcisèd dog' (*Othello* 5.2.352, 364). But the subplot of *Women Pleased* belongs to the domain of comedy, not of tragedy, and there is no gloomy pit of shattered identity into which Lopez can fall. He does momentarily doubt his own senses, but he never loses control of himself completely. Lopez's misgivings are circumstantial, as they originate from plot twists, from

---

[19] See, for example, Donald C. Freeman, '*Othello* and the "ocular proof"', *Shakespearean International Yearbook* 4 (2004), 56–71.

errors in a comedy, and they cannot lead to any deep tragic realization. In addition, Lopez is not as gullible as Othello. When Lopez and Isabella remain alone onstage towards the end of the scene, the audience realize that he must have known all along that there has been some sort of trick afoot, as he forcefully confronts her:

> Now, Isabella, tell me truth, and suddenly,
> And do not juggle with me nor dissemble,
> For, as I have life, ye die then. I am not mad,
> Nor does the devil work upon my weakness.
> Tell me the trick of this, and tell me freely.
>
> (*WP* 3.4.187–91)

This is a level of resolution in the face of public humiliation that Othello would have never been capable of: as Colin Burrow argues, 'Othello wants a degree of certainty which is incompatible with comedy as written by Plautus and Terence and as explored by Shakespeare in the years leading up to the composition' of *Othello*; by contrast, Lopez is perfectly at ease in the realm of comedy, in which the differences between evidence and belief, between opinion and truth, are constantly blurred.[20] Lopez therefore cannot be as devastated as Othello by the shifting reality around him, and he is easily satisfied with Isabella's reply, even though she never tells him what actually happened but in fact tricks him into believing that the lover awaiting her was Bartello rather than Ruggio (i.e., Claudio in disguise). Truth is not such an important concern in *Women Pleased* after all.

Fletcher thus appears to have tried to create some dramatic effect for the audience by self-consciously responding to *Othello*'s comedic roots, while at the same time identifying and making some important thematic concerns of the play stand out in his theatrical riposte to Shakespeare. The different, intertwined ways in which Fletcher reworks the Shakespearian matrix in his own play bring to the fore his sharpness in identifying the structural roots of *Othello* and some of the key issues around which the most profound meanings of the play accrue. There is yet one further facet of *Othello* on which Fletcher appears to reflect in *Women Pleased* – namely, the conditions of its performance, and it is to this aspect that the article now turns.[21]

'I SHALL STUMBLE TO YE': *OTHELLO* AND CANDLELIT PERFORMANCE

The words that Lopez yells at the hapless Jaquenet as he enters the darkened bedchamber before attacking her – 'Have you put your light out? I shall stumble to ye, / You

whore, you cunning whore!' (*WP* 3.4.92–3) – already quoted above, seem to serve an additional purpose to cementing the parallel between Lopez and Othello. The central, original bit, in particular – that is, 'I shall stumble to ye' – is sandwiched between two quasi-verbatim quotations from *Othello* and would have thereby acquired added relevance for playgoers, whose attention would have been inevitably drawn to it. Again, Fletcher not only identifies a crucial moment in the play in terms of stage business (i.e., the putting out of the candle), but also as regards thematic concerns, the symbolism of Othello's candle having been variously scrutinized by scholars.[22] In this case, however, Fletcher seems to be exclusively interested in the practicalities of how that sequence was realized onstage, rather than in its metaphorical value.

When *Othello* was first performed in London around 1604, it was staged at the Globe, in broad daylight. Probably the final scene would have started around 4 p.m. if the performance had begun around 2 p.m., and the idea of a darkened bedchamber only lit by a flickering candle would have had to be entirely imagined by the audience. Yet, after the King's Men started using the Blackfriars around 1608/1609, the new indoor space would have offered the company fresh lighting possibilities that might have had an impact on successive performances of *Othello*. True, the play had been already staged indoors at court as early as November 1604, but court performances were a very special kind of indoor performances and would have been different from performances at the Blackfriars in terms of illumination.[23] As

---

[20] Burrow, *Shakespeare and Classical Antiquity*, p. 160.

[21] That Fletcher was particularly attentive to the stage business in *Othello* seems to be borne out by another reversal in *Women Pleased* of what occurs in *Othello*. In Shakespeare's play, Othello, after murdering Desdemona, closes the bed curtains before unlocking the door for Emilia in order to hide his violence, while Lopez cannot wait to show everyone what he has done, (comically) proud as he is of his actions. Once again, Fletcher identifies an important connection between staging and deeper layers of meaning, in that the protracted stage business in the final scene of *Othello*, which involves repeatedly opening and closing the bed curtains, as well as locking and unlocking the door, has been compellingly discussed by Michael Neill, 'Unproper beds: race, adultery, and the hideous in *Othello*', *Shakespeare Quarterly* 40 (1989), 383–412, as a dramatic literalization of the theme of discovery in a play that is pervaded with hidden wickedness and intolerable secrets.

[22] See, especially, Robert F. Willson Jr, 'Symbol and character: the function of Othello's candle (V.ii.122)', *Literatur in Wissenschaft und Unterricht* 14 (1981), 29–35.

[23] R. B. Graves, *Lighting the Shakespearean Stage, 1567–1642* (Carbondale, IL, 1999), pp. 158–74.

Sarah Dustagheer argues, dramatic texts written for the company after 1608 can be said to have been 'marked by a performance duality', combining 'practices from both playhouses to produce performances with valuable and distinct spatial resonances at the Globe and Blackfriars, respectively'.[24] Yet there remain discordant views on the use of lighting at the early modern indoor playhouses, and the issue is still debated, as not enough evidence has survived to enable scholars to settle the matter.[25]

First, it is impossible to establish whether Blackfriars performances ever took place in almost total darkness or not, given that, as Robert Graves contends in his pioneering study of lighting on early modern stages, 'such evidence as we have indicates the auditoriums were well provided with windows, admitting substantial amounts of sunshine', and there exists 'no specific evidence of windows being closed at the professional indoor theatres'.[26] In the 2010s, however, Martin White started reconsidering aspects of Graves's work, suggesting that the operation of the lighting in an indoor playhouse would have been somewhat more flexible and would have been susceptible of producing more scenic effects than Graves argues. While Graves sounds a note of caution against 'think[ing] of the [early modern] stage as a modern showcase where the audience's attention was drawn toward beautiful pictures behind a proscenium frame', White shows that a well-organized and creative use of artificial lighting during indoor performances may have had a meaningful impact on the audience by adding emphasis to certain elements of staging that would not have stood out with the same effectiveness in outdoor playhouses.[27]

Examining *Othello*, act 5, scene 2, Graves wonders if, when Othello enters Desdemona's bedroom '*with a light*' (*Othello* 5.2.0.1 SD), we are supposed to see 'this lonely candle burning in a darkened hall, ironically signaling her true chastity in a nasty world'; he also notes, however, that, if the scene was ever 'presented illusionistically at the indoor theaters with only Othello's flickering candle lighting the stage', this would have been likely to create problems, as 'the audience might have [had] difficulty seeing Desdemona's horrified reaction to Othello's accusation'.[28] That the darkness should be viewed as purely metaphoric is Alan Dessen's firm conviction. He believes that the 'putting out of a light in this scene ... has little if anything to do with stage illumination' and that, 'when we assume that figures onstage do not see each other *because* it is dark, we are in danger of translating the action into our own idiom and theatrical language at the expense of the original metaphors'.[29] What really matters, he argues, is that the presence and use of the light of the candle in the final scene

of *Othello* 'can generate metaphoric possibilities' that 'can help us to grasp more fully the inner darkness and the failure in vision' that pervade the play.[30] By contrast, Goran Stanivukovic and John H. Cameron are more inclined to countenance at least the idea that the 'Blackfriars would have enhanced the sense of intimacy and even augmented the effect of "close-up" moments' in *Othello*, especially in act 5, scene 2.[31] More specifically, Stanivukovic and Cameron believe that the fact that 'the meaning of these lines is built around the image of a lit candle, and around changes between light and darkness depending on whether the candle is lit or extinguished, makes the candlelight not just a metaphor', but it 'suggests that any signification attached to light and dark should take into account how such changes might have been enhanced ... in a smaller, indoor theatre'.[32]

The conundrum is difficult (perhaps impossible?) to solve, and what follows is by necessity highly conjectural in the absence of any external evidence, but my immediate reaction to Lopez's 'I shall stumble to ye' was that those words can be interpreted critically in two different ways. The most straightforward level of reading is that Fletcher is perhaps using Lopez to mock the theatrical convention at the Blackfriars: if the bedroom had been lit exclusively by a candle before Isabella extinguished it, then putting that light out would have meant for Lopez to be finding his way to Jaquenet in complete darkness; that way, he would have easily stumbled in the process. By analogy, if the stage were *really* that dark, then Othello, too, should have stumbled or at least groped his way with difficulty to Desdemona's bed. While the

[24] Sarah Dustagheer, *Shakespeare's Two Playhouses: Repertory and Theatre Space at the Globe and the Blackfriars, 1599–1613* (Cambridge, 2017), p. 3.

[25] Graves, *Lighting*; Martin White, '"When torchlight made an artificial noon": light and darkness in the indoor Jacobean theatre', in *Moving Shakespeare Indoors: Performance and Repertoire in the Jacobean Playhouse*, ed. Andrew Gurr and Farah Karim-Cooper (Cambridge, 2014), 115–36; Dustagheer, *Shakespeare's Two Playhouses*; Martin White, '"By indirections find directions out": unpicking early modern stage directions', in *Stage Directions and Shakespearean Theatre*, ed. Sarah Dustagheer and Gillian Woods (London, 2018), 191–211.

[26] Graves, *Lighting*, pp. 125, 153.

[27] Graves, *Lighting*, p. 195; White, 'Light and darkness'; White, 'Unpicking'.

[28] Graves, *Lighting*, p. 8.

[29] Alan C. Dessen, *Elizabethan Stage Conventions and Modern Interpreters* (Cambridge, 1984), pp. 82, 83.

[30] Dessen, *Elizabethan Stage*, p. 82.

[31] Goran Stanivukovic and John H. Cameron, *Tragedies of the English Renaissance* (Edinburgh, 2018), p. 121.

[32] Stanivukovic and Cameron, *Tragedies*, p. 122.

potential stumbling would be a source of laughter in comedy, it would be ridiculous and inappropriate in tragedy. Fletcher would thus be sneering at the absurdity of the convention (i.e., 'It should be pitch dark, but it's not; can't ye see that?'). A second possibility – much more speculative, albeit not entirely far-fetched, I hope – is that Fletcher may have been reflecting on certain aspects of some recent performance(s) of Shakespeare's tragedy staged at the Blackfriars, in which the concluding scene was *actually* staged in almost complete darkness, in an (isolated?) experiment – which would have left no other trace – to augment the metaphorical signification of the light of Othello's candle by taking advantage of the lighting possibilities of the Blackfriars to stage the sequence illusionistically. In this scenario, Fletcher would be referring in an aslant, tongue-in-cheek way to said attempt – probably a failure, if Othello did 'stumble' his way to Desdemona. Again, there survives no direct evidence for any of this (though we do have evidence for *Othello*'s currency in the period between 1610 and 1640 – namely, the quarto edition published in 1622 and the documented revivals in 1610, 1612–1613, 1629, 1635 and 1636), but I believe this suggestion – bold as it is – ought at least to be pondered over, especially in light of Fletcher's characteristic self-consciousness in terms of staging techniques as displayed across his oeuvre.

AN OVERLOOKED INSTANCE OF *OTHELLO*'S EARLY RECEPTION

One can find traces of the fact that *Othello*'s concluding scene had made an impression on Fletcher rather early in his playwriting career. As Harry McCarthy remarks, the bed scene in Beaumont and Fletcher's *The Maid's Tragedy*, in which Evadne kills the King, 'perversely inverts the physical dynamics of the murder of Desdemona in *Othello* (which ... was in the King's Men repertory in 1610)'.[33] Was Fletcher's interest in *Othello* somehow rekindled, roughly ten years later, by a recent revival of the play? If the answer is yes, as seems likely, then the role of Othello would have been assigned to a different actor from

Richard Burbage, the original Othello, who had died just over a year earlier, in March 1619. Did the change of the main actor (the company having now given the role probably to Joseph Taylor) help Fletcher view *Othello* under a new light? Given that Fletcher seems to have authored a poignant 'Elegy on the Death of the Famous Actor Richard Burbage', which survives in manuscript (and in which Burbage is duly mentioned as having played 'the grieved Moor' onstage), the notion that the inevitable change in casting would have made an impact on Fletcher is not implausible.[34]

Whatever the answers to these questions may be, unearthing Fletcher's engagement with *Othello* in *Women Pleased* has been important for several reasons. First, this article has drawn attention to an overlooked instance of the early reception of *Othello*, which provides further proof of its enduring power on Shakespeare's fellow playmakers and playgoers alike. Second, it has provided fresh insights into the dynamics of the King's Men's repertory by complicating our understanding of the range and complexity of what Wiggins has described as the 'King's Men style'.[35] Third, it has cast new light on Fletcher's sharp, competent and informed eye on the plays of his time, as well as into his knack for deconstructing Shakespearian drama to its most significant constitutive elements, both structural and thematic. In more than one way, *Women Pleased* feels like an act of loving criticism of *Othello*, as the profound and extensive engagement with Shakespeare's tragedy that Fletcher's tragicomedy exhibits on so many levels – namely, in terms of dramatic structure, generic development, character construction, thematic concerns and staging practices – cannot but be that of a very attentive and enthusiastic admirer.

---

[33] Harry R. McCarthy, *Boy Actors in Early Modern England: Skill and Stagecraft in the Theatre* (Cambridge, 2022), p. 180.

[34] On the elegy commemorating Burbage's death and its attribution to Fletcher, see Lucy Munro, *Shakespeare in the Theatre: The King's Men* (London, 2020), pp. 17, 197n9.

[35] Martin Wiggins, *Shakespeare and the Drama of His Time* (Oxford, 2000), p. 127.

POWER, HOROLOGY AND IMPERIAL DOUBT: REIMAGINING TIME IN SHAKESPEARE'S *A MIDSUMMER NIGHT'S DREAM*

COURTNEY NAUM SCURO[1]

Look closely at how the fairies account for time in *A Midsummer Night's Dream* and you will find plenty of natural allusions, as one likely expects, but also something a bit more surprising: references to minutes, seconds and celestial orbits more evocative of mechanized timekeeping and contemporary astronomy than supernatural forest. Oberon may measure out time via marvellous allusions – to mermaid song, and wandering stars, and 'the leviathan . . . swim[ming] a league' – but Puck starkly measures his time to 'girdle' the earth as a mere 'forty minutes', while the first fairy quantifies its pace as 'Swifter than the moones sphere' (2.1.175–6, 6–7). Titania instructs her fairies to finish their forest chores in 'the third part of a minute', demanding a degree of precision beyond the capabilities of most contemporary timekeeping devices while, like Puck, simultaneously engaging in a clock-like quantification of time (2.2.2). The fairies' talk about time seems to 'wander everywhere / Swifter than the moones sphere', to borrow a line from Shakespeare's first fairy, by invoking phenomena in ways which defy the kinds of ontological tensions like nature/technology, city/forest, mundane/magical that previous scholarship has focused upon (2.1.6–7). Closely reading the play's references to timekeeping alters our sense of their significance: it surfaces the speculative potential of timekeeping animated through England's shifting time-practices; it reveals temporal acumen to be an important (if overlooked) source of agency in the play; and it exposes intersections between timekeeping and the politics of place, empire, class and technology which preoccupy Shakespeare in *Dream*. By digging into allusions to time-keeping, this article demonstrates the ways in which competing strategies for quantifying, conceptualizing and communicating time's passage raise questions not only about the nature of time, but about who has influence over whom, why and when.

Shakespeare's views on time are far from unique, but surfacing the politicized dynamics that shape early modern timekeeping will require more scholarship that connects visual, material and literary cultures. In their recent Introduction to *Seeing Race before Race: Visual Culture and the Racial Matrix in the Premodern World*, Noémie Ndiaye and Lia Markey open with an incisive reading of Nikolas Rugendas the Elder's 1620 'Figure Clock with an African Man'.[2] The device 'features a Black-skinned Moorish man holding a long rod . . . which directs our attention to a rotating sphere . . . which turns to indicate the hour' as the figure simultaneously turns its head as if to observe the viewer. Like the swan-shaped, skull, and mechanized galleon clocks that also survive from this period, Rugendas's device embodies a bit of clockmaker whimsy, but with graver implications. As Ndiaye and Markey observe, this 'Racially charged automata overtly confront viewers in today's museum, forcing us to think about the role of enslaved Africans and Turkish soldiers in European courts as well as other power relations across the premodern globe'; and, as they go on to assert 'It is about time', we recognize the racialized discourses manifested through such objects. Timekeeping and racist ideologies intertwine in the clock's material form, just like Ndiaye and Markey say, but also through

[1] I would like to thank Mary Floyd-Wilson and members of the Shakespeare Association of America (SAA) 2019 Seminar 'Occult Agents in Shakespeare' for their feedback and encouragement on an early version of this project. Also, big thanks to Heidi Brayman who will always be my most incisive and enthusiastic reader (not to mention, valued mentor). Finally, to Ian Smith, your call for 'worldly care' has given my humanist labours fresh purpose – much respect and appreciation for you, sir.

[2] Noémie Ndiaye and Lia Markey, eds., *Seeing Race before Race: Visual Culture and the Racial Matrix in the Premodern World* (Phoenix, 2023), https://asu.pressbooks.pub/seeing-race-before-race.

this object's terms of use. One must quite literally *animate* the cultural scripts that this automaton's operation encodes in order to use it. Not only impacting time's objects, social constructs such as race shape the culturally defined timekeeping practices that devices such as Rugendas's clock serve. Early modern writers pick up on the potentiality of that relation. In many texts, time-practices probe and manipulate concepts of difference such as race, as Shakespeare and his contemporaries engage a range of identities and social prejudices in order to explore individuals' places within a given community, hierarchy or history. Through *A Midsummer Night's Dream*, I draw out a methodology for reading these dynamics and show how timekeeping can shift our understanding of a text – even one we may think we know well.

Like the play itself, I begin with Theseus and Hippolyta whose disagreements over time's passage encode an ongoing struggle for authority in *A Midsummer Night's Dream*. Shakespeare picks up their well-known classical tale midway through: after Theseus's conquest of the Amazonians and his return to Athens with their queen, Hippolyta, in order to wed her.[3] *A Midsummer Night's Dream* may not start until the wedding part, but troubling themes of imperial conquest, patriarchy and racial privilege nevertheless accompany this pair's entry into the play – and shape their conflicts over time.[4]

DRAW ON APACE (OR NOT): MISALIGNING TIME IN THESEUS'S COURT

A Midsummer Night's Dream begins:

THESEUS Now, fair Hippolyta, our nuptial hour
Draws on apace. Four happy days bring in
Another moon – but O, methinks how slow
This old moon wanes! She lingers my desires
Like to a stepdame or a dowager
Long withering out a young man's revenue.

HIPPOLYTA Four days will quickly steep themselves in night,
Four nights will quickly dream away the time;
And then the moon, like to a silver bow
New bent in heaven, shall behold the night
Of our solemnities.

(1.1.1–11)[5]

In her very first line, Hippolyta counters her recent conqueror and soon-to-be-spouse's claim about time's passage; she contends that 'Four days will quickly steep

themselves in night', in direct opposition to Theseus's lament over 'how slow / This old moon wanes!' They feel time's passage differently, but more importantly, they disagree epistemologically. Theseus constructs his sense of time out of the *now* of his verbs' present tense ('bring', 'lingers'), while for Hippolyta, time's meaning emerges from what *will happen* in the time-to-come of future tense ('will quickly', 'will quickly', 'shall behold'). Their relationships to time in this opening scene are distinct on both a semantic and structural level. Thus, the play's first moments stage a debate over how to mark, articulate and understand time's passage; and that debate establishes the Athenian court as a place comprised of multiple, incompatible orientations to time that must compete for the right to define events and lived experiences.

Theseus's opening lines feature heavily in scholarship on time in *A Midsummer Night's Dream*, but for entirely different reasons from those I have highlighted here. Instead, criticism has focused upon the 'four days' that Theseus's speech claims must pass before his act 5 'nuptial hour', and how this constitutes a longer stretch of time than that covered by the play's intervening scenes (1.1.1–2) – somewhere we lose a day. Time is notably problematic in this play as a formal component of dramatic structure, in other words. Scholars including Brian Richardson and Matthew Wagner have argued that

---

[3] On Shakespeare's sources for Theseus, see especially Loren Cressler, 'Asinine heroism and the mediation of empire in Chaucer, Marlowe, and Shakespeare', *MLQ* 81 (2020), 319–47. Scholars have given much attention to the political critique possibly scripted into the play's treatment of Theseus. See also Mary Floyd-Wilson, 'The habitation of airy nothings in *A Midsummer Night's Dream*', in *Geographies of Embodiment in Early Modern England*, ed. Mary Floyd-Wilson and Garrett A. Sullivan Jr (Oxford, 2020), 243–61; A. D. Nutall, '*A Midsummer Night's Dream*: comedy as apostrophe of myth', in *Shakespeare Survey 53* (Cambridge, 2000), 49–59; Peter Holland, 'Theseus' shadows in *A Midsummer Night's Dream*', in *Shakespeare Survey 47* (Cambridge, 1994), 139–151; and Peter Herman, 'Equity and the problem of Theseus in *A Midsummer Night's Dream*: or the ancient constitution in ancient Athens', *Journal for Early Modern Cultural Studies* 14 (2014), 4–31.

[4] Dympna Callaghan, *Shakespeare Without Women* (New York, 2000), p. 7. Callaghan observes, 'One only has to think of Cleopatra, who serves simultaneously as a symbol of woman, of female sovereignty, of racial difference, and of subjected nationhood, in order to recognize that race is not an ancillary representational category.' The same could be said of Hippolyta.

[5] Both the First Folio and the First Quarto of 1600 read 'Now bent', but modern editors typically substitute 'New'. In either case, how Theseus and Hippolyta each relate to time in this scene remains distinct.

Shakespeare utilizes the narrative's time-discrepancy to construct 'two internally consistent but mutually incompatible time schemes': that of Theseus's court and of the fairies' forest.[6] Building on Richardson's reading of *A Midsummer Night's Dream* as an antagonistic competition between temporal modes, Wagner argues that, in *A Midsummer Night's Dream*, Shakespeare creates a 'temporal collision' intent on rendering time into something multiple and incompatible, but still not 'arbitrary'.[7] In other words, time remains significant in *A Midsummer Night's Dream*, according to Wagner, despite the fairy-world's intervention into the 'duration, measure, orderliness' of Theseus's court which generates a temporal multiplicity that turns time into something that is ultimately incomprehensible in the world of the play, as evidenced by its breakdown of narrative time.[8]

Richardson's and Wagner's argument depends upon our ability to see fairy-land and courtly-land operating as 'mutually incompatible time schemes' that are each 'internally consistent', but that collide to create conflicts over time *between* them. Certainly, there is compelling evidence to support their conceptualization of the play's spatio-temporal scheme, as their arguments deftly unpack. But I would like to suggest that the text offers up an equally compelling argument *not* to conceptualize the world of the play as Richardson and Wagner have done. First, there is the temporal multiplicity and misalignment that surfaces in the court through Theseus and Hippolyta's opening exchange (which undermines ideas of the court's temporal orderliness and internal cohesion). Second, there is the capacious sense of place attributed to the fairies in several instances, which runs counter to Richardson's and Wagner's characterization of the fairies as courtly interlopers and outsiders.[9] 'I do wander everywhere', the first fairy announces, claiming a space for his elemental interventions that undoes spatial distinctions. And through Titania's description of the ecological catastrophes inflicted on an entire 'mazed world', thanks to her and Oberon's quarrel, their special agency which Titania describes defies restriction to the forest: the fairy-rulers' fight affects crops and floods rivers (like the kind that runs through London), pushing fairy-effect out far beyond the tree line (2.1.81–117). Finally, there is the play's ending where we hear the fairies will 'stray' to each 'bride-bed' to 'bless[]' the 'issue there create' (5.2.32–51). With these final lines, the fairies set the story's sense of resolution in order through their intimate familiarity with the court, its inhabitants and nuptial practices. Additionally, through Oberon's directive to 'the issue there create', fairies offer the final act

which sets time right in the court by establishing a clear expectation of lineal 'duration' (to borrow one of Wagner's terms).[10] By ensuring 'the blots of nature's hand / Shall not in their issue stand. / Never mole, hare-lip, nor scar, / Nor mark *prodigious* … ', Oberon even goes so far as to head off any monstrous disturbance to a neat and orderly concept of temporal, ancestral and social progression (5.2.39–42, italics mine).[11] In other words, place-ness and timeliness intersect in ways which confuse the discrete spatial identities key to Wagner's and Richardson's arguments – and especially Wagner's concept of court-time as defined by 'duration, measure, orderliness' which the fairies *disturb*. The point is that I see time as everything that Richardson and Wagner claim – tense, multiple and deeply tied to formations of place and power in *A Midsummer Night's Dream* – but in ways which ultimately defy the tight spatial schema that the text in many instances appears to be advancing (and that their argument focuses on). All things considered, I see that the play's fraught, politically charged explorations of time are really about exploring the relative power of its various agents as they move, relate and attempt to control one another through *A Midsummer Night's Dream*'s multiple, mutual, but not entirely compatible 'schemes'. More specifically in Theseus and Hippolyta's case, conflicts over keeping time define an

---

[6] Brian Richardson, '"Time is out of joint": narrative models and the temporality of the drama', *Poetics Today* 8 (1987), 299–309; p. 299.

[7] Matthew Wagner, *Shakespeare, Theatre, and Time* (New York, 2013), p. 129.

[8] Wagner, *Shakespeare, Theatre, and Time*, p. 128.

[9] Recently, several scholars have challenged tendencies to read *Dream* dialectically. Though my reading does not directly engage theirs, my view of *Dream* has certainly been influenced by their insights. See, especially, Adam Rzepka, '"How easy is a bush supposed a bear"?: differentiating imaginative production in *A Midsummer Night's Dream*', *Shakespeare Quarterly* 66 (2015), 308–28; Louise Gedde, 'Playing no part but Pyramus: Bottom, celebrity and the early modern clown', *Medieval and Renaissance Drama in England* 28 (2015), 70–85; and Christopher Thurman, 'Fine frenzies: Theseus, Shakespeare and the politics of their poets', *Shakespeare* 11 (2015), 115–34.

[10] David Kastan argues the 'shape' of narrative time to be a defining generic feature in Shakespeare's oeuvre, with comedy's time structurally characterized by its opening out through the promise of renewal and continuity offered through a story's resolution. See David Kastan, *Shakespeare and the Shapes of Time* (London, 1982).

[11] Elsewhere, I have written more on monstrosity as disruptive to orderly concepts of time in Shakespeare, see Courtney Naum Scuro, 'Temporo-corporeal politics in Shakespeare's *Henry V* and other monster texts', *Shakespeare* 17 (2021), 184–209.

ongoing negotiation for authority beginning in act 1 and continuing when these two retake the stage later in the play.

Act 4, scene 1 sees Hippolyta, Theseus and assorted courtiers travelling through the forest on their way to a hunt. Once again, Hippolyta disagrees with Theseus's sense of time. Theseus boasts about the excellence of his hounds, proclaiming, 'We will . . . up to the mountain's top / And mark the musical confusion / Of hounds and echo in conjunction' (4.1.108–10). Hippolyta responds by recounting another hunt she once went on, one with Hercules where 'Never did [she] hear/ Such gallant chiding . . . so musical a discord, such sweet thunder' as *his* hounds performed that day (4.1.113–17). Theseus then counters with a long and effusive description of his dogs' pedigree and orders Hippolyta, 'Judge when you hear' (4.1.126). Struggling to maintain a position of privilege in the face of Hippolyta's praise for Hercules, Theseus defends his hounds' reputation by insisting that judgement cannot be made *yet*. In other words, Hippolyta cannot know *now* which are the better hounds, according to Theseus. When the party suddenly spies a sleeping Hermia, Lysander, Helena and Demetrius nearby, the scene's focus abruptly shifts and this dog-inspired discord is left to hang in the air unsettled.

So, is this incident meant to take Theseus down a notch or two? Does Hippolyta manage to undermine Theseus's self-aggrandizing bravado by suggesting the prestige that he presumes for his hounds (and, consequently, himself) instead belongs to another hunt, another set of animals, and another man in another time? Was that Shakespeare's intention? It is impossible to say, of course – and may award Shakespeare more feminist and anti-imperial sympathies than he truly deserves – but entertaining the possibility that Shakespeare sought to question Theseus's prerogative to unilaterally define the significance of that present-moment in time would help to explain why Shakespeare includes this otherwise bizarre exchange. Along with an earlier allusion to May Day rites in Theseus's lines, the hunt helps to establish why the royal party would be out in the woods and subsequently discover the lost, slumbering pairs of young lovers. Otherwise, the twenty or so lines we get on the hounds seem to serve little purpose. Previous scholarship emphasizes the sense of harmony arising from the hounds' cacophony to argue that these lines participate in the play's attempt to present an image of natural and social concord ultimately triumphing over states of conflict.[12] However, such explanations displace Theseus and Hippolyta's discord onto the hounds. If we resist this parallel (as I do), what are we left with? We get a scene whose focus shifts prior to the text providing a clear indication that Hippolyta has acquiesced to Theseus's perspective and, through her accord, established a clear resolution to their conflict over how to distinguish the significance of this time-of-the-hunt from other moments and experiences in time. Theseus and Hippolyta's potentially fraught exchange more or less ends with Theseus's demand to her to 'Judge when you hear'. Theseus's directive defers, rather than rectifies, the rift that arises from their competing evaluations and expectations for what this soon-to-commence hunt will mean *in time*, and so exposes an ongoing struggle not just to synchronize their perspectives, but over who ultimately has the right to dictate the significance of their shared lived experience and, in time, their history.

There is also another angle to consider to account for this episode of the hounds: that Hippolyta's description of Hercules' hunt grants Shakespeare an opportunity, if only briefly, to mull over the role past experience can play in shaping present temporal perspectives and expectations. Unlike the majority of classical references littering early modern texts, Hippolyta's invocation of Hercules refers to her actual experience of another time. It is, therefore, not figurative in the same sense that a comparison between an *imagined* distant past and present moment would be, but phenomenological in the sense that it derives from Hippolyta's recollection of her own lived experience. In making her comparison, Hippolyta relies on the power of memory and, more specifically, leverages her ability to recall another time as a way to evaluate and mark experience in the present moment. Theseus disputes the validity of her time-practice, but not on the basis of its rhetoric of relativity, but because Hippolyta has compared the wrong moments. Hippolyta cannot judge *yet*, according to Theseus, but should 'judge when [she] hears'. In other words, Hippolyta's comparison should not occur between past and present, but between past and the future moment of the hunt which this scene anticipates. Theseus does not appear to believe this same requirement should apply to his temporal practices, however, as his initial boast assumes absolutely what significance his

12 For example, see Maurice Hunt, 'The voices of *A Midsummer Night's Dream*', *Texas Studies in Literature and Language* 34 (1992), 218–38; William E. Slights, 'The changeling in a dream', *Studies in English Literature* 28 (1988), 259–72; Leon Guilhamet, '*A Midsummer Night's Dream* as the imitation of action', *Studies in English Literature* 15 (1975), 257–71.

hounds *will* have in that future moment.[13] Thus, Theseus attempts to claim special agency over the meaning and definition of these unfolding moments in time, but in ways that the play arguably fails to affirm, thanks to the deferral of judgement which leaves this disagreement around his hounds ultimately unresolved: the stuff not of dreams, but of an unstaged future moment.

While obviously gendered, the power struggle happening in this scene is just as much about the concepts of empire, conquest and race that infuse Hippolyta and Theseus's origin story. Through this debate over time, we witness Theseus's attempt to impose a hegemonic worldview that erases differentiated perspectives and lived experiences by resituating all points of temporal comparison within the bounds of imperial time. His argument also attempts to negate the significance of the pre-conquest past that Hippolyta invokes and render it inconsequential to the present-moment and to the future that Theseus anticipates in this scene, a future marked by imperial pre-eminence and prestige which his hounds synecdochally signify. Understood in this way, this scene provides additional evidence to support Margo Hendricks's claim for Shakespeare's *A Midsummer Night's Dream* being 'complicit[] in the racialist ideologies being created by early modern England's participation in imperialism' and the practices of subjugation such politics activate, as Hendricks has so convincingly argued through tracing references to India found in *A Midsummer Night's Dream*.[14] According to James W. Stone, India and Amazon carry striking symbolic similarities, both equally 'barbarian' and threateningly feminine according to the Hellenic culture serving as Shakespeare's backdrop in *A Midsummer Night's Dream*. They serve, alongside the play's various Orientalist allusions, as 'a measure of what falls short of the Greek male cultural ideal'.[15]

'[B]ut there are gaps in the play as well', Stone goes on to explain, that 'valorize' these othered cultures 'as a place for escaping the rigors and prejudices of patriarchy'.[16] Here in act 4, scene 1, we see another such gap (in addition to those identified by Stone). However, I would argue that this gap offers more than momentary 'escape' from the kind of patriarchal-imperialist culture Theseus embodies; it introduces lingering, unresolved doubt over the extent of his power. There is a notable, albeit subtle, silence and deferral that follows Theseus's directive to 'judge when you hear'. Instead of any sort of vocalized acquiescence or reiteration of Theseus's imperial agenda by Hippolyta or any of the rest of the gathered courtiers, the play suddenly shifts to the sleeping young

lovers. This omission speaks volumes. Male, ruler, conqueror: despite the several intersects suggesting Theseus's authoritative privilege, he does not clearly win this debate. He falls short of imposing his will over how moments in time get marked out and their meaning measured by his (supposed) subordinates.

Empire-making comes with its own kind of time, as Supriya Chaudhury explains: 'The colonial project [and I would say more broadly, that of conquest] was itself an interruption of, perhaps an assault upon, notions of time and history' that 'required the supersession of earlier kinds of temporal knowledge' in order to institute values and beliefs that would serve an imperialist agenda.[17] As Chaudhury's study of Shakespeare's afterlives in India examines, we still live today with the consequences of a Western, imperial, colonial imperative to impose what Christopher Prendergast, building on Arjun Appadurai's term, calls 'Eurochronology': a worldview so predicated upon European knowledge-systems and narrative forms that it cannot recognize the value of anything out of alignment with the West's very limited perspective.[18]

Chaudhury, Prendergast and Appadurai's insights emerge from their careful study of centuries-long histories of coercion and violent revisionism – a majority of which come after Shakespeare's lifetime. Similar dynamics are nevertheless evident in *A Midsummer Night's Dream*, which grapples with uncertainties around the capacity for that imperial power which Theseus

---

[13] For more on the hunt as a performance of power dynamics, and exploration of the same in the Mechanicals' entertainment, see Patricia Akhimie, '"Hard-handed men": manual labor and imaginative capacity in A Midsummer Night's Dream', in *Shakespeare and the Cultivation of Difference: Race and Conduct in the Early Modern World* (New York, 2018), 117–50.

[14] Margo Hendricks, '"Obscured by dreams": race, empire, and Shakespeare's *A Midsummer Night's Dream*', *Shakespeare Quarterly* 47 (1996), 37–60; p. 43. For foundational readings of race in the play, also see Kim F. Hall, *Things of Darkness: Economies of Race and Gender in Early Modern England* (London, 1995).

[15] James W. Stone, 'Indian and Amazon: the Oriental feminine in *A Midsummer Night's Dream*', in *The English Renaissance, Orientalism, and Ideas of Asia*, ed. Debra Johanyak and Walter S. H. Lim (London, 2010), 97–114; p. 98.

[16] Stone, 'The Oriental feminine', p. 98.

[17] Supriya Chaudhury, 'Remembering Shakespeare in India: colonial and postcolonial memory', in *Celebrating Shakespeare: Commemoration and Cultural Memory*, ed. Clara Calvo and Coppelia Kahn (Cambridge, 2015), 101–20; p. 107.

[18] Christopher Prendergast, 'The World Republic of Letters', in *Debating World Literature*, ed. Christopher Prendergast and Benedict Anderson (London, 2004), 1–25.

personifies to impose its understanding of time and history universally. In the play's opening, as well as here in act 4, that ambivalence emerges in silence; it emerges in a *lack* of affirming words to secure Theseus's imperial temporal prerogative and subdue the states of temporal heterogeneity that instead persist through this absence.

However, while Hippolyta's use of memory in this scene certainly invokes larger questions of history in line with Chaudhury, Prendergast and Appadurai's arguments, her disagreement with Theseus is just as much about time *in the present* and, in particular, how one can and should go about measuring time's passage *now*. This idea, I admit, is easier to see in act 1, scene 1, when Theseus and Hippolyta's disagreement centres on how to account for a specific quantity of time – four days – by offering competing approaches to qualifying the experience of a specific quantity of time passing. Their act 4 debate is similarly about measuring time – however, in a slightly different way. Here, their disagreement involves how to identify, differentiate and mark a specific moment in time in the face of an ongoing and successive flow of lived experiences. In his detailed study of timekeeping devices and techniques, Gerard Dohrn-van Rossum explains that measuring time essentially boils down into two different activities: one, marking a particular point in time (like 2 p.m. or, I would add, the occurrence of an exemplary event); two, tracking the passage of a specific quantity of time, like three hours or three days.[19] These two timekeeping activities have become conflated for those of us today who live amongst a rich array of reliable, visual timekeeping devices, but for earlier horologists, they presented very different problems. Thus, we can see Hippolyta and Theseus's disagreements imaginatively engaging a range of timekeeping tasks that, thanks to horological advancements happening in Shakespeare's lifetime, were undergoing significant change.

Watches, improved sun- and equinoctial dials, tower clock-faces, printed almanacs, changing calendars: the period sees a slew of technological innovations which rattle incumbent timekeeping practices and infuse individual relationships to time with fresh senses of power and possibility. In his long-printed English almanac *A Prognostication Euerlasting of right good effect*, Leonard Digges declares to his reader 'thus I saye and trewly, the ingenious learned, and well experienced circu[m]spect student *mathematical* receyueth dayly in hys witty practices, more pleasant ioye of mynde, then all thy goodness (how rych so euer thou be) canne at any tyme purchase'.[20] These 'witty practices' mathematical are in fact a series of tools, tables and accompanying techniques for tracking the timing of holidays, new moons and sunrises – in other words, for keeping time. But Digges's new timekeeping strategies also come with a promise that their regular use will lead to 'wonderfull unknowen pleasant profites': in other words, Digges claims they will significantly improve one's lived experience. As Carlo M. Cipolla explains in his seminal study *Clocks and Culture: 1300–1700*, 'most people believed that a correct knowledge of the conjunction of heavenly bodies was essential for the success of human enterprises', and that pursuit was inextricably intertwined with early moderns' pursuit of better timekeeping technologies and techniques.[21] Theseus and Hippolyta's temporal disputes are all wrapped up in the period's developments in horology: firstly, because their arguments engage two essential questions of horology – measuring duration and distinguishing specific moments in time – and, secondly, because their scenes are infused with allusions intimately tied to timekeeping for Shakespeare and his contemporaries – in act 1, scene 1, the sun and moon; in act 4, scene 1, the arrival of May Day.[22]

However, when it comes to this play's preoccupations with timekeeping, power and what uncertainties the period's horological advancements might instigate, Theseus and Hippolyta are just the beginning. Turning next to the Mechanicals' commotions, we can see how conversations on timekeeping in *A Midsummer Night's Dream* envelop a much wider political sphere: impacting the whole of this play's social hierarchy from top to Bottom and affecting what would surely have been a more familiar and relatable representation of power and influence for most of its first audiences, the trade guilds.

---

19 Gerhard Dohrn-van Rossum, *History of the Hour: Clocks and Modern Temporal Orders* (Chicago, 1996). For more on the connection between marking time and truth-claims in accounts of exceptional events in the period, see David Cressy, *Travesties and Transgressions in Tudor and Stuart England: Tales of Discord and Dissension* (Oxford, 2000).

20 Leonard Digges, *A Prognostication Euerlasting of Ryght Good Effecte* (London, 1556).

21 Carlo Cipolla, *Clocks and Culture: 1300–1700* (New York, 1967), p. 41.

22 Happening halfway between the spring equinox and summer solstice, May Day's timing would have been perceived by early moderns to be intimately linked to the movements of celestial bodies. For more on early moderns' changing attitudes towards calendars, holidays and, as a result, temporality, see David Cressy, *Bonfires and Bells: National Memory and the Protestant Calendar in Elizabethan and Stuart England* (London, 1989).

THE MECHANICALS, MOONSHINE AND THE POWER OF KEEPING TIME

The Mechanicals' two rehearsal scenes start with essentially the same question: in act 1, scene 2, 'Is all our company here?'; and in act 3, scene 1, 'Are we all met?' (1.2.1, 3.1.1). Essentially, each rehearsal opens by seeking confirmation that the Mechanicals have all successfully kept time: that they have effectively coordinated their actions in order to arrive in this same place, at this exact moment. Near the close of the first rehearsal in act 1, Quince's plea to the gathered company suggests this accomplishment should not be taken for granted.

QUINCE But masters, here are your parts, and I am to entreat you, request you, and desire you to con them by tomorrow night, and meet me in the palace wood, a mile without the town, by moonlight. There will we rehearse ... I pray you fail me not

(1.2.90–9)

Quince implores his fellows to 'fail ... not' to put their time to good and similar use, first by learning their lines within the span of time until their next meeting and, second, by arriving at that next meeting where and when designated. Achieving such synchronization is no easy task, Quince's lines suggest, but requires forethought, administration and, apparently, quite a bit of goading by someone willing and able to take the lead. When the Mechanicals convene for their second rehearsal, Quince will emerge as the group's timemaster once again, but in a manner which more explicitly connects Quince's attentive timekeeping to the sway that he holds over his peers.

QUINCE ... but there is two hard things: that is, to bring the moonlight into the chamber – for you know Pyramus and Thisbe meet by moonlight.
SNOUT Doth the moon shine that night we play our play?
BOTTOM A calendar, a calendar – look in the almanac; find out moonshine, find out moonshine.
QUINCE Yes, it doth shine that night.
BOTTOM Why, then may you leave a casement of the great chamber window where we play open, and the moon may shine in at the casement.

(3.1.43–50)

Does Peter Quince have an almanac? Does he pull it out in response to Bottom's frenzied cries? Or does Quince travel around with an astronomical compendium of some sort, with phases of the moon engraved into its inner shell?[23] Or maybe Quince, knowing he would be on the road the night of the play, already looked up and/or calculated the status of the moon on that date in preparation for his impending travels?[24] The play does not make explicit *how* Quince knows, only *what* Quince knows: '[the moon] doth shine that night'. Perhaps this is part of the point; when it comes to keeping time, the *what* matters more than the *how*. Regardless of how he manages it, Quince demonstrates a temporal adroitness to outdo his companions. Knowing *when* the moon will be in fuller phase, Quince is empowered to intervene following Bottom's frantic call for 'a calendar, a calendar' to effectively diffuse the group's anxieties around plans for their play, at least for the moment.

Adam Smyth reads this same moment from *A Midsummer Night's Dream* quite differently. Citing Bottom's line, Smyth asserts a character calling for an almanac represented, broadly, the same thing across the Elizabethan period, and that thing was some combination of gullibility, doomed social ambition, provincialism and ignorance. Literary representations of almanacs, in other words, become early modern shorthand for representing a particular kind of the popular, defined against the elite, the urbane or the informed.[25]

Now, surely Bottom as a character emerges as the epitome of those very characteristics Smyth lists, but Bottom's call for an almanac, given its contexts, nevertheless deserves some defence. Certain almanac practices will increasingly inspire contempt as we move into the seventeenth century – judicial prognostication, in particular – but right when Shakespeare is writing

---

23 Astronomical compendiums were typically maritime tools, but surviving examples with tables of latitudes for landlocked cities (latitudes were needed to correctly configure the instrument to work at different locations) suggest these tools were also used by those engaged in extensive land travel. However, it seems unlikely a carpenter like Quince would have the economic means to afford such a piece of equipment or the training to use it. Shakespeare likes taking some dramatic licence in these respects, however, as Touchstone and the watch he supposedly pulls from his pocket readily attests to in *As You Like It* (2.7.23, 26).

24 With our ready access to incandescent lighting, it can be easy to forget how important the moon's illumination was for centuries. Even into the nineteenth century, social events – such as a ball given at a country manor house – would often be planned around the full moon if guests would be travelling at night.

25 Adam Smyth, 'Almanacs and ideas of popularity', in *The Elizabethan Top Ten: Defining Print Popularity in Early Modern England*, ed. Andy Kesson and Emma Smith (Burlington, 2013), 125–33; p. 128.

A Midsummer Night's Dream, an almanac is really a fairly accessible and accurate tool for determining something like the moon's phase on a specific date.[26] So criticize Bottom and all his buffoonery, certainly, but not because he seeks out an almanac to '[f]ind out moonshine'. Instead, it is perhaps the most reasonable act we witness Bottom performing.

However, I do not really indulge in this brief apologetics for the weaver's calendric mania for his sake, but for the carpenter's. Quince's time-knowledge allows him to shift the emotional thrust of this scene – if only briefly – by diffusing the affective flurry activated by Bottom's clamouring. It is Quince's ability to effectively leverage newer timekeeping technologies, such as an almanac's astrological calendar, which gives him greater insight into the operations of the natural world (at least compared to Bottom) and grants him special authority in this exchange. Here in the Mechanicals' scene, such time-knowledge translates into power, and is therefore a source of 'wonderfull unknowen pleasant profites', just as almanac-writer Leonard Digges claims.

In a moment, I will move on to Shakespeare's fairies. Through them, these themes of time, technology and power beginning to take shape through the Mechanicals will acquire additional dimensions as we delve into the speculative and wondrous possibility that Shakespeare explores through fairy-timekeeping. But first, there is a timekeeping trait of the Mechanicals deserving additional attention: their synchronicity. While subtle, the Mechanicals' ability to align their individual movements through time in order to successfully meet at the place and moment of each of their two rehearsals demonstrates their ability to keep and manage time. Given the difficulties with accounting for time which plague Theseus's court and, as I will later discuss, confuse the young lovers' plans, the Mechanicals' ability to meet without much confusion or consternation is itself notable. Once again, when it comes to the trouble with time in *A Midsummer Night's Dream*, there is as much to be gleaned from what is *not* present in the text as what is.

Registering little in the way of conflict (at least over time), the Mechanicals appear to operate under a fairly unified or singular approach to timekeeping. In other words, the Mechanicals do not appear bothered by the kind of irreducible multiplicity causing troubles at court between Theseus and Hippolyta. Taking just these two perspectives from the play, Mechanicals and court, it would be easy to make a couple of assumptions: that homogeneity is the key to establishing effective communal timekeeping strategies, or that competing temporal attitudes always pose a threat – hence why imperialist anxieties about cross-cultural exchange and influence get encoded as competing temporal orientations. Neither of these assumptions holds up, however, once we take into account the additional layer of complexity and possibility presented through fairy-time in *A Midsummer Night's Dream*.

FAIRY-TIME AND THE NATURE IN/ OF EARLY MODERN HOROLOGY

Timekeeping amongst the fairies does not introduce the kind of discord legible in Theseus and Hippolyta's exchanges, despite the multiple orientations to time that the fairies pursue. Effectively navigating multiple ways to convey and manage time, the fairies possess privileged insight and agency over it: an agency that aligns with their special command over other natural systems. Soon after the fairies' arrival onstage at the top of act 2, Oberon talks to Puck about discovering 'love-in-idleness' (the flower he will later use to enchant Titania and the young lovers). Oberon marks out that specific moment in time through a dense and heady weave of allusions. He begins by asking Puck if he 'rememb'rest' the time Oberon

> ... heard a mermaid on a dolphin's back
> Uttering such dulcet and harmonious breath
> That the rude sea grew civil at her song
> And certain stars shot madly from their spheres
> (2.1.150–3)

Oberon goes on to explain it was then he witnessed 'young Cupid's fiery shaft / Quenched in the chaste beams of the wat'ry moon' hit the 'little western flower' that he now orders Puck to fetch 'Ere the leviathan can swim a league' (2.1.155–70). A few lines later, Oberon will direct Puck again, asking Puck to meet him 'ere the first cock crow' (2.1.267). Oberon constructs a sense of time – past-event, call to present action, and future injunction – through a mix of references to marvellous creaturely actions, celestial bodies, and also more mundane natural-temporal rhythms (the cock's crow). It is

---

[26] On almanac culture in early modern England, see Bernard Capp, *English Almanacs, 1500–1800: Astrology and the Popular Press* (London, 1979); Alison A. Chapman, 'Marking time: astrology, almanacs, and English Protestantism', *Renaissance Quarterly* 60 (2007), 1257–90; Lauren Kassell, 'Almanacs and prognostications', in *The Oxford History of Popular Print Culture*: vol. 1: *Cheap Print in Britain and Ireland to 1660*, ed. Joad Raymond (Oxford, 2011), 431–42.

the sort of temporal awareness we most likely expect from the fairies: offering a strange and pleasantly disconcerting blend of relatable phenomenon like moon and cock with more marvellous invocations of mermaid, Cupid and sea-monster that together work to conceive of a natural world that simultaneously feels both familiar and fantastically alien.

Given Oberon's speech, Puck's response part-way through the scene seems oddly sparse: 'I'll put a girdle round about the earth / In forty minutes' (2.1.175–6). Puck's succinct, clear and empirical quantification of time seems out of step with Oberon's fantastical creatures and watery moon, and yet Oberon shows no sign of balking at this shift in temporal discourse; his lines carry on, failing to register the sort of temporal discord we earlier witness between Theseus and Hippolyta. Nor do these shifts in Oberon and Puck's talk about time generate a conflicting sense of present-time or passing time, as we also see occurring between Theseus and Hippolyta.

While dissimilar from his master's, Puck's line also establishes a temporal mode that is steeped in imaginative suggestiveness. Like Titania's line at the start of the next scene, when she sends her fairies 'for the third part of a minute' to complete their fairy chores, Puck's line is surprisingly evocative of clock-time (2.2.2). And yet, both his forty minutes and Titania's twenty seconds speak to a level of temporal measurement and management still fairly untenable for Shakespeare's audience. Most personal timepieces still lacked a minute hand, let alone a second hand. These devices simply were not precise enough for that level of calculation – especially the portable kind of timepiece capable of being taken into a forest or on a trip. Titania's twenty seconds arguably would be much like twenty milliseconds are to us today: understandable theoretically, but difficult to actually measure. Thus, here, Titania and her fairies evidence their ability to track, manage and experience time at a level beyond mortal ken, but yet in form and language aligning with humankind's more recent horological advancements.

Fairy-time is remarkably multi-modal, moving between mechanical and natural orientations to timekeeping quite effortlessly and refusing bipartite models of thinking (like nature/technology) by suggesting flexibility and temporal agency to be closely linked. But rather than see this attitude as yet another Shakespearian invention that we encounter in *A Midsummer Night's Dream*, I would like to suggest that this close affinity we find in fairy-time between technology and nature actually reflects early moderns' views on

horology. To be clear, I am not suggesting that the fairies themselves represent new timekeeping instruments or practices. Instead, I see the fairies as embodying something more along the lines of the wonder and magic generated as an *effect* of humankind's newest timekeeping strategies and technologies, advancements which seem as though they promise that, one day, humankind may achieve mastery and sway over nature's most influential temporal motions.[27] Nature's movements and those of the timepiece go hand in hand, as instruments like the period's popular astronomical clocks visually attest. Take the table clock (Figure 13), for instance, whose series of dials track the numerical passing of the hours along with the phase of the moon and even the rise and fall of the Thames's tide. As is also the case with the many other examples of astronomical timepieces produced in this period, the mechanical and natural coincide to suggest that, through innovation, humankind has come closer to unveiling the mysterious and influential inner workings of nature by mimicking them.[28] In other words, human technology does not supersede nature (although one might certainly argue this attitude arises in later centuries); instead, technology allows humans to achieve a new and fantastic kind of harmony with nature's powerful forces, such as the passing of time (and the moon, stars and tides which go with it – Figure 14).

Early moderns' pursuit of better strategies for keeping time simultaneously occur through multiple technologies, along multiple trajectories and through various types of devices – as do debates around timekeeping in *A Midsummer Night's Dream*. The most notable development in the period arguably comes through domestic

---

27 For more on wonder and technology, see Wendy Beth Hyman, 'Introduction', in *The Automaton in English Renaissance Literature*, ed. Wendy Beth Hyman (New York, 2011), 13–27. According to Hyman, the mechanical can often serve as 'a source of wonder, suggestive of magic . . . just as likely to unsettle the divide between man and divinity as between man and matter'. On the machine-imaginary, also see Adam Max Cohen, *Technology and the Early Modern Self* (New York, 2009); Jonathan Sawday, *Engines of the Imagination: Renaissance Culture and the Rise of the Machine* (New York, 2007); Jessica Wolfe, *Humanism, Machinery, and Renaissance Literature* (Cambridge, 2004).

28 According to Henry Turner, rather than disrupting one's relationship with and reliance on natural orders, early moderns saw new techniques and knowledge practices as renegotiating the terms of that interaction – ideas Turner relates to *Dream* in his *Shakespeare's Double Helix* (New York, 2007). Also see Turner's *The English Renaissance Stage: Geometry, Poetics, and the Practical Spatial Arts, 1580–1630* (Oxford, 2006) for discussion of the effects of 'new science' on the early modern imaginary – and drama, in particular.

13 Astronomical tabletop clock built by Francis Nowe, 1588, which includes devices for calculating the phase of the moon and time of high water at London Bridge (© Victoria and Albert Museum, London).

14 Astronomical watch and watchcase made by H. Roberts, 1600–1610, which also includes devices to track the age and phase of the moon (© The Trustees of the British Museum. All rights reserved).

clocks and watches: timekeeping devices exceedingly more personal and portable than their technological predecessor, the massive tower clock, and which instigate a slow shift towards more individualized and mechanized methods for keeping track of time. As Carlo Cipolla explains, 'The first watches made by English craftsmen in the last two decades of the sixteenth century were unimaginative but diligent replicas of French and German models' and, while 'there is no record of an English watch before 1580 … before the century was over signs of improvement and change were abundantly clear'.[29] Delicate, temperamental and still requiring specialized skills and daily management to keep them running, these new devices nevertheless helped to tie mechanized timekeeping to significant bodies, rather than significant buildings, as it became feasible for members of the upper classes to take these newest markers of privilege and prestige with them. But while actual ownership of these new technologies may be restricted to a select few for more than a century to come, the possibilities suggested by these temporal-technical developments had much wider influence on how early moderns thought about time. *A Midsummer Night's Dream* and its fairies offer one example. Shakespeare imagines his fairies' remarkable timekeeping acumen as a powerful, personal and embodied quality which works right alongside the fairies' special insights into nature's operations. In other words, fairy-time follows the great paradigm shifts accompanying advancements in horology at the turn of the seventeenth century by animating a new sense of imaginative possibility which these advancements inspire.

Puck's 'forty minutes', like Titania's 'third of a minute', works by engaging inchoate modes of temporal relationality in an unexpected and imaginative way. However, where Titania goes small, Puck goes big: pushing the suggestive

---

[29] Cipolla, *Clocks and Culture*, 69.

potential of time's new mobility out to its geographical extremes. With his promise to 'put a girdle round about the earth / In forty minutes', Puck collapses the whole world into the breadth of his temporal command. It is a grand claim, but one positioning Puck's spatio-temporal manoeuvrability *just outside* the limits of possibility in seventeenth-century England, not leagues beyond.[30] Coming about twenty-five years after Sir Francis Drake's successful circumnavigation, Shakespeare writes *A Midsummer Night's Dream* at a moment when advancements in navigation have indeed made it possible for the earth to be 'girdled', albeit not in under an hour. Here we surface yet another spectre of imperialism and conquest at work within this play's talk about timekeeping. Gitanjali Shahani has argued that, while Shakespeare's fairies align with traditional English folklore in many respects, they also repeatedly allude to England's changing networks of commerce and exchange; ultimately, through them, Shakespeare 'invokes England's precapitalist, folkloric past only to imbricate it in England's proto-colonial, mercantile present'.[31] In addition to the allusions to India and colonial labour which Shahani identifies, Puck's timekeeping provides further evidence to support claims made by Shahani, Hendricks and other scholars that the '*Dream* text participates in early modern racial, imperial, and mercantilist discourses' in subtle yet revealing ways.[32]

Closely linked to sociopolitical developments in England on the one hand, on the other, Shakespeare's fairy-time possesses quite the speculative quality. Shakespeare writes *A Midsummer Night's Dream* at a time when one could presumably track the duration of one's travel, perhaps even in quantities as small as minutes. However, while certainly much longer than Titania's third of a minute, Puck's two-thirds of an hour would still have been a duration of time somewhat difficult for contemporary audiences to track. Most watches had some sort of hash mark to help indicate half hours, but with only an hour hand, to track any other quantity of passing minutes with decent precision would have been difficult without another device, like a sand-glass, specifically manufactured to track that quantity of time.[33]

Paul Glennie and Nigel Thrift's detailed study of time practices, *Shaping the Day: A History of Timekeeping in England and Wales 1300–1800*, provides some helpful contextualization. Tracing references to time in letters, diaries and other private writing, Glennie and Thrift argue that certain quantities of time remain much easier to comprehend than others all the way up into the early nineteenth century. Particularly relevant to Puck's 'forty minutes' is their analysis of Thomas Turner's diary from

the 1750s and 1760s. Despite Turner's fairly frequent references to portions of an hour, especially between the hour and the half-hour, the 'scarcity of [recorded] times between half past and the hour suggests some difficulty in keeping track of time' in those quantities, according to Glennie and Thrift.[34] Given the increase in 'precision and availability of clock-time information' throughout English cities between *A Midsummer Night's Dream*'s first performances and Turner's diaries, if for Turner forty minutes was a somewhat illegible duration of time, one can only imagine what it might have felt like for Shakespeare's audience.[35]

Thus, Puck's ability to comprehend space and time surpasses mortal capacities while still alluding to recent scientific and technological achievements which would have been top of mind for the average Londoner.[36] Caught in this tension between similarity and disparity, Puck's enhanced agency and manoeuvrability becomes a vehicle to explore the imaginative possibilities that new discoveries and technologies bring tantalizingly into view, but that still remain out of reach.[37] In other words, Puck's forty-minute girdling moves away from what *is* to compel

---

[30] For more on allusions to travel and geography in the play, see Laura Aydelotte, 'Mapping women: place names and a woman's place', in *Travel and Travail: Early Modern Women, English Drama, and the Wider World*, ed. Patricia Akhimie and Bernadette Andrea (Lincoln, NE, 2019), 181–98.

[31] Gitanjali Shahani, *Tasting Difference: Food, Race, and Cultural Encounters in Early Modern Literature* (Ithaca, 2020), p. 41.

[32] Shahani, *Tasting Difference*, p. 42. Having little to add on the issues of India, Empire and the fairies so incisively argued by scholars including Hendricks, Stone and Shahani, as well as R. W. Desai, Ania Loomba, Shankar Raman, Kevin Pask and Hugh Grady, I direct this article's arguments elsewhere.

[33] That is, an hourglass, which was still the go-to device for measuring a specific duration of time. Produced to track quantities of time from as little as a minute to more than an hour, they were used in everything from counting a ship's watch, to timing court proceedings, to cooking. For more, see Paul Glennie and Nigel Thrift, *Shaping the Day: A History of Timekeeping in England and Wales 1300–1800* (Oxford, 2009), and Gerard Dohrn-van Rossum, *History of the Hour: Clocks and Modern Temporal Orders* (Chicago, 1996).

[34] Glennie and Thrift, *Shaping the Day*, p. 264.

[35] Glennie and Thrift, *Shaping the Day*, p. 263.

[36] My language here borders on the teleological not to imply we should value these transitions as progress, but rather to reflect contemporary attitudes especially prevalent around a figure such as Drake and his circumnavigation.

[37] For more on how exploring the '"possible" . . . enabled [early modern English] writers to grapple with the challenges of constructing knowledge in and about an incomprehensible world', see Debapriya Sarkar, *Possible Knowledge: The Literary Forms of Early Modern Science* (Philadelphia, 2023), p. 2.

us to consider what *might be next*. Couched in all the enticing, fantastical, imaginative potential that the fairy-world has to offer, the fairies' engagement with powerful natural forces – such as time – invest still developing modes of temporal relationality brought about by recent horological and navigational advancements with intoxicating, wonder-inducing and invigorating possibility. Importantly, these possibilities are closely linked to the fairies' special capacity to direct natural processes, access magical resources and shape the course of events affecting the human characters of the play. Put simply, keeping time equates to power, authority and influence once again in *A Midsummer Night's Dream*.

WHAT ABOUT THE YOUNG LOVERS?

It seems impossible to talk about this play without mentioning its young lovers. Where do they fit into this array of temporal dynamics? The four characters around whom much of this play's plot revolves – Hermia, Lysander, Helena and Demetrius – are crucial to narrative time in the sense that it is their storyline which provides the play's marriage plot with its structure. However, they otherwise offer fairly little to a discussion on time; they just provide another facet to questions and schemes which Shakespeare more vigorously takes up through other characters and plotlines. Nevertheless, it is worth briefly discussing the lovers' relationships to time since the additional facet that they provide helps to demonstrate overlaps between various models of timekeeping simultaneously in motion in *A Midsummer Night's Dream*.

With her father attempting to force her into marrying Demetrius, Hermia makes plans to run away and elope with her love, Lysander, instead. Like the Mechanicals, the lovers intend to utilize the forest for activities best kept away from prying Athenian eyes. Also like the Mechanicals, the success of their woodland endeavours will require coordinating their individual motions through space and time. Lysander directs Hermia saying,

LYSANDER Steal forth thy father's house tomorrow night,
And in the wood, a league without the town,
Where I did meet thee once with Helena
To do observance to a morn of May,
There will I stay for thee

(1.1.164–8)

Hermia responds by dutifully swearing to meet him. Lysander's instructions have some basic similarities to those Quince gives the Mechanicals in act 2, scene 1.

Like Quince, Lysander lays out in fairly specific terms a period of time and location to meet which require confirmation and commitment from other participants in the scheme before moving on. What Lysander does which Quince does not, however, is work comparatively: Lysander refers to a shared past moment in order to establish his future act of temporal and spatial alignment with Hermia. In act 2, we will see Oberon similarly leveraging memory to designate which flower he wishes Puck to retrieve for his future use. As with Lysander, Oberon's temporal comparison utilizes the past to create a shared understanding in the present in order to, ultimately, direct actions in the future. These characters perform a sort of timekeeping which we might not instantly think of as timekeeping, but it does in fact serve one of the two basic tasks of horology by working to mark out specific moments in the ongoing flow of time. We also see this comparative strategy at yet another point in the play – however, that time inspiring discord. At the hunt, Hippolyta utilizes her memory of past experience to resist Theseus's present sense of superiority based on the future performance of his hounds. In doing so, she undermines his presumed time-defining privilege. What is similar in all these cases is that past experience helps to mark out time, its significance and the actions still to take place. As Charlotte Scott has argued, with the play's use of story, the significance of 'both the past and present are still in contention' because, I would add, their meaning depends on what happens next: significance takes shape by relation, partially deferred and obscured by a time that is still unfolding.[38] Thus, in multiple instances, we see Shakespeare playing with the capacity for past personal experiences to shape our understanding of that which *is* as well as that which *will be*.

A few lines later, Helena will wander into Lysander and Hermia's scheming and allow us to see how differently our young lovers conceptualize time. Lysander and Hermia share their newly hatched plan with Helena:

LYSANDER Helen, to you our minds we will unfold.
Tomorrow night, when Phoebe doth behold
Her silver visage in the wat'ry glass,
Decking with liquid pearl the bladed grass –
A time that lovers' sleights doth still conceal –
Through Athens' gates have we devised to steal.

---

[38] Charlotte Scott, '"The story shall be changed": antique fables and agency in *A Midsummer Night's Dream*', in *Shakespeare Survey 73* (Cambridge, 2020), 119–28, p. 120.

HERMIA And in the wood where often you and I
Upon faint primrose beds were wont to lie,
Emptying our bosoms of their counsel sweet,
There my Lysander and myself shall meet . . .
Keep word, Lysander. We must starve our sight
From lovers' food till morrow deep midnight.

(1.1.208–17, 222–3)

Lysander's description, with its heavy reliance on myth-ical and natural imagery, bears some similarity to Oberon's approach to delineating specific moments and places in time. Following him, Hermia's explanation that the lovers will meet – 'in the wood where often you and I / Upon faint primrose beds were wont to lie' at 'morrow deep midnight' – lacks Lysander's poetic flair or verbosity. Like with Oberon and Puck, here we see a distinctive shift in the discursive mode being engaged by speakers who together seek to define and align movements through space and time. However, unlike Oberon and Puck, Lysander and Hermia's planning proves only *partially* effective. For one, Lysander's description does not manage to convey all the necessary details: despite his effusiveness, he only manages to cover the when, leaving Hermia to jump in with the where. But, most importantly, while Lysander and Hermia's entrance in act 2, scene 2 implies that these two do manage to meet up, Helena's failed attempt (with Demetrius in tow) to sync up with these two suggests Lysander and Hermia's ability to effectively either describe or follow their own temporo-spatial instructions leaves something to be desired. Or, perhaps, the fault is Helena's. Either way, something gets lost – and then so does Helena. The lovers' movements through the forest accidentally become misaligned, providing Puck an opportunity to mistake one pair of Athenians for the other, which then leads these flower-crossed lovers to spend the next several acts wandering in the woods. Importantly, *how* Hermia and Lysander plan and communicate movements through space and time has strong similarities to what we see with effective timekeepers in the play. Less about the strategy than the execution, then, what is it *exactly* that goes wrong here? What is it that determines one's temporal acuity (or a lack thereof)? Shakespeare never quite makes it clear.

FINDING OUT FAIRY-TIME AND COMING TO CONCLUSIONS

Like the play itself, I end with the fairies. Seamlessly traversing multiple temporal discourses and demonstrating abilities to track, measure and keep time with a precision unattainable by mortals (for now, at least), the fairies invig-orate our sense of time's capacity to amaze and enchant us. Previous scholarship has tended to read court-time in *A Midsummer Night's Dream* as representing the play's most desirable model of time management – laudable, as Richard Wagner says, for its 'duration, measure, orderli-ness'. However, I would argue it is instead the fairies who are Shakespeare's most ideal timekeepers. Puck and Titania's lines in particular extend the naturally aligning and enthralling possibilities presented by the times to imagine what other 'wonderfull unknowen pleasant prof-ites', as Leonard Digges says, could possibly come next?

By leveraging the language of instrumentalized, mechanized horology – and, thus, gesturing towards some of the latest and greatest in timekeeping technolo-gies hitting London's streets – Shakespeare places what might seem to us today to be fairly mundane allusions to clock-time inside a nexus of wondrous potential in *A Midsummer Night's Dream*. The fairies suggest entanglements of space, time, bodies (human and celes-tial) which defy the kinds of binaries prevalent in scholars' thinking on time in this period and in this play – such as nature/technology, forest/court, etc. Instead, the fairies seem to ideologically and experien-tially 'wander everywhere': amongst several discourses as well as several timescapes, as past, present and future actions all contribute to our understanding of what is *now*. The play's mortal agents attempt something simi-lar – crossing times through various comparative strat-egies – but often with noticeably less success. The fairies' different ways of relating to time and through time intertwine, overlap and symbiotically work to create a flexible but still fairly unified sense of time and move the action of the play forward. Looking closely, we begin to see that *A Midsummer Night's Dream*'s vision of time-keeping does not emerge from an adversarial tension between mechanical/natural time, or court/forest time, but through an interconnected, complementary array of temporal understandings and strategies which encompass an expanding range of marvellous possibilities.

As intoxicating and alluring as Shakespeare's specula-tive engagements with time through the fairies might be in *A Midsummer Night's Dream*, however, his play's sim-ultaneous investments in fictions of power and false authority – most notably, of imperialism – also must give us pause. One aim of this article has been to surface the place of timekeeping, specifically, in such conversa-tions. Another has been to demonstrate what close and careful reading of a text's sometimes seemingly mundane references to keeping time can yield. There is still much more work to be done in order to truly understand how Shakespeare's ideas about timekeeping and those of his contemporaries influence perceptions of agency, nature and temporality in ways which impact the constitution of political systems of power in this period. Such work will require close attention to the links between time-keeping, race and Empire. It also will require attention to additional identity constructs closely linked to the constitution and maintenance of social hierarchies, such as age, gender, nationality, class and ability. 'It is about time', Noémie Ndiaye and Lia Markey recently wrote, about confronting the racist dynamics infusing early modern cultural artefacts such as Rugendas's clock.[39] I concur, but in more than one respect; it is *about time* that we recognize it *is* about time.

---

[39] Ndiaye and Markey, eds., *Seeing Race before Race*.

'BY THE BOOK': SOURCE STUDY
AND THE PLOT OF *ROMEO AND JULIET*

PATRICK DURDEL

Romeo and Juliet is a play of many books. Books are a tool of learning in the Servingman's speech (1.2.59) and in Romeo's simile of the schoolboys (2.1.201); Mercutio calls Tybalt 'a villain who fights by the book of arithmetic' (3.1.101–2). Books are also identified as part of theatrical practice: when Mercutio imagines their imminent arrival at the Capulet's ball, he tells Romeo that they will have 'no without-book prologue, faintly spoke / after the prompter, for our entrance' (1.4.7–8). There are school-books, fencing manuals, prompt books, and Count Paris who is a 'precious book of love' (1.3.89). His face, suggests Lady Capulet, should be read and admired like a book: 'Read o'er the volume of young Paris' face, / And find delight writ there with beauty's pen' (1.3.83–4). Later in the play, Juliet picks up her mother's metaphor to describe Romeo after she has heard of his role in Tybalt's death: 'Was ever book containing such vile matter / so fairly bound' (3.2.83–4). In this library of different books, what exactly does it mean when Juliet tells Romeo, 'You kiss by th' book' (1.5.109)?

Shakespeare, as we know, writes his tragedy of the star-crossed lovers 'by the book': he adapts it from a source. His Romeo kisses just like Arthur Brooke's Romeus did, just like Pierre Boaistuau's Rhomeo kisses Juliette, and Matteo Bandello's Romeo kisses Giulietta. When the first and second quarto of Shakespeare's *Romeo and Juliet* were published in the 1590s, they were books among others. His contemporaries could read two English versions of the story of Romeo and Juliet: Arthur Brooke's narrative poem *The Tragicall Historye of Romeus and Juliet* (1562) and William Painter's version in the second volume of his *The Palace of Pleasure* (1567). Both were translations of Pierre Boaistuau's French version in *Histoires tragiques* (1559), itself a translation of Matteo Bandello's ninth novella in the second volume of his *Novelle* (1554), an adaptation of Luigi da Porto's

Historia novellamente ritrovata di due nobili amanti (1531). Books, books, books.

Laurie Maguire and Emma Smith, in their article amend to 'What is a source?', observe that 'we continue to look for sources even as methodology for assessing or admitting them remains undertheorized'.[1] Such a lack would explain, too, why, as Catherine Belsey puts it, 'the sources identified have so often remained inert in the process of interpretation'.[2] Without a clear understanding of how we construct the connections between texts, the status of those identified as sources remains, somewhat, unclear. This is still the case, despite recent endeavours to revisit source study and understand its value and importance in our present.[3] In this article, I want to make a small contribution to this theoretical project. While others, such as Maguire and Smith or John Kerrigan, have offered novel ways of conceiving of the texts Shakespeare consulted for his work and of the relationships between them, I turn to the practices of source study.[4] The question, in very general terms, is:

[1] Laurie Maguire and Emma Smith, 'What is a source? Or, how Shakespeare read his Marlowe', in *Shakespeare Survey 68* (Cambridge, 2015), 15–31; p. 16.

[2] Catherine Belsey, 'The elephants' graveyard revisited: Shakespeare at work in *Antony and Cleopatra*, *Romeo and Juliet* and *All's Well That Ends Well*', in *Shakespeare Survey 68* (Cambridge, 2015), 62–72; p. 62.

[3] See, for example, the contributions in Dennis Austin Britton and Melissa Walter, eds., *Rethinking Shakespeare Source Study: Audiences, Authors, and Digital Technologies* (New York, 2018). For an overview of recent work in source studies, see Melissa Walter and Sarah Klann, 'Shakespeare source study in the early twenty-first century: a resurrection?', *Literature Compass* 15 (2018), 1–9.

[4] See, for example, Maguire and Smith, 'What is a source?', pp. 24–7; John Kerrigan, *Shakespeare's Originality* (Oxford, 2018), pp. 1–4. For a list of alternative terms for relationships between texts in recent scholarship, see Maguire and Smith, 'What is a source?', p. 16.

what does it mean to work with a source? We know very little about this when it comes to the writing of early modern drama, at least beyond the fact that it did happen. But what I want to suggest here is that later work, equally concerned with sources and how they relate to the writing of drama, can help us understand what it means to write a play 'by the book'. The work is that of three scholars, Edward Capell, Rudolf Fischer and Jill L. Levenson, who at different moments in time (the 1780s, 1920s and 1980s) turned their attention to Shakespeare's sources for *Romeo and Juliet*. I will show how the source is constructed through the work of these scholars, and what role 'plot' plays in this. Ultimately, I hope that such an enquiry into 'plot' as part of the scholarly practices of source study can add to our understanding of what a source is and what we can do with it. Every methodology, source study included, favours some questions over others, delineating what is and what is not part of its purview. This article shows new ways to ask questions about familiar texts and the connections between them.

BY THE BOOK

Throughout the Tudor period, adaptation was a mainstay of dramatic writing: Henry Medwall's *Fulgens and Lucres* (*c*.1495, printed *c*.1512–16), the earliest surviving printed play in English, is adapted from a pseudo-Ciceronian text, John Tiptoft's English translation of a French translation of Niccolò di Buonaccorso's Latin debate *De vera nobilitate*.[5] Thomas Preston drew on Richard Taverner's *The Garden of Wysedome* (1539) for his play *Cambises* (*c*.1561) and Richard Edwards based his humanist tragi-comedy *Damon and Pithias* (1571) on a classical story, probably taken from Thomas Elyot's *The Gouernour* (1531). Hence, when Marlowe wrote *Tamburlaine* and Shakespeare his first history plays, using other texts as their basis was hardly an innovation. And while the commercial theatre might have offered further incentives to draw on (more or less) well-known stories, such acts of adaptation were already well established as a mode of dramatic production in sixteenth-century England. Emma Smith points out that 'to be a writer in the early modern period was to be an adaptor' and that 'every guide and protocol, every schoolroom exercise, every expectation from readers, aligned in anticipating the postmodernist axiom that all writing is rewriting'.[6] In a similar vein, John Kerrigan suggests that Shakespeare's 'originality is partly original-ity, a drawing upon originals' and that Shakespeare's audiences would have understood, and perhaps even looked for, allusions

to prior texts.[7] In many cases, these texts were novellas. Melissa Walter counts sixty-six sixteenth- and seventeenth-century plays, in addition to Shakespeare's, that were based, at least partially, on Italian and French novellas or their contemporary English translations, as well as thirteen lost plays with titles 'suggesting a novella source'.[8]

What the source for a particular play was might tell us something about the general cultural context of the time, about education, literary reception and the international networks of writing, reading and printing, as well as the book trade in early modern Europe.[9] But that does not answer the question of what it means to write a play 'by the book'. A partial answer to this question, or a step towards one, lies in the historically specific meanings of the word 'plot'.

PLOTS (PL.)

With W. W. Greg's study of Elizabethan dramatic documents, 'plot' took on a specific meaning in the context of early modern English drama and performance. 'Theatrical plots', Greg writes, 'are documents giving the skeleton outline of plays, scene by scene, for use in the theatre.'[10] Plot is, for Greg, a 'highly specialized term of the early playhouse' and thus not fully congruent with what he calls 'non-technical' uses of the word, such as 'speaking of the plot of a play or novel' or a playwright's 'outline sketch serving as a guide for the composition of the play'.[11] It is helpful to try to understand this distinction between 'technical' and 'non-technical' here. What we encounter

---

5 I call this text 'pseudo-Ciceronian' because William Caxton originally printed it in 1481 as part of a volume with English translations of Cicero.

6 Emma Smith, 'Shakespeare as adaptor', in *The Arden Handbook of Shakespeare and Adaptation*, ed. Diane E. Henderson and Stephen O'Neill (London, 2022), 25–37; p. 25. The volume contains only one chapter on Shakespeare's adaptations of other texts, the remaining chapters are concerned with later adaptations of Shakespeare.

7 Kerrigan, *Shakespeare's Originality*, pp. 2–3.

8 Melissa Walter, *The Italian Novella and Shakespeare's Comic Heroines* (Toronto, 2019), pp. 153–9. Geoffrey Bullough's eight-volume *Narrative and Dramatic Sources of Shakespeare* (New York, 1957–75) is perhaps the most prominent and important product of the efforts to identify Shakespeare's sources.

9 See Karen Newman and Jane Tylus, 'Introduction', in *Early Modern Cultures of Translation*, ed. Karen Newman and Jane Tylus (Philadelphia, 2015), 1–24; pp. 18–19.

10 W. W. Greg, *Dramatic Documents from the Elizabethan Playhouses* (London, 1931), p. 1.

11 Greg, *Dramatic Documents*, p. 1.

in the first lines of Greg's chapter are in fact three different kinds of plots, semantically and functionally connected, but conceptually separate: 'plot of a play', 'outline sketch' and 'stage or theatrical plot'.

The 'plot of a play or novel' is a general category, perhaps best understood as a descriptive or illustrative one, just like the 'ground-plan' Greg identifies as its semantic origin.[12] This kind of plot emerges as an important property of what Lorna Hutson terms the 'invention of suspicion' in sixteenth-century literature. Very generally speaking, plot is 'the why, where, when, how, and who of fictional representation'.[13] The seemingly simple definition is complicated, though, by overlapping meanings of 'plot'. In Hutson's reading of *Titus Andronicus*, plot 'fluctuates between spatial and rhetorical senses';[14] in her discussion of 'detective plots' in early modern drama, including *Hamlet*, the plot of the play at times seems indistinguishable from the plots hatched within the play.[15] This agency to interact with and manipulate the plot is articulated very clearly in Hutson's earlier article 'Fortunate travelers', where she discusses what it means to 'read for the plot' in the sixteenth century.[16] Hutson describes the ways in which characters use rhetoric to 'reemplot' their actions – that is to reframe circumstances to serve a new or different kind of narrative, just like, according to Hutson, Pierre Boaistuau 'reemplotted' Bandello.[17] It seems likely that Hutson would call these uses of plot 'technical' as well: it is an essential part of her argument, both in 'Fortunate travelers' and *The Invention of Suspicion*, that the technical uses of rhetoric shape early modern narrative and drama. It is also easy to see how such an understanding of 'technical' would differ from the one suggested by Greg. As we will see, the theatrical plot embeds the dramatic text within the practices of performance, both on and off the stage. Hutson's understanding of plot, on the other hand, likens authorial plotting to the plotting of characters: how they interact with and shape plots which are not just representations of actions but active in structuring the narrative at hand. In this account, plot is clearly a property of the text.

Greg's theatrical plots are technical because they are practical. The plots discussed in *Dramatic Documents from the Elizabethan Playhouses* once served a clear function: they were 'prepared for the guidance of actors and others in the playhouse'.[18] Fundamentally, a plot in Greg's 'technical' sense 'consists of the record of the successive entrances of the characters of a play' and might 'in very varying degrees' include information about 'properties and other requirements of the stage', as well as about 'the

actors assigned for the individual parts'.[19] Therefore, Greg concludes, the 'Book or prompt copy of the play' must have been the basis for the creation of a theatrical plot, which seems to follow relatively stable formal conventions that dictate the material layout of the plot as a document used in the theatre.[20] This is, essentially, both a temporal and material relationship between different kinds of practical documents. In the context of performance, neither prompt book nor stage plot are simply texts – they represent and produce the order of events unfolding on the stage. But in Greg's understanding, the plot is clearly posterior to the prompt book; it summarizes concisely, for the concrete purpose of getting 'the actors on to the stage at the right point', information about the intended performance of a play.[21]

The playwright's 'outline' might share some features with such a theatrical plot – for example, 'a list of scenes with the characters appearing in each' – but is, in Greg's eyes, not 'technical' in the same sense as the documents he goes on to analyse.[22] What seems to prompt this differentiation is, it appears, an ambiguity of nomenclature in the specific context of early modern drama and performance. 'Plot', as Greg uses it, shares an origin with the 'plot of a play', but as a material object it is markedly different from the plots discussed by Hutson: Greg's plots are both documents and objects of the Elizabethan playhouse.

To make such a distinction for the third kind of plot, the 'outline sketch', is not quite so easy, since this plot, too, is a theatrical document. Greg encounters it in

---

[12] Greg, *Dramatic Documents*, p. 1.

[13] Lorna Hutson, *The Invention of Suspicion: Law and Mimesis in Shakespeare and Renaissance Drama* (Oxford, 2007), p. 114. Following this definition, plot is most easily represented as a list (of answers to these questions), a fact that resonates well with my analysis later in this article.

[14] Hutson, *Invention*, p. 95.   [15] Hutson, *Invention*, p. 68.

[16] Lorna Hutson, 'Fortunate travelers: reading for plot in sixteenth-century England', *Representations* 41 (1993), 83–103. Hutson's title deliberately echoes Peter Brooks's *Reading for the Plot: Design and Intention in Narrative* (New York, 1984).

[17] Hutson, 'Fortunate travelers', pp. 94–6.

[18] Greg, *Dramatic Documents*, p. 3.

[19] Greg, *Dramatic Documents*, p. 73.

[20] Greg reiterates this conclusion about the relationship between 'Book' and 'Plot' later in the chapter; see Greg, *Dramatic Documents*, p. 86. For the material description of extant plots according to an assumed 'uniform plan', see Greg, *Dramatic Documents*, pp. 70–2.

[21] Greg, *Dramatic Documents*, p. 77.

[22] Accordingly, Greg uses 'Plot' with a capital P to distinguish the theatrical documents he discusses from other uses of the term.

Henslowe's diary (which he had edited for publication in 1904). In Henslowe's accounts, the word 'plotte' appears three times (and only in this spelling); in all three instances, Ben Jonson is identified as a writer of plots. On 3 December 1597, Jonson received money from Henslowe for a 'boocke which he was to writte for vs', and for which 'he showed the plotte vnto the company'.[23] On 23 October 1598, 'Robart shawe & Jewbey' receive money to give to George Chapman for 'one his playe boocke & ij ectes of a tragedie of bengemens plotte'.[24] Greg quotes and briefly discusses these instances of 'plot', concluding that 'in these cases we must suppose that the plot meant a written sketch of the play', but he quickly discards these instances of plot as irrelevant to the discussion of theatrical plots.[25] To him, these documents are fundamentally different from the plots he wants to discuss, partially – perhaps – because they are not materially present to him in the same way the stage plots are.

Tiffany Stern's work adds important nuance to such an assessment, in particular by highlighting the ways in which the work of outlining, the creation of a 'plot-scenario', can be technical in Greg's sense as well. In her study of early modern English documents of performance, Stern dedicates the first chapter to what she calls 'plot-scenarios': documents outlining the plot of a play to be written. She writes, '"structure", in this period, was created before the rest of the play was, and was called in its initial formation "the plot": these days it would be called a "scenario"'.[26] Several observations from Stern's chapter seem important here: plot and play 'were created as, initially, separate documents: they were different texts'.[27] These plot-scenarios were supposedly 'primitive and messy in the form in which they were first written: ... private documents made for the personal use of a small number of people'.[28] But it is important that the plot as a document that can be shared also enabled collaborative work on a play: 'talented plotters were ... cherished and revered' both by theatre companies and spectators.[29] Writing the plot of a play was considered an act of co-authorship, and plots allowed 'non-linear writing' of a play, potentially by more than one author.[30] In its material form, then, the plot-scenario is no less practical and technical than Greg's stage plots. It, too, enables the collaborative practices that shaped early modern drama in performance. Stern summarizes, 'Plots were the backbone of a good play; they preceded plays, but were also visible within them, setting up the notion that a play in its final performance form could still be stripped down to the root document that made it up'.[31] There is, thus, an inherent connection between the two kinds of plots. The work required for them, we come to realize, is identical: plotting 'turns a play into a series of separate units' in which 'the breaks and stops in the narrative are as prominent as the action'.[32] The two different kinds of 'theatrical documents' (Greg) or 'documents of performance' (Stern) represent, materially, two similar kinds of practices with their own 'technical' purposes. They share an orientation towards the dramatic text, though from different directions: Stern's plot-scenario is prior to the writing of the play, Greg's stage plot is posterior to it.

From the material collected by Stern, it becomes clear that early modern writers were more than comfortable using the terms 'plot' and 'narrative' in discussing the work of the playwright. Importantly, for the purposes of this article, Stern adds in a footnote that 'at least two other printed plot-scenarios survive but before poems rather than plays' – one of these poems is Arthur Brooke's *Tragicall Historye of Romeus and Iuliet*. Both, Stern writes, 'have "arguments" different enough from the story then told to suggest that they are the printed form of summaries that preceded writing'.[33] This is an intriguing suggestion, not just for the reasons implied by Stern, because short summaries appear before the individual novellas in Giovanni Boccaccio's *Il Decamerone*, and later in Matteo Bandello's *Novelle*. The second volume's ninth novella, this short summary tells us, is about 'The unfortunate death of two most unlucky lovers, one of whom dies of poison, the other of grief, with various accidents'.[34] In Bandello, who does not employ a framing story as Boccaccio did, the novellas are also accompanied by dedication letters which often touch on the content of the respective novella. Pierre Boaistuau, in his translations, includes a short summary at the beginning of each novella, but also a paratext he calls 'sommaire', which seems to structurally replace the dedication letter accompanying Bandello's novella. In the case of his

---

[23] Philip Henslowe, *Henslowe's Diary*, ed. W. W. Greg (London, 1904), p. 70. An almost identical entry appears two pages later.

[24] Henslowe, *Diary*, p. 89.

[25] Greg, *Dramatic Documents*, p. 1, n. 2.

[26] Tiffany Stern, *Documents of Performance in Early Modern England* (Cambridge, 2009), p. 10.

[27] Stern, *Documents*, p. 9. [28] Stern, *Documents*, p. 18.

[29] Stern, *Documents*, pp. 18 and 27.

[30] Stern, *Documents*, pp. 29 and 32.

[31] Stern, *Documents*, p. 35. [32] Stern, *Documents*, p. 15.

[33] Stern, *Documents*, p. 259, n. 18.

[34] Matteo Bandello, *Tutte le opere*, ed. Francesco Flora (Milan, 1952), p. 727 (translation my own).

third novella, Boaistuau's 'sommaire' is about a page in length, but only about two lines of prose are dedicated to a summary of the story.[35] The novella tells the story 'of two lovers, one of whom dies of poison, the other of sadness'.[36] (This is, as we will see later, not an entirely truthful representation of the ending of Boaistuau's version.) Brooke's 'argument' accompanying his *Tragicall Historye of Romeus and Iuliet*, the one mentioned by Stern, is fourteen lines long and offers an adequate and concise summary of the Romeo and Juliet story.

Brooke stands as an intermediary between Shakespeare and his narrative sources; he is an adaptor as well as a translator.[37] If we follow Stern, the plot-scenarios of early modern drama are, through Brooke, only one degree removed from the paratextual summaries accompanying sixteenth-century novellas. In this constellation, plot emerges as a shared property of the material processes of translation and adaptation that connect the different versions of the Romeo and Juliet story in early modern England and Europe.

There is no concrete material evidence of sixteenth-century playwrights' practices of adaptation apart from the resulting dramatic texts themselves. What do playwrights do when they adapt a play? How do they engage with their sources? How do the 168 pages of Brooke's 'tragicall historye' turn into a 'lamentable tragedy'?[38] The plot-scenarios discussed by Stern suggest that some kind of practical document might have been part of this work – in other words, that there would have been a material trace connecting the two texts. In the absence of such evidence, I will instead look at three instances of scholarly engagement with Arthur Brooke's *Tragicall Historye of Romeus and Iuliet* and its French and Italian precursors. Each of these critical encounters is ultimately motivated by an interest in Shakespeare's play: the handwritten notes in the copies of Brooke and Boaistuau in the library of eighteenth-century Shakespeare critic Edward Capell, now held in the Wren Library (Trinity College, Cambridge, UK); a 1922 German anthology of the Romeo and Juliet novellas in translation; and Jill L. Levenson's work on Shakespeare's sources for *Romeo and Juliet*, in particular her 1984 article 'Romeo and Juliet before Shakespeare'.

CAPELL'S ANNOTATIONS

The eighteenth-century Shakespeare critic Edward Capell, after editing a ten-volume octavo edition of Shakespeare's plays (1768), devoted himself to an extended commentary on the plays which appeared between 1779 and 1783 under the title *Notes and Various Readings to Shakespeare*. The third and final volume, published posthumously, speaks to Capell's interest in the cultural and literary background against which Shakespeare was writing his plays. Aptly titled *The School of Shakespeare*, it collects extracts 'from divers English Books, that were in Print at that Author's Time; evidently shewing from whence his several Fables were taken, and some Parcel of his dialogue'.[39] The material I discuss in the following is clearly connected to Capell's efforts to identify Shakespeare's sources.[40]

In Edward Capell's copy of Arthur Brooke's *The Tragicall Historye of Romeus and Iuliet* (Wren Library, Trinity College, Cambridge, Capell X.4), we can see the material traces of this work: the book is annotated throughout with numbered brackets.[41] These brackets isolate parts of the text of varying length, sometimes only a few lines, sometimes several pages long. They are either neatly aligned with the beginning of a line on the left-hand side of the page or are meticulously inserted into the line, between two words. Added to the left of the bracket or line are small crosses with accompanying numbers, starting with the second cross, thus ranging from '2' on fol. 2r to '81' on the final page of the poem. Capell's copy also includes a multitude of unnumbered brackets, usually highlighting short passages of the text.

To give one example: Capell's handwritten '40+ [[' is followed by Brooke's lines 'And that I may discharge /

---

[35] The rest of the 'sommaire' establishes a classical and historical precedent for deathly love (Pliny, Valerius, Plutarch), concluding that the story to follow is not just 'admirable' but also 'true': Pierre Boaistuau, *Histoires tragiques*, ed. Richard A. Carr (Paris, 1977), pp. 61–2. In the following, I quote from this edition when not referring to specific archival material.

[36] Boaistuau, *Histoires*, p. 63.

[37] Curiously, Brooke claims on his title page to have translated Bandello's Italian novella, 'written first in Italian by Bandell, and nowe in Englishe by Ar. Br.', neglecting to mention Boaistuau whose French version he actually consulted and translated: Arthur Brooke, *The Tragicall Historye of Romeus and Iuliet* (London, 1562), sig. ¶1r.

[38] Q1 of *Romeo and Juliet* (1597) is not lamentable yet, but 'excellent conceited'.

[39] Edward Capell, *Notes and Various Readings of Shakespeare*, vol. 3: *The School of Shakespeare* (New York, 1970 [1783]), title page.

[40] See, for example, Capell's argument for Brooke's poem as the immediate source for Shakespeare's play at the very end of the passage from Brooke's *Tragicall Historye* printed in Edward Capell, *School of Shakespeare*, p. 525; or the discussion of the meaning of 'Freetown' in Edward Capell, *Notes and Various Readings to Shakespeare*, vol. 2: Part 4 (New York, 1970 [1780]), pp. 2–3.

[41] I am very grateful for the invaluable support of the library staff at the Wren Library.

15 Arthur Brooke, *The Tragicall Historye of Romeus and Iuliet* (London, 1562), fols. 10v–11r, Capell X.4, Wren Library, Trinity College, Cambridge. Reproduced with permission of the Master and Fellows of Trinity College, Cambridge.

your hart of heavy care';[42] there is also, which is unusual, a short annotation on the right-hand side of the page: '(v. F.3.$^{b.}$)'. Capell's annotation serves as an aid to finding the end of the bracketed passage, seventeen pages later, after Brooke's 'My Juliet, my loue, / my onely hope and care'.[43] He uses double brackets, here, to distinguish between two layers of emphasis: contained within the seventeen pages of bracket 40 is one other bracket, unnumbered, on fols. 35v–36r.[44] Only once, displaying his philological care, he uses a different colour for his brackets and adds on the side of the page the short note 'n.b. all the lines between the red hooks, twenty in number, are missing in the edition of 1587' (fol. 11r) (see Figure 15).

Capell's copy of Brooke's narrative poem is bound together with Da Porto's Romeo and Juliet novella (the first part of the bound volume) and John Taylor's

Taylor's Motto (the last part of the bound volume). In fact, Capell X.4 includes a fourth element not listed in the library's catalogue:[45] Brooke's poem is followed by five sheets of paper containing a manuscript list that matches each numbered item in Brooke's poem with the corresponding passage in its source, Pierre Boaistuau's French translation of Matteo Bandello's Italian novella.

---

42 Brooke, *The Tragicall Historye of Romeus and Iuliet*, fol. 35r, Capell X.4, Wren Library, Trinity College, Cambridge.
43 Brooke, *Tragicall Historye*, fol. 43v.
44 This is not the only time Capell makes such a distinction; bracket 62, to name just one further example, contains four unnumbered brackets on fols. 70r–71r.
45 The current entries appear to be based on W. W. Greg, *Catalogue of the Books Presented by Edward Capell to the Library of Trinity College in Cambridge* (Cambridge, 1903).

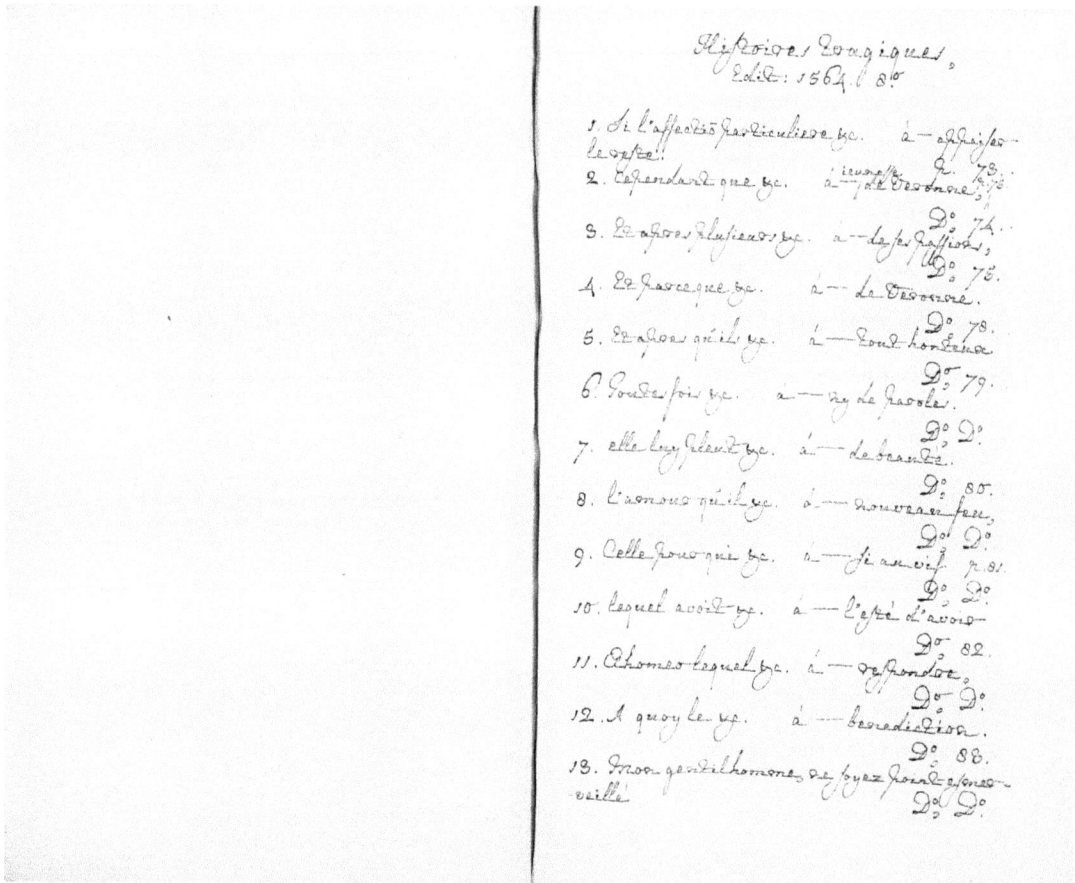

16 Manuscript page from Capell X.4, Wren Library, Trinity College, Cambridge, n.p. Reproduced with permission of the Master and Fellows of Trinity College, Cambridge.

The exact edition of Boaistuau's novella used for this comparison is identified in the title of these added, handwritten notes: it is the sextodecimo version printed in 1564 by Gilles Robinot.[46] These sheets of eighteenth-century paper are slightly larger and thicker than those of the printed sixteenth- and seventeenth-century books surrounding them. The list of page references for the eighty-one passages highlighted in Brooke is written in a neat hand and each page is meticulously structured after a general scheme, evoking the accuracy of a typeset page (see Figure 16). The references to the French text in the manuscript notes are made by indicating both the beginning and the ending of a passage, as well as the corresponding page numbers in the 1564 edition of the first volume of the *Histoires tragiques*.

Capell's copy of the 1564 *Histoires tragiques* (Wren Library, Trinity College, Cambridge, Capell ★.21) bears similar annotations to those found in his copy of Brooke:

brackets and small crosses.[47] In this copy, Capell marks only passages in the third of eighteen novellas, Boaistuau's translation of Bandello's novella. This gives us a good sense of how and for what purposes Capell read the *Histoires tragiques*: he is reading the book not for entertainment, not for stories of tragedy and gore – instead, he singles out the one narrative connected to Shakespearian drama and reads it carefully. The brackets in the Boaistuau novella, however, do not match the list of passages accompanying Brooke's poem. While Capell's copies of the two texts clearly share a system of referencing, they are not made to reference each other. The annotations do not construct a closed

---

46 In the heading of this list, Capell describes the edition as an octavo, which seems to be a mistake.

47 Pierre Boaistuau, *Histoires tragiques* (Paris, 1564), Capell ★.21, Wren Library, Trinity College, Cambridge.

system of mutual reference. Chronologically, Capell's work points us backward in time. Brooke, whom Capell determined to be the immediate source for Shakespeare,[48] points the editor and critic to an earlier version of the story, and Capell adds his version of Boaistuau, shortened to eighty-one referential links, to his copy of Brooke's narrative poem. For Capell, as far as we can reconstruct this from his library, this referential movement from source to source stops with Boaistuau. The passages highlighted in the third novella of the *Histoires tragiques* do not explicitly point to any of the other books in Capell's library (at least not in the state that can be accessed and reconstructed today).

Capell also owned copies of Bandello's *Novelle*, Da Porto's novella (bound with Brooke's narrative poem), and the second edition of Brooke, as well as Painter's *The Palace of Pleasure*.[49] But there is no indication in any of these books that they connect to either the annotations and list in Capell X.4 or to the annotated version of Boaistuau in Capell ★.21. We can find, however, the published results of this practice of annotating in Capell's *School of Shakespeare*. There, the passages selected from Brooke's poem are interspersed with comments, set apart typographically, which point out, for example, an 'addition of the poet' or 'this author's invention; there being nothing of it, either in *Boistuau*, (who was his original) or in the *Italian* novelists'.[50] Capell's annotations in Brooke's narrative poem and his manuscript list of references are the material traces of a mode of reading: a reading for connections, for parallels between different texts, and a reading directed both towards the past and the future of a text that is part of a history of transformations.

In the following, I will discuss two further instances in which scholarly engagement with the sources for Shakespeare's *Romeo and Juliet* lead scholars to compile a list. Rudolf Fischer, in an anthology of Shakespeare's sources, compiles a list of headings delineating presumably equivalent sections in the novellas and Brooke's poem.[51] Jill L. Levenson, in an article, presents an 'essential narrative' in the form of a list of twelve sequential events.[52] As we will see, these accounts of the relationship between texts is much less interested in transformations: both emphasize, in different ways, the stability of the Romeo and Juliet stories.

FISCHER'S HEADINGS

As the second volume of a series that was never continued afterwards, the German anthology *Shakespeares Quellen: Romeo und Julia* ('Shakespeare's Sources: Romeo and Juliet') testifies to a philological and pedagogical interest

in Shakespeare's sources in the early twentieth century. In his foreword, the Austrian-German philologist Alois Brandl, a former president of the German Shakespeare Association, expresses delight in knowing young students will have access to the earlier volume with sources for *King Lear*.[53] The present volume, edited by Rudolf Fischer, who also undertook most of the translations, contains German translations of the Italian novellas by Luigi da Porto and Matteo Bandello, and of Pierre Boaistuau's French translation, as well as Arthur Brooke's narrative poem in English and German on facing pages.[54] That is, it contains all the versions of the Romeo and Juliet story available at the time when Shakespeare was writing his play, except for William Painter's translation. Apart from Brandl's foreword, there is no accompanying material to be found in the volume: no footnotes, no commentary, no critical introduction or conclusion. Brandl makes some general statements about these texts and about how this material differs from that in the prior volume on *King Lear*, but none of his remarks, even when they seem to build on the scholarship of others, contains references of any kind.[55] Clearly, *Shakespeare's Sources* is not meant to be a critical edition of the Romeo and Juliet novellas, and neither does it advance a sustained argument about Shakespeare and his work as an adaptor.

Beyond the act of translation itself, the volume engages and interferes with these texts only in one significant way. Starting with Da Porto's version of the story, the first one that uses Verona as its setting and that calls its protagonists Romeo and Giulietta, headings and subheadings are added throughout the texts. These headings follow a general scheme. Fischer uses the same headings and subheadings to divide the versions of the Romeo and Juliet story written by Da Porto, Bandello, Boaistuau and Brooke. The novellas and the narrative poem are divided into

48 Capell, *School*, p. 525.
49 Capell also owned translations of Bandello by Geoffrey Fenton, perhaps hoping to identify more versions that could potentially have been Shakespeare's source.
50 Capell, *School*, pp. 522 and 518.
51 Rudolf Fischer, ed., *Shakespeares Quellen, 2. Bändchen: Romeo und Julia* (Bonn, 1922).
52 Jill L. Levenson, 'Romeo and Juliet before Shakespeare', *Studies in Philology* 81 (1984), 325–47; p. 329.
53 Fischer, *Shakespeares Quellen*, p. v.
54 Fischer also includes a novella by Masuccio Salernitano usually considered a source for Da Porto's version of the Romeo and Juliet story; in Salernitano's version, the protagonists are called Mariotto and Ganozza.
55 Fischer, *Shakespeares Quellen*, pp. vi–viii.

four parts with further subdivisions. Typographically, the anthology prioritizes the subheadings over the four parts; both are set equally large, but the subheadings are in bold type. All these novellas, the German anthology suggests, share twelve constituent sections: Strife in Verona ('Streit in Verona'), Love ('Liebe'), Engagement ('Verlobung'), Marriage ('Heirat'), Romeo's Banishment ('Romeos Verbannung'), Separation ('Trennung'), Juliet's Distress ('Juliens Bedrängnis'), The Friar as Saviour ('Der Mönch als Retter'), Juliet's Apparent Death ('Juliens Scheintod'), Romeo's Willingness to Die ('Romeos Todesbereitschaft'), Death ('Tod'), Peace in Verona ('Friede in Verona'). With titles set in smaller type, some of these sections are divided further: 'Strife in Verona', for example, contains 'Verona' and 'The Noble Houses' in most of the novellas; 'Love' contains 'The Aloof Beloved', 'Ball' and 'Juliet's Doubts'.

The business of structuring the play is slightly puzzling and it remains unclear what the rationale behind the headings and subheadings is. Since Fischer never explains why he makes these additions, all we can do is infer from the texts themselves. The headings do not follow any kind of exterior principle: they do not mirror the five-act structure imposed on Shakespeare's tragedy, for example, and neither do the titles and their sequence derive from the prior translation consulted for Da Porto's novella in the volume.[56] The headings do not establish an interior principle, or any kind of internal coherence. In fact, a closer look reveals the disparity of the structure. The novellas are not, strictly speaking, divided into units of action. To name a few examples: some of the headings are concerned with setting (such as 'Verona'), others with mental states ('Juliet's Doubts', 'Romeo's Willingness to Die'), character and characterization ('The Aloof Beloved', 'The Friar as Saviour') or a rather abstract notion ('Love' as opposed to 'falling in love'). 'Lament' describes a mode of speech, or poetic mode, as well as the action of lamenting; and 'Ball' metonymically merges scene and action. Therefore, the headings remain idiosyncratic: they isolate parts of the action of the novellas, some of the setting, some characters and their function, some speeches, and disregard others. Since the anthology does not include these titles in its table of contents, it seems like this structuring is also not meant to facilitate easier navigation for the reader within any given novella. So, what do they do? The titles highlight and signpost connections between the novellas for a reader who is reading not one but several novellas in the volume (or, ideally, all of them). Effectively, the inserted titles create links between the novellas, similar

to how Capell's annotations create a link between the versions by Brooke and Boaistuau. The headings are not specific to any of the novellas but try to generalize the component parts of all of them. Highlighting, for example, Romeo and Juliet's wedding in this way allows the reader of the volume to easily identify comparables: how does Bandello handle this scene, how does Boaistuau, how does Brooke? But because the selection is essentially arbitrary, Fischer's way of dividing up the text tells us something about which parts of the novella he considered worthy of such comparisons. It also indicates how to understand the lack of the sub-headings 'Verona', 'The Aloof Beloved', 'Wedding Night' and 'Lament' in the translation of Da Porto's version: Bandello added some details, and the structure of the novella as Fischer sees it remains stable afterwards. This stability is a convenient fiction. The act of establishing a general structure of the Romeo and Juliet novellas must necessarily disregard the shifting and changing that characterizes the work of the Italian *novellieri*, the French translator and the English poet.[57]

Fischer's anthology shows us that devising a structure for these novellas is, inherently, an act of judgement and interpretation. If we take a step back, the titles help us see what an early twentieth-century scholar deemed important about the narrative sources of Shakespeare's tragedy: setting and context, a relationship arc from love to marriage, the externally enforced separation of the lovers, the (more or less) causal chain of events that leads from Juliet's distress to the death of Romeo and Juliet (including, explicitly, the role the friar plays in this), and ultimately the resolution of the initial 'strife in Verona'. The sequence of titles forms one version of the Romeo and Juliet story, one that suggests general applicability, but it foregrounds some aspects of the story just as it ignores others. Structuring means judging which parts are important, and applying such a measure of importance is unavoidably an act of interpretation. In the case of

---

[56] For the translation of Da Porto's novella, Fischer consulted and then modified a German translation by Karl Simrock. Simrock worked extensively on Shakespeare's sources – see, for example, the English version of his earlier work in German: Karl Simrock, *The Plots of Shakespeare's Plays* (London, 1850). For Simrock's role in the history of European source study, see Lori Humphrey Newcomb, 'Toward a sustainable source study', in *Rethinking Shakespeare Source Study*, ed. Britton and Walter, 19–45; pp. 21–2.

[57] Menninghaus points out some of these instances, but he does not discuss them in detail: Winfried Menninghaus, 'Zwischen Bandello und Shakespeare: Pierre Boaistuaus Romeo und Julia-Version', *Poetica* 19 (1987), 3–31; p. 13.

Shakespeare's Sources, it is one that emphasizes stability over change, and one that creates an almost archetypical version of the Romeo and Juliet story, reminiscent of later formalist and structuralist work such as Vladimir Propp's *Morphology of the Folktale* (1928). We can see, in the following, an even stronger assertion of narrative stability in Jill L. Levenson's work on Shakespeare's sources.

LEVENSON'S SEQUENCE

While there is a long history of critical engagement with Shakespeare's sources, of which Capell's work is one of the earliest examples, detailed analysis of their formal and stylistic influence on Shakespeare's *Romeo and Juliet* has been relatively scarce. Most notable is Jill L. Levenson's work, in particular her 1984 article 'Romeo and Juliet before Shakespeare' which also informs her later work on *Romeo and Juliet*, such as the article 'Echoes inhabit a garden: the narratives of *Romeo and Juliet*' or the introduction to her Oxford Shakespeare edition of the play.[58]

'Romeo and Juliet before Shakespeare' sets out to analyse 'the structure and tone of the narrative in its novella form' in order to gain 'a new perspective from which to view ... Shakespeare's dramatic method in *Romeo and Juliet*'.[59] Levenson argues that the Romeo and Juliet story was well known to an early modern English audience, but later stresses that the novellas' style had become 'outmoded' by the time Shakespeare started working on the play.[60] Levenson herself does not hesitate to unfavourably judge the novellas: she writes, 'the five novellas which house the Romeo and Juliet narrative do not qualify as literary masterpieces'.[61] It is significant that the novellas (plural) turn into a narrative (singular) here. This idea of an emphatically singular narrative is a cornerstone for her interpretation of Romeo and Juliet 'before Shakespeare'. Early on, Levenson suggests that 'through its extensive journey, the narrative steadfastly resisted alteration'.[62] The singular 'narrative' allegedly 'arranged the same characters, situations, and events in the same order'.[63] (The veracity of this statement depends, I suppose, on how closely we look at the texts, and at which combination of texts.) Tellingly, Levenson calls this the 'essential narrative' of the Romeo and Juliet novellas;[64] and in the introduction to her edition of the play, she expounds on 'myth' as the 'primary origin' for the story of Romeo and Juliet.[65] Levenson's notion of an 'essential narrative' removes the story of Romeo and Juliet from their sixteenth-century

authors, translators and adaptors, and paves the way for her panegyric on Shakespeare's tragedy in the second half of her article: the neutral, singular, archetypal narrative, Levenson's framing suggests, is waiting for Shakespeare to be brought to perfection and, ultimately, canonization.

Levenson's analysis of Shakespeare's sources neutralizes, through abstraction and generalization, the unruly processes of transformation, across languages and genres, that enabled Shakespeare to write about two star-crossed lovers in a small city in what is now northern Italy. For Levenson, Romeo and Juliet 'before Shakespeare' boils down to a 'sequence ... of twelve incidents' that can be 'extracted' from the novellas.[66] The resulting list appears in 'Before Shakespeare' and is later repeated in 'Echoes inhabit a garden' and in Levenson's 'Introduction':

Romeo's initial, abortive love affair; the Capulet feast, where Romeo and Juliet first encounter each other and immediately become enamored; the meeting at Juliet's house, when they plan to marry; the carrying out of these plans with the assistance of a friar; the brawl between Montagues and Capulets which leads to Romeo's banishment; Romeo and Juliet's leave-taking of each other; the Capulets' arrangement for Juliet to marry a man of their choice; Juliet's appeal to the friar for help, resulting in the potion scheme; Juliet's false death, reported to the exiled Romeo as true; the scene in the tomb, where both lovers die; the governor's distribution of justice; and the reconciliation of the two families.[67]

The similarities between Fischer's headings and Levenson's list are not surprising as both Fischer and Levenson share a knowledge of Shakespeare's play. Their ways of structuring the Romeo and Juliet stories might not mirror the structure of the tragedy in any obvious way, but Shakespeare's version certainly constitutes a moment of

---

58 Jill L. Levenson, 'Echoes inhabit a garden: the narratives of *Romeo and Juliet*', in *Shakespeare Survey 53* (Cambridge, 2000), 39–48; Jill L. Levenson, 'Introduction', in William Shakespeare, *Romeo and Juliet*, ed. Jill L. Levenson (Oxford, 2000), 1–125.

59 Levenson, 'Before Shakespeare', p. 325.

60 Levenson, 'Before Shakespeare', pp. 326 and 344.

61 Levenson, 'Before Shakespeare', p. 328. Levenson reiterates this judgement, word for word, in the introduction to her edition of the play – see Levenson, 'Introduction', p. 6.

62 Levenson, 'Before Shakespeare', p. 327.

63 Levenson, 'Before Shakespeare', p. 327.

64 Levenson, 'Before Shakespeare', p. 327.

65 Levenson, 'Introduction', pp. 2–4.

66 Levenson, 'Before Shakespeare', pp. 329 and 327. Levenson bases her notion of sequence on the definition in Earl Miner, *To Tell a Story: Narrative Theory and Practice* (Los Angeles, 1973), pp. 7–8.

67 Levenson, 'Before Shakespeare', p. 329; also in Levenson, 'Introduction', p. 5; and Levenson, 'Echoes', p. 42.

narrative solidification. Just as in Fischer's headings, Shakespeare's play serves as the standard for the names of characters. In Levenson's 'sequence', there is no difference between 'Rhomeo' and 'Romeo' or between 'Giulietta' and 'Juliet'. The perceived stability of the Romeo and Juliet story, implicit in Fischer's anthology and explicitly proclaimed in Levenson's article, is not an inherent quality of Shakespeare's sources, but rather an effect of the unprecedented canonization of Shakespeare and his works. After Shakespeare, the novellas have become a unified narrative 'before Shakespeare'.

Levenson does not ignore the differences between the Italian versions and the subsequent translations and adaptations, but she locates these differences primarily on a stylistic level. The plot remains the same, the execution differs. Levenson points out the quick pace of Da Porto's version of the story, speaking quite favourably of its 'dynamic, uncluttered narration of events' and his approach which 'allows the story now and again to slip into the realm of ambiguity'.[68] Accordingly, what she finds fault with in the later novellas is that they 'borrow [Da Porto's] plot and viewpoint but disregard his method', with, for Levenson, disastrous effects: 'Handy-dandy, a lithe novella grows into a tome, a gazelle becomes a gnu.'[69] Simply put, they explain too much, they 'explain everything'.[70] They are interested, it seems to Levenson, not in 'telling a story' but in 'building an incontestable argument'.[71] In a later article, Levenson characterizes the novellas as 'rhetorical compositions based on the story as da Porto had arranged it', in which 'the dozen plot elements' – Levenson's 'twelve incidents' – are used as 'a *res* or subject-matter'.[72] Clearly, the plot of Romeo and Juliet is understood as something stable here; the differences between the novellas do not affect the 'essential narrative' of Romeo and Juliet. This becomes perhaps most apparent in Levenson's talk of a 'lineage of Shakespeare's *Romeo and Juliet*' and of a 'main line of descent'.[73] Eventually, that is what the novellas do in Levenson's eyes: they 'transmit' a set of twelve incidents 'from Italy across the Alps to England'.[74] The 'Romeo and Juliet fable' is on an 'unchanging course' until it is picked up by Shakespeare.[75] This idea of movement without change is one that emphasizes the 'twelve incidents' she 'extracts' from the novellas as something that lies outside the text. For Levenson, plot is not so much a property of the novellas as it is a precondition for them.

Thus, when Levenson goes on to compare Bandello, Boaistuau, Brooke and Painter to 'describe the story of the Veronese lovers',[76] the stage is already set: describing is an act of interpretation, and describing the novellas as variations on a common theme means interpreting them in

relation to an abstraction.[77] Levenson's description is, just like Fischer's headings in his anthology, an act of constructing plot as a set of comparables. It is Levenson's way of describing and interpreting the relationship between these texts.

COMPARISONS

Comparison is the essential mode of source study. Maguire and Smith state that 'in most cases of source study ... the strength of any claim to have identified a potential source – its proof of concept – is based on the evident continued legibility of that source in the text'.[78] This 'continued legibility' is established, usually, through comparison. In Belsey, this observation almost sounds like a definition, 'A source is a source to the degree that it resembles Shakespeare's text. But it is a source, and not the work itself, to the degree that it differs from that text.'[79] A source, in these terms, always hinges on a perceived stability of similarities and differences between two (or more) texts. Plot, as presented by Levenson and Fischer, is one formulation of this stability.

In the following, I want to look at three examples to trace this subtle balance between similarity and difference which characterizes the relationship between a text and its source. In the case of the Romeo and Juliet stories, there are, of course, sources of sources, and it is therefore possible to trace similarities and differences through multiple iterations of adaptation.

The changes revealed by comparison, made in the process of translation and adaptation, can be easily construed as traces of an authorial intention. Belsey proposes that 'Comparison with the source is where we catch

---

68   Levenson, 'Before Shakespeare', p. 330.

69   Levenson, 'Before Shakespeare', p. 330.

70   Levenson, 'Before Shakespeare', p. 331.

71   Levenson, 'Before Shakespeare', p. 331.

72   Jill L. Levenson, 'Shakespeare's Romeo and Juliet: the places of invention', in *Shakespeare Survey 49* (Cambridge, 1996), 45–56; p. 45; Levenson, 'Introduction', p. 10.

73   Levenson, 'Before Shakespeare', p. 327; and Levenson, 'Introduction', pp. 5 and 6.

74   Levenson, 'Before Shakespeare', p. 327; and Levenson, 'Introduction', p. 5.

75   Levenson, 'Before Shakespeare', p. 328.

76   Levenson, 'Before Shakespeare', p. 331.

77   See John Frow, *On Interpretive Conflict* (Chicago, 2019), pp. 20–1.

78   Maguire and Smith, 'What is a source?', p. 18.

79   Belsey, 'Elephants' graveyard', p. 63.

Shakespeare at work. It's what he changes that throws into relief what makes him Shakespeare.'[80] But ascribing certain intentions to certain changes is always a work of conjecture.[81] The changes, however, are visible as such. We do not know why exactly Boaistuau chose to change the scene when Rhomeo and Juliette first meet at the Capellets' ball, but we can observe and describe this change.

In Bandello, Giulietta sees Romeo from a distance and determines him to be 'the most beautiful and graceful young man' at the ball.[82] She wishes that Romeo would dance, so that she can both see him better and hear him speak when he comes closer.[83] When the dancing part of the ball is about to end, the guests come together for one last dance. Through the logic of this dance, Giulietta and Romeo end up together: she takes his hand 'with inestimable pleasure for both parties'.[84] On her other side is someone introduced as Marcuccio in the text, who is characterized primarily by his cold hands, thus setting up a dichotomy between cold and hot which gives the cue for a dialogue of passion between Giulietta and Romeo.

Boaistuau keeps the setting for the meeting of the two lovers, including the third character, who is called Marcucio here. But in his version, Juliette and Rhomeo do not dance together. While Boaistuau's Juliette assesses Rhomeo's beauty in close correspondence to Bandello's Giulietta, the latter's explicit wish to see Rhomeo dance is nowhere to be found in the French translation. There, Juliette is taken by 'some gentleman' to dance (at which she apparently excels).[85] Rhomeo remains physically inactive, but mentally anticipates where Juliette will be when the dance finishes: she ends up sitting between Rhomeo and Marcuccio, and they can finally speak to each other. The situation, although expressed in rhymed couplets, is identical in Brooke's version; the lovers meet off the dancefloor:

> With torche in hand a comly knight
>   did fetch her foorth to daunce.
>
>   . . .
>
> The whilst our Romeus,
>   a place had warely wonne:
> Nye to the seate where she must sit,
>   the daunce once beyng donne.
> Fayre Iuliet tourned to,
>   her chayre with pleasant cheere:
> And glad she was her Romeus
>   approched was so neere.[86]

In Q1, Q2 and F of *Romeo and Juliet*, there is no indication that Romeo and Juliet dance together. An earlier stage direction, 'Music plays, and the masquers, guests,

and gentlewomen dance' (1.5.26 SD), confirms that there is dancing at the ball, and so does Capulet's 'Nay, sit, nay, sit, good cousin Capulet, / For you and I are past our dancing days' (1.5.30–1). The dialogue between Romeo and the Servingman suggests that Romeo is not dancing; he asks, 'What lady's that which doth enrich the hand / Of yonder knight?' (1.5.41–2). In Shakespeare's play, it remains unclear when exactly the dance ends and how exactly Romeo and Juliet end up positioned so they can speak their famous sonnet together. Shakespeare took this scene and turned it into one, in Hester Lees-Jefferies's words, of 'extraordinary intimacy'.[87]

Is this a small change? If we look at the novellas and the play in terms of plot in Levenson's sense, this is but a slightly different treatment of the *res* or subject matter 'Capulet feast' (or Fischer's 'Ball'). Theatrically, the difference would be more pronounced. For a plot in Greg's sense, it matters who is dancing when and where, but in this, Shakespeare's play does not differ from Brooke's poem. Finally, in Lees-Jefferies's argument about poetic language in the play, Shakespeare's treatment of Romeo and Juliet's encounter at the Capulet ball is strikingly different from the one in his source. She concludes that 'Shakespeare's transformation of his sources is simultaneously a radical poetic metamorphosis and a theatrical one' because the sonnet makes theatrically legible the tension and passion of the first encounter between Romeo and Juliet.[88]

Things get slightly more complicated when we look at another scene: the two lovers' wedding night. In Bandello, Boaistuau and Brooke, the consummation of the marriage is narrated in the text; in Shakespeare's play, it is not depicted at all. Bandello's novella describes Romeo and Giulietta's wedding night in a short passage, and quite succinctly:

They then retreated to one of the corners of the garden where there were certain benches on which they, lovingly lying

---

[80] Belsey, 'Elephants' graveyard', p. 63.

[81] Ultimately, in the case of translation and adaptation, change is not more or less a site of intention than any other part of the text, it is simply more visible as one.

[82] 'Il più bello e leggiardo giovine'; Bandello, *Opere*, p. 731.

[83] Bandello, *Opere*, p. 731.

[84] 'Piacer inestimabile di tutte le parti': Bandello, *Opere*, p. 732.

[85] Boaistuau, *Histoires*, p. 69.

[86] Brooke, *Tragicall Historye*, fol. 7v.

[87] Hester Lees-Jefferies, 'Body language: making love in lyric in *Romeo and Juliet*', *Review of English Studies* 74 (2023), 237–53; p. 240.

[88] Lees-Jefferies, 'Body language', p. 242.

together, consummated the holy matrimony. And since Romeo was a youth of strong backbone and much in love, many and many times he went back to this pleasure with his beautiful wife.[89]

It is an outdoor scene: Romeo, with the help of his servant, climbs the wall and meets Giulietta in the garden. Before, he had used a rope ladder to climb to Giulietta's window and hatch a plan for their wedding, but since this window is barred, the two newly-weds must meet elsewhere for their wedding night. Bandello emphasizes the two lovers' shared sexual pleasure in the idyllic setting of the garden. In Boaistuau, Rhomeo uses the ladder to climb to Juliette's window and enter her room. This resonates with how the events of their wedding night are described: 'Rhomeo, breaking the holy ties of virginity, took possession of the place which so far no one had besieged.'[90] Brooke expands on this militaristic imagery of sexual conquest. From the very start, the site of consummation is framed as one of battle. The Nurse tells Romeus and Iuliet, 'And eche of you hath been the cause of others wayled woe, / Loe here a fielde, (she shewd a fieeldbed ready dight) / Where you may, if you list, in armes, reuenge your selfe by fight'.[91] Later, Brooke describes Romeus as 'Mars himself', and calls him 'warlike Romeus' who conquers 'the virgins fort . . . In which as yet no breache was made by force of canon shot'.[92] At the same time, Brooke also admits that he has no idea what he is talking about: 'Fortune such delight as theyrs dyd neuer graunt me yet', therefore, 'By proofe no certain truth can I vnhappy write: / But what I gesse by likelihod that dare I to endite'.[93] In Shakespeare, no corresponding scene exists.

Accordingly, neither Levenson in her sequence of events nor Fischer in his headings include the wedding night. It is subsumed, in both cases, under preceding events: 'the carrying out' of the 'plan to marry', or simply 'Marriage'. Because the play does not include a sex scene, it might appear that there is, at least in terms of plot, no way to engage with this passage in Brooke's poem in relation to Shakespeare's play. Absence itself constitutes difference, and it impedes the assessment of similarity. Brooke's turn to the language of Roman deities (Mars, Venus) finds an echo perhaps in what Julia Reinhard Lupton has termed Juliet's 'cute classicism' in the scene in which she anticipates Romeo's arrival in her room.[94] But, ultimately, any immediate comparison seems difficult, here, when attempted from the position of Shakespeare source study, as there is no initial point of comparison in *Romeo and Juliet*. From the opposite perspective, however, Brooke's representational dilemma seems to foreshadow the absence in Shakespeare's

play: Romeo and Juliet cannot be shown to have sex, just as they cannot be mimetically described as having sex in Brooke's poem or in Boaistuau's French translation with its elevated style.[95]

A third and final example: Juliette's manner of death in Boaistuau's version differs significantly from Giulietta's in Bandello's novella. In Bandello, the short summary at the beginning of the novella proclaims that one of the lovers dies of poison, the other of pain.[96] This is precisely what happens towards the end of the novella. Giulietta, holding the dead Romeo in her arms, practically rejects life: overcome with grief, she simply stops breathing and dies.[97] In Boaistuau, Rhomeo's servant prompts the Friar to leave the cell; Juliette, now all alone, grabs Rhomeo's dagger and repeatedly stabs herself.[98] Brooke's Iuliet does the same: 'With hasty hand she did draw out, the dagger that he ware', speaks a lengthy speech and, eventually, 'These said, her ruthlesse hand through gyrt her valiant hart'.[99] Caught in the gravitational pull of canonicity, we expect this to happen. We know that, in Shakespeare, Juliet stabs herself: 'Yea, noise? Then I'll be brief. O happy dagger / This is thy sheath! There rust, and let me die' (5.3.168–9).

This speech signals a pronounced difference between Shakespeare and his source. In Brooke, Iuliet's speech after taking Romeus's dagger and before stabbing herself is eight rhymed couplets long. When Shakespeare's Juliet says 'I'll be brief', she does so not just out of dramatic and theatrical necessity, but because of Iuliet's precedent in Brooke's poem. In terms of plot, as outlined by Levenson and Fischer, these are minor changes; the narrative unit 'death' is still intact. Superficially, it does not matter how exactly Juliet dies. Reading the play alongside its source (and the sources of its source), however, we can see that the manner of Juliet's death is not coincidental: it follows Brooke who follows Boaistuau.

Juliet dies more than one death in the sources. Paul A. Kottman, in an article highlighting Romeo and

[89] Bandello, *Opere*, p. 739. [90] Boaistuau, *Histoires*, pp. 81–2.

[91] Brooke, *Tragicall Historye*, fol. 25v.

[92] Brooke, *Tragicall Historye*, fols. 26r–26v.

[93] Brooke, *Tragicall Historye*, fol. 26r.

[94] Julia Reinhard Lupton, '"Cut him out in little stars": Juliet's cute classicism', in *Shakespeare Survey 70* (Cambridge, 2017), 240–8; pp. 243–6.

[95] For the intention behind differences in style between Bandello and Boaistuau's translation, see Boaistuau's address to the reader in the beginning of *Histoires tragiques*: Boaistuau, *Histoires*, pp. 6–7.

[96] Bandello, *Opere*, p. 727. [97] Bandello, *Opere*, p. 765.

[98] Boaistuau, *Histoires*, p. 113.

[99] Brooke, *Tragicall Historye*, fols. 77v–78r.

Juliet's 'struggle for freedom', has pointed out that 'venerating their struggle as a kind of *Liebestod*, we mistake these individuals for a single pair . . . The two suicides are treated as if they were one death.'[100] This is equally true for Levenson's and Fischer's ways of structuring the plot of the Romeo and Juliet stories. Death, here, is always the death of Romeo and Juliet.[101] But, tracing this moment through the different versions of the story, we can distance ourselves from the familiarity of the play's ending and see this scene as what it is: a bloody scene of a self-inflicted, fatal wound; a scene of suicide; a scene of violence originating from adaptation.

Plot is designed to cover both the similarities and differences between texts. It covers up that Giulietta, Juliette, Iuliet and Juliet are not the same – how differently they are treated in the three texts. When Nora J. Williams writes that 'early modern plays have misogyny baked in as an essential part of their dramaturgies' and that the 'misogyny of these works goes . . . down to the structures, logics, and assumptions that hold these plays together', we can understand the novellas, their translations and their adaptations as a part of that baking process.[102] The three scenes help us see the functioning of plot: what it emphasizes and what it obscures – that is, which questions it encourages and which questions it makes impossible. The comparisons between the novellas, the poem and the play have shown us: plot is not an innocent thing; it is abstract, but not neutral. There is a reason why Romeo does not dance, a reason why there is no sex in *Romeo and Juliet*, and a reason why Juliet stabs herself. The consequences of these questions for our understanding of Shakespeare's play lie outside of the purview of source study as it is outlined by Capell, Fischer and Levenson.

PLOT AND DRAMATURGY

As a product of adaptation, Shakespeare's tragedy emerges not from and on the empty page, but from a book that comes from a line of books. The three examples of scholarly engagement with the novellas have shown us something akin to this act of adaptation – namely, the acts of interpretation that seek to establish what is most important about a source. The solidified plot presented in Levenson's article, similar to what Capell calls the

'fable' on the title page of *The School of Shakespeare*, is the result of a work of abstraction and generalization, just like the headings in Fischer's anthology.

It is important to point out this role of plot in the practices of source study because it allows us to understand what happens beyond the legible results of abstraction. What my comparisons of the different versions of the Romeo and Juliet story have shown is that plot necessarily subsumes differences as much as it constructs comparables. Williams proposes to understand dramaturgy 'as the system that holds the play together: its organizing structures and principles, as well as the discussion and realization of those principles through the processes of rehearsal and performance'.[103] With Capell, Fischer and Levenson, we can begin to understand that such a notion of dramaturgy, one that emphasizes the work with and around the dramatic text, can be mirrored backwards. Plot emerges in the three examples as the result of a work with texts, leaving traces in both manuscript and print. Because plot is conceptual (in Hutson's sense), it replicates the narrative systems of domination of their sources; because plot is material and practical (in Stern's sense), it continues to matter.

Williams's focus on performance and theatrical practice seeks to disconnect 'our conception of "Shakespeare" from a fixed, unchanging text and canon'.[104] I have shown that paying attention to the practices of source study can have the same effect: instead of subscribing to a narrative of teleological development in which Shakespeare realizes the full potential of an 'essential narrative' or 'myth', an awareness of the shifting and changing that is so characteristic of early modern translation and adaptation shows us the procedural quality of Shakespeare's tragedy as a work 'by the book'. Dramaturgy does not end with Shakespeare, and it also does not start with him.

[100] Paul A. Kottman, 'Defying the stars: tragic love as the struggle for freedom in *Romeo and Juliet*', *Shakespeare Quarterly* 63 (2012), 1–38; p. 36.

[101] Levenson mentions 'Liebestod' as a 'mythical component' of Shakespeare's 'narrative sequence': Levenson, 'Echoes', p. 45.

[102] Nora J. Williams, 'Incomplete dramaturgies', *Shakespeare Bulletin* 40 (2022), 1–22; p. 1.

[103] Williams, 'Incomplete dramaturgies', p. 2.

[104] Williams, 'Incomplete dramaturgies', p. 3.

WAR, HUNGER AND GLUTTONY IN SHAKESPEARE'S ENGLISH HISTORIES: SIR JOHN OLDCASTLE AND JACK CADE

JOAN FITZPATRICK

In the plays featuring the reign of Henry VI, in the first tetralogy, Shakespeare dramatizes England's medieval wars in France and insurrection closer to home: Jack Cade's uprising in England and his role in rebellion in Ireland. The second tetralogy, depicting what happens before this, culminates in a return to England's wars in France under the reign of King Henry V, following his adventures as a young man under the influence of his companion Sir John Oldcastle (Falstaff) and his negotiation of responsibilities as king in the context of this relationship. In all these plays, Shakespeare explores the catastrophic impact of war upon the most basic human need: having enough food to eat.

This article will explore the role of hunger and gluttony in Shakespeare's first tetralogy, the play's debt to the medieval penitential tradition, and the impact this might have had upon his subsequent English history plays. These are connections hitherto neglected by critics. Hunger was, and remains, a weapon of war, but for Shakespeare it also provided the precondition to signal English heroism: the productive hunger of the brave soldier in the face of gluttony and cowardice. Shakespeare apparently re-read his first tetralogy when writing the second to further develop connections between English heroism, bravery and hunger. He might also have been informed by the medieval view of hunger as morally beneficial. These connections to the past, in his own writing and earlier traditions, are especially relevant to hitherto overlooked parallels between the cowardly and gluttonous knight Sir John Oldcastle and the brave, though ignominious, English rebel Jack Cade.

At the beginning of Shakespeare's *Henry V* the Chorus refers to 'the warlike Harry' who 'at his heels, / Leashed in like hounds' has 'famine, sword, and fire' (Prologue 5–8). In his threats before the gates of Harfleur, Henry characterizes 'impious war' as hell on earth – 'Arrayed in flames like to the prince of fiends' – warning that the consequences of continued defiance will be the rape and murder of the weak and innocent. Later in the play, the Chorus alludes to the return of Elizabeth's Lord Deputy from Ireland:

> Were now the General of our gracious Empress –
> As in good time he may – from Ireland coming,
> Bringing rebellion broached on his sword,
> How many would the peaceful city quit
> To welcome him!
>
> (5.0.30–4)[1]

The allusion is probably to Essex, who had been sent to Ireland on 27 March 1599 and returned in disgrace on 28 September the same year, and so the play was presumably written before his disgrace, in the spring or early summer of 1599. The allusion might refer to the return of Charles Blount, Lord Mountjoy, following his victory in Kinsale in the winter of 1601, but critical consensus is for placing *Henry V* in 1599.[2] Early modern playgoers in London, like their modern counterparts, might have experienced the kind of violence threatened against the people of Harfleur as combatants in, or refugees from, a foreign war, but they would have had no experience of this sort of mass slaughter by an invading army at home. Yet London was not exactly a 'peaceful city', having experienced riots by apprentices, primarily over the high cost of food, as recently as the summer of 1595. Henry's threats that the city of Harfleur will 'in her ashes ... lie buried', becoming a place of 'waste and desolation' if it

---

[1] All quotations of Shakespeare's plays are from William Shakespeare, *The Complete Works: Compact Edition*, ed. Stanley Wells, Gary Taylor, John Jowett and William Montgomery (Oxford, 1988).

[2] Gary Taylor and Gabriel Egan, eds., *The New Oxford Shakespeare Authorship Companion* (Oxford, 2017), p. 527. Performance and publication dates for plays are also indebted to the electronic resource 'Database of Early English Playbooks', or 'DEEP', created by Alan B. Farmer and Zachary Lesser and hosted by the University of Pennsylvania.

does not surrender (3.3.92, 101), allow an audience to imagine the horrors of siege warfare, including the consequences of exhausting stored food supplies, but it might also provoke recollection of more recent food-related violence in London. In *1 Henry VI*, too, the great English warrior Talbot, like Henry V in his threats against the people of Harfleur, might remind playgoers of the dangers of food instability when he tells the General of Bordeaux that his refusal to submit will 'tempt the fury of my three attendants – / Lean famine, quartering steel, and climbing fire' (4.2.10–11).

During the sixteenth century, stories emerged from Ireland of the famine suffered as a result of war. In Holinshed's *Chronicles*, John Hooker describes the famine that followed the Desmond rebellion being so severe that people were 'driuen to eat horsses, dogs and dead carions; but also did deuoure the carcases of dead men, whereof there be sundrie examples'.[3] Similarly, Fynes Moryson reports that, following the destruction of Irish corn by English forces, he witnessed 'a most horrible spectacle of three children ... all eating and knawing with their teeth the entrals of their dead mother'.[4] Reports of famine in Ireland emerged from other sources also. In Edmund Spenser's *A View of the Present State of Ireland* – not published until 1633, but written in 1595 and presumably circulating in manuscript – Irenius describes the consequences of the scorched earth policy implemented by English forces against the rebellions led by the Earl of Desmond in Munster:

Out of euerie Corner of the woode and glinnes they Came Crepinge forthe vppon theire handes, for theire Leggs Coulde not beare them, they loked like Anotomies of deathe, they spake like ghostes, Crying out of theire graues; they did eate the dead Carrions, happie wheare they Could finde them, Yea and one another sone after, in so muche as the verye carkasses they spared not to scrape out of theire graues. And if they founde a plotte of water Cresses or Shamarocks theare they flocked as to a feaste for the time, yeat not able longe to Continue thearewithall, that in shorte space theare weare non allmoste lefte and a moste populous and plentifull Countrye sodenlye lefte voide of man or beastr, yeat sure in all that warr theare perished not manie by the sworde but all by the extreamitye of famyne which they themselves had wroughte.[5]

Spenser relates what happened in Munster, via the fictional Irenius, in order to persuade his reader that famine is a useful weapon of war, one that might also be used to suppress the ongoing rebellion in Ulster.

Extreme hunger was a reality of war in Ireland but, as is clear from the actions of London's apprentices, a lack of ready access to food was also an issue during peacetime. In

The Second Part of the Anatomie of Abuses (published in 1583), Phillip Stubbes, in the voice of Philoponus (and sounding rather like Spenser's Irenius), describes the fate of the poor English who cannot work and provide for themselves:

[They] die some in ditches, some in holes, some in caves and dens, some in fields ... rather like dogs than Christian people. For notwithstanding that they be never so impotent, blind, lame, sick, old or aged, yet are they forced to walke the countries from place to place to seeke their releefe at every mans doore, except they wil sterve or famish at home ... Yea, in such troups doe they flocke, and in such swarmes doe they flowe, that you can lightlie go any way, and you shall see numbers of them at everie doore, in everie lane, and in everie poore cave.[6]

The sick, disabled and old might have to beg for food but even the able-bodied poor were at risk of food shortages. Before the early sixteenth century, food was relatively plentiful and wages comparatively high, mainly due to the disastrous effect of plague upon England's population, but around 1520 the population of England had begun to rise and a higher demand for food led to higher prices that many people could not afford because inflation had outstripped wages.[7] This situation was exacerbated by three bad harvests in the 1560s and a particularly bad harvest in 1573. Food was also scarce in 1586, but because the early 1590s saw four good harvests, the government repealed the tillage act of 1563 (an anti-enclosure measure) and allowed the export of wheat. The year 1594 saw the first of four consecutive bad harvests leading to widespread starvation, the threat of popular rebellion in various parts of England, and the apprentice riots that erupted in London in 1595.[8] Ian Archer observed that, although

[3] Raphael Holinshed, *[Holinshed's Chronicles] The First and Second Volume of Chronicles ... Newlie Augmented and Continued By J. Hooker Alias Vowell Gent. and Others*, STC 13569, 3 vols. (London, 1587), vol. 2: *The Description of Ireland*, sig. R1v–R2r.

[4] Fynes Moryson, *An Itinerary Written By Fynes Moryson Gent. (Containing His Ten Yeeres Travell Through the Twelve Dominions of Germany, Bohmerland, ... France, England, Scotland, and Ireland)*, STC 18205 (London, 1617), sig. Bbb2r.

[5] Edmund Spenser, *The Works of Edmund Spenser: A Variorum Edition*, vol. 10: *Prose Works*, ed. Rudolf Gottfried (Baltimore, 1949), p. 158.

[6] Phillip Stubbes, *The Second Part of the Anatomie of Abuses* (London, 1583), G1r.

[7] Y. S. Brenner, 'The inflation of prices in early sixteenth century England', *Economic History Review* 14 (1961), 225–39, pp. 235–6; Marjorie K. McIntosh, 'Poverty, charity, and coercion in Elizabethan England', *Journal of Interdisciplinary History* 35 (2005), 457–79; pp. 459–60.

[8] W. G. Hoskins, 'Harvest fluctuations and English economic history, 1480–1619', in *Essays in Agrarian History*, ed. W.E. Minchinton (Newton Abbot, 1968), vol. 1, 93–115; pp. 106–8;

'the fundamental stability of the City' was not in question, these riots made for a distinctly nervous elite and the 'sense of perceived crisis' was significant.[9]

As the agricultural historian Joan Thirsk pointed out, the reality of food shortages 'set writers thinking on new lines. Their books actually discussed how to survive starvation, in novel ways that had not been discussed before.' One of these was Hugh Platt's *Sundrie New and Artificiall Remedies against Famine*, printed in 1596. Here Platt:

offered advice on making various plants palatable in emergency. Among those he named were beans, peas, beechmast, chestnuts, acorns and vetches, and his detailed instructions revealed his own many practical experiments, some of which were entirely sensible, like cooking out the bitterness of acorns before mixing the pulp with flour, grinding more bran into meal than usual, or adding herbs to disguise a disagreeable taste.[10]

The threat of starvation meant that foods previously regarded as undesirable were 'viewed in a fresh light as the life-saving foods that could insure against starvation'. People also became more self-sufficient: they 'grew roots on dunghills outside London, and public officials urged local authorities to promote their growing by the poor'. The better-off too 'heeded the importance of growing "cabbages and roots" as an insurance against lean times and looked more appreciatively at those vegetables'.[11]

Might the reality of food shortages at home and in England's war against the Irish abroad also have had an impact upon Shakespeare's writing, specifically in his English history plays? Sir John Oldcastle and his exploits in the second tetralogy are often the focus of critical attention when it comes to the topic of food and eating in Shakespeare; Prince Hal must reject this figure of vice, a man given to gluttony and other failings, if he is to become an effective leader.[12] Yet there are important moments relating to hunger and gluttony in the Henry VI plays of the first tetralogy, pertaining to England's military engagements abroad as well as rebellion at home, that prefigure Shakespeare's gluttonous Sir John in the second tetralogy. Crucially, his English history plays also reveal Shakespeare's debt to medieval views regarding hunger and gluttony beyond the commonly acknowledged allusion to Sir John as the Vice of old morality plays, by specifically connecting Sir John's gluttony with his cowardice.

In Shakespeare's time, gluttony was widely considered bad for the soul as well as the body. In the Church of England's *Homily Against Gluttony and Drunkenness* (1563), the good Christian is told 'howe destesttable and hatefull all excesse in eatyng and drinkyng is, before the face of almightie God'.[13] Gluttons are deemed 'belly gods' and the biblical Gospel according to Saint Luke invoked as evidence that they will receive appropriate punishment from God: 'Wo be to you that are full, for ye shall hunger.'[14] Yet the other extreme of fasting was acceptable only if it was not overly indulgent or ostentatious,[15] since fasting invoked the old Catholic monastic tradition and Catholic fast days. Early modern dietary literature, a popular and influential genre indicating how to live a healthy life, also advised against gluttony. In William Bullein's *Government of Health*, the sober Humphrey offers advice to the riotous John who is keen to reform his ways: 'those bellies that follow the lust of the eyes (in meats) in youth shall lack the health of all their bodies in age if they live so long'.[16] Here the focus is mainly on physical health rather than moral wellbeing. Similarly, Andrew Boorde's observance that 'abstinence . . . is the most best and the perfect medicine that can be'[17] is typical of the genre's concern with the body rather than the soul.

Yet, as I hope to demonstrate here, Shakespeare's conception of gluttony and hunger in his English history

---

Roger B. Manning, *Village Revolts: Social Protest and Popular Disturbances in England, 1509–1640* (Oxford, 1988), p. 220; Ian W. Archer, *The Pursuit of Stability: Social Relations in Elizabethan London* (Cambridge, 1991), pp. 1–9.

[9] Archer, *The Pursuit of Stability*, p. 9.

[10] Joan Thirsk, *Food in Early Modern England: Phases, Fads, Fashions 1500–1760* (London, 2007), p. 34; Hugh Platt, *Sundrie New and Artificiall Remedies against Famine*, STC 19996 (London, 1596), sig. D1v–D3v.

[11] Thirsk, *Food in Early Modern England*, pp. 34–5.

[12] Joan Fitzpatrick, *Food in Shakespeare: Early Modern Dietaries and the Plays* (Aldershot, 2007), pp. 11–36; Elena Levy-Navarro, *The Culture of Obesity in Early and Late Modernity: Body Image in Shakespeare, Jonson, Middleton, and Skelton* (Basingstoke, 2008), pp. 67–109; Joshua B. Fisher, 'Digesting Falstaff: food and nation in Shakespeare's *Henry IV* plays', *Early English Studies* 2 (2009), 1–23; Christine Hoffmann, 'Biting more than "we" can chew: the royal appetite in *Richard II* and *1* and *2 Henry IV*', *Papers on Language and Literature: A Journal for Scholars and Critics of Language and Literature* 45 (2009), 358–85.

[13] Church of England, *The Seconde Tome of Homelyes of Such Matters as Were Promised and Intituled in the Former Part of Homelyes, Set Out By the Aucthoritie of the Quenes Maiestie: and to be Read in Every Paryshe Churche Agreablye*, STC 13664 (London, 1563), Oo2r.

[14] Church of England, *The Seconde Tome of Homelyes*, Oo2v; Luke 6.25.

[15] Church of England, *The Seconde Tome of Homelyes*, Nn1v.

[16] Joan Fitzpatrick, *Three Sixteenth-Century Dietaries: A Critical Edition*, The Revels Companion Library (Manchester, 2017), p. 222.

[17] Fitzpatrick, *Three Sixteenth-Century Dietaries*, p. 173.

plays appears to have been informed not only by early modern descriptions of and proscriptions against excess and lack – due to Ireland's wars, rising food prices and crop failures, early modern sermons and dietary literature – but also by what we might term the 'morally productive hunger' of an older tradition.

In *Piers Plowman*, William Langland's important and highly influential medieval, allegorical, dream-vision poem, gluttony is repeatedly invoked as a sign of moral corruption.[18] Early in the poem, Holy Church warns Will the Dreamer that 'Mesure [moderation] is medcyne' (1.35) for the soul as well as the body since 'þe fende and þi flesch folowethe þe to-gidere' (in modern English, 'the fiend and the flesh follow thee together') (1.40). Gluttony is present at the wedding of Lady Meed (the enemy of Holy Church) and, with his pal 'Great Oaths', spends all day drinking and eating in taverns. It is this physical excess that prompts a drunken sleep and the sin of despair: 'And þanne wanhope to awake him so with no will to amend, / For he leueth be lost – þis is here last ende' ('And then Despair to awaken them so with no will to amend; / They believe themselves lost: this is their last end') (2.99–100). Later, Gluttony will visit another tavern, diverted from the Church to which he is heading to make confession, where he vomits and is helped home to bed by others.

Although Langland is concerned with the physical effects of gluttony (sleeping, vomiting, temporary physical incapacity), he does not mention the long-term physical consequences of disease upon the body, which dominates the early modern dietary genre, since his main objective is to highlight gluttony as a moral and social ill. Yet it is in his treatment of hunger and famine that Langland's allegory is furthest from early modern notions of gluttony. When the Christ-like Piers sees that some of his fellow pilgrims refuse to work the land alongside him, he asks Hunger to punish them, and he obliges: 'He bette hem so bothe he barste nere here guttes' (in modern English, 'He so beat them both that he nearly burst their guts') (6.180). When, come harvest-time, the people have enough to eat, they again refuse to work, and we are told that Hunger will return: 'and derthe be iustice' ['and dearth be justice'] (6.330). Clearly, the people have not truly repented their former idleness, and hunger is their punishment. Medieval monks were encouraged to follow the example of the early Christian saints who practised fasting, as described in the widely read hagiographies contained in Jacobus De Voragine's *The Golden Legend*, and to adhere to the Rule of Saint Benedict that forbade certain foods.[19] Outside the walls of the

monastery too, hunger was a means by which the good Christian might, of his or her own volition, reach or maintain spiritual integrity, but in Langland it is specifically a penalty that serves to remind the common people of their moral and social duty to God and each other.

In *1 Henry VI* too, hunger is morally good since it makes for tenacious and valiant soldiers: Charles the Dauphin describes 'the famished English, like pale ghosts [that] / Faintly besiege us one hour in a month' (1.1.7–8). Although weak and exhausted, they will not give up. They are 'like lions wanting food' who 'rush upon us as their hungry prey' (1.3.6–7), and 'Lean raw-boned rascals' full of 'courage and audacity' whereby 'hunger will enforce them to be more eager' so that 'rather with their teeth / The walls they'll tear down, than forsake the siege' (1.3.14–15, 18–19). Earlier in the play an English Messenger reports Talbot's bravery before his capture:

> More than three hours the fight continued,
> Where valiant Talbot above human thought
> Enacted wonders with his sword and lance.
> Hundreds he sent to hell, and none durst stand him;
> Here, there, and everywhere, enraged he slew.
> The French exclaimed the devil was in arms:
> All the whole army stood agazed on him.
> His soldiers, spying his undaunted spirit,
> 'A Talbot! A Talbot!' cried out amain,
> And rushed into the bowels of the battle.
>
> (1.1.120–9)

The actions of Fastolf undermine the bravery of Talbot and his men against the French:

> Here had the conquest fully been sealed up,
> If Sir John Fastolf had not played the coward.
> He, being in the vanguard placed behind,
> With purpose to relieve and follow them,
> Cowardly fled, not having struck one stroke.
>
> (1.1.130–4)

Here in the figure of Fastolf we seem to have an antecedent of the cowardly knight Sir John Oldcastle,

---

[18] William Langland, *The Vision of William Concerning Piers the Plowman*, ed. Walter W. Skeat (London, 1869).

[19] For example, *The Golden Legend* relates that Saint Giles only occasionally drank milk from a female deer, and the Rule of Saint Benedict did not allow the consumption of animal flesh and wine except for the sick and weak (Jacobus De Voragine, *The Golden Legend: Readings on the Saints*, trans. William Granger Ryan with an introduction by Eamon Duffy (Princeton, 2012), ch. 130; Saint Benedict, *The Rule of Saint Benedict: In Latin and English*, trans. and ed. Justin McCann (London, 1952), chs. 39, 40).

later renamed Falstaff, who appears in the second tetralogy. Although Fastolf is not a major character in the first tetralogy – and he has neither Falstaff's girth nor what Edward Burns referred to as his 'calculated dishonesty'[20] – the cowardice of Fastolf makes for a clear thematic connection between the two figures.

In addition to the Messenger's report of Fastolf's cowardice, Talbot himself complains: 'But O, the treacherous Fastolf wounds my heart, / Whom with my bare fists I would execute / If I now had him brought into my power' (1.6.13–15). Fastolf appears again when, for a second time, he runs away from battle:

CAPTAIN Whither away, Sir John Fastolf, in such haste?
FASTOLF Whither away? To save myself by flight.
We are like to have the overthrow again.
CAPTAIN What, will you fly, and leave Lord Talbot?
FASTOLF Ay, all the Talbots in the world, to save my life.
    Exit
CAPTAIN Cowardly knight, ill fortune follow thee!

(3.5. 63–8)

Michael Hattaway suggested that the name Fastolf 'may have been punningly pronounced "Fast-off"';[21] George Walton Williams noticed the pun fifteen years earlier, but thought it either unintentional or non-existent.[22] If Hattaway is nearer the mark, then might Shakespeare have extended his pun to suggest gluttony (he is off his fast) as well as cowardice in the second tetralogy? Michael Taylor's observation that Fastolf has 'nothing in common' with 'the later and greater comic creation' seems overstated and rather odd since elsewhere Taylor acknowledges the 'self-preservation' of both figures.[23] If Fastolf's name might be considered a pun on moving quickly to save his own skin, it is plausible that Shakespeare should subsequently think of the pun in the sense of both Sir John Falstaff's cowardice and his gluttony (his 'fast' is always 'off'), making him a doubly dubious figure.

Delivering a letter to Gloucester from the Duke of Burgundy, Fastolf is confronted by Talbot – 'I vowed, base knight, when I did meet thee next, / To tear the Garter from thy craven's leg' and, explaining to those present how Fastolf fled from battle, Talbot denounces him as a 'dastard' and a coward (4.1.14–15, 19). Gloucester refers to Fastolf's running away as 'infamous' and especially heinous in a man of rank, with Talbot agreeing that he 'Doth but usurp the sacred name of knight, / Profaning this most honourable order' (4.1.30, 4.1.40–1) before Fastolf is denounced by the king:

Stain to thy countrymen, thou hear'st thy doom.
Be packing, therefore, thou that wast a knight.
Henceforth we banish thee on pain of death.

(4.1.45–7)

Talbot's denunciation of Fastolf as a coward stems from the historical Fastolf's behaviour during the Battle of Patay in June 1429 when, having made too far an advance, Fastolf was forced to retreat and Talbot was captured. In the chronicles of Edward Hall and Raphael Holinshed, Fastolf is praised for his bravery in the wars against the French before this incident, with Hall listing him amongst 'diverse other valiaunt knightes and esquiers', and he retained the respect and trust of John, Duke of Bedford, whose inquiry cleared him of cowardice.[24]

It is only in the second tetralogy that Shakespeare fully develops a link between cowardice and gluttony, although there is a link between Fastolf and food since the historical Fastolf commanded the convoy that brought supplies to English soldiers during the siege of Orléans. The French attempted to prevent the delivery of provisions to English soldiers but were defeated in what became known as The Battle of the Herrings, in which Fastolf used barrels of fish as a stockade.[25] Salted herring was a food with which any glutton who has 'addict[ed] themselves to sack' like Sir John (*2 Henry IV* 4.2.120–1) would be familiar since it was often sold in taverns, as was the 'pickled herring' consumed by Sir Toby Belch in *Twelfth Night* (1.5.116–17). There is also a link between the historical Fastolf and hunger since, in 1435, he advocated a scorched-earth policy (what he termed 'sharpe and cruelle war') along the borders of

20 William Shakespeare, *King Henry VI Part 1*, ed. Edward Burns, Arden Shakespeare (London, 2000), 112n31.

21 William Shakespeare, *The First Part of King Henry VI*, ed. Michael Hattaway, New Cambridge Shakespeare (Cambridge, 1990), 132n104.

22 George Walton Williams, 'Fastolf or Falstaff', *English Literary Renaissance* 5 (1975), 308–12; 311n9.

23 William Shakespeare, *Henry VI, Part One*, ed. Michael Taylor, Oxford Shakespeare (Oxford, 2003), 93, 180n106.

24 Edward Hall, *The Union of the Two Noble and Illustre Famefies of Lancastre [And] Yorke Beeyng Long in Continual Discension for the Croune of This Noble Realme ... Beginnyng at the Tyme of Kyng Henry the Fowerth, the First Aucthor of This Deuision, and so Successiuely Proceadyng to the Reigne of the High and Prudent Prince Kyng Henry the Eight ...*, STC 12721 (London, 1547), A6r; Williams, 'Fastolf or Falstaff', p. 308; G. L. Harriss, 'Fastolf, Sir John (1380–1459)', in *Dictionary of National Biography*, ed. H. C. G. Matthew, Brian Harrison and Lawrence Goldman (Oxford, 2004–13), n.p, https://doi.org/10.1093/ref:odnb/9199.

25 Harriss, 'Fastolf, Sir John (1380–1459)'.

Normandy in place of the siege warfare hitherto adopted by the English in France.[26] If Shakespeare was aware of this, it might well have triggered the connection he makes in the second tetralogy between Sir John and food.

Critics have claimed that Shakespeare's lampooning of the proto-Protestant martyr Oldcastle – which got him into so much trouble with Oldcastle's relatives and compelled him to change the name to Falstaff – may indicate Shakespeare's Catholic sympathies or his criticism of non-conforming Protestants.[27] Geoffrey Bullough pointed out that, in a book praising Oldcastle, John Bale reported the knight's repentance before the Archbishop of Canterbury 'that in my frail youth I offended the Lord, most grievously in pride, wrath and gluttony, in covetousness and in lechery', and so Shakespeare might have fixed upon this reference to gluttony, making it a dominant character trait.[28] But it is also possible that Shakespeare returned to the earlier play 1 Henry VI to reuse the name Fastolf and, upon doing so, decided that just as connections in the earlier play had been drawn between English bravery and hunger, so he might also make connections between English cowardice and gluttony, something perhaps suggested to him by the historical Fastolf's role in The Battle of the Herrings. 1 Henry VI was probably written by Thomas Nashe, Christopher Marlowe and another (as yet unknown) playwright around 1592, and later adapted by Shakespeare, sometime between 1592 and 1599, with the year 1595 being most likely.[29] In the early 1590s food was not especially scarce (as noted above, these years saw four good harvests), but when composing 1 Henry IV, and the figure of Oldcastle as a cowardly and gluttonous knight, in the late 1590s (the period that also saw Shakespeare change the name Oldcastle to Falstaff), the bad harvests of 1594 to 1597 inclusive, and the hunger and rebellion that accompanied them, would be fresh in many people's memories. It is around the time when England suffered significantly from hunger that a specifically gluttonous coward appears; no mention of cowardice is made by the historical Oldcastle in his confession, so it is likely the figure of Fastolf who suggested this aspect of the characterization to Shakespeare.

In 1 Henry VI, Talbot attacks the French when their guard is down, after they have 'all day caroused and banqueted' (2.1.12), and Charles and Joan are characterized as cowardly when Burgundy asserts that he has 'scared the Dauphin and his trull' (2.2.28). Although brave men in the play are not averse to food – as when Talbot asks the Countess of Auvergne for wine and cates, 'For soldiers' stomachs always serve them well' (2.3.80) – they eat moderately and only when the timing is right (the French having just fled). Returning to the first tetralogy appears to have focused Shakespeare's mind on the moral merits of a healthy hunger and its corollary: an unhealthy gluttony. Whether Shakespeare originally wrote parts of 1 Henry VI or was responsible for adapting an earlier play[30] is irrelevant to my argument that the first tetralogy and its treatment of appetite influenced Shakespeare in his portrayal of Sir John in the second tetralogy who, though an attractive figure at times, especially in the first half of 1 Henry IV, is ultimately a pathetic man made ill and morally corrupt by over-indulgence.

The historical Fastolf's role in the Battle of the Herrings makes for a curious connection between Shakespeare's delineation of Sir John in the second tetralogy and his earlier portrayal of Jack Cade. In 2 Henry VI, Dick the Butcher suggests Cade is so named for 'stealing a cade of herrings' (4.2.34–5), a 'cade' being a barrel containing 720 – later 500 – herring. In Lenten Stuffe (published in 1599), Thomas Nashe observes, 'The rebel Jacke Cade was the first, that devised to put redde herrings in cades, and from hym they have their name', but Nashe's work is ironic and the OED records use of the word to mean 'a barrel of herrings' prior to Cade's rebellion.[31] The herring–Cade–Nashe connection is of special interest because Nashe is widely accepted as one of the authors of 1 Henry VI, although he is thought to have written most of act 1, not act 4 where the reference to herring comes up.[32] Nashe is more usually noted for his praise of the play's presentation of 'brave Talbot (the terror of the French)' in Pierce Penniless,[33] which of

26 Harriss, 'Fastolf, Sir John (1380–1459)'.
27 Fitzpatrick, Food in Shakespeare, p. 20.
28 Geoffrey Bullough, Narrative and Dramatic Sources of Shakespeare, 8 vols., vol. 7: Major Tragedies: Hamlet; Othello; King Lear; Macbeth (London, 1973), pp. 169–70; Fitzpatrick, Food in Shakespeare, p. 20.
29 Gary Taylor and Rory Loughnane, 'The canon and chronology of Shakespeare's works', in The New Oxford Shakespeare Authorship Companion, ed. Taylor and Egan, pp. 417–602; 513–17.
30 Taylor and Loughnane, 'The canon and chronology', pp. 516–17.
31 Thomas Nashe, The Works, ed. Ronald B. McKerrow, 5 vols. (Oxford, 1904), vol. 3, p. 221; Joan Fitzpatrick, Shakespeare and the Language of Food: A Dictionary, Continuum Shakespeare Dictionaries (London, 2010), 'herring'; OED Online, 'cade n.1 2'.
32 Taylor and Loughnane, 'The canon and chronology', pp. 513–14.
33 Thomas Nashe, The Works, ed. Ronald B. McKerrow, 5 vols. (Oxford, 1904), vol. 1, p. 212.

course was self-praise. More relevant to Shakespeare's characterization of Sir John in the second tetralogy might be the links that emerge between Cade, dishonourable conduct and gluttony.

In *2 Henry VI*, Jack Cade ('that coistrel', 3.1. 381) promises excess, urging his followers 'Be brave, then, for your captain is brave and vows reformation' (4.2.66–7). His vision of revolution consists of a land of plenty: 'There shall be in England seven halfpenny loaves sold for a penny, the three-hooped pot shall have ten hoops, and I will make it felony to drink small beer' (4.2.67–9). He promises, moreover, that 'there shall be no money / All shall eat and drink on my score' (4.2.74–5) and that 'the Pissing Conduit will run nothing but claret wine this first year of our reign' (4.6.3–4). As Ellen C. Caldwell observed, Cade's promise that the Pissing Conduit – a place from where the lower classes drew water – will run with wine strikes most critics as ludicrous.[34] For example, Eklund, whilst acknowledging that Cade's proposal to have the conduit run with wine should be read in the context of the hungry poor, inviting 'contemplation of a system where food and drink are, like water, a kind of public commons', nevertheless described it as a 'laughable programme'.[35]

Yet, as Caldwell noted, 'it was customary for the city of London to celebrate the coronations and victories of kings and queens by staging pageants at the conduits and having those conduits run wine'.[36] She added that 'the demand for wine itself is unusual only in the length of time and for whom it should flow, an exaggeration that underscores rather than undercuts the seriousness of the proposal', so that, by proclaiming himself king, 'Cade arrogates to himself the traditional ceremonies of accession.'[37] Chris Fitter thought that Caldwell underplayed the comic potential of Cade's exaggeration,[38] but her point nevertheless makes his promise of wine instead of water less ludicrous than it might at first appear, although the early audience would have understood it as gluttonous, with a possible nod towards Catholic transubstantiation (water into wine), which would be in keeping with Cade's medieval origins.

The Cade scenes are darkly comic – and there are moments when his proclamations are contradictory, such as 'all the realm shall be in common ... when I am king' (4.2.70–1) – but he is not merely a fool. For Roger Warren, the laughter in these scenes is not necessarily carnivalesque and we should not assume that the comments made by his fellow rebels are mocking asides heard only by the audience. Rather, the comments made following Cade's claim to be a Mortimer

might well be 'overt, mocking statements, heard and relished by all'.[39]

Before the audience encounter Cade, York characterizes him as a brave fighter:

> In Ireland have I seen this stubborn Cade
> Oppose himself against a troop of kerns,
> And fought so long till that his thighs with darts
> Were almost like a sharp-quilled porcupine;
>
> (3.1.360–3)

Cade is a shape-shifter, not only fighting the Irish enemy but passing himself off as 'a shag-haired crafty kern' (3.1.367) (a 'kern' was an Irish footsoldier) in order to move amongst them and act as an informant for York. Cade's impersonation of the dead Sir John Mortimer, whom he resembles (3.1.358–9), similarly enables York to 'perceive the commons' mind, / How they affect the house and claim of York' (3.1.374–5). Although York describes Cade as brave and loyal – 'I know no pain they can inflict upon him / Will make him say I moved him to those arms' (3.1.377–8) – we witness mainly rabble-rousing and bullying. In Hall's *Chronicle*, as Geoffrey Bullough pointed out, during his rebellion Cade was in control of his men, at least at first, and engaged reasonably with representatives sent from the king. Hall notes 'These lordes found him sober in communicacion, [and] wyse in disputyng', although 'arrogant in hart and styfe [stiff] in his opinion', and Cade prohibited 'to all men, Murder, Rape, or Robbery'.[40] As with Sir John Oldcastle, the dramatic character exhibits characteristics not evident in the historical figure upon whom he is based. In *2 Henry VI*, the characterization of Cade as bravely loyal and also a rebel might be explained by the presence of more than one hand in the play.[41] Yet the

---

34 Ellen C. Caldwell, 'Jack Cade and Shakespeare's *Henry VI, Part 2*', *Studies in Philology* 92 (1995), 18–79; p. 52.

35 Hillary Eklund, Revolting Diets: Jack Cade's "Sallet" and the politics of hunger in *2 Henry VI*, *Shakespeare Studies* 42 (2014), 51–62; pp. 58, 57.

36 Caldwell, 'Jack Cade and Shakespeare's *Henry VI, Part 2*', p. 53.

37 Caldwell, 'Jack Cade and Shakespeare's *Henry VI, Part 2*', p. 54.

38 Chris Fitter, '"Your captain is brave and vows reformation": Jack Cade, the Hacket Rising, and Shakespeare's vision of popular rebellion in *2 Henry VI*, *Shakespeare Studies* 32 (2004), 173–219; p. 176.

39 William Shakespeare, *Henry VI, Part Two*, ed. Roger Warren, Oxford Shakespeare (Oxford, 2003), p. 52.

40 Hall, *The Union of the Two Noble and Illustre Families of Lancastre [And] Yorke*, m5v; Bullough, *Narrative and Dramatic Sources of Shakespeare*, vol. 3: *Earlier English History Plays: Henry VI [Parts 1–3]; Richard III; Richard II* (London, 1960), pp. 96, 115.

41 Taylor and Loughnane, 'The canon and chronology', pp. 493–6.

apparently contradictory characterization of Cade across the rebellion scenes might well be deliberate. Although it is beneficial to York and the English forces in Ireland that Cade can retrieve information from the enemy, his bravery is undercut rather by the ease with which he can so easily impersonate an Irish rebel and, later, a man of rank (Mortimer), suggesting that duplicity comes easily to him.

The excess promised by Cade to his followers is prefigured in an earlier scene, when the apprentice armourer Peter Thump fights with his master Horner, whom Thump has accused of treason. Horner is already drunk and continues to accept a range of strong drinks from his neighbours: the wines charneco and sack, and 'a pot of good double beer' (2.3.64–5). Double beer was especially strong, unlike weak small beer, and in Holinshed's *Chronicles* the selling of strong beer in England's weekly markets is condemned as especially harmful:

there is such headie ale & béere in most of them, as for the mightinesse thereof among such as séeke it out, is commonlie called huffecap, the mad dog, father whoresonne, angels food, dragons milke, go by the wall, stride wide, and list leg, &c. And this is more to be noted, that when one of late fell by Gods providence into a troubled co[n]science, after he had considered well of his reachlesse [reckless] life, and dangerous estate: another thinking belike to change his colour and not his mind, caried him straightwaie to the strongest ale, as to the next physician.[42]

In the anonymous play *The Life and Death of Jack Straw*, identified by Bullough as an analogue to *2 Henry VI*,[43] one of the rebels, Tom Miller, claims that Parson Ball, the radical priest and fellow rebel, is given to drunkenness: 'Find him in a pulpit but twise in the yeare, / And Ile find him fortie times in the ale-house tasting stronge beare'. Later in the play, Miller announces himself a regular consumer of strong ale.[44] In *2 Henry VI*, Thump refuses all offers of drink, and wins the fight with his master, Horner, even though Horner is skilled at fencing. Having been defeated, Horner admits his treason; the drunkard who drinks to excess is thus shown to be ignoble. It is possible that just as he returned to the cowardly Fastolf to develop the figure of Sir John in the second tetralogy, Shakespeare also returned to this scene (whether or not he actually wrote it), to develop the concept of the dishonourable man of high rank who drinks sack to excess and is exposed as an immoral fraud. Ronald Knowles characterized the Thump–Miller scene as 'a burlesquing of the chivalric code',[45] something Shakespeare will develop more fully, via the figure of Sir John, in the second tetralogy.

Although, at the height of his power, Jack Cade, accompanied by Dick the Butcher amongst others, promises abundant food and drink, he is ultimately driven to forage for food in the garden of Alexander Iden, whose name may pun on the biblical Eden (and is spelt as Eden in Holinshed). That the historical Cade was found lurking in the garden of Eden allows the drama to develop in the spirit of the medieval, allegorical tradition of Langland's *Piers Plowman*. Before encountering Cade, Iden asks 'who would live turmoiled in the court / And may enjoy such quiet walks as these?' (4.9.16–17), only to have his beloved idyll destroyed by Cade's sinister presence. Earlier in the play, York praised Cade as a 'devil' (3.1.371), something picked up in a rather subtle way later when Cade claims his followers will 'worship me their lord' (4.2.77). Remarking upon the irrelevance of his modest ancestry, he observes 'And Adam was a gardener' (4.2.133), alluding to the proverbial question 'When Adam delved and Eve span who was then a gentleman?', used also by the rebel priest John Ball and recorded in Holinshed's *Chronicles* and in *The Life and Death of Jack Straw*.[46] As William Montgomery observed, when Cade proclaims 'our enemies shall fall before us' (4.2.36), he 'may be punning implicitly on his name and the Latin verb *cadō, cadere*, meaning *fall*'.[47] Like Satan, the first rebel, who encouraged Eve to eat the forbidden fruit that brought about the Fall of humankind, Cade promises his followers transformation by consumption, but his promises prove to be empty.

In his fight with Alexander Iden, Cade threatens to 'cut ... out the burly-boned clown in chines of beef' (4.9.57). It is fitting that the famished Kentish man should, in the county long termed the garden of

[42] Holinshed, *[Holinshed's Chronicles] The First and Second Volume of Chronicles*, vol. 1: *The Description of Britaine; The Description of England; The Historie of England*, S4v.

[43] Bullough, *Narrative and Dramatic Sources of Shakespeare*, vol. 3: *Earlier English History Plays*, pp. 138–50.

[44] Anon, *[Jack Straw] The Life and Death of Jacke Straw, a Notable Rebell in England: Who Was Kild in Smithfield By the Lord Major of London*, STC 23356 (London, 1593), A4r, D4r. *The Life and Death of Jacke Straw* was first published in 1593, a year before *2 Henry VI*, and both plays were probably first performed in 1591.

[45] William Shakespeare, *King Henry VI Part 2*, ed. Ronald Knowles, Arden Shakespeare (London, 1999), p. 88.

[46] Bullough, *Narrative and Dramatic Sources of Shakespeare*, vol. 3: *Earlier English History Plays*, p. 133; Anon, *[Jack Straw] The Life and Death of Jacke Straw*, A4r.

[47] Stanley Wells, Gary Taylor, John Jowett and William Montgomery, *William Shakespeare: A Textual Companion* (Oxford, 1987), p. 188.

England, imagine a specifically English foodstuff; the dietary author Andrew Boorde considered beef 'good meat for an Englishman', observing that young, salted beef from the male animal 'doth make an Englishman strong'.[48] Yet the focus here is not physical strength but moral degeneracy. Where, in *1 Henry VI*, Talbot and his men are described as 'Lean raw-boned rascals' full of 'courage and audacity' (1.3.14–15), their 'productive hunger' making them good soldiers, Cade's gesture towards cannibalism (Iden's flesh is imagined as a 'chine' or joint of meat) is part of a wider confluence between savagery and unnatural consumption in the first tetralogy.[49] There is a clear sense that war drives men to savagery and, in some cases, acts of cannibalism such as those reported from the wars in Ireland, perhaps gesturing to Cade's role in the Irish wars, when he is said to have both fought the kerns and disguised himself as a kern (*2 Henry VI* 3.1.360–1, 367–8). In *Sundrie New and Artificiall Remedies against Famine*, Hugh Platt suggests 'Certaine strange and extraordinarie waies for the relieuing of a prisoner, or other poore distressed creatures, when al hope of usual victual is taken from him', one of which is that 'a man may liue 10. or 12. daies by sucking of his owne bloud'.[50] During such desperate times, consuming the blood or flesh of another might well be a logical next step. It is perhaps unsurprising that the famished Cade should hint at cannibalism, a nod towards the Catholic transubstantiation suggested in his earlier promise to transform water into wine.

In Iden's garden, Cade puns on the word 'sallet' as a foodstuff (our modern 'salad') and a soldier's helmet: 'many a time, but for a sallet, my brain-pan had been cleft with a brown bill; and many a time, when I have been dry, and bravely marching, it hath served me instead of a quart pot to drink in' (4.9.10–14). Cade thus reminds the audience that he is a former soldier (a 'brave' one at that), which Fitter thought 'would bond Cade to many in his commons audience' – specifically, those veterans who remained unpaid by the Queen for their services – allowing for what Eklund characterized as a broadening of 'the commensality of hunger beyond his own criminally-induced starvation'.[51] As Fitter noted, there is nothing in the chronicle sources to suggest Cade was famished at the time of his death. He argued that Cade's hunger and the 'heavy-handed proprietorial aggression' of Iden works to encourage audience sympathy: 'a small, starved, undaunted man, he is done to death by a huge, unpitying, well-fed one'.[52] It is a convincing point, yet the heavily allegorical nature of the scene in Iden's garden arguably also encourages the audience to regard Cade as a symbol of vice that must be banished, just like the gluttonous Sir John in the closing scenes of *2 Henry IV*. As in *1 Henry VI*, where Talbot and his men stand for productive hunger, Shakespeare is here too apparently invoking the concept of hunger as a means of moral correction. It is an aspect of spiritual instruction rooted in England's medieval past, and evident in Langland's *Piers Plowman*, rather than an early modern culture that sought to distance itself from monastic self-denial.

Discussing the absence of any scenes featuring the lower orders in *1 Henry VI*, Michael Taylor observed how, in *2 Henry VI*, 'Cade's comic cruelty anticipates the superbly balanced tavern scenes in the two parts of *Henry IV* where the comedy only thinly camouflages a sinister nihilism.'[53] The Cade rebellion scenes might also have prompted Shakespeare to draw a connection between dishonourable conduct in war and gluttony when developing the character of Sir John in the second tetralogy. This is especially pertinent given the historical Fastolf's connections with food and hunger: commanding the convoy that brought supplies to English soldiers during the Battle of the Herrings and urging a scorched earth policy in the French wars, the same policy that would be made use of in Ireland where Cade has served York. In *1 Henry VI* valiant English soldiers are hungry where the duplicitous French, advantaged by the witchcraft of Joan La Pucelle, are given to excess, and in *2 Henry VI* a sober Horner defeats his gluttonous, dishonest, master. Before his death, Cade proclaims: 'Tell Kent from me she hath lost her best man, and exhort all the world to be cowards. For I, that never feared any, am vanquished by famine, not by valour' (4.9.72–5). The same cynicism towards honour will be expressed by Sir John in his 'catechism' in *1 Henry IV* – 'Can honour set-to a leg? No... Honour is a mere scutcheon' (5.1.131–2, 140) – and his exhortation that others (his imagined 'thousand sons', humanity as

[48] Fitzpatrick, *Three Sixteenth-Century Dietaries*, p. 185.
[49] For example, the references to drinking blood in the Temple Garden scene (*1 Henry VI* 2.4.108, 134); the characterization of Suffolk as a cannibal who has 'overgorged' on the heart of his mother, England (*2 Henry VI* 4.1.85); and Margaret's description of her son's murderers as 'Butchers and villains! Bloody cannibals!' (*3 Henry VI* 5.5.60).
[50] Platt, *Sundrie New and Artificiall Remedies against Famine*, B1r.
[51] Fitter, '"Your captain is brave and vows reformation"', p. 207; Eklund, 'Revolting diets', p. 59.
[52] Fitter, '"Your captain is brave and vows reformation"', pp. 208, 210, 211.
[53] Shakespeare, *Henry VI, Part One*, ed. Taylor, p. 62.

a whole) should 'addict themselves to sack' (4.2.118–20). Neither Cade nor Sir John repent their wicked ways, and in this they resemble the idle commons in Langland's poem who suffer punishment as a consequence of their sinful recidivism. As in the earlier poem, the wider social, political and national good is at stake, since vice – in the shape of rebellion against or corruption of a leader – cannot be tolerated.

Unlike Sir John, Cade is not a glutton, although by promising his followers an unlimited supply of bread and strong drink he appeals to their impulse towards gluttony. Instead, he suffers hunger, recalling Langland's use of Hunger in *Piers Plowman* as a means to punish wrong-doing. Shakespeare's comic actor Will Kempe would likely have performed the role of Falstaff in the second tetralogy, and if Kempe also played the part of Cade, drawing upon his skills as a Morris dancer (as suggested by Richard Helgerson), as well as his talent for comedy,[54] then a connection between Sir John Falstaff and Jack Cade emerges, part of a larger connection between the first and second tetralogy – one that is predicated on war, hunger and gluttony and clearly indebted to the medieval penitential tradition.

---

[54] Shakespeare, *King Henry VI Part 2*, ed. Knowles, pp. 65–6; Richard Helgerson, *Forms of Nationhood: The Elizabethan Writing of England* (Chicago, 1992), p. 216.

SOME DEEPER THING: VISUALIZING COMPLEXITY IN *HAMLET* THROUGH THE PYRRHUS SPEECH

ROCCO CORONATO

BEHIND THE ARRAS: A DIVE INTO MULTIDIMENSIONALITY

After delivering a concise rendition of 'To be or not to be' in the First Quarto (1603), Hamlet resumes his role as the ever-delaying revenger with a remarkable declaration: 'Let me alone / To find the depth of this' (Q1 7.204–5). He also promises to uncover '[s]ome deeper thing' (Q1 7.200).[1] Some deeper things do impact a crucial aspect of the tragedy – the interplay between acting and hesitation. This becomes more apparent when examining the relationships of *Hamlet* to its major sources, Saxo Gramaticus's *Historia Danorum* and François de Belleforest's *Histoires tragiques*, individually in its three texts: Q1 from 1603, Q2 from 1604–1605, and F from 1623. Q1 aligns more closely with Saxo's densely paced sequence of actions, while both Q2 and F expand on hesitation and the disconcerting association with melancholy that Belleforest had already magnified.[2] Hesitation in *Hamlet* emanates from this 'depth'.

Hamlet encompasses a tightly woven textual sequence that, despite its hyperbolic nature, provides a means to explore its depth: the Pyrrhus Speech.[3] The story of Pyrrhus, Achilles' vengeful son who ruthlessly murders Priam during the fall of Troy, had been extensively depicted in ancient, medieval and Renaissance literature and art. All three texts of *Hamlet* commence with Pyrrhus mercilessly slaughtering Greeks, proceed with his savage killing of Priam, and culminate in the spectacle of a distraught Hecuba vainly crying out to the heavens for mercy. Only Q2 and F include an intermediate section where Pyrrhus momentarily pauses (Q2 2.2.412–20; F 2.2.470–8). Following this brief intermission, he returns to violence and slays Priam.

I aim to utilize the Pyrrhus Speech as a significant entry point into the 'deeper things' of hesitation and action in *Hamlet*. This approach involves a distinct form of interpretation, focused on multiplicity and its visualization – an interweaving similar to the way the Troy story appeared in the popular late fifteenth-century Franco-Flemish tapestries originally sold by Pasquier Granier and later by his son Jean.[4] In these tapestries, various subplots are 'carefully interwoven, with extra figures and linking movement from one to the other'.[5] A richly storied sequence of events thus unfolds,

---

[1] Quotations from the three texts of Hamlet are parenthetically inserted in the text and are sourced from William Shakespeare, *Hamlet*, ed. Ann Thompson and Neil Taylor, Arden Shakespeare (London, 2007), for the second Quarto (Q2); and from *Hamlet: The Texts of 1603 and 1623*, ed. Ann Thompson and Neil Taylor, Arden Shakespeare (London, 2007), for the First Quarto (Q1) and the Folio (F).

[2] While it is beyond the scope of this discussion to take a stance on the status of Q1 – whether it is a partially memorial reconstruction, a germinal text, an authorial first version or a version edited for performance – from the perspective of revenge and hesitation, Q1 provides little hindrance to the enactment of revenge aside from the conventional delays that obstruct the revenger. On the other hand, Q2 and F significantly delve into a deeper and more introspective hesitation, characterized by an internal state of pause that entails suspension and the consideration of all options. This expanded treatment of hesitation is not surprising for a more philosophical rendition of the story to be staged at the two universities, as also indicated by the frontispiece of Q1. See *Shakespeare and the First Hamlet*, ed. T. Bourus (New York, 2022).

[3] Q1 7.342–50, 354–9,366–75; Q2 2.2.388–402, 406–35, 443–56; F 2.2.449–61, 464–93, 501–14.

[4] The story of Troy was the most popular secular object in late medieval tapestries. For further insights, see Scot McKendrick, 'The great history of Troy: a reassessment of the development of a secular theme in late medieval art', *Journal of the Warburg and Courtauld Institutes* 54 (1991), 43–82. An idea of the grandeur of these tapestries can be gleaned from the surviving arras at the Cathedral of Zamora in Spain. From the late fifteenth century to the sixteenth century, these tapestries enjoyed widespread popularity across the courts of Europe, including England.

[5] McKendrick, 'The great history of Troy', 77.

featuring Pyrrhus as a central figure. Juxtaposed nearly simultaneously, the scenes seamlessly progress from left to right: on the left, Pyrrhus enters the Temple of Apollo, raising his sword towards Priam, who clings to a pillar in desperation; in the centre, the raving Hecuba attempts to bite a Greek's ear as she watches Pyrrhus preparing to behead her daughter Polyxena, who kneels on Achilles' tomb on the right.

Shakespeare appeared to be well acquainted with the multiple organization of Troy-themed tapestries. The distressed Lucrece temporarily finds solace by gazing at a 'piece / Of skilful painting' on the Fall of Troy, characterized by 'a press of gaping faces'.[6] Tapestries served as helpful reminders of an era where intertextuality relied heavily not only on reading but also on what Lyne calls the interplay between implicit and explicit poetic memory.[7] Moreover, early modern sources often offered themselves in a textual tapestry, rather than as separate entities. There was no single compelling Elizabethan translation of the *Aeneid* in Shakespeare's time; instead, many relevant passages were found in florilegia and commonplace books, which early modern authors, including Shakespeare, frequently used as handy substitutes for the actual texts.[8] In the case of the Pyrrhus Speech, my favourite contender for the catalyst behind Shakespeare's passage is the *Symbolarum libri XVII* (1599), an extensive commentary on the *Aeneid* by the Jesuit Jacobus Pontanus (Jakob Spanmueller, 'the bridge-maker'), which was also used by Ben Jonson (a probable source of books for Shakespeare).[9]

The Pyrrhus Speech is frequently interpreted in a linear fashion as a parody of both Marlowe's and Edward Alleyn's style, while also echoing a past tradition of action and rhetoric that Hamlet fails to replicate.[10] However, there appears to be an unusual amalgamation of parody, pastiche and homage, raising questions about the unidirectional intentions.[11] Alongside the themes of action, revenge and inaction, the Pyrrhus Speech, particularly in Q2–F, contains contradictory and open-ended resonances that challenge the image of *the* source and instead suggest a new perspective based on multiplicity.

Recent approaches to Shakespeare have emphasized the importance of exploring 'endlessly complex, multilayered fields of interpretation'.[12] It is not merely the recognition of new sources, particularly new forms of the source, that is essential for a fresh and 'sustainable' source study, as argued by Newcomb.[13] The utilization of sources is a process that involves originality and complexity, rather than a linear operation. Shakespeare often engages in what Kerrigan punningly terms 'original-ity,

a drawing upon originals', enabling a means of going back to origins while also being generative.[14] The interplay between similarity and difference is also significant. Belsey has observed that a source becomes a source precisely due to its divergence from Shakespeare's texts, despite their resemblance; it is through the contrast with the sources that we see Shakespeare at work.[15]

The 'deeper things' that I aim to demonstrate in *Hamlet* are rooted in the inherent multiplicity of Shakespeare's work.[16] Mapping these multiple and often contradictory connections necessitates a different approach. Instead of the source, Drakakis intriguingly puts forth the concept of the resource, which relies on a 'complex interweaving of texts' and unravels a 'complex web of representations'.[17] It is this intricate web that I strive to identify and visualize.

---

[6] William Shakespeare, *The Rape of Lucrece*, in *Complete Sonnets and Poems*, ed. Colin Burrow (Oxford, 2002), p. 1408. An identical *descriptio* of the war of Troy arrests Aeneas' attention when looking at the decorated walls of Dido's palace (Virgil, *Aeneid* I.455–93).

[7] See Raphael Lyne, 'Moving between sources: Ovid and Erasmus in Shakespeare's Sonnets', in *Memory and Intertextuality in Renaissance Literature* (Cambridge, 2016), 76–112. On the interplay between orality and print culture, see Jennifer Richards, *Voices and Books in the English Renaissance: A New History of Reading* (Oxford, 2019).

[8] See Charles Martindale, 'Shakespeare and Virgil', in *Shakespeare and the Classics*, ed. Charles Martindale and A. B. Taylor (Cambridge, 2004), pp. 93, 100; David Scott Wilson-Okamura, *Virgil in the Renaissance* (Cambridge, 2010), p. 199.

[9] On Jonson's copy at Cambridge University Library, see David McPherson, 'Ben Jonson's library and marginalia; an annotated catalogue', *Studies in Philology* 71 (1974), 96.

[10] See Jonathan Bate, *The Genius of Shakespeare* (Oxford, 1997), p. 128; Andrew Hiscock, '"What's Hecuba to him … ": Trojan horses and rhetorical selves in Shakespeare's Hamlet', in *Fantasies of Troy: Classical Tales and the Social Imaginary in Medieval and Early Modern Europe*, ed. Alan Shepard and Stephen D. Powell (Toronto, 2004), 161–75.

[11] R. S. Miola already recognized underneath the passage a multiple range of references – 'Aeneas and Hamlet', *Comparative and Modern Literature* 8 (1988), p. 278.

[12] Stephen Lynch, *Shakespearean Intertextuality: Studies in Selected Sources and Plays* (Westport and London, 1998), p. 2.

[13] L. H. Newcomb, 'Toward a sustainable source study', in *Rethinking Shakespeare Source Study: Audiences, Authors, and Digital Technologies*, ed. D. A. Britton and M. Walter (New York and London, 2018), 19–45.

[14] John Kerrigan, *Shakespeare's Originality* (Oxford, 2018), p. 2.

[15] Catherine Belsey, 'The elephants' graveyard revisited: Shakespeare at work in *Antony and Cleopatra*, *Romeo and Juliet* and *All's Well That Ends Well*', in *Shakespeare Survey 68* (Cambridge, 2015), 62–72.

[16] Brian Gibbons, *Shakespeare and Multiplicity* (Cambridge, 1993).

[17] John Drakakis, *Shakespeare's Resources* (Manchester, 2021), pp. 187, 188.

I will compare the various components of the Pyrrhus Speech, particularly in Q2–F, as a key that can unlock the deep receding structures of action and hesitation. Through a counterpoint between Hamlet and Pyrrhus, I will begin with the most basic and apparent strand of the story: Pyrrhus representing impulsive action and revenge, and Priam embodying helplessness and pity, which form the initial deep structure. Each subsequent level of depth is characterized by the infiltration of an embedded character, either directly quoted in *Hamlet* (Hecuba) or present in the sources (Polyxena and Aeneas). This progression reveals a succession of receding depths:

1. *couple*: opposition between Pyrrhus and Priam (action/inaction)
2. *emergence*: the embedded Hecuba (madness)
3. *interference*: Polyxena (pause and suspension)
4. *synthesis*: Aeneas (pause, deliberation and action)

My intention is to propose how multidimensionality can be visualized in literary texts and how we can grasp the deeply multilayered nature of early modern texts through their networks of resonances. The Pyrrhus Speech exhibits a rich texture that somehow aligns with Riemann's notion of the manifold (*Mannigfaltigkeit*): continuous manifolds are developed from points and allow for a continuous transition from one to another of these specializations.[18] In essence, what I aim to do is explore the concept of the *pli*, the fold that Deleuze so astutely identified in the Baroque age, which bends and rebends the folds, pushes them to infinity, fold upon fold, fold according to fold.[19] Unravelling these folds calls for a different approach: complexity emerges as an apt term to describe these intricate, open-ended structures of thought. In due course, I will present a few principles of literary complexity as they can be discerned in *Hamlet* through the lens of the Pyrrhus Speech.

THE COUPLE (PYRRHUS AND PRIAM)

During the Middle Ages, the dissemination of the Trojan story primarily occurred through non-Homeric narratives in Latin and vernacular languages.[20] The absence of the Homeric poems until at least the Renaissance (with the first edition being published in Florence in 1488) and the presence of numerous questionable editions of Virgil meant that the Trojan tradition relied heavily on the apocryphal books of Dares the Phrygian and Dictys of Crete. These works portrayed themselves as fictional eyewitness accounts of the fall of Troy (both Latin works were likely based on lost Greek texts). Despite Troy not being an empire, it became the model for imperial ideals in many European traditions. In their own *translatio imperii*, the Elizabethans exhibited exceptional and lasting interest in the Trojan legend, appropriating it to legitimize royal power and national identity, particularly during times of entrenched controversy.[21] The first English printed text (though not printed in England) was *The Recueil of the Histories of Troie* (1473–1474), which was an English translation by Caxton of Raoul Lefèvre's *Recoeil des histoires de Troyes*. The popularity of the Trojan cycle was also evident in drama. *Hamlet* was preceded by several plays centred around the Trojan theme.[22] Within the Trojan story, the tale of Dido and Aeneas, also present in Ovid (*Heroides* 7), was highly favoured in England. Chaucer mentions it as a canonical story in the *House of Fame*, when the dreamer narrator reads about the fall of Troy and Aeneas' journey 'writen on a table of bras' in Venus' temple.[23]

Yet Pyrrhus played a marginal role in this tradition. Homer mentions him only once in passing, during Achilles' speech on the death of Patroclus (*Iliad* 19.326–33). The name Pyrrhus, which means 'flame-coloured' or 'red-headed', evokes the symbolism of fire

---

[18] Becky Vartabedian, *Multiplicity and Ontology in Deleuze and Badiou* (London, 2018), pp. 57–60.

[19] Gilles Deleuze, *Le pli. Leibniz et le baroque* (Paris, 1988), p. 5.

[20] Marilyn Desmond, 'Trojan itineraries and the matter of Troy', in *The Oxford History of Classical Reception in English Literature, I (800–1558)*, ed. Rita Copeland (Oxford, 2016), 251–68.

[21] See Heather James, 'Shakespeare and the Troy legend', in *Shakespeare's Troy: Drama, Politics, and the Translation of Empire* (Cambridge, 1997), 7–41; Sylvia Federico, 'Late-fourteenth-century London as the new Troy', in *New Troy: Fantasies of Empire in the Late Middle Ages* (London and Minneapolis, 2003), 1–28.

[22] A production of *Troilus and Pandarus* was staged at court on 5 January 1517. Other plays based on the Trojan war included Thomas Heywood's *Iron Age* (Part I, written after 1593, printed in 1632), a Troy play performed at the Rose Theatre in 1596, and the popular tragicomedy *The Siege of Troy*. According to Henslowe's Diary, a payment was made to Ben Jonson on 3 December 1597, for a plot related to Troy. Additionally, there were plays centred around Dido, such as performances at Cambridge in 1564 and at Oxford in 1583. In 1598–1599, Dekker and Chettle produced a series of Dido plays. See Władysław Witalisz, 'The literary transmission of Troy', in *The Trojan Mirror: Middle English Narratives of Troy as Books of Princely Advice* (Frankfurt am Main, 2011), 37–73.

[23] Geoffrey Chaucer, *The House of Fame*, in *The Riverside Chaucer*, ed. Larry Benson (Oxford, 2008), l.142.

and its destructive power. In Shakespeare's era, the orange or yellow hue associated with a fiery complexion still denoted a choleric temperament.[24] This thematic association connects Pyrrhus with the fire that ultimately razes Troy.[25] The description of Pyrrhus as 'burning' ('ardens', *Aeneid* II.529) also links him to passionate and vehement speech, a characteristic Aristotle attributes to youthful lack of self-control (*Rhetoric* II.12). The association with choler or anger persisted in Pyrrhus' descendants as well. Plutarch recounts how Neoptolemus, Pyrrhus' son, conquered Epirus and established a dynasty of kings known as the Pyrrides. Among them, Pyrrhus, the author of the infamous victory, was notorious for his volatile temperament: he was described as being ready to turn 'all on a fire with choller, and his face al bloody and terrible to behold'.[26]

Signs of this hyperbolic inflamed action are evident in the first part of the speech concerning the 'rugged Pyrrhus', and in the second part regarding Priam's futile resistance. The two passages remain nearly identical in all the three texts of *Hamlet*:

> The rugged Pyrrhus, he whose sable arms,
> Black as his purpose, did the night resemble
> When he lay couced in th'ominous horse,
> Hath now this dread and black complexion smeared
> With heraldry more dismal, head to foot.
> Now he is total gules, horridly tricked
> With blood of fathers, mothers, daughters, sons,
> Baked and impasted with the parching streets
> That lend a tyrannous and a damned light
> To their lord's murder; roasted in wrath and fire,
> And thus o'ersized with coagulate gore,
> With eyes like carbuncles, the hellish Pyrrhus
> Old grandsire Priam seeks
> (Q2 2.2.390–402; cf. Q1 7.342–50, F 2.2.449–61)

> Anon he finds him
> Striking too short at Greeks. His antique sword,
> Rebellious to his arm, lies where it falls,
> Repugnant to command. Unequal matched,
> Pyrrhus at Priam drives, in rage strikes wide,
> But with the whiff and wind of his fell sword
> Th'unnerved father falls.
> (Q2 2.2.406–12; cf. Q1 7.354–9, F 2.2.464–709)

Other instances of this fundamental opposition are scattered throughout the text. The realm of *action* finds embodiment in references to King Hamlet's fiery rage and prowess in combat (1.1.46, 1.1.61–2, 1.1.1143, 1.2.199), the impulsive nature of young figures like Fortinbras and Laertes (and even Hamlet himself, previously described as a 'toy in blood' before his mourning,

1.3.6). On the other hand, *inaction* characterizes the older fathers (1.2.29, 2.2.65, 2.2.194–201), as well as the present Hamlet, burdened by grief (1.2.66–133). Unlike Pyrrhus, Hamlet does not seem prone to 'splenative rash' actions (Q2 5.1.250). He is plagued by a 'brainish apprehension' (Q2 4.1.11) and remains 'unpregnant' of his cause (Q2 2.2.503).

The couple *action/inaction* is also reflected in the sources. The Pyrrhus Speech clearly draws from Aeneas' tale to Dido in the *Aeneid* (II.438–558), which focuses on the wrathful Pyrrhus, and the aged, pitiful Priam futilely attempting to wield his arms.[27] Hecuba tries to dissuade the king from fighting, while he stands by the altar, vainly engaged in combat (a detail retained by Shakespeare).[28] Pyrrhus violently plunges his sword into Priam,[29] who meets his end within the *sancta sanctorum* of Troy. A coruscated, resplendent Pyrrhus emerges triumphant, adorned in gleaming armour and a burnished brass helmet,[30] a chromatic detail that Shakespeare shifts to when Pyrrhus enters Troy in 'a tyrannous and a damned light' (Q2 2.2.398; F 2.2.457).[31] Virgil's Pyrrhus assumes a symbolic role as a reborn Achilles (*rediuiuus*), embodying a malevolent bestial nature. For Elizabethan readers, Virgil

---

24 Gail Kern Paster, *Humoring the Body: Emotions and the Shakespearean Stage* (Chicago and London, 2004), pp. 35, 37.

25 James J. O'Hara, *True Names: Virgil and the Alexandrian Tradition of Etymological Wordplay* (Ann Arbor, 1996), p. 106.

26 Plutarch, 'The life of Pyrrhus', in *The Lives of the Noble Grecians and Romanes, compared together by that grave learned philosopher and historiographer, Plutarke of Chaeronea* (London, 1595), pp. 422, 438.

27 '[A]rma diu senior desueta trementibus aevo, / circumdat nequiquam umeris et inutile ferrum / cingitur ac densos fertur moriturus in hostis', *Aeneid* II.509–11; 'the aged King did bind / his rusted armor to his trembling thews, – / all vainly, – and a useless blade of steel / he girded on; then charged, resolved to die encircled by the foe'. Translations are from Virgil, *Aeneid*, trans. Theodore C. Williams (Boston, 1910).

28 '[S]enior telumque imbelle sine ictu / coniecit, rauco quod protinus aere repulsum / et summon clipei neiquiquam umbon pependit' (II.544–6); 'the aged warrior hurled with nerveless arm / his ineffectual spear, which hoarsely rang / rebounding on the brazen shield, and hung / piercing the midmost boss, – but all in vain'.

29 '[D]extraque coruscum / extulit ac lateri capulo tenus abdidit ensem' (II. 552–3); 'a glittering sword / his right hand lifted high, and buried it / far as the hilt in that defenceless heart'.

30 'Vestibulum ante ipsum, primoque in limine Pyrrhus / Exultat, telis, et luce coruscus aëna' (II.469–70).

31 The reference to Priam's sacrifice on the altar imbibed with his blood also occurs in Ovid (*Metamorphoses* 422–577, 494–531). The detail of the 'flowing streames of blood' is kept in Surrey's translation – Henry Howard, Earl of Surrey, *Aeneid*, ed. Florence H. Ridley (Berkeley and Los Angeles, 1963), p. 718.

held authority in both eloquence and moral guidance.[32] Shakespeare likely encountered Virgil through editions or translations and may have been familiar with the medieval Latin apocryphal tradition.[33] Priam is depicted as 'unequal match'd', closely echoing Virgil's words ('impar congressus', 1.475).[34] Hamlet compares Pyrrhus to the 'Hyrcanian beast' (2.2.453), the same expression used by Dido to describe Aeneas in her final speech (*Aeneid* 4.366–7).[35]

Virgil's depiction of Pyrrhus portrays him as an unhesitant slayer of Priam. The medieval tradition inherits this portrayal of a relentless and fiery Pyrrhus.[36] Both Dares and Dictys include the sequence of brutal actions performed by Pyrrhus, who indiscriminately kills Trojans, infiltrates the royal palace, pursues Priam and dismembers his body before the altar, while Hecuba escapes with Polyxena. Pyrrhus' unwavering ruthlessness is a consistent theme in medieval texts. This hyperbolic portrayal of his nature, characterized by excessive cruelty, returns in most Renaissance translations of Virgil.[37] It is also condensed in Peele's *A Tale of Troy* (1589), which likely provided a stylistic example of hyperbole for Marlowe and indirectly influenced Q2–F1:

> he whose bloodie mind and murdring rage,
> Nor lavve of Gods, nor reuerence of age,
> Coulde temper from a deede so tyrannous,
> *Achilles* sonne, the fierce vnbridled *Pyrrhus.*
> His fathers ghost belike entycing him,
> With slaughtring hand, wyth visage pale and dim.
> Hath hent this aged *Priam* by the haire,
> Like Butcher bent to sley.[38]

The episode of Pyrrhus and Priam became a symbol of excessive descriptions of passion. This is evident in the 1602 additions to the *Spanish Tragedy*, one of which may have been written by Shakespeare himself: 'There you may show a passion, there you may show a passion. Draw me like old Priam of Troy, crying "The house is a-fire, the house is a-fire as the torch over my head!"'[39]

My first network clarifies this simple, starting opposition. Each network clearly shows character relationships and key plot points, themes and emotions, gradually increasing in complexity.

As illustrated in Figure 17, the initial deep structure is a simple *couple*, a contrast between two elements, primarily focused on the first two acts of the play before the actors' arrival. Pyrrhus represents the first core, which is the realm of *action* fuelled by his desire for *revenge* for the killing of his deceased father Achilles.

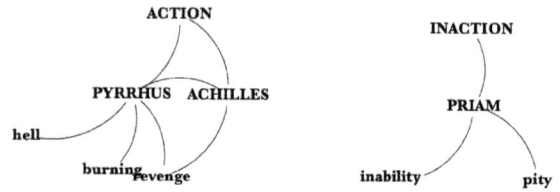

17 The couple (Pyrrhus and Priam).

[32] See Margaret Tudeau-Clayton, 'English Readers' Virgil', in *Jonson, Shakespeare and Early Modern Virgil* (Cambridge, 1998), 21–43.

[33] Colin Burrow, *Shakespeare and Classical Antiquity* (Oxford, 2013), pp. 23–4.

[34] Miola, 'Aeneas and Hamlet', pp. 278, 282, 285.

[35] Martin Mueller, 'Hamlet and the world of ancient tragedy', *Arion* 5 (1997), 22–45 p. 37;. See also Sarah Knight, 'Pyrrhus and the tiger', *Modern Language Notes* 135 (2020), 1062–77.

[36] In Phrygius, the death of Priam is a sign of an utter destruction (Dares Phrygius, *Excidium Troiae*, ed. E. Bagby Atwood and Virgil K. Whitaker (Cambridge, MA, 1944), p. 19). The killing of Priam on the altar returns in Benoit de Sainte-Maure's *Roman de Troie* (1160–1170), which, drawing on Dares and Dictys, claims that Pyrrhus made the altar bleed and thus satisfied the infernal furies of revenge: Benoit de Sainte-Maure, *Le Roman de Troie par Benoit de Sainte-Maure*, ed. Léopold Constans (Paris, 1908), IV.26145–8, 26391–4. In Guido delle Colonne's *Historia destructionis Troiae* (1287), a translation into Latin prose of the Roman de Troie that was to influence a significant body of English vernacular writing in the fourteenth and fifteenth centuries (see James Simpson, 'The other book of Troy: Guido delle Colonne's Historia destructionis Troiae in fourteenth- and fifteenth-century England', *Speculum* 73 (1998), 397–424), Priam drenches the altar with his blood (Guido delle Colonne, *Historia destructionis Troiae*, ed. N. E. Griffin (Cambridge, MA, 1936), sig. 111v). The gory detail returns in The '*Gest Hystoriale*' of the Destruction of Troy, a thirteenth-century English alliterative romance based on Guido, and in the anonymous *Laud Troy Book* (c.1400): *The Laud Troy Book, A Romance of about 1400 A.D.* (London, 1902), pp. 18298–300. The desecration of the temple perpetrated by Pyrrhus also occurs in John Lydgate's *The hystorye / Sege and dystruccyon of Troye* (London, 1513), IV.xxxiv, 6411–12, translated and versified from Guido delle Colonne; and in William Caxton, *The Recueile of the Histories of Troie* (London, 1553), sig. xliiiir.

[37] In Caxton's *Eneydos* (1490), there is no reference to Aeneas' tale: *Eneydos 1490, Englisht from the French Liure des Eneydes, 1483* (London, 1890), XIX, 30–3. Translations of Virgil were made by Gavin Douglas (1513), Surrey (c.1540), Phaer (1558) and Stanihurst, along with a new edition by Phaer-Twyne. See Colin Burrow, 'Virgil in English translation', in *The Cambridge Companion to Virgil*, ed. Charles Martindale (Cambridge, 1997), 21–37. In all of them, Pyrrhus ruthlessly acts with his father's might.

[38] George Peele, *A Tale of Troy*, in *A Farewell* (London, 1589), sigs. 19v, 20r.

[39] Thomas Kyd, *The Spanish Tragedy*, ed. C. Calvo and J. Tronch, Arden Shakespeare (London, 2013), 3.12A.152–5. For the attribution of the addition to Shakespeare, see pp. 319–28.

This core is also associated with the *burning* and destruction of Troy, Pyrrhus' fiery temperament, grotesque exaggeration, as well as the *hell* from which Achilles drives him to revenge. Priam embodies the second core, *inaction*, as he is *unable* to wield his weapons and becomes an object of *pity*. The presence of the first core attracts characters such as the impulsive youths (including Hamlet before his mourning period) and King Hamlet in his prime. On the other hand, the distinct core of *inaction*, influenced by the feeble and pitiable Priam, aligns with Hamlet's own inability to act due to his grief and mourning.

According to Aristotle, 'pity is occasioned by undeserved misfortune' (*Poetics* VI.35). No one probably deserved pity more than the rather unfortunate Hecuba, an embedded character in the story.

EMERGENCE (HECUBA)

One notable difference among the three versions of the Pyrrhus Speech is that Pyrrhus, albeit briefly, hesitates in Q2–F during the ongoing destruction of Troy:

> Then senseless Ilium
> Seeming to feel this blow, with flaming top
> Stoops to his base and with a hideous crash
> Takes prisoner Pyrrhus' ear. For lo, his sword
> Which was declining on the milky head
> Of reverend Priam seemed i'th' air to stick.
> So as a painted tyrant Pyrrhus stood
> Like a neutral to his will and matter,
> Did nothing.
>
> (Q2 2.2.412–20; F 2.2.470–8)

Pyrrhus' momentary hesitation in Q2–F aligns with Marlowe and Nashe's *Dido*, which amplifies the Virgilian theme of exaggerated horror ('Young infants swimming in their parents' blood, / Headless carcasses pil'd up in heaps, / Virgins half-dead, dragg'd by their golden hair', 193–5).[40] Furthermore, *Dido* foreshadows the Shakespearian detail of Hecuba staring at Priam (2.1.244–6; cf. *Hamlet* Q2 2.2.451–2, F 2.2.509–10; *Lucrece* 1447–9), which is absent in Virgil's account.

In *Dido*, there are two instances of brief hesitation. The first occurs when Pyrrhus raises his sword towards the royal couple and stares at them: 'He, with his falchion's point rais'd up at once, / And with Megaera's eyes, star'd in their face, / Threatening a thousand deaths at every glance' (*Dido* 2.1.229–31). Priam pleads for mercy and clumsily attempts to engage in combat, only to be savagely slain by Pyrrhus:

> Wherat he lifted up his bed-rid limbs,
> And would have grappled with Achilles' son,
> Forgetting both his want of strength and hands;
> Which he disdaining, whisk'd his sword about,
> And with the wound [1594 Q: wind] thereof the
>   king fell down.
>
> (*Dido* 2.1.250–5)

The final line echoes the phrase 'the whiff and wind of his fell sword' (Q2 2.2.411; the phrase is present in all three texts), possibly emphasizing its increased grotesqueness. The second hesitation occurs after the dismemberment of Priam and the desecration of the altar by dipping Achilles' flag in the king's blood. Pyrrhus pauses to observe the devastation: 'So, leaning on his sword, he stood stone still, / Viewing the fire wherewith rich Ilion burnt' (*Dido* 2.1.263–4).

The emergence of a new core, hesitation, slightly anticipates the introduction of an embedded character within the Troy story, who appears in the conclusion of the Pyrrhus Speech:

> Run barefoot up and down, threatening the flames
> With bisson rheum, a clout upon that head
> Where late the diadem stood and, for a robe,
> About her lank and all-o'erteemed loins,
> A blanket in the alarm of fear caught up.
> Who this had seen, with tongue in venom steeped,
> 'Gainst Fortune's state would treason have pronounced.
> But if the gods themselves did see her then,
> When she saw Pyrrhus make malicious sport
> In mincing with his sword her husband limbs,
> The instant burst of clamour that she made
> (Unless things mortal move them not at all)
> Would have made milch the burning eyes of heaven
> And passion in the gods.
>
> (Q2 2.2.443–56; F 2.2.501–14)

Hecuba, universally symbolizing grief and passion, embodied the emotional intensity generated by suffering women.[41] Her capacity for pathos, stemming from countless sorrows, intensified in post-Homeric tradition. In Ovid's *Metamorphoses*, while mourning the loss of Polyxena and Polinestor, she becomes a symbol of tragic characters who have lost everything ('omnia

---

[40] Quotations are from Christopher Marlowe, *Dido, Queen of Carthage*, ed. Ruth Lunney (Manchester, 2023). See Laurie Maguire and Emma Smith, 'What Is a Source? Or, How Shakespeare Read His Marlowe', in *Shakespeare Survey 68* (Cambridge, 2015), 15–31.

[41] Tanya Pollard, 'What's Hecuba to Shakespeare?', *Renaissance Quarterly* 65 (2012), 1065–6.

perdidimus', XIII.527) and abandons all decorum.[42] Her transformation into a symbol of absolute loss and a model for complaint is evident in the Renaissance. She appears as an exemplary victim of fortune in Jasper Heywood's 1559 translation of *Troas*.[43] Peele describes Hecuba as having 'suruiude the last, / Till Fortunes spight and mallice all was past / And worne with sorrow, wexen fell and mad'.[44] She also plays a prominent role in *The Rape of Lucrece*, representing female complaint and vulnerability.[45] Her potential for pathos is also evident in Thomas Fenne's *Hecubaes mishappes* (1590), where the slumbering poet envisions her as 'A woman vext with eager lookes in frantike fierie moode', 'perplext / In minde and soule'.[46] Marlowe also mentions Hecuba's frantic behaviour, depicting her being carried away by soldiers 'howling in the empty air' (*Dido* 2.1.247).

Alongside grief, madness and metamorphosis, Hecuba was associated with the profound pathetic effects of a masterful speech on both the audience and the speaker delivering it. The actor is the first to be moved by the speech, as observed first by Polonius and later reflected upon by Hamlet in his monologue ('What's Hecuba to him', Q2 2.2.494ff.). Plato refers to Hecuba and Priam as examples of those pitiful passages whose recitation makes the actor seem to be rapt, as Ion states: 'whenever I recite a tale of pity, my eyes are filled with tears, and when it is one of horror and dismay, my hair stands up on end with fear, and my heart goes leaping', evoking an emotional response that is also stirred in the spectators who are 'weeping, casting terrible glances, stricken with amazement at the deeds recounted'.[47] Hecuba's paradigmatic value is exemplified in a treatise by the rhetorician Aphthonius of Antioch, translated into English in the mid sixteenth century, where she serves as an illustration of *pathopoeia*, 'which expresseth the emotions, what they pertain to in short, what the motion of the mind signifies; for example, what words Hecuba might utter after Troy's destruction'.[48] In Richard Rainold's *Foundation of Rhetoric* (1572), Hecuba's 'patheticall and dolefull oracion' signifies her as a symbol of fickle fortune, whose fate changes as 'stone doth roule, as floodes now flowe, floodes also ebbe'.[49] A *scolium* to Aphthonius quotes a passage from Quintilian that mentions the tears evoked by the forceful portrayal of characters' passions. Quintilian urges the skillful orator to utilize description of war-ravaged cities such as Troy as a means of eliciting pity (*Institutio oratoria* 8.3).

The association between Hecuba's sufferings and the profound mollifying impact of pathos even on a hardened murderer (for example, Claudius during the murder of Gonzago) is reflected in an anecdote reported by Plutarch about Alexander, the tyrant of Pherae. Plutarch recounts how Alexander almost punished the actor who had moved him to tears by evoking the suffering of Hecuba and Polyxena, referencing Euripides' play *Hecuba*. Alexander

suddenly left the theater, made haste away, & went faster than an ordinary pace untill he was out of sight withall, that it were a great indignity for him to weepe and shed teares, in compassion of the miseries and calamities of queene Hecuba or lady Polyxena, whoever he any day caused so many citizens and subjects thoats to be cut.[50]

A possible link is Cicero, who, discussing the ineffectual nature of rule by fear, mentions Alexander in a sequence of tyrants that also includes Pyrrhus, the king of Epirus (*De officiis* II.7.23–6).

Hecuba's underlying element of madness further develops the theme of inaction and pity. It can be connected to other forms of mental disturbance, particularly Hamlet's melancholy, his 'antic disposition' (1.5.170), the 'ecstasy of love' proposed by Polonius as an explanation for his 'transformation' (2.2.5), his 'diseased' wit (3.2.314) and the loss of all his joy (2.2.261–76). Figure 18 illustrates the emergence of the embedded character Hecuba, linked to Priam and Pyrrhus in the sources. Supported by the account of Alexander, she expands the theme of

---

[42] *P. Ovidii Nasonis opera ... Henrici Galreanus annotationes* (Basle, 1523), sig. 171v.

[43] *The Sixt Tragedie of the Most Graue and Prudent Author Lucius, Anneus, Seneca, Entituled Troas, with Diuers and Sundrie Addicions to the Same* (London, 1559), sig. B1v. See Jessica Winston, 'Seneca in early Elizabethan England', *Renaissance Quarterly* 59 (2006), 29–58.

[44] Peele, *A Tale of Troy*, 19–20.

[45] Mary Jo Kietzman, '"What is Hecuba to him or [s]he to Hecuba?" Lucrece's complaint and Shakespearean poetic agency', *Modern Philology* 97 (1999), 21–45; p. 26.

[46] Thomas Fenne, *Fennes Frutes ... whereunto is added Hecubaes mishaps, discoursed by way of apparition* (London, 1590), sig. Bb3v.

[47] Plato, *Ion*, in *Plato in Twelve Volumes*, trans. W. R. M. Lamb, vol. 9 (Cambridge, MA and London, 1925), 535b–c.

[48] Aphthonius, *Progymnasmata*, trans. E. Lorich (1542), quoted in C. O. McDonald, *The Rhetoric of Tragedy: Form in Stuart Drama* (Amherst, 1966), p. 84.

[49] Richard Rainolde, *A Booke called the Foundacion of rhetorike* (London, 1563), sigs. xlixr, lv. See Andrew Wallace, '"What's Hecuba to Him?" Pain, privacy, and the ancient text', in *Ars Reminiscendi: Mind and Memory in Renaissance Culture*, ed. Donald Beecher and Grant Williams (Toronto, 2009), 231–43.

[50] Plutarch, *The Morals*, trans. Philemon Holland (London, 1603), 1273. Elsewhere, Plutarch reports the episode in connection with Euripides' *Troades* (*Life of Pelopides* II.324–5).

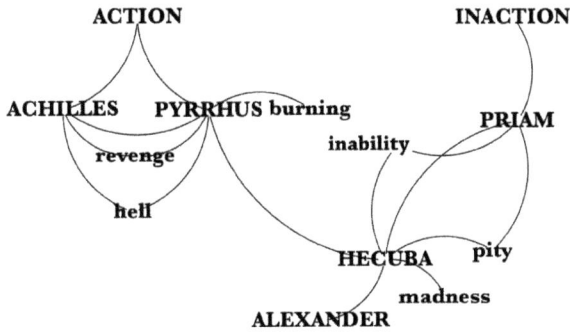

18 Emergence (Hecuba).

inaction and, with its element of *madness*, establishes a connection with the concepts of *inability* and *pity*.

The connections delve deeper, extending beyond the explicitly mentioned sources to other embedded characters within the story of Pyrrhus. In later traditions, Hecuba's intense passion transformed into madness. However, the cause of this emotional outburst was not the sight of Priam being maliciously ravaged, but rather witnessing the killing of her daughter Polyxena. As shown in the Flemish tapestries, Hecuba became mad and 'began to renne vagabond and all araged', to quote Caxton.[51] This madness was made manifest by a series of deranged actions that Shakespeare shifted to the killing of Priam ('run barefoot vp and down', Q2 2.2.443; F 2.2.501). Interestingly, even Pyrrhus hesitated while killing Polyxena, a detail that was absent in many medieval and Renaissance texts but prominently featured in a likely analogue, Euripides' *Hecuba*, mentioned in the Alexander episode.[52] In this context, Shakespeare introduces a third deep structure, *interference*.

INTERFERENCE (POLYXENA)

While all three texts of *Hamlet* incorporate elements of action, inaction and madness, their differences are further accentuated by the inclusion of pauses. Preceded by Pyrrhus' moment of pause, suspension becomes prominent at the centre of the play in act 3. It is during this act that Hamlet learns the practice of suspension and refrains from immediate action twice: in the soliloquy 'To be or not to be' ('that must give us pause', 2.2.67), and during the prayer scene ('that must be scanned', 3.3.75). As stated only in Q2, following the passing of Fortinbras's army, the question arises of how to act boldly like Pyrrhus but 'without great argument' (Q2 4.4.53). Pyrrhus' moment of pause resonates with various instances in *Hamlet* that are present in Q2–F but absent

in Q1: for example, Claudius' court speech discussing the equal weighing of 'delight and dole' (1.2), Hamlet's praise of Horatio as a man that has taken 'Fortune's buffets and rewards ... with equal thanks' (3.2.62–4), Claudius' bifold suspension during the prayer scene as he stands in 'pause ... like a man to double business bound' (Q2–F 3.3.42, 41), torn between repentance and the enjoyment of the benefits gained from murder.

The result is a complete suspension of judgement, as expressed in a philosophical aphorism present only in F: 'there is nothing either good or bad, but thinking makes it so' (F 2.2.247–8). The connection between Pyrrhus and hesitation is perhaps extended by mere phonetic similarity with the name of the ancient philosopher Pyrrho (*c*.360 – *c*.270 BC), the sceptical advocate of suspension. Pyrrho establishes an opposition between the immobile divine mind and the constantly moved human mind.[53] He embraces suspended hesitation, 'hesitans suspenso', as a means to attain the unmoved ('imperturbatum') state of mind.[54] Recognizing the fallibility of human judgement, he seeks to remain in a perpetual state of balanced suspension and indifference to all things; for Montaigne, the 'mot sacramental' of this philosophical sect is ἐπέχω, meaning 'I hold, I do not move.'[55]

Hesitation can lead to a momentary pause of suspension, akin to Pyrrho's philosophy, and subsequently

---

[51] Pyrrhus 'cut her al in peeces, and cast hem all aboute the sepulture of hys father' (Caxton, *The Recueile of the Histories of Troie*, sig. xlvr).

[52] Phrygius reports that Antenor delivered Polyxena to Pyrrhus, who mercilessly put her to death (*The faythfull and true storye of the destruction of Troye*, sigs. 54r, 55v). In the *Excidium Troiae*, Pyrrhus binds her and lays her alive inside the tomb (20, 1–4). Guido Delle Colonne (*Historia destructionis Troiae*, lib. XXX, sig. 113r) states that, despite her noble speech, Pyrrhus does not relent and immediately kills her ('statim') impiously ('impie'). A similar lack of hesitation appears in *The 'Gest Hystoriale' of the Destruction of Troy* (1214–1459) and in the *Laud Troy Book* (18567–70). Lydgate vividly describes Pyrrhus dismembering the girl, behaving even more wildly than a lion (*The hystorye/Sege and dystruccyon of Troye* IV. xxxiv). The transformation of Polyxena into an icon of virtue is complete when, in the *Laud Troy Book*, facing death, she prays 'so Christ me spede' (18558).

[53] See Nicola Panichi, 'Montaigne and Plutarch: a scepticism that conquers the mind', in *Renaissance Scepticisms*, ed. Gianni Paganini and José R. Maia Neto (Dordrecht, 2009), 183–211.

[54] *Sexti philosophi Pyrrhoniarum hypotypωseωn libri III* (Paris, 1562), I. iii.10, 15, 16.

[55] Michel de Montaigne, *Essais*, ed. Maurice Rat (Paris, 1952), II. xii, 559, 560. Epistemological questions at Oxford and London's Inns of Court also explored this suspended examination of both sides of a topic. In 1562, Henri Estienne produced a Latin

divide into either prolonged suspension or the contemplation of taking action. Another division pertains to action itself, which can manifest itself as either impulsive or virtuous. The act of killing Polyxena, as depicted in the sources, presents an unexpected opportunity for even the cruellest warrior to pause, reflect and encounter unfamiliar emotions. Pyrrhus' pause precedes his gruesome act of drenching another monument, his father Achilles' tomb, with the blood of his victim: Polyxena, the daughter of Priam and Hecuba, for whom Achilles had been killed. Virgil does not mention her in his account. The inclusion of Polyxena's fate is a variation to the speech passingly introduced by Marlowe, whose Aeneas reports that she was 'sacrific'd' by Pyrrhus (*Dido* 293).

Polyxena's sacrifice represents the nearly inexpressible. Quintilian cites it as an example of the Greeks' ability to evoke pathos, when we attempt to show that what we have suffered is of a more horrible nature than what are usually regarded as great evils (*Institutio oratoriae* VI.2, 22–3). The episode holds significant prominence in Euripides' *Hecuba*, a tragedy that experienced immense popularity in the sixteenth century due to numerous editions and Latin translations.[56] Notably, Erasmus's translation (1507) played a significant role, likely making it part of Elizabethan syllabi, particularly in the absence of a Senecan version of *Hecuba*.[57] *Hamlet* contains a distinct echo of the tragedy in the passage on the 'mobbled queen': Erasmus describes Hecuba as 'circum operta linteis'.[58]

In Euripides' play, the death of Polyxena is conveyed by a messenger in a passage (*Hecuba* 484–628) praised by Erasmus as an example of *enàrgeia* or *evidentia*. Erasmus argues that it employs amplification, ornamentation and delight to not only depict a scene but also present it as a vividly painted picture. The reader or listener, transported beyond themselves ('extra se positum'), will believe that they are in a theatre.[59] In Euripides' portrayal, Polyxena bares her breast and kneels before Pyrrhus, offering herself to him, and he is both willing and unwilling to kill her.[60]

Pyrrhus' brief hesitation is exclusive to Euripides and his Latin and Italian translations or adaptations. In Ovid, Pyrrhus stands with his sword, gazing ('Neoptolemum stantem', XIII.455). Moved by Polyxena's dying words, he himself weeps and reluctantly carries out his task against his will.[61] Seneca's *Troades* also emphasizes the crying provoked by Polyxena, the imagery of the grave flooded with blood, and Pyrrhus' unexpected and monstrous slowness in executing the deed.[62] Hesitation reappears in Renaissance translations of Euripides, often with significant expansion. In Erasmus's translation, Polyxena's offer

of her bare breast leads Pyrrhus to relent, described as 'volensque et non uolens: atque hesitans'.[63] In Lodovico Dolce's 1563 translation, possibly known by Marlowe, Pyrrhus initially acts without delay ('senza porui altra dimora'), but eventually he is moved and lingers hesitantly between yes and no.[64] The Senecan *monstrum,* Pyrrhus' unnatural reluctance to kill, which almost foreshadows divine intervention, resurfaces in Heywood's translation of the play with words that may have influenced Marlowe: 'a strange thing monstruouse like, / That Pyrrhus even himselfe stoode styll, / For dread, and durst not stryke'.[65] In Heywood's translation of Seneca's *Troades*, Pyrrhus, who appears relentless in Seneca's *Agamemnon* and in Marlowe's own work, exhibits reluctance.

---

translation of the outlines of Pyrrhonism. Thomas Nashe refers to a lost English translation of Estienne in his preface to Sidney's *Astrophil and Stella* (1591). In his *History of Philosophy* (1655–61), Thomas Stanley includes a complete translation of Sextus' *Hypotiposes* which might well depend on this lost English version: 'For he who is Opinion there is something Good or Bad in its own nature, is continually disturbed ... Whereas he who defines nothing concerning Things naturally Good or Bad, neither flyeth nor pursueth any thing eagerly, so that he remains undistrubed' (quoted in Ronald Knowles, 'Hamlet and counter-humanism', *Renaissance Quarterly* 52 (1999), 1055).

56 See L. Schleiner, 'Latinized Greek drama in Shakespeare's *Hamlet*', *Shakespeare Quarterly* 41 (1990), 29–34.

57 See Frank N. Clary Jr, 'Hamlet's Mousetrap and the play-within-the-anecdote of Plutarch', in *Reading Readings: Essays on Shakespeare Editing in the 18th Century*, ed. Joanna Gondris (Madison, NJ and London, 1997), pp. 164, 166, 177.

58 Euripides, *Hecuba*, in *Hecuba & Iphigenia in Aulide*, trans. Erasmus (Venice, 1507), sig. Ciiir.

59 Erasmus, *De duplici copia verborum ac rerum*, in *Desideri Erasmi opera omnia* (Ludguni Batavorum, 1703), I, 77, 75, 78.

60 'ὃ δ' οὐ θέλων τε καὶ θέλων οἴκτῳ κόρης' (Euripides, *Hecuba*, corresponding to l.566).

61 'Ipse etiam flens invitusque sacerdos / praebita coniecto rupit praecordia ferro' (Ovid, *Metamorphoses* XIII.475–6).

62 'Uterque flevit coetus; at timidum Phryges / misere gemitum, clarius victor gemit'; 'obduxit statim / saevusque totum sanguinem tumulus bibit'; 'novumque monstrum est Pyrrhus ad caedem piger' – Seneca, *Troades*, in *Troades: Introduction, Text and Commentary*, ed. Atze J. Keulen (Leiden, 2001), 1000, 1154, 1160–1, 1163–4.

63 Euripides, *Hecuba*, sig. Ciiiir.

64 'Al fin di questi accenti alta pietade / Punse di Pirro il giovanetto core; / E fuor la dimostrò: che lungo spatio / stette fra'l sì e'l no d'occider lei': Lodovico Dolce, *La Hecuba* (Venice, 1560), sig. 38v. See Mary E. Smith, 'Marlowe and Italian Dido drama', *Italica* 53 (1976), 233.

65 *Jasper Heywood and His Translations of Seneca's Troas, Thyestes and Hercules Furens. Edited from the Octavos of 1559, 1560 and 1561*, ed. H. De Voht (Louvain, 1913), fol. iiir, vv. 2522–4.

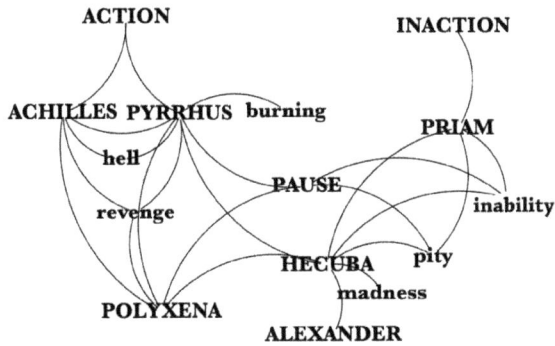

19 Interference (Polyxena).

As depicted in Figure 19, the embedded Polyxena interferes with both *action* and *inaction*, expanding and blending the two opposites. She interferes with both core 1, *action* (as Polyxena is the true target of the *revenge* connecting Pyrrhus and Achilles), and core 2, *inaction* (as she elicits profound *pity* and briefly halts Pyrrhus). Moreover, Polyxena introduces a *pause*, inserting it between *action* and *inaction*. While *emergence* (Hecuba) mitigates the pair of opposites, *interference* (Polyxena) introduces a new element that further dissolves this dichotomy and interacts with both poles.

Another aspect of multiplicity in the Pyrrhus Speech and of its echoes in *Hamlet* is the duality of the same element (pause) being simultaneously present and absent, and then becoming a precursor to a renewed cycle of senseless violence or to thoughtful deliberation and virtuous action. In the last deep structure, *synthesis*, the Pyrrhus Speech unveils even more contradictory connections and offers a new resolution to the first pair of opposites.

SYNTHESIS (AENEAS)

After a momentary pause, Pyrrhus resumes his destructive actions in Q2–F:

> But as we often see against some storm
> A silence in the heaven, the rack stand still,
> The bold winds speechless and the orb below
> As hush as death, anon the dreadful thunder
> Doth rend the region, so after Pyrrhus' pause
> A roused vengeance sets him new a-work
> And never did the Cyclops' hammers fall
> On Mars' armour, forged for proof eterne,
> With less remorse than Pyrrhus' bleeding sword
> Now falls on Priam.
>
> (Q2 2.2.421–30, F 2.2.479–88)

The killing of Priam exemplifies how action follows a brief pause and highlights Pyrrhus' degeneracy. According to Virgil, one must show pity towards the conquered and defeat the haughty ('parcere subiectis et debellare superbos', *Aeneid* VI.853). However, both virtues are conspicuously absent not only in Pyrrhus' action but also in his words. Interestingly, the Virgilian Pyrrhus responds to Priam's accusation of being less noble than Achilles with a sarcastic retort, which bears some resemblance to Hamlet's scathing replies when questioned about the location of Polonius's body. Pyrrhus sends Priam to hell, allowing him to personally inform his father of his degeneracy.[66]

Pyrrhus' proud embrace of his degeneration is also amplified in medieval texts and early modern translations and adaptations. He is conventionally portrayed as a swerver from virtue and a symbol of degeneration in contrast to his father. Luther, in his interpretation of the Hebrews who attacked Christ as vain imitators claiming to be sons of Abraham, cites Pyrrhus as an example of the disparity between father and son, asserting that spiritual virtues do not propagate themselves like natural ones due to original sin: Pyrrhus is not equal to his father Achilles ('Pyrrhus non aequat patrem Achillem').[67] The scene between Pyrrhus and Priam also raises the question of the absence of pity, a topic frequently debated in chivalric literature.[68] Pyrrhus violates the obligations of restraint and moderation emphasized in Renaissance chivalric treatises, as gentlemen are not expected to be 'by bloud . . . [i]nflamed, or on choler kindled presently', two things which should 'not be in Men of discretion' as they lead one 'to Degenerate'.[69]

Echoes of the association between Pyrrhus and filial degeneration can be discerned in Hamlet's monologue on Hecuba and the player (Q2 2.2.511–22; F 2.2.570–82), as well as in the Q2-only monologue on occasions (4.4.55–64). The hell to which Pyrrhus sends Priam becomes a metaphor in Q2–F, with the 'Cyclops hammers' serving as an exaggerated backdrop to the '*hellish*

66 '[I]lli mea tristia facta / degeneremque Neoptolemum narrare mento' (*Aeneid* II.548–9).
67 Martin Luther, *Enarrationes in primum librum Mose* (1535), in *Exegetica opera latina*, ed. H. Schmid (Erlangae, 1846), IX.47.
68 Richard W. Kaeuper, *Chivalry and Violence in Medieval Europe* (Oxford, 1999), pp. 45–62.
69 George Silver, *Paradoxes of Defence* (1599), in *Three Elizabethan Fencing Manuals. Giacomo di Grassi, His True Art of Defence (1594). Vincentio Saviolo, His Practice (1595). George Silver, Paradoxes of Defence (1599)* (New York, 1972), p. 79.

Pyrrhus' (Q2 2.2.427, 401; F 2.2.485, 460). It also fore-shadows Hamlet's depiction of his own 'imaginations', which may be as 'foul / As Vulcans stithy' (Q2 3.2.80; F 3.2.82). The epic motif of the restoration of the body enables this hellish framing: hell is now the 'other place' (Q2 4.3.33), not a transitional space in which to offer a filial sacrifice.

Hesitation and suspension should ultimately enable decision and action, yet indications of deliberation do arise quite belatedly in *Hamlet*. The soliloquies vividly depict the gradual emergence of deliberation amidst doubt and suspension. Upon witnessing the actor's emotional performance for Hecuba, Hamlet perceives his own shortcomings, given 'the motive and that for passion' that he has (Q2 2.2.495–7; cf. F 2.2.55–6). Prompted to revenge by heaven and hell, Hamlet unpacks his heart 'with words' (Q2 2.2.520; F 2.2.580; cf. Q1 7.426). In act 3, there is a growing realization of the necessity, even while ostensibly providing instructions to the actors, to 'suit the action to the word' (Q2–F 3.2.17), whereas Q1 merely insists on examples of preposterous overacting. Following the play-within-the-play, Hamlet states (with a revealing choice of the modal verb) that he 'could … drink hot blood / And do such business as the bitter day / Would quake to look on' (Q2–F 3.2.380–2). Surprising the King while he is praying, Hamlet recognizes the possibility of taking action before contemplating it: 'Now I might do it' (Q2–F 3.3.73). External events and characters further accentuate Hamlet's state of suspension: the appearance of the Ghost serves as a reproach to a 'tardy son' (Q2 3.4.103; F 3.4.96; Q1 11.60), and the sight of Fortinbras's army leads him to see himself as one who yet lives 'to say this thing's to do' (Q2 4.4.43). Preceded by Pyrrhus' resolute return to action after his momentary pause (2.2.421–30), indications of impulsive deliberation reach their pinnacle in Hamlet's conversation with Horatio concerning indiscretion. The encounter with the pirates marks the end of suspension and the commencement of purposeful rashness, in a passage that is completely absent in Q1. Initially, Hamlet remains internally suspended in 'a kind of fighting / That would not let me sleep' (Q2–F 5.2.4–5), until he decides to act, and act

> rashly –
> And praised be rashness for it – let us know
> Our indiscretion sometime serves us well
> When our deep plots fall
>
> (Q2–F 5.2.6–9)

Clearly, the suddenness of Hamlet's new-found deliberation in act 5 is more pronounced in Q2–F.

This virtuous form of hesitation is contrasted in the sources with Pyrrhus' lack of chivalric discretion, particularly when compared to the final pause experienced by the last embedded infiltrator, Aeneas. Before slaying the violent Turnus and becoming *fervidus* (12.951), the Virgilian Aeneas, the virtuous practitioner of pity and the dutiful son, 'suffers the type of hesitation that must be endured before a power over which a viewer has no control'.[70] His brief hesitation embodies Aristotle's *proairesis*, the moment of deliberated choice: virtue and virtuous acts are the intentional culmination of deliberation (*boulesis*).[71] Epic heroes often pause to deliberate: 'Tra se volve Ruggiero e fa discorso, / se restar deve, o il suo signor seguire.'[72] Following this hesitation, Aeneas is consumed by fury at the sight of Palladis' belt on Turnus.[73]

Aeneas' final eruption of fury was the subject of extensive debate.[74] Subsequent reimaginings of the story, such as the thirteenth book added by the Italian humanist Maphaeus Vegius, amplify Turnus' rage and identify him as the fury of war, redirecting Aeneas' *pietas* towards the goal of peace.[75] This emphasis on Aeneas' *pietas* is also present in Lodovico Dolce, whose Turnus nearly elicits pity from Aeneas and transforms him into a 'religiosissimo, e Christianissimo Principe'.[76] In Virgil, Aeneas, while hesitating with his spear ('Cunctanti telum', *Aeneid* XII.919), hurls it with a rumble likened to the gathering of a storm ('nec fulmine tanti / dissultant crepitus', XII.922–3). The spear flies like a thunder ('atri turbinis instar', XII.923), which echoes a Q2–F passage, the 'storm' preceding Pyrrhus' furious action:

> A silence in the heaven, the rack stand still,
> The bold winds speechless and the orb below
> As hush as death, anon the dreadful thunder
> Doth rend the region
>
> (Q2 2.2.422–5; F 2.2.480–3)

---

70 Michael C. J. Putnam, *Virgil's Aeneid: Interpretation and Influence* (Chapel Hill and London, 1995), 156, 160. The scene likely recalls Achilles' hesitation in killing Agamemnon (*Iliad* I.189).

71 James Lawrence Shulman, *'The Pale Cast of Thought': Hesitation and Decision in the Renaissance Epic* (Newark and London, 1998), 13.

72 Ludovico Ariosto, *Orlando furioso*, ed. Emilio Bigi (Milan, 2002), 40.66.1–2.

73 'Furiis accensus et ira / terribilis': *Aeneid* XII.946–7.

74 Theodore Ziolkowski, *Hesitant Heroes: Private Inhibition, Cultural Crisis* (Ithaca and London, 2004), pp. 14, 33.

75 James D. Garrison, *Pietas from Vergil to Dryden* (University Park, PA, 1992), p. 162.

76 Lodovico Dolce, *L'Enea*, in *L'Achille e l'Enea* (Venice, 1571), 526.

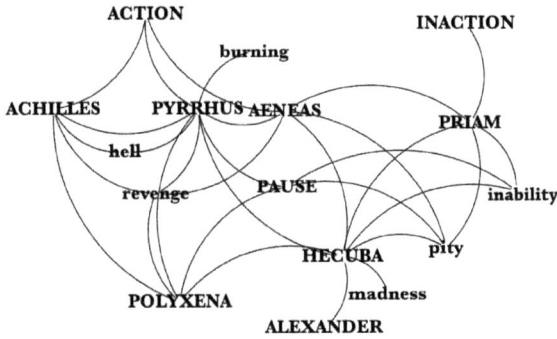

20 Synthesis (Aeneas).

Aeneas' interplay of hesitation and deliberation eventually transforms into furor, which justifies the 'rash and bloody deede' of killing Polonius, as well as the calculated promptness exhibited by Hamlet aboard the ship, and his ultimate acceptance of indiscretion and readiness.

Figure 20 illustrates how the combination of rage and degeneration, in contrast, leads to the emergence of genuine virtuous action by expanding upon the pause introduced by Polyxena. The core of *action* is fragmented, and two elements (*rage* and *revenge*) are connected to the last core (*pause*). Two contrasting possibilities are presented for the *pause*: Pyrrhus halting before plunging into further destruction, and Aeneas stopping before deliberating on virtuous revenge. Virtuous action arises after Polyxena's interference. This sequence of three infiltrators (Hecuba, Polyxena, Aeneas) is brought to a new synthesis, action led by 'readiness' after the pause of suspension.

SHAKESPEARE AND COMPLEXITY

The analysis of this network of sources highlights the disparities between Q1 and Q2–F, indicating a growing divide between the performable text depicted in Q1, which probably underwent cuts and revisions, and the deeper philosophical dimension found in Q2–F. I also hope to have shown how this interwoven tapestry of sources highlights the open-ended nature of the Pyrrhus Speech and its reverberations in *Hamlet*. The Pyrrhus Speech not only enfolds contrasting themes and is simultaneously associated with multiple elements: its effectiveness lies precisely in its ability to encompass divergent concepts such as virtue and degeneration, revenge and hesitation, choice and action. The 'deepest thing' that can be observed in *Hamlet* is its complexity. When reviewed through the lens of isomorphism, the Pyrrhus

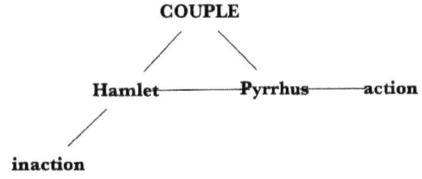

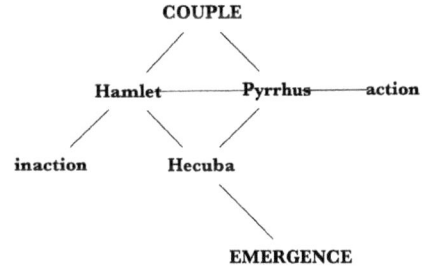

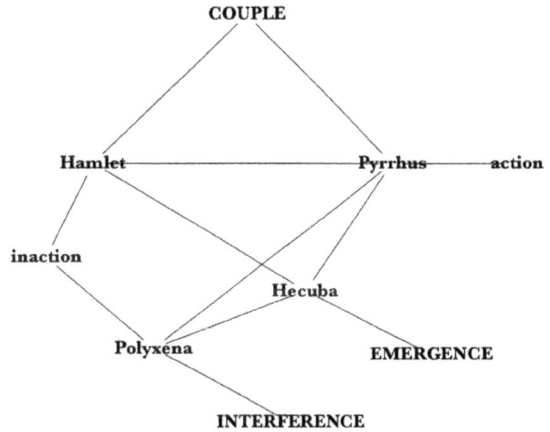

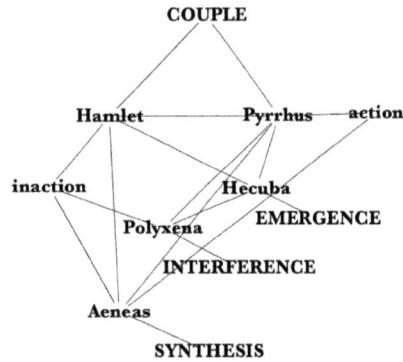

21 Complexity in *Hamlet*.

Speech becomes a token representation of *Hamlet*, revealing the same pattern of feedback at any level of the system itself. Such self-similarity, or scale invariance, characterizes complex systems.

Complexity is distinguished by a similar isomorphism between systems of different types and components, where each element performs a function within the larger whole and is not independent.[77] It means that meaning is not derived from a one-to-one correspondence, but rather from the relationships between the components of the system. Multiple things coexist at a single moment, demanding new ways of describing the world 'while keeping it open'.[78] The mutual interaction among the fundamental elements is arguably the defining quality of complexity: complex systems 'consist of large networks of individual components, each given relatively simple rules and with no central control, whose collective actions cause complexity'.[79] The networks I have utilized hopefully demonstrate how the diverse entities of the Pyrrhus story interact in such a non-linear manner.[80]

The recursive mechanisms of rich interaction and mutual influence, which trigger the connection between the different elements of the Pyrrhus story and its resonances, also exemplify complexity. This intertwined multiplicity can be exhibited and interpreted through a concept that underlies complexity, namely the feedback resulting from the introduction of a few basic operations that cause different states. The multidimensionality of *Hamlet* appears to be the complex outcome of three simple, incremental procedures, as can be seen in Figure 21 once Hamlet has been placed at the centre of the opposition with Pyrrhus:

- *deepening*: each new infiltrator initiates a deeper level connected initially to only one core (Hecuba), then to two (Polyxena), and ultimately to the previous ones, culminating in a synthesis (Aeneas).
- *feedback*: each infiltrator intersects with the preceding ones.
- *interlocking*: each infiltrator is linked to the previous one(s) and introduces a new layer (Hecuba: halting the action; Polyxena: pausing the action; Aeneas: pausing the action and subsequently choosing another course of action).

Suspended by his conscience between surrendering the fruits of his murder and still enjoying them, Claudius argues for the 'twofold force' of prayer, which can forestall our downfall or pardon us when we are 'down' (Q2 3.3.48). Scarcely repentant, the manifold force of Shakespeare's imagination likely envisioned the sources on Pyrrhus as a tapestry, where complexity dismantles all conventional oppositions.

---

[77] Franco Heylighen, Paul Cilliers and Carlos Gershenson, 'Philosophy and complexity', in *Chaos, Science and Society*, ed. Jan Bogg and Robert Geyer (Oxford and New York, 2007), 117–34; p. 121.

[78] Annemarie Mol and John Law, 'Complexities: an introduction', in *Complexities: Social Studies of Knowledge Practices*, ed. John Law and Annemarie Mol (Durham and London, 2002), 1–22; pp. 1, 16.

[79] Melanie Mitchell, *Complexity: A Guided Tour* (Oxford, 2009), pp. 12–13.

[80] Scott E. Page, *Diversity and Complexity* (Princeton and Oxford, 2011), pp. 3, 6–7, 25–6.

LUCRECE AND LEONARD BECKET, 1614–1633

CHARLES CATHCART

Lucrece attained its ninth edition in 1655. Clearly, it was a book in demand, even if it was not quite so popular an offering as Shakespeare's earlier narrative poem, *Venus and Adonis*.[1] But for several decades before and after the 1650s, the reading public would have been less likely to come across lines from *Lucrece* through its various quarto publications than by means of a compilation – half conduct book and half miscellany – released by the stationer Leonard Becket and his successors. From 1623 to 1682, readers of *A Help to Discourse; or, A Miscellany of Merriment* were able to encounter the poem.[2] A single couplet from *Lucrece* was added to *A Help to Discourse* in the fifth edition of 1623; and following the book's major expansion of 1627, three excerpts appeared. Each was still present in the seventeenth and last edition of 1682. *A Help to Discourse* was published by Becket until 1631, then by his successor Nicholas Vavasour, and later by others. It held a sustained place in the book trade for most of the seventeenth century and helped to shape the Protectorate and Restoration taste for miscellany publication.[3]

Although the exceptional prominence of *A Help to Discourse* made it into a powerful motor for transmitting excerpts from *Lucrece* during those sixty years, it was not the only, the first, or even the principal vehicle for disseminating material from *Lucrece* within the publishing business that Becket developed. A spin-off venture – *A Help to Memory and Discourse* – ran through three editions between 1620 and 1630, and the last of these, comprising the most wide-ranging and extensive miscellaneous material released by Becket, introduced two further passages from *Lucrece*.[4] However, it was the third and the originating work of this type, *The Philosopher's Banquet*, that began the publishing house's signature gambit of elaborating prose observations by means of illustrative verse quotations. Hence *The Philosopher's Banquet*, billed in 1609 as the translation

of a work by Michael Scot, reappeared five years later in an expanded edition.[5] This revamped version of 1614 introduced passages of verse from Michael Drayton, Samuel Daniel, John Donne and Sir John Davies, and quoted items of dialogue from *Hamlet* and *Richard II*.[6] Also to feature was a seemingly self-contained nine lines of verse from *Lucrece*, comprising one full stanza alongside a couplet from elsewhere in the poem. Nineteen years later – in 1633 – as the first publication of Nicholas Vavasour, Becket's former apprentice and the husband of his widow, the third and final edition of *The Philosopher's Banquet* appeared.[7] This added three new extracts from *Lucrece*, presenting in total forty-nine of the poem's lines.

The Philosopher's Banquet identified its translator of 1609 as 'W. B.' In 1614 'W. B.' gained a new designation as the book's 'author'.[8] Given that *A Help to Discourse* used the same initials to designate its principal composer in all editions from 1619 to 1631 (it had a second part, *The Countryman's Counsellor*, by an 'E. P.'), and as *A Help to Memory and Discourse* indicated that 'our vnwearied author' was providing 'for Discourse a second new supply', it

---

[1] See Katherine Duncan-Jones and Henry Woudhuysen, eds., *Shakespeare's Poems* (London, 2007), p. 73.

[2] W. B. and E. P., *A Help to Discourse; or, A Miscellany of Merriment* (London, 1623); *A Help to Discourse; or, A Miscellany of Merriment* (London, 1619).

[3] See Charles Cathcart, 'Leonard Becket, stationer, and *A help to discourse*', *The Library* 19 (2018), 301–24.

[4] *A Help to Memory and Discourse* (London, 1620); *A Help to Memory and Discourse* (London, 1630).

[5] W. B. (trans.), *The Philosopher's Banquet* (London, 1609); W. B., *The Philosopher's Banquet* (London, 1614).

[6] See Cathcart, 'Leonard Becket', 318–19.

[7] W. B., *The Philosopher's Banquet* (London, 1633).

[8] W. B., *The Philosopher's Banquet* (1614), sigs A5r, S4v.

becomes clear that all three works were claiming a common authorship.[9] 'W. B.' is often identified as William Basse, and yet the attribution is a speculative one.[10] Nevertheless, one might reasonably detect in the sustained pattern of quotation from *Lucrece* the signs of a single redactive agent. Within the output of Becket's publishing business, however, it was not only the works associated with 'W. B.' – that is, *The Philosopher's Banquet*, *A Help to Discourse* and *A Help to Memory and Discourse* – that displayed an interest in *Lucrece*, for a couplet from the poem illustrated an observation in Alex Niccholes's *A Discourse of Marriage and Wiving*.[11] This was a conduct book aimed not at conversational skills (like *A Help to Discourse* and its companion) but at successful matrimony for men. *Marriage and Wiving* was released in 1615, the year after the second edition of *The Philosopher's Banquet* and therefore the year after the first direct citation of lines from *Lucrece* in any Becket volume. The close association between these two publications is shown by their shared inclusion of the same lines from *Hamlet*.[12] *Marriage and Wiving* also bears testimony to a more informal connection with *Lucrece* amongst Becket's authors, one that operates on the level of echo or influence rather than of direct quotation, and this in turn invites the question of what the imaginative association between *Lucrece* and Becket's author-compilers might have been.

This article will illustrate and review the ways in which these anthologizing writers made use of *Lucrece*. In doing so, it will pursue a twin line of enquiry. First, the appropriations of *Lucrece* in *The Philosopher's Banquet* and elsewhere offer an insight into the afterlife of *Lucrece*; indeed, as argued above, Becket's miscellanies display an encounter with the narrative poem that is textually rich and extensive in its reach: I suggest, quite simply, that it formed the seventeenth century's most sustained literary engagement with *Lucrece* and promoted that century's most pervasive dissemination of the poem. And second, the same appropriations, viewed from another angle, say much about the creative and anthologizing efforts of the redactive agents who worked for Becket. The reflective observations of *Lucrece* help to shape the conduct literature that the stationer sponsored, and *Lucrece* emerges as a means by which Becket's author-compilers were able to comment upon the transience of life even as they created varied and light-hearted works for a popular readership. More broadly, the deployment of *Lucrece* in Becket's miscellanies constitutes a vivid example of the commonplacing practices and the inventive forms of textual transmission that inspire current approaches to book history and the use of quotation.[13]

I will proceed by presenting a straightforward narrative account of the uses of *Lucrece* made by 'W. B.' and by Becket's other authors. In doing this, I set out what I hope is a comprehensive documentation of the excerpts to appear in the books published by Becket and his successors.[14] Naturally, some aspects of *Lucrece*'s afterlife will come into relief as I sketch this history, and the appropriating style and technique of the various compilations will emerge at the same time; and the delicacy of assessing the echoes that fall short of quotation will become apparent too. The documentary tale will form a basis for examining the distinctive agencies at play in the handling of *Lucrece* and the miscellaneous nature of the way in which *Lucrece* gained a popular outlet.

* * *

In the second book (or 'course') of *The Philosopher's Banquet*, the focus shifts from what may be eaten at a banquet to who might be present at the feast. The third chapter bears the title 'Of Princes'. This chapter – like so many others – altered and grew in the book's second edition. In 1609, the chapter ended with a statement on the importance to rulers of wisdom; five years later, wisdom is bracketed with 'the practice of Vertue', and the chapter concludes:

For as the least sparke or scruple of merite in them, is more spread and blowne by the breath of Rumour, then whose flames, whole ounces, in persons of lesser eminencie.

---

9 *A Help to Memory and Discourse* (1620), sig. A4r.
10 See, for example, Ernest Sullivan, II, *The Influence of John Donne: His Uncollected Seventeenth-Century Printed Verse* (Columbia, MO, 1993), pp. 86–90, who identifies Basse as one of Donne's early readers.
11 Alex Niccholes, *A Discourse of Marriage and Wiving, and of the greatest mystery therein contained: how to choose a good wife from a bad* (London, 1615).
12 W. B., *The Philosopher's Banquet* (1614), sig. L3v; Niccholes, *Marriage and Wiving*, sig. F4v.
13 See, for example, Laura Estill, *Dramatic Extracts in Seventeenth-Century English Manuscripts: Watching, Reading, Changing Plays* (Lanham, MD, 2015); Jeffrey Todd Knight, *Bound to Read: Compilations, Collections, and the Making of Renaissance Literature* (Philadelphia, PA, 2013); and Julie Maxwell and Kate Rumbold, eds., *Shakespeare and Quotation* (Cambridge, 2018).
14 Most of the quotations to appear within Becket's various publications feature in John Munro, ed., *The Shakspere Allusion Book*, 2 vols. (London, 1909), or in Roland Mushat Frye's essays 'Shakespeare's composition of *Lucrece*: new evidence', *Shakespeare Quarterly* 16 (1965), 289–96, and 'Five Shakespeare allusions: 1621–1630', *Shakespeare Quarterly* 20 (1969), 81–3.

So likewise their errors and corruptions: To which effect these seeme to accord, as with their Authour.

> *The Crowe doth bathe his cole-blacke wings in myre,*
> *And vnperceiued flye with filth away:*
> *But if the like the snowe-white Swan desire,*
> *The stayne vpon her siluer-Downe will stay,*
> *Poore groomes (are sightlesse night) Kings glorious Day.*
> *Gnattes are vnnoted where soere they flye,*
> *But Eagles gazde vpon with euery Eye.*
> *And Princes are the Glasse, the Schoole, the Booke;*
> *Where Subiects eyes doe learne, doe reade, doe looke.*[15]

The Philosopher's Banquet concerns itself at this point with the need for princes – and, by extension, any figure of authority and prominence – to avoid those faults that may adversely affect their standing. The lines yoke the full stanza at *Lucrece* 1009–15 and the couplet at 615–16.[16] That couplet operates as a closing tag to the whole portmanteau extract, relegating the contrast between gnats and eagles to a subsidiary position. The fit is neat, and an altered meaning emerges, one that accentuates the exemplary office of 'princes'. As Sasha Roberts puts it, the compiler 'creates a new literary piece out of Shakespeare's poem for a new rhetorical context'.[17]

Becket's next release was *A Discourse of Marriage and Wiving*. In urging married couples to seek 'vnity and concord', Niccholes advises partners against aggravating matrimonial difficulties by making a truculent response to any domestic 'crosses' that they may face:

Who is so weake in discretion, that by some disaster hauing blemished one eye, for griefe thereof, will weepe out the other. That mother tries a mercilesse conclusion:

> Who hauing two sweet Babes, when death takes one,
> Will slay the other, and be nurse to none.[18]

The couplet is reproduced verbatim – but Niccholes uses not two but three lines from *Lucrece* (1160–2), for 'The mother tries a merciless conclusion' is Shakespeare's lead-in to the couplet. The extravagant thought experiment, delineating Lucrece's debate over suicide, is seemingly excessive in its new setting. Even so, it fits with the solemn significance that Niccholes accords to his own project, for he describes a man's choice of marriage partner as a matter 'Of the deareest use, but the deepest cunning that man may erre in: which is, to cut by a Thrid betweene the greatest Good or euill in the world'.[19]

Niccholes almost certainly quarried *Lucrece* further, and in a different manner, and here the debt – if such it is – operates in a slighter and less explicit way. *Marriage and Wiving* concludes with a long poem titled 'Discontents in all Ages, Sexes, States, Conditiones'. The poem addresses the human tendency to long for what is not possessed. Niccholes applies this to his subject; the 'single man' must snatch his sexual adventures briefly, uncomfortably and sometimes not at all:

> Bannish't like Tantalus in his forc'd hast,
> To touch the sweetnesse that he may not taste.[20]

The married man, conversely, may find that 'all these dainties cloy'. Niccholes extends his thesis elsewhere:

> Noting the Marchant, how from forraine shores,
> The winds and waves land wealth vnto his dores:
> That where he sleepe, or wake, or rest, or play,
> So Aires be prosperous, he growes rich that way,
> Dislikes his choyce, the Marchant he in danger,
> T'whom Rockes, and Shelues and Pyrates are no stranger:
> That try the wonders of the vnknowne deepes,
> Whom but a three inch't board from danger keepes:
> Traffiques with vnknowne Aires, and vnknowne friends
> Leauing his wife at home to doubtfull ends.
> VVho in his watry Pilgrimage is sed
> To be with neither liuing nor the dead.[21]

Shakespeare's Tarquin had concluded his stanza on the ways in which troubles or complications may enhance satisfaction with this couplet:

> Huge rocks, high winds, strong pirates, shelves and sands,
> The merchant fears, ere rich at home he lands.
>
> (335–6)

That *Marriage and Wiving*'s 'Marchant' should face 'Rockes and Shelues, and Pyrates' strongly suggests a debt, especially as Tarquin's thoughts are uttered as he reaches 'the chamber-door / That shuts him from the heaven of his thought' and that 'Hath barr'd him from the blessèd thing he sought' (337–8, 340), much as Niccholes's bachelor longs unrequitedly for 'the sweete fruition of a wife'.[22] Possible, but less likely, is that the allusion to Tantalus drew its shape from Tarquin's lines about the 'agèd man that coffers up his gold' and who

---

[15] W. B., *The Philosopher's Banquet* (1614), sigs. H3v–H4r.

[16] Citations of *Lucrece*, *Hamlet* and *Romeo and Juliet* are to *William Shakespeare: The Complete Works*, ed. Stanley Wells, Gary Taylor, John Jowett and William Montgomery, 2nd ed. (Oxford, 2005).

[17] Sasha Roberts, *Reading Shakespeare's Poems in Early Modern England* (Basingstoke, 2003), p. 134.

[18] Niccholes, *Marriage and Wiving*, sigs. Gv–G2r.

[19] Niccholes, *Marriage and Wiving*, title page.

[20] Niccholes, *Marriage and Wiving*, sig. H2v.

[21] Niccholes, *Marriage and Wiving*, sig. H3r.

[22] Niccholes, *Marriage and Wiving*, sig. H2v.

'scarce hath eyes his treasure to behold, / But like still-pining Tantalus he sits' (855, 857–8); and at that point Tarquin – anticipating the line of thought that Niccholes would develop – reflects that:

> The sweets we wish for turn to loathèd sours
> Even in the moment that we call them ours.
>
> (867–8)

When *Marriage and Wiving* gained its second – slightly expanded – edition in 1620, a new prefatory poem offered 'An Admonition to such as hereafter intend to marry':

> Ile tell them of the dangers in the way,
> Ile tell them there are shelues, and rocks, and sands,
> *Scylla* and *Charibdis* vpon both their hands.[23]

As in *Lucrece*, 'sands' is joined to the dangerous 'shelves' and 'rocks', suggesting a continued – and slightly varied – allegiance to Tarquin's words. In the same year, *A Help to Memory and Discourse* came out, and its closing poem, 'Of money and the quallity thereof', features:

> It like the Sea continuall ebbes and flowes,
> And is of such strong power, such secret might
> It makes the Lady as it bought the Knight,
> [It] sends the Marchant ouer shelues and sands,
> To forraigne Regions and farre distant lands;
> Who in his watry pilgrimag is sed
> To be with neither liuing nor yet dead,
> To deale with doubtfull foes, for firmest friends
> Leauing his wife at home to doubtfull ends.[24]

This poem is clearly related to the verses of 1615 from *Marriage and Wiving*, for it reproduces three lines from the passage cited above and shifts 'Leauing his wife at home to doubtfull ends' to a later position. And it also speaks of sending 'the Marchant ouer shelues and sands, / To forraigne Regions', again reuniting 'shelves' and 'sands', and this time doing so in relation to a 'merchant'. It seems very likely that a continuing engagement with the lines from *Lucrece* extended from 1615 to 1620.

To that date, the appropriations of *Lucrece* by Becket's authors were brief, occasional, and in some cases in the realm of echo rather than quotation. From 1623 onwards, however, the story is of increasingly profuse citations of Shakespeare's poem. (Between 1615 and 1623, the only surviving direct quotation from *Lucrece* within the Becket corpus occurred in the 1620 edition of *Marriage and Wiving*, for that again featured the couplet about 'two sweet babes'.) In 1623 Becket's most popular venture, *A Help to Discourse*, was 'for the fift time published, and much *inlarged by the former authors*'. As well as *A Help to Discourse*'s first citation of *Lucrece*, lines from *Hamlet*, *Love's Labour's Lost* and *Romeo and Juliet* appear.[25] The quotation from *Lucrece* occurs within the question-and-answer passages that form the greater part of the book:

Q: Who are those that fortune seldome favours?

A: The ouer timerous man; for, his own feare presents some difficulty to discourage euen in matters of most easie atchieument: and therefore as the Poet said:

> *Qusiquis apes, vndasque timet, spinasq; roseti,*
> *Non mel, non pisces, non feret ille rosas.*
> Who feares the Bee, the Water, pricke o'th Rose,
> Shall haue no Hony, Fish, nor Flowers for's nose.

Or thus:

> Who feares a Sentence, or an old mans Saw,
> Shall by a painted cloth be kept in awe.
> And therefore, *Audaces fortuna juvat.*[26]

Here the illustrative quotation from *Lucrece* – if considered in isolation from its source – possesses a certain fit with its new context. Verbally, it chimes with the 'Who feares' that rendered 'timet' in the preceding couplet. In tone, it accords with the light-hearted injunction to be daring. In *Lucrece* the couplet had presented the implied thoughts of Tarquin as he persuades himself to commit the rape he contemplates; and in that context, the casual, even flippant, tone is gross; and yet the inappropriateness is one that *Lucrece* itself leans towards, for Tarquin is minimizing in his own mind the abhorrent nature of the act he plans. Like each of the quotations from *Lucrece* to feature in *A Help to Discourse* (and indeed in Becket's other publications), it retained its place in all later editions; by the time its last readers encountered it afresh, the libertine ethos of so much Restoration verse and the often relaxed attitude to sexual coercion depicted in the period's drama meant that the lines from *Lucrece* were appearing in an altered cultural world.

The phrase 'kept in awe' may have been echoed previously within the Becket corpus. At this point I turn back in time to a Becket publication that precedes the 1614 *Philosopher's Banquet* and its first quotation from *Lucrece*. William Crashaw's *The Ambassador between Heaven and Earth* (1613), like *Marriage and Wiving*, contained a long

---

23 Niccholes, *A Discourse of Marriage and Wiving* (London, 1620), sig. B2r.
24 *A Help to Memory and Discourse* (1620), sig. F7v.
25 W. B. and E. P., *A Help to Discourse* (1623), sigs. M5v, F11r, N3r–v.
26 W. B. and E. P., *A Help to Discourse* (1623), sigs. O4v–O5r; see *Lucrece* 244–5.

concluding poem: 'A short Memoratiue of the mortality of our life, and the folly of our liuing'. The final lines of Crashaw's verses would be commandeered to end the tribute to King James added to *A Help to Discourse* in 1627.[27] Like many other Becket publications, it echoed *Hamlet* ('Angels & Ministers of love and grace').[28] The poem also contains these lines:

> Where if the righteous scarce shall fauour finde,
> What place for gracelesse sinners is assignd?
> Such as thy precepts haue not kept in awe,
> But broke each text, & canon of thy law.[29]

The phrase ('kept in awe') is not itself so rare as to establish that these lines are indebted to *Lucrece*. However, *Lucrece*'s couplet is immediately followed by 'Thus, grace-less', seemingly the inspiration for Crashaw's '*gracelesse sinners*', whilst Crashaw's 'precepts' holds the place of 'a Sentence, or an old mans Saw'. It is at least possible that the lines of 1613 were indebted to those of 1594, and that Tarquin's insouciant disregard for moral sanctions reappears in a more solemn light. Less than twenty lines previously, '*What shelues, and sands, and windes, and waues with-stood*' had appeared in Crashaw's poem, again in a context of spiritual peril – and this may be another debt that anticipates those of the later publications, on this occasion responding to the 'Huge rocks, high winds, strong pirates, shelves and sands' that Tarquin's merchant fears.

Four years after the addition of this couplet, *A Help to Discourse* acquired two further extracts from *Lucrece*. In 1623 the question '*What is that which being the heauiest and hardest of all things, yet yeelds both to the extremity of fire and water?*' received the bald answer 'A stone'; and in 1627 this answer was expanded to read:

> A Stone, that Fire melts, that Water weares, that Time
>   consumes.
> *Which cheares the Ploughman with increasefull crops?*
> *And wastes huge Stones with little water-drops.*[30]

As the preamble signals, these lines originally formed a halt to the fifth stanza of Lucrece's great disquisition upon 'Time'. And the other new extract, though appearing later in the edition of *A Help to Discourse*, is formed of eight lines drawn from the poem's two previous stanzas. The answer to the question, '*What may the Memory bee compared vnto?*' became longer, and the added material runs:

Against whome, time and obliuion euer make warre to deface her Register, that the most famous things euer done; the greatest wonders euer acted; the stateliest Monument euer raised; the mightiest Monarches that euer raigned should

haue here no perpetuitie, but bee interred in ruine and for-getfulnesse, for as one saith of Time:

> *Time ruinates proud buildings with her howres*
> *And smeares with dust the glittering golden Towers.*
> *Time fills with wormholes, stately Monuments*
> *And feedes obliuion with decay of things:*
> *Shee blots old Bookes, and alters their contents,*
> *And pluckes the quills from auncient Rauens wings.*
> *Shee spoyles Antiquities of hammered steele,*
> *And turnes the giddy round of fortunes wheele:*
> *She weares out Brasse, and Marble, and decayes*
> *Stones to drop downe, that spoke their raysers praise.*[31]

This extract has undergone significant changes. Some are minor: *Lucrece* reads 'To fill', 'To feed', 'To blot' and 'To pluck', for instance. But one line is omitted completely: the fifth line of the stanza beginning 'To fill with worm-holes' – that is, 'To dry the old oak's sap and blemish springs' (950). And the extract proper concludes with '*fortunes wheele*'. In short, a couplet from one stanza, a quatrain formed by the first lines of the next stanza, and that same stanza's closing couplet form the borrowed material, and an added pair of lines round off the ten lines of verse. Those final two lines operate much as the couplet about 'Princes' and 'Subiects' does in forming a finale to the twinned extract that appeared in *The Philosopher's Banquet*; and on this occasion the compiler seems to have drafted the closing couplet.

The significance of this appropriation lies squarely in its emphatic treatment of the *tempus edax rerum* theme: the notion that the passage of time will destroy all things. This is a dominating feature of many of the works Becket published. Crashaw's 'A short Memoratiue of the mortality of our life', the much-anthologized 'A memento for mortality' to appear in every edition of *A Help to Discourse*, the 'heape of Sculles' that addresses the reader in *A Father's Blessing*, and *The Curtain-Drawer of the World*'s 'A meditation of the vanity of all vanity': these are

---

27 Charles Cathcart, '"A memento for mortality", the publications of Leonard Becket, and the afterlife of *Hamlet*', *Review of English Studies* 67 (2016), 290–1.
28 William Crashaw, *The Ambassador between Heaven and Earth* (London, 1613), sig. Q10r; see *Hamlet* 1.4.20.
29 Crashaw, *The Ambassador*, sig. Q10r.
30 W. B. and E. P., *A Help to Discourse* (1623), sig. D7r; *A Help to Discourse; or, A Miscellany of Merriment* (London, 1627), sig. D9r; see *Lucrece* 958–9.
31 W. B. and E. P., *A Help to Discourse* (1627), sigs. E11v–E12r; see *Lucrece* 944–9, 951–2.

simply some of the most striking examples of the tendency to write on 'memento mori' topics.[32] This glances back at *Lucrece* itself, highlighting a prominent feature of Shakespeare's poem and one that helped to render it so fitting a resource for Becket's agents. The selection of the lines on 'Time' and its depredations enabled *A Help to Discourse* to develop its distinctive and meditative character. Moreover, it was this last inclusion that formed the single most intensive means by which the 'W. B.' publications disseminated *Lucrece*, for *A Help to Discourse* outstripped all other vehicles through which *Lucrece* reached Becket's readership.

By 1627 *A Help to Discourse* had reached its maximum extent, something which it maintained until 1631 and its eighth edition; the subsequent omissions did not involve the excerpts from *Lucrece* and these held their place until the final edition of *A Help to Discourse* in 1682.[33] Meanwhile – in 1630 – *A Help to Memory and Discourse* attained its last and longest manifestation. This third iteration formed the richest and most varied verse miscellany of Becket's entire output. In two long added sections appeared extracts from authors and works previously quarried, and others that were altogether new.[34] Many are of great interest in themselves, and they include the first print versions of two of John Donne's best-known lyrics.[35] The two new inclusions of material from *Lucrece* occur in the first group of additions. They illustrate the book's mix of light-hearted and solemn observations, and the eclectic nature of its appropriations. The question is posed: '*Whether are men of short and little statures, or those of the more ample and spacious, commonly the wisest or the longest liued?*' In offering an answer, the author turns to Homer, who:

doth describe *Vlisses* to be short and wise, and *Aiax* long and a foole.

> In *Aiax* and *Vlisses* what Art
> Of Physiognomy might one behold?
> The face of either cypher eithers heart,
> Their face, their manners, most expresly told:
> In *Aiax* eyes blunt rage and rigor rold,
> But the mild glance that sly *Vlisses* lent,
> Shew'd deep regard, in smyling merriment.[36]

This generally close citation of *Lucrece* 1394–1400 contains one notable alteration. Shakespeare's stanza concluded with 'smiling government', not 'merriment'; and all the uneasy intimations of how the 'sly' Ulysses bore himself have disappeared. For 'W. B.', the contrast

is between ill humour and equanimity; for Shakespeare (or for Lucrece), it involved intemperate anger and calculating self-control. Beyond this, though, *Lucrece* seems to be cited for essentially trivial reasons; the miscellanist commandeered the lines for anecdotal purposes to develop a curio of a question.

The other new inclusion, however, accords with the kind of meditative content seen in the attention to 'Time' and its power to waste, three years previously. It also shows *Lucrece* in conversation with a dramatic extract. The passage runs:

Q: There are three things especially, that are enemies to sleepe (deaths Image) and what are they?

A: An vnquiet bed, vnrestlesse cares, a troubled mind.

And therefore as the Poet saith:

> *When all things else to rest themselues betake,*
> *Then theeues, and cares, and troubled mindes they wake.*
> And so the contrary.
> *Where vnbrused youth with vnstuft braine*
> *Doth couch his golden limbes, there sleepe [doth] raigne.*[37]

Here the context for the quotation from *Lucrece* is one of an explicit awareness of mortality, for sleep is '*deaths Image*', whilst the 'answer' picks up on the '*cares*' and the '*troubled mindes*' of the extract. This is one of the more extensively amended of the *Lucrece* passages; the lines of 1594 ran: 'And every one to rest themselves betake, / Save thieves, and cares, and troubled minds, that wake' (125–6). The changes intensify the couplet's function as a *sententia*. When the compiler turns towards the converse – the repose that comes easily to the young and untroubled person – it is *Romeo and Juliet* that supplies the 'contrary' claim. This choice again shows the tendency to gravitate to a consistent pool of material, for this appropriation from Friar Lawrence's second speech had been preceded by *A Help to Memory and Discourse*'s edition of 1621 and the *Help to Discourse* of 1623, both of

---

[32] Crashaw, *The Ambassador*, sigs. Q9r–Q12r; W. B. and E. P., *A Help to Discourse; or, A Miscellany of Merriment* (London, 1619), sigs. I10r–I11r; *A Father's Blessing* (London, 1616), sigs. D2v–D3r; William Parkes, *The Curtain-Drawer of the World* (London, 1612), sigs. H4v–I3v.

[33] *A Help to Discourse* (1682), sigs. Cr, C9r–v, K5v.

[34] *A Help to Memory and Discourse* (1630), sigs. A12v–C7v, and sig. F3r onwards.

[35] *A Help to Memory and Discourse* (1630), sigs. C2r–v, G3r.

[36] *A Help to Memory and Discourse* (1630), sig. B6v.

[37] *A Help to Memory and Discourse* (1630), sig. D3r.

which deployed several lines from the Friar's opening soliloquy.[38]

If the inclusions of 1630 in *A Help to Memory and Discourse* constitute the single most ambitious range of commonplacing within the Becket corpus, the final edition of *The Philosopher's Banquet* three years later supplies the most intensive recourse to *Lucrece* itself. Technically, this was not a Becket publication; the publisher had died, and the final *Philosopher's Banquet* was released by Vavasour. In practice, it displays exactly the same characteristics, and in this final edition *Lucrece* becomes the dominant inclusion.

The twinned extract about the reputation of princes is retained from 1614, and several extended passages appear anew. The first reprises the extract on 'Time':

Q. What is the wisest of all things?

A. Thales Milesius answered, Time; for it finds out, teacheth and altereth all things. But one of *Pythagoras* Schollers of late time said the contrary, and that it was the most rude and unknowing, and the master of all ignorance: for with his owne long waste, it wrapt all things in ignorance.

Times office, saith one, is

> To shew the Beldam daughters of her daughters,
> To make the child a man, the man a child,
> To slay the Tyger, that doth live by slaughter,
> To tame the Vnicorne, and beasts most wild:
> To fill with worme-holes stately Monuments,
> To feed Oblivion with decay of things,
> To blot old books, alter their contents,
> To plucke the quils from ancient Ravens wings:
> To spoyle Antiquities of hammerd steele,
> And turne the giddy round of Fortunes wheele.[39]

Although the compiler has looked towards the same passage from *Lucrece* that circulated almost annually since 1627 in *A Help to Discourse*, the exact selection of lines (953–6, 946–9, 951–2) and their arrangement are subtly different. The couplet beginning '*Time ruinates proud buildings*' is absent; the added and manufactured lines about decayed stones that had once '*spoke their raysers praise*' are also gone; and the line about 'stately Monuments' is relegated to the middle of the extract, now following those on 'the Beldam', 'the child', 'the Tyger' and 'the Vnicorne'. The effect is to downplay the impact upon buildings and to accentuate the instructive role of 'Time'. In one regard the use of the passage follows that of 1627 exactly, for the last six lines comprise a full *Lucrece* stanza – but with, as before, the omission of the fifth line. This makes the seven-line rhyme royal form turn into *sesta rima*. This alteration formed the basis for Roland Mushat Frye's inventive but improbable theory that the Becket appropriations reflect an early draft of *Lucrece*, one that had used the same form as *Venus and Adonis*.[40] This amendment of the rhyming pattern also partly corresponds with some, but not all, of the other inclusions.

As part of an answer on '*the most industrious*' man, the following appears:

hee is accounted the true wise man that learnes from every man, hee the strong man that masters his owne affections: hee the true rich man, that rejoyceth in his owne store; which is the levell many misse, which makes their life miserable, according as a learned writer thus delivers it:

> The aged man that coffers up his gold,
> Is plagu'd with cramps, and gouts, and painfull fits,
> And scarce hath eyes his treasure to behold,
> But like to stil pining *Tantalus*, he sits
> Having no other pleasure of gaine,
> Then torment that it cannot cure his paine.
>
> So then he hath it when he cannot use it,
> And leaves it to be mastred by his yong,
> Who in their pride doe presently abuse it:
> Their Father was too weake and they too strong
> To hold this blessed, cursed fortune long.[41]

Uniquely, the layout of 1633 indicates the stanza break, and the absence of 'And useless barns the harvest of his wits' (859) from the first stanza quoted becomes more obvious. The fifth line of the next stanza, however, is present, thus allowing the extract to conclude with a rhyme. This is part of the passage that may have drawn the attention of Niccholes as he drafted his lines about the human tendency to yearn for what is not possessed; but the passage of 1633 is not particularly concerned by this, and hence, perhaps, the omission of the final couplet from the Lucrece stanza: 'The sweets we wish for turn to loathèd sours / Even in the moment that we call them ours' (867–8). Also without precedent in this history is the description of *Lucrece*'s author as a 'learned writer', for otherwise he is simply 'the Poet', 'one' or even 'another'.

---

[38] *Romeo and Juliet* 2.2.37–8; *A Help to Memory and Discourse* (London, 1621), sig. E9r; W. B. and E. P., *A Help to Discourse* (1623), sig. N3r–v; *Romeo and Juliet* 2.2.15–22.

[39] W. B., *The Philosopher's Banquet* (1633), sigs. Ov–O2r.

[40] Frye, 'Shakespeare's composition of *Lucrece*'.

[41] W. B., *The Philosopher's Banquet* (1633), sigs. P10v–P11r; see *Lucrece* 855–8, 860–6.

The most extensive single recourse to *Lucrece* is the final new inclusion of 1633:

Q. *What is the most guilty part of Time?*

A. Opportunity: which if neglected, maketh the best thing unrespected, according to the Poet:

> Like to a poore man so befriended,
> Or Summers Chimneys, Winter ended;
> Or like to Souldiers, warres being done,
> Or like to Dogges, their races runne,
> Or like to beauty wrinkled old,
> Or like a secret knowne, and told,
> So Time of all the dearest cost,
> Not taken by the fore-top, lost.

And for the guilt, another thus,

> O Opportunity, thy guilt is great,
> 'Tis thou that executes the Traytors treason,
> Thou setst the Wolfe, where hee the Lambe may get,
> Whoeuer plots the sinne, thou points the season:
> And in thy shady cell, where none may spy him,
> Sits sinne to seize the soules that wander by him.
> Thou mak'st the Vestal violate her oath,
> Thou blow'st the fire when temperance is thaw'd,
> Thou smotherest honesty, thou murderest truth,
> Thou foule abettor, thou notorious baud:
> And to expresse thy nature here in briefe,
> Thy honey turnes to gall, thy joy to griefe.
> When wilt thou be the humble suppliants friend,
> And bring him where his cause may be obtain'd;
> When wilt thou sort an howre great strife to end,
> Or free the soule that wretchednesse hath chain'd,
> Give Physicke to the sicke, ease to the pain'd?
> The poore, lame, blind, halt, creep, cry out to thee,
> But they ne're meet with Opportunitie, &c.[42]

As with the passage that linked couplets from *Lucrece* and *Romeo and Juliet*, here *Lucrece* again has a partner extract. I cannot identify the lines about a 'poore man' and include them here simply to display the immediate context for the long verse passage from Shakespeare's poem. The introduction brings together guilt, opportunity and time, directing attention therefore to three of the concepts most insistently explored in *Lucrece*. The extract comprises three stanzas. The first two display the amendment to the *sesta rima* form; the last appears in rhyme royal. The substitution of 'And to expresse thy nature here in briefe' in place of Shakespeare's 'Thou plantest scandal and displaceth laud. / Thou ravisher, thou traitor, thou false thief' (887–8) constitutes by far the greatest departure from the original lines of *Lucrece* in any of the direct quotations introduced by Becket's compilers. The

extract concludes with an ampersand, thereby hinting that a still longer quotation might have been furnished.

That, then, is the trail of *Lucrece*'s afterlife within the redactive and commonplacing activities of Becket's authors. By terminating this history in 1633 upon the release of the final, expanded *Philosopher's Banquet*, a line is drawn at the last new appropriation of Lucrece to appear with the series of publications that Becket initiated. And yet, given that *A Help to Discourse* experienced numerous further editions – 1635, 1636, 1638, 1640, 1648, 1654, 1663, 1667 and 1682 – the reach of Shakespeare's poem, and in particular the long excerpt upon 'Time', with its portentous preface and its closing embellishment, was both wide and long-standing, continuing for almost fifty additional years.

The date of 1633 concludes two decades of appropriative play with Shakespeare's *Lucrece*. In reviewing this activity, I turn first to the issue of authorial agency. Of course, by directing attention so often to 'Becket's compilers', or to a similar formula, whilst setting out this chapter in *Lucrece*'s afterlife, a history emerges that looks not towards the writers involved but at the commercial context of their activity. And certainly, by focusing attention squarely upon a specific corporate culture – that of the publishing business of the stationer, Leonard Becket – this article has attempted a manoeuvre away from the author and towards the environment in which individual agents operated.

But individual agents there were, and one feature of this two-decades-long activity is that an idiosyncratic agency seems at play. To look towards 'W. B.' (whoever 'W. B.' may have been) is one obvious avenue. And, indeed, the 1614 and 1633 editions of *The Philosopher's Banquet* book-end the formal quotations from *Lucrece*, and these are editions that identify 'W. B.' precisely as author, and nearly all the intervening inclusions, and all that remained in print after 1633, are those of *A Help to Discourse* (by 'W. B.' and E. P.') or *A Help to Memory and Discourse* (which claims the agency of the same author). Who 'W. B.' was – and even whether the initials point to a single individual – is uncertain. Nevertheless, the consistent, ruminative, deviating style of the three collections, with their embellishments, their jackdaw-like appropriations, and their erection of solemnity upon a framework of light-heartedness, does seem to reflect the taste and the manner of a distinctive composing and coordinating agent.

---

[42] W. B., *The Philosopher's Banquet* (1633), sigs R4v–R5v; see *Lucrece*, 876–9, 881–6, 889, 897–903.

On the other hand, the dependency upon *Lucrece* of *A Discourse of Marriage and Wiving* and – less distinctly – *The Ambassador between Heaven and Earth* displays some of the same qualities. Given that Niccholes is quite unknown, the named authorship of *Marriage and Wiving* offers little assistance; indeed, the conduct book's modern editor suggested that the name might be a pseudonym.[43] *The Ambassador* and its author William Crashaw at first sight appear much more promising. Crashaw leaves a strong trail through his many publications and his public roles, and there too a distinctive personality is evident.[44] However, the indications that *The Ambassador* in 1613, *Marriage and Wiving* in 1615 and 1620, and *A Help to Memory and Discourse* in 1620 all gravitated in similar ways towards Lucrece's line about the 'merchant' and his fear of 'Huge rocks, high winds, strong pirates, shelves and sands', and that *The Ambassador* as well as *A Help to Discourse* may have responded to the lines about 'a Sentence, or an old mans Saw' present a conundrum. We might posit that the poems that conclude both *The Ambassador* and *Marriage and Wiving* were composed by the same person who contributed 'Of money and the quallity thereof' to the first edition of *A Help to Memory and Discourse*. But the shared sense of mortality appears freely in Crashaw's translations too. In his rendering of the dialogue between 'The Soule and the Bodie of a damned man' he writes that:

> Those turrets gay of costly masonry,
> And larger Palaces are not now thy roome,
> But in a coffin of small quantity,
> Thou lyest interred in a little tombe.[45]

This pooled recourse to the couplet in *Lucrece* may best be approached in the light of the links between, on the one hand, *The Ambassador*, *The Curtain-Drawer of the World* and *The Father's Blessing*, and, on the other, 'A memento for mortality' and its partner poems as they appear and even alter in the 1619, 1623 and 1627 editions of *A Help to Discourse*.[46] There a common dependency upon *Hamlet's* graveyard scene is one of the features that offers a context for what is a clear case of borrowing and textual transmission within the corpus of Becket's publications.

An alternative way of making sense of the place of *Lucrece* within these publications is to look outwards from Becket's enterprise and view them in the light of the developments within the book trade. In commenting on the afterlife of *Lucrece*, commentators are often quick to examine *England's Parnassus* and *Belvedere* – and with very good reason too, for the prominence of *Lucrece* within these collections is conspicuous and shows the salience that the poem had gained just a few years after its first print publication.[47] Thomas Middleton's quasi-sequel, *The Ghost of Lucrece*, is a very explicit response to Shakespeare's poem; and so, in a different way, is Thomas Heywood's play *The Rape of Lucrece*. Scholars have also examined the afterlife of *Lucrece* in Protectorate and Restoration times in charting the poem's reception.[48] This article has sought to delineate a progressive or developing impact within a single creative context: Becket's publishing house, with the three aggregative miscellanies linked to 'W. B.' at its heart. However, the nineteen years between two *Philosopher's Banquet* editions of 1614 and 1633 marked a period during which the practice of composite publication was transformed. In the first of these years, Laurence Lisle released Sir Thomas Overbury's poem *A Wife*, and by the end of that year the long run of new editions was well under way, with its accretion of commendatory tributes, characters and news items.[49] It would be a publishing phenomenon even more extensive in its number of versions than Becket's *A Help to Discourse*, and much more compressed in time. John Stephens, originally a contributor to *A Wife*, was the principal composing agent in a parallel venture, one backed by different publishers and sporting more than one title.[50] Stephens was involved also in Henry Fitzgeoffrey's *Satires*

---

[43] Lloyd Davis, ed., *Sexuality and Gender in the English Renaissance: An Annotated Edition of Contemporary Documents* (New York and London, 1998), p. 213.

[44] P. J. Wallis, *William Crashawe: The Sheffield Puritan* (n.p., 1963). See also R. M. Fisher, 'The predicament of William Crashawe, preacher at the Temple, 1605–1613', *Journal of Ecclesiastical History* 25 (1974), 267–76.

[45] Crashaw, *Querela sive, dialogus animae et corporis damnati* (London, 1613), sigs. A6r, A7r.

[46] See Cathcart, '"A memento for mortality"'.

[47] Duncan-Jones and Woudhuysen, eds., *Shakespeare's Poems*, pp. 73–4; Jeffrey Paxton Hehmeyer, 'Heralding the commonplace: authorship, voice, and commonplace in Shakespeare's Rape of Lucrece', *Shakespeare Quarterly* 64 (2013), 160–1; Kate Rumbold, 'Shakespeare anthologised', in *The Edinburgh Companion to Shakespeare and the Arts*, ed. Mark Thornton Burnett, Adrian Streete and Ramona Wray (Edinburgh, 2011), 89–90; Peter Stallybrass and Roger Chartier, 'Reading and authorship: the circulation of Shakespeare 1590–1619', in *A Concise Companion to Shakespeare and the Text*, ed. Andrew Murphy (London, 2007), 35–56; pp. 45–53.

[48] Adam G. Hooks, 'Royalist Shakespeare: publishers, politics, and the appropriation of *The Rape of Lucrece*', in *Canonising Shakespeare: Stationers and the Book Trade*, ed. Emma Depledge and Peter Kirwan (Cambridge, 2017), 26–37.

[49] See Alastair Bellany, *The Politics of Court Scandal in Early Modern England* (Cambridge, 2002), pp. 117–31.

[50] Thomas Overbury, *A Wife, now The Widow*, 1st ed. (London, 1614), sig. A3r; John Stephens, *Satirical Essays, Characters, and Others* (London, 1615), and *Essays and Characters, Ironical and Instructive* (London, 1615).

and Satirical Epigrams, and this too ran to multiple volumes and accumulated accretions.[51] The social networks that lay behind these enterprises were largely formed through the Inns of Court, with Lincoln's Inn and the Middle Temple to the fore. The same is true of other portmanteau publications that came out just as Becket was taking his own first steps as a publisher with a shop close to the Inner Temple and an early association with Crashaw, who held the post of Reader at both the Inner and the Middle Temple. In 1613, the verse of two Innsmen, John Marston and Samuel Page, was appended to the reissued *Alcilia; or, Philoparthen's Loving Folly* in a collection that looked back to the 1590s.[52] It was released again in 1619 and 1628. In 1611, the mass of spoof commendatory poems in good-humoured mockery of Thomas Coryate appeared; and this too was a venture deeply shaped by the friendship associations forged through the Inns of Court.[53]

These are only some of the publishing enterprises that offer a context and furnish analogues for *A Help to Discourse* and its fellow publications. In the two decades between the first and last illustrative quotation from *Lucrece* to appear in a Becket publication, the cultural context in which London's printing houses operated had undergone substantial changes. Becket's commercial activities were distinctive in that they identified, exploited and whetted the market for popular works that presented themselves as conduct books, but which actually offered a leisurely journey through philosophical and religious speculations, often in a question-and-answer format, and increasingly edging into the genre of miscellany. The practice of embellishment – fresh inclusions designed to attract new customers and thereby to sustain a successful formula – however ingeniously prosecuted in *A Help to Discourse*, holds an obvious resemblance to the efforts of Lisle. So does the loose notion of authorship that underpins the venture: if 'W. B.' is elusive, and perhaps a token for a corporate effort, so 'Thomas Overbury' was decreasingly the true agent of *A Wife*.

Anyway, between 1614 and 1633, Shakespeare died, the first and second Shakespearian Folios (which excluded *Lucrece*) appeared, Jonson's *Works* saw print, and in 1633 so did the first collection of Donne's verse, and this included items that had first been printed in the two *Help* volumes. Within this changed print and reading culture, Becket's output seems to have targeted a rather different market from that of these Folios and collections, and even from the London-centric and Inns-based products of Lisle's operation. The tendency to present extracts as an illustrative companion to remarks about 'Time' or

'Opportunity' loosely accords with the organizing principle used in *England's Parnassus* or *Belvedere*, but this is deceptive: Becket's writers offer their passages from *Lucrece* almost as afterthoughts; indeed, often they were actual afterthoughts, tacked on to pre-existing passages. Becket seems to have aimed at a less elite and a less metropolitan readership; and in this his publications look towards later developments in miscellany publication. Adam Smyth suggests that 'Elizabethan collections often had an overt seriousness of purpose largely absent in their mid-seventeenth-century relatives.'[54]

Perhaps it is a modern analogy that best explains the reach of *Lucrece* through Becket's publications. Clips from movies and television dramas often present iconic screen moments – Darcy plunging into the lake at Pemberley, the playing of the piano in *Casablanca*, the opening shots of *The Searcher* – as short clips within a wider compilation, often introduced through a commentary. In this way, a shared cultural heritage grows, and people who would rarely view a film of the 1940s or a classic Western, or sit through several hours of an Austen dramatization, share a familiarity with these brief episodes. Naturally, this analogy should not be pushed too far: the huge reach of that digital access to such familiar screen moments creates a shared cultural heritage of a depth that exceeds anything that a printed excerpt might attain in, say, the 1620s. Nevertheless, the popularity of Becket's miscellanies had something of this effect, I would argue, and certainly the dissemination of the *Lucrece* extracts through *The Philosopher's Banquet* and the two *Help* volumes looks to a wider, and perhaps a more diverse, readership than the verse of *Lucrece* otherwise obtained.

What perception of this verse might Becket's readers have gained? The lines on the depredations of time may have gained the greatest purchase. When, in 1627, 'W. B.' first cited the lines beginning '*Time ruinates proud buildings with her howres*', readers encountered the longest of those quotations that persisted from the 1620s to

[51] Henry Fitzgeoffrey, *Satires and Satirical Epigrams, with Certain Observations at Blackfriars* (London, 1617), sigs. E4v–Cv, E5r, F8r–v.

[52] I. C., *Alcilia: or, Philoparthens Loving Folly, whereunto is added Pygmalion's Image with The Love of Amos and Laura, and also Epigrams by Sir I.H. and others* (London, 1613).

[53] *Coryate's Crudities* (London, 1611). See Michelle O'Callaghan, *The English Wits: Literature and Sociability in Early Modern England* (Cambridge, 2006), pp. 102–10.

[54] Adam Smyth, *'Profit and Delight': Printed Miscellanies in England, 1640–1682* (Detroit, 2004), p. 22.

the 1680s. This quarried the lines that would also emerge in the final edition of *The Philosopher's Banquet* – the only *Lucrece* passage to be quoted directly in two separate Becket compilations. *England's Parnassus* had reproduced the full three stanzas from *Lucrece* (939–59) that include not only the lines mentioned above but also the couplet that illustrated the impact of 'Time' upon 'A Stone' and that formed the other new acquisition of 1627. The legacy of *Lucrece* – at this point – is a concentration upon the decay of buildings and of the stones that formed them. As W. B.'s summarizing couplet puts it, Time *'weares out Brasse, and Marble, and decayes / Stones to drop downe, that spoke their raysers praise'*. The emphasis here is very strong; *Lucrece*'s 'stately Monuments' finds its way into the passage's preamble too, where 'the stateliest Monument euer raised' appears. This stands alongside 'the greatest wonders euer acted' and 'the mightiest Monarches that euer raigned' as phenomena to be 'interred in ruine and forgetfulnesse'. *Lucrece* therefore furnishes what is a signature statement of *A Help to Discourse*, and one that articulates a central perspective offered within Becket's ouevre: the fragility and evanescence of the earthly world.

AUDIO SHAKESPEARE

THOMAS MIDDLETON ON BBC RADIO

MICHAEL P. JENSEN[1]

This group of articles shows the study of Shakespeare audio growing out of its infancy, but audio studies of other early modern English playwrights still await conception. Aside from one faulty list,[2] nothing has been published about audio performances of plays by Thomas Dekker, John Ford, Thomas Heywood, Ben Jonson, Thomas Kyd or their contemporary playwrights, including the subject of this article, Thomas Middleton.

I begin this expansion with Middleton for two reasons. Audio performances of his plays are confined to the British Broadcasting Corporation (BBC) radio, making the amount of data manageable in a short article, and, while I am unconvinced that Middleton contributed to *All's Well That Ends Well*, his contributions to *Macbeth* – however those were added[3] – and collaboration on *Timon of Athens* are a natural transition between Shakespeare and Middleton audio studies. There are many programmes with readings excerpted from *Macbeth* and *Timon*, but we shall concentrate on adaptations. There are at least forty-six *Macbeth* radio adaptations worldwide, starting with the BBC's 1923 broadcast directed by Cecil A. Lewis.[4] Most of these are abridged. Seventeen commercial audio recordings were released, starting in 1940 with Orson Welles's abridgement,[5] although most commercial recordings are unabridged. Some are superb, such as Martin Jenkins's[6] and Richard Eyre's[7] broadcasts for the BBC, the Old Vic Company audiobook directed by Frank Hauser,[8] and Fiona Shaw's audiobook in which she also plays Lady Macbeth.[9] English-language radio broadcasts of *Timon of Athens* are not in circulation and so are difficult to study, but there were five starting with Peter Watts's in 1953.[10] There were five known commercial recordings between 1954 and 2022, starting with a German translation produced by Ludwig Berger, first broadcast on radio and later given commercial release.[11] The language barrier prevents me from evaluating that

show, but those by George Ryland[12] and Clive Brill[13] are worth hearing. Most *Macbeth* and *Timon* audio performances are documented by Michael P. Jensen and the Learning On Screen Shakespeare Database.[14]

Ten other Middleton plays received sixteen productions on various BBC radio services between 1950 and 2009. This article introduces these under-known performances. No attempt is made to theorize these broadcasts; the goal is to get them into the Middleton performance history so proper study may begin. To understand the context of these broadcasts, we must

---

[1] This article is dedicated to my colleague, friend, and fellow contributor Alden T. Vaughan. Flights of angels.

[2] Janet Clare, 'Theatre of the air: a checklist of radio productions of Renaissance drama, 1922–1986, with an appendix of television productions (excluding Shakespeare)', *Renaissance Drama Newsletter*, Supplement 6 (1986).

[3] The popular 'Middleton revised *Macbeth*' theory should be replaced by musical additions as explained by Tiffany Stern in *Shakespeare, Malone and the Problems of Chronology* (Cambridge, 2023) p. 49.

[4] BBC Radio, 18 October 1923, 120 minutes.

[5] Mercury Text Records, 1940, 78 minutes.

[6] BBC Radio Three, 23 April 1984, 130 minutes.

[7] BBC Radio Three, 10 September 2000, 110 minutes.

[8] EMI, 1953, 106 minutes. [9] Naxos, 1988, 144 minutes.

[10] BBC Third Programme, 18 January 1953, 110 minutes.

[11] SFB, 16 October 1954, 81 minutes.

[12] Marlowe Dramatic Society, 1961, 123 minutes.

[13] Arkangel, 1999, 138 minutes.

[14] Michael P. Jensen, *Shakespeare after Shakespeares: An Encyclopedia of the Bard in Mass Media and Popular Culture*, ed. Richard Burt, vol. 2 (Westport, CT, 2007): *Macbeth*, pp. 538–44; *Timon of Athens*, p. 570. The Learning on Screen Shakespeare Database may be accessed at http://bufvc.ac.uk/shakespeare. Counts for *Macbeth* and *Timon of Athens* were derived by the subjective process of examining the entries in this database to determine which were full-length plays, defined below, and adding known performances not in the database. Some productions may have been missed.

understand BBC play adaptations, which takes us on a detour through some other early modern playwrights.

The BBC is by far the most prolific broadcaster of their plays worldwide in every decade since *Scenes from Shakespeare*, its first Shakespeare broadcast in 1923, a programme of excerpts from three plays produced by Lewis[15] who, with Cathleen Nesbitt, co-led a dedicated Shakespeare unit in the early years.

The Corporation soon produced what they called 'full-length plays', meaning the plot was essentially intact, although there were cuts and light revisions with narration added to the earliest broadcasts, all done to compensate for the limitations of this non-visual medium. More on that below. The Corporation's first full-length play was *Twelfth Night* directed by Nesbitt that same year,[16] followed by dozens more Shakespeare broadcasts. The first verifiable early modern play broadcast not written by Shakespeare is one scene from Marlowe's *Doctor Faustus* in a 1929 programme called *Three Great Playwrights*.[17] The other writers were not early modern. A dozen more Marlowe broadcasts were given over the next fifteen years, but the BBC was slow to embrace most early modern playwrights. Jonson's *Volpone* was directed by John Burrell and broadcast in 1944[18] followed by a 1947–1948 surge when M. R. Ridley produced Heywood's *A Woman Killed with Kindness*,[19] Felix Felon produced John Webster's *The Duchess of Malfi*[20] and *The White Devil*,[21] and John Richmond produced Philip Massinger's *A New Way to Pay Old Debts*.[22] The BBC continued to expand its roster of early modern playwrights in the years that followed, and that takes us to Middleton.

This article uses the terms 'producer' and 'director' interchangeably because these were usually one job at the BBC. The show descriptions below are in three parts. First are basic facts such as the year broadcast and the name of the director. Second, adaptive strategies are described for programmes in circulation. Most scholars neglect the marketing of Shakespeare media performances, so the third part describes material the BBC created to attract listeners to each play. A second but not always reliable aspect of marketing is casting. Stars draw audiences, but a programme's intended prestige is unclear when a star is not cast, since first actor choices are not always available. Nevertheless, casting informs public perception of a programme's prestige – therefore, principal members of the cast are listed with notes on their impact at the time of each broadcast, in an imperfect glance at contemporary impressions of each show.

The first two Middleton plays were adapted and directed by Frank Hauser. *The Changeling* was presented in 75-minutes.[23] This 1950 broadcast eliminated the subplot written by William Rowley and probably thinned the dialogue of the main plot, a strategy for shortening plays still common today. Hauser was a general-assignment producer with the BBC from 1948 to 1952, mostly directing classic plays, poetry readings and children's serials. The BBC called *The Changeling* 'A Jacobean drama of "blood and poetry"'. The radio listing was accompanied by a striking illustration of the principal characters to draw attention to the listing.[24] Peter Finch starred as De Flores and Jill Balcon as Beatrice-Joanna. Both were enjoying fame on the London stage at that time and the rest of the cast is also very strong, marking this as a prestige broadcast. Unfortunately, no recording is in circulation, a frequent frustration for radio researchers.

The BBC did not always know it was producing Middleton. Hauser directed *The Revenger's Tragedy* the next year.[25] The play was then attributed to Cyril Tourneur, an attribution often doubted even before Middleton's authorship was established in the 1980s.[26] The BBC names Tourneur as the author in the *Radio Times* and would have on the air, so this show should not be understood as an exploration of Middleton's works but as part of the Corporation's effort to broadcast more early modern playwrights. At 110 minutes, the play is probably fairly complete. The programme is not described in the *Radio Times* listings, but a feature article claims that Tourneur was an impressive and 'much under-rated dramatist'.[27] Four of the actors were prestigiously named above the title in the broadcast listing, Walter Fitzgerald (the Duke), Hugh Burden (Lussurioso), Rita Vale (the second Duchess) and William Devlin (Vindice).[28] All were busy in film, television and on the stage. Only Devlin

---

[15] BBC Radio, 16 February 1923, 105 minutes.

[16] BBC Radio, 28 May 1923, 110 minutes.

[17] BBC Radio, director unknown, 22 May 1929, 60 minutes.

[18] BBC Home Service, 19 March 1944, 90 minutes.

[19] BBC Third Programme, 13 April 1947, 130 minutes.

[20] BBC Third Programme, 11 August 1947, 105 minutes.

[21] BBC Third Programme, 15 February 1948, 135 minutes.

[22] BBC Home Service, 18 October 1948, 90 minutes.

[23] BBC Home Service, 20 November 1950, 75 minutes.

[24] *Radio Times*, 19 November 1950, p. 22.

[25] BBC Third Programme, 16 September 1951, 110 minutes.

[26] Several articles preceded MacDonald P. Jackson's decisive edition *The Revenger's Tragedy, Attributed to Thomas Middleton: A Facsimile of the 1607/8 Quarto* (Rutherford, NJ, 1983).

[27] Basil Ashmore, 'A thunderstorm of a play', *Radio Times*, 14 September 1951, p. 13.

[28] *Radio Times*, 16 September 1951, p. 21.

had extensive experience broadcasting early modern plays, mostly Shakespeare. The programme was repeated three times through 1952.

The 1955 *Women Beware Women* also received a feature story now promoting Middleton by name.[29] R. D. Smith adapted and produced the 140-minute programme.[30] While the cast was not well known outside of broadcasting, the London Chamber Orchestra was promoted for playing incidental music composed for this broadcast by Anthony Bernard. Smith produced literary programmes for the BBC from 1946 to 1973, including adaptations of Shakespeare, Jonson and Kyd. *Women Beware Women* was rebroadcast twice.

A short version of *A Yorkshire Tragedy* was broadcast to the Manchester region in 1955.[31] That programme, starring the well-known theatrical couple Donald Wolfit and Rosalind Iden, was introduced by early modern scholar G. Wilson Knight and directed by Colin Shaw, who called Wolfit 'a boyhood hero'.[32] We now know the play is Middleton's, but as the *Radio Times* notes, the 1608 quarto edition misattributes the play 'to William Shakespeare'.[33] That attribution became the point in a 1957 Middleton broadcast, which we examine out of chronological order.

The BBC produced a 1956–1957 series based on five plays in the Shakespeare Apocrypha – plays that have been attributed to Shakespeare, often dubiously – starting with the Shakespeare / John Fletcher collaboration *The Two Noble Kinsmen* produced by Michael Bakewell.[34] The fourth episode was an abridged *Yorkshire Tragedy*.[35] The broadcast was directed by Peter Watts, who produced and introduced the last three plays in this series. The evidence suggests this was a first-class production, starting with an anonymous note in the *Radio Times* previewing that Watts's on-air introduction would give reasons the play is not Shakespeare's – Middleton is not mentioned – and tells readers that the story is based on historical events.[36] Star Michael Hordern's name is listed above the title in the radio listings.[37] He recently had lead parts at the Shakespeare Memorial Theatre and the Old Vic. Watts directed hundreds of BBC broadcasts, largely literary, including more than twenty-five adaptations of plays by Shakespeare and his contemporaries.

Returning to chronological order, there were two Middleton adaptations in 1956, starting with an abridged *Roaring Girl*, the Middleton / Thomas Dekker collaboration.[38] The listing in the *Radio Times* describes *The Roaring Girl* as 'light-colour stuff ... good to keep you in an afternoon from dice at home',[39] revealing how differently this comedy was perceived compared

to how seriously it is taken today. The programme stars Fay Compton, a star on stage and screen. *Radio Times* spotlighted Compton's appearance in a small note accompanied by an illustration that modernizes the frontispiece from the quarto edition of the play.[40] Smith adapted and directed. The show was repeated twice.

Another Middleton/Dekker collaboration, *The Honest Whore, Part One*, was broadcast a month later.[41] The BBC's radio listings emphasize Dekker, although Middleton is mentioned in the description:

Thomas Dekker is believed to have contributed to as many as forty plays in that astonishing era of collaborative dramaturgy around the turn of the seventeenth century, but there survive less than a dozen works of which he can be said to have been the sole or principal author. *The Honest Whore* is one of them. Thomas Middleton is acknowledged to have had a hand in Part I, but Part 2, altogether more skilfully constructed and felicitously written, is probably Dekker's own unaided work. The two parts contain virtually the same characters and are almost continuous in time, but each forms a complete play in itself.[42]

Part Two went out the next day with the same cast. Top billed were the highly respected actors Mary Wimbush and Maurice Denham. Wilfrid Grantham adapted and directed these broadcasts. Grantham usually produced literary adaptations and had several Shakespeare credits. The broadcasts were repeated three times.

The BBC returned to Middleton in 1960 with a new *Changeling* as part of an eight-episode series called *British Drama: 1600–1642*.[43] The radio listings mention that 'The principal source of *The Changeling* is John

---

[29] H. A. L. Craig, 'Poison, poetry, and passion', *Radio Times*, 4 March 1955, p. 6.

[30] BBC Third Programme, 6 March 1955, 140 minutes.

[31] BBC Home Service North, 27 March 1955, 55 minutes.

[32] https://connectedhistoriesofthebbc.org/data/north/ColinShaw/interview1/LR003248Transcripts1.pdf.

[33] *Radio Times*, 27 March 1955, p. 12.

[34] BBC Third Programme, 12 October 1956, 110 minutes.

[35] BBC Third Programme, 21 April 1957, 60 minutes.

[36] 'A Yorkshire Tragedy', *Radio Times*, 21 April 1957, p. 25.

[37] *Radio Times*, 21 April 1957, p. 28.

[38] BBC Third Programme, 15 January 1956, 95 minutes.

[39] *Radio Times*, 13 January 1956, p. 11.

[40] 'The Roaring Girl', *Radio Times*, 13 January 1956, p. 5.

[41] BBC Third Programme, 9 February 1956, 115 minutes.

[42] *Radio Times*, 5 February 1956, p. 29.

[43] BBC Home Service, 6 April 1960, 127 minutes.

Reynolds' *The Triumphs of God's Revenge against ...
Murther* (1621) and sections from this book will be read
by David Bird before each of the five acts.'[44] Narration
in play adaptations was unusual by 1960 so the BBC
emphasizes this to authenticate the broadcast. The passages from Reynolds were, in fact, greatly condensed
and paraphrased, though occasional lines are
recognizable.[45] Producer Raymond Raikes adapted the
narration, the play, and directed the performance. This
show and all those following are in circulation. An
analysis follows.

BBC Radio developed adaptation strategies starting
with their earliest full-length Shakespeare broadcasts.
Cuts shortened running times and focused waning attention spans. Raikes made many cuts in this *Changeling*.
Rowley's madhouse scenes are again removed and there
are single and multiple lines cut throughout the play, the
first being lines 7–8 of Alsemero's opening speech.
Words and phrases are revised when original meanings
are obscure. Beatrice-Joanna's aside in 2.1.105–6 is completely rewritten along with several other lines, and some
whole speeches from all parts of the play. Adapters may
move speeches to a different part of a scene and sometimes transpose scenes. Transpositions are sometimes
done for emphasis, or dramatic contrast, but often to
keep one group of actors at the microphone longer
instead of having them leave then return after an intervening scene. There are just a few transpositions in this
broadcast, such as 2.2.40–52, a conversation between
Beatrice-Joanna and Alsemrero, moved earlier in their
dialogue. New lines are added most often when characters enter a scene in progress because listeners cannot see
characters enter and so do not know who is now speaking. This begins early in *The Changeling*. Alsemero finishes his initial monologue, then, in an added line, calls
to Jasperino twice to get his attention in a public place (a
bustling sound pattern supports this). Listeners now
know who speaks when they hear Jasperino's first line,
1.1.13.

The performances seem dated today, but the actors
hold listener attention through some very dense dialogue. The lead actors have a lot of radio experience.
Michael Gough (De Flores) was one of England's busiest
film, radio and television actors. June Tobin (Beatrice-
Joanna) appeared on hundreds of radio broadcasts,
including ten of Shakespeare's plays. Norman Shelley
(Vermandero) was another of the Corporation's busiest
radio actors; his first radio role was in 1926, and over
a fifty-year career his credits numbered in the thousands.
Raikes produced hundreds of literary broadcasts

including more than two dozen productions of
Shakespeare and other early modern writers. The programme was repeated twice. Ancillary to this broadcast
was the 21 April 1960 episode of the weekly arts programme *Comment*, directed by George MacBeth, that
featured literary critic Christopher Ricks who critiqued
this adaptation between its first and second airings.[46]
Ricks expressed his displeasure with some of the cuts,
additions, and the resulting change in emphasis: '*The
Changeling* is a great play ... not even this production
quite managed to disguise that'.[47]

Raikes produced and adapted a 105-minute *Women
Beware Women* two years later.[48] The BBC did not
promote it strongly, simply calling the play 'A poetic
tragedy of passion and intrigue'.[49] The most notable
member of the cast is Margaret Rawlings as Livia.
Though best known on stage and film for modern
roles, Rawlings was a prolific radio and television actor
whose broadcasts included a dozen radio and television
Shakespeare programmes between 1934 and 1969. The
less-known Diana Olsson was Bianca. This show was
repeated three times, the last Middleton broadcast until
a new *Honest Whore* in 1970.

Both parts were broadcast on the same day with *Part
One* running 60 minutes and *Part Two* 63 minutes.[50] The
programme description is purely factual, 'The First Part
of *The Honest Whore* by Thomas Dekker and Thomas
Middleton was printed in 1604: the Second Part (presumably Dekker's unassisted work) was not printed until
1630. Both parts contain plot and sub-plot: for this
broadcast the sub-plot, which has little connection
with the main plot, is omitted.'[51] Only Dekker's authorship is mentioned on the air. While the dialogue of the
main plot is thinned in *Part Two*, *Part One* is cut more
severely with most latter scenes deleted. Those remaining are greatly condensed. The announcer tells listeners
that the setting is Milan, but they should think of it as
Eastcheap. Raikes's script is inconsistent in creating

---

44 *Radio Times*, 3 April 1960. *Radio Times* online listings do not give
    page numbers after 1959.
45 John Reynolds, *The Triumphs of God's Revenge Against Murther*
    (London, 1621).
46 BBC Third Programme, 21 April 1960, 20 minutes.
47 Script for *Comment*, no. 16, BBC, 21 April 1960, p. 3. My thanks to
    Professor Ricks for sending a copy of his *Comment* script to me.
48 BBC Third Programme, 14 September 1962, 105 minutes.
49 *Radio Times*, 8 September 1962.
50 BBC Radio Three, 6 September 1970, 60 and 65 minutes.
51 *Radio Times*, 5 September 1970.

dialogue to indicate entering characters, so both parts are sometimes clear and sometimes muddled. The cast are virtually unknown today, except for Michael Hordern as Orlando. Up-and-coming actor Joss Ackland played the Duke with stern menace (*Part One*) and good governance (*Part Two*). Raikes gives Madi Hedd as Bellafront a strong scene in 3.3. Hipolito (John Rye) excites her with his hand, justifying the line 'honest wenches turn strumpets with a wet finger'. Ashamed at giving in to him, Bellafront determines to become strong and honest. This show had one repeat. It was a long time before the BBC returned to Middleton, but when they did Middleton was given a regular adapter.

Peter Barnes was a successful playwright and screenwriter when he began adapting early modern plays for the stage in 1970. Producer Martin Jenkins commissioned Barnes to adapt *A Chaste Maid of Cheapside* for radio in 1979.[52] Barnes includes nearly the entire play, with some new dialogue so listeners will understand the action described in stage directions. This faithful adaptation had a surprisingly short running time of 98 minutes. The *Radio Times* enticed listeners with 'a richly sensual world of sexual hypocrisy and deceit in which "wit" and blatant self-interest become the accepted standards for success and where all forms of authority are discredited'.[53] The stars are Siân Phillips (Lady Kix), Peter Jeffrey (Sir Oliver) and Norman Rodway (Sir Walter), actors very well known in the UK.

Barnes adapted several other plays for the BBC, including two by Thomas Otway and one by John Marston, before his next Middleton assignment in 1983, a 95-minute broadcast of *A Mad World My Masters* produced by former radio writer Penny Gold:[54] her 1985 adaptation of *Sir Thomas More* for director Martin Jenkins makes dramatic that rambling manuscript.[55] Gold became a producer of original radio plays before directing several Shakespeare broadcasts.

Barnes changed his adaptive approach, making major cuts and revising dialogue more than is usual in BBC adaptations. The first description in *Radio Times* is sparse: 'A rare revival of one of Middleton's greatest Jacobean city comedies',[56] greatly expanded when the broadcast was repeated fifteen months later:

A rare revival of one of Middleton's greatest Jacobean city comedies. Follywit, kept penniless by his rich grandfather Sir Bounteous Progress, is determined to get his hands on some of his future inheritance while he is still young enough to enjoy it. With the help of wit and disguise things seem to go his way but, in the end, perhaps, the biter bit.[57]

The strong cast featured current and future stars of stage and screen such as Roy Marsden (Follywit), James Villers (Sir Bounteous Progress), Ian McDiarmid (Master Penitent Brothel) and Brenda Bruce (Francesca's Mother). The show was repeated the next year and twice on the BBC's streaming service in 2021, which reused the second description[58] – a total of four broadcasts.

Barnes remains heavy-handed in substituting words and rewriting speeches in his 94-minute adaptation of *A Trick to Catch the Old One*, and the play is more heavily cut than his previous Middleton adaptations.[59] One cut may have been understandable censorship: 'No, rather of a Jew' was removed from 1.3.17. The *Radio Times* simply described the play: 'The themes of this comedy are avarice, the power of money, and the gullibility and greed of those who pursue it.'[60] Alan Rickman, then making his name at the Royal Shakespeare Company, is a brilliant Witgood; Maurice Denham returns to Middleton as Pecunius Lucre; and the always excellent but under-known Peter Bayliss is Walkadine Hoard. This fine revision of the play was initially broadcast in 1985 and repeated once in 1989. Director Ian Cottrell produced music and personality profiles before becoming one of the Corporation's top producers of plays and other dramatic programmes. This was Cottrell's first Middleton broadcast.

The second was *The Old Law* in 1986.[61] Barnes so heavily adapted the text that he is credited as co-author, the on-air credits being 'by Thomas Middleton, William Rowley, Philip Massinger, and Peter Barnes'. Well over half the lines are cut or paraphrased. Most of the scenes featuring the Bailiff, Butler, Cook and Taylor are radically condensed, with all the dancing, drinking and music scenes rewritten to eliminate visuals. This isn't exactly Middleton, Rowley and maybe Massinger's play,[62] but

---

[52] BBC Radio Three, 24 June 1979, 98 minutes.
[53] *Radio Times*, 21 June 1979.
[54] BBC Radio Three, 21 July 1983, 95 minutes.
[55] BBC Radio Three, 27 February 1985, 122 minutes.
[56] *Radio Times*, 16 July 1983.
[57] *Radio Times*, 6 October 1984.
[58] https://genome.ch.bbc.co.uk/po9kgzll.
[59] BBC Radio Three, 25 September 1985, 94 minutes.
[60] *Radio Times*, 27 September 1985.
[61] BBC Radio Three, 13 May 1986, 115 mins.
[62] The Massinger attribution on the title page of the 1656 first edition has long been doubted. These doubts are summarized by Taylor in 'Works included in this edition: canon and chronology', in *Thomas Middleton and Early Modern Textual Culture: A Companion to the Collected Works*, ed. Gary Taylor and John Lavagnino (Oxford, 2007), 405–8.

Barnes delivered a masterpiece of light-hearted radio entertainment. The cast is filled with stars of the time, such as Michael Maloney (Cleanthes) and Gerard Murphy (Prince Evander), supported by June Tobin (Antigona). The description orients: 'The ruler of a small Greek state resurrects an old law which decrees that all men on reaching the age of 80 and all women on reaching the age of 60 are to be put to death as no longer being of use.'[63] *The Old Law* was repeated in 1989.

It was a long time before the BBC broadcast Middleton again, but it was a triumph. No adapter is credited for the 2003 *Women Beware Women*.[64] Aside from some light cutting and lighter word substitutions, the play is given pretty much intact in 133 minutes. The *Radio Times* described it as 'Thomas Middleton's Jacobean tragedy in which the women are the worst betrayers. When Leantio's beautiful wife Bianca catches the eye of the duke, the worldly Livia arranges an assignation, plunging Bianca into the vice and corruption of the court.'[65] This faithful adaptation works very well under the direction of Alison Hindell, then a prolific director of plays written for radio, though she has broadcast many stage plays since. The cast includes Penny Downie as Livia, then impressing critics with her work at the Royal Shakespeare Company, and Nigel Terry from Derek Jarman's films as the ravenous Duke.

The Corporation's most recent Middleton is a third *Changeling* in 2009.[66] Adapter/director Jeremy Mortimer often leaves listeners bewildered as to who is at the microphone. In a break from better Middleton broadcasts, little effort is made to identify new characters when they enter, thus there is no calling to Jasperino before he speaks at 1.1.13. The ghost in 4.3 is indicated by the sound of wind, and De Flores gasps before speaking line 58, but nobody mentions the ghost to help listeners understand the wind and the gasp. Mortimer adds unnecessary sound patterns. We hear De Flores and Beatrice-Joanna have sex in the bridge between 3.4 and 4.1, and again when locked in the closet at 4.3.138 before she exits dying, making too graphic the cliché associating sex with death. The madhouse scenes are finally included. The BBC's description: 'A new radio production of Thomas Middleton and William Rowley's Jacobean classic, set in Alicante, Spain, in the 1920s. Beatrice-Joanna is due to marry Alonzo e Piracquo, until she falls in love with Alsemero and seeks the help of her father's man, De Flores.'[67] Few sound patterns indicate the 1920s setting so there is little point to it. The cast is less well known than usual. Nicky Henson (Vermandero) and Alex Hassell (Tomazo) may be the most recognizable actors. Anna Madeley plays

Beatrice-Joanna and Zubin Varla is De Flores. The show has not been rebroadcast.

These Middleton programmes vary in quality, apparent prestige and faithfulness to the printed texts. The BBC's approach changed from producer to producer, each with his or her own way of broadcasting Middleton. The only constant in the circulating broadcasts is the excellence of the performers, well known or not. I find no other audio Middleton worldwide besides *Macbeth* and *Timon of Athens*.

Other broadcasts have Middleton content, such as Christopher Ricks's *Comment*, already mentioned. Similar Middleton content is heard as segments on arts programmes that share time with news about books, films, gallery shows and forthcoming or recently opened plays. There is no space to mention all that are known, so we note four arts programmes that mention *Women Beware Women* to understand what these segments are like.

Royal Shakespeare Company director Terry Hands discussed his staging on *The Arts This Week* in 1969,[68] and Howard Baker commented on his Royal Court Theatre staging on *Critics' Forum* in 1986.[69] Both broadcasts were produced by Philip French. *Saturday Review* covered the play twice. Torque MacLeod produced the review of the National Theatre's production in 2010,[70] and Oliver Jones produced the review of the Globe Theatre's modern dress production in 2020.[71] Other Middleton plays discussed on similar shows are *The Changeling*, *The Honest Whore*, *The Revenger's Tragedy* and *The Roaring Girl*.

At least three additional programmes have Middleton content. The earliest found is *The English Poets: From Chaucer to Yeats*, a 1971–1972, 26-part anthology series of poetry readings produced by George MacBeth and introduced by Peter Porter.[72] The programme was 'a serious attempt to give the listener a sense of the range and development of English poetry over 500 years'.[73] Works by Jonson, Webster, Tourneur, Ford and Middleton were read on the seventh episode.

[63] *Radio Times*, 10 May 1986.
[64] BBC Radio Three, 30 March 2003, 133 minutes.
[65] *Radio Times*, 29 March 2003.
[66] BBC Radio Three, 29 November 2009, 119 minutes.
[67] *Radio Times*, 28 November 2009.
[68] BBC Radio Three, 9 July 1969, 30 minutes.
[69] BBC Radio Three, 15 February 1986, 50 minutes.
[70] BBC Radio Four, 1 May 2010, 45 minutes.
[71] BBC Radio Four, 29 February 2020, 49 minutes.
[72] BBC Radio Four, 10 November 1971, 19 minutes.
[73] *Radio Times*, 25 September 1971.

The 'Elizabethan Revenge' episode of *In Our Time* was broadcast in 2009.[74] Jonathan Bate, Janet Clare and Julie Sanders discuss various plays with host Melvyn Bragg. Most thoroughly covered early in the programme are Thomas Kyd's *The Spanish Tragedy* and Shakespeare's *Hamlet*, but *Titus Andronicus* and Shakespeare's history plays also receive mention. Middleton's *Revenger's Tragedy* fills the last ten minutes. Bate says that the play 'bears the same relationship to the inherited form [of revenge tragedy] as, say, a Quentin Tarantino film does to a Clint Eastwood film'.

The most recent show found was broadcast the next year. *The Tudor Tarantino* is a radio documentary about Middleton's life and works.[75] The broadcast website calls Middleton the 'bad boy of the Renaissance', though the programme is quite balanced. The voice with the most impact at the start is Gary Taylor's, who with John Lavagnino led the team that published Middleton's *Collected Works*.[76] Other speakers are the actor Harriet Walter, Jonathan Bate again, and Brian

Vickers, who corrects some of Taylor's excessive claims. It is an entertaining and fast-paced half-hour hosted by Dominic Arkwright and produced by John Byrne.

Finding these programmes can be a matter of luck. The *In Our Time* website does not mention Middleton so the 'Elizabethan Revenge' episode would not be included here had I not heard the programme and remembered it. There may be, and are likely to be, other arts programmes and radio documentaries with Middleton content not found by internet searches.

Audio opens the field of Middleton performance studies considerably. I hope this beginning will lead to a fulsome study of Middleton audio.

---

[74] BBC Radio Four, 18 June 2009, 43 minutes. My thanks to Andrea Smith for identifying director Paul Tinline.

[75] BBC Radio Four, 4 May 2010, 30 minutes.

[76] Thomas Middleton, *The Collected Works*, ed. Gary Taylor and John Lavagnino (Oxford, 2007).

JOHN GIELGUD ON AIR: 65 YEARS OF PERFORMING SHAKESPEARE ON RADIO

ANDREA SMITH

Sir John Gielgud was one of the twentieth century's most highly regarded Shakespearian actors. For generations, his stage performances were considered the peak of excellence, inspiring those who followed him. His influence on the stage and his work at London's Old Vic Theatre and Stratford-upon-Avon are well documented. What is far less well recognized is his work on radio. He was the most prolific Shakespearian leading actor on British radio, as well as giving performances in America and for the BBC World Service. During his 65-year radio Shakespeare career, he moved through four main periods: pioneer, star, sage and national treasure. This article will concentrate on his domestic BBC radio broadcasts, examining his legacy and the impact it has had with reference to extant recordings and contemporary writing. It will show that, as well as being one of the pre-eminent stage Shakespearians, he was also instrumental in the formation, development and continuing production of Shakespeare's work on radio.

Gielgud first performed Shakespeare on the stage of the Old Vic in 1921, aged just seventeen.[1] He was still in his teens when he appeared on radio for the first time, and not quite twenty-one when he first performed Shakespeare on the BBC.[2] He quickly became established in both media: Sheridan Morley noted that 'he was among the very first stage stars to welcome radio'.[3] Gielgud played his first leading Shakespearian role on radio in 1929: his rise to prominent radio roles coincided with his brother, Val, becoming head of radio drama. These two events may not have been connected – Gielgud was a rising theatrical star and the BBC regularly poached from the stage – but Val was a constant employer of his brother in his Shakespeare productions and other plays. From this point on, John Gielgud's appearances in Shakespeare on radio were fairly continuous, almost to his death,

culminating in his final role as Lear in 1994, broadcast to mark his ninetieth birthday.

Despite his frequent work on radio, and the plaudits he received for them, Gielgud was always fairly dismissive about the medium. At times he was clearly frustrated with radio, writing to his secretary Kitty Black in 1941:

I am thoroughly bored by the whole BBC ... and I shan't do another for a long time if I can help it.... It's the same trouble as the cinema, they buy your name and time and don't attempt to reach your standard because they won't take the trouble and patience to work properly and consult you about the obvious details which should be considered.[4]

Hallam Tennyson, who directed Gielgud for the BBC's World Service, believed that the actor, 'like a lot of his generation ... looked on radio as a secondary art-form'.[5] And Gielgud himself admitted as much: 'I was never keen on radio, except as easy money on the side ... You've got to be very sympathetic to the medium, and treat it gently, which is not easy for me, as I'm very impatient.'[6] Writing in the year 2000, Alan Beck stated that another World Service drama producer, Gordon House, had told him that 'Twenty years ago, Sir John was asked whether he worried that the onset of old age

---

[1] John Gielgud, *An Actor and His Time* (Harmondsworth, 1979), p. 62.
[2] Alan Beck suggests this was on 2 March 1925 ('John Gielgud – the longest radio career', *Studies in Theatre and Performance* 20 (2000), 211; p. 211). However, BBC listings give the date as 3 March 1925 ('Popular excerpts from Shakespeare', *Radio Times*, 27 February 1925, p. 441).
[3] Sheridan Morley, *John G: The Authorised Biography of John Gielgud* (London, 2001), p. 129.
[4] John Gielgud, *Sir John Gielgud: A Life in Letters*, ed. Richard Mangan (New York, 2004), p. 63.
[5] Jonathan Croall, *John Gielgud: Matinee Idol to Movie Star* (London, 2011), p. 331.
[6] Quoted in Croall, *John Gielgud*, p. 331.

would make learning lines difficult, and thus put an end to his stage career. "Oh well – if the worst comes to the worst," he said, "there's always the wireless ... ".[7] Gielgud was not alone in his attitude to radio, but it is perhaps surprising that someone so well regarded as a performer in the medium seemed to lack any enthusiasm for it.

The main reason Gielgud was praised so much for his work may well have been his voice. Radio is reliant on sound and therefore the qualities of an actor's voice are more important than in a visual medium, where gesture, movement and costume can play a large part in the performer's interpretation. In addition, particularly in the earliest days of radio where sound quality could be poor, enunciation was valued very highly. Stanley Wells comments that 'Famous for beauty of speech, he had inherited what is sometimes called "the Terry voice", a musical resonance of perfectly controlled vocal quality guided in his case by keen intelligence and deep understanding of his lines and responsiveness to the dramatic situation.'[8]

He notes that, to modern tastes, Gielgud's 'speaking on early recordings is susceptible to a charge of self-indulgence'.[9] There is some justification for this – listening to Gielgud's surviving radio work now, it is clearly from another era – but it also continues to have the power to move.

The first period of Gielgud's radio work dates back almost as far as Shakespeare on radio itself and continues through to World War II. During this time, nearly 200 productions of Shakespeare were broadcast on BBC radio. These varied in duration and quality as producers tried to work out how best to create radio drama and how to take the visual medium of theatre and present it in sound only. Technology and facilities were limited too, although these improved greatly when the BBC moved to its current headquarters, London's Broadcasting House, in 1932. As such, Gielgud's formative broadcasts put him among the early radio drama pioneers.

The BBC began presenting Shakespeare plays of around two hours in length in 1923, although Gielgud did not initially appear in these and instead performed poetry readings or shorter excerpts from Shakespeare. He played Romeo at least twice at this time, once in 1925 and then a year later in the landmark series *Shakespeare's Heroines*, 'short dramatic Shakespeare recitals (fifteen minutes in length) by well-known actresses from London's theatres'.[10] The male actors in these were treated as subsidiary players and Gielgud continued largely to only give short readings for the

next three years. He also lacked confidence in his abilities at the time: 'I was struck by the brilliance of the radio actors of the day ... They seemed to do so little, yet get it absolutely right. When I listened to myself in those early days I was appalled at how much I was over-acting!'[11] In 1928 he began to appear in longer drama productions, and then in 1929 he took on his first leading Shakespeare role on radio, a part he had just started playing at the Old Vic: Antonio in *The Merchant of Venice*.[12] Admittedly, this was a very much truncated production for schools, running for just forty-five minutes. But from this point on, he would go on to appear on BBC radio in all the major roles he became associated with onstage.

Just over a year later, he appeared as a character which would continue to be part of his repertoire for the next sixty years: Prospero in *The Tempest*. Broadcasts were live and no BBC recordings of Gielgud exist from this period. However, newspaper and magazine articles can help give an impression of his work at this time. For example, the reviewer 'Philemon' wrote in *Popular Wireless*: 'The performance of this play was distinguished by the presence of Mr John Gielgud in the cast. It is always a delight to hear Shakespeare so beautifully spoken; every word clear; every sentence properly phrased; and every ounce of meaning drawn from the familiar lines.'[13]

The writer went on to note the importance of voice casting 'for, unless the voices communicate the parts, you get a piece of elocution and not a play'.[14] This was perhaps the key to Gielgud's success: not only did he enunciate clearly and deliver the verse as poetry, but he also imbued his characters with personality through his

[7] Beck, 'John Gielgud', p. 211.

[8] Stanley Wells, *Great Shakespeare Actors: Burbage to Branagh* (Oxford, 2015), p. 172.

[9] Wells, *Great Shakespeare Actors*, p. 172.

[10] Eve-Marie Oesterlen, 'Full of noises, sounds and sweet airs: Shakespeare and the birth of radio drama in Britain', in *Shakespeare on Film, Television and Radio: The Researcher's Guide*, ed. Olwen Terris, Eve-Marie Oesterlen and Luke McKernan (London, 2009), 51–73; p. 58.

[11] John Gielgud quoted in David Gillard, 'A prince among Hamlets', *Radio Times*, 6 April 1989, p. 58.

[12] 'Play to schools', *Radio Times*, 4 October 1929, p. 50; Robert James Frost, 'The Shakespearean performances of Sir John Gielgud', unpublished doctoral thesis (University of Birmingham, 1983), p. 524.

[13] 'Philemon', 'For the listener', *Popular Wireless*, 7 March 1931, p. 1182, pp. 1211–12; p. 1211.

[14] 'Philemon', 'For the listener', p. 1211.

voice. In some ways, Gielgud was better suited to radio than the stage when it came to certain parts in the pre-war years. As the reviewer in *The Times* wrote of his performance at the Old Vic in 1930, 'the only fault to be found with this Prospero is a youthfulness'.[15] However, the reviewer went on to add that Gielgud's 'voice has the weary cadence of an embittered maturity'.[16] While his looks may have betrayed his age, his voice did not and as radio relies on vocal performance, he may have made a more convincing Prospero on air than onstage.

Before and during World War II, Gielgud played a succession of leading Shakespearian men on radio, including Hamlet (1932 and 1940), Iago (1932) and Lear (1941). None of these performances was preserved, even though excerpts of some Shakespeare plays were being archived as early as 1938. At the outbreak of the war, BBC radio was still only a teenager, with technology and techniques that were continuing to develop. During the conflict, the drama department had to leave Broadcasting House and many radio plays were performed in 'lash-up' conditions.[17] Actors taking part throughout these early decades had to constantly evolve and adapt to their working environment, something that Gielgud appears to have done very successfully, based on the reception reviewers gave his work.

Gielgud's second era of radio Shakespeare began at the end of World War II. His career, across all media, was at its peak, and he received a knighthood for his work in 1953. From 1949 onwards, he starred in or directed (sometimes both) a string of productions at the Shakespeare Memorial Theatre in Stratford-upon-Avon, as well as appearing in films of Shakespeare plays including *Julius Caesar* (1953), *Romeo and Juliet* (1954) and *Richard III* (1955), although he was never the lead. On radio, however, he took on starring roles, including bringing performances of some of his most famous parts to the air: Hamlet, Lear and Richard II.

The most successful of these was his 1948 Boxing Day performance in *Hamlet*. The production was virtually full-text and lasted for 4 hours 20 minutes, including two intervals. Although it was broadcast in the same year that Olivier's film of the play was released, there was no mention of this in the pre-broadcast media coverage. Instead, it was suggested that listeners would have the opportunity to judge whether Gielgud might be the finest Hamlet of his generation.[18] The production became such a hit that it was repeated at least eight times over the following decades. By the 1959 broadcast, it was no longer a question of *if* Gielgud was the finest; he was

billed as 'The best Hamlet of our time'.[19] Of all Gielgud's performances in Shakespeare on radio, this was the most successful and enduring. His delivery of the text seems to have been at the heart of this. A week before the broadcast he appeared as Prospero in another production of *The Tempest* (1948). Phillip Hope-Wallace, reviewing that production for the magazine *The Listener*, wrote: 'Mr Gielgud managed to extract the fullest music and the fullest meaning from [the] part ... What poetry! And how lucid, sad and sweet.'[20] And he had similar words of praise for Gielgud's Hamlet, stating that the actor's delivery of the text showed 'a superb understanding of what makes the sound of Shakespeare unmatchable' with 'emotion *sans* emotionalism, the heart's voice itself – classical'.[21] Later repeats continued to praise Gielgud. Peter Forster wrote that 'many consider [his performance] as near the definitive as we are likely ever to get', adding that 'Here *in excelsis* are all Sir John's supreme qualities – the pathos, the Terry voice, the poetry.'[22] Both at the time of original broadcast and subsequently, Gielgud's radio Hamlet was held up as the exemplar for others to strive for. This may be why there were relatively few other productions of *Hamlet* in the mid twentieth century, compared to some of Shakespeare's other popular plays.

The initial broadcast of this production was also at a time when radio was at its peak. Television had not yet taken off and popular plays received 'an average audience of over 12 million in 1948'.[23] While it is reasonable to assume that a Boxing Night airing might not gain quite such high listening figures, this broadcast and its many repeats (as well as a release on CD, and finally streaming in the twenty-first century) suggest that many millions of people have heard this production. In addition, Susanne Greenhalgh notes that 'All the *Hamlet*-related programmes

---

[15] 'Old Vic Theatre', *The Times*, 7 October 1930, p. 12.

[16] 'Old Vic Theatre', p. 12.

[17] Val Gielgud, *Radio Theatre: Plays Specifically Written for Broadcasting* (London, 1946), p. viii.

[18] Stephen Williams, '"Treasure Island": a tale that will always be loved', *Radio Times*, 24 December 1948, p. 6.

[19] Peter Forster, 'The best Hamlet of our time', *Radio Times*, 17 April 1959, p. 7.

[20] Philip Hope-Wallace, 'Broadcast drama: cloud-capp'd towers', *The Listener*, 23 December 1948, p. 983.

[21] Philip Hope-Wallace, 'Critic on the hearth – broadcast drama: Uncle, Uncle!', *The Listener*, 30 December 1948, p. 1024.

[22] Forster, 'The best Hamlet', p. 7.

[23] Asa Briggs, *The History of Broadcasting in the United Kingdom*, vol. 4: *Sound and Vision* (Oxford, 1995), p. 632.

on the Third [the Third Programme, now BBC Radio 3] in the next few years would in some sense be in dialogue with this "entirety" production.'[24] This includes special programming alongside the repeats in 1949 and 1951. In 1954, Gielgud also gave a talk on the Third Programme, apparently off the cuff, entitled 'Hamlet: The Actor's View'.[25] This survives in the BBC archives and his authoritative examination of both the role and the play demonstrates his deep level of knowledge. He spoke again about *Hamlet* in a half-hour interview with George Rylands on the Third in 1964.[26] The 1975 repeat of the play was previewed with a lengthy article in the *Radio Times*, and the production's final airing in 1989, to mark Gielgud's eighty-fifth birthday, was accompanied by a half-page article including two photographs. The number of repeats, and the high profile that these were given, is unprecedented in the history of BBC radio drama and highlights the very high regard with which his performance in this production has been held.

Hamlet was by no means Gielgud's only leading Shakespearian role for BBC Radio during this period. In 1961 he gave his only radio performance as Richard II. And it was trumpeted as an important production:

Most theatre-goers would agree that among Sir John Gielgud's many memorable Shakespearian roles two in particular have become the definitive performances of our time: his Hamlet and his Richard II. A recording of Gielgud's *Hamlet* has existed in the BBC archives for some years ... but there was no complete recording of his *Richard II*. It was felt that this was a serious omission which should be remedied.[27]

The play's producer, John Richmond, who was also responsible for *Hamlet* (1948), stated that the aim was 'to secure a permanent record of an outstanding performance'.[28] However, not everyone was convinced. Reviewer Ian Rodger complained that 'It was a congenial idea to make a record in sound of a great performance but I suspect that posterity will realize sadly that Sir John's Richard had to be seen as well as heard.'[29] He did have some praise, though, stating that Gielgud 'was bravely close to his great stage performance and his voice mounted splendidly to the moment of anguish when the King knows that he has utterly lost'.[30] Despite Rodger's reservations, the production was very much sold to audiences on Gielgud's reputation as a performer of Shakespeare, consolidating his status as a star of radio drama.

Gielgud also returned to King Lear twice in this period. Ahead of his 1951 broadcast, his brother, Val, wrote that: 'Peter Watts presents John Gielgud in *King*

Lear: a performance generally acknowledged as the highlight of the season, and possibly the peak achievement to date of this finest of our Shakespearean actors.'[31] Val was always one to talk up any radio drama production, but even by his standards this was quite a claim. Although other actors had played Lear on radio before, Gielgud's starring role drew more attention than his predecessors. His 1967 production was greeted less triumphantly, although the *Radio Times* did include a large display box on the listings page with a picture of Gielgud in costume from his 1950 performance at Stratford-upon-Avon.[32] By this point, radio was getting less attention in the press and even *The Listener*, which had traditionally championed radio drama, chose to devote its entire radio review that week to the newly launched BBC Radio 1. Gielgud, however, gives possibly his best radio performance in the role. He still used his poetic style of delivery, but he was now more subtle and sympathetic. And having first played Lear onstage in his twenties, at the age of sixty-three he was also much closer to Lear's age, 'fourscore and upward' (*Lear* F 4.6.54), and his voice reflected that. This was the last major Shakespearian role he would play on BBC radio for nearly three decades, but he did still appear occasionally, albeit in smaller parts.

By the mid-1970s, Gielgud had become an elder statesman of both the theatre and radio. A profile in the *Observer* to mark his seventieth birthday noted: 'Gielgud remains primarily a stage actor and, coming a fair second, a stage director. He has done very little television and only a smattering of films.'[33] His radio career was not acknowledged. As he grew older, he took on fewer roles in all media and other actors began to stake claims on the parts he had called his own for so long. Acting styles were

---

[24] Susanne Greenhalgh, '"A stage of the mind": Hamlet on post-war British radio', in *Shakespeare Survey 64* (Cambridge, 2011), 133–44; p. 137.

[25] 'Hamlet: the actor's view', *Radio Times*, 14 May 1954, p. 13.

[26] Carl Wildman, 'Gielgud on acting Shakespeare', *Radio Times*, 9 January 1964, p. 15.

[27] John Richmond, 'The life and death of King Richard II by William Shakespeare', *Radio Times*, 1 June 1961, p. 37.

[28] Richmond, 'The life and death', p. 37.

[29] Ian Rodger, 'Drama: quick work', *The Listener*, 15 June 1961, 1063–4; p. 1063.

[30] Rodger, 'Drama: quick work', p. 1063.

[31] Val Gielgud, 'The purpose of "World Theatre"', *Radio Times*, 5 October 1951, p. 13.

[32] 'The tragedy of King Lear', *Radio Times*, 21 September 1967, p. 62.

[33] 'The old master of rhetoric and robes', *Observer*, 14 April 1974, p. 9.

also changing; vocal delivery was becoming less poetic. Radio producers were looking for actors to inhabit the roles. Around this time, Gielgud's relationship with radio Shakespeare shifted again. His name, and voice, still carried a cachet and his presence brought additional grandeur to the productions. As such he became a Shakespearian sage, a revered interpreter of the texts, rather than leading man. Writing about this period of Gielgud's stage career, Benedict Nightingale commented that the actor 'seemed also to be Shakespeare himself'.[34] Two radio productions in particular used this to their advantage. In 1976 he led the cast of *Henry V* as The Chorus, and nearly six years later he played Time in *The Winter's Tale* (1982). In both these parts, Gielgud could almost be said to be talking directly to the listeners as Shakespeare the narrator; certainly, they were roles set apart from the rest of the ensemble, acting as a conduit between the main action and the audience.

Before he even appears in *Henry V*, the opening of the play sets up the high esteem in which he was held. In a similar way to Olivier's film of the play, which begins with the Chorus speaking at the Elizabethan Globe Theatre, the radio production starts with people chattering in a modern theatre. Following the announcement 'Ladies and gentlemen. *Henry the Fifth* by William Shakespeare', sixteen cast members are listed, during which a hush descends over the 'audience'. It culminates with a slight pause and a final name, spoken in reverential tones: 'With John Gielgud as Chorus'. This is immediately followed with his delivery of 'Oh, for a muse of fire' (*Henry V* Prologue 1) in highly dramatic tones, projected to the imaginary theatre and very unlike much of the more contained Shakespearian acting on radio at the time. It is also unlike previous radio narrators, who usually speak newly written, explanative text in unobtrusive tones so as not to disrupt the flow of the play. Reviewer Derek Parker commented that Gielgud was among the 'virtues' of the production, 'gifting us all his intelligence and vocal command'.[35] The use of Gielgud here is clearly a very definite choice: not only does his name add prestige, but his poetic, almost melodramatic, delivery sets The Chorus apart from the action of the play as well as making the narration a compelling listen.

In a similar way, he appears as Time in *The Winter's Tale* (1982). The character only has thirty-two lines but provides the vital bridge between the first and second halves of the play. His voice is warm and avuncular, and while it retains the poetic delivery he was famous for, he does not end-stop the lines, reading the speech almost as

prose and creating an effect similar to a child's bedtime story. Christopher Reid in *The Listener* claimed the continuity announcer at the beginning said: 'A pretty good cast . . . plus Sir John Gielgud thrown in'.[36] If true, this is a surprisingly flippant way to describe both the production and Gielgud's role within it, although it does sum up Reid's own take on the play. However, the use of Gielgud is perhaps as a garnish, as Time could easily have been played by another member of the cast. As with his role as The Chorus, his presence seems very much to be there to increase the appeal of the production and perhaps as a sign of quality. These are the only two parts of this kind that he played for BBC radio, although his final audio performance was in a similar role, as Gower in *Pericles* (1999) for Arkangel Shakespeare.

As the millennium approached, Gielgud entered his final era of Shakespeare on BBC radio: that of national treasure. Ten years after *The Winter's Tale*, he played the Ghost of Hamlet, the late King of Denmark, with Kenneth Branagh as his son. It led to the first photograph on the front page of the *Radio Times* for a radio Shakespeare production since 1958.[37] The picture features a beaming, eager, young Branagh with Gielgud slightly above and behind, serious and intense with just a hint of a smile, and is headlined 'Heir to the throne'.[38] Charles Spencer noted that 'it almost looked as though our greatest actor-knight was appointing Branagh as his natural successor'.[39] And as Val Arnold-Forster commented: 'The publicity machine has been in overdrive. Features, pictures; the Hamlet of Hamlets'.[40] Spencer was also aware of the 'tidal wave of hype', adding that 'you'd have thought Kenneth Branagh's Hamlet for Radio 3 was a major new movie or at the very least, the start of a twice-weekly TV soap'.[41] However, as Jack Tinker wrote:

[34] Benedict Nightingale, 'He was such stuff as dreams are made on', *The Times*, 23 May 2000, p. 3.

[35] Derek Parker, 'Radio: the words rule – OK?', *The Listener*, 29 April 1976, p. 543.

[36] Christopher Reid, 'Unique Joyce', *The Listener*, 28 January 1982, p. 26.

[37] 'Romeo and Juliet', *Radio Times*, 14 November 1958, p. 1.

[38] 'Heir to the throne', *Radio Times*, 23 April 1992, p. 1.

[39] Charles Spencer, 'A mind's-eye vision of Elsinore', *Daily Telegraph*, 27 April 1992, p. 15.

[40] Val Arnold-Forster, 'Prince charming', *Guardian*, 1 May 1992, p. 32.

[41] Spencer, 'A mind's-eye', p. 15.

[T]he event turned into a media circus, this time hijacked by the fact that Sir John Gielgud, one of the great Hamlets of the century, was now playing the ghost to Branagh's Prince. A great deal of nonsense was talked about pretenders to the throne and heirs apparent, which Sir John treated with his customary Olympian loftiness.[42]

That loftiness was apparent in the interview the pair gave to the *Radio Times*. Gielgud arrived late and, after asking Branagh what he was working on, 'cheerfully' commented: 'You're doing Coriolanus? I hate the play. At Chichester? Nasty theatre'.[43] The BBC, and some of the media, may have felt the baton was being handed over, but there was no evidence of it between the two actors. And while Branagh has appeared in three more Shakespeare productions, he has never made it his medium as Gielgud did.[44] As for Gielgud, perhaps surprisingly, his famous voice is not very much in evidence in the production as it is masked by a lot of distortion to create the sound of the ghost. This suggests that what was most important was his presence – his status – and less so his actual performance.

The following year Branagh returned with *Romeo and Juliet* (1993), again casting Gielgud, this time as Friar Laurence. And in 1994 the pair were united for a final time in *King Lear*. Two years on from *Hamlet*, comparisons between them were still being made. Andrew Duncan, in an interview with Gielgud, wrote:

How, I wonder, does the New Pretender, Branagh, whose Renaissance Theatre Company co-produced *King Lear*, compare with the greats of the past? [Quoting Gielgud] 'You can't call him "great". In a way he's a better organiser and director than actor, but he's very good as Edmund and I thought his *Henry V* film was remarkable, too.'[45]

Gielgud was also rather dismissive about the experience of returning to the radio studio – or 'laconic', as Duncan describes him: 'I didn't enjoy doing it very much. I know my own voice too well and found it boring to listen to.'[46] Perhaps the experience was not all it might have been for Branagh too, who was reported as saying that 'Sir John practically directed himself in the play: "He's already thought of all the suggestions you offer. All you do is provide a reminder service."'[47] Nevertheless, it received rapturous reviews, including 'a treasurable and deeply moving performance', and 'a version which surely won't be bettered'.[48] Much emphasis was placed on Gielgud's age and status. Charles Spencer noted:

At 90, Gielgud was never going to be the most thunderous of Lears . . . But this Lear was far more than a demonstration of the voice beautiful. Throughout the evening one was aware of the pressure of emotion behind the words, and during the longer speeches you could sometimes hear Gielgud struggling for breath, bringing Lear's frailty almost unbearably close to home.[49]

Jack Tinker commented: 'Age has merely added its own haunting timbre.'[50] He also referred to the professional rivalry between Gielgud and Laurence Olivier: 'Whereas Olivier, the arch-competitor, the athletic usurper of Gielgud's pre-war throne, the jealous custodian of his reputation's crown, endured a painful winter of discontent towards his own final curtain – the faculties more or less flown on ahead – Gielgud has been left to bask in a glorious golden autumn.'[51]

Gielgud was being hailed as *the* Shakespearian actor of the century – and the final consolidation of that status was through a performance on radio.

This was Gielgud's last Shakespeare play for the BBC. He performed in twenty productions in total on the domestic channels, playing more leading Shakespearian roles on BBC radio than anyone else and over a much longer time span. Over the decades his status in these productions changed, but from quite early in the BBC's existence he was an important and influential figure. He may have made his name initially on the stage, but for millions of British people he would be much better known through his broadcasts. From pioneer to star, Shakespearian sage to national treasure, he maintained a huge influence on the medium for more than six decades. And yet his contribution is rarely acknowledged. Hopefully, in future, his radio work will be recognized alongside his stage performances for the way it shaped Shakespeare for many people in the UK in the twentieth century.

42 Jack Tinker, 'Alas, poor Kenneth', *Daily Mail*, 9 May 1992, p. 22.
43 Libby Purves, 'The king and I', *Radio Times*, 23 April 1992, pp. 20–2; p. 22.
44 As well as *Hamlet* (1992), *Romeo and Juliet* (1993) and *King Lear* (1994) discussed here, Branagh also appeared in *Antony and Cleopatra* (2014).
45 Andrew Duncan, 'People expect me to be outrageous and say frightful things', *Radio Times*, 7 April 1994, pp. 28–31; p. 31.
46 Duncan, 'People expect me', p. 28.
47 Susannah Herbert, 'Gielgud admits: "I'm bored with Bard"', *Daily Telegraph*, 13 April 1994, p. 7.
48 'Peerless prince of many parts', *Observer*, 3 April 1994, p. 19; Gillian Reynolds, 'They can't take any more', *Daily Telegraph*, 12 April 1994, p. 18.
49 Charles Spencer, 'Moved by the magnificent Sir John', *Daily Telegraph*, 11 April 1994, p. 21.
50 Jack Tinker, 'John the giant killer', *Daily Mail*, 16 April 1994, p. 26.
51 Tinker, 'John the giant', p. 26.

'DIDST THOU NOT HEAR A NOISE?': SHAKESPEARE WITH HEADPHONES

SHEILA T. CAVANAGH[1]

Max Webster's *Macbeth* at London's Donmar Warehouse, starring David Tennant and Cush Jumbo, was a significant draw in 2023. Tickets sold out immediately, with many would-be patrons left waiting for its 2024 transfer to the West End. Unfortunately, for international audiences, the show's trademark technology (headphones with binaural sound) makes it an unlikely fit for avenues such as National Theatre Live. This show needs to be experienced in person. Notably, however, the technology also creates controversy. Personally, I was thrilled to nab a ticket, although sceptical about the headphones. The production's audio transmission, however, presented by talented actors, dominates this *Macbeth*'s conceptualization. As this show indicates, sound design is developing in significant new directions, which promise innovative audio possibilities, while simultaneously unsettling patrons desiring more familiar stagings.

Not surprisingly, therefore, not all critics were impressed. Fiona Mountford, for example, proclaims that 'David Tennant is magnificent – but this production is style over substance.' She complains that 'Tennant is paired with a powerful Cush Jumbo as Lady Macbeth – but the production often wastes their talents.'[2] Nick Curtis from the *Evening Standard* offers a similar assessment: 'With the excellent David Tennant and Cush Jumbo as Shakespeare's murderous couple, this show promptly sold out its whole run at the 251-seat Donmar. If you didn't get tickets, take comfort, a potentially great production is coarsened by an overreaching gimmick.'[3]

Not everyone offered an irritated account of the production, but those disliking the show consistently aimed their vitriol at the headphones. The Donmar website noted 'This production of *Macbeth* uses binaural stereo to create a 3D soundscape, and wearing headphones is a critical aspect of the show.' The Donmar also provided diverse ways to receive appropriate sound through the headphones and they offered captioning. It

seems unlikely that Max Webster and the Donmar team, including sound designer Gareth Fry,[4] viewed the headphones as a gimmick. They designed the entire production around their use.

Fry is an accomplished sound designer with extensive experience, including work on Ian McKellen's 2024 UK tour as Falstaff in *Player Kings*.[5] As his website indicates:

Gareth Fry is a sound designer, best known for his cutting-edge work in theatre. His work includes productions for Complicité, National Theatre of Scotland, at the National Theatre, Royal Court, Bridge Theatre, Old Vic, Young Vic, in the West End and many more. He has also designed numerous exhibitions, such as … the Opening Ceremony of the 2012 Olympic Games. He is a specialist in the use of spatial and binaural sound, used in Complicité's *The Encounter,* the BBC's *The Dark Is Rising*, numerous VR experiences, podcasts and advertising campaigns, including for Bose, Volvo and Land Rover.[6]

Despite the qualms of some audience members, who would presumably disagree, appointing Fry as Sound Director, with his expertise in binaural sound, seems to make audiological and interpretative sense for a play that often blurs boundaries between what is real and what may be imagined or created by supernatural or pharmaceutical powers (the "insane root" cited by Banquo in 1.3). Routing some of the dialogue exclusively through

---

[1] This article is dedicated to the memory of Alden Vaughan, a wonderful man, skilled researcher and talented teacher. Condolences to Ginger.

[2] https://inews.co.uk/culture/arts/macbeth-donmar-warehouse-review-david-tennant-magnificent-style-over-substance-2812821.

[3] www.standard.co.uk/culture/theatre/macbeth-donmar-ware house-review-david-tennant-cush-jumbo-b1127257.html.

[4] Webster and Fry discuss the sound design in this interview: www.westendtheatre.com/214145/news/show-photos/videos/video-macbeth-starring-david-tennant-sound-designer-gareth-fry-director-max-webster-talk-the-sound-technology-behind-macbeth.

[5] https://playerkingstheplay.co.uk. [6] www.garethfry.co.uk.

headphones enables the production to nudge the playgoers off-kilter, just as Macbeth, Lady Macbeth and others occasionally lose psychic balance during the drama. Binaural sound, which directs different auditory messages into each ear of those listening, seems particularly appropriate for spreading disorienting sensations among audience members.[7] Webster and Fry, for instance, transfer the three witches from characters on the stage to sounds within headphones, making it impossible to determine whether the voices come from figures within the play or whether they represent sounds emanating within the heads of Macbeth, Banquo and/or the audience. This decision helps maximize an aural effect, not specific to this production, described by sound designer Victoria Deorio:

because we hear in 360 degrees, the shape of the field is dependent upon where we are within it. It can be imagined as a sphere with the human body positioned at the center. What is happening to the left, right, behind, in front of, above, or below is detectable because the auditory field surrounds the listener's perspective. Human beings use directional listening within omnidirectional hearing.[8]

As Deorio intimates, creating an unexpected spatial-audio field in a theatrical environment can prompt listeners to pay more attention to perceived sources of the sound being transmitted in ways that can enhance the power of the audio being presented, as it is in this *Macbeth*.

Expanding upon such human usages of directional listening and omnidirectional hearing, which binaural sound caters to, prominent audio phenomenologist Don Idhe notes how the disruption of common hierarchies which place sight over sound can also bring new ideas and realizations into play:

A turn to the *auditory dimension is* [sic] thus potentially more than a simple changing of variables. It begins as a deliberate decentering of a dominant tradition in order to discover what may be missing as a result of the traditional double reduction of vision as the main variable and metaphor.[9]

Deorio's and Idhe's observations draw attention to important interacting features in the sound, set and costume design of Webster's *Macbeth*. The lack of colourful costumes and the absence of elaborate or distracting props and set design elements encourage audience members to focus intently on the actors in front of them and the sounds emanating through each set of headphones. While some audience members were uncomfortable or annoyed with the sound design, the decision to incorporate binaural sound supports a consistent range of choices made by the production team.

Given the accusations of 'gimmickry' levelled against this production, moreover, it is noteworthy that binaural sound technology is, in fact, not a new-fangled invention. As Gascia Ouzounian relates in *Stereophonica*, experimentation with binaural technologies was prominent in the nineteenth century. Treatises devoted to 'propagation of sound', moreover, appeared regularly in scientific publications.[10] In addition, she notes that, in earlier texts, it was the physiology of the *single* ear that was under scrutiny in Western anatomy and medicine. Influential texts made scant, if any, reference to the action of hearing with both ears – what is now called 'binaural audition', and what is widely understood as a fundamental aspect of 'spatial hearing'.[11]

Over time, of course, technological and scientific advances, such as binaural audio, contributed to people's growing interest in immersive experiences, as Ouzounian also notes:

the increasingly common desire to 'immerse' the listener in three-dimensional auditory space, as with VR audio. In these ways, the sonic spatial pursuits of nineteenth-century scientists and inventors – transmitting sound across a distance, establishing the principles of binaural audition, mapping auditory space perception, broadcasting music and theater in three dimensions – would have enduring repercussions in a number of contexts. They would anticipate and set the stage for a new century in which spatial hearing would not be remarkable, but normalized and would even come to dominate cultures of listening.[12]

While disgruntled patrons at Webster's *Macbeth* might balk at the notion that the spatial hearing presented through headphones in this production represents 'normalized' theatrical sound, Ouzounian rightly observes

---

[7] Pete Malkin, a frequent collaborator with Fry, uses binaural sound in Factory International's 2024 production of *Robin/Red/Breast*, starring Maxine Peake, directed by Sarah Frankcom. Here, the audience wears the headphones only for the first half of the play when all the words are presented solely through this sound technique, making it clear that these are the character's internal thoughts.

[8] Victoria Deorio, *Art of Theatrical Sound Design: A Practical Guide* (London, 2018), p. 19.

[9] Don Idhe, *Listening and Voice: Phenomenologies of Sound* (New York, 2007), p. 13.

[10] Gascia Ouzounian. *Stereophonica: Sound and Space in Science, Technology, and the Arts* (Cambridge, MA, 2020), p. 3.

[11] Ouzonian, *Stereophonica*, p. 11. Here she is alluding, in part, to the work of Jens Blauert, notably, *Spatial Hearing: The Psychophysics of Human Sound Localization* (Cambridge, MA, 1983).

[12] Ouzonian, *Stereophonica*, p. 36.

the increasing interest in immersive productions among many potential theatregoers.

Binaural sound contributes significantly to the creation of the immersive aspects of this *Macbeth*. As Jens Blauert and Jonas Braasch suggest, it is the combination of sound, meaning and spatial awareness produced through binaural technology that offers to increase audience immersion in plays such as *Macbeth*:

Sound, devoid of *meaning*, would not matter to us. It is the information sound conveys that helps the brain to understand its environment. Sound and its underlying meaning are always associated with time and space. There is no sound without spatial properties and the brain always organizes this information within a temporal-spatial framework. This book is devoted to understanding the importance of meaning for spatial and related further aspects of hearing, including cross-modal inference.

People, when exposed to acoustic stimuli, do not react directly to what they hear but rather to what they hear means to them.[13]

Despite the ways in which varying modes of aural transmission can increase meaning for listeners, however, audience members often attach meaning to the way that sound is conveyed to them, frequently with dismay. In 1999, for example, famed Shakespearian director Trevor Nunn, then Artistic Director at London's National Theatre, provoked outrage for equipping actors with microphones for a production of *Troilus and Cressida*, as many theatrical professionals complained in the *Guardian*:

Graham Sheffield, artistic director of the Barbican theatre, said: 'Using microphones for special sound effects is one thing, but it is quite another if they become a general support mechanism for lazy actors. It does destroy the intimacy and naturalness between actors and an audience. However well it is done it will always sound slightly artificial – it has the effect of flattening out the modulations in an actor's voice.'[14]

While some current theatre attendees would agree with such sentiments, the use of microphones is now extremely common. It is striking, however, that the criticism directed at Trevor Nunn closely resembles the attacks hurled at Webster's inclusion of binaural sound in *Macbeth*. The objecting theatre patrons want to feel a connection with each other and with those on the stage and believe that modern sound technologies deprive them of that experience. Agnieszka Roginska, however, describes these related kinds of sounds in ways that explain the effects binaural sound is intended to achieve. Here, for instance, she differentiates stereo from binaural sound: 'in contrast to *stereo* reproduction

over headphones, binaural signals contain embedded spatial cues in the form of time, intensity and spectral coloration – cues that mimic and enhance natural human localization. The target reproduction system for binaural signals is headphones.'[15]

Roginska further describes this process in terms correlating with the Donmar production:

Binaural sound refers to the two-channel sound that enters a listener's left and right ears. Although many could argue that all stereo sound is binaural, the term *binaural* is reserved for sound where the two-channel sound entering a listener's ears has been filtered by a combination of time, intensity, and spectral cues intended to mimic human localization cues.[16]

Roginska's description of binaural audio reflects the sound-based experience this *Macbeth* offers. Before the show, the headphone tests demonstrate how the right and left ear are receiving different input. While audience members may not understand how the technology is operating, they presumably recognize that these sounds have been processed in a way that can facilitate the kind of immersive experience intended. For those appreciating such techniques, the production rises far beyond gimmickry.

Still, as noted, responses to the incorporation of binaural sound into *Macbeth* were decidedly mixed, suggesting that such audiological innovation is either ahead of its time for some individuals or that this design does not reach every ear equally. Mountford, for instance, admitted that 'I must confess that I swiftly started to take the headphones off for extended periods, so as to restore that all-important connection between voice and corporeal action.'[17] Mountford also objected to a perceived sense of being distanced from others in the audience, resembling what some others experienced here and at Nunn's *Troilus and Cressida*: 'What remained missing, though, was that electric sense of audience members having a shared experience and registering each other's

---

[13] Jens Blauert and Jonas Braasch, eds., *The Technology of Binaural Understanding* (Cham, Switzerland, 2020), p. v (emphasis in original).

[14] Amelia Gentleman and Fiachra Gibbons, 'Outcry at Nunn's use of mikes in theatre', *Guardian*, Wed. 31 Mar 1999.

[15] Agnieszka Roginska and Paul Geluso, eds., *Immersive Sound: The Art and Science of Binaural and Multi-Channel Audio* (New York, 2018), p. 92.

[16] Roginska and Geluso, eds., *Immersive Sound*, p. 88.

[17] https://inews.co.uk/culture/arts/macbeth-donmar-warehouse-review-david-tennant-magnificent-style-over-substance-2812821.

reactions. Instead, we remain forlornly isolated in our own private sound world bubble.' In contrast, I was so excited to be seated at this production that I never felt forlorn. Curtis, however, also reports feeling distanced, even though, in apparent contradiction, they purport to be 'open to any tech that enriches a live theatrical experience'.[18] This review indicates that 'this is like listening to a very good audio production of *Macbeth*, while watching very good actors mime to it. Interesting, but not something you'd necessarily choose to experience.' Surprisingly, after this derogatory description, they maintain that the production 'features the most emotionally committed Shakespearian performance I've seen Tennant give'. They also indicate that Jumbo and Tennant 'have a fierce intimacy', so it remains unclear why this review is so testy.[19]

Despite these multiple complaints, not all reviewers respond negatively to the headphones, suggesting that many became immersed in the experience as it was intended. Mert Dilek in the *Theatre Times* applauds the sound design, noting that the play's 'central deployment of binaural stereo paves the way to a unique and well-executed re-visioning of Shakespeare's tragedy'.[20] Dilek then offers a lengthy explanation of why he found this technique so compelling: 'There are many aspects to commend in Webster's resonantly stark *Macbeth*, but nearly all of them gain their sustained force from their interaction with the production's aural intimacy and layering.' Dilek further reports that 'the auditory life on stage becomes invasive, granular, and haunting' and that: 'Many of Shakespeare's familiar lines acquire new vibrancy when whispered or delivered inwardly, and the production's decision not to show the Weird Sisters . . . demonstrates a thoughtful engagement with the play's, and Macbeth's, questioning of reality and delusion.' Dilek also praises the actors, determining that 'Tennant is terrifically fresh in his take on the leading part', while Jumbo 'presents a supremely calibrated performance'. Dilek appears to have seen the same production I enjoyed, which differs significantly from those denouncing binaural sound as a 'gimmick'.

It may also be relevant (or at least entertaining) to note that the headphones transform the theatrical experience for the actors, as well, according to a *Times* article including an interview with Cush Jumbo:

The experience is designed to be immersive, with the headphones magnifying every stage whimper and whisper. But, Jumbo explains, it also means that the audience is unaware of how loud they sound to the headphone-less actors on stage.

The Donmar is tiny and they are thinking, 'Well no one else can hear me, they've got their headphones on.' They can't hear themselves rustling a sweet packet, but we can. And they fart.[21]

Notably, these additional multi-sensory aspects of the production have not yet attracted widespread critical interest.

Bodily noises aside, however, it may be that comfort with binaural sound and other immersive technologies faces generational, cultural and other barriers that impede some patrons' comfort. Accordingly, even those praising the production, including the technology, sometimes need to become accustomed to the experience. Andrzei Lukowski, for instance, in his *Time Out* review, acknowledges that 'for about half an hour I hated it, or was at least very unsure'.[22] At the same time, he eventually recognizes the effect that the binaural sound is meant to create: '[the headphones] allow a constant stream of 3D sound to be relayed to your ears: the screeches of birds, music from musicians . . . and most impressively a three sisters who are wholly physically absent, just disembodied voices whose location we feel we can "see" thanks to the pinpoint design'.

Neil Durham, in contrast, never acclimatized to the headphones, instead deciding not to wear them: 'we chose not to wear the headphone for much of the production because we felt that technology should not be relied upon to enhance the live theatre experience'.[23] He admits, however, that someone in his party had a completely different experience: 'Our companion however wore the headphones throughout and felt it was 1 of the best productions of *Macbeth* that he'd ever seen because the audio experience was exemplary and the edit of the text was so strong.'[24] Like some of the other critics, Durham appears to have decided in advance that

[18] www.standard.co.uk/culture/theatre/macbeth-donmar-warehouse-review-david-tennant-cush-jumbo-b1127257.html.

[19] This reviewer also remarks on a 'glitch' whereby the witches are 'wayward' rather than 'weird'. They surmise that this language suggests that the trio got 'tattoos without telling their dads'. This segment of the review seems to indicate that the reviewer is not familiar with Shakespearian textual scholarship.

[20] https://thetheatretimes.com/macbeth-at-the-donmar-warehouse.

[21] www.thetimes.co.uk/article/cush-jumbo-theatre-audience-behaviour-is-getting-weirder-but-i-never-expected-this-87qzqwq7q.

[22] www.timeout.com/london/theatre/macbeth-83-review.

[23] Durham does not indicate whether or not he is using the 'royal we'.

[24] https://monstagigz.com/2023/12/10/theatre-review-macbeth-starring-david-tennant-cush-jumbo-at-the-donmar.

this technology remains antithetical to the experience he prefers to have with live theatre. It is noteworthy, however, that such criticism often comes from those who chose not to wear the headphones that were an integral part of the production's design. Such hesitation against theatrical innovation can be warranted, of course, but it frequently occurs when audiences encounter unfamiliar technologies. When Lev [Leon] Theremin presented his eponymous music machine in the early twentieth century, for instance, many people were captivated by it. George Bernard Shaw, however, apparently said that 'he had heard better noises on a comb covered with tissue paper.'[25] Such disparate responses are not surprising, given the role of sound in performance. As sound theorist Brandon LaBelle reminds us, 'Sound is intrinsically and unignorably relational. It emanates, propagates, communicates, vibrates, and agitates; it leaves a body and enters others; it binds and unhinges, harmonizes and traumatizes; it sends the body moving, the mind dreaming, the air oscillating. It seemingly eludes definition, while having profound effect.'[26]

Caspar Henderson, moreover, strikingly draws from Shakespeare in order to suggest that what we perceive as 'noise', rather than welcome 'sound', 'in a technical sense makes variation and hence innovation possible. In both everyday speech and poetic imagination it can speak of wonders.'[27] Alluding to Caliban's reference to 'sounds and sweet airs' and Macbeth's invocation of 'sound and fury', Henderson suggests that sound remains open to shifting interpretations and that negative associations ('noise pollution', but not 'sound pollution', for instance)[28] disregard the way that changes in sound can lead to important advances in our ability to discern what we experience from innovative positions. Whether binaural sound such as that offered in Webster's *Macbeth* ultimately wins over those preferring more conventional theatrical practices may be less important than achieving the advances possible through skilled experimentation, however controversial it may be.

Given this level of disagreement, Deorio strikingly maintains that a sound designer should strive for both a 'unique' and a 'universal' response to the audio-based facets of a production:

The most challenging part of a sound designer's work is to create an emotional response that is perceived and interpreted both uniquely and universally. It should be unique to the artist creating it, as well as unique to the production in which it is contained. And yet, it should be universally understood by an audience to produce a similar collective response, even if the individuals within that audience interpret the meaning slightly differently due to their own separate experience and perception.[29]

The Donmar *Macbeth*, however, indicates why this goal could be unattainable in some instances. It could take time for people to adjust to such technology, or it may be that universal satisfaction may remain elusive.

Despite the wide range of opinions generated by the Donmar *Macbeth*, where expectations about 'normal' theatrical experiences clashed with technical innovation, however, numerous other theatrical artists are concurrently focusing on the ways in which advances in sound technology can invigorate Shakespearian performance. Knock at the Gate productions (KATG), for example, began creating immersive Shakespeare during the COVID-19 pandemic. Artistic Director Joe Discher and Artistic Producer Sean Hudock have created three productions presented solely through sound, designed to be experienced in the dark while wearing headphones: *Julius Caesar*, *Macbeth* and *The Tempest*.[30] Both Discher and Hudock have extensive professional backgrounds in theatre, as these performances clearly indicate. When providing KATG recordings to Emory undergraduates, they meticulously take care with many details in addition to those focused upon in production. Before my students listen to these productions, for instance, they receive beautifully crafted letters from characters in the play. For *Macbeth*, one of these missives was signed by the Porter, who instructed them to 'Gather your headphones, dim your lights as we prepare to test the boundaries of immersion and resonance through sound alone.'[31] This epistle also includes the text of Macbeth's letter to his wife, announcing the approach of Duncan to their castle. These letters caught my students' interest and encouraged them to follow the instructions closely. Like at the Donmar Warehouse, with its admonition to wear the headphones, these productions are designed for audience members to listen in

25 Albert Glinsky, *Theremin: Ether Music and Espionage* (Champaign, IL, 2005), p. 65.
26 Brandon LaBelle, 'Auditory relations' in *The Sound Studies Reader*, ed. Jonathan Sterne (London, 2013), 468–74; p. 468.
27 Caspar Henderson, *A Book of Noises: Notes on the Auraculous* (Chicago, 2023), p. 6.
28 Henderson, *A Book of Noises*, p. 6.
29 Deorio, *Art of Theatrical Sound*, p. 16.
30 www.knockatthegate.com.
31 KATG unpublished materials.

the dark, wearing headphones. The immersive sound technology does not translate as powerfully for those who listen in other settings.

The production was created using practices now familiar due to the pandemic. Actors rehearsed and performed from their individual locations rather than together at one site. According to KATG's website, 'Macbeth was rehearsed & recorded in isolation over 24 hours September 18–October 2, 2020.'[32] Since there were numerous recordings of each portion of the text, the producers and sound designer Will Padilla (Leigh Roberts in *Julius Caesar* and *The Tempest*) could interweave segments from diverse presentations, in addition to adding pertinent sound effects and appropriate audio techniques. According to Discher: '[we] recorded individually on actors' computers in different acoustic spaces with varying equipment and geographical locations from New York to Los Angeles to New Zealand, added a soundscape and edited into what is now our production of *Macbeth*'. Like the Donmar *Macbeth*, this version of the Scottish play uses audio in order to create the illusion that listeners are embedded within the action presented. My students report that this design is extremely effective, particularly during scenes with the witches. Several of them remarked about feeling frightened during supernatural segments of the production, even though they knew the narrative and clearly realized it was a play. They indicated that the lines between fiction and reality became blurred for them and that they regularly found themselves looking over their shoulder even though they knew the characters existed only on audio.

Hudock explains the power he finds and tries to create while encouraging people to listen to this performance in the dark, as he indicates in an interview with Adron McCann from Georgia radio station WABE:

It didn't dawn on me, truly, the power of [Shakespeare's] language, until I sat in the dark the first time . . . I know sounds a little creepy, but I know there is scientific research that I've been looking into that has been studying the effects of darkness on sound and how we interpret sound . . . your hearing is actually piqued in the dark.[33]

He further suggests that listening in the dark enables audience's 'ears [to be] even more activated and tuned to the language Shakespeare's given us'.

January Lavoy, who plays Lady Macbeth in the Emory / Knock at the Gate version of this show, admits that her 'expectations were not super high' when she was first invited to participate in the recording, because Zoom theatre had been a mixed experience for her. She quickly changed her mind, however and became 'totally engaged'.[34] According to Lavoy, KATG creates a similar immersive experience to that presented by the Donmar production's sound design: 'One character was talking in one ear, the other character was talking in my other ear, and I truly had the experience of feeling like I was in the scene with them and sort of powerless to do anything about it.' Discussions with Discher and Hudock make it clear that Lavoy's experience of the audio play represents exactly the effect they are aiming for.

The creation of these productions requires meticulous time, attention and collaboration. Discher, for instance, listens to innumerable versions of the recorded lines and prepares detailed dramaturgically informed notes for the sound designer. Choosing precise excerpts from various renditions of the text, Discher offers a carefully choreographed intersection of dialogue and expressions gleaned from actors recording in far-flung spaces. The sound designer brings other creative aspects into the process, based on Discher's notes, the designer's experience with sound, and the creativity of all involved. These combined efforts produce an immersive drama that could not be recreated on a traditional stage. The team pay close attention to where the audience will be situated during each moment of the play, for example, so that individual listeners regularly feel themselves in the centre of the action, whether placed between two characters who are speaking to each other or when presented with the distinctive positions of the three witches around the cauldron – even though, in KATG's production, one actor, Laila Robins, voices all of these characters. Other sounds reflect individual aspects of the setting or facets of specific figures in the plays. When the Macbeths become monarchs, for example, the soundscape of their scenes reflects the plush accoutrements of their chamber, in

32 www.knockatthegate.com.

33 www.wabe.org/knock-at-the-gate/?gclid=CjoKCQiA5fetBhC9 ARIsAP1UMgELotb Ojo79PZyB3OS-T47HBlHUCoqA4 ZIpW_8Z5NCrKOnOXTkgPdEaAuJqEALw_wcB.

34 www.wabe.org/knock-at-the-gate/?gclid=CjoKCQiA5fetBhC9 ARIsAP1UMgELotbOjo79PZyB3OS-T47HBlHUCoqA4ZIp W_8Z5NCrKOnOXTkgPdEaAuJqEALw_wcB. Knock at the Gate produced a version of this recording with professional actors in 2020, as well as one in conjunction with Theater Emory in 2022. The Emory production also included student actors. The productions are similar, but distinctive. Information included here comes from numerous Zoom conversations with Discher and Hudock and a Zoom interview with Roberts in June 2024.

contrast to the barer space of the Great Hall in which they conversed before their coronation. In *Julius Caesar*, conversations are sometimes sonically placed under a viaduct during a storm, while rain in *The Tempest* requires the sounds of 'big drops on big leaves'. Also in this play, disparate footsteps occur either on stone or on sand, such as when Ferdinand runs towards his father. The team consider what an airy spirit such as Ariel would sound like and determine that Prospero will always summon him by whispering. Caliban, on the other hand, who is referred to in the text as a 'fish' is accompanied by the sound of gills to augment his breathing within a very wet environment (*Tempest* 2.2.24), although they occasionally drop all external sound effects in order to delve into Caliban's mind. Each choice emphasizes the centrality of sound over absent visuals in these performances.

Leigh Roberts, the sound designer for KATG's *Julius Caesar* and the *Tempest*, is not a Shakespearian, but he and Discher agree that his perspective often brings new insights into the process since he hasn't been involved in productions of these particular plays before. Noting that the Logic Pro technology they use works well for creating such immersive drama, Roberts also describes the many challenges attendant upon the need to make it sound as though all the actors are in the same place, which is far from the reality of this composition process. For the sound to work well, the director and designer need to interweave segments with extremely subtle differences, making sure that the sound doesn't overwhelm the plot and the story. As they work, they continually close their eyes in order to 'see' what is happening with their ears, asking, for example: how far away is the ocean in this scene? Can the characters see the ocean? What time of day is it? During the day, there would be sounds of insects in the mix, while at night, cicadas, crickets and frogs might make their presence subtly known. They need to determine where the listener will be within the scene: which character(s) are nearby and in which direction? While the auditors may not be consciously aware of the minutiae associated with such decisions, the end result depends on mixing the sound appropriately. Roberts notes that *The Tempest* was harder, in many respects, than *Julius Caesar*. Acknowledging that the sounds of armour, shields and swords are well known, Roberts contrasts that with the inability to determine precisely what Prospero's magic sounds like. Given Caliban's uncertain physicality, what kind of breathing apparatus might he have? Since Prospero's staff makes no sound, how can its presence be indicated? When should vocal sounds, such as exhalations, that are not identified in the text, be included? Roberts describes innumerable lengthy discussions with the rest of the production team in order to create the precise sound needed in each moment. He recognizes that there is a fine line between art and gimmick that needs to be navigated with great care. Thus, when Caliban is in his cave, there is a reverberant echo present that disappears when Caliban goes outside. Such distinctions remain subtle, but key to the production's success. Determining where not to place sound is as significant as deciding where sound will work well. Accordingly, at the end of *The Tempest*, there is pure silence, but the audience may or may not realize what has happened. The creation of this sound regularly demands close attention to detail that may elude the conscious recognition of the auditors.

All the productions included here have emerged since the pandemic. As immersive experiences grow in popularity and sophistication, these kinds of performances are likely to proliferate. As the hesitancy of some Donmar critics indicates, this trend is not welcomed by all, but the artistic ability and technical proficiency associated with these audio-centric Shakespearian productions suggest that even the sceptics would be well served by allowing themselves to be drawn into these immersive theatrical experiences. Notably, Shakespearian directors continue to emphasize the importance of audio in their productions. Jamie Lloyd, for example, draws attention to headphones and sound in his 2024 production of *Romeo and Juliet*, starring Tom Holland and Francesca Amewudah-Rivers. Here, the young couples' earbuds are removed at the end of the play to signal their deaths, after a staging where audio remains central. While the headphones handed to audiences during productions using binaural sound may confound some current audiences, it seems likely that sound design will continue to play an increasingly important role in 21st-century Shakespearian performances.

'STRIKE THEIR SOUNDS TOGETHER': RADIO AND TELEVISION IN THE TEACHING OF SHAKESPEARE IN TWENTIETH-CENTURY AMERICA

JOSEPH P. HAUGHEY [1]

The story of radio in the teaching of Shakespeare in American high schools is but one chapter in a larger, ongoing narrative of Shakespeare's part in education. The radio era, which flourished particularly in the 1930s and 1940s, had its roots in the nineteenth century when Shakespeare's plays first firmly established themselves atop the secondary school canon. This ongoing narrative, which continues to unfold as schools adapt to Shakespeare's ever changing role in their curricula, remains forever intertwined in historical context, sociocultural shift and technological advancement. Throughout most of the twentieth century, *English Journal* (*EJ*), the cornerstone publication of the National Council of Teachers of English (NCTE), which began publication in 1910, provided American English teacher-scholars a platform for sharing pedagogical perspectives and practices and, as a result, recorded that evolution. This study analyses the pivotal role that radio and its descendant, television, played in the evolution of Shakespeare's place in a technology-driven, student-centred, project-based curriculum through the lens of these educators.

Before radio, the phonograph had already provided teachers with a groundbreaking tool for bringing recorded music and performance into their classrooms. The first phonograph recordings had been made in the 1890s – one of the first known Shakespeare phonograph recordings was Mark Antony's Curse in 1894/1895 – and by the 1910s, teachers were using these recordings to supplement lessons with music, most commonly Mendelssohn's *A Midsummer Night's Dream*. Soon after, teachers used phonographs to bring professional actors' voices into classrooms. Early Shakespeare recordings, such as Mark Antony's Curse, had been just snippets meant to preserve well-known voices for posterity; however, by the 1930s and 1940s, innovative Shakespearians including Orson Welles and Maurice Evans pushed the boundaries by producing full plays (albeit abridged) in multi-record sets that brought whole performances into schools and homes. By the time radio entered the American classroom, phonograph technology had already forged a curricular path that radio would trace.[2]

Radio likewise paved a road for later technologies. The pedagogical conversations surrounding radio in *EJ* – for example, how to influence students to choose high-quality productions, methods for using radio in the classroom, having students create mock programmes, etc. – would establish methodological foundations for later audio and visual media in the classroom: television and 16 mm / 8 mm film technologies beginning in the late 1940s; cassette and VHS tapes in the 1980s; CDs, DVDs and computers in the 2000s; down to the digital technologies that permeate today's educational landscape – artificial intelligence, virtual reality, social media, learning apps, multimedia mashup retellings, etc. These technologies – those of the past and those today – all interconnect in that larger ongoing narrative, advancements building on one another as each trailblazes pedagogical space for the next. The consideration of the place of radio in the teaching of

---

[1] This article is dedicated to the memory of Alden Vaughan.

[2] As I have argued elsewhere, even before the phonograph, school texts in the early nineteenth century provided students with passages from Shakespeare, not whole plays. In the 1870s, though, the first American single-play editions provided full plays. Thus, the transition from studying Shakespearian passages to whole plays is a trend that repeats itself across textbook, phonograph, radio and television. See Joseph Haughey, '"It is worth the listening to": the phonograph and the teaching of Shakespeare in the early twentieth-century America', in *Broadcast Your Shakespeare: Continuity and Change across Media*, ed. Stephen Neill (London, 2018), 123–40.

Shakespeare, thus, is not an isolated moment but rather part of a rich, continuous process that has kept classroom experience with Shakespeare ever evolving.

To tell the story of radio in the teaching of Shakespeare, this article turns next to radio's historical and technological contexts. The 1930s were a markedly different decade from the 1910s and 1920s. Mired in economic collapse but simultaneously illuminated by the advance of rich critical and technological innovation, the decade witnessed stock markets crash, banks close and families driven from their homes and farms by foreclosure and bankruptcy, but at the same time saw the advance of new theoretical approaches to understanding literature, as well as the rise of the motion picture and radio, institutions that would reshape not only the classroom and methods through which students learned Shakespeare, but also the very fabric of American culture as the nation healed from the stranglehold of the Great Depression. At the 1933 NCTE convention, one speaker declared:

[Radio] programs are valuable in so far as they supply something which the teacher cannot give the pupils. They are invaluable as illustrative material. Is the English lesson on Shakespeare? Then the radio program can bring excerpts from his plays to illustrate the specific points the teacher wishes to make. The effect of hearing these plays properly read is worth much to the pupil who might otherwise only know them through the printed page.[3]

As the 1930s turned to the 1940s, Asia and Europe tangled themselves in a catastrophic war, and the United States, for the second time in the century, found itself pulled again towards world war. This time, though, Americans at home experienced the war through radio, and *EJ* contributions made the war their focus too. When Germany seized Austria in 1938, one speaker at a meeting of the New Jersey Association of Teachers of English spoke about how radio broadcasting brought the fight directly into Americans' living rooms. He added, though, that 'radio has no morals at all. It is a *means* and can be equally effective for maintaining democracy or perpetuating dictatorship'; he argued that English classrooms have a responsibility to foster a 'critical and discriminating public of listeners [who] will not be taken in by the tricks and devices of fascist propagandists'. His speech was subsequently published in *EJ*.[4]

Within three years, many teachers would leave their positions for military service, while their colleagues who stayed behind struggled to help their students (and themselves) understand America's place in the war.[5] At the

1941 NCTE annual convention over the Thanksgiving holiday, Robert Pooley, the NCTE president, in his annual address, referred to a recent conversation with another convention-goer: this fellow English teacher had been too young to serve in World War I and was too old now to serve in this one; he felt left behind 'teaching freshman English and Shakespeare' while his younger peers and students enlisted, leaving him having 'never felt so useless'; the NCTE president, though, after telling his colleague's story, reminded convention-goers of the importance of the work of the English teacher:

We must teach how to listen and read . . . This is a difficult task. It carries no glory, nor will it ever be publicly recognized. But I assert with all the force of which I am capable that this task is more important to the health, spirit, and continuity of our democracy than airplanes, guns, tanks, or even food itself.[6]

Two weeks after the 1941 convention, Japan bombed Pearl Harbor. There would be no annual convention in 1942 or 1943; however, NCTE served in these war years as the collective voice of English teachers through its *EJ*.[7] By the end of the 1940s, the world map had shifted even as many pedagogical questions regarding Shakespeare echoed: which plays should be taught? With what methods? Where do art and performance fit? What makes an appropriate school text of Shakespeare? How do teachers assess Shakespeare instruction; how do they know if students have learned? What about motion pictures? What about radio?[8]

---

[3] F. H. Lumly, 'The English teacher and radio broadcasts', *EJ* 23 (1934), 478–85; pp. 481–2.

[4] Keith I. Tyler, 'What can we do about the radio?' *EJ* 27 (1938), 556–66; p. 559.

[5] J. N. Hook, *A Long Way Together: A Personal View of NCTE's First Sixty-Seven Years* (Urbana, IL, 1979), pp. 130–1.

[6] Robert C. Pooley, 'One people, one language', *EJ* 21 (1942), 110–20; pp. 117–19. Robert Pooley was honoured as one of ten teachers/scholars who most influenced the development of the secondary English curriculum. See Ken Donelson, 'Ten teachers and scholars who influenced the secondary English curriculum, 1880–1970', *EJ* 73 (1984), 78–80; p. 79. For further NCTE wartime justifications for teaching English, also see Hook, *A Long Way*, pp. 131–6.

[7] See Thomas Pollock, 'The profession in perspective: two reminiscences of the NCTE', *EJ* 66 (1977), 6–9.

[8] War themes would also reverberate in *EJ*. Matilda Bailey, in 1942, for example, joined an ongoing discussion in newspapers that compared Rudolph Hess's English journey to that of Malcolm in *Macbeth*: Matilda Bailey, 'Conscripting literature for a present emergency', *EJ* 31 (1942), 130–6. Towards the end of the war, Marion Kaplan, in 1945, wrote that 'perhaps the radio offers the most direct method of inculcating democratic ideals, for the radio

Radio had been kept a military secret during World War I but had become commonplace by the mid-1930s; it was rare to find children who did not listen regularly. The NCTE had established a Radio Committee and in 1935 its chair, Max Herzberg, wrote in *EJ*:

Within an astonishingly short time – hardly more than a decade – the American people have acquired a new folkway – listening to the radio. The number of hours of time each day when the radio is on in American homes, places of business, offices, and school must reach figures of astronomical vastness.[9]

He commented on people listening even in automobiles and semi-correctly predicted that, one day, there would be 'people walking our streets with minute radio sets hung from their hats and going full blast as they step along'.[10] Radio programming then, though, was not like radio today. It more closely resembled what television would become later in the twentieth century with mostly spoken-word programming: dramas, sports and news programmes, all designed to fit into half-hour, 45-minute, and hour-long time slots.

In 1936, a study of 3,345 New York schoolchildren, ages 10–13, found that 'boys and girls spend over six hours a week listening to radio programs; ... [and] that this listening was the greatest principal activity outside school except outdoor play'.[11] Two years later, in 1938, Joseph Mersand contributed an analysis of a recent survey of 150 high school juniors that found nearly all had a radio at home and concluded that radio dramatizations inspired students to read the books from which they were derived. These included six recent broadcasts of Shakespeare: *Hamlet, Macbeth, Merchant of Venice, A Midsummer Night's Dream, Othello* and *Taming of the Shrew*. He writes that the 'progressive teacher who is anxious to adopt new devices for the improvement of his skill in the classroom [but who would] ... refuse to accept the radio as such a medium would seem to indicate a narrowness of pedagogical philosophy'.[12] That same year, one *EJ* contributor declared:

This is the age of radio. All of us are radio-minded. The youth now in our high schools is truly a radio generation. They were born with the birth of radio, and the two have grown up together. Many of us are so bewildered by these rapid changes in the habits of the whole population that we fail to grasp the significance which they have for us in our daily work of educating America's youth.[13]

Replace the word 'radio' above with 'artificial intelligence' or 'social media', and his observation mirrors today's 21st-century education landscape. The same contributor follows up in a 1939 contribution: 'young as radio

is, its educational potentialities are fairly well established. Radio education is no fad today. No longer can it be disregarded by the intelligent teacher'.[14] Thomas Rishworth, a Minneapolis educator, in 1941 championed the no-longer-new medium: 'radio has an opportunity unequalled throughout the history of man for the stimulation of intellectual curiosity, the development of appreciation of beauty, truth, and goodness, and the inculcation of a sense of participating citizenship endowed with rights and duties without which this world as we know it cannot survive'.[15] Radio had replaced the lowbrow version of stage theatre, which had been abandoned almost entirely to the highbrow decades before but had not yet been displaced by television.[16] In tandem with motion pictures,

---

thrusts deep into the consciousness of our students. The democracies have learned from the Axis how potent an instrument for propaganda radio can be. In our own country it was used effectively before the war ... which warned against Fascist aggression. After the outbreak of the war radio became an even more powerful means of attack ... roused the people to patriotic fervor'; Marion Kaplan, 'Radio technique in high-school dramatics', *EJ* 34 (1945), 88–93; p. 88. After the war, in 1946, Dora Palmer and Ruth Weeks each authored a contribution suggesting new methods of teaching tolerance through *The Merchant of Venice* in response to early reports of the atrocities that had been inflicted in what would later be called the Holocaust: Dora E. Palmer, 'A good deed in a naughty world', *EJ* 35 (1946), 370–5; Ruth Weeks, 'Teaching tolerance through literature', *EJ* 35 (1946), 425–32.

9 Max Herzberg, 'Tentative units in radio program appreciation', *EJ* 24 (1935), 545–55; p. 545. Two years after Pooley, in 1943, Herzberg would serve as another wartime NCTE president. Over the course of his career, he authored several books and articles on teaching with mass media and edited school editions of *Julius Caesar* and *Hamlet*. He was also honoured by Donelson, 'Ten teachers', p. 79.

10 Herzberg, 'Tentative units', p. 546.

11 Richard Hurley, 'Movie and radio – friend and foe', *EJ* 26 (1937), 205–11; p. 208. Hurley suggests that the movies are a friend to schools while radio is a foe.

12 Joseph Mersand, 'Radio makes readers', *EJ* 27 (1938), 469–75; p. 469. Joseph Mersand would also serve as NCTE president.

13 Tyler, 'What can we do about the radio?', p. 557.

14 Keith Tyler, 'Recent developments in radio education?' *EJ* 28 (1939), 193–9; p. 193.

15 Thomas Rishworth, 'Responsibility of the school in educational broadcasting', *EJ* 30 (1941), 287–93; p. 287.

16 Lawrence Levine illuminates the evolution of American stage Shakespeare. Early in the nineteenth century, stage Shakespeare served as lowbrow entertainment, often paired with juggling and other entertainments, and catered to the masses; however, as the nineteenth century advanced, it underwent a significant transformation, becoming increasingly highbrow and targeting the upper socio-economic echelons; see Lawrence Levine, *Highbrow/Lowbrow: The Emergence of Cultural Hierarchy in America*

it re-shaped how Americans received and consumed entertainment, art and news.[17]

Although contributions to *EJ* would often complain that they did not do enough, radio producers were at least partially attentive to listeners' intellectual development. Though it was less lucrative, they strived to include educational and artistic programming, including Shakespeare, amongst their offerings.[18] These early Shakespeare radio broadcasts attempted to recreate the experience of attending a performance in a theatre; however, they were typically cut to fit the standard time slots and employed a narrator to help contextualize the reduced text.[19] Orson Welles, before recording phonographs for schools,[20] earned fame as a radio celebrity and starred in several Shakespeare radio broadcasts. He produced and starred in *Hamlet* in two parts in 1936, each cut to thirty minutes; however, his most oft-referenced Shakespeare radio broadcast was his 1938 *Julius Caesar*, based on his groundbreaking, albeit financially unprofitable, stage version the prior year. Set in fascist Italy – even employing CBS's revered news reporter, H. V. Kaltenborn, to narrate events between dialogue – the radio production alluded to the events leading up to World War II. There would be no attempt to recreate this politicized reading in his later school phonographs, though; Welles differentiated his work for schools from that for general audiences. Other examples of Welles's radio credits include multi-part performances in 1941 in *Julius Caesar*, *Twelfth Night* and *The Merchant of Venice*, and a thirty-minute *King Lear* in 1946 that he adapted and produced for the *Mercury Summer Theater on the Air*.[21] Other radio programmes also took on Shakespeare. NBC's *Radio Guild*, for example, presented forty Shakespearian dramatizations between 1929 and 1940, including a cycle of Shakespeare's history plays in December 1935 and January 1936.[22]

Perhaps the climax of Shakespeare radio came in 1937 with two competing series of summer Shakespeare offerings on NBC and CBS, each airing on Monday evenings, and pitting an ageing John Barrymore for NBC, who played the lead, against a host of Hollywood celebrities acting for CBS (including Orson Welles, who took on Orsino in *Twelfth Night* on 30 August).[23] Despite playing in the summer, the programmes proved popular with English teachers: education professor Elizabeth Carney helped her student teachers organize out-of-school weekly Shakespeare dinner parties for high-schoolers to listen to and discuss the dramatizations together every Monday evening, which lasted through the summer. She hosted the first herself in her home, and her student

teachers and their students hosted the rest; she proudly reports, 'Never in my career of teaching have I witnessed so much enthusiasm for Shakespeare.'[24] NBC's *Great Plays* series was also popular with teachers. Its producers

---

(Cambridge, 1990). Susanne Greenhalgh notes that in the twentieth century, Orson Welles 'showcased Shakespeare ... in countless anthologies and variety programmes ... Welles' radio Shakespeare represents both artistic achievement and a politically liberal attempt to appropriate Shakespeare in the service of uniting popular and elite culture, theatre and mass media'; see Susanne Greenhalgh, 'Shakespeare and radio', in *The Edinburgh Companion to Shakespeare and the Arts*, ed. Mark Thornton Burnett, Adrian Streete and Ramona Wray (Edinburgh, 2011), 541–57; p. 553. For further exploration of Welles through this highbrow/lowbrow lens, also see Michael Anderegg, *Orson Welles, Shakespeare, and Popular Culture* (New York, 1999), pp. 6–9.

[17] See Michael P. Jensen, *The Battle of the Bard: Shakespeare on U.S. Radio in 1937* (Amsterdam, 2018), p. ix.

[18] See Douglas Lanier, 'WSHX: Shakespeare and American radio', in *Shakespeare after Mass Media: A Cultural Studies Reader* (New York, 2002), 195–219, pp. 199–201; Jensen, *The Battle of the Bard*, pp. 2–3; Greenhalgh, 'Shakespeare and radio', p. 552.

[19] Greenhalgh, 'Shakespeare and radio', pp. 544–7; Jensen, *The Battle of the Bard*, p. 9; Lanier, 'WSHX', pp. 195–8.

[20] Among Orson Welles's notable contributions were his Mercury Shakespeare Records, which included *Julius Caesar*, *Twelfth Night*, *The Merchant of Venice* and *Macbeth*. Anderegg points out that 'In virtually every media open to him – including but not limited to books, stage, radio, recordings, film, and television – Welles turned again and again to Shakespeare's plays with an energy and enthusiasm that suggests a paramount need both to express himself through Shakespeare and to make Shakespeare's plays and characters, themes and motifs, available to a wide popular audience': *Orson Welles*, p. 17. This underscores Welles's lifelong alliance with Shakespeare's plays, which 'simultaneously reached backward to the nineteenth century and forward to the world of the postmodern': p. 19. Also see Anderegg, *Orson Welles*, pp. 24–8, 39–56; Haughey, '"It is worth the listening to", p. 132; Lanier, 'WSHX', pp. 197–8; Robert Sawyer, 'Broadcasting the Bard: Orson Welles, Shakespeare and war', in *Broadcast Your Shakespeare: Continuity and Change Across Media*, ed. Stephen Neill (London, 2018), 47–65.

[21] Anderegg, *Orson Welles*, p. 30; Greenhalgh, 'Shakespeare and radio', pp. 552–3; Lanier, 'WSHX', pp. 201, 213.

[22] Greenhalgh, 'Shakespeare and radio', pp. 552–3; Jensen, *The Battle of the Bard*, pp. 10–13; Lanier, 'WSHX', p. 200.

[23] Jensen details the competing 1937 programming; see *The Battle of the Bard*, pp. 25–42 for his analysis of NBC's programming, and pp. 43–66 for CBS. Also see Greenhalgh, 'Shakespeare and radio', pp. 545–6; Lanier, 'WSHX', pp. 202–3.

[24] Elizabeth Carney, 'Experiencing Shakespeare through the radio theater party', *EJ* 27 (1938), 134–5. Also, Jensen reports that a University of California professor, Alfred E. Longeuil, in June 1937, 'was so impressed by the first broadcast that he asked NBC for the scripts to study in class'. Jensen muses he would like to 'have been a fly on that classroom wall' – see *The Battle of the Bard*, p. 42. I would too.

even made available an accompanying teaching guide, and the programme and its guide received notice in the pages of *EJ*, urging teachers to use its productions in their teaching.[25]

Teachers responded. Through the 1930s and 1940s, they crafted lessons inspired by radio Shakespeare, often having students produce their own mock radio programmes. A Georgia teacher, in 1934, wrote about her tenth-graders' productions of a scene from *Merchant of Venice*: one half of the class read out the scene the first day while the other half served as an audience, and on the second day, the two groups switched roles. There was no actual radio equipment, only the students' imaginations as they read out the parts of the narrator and actors, adding music as appropriate from a phonograph.[26] One New York teacher planned a Play Festival Week at her school the same year. Students drafted scripts from novels they had previously read, which they then performed before classmates and guests.[27] Another teacher spent four weeks with his students in 1944 listening to Orson Welles's phonograph recordings and reading from his accompanying texts in preparation for what he called a 'reading production', a formal staged reading of *Macbeth* in the style of a radio production – on the school stage with peers and parents in the audience – complete with a narrator, sound effects and music, but without a set, costumes or blocking.[28] Through the 1940s, other teachers crafted similar mock radio projects that they argued worked with mainstream, special needs and vocational students.[29]

The overwhelming response in *EJ* to radio's growth reverberated the need to teach students the skills to differentiate good programming from bad. Although some teachers saw radio's possibilities, there remained significant criticism. It echoed an old struggle, an offshoot of the profession's never-ending task of redirecting students towards worthwhile material. Even those in the radio industry saw schools as the grindstone for shaping public taste; Raymond Knight, a popular radio personality, addressed the NCTE at its 1933 convention:

In my humble opinion we can do better ... I'm no Shakespeare, and perhaps some of my stuff is as bad as that ... All I say is that if *you* and *you* and *you* [the English teachers in attendance at the convention] educate the public's taste to the point where it will brand such stuff as tripe, then, of necessity, those of us who feed the air waves will have to turn out better material ... The problem of education has always been to educate students to appreciate and demand the best ... students can be taught to demand the best ... in radio.[30]

The collective theme was that radio had great potential – which became even more enthusiastic during World War II as radio became seen as a means for instilling democratic values – and often individual teachers reported great successes with their students, but overall, those ambitions were perceived as unachieved on a larger scale.

Given the cry for better programming that continued through *EJ*, as radio settled in, successes were often peppered against perceptions that the public's listening habits had become worse, and even Lee de Forest, one of the inventors of radio, acknowledged its shortcomings in a 1947 letter to the National Association of Broadcasters, which was subsequently printed in *EJ*: 'What have you gentlemen done with my child? He was conceived as a potent instrumentality for culture, fine music, the uplifting of America's mass intelligence. You have debased the child ... you and your sponsors believe the majority of listeners have only moron minds.'[31]

Teachers collectively saw themselves as the guardians of literary taste but did not know how to defend it, and the collective complaint continued to echo. Many threw their hands up at what most Americans listened to on their radios. At the 1947 annual convention in San Francisco later that year, one speaker described the trouble:

The problem of both movie and radio director is the age-old one of the theater manager: Shall he give to the public what it wants, yield to its taste, or give to the public what, presumably, it ought to have? That which brings in the money ... wins every time – and apparently is going to win for some time to come unless a much larger number of persons than now do, boycott the drivel. That is our challenge: How can we increase

[25] In March 1939, one contributor wrote, 'The English teacher finds the air filled with good listening for his students. There is the "Great Plays" series of the National Broadcasting Company for which a helpful teacher's manual is available'; see Tyler, 'Recent developments', p. 195.

[26] See Virginia Tanner, 'Broadcasting Shakespeare', *EJ* 23 (1934), 677–9.

[27] See Abigail Crawford, 'A radio drama festival', *EJ* 30 (1941), 403–4.

[28] See William Ladd, 'Macbeth – as a reading production', *EJ* 33 (1944), 374–7.

[29] See Kaplan, 'Radio technique', pp. 88–93; Gertrude Mescall, 'A radio reading project', *EJ* 30 (1941), 236–8; Delight Phillips, 'A unit on the use of radio', *EJ* 26 (1937), 33–8; Rishworth, 'Responsibility of the school', pp. 287–93.

[30] Raymond Knight, 'Radio and the English teacher', *EJ* 23 (1934), 504–6; p. 506.

[31] As quoted in Carlton Larrabee, 'Radio, a public servant', *EJ* 38 (1949), 92–4; pp. 92–3.

that number? How can we more effectively improve the public taste, and how quickly?[32]

Good programming was available, but radio privileged more profitable shows in their schedules. Advertising dollars trumped literary quality.

A New York teacher, in 1948, was still complaining: 'When you discover that ... young people are spending ... hours a day listening to programs that in most part are little more than trash, you will conclude that constructive steps ought to be taken in school to develop something resembling taste in radio listening.'[33]

Her message, though, at least regarding her own students, was one of optimism: she designed a series of projects in which her classes developed their own radio listening schedules covering sports, drama, news and music, and at its conclusion, in the same vein as those mentioned above, had students create mock radio programmes and long-term listening plans. One Wisconsin teacher in 1949 similarly organized for his students subscriptions to *Let's Learn to Listen*, at 25 cents an issue, and *Radio Listening*, at 35 cents an issue, both published by the Wisconsin Association for Better Radio Listening, and then surveyed students before and after. For four months, students selected programmes based on these guides and wrote letters to radio stations regarding the shows they thought most worthy of airtime. Anderson reports anecdotally how his students, over the course of a semester, improved their listening choices, as did their families at home.[34] The most common student radio assignments detailed in *EJ* involved students evaluating their own listening behaviours and creating their own mock radio programmes, assignments that would evolve in subsequent decades alongside later technologies.

As the 1940s came to an end, the contradiction remained. Individual teachers were winning battles with their own students but were sure they were losing the larger struggle of getting the public, long term, to make better listening choices. Radio's potential remained unrealized. An assistant professor of English at Fresno State College, in 1949 bemoaned: 'We teachers of English ... have for almost two decades been conscientiously wrestling with many a problem presented to our profession by radio. For twenty years we have been struggling ... to bring into our classrooms appropriate programs and transcriptions and thus to make of radio an assistant teacher.'[35]

This question of radio, though, had already started to transform into a question of television by the late 1940s. The decade after World War II witnessed television gradually replace radio, quite literally changing how the nation saw its own customs, traditions and perspectives.

And as popular radio programmes morphed into television programmes, radio Shakespeare transformed into television Shakespeare,[36] and school radio assignments became television assignments. As early as September 1938, Orson Welles had prophetically announced live to his radio listeners in the introduction to *Julius Caesar* for *Mercury Theater on the Air* that he himself 'wish[ed] for the extra dimension of television' for that night's radio broadcast. The first full-length Shakespeare television production, an abridged *Julius Caesar*, had been broadcast the previous July, a 70-minute production that had drawn on the antifascism of Welles's 1937 staging. In 1953, Welles acted in his first (and only) Shakespearian television role, under the direction of Peter Brook, as King Lear. By the mid-1950s, students were watching television in droves, and it would prove as moving a force mid-century as radio had in the 1930s and 1940s.[37]

Hundreds of Shakespearian telecasts peppered these many hours of teenage television viewing. Television Shakespeare in the 1950s provided the visual element, the 'extra dimension' that Welles had wished for, but remained an extension of radio Shakespeare. American television producers, for example, shortened and formatted Shakespeare's texts to fit allotted time slots, just as their predecessors in radio had. They also attempted to replicate live theatrical conditions, with actors performing live stage Shakespeare for the television camera as they might onstage. Several early television performances were broadcast live from national theatres, bringing the visual experience of theatre into American living rooms for the first time. NBC and CBS likewise cast Shakespeare on television in the 1950s much like they had on the radio in

---

[32] Milton Fadiman and Arnold Marquis, 'The San Francisco Convention', *EJ* 37 (1948), 97–102; p. 99.

[33] See Marion Tallman, 'Teaching discriminating radio listening', *EJ* 37 (1948), 408–12; pp. 408–9.

[34] See Borghild Anderson, 'Are good radio listeners made?', *EJ* 38 (1949), 391–4.

[35] See Larrabee, 'Radio, a public servant', p. 92.

[36] H. R. Coursen makes the case that television Shakespeare derived from radio Shakespeare, differentiating film and television technologies. Film evolved from the silent screen tradition, whereas television evolved from the radio tradition; see H. R. Coursen, 'The Bard and the tube', in *Shakespeare on Television: An Anthology of Essays and Reviews*, ed. James C. Bulman and H. R. Coursen (Hanover, NH, 1988), 3–10; pp. 6–7. For more on the transition from radio to television, see Lanier, 'WSHX', p. 211.

[37] See Michael Barry, 'Shakespeare on television', *BBC Quarterly* 9 (1954), 145–9; Stephen Purcell, 'Shakespeare on television', in *The Edinburgh Companion to Shakespeare and the Arts*, ed. Thornton Burnett, Streete and Wray, 522–40.

the 1930s. NBC and its *Hallmark Hall of Fame* series again emphasized a single actor in their television Shakespearian programming, much like they had on radio in 1937, this time featuring Maurice Evans against a backdrop of supporting actors for *Hamlet* in 1953, *Richard II* and *Macbeth* in 1954, *Taming of the Shrew* in 1956, *Twelfth Night* in 1957, and *The Tempest* and *Macbeth* (again), both in 1960. CBS, on the other hand, just as they had for radio in the summer of 1937, cast a variety of leading actors in their competing series of Shakespeare telecast productions.[38] Television in the 1950s would likewise use Shakespearian productions and allusions to heighten its highbrow image, and NCTE contributions then, just as with radio, would debate how best to incorporate the new technology in their teaching.

Shakespeare on television was a common topic amongst mid-century *EJ* contributions. Some, remembering the old radio programmes with nostalgia, complained that the added visual element of television privileged the visual at the expense of the auditory, resulting 'in a dulling of imagination's ear'.[39] Squeezing Shakespeare into sixty- and ninety-minute time slots drew the ire of others; one English teacher in 1959, for example, echoed his teacher ancestors, complaining that he preferred 'an average Sunday with Camera Three [more] than any ninety-minute thumbnail version of Shakespeare'.[40] Others complained of the added demands of incorporating televised Shakespeare in their teaching: 'Usually I must devote hours after the night telecast to planning classroom follow-up'.[41] One particularly cynical teacher complained: 'If Shakespeare's Henry V had lived in our day, he might not have been so envious of the common man, ... cramm'd with the distressful images of half-a-dozen television shows and who next morning rises with a vacant mind, eager to consume another dozen shows'.[42] Perhaps most of all, English teachers continued to see themselves as guardians of taste and remained concerned with directing their students towards, and encouraging the production of, higher-quality offerings; one New York teacher advised that 'you can devise many ways of helping ... pupils develop an active and intelligent interest in good programs instead of the passive and indiscriminate soaking-up of entertainment that now absorbs their time'.[43]

Radio and television both had the advantage of better encapsulating the immediacy of theatre. Unlike the phonograph or other later recorded visual technology, radio and early television presented performances live. There could be glitches. There could be mistakes. It had the same appeal that drew audiences to a stage production. However, radio and television remained limited regarding classroom use due to scheduling conflicts and their ephemeral nature. Because they lasted only as long as their scheduled time slot, they left teachers no means to review a broadcast or parts of a broadcast with students in class the next day and no way the following year, except for occasional repeat broadcasts, to make use of a broadcast with future students. Coordinating school and radio/television schedules was challenging and naturally imperfect. Radio Shakespeare had been a force in education, but it had been secondary to phonograph Shakespeare. Likewise, television Shakespeare was a force, but it was secondary to the century's various recorded visual technologies. These were far more flexible to the classroom needs of teachers. They provided more complete versions of Shakespeare, which could be divided as desired into specific passages or scenes, easily reshaping a production to align with a lesson. They started precisely when called upon to do so, could be paused and repeated as necessary, and adapted to fit within the school bells. As a result, recorded media proved historically more influential in education than live media such as radio and television.

That said, the story of radio and television Shakespeare in schools remains a fascinating study in the intersection of Shakespeare and educational technology. The two technologies mark the first time that a whole population could experience a play simultaneously with the energy of live performance, and that energy seeped into classroom study.[44] It centred viewers

---

[38] See Purcell, 'Shakespeare on television', pp. 524–5.

[39] See Robert Lambert, 'Pitfalls in reading drama', *EJ* 53 (1964), 592–4; p. 602.

[40] See Patrick Hazard and Mary Hazard, 'What's TV doing to English? – Part II', *EJ* 48 (1959), 491–3; p. 492.

[41] See Miriam Goldstein, 'Humanities through television', *EJ* 49 (1960), 250–5; p. 250.

[42] See Stuart Stengel, 'What is the high school teacher of English doing about television?' *EJ* 43 (1954), 120–4; p. 121.

[43] See Sarah Roody, 'Effect of radio, television, and motion pictures on the development of maturity', *EJ* 41 (1952), 245–50; p. 247. For other *EJ* contributions on television, also see William Boutwell, 'What can we do about movies, radio, television?' *EJ* 41 (1952), 131–6; Edgar Dale, 'Child welfare and the cinema', *EJ* 26 (1937), 698–705; Henry Maloney, 'The public arts: half a *Hamlet* better than none?' *EJ* 48 (1959), 94–6; Richard Mueller, 'A groundling's approach to Shakespeare', *EJ* 53 (1964), 584–8; Milton Kaplan, 'Television drama: a discussion', *EJ* 47 (1958), pp. 549–61.

[44] Jensen addresses the debate at the time about whether a heavily abridged live performance really counts as Shakespeare; see *The Battle of the Bard*, pp. 44–5. Greenhalgh does not address significant cutting but has pointed out that, while 'criticism of radio drama has always been haunted by the idea that it can give only an "impoverished", "incomplete", representation, especially of artworks originally designed for audiovisual perception in the theatre, early

in a way no performance could before, with the whole country listening together and then spending the following days in shared reflection. It buzzed outside and inside classrooms. Live performance before could not do that; at most, a live show could seat just a few hundred at a time, maybe a few thousand in some of the largest American theatres – but even there, its reach was limited to a specific geographic region, paltry compared to mass media that could connect millions of listeners to Shakespeare at the same time coast-to-coast. Later recorded media, even with its flexibility, could not do that either. Recordings scatter the attention of masses across time. Audiences do not watch together but at their convenience. With no sense of immediacy, some do not watch at all. And in the current century, with a plethora of digital options, nothing brings an audience together in concentrated viewership in that same way.

Radio and early television, though, did that. They made a performance a nationwide spectacle in which a significant chunk of the country could focus on a single production. And when networks turned single shows into a season of Shakespeare as NBC and CBS did with radio in the summer of 1937, they took that energy and extended it over a summer, with families, communities and a whole nation listening together at the same time, Shakespeare's words all bobbing about in America's collective heads simultaneously – a series of productions, albeit significantly reduced, reaching more Americans over the summer than any theatre season before or since. That had never happened before and will not happen again. Radio and television, by their very limits, generate mass collective interest. And when that energy turned to Shakespeare, it concentrated the nation's energies in ways that made classroom Shakespeare topical and pressing, an energy teachers could and did make manifest in their teaching.

In the larger narrative of the history of classroom Shakespeare, these stories of radio and television reinforce time-tested, pedagogical approaches that balance the close study of text against a contextualized analysis of authentic engagements with Shakespeare outside of the classroom, i.e., what actual people are doing with Shakespeare out in the real world. Students learn best from engaging with the plays in the same ways as professional and amateur Shakespearians. In the case of radio, that meant juxtaposing traditional language-based study against considerations of how radio and television personalities – such as Orson Welles, John Barrymore, or Maurice Evans – shaped Shakespeare in their own historical and technological contexts: connecting Shakespeare to current world

events, creating mock performances, and evaluating networks' production and programming choices. In the case of early phonograph technology, that history and context had meant something different: connecting Shakespeare to music – think Mendelssohn – and preserving Shakespearian actors' voices for perpetuity. In the years after radio and television, that context expanded and evolved to encompass other contexts and technologies, but the central tenet would remain that students learn best through methods based on authentic engagements with Shakespeare modelled after the things modern-day Shakespearians – whether performers, scholars, artists or just enthusiasts who care about the work – are actually doing with Shakespeare.

Such approaches are myriad. Some Shakespearians are exploring and blending new media today as Orson Welles did with old media a century ago. Alongside television in the 1950s, some Shakespearians started making his plays into comic books and graphic adaptations, and though today's graphic adaptations look quite different from those, the tradition persists with graphic novels, and innovative teachers have crafted lessons in which students create their own graphic versions of Shakespeare. More traditional visual arts, such as painting, drawing and illustrating, have taken inspiration from Shakespeare even longer, for centuries, and today's creative teachers likewise make space in the classroom for their study and for students to create in their own visual art. Similarly, creative writers gathered inspiration from Shakespeare and re-moulded his stories into their own. The list goes on.

This is not to suggest skipping the study of Shakespeare's language; that has always been the foundation of best practice. However, that study best takes on enduring shape when teachers allow students to craft their

---

attempts at constructing a poetics of radio frequently envisaged it as a mode of performance analogous to the Shakespearean ideal stage evoked by the opening Chorus speech of *Henry V*, in which the "imaginary forces" of the listener called up an "inner vision", variously likened to the workings of the mind in dreams, reading, stream of consciousness, or the process of memory' – see 'Shakespeare and radio', p. 544. Lanier had drawn similarly on the prologue to *Henry V*, alluding to the perceived weakness of the stage as a medium as a parallel to a perceived weakness of radio, but Lanier suggests, 'Yet what at first seems an insurmountable deficiency turns out to be an advantage. The very inadequacy of the medium – with some help from the Prologue's repeated exhortations – prompts the audience to "piece out our imperfections with your thoughts"'; see 'WSHX', p. 195.

own interpretations, taking an image, character, passage or scene from Shakespeare as a spark for their own analytic and creative energies. There are many guises through which lovers of Shakespeare engage, both personally and professionally: as readers, theatregoers, actors and directors, literary and theatre critics, editors, video game designers, set and costume designers, and dozens of others, each presenting opportunities in the classroom for invention. The best teachers of the 1930s and 1940s used radio to this end. The best teachers today use the technological, cultural and creative milieu about them to a similar end: providing classroom opportunities for students to engage deeply in Shakespeare's originals and then analysing the various ways contemporary Shakespearians engage with that text, ultimately integrating these into their students' own intellectual pursuits through project-based activities that push students' evaluative and creative skill to their highest levels.

'SAY WHAT THOU SEEST YOND!': MUSIC, SPECTACLE AND THE ACTOR'S VOICE IN AUDIO PRODUCTIONS OF *THE TEMPEST*

VIRGINIA MASON VAUGHAN AND ALDEN T. VAUGHAN†[1]

Shakespeare's *Tempest* is frequently described as his most musical play. Like his other comedies, the text requires songs: Ariel performs four; Stephano, Trinculo and Caliban share a 'freedom' catch; and Juno and Ceres sing a marriage blessing during the masque.[2] More unusual are the Folio's stage directions that call for music '*dispersedly*' (1.2.383) around and under the stage, creating a sort of early modern soundtrack to bring Prospero's magical island to life. Especially at the Blackfriars, where Shakespeare had access to an organ and a musical consort hidden in an alcove behind the stage, spectators were treated to 'sweet airs that give delight and hurt not' (3.2.139). Of course, some of the play's sounds were not so pleasant. Loud noises are crucial to the tempest that opens the play, as well as for Caliban, Stephano and Trinculo's drunken antics, the Harpy's appearance in 3.3 and, perhaps most important, the antimasque that follows the elaborate court masque of act 4. Shakespeare's reliance on musical interludes and other sound effects, particularly thunder and lightning, make *The Tempest* an ideal text for a radio broadcast or an audiobook.

Yet *The Tempest* is also one of Shakespeare's most spectacular plays. As Andrew Gurr observed long ago, *The Tempest* requires more special effects 'than any play in the canon'.[3] Spectacles, interspersed between lengthy passages of exposition – such as Prospero's detailed explanation of his arrival on the island – constitute much of the action. The opening storm is the first such 'show', enacted at the Blackfriars with a sea machine (pebbles rolling in a drum), a wind machine (shaken loose pieces of canvas), a thunder sheet or rolled cannonball to create waves, wind and thunder. Audio productions can present these sounds effectively, but blocking is another matter. On the Blackfriars stage, the ship's Master could be seen on the upper stage, speaking as if

from the boat's mast, the court party yelling from the stage below the ship's deck: spacing that highlights the debate about who's in charge.

Sight gags and visual spectacles are a particular challenge for audio producers. The comic stage business in 2.2, as Trinculo crawls underneath Caliban's gaberdine to form what seems to Stephano to be some kind of monster, depends primarily on what the audience sees. Two actors crawl under a cloak and then move around the stage like a giant crab. The scene's hilarity is muted if we can't see these shenanigans. The 'strange shapes' who prepare a banquet in 3.3 interrupted by Ariel's descent from the heavens as a harpy were calculated to startle the audience as well as the onstage Neapolitan party, but if we can't envision the spectacle, the effect is lost. Prospero's masque of act 4 – staged with Juno also descending from aloft, joined by elegantly clad goddesses, and a dance of nymphs and reapers – also depends on visual display, particularly the goddesses' elegant costumes and the choreographed dance. Similarly, the act 4 antimasque, when Caliban, Stephano and Trinculo don Prospero's clothing and hounds chase them around the stage, has less effect if we cannot see drunks cavorting in borrowed robes as a comic parody of the formal masque

---

[1] Alden T. Vaughan was an active collaborator on this project until his death on March 19, 2024. Virginia Mason Vaughan compiled the final draft; she is grateful for the assistance received throughout the project from Mike Jensen. Quotations from *The Tempest* are from *William Shakespeare: The Complete Works*, ed. Stanley Wells, Gary Taylor, John Jowett and William Montgomery (Oxford, 2005).

[2] Settings of 'Full Fathom Five' and 'Where the Bee Sucks' by Robert Johnson, a composer active during James I's reign, are extant. For a thorough discussion of Shakespeare's songs, see David Lindley, *Shakespeare and Music* (London, 2006).

[3] See Andrew Gurr, 'The Tempest's Tempest at the Blackfriars', in *Shakespeare Survey 41* (Cambridge, 1988), 91–102; pp. 91–2, 95.

that precedes it. These 'shows' present a series of challenges for audio productions of *The Tempest*.

Let's begin with the 1.1 shipwreck. Early radio productions often relied on narrators to explain what a stage audience would see. NBC's 1940 one-hour *Tempest* opens, for example, with the Narrator's description of Prospero's arrival on the island, framing Shakespeare's magical story as a frightening bedtime story. He reports that after he arrived on the island, Prospero met Caliban – 'more like an animal than a man' – who inherited 'the marks of evil' from his mother Sycorax. Then he briefly refers to the shipwreck. Fortunately, many later broadcasts and audiobooks (which follow the text more consistently) exploit 20th-, and eventually 21st-, century technology to make the listener feel the storm. They begin with waves breaking, shouting, thunder and lightning, and a variety of additional effects. The 1962 BBC radio production opened with the sailors singing Stephano's sea chanty, which is interrupted by a sudden crescendo of thunder and lightning, the sailors howling as they drown. Later productions add other noises: seagulls, bells, the Master's whistle, the cracking of the mast, and the pull of ropes. Two productions from the twenty-first century do even more. The 2011 BBC Radio 3 production framed the storm scene with the sound of a cello. We hear Prospero speak to Ariel – 'Bestir. Bestir' – followed by bells, wind and water, as the cello continues playing. A downside is that the Boatswain and Gonzalo's exchange gets lost. The BBC Radio 3 production of 2021 opens with a statement relating Shakespeare's play to ecological issues, including land rights, stewardship and biodiversity. The storm, it would seem, is nature's revenge on humankind for its abuses, including perhaps the deforestation of Prospero's island. Of the many spectacles in Shakespeare's text, the initial storm's tumult is the easiest to convey through sound, and the play's opening scene in most productions is quite effective. Most audio *Tempest*s introduce thunderous sound effects not simply at the beginning, but intermittently through the entire play, even at places not indicated by the Folio stage directions. After all, the entire play is *The Tempest*.

The storm continues in act 2, scene 2, the 'gaberdine scene'. The Folio stage direction reads, '*Enter Caliban with a burden of wood; a noise of thunder heard*', and accordingly thunder and splashing waves inevitably introduce the scene. Different audio producers have found aural ways of following these stage directions. The 1960

Caedmon recording announces that Caliban is on a barren upland, and his approach is signalled in the 1974 BBC Radio 3 version by the sound of the chains he wore in 1.2. In the 2011 Blackstone audiobook, we hear Caliban drop his logs to survey the brewing storm, while the 2006 Arkangel recording adds the creepy sound of crickets.

Fortunately, much of 2.2's action is conveyed through Caliban, Trinculo and Stephano's lines, and in the best audio productions their words are embellished with groaning, sniffing, guzzling, burping and other noises. Afraid of being tormented by a spirit, Caliban announces that he will 'fall flat' when he hears someone coming. In the 2012 BBC 3 performance, Trinculo enters whistling. He describes what he sees, noting that there is 'neither bush nor shrub' to protect him from the gathering storm. When he notices Caliban, he sniffs and describes the creature under the gaberdine as a 'strange fish'. Then the thunder sounds again (the 2021 BBC Radio 3 broadcast adds the sound of raindrops), and Trinculo decides to creep under the gaberdine with Caliban. With these lines in mind, a radio audience can picture a large cloak spread over Trinculo and Caliban. Only later does the text make clear that the two actors lie across each other, so that each side of the gaberdine sports two legs. As Stephano notes, 'This is some monster of the isle, with four legs' (2.2.65–6). Frequently the actors embellish with groans and moans. When Stephano pulls Trinculo out from under the gaberdine, we can hear Trinculo's body scraping the ground (1979 CBC Festival Theatre), or a thud as the bodies tumble out (2012 BBC Radio 3). Once Trinculo and Caliban are out from under, sounds of corks popping, guzzling as Stephano pours wine down Caliban's throat, belching and slurred words prepare for the drunken song that ends the scene. If the actors who impersonate Trinculo and Stephano improvise with enthusiasm, the scene works even though we cannot see it.

Act 3, scene 3's banquet and Ariel's descent as a harpy are more challenging. In most productions, music is key to the appearance of 'strange shapes' presenting a banquet, whether it be majestic (1960 Marlowe Society) or cacophonous (1962 Living Shakespeare). Still, music can't convey what the stage directions describe: '*Solemn and strange music, and* Prospero *on the top (invisible). ... Enter spirits, in several strange shapes, bringing in a table and a banquet, and dance about it with gentle actions of salutations, and inviting the King and his companions to eat, they depart*' (3.3.19). Performed onstage, these stage directions call for specific gestures, movement and dance. Unlike in the gaberdine scene, Shakespeare provides little in the spoken text to tell us what is seen. We hear strange music, and the court party's comments are suggestive, but only that. Sebastian calls what he sees 'A living drollery!' and Gonzalo refers to the islanders being of 'monstrous shape', who yet display manners that are gentle and kind. Alonso marvels over their 'shapes, such gesture, and such sound, expressing … a kind / Of excellent dumb discourse' (3.3.21–38). The court party's partaking of the banquet is seldom clear, but the 1979 CBC Festival Theatre broadcast at least adds the sound of plates crashing as the banquet ends and Ariel appears.

Thunder and lightning accompany Ariel's descent, but not until Ariel vanishes do we learn from Prospero that he was attired as a harpy (3.3.83). During Ariel's speech, we can hear the startled court party drawing their swords, the swords falling to the ground, and moans of terror. The 2012 BBC 3 production adds an explosion and whirlwind as Ariel descends, but despite the court party's fearful moans, the terror of Ariel's sudden appearance is lost. In the audio presentations we accessed, this scene was clearly the least effective in helping the audio audience visualize the actions mentioned in the text.

Shakespeare's act 4 masque to celebrate the betrothal of Ferdinand and Miranda is a shortened rendition of the popular Jacobean court masque, a spectacle that required all the bells and whistles James I's money could buy. But after so many centuries, audiences are no longer able to interpret the significance of the elaborate stage effects, stylized language and extravagant costumes of the Jacobean court masque. In 2007 Libby Appel, then the Artistic Director of the Oregon Shakespeare Festival, directed *The Tempest*. When asked why she substituted the recitation of several Shakespearian sonnets for Shakespeare's masque, she replied that the scene as Shakespeare wrote it is impenetrable and boring to contemporary audiences. In most recent stage productions of *The Tempest*, the masque is drastically cut, and the text modified.[4] So it is not surprising that this scene is changed in most audio productions of the play. Two abridgements, the NBC 1940 broadcast and the 1962 Living Shakespeare, eliminate it entirely, solving the two problems of reducing the running time and of making the masque intelligible when it cannot be seen. Others shorten the text and add extra music; the early broadcasts rely on period musical settings. The 2011 Blackstone audiobook uses Robert Johnson's contemporary setting for Ariel's song 'Full Fathom Five', and period music for the masque. Sometimes audio productions introduce original musical arrangements. Whatever the style, music is the tool most audio *Tempest*s exploit to convey the masque's grandeur. The 1960 Caedmon recording, for example, begins the masque with lute music in the background as Iris and Ceres speak. Then Juno and Ceres sing their blessing in operatic tones to the accompaniment of violins, and the nymphs and reapers' appearance is simply signalled by Baroque dance music. In contrast, the 1979 CBC Festival Theatre broadcast employs march music to introduce the dancers. The 2006 Arkangel audiobook's concluding credits list the instruments used in the production: double bass, cello, violin, oboe, flutes, soprano sax, steel pan, guitar and various percussion instruments. The 2011 Blackstone audiobook lists the violin, recorder, lute and viola de gamba. Such musical consorts are one of the delights of listening to audio *Tempest*s.

At the beginning of 4.1, Prospero explains to Ariel that he intends to show 'some vanity of my art' (4.1.41). He asks Ariel to 'bring a corollary / Rather than want a spirit' (4.1.57–8). Like King James, he intends this performance to show off his royal status and power. The masque's language is highly stylized and based on classical myth. Iris is the rainbow, and presumably would enter with a colourful costume suggesting her status as Juno's messenger. Ceres is the goddess of plenty, while Juno, queen of the gods, represents marriage. Iris enters at l. 60, calling for Ceres. While she speaks, the Folio stage direction reads, '*Juno descends*'. At the Blackfriars, Juno would be lowered from the heavens on a 'machine' – a chariot decorated with her signature peacock. The Blackfriars audience, most of whom had never experienced the splendour of a court masque, must have been astonished at the sight.

Ceres' worries that blind Cupid might show up to disturb the celebration of Ferdinand and Miranda's betrothal reflect Prospero's concern that no 'bed-right be paid / Till Hyman's torch be lighted' (4.1.96–7) – that the besotted lovers might engage in sex before marriage. The goddesses' lines were meant to be spoken until line 106, where the Folio stage direction reads, '*They sing*'. The 1962 Living Shakespeare keeps much of Iris and Ceres' initial dialogue but sets it to music for an operatic interlude. The 1979 CBC Festival Theatre broadcast skips those lines and goes right to line 106, and then we hear the beat of a march, dance music and laughing.

---

4 See Virginia Mason Vaughan, 'Un-masquing *The Tempest*: staging 4.1.60–138', *REAL* 21 (2013), 283–95.

Unfortunately, in this production, the dialogue between Iris and Ceres that underscores Prospero's desire for a marriage whose legitimacy will unite Milan and Naples is cut.

Nearly all productions retain Juno's song that pronounces her blessing upon the marriage and Ceres' response that promises the lovers fruitfulness and prosperity (lines 106–17). This blessing is, of course, the whole point of the masque, and it varies only in the musical score and the instruments used – recorders, Renaissance brass, lutes or violins. In the earlier audio productions, the masque favours the Baroque style of Thomas Arne. Later productions use simpler scores, and the most recent draw upon original compositions not only for the masque but for Ariel's songs as well. The 2021 BBC 3 broadcast proudly offers 'original Scottish music composed by Pippa Murphy', using binaural recording methods throughout 'to ethereal and magical effect'. Since the actors in this production spoke with Scottish accents, this musical timbre seemed appropriate.

Ferdinand interrupts the masque to tell Prospero how impressed he is, but his future father-in-law replies, 'Sweet now, silence / Juno and Ceres whisper seriously' (4.1.124–5). After that brief interruption, Ceres and Iris continue the theme of fertility by calling for a dance of nymphs and reapers. The Folio stage direction reads: 'Enter certain Reapers, properly habited. They join with the Nymphs in a graceful dance, towards the end whereof Prospero starts suddenly and speaks: after which to a strange hollow and confused noise, they heavily vanish' (4.1.138). The strange and hollow noise is easily conveyed by audio, but the elaborate footwork of the nymphs and reapers is lost. Most audio productions shorten the dance, if they present it at all (BBC Radio 3's 2012 and 2021 broadcasts eliminate it). When they do include the dance, they use fiddle music to suggest its rustic flavour.

When Prospero recalls Stephano, Trinculo and Caliban's plot to murder him and take over the island, he shouts, 'Avoid, no more!' (4.1.142). Ariel reports that they are 'red-hot with drinking, / So full of valour that they smote the air . . . [and] beat the ground' (4.1.171–3). Ariel's charm has led them into a 'filthy-mantled pool' (4.1.182) where they were up to the neck in brackish water. This revelation inspires the 'antimasque'; Jacobean masques opposed their stately presentation of mythical and royal personages with contrasting performances by witches, goblins, even the ingredients in a cooking pot. Prospero's antimasque is a parody of the goddesses' performance. Prospero tells Ariel to go into his cell and retrieve some 'trumpery' – fancy garments – and hang them on a line nearby where the drunken knaves will see them. So, instead of goddesses dressed in their celestial splendour, here we have an antimasque: two drunks dressing in stolen finery and quarrelling about who gets to wear what.

Clearly, a little narration can help with this scene. The 1979 CBC Festival Theatre broadcast has Prospero tell Ariel to get 'the garments that I wore in Milan'. The 1996 BBC radio production also has Prospero interject, 'This fine apparel will draw them in.' The other Tempest audios we accessed used a variety of sounds to clarify the action: Prospero and Ariel pulling the line and hanging the clothes, the drunks staggering through the brush, or the clothes thrown around or rustling. The 1996 BBC Radio 3 broadcast had Trinculo and Stephano hit Caliban with the clothes as he tries to get them to focus on murdering Prospero. The 2012 BBC Radio 3 version adds the voices of spirits, who name the types of clothing being tried on: doublet, jerkin, garters and cloaks. Similarly, in 2021, BBC 3 has the drunks exclaim, 'Here's a jacket!', 'Here's another garment.' All versions follow the Folio's stage direction, 'A noise of hunters heard. Enter diverse Spirits in shape of dogs and hounds, hunting them about, Prospero and Ariel setting them on' (4.1.266). Some add trumpets and dissonant music to accompany the hounds' frantic baying. And as those sounds fade, they quickly move into 5.1, where the only spectacles are Prospero's donning of his ducal attire and the seemingly miraculous appearances of Ferdinand and Miranda, and the Boatswain.

Our sampling of Tempest audios also revealed some changes The Tempest has undergone since radio performances were first aired. The great advantage of audio is the opportunity to focus on the most important sound of all, the actors' voices and their reading of the lines. Over the decades, these radio broadcasts and audiobooks offer a spoken record of how several of the greatest actors of the twentieth and twenty-first centuries envisioned Prospero's role. The Narrator describes the 1940 NBC Prospero (Cedric Hardwick): 'He was not the type of ruler to thrive in a corrupt court'; '[He was] a scholar who put his faith in his brother Antonio'; and 'in his kindness he taught Caliban how to speak'. Throughout this short version, Prospero was fatherly and kind. Subsequent Prospero's were not so gentle. Michael Hordern's Prospero (1960 Marlowe Society) starts out calmly and is gentle with Miranda, but his anger at Caliban soon makes him tetchy. Michael Redgrave's 1960 performance for Caedmon Records takes a schoolmaster's tone; he is clearly angry at both Ariel and Caliban in 1.2. When it comes to Prospero's most famous speeches – the 'arias' beginning with 'Our revels now are ended' (4.1.148–58) and 'Ye elves of hills' (5.1.33–57) – Redgrave nearly sings the lines. So does Donald Wolfit in the 1962 Living Shakespeare. Paul Scofield (1974 BBC Radio 3) is more subtle; he speaks the revels speech calmly, but in 'Ye elves' he builds gradually to a climax, then decrescendos to a resolution in the last lines. By 2004, acting styles had become less operatic, more naturalistic, as demonstrated in Ian McKellen's soft-spoken, conversational Prospero (2004 Naxos). Bob Peck's 2006 Arkangel Prospero is somewhat nasty in the exposition of 1.2, whereas David Warner (2012 BBC Radio 3) is affectionate with Miranda, and presents the final speeches more subtly. Ian McDiarmid's Scottish burr in the 2023 BBC Radio 3 production softens the magician's voice. As these audio performances attest, over the decades, Prospero has moved from righteous anger at the disobedience of his servants to a more problematic, often unjust, master in charge of subordinates who wish to be free.

Just as interpretations of Prospero changed over the decades, so too did ways of presenting Ariel. With a couple of exceptions, the twentieth-century Ariel was a childlike female soprano who could deliver Ariel's songs with a light touch. Jessica Tandy is described in the 1940 NBC abridgement as a 'childlike sprite' who provides 'dainty service'. She is a 'featherless' angel, and Tandy speaks Ariel's lines and songs accordingly. Margaret Field-Hyde is more animated in the 1960 Marlowe Society audiobook, and Vanessa Redgrave's Ariel (performing opposite her father's Prospero) in Caedmon's 1960 recording is decidedly girlish and childlike. Mai Zettering's Ariel (1962 Living Shakespeare) is accompanied by the buzzing of bees, perhaps an association with her 'freedom song' – 'Where the Bee Sucks'. The male actor Ronnie Stevens performed Ariel in the 1974 BBC 3 production with a whispery tone that was amplified as if in an echo chamber. CBC's 1979 Festival Theatre broadcast reverts to a female Ariel, who is accompanied in the masque by a chorus of female sprites. In its 1996 production, BBC's Ariel was Nina Wadia, who frequently giggled to underscore her spriteliness.

As the twenty-first century began, Ariel morphed from a childlike girl to a young male. Scott Handy's Ariel sings his songs in a clear countertenor (2004 Naxos), and Adrian Lester's Ariel (2006 Arkangel) enters whistling. Ira Burts's Ariel speaks in an electronically modified voice that sounded as if he were in a wind tunnel, and when he appears as a harpy, he lisps (2011 Blackstone). Carl Prekopp's Ariel is a gifted singer who can tackle contemporary arrangements of Ariel's songs, including 'Where the Bee Sucks', which is set to country music (2012 BBC Radio 3). The BBC 3's 2021 Tempest may suggest further changes yet to come as audio productions seek to be more inclusive, and as attitudes towards gender identity become more complex. Ariel's lines are spoken by Madeleine Worrell. Describing her interpretation of the role, Worrell echoes the production's environmental theme: Ariel is 'a liminal creature, born in the salty marshlands between land and sea, where reeds thrive, or else beside a river. He is of air, but he is of water, too – straddling the elements in all his forms.'[5] In this most recent production, Ariel is he and she, and female actors also take over the roles of Sebastian, Gonzalo and Stephano, and their pronouns are changed accordingly.

Shakespeare's text sets up a binary opposition between Ariel and Caliban. Light as air, Ariel can fly and change shapes; Caliban is a creature of the earth, stied in a cave. With radio we cannot see what the text describes: Caliban's monstrous earthbound form, Ariel's flights – but sounds can indicate the contrast between him and Ariel. For the most part, the actors who read Ariel's lines have light, even girlish voices. In contrast, the actors cast as Caliban speak with a deep bass or baritone. Louis Hector, Caliban in the 1940 NBC production has a low raspy voice, and intersperses his lines with diabolic laughs. Patrick Wymark (1960 Marlowe Society) is also a bass. His voice is angry and harsh, and he sometimes spits. Caedmon's 1960 Caliban, Hugh Griffith, is a baritone who spits and laughs devilishly. Changes of accent can also mark Caliban's difference. Denis Shaw (1962 Living Shakespeare) has a gravelly tone and speaks in a Cockney accent. In the 1996 BBC radio Tempest, Caliban growls, laughs lasciviously, yet in his most famous speech (3.2.138–46), his voice switches from drunken slurs to the soft tones of a dreamer. Ben Onwuke's deep bass voice has a slight African accent, a casting decision that suggests a postcolonial interpretation of his relationship with Prospero (2004 Naxos). The 2006 Arkangel version offers another variation: Richard McCabe's Caliban has something of a lower-class accent but speaks his words carefully and slowly. Similarly, Paul Spira's 2011 Blackstone Caliban is slow

---

5   See her guest blog, 'Madeleine-Worrall-on-THE-TEMPEST-on-BBC-Radio-3–20211105' at www.broadwayworld.com.

and careful with his enunciation, with emphasis on consonants. This deliberateness could suggest a learning disability, but more likely it reminds us that Caliban was taught to speak, and if he did have a language of his own before Prospero's arrival, it was not English. The initial introduction in the 2021 BBC Radio 3 production also reminds us that Caliban was enslaved, yet his Scots accent is similar to that of the other characters. From the recordings we accessed, it was clear that differences – sometimes obvious, sometimes subtle – in the actors' mode of speaking the lines, especially with Caliban and Prospero, suggest changing interpretations of Shakespeare's text.

Indeed, listening to the spoken text, undistracted by costumes and sets, we can focus on what we hear. The actors who participate in audio productions of *The Tempest* bring with them a variety of techniques and choices. Should Miranda be mature or girlish? Should Alonso seem genuinely sorry at the end? An actor's way of speaking shapes the role and how we respond to it. Take Gonzalo, for example. How old should he be? Is he old and doddering – as Sebastian and Antonio suggest – or a competent counsellor? In the 1960 Marlowe Society recording, Gonzalo speaks with a lisp, and it sounds as if he has loose false teeth. The 1974 BBC radio broadcast

also gives Gonzalo a thin, reedy voice that makes him sound old. Do we decide not to take him seriously and, with Sebastian and Antonio, say to ourselves, 'There he goes again?' By way of contrast, the 2006 Arkangel recording's Gonzalo speaks with an Oxbridge accent worthy of a British politician.

Other choices abound. How drunk should Stephano be? In the 1979 Festival Theatre broadcast, Stephano enters singing and playing the guitar; the 1974 BBC 3 Stephano is more sodden. He burps as he drinks, and when Caliban describes scamels he finds in the rocks, he mutters 'Yuck!' How silly should Trinculo be? In the 1960 Marlowe Society audiobook, Miles Malleson's quick little laughs and reedy voice are reminiscent of the comedian Stan Laurel. For us there was a pleasure in that recognition, but would a younger listener recognize the similarity? Audio performances make the listener aware of the many choices actors make simply in the ways they speak Shakespeare's lines. Even without *The Tempest*'s spectacles – the disappearing banquet and strange shapes, the harpy, the masque of goddesses, the dance of nymphs and reapers – audio productions focus squarely on the actor's spoken words and allow us to 'see' the characters Shakespeare created in all their infinite variety.

SHAKESPEARE PERFORMANCES IN ENGLAND, 2024

HESTER LEES-JEFFRIES, *London Productions, 2024*

In my first year reviewing London productions, I resolved to see everything that I could, including adaptations – a total of nineteen shows in thirteen different spaces: two *Romeo and Juliets*, three *Lears* (or versions thereof), three *Macbeths* (or versions thereof), and among the others only four comedies (three of them at the Globe) and two histories. What follows pays particular attention to design and attempts to take the temperature of the London professional theatre scene, an environment that is precarious even as it is varied, resilient, sometimes puzzling, sometimes frustrating, but almost never less than interesting in its engagement with Shakespeare's plays.

TWO *ROMEO AND JULIETS*

Almost the first show I saw in 2024 was *Romeo and Juliet*, at Shakespeare's Globe. While this 'Playing Shakespeare' production (performed for free for around 14,000 school students) had some features in common with Ola Ince's 2021 Globe production (its concern with knife crime, its streetwear wardrobe), it was bleaker. It was also less witty, and its leads were not as strong, although this was emphatically an ensemble production, and a tight one. As well as graffiti art panels, there were 'shrines' either side of the stage, with flowers, candles and photos. The prologue was spoken chorically as if at a protest vigil, led by the mothers, although the Montague parents were otherwise absent. Mantua was marked by a London Underground sign implying that this was the end of the line, and also that Romeo was unambiguously out of his postcode; the apothecary was convincingly a dealer with a repurposed Just Eat pack, the fatal drug a few inches in a plastic bottle. Benvolio (Saroja-Lily Ratnavel) took the role of Balthasar in conveying the news of Juliet's 'death'. Friar Lawrence (Marième Diouf) was running a gardening project for at-risk youth, and a food bank. Samson and Gregory weren't any great loss, and their edgy, latently violent energy (if not their comedy) was present in the BMX riders doing tricks, who added both menace and the ticking of a clock, fate, death: Owen Gawthorpe was described as 'Fate / The Cyclist' in the cast-list. Played without an interval and with a running time of around 1 hour 45 minutes, the text was skilfully cut (textual consultant, Sophie Duncan), although inevitably there were losses, the most significant probably 'Gallop apace' in its entirety and much of the scene between Juliet and the Nurse after Tybalt's death and Romeo's banishment, as well as parts of the balcony scene and the tomb scene. Juliet's bounty was not as boundless as the sea. I regretted most the cuts from the lovers' scenes, because this relationship, although touchingly played by Felixe Forde and Hayden Mampasi, did seem extraordinarily slight after their initial meeting, which was beautifully done. Juliet's physicality in particular was recognizably adolescent, with habitually folded arms; she opened up in the balcony scene, however, and the dawn scene was sweet, as the lovers took selfies and snuggled.

Miriam Grace Edward's Nurse was an NHS paramedic, family friend rather than servant; she was tough and weary. She wasn't the only paramedic: stab vests and police incident tape featured, and the helicopters sporadically overhead made complete sense. The production was uncompromisingly bloody in its violence: by the relatively late point in the run when I saw it, stains on the stage were clearly visible, marking the murder sites downstage left and right. The knives were recognizably kitchen knives, produced from waistbands, and there was nastiness not just in the violence but in the selfies that were taken with Mercutio's body (Ashley Byam) and the way that the cyclist jumped his bike over it.

CLEOPATRA
'Tis sweating labour
To bear such idleness so near the heart
As Cleopatra this. But, sir, forgive me;

22 Nadia Nadarajah as Cleopatra in *Antony and Cleopatra* at
Shakespeare's Globe (© Ellie Kurttz / ArenaPAL).

Simeon Desvignes was a vicious, bullying Paris, Andrew Tate-adjacent, rather than a dupe, first ingratiating himself with Capulet (Gethin Alderman) and then dominating him. When Friar Lawrence described the effects of the drug to Juliet, it was intercut with the scene of her awaking; the drug made her hallucinate a fantasy sequence of her marriage to Paris, which began as a comic hen-night dance sequence but then became much more threatening, Paris posturing in a silver tracksuit before stripping off to reveal leopard-print boxer shorts as Juliet cowered on the bed. There was an edge of sexual violence and real fear, repeated in the encounter at Friar Lawrence's.

The tomb scene was relocated to a morgue, with Tybalt (Liam King) and Mercutio on gurneys as well as Juliet, and Romeo arriving in scrubs; Paris was visiting more officially. This setting was the production's choice about which I was least convinced; there was little opportunity for intimacy or for the lovers to die in each other's arms (perhaps that was the point): a gurney is too high and too narrow, and somehow a morgue activates the tomb scene's latent necrophilia more than the actual tomb. Romeo killed Paris with a scalpel, before Juliet killed herself with another scalpel, and the realism of the setting jarred with that detail in particular: why were scalpels there in the first place? At the scene's end, all five bodies (including Paris) were zipped into body bags. The mothers came back to deliver the final lines: this story of woe had been that 'of Juliet – Mercutio, Tybalt, Paris – and her Romeo'. Notably, this production met the challenge of mobile phones head on and with some wit; they're central to contemporary youth culture but tricky in a tragedy precipitated by an undelivered letter: as well as the selfies, Romeo and his friends learned of the Capulet party when a boy on a bike stole Paris's phone and delivered it to Mercutio; Romeo had his phone nicked in Mantua; and Friar Lawrence was shown failing to get through. On the Saturday afternoon when I saw it, there were plenty of young people in the audience, gripped by the strong visuals, physicality and clear storytelling.

At least superficially, *Romeo and Juliet* directed by Jamie Lloyd for his eponymous company at the Duke of York's was also aimed at the youth market in its casting of Tom Holland, now better known as Spiderman, as Romeo, although its ticket prices (bar some deals for young people and other groups) were eye-watering. There was very loud music before the show began, heavy haze, and no curtain. Instead, there was what appeared at first to be an industrial grille on a gantry; there was vertical strip lighting in the shell of the stripped-out stage space, with visible lights and mikes, wiring and hard surfaces, and a staircase stage right, down from a door halfway up the back wall (designer Soutra Gilmour). The grille was a screen, used to project first '1597' (incongruous in this resolutely contemporary setting), then 'Sunday', 'Monday', etc, before being used for live video footage; it could also have scenes played behind it with simultaneous projection. The production was entirely prop-less, and costumes were more or less monochrome, with Romeo and Juliet (Francesca Amewudah-Rivers) both in dark jeans, white vests, hoodies, and the other characters mostly in black; no dog-collar for Friar Lawrence (Michael Balogun), who had much less of a presence than the Nurse (Freema Agyeman). Every actor had a mike visibly taped to his or her face, and there was extensive use of other mikes, on stands or hand-held. The delivery was often very quiet and notably slow; all of the ensemble knew how to do stillness and slowness.

Throughout, there were integrated camera operators, a Jamie Lloyd trademark, projecting live footage both of onstage action and from other spaces around the theatre. In the substantially cut 1.1, Romeo was filmed, hood up, with a cigarette, mooching under the stage: this meant that his first entry was virtual, perhaps cleverly forestalling a disruptive entry round. The cameras worked particularly well for the party, which was taking place in the theatre foyer bar, all gold and mirrors. There was no attempt to stage dancing or any kind of crowd; it was a tiny cast, with no supernumeraries. First Paris (Daniel Quinn-Toye) was shown ineptly flirting with Juliet, throwing peanuts in the air to catch in his mouth; he was very young, with enormous baby eyes, out of his depth, too juvenile to be creepy or threatening (meeting Juliet after their marriage had been agreed, he didn't even attempt to kiss her, kissing his fingers to her instead). As the lovers 'met', Romeo was on the main stage; Juliet was looking at him via her reflection in the foyer mirror. 'Gallop apace' was heavily cut, with Amewudah-Rivers's face in close-up on the screen: having been subject to appalling racist abuse online before and during the production's run, the actor subsequently commented on how vulnerable such close-ups had sometimes made her feel.

The first half lasted around seventy minutes, with the interval falling just after the Prince (who never appeared) had banished Romeo in voice-over, so the 'banishing' scenes began the second half, with the Nurse, Romeo, Juliet and the Friar standing at mikes across the stage; the scenes were strikingly intercut, bringing out the echoing repetitions of 'banished'. The dawn scene was filmed from above, the lovers lying head-to-head mid-stage behind the screen; Romeo got up and his face was lit through the screen more or less as Juliet's nose, but it worked. There was no suggestion of a bed or getting dressed, let alone anything as effete as birdsong or a brightening light, and there was very little physical contact. As they parted, Juliet was filmed slightly from below and Romeo from above; they were projected on the screen as they spoke. The conversation between Paris and Capulet (Tomiwa Edun) was also filmed backstage, and when Benvolio (Nima Taleghani, who also edited the text) went to Mantua, he rendezvoused with Romeo on the roof, 'MANTUA' projected, and the evening sky, the ENO, and the London Eye in the background. Romeo re-entered the building as if talking to the apothecary, a disembodied voice behind the camera.

The balcony scene was idiosyncratic but effective: the lovers sat side by side downstage; the effect was very intimate and perhaps surprisingly created real tension, despite the lack of distance between them; it played a full text. By contrast, the marriage scene was heavily cut, although there was enough passion for an audience predisposed to sigh and laugh indulgently. Amewudah-Rivers as Juliet was very good, with a wonderfully expressive face and hands (which she sometimes seemed to be working to keep still, like the other actors), lots of detail, and convincingly teenage. She played most of the potion speech, almost relishing the gothic fantasy of her vision; it was a lovely, fine-grained interpretation. Asking herself if she would marry Paris, she interpolated a definite 'Nope!!' Holland's Romeo was fine, albeit light-voiced, with perhaps a little vocal strain by the point in the run when I saw it. Like the production in general, he resisted glamour, and was snottily weepy in the first scene in particular; there was genuine and effective shock when, sitting with Benvolio later in the same scene, he put his hand in a pool of blood. Queen Mab was done well, but substantially cut, as was the Nurse's banter with the boys, and Mercutio's role was much diminished, as was Tybalt's (Joshua-Alexander Williams, Ray Sesay). There was no physical action for the fights: rather, there were two loud blackouts, following which the boys appeared heavily bloodied.

Capulet was both Capulet parents, with the Nurse speaking the few Lady Capulet lines that remained essential, and he was genuinely frightening, with Paris in particular seriously intimidated by this big boss; there was no Lady Montague and Montague's role was tiny. The Nurse was very young, and it was a tough, passionate, sometimes teary performance, powerful and moving. She was almost the only character who occasionally paraphrased or modernized (the 'cockerel's stone' became a bollock); she was highly dubious about the marriage, with a sceptical, foreboding tone for 'this afternoon?', and it was she who had failed to deliver the letter – no mention of plague, Capulet simply hadn't allowed anyone to leave the house, entirely plausible given his menacing power. There was kissing in the party scene and the marriage, but particularly in the tomb scene there was almost no touching. It was heavily cut, with no Paris and not even 'my love, my wife!', usually guaranteed to reduce me to sniffles. There were no embraces: Romeo sat beside Juliet (who had remained in the same position, sitting at the front of the stage, since her potion speech) but they didn't interact at all. His last line was 'Thus with a kiss I –' at which he untaped his microphone. The Friar didn't appear; Juliet's lines were brief, before she too untaped her mike. They sat beside each other, eyes closed, and there was a blackout. Then the Friar was sitting with them slumped on his lap, as he spoke the last few lines.

I wasn't convinced by the Jamie Lloyd 'house style' for this production, at the same time as I was impressed by it. The company certainly went all in, with tremendous commitment and technical accomplishment (the camera work was often brilliant: operators Callum Heinrich, Kody Mortimer, Harriet Bunton, design and cinematography Nathan Amzi, Joe Ransom) but it was disconcerting to see this tactile play performed in such a disembodied idiom. There was no evocation of a world, or of what might be behind the feud, or much sense of what was at stake, and there was almost no action or even physical contact after the wedding scene. The lovers were convincingly young, and they made sense of the text. But it was oddly detached, and in particular I missed the synthesis of words and bodies which I think is so central to the play; there was little reaction or interaction between characters, even, with so much of the text being played out front, and with so little gesture. In some respects, it was not unlike Izzard's *Hamlet* (see below) in its lack of affect, although it was far more interesting as a version of the play. I wasn't unmoved but I didn't want to cry. It had great integrity within its own idiom. But it sometimes felt like a waste of good actors, especially good young actors.

FOUR COMEDIES

Twelfth Night at the Open Air Theatre, Regents Park (directed by Owen Horsley), had a deep-blue-painted set (designer Basia Binkowska), with large letters on the roof spelling out 'Olivia' (in reverse): it was a café bar / club / jazz dive, with chairs and tables, a bar and two sets of double doors, as if to kitchens as well as outside, and a platform for the band, with piano and bass. A pianist began, joined one by one by violin, accordion, bass (later sax and clarinet also featured; music Sam Kenyon), as Orsino (Raphael Bushay) in quasi-naval dress uniform sat at a table and smoked. Then, in a preset, Malvolio (Richard Cant) arrived with ever larger bouquets of flowers, presumably from Orsino, which he gave to Maria (Anita Reynolds), behind the bar. Parrots played in the trees and squawked noisily as the sun went down. The four musicians were in blue striped trousers, sailor jackets and hats, a camp crew of courtiers and waiters, as

well as musicians; sometimes the more choric lines were split between them, or the lines of minor characters such as Fabian. They were in effect a chorus, present throughout, more Dolce e Gabbana than HMS *Pinafore*, just, owing something perhaps to the Frecknall *Cabaret*.

Toby (Michael Matus) made his first appearance in drag – in a gold sequined dress, gold boots, and a pink wig which he removed, padded underwear and a fur coat – definitely and grotesquely drunk rather than cheerily tipsy. Andrew (Matthew Spencer) was much younger, with floppy blond hair, a green shirt and coloured glasses. Feste (Julie Legrand) walked with a stick, her foot in a moonboot, presumably a late accommodation of an actor's injury; she was a mean chanteuse. Malvolio was cross and petulant from the beginning, although not wholly without dignity. Viola (Evelyn Miller) first appeared in a silk dress, with bare feet and a life jacket; she was brought in by the Irish captain (Nicholas Karimi, doubling Antonio) and given a drink, and there was a slight principal boy quality to her Cesario, in cream wide-legged trousers with a laced back, a cropped sailor jacket, cream top and sailor hat. Her performance was properly good, detailed and clear, as well as attractive and touching. Antonio's initial parting from Sebastian (Andro Cowperthwaite) was passionate, Antonio already devastated at the prospect.

Olivia (Anna Francolini), however, was sometimes undignified, and she had to work hard against a very big black frock; she made her first appearance with a large, jewelled urn evidently containing her brother's ashes, which she addressed when sending Malvolio after Cesario. I could have wished her more dignity in both love and grief, and a little less tulle. For the revels scene, Toby wore a gold plastic fringe and Andrew was also in drag, a pink dress with a big bow, silver sandals over socks. It was his birthday; party hats were being worn and Feste presented him with a cake, which ended up being wiped on Malvolio, in mustard pyjamas and a brown dressing gown. As will perhaps be apparent, the production used bold colour very well, Cesario and the similarly creamy Chorus and Olivia's black tempering the more acid notes (costumes, Ryan Dawson Laight).

'Come Away Death' was definitely a torch-song, to the accompaniment of accordion, bass, triangle, with Orsino and Cesario at a table in a spotlight, with a lingering eye-meet, clasping hands and leaning in, before Cesario moved to another table; for once, the band left with Feste (they were mostly onstage throughout). The scene was very well done, with great tenderness, and almost an embrace at the end. The whole Chorus were part of the box tree scene, which was a 'privy' – one of the doors, all going in and then coming out. Many gags: Malvolio sat on Andrew's hand on a bar stool, for instance; he did the now-near-inevitable 'revolve', and the conspirators had to freeze frame when he returned (having exited) for the postscript.

The second half began under a fingernail moon; Orsino was up on the roof by the neon sign, smoking. In general, he was rather sidelined by the production concept, because it was Olivia's place and mostly her show, and even the Chorus seemed her people more than his. Olivia's big number in the second half was another bravura torch-song setting of 'Make Me a Willow Cabin'. Malvolio's yellow stockings became yellow socks with elastic garters, worn with yellow lederhosen, and it was Andrew who released him at the end. The show had a dreamy quality, in-between and out of time, melancholy without being bleak, although there were flashes of cruelty in Toby in particular. Antonio and Sebastian were allowed a happy ending, leaving together, and Malvolio had dignity and pathos in his beige restraint. There was a slight 'Tales of the City' vibe: suitcases were a poignant motif throughout, as if everyone were only passing through, but always hoping for a place to stay. At the end they did: Olivia, Feste, Fabian, Maria, Toby and even Malvolio, a chosen family, making more than the best of things.

The other three comedies were all part of the Globe's summer season. I saw *The Comedy of Errors* (directed by Sean Holmes / Naeem Hayat) on a beautiful evening with a buzzy audience; this was a revival of the 2023 production, with significant overlap between the casts, although both the Antipholuses (Daniel Adeosun, Caleb Roberts) were new. It was a perfectly good, solid, lively show, making the most of physical comedy, and its costumes (designer Paul Wills) were a particular pleasure, as was the music. I continued to think (as I did on my first viewing) that it didn't need its splatter comedy knockabout prologue, in which a condemned man was messily beheaded by an executioner straight out of the London Dungeon as the citizens of Ephesus bayed for his blood, chanting 'Ephesus!', but it established Ephesus as a violent place, efficiently raising the temperature and the stakes before the very long expository speech by Egeon (Paul Rider, always one of the most elegant and subtle actors in this space). (It still seemed a lot of hassle.) The strong double act from Luciana and Adriana (Shalisha James Davis and Gabrielle Brooks) was one of its best features, as was the clever, sly joke in having so many of Ephesus's citizens doubled or tripled (largely by

Phoebe Naughton and Danielle Phillips); it made it feel properly uncanny as well as bravura theatre in its quick changes. The ending is always unexpectedly moving – it *is* striking to leave it to the Dromios (Martin Quinn, Sam Swann) – and Egeon and Emilia (Anita Reynolds) seemed especially prescient of *Winter's Tale* in this production, which was not startling, let alone profound, but still cheerfully entertaining.

In some respects, the Globe's *Much Ado* (also dir. Sean Holmes) was reminiscent of a Globe on Tour production many years ago, with baskets of oranges onstage as well as very beautiful orange trees on the tiring house façade. (This facilitated various bits of orange-related business, including Beatrice catching one on a knife's point, to audience cheers.) There were cobalt blue 'iron-work' galleries around the stage pillars, and brightly painted benches. The set worked well but it wasn't *used* much, lovely to look at rather than hugely inter-active; the costumes (designer Grace Smart) were beautiful, at once Renaissance and Mediterranean without being fussy or pedantic. It played a very full text.

Performances were sometimes rather too reliant on 'comedy' gestures and delivery, including on occasion from Beatrice (Amalia Vitale, generally sweet and sharp, and with excellent timing) and Benedick (Ekow Quartey), and it was not entirely believable that they could fall in love 'for real'. Claudio (Adam Wadsworth) was extremely callow and properly mocked for it; he wasn't even an ingénu, really, but out of his depth. Definitely a beardless boy, he was almost more thrilled to be reconciled with his mate and mentor Benedick than with Hero's 'resurrection'. The overhearing scenes felt undercooked, almost as if they were resisting adding the kinds of gags that have become common: Beatrice was in the yard for some of it, gamely, with the odd interjection ('Harsh!') as her reputation was traduced. Benedick was mostly in one of the galleries on the pillars, although he did move along, 'hiding' among the trees at the back too. There was a lot of fine dancing in the masquerade, and excellent masks, some recycled from another previous Globe *Much Ado*: Claudio was a ridiculous, grumpy bear; Don Pedro (Ryan Donaldson), a lion; Hero (Lydia Fleming, not at all mimsy, in fact a bit coarse), a devil. Benedick was a fine comic pigeon, and Beatrice a jaguar; it was a nice gag to have Antonio as a preening butterfly.

Leonato, played young by John Lightbody, was calculatingly ambitious; he sang 'Sigh No More' Tom Jones-style, milking the crowd for encores, and there was good comedy as Benedick plugged his ears with orange-peel, making him look like Shrek. He was clever at the physical comedy and especially with the challenge and took sly pleasure in his costume throughout; he was tender and touching in the chapel scene. Don John (Robert Mountford) was posh and older, gleefully embracing his plummy ridiculousness, a pantomime villain rather than a threatening machiavel; Borachio was actually shown as a perfumer, with a censer, gladdening the heart of material-culture aficionados everywhere. Dogberry (Globe stalwart Johnnie Broadbent) had steely determination in the comedy, which was efficient and amusing but did nothing surprising. Overall, the delivery was a bit shouty, and too often the characters broke out into dance steps at moments of self-realization or revelation. I have seen far more subtle and lyrical *Much Ado*s, including at the Globe, and there was a little too much playing for easy laughs, but it was generally sunny.

For *The Taming of the Shrew* (directed by Jude Christian), the Globe's stage was covered with white fabric, including much of the central part of the stage and the front of the tiring house, with an enormous white teddy-bear with an opening down its front through which characters sometimes entered. Costumes were incoherent: why did Baptista (Simon Startin) have paws? Why was Biondello (John Cummins) wearing a satin babygro? It seemed wilfully ugly in its design, and the actors looked uncomfortable. The fabric covering of the stage badly affected audibility, not helped by a helicopter overhead for most of the wedding scene; Petruchio (Andrew Leung) and Lucentio (Yasmin Taheri), in particular, had problems. A puppet for Bianca (Sophie Mercell) made sense, sort of, but *commedia dell'arte* masks on an enormous scale worn as belly puppets by Grumio (Eloise Secker) and Hortensio (Lizzie Hopley) didn't, although their manipulations of the mouths and tongues were sometimes grossly effective, but it meant that they couldn't gesture easily. Tranio (Tyreke Leslie) had lovely presence, but why he became a comedy Nigerian prince (with ad libs) as 'Lucentio' was opaque, if uncomfortably amusing.

Christopher Sly (Nigel Barrett) was drunkenly effective, coming through the yard (he later played Gremio, rather than Petruchio – and Sly as an abusive drunk in the theatre is old news), as was the device of 'Marian' (Thalissa Teixeira) being picked out of the audience, first for a confrontation with Sly and then to play Katharina. The actors lined up, orchestrated by the actor playing Vincentio (Jamie-Rose Monk, who mostly sat reading a magazine and occasionally rudely interjecting), and were given slips of paper with their roles, which they read out with brief character descriptions; it helped exposition, marginally.

The final scene was played fairly straight, with Katharina's speech well done – after she had climbed out of the shrew costume, complete with tail, and was back in her 'Marian' clothes. Teixeira was strong and charismatic, and largely wasted in this incoherent production. When 'Vincentio' had earlier shot Biondello, bloodily, I thought this otherwise inexplicable action (Biondello is annoying, but most of the characters are annoying) suggested that Katharina might shoot Petruchio, or indeed vice versa, in the final scene, but no. One of the production's many problems was that it wasn't clear how the frame worked; the actors were game and hard-working but it was an inexcusably impenetrable and incoherent production of what is now a pretty inexcusable play. I was surrounded by utterly baffled (English-speaking) tourists and was particularly sorry for those responsible for wrangling and maintaining the unwieldy set.

THREE *MACBETH*S

My first show of the year was an adaptation: Zinnie Harris's *Macbeth (An Undoing)*. This production, directed by the playwright, which I saw at the Rose Theatre, Kingston, began life at the Royal Lyceum in Edinburgh in 2023. Tom Piper's design with rafters, girders and mirrored panels brought out the uncanniness of both empty house and empty theatre. It managed to evoke the kind of space in which it was impossible ever to feel properly warm, and there was brilliant use of haze, pouring across the stage at floor level or hanging thickly in mid-air like a murmuration (lighting, Lizzie Powell). There was menace in the soundscape (sound and composition, Pippa Murphy, Oğuz Kaplangi), a drone off-set with jazzy party music and the sound of a trapped bird.

To my mind this was an excellent production of a play that is interesting and suggestive, a resonant companion piece to *Macbeth*, rather than a play that entirely succeeds on its own terms. It is a multifariously haunted play, with many powerful images which might work better as a single unbroken act. Nicole Cooper's excellent Lady Macbeth reminded me a little of Camille O'Sullivan's Lucrece in her intensity and isolation, constantly renegotiating what agency – not even power, by the end – might look like in this strange, in-between space. Seen a week before the Godwin *Macbeth*, it was striking to be made to think about Scottishness and borderlands, through the cadences of speech, the listing of many more thanes than Shakespeare ever considered, and a variety of tartans: James Robinson's Banquo was particularly striking in his immaculate heather-toned Highland dress, with a nice cabled jumper for the morning after. He was having an affair with the very pregnant Lady Macduff (Emmanuella Cole); she was Lady Macbeth's sister, or cousin, or friend, theirs a shifting alliance shaped by rivalry as much as any residual trust; Macduff (Thierry Mabonga) barely appeared, although there was more sense of his identity as a soldier than Macbeth's (Adam Best). The latter's delivery was colloquial, sometimes incredulous; he was a man caught up in events, hardly able to believe what was going on, a note which Malcolm (Star Penders) took to extremes in a grotesque caricature, drunkenly vomiting at the banquet. The Macbeths' childlessness was a wretched, ongoing grief, with the desperate hope that there might yet be time, that other children might yet be saved.

The witches/servants, led by Liz Kettle as porter / stage manager / director, were not Downtonesque and neither were they straightforwardly Grace Poole or even Mrs Danvers, although all of these too had a ghostly presence. *Retainers*, I thought. In the play's closing scenes, there was one of its best, most uncanny effects: a whole rack of white wedding dresses brought on by stage management but no sooner quick-changed into than bloodied, evoking that other Scotswoman, Lucy, Bride of Lammermoor. The play, powerful in performance and emphatically good to think with, reminded me (among many other things) that *Macbeth*, too, is a play full of rapid political calculations being made on the fly and being got wrong more often than not, rather than the inexorable unfolding of a grand masterplan.

On a sunny spring evening, I braved Canada Water in London's redeveloped East End docklands for Simon Godwin's touring production of *Macbeth*, with Ralph Fiennes in the title role, finishing its London run before performances in the US. The location was a cavernous (modern) warehouse, its foyer spaces dimly lit and black-hung, with a battlefield/supernatural soundscape (Christopher Shutt) already running. When the house opened, entry was through a space evoking the aftermath of battle, with trees, rubble, smoke, soldiers, and a burning car, the latter the image central to the production's publicity. The auditorium proper surrounded the reasonably small, shallow thrust stage on three sides, the pre-set entry space being behind the stage's back wall. The set (Frankie Bradshaw) was powerful and flexible: wide concrete-effect steps led up to central opaque glass

doors, two entrances above, two below. Jai Morjaria's lighting was terrific, including a flare/blackout effect which really did make the witches vanish into the air; beyond this, there were few 'illusions', the apparitions being performed as if channelled in a trance by the murderers (Michael Hodgson, Jake Neads) and Seyton (Jonathan Case), all three portrayed as weak and suggestible, but increasingly appalled by what they were being asked to witness or perform. The sole 'supernatural' effect, bar the vanishing, was the back wall of the set 'bleeding' from top to bottom after the apparition scene; there were spectacular explosions when Malcolm's forces took the castle.

There was no porter and no third murderer; I missed the latter slightly and the former very little indeed. As seems to have become conventional, however, Lady Macduff (Rebecca Scroggs) and the children (small boy and girl, no baby) were present at the castle as part of Duncan's entourage; the little girl presented Lady Macbeth (Indira Varma) with a diamond pendant on Duncan's behalf (Keith Fleming as Duncan, doubling Siward). There was considerable cutting of the witches' scenes and the England scene, and some combining of roles among the thanes (although Ross didn't gain the prominence and specificity that he has in some productions), but in general it was quite a full text (Godwin's regular collaborator Emily Burns). The witches were feral, threatening and fierce, but also somehow matter of fact, unremarkable in charity shop clothes, and certainly no cackling; they were all young women, not teenagers or children, and they sometimes appeared through the auditorium (Lucy Mangan, Danielle Fiamanya, Lola Shalam; Rose Riley was on for the latter in the performance I saw). The uniforms were carefully non-specific; the Scots and the English were differentiated in their camouflage but the formal mess dress didn't suggest particular services (in contrast to Godwin's National Theatre *Antony and Cleopatra*), although there was quite a lot of maroon; Malcolm and Donalbain (Ewan Black, Jake Neads) never appeared in uniform but wore maroon polo-necks under coats on their first appearance, and maroon pyjamas. There was no attempt at conjuring Scottishness, to the extent that Steffan Rhodri's excellent Banquo was Welsh. There was no crown, which I did regret a little: Duncan, then Macbeth, wore a gold chain of office, and Macbeth had a purple velvet coronation robe, while Lady Macbeth had an excellent tiara and emerald-green cloak and matching shoulder-robed dress.

This was a bloody production, with much staining and spurting: a large bowl of water was produced for Macbeth to wash his face on his return to the castle, and this remained for both Macbeths to wash their hands after Duncan's murder, its water turning scarlet. Commando knives were the weapon of choice, with machete-like blades for the final duel between Macbeth and Macduff (Ben Turner) and there was a sense that every man was a trained killer, or had become one, in a civil war scenario. There wasn't much hope at the end that this was a peace that would last, not because Malcolm (and Macduff) were notably weak, but because the state of war seemed normalized. It was not, however, as sadistic or graphic in its violence as some productions, and this was especially the case in the murders of Macduff's family, performed by Banquo's murderers, visibly uneasy, after Seyton had given the warning. Fleance (Ethan Thomas) was an adult in uniform.

Varma was a powerful, smart, yet brittle Lady Macbeth, taking her time over the letter scene in particular; there was pathos in her mid-length nightdress, not quite M&S but tending that way, after her slinky emerald evening wear. Seyton was initially her creature, very young, smart and sinister in his black suit with necklace and a pearl earring. Although there was less specificity over her implied history as a mother in the play than in some recent productions, that the couple had lost a child, children or pregnancy/pregnancies was made clear, and Macbeth's 'bring forth men children only' had a bittersweet desperation to it. Macbeth was in thrall to his wife, but she was increasingly alienated by him, and rejected him sexually before Banquo's murder, as if spooked by 'Light thickens'. In general, Fiennes delivered the soliloquies and other 'big' speeches with thoughtful clarity, measured and reflective; he made some resonant pauses ('my thought, whose – murder – yet is but fantastical'; 'if the – assassination – could trammel up the consequence') which for me remained on the right side of mannered, and 'is this a dagger' was particularly fine, with a real sense of hallucination; 'Tomorrow and tomorrow' was, by contrast, perhaps a little too low key, although still affecting in its exhaustion. This was a Macbeth who went mad quite early on, paranoid and vacillating; he whimpered and moaned, choking over his words, after Duncan's murder, as his wife rebuked him and took charge.

Godwin is a director who is skilled at working on a grand scale, notably in the National's Olivier. This was a high-concept show in many respects, with headline casting, but also exceptionally carefully conceived for

touring (albeit not on a shoestring) in its flexible set, versatile ensemble and carefully edited text. It will be interesting to see how it translates to film.

My final 2024 Shakespeare was another *Macbeth*. Apart from its headline casting (David Tennant as Macbeth, Cush Jumbo as Lady Macbeth), the main pitch for this show, which transferred to the Harold Pinter Theatre after a sell-out run at the Donmar, was its use of binaural sound, via headphones worn by everyone in the audience. I had expected something much more radical and immersive: the witches (who really only existed sonically) worked well, chattering and echoing, moving uncannily from ear to ear, and there were some nice moments with birdsong and the sound of birds taking flight, and of a crying child, as well as occasional echoes and whispers. An odd aspect of the soundscape was that the elegant, near-outsize broadswords in the final scene did not clash; they sounded almost wooden. The music was beautifully performed, with elements of chant and song, as well as instrumental, and I enjoyed the exuberant and recognizably Scottish dance sequence at the victory feast. The ensemble was small: Lady Macduff (Rona Morison) was fully integrated from the beginning and the implication was that both she and Ross (Moyo Akandé), playing as female, were involved in the fighting too. It ran a shade over two hours, with no interval.

Rosanna Vize's set was a black box with a floating white platform forming the main acting area; there was a simple glass basin full of water in the middle, which Macbeth used to wash his hands and face at the beginning, changing from a bloodstained top into a clean one. It was still recognizably Donmar in its outlines (black box, a shallow acting area, considerable attention to the upstage space, here on an upper level behind sliding glass panels). With the exception of Lady Macbeth, who wore white (fitted top and long skirt, anticipating the not dissimilar but shorter nightdress that she wore for the sleep-walking scene), all the company were in black kilts, black boots and socks, and tops in blacks and greys, sometimes with an asymmetric slightly cropped black jacket, fastened with two off-centre buttons (this was Duncan's uniform), sometimes a singlet (notably Macduff in the battle scene).

The child who appeared as Fleance, Young Macduff and Young Siward, as well as in other roles, had a kilt and top which were pale grey and knitted, giving a slightly larval, ghostly effect, but cuddly. He appeared first sitting behind the glass panels, banging on them, a moth on a window, and so at times seemed the Macbeths' child too: Macbeth killed him (as Young Siward) after embracing him, something he'd also done with Fleance. The boy also spoke the prophecies: the scene involved a number of the ensemble, lying on the ground shuddering and rearing as they shared out the lines of 'Double double' between them: most of it was played, with the odd tweak to the lines (no 'blaspheming Jew', for instance, and the 'babe, ditch-delivered by a drab' had become the 'baby' of a 'lady'). They were dimly lit in red with a plume of haze, rising at the end to criss-cross the stage in crowns, as Banquo (Cal MacAninch) looked on, bloodily, from behind glass.

In terms of particular choices in this production: Lady Macbeth warned Lady Macduff (as in the Farber version at the Almeida). There was no third murderer, and the scene of Banquo's murder was substantially cut, as was that of the Macduffs' murder; there were some nastily ambiguous sounds in a blackout, not protracted, which could have suggested sexual violence. The England scene was heavily cut, although some of the description of the kingly virtues was spoken by Duncan (Benny Young, doubling the Doctor) as he invested Malcolm (Ros Watt) as Duke of Cumberland. The Porter (Jatinder Singh Randhawa), however, was fully present, blending scurrilous Glaswegian improv with quite a lot of the text: the house lights came up to reveal him slumped over the edge of a box, later bantering – in audio form – with a supercilious usher (*no readmission if you leave, sir, that'll be £17.50 for a programme, sir*) as he made his way to the stage. There were good gags (*look at you in your headphones, paying £800 for a radio play; [crashing into a wall] that's the 4th wall I've broken today*).

David Tennant was a wiry, jumpy, intense Macbeth, perhaps not hugely believable as a great warrior but convincing in his kamikaze madness and intelligence; there was sometimes a tendency to irascibility rather than rage. He had a good rapport with Banquo (whose ghost didn't appear, it was all done via the headphones) and the relationship with Lady Macbeth was convincingly intimate, although less sexually charged than in some recent productions. The headphones did work well for the murder scene, and its panicked imagining (or not) of noises off. Tennant's delivery was speedy, his accent broad, but it was clear and often detailed, although there could have been a little more variation in pacing, which he did find in 'Tomorrow'. He did some interesting things with the floor, crawling, working with his shadow, especially in the 'Dagger' speech; the implication was that he was seeing it lying on the ground, a persuasive thought. His final stand-off with

Macduff was keenly observed, come-and-have-a-go defiance; he knew the game was up. Jumbo had tremendous presence, her accent and white costume setting her apart in this tight-knit Scottish ensemble; her delivery was poised and focused, with a steely watchfulness rather than a clear sense that she was the driving force of the relationship, although it was she that crowned him. That her sleep-walking scene, complete with candle, was observed by the Gentlewoman and Doctor from behind the glass wall emphasized her isolation. The ending was slightly downbeat – Malcolm fearful, a bit querulous; Macduff (Noof Ousellam, good in his grief, but diminished by cuts in the last few scenes) not much of a presence. Most effective was the filling of the area behind the glass wall with lush, green-gold-lit forest, a promise of renewal and the first colour in this relentlessly monochrome world.

I wished I had seen it at the Donmar, although its atmosphere as a performance space was pretty closely recreated. By the end I was fighting the urge to take off the headphones (which were perfectly comfortable, unlike my seat) to hear these actors 'properly' in the space (they were of course all miked); the staging was intimate enough that it didn't seem to add much to have the headphones. The technology was impressive, but more at the level of mixing, seamless switching between mikes (the neat cut so that any squelch of a kiss on Macbeth's arrival at Glamis went unamplified, for instance), than as an addition to the experience. I wondered if it was cutting the actors off from each other, sometimes, and would have been fascinated to see them play it without mikes.

THREE *LEARS*

Yaël Farber's *King Lear* at the Almeida was deeply moving and deeply sad, performed by an ensemble who at times seemed to think – and at the end sang – as one. Danny Sapani's Lear never had a crown, instead sharing out his many chunky silver rings between his sons-in-law. But the sparse set (Merle Hensel) hung chain metal curtains around the stage's curved back wall, its signature brick visible through the 'rain', and briefly gained a crenellation or crown effect from its downlighting, and the stage's curved apron and balconies, the latter similarly curtained, presented a pattern of repeating circles that worked almost subliminally. The floor was a mottled dark mirror, initially holding only a stylized metal globe on a stand, and increasingly strewn with earth as the performance progressed, elementally

23 Min Eun-kyung as the Fool and Kim Jun-su as King Lear in *Lear*, performed by the National Changgeuk Company of Korea at the Barbican Theatre (© Tristram Kenton).

recalling the water which flooded the stage in Farber's Almeida *Macbeth*.

Sapani's Lear's apparently robust health and strong physicality were almost defiantly displayed in a pre-set in which he appeared, back to the audience, stripped to the waist, to be dressed in a smart blue suit, white shirt and black tie by his daughters. (Lear's breakdown was all the more moving because of his apparent physical strength; at his reunion with Cordelia he was utterly reduced, without being 'frail', in hospital gown and wheelchair.) Lear was dressing for a television press conference with a small studio audience, which included Fra Fee's confident, affable, entitled Edmund, seating himself among the courtiers in his leather jacket, rucksack still in hand. With Gloucester (Michael Gould), Kent (Alec Newman) seemed to be the aide-de-camp in charge of the event, the only one in uniform; his beret later appeared as an identifying token sent to Cordelia. Lear and then his daughters spoke within a circle of microphones to an invisible camera. When he lost his temper, he violently scattered the microphones across

the stage, their height giving them a fleetingly human quality.

Camilla Dely's costumes and Sophia Khan's hair, especially for the daughters, were brilliantly nuanced, rich textures and shades enhanced by Lee Curran's lighting. Goneril (Akiya Henry) and Regan (Faith Omole) were neatly differentiated, the latter favouring slinky silks and satins and fine knitwear, her long hair straightened and waved, while the former had her hair elaborately braided and she favoured draped cotton, linen and mohair in coarser weaves; both sisters began the play in shades of cream, moving through camel, caramel, and coffee to khaki, albeit still luxe, by the end. Cordelia (Gloria Obianyo) wore her hair in short braids; she wore wide-legged cream canvas trousers with a cropped vaguely naval jacket in the opening scene, black fatigues when she reappeared. Her performance in the opening scene was self-contained to the point of defiance: this was not a misunderstanding or a game gone wrong but a considered position. The three sisters seemed close, huddling for comfort after Cordelia's banishment,

Goneril and Regan consoling their sibling with apparently genuine concern.

One wonders if this is the only time that an actor playing Edmund has recently starred as the EmCee in *Cabaret*? Fra Fee began his first solo scene seated at the piano, playing and singing (the opening of Bob Dylan's 'A Hard Rain's A-Gonna Fall'; he was, of course, the blue-eyed son) with panache and worldly cool as he dug out first his cigarettes and then a tin from which he produced a joint. In a strikingly original and successful interpretation, he delivered his first soliloquy to Edgar (Matthew Tennyson), nerdy and fascinated, chasing him around the room and making him inhale: Edgar became the bastard's first seduction. (And certainly not his last; there was considerable army-cot coupling in the later scenes, between Edmund, Goneril and Regan.)

Edgar had been so apparently weak that his transformation into Poor Tom seemed less a disguise than a total metamorphosis, stripped to underwear (and knee pads), white body paint, black streaked face, mud, deep cover tested when he was caught by guards with torches and managed to convince them that yes, 'Poor Tom's a-cold'. There were no traces here of the too-familiar stigmata or crown of thorns, but Poor Tom was a mystical figure, strange and self-contained; it didn't seem completely absurd to imagine him as a 'philosopher'. Despite his initial weakness, Edgar was convincingly authoritative in the final scene, a black hoodie concealing his identity. Gloucester was less prominent a character than in some productions, with less sense of his story mirroring Lear's, although their meeting on the heath was still profoundly moving.

The play's violence was considered and matter of fact, an apparently unremarkable feature of life in this place. The disguised Kent's stocking, potentially tricky in modern dress, found a perfect expression when he was forced, efficiently, onto an ordinary plastic stool, his ankles and wrists secured to its front legs with cable-ties in an apparent stress position and then laid on his side on the ground. Gloucester was blinded in his own sitting room, the act's petty cruelty increased by his rather unassuming interpretation of the role, a genial, slightly fussy functionary, not Lear's double; there were no Grand Guignol additions of corkscrews or stiletto heels, just Oswald (Hugo Bolton, a wonderfully detailed, watchful, nasty characterization) wordlessly covering the sofa with a large sheet of plastic as the scene began. It was a bloody blinding, though, as was Cornwall's stabbing, and Regan strangled the servant who killed him. Lear and Cordelia were brought on as prisoners in blue jumpsuits, black cloth bags on their heads, tied back-to-back. The final duel was a vicious knife-fight.

The piano reappeared on a number of occasions, played and as a piece of set: Edgar and Gloucester climbed over it on Dover Cliff, although Gloucester jumped from centre stage. The hovel was a tractor tyre, dragged on to the stage and for a time topped with a tattered picnic umbrella against the storm, which was loud in both Sapani's delivery and in its sound effects: the chains at the rear of the stage were animated into swaying torrents of wind-driven rain and Poor Tom ran around the stage, trailing a long piece of waste plastic behind him. There were flashing lights but no strobe. Lear had apparently adjusted to life on the road, his respectable hooded anorak matched with a woolly hat and layers of plastic taped on to his feet. He looked bewildered, battered, lost, a giant brought low, and his scenes with the Fool (Clarke Peters) were great, two old companions, friends and apparent equals, trying to make sense of things. Peters was loose-limbed and cool, his long grey locks tied back, his scarf still natty; he was a jazzman, not a jester. There was no attempt made within the play's action to 'explain' his disappearance: rather, he sang the prophecy, full-voiced, and it was then repeated by Cordelia, sitting centre stage, both of them replacing 'Merlin' with 'the unborn', before he walked slowly offstage. The effect was mystical, as if he were ceding the space to her.

All the actors were miked and there was music/sound throughout (Peter Rice; composer Max Perryment), sometimes a drone, which was on occasion played live on violins by Oliver Cudbill and Steffan Rizzi (who also played Burgundy and France, knights, soldiers, servants, as required). Their tenacity in playing while lying on the ground, running, and shielding their instruments in fights was impressive. In a final *coup de théâtre*, the metal globe from the opening scene reappeared at the end and burst into flames amid the bodies; the dead arose and, led by first Faith Omole and then Fra Fee, sang an impassioned version of 'A Hard Rain's A-Gonna Fall', again, a cappella. It was a devastating end to a devastating production, rich in detail without ever falling into any kind of mimetic realism or evoking a particular setting in time and place, save 'now' or 'soon' and 'anywhere': a *Lear* not so much apocalyptic as one for the end of the world.

At the Riverside Studios in May, the Tang Shu-wing Theatre Studio, based in Hong Kong, presented a wordless (not silent) *King Lear*, directed by Tan-shu Wing, with actors from Hong Kong and Romania – nine in total (Figure 23). There was a pale grey floor with a neon-effect border around its edge, which glowed white, red or orange, and a white cotton drape over the stage, parachute-like, lit from above. The drapes at the back of the stage rose and fell like a Roman blind and were also backlit; there was some impressive shadow work (design, Hon-wai Yuen). In the all-female cast, Lear (Cecilia Yip; other roles were not identified) was all in white, initially elegant in wide-legged, pleated trousers. His hair started the show in a neat chignon and gradually came down. The sisters were in tailored, corseted black, with flashes of red; Gloucester in tweed; Cordelia in flowing white, with Doc Martens and a choker, a manic pixie dream girl; at one point, she sang. She doubled the Fool, cartwheeling in jeans, beanie, heavy chains around her neck. (That she was in disguise as the Fool was strongly suggested.) Edmund and Edgar were near doppelgangers and looked like land-girls, at least in silhouette (jodhpur-like trousers, etc.).

Gloucester was blinded very early, hair loosened and eyes smeared with red. Edgar as Poor Tom stripped to underwear, with a mask: his first appearance was very effective, crawling under bentwood chairs; it was one of the very few recognizable 'images', the snail carrying its house on its back. A chair continued to be used effectively, for instance as the cliff, but it was especially striking when placed precariously as a throne on top of the wooden stepladder, which had also been the hovel. *Walking* was one of the most striking elements of the production's movement: it was audible, rhythmic and often very slow. There were some great subtleties of gesture and facial expression, especially from Lear. The storm was not especially spectacular: I was waiting for the cloth over the stage to billow and fall, but it didn't; the main storm effect was red laser beams, whirling in chaotic lines, giving the effect of tracer fire. It was very far from silent – there was moaning, chattering and screaming – and the soundtrack was painfully loud, with machinegun fire and electronic noise. It was, however, very literal and traditional in its storytelling and characterization, although Lear himself was compelling, a performance of intense complexity, charisma and pathos.

For the performance of *Lear* by the National Changgeuk Company of Korea, directed by Jung Young-doo, the stage of the Barbican Theatre was flooded, with boardwalks and stepping stones; there

24 Ken Nwosu as Othello and Ralph Davis as Iago in *Othello* in the Sam Wanamaker Playhouse at Shakespeare's Globe (© Johan Persson / ArenaPAL).

were later some beautiful effects of splashes and ripples (designer Lee Tae-sup). Throughout, the lighting was not very subtle, with heavy use of spots and some strobe. The costumes were largely in earth tones, tending to grey and dark. This was an adaptation of the play by the Korean playwright Pai Sam-shik, 'intertwining Shakespeare's tale of a powerful king's descent into madness with Lao-tzu's ancient philosophy of water, the natural world and balance, connecting with the deep Korean emotion of "han" (symbolising grief and sorrow)' (from the press release). Much of the dialogue was sung, rather than spoken, in a musical idiom that blended Changgeuk, a traditional Korean opera form, Pansori, another form of musical storytelling, and K-pop, played live (but offstage) by a thirteen-piece orchestra on both Western and traditional Korean instruments. As someone wholly unfamiliar with Korean dramatic and musical traditions, it was difficult to get a handle on these idioms: it was almost through-sung, with additional songs and often very loud, with segments more akin to rock opera; some of the vocals were deliberately strained, apparently a feature of the Pansori idiom.

Cordelia seemed to disguise herself as the Fool in breeches and a distinctive tall hat, with red spots on her cheeks; I wondered if this was a traditional type. Poor Tom wore black and grey rags and carried a leaf-shaped mask; he was mostly played for laughs and also seemed a type, with a distinctive splayed-legged, skipping walk; the audience clapped along with his first song. The scene between him and Lear was oddly joyous. Albany was quickly established as the good guy; he had a bird on his shoulder and sang about wanting to retire to his garden. Edgar and Edmund were almost interchangeable. In an odd plot point, the question of Cordelia's marriage disappeared so there was no sense that she had gone abroad; instead, there was a plot to provoke civil war and present Cordelia as a rebel. Some of the visual effects were very beautiful, as when the Chorus entered with white puppet geese on short stakes, wheeling and fluttering. The Chorus made the storm (alongside sound/lighting effects and haze) with long boards across their shoulders, almost a crucifixion effect, or held vertically, as if a forest or palisade, and it was a snowstorm: snow floated on the water afterwards, and there was an enormous mobile of curved white lines, like time-lapse photography of windblown snow. A seasonal pattern underpinned the show, moving from autumn to winter to spring.

The second half seemed closer to paraphrase or a more literal translation, including in the moving reunion scene (there was no suggestion of special music, however) but the pacing became strange at the end: Edmund was at the point of death, the messenger had been sent, Goneril killed herself, and then there was another song. There was no 'howl' and the stage was otherwise clear for Lear and Cordelia at the end, having been flooded for the battle – which was elaborate and extended, with flags, spears and swords, dimly lit, with much splashing. At the end, Cordelia lay in the water for a long time. There was no attempt to render the last lines, but rather a recapitulation of the Chorus about a flowing river which had opened the show, which ran for three hours. I was glad to have seen it, but at the same time puzzled by its plotting and idiom.

TWO (OR THREE?) HISTORIES

One of the year's hottest tickets was Rob Icke's staging of *Player Kings*, his own adaptation of the two parts of *Henry IV*, which I saw during its West End run at the Noel Coward before Ian McKellen, playing Falstaff, had to withdraw from the production following a fall. The first half lasted two hours, beginning with the coronation in dumb show, then into the King's opening speech as his regalia was removed (Richard Coyle as the King). Eastcheap was debauched and druggy, exposing any sentimental nostalgia for an old 'gangland' East End, fostered by Falstaff; I have never before seen *quite* so much of Hal (excellent Toheeb Jimoh), who was first seen breaking into a stolen cash register with an angle-grinder. Falstaff's relationship with Hal was particularly rich: Hal recognized Falstaff's nasty streak and learned from it, but there was also deep affection, expressed in a warm embrace after Falstaff's 'resurrection' at Shrewsbury. Lovely Geoffrey Freshwater was Bardolph, no longer really able to keep up, happiest nursing a pint, but still game to be there playing his part.

Its world was emphatically contemporary: Hildegard Bechtler's set featured a back wall of bare grey brick, which felt initially a little like an underpass or a carpark, and also a nod to the Almeida, now surely in Icke's DNA. Later there was a tan traverse, behind which there were very rapid scene changes, and also a drop with projections of locations, occasionally details of history or plot. Bits of the back brick wall were blown out and backlit for Shrewsbury, and a familiar Icke device returned, debris blowing in from the side for the battle, which was nastily violent urban warfare, its weapons pistols and knives. It was also ruthless and indeed had no place for honour: Hal killed Hotspur (Samuel

Edward-Cook) by stabbing him in the back as the Last Post sounded. Such brutality had been anticipated by the violence of Gad's Hill: after a blackout there was a security guard motionless on the floor, his head in a pool of blood, which vanished with impossible speed in the next blackout.

The court/political scenes particularly featured Warwick (Annette McLaughlin), and there was good use of conference calls as negotiations between the rebels and the King, trying Hotspur's patience. He was compulsively striking matches before the battle; there was no map scene and his comedy wasn't really allowed to flourish, although the scene with Kate Percy (Tafline Steen) was touching, with an implied pregnancy. There was no Glendower, the adaptation's most significant cut – perhaps there was simply no room for his mysticism and eloquence in this world. Accents were strong. There was an emerging sense of family as much as 'Household' among the courtiers, and especially Warwick's care for Henry, particularly in Part II when she abandoned her Liz Truss / Thatcher blue; Eastcheap was by no means the only source of human warmth in this world.

The second half began not with Rumour but with a bravura set piece, Falstaff having a quick touch-up of his make-up before delivering the sack speech in a spotlight as if for a television commercial, in a terrible British Legion blazer, too many medals, and a Garrick tie. Hotspur had become Pistol, with an appalling permed mullet on his hitherto shaved head, and Lady Percy became Doll, who was (rather lazily) Eastern European; again, she was possibly pregnant. Part II wasn't as tight as Part I, perhaps inevitably. But it did include Shallow (Robin Soans) and Silence (James Garnon, also playing Worcester) and an apple branch, although not the recruits; their scenes were properly elegiac, with an emphasis on *old*, old. Falstaff had already been in a wheelchair, mostly to enable a gag whereby he and his cronies stole all the sack at the product launch, stowing it in the chair. He aged, his hair fluffy by the end; he seemed somehow thinner, and had a funny turn in the pub.

It was very good around the succession, the death scene and the Lord Chief Justice (Joseph Mydell). The King had been carefully established as a smoker; he was not *not* George VI. There was a moving moment when Hal picked up his frail, dying father and carried him back to bed, and a lovely vignette after the King's death, which seemed a snapshot from a more mystical play: a beekeeper appeared, to tell the bees. The rejection, on the coronation red carpet, was very affecting, with Falstaff on his knees. It segued into his death from *Henry V*, spoken by Clare Perkins's excellent Mistress Quickly with the Eastcheap people lined up along the edge of the stage, Falstaff standing behind them. The play ended by restaging the coronation opening, with a blackout at the end.

What was especially notable in the outstanding music (composer Laura Marling) was its a cappella bareness, familiar tunes cutting through in a beautiful, unearthly countertenor. Their principal singer was sometimes part of the action (Henry Jenkinson, in various minor roles), sometimes strolling serenely across the stage: a dissonant 'God Save the King', 'O Peaceful England', 'Jerusalem' and, most slyly moving, 'I Vow to Thee My Country' as the curtain began to fall on the 'dead' Falstaff at Shrewsbury, with a decent pause until his enraged 'embowelled?!' But there was also a sense of what *wasn't* being heard: no 'Zadok', no Elgar or Walton; it reached for something at once more elegiac and also slightly more folky. All Falstaff's set-pieces were there, with the 'honour' speech a particular tour de force. He was not a nice man, but he was a charismatic one, and McKellen's performance combined astonishing technique and physical stamina with layers of complexity – no easy phone-in by a 'national treasure' here. Thank goodness that his fat suit apparently saved him from more serious injury than that which he still sustained.

Richard III at the Globe, directed by Elle While, designed by E. M. Parry, and performed by a cast of women and non-binary people, began with a prologue approximating the Wars of the Roses as a dance battle, at the end of which Richard (Michelle Terry) killed Henry VI. Red roses on the tiring house doors were ripped off to reveal white, and purple banners of Edward IV and Queen Elizabeth dropped from the gallery. James Maloney's cool, grunty score was percussion heavy, with sax. The stage's central trap was covered with a grille, into which the condemned, or bodies, were tipped by sinister attendants, wearing black corsets over white shirts, black breeches – governesses or dominatrixes (Rosalind Blessed, Ayla Wheatley): it was a good solution to the idea of 'The Tower', and meant that bodies didn't have to be got off. Costuming was very mixed: Helen Schlesinger's Buckingham was the only major character entirely in modern dress (initially a neat three-piece suit); most were in composite, some from stock, with quite a lot of ruffs and mostly trainers (which do look surprisingly good with 'Elizabethan' dress) on their feet. After her marriage to Richard, Lady Anne (Katie Erich) was redressed in a parodic crinolined shepherdess style, with a beehive hairstyle, lots of gold, and silver shoes; she was explicitly poisoned. Queen Elizabeth (Marianne Oldham) was passionate, steely, beautiful, wearing pearls, black, an Elizabethan bodice over trousers; shades of Diana in her dark glasses, a performance of grief that was at once heartrending and calculated.

There was a particularly good effect when the shrouded, red-ribboned corpse of Henry VI indeed began to bleed, and a horribly convincing head for Hastings (Catrin Aaron), played as a dim genial posho in moleskins and a padded gilet (with chameleon doubling as Tyrell, punk and traumatized). Clarence's murderers had rubber pig masks, which ramped up the comedy perhaps a fraction too long, and Clarence's dream was almost entirely cut, bar a few lines when he was being drowned in a barrel. The stabbings were all very bloody. There were (excellent) children playing the princes, and their deaths were horrific, smothered in their sleeping bag and dragged off, reminiscent of the McCrory *Medea*. At the interval, distorted pictures of Richard were roughly taped to the pillars, and the second half began with a line dance, everyone in MAGA red hats, as 'RIII' and a crown (the production's logo, a touch of Basquiat) were spraypainted on the central doors. There was a sense throughout the show of scribbling on the space and on the play.

Michelle Terry's Richard was a powerhouse, fearlessly creepy, properly *weird*, baby voice and robot dancing, working the asides and drinking a lot; there was malice and mayhem in every twitch of his tiny, tiny hands, and always the question: what would he wear next? Richard's body gained a plastic quality, explicitly when he added a false torso, covering chest and neck almost to jaw level (it deserved its own credit): his costume became progressively more outrageous and less 'period', although there was a lot of emphasis on the codpiece. The production had been highly controversial in some quarters for its casting of an actor without a visible disability in the title role. In fact, all the text's references to deformity and disability were cut, and there was considerable collaging and interpolation; all the textual changes were thought-provoking. Anne spoke in part in BSL, and in particular cursed in BSL, which was extremely powerful. The scenes of lamentation with the women were ultimately good, although their power was perhaps diminished by having Margaret (Poppy Miller) on the gallery above and the Duchess and Elizabeth below, although it emphasized their isolation.

The scene of Richard being 'forced' to take the crown made complete sense being played out front,

with Richard above (with two prostitutes dressed as bishops) and Buckingham working the crowd below. Buckingham's energy in the London scene was far more apparent from the yard, especially his muttering. He was complex, smooth, a fixer, pivotal to the show and to Richard; his fall was genuinely shocking. The Mayor (Sarah Finigan, also playing King Edward) in a pussy-bowed blouse encouraged the yard to kneel (successfully at the Saturday evening performance but not at the weekday matinee, possibly because there had been some rain and the ground was wet?). When Richmond (Sam Crerar) arrived, he was 'normally' dressed, in jeans, boots, bomber jacket; the actor had been doubling Catesby, among others, and so Catesby had to be explicitly killed off; there was dark humour in Richard's calling for him when Catesby was dead. He gave his first speech from the yard. There was a full complement of ghosts, bloodied, Hastings with his head, and the nightmare speech was excellent, with a cabaret quality. But Bosworth felt perfunctory, and Richard had no final line. Richmond's final speech interpolated 'we have more in common than that which divides us', quoting the maiden speech of the murdered MP Jo Cox: it was played movingly straight. This was an uneven production, mostly held together by a compellingly bizarre rockstar performance by Michelle Terry — but after all the grotesquery, the sense of release at the end, as a stage full of women and non-binary people of all ages absolutely rocked out, was a joyful thing.

At *Othello* in the Wanamaker (Figure 24), directed by Ola Ince with design by Amelia Jane Hankin, no candles had been lit before the show began, and the theatre's 'daylight' shutters were fully open. The back wall of the stage was covered with blue-green vertical timbers, with ventilation panels above head height all along. The central doors and left-hand doors to the tiring house were open, but the right blocked with a diagonal rusty stair to the gallery. There was very little furniture (people sat on plastic crates) and a central grating in the floor, out of which Cassio and then Othello appeared, as if they'd dived through sewers to get to 'Cyprus'. This was a high-concept show, its world carefully imagined, performed to a luscious, sometimes funky, sometimes lyrical score from Renell Shaw (musical director, Rio Kai).

The play opened with the sound of crackling police radios and half-heard racial slurs, clearly recalling Metropolitan Police scandals, past and recent: it cut the opening scene with Roderigo and Iago at Brabantio's house. Instead, to a lively soundtrack reminiscent of police procedurals, above all Jed Mercurio's *Line of*

Duty, it showed Othello (Ken Nwosu) arresting a dangerous criminal and being given a commendation by the 'commissioner' (the Duke; Brabantio became 'commander'), the naming of Cassio as 'inspector', and then the marriage of Desdemona (in white satin) and Othello (in tux, with buttonhole); she threw the bouquet and it was caught by Roderigo (Sam Swann) in the pit. Othello was 'commander' but more usually 'guvnor', and not noticeably older than the other characters. Cyprus was the docklands or the docks, Venice was Chelsea or the King's Road or Scotland Yard (this became incoherent) and the Turks were the 'Lurks', a 'criminal cartel'. As in other recent productions with a modern military setting, it brought out the sense of the barracks – here downtime on a dangerous undercover surveillance op, although the outlines of this remained fuzzy: after all, in the play the Turks are defeated early on, and so it wasn't quite clear the roles being played, what kind of activity they were actually engaged in; there were a couple of 'montage' sequences with images of suspects on boards, suggestions of raids or of monitoring cameras. To my ear, the production could have dialled back its textual changes: did the Turks really need to become the Lurks, would 'Venice' and 'Cyprus' really jar so much? Odder was that 'thou' was changed to 'you' throughout, but other forms (especially 'dost') remained. Was the aim accessibility? (It kept the Propontic and the Hellespont.) The setting and resonances would have been clear enough without the changes: it was London and it was now.

The drinking scene combined a welcome/wedding celebration for Desdemona and Othello, with drinking, dancing and singing (into which the 'Willow Song' was added; Cassio joined in on guitar), into a kind of hazing for Cassio's promotion to inspector, with forced drinking, etc. Cassio (Oli Higginson) was a posh boy, flirty and tactile with everyone; the description of him as an 'arithmetician' was accompanied by a typing-at-keyboard gesture: he's a techy, backroom, not front line. Ralph Davis's Iago was young, tall and fit, physically not unlike Cassio; he was very matter of fact in the soliloquies, with something of a defiant direct address to the audience – the occasional 'what?' Emilia (Charlotte Bate) seemed suspicious of him very early on. Roderigo was first in a burgundy suit over a t-shirt, chains, loafers, no socks; he arrived in the 'Docks' undercover in forensics overalls, white boots, etc., and came to the drinking session to pick a fight as a Deliveroo rider; then it was filthy hi-vis for his third appearance. (All of these were slightly too big, as if Iago was mocking him.)

The production's most radical innovation was the 'subconscious' who sometimes accompanied Othello, played by Ira Mandela Siobhan. This became more convincing as the play developed, although I never entirely took to it; it was more successful when text was shared, or when it was clearly legible in its actions and movement (which was always interesting, and frequently beautiful to watch) – as the traumatized recruit, for instance, or as a form of internalized racism, or its damage, which Othello was constantly having to suppress or mask. At one point the subconscious was on the gallery in clownface/whiteface, in the madness scene, as if a manic presence unable to be suppressed; Cassio also appeared and partly acted out the 'dream'. Where the device was particularly effective was in the final scene, when Othello entered pulling his subconscious after him, the subconscious once again in the wedding suit; he died too. Nwosu's delivery was strikingly direct, London accented. The police radio slurs reappeared in Othello's madness, delivered by actors in balaclavas, as if they were inner voices but also a non-stop background chatter of systemic institutional racism. There was also the suggestion that these voices predisposed Othello to listen to Iago, that Iago was as it were just saying the quiet part out loud? Othello as an inspiring, charismatic leader wasn't entirely clear ('put up your bright swords' was cut); his backstory had no mystical edge but rather was about hardship overcome. His trajectory seemed both clear and inevitable, as if he had been set up to fail from the start.

The handkerchief was a large dark silk scarf. I really liked the 'Willow Song' scene (here without song) from Emilia in particular: the two women crouched on the floor, knowing they were in danger, and it was clear and cynical and broken; it really brought out the resonances with *Shrew*. In a futile gesture, Emilia gave Desdemona her police radio. The bed, part of an old boat, was framed with candles, which Othello lit for the final scene; the bed didn't quite work, the candles did. Desdemona wore practical leggings and put her boots back on to fight for her life – and she really fought. He strangled her on the floor; it wasn't sexualized, although the kisses were lingering; she didn't revive at all. Roderigo shot Cassio offstage, and Iago killed Emilia with a tiny, concealed blade. In a final, devastating *coup de théâtre*, Othello was delivering his last speech prior to shooting himself (no 'base Judean', no 'med'cinable gum', no 'Aleppo') when Cassio appeared, shouted 'Tazer Tazer' and shot him. Othello and Iago were both cuffed and paraded for mugshots and the press, Othello described in voiceover (as if in tabloid headlines) as 'Black beast Nigerian cop' and Iago as evidence of a crisis in 'Police mental health'. The production was good at class: Cassio's privilege ensured that he still came out on top at the end, and he was the one taking the photos.

ROMANS (IN EGYPT)

The central production of the Globe's summer season, and the most anticipated, was *Antony and Cleopatra*, directed by Blanche McIntyre (with Charlotte Arrowsmith as AD), with a wholly signed (BSL) performance by Nadia Nadarajah as Cleopatra and a mixture of speech and signing from the rest of the company (Figure 22). It was thought-provoking, impressive and enjoyable both as a version of the play and as a theatrical event; there were moments of tremendous power and beauty. I am not qualified to comment on the BSL aspects of the performance or the production's significance in d/Deaf theatre and culture, and here link to an article by Charlie Swinbourne for *The Limping Chicken*.[1] I saw the production twice, once on press night from a seat in the gallery, around to the side, and then later in the run from the yard.

Among the cast, signing was employed in different ways: Dolabella (Mark Donald) could translate, as could Antony (sometimes) and even Enobarbus (Daniel Millar) a little, and Antony (John Hollingworth) and Cleopatra signed to each other. Charmian (Zoë McWhinney) only signed, and her gestures were the most flamboyant, with some vocalization in the final scene; Iras (Gabriella Leon) both signed and spoke (and doubled Octavia). The Soothsayer (William Grint) signed and also vocalized; he played many roles and had brilliant comic timing. The use of 'home signs' (locally devised signs, intelligible among a particular group) and hence the sense of shared language was striking and often moving, as was Antony not signing when he was angry with Cleopatra – a deliberate, painful gesture of exclusion. Characters (especially Antony and Cleopatra) interrupted and drew each other's attention by stamping. There was very little throughscoring, much less than is now usual, although there were moments of great visual impact from the musical instruments, long dragon-headed trumpets, for instance, played from the galleries. One effect of the integrated BSL was on the blocking, which tended to be quite linear and horizontal, with the ensemble often playing in a line across the front, allowing for sightlines between them. The action and dialogue were much more readily intelligible from the yard; the fluency and detail of the signing was lovely.

There was a lot of doubling, with (for instance) Seleucas present as a third woman throughout, a smart solution in this sprawling cast-of-thousands play. The comedy had become slightly less broad on my second viewing, although Mardian (Nadeem Islam, also playing Alexas and many messengers) was still scene-stealing, a wonderful comic. In general, the text was heavily cut: the burning barge mostly survived but there was only half the crocodile and no mention of Cleopatra wearing Antony's sword Philippan, and the Roman scenes seemed particularly stripped out, with Pompey, Lepidus and even Octavius Caesar (Bert Seymour) becoming fairly notional as characters and Menas even more so. It was interesting in effect to 'hear' Antony more than Cleopatra: parity was clearly tricky, as the Romans could 'say' more in less time than in the (mainly signed) Egyptian scenes, although the pacing had settled later in the run.

The gallery was slightly built out with a curved platform, supported by pillars (designer Simon Daw), and the tiring house wall was covered with patched indigo cloth, with ropes giving the effect of sails; the 'masts' supporting some of the blue drapes collapsed after Antium. For his death, Antony was hauled up on ropes to the gallery, and his body was then gently rolled below the canvas at the back, a good solution to a tricky moment. Above the gallery, there was a large central roundel, which proved to be the screen for captions (there were three other screens on the auditorium galleries); it was also a sun and a moon, rising and setting, with the odd visual joke: the words moved drunkenly in the bacchanal scene, and Cleopatra's final lines disappeared as a shower of sparks, surprisingly moving. The text that they displayed was the complete (cut) text, not a re-translation of the BSL.

The women's costumes were pleated and floor-length, Charmian in blue, Iras in green (costume supervisor, Natalia Alvarez). Cleopatra began in a gold cross-over halter-neck top with a white skirt, but also wore bright sun-yellow pleats with green accents, and a blue skirt with an overlapping leather 'armour' bodice. Romans were standard-issue, leather or metal armour over rose or maroon; Antony began in blue but added a maroon

---

[1] https://limpingchicken.com/2024/09/05/i-cant-believe-im-on-that-stage-again-nadia-nadarajah-on-starring-as-cleopatra-at-shakespeares-globe-bsl.

cloak. It was striking in a (partially) Roman play, that there was almost no white, and no black at all. The snakes were golden and articulated, making no attempt at realism, and Cleopatra died on a throne mid-stage; her 'robe' was in effect a collar and a cloak of turquoise beads, authentically 'Egyptian' but lacking in visual impact as it mostly hung down behind her, and she had a golden diadem. Nadarajah was mesmerizing; she didn't play out front much but when she did it was very effective, and it was particularly powerful when, in desperation, she vocalized as well as signing, protesting that she could not go to Rome in the 'waterfly' speech. Her gold nails added to the detail and beauty of her signing, and her speech to Dolabella about Antony, one of the most closely translated passages, was especially beautiful to watch, with Nadarajah's delicate gestures and ecstatic face, filled with reverie. Even after twenty-five years seeing shows at the Globe, it's rare that I am not moved by the final dance, and that was particularly the case in this landmark production, which brought genuinely fresh perspectives to the play.

When the house opened for *Coriolanus* (directed by Lyndsey Turner) in the Olivier at the National, there was centre-stage a colossal near-cube apparently made of concrete columns, covered with projections, as if looking at black-and-white satellite or drone footage of a city: a crowd was gradually gathering, casting long shadows, filling the surfaces. It seemed to gesture at the Arab Spring, but also gave an impression of pigeons, or ants in a formicary. There were searchlights, sidelighting, haze, a drum beat and a drone. For the first scene, the cube moved upwards to reveal plinths in a museum, displaying antiquities, including Romulus and Remus. Throughout, its 'blocks' were raised and lowered in different configurations; there were many different concrete interiors, sometimes giving the sense that the theatre's own concrete construction had been brought onstage. Its elegance and flexibility were quintessential Es Devlin, thinking hard about Rome and Romanness but not through marble, ruins or columns – after all, concrete too was a Roman invention. Later, the Volsces had a shattered Parthenon frieze on the wall of Aufidius' dining room.

In what could have been a nod to the 2012 Hytner *Timon*, in the opening scene there was clearly a patrician 'function' going on offstage at the rear; there were champagne glasses, flower arrangements, 'buzz'. The plebs had sneaked in; they had placards, and there was a bit of half-hearted graffiti of the Romulus and Remus statue. Throughout, the plebs were a little underpowered: there could simply have been more of them – there was no sense of mob, although they were expertly differentiated with a real sense of characters and they did manage to be threatening. They filmed everything, and set up the stylish use of video projection throughout; big scenes were played out front and sometimes projected too. Plum/maroon was the regime colour, including for the women (costumes, Annemarie Woods). In the opening scene Menenius (Peter Forbes) appeared from the museum function in black tie, followed by Coriolanus in elegant double-breasted plum velvet; it was the only slightly off note – why not dress uniform? Perhaps that was the point, his first attempt at 'doing' politics. Later, the tribunes (Jordan Metcalfe, Stephanie Street) also had a sartorial upgrade, with him being measured up by a tailor, a better haircut and new glasses (this was at the height of 'controversy' over Keir Starmer's new designer eyewear); she had had a proper blow-dry.

Despite such modernity, the fighting was done with swords and round shields: when Coriolanus and Aufidius (Kobna Holbrook-Smith) fought, Coriolanus began with two swords, and they eventually fought bareknuckle, with some kickboxing moves. In the Volsce scenes, there were 'classic' army great coats, but in the earlier battle there was what was in effect body armour, and the fight sequences were high octane. In this place, war was something out of time, a ritual as much as a reckoning in a political or strategic conflict. Those familiar with the text might have noted that in this production Aufidius and Coriolanus had not 'been down together in [their] sleep, | Unbuckling helms, fisting each other's throat' (4.5), and in general the potential for homoeroticism in the text was played down.

The marketplace scene worked very well: there was ritual not just in Coriolanus' actions and dress but in the actions of the plebs themselves; they too had a culture and hierarchy, with old, faded banners, something like miners' banners, as if each one represented a union or guild – a good way around the crowd problem. They weren't quite sure what they were doing, within the play's world, but knew it still had to be taken seriously. The women in the supplication scene were strange, ritual, ancient, in black 'classical' draperies and elaborate, very tall gold headdresses; there was a slight suggestion of behatted church ladies, a formidable tribe. But their roles were trimmed throughout the play, flattened into the ensemble, and Volumnia (Pamela Nomvete), in

25 Conor McLeod as Gallus and Anushka Chakravarti as Alba (two of the plebs) in *Coriolanus* at the National Theatre (© Misan Harriman).

particular, lacked impact relative to some productions; there was no trace of the Folio SD 'she holds him by the hand silent', either.

As Coriolanus, David Oyelowo was charismatic and articulate, although sometimes could have let rip a bit more; the banishment scene, however, was tremendous, as he went up the central aisle of the theatre like a furious rocket. The projections sometimes distracted, as did the sound design, occasionally a little intrusive; everyone was miked and there was the odd balance problem. There was no use of the Olivier revolve at all but no wings either; it was a vast stage and the fight scenes used nearly the whole depth; there may have been some sightline problems. But it was spectacular, clever and thought-provoking, as a piece of theatre and as a production of this fascinating, sometimes recalcitrant play. Despite the bare-torsoed poster splashed around the Tube, Coriolanus' body was not framed as an object until the very end, at the moment of his killing and when there was a clever suggestion that he became (in monumental terms) just another museum exhibit like the rest, a Black body displayed behind a golden shield, looked at by a small child who might have been his own, being exhorted to exit through the gift-shop.

At the other end of the scale, in terms of budget, cast size and performance space, was *Julius Caesar*, performed by the Icarus Theatre Collective and directed by Max Lewendel at the Southwark Playhouse (Borough), foregrounding 'creative captioning' and set in 'the future', which meant a Mad Max-ish aesthetic with big coats,

328

metal, braids and blacked-out eyes (designer Flavio Graff). It also meant complicated projected captions (characters interacted with them, zooming, muting or swiping) as well as some pre-recorded material (captions, Samantha Baines; projections, Will Monks). There was a sense of VR/AR, social media and gaming (especially in its scoring – the epic ambience of gaming soundtracks); there was effective use of neon scribbles and animations, but it was visually very busy and would perhaps have been difficult to follow for someone dependent on the captioning. The whole system had to be rebooted half an hour in at the performance I saw. The stage was a dimly lit space with haze; hanging panels over the stage were used for the captions and other projections, and the set's main feature was three panelled 'booths' which were constantly moved about, rotated and opened.

Marullus was projected as a shock-jock-type video DJ, with the Lupercal represented downstage as a decadent party. The expository passages (Cassius on Caesar's weaknesses, the offstage presentation of crowns) were effective as stick-figure projections; Brutus' key soliloquy was accompanied with a cool snake and egg projection, but she did have to deliver it from inside one of the booths. Brutus, Casca, Trebonius (upgraded, as one of the central conspirators, played by Eleanor Crosswell, doubling Calphurnia) were all played as female, and Brutus (Rowan Winter) was in a relationship with Portia (Gabrielle Sheppard, doubling Casca); replacing Eros with Metellus Cimber (Gareth Cooper, doubling Lepidus) – who appeared multiple times as an all-purpose, sometimes comic, servant – diminished Brutus' complexity.

Caesar (Will Travis) *only* appeared as a projection, which was reasonably effective, even for the killing, where he became pixellated and distorted. (Alongside all the digital material, there were real knives and blood.) What really didn't work, however, was that the conspirators then produced as Caesar's 'mantle' the red fake-fur coat he'd worn on screen, which was rather too closely reminiscent of Sesame Street's Elmo. Overall, it didn't quite come off, especially in the second half, although the 'pricking' was chillingly efficient in the digital environment. It didn't need its rather clunky 'futuristic' setting to justify its digital effects, which might have been more powerful had they not been applied to such a busy set. But its young cast worked hard, with careful doubling and a skilfully constructed text, and it had some interesting things to suggest about power and its operation, as well as about what accessibility in theatre might look like now and in the future. It was thought-provoking to see it in the same season as the Globe's *Antony and Cleopatra*: the production had originally intended to integrate BSL too, but abandoned this during the R&D period.

Perhaps the oddest show I saw in 2024 was Eddie Izzard's solo *Hamlet* (directed by Selina Cadell) at the Riverside Studios. Tom Piper's set was a white box with two slit windows, lit from within. Scene changes and any effects were done with lighting: the ghost in turquoise green, warm golden light for the play scene. The house lights were up from time to time and a number of scenes were played from the audience, including some of the soliloquies and Ophelia's mad scene. Izzard wore stacked heel boots, leather trousers, and a tailored jacket in black brocade which sometimes lit green, with padded shoulders and a single button; heavy false eyelashes meant that her eyes were often lost.

The first half lasted around eighty minutes, with the interval coming after the closet scene. The cutting (text by Mark Izzard) was quite skilful; the modernization was mostly at the level of the odd word: 'beaver' became 'visor'; 'arras', 'curtain'; etc. As one might expect, the more stichomythic passages were the least successful, except for Rosencrantz and Guildenstern, who were played as if sock puppets, Izzard's long red nails clattering drily, like bloody mouths. There was little startling in the characterizations: Claudius was a smooth bounder, Polonius a gabbling fusspot, Laertes suave, and Ophelia and Gertrude were particularly underpowered. The play scene was much abbreviated, although the audience reactions worked quite well. Izzard's physicality was odd: in some dialogue, she changed position, whirling around from left to right as she swapped characters; in the graveyard scene, in particular, as she changed characters, she looked as if she were 'doing a twirl'. There were no props, not even letters (mimed as scrolls being unrolled); swords were unsheathed in a rather wafting way, with no sense of their having weight or length (movement, Didi Hopkins).

The second half felt more perfunctory, and the solo format brought out how much more *dialogue* there is. The gravediggers had a bit of paraphrase and improv; it was the show's most recognizable comedy in its idioms and rhythms. Osric was heavily cut (and sounded vaguely Spanish); Fortinbras was vaguely Scottish. For all the thinness of Ophelia's characterization, the mad scene was quite effective, with repeated snatches of 'how should I your true love know?', much of it delivered from the auditorium. The final fight was, unsurprisingly, odd – carefully choreographed, active and extended, but it really underlined how much dialogue there is and how little of it is spoken by Hamlet and Laertes. (There is good reason why one actor having a fight is a comedy cliché.) Izzard made a short speech at the end, exhorting the audience to 'tell all your friends' – that this was for 'the people' not the critics. But I was left asking, what was the point? It was certainly an impressive feat of memory; oddly, it might have worked better as a radio play – because what one missed, especially in the final scene, were the reactions, the sense of thought and dawning realization, the unarticulated decision-making. There was nothing particularly startling about the soliloquies, which I had thought might be distinct-ive; I learned little about the play and its possibilities.

What did Shakespeare look like on London stages in 2024? Pretty dark, in the mirror it was holding up; relatively little comedy and not a single late play. Solid in its commitment to diversity of casting – London stages look (and sound) a lot like London streets, at least superficially – but also quite male, in its auteur directors and star power (Icke, Lloyd, Godwin; McKellen, Tennant, Fiennes, Oyelowo), with the honourable exception of the Globe, especially Blanche McIntyre – although work by Yaël Farber and Rebecca Frecknall (no Shakespeare from her this year) and from the Almeida in general is hugely influential across a variety of spaces. High concept and eclectic in design, not always successfully, although sometimes to thrilling effect (as at the Almeida and the National, and out in the Docks), with any attempt at coherent period settings largely skewing to the here and now. Confident in its incorporation of technology, in re-gendering characters, tweaking the text, and in exploring the dramatic potential of accessibility. Complex soundscapes and underscoring are now the norm; so, increasingly, is miking actors. I was thrilled to get out of my West End / South Bank comfort zone into some different spaces and to see shows in so many different idioms. Shakespeare, at least on this showing, can still be reliably box-office.

Despite the amount of innovation and creativity in evidence, reviewing Shakespeare productions outside London in 2024 was a somewhat gloomy experience. The first performance under consideration, Tim Crouch's *Truth's a Dog Must to Kennel*, was performed as part of the Mayfest festival, originally founded in 2011 by Kate Yedigaroff and Matthew Austin. This biennial festival is one of the best places to find new work in the country, bringing world-class, international live performance to Bristol, and has long been a force for good in the city. This year, for example, it operated a 'pay-what-you-can' ticketing structure to encourage those without economic means to access performances and build new audiences. Sadly, in November 2024 Mayfest announced that they would have to take an organizational hiatus until 2026 for financial reasons, evidence of a cultural sector in crisis that could be witnessed up and down the country. In Sheffield, for example, I was fortunate to see Northern Ballet's *Romeo and Juliet* at the Lyceum where Prokofiev's outstanding score was played by the Northern Ballet Sinfonia. However, financial restrictions meant that the subsequent tour used recorded music, a sign of the impact that the pandemic and the outgoing Conservative government's neglect of the sector were having across the creative industries. As I entered the theatre I was given a flyer by a member of the Musicians' Union urging the government to 'Save Our Orchestras', and the news that very day reported that English National Opera (ENO) musicians had been 'fired and rehired' onto casual contracts. Around the UK, it seemed, venues were scrambling to stay afloat under severe economic pressure. The future for artists and theatres and the cultural industries generally remains uncertain as we head into 2025. It really is a wretched time for the arts, and yet their capacity to provide space for alternative voices and viewpoints has never been more important.

BRISTOL SHAKESPEARE

TRUTH'S A DOG MUST TO KENNEL, DIR. TIM CROUCH, TOBACCO FACTORY THEATRE, 19 MAY 2024

Strangely for Bristol – known more for its contemporary arts than classical theatre – two Shakespeare productions toured to the city in 2024. Typically for Bristol – given its quirky and rebellious character – the first's connection to Shakespeare was orthogonal, to say the least. Audiences, then and now, social and theatrical, were the theme of *Truth's a Dog Must to Kennel* . . . but how to write about a Tim Crouch performance? For over twenty years he has been exploding ideas around theatre, the performer, the writer, the audience and the contract which binds them together, via works such *My Arm* (2003), *An Oak Tree* (2005) and *The Author* (2009). His concerns are often explored through the prism of Shakespeare, whether as a performer – *I, Malvolio*; *I, Cinna*; *The Complete Deaths* – or as a director – *The Taming of the Shrew*, *King Lear*. Crouch returns to *Lear* in *Truth's a Dog*, but indirectly, using the horrors of a seventeenth-century play to explore those of our contemporary moment.

This is achieved through two modes of performance. The first involves Crouch donning VR goggles (Figure 26) to observe an imagined, past production of *Lear* in which he played the Fool, but left the stage in disgust at the play's cruelty. Ironically, this 'modern-dress' performance is situated as a 'live, interactive, immersive experience', which was, in actuality, always mediated by Crouch's narration of events. Despite the two removes of headset and description, Crouch managed to conjure a vivid playworld for this imagined performance, one in which privilege was emblematized by Bentleys and Range Rovers and country houses, countered by a more dominant natural world of chalk,

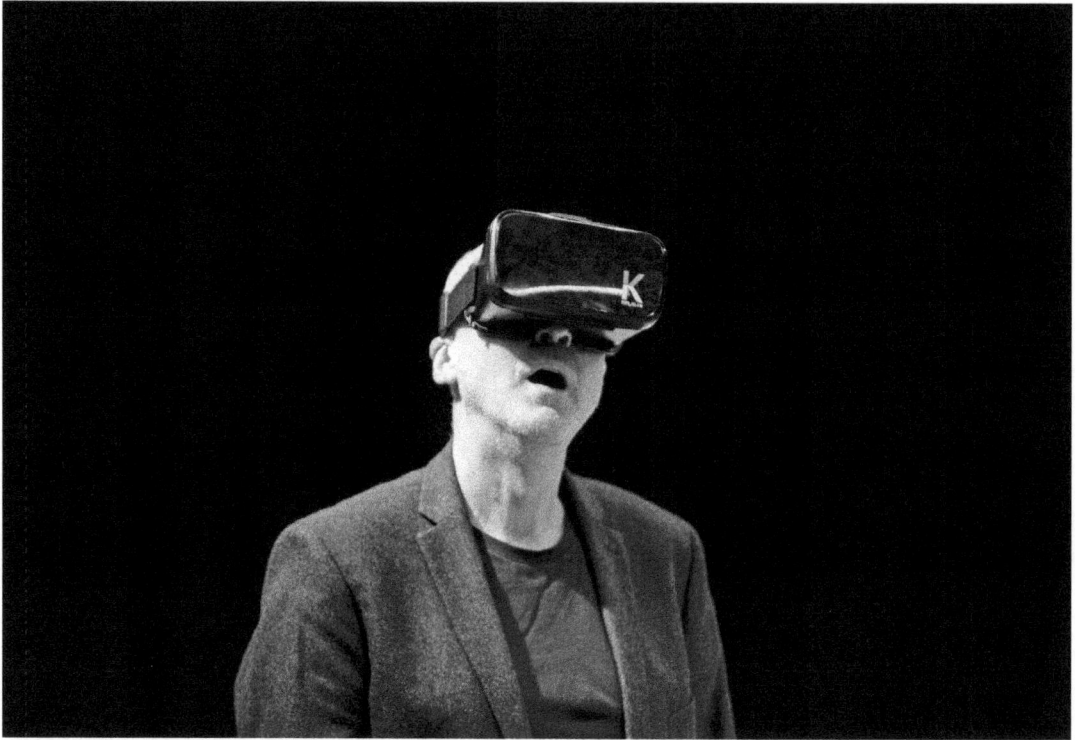

26 Tim Crouch in *Truth's a Dog Must to Kennel* (© Stuart Armitt).

flint, nettles, bracken, a kestrel, crows, some gorse. He also turned towards us – an audience exposed with houselights up – using his VR goggles to re-cast us into a proscenium arch theatre, pointing out who was the independent school theatre trip, who had come from the corporate away day, who was the woman in the access seat with the carer, and who was the man who paid £135.50 for the theatre/dinner package.

The second performance mode, initiated whenever Crouch removed the goggles, drew on the perceived spontaneity of stand-up comedy; though presumptions of the directness of the comic mode and the distance of historical plays were toyed with. While the 'comedy' sections proved increasingly alienating as Crouch's monologue unfurled, the performance of *Lear* came too close for comfort. This was particularly the case when Gloucester's eyes were gouged out, which Crouch relayed as if he – and we – were witnessing it for the first time; and it is almost intolerable. After the event, his blank, black goggles stood in for Gloucester's 'sightless sockets' as he turned to face the audience, bewildered that such a thing could happen. A little

later, a frenzied retelling of the 'Aristocrats' joke (punchline replaced with 'Royalty') repels us in a different way. The wild depictions of incestuous, orgiastic deviance, in which 'you know' euphemistically replaces the cavalcade of sexual practices and body parts involved, left us scrambling to figure out what we probably really don't want to know. Though of course it dawns on us, at some point, that it is the plot of *Lear*.

In testing these different theatrical modalities, performance histories, levels of personae, knowledge and imagination, and the audience's own reactions and boundaries, Crouch interrogated audience complicity in theatrical and social systems. The woman in the access seat is so deeply affected by the scene of eye-gouging that she starts to yap (like a dog?), but the audience shush and hush her: this is not appropriate theatrical behaviour. Later, in the finale of deaths, a real death occurs – the man who has enjoyed the dinner package suffers a heart attack and has to be carried from the auditorium. The distinction between theatre and reality, between then and now, imaginatively collapses – as Crouch puts it, 'time cracks apart'. But an audience who should be trained in the arts of empathy find no space in their hearts for this loss, to lament a clod as much as a promontory. Instead, it is a rupture of their pleasant experience: 'A disturbance! A disturbance!', Crouch exclaims.

Lear thus became a template for considering the effects and purpose of theatrical experiences, whether they develop our humane understanding, and indeed whether they have any place at all in this moment of history. Crouch terms what we are engaged in as 'necrotheatre', 'a morgue', 'an arcane anthropological object of study'. Surpassing even 'the Aristocrats' – who at least don't commit necrophilia in their terrible act – we are accused of 'fucking a corpse' when we watch Shakespeare. Why are we all here anyway, sitting and observing imagined atrocities – what purpose does it all serve? And why is the lowly servant the only one to step up to defend Gloucester, losing their life in the process? These questions reflect back onto us uncomfortably as truth tries to find its kennel. At times Crouch was implicated in the same systems that he was critiquing, as when he called out an usher for letting in latecomers at an inopportune moment – the show's own rupture – even though ushers are themselves probably the lowliest, and most poorly paid, in the theatrical event.

How to write about a Tim Crouch performance? In a mixture of tenses, it seems – because there is something utterly alive and present and vital about this work. The word 'genius' gets bandied around a lot in Shakespeare studies, but it is hard not to feel that you are in the presence of theatrical genius here. The vocabularies of the performance are shifting sands; we lose our footing; direct address signposts multifaceted and oblique possibilities. 'Who's speaking now?', Crouch asks. 'I am!', he replies – as if that in any way answers his question. After the eye-gouging, Crouch asks, incredulous 'Who *wrote* this?'. Shakespeare, your brain replies, until you consider that he was working from the anonymous *King Leir*. And, in fact, Crouch wrote this bit, didn't he? And, actually, aren't we all working from a collective memory rather than a text at this moment? And, *actually*, who is the 'author' of the performance of Gloucester's torture anyway – the actor(s) or the dramatist(s)? Crouch's questions, hydra-headed, generate more questions, their singularity always belying possible plural responses.

Crouch also employed recursion, returning to ideas but to produce different effects, the simplicity of conceits becoming more complex, twisted and meaningful each time they were repeated. Refrains such as 'above my paygrade' – put into the mouths of the Fool, of Crouch-as-Fool, of us-as-audience – move us from imagined pasts to our current, unbearable present as they are reiterated and recontextualized. It does Crouch a disservice to say what his performances are 'about' – they are about many things – but what *Truth's a Dog* encourages us to reflect on is our role as social audience to the events that surround us. Fascism and genocide and massacre and poverty are never mentioned, but they are the obscene undercurrent – the 'you know' – of the performance. 'When it's threatened it's one thing', Crouch says about the eye-gouging; 'When it's here, it's here.' And it's here.

What are we going to do as time cracks apart, Crouch asks, as things falls apart, as the cruelties that we thought were consigned to history resurface in the present? What do we do when the cosy scenes experienced in darkened auditoria are disturbed by real events, when there is a rupture in the liberal framework of continual progression? What kind of folly is this, and what is the ugly truth that must be driven home as we sit in the glare of house-lights? The VR goggles provide a lens through which to see objectively that to which we have become inured, whether the virtual reality of Gloucester's blinding, or the actual reality of the parlous state of the world. The predictability of an audience disgusted by Gloucester's torture is lampooned: 'We liked it before', they are imagined to say, but it is *our* predictability really – because we haven't been overlaid with another audience *really*. As the performance modes merge and meld, the levels of dissociation become smaller and smaller until it is inescapable that it is us that Crouch can see through his goggles, our own sightless sockets swerving the disturbance taking place right before our eyes.

MACBETH, DIR. RICHARD TWYMAN, BRISTOL OLD VIC, 9 FEBRUARY 2024

The other significant Shakespeare in Bristol's theatrical year was the English Touring Theatre (ETT) version of *Macbeth*, a stalwart of the UK theatre due to its status as a set GCSE text and commercial viability. Guesting on the podcast 'Codeswitch', Ayanna Thompson argues that Shakespeare is perceived in the West as 'intellectual spinach', assumed to be 'good for you. He's universally good for you.'[1] Thompson questions this idea with regard to minoritized peoples, with the implication that spinach is something to be endured rather than enjoyed, as any schoolchild might attest. Her words popped into my head during ETT's *Macbeth* at the

---

[1] www.npr.org/transcripts/752850055.

Bristol Old Vic as the audience suffered, sighed and sniggered their way through the performance. I was left wondering why exactly they had stuck around if not the belief – at least for some – that Shakespeare is intellectual nutrition to be unenthusiastically imbibed.

Much of the commentary surrounding this production has centred on the decision to delete scenes involving the three witches. There was a general equivocation over whether the witches were real – as intimated by an opening news report (barely audible from the Upper Circle) implying that witchy business was afoot locally – or imagined – 'emerging from the psychology of the characters', as the director Richard Twyman writes in the programme note. Lady Macbeth seemed to call them from beyond when she flung open the doors of the balcony to welcome spirits into the slick interior of the Macbeths' flat. But when the witches' prophecies were later voiced by Banquo in a creepy dream-like sequence, it couldn't be determined in whose voice he was speaking – was he rehearsing an earlier meeting with the witches, or had he been possessed? And did Lady Macbeth's opening incantations mean that she was, in fact, the source of all the strange activity? Twyman states that the supernatural layer of the play was therefore 'explored from two directions', but it seemed more like having your cake and eating it. The play itself provides ample opportunity to explore whether the witches are 'within' or 'without' through the complex interplay of free will and determinism in the Macbeths' actions. It is entirely possible to examine this concern without enacting a profound dramaturgical intervention which only makes sense if you are familiar with the play, or able to buy a programme, both of which militate against inclusion.

In a particularly tricksy and tiresome conclusion to the witch question came the 'twist at the end' in which Ross, Lennox and Macduff suddenly conspired on the final line, 'When shall we three meet again?', before an abrupt blackout – insinuating that they had been the witches all along. If so, there had been no indication that this was the case. While it is not an issue to keep the undecidabilities of the text in play in performance, the confusion over the witches simply added to the clutter of ideas in the production. Beginning with 1.5 appeared to herald Twyman's decision to foreground Lady Macbeth's (Laura Elsworthy) story and the domestic dimensions of the play. However, it also meant that we were flung almost straight into the plan to murder Duncan, with little opportunity for the Macbeths to reflect on the seriousness of committing regicide, or,

indeed, to establish their marital relationship. The condensing of the opening matter meant that we were catapulted directly into the tedious cliché of their sexy *folie à deux*, which consequently meant that their marriage did not ring true (the Macbeths' general disconnection was not helped by a mannered performance by Mike Noble in the title role). The reorganization of the text also threw the exploration of masculinity and political structure, meaning that the hierarchies of soldiers and the rulers were not sufficiently established. This confusion was heightened by a preponderance of beards and shaved heads onstage, meaning that one masculine role bled into another, making it unclear who was who or what they wanted. Not ideal for a production aiming to elucidate the play for schoolchildren.

Presumably the limitations of touring informed the single-set design of the Macbeths' apartment, and, in her programme note, the designer, Basia Bińkowska, identifies the complications of starting the tour among the reconstructed historical architecture of the Shakespeare North Playhouse before moving on to other venues. Nevertheless, the flat itself – situated somewhere between the 1920s, the 1970s and the contemporary moment – seemed to be aiming for class and simplicity, though its ghastly green carpet was more Travelodge Conference Room. A glass fronted bathroom gave us a helpful window onto the Macbeths' bickering, but was undermined by the fact that a fridge lived improbably next to a shower. More illogically, the continuance of domestic scenography was at odds with the splitting of the performance into titled parts, two of which were 'Kingdom' and 'Nation' – despite the fact that action was almost always located in the flat. A curtain was sometimes pulled across the set to attempt to 'neutralize' the space, but inconsistently – and, weirdly, not when the play moved to England, when it would have been most useful to relocate the action. Bińkowska's programme note tells us that the design was intended to move from the home towards a more 'abstract world' by the end of the play, signalled, for instance, by the bottom half of a tree lowered from the fly tower as Birnam Wood moved to Dunsinane. However, the dominance of the apartment's interior defied a non-representational logic of space, and meant that the performance came to crudely rely upon ill-judged spurts of bagpipes to tell us which side of the border we were on.

The use of multi-media technology was equally inconsistent. Influenced by contemporary theatre techniques, live filming was used frequently onstage, but never convincingly integrated into the performance grammar as a whole. At times, it seemed to allude to home video; at others, the interdependence of the public and private sphere; sometimes what was happening onstage seemed to be projected for no other reason than because it could be. Trying to interpret the significance of video thus proved more of a hindrance than a help to interpreting the production; it was only used truly effectively once, in order to materialize Banquo's ghost at the feast. Other contemporary techniques in evidence included miked sound, and the microphone made a memorable appearance when used by Malcolm (Hayley Konadu) to sing 'Yes sir, I can boogie' at the beginning of 4.3 – a welcome moment of theatricality in an otherwise dramatically inert scene.

The final nod to contemporary practice entailed the use of audience participation in the banquet scene. The production again revealed its origins in the Shakespeare North Playhouse (SNP) as it compelled audience members onto the stage, a device which perhaps worked better in the reduced distances between spectator and actor at the SNP than in the traditional proscenium arch theatre of the Bristol Old Vic. It was painful to watch the participants' stilted awkwardness and confusion about what they were meant to do. In fact, it's unclear whether Twyman was trying to harness their embarrassment as a comment upon Macbeth's public breakdown, or whether this was an unintended side effect.

Writing a poor review inevitably feels uncharitable because theatre productions take effort, time, money and collaborative, creative energy, and there *were* positive moments to be found, including Leo Wan's Porter, and a couple of eerie moments, such as the shadowy materialization of three silhouettes behind a shower curtain. However, it is arguably more important to candidly critique schools-facing Shakespeare at a moment when the values upheld by staging his works are under scrutiny: identifying good and bad practice can only help to build the resilience of the industry in both its pressured present and possible future. For a generation of young people encountering one of their GCSE texts in performance for possibly the first time, there is a greater chance of them being turned off rather than turned on to Shakespeare by this production. Shakespeare shouldn't be something that *has* to be done, a form of cultural spinach. We must instead embrace the alternative which Thompson proposes: performances of Shakespeare with clear purpose, which rigorously interrogate whether Shakespeare is something that we *should* be doing, which questions

whose stories are told, and whose – like the witches here – are left out.

NORTHERN SHAKESPEARE

MACBETH, DIR. AMY LEACH, LEEDS PLAYHOUSE, 12 MARCH 2024

One wonders whether Raymond Williams's theory of 'structure of feeling' can be detected in the glut of *Macbeth*s in the last few years. *Macbeth* is always popular, of course, but the preponderance of productions at the moment perhaps also point to 'a particular quality of social experience and relationship' articulated by the play, an exploration of 'meanings and values as they are actively lived and felt' which *Macbeth*, today, seems to express.[2]

In contrast to the noise of the ETT production was Amy Leach's pared-back revival at the Leeds Playhouse, which also targeted schools audiences (Figures 27 and 28). The production highlighted storytelling over concept, even adding extra bits of text to clarify what was happening – an opening section of exposition accompanied with thumping music and stylized battle scenes, and a fleshed-out inauguration, for example – as well as an added backstory about child loss for the Macbeths. Their marital relationship was underpinned by the kind of quiet understanding characteristic of long-term coupledom; the knocks that they had taken were emphasized in an attempt to provide a credible context for their actions. This worked in large part because of an authoritative performance by Ash Hunter in the title role, and an especially noteworthy one by Jessica Baglow as Lady Macbeth. Both actors delivered their parts with clarity and comprehension, but Baglow, in particular, shone as a women initially contented, but whose goals and outlook fatally changed following the witches' prophecy.

The witches were very 'witchy', dancing roundels, casting spells, moving strangely and wearing rags. While their performance was not especially weird, it had a simplicity, and the trio's omnipresence as servants in the Macbeth household underscored their manipulation of the action in a more sophisticated way. But, overall, simplicity was the keyword for Leach's production. Hayley Grindle's set design consisted of a single set: a forest-like floor of woodchip, stones, and puddles with a vast black ramp at

---

[2] Raymond Williams, *Marxism and Literature* (Oxford, 1977) pp. 131, 132.

27 The cast of *Macbeth* at Leeds Playhouse (© Kirsten McTernan).

28 Adam Bassett (Macduff) and Paul Brown (Lennox) (© Kirsten McTernan).

its centre, surrounded by lighting towers topped with searchlights, which served for trees when necessary. The front of the ramp was hoisted up to form an upper stage at points, which worked especially well during scenes of hospitality, meaning the Macbeths could plot and fret in privacy 'above' while Duncan and his entourage, and later the banquet guests, could convey conviviality through stylized movement below: the feasting and quaffing well realized by movement director, Georgina Lamb. Costume was situated as vaguely early modern, but the added text tended towards the contemporary, as did the bro-like behaviour and complicated handshakes of the soldiers.

The original text was streamlined in order to bring the whole production in at around 2 hours and 20 minutes, risking detailed engagement with the play's concerns at times – the dialogue between Malcom and Macduff was more or less excised, for example – but also sharpening its trajectory. Where the production did push boundaries was in its inclusive casting of Deaf actors, notably Shakespeare stalwart Charlotte Arrowsmith as Witch / Lady Macduff, and Adam Bassett as an excellent Macduff, whose frustrations at trying to find words for actions in the play – whether Duncan's slaying or his own family's massacre – were movingly communicated through BSL. Arrowsmith, too, found the visual poetry in sign language for her dual roles of hurt wife and spell-casting witch. As is often the case, the visuality of BSL proved an especially effective way of communicating Shakespearian text: given that some speeches were sometimes only half-translated into spoken language by characters, however, subtitles might have been used to make the production inclusive for all.

As it moved towards its climax, the production started to lose power, culminating in a fairly standard encounter between Macbeth and Macduff. The performance did slightly unravel the containment of its ending, having Fleance (Jayden Jhermaine / Candala Seidi Dias / Josh Ndlovu) return to the stage to herald the Stuart line with 'Long live the King!', undermining Banquo's assertion of the same line only seconds before and gesturing towards further strife to come. While the commitment towards straightforward storytelling made the performance a little pedestrian at times, the creative decisions made by Leach and the production team were entirely justifiable given its target audience, and the more experimental aspects around casting lent enough interest to ensure that it didn't become a painting-by-numbers *Macbeth*. Given the pressures on the arts which seem to be a feature of local council budgets this year, the Playhouse's decision to revive a successful and viable production of a KS3/KS4 text seemed entirely legitimate in the context.

TWELFTH NIGHT, DIR. JIMMY FAIRHURST, SHAKESPEARE NORTH PLAYHOUSE, 11 JUNE 2024

Not Too Tame's high-octane *Twelfth Night* was framed through the carnivalesque conceit of the 'music industry', the performance's holiday humour sustained by live music including a rousing rendition of the Rolling Stones' 'Gimme Shelter' by Viola (Georgia Frost) and Sebastian (Tom Sturgess) at the opening of the play, as well as a beautifully sung cover of Shakespears Sister's 'Stay' by Olivia (Purvi Parmar) in the first half. The set, designed by Good Teeth, was dotted with amps, flight cases, and festival fencing to further the industry theme, and included a scene in which a red velvet rope had to be unclipped between stanchions to get on- and offstage, an obstruction milked for comedy. Problems were produced, however, by the fact that it remained resolutely unclear whether this music industry milieu consisted of a tour, a gig venue, or a festival – as suggested by the wristbands that we were offered on the way into the theatre, as well as the gender-swapped role of Antonia (Kate James) as a St John's Ambulance paramedic, apparently hailing from a medical tent.

In this overlaid narrative, Antonia meets Sebastian following a drug-induced collapse, an event which causes his separation from Viola, but which also allows a romantic relationship to blossom between the medic and patient. Leaving aside the improbability and troubling ethics of this decision, there is a timing issue – a festival tent suggests a three-day event, rather than the three-month timeframe of the play (which 'MC' Feste (Louise Haggerty) herself acknowledged through the interpolated line, 'Tomorrow and tomorrow and . . . a few months later'). So perhaps the framing device invoked a tour rather than a festival, one in which the star power of diva-singer Olivia was matched by Orsino (Reuben Johnson) as a rapper who turned soliloquies into bars, his hip-hop persona convincingly expressing the fine line between charisma and narcissism of the character. However, the choice to make Olivia a popstar didn't quite square with her period of mourning and separation from society. Also, why did Orsino have such a beef with a paramedic, and why did he call her a 'notable pirate'? The framing device was thus stretched beyond utility – the retained plot of the shipwreck tussling with the interpretation, and jarring awkwardly with the imposed plots and timescales of the performance.

According to the programme, Malvolio (Les Dennis) was a 'tour manager', an identity which, if not entirely clear, helped to account for his out-of-placeness in terms of age and attitude from the rest of the cast. While Dennis didn't quite scale the heights of Malvolio's hubris, he absolutely plumbed the depths of his pathos, particularly during his discovery of 'Olivia's' letter, following the reading of which he simply, sweetly concluded 'I am happy' (2.5.176). Dennis brought an unexpected amount of anguish to the role, mining it for empathy when he sang an acapella version of 'Smile' in the darkness of prison, and cutting a pathetic figure, make-up running down his face, in the final scenes. The casting was therefore no celebrity gimmick – Dennis was utterly in control of the role's comedy during the performance, particularly the yellow stocking reveal conducted to the soundtrack of 'You Sexy Thing', but also its pity, and the audience clearly felt for Malvolio as the victim of a cruel joke that goes too far. His lack of understanding about how he has deserved such maltreatment, delivered memorably through the line 'Tell me why' (5.1.366), was heartbreakingly plaintive.

On their website and in the programme, Not Too Tame communicate their mission to democratize theatre and make it accessible, a feat partly achieved in *Twelfth Night* through the reappropriation of Shakespearian axioms – such as an added prologue which cued us to observe 'Two twins, both alike in revelry' – and through inclusive additions such as the 'golden brown which nature's own cunning hand laid on' Parmar's face. However, too often 'accessibility' meant adding swear words. Calling Sir Andrew Aguecheek (Reuben Johnson again) a 'very fool and a massive bellend' was innocuous enough, but the implications of Olivia's Cs, Us and Ts were unnecessarily spelled out in 2.5. The most egregious example was the immediate undercutting of the reconciliation of Viola and Sebastian when the latter exclaimed, 'What the fuck is going on?' The audience laughed – as they often do when they perceive the 'high' culture of Shakespeare to be pricked – but all emotional depth, all consideration of grief, loss and rebirth, was instantly whipped away from the scene. My concern doesn't emerge from stuffiness but from a propensity of 'accessible' productions to seek cheap laughs, and to patronize their audiences in the process, forgoing lyricism, allusion and poetry in the service of 'relatability'. In the case of this performance, it meant that the more beautiful passages of dramatic verse – such as Antonia's soliloquy, 'My desire / More sharp than filèd steel'

(3.3.4–5) – were rushed through. It also manifested in a flattening of characterization: Frost gave an intelligent and sparky performance as Viola and Parmar a lively one as Olivia, but both lacked the vulnerability of nuanced portrayals of the roles, and I suspect this was a consequence of direction rather than ability.

This was an energetic and agile production nonetheless, one in which MC Feste took on a much more central role as chief of revelry, and whose success was hugely contingent on the comic double act of toffs, a feckless Sir Toby Belch (Jack Brown) in an array of festival garb, and a remarkably stupid Andrew Aguecheek, whose daft interventions frequently produced the funniest moments of the evening. Fairhurst directed the play skilfully in the round, the stage configuration mirroring its desired communality, and – barring the swearing – additions to the text seemed less anxious about appealing to working-class audiences than last year's *Midsummer Night's Dream*, emerging more organically from a developing 'house style' and the flamboyant playworld than from a contrived desire to appeal to 'locals'. However, as with the production of *A Midsummer Night's Dream*, there was a similar overabundance of ideas, and a tendency to gallop through the play rather than to seek out its light and dark.

Audience participation remained a crucial feature of Not Too Tame's approach, and the audience who joined in were game. The line between 'us' and 'them' was more generally blurred through direct address as well as the use of vom exits and entrances. Overall, the audience were completely engaged by this accomplished and versatile *Twelfth Night*, which demonstrated a strengthening of the signature style of both the company and the playhouse.

TOURING SHAKESPEARE

ROMEO AND JULIET, NORTHERN BALLET, SHEFFIELD LYCEUM THEATRE, 4 APRIL 2024

Also originating in the North, but touring nationally, was Northern Ballet's revival of Christopher Gable's and Massimo Moricone's 1991 ballet, *Romeo and Juliet*, including the painstaking remaking of costumes and sets destroyed by floods in 2015. Against the somewhat depressing background of cuts to live orchestras considered in the introduction, this adaptation of *Romeo and Juliet* served as a beacon of what performance can do, illuminated by stunning principal performances from Joseph Taylor and Dominique Larose (Figure 29). It concentrated on the central romance of the couple, or rather the love triangle involving Romeo, Juliet and Paris (Jackson Dwyer) – and its revelations about the dynamics of that triangle were traced through a series of repeating *pas de deux*. When we first saw Juliet meeting Paris, she took his hand and danced in glassy-eyed fashion, a ballerina in a music box, pretty and empty. She was thrilled to be touched by a suitor nonetheless, and beamed as he elevated her – a new bodily experience – yet she also continually checked in with her familial audience for confirmation that she was performing 'being wooed' correctly.

Everything changed after her metamorphic encounter with Romeo. At first sight, she was unable to stop staring, her studied postures replaced with yearning lines as they began to move together. Following their meeting at the ball, it was as if Juliet began to feel her body in a wholly new way – waves of butterflies rose up from her stomach to engulf her upper body, convulsing her torso forward with pleasure, or curling her backwards over the balcony. Juliet touched her bare shoulders and neck as if they were brand new. At the same time the homosociality between Romeo, Mercutio (Aaron Kwok) and Benvolio (Filippo Di Vilio) was also irrevocably changed. The masculine bonds that had been symbolized through movement that cannoned across the trio, or with arms slung laddily around each other's shoulders, disappeared. Following the balcony scene, the boys' corporeal synchronicity was disrupted, and Mercutio found himself unable to entice a distracted, lovelorn Romeo back to the crew.

The choreography of Romeo and Juliet's *pas de deux* involved stretched and extended limbs, the couple undulating together and hanging from each other, their movement increasingly erotic and less prettified as the relationship became more sexual. In Juliet's bedroom they overlaid and melted into each other, grabbing the other's hand to rub against their mouth and over their scalp in post-coital intimacy. This focus on hands would pay dividends when Juliet's was placed again into Paris's by Lord Capulet (Jonathan Hanks). Juliet's abject horror that a part of her body that had touched Romeo should be violated through contact with another man precipitated an emotional outburst, invoking the fury of her father, and leading her to re-accept Paris's hand in marriage under threat of a thrashing. Paris and Juliet's initial *pas de deux* was revisited, but was now emptied out, Larose lethargically pulling her body through the

29 Dominique Larose and Joseph Taylor in *Romeo and Juliet* (© Emily Nuttall).

motions of romance, devoid of feeling, desultory and shattered, Paris increasingly hurt and befuddled by her disgust.

Romeo and Juliet's *pas de deux* was also restaged in the tomb, as Romeo heartbreakingly tried to revive the lifeless body of Juliet through repeating their dance of love, hauling her into their former lifts, devastated as he brought her limp hand to his mouth. The repeated performance of *pas de deux* thus inventively served as a barometer of emotion in the production. Using bodies rather than words to measure these changes was an effective and refreshing way of engaging with the play, helped by a taut adaptation of narrative and unambiguous choreography. The ballet's focus on the romantic dynamics meant that a number of other characters were minimized, including (at no great loss) Friar Laurence (George Liang). The roles of Mercutio and Tybalt were also pared back, but were nevertheless brilliantly danced by Kwok and Harry Skoupas. Mercutio was a cheeky, impish rogue, capable of intricate footwork and impossibly high jumps, provocatively blowing kisses at Tybalt as he was thrown out of the Capulet's ball. While there were edits, aspects of story were also added to complicate the relationships: Lady Capulet (Amber Lewis) was having an affair with Tybalt, and was left bereft and in despair by his death. Her identification of Romeo as his murderer triggered a lightning strike before a sheet of rain poured down onto the stage in a sensational *coup de théâtre* before the second interval.

The ballet played out on Lez Brotherston's reconstructed set of stone plinths, invoking ancient Rome as much as Renaissance Verona, with a palette connecting evil to darker colours and virginity and goodness to whiteness, somewhat binarily. Gable and Moricone introduced a clear class dimension to the narrative: the Capulets were marked out as the cold and oppressive villains – elite, wealthy, draped in elaborate Renaissance garbs of reds, golds and black, made of luxurious velvets and furs alongside leather and studs. During the Dance of the Knights some wore skull masks, mobile *memento mori*, and their bolshy dancing was characterized by grand, statuesque poses and staccato choreography (Figure 30). Staffs were used to control movement – and women, with the violent masculinity which undergirded the family epitomized by Skoupas's grand and arrogant Tybalt. The Montagues were lighter – in both clothing and movement – dressed as gypsies during the Veronese Carnival which served as the general conceit for the action. Their family insignia of an eagle was waved on poles with fluttering ribbons; their association

with flight manifested in choreographic fluidity. The stakes of the conflict between the families were high and weapons appeared casually and often: the Duke's opening injunction against further fighting was issued after their brawling had caused a child's death, while the fight that would end the lives of Mercutio and Tybalt occurred after the latter had sexually and physically assaulted one of the Montague women.

Problematically, in order to adhere to a scheme in which the Capulets were 'baddies' and the Montagues 'goodies', the sexual assault of the Nurse (Heather Lehan) was passed off as simply light-hearted banter in contrast to the 'proper' assault conducted against the Montague woman. As a result, the public humiliation of the aged body of the Nurse – who was also presented as fat because of a bustle which padded her posterior – was seen to somehow matter less than the younger, slimmer woman's, and played into an overall conception of the femininity of the mature, overweight Nurse as an object of humour and ridicule. A rigid sense of right and wrong was thus allied to 'good' or 'bad' versions of femininity to either exacerbate or excuse gender-based violence. In a way, these differentiations were a consequence of the homogeneity of balletic bodies – uniformly youthful and light in this company's case – and the resulting necessity of producing alterity through costume, wigs and make-up. However, this risked caricature and, given the growing recognition of the body-shaming that took place in dance schools from at least the 1990s, revivals of ballets from that time might pay closer attention to how the choreography and designs of the past contribute to a world in which some bodies are viewed as valuable, and others are not.[3] While it was a remarkable feat to reconstruct the production of 1991, perhaps the Northern Ballet should also have reimagined some conceptual elements of that work for a more progressive era.

This criticism does not detract from the utterly compelling and frequently mesmerizing vision of the play. The adaptation creatively telescoped Shakespeare's *Romeo and Juliet*, propelling us through a concentrated version of the story told through superb dancing and skilful choreography, buoyed throughout by Prokofiev's dramatic score. The tragedy of the final scene was particularly heightened because of the form: the lack of words made the final sequence of deaths appear even more impetuous and

---

[3] In 2023, a BBC *Panorama* documentary explored 'The dark side of ballet schools', finding widespread evidence of bullying and body-shaming taking place in such institutions.

30 Northern Ballet dancers in the Capulet Ball (© Emily Nuttall).

pointless. A final embrace between Montague and Capulet signalled rapprochement, but could not balance out the waste of youth and hope and strength that plagued the stage.

PLAYER KINGS, DIR. ROBERT ICKE, MANCHESTER OPERA HOUSE, 19 MARCH 2024

Player Kings was a sure contender for Shakespearian 'event theatre' of 2024, not least because of the casting of Sir Ian McKellen as Falstaff under the direction of zeitgeisty Robert Icke. It is a huge shame that so many audiences who booked tickets for the national tour therefore missed out on McKellen's Falstaff, who was a clear highlight of the production (Figure 31). A quick google at the time of writing produces tabloid reports that he was last seen partying the night away, however – so hopefully he has made a good recovery since his fall from the Noel Coward Theatre stage in June.[4]

When Sir Ian kindly invited University of Bristol students to a preview of his one-man show at the Bristol Old Vic in 2019, he made it clear that Falstaff was the one Shakespearian part that he didn't 'get' and had no desire to play – yet there was no trace of such reluctance in a performance which seemed to relish and revel in the role. Making the most of the character's delight in chiasmus and absurdity, McKellen was a very funny Falstaff who rinsed the comic potential of his lines, but he was also a thoughtful one, especially in *Part Two*, in which his elderliness proved indivisible from Sir John's reflections upon ageing and the inevitability of death. McKellen's ability to inhabit both registers was key to the complexity of a performance in which there were many high points, such as his Captain Tom-like appearance as the returning war hero at a 'Falstaff's Back' event, during which he used his wheelchair to steal the wine. McKellen's Falstaff was absolutely a 'trunk of humours', sniffing and wheezing and blowing his nose throughout a very phlegmy performance. In terms of actorly craft, it was wonderful to see skills borne of decades of experience in action: for those of us sitting way up in the gods of Manchester's Opera House, Sir Ian's ability to include us during direct address sequences was remarkable.

---

4 https://instinctmagazine.com/adorable-sir-ian-mckellen-85-parties-at-gay-club; www.dailymail.co.uk/tvshowbiz/article-13957845/Ian-McKellen-gay-club-night-shaking-stage-injury.html.

31 Ian McKellen as Falstaff in *Player Kings* (© Manuel Harlan).

At the same time, Icke's production was a feat of endurance for actor and audience alike, combining *Henry IV, Part One* and *Part Two* over 3 hours and 40 minutes. At points, in this early part of the run, it felt too long – there were drops in energy and moments of patchy direction which affected the pacing, especially in the second half. At others, the bringing together of the two plays allowed for points of connection and refraction that were conceptually rich, particularly with regard to representations of masculinity, ageing and – as the title suggests – the rightful basis of rule. Icke's vision for the play was modern: Mistress Quickly (Clare Perkins) exhibited tinges of the 1980s, but otherwise the costume was millennial, showing the clear influence of British gangster films in the Eastcheap scenes. The production contemporized the arenas for the plays' depictions of politics, warfare, monarchy, city and country, and Hildegard Bechtler's set design initially seemed spare, the stage encompassed by bare brick walls. However, it was frequently and inventively transformed through an ingenious use of curtains that both concealed and revealed, enabling complex set changes to take place while action happened elsewhere on the stage. At one

point, the erection of an entire brick wall which subdivided the stage and served as a backdrop for 'a road outside Coventry' seemed to happen in a matter of seconds, verging on the magical. The multiple locations of the plays were stylishly facilitated by the design – such as a 'split screen' stage for a conference-call encounter between Henry IV and Hotspur in 1.3 of *Part One* – as well as some stunning set reveals, notably the detailed scenography of The Boar's Head with its pool tables, crates, chairs, tables, bottles and pub clutter, which always seemed to be assembled in an unfeasibly short amount of time.

The Boar's Head itself was a febrile environment, characterised by drinking, partying, fighting, fornicating, kinkiness and knife violence. The Eastcheap fellows were defiantly criminals rather than high-spirited youths, their world sustained by lawbreaking and aggression (Figure 32). Blackouts lifted to expose snatches of vicious action during the robbery at Gad's Hill, for instance, such as one of its victims lying face down in a pool of his own blood. The word 'lads' took on new resonances in this context – throwing us back to the glamorization of gangster culture in masculine discourse of the 1990s – and the delinquency

32 Eastcheap gang at Gad's Hill (© Manuel Harlan).

was sometimes underscored, and arguably romanticized, by a jazzy soundtrack. Yet there was also a real warmth and community to this world, which contrasted with the stark and lonely existence of Henry IV (Richard Coyle), frequently depicted alone onstage except for when conducting business with Warwick (Annette McLaughlin) and Sir Walter Blunt (Hywel Morgan), both of whom were imagined as modern politicians advising the King of the next crisis in need of resolution.

As the title *Player Kings* suggests, the production examined the theatricality of kingship, whether through Falstaff and Hal (Toheeb Jimoh) role-playing father and son at the Boar's Head in 2.4 of *Part One*; the contrapuntal representations of feckless Hal and warlike Hotspur (a compelling Samuel Edward-Cook); the proliferation of Kings on the battlefield of Shrewsbury; or the Lord Chief Justice (Joseph Mydell) representing 'the person' of Hal's father in *Part Two* (5.2.74). This last moment directly recalls Douglas's dismay at the counterfeiting of kingship on the Shrewsbury battlefield, of course (5.4.28), highlighting the echoes that make the staging of both parts of *Henry IV* such a worthwhile endeavour. Kingship, in both the texts and *Player Kings*, is represented as a series of substitutions, its assumption either unwelcome or vexed, with the authenticity of masculinity always under interrogation. In a particularly stark theatrical invocation of these concerns, lighting was used to cast vast shadows of Prince Hal against the brick walls when he 'usurped' the crown of his dying father in *Part Two*: 'the shadow of succession' materialized (3.2.102). However, Hal's continued disavowal of hereditary destiny is punished by a father who uses his last vestiges of strength to wrestle his wayward son onto his deathbed while rebuking him for 'mock-[ing] at form' (4.3.272). Henry IV's own reign was repeatedly haunted by illegitimacy, and the stage appearance of Richard II at the beginning and end of *Part One* emphasized this by identifying his monarchical role as a performative act based on a murder for which he could never fully atone, redemption for which was as out of reach as his proposed pilgrimage to Jerusalem.

Interpolations from other history plays thus helped to situate and contextualize the adaptation, working well in this instance to underscore the idea of men playing at being monarchs, whether the 'skipping' kingship of Richard or the usurped bloodline of

Henry. Sections from early scenes of *Henry V* were also inserted at the end of the production, pointing us forwards towards Falstaff's death, Hal's reform, and the wars in France – though this felt like rather too neat a conclusion. If the performance had ended immediately after the banishment of Falstaff, Hal would have been shown fatherless and alone, as his own father had been, facing a similarly uncertain future in a monarchical role which separates men from community and denies them affection and comfort.

Not that the relationship between Hal and Falstaff wasn't troubled in this production; in fact, it was shown to be at the point of dissolution from the outset of the performance, Hal spitting out fatphobic insults at a father-figure who seemed to actively disgust him (Figure 33). His antipathy was focused in the foreshadowing of his rejection of Falstaff in 2.4 of *Part One*, with Jimoh squarely landing his intention to banish Falstaff, 'I do, I will' (2.4.298), squarely at 'plump Jack'. Hal was thus shown to be rebelling against two fathers in the play. However, the depth of his feeling for Falstaff was also revealed when he believed that the knight had been killed at Shrewsbury, and his final rejection was an emotional one – Hal/Henry wiping away tears as he claimed to not know the old man. Jimoh and McKellen thus traced a complex and nuanced bond – each hurting the other through lies and betrayal during the course of the performance.

Jimoh was often found at the margins of the stage or on the apron, rehearsing his separation from others that would be an inevitable consequence of kingship. However, sovereign disconnection was examined within a wider consideration of existential loneliness. The explosions and falling rubble of an ambitiously staged Shrewsbury were accompanied by subtitles that relayed a contemporaneous account of the battle, including a report that the royal army fell like 'apples . . . in the autumn'. The idea was picked up again in the scenes between Falstaff, Silence and Shallow (James Garnon and Robin Soans) in *Part Two*, over which an apple tree ominously dropped her fruit, a harbinger of the trio's own autumnal existences and impending mortality as they drew together against their imminent winters. The set thus alluded to the exploration of longevity and transience, genealogy and memory, and family and friendship in the old men's conversation. Unfortunately, the somewhat plodding performances of these scenes did not match Bechtler's shrewd design, and the production – as well as the characters – lost vitality in its third age. Icke's yoking of *Part One* and *Part Two* ultimately ran into the familiar trouble that the second play is a very different beast from the first: messier, stranger and more philosophical.

33 Ian McKellen and Toheeb Jimoh as Falstaff and Hal
(© Manuel Harlan).

Whatever magic Orson Welles performed in *Chimes at Midnight* was missing in this stage version, in which the numerous benefits of bringing the plays together for their conceptual similarities were undermined by their dramaturgical and affective differences.

ROYAL SHAKESPEARE COMPANY SHAKESPEARE

THE MERRY WIVES OF WINDSOR, DIR. BLANCHE MCINTYRE, ROYAL SHAKESPEARE THEATRE, 21 JUNE 2024

The Merry Wives of Windsor is a peculiar outlier in the Shakespearian canon, arguably the most 'seventeenth-century' and citizen comedy-like of his plays, yet also written in the very last years of the sixteenth. Without wading into the weeds of its problematic dating – Liz Schafer suggests *c.*1598–1599 – there is something very strange about the timeline of the play in terms of dramaturgical allusion and its trenchant intertextuality. It sits, theoretically, between *Henry IV, Part One* and *Part Two*, referring to these earlier plays in its resurrection of Falstaff alongside Pistol, Bardolph, Nym and Shallow. Its joke structure and reliance on national stereotypes also align with these plays, as well as others of the tetralogies, most notably *Henry V*. But then the faery masque with which it culminates seems to be a revenant of *A Midsummer Night's Dream*, and both *Dream* and *The Merchant of Venice* reverberate through its depictions of controlling fathers and marital choice in the figures of Master Page, his daughter Ann, and her multiple, unworthy suitors. Ann's elopement against her parents' choice, and Master Page's complaint that Fenton, Roderigo-like, 'haunt[s] my house' (3.4.71), also point us forwards to Brabantio and Desdemona in *Othello*, as does the play's central concern with Master Ford's suspicion of his wife, which invokes a host of later plays concerned with jealousy, including *Much Ado* and *The Winter's Tale*. Then Falstaff's punishments at the very climax of the play – involving pinching and oak trees – swerve us towards Caliban and Ariel's tortures in *The Tempest*, which Shakespeare presumably was over ten years away from writing, while Falstaff hiding behind the arras anticipates Polonius. In many ways, the play feels like a revue or satirical sort of Shakespeare 'greatest hits', which is impossible given the career point at which it was written.

The play's most persuasive intertext is *Othello*, with line-for-line connections between the plays almost registering a call-and-response relationship between them. Evans tells Ford, for instance, that he thinks 'your wife is honest' while Othello 'think[s] my wife be honest, and I think she is not', in the same acts and scenes from their respective texts (3.3.216; 3.3.439). A similarly striking parallel between the plays occurs when Master Ford, disguised as Brook, rails against female duplicity in an Othello-like rage, and Mistress Ford, expresses a wish that 'heaven make you better than your thoughts' (3.3.201), an almost direct retort to Othello's demand to Iago, 'By heaven, I'll know thy thoughts' (3.3.191). Men's thoughts about women therefore dominate both texts, but, in *Merry Wives*, it is as if Mistresses Ford and Page get their own back on the men who aim to control their minds, or erase their bodies.

Despite the elements of feminine empowerment in *Merry Wives*, there are deep threads of sexism and coercive control running through it, most notably in Ford's disguising as Brook in order to catch out his wife. Played twitchily by Richard Goulding, it proved

difficult to forgive him for the emotional violence directed against his wife, even if she could. The forces of misogyny swirled around the town of Windsor until they were channelled through the Witch of Brentford, a figure who reveals much about male attitudes to women in the play. Only spoken about, but never seen, the scale of deviance which snowballed her from 'the fat woman of Brentford' to 'the old woman of Brentford' to the 'witch of Brentford' was surprising in both its speed and hatred (4.2.75, 84, 97). Tellingly, Simple (Jessica Alade) calls her the 'wise woman of Brentford' (4.5.25) shortly after her supposed beating – a synonym for a witch, but one which exposes that her offence might actually be one of knowledge. Simple's descriptions enable us to interpret her as a woman who does not express her cunning 'merrily' enough – her continual body- and age-shaming making it clear that she sits outside of feminine ideals.

Blanche McIntyre's production for the RSC expressed these concerns through reimagining the play as a 1980s sitcom, with all of the sexism and xenophobia that the genre involves. Robert Innes Hopkins's hilariously bourgeois-kitsch set design was characterized by mock Tudor housing and Yale alarm boxes, trim hedgerows and prim lawns with 'please do not let your dog foul on the grass' signs. Housefronts niftily became pubs or domestic interiors courtesy of a central revolve, and symbols of late modernity were in abundance, from bunting to plastic pigeons atop TV ariels. It was a canny and generative setting for the play, helping to manifest its quaintly local comedy in a town which felt more like an English village than a town, with a well-defined social hierarchy and inability to integrate 'outsiders'. McIntyre fruitfully used the immediate context of the 2024 Euros to think through cultural differences at both national and European levels, and yet these hierarchies were very broad in their conception: the lower order consisted of a beer-swilling, drug-taking, petty criminal working class in sportswear, countered by an upper-middle class of yummy mummies and Barber-jacketed, flat-capped, chino-wearing gents. The social mapping was therefore problematic in terms of generalization, but did work in the sense of reproducing the text's reliance on recognizable archetypes, and played well to the typically white and middle-class RSC audience.

The world of Windsor felt full, and this was helped by a lively supporting cast of 'working-class' characters including David Partridge, Omar Bynon and Yasemin Özdemir as Bardolph, Pistol and Nym. Dr Caius (Jason Thorpe) was imagined as a dentist and drew heavily from Officer Crabtree in *'Allo 'Allo* – 'ears' misprounounced 'arse', and 'third' as 'turd'– while Hugh Evans (Ian Hughes) reincarnated elements of *Henry V*'s Fluellen: both appealed to the audience's apparent desire to laugh at 'funny' accents. In terms of the play's sexism, the bored housewife typology helped to resituate the control of early modern women within the constraints of late twentieth-century suburban femininity. Mistresses Ford and Page (Siubhan Harrison and Samantha Spiro: Figure 34) were incredibly well turned out in pastels and florals – 'fragrant' women to use

Justice Caulfield's term for Mary Archer – but shrewdly able to manipulate their limited options, using their objectification under the male gaze to tame and shame grandees of the Windsor patriarchy. Ultimately, the imbalance that they restored was heteronormativity, but their craftiness during this rebalancing found some space for feminine agency within rigid strictures. According to this revenge comedy, it is men whose name is 'frailty', not, as Hamlet would have it, women (3.5.50).

The concept of 'hosting' itself emerged strongly in the production, as did spaces of hospitality: there is The

34 Siubhan Harrison and Samantha Spiro in *Merry Wives of Windsor* (© Manuel Harlan).

Garter of course, but Falstaff (John Hodgkinson) was also appointed at various times to be hosted in Mistress Ford's house, and, he hoped, her bedroom, whose sexual possibilities were always rather coy, their 'fnar fnar' nature befitting the sitcom context. There was also a failure of hosting in the expulsion of the Old Woman of Brentford when Ford beat her from his tidy living room in order to cleanse the household. Her crime is explicitly one against gender – 'I like it not when a woman has a great beard', Evans says (4.2.192), though in fact the clothing which Falstaff appropriated was a pink dress and netted hat, suitably feminine, albeit criminally 'large' compared to the small and neat Windsor wives. 'Her' public humiliation exposed how compulsory heterosexuality entails the banishment of non-reproductive elements from early modern comedy, helping to explain why the body-shaming of older characters in the play is so depressingly constant. For all of the fun and empowering potential of Mistresses Ford and Page, it is difficult to recuperate *Merry Wives*: this is a conservative text whose various revenge plots are predicated on the creation of communities – local, national, age-based and gendered – which rely upon the identification and casting out of others. The Host of the Garter (Emily Houghton), for instance, orchestrates dissension between the Welsh and French characters – manufacturing a duel between them – only to smooth over the argument and facilitate their reconciliation in a show of political strength. But community is always premised on scapegoating.

If that all sounds a bit serious, McIntyre's production certainly wasn't. Spiro and Harrison were fizzing balls of farcical fun in their gulling of Falstaff (Figure 35); Patrick Walshe McBride was an excellent Slender in the mode of Mr Bean; and Hodgkinson as Falstaff, oscillating between oily used-car salesman and local big-wig, fully inhabited the role of town lech. The audience audibly groaned when he told Mistress Ford that she 'deservest' his round belly, but Hodgkinson was also able to produce a certain amount of pity for the shamed knight, reacting boyishly to being told that he has 'charm', and later telling us, sadly, 'I am dejected', and 'I am made an ass' (5.5.169, 126). In his failure to win over the wives, Falstaff as 'an old, fat fellow' (4.4.16) is elided with the old, fat witch – cruelly ejected from Windsor society, though of course only pinched rather than half beaten to death like the Brentford woman (4.2.163–4). By the end of the play, and via its various plots, the Windsor residents banish 'sluts and sluttery' (5.5.50) from their borders, restoring non-violent heteropatriarchy – for the time being. Even Falstaff is ultimately recuperated,

35 Siubhan Harrison and John Hodgkinson in *Merry Wives of Windsor* (© Manuel Harlan).

invited by Page to eat a posset and 'laugh at my wife' (5.5.180). However, the line reveals that women have managed to merrily reinstate an order which subjugates them, the 'at' situating them as possible objects rather than equals. It is only the strange figure of Dr Caius's servant, Rugby (David Mara), that the play, and this production, cannot quite find a space for, continually traversing the village green of Windsor but never really finding a home within it, neither claimed by the town nor outcast from it, a social phantom.

McIntyre's *Merry Wives* performed the play with a decided emphasis on levity. As a result some of the darker echoes of the play – the way in which 'Brook' offers Falstaff money for sexual access to Mistress Ford (foreshadowing the interactions of Roderigo and Iago), and later, more sinisterly, Mistress Quickly's report that Ford has beaten his wife 'black and blue, that you cannot see a white spot about her' (4.5.92–4) – were incorporated and subordinated to the comedy. This enabled the performance to revel in the plays' explorations of female friendship and the love between women – and the triumph of the wives goes some way to correct the violence directed towards them in both the play and its intertexts. Unlike Kate in *The Taming of the Shrew*, it is men who are tamed here, Falstaff and also Ford, who concludes, in a direct reference to *Shrew* that 'I rather will suspect the sun with cold than thee with wantonness' (4.4.8). But it's a delicate balance. While Ford's contrition partially redresses Petruchio's gaslighting when he makes Kate claim the exact opposite in *Shrew*, *Merry Wives*' very intertextuality continually raises the spectre of what can and does happen when women don't conform, or when they aren't sufficiently merry about needing to.

A MIDSUMMER NIGHT'S DREAM, DIR. ELEANOR RHODE, ROYAL SHAKESPEARE THEATRE, 8 MARCH 2024

The Royal Shakespeare Company's (RSC's) *A Midsummer Night's Dream*, Eleanor Rhode's second outing as RSC director, centred its interpretation of the play on the disturbed boundaries between reality, sleep, dreams and theatrical fantasy. Magic was key to Rhode's vision, whether sleight-of-hand work with small lights or higher-tech projections and Augmented Reality (AR) under the direction of Illusion Designer, John Bulleid. In terms of set design, Lucy Osborne suspended paper orbs of varying sizes from the roof, which seemed to signify both clouds and planets, but were also lit colourfully to become the fairies of the woods. Indeed, a monochrome Athens was contrasted with the technicolour forest, and the design made reference to the last decades of the twentieth century through costumes which ranged from the 1960s to the 1980s, as well as an opening video sequence which featured the test card. The palette of the playworld changed in a *Wizard of Oz*-like way following the lovers' experiences in the woods, contrasting their colourful freedom with black-and-white austerity.

In many ways, this accessible production was a vehicle for Matthew Baynton's mod-styled Bottom, the actor bringing his wide-eyed guilelessness to the role in a typically appealing way. However, Rosie Sheehy was also outstanding as a strange, original and grotesque Puck (Figure 36). Her muscular, athletic Robin Goodfellow grimaced and gurned at us, exhibiting an oddly protruding tongue and twisted hands.

36 Rosie Sheehy as Puck in *A Midsummer Night's Dream* (© Pamela Raith).

Beyond gender, Puck's costume combined Heath Ledger's Joker with the Artful Dodger, their gait and movement both heavy and light, their diction over-enunciated and in tension with unkempt blue locks and messy make-up. Sheehy's Puck trod a fine line between entertaining us and utter disdain – her virtuosic dance as she chased the lovers through the woods was always on the verge of both magnificence and loss of control, but the choreography ended abruptly when the music stopped, and she turned to curl her lip at us. Another highlight came in the form of Premi Tamang's show-stopping performance as a terrifying moon. Despite all of the concern about the lion scaring the ladies, nobody predicted Starveling's horrifying embodiment of a Ring-like Moonshine. Face and body contorted, flashlight flicking on and off below her chin, Tamang cast genuine darkness rather than sunny beams over *Pyramus and Thisbe*.

This was an amusing and imaginative *Dream* which zipped along and was played entirely for laughs, much like McIntyre's *Merry Wives*. However, this was also its weakness. Bucking the trend of many recent productions, the troubling sexual politics of the play were glossed over, and the various instances of gender-based violence in the play wholly subsumed into the comedy. A mainly neutered Hippolyta (Sirine Saba) was shown to shrug off her coercion into marriage, mouthing 'well' and shrugging in response to a hapless and harmless Theseus's (Baly Gill) talk of wooing her with his sword and 'doing thee injuries' (1.1.17–18). She was watchful of proceedings and indicated that her mind was blown by the argument between Egeus (Neil McCaul), Hermia (Dawn Sievewright) and the Duke in 1.1, but didn't do anything to comment on the sentence of death or immurement passed upon Hermia, instead mutely following her husband-to-be off the stage. The first scene was thus wrung for comedy, establishing a general tone of heightened exuberance which would be the hallmark of the production, alongside its deliberate disavowal of the play's darker themes.

While there is often not the leeway within the text itself for female characters to comment on the problematic gender representations of early modern drama, theatre-makers usually take the opportunity of performance to introduce action, or to reassign dialogue, that affords Shakespeare's women more agency and control. In productions of *Dream*, this often takes the form of marginalized characters responding to the violent norms which underlie its heteropatriarchy. Such comment was not only absent in Athens, but also in the woods, in which Oberon's drugging and humiliation of Titania (Figure 37) was instantly accepted by the faery queen upon waking, while his abduction of the Indian Boy remained uninterrogated through either colonial or pederastic frameworks. Indeed, the fact that the Boy was not staged at all exacerbated the silencing of his trafficking, reducing him to a mere plot device. Meanwhile, Demetrius's warning that he will do Helena 'mischief in the wood' (2.1.244) was doubly minimized – in delivery as well as in the fact that the pair nearly kissed at one point of the argument, a reading of their relationship which is difficult to sustain given his contemptuous treatment and threatening of her.

Not every production of Shakespeare has to take on every ethically dubious element, and this populist *Dream* played well to the audience, with its preponderance of Pythonesque silly walks and nods to national treasures such as Rick Mayall in Ryan Hutton's Lysander. However, to deliberately disengage with the known shadows of the play in favour of such a light

37 Matthew Baynton as Bottom and Sirine Saba as Titania
(© Pamela Raith).

interpretation led to a production which lacked contrast, downbeats or pauses to temper the dialogue, resulting in some scenes, such as the lovers' four-way argument in 3.2, that became wearying sequences of comic overtopping that swelled to near-hysteria. While the broadsheets adored this fun and frivolous, politics-free iteration of the play and the audience appeared to be thoroughly entertained, I suspect that in the longer-term production history of the play this version (which transferred to the Barbican in winter 2024) will also have the fading impermanence of a dream.

PERICLES, DIR. TAMARA HARVEY, SWAN THEATRE, 2 SEPTEMBER 2024

More magic was in evidence in Tamara Harvey's sweet and wondrous *Pericles*, most especially in the reunion between father and daughter (Alfred Enoch and Rachelle Diedericks) at its climax. Another peripheral work, *Pericles* has not been staged in Stratford for eighteen years; the fact that it was programmed in their opening season perhaps indicates a welcome commitment from the new Artistic Directors to showcase lesser-known as well as oft-staged works. Shakespeare's *c*.1607–1608 collaboration with George Wilkins certainly throws down a number of theatrical gauntlets due to its uneven text, sheer number of characters, the longue durée of its narrative action and, perhaps chiefly, its diffuse geography. Harvey's response to this last problem was a set consisting mainly of ropes that gestured simultaneously to both maritime and theatrical rigging, as well as a neutral, terracotta-toned North African or Levantine backdrop, whose scenography was studded with rich hues and gem-coloured costumes to represent the locational shifts between Tyre, Antioch, Tarsus, Pentapolis, Ephesus and Mytilene. The design enabled an underlying motif of the play to emerge in terms of its concern with base materials such as 'metals, stones' (3.2.40), alongside multiple references to diamonds and jewels, and its placemaking solution was theatrically deft, though sometimes led to a blurring rather than clarification of setting.

The production utilized an ensemble playing style in which a limited number of actors took on many roles, with some cast members rising admirably to the challenge, including Jacqueline Boatswain as Cerimon and Bawd, and Sam Parks who was covering the role of Simonides, in addition to Escanes, Leonine and Fisherman, on the night that I saw it. The multi-roling produced some resonant comparisons, as when Chyna-Rose Frederick doubled as Lychorida – Marina's midwife – as well as the daughter who is incestuously defiled by Antiochus (Felix Hayes): a tragic pairing of child care and abuse. The ensemble's slowed-down movement sequences had the choric effect of setting scenes, and the cast ingeniously created events such as tempests and shipwrecks through choreography. However, the communal storytelling approach also led to some roles being sketched rather broadly, proving most problematic when lower-class characters were voiced with either cockney or country bumpkin accents. More care might

also have been taken over the presentation of Myteline's sex workers as grotesque, especially given that they were as likely to have been trafficked as Marina.

The effect of the whole was therefore sometimes stronger than individual contributions; however, the sheer commitment across the cast to knit together the play's patchiness was clear. The production did not make the usual cuts to acts 1 and 2, and so Pericles's (dis)connection with Tyre, and the relationship between Pericles and Helicanus (Philip Bird), could be more fully examined. Changes were made to the text insofar as Gower's function was reascribed to Marina, a dramaturgical decision which helped to resituate the play as more of a family drama and personal history, and undoubtedly fuelled the emotional weight of the eventual reunion with her father.

Another key difficulty of *Pericles* centres on the casting of the same actor over decades of plot, which Enoch handled well by freezing himself into a sort of catatonic, post-traumatic timescape after the loss of his wife and daughter, wandering the stage in shock and silence. Leah Haile, though ideal as his radiant young bride in a relationship marked by a gentle and romantic sensuality, lacked the age and emotional maturity to reconnect with her daughter in the same powerful way as Enoch. Nevertheless, the reunion between Pericles and Marina really was the focal point of Harvey's production, father and daughter moving infinitesimally closer together until the moment that any grief-stricken person longs for – the ability to touch their lost loved one again. So tender and full of marvel was the meeting of their hands, that it made me appreciate all over again what makes theatre the superlative artform: the fact that – unlike any other medium – it can make all of our ideas, our fears, our relationships, and our desires flesh. It is a capacity that Shakespeare seemed repeatedly drawn to in his later works, works which reunite bodies across impossible gulfs of time, space and even death.

PROFESSIONAL SHAKESPEARE PRODUCTIONS IN THE UK, JANUARY–DECEMBER 2023

JAMES SHAW

Most of the productions listed are by professional companies but some amateur productions are included. The information is taken from listings, company publicity and published reviews. The websites provided for theatre companies were accurate at the time of going to press.

ANTONY AND CLEOPATRA

The Etheric Players. Questor's Theatre, London, 16–20 May; Ealing Project Cinema, 9–11 July.

AS YOU LIKE IT

Soho Place, London, 6 December 2022 to 28 January.
https://sohoplace.org
Director: Joise Rourke
Rosalind: Leah Harvey
Celia: Rose Ayling-Ellis
Rosalind and Celia communicated primarily using sign language with surtitles.

Three Inch Fools. The Festival Theatre, Hever Castle, 27 May and tour to 13 September.
www.threeinchfools.com
Company of five.

Royal Shakespeare Company. Royal Shakespeare Theatre, Stratford-upon-Avon, 17 June–5 August.
www.rsc.org.uk
Director: Omar Elerian
Rosalind: Geraldine James

Shakespeare's Globe. The Globe Theatre, 18 August–29 October.
www.shakespearesglobe.com
Director: Ellen McDougall

Rosalind: Nina Bowers
Gender-neutral casting with modern text insertions.

THE COMEDY OF ERRORS

Shakespeare's Globe. The Globe Theatre, London, 12 May–29 July.
www.shakespearesglobe.com
Director: Sean Holmes

Rain or Shine Theatre Company. Brighton Open Air Theatre, 19 July and tour to 7 September.
www.rainorshine.co.uk

The Pantaloons. The Maltings, Farnham, 28 July and tour to October.
https://thepantaloons.co.uk
Director: Steve Purcell
Cast of four.

Adaptation

The Comedy of Errors (More or Less)
Shakespeare North Playhouse, Prescot, 3–25 March; Stephen Joseph Theatre, Scarborough, 30 March–15 April.
Director: Paul Robinson
The twins hail from Prescot and Scarborough in a joint production between theatres from Prescot and Scarborough.

CORIOLANUS

The Wet Mariners. The Willow Globe, Llanwrthwl, Powys, 26 August.

www.wetmariners.com
Performed at Folio Festival, a weekend celebration of the First Folio.

CYMBELINE

Royal Shakespeare Company. Royal Shakespeare Theatre, Stratford-upon-Avon, 28 April–27 May.
www.rsc.org.uk
Director: Gregory Doran
Imogen: Amber James

HAMLET

Lazarus Theatre Company. Southwark Playhouse Borough, London, 12 January–4 February.
www.lazarustheatrecompany.co.uk
Director: Ricky Dukes
Older characters cut – Gertrude, Claudius, Polonius.

National Theatre. Dorfman Theatre, London, 20–28 March.
www.nationaltheatre.org.uk
Director: Ellie Hurt
Reimagined for young audiences, ages 8–12.

Next Generation Hamlet
RSC Next Generation Act Company. The Other Place, Stratford-upon-Avon, 28–29 July.
www.rsc.org.uk
Director: Paul Ainsworth
RSC's young company.

Adaptation

Inspired by Hamlet: Hamlette
Drama on 3. BBC Radio 3, 5 November.
Director: Emma Harding
Adaptation for radio. A politician avenges the rape of her sister.

HENRY IV

Bard in the Botanics. Glasgow Botanical Gardens, 22 June–8 July.
www.bardinthebotanics.co.uk
Director: Gordon Barr
Conflation of *Henry IV* pts. 1 and 2.

HENRY V

Headlong Theatre and Shakespeare's Globe. Sam Wanamaker Playhouse, 10 November 2022–4 February; Leeds Playhouse, 9–25 February; Connaught Theatre, Worthing, 28 February–4 March; Royal and Derngate, Northampton, 7–18 March.
www.headlong.co.uk
Director: Holly Race Roughan

JULIUS CAESAR

Royal Shakespeare Company. Royal Shakespeare Theatre, Stratford-upon-Avon, 18 March–8 April and tour to 24 June.
www.rsc.org.uk
Director: Atri Banerjee
Cassius and Brutus played as women.

The Factory. Marylebone Theatre, 14 May–12 July.
www.factorytheatre.co.uk
Director: Scott Brooksbank and Reuben Grove
Billed as: A changing squad of actors. No costumes. No blocking. Different every time.

Bard in the Botanics. Glasgow Botanical Gardens, 23 June–8 July.
www.bardinthebotanics.co.uk
Director: Jennifer Dick

Adaptation

Julius Caesar: the Musical
Mission Theatre, Bath, 21 July.
www.missiontheatre.co.uk
Comic adaptation with pop-music soundtrack.

KING LEAR

Wyndham's Theatre, London, 21 October–9 December.
Director and King Lear: Kenneth Branagh
Abridged to two hours without interval. Cast predominantly recent RADA graduates.

Adaptation

Truth's a Dog Must to Kennel

York St John University Creative Centre Auditorium and Atrium, 29 April.
Performer: Tim Crouch
Solo show. An actor wearing a VR headset describes watching a production of *King Lear*.

Oddbodies. Arena Theatre, Wolverhampton, 4 May and intermittent tour to November. Revival of 2019 Brighton Fringe Festival production.
https://oddbodies.com
Director: John Mowat
Playwright: Susanna Hamnett
Solo performance from the perspective of the Fool.

Lear
Unseemly Women and Girl Gang. Hope Mill, Manchester, 7–18 June; Shakespeare North Playhouse, Prescot, 21–24 June.
Director: Kayleigh Hawkins
All-female production.

Nearly Lear
The Fringe Office, Edinburgh, 10–19 August; The Playground Theatre, London, 23–25 November.
Director: Edith Tankus
One-woman show from the perspective of the Fool.

LOVE'S LABOUR'S LOST

Changeling Theatre. Eltham Palace, London, 15 July and summer tour.
https://changeling-theatre.com

MACBETH

The Bridge Theatre Training Company. Cockpit, London, 15–25 February.
All-female cast 15–18 February; mixed cast 22–25 February.

Imitating the Dog. Cast, Doncaster, 22–23 February and tour to 6 May.
www.imitatingthedog.co.uk
Director: Andrew Quick
Including flashbacks to the Macbeths' childhoods. Cast of five.

Flabbergast Theatre. Southwark Playhouse, London, 14 March–8 April and tour.
www.flabbergasttheatre.co.uk

A company specializing in puppetry, clown, mask, physical theatre and ensemble.

Dickens Theatre Company. Brentwood Theatre, Brentwood, 17–19 April and tour to May.
www.dickenstheatrecompany.co.uk
For schools.

Elysium Theatre Company. Assembly Rooms, Durham, 12–22 July and tour to 27 September.
https://elysiumtc.co.uk
Director: Jake Murray

Shakespeare's Globe. The Globe Theatre, 21 July–28 September.
www.shakespearesglobe.com
Director: Abigail Graham

Royal Shakespeare Company. Royal Shakespeare Theatre, Stratford-upon-Avon, 19 August–14 October.
www.rsc.org.uk
Director: Wils Wilson

English Touring Theatre. Shakespeare North Playhouse, 1–23 September and non-continuous tour to Lyric Hammersmith Theatre, 28 February–29 March 2025.
https://ett.org.uk
Director: Richard Twyman

Watermill Theatre, Newbury, 31 October–4 November.
Director: Abigail Pickard Price

Underbelly in association with Shakespeare Theatre Company. The Depot, Liverpool, 18 November–16 December; Royal Highland Centre, Edinburgh, 13–27 January 2024; Dock X, Canada Water, London, 10 February–23 March 2024.
Director: Simon Godwin
Macbeth: Ralph Fiennes
Lady Macbeth: Indira Varma

Donmar Warehouse, 8 December–10 February 2024.
Director: Max Webster
Macbeth: David Tennant
Lady Macbeth: Cush Jumbo
Headphones distributed to the audience to experience the production.

Adaptation

Macbeth (An Undoing)
Royal Lyceum Theatre Edinburgh, 4–25 February.

Director: Zinnie Harris
Feminist retelling from the perspective of Lady Macbeth.

Partners of Greatness
Faction Theatre. Northcott Theatre, Exeter, 20–21 February.
www.1623theatre.co.uk
Fifty-minute adaptation with cast of two.

Romeo and Juliet and Macbeth: An Unhinged Comedy Double Bill
Four Forty. Joseph Rowntree Theatre, York, 29 July and tour.
www.440theatre.co.uk
Both plays abridged to forty minutes.

Opera

Uncovered Opera Company. Hoxton Hall, London, 23 February–5 March.
www.uncoveredoperacompany.com
Director: Valeria Perboni
Composer: Verdi

MEASURE FOR MEASURE

Moving Stories in partnership with West Cornwall Women's Aid. Minack Theatre, Penzance, 3–fs6 July.
www.movingstories.org.uk
Director: Emma Gersch

Stamford Shakespeare Company, Tolethorpe Hall, 13–29 July.
www.stamfordshakespeare.co.uk

THE MERCHANT OF VENICE

Wick Theatre Company. Barn Theatre, Southwick, 8–11 March.
https://wicktheatre.co.uk
Director: Sam Razavi

Poetic Justice. JW3 Arts & Culture Jewish Community Centre, London, 29 October and tour to 2 December.
www.poeticjustice.eu
Director: Alex Pearson

Adaptation

The Merchant of Venice 1936
Trafalgar Theatre Productions. Watford Palace Theatre, 28 February–11 March and tour to 2 December.
Director: Brigid Larmour
Shylock: Tracy-Ann Oberman
A single mother and survivor of attacks on Jewish people in Russia runs a small business from her home in Cable Street.

THE MERRY WIVES OF WINDSOR

Folksy Theatre. Boiling Wells Amphitheatre, 4 August. Bristol Shakespeare Festival and tour to September.
https://folksytheatre.co.uk

Opera

Falstaff
Opera North. Grand Theatre and Opera House, Leeds, 28 September–25 October and tour to 19 November.
Director: Jo Davies

A MIDSUMMER NIGHT'S DREAM

Shakespeare's Globe. The Globe Theatre, 27 April–12 August.
www.shakespearesglobe.com
Director: Elle While
Puck: Michelle Terry

Stafford Shakespeare Festival. Gatehouse Theatre, Stafford, 23 June–9 July.
www.gatehousetheatre.co.uk
Director: Sean Turner
Stafford Shakespeare Festival first indoor production.

The Handlebards. Dorchester Arts Centre, Dorchester, 23 June and tour to 8 September.
www.handlebards.com
Director: Nel Crouch

Figure. Opera Holland Park – Open Air Theatre, London, 29 June–1 July.
Composer: Mendelssohn
Director: Samuel Rayner

Live orchestra accompanying with Mendlessohn's incidental music.

Grosvenor Park Open Air Theatre, Chester, 15 July–27 August.
Director: Elvi Piper

Out of Chaos. Theatre Royal, Bury St Edmunds, 12 September.
www.out-of-chaos.co.uk
Company of two.

Flabbergast Theatre. Malvern Theatres, 21–25 November and tour.
www.flabbergasttheatre.co.uk
Director: Henry Maynard

Adaptation

Midsummer Mechanicals
Splendid Productions. Shakespeare North Playhouse, Knowsley, 15–18 July; The Globe Theatre, 28 July–21 August.
https://splendidproductions.co.uk
Director: Lucy Cuthertson
The mechanicals stage another play.

Opera

Glyndebourne Opera, 1 July–22 August.
www.glyndebourne.com
Director: Peter Hall
Composer: Benjamin Britten

The Fairy Queen
Longborough Festival Opera, 29 July–3 August.
https://lfo.org.uk
Composer: Henry Purcell

MUCH ADO ABOUT NOTHING

Questor's Theatre. Judi Dench Playhouse, London, 28 April–6 May.
http://www.questors.org.uk
Director: Anne Neville

Creation Theatre. South Oxford Adventure Playground, Oxford, 12 July–19 August.
https://creationtheatre.co.uk
Director: Helen Tennison

Oddsocks. Markeaton Park – Craft Village, 13 July and tour to September.
www.oddsocks.co.uk

Unbound Theatre. Limelight Theatre, Aylesbury, 14–15 July and tour to 28 July.
https://unboundtheatre.co.uk
Part of Buckinghamshire Shakespeare Festival.

Opera

Beatrice & Benedict
Mid Wales Opera, SpArC, Bishop's Castle, 13 October and tour to 10 November.
www.midwalesopera.co.uk
Composer: Hector Berlioz

OTHELLO

Frantic Assembly. Curve Theatre, Leicester, 19 September–1 October 2022 and tour to Lyric Hammersmith, London, 19 January–11 February.
www.franticassembly.co.uk
Director: Scott Graham

National Theatre. Lyttelton Theatre, London, 23 November 2022–21 January.
www.nationaltheatre.org.uk
Director: Clint Dyer
Othello: Giles Terera
Iago: Paul Hilton
First black director to stage *Othello* at a major British theatre.

Sixty Hour Shakespeare. Abbey Ruins, Reading, 13 August.
www.60hourshakespeare.com
Performed after sixty hours of rehearsal.

Riverside Studios, London, 4–29 October.
Director: Sinead Rushe
Iago shared between three performers.

PERICLES

Flute Theatre. Riverside Studios, London, 24–27 October and UK tour.
www.flutetheatre.co.uk

Director: Kelly Hunter
Production for autistic individuals and their families.

RICHARD III

York Shakespeare Project. Friargate Theatre, York, 26–29 April.

Rose Theatre and Liverpool Everyman & Playhouse. Everyman & Playhouse, Liverpool, 6–22 April; Rose Theatre Kingston, 26 April–13 May.
Director and Richard III: Adjoa Andoh

Tower Theatre Company. Tower Theatre, London, 17–27 May.
www.towertheatre.org.uk
Director: Kornelia Adelajda

Brite Theatre. Brockley Jack Studio, London, 6–10 June and tour.
Director: Kolbrun Bjort Sigfusdottir
One-woman show.

ROMEO AND JULIET

Actors From The London Stage. The Cockpit, London, 23–24 March.
Cast of five.

The Lord Chamberlain's Men. Tour May–September.
https://tlcm.co.uk
Director: Peter Stickney

Handlebards. JAGS Sports Club, London, 18 May and tour to 5 August.
www.handlebards.com
Travelling between venues by bicycle.

OVO. Roman Theatre, St Albans, 5 June–29 July.
https://ovo.org.uk
Director: Adam Nichols
Set in Belfast in 1998.

Almeida Theatre, London, 6 June–29 July.
Director: Rebecca Frecknall
Two hours without interval.

East London Shakespeare Festival, Higham Hill Hub, London, 16 June–13 August.

Sun & Moon Theatre. Penlee Park Open Air Theatre, Penzance, 23 June and tour to 13 August.

https://sunandmoontheatreuk.com

Troubadour Stageworks. St Paul's Church (The Actors Church), London, 5–8 July and tour.
https://troubadourstageworks.com

Dickens Theatre Company. Waterside Theatre, Aylesbury, 9–14 October.
www.dickenstheatrecompany.co.uk

Royal Exchange, Manchester, 20 October–18 November.
www.royalexchange.co.uk
Director: Nicholai La Barrie

Adaptation

Romeo and Julie
National Theatre and Sherman Theatre. Dorfman Theatre, London, 14 February–1 April; Sherman Theatre, Cardiff, 13–29 April.
Director: Rachel O'Riordan
Playwright: Gary Owen
Modern adaptation.

Romeo + Juliet
Backyard Cinema. Alexandra Palace, London, 30 May–4 June.
Screening of Baz Luhrmann's film with live orchestral and choir accompaniment.

Rubbish Shakespeare Company. St Luke's Bombed Out Church, Liverpool, 27 July.
www.rubbishshakespearecompany.com
Director: Lee Hithersay
Slapstick version for younger audiences.

Romeo and Juliet and Macbeth: An Unhinged Comedy Double Bill
Four Forty. Joseph Rowntree Theatre, York, 29 July and tour.
www.440theatre.co.uk
Both plays abridged to forty minutes.

Shakespeare's R&J
Reading Rep Theatre, Reading, 11 October–4 November.
www.readingrep.com
Director: Paul Stacey
Playwright: Joe Calarco
Four boarding-school students discover a secret version of *Romeo and Juliet*.

Ballet

Ballet Theatre UK. New Theatre Peterborough, Peterborough, 25 March and tour to 26 May.
www.ballettheatreuk.com

Matthew Bourne's Romeo + Juliet
New Adventures. Curve, Leicester 3–8 July and tour to 4 November. Revival of 2019 production.
www.new-adventures.net
Director: Matthew Bourne
Composer: Prokofiev

THE TEMPEST

Royal Shakespeare Company. Royal Shakespeare Theatre, Stratford-upon-Avon, 16 January–4 March.
www.rsc.org.uk
Director: Elizabeth Freestone
Prospero: Alex Kingston

Playing Shakespeare with Deutsche Bank. The Globe Theatre, London, 2–30 March.
Director: Diane Page
Ninety-minute adaptation.

Adaptation

Return to the Forbidden Planet
Brentwood Operatic Society. Brentwood Theatre, Brentwood, 23–27 May.

The Tempest Re-imagined for Everyone Aged Six and Over
Open Air Theatre, Regent's Park, London, 30 June–22 July.
https://openairtheatreheritage.com

The Tempest: Re-rigged
Portland Players and Offshoot Collective, Portland, Dorset, 15–17 September.
Three devised plays developed with community groups: *Wilderland*; *Red Moon*; *Book of Sycorax*.

TITUS ANDRONICUS

Shakespeare's Globe. Sam Wanamaker Playhouse, London, 19 January–15 April.
www.shakespearesglobe.com
Director: Jude Christian
Titus: Katy Stephens

TWELFTH NIGHT

Dukes Theatre Company. BOAT (Brighton Open Air Theatre), Brighton, 8–10 June; Wilton's Music Hall, London, 10–11 July and tour.
www.thedukestheatrecompany.co.uk
Director: Martin Parr

Shakespeare in the Squares. St Paul's Church (The Actors Church), London, 30 June–1 July and tour to 7 July.
https://shakespeareinthesquares.co.uk

Immersion Theatre Company. Tour July–August.
www.immersiontheatre.co.uk
Director: James Tobias

Open Bar Theatre. Longfield Hall 2 July and tour.
www.openbartheatre.com
Director: Nicky Diss

Illyria Theatre Company. The Hawth, Crawley, 6 July and tour to 3 September.
www.illyria.co.uk

Lakeside and Nottingham Playhouse. Lakeside Arts Centre, Nottingham, 8–9 July; Playhouse, Nottingham, 19–29 July.
Director: Martin Berry

Petersfield Shakespeare Festival. Wylds Farm, Petersfield, 18–23 July.
https://psfest.co.uk
Director: Chris Hollis

The Mill at Sonning, 1–5 August.
https://millatsonning.com
Director: Tam Williams
Sixty-minute adaptation.

Adaptation

I, Malvolio
Sam Wanamaker Theatre, London, 30 November–9 December.
Performer: Tim Crouch
One actor retelling from the perspective of Malvolio. Premiered at Brighton Festival 2010.

THE WINTER'S TALE

Shakespeare's Globe. The Globe Theatre, London, 9 February–16 April.

www.shakespearesglobe.com
Director: Sean Holmes
First Globe production to use both Sam Wanamaker Playhouse (Sicilia) and the Globe Theatre (Bohemia) stages.

Eastbourne Operatic & Dramatic Society. Devonshire Park Theatre, Eastbourne, 26 July–6 August.

MISCELLANEOUS

The Book of Will
Queen's Theatre, Hornchurch, 27 April–13 May; Octagon Theatre, Bolton, 17 May–3 June; Shakespeare North Playhouse, Prescot, 19 October–11 November.
Playwright: Lauren Gunderson
Following Shakespeare's death, Heminges and Condell undertake the publication of his complete works.

A Bunch of Amateurs
Archway Theatre Production, Horley, 28 March–8 April.
https://archwaytheatre.co.uk
Director: Chris Yeldham
Playwrights: Nick Newman and Ian Hislop
A fading Hollywood action hero plays King Lear for a village amateur troupe.

Compositor E
Omnibus Theatre, Clapham, London, 19 September–7 October.
Playwright: Charlie Dupré
The printing of the First Folio.

Dead Poets Live – Shakespeare
Dead Poets Live. The Coronet, Inner London, 11 June.
https://deadpoets.live
Regular themed poetry event.

Doing Shakespeare
The Northern Comedy Theatre. Questor's Theatre, London, 20–22 April.
https://northerncomedytheatre.com
Director: Shaun Chambers
Playwright: David Spicer
Six actors, rehearsing separately only with cue scripts, discover they have been given six different plays and press ahead with a performance.

Falstaff
Mike Stoneham. The Stables Theatre and Arts Centre, Hastings, 28 September.
Director: Peter Mould
Adapted from the Robert Nye novel.

Fix the Folio
Troubadour Stageworks. London tour July–August.
https://troubadourstageworks.com
Playwright: Mingma Hughes
Isaac Jaggard races to get the First Folio manuscript ready for the printing deadline.

Folio Festival
Shakespeare Link and The Wet Mariners. The Willow Globe, Llanwrthwl, Powys, 26–28 August.
Folio-themed weekend with letterpress, calligraphy, movement workshops, a scavenger hunt, talks, films and games.

MachHamLear
Heartbreak Productions. Jephson Gardens, Leamington Spa, 2 June and tour to 1 September.
www.heartbreakproductions.co.uk
Playwright: Michael Davies

The Motive and the Cue
National Theatre. Littleton Theatre, London, 20 April–15 July.
Director: Sam Mendes
Playwright: Jack Thorne
John Gielgud directs Richard Burton in the 1964 Broadway *Hamlet*.

Mr. William Shakespeare's Plays
Fluellen Theatre Company. Grand Theatre, Swansea, 12 October and tour.
Celebrating the 400th anniversary of the First Folio.

Nay, Remember Me!
Malvern Theatre Players. The Coach House Theatre, Malvern, 5–11 November.
Playwright: Amelia Marriette
The story of the making of the First Folio, part of Malvern Folio 400 Festival.

Not Such Stuff
Chelmsford Theatre Workshop. Meadows Shopping Centre, Chelmsford, 4–9 July.
https://notsuchstuff.co.uk
Director: Ria Milton
Playwright: Chris Wind

Shakespeare's female characters organize a press conference to set the record straight.

Queer Folio
1623 Theatre Company. Museum of Making, Derby, 5 May.
www.1623theatre.co.uk
Thirty new pieces co-created by LGBTQ+ artists and community groups inspired by the First Folio.

ShakeItUp: The Improvised Shakespeare Show
The Turbine Theatre, London, 31 October–4 November.

Shakespeare in the Abbey
Shakespeare's Globe. Westminster Abbey, 29–31 March.
www.shakespearesglobe.com
Director: Darren Raymond
A promenade performance with extracts performed at various locations in Westminster Abbey.

Shakespeare's Fool
Tortive Theatre. Queen's Hall Arts Centre, Hexham, 19–20 September and tour to 21 October.
www.tortivetheatre.com
Director: Ben Humphrey

The story of Will Kempe.

Sheldrake on Shakespeare: Live!
James Sheldrake. Etcetera Theatre, London, 2 June and tour to 23 July.
Stand-up comedy.

POEMS

Shakespeare Sonnet Marathon
York International Shakespeare Festival. The Garden, York Theatre Royal, 22 April.
The sonnets read in order by volunteers.

Lucrece
York International Shakespeare Festival. Friargate Theatre, York, 23 April.
A semi-staged adaption of *The Rape of Lucrece*.

Venus and Adonis
Noontide Sun. Riverside Studios, London, 9–21 May.
https://thenoontidesun.com
Director: David Salt
One-actor show.

THE YEAR'S CONTRIBUTION
TO SHAKESPEARE STUDIES

1. CRITICAL STUDIES
reviewed by EZRA HORBURY

With the slow metabolism of academic publishing, we are only now seeing in print those works produced during or shortly after Trump's tenure as 45th president of the United States. Encountering these books now is curiously temporally displacing. On the one hand, such books offer the promise of reflecting soothingly, perhaps therapeutically, on a time confined to the past. The writing of history is a way of telling ourselves that certain things are over. But reading a book that engages in such reflection on the eve of the 2024 presidential election, then attempting to review it the day after forces a dislocation in perspective. Simultaneously, one looks at the past that was safely confined to the narrative of history, and one must also reckon with the traumatic intrusion of that past once again. It is hard not to read these books hauntologically.

The question of history, who tells it and how, does not just permeate these works but runs scar-deep in many of them. I did not consciously select a shortlist of books to think with the 2024 presidential election, but the event itself and the legacy of US imperialism seems to continually recur. These are books about how history is embodied in children and in women, how consent is politicized to shape a preferred historical narrative, about how history and nationalism are embodied in cultural appropriation, about who tells the stories of trans people, about how we are embodied in history, and about the work of critical race studies against the current landscape. Shakespeare has been used to write and rewrite history for centuries

and this practice shows no sign of stopping – not even in Trump's America. At the precipice of another uncertain time, these works offer us ways to use Shakespeare to think about and think through these writings of history, perhaps to some path for continued survival – both for Shakespeare and for ourselves.

In his enduring work on queerness and the political strategies of US imperialism, Lee Edelman writes, 'the image of the Child, not to be confused with the lived experiences of any historical children, serves to regulate political discourse – to prescribe what will count as political discourse – by compelling such discourse to accede in advance to the reality of a collective future whose figurative status we are never permitted to acknowledge or address'.[1] As Trump ran a platform substantially based on protecting children from the 'Left-Wing Gender Insanity' that causes 'the chemical, physical, and emotional mutilation of our youth', the phantasmatic Child once again became central to US discourse on who deserved political protection.[2] In Joseph Campana's *Shakespeare's Once and Future Child: Speculations on Sovereignty*, Campana returns to Edelman's axiom to consider 'the process by which the child comes to be

---

[1] Lee Edelman, *No Future: Queer Theory and the Death Drive* (Durham, 2004), p. 11.

[2] Donald J. Trump, 'President Trump's plan to protect children from left-wing gender insanity', 1 February 2023, www.donaldjtrump .com/agenda47/president-trumps-plan-to-protect-children-from-left-wing-gender-insanity.

a privileged figure for speculations on potential political futures from the cyclically rejuvenated ruins of sovereignty' (1). In demonstrating the still untapped valences of children as cultural objects, Campana's book considers the uneasy vulnerability and potent metaphoric potential of the child in relation to sovereignty in Shakespeare's work. The book meditates on these tensions between flesh and metaphor across *Richard III*, *King John*, *Richard II*, *Macbeth*, *The Rape of Lucrece*, *Titus Andronicus*, *Coriolanus*, *Antony and Cleopatra*, *The Comedy of Errors* and *Twelfth Night*. Following Edelman, Campana argues how 'Shakespeare's figurations of children and childhood expose the parameters of imaginable political futures' (14). As we reconsider what political future we now can, and indeed must, imagine for the next four years and beyond, Campana supplies an important and timely contribution to our rethinking of literary and historical attitudes towards, and uses of, children. The child's vulnerability emerges here as a necessary 'balance [to] the potency of the sovereign', and it remains urgent for us to interrogate how that vulnerability is utilized and the dynamic constructed between it and our political rulers today (44).

Campana also addresses throughout the sentiments provoked by the representations of real children in the plays, not just their metaphoric potential: the desire to kill, to protect and to eroticize the child in readings facilitated by Foucault, Agamben and Edelman. An analysis of the rhetoric of Lucrece produces an excellent reading of how 'increase, often embodied by children, was imagined simultaneously as a threatening multiplicity that may require culling and a necessary proliferation of life that must be protected from corruption' (94). This thread is picked up in different manifestations in considering the inhuman multiplicity of hive-like reproduction in Shakespeare's Rome, 'which reveal the tenuous humanity especially of children but ultimately of all subjects to sovereignty' (109). This comparative analysis of the impartial citizenship of commoners and children in the Roman plays reads rewardingly when positioned alongside analysis of the children's animalistic nature – as explored by Lucy Munro[3] – or their artificiality, as Michael Witmore has so usefully charted.[4]

Campana's turn to the trafficking of children in the shipwreck plays is especially provocative and usefully reframes a series of episodes around those 'frequently lost and (sometimes) found children who populate early and late comedies . . . as figures for loss and recovery, profit and risk in a world of maritime exchange' (143). Campana closes with a gesture to Urvashi Chakravarty's *Fictions of Consent* and its reading of

children as part of an ideology of slavery, and there is certainly much to be explored too in how the racialization of children inflects their relation to sovereignty (Titania's Indian boy appears only in the epilogue).[5] The racialization of childhood may be a topic more appropriate for subsequent work. But in considering the inflection of childhood along other vectors, the issue of age is neglected to a surprising degree. Although the focus is on children, Campana does not dedicate much thought to the taxonomy of age encompassed by this term. Aaron's unnamed babe and Sebastian and Viola may all be young, but an infant and these employable youths occupy distinct categories of youth. This is an idea that could be challenged more productively, and the book may well lay the groundwork for such interrogations in future. There are moments when Campana brushes against these ideas – his conceptualization of Richard III as both 'the monstrous child and the monstrous child-killer' (32) – but overall the central notion of 'childhood' is not much unpacked in relation to the vastly different ages (and classes, and races) of children that fall under that banner. In accepting Sebastian and Viola as shipwrecked children of marriageable age, what additional readings of the issues of agency and consent does this open up?

Campana's work is an ambitious and far-reaching text that delves deeply into the Shakespearian canon, offering both fresh readings of less popular works and effective reevaluations of more familiar texts. The continued use to which children and the Child are put in political discourse remains in need of urgent interrogation.

While the Child continues to endure as the metaphoric repository of history and futurity, Hailey Bachrach's excellent debut monograph *Staging Female Characters in Shakespeare's English History Plays* demonstrates too the centrality of women to constructing ideas of history. This work considers the gendering of history and the history play – specifically, how the marginalization of female characters is crucial to how we gauge the authenticity of Shakespearian history. It offers a thrilling analysis of Shakespeare's history plays, valuably

---

[3] Lucy Munro, 'Coriolanus and the Little Eyases: the boyhood of Shakespeare's hero', in *Shakespeare and Childhood*, ed. Kate Chedgzoy, Susanne Greenhalgh and Robert Shaughnessy (Cambridge, 2009), 80–95.

[4] Michael Witmore, *Pretty Creatures: Children and Fiction in the English Renaissance* (Ithaca, 2007).

[5] Urvashi Chakravarty, *Fictions of Consent: Slavery, Servitude, and Free Service in Early Modern England* (Philadelphia, 2022).

re-examining some of the least studied of Shakespeare's women, as well as a highly productive re-gendering of the genre of the history play as Bachrach argues for 'a distinctive feminine structural position in Shakespeare's history plays, a facet of his historical dramaturgy that is deliberately gendered and specifically associated with women and feminine men' (4).

Alongside Bachrach's work on women and Campana's on children, Victoria Sparey has also published *Shakespeare's Adolescents: Age, Gender and the Body in Shakespearean Performance and Early Modern Culture*. Last year saw the publication of Victoria L. McMahon's book on *Shakespeare, Tragedy and Menopause*, which offered the first full-length definition of early modern menopause. Now Sparey presents a book with similar methodological goals on adolescence, taking the central premise to prioritize age rather than gender as the category of analysis. This offers a usefully comparative approach to read male and female bodies together rather than apart, one not usually taken by existing scholarship. It is a four-chapter work with a substantial introduction that offers an extremely thorough synthesis of scholarship, so will be of particular use to readers wanting to get to grips with the field.

Chapter 1 of Sparey approaches floral imagery and the concept of ripening in adolescence, perhaps most intriguingly highlighting the common positioning of 'adolescent ripening promise' alongside old age and decay (41). Sparey emphasizes the imagery of rot found in agricultural metaphors of adolescence for a usefully intersectional comparison. There is an important consideration of the importance of *potential* in relation to adolescence – to consider not just the current state of the body but what physical states it might soon enter or acts it might undertake. This develops in chapter 2 as Sparey considers breathlessness not as a static condition, but as also the potential for beardedness, and that 'timely beards' offer a promise of forthcoming 'masculine vitality' (81). This reconfiguration of the body positioned on the edge of adolescence as one of potential offers new ways of thinking about the boundaries between life stages, to re-evaluate watersheds as instead part of an atemporal narrative that is always forward looking.

Chapter 3 is concerned with the voice, not the unbroken voice but the role of 'humoral heat thought to inform how adolescents spoke' and its role in 'promot[ing] mental agility' (102). This is a refreshing approach. We care too much about the timbre of the voice. This is particularly useful for thinking about female wittiness and how adolescence 'presented

opportunities for girls to demonstrate a flair for speaking' (119). This reads well alongside Bachrach who considers female cursing as a verbal means to enable historical intervention, and there is a useful comparative reading of the relationship between the social values placed on different speech acts (or their role in a narrative) and the construction of embodied age. After all, while curse and prophecy is most often associated with old age, it can also be born of childhood, as Campana emphasizes in his analysis of the phantom children in *Macbeth*. Sparey also offers a rich engagement with differing heights *within* adolescence: that it is not a stage of equal sameness but one contrarily marked by intense differences in heights, as obviously and visually represented in the differing heights of various boy players. Shakespeare thus offers 'altering perspectives to calibrate the singularity of a "normative" measure for adolescent selves' (162).

There are some readings with which I struggled to agree, and given the emphasis on these elements it is worth questioning. A reading of beardedness in *Coriolanus* very valuably highlights Coriolanus' beardless youth, which must, presumably, contrast with a bearded adulthood – an element often dropped from modern productions which associate a clean-shaven jaw with a military aspect. But when Coriolanus 'with his Amazonian chin he drove / The bristled lips before him' (2.2.84–5), Sparey reads the 'bristled lips' as those of Coriolanus – with a budding moustache, yet beardless; however, surely the 'bristled lips' refers here to those enemies that Coriolanus drives before him (i.e., repulses in battle)? And in an important reading of pubic hair, Sparey argues for the early modern belief that 'After the initial "ripening" stage of their lives, women seem to have been thought to produce less pubic hair' (83). Yet the evidence for this in Jane Sharp states that married women's pubic hair is 'more curled in women than the hair of maids' (83). This to me does not suggest a *lessening* of pubic hair, but a curling or textural change. Hair curling, as opposed to diminishing, is an important distinction. These are small nitpicks, but important to consider.

Returning to Bachrach, her work advocates throughout for the concept of 'historical dramaturgy', 'the artistic process by which historical material is adapted for dramatic representation' (4). This considers the contexts of production of these plays, clearly showing Bachrach's background in theatre, and is not purely textual. Bachrach argues for 'a distinctive feminine structural position in Shakespeare's history plays . . . that is deliberately gendered and specifically associated with women and feminine men' (4). Bachrach distinguishes herself from engaging purely formalistic approaches in the interdisciplinarity of this dramaturgy, but there is a strong formalist thread in 'argu[ing] that we must think of characters structurally, not as fictionalised people' (169).

In chapter 1, Bachrach argues for a more expansive definition of the history play, considering these works as participants in as well as depictions of history, and the importance of the comic mode in such constructions. Although Bachrach does not extensively interrogate questions of canonicity and whose history is told (white history, men's history, etc.), this analysis of the comic mode offers an important consideration of how 'All onstage history is necessarily fictionalised: the question is merely what type and degree of fiction we deem acceptable' (28). Considering the symbolic treatment of the female subject and of the foreigner, she argues for a 'multi-vocal depiction of history' (44).

Silence and voice are central to chapter 2, a theme which is also essential in Sparey's work. For Sparey, the focus is on the garrulity of humorally hot adolescent speech, but her work offers some similarly useful ways to reconfigure the relationship between restraint of female speech and social participation. As Sparey writes, 'although *The Taming of the Shrew* ascribes to cultural forces that limited female speech, the play's framing of Katherine's "unruly" voice as adolescent may explain why Katherine is not yet regarded as sexually licentious because she talks' (125). Back in Bachrach, in chapter 2 the emphasis is on women's failed interventions, where Bachrach argues that 'failed participation is not lack of participation, and characters who operate in settings parallel to and apparently separate from the main political plot can still be agents of profound literal and symbolic change' (56). Joseph J. Fischel's emphasis in *Screw Consent*[6] on pressuring the concept of consent and challenging its primacy in determining sexual pressure offers a useful further way to think with Bachrach's important defence of failed consent: 'Shakespeare deliberately embeds quiet resistance – including Catherine's resistance to just saying *yes* – that should not be overlooked simply because it is ineffectual' (78). For Fischel, our cultural fetishization of sexual consent fails to adequately support healthy and positive sexual experiences in that it fails to acknowledge the existence of bad consensual sex (and, more complicatedly, that we might find non-consensual sexual experiences enjoyable). For Bachrach, the refusals of no are 'moments of failed intervention and elided consent as examples of curtailed agency rather than bland submission' (78). I think too of Jack Halberstam's work on failure – not failure of consent but failure of ambition – and the importance of celebrating failure in how it 'preserves some of the wondrous anarchy of childhood and disturbs the supposedly clean boundaries between adults and children, winners and losers'.[7] There is value to be found in locating and highlighting these marginal, 'failed' characters in Shakespeare's history plays and beyond – a theme that will recur in Amanda Bailey's work. In ignoring their value due to their failures, as Bachrach argues, 'These characters are thus doubly disempowered, separated both from in-play political power that would enable them to meaningfully intervene in the events they seek to alter, and from the extra-textual structural power that would allow them to act as agents, not victims, of the demands of history' (78). It is hard not to identify with such failed warnings from women as the US faces another rollback of reproductive rights, and indeed human rights in general.

Chapter 3 of Bachrach treats how 'female characters narrate or otherwise attempt to rewrite history within the plays' (102). This offers a lovely consideration of how acts such as mourning, cursing, prophesying are 'moments in which female characters act as historians' (103). This includes a fantastic examination of cursing and genealogy: 'Because the ability to curse is dependent on marginalisation, it is always prefaced with some kind of mourning, and this mourning calls upon genealogy to demonstrate the specific terms of one's disrupted connection to the masculine historical chronologies and lines of succession that such genealogies traditionally represent' (109). This offers such rich ways to think about cursing of other marginal figures who must make similar attempts to define themselves against such genealogies even outside of the history plays: Caliban's cursing, Shylock's biting, Lear's invocations. And there is important emphasis here on the role of identification between audience and reader: 'The history these women narrate is a version of one that we have seen enacted – and often have seen them explicitly excluded from' (118–19).

Chapter 4 was for me one of the most rewarding chapters, with its turn to effeminacy in the overlooked

---

6 Joseph J. Fischel, *Screw Consent: A Better Politics of Sexual Justice* (Los Angeles, 2019).

7 Jack [Judith] Halberstam, *The Queer Art of Failure* (Durham, NC and London, 2009), p. 3.

early modern sense, as a lack of temperance. Hotspur's rashness in contrast to Hal's moderation offers the most overt example of this, but Bachrach draws on Meghan C. Andrews's compelling reading of Henry IV, who reads that character as humorally cold, militarily unsuccessful and prone to crying.[8] Building on this, Bachrach sees effeminate men such as Henry IV and Gaunt as being associated with prophecy. This was exciting, transformative material and forced me to reconsider the role of all such omen-speaking in early modern drama. Children, women and the old are all sites of prophecy, all filling prophecies of the future with death. In contrast to the image of the Child, embodying an always deferred futurity, these children, women and old men speak of futures filled with death. Now more than ever, we need to heed them.

Bachrach's conclusion argues for complicating the vision of masculine, tragic history as 'a means of undermining this patriarchal dramaturgy at its root' (175). Such challenges are urgent. Convincing, compelling and hugely productive, Bachrach's work is an important contribution to thinking about history and history-making.

As an early modern trans studies scholar, one of my most anticipated books this year was Colby Gordon's *Glorious Bodies: Trans Theology and Renaissance Literature*. Medieval and early modern trans studies has made exceptional strides in the past five years, with the publication of the *Journal of Early Modern Cultural Studies'* special issue on 'Early Modern Trans Studies', Leah DeVun's *The Shape of Sex*, the edited collection *Trans and Genderqueer Subjects in Medieval Hagiography*, and a vibrant range of articles by predominantly early-career scholars that have created such a rich field in such a short space of time. Colby Gordon's *Glorious Bodies* is an extremely worthy contribution to this field, focusing on the theological and religious contexts for transness in Sonnet 20, *The Duchess of Malfi*, John Donne and *Samson Agonistes*. Versions of the first two chapters have been previously published as articles and have already left a significant imprint on scholarship, so I will focus on the brand new material and use the book to think through some contemporary issues in early modern trans studies.

I will first briefly treat Gordon's chapters on Sonnet 20 and *The Duchess of Malfi*. Gordon's reading of trans technogenesis in Sonnet 20 has frequently been core reading for my teaching on queer approaches to sonnets. Gordon reads the 'prick' of Sonnet 20 as 'a scene

of collaborative labor and feminized artisanship ... that reclaims trans embodiment as prosthetic, hand-crafted, and technically fabricated' (35). In a work so much engaged with fleshy embodiment, it is extremely useful to offer this additional engagement with the prosthetic aspects of trans identity – even if only through the metaphorization of Nature's designs. In his reading of *The Duchess of Malfi*, Gordon highlights the animality of trans studies and the slippery exchanges between human and animal bodies in transition. The zoology of cosmetics is fascinating here, with the make-up of a woman's face drawn from a range of animals, while Gordon also argues for a trans reading of the metaphoric hyena imagery (an animal known for its supposed sexual disorder) associated with the Duchess.

In his new material, Gordon throws down a gauntlet, arguing 'that trans embodiment in the Renaissance was not chiefly understood as a question of clothing or a fantasy explored through the fictions of the stage. Instead, this book insists that transition *happened*, both socially and surgically, and that the significance of such alterations was glossed through the categories provided by theology' (3). This marks a difficult question in trans studies, as trans scholars are awkwardly positioned between two currents. On the one hand, there is the widespread desire to shift readings of transness away from the purely vestimentary (Sawyer Kemp's influential article on this topic reflected long-felt discomforts, particularly by trans scholars).[9] On the other, the practical, pedagogical and populist forces of Shakespeare's dominance make the centrality of 'cross-dressing plays' difficult to dislodge.

Gordon takes well-deserved aim at the dominance of sexology in twentieth-century readings of early modern gender. Gordon writes, 'My concern here is not with Shakespeare's comfort, but with the comfort of Shakespearians: the pleasures they have taken in discussing gender-variant bodies, their ease with the fetishistic language of "crossdressing" and "transvestism," and their pronounced discomfort with trans scholarship and trans people. What does the Shakespearean know of trans

---

[8] Meghan C. Andrews, 'Gender, genre, and Elizabeth's princely surrogates in *Henry IV* and *Henry V*', *Studies in English Literature, 1500–1900* 54 (2014), 375–99.

[9] Sawyer Kemp, 'Shakespeare in transition: pedagogies of transgender justice and performance', in *Teaching Social Justice through Shakespeare: Why Renaissance Literature Matters Now*, ed. Hillary Eklund and Wendy Beth Hyman (Edinburgh, 2019), 36–45.

life?' (18). There is a real and damaging issue in scholarship on the history of transness and gender variance, not just in early modern history but, of course, in the medical discourses that shaped trans people's lives often against their best interests in the twentieth century. The unwillingness of early modern academics to engage with the work of trans scholars, turning instead to sexology, is a major problem that requires redress. Even in works published this year, there is a lack of engagement with the work of queer and trans theorists on gender. Indeed, this is an instance where I wish Sparey had ventured more critical interrogation of one of her basic axioms, choosing to approach sex and gender as '"sex" refers to biological difference that was used to distinguish between male and female, and "gender" refers to cultural expectations and stereotypes that were attached to the sexes' (14). For a work that engages so extensively and so importantly with the comparisons between different gendered embodiments, it is surprising to see no reflection at all on the now 34-year-old challenge to those distinctions offered by Judith Butler, and subsequently significantly complicated. Trans studies ought to be central to these discussions, not absent entirely.

Gordon provides a very useful genealogy of how 'trans possibility was safely cordoned off from the Renaissance' that is well worth reading for any scholars not familiar with this field (24). I also want to highlight the important work here on tracing early anti-semitic transphobic discourse. The interlinking of transmisogyny with anti-semitism in contemporary politics has been widely acknowledged, but the historians among us are aware that this strand goes back far further (a highly offensive book even argued for medieval origins of the Jewish transgenderist cabal).[10] Gordon engages with the important strand of racialized gender as 'closely keyed to the historical development of white supremacy, anti-Semitism, Islamophobia, imperialism, and settler colonialism' (5), a theme that builds most immediately on the work of Riley C. Snorton's *Black on Both Sides* and Gil-Peterson's *Histories of the Transgender Child*, but which stretches back to ideas of feminine whiteness explored in an earlier form in Kim F. Hall's 1990s work *Things of Darkness*. This is richly tackled through Donne's incarnational theology, which imagines the resurrected body after Judgment Day as beyond not only sexual difference but also racial difference. The gleaming white, sexless body is the apotheosis of Christian perfection, and this is rewardingly explored through Donne's poetry. This does important work in turning away from the stage in thinking about transness,

especially in rooting it in embodiment. Both the resurrected body and Christ's vaginal, lactating body make particularly excellent positions for this. One of the most useful observations here is the treatment of Donne's gender in the scholarship. As Gordon argues, 'It is not a coincidence, I think, that the same slate of incoherent, contradictory accusations levied against trans women accrue to Donne as well: he is "hypermasculine," a "bully," and a misogynist, but also effeminate and weak, almost an incel *avant la lettre* . . . like the autogynephile, he gets off on imagining himself as a woman' (122). Here, Gordon's excellent grasp of contemporary transphobia and early modern prejudices come into extremely effective focus.

The reading of *Samson Agonistes* also offers a wonderful examination of maiming and mayhem that thinks about Samson's hair-cutting in terms of castration and concludes that 'the claim here is not that Samson is transgender, if we take that to mean that he identifies as a woman. Rather, what *Samson Agonistes* clarifies is that criminal mayhem is a legal device that folds together racialization, transition, and physical impairment into the figure of a defiling cut that constitutes a threat to the nation-state' (157–8). This is excellent, and I think its efficacy is particularly enabled by its shift away from identificatory discourses towards the rhetorical.

On egg theory, I am more split with Gordon. Gordon draws on 'egg theory' to re-evaluate Donne's gender identity, arguing that 'It is time that we let go of the transphobic assumption that the genders of the long-dead authors we study are self-evident and stable' (123), and 'it should be clear that I do not think that Donne was a man' (119). Gordon excellently reads Donne through egg theory, a concept that circulated in predominantly online transgender discourse and which was brought to academia through Grace Lavery's 'Egg theory's early style'.[11] The opening sentence of Lavery's piece is important to emphasize, and one often overlooked in application of the term 'egg': 'One only becomes an egg in retrospect, when one has hatched, and the chick has emerged.' And, also importantly, 'An egg is displaced in time, "retconned" back into one's own being; a protocol for a new, and newly

---

[10] Eric Striker, 'New book exposes history and money behind the transgender lobby', *National Justice*, 23 November 2020, www.nationaljustice.com.

[11] Grace Lavery, 'Egg theory's early style', *Transgender Studies Quarterly* 7 (2020), 383–98.

incommensurable, sense-making procedure.' For Gordon, an egg 'is a latent trans person who is attempting to indefinitely defer transition' and he 'argue[s] that Donne's stylistic quirks, as well as his resurrection fetish, make him an egg theorist, or rather, an egg lyricist' (36). Gordon's reading of Donne's 'egg theology' is deeply rewarding, compellingly argued, deeply evidenced, and both effective and moving (97). But I do want to emphasize this shift in the meaning of egg theory in the locus of identification: away from the self to the observer or interpreter. I do fully reject the assumption that all people (in this case, dead historical figures) are cisgender until proven otherwise, and there is no moral objection to reading such figures as trans. But I wonder about the hermeneutic implications of applying concepts for the *self-reflexive* means of exploring gender onto other selves. What kind of an interpretation do we perform when centring an other in a self-reflexive theory? Such approaches may construct gender identities where the subject cannot, and though I place no critical judgement on this, I want to highlight its existence. This relates to how we think about literary characters too, and the methods we use to construct gender identities for them. Trans studies is a discipline built on the lived experiences of trans people, and literary trans studies imports these methods to a literary medium. I want us to continually probe the implications of such methods. This is not to reject them, but simply to ask how we as literary scholars should navigate the unliterariness of trans studies and the implications this has for our own field.

In what will likely make a major and substantial addition to undergraduate syllabi, the Oxford *Handbook* series adds to its collection *The Oxford Handbook of Shakespeare and Race*, edited by Patricia Akhimie (Oxford, 2024). The volume offers forty-two chapters split between three sections on 'Shakespeare and Race: An Overview', 'Archives and Intersections' and 'Shakespeare and Race Now'. These three sections have discrete aims: to 'demonstrate the ways in which feminist, postcolonial, and critical race theory . . . and the histories of Shakespeare performance and adaptation, have broadened our understanding of the definitions and discourse of race and racism to include not only phenotype, but also religious and political identity, regional, national, linguistic, and biological difference, and systems of differentiation based upon culture and custom' (3); 'to offer readers already familiar with premodern critical race studies a look at new methodologies and new archives' (4); and 'to discover the ongoing conversations about race in our current historical moment, in the worlds of contemporary performance, appropriation, pedagogy, and activism' (6).

The collection has marshalled a range of scholars from early to late career, including major names such as editor Patricia Akhimie, Urvashi Chakravarty, Jean E. Howard, Farah Karim-Cooper, Mario DiGangi and Kim F. Hall, although it remains encouraging to see earlier career scholars also platformed in a major collection such as this. There is too much material to cover thoroughly so I will touch on some highlights. In the first chapter, Chakravarty 'considers the meaning and role of critical race theory to our understandings of race (as structural, cultural, and strategic), and explores the role of critical race theory . . . within a genealogy of scholarship on race in Shakespeare' (11). This overview of critical race theory disentangles it from the politicized misuse of the term in, particularly, contemporary America, and outlines its legal background and its history in the field of Shakespeare. It then provides a close reading of *The Merchant of Venice* and *Measure for Measure*, wherein Portia's question ('Which the merchant and which the Jew?') 'traffics in the fiction of "colour blindness" – the fiction that one refuses to "see race" – that ratifies the law even as it perpetuates systems of racial inequity' (22), and Isabella's silence in response to the Duke's demand of marriage, 'comprises the prospect of rupture, and the promise of exposing the complicity of systems of justice – and other institutional structures – with the operations of power' (27).

Howard focuses on an overview of the handkerchief and its differing meaning in scholarship, from metonymic representation of the blood-stained bridal sheets to Othello's black-dyed token of his own body, but also includes an incisive reading of kinship in *The Two Noble Kinsmen*, which Howard argues 'uses a quasi-classical, quasi-chivalric romance setting to explore these issues, eventually elaborating, iteratively, a set of practices and qualities that become the basis for consolidating a "fair" kind' (40). Karim-Cooper turns to the failures of 'colour-blind casting' in contemporary performance, asking instead for a 'Race consciousness' that 'asks us to be more intentional in the way directors and artists think about bodies on stage' (88). Meanwhile, Joyce Green Macdonald contributes here on adaptation, with an exciting chapter on minstrelsy Shakespeare adaptations in the US. Such performances' 'use of Shakespeare demonstrates a special kind of adaptation that re-racializes its original texts in ways that recognize and mediate racial and other social tensions' (111). DiGangi provides a highly accessible overview of the entanglement of race and queer studies scholarship in Shakespeare, while also providing an illuminating reading of Iago: 'by sharing his foul (racist) thoughts with Othello and suggesting that Desdemona hides foul (racist) thoughts of her own', Iago is able to construct 'erotic racism' (165). Alexa Alice Joubin considers what 'trans-inclusive and antiracist campaigns have in common beyond their cognate agendas of social justice' (196). Joubin and Abdulhamit Arvas adopt contrasting positions on *Twelfth Night*, where for Joubin Viola offers a 'transgender expression' (195) whereas Arvas considers the more specific 'Does Viola's desire to transform into a eunuch signify her desire to transition into a new distinct gender that is not a man or boy?' (220). Against the backdrop of the Ottoman eunuch and *köçek*, Arvas also demonstrates 'intricate entanglements between imperial violence and desire in the production, objectification, and consumption of these gender-nonbinary figures in early modernity' (216) before interrogating Othello's gender and calling for us 'to trace how cis-genders are constructed in any given play' (220). I think the material here is excellent and important, though it raises the question of why we should assume such characters are cis in the first place. Nonetheless, this is strong. M. Lindsay Kaplan provides an excellent background on early and medieval Christian racial discourses, arguing: 'An analysis of *The Merchant of Venice* through the lens of persisting Christian racializing discourses reveals the extent to which they connect Jews, Muslims, and Africans in shared concepts of sinful inferiority' (270). Holly Dugan then considers animal studies in *King Lear*, where 'metaphors of slavery and animality work to bolster humanist, universal ideals about tragedy and art' (343).

Beyond these highlights, Part I additionally considers colonial race-making in *The Tempest*, the sexual irresistibility of hyper-whiteness in *Venus and Adonis*, and presents oral histories on artists' experiences with Shakespeare. Part II, a more substantial section, covers a wider range of topics. It opens with oral histories on identity, then considers intersections between Shakespeare studies and critical Indigenous studies, Othello's disabling condition as a non-white immigrant, procreative racial mixing in *Titus Andronicus*, the implications of locating *Antony and Cleopatra* within an Eastern Mediterranean context, Spain's racialized slavery and imperial territories, constructing whiteness in *The Comedy of Errors*, race-thinking through *Macbeth*'s witches, oral histories on corporeality, how race-making expanded the protections and rights for some disenfranchised people but through the exclusion of others, the intertwining constructions of both race and early scientific endeavours, repertory studies and ink culture. Part III opens with an interview with Fred Wilson on Shakespeare and Black racial identity, then turns to post-independence Indian film adaptations of Shakespeare, casting and intersectional identities. It then offers oral histories on conversations about race, and race and appropriation, as well as concept productions, and considers how textual editing privileges white racial structures, and how translations function as an archive that tracks the dissemination of Shakespeare 'beyond the limits of Anglocentric, monolingual studies' (546). Further oral histories approach directing and performing Shakespeare, teaching race and Shakespeare in secondary schools, considering pedagogies that offer a 'student-centred and culturally responsive approach to studying Shakespeare' (594), how to think beyond *Othello* in considering the anti-blackness of cinema, reading Shakespeare while white, linguistic identity on *la frontera* in Texas, and conversations with artists about their connections to Shakespeare.

The collection does not seem to be aimed at one particular demographic in terms of expertise or subdiscipline. Some chapters, like those that dominate Part I, for example that of Mario Digangi on 'Shakespeare, race, and queer studies', provide thorough geographies of the scholarly landscape that will be of particular use to undergraduates who are seeking a means to navigate the wealth of scholarship on that particular theme. Other chapters, such as Kim F. Hall's discussion of '"Reading" Shakespeare as political activism', offer close analyses of specific performances or adaptations and will be of more interest to those working in the relevant fields. Other chapters still strike a balance between the two, such as Karim-Cooper's 'The imperatives of race consciousness in 21st-century Shakespearean performance'. As the introduction states, the different sections of the book aim to provide an overview to newcomers as well as 'to offer readers already familiar with premodern critical race studies a look at new methodologies and new archives' (4). While both approaches – the broad literature review and the specific analysis – are of value, it means that this handbook will be of less use as a singular coherent text. This is not necessarily a criticism; handbooks are rarely required reading in their entirety, after all, but it does mean this is a book that might be more comfortable in a library than on one's personal bookshelf.

Also tackling many of these elements of critical race studies, *Shakespeare/Skin: Contemporary Readings in Skin Studies and Theoretical Discourse*, an edited collection by

Ruben Espinosa, crystallizes such themes onto the topos of skin. This accompanies a second work on surfaces, epidermal and otherwise, in Liz Oakley-Brown's *Shakespeare on the Ecological Surface*. Espinosa's collection considers skin's (im)permeability, markability, rewritability, interiority and exteriority, animality, signification, representability, readability, transformation, and reveals a network of overlapping epidermal semiotics chiefly contextualized within the approaches of critical race and postcolonial studies. In Oakley-Brown's work, which is steeped in its contexts of production as it was written in relative isolation during the height of the COVID-19 pandemic, surfaces such as steam, snails, smoke, silk and soil are treated through a sparky, corona-viral lens. These two different works introduce new lines of inquiry into skins and surfaces in Shakespeare, primarily inflected through racial identity and infection.

In Oakley-Brown's short work, we encounter the smokelessness of *The Taming of the Shrew*; snails defined not by slime but by their blindness and 'experiential rather than visual mode of existence' (142); the skyward thoughts of Hamlet and Antony who want to colonize the heavens; the literal steaminess of *Venus and Adonis*; and how *Richard II*, *Hamlet* and *Timon of Athens* ought to be approached as 'Soilscape Tragedies' (118). Tightly, clingingly rooted in the pandemic conditions that shaped it, the work in many ways is most fascinating for exploring the kinds of thought and experience produced by doing scholarship in such isolating, infectious conditions. It offers inventive connections between Shakespeare and the surfaces of things, sliding and sticking between plays and ideas as it considers Shakespeare and our contact with ecological 'skins'.

Skin is the often permeable surface treated in Espinosa's work. Skin, Espinosa writes, 'should point us purposefully at understandings of the way skin touches on our relationship – both in positive and in destructive ways – to our world and those who surround us' (2). Writing prior to the 2024 American presidential election, Espinosa argues, 'When it comes to considering how notions of one's value, legitimacy, citizenship, human rights and belonging are often tethered to the color of one's skin, the stakes could not be higher in interrogating these interconnections and in considering how structures of white supremacy function therein' (3). Along with Bailey and many essays in the *Oxford Handbook to Shakespeare and Race*, these analyses of white supremacy are about to become more relevant than ever.

Titus Andronicus unsurprisingly features significantly in this collection, highlighting Aaron's blackness as well as the play's spectacular approach to victimhood. For Sandra Young, 'it is the position of the witness when bodily violation is rendered spectacular: to what extent might the witness be implicated in the violence that has been brought into view along with the victim's violated body' (253). For Karen Raber, in considering Aaron, 'the multiplicity of species used to reflect his racial status and attach it to his scheming nature ... threaten to become, in the end, merely illegible' (45). Across illuminating analyses of Aaron's hair, Queen Mab's locs, and comparisons between Portia and the golden fleece, Raber demonstrates the importance of hair in drawing national boundaries, and demonstrates how 'Racializing fictions and anthropocentric fictions ... cooperate in manufacturing the bestialized racialized characters that populate early modern European texts', which 'does not reliably result in their mutual reinforcement; more often, the consequence is their mutual subversion' (44).

Hermione in *The Winter's Tale* presents another focus for thinking about skin. In an excellent analysis of Hermione's wrinkles, DiGangi considers how this skin 'serve[s] as a point of convergence for early modern ideologies of race, gender, and sexuality' (97). This reinterpretation of Hermione's skin as '"un-faired" or age-darkened beauty' offers an important analysis of the racialization of different shades of whiteness as considered through the lens of ageing (97). Jennifer Park presents a fascinating examination of 'Shakespearean skincrafts', considering how 'recipe and crafting culture ... informed early modern English ideas about the skin as manipulable' (228). Through Hermione's white-faced statue, Park thrillingly argues how 'Whiteness can transform into whiteness and be celebrated. To any other ends without whiteness, Shakespearean skincrafts can only safely cover, preserve, transmit' (248). Also covering Celia's umber in *As You Like It*, candying and dis-candying in *Antony and Cleopatra*, and how Othello's handkerchief transmits blackness, the theorization of skincrafts is an exciting means of specifying other forms of early modern race-making.

Elsewhere, Craig Koslofsky and Sachini K. Seneviratne ask how skin became so important on the early modern stage, arguing that 'two sets of developments started to transform the place of skin in Western European thought, culture and practice. One was rooted in medicine – specifically anatomy and pathology – and the other in European expansion into the wider world' (13). The intertwining of such developments gives rise to their concept of the Möbius skin, where 'early modern skin was epistemologically ungrounded, struggling to be both "open" and "closed"' (15). This chimes well with many of Oakley-Brown's reconsiderations of where the boundaries might lie between one surface and another. Another way in to thinking about such boundaries is in Bernadette Andrea's consideration of Caliban as a hinge to whiteness, one that facilitates thinking about Islamophobia as 'an amalgam of residual and emergent modes of racism' (272). Meanwhile, in *Love's Labour's Lost*, Darryl Chalk questions 'What might the plethora of pale, predominantly white, young lovers that adorn Shakespeare's comedies tell us about early modern conceptions of skin?' (70), and, in doing so, demonstrates the lack of whiteness's neutrality in this text and the deranging impact of love melancholia on deciphering such whiteness.

Finally, Wendy Lennon argues in 'Skin/Pedagogy' for three principles to confront race and improve racial literacy: to 'root teaching and learning in hope', and for 'educators and learners . . . to reflect on their own positionality', and to 'be aware of and actively confront the continuing professional development of our staff' (212–13). In a useful complement to several essays on similar themes in the *Oxford Handbook to Shakespeare and Race*, Amrita Sen, Boram Choi, Katherine Gillen and Alfredo Michael Modenessi consider appropriations of Shakespeare across Indian, Japanese, US-Mexican and Spanish adaptations. Concluding with a final discussion on Indigenous theoretical response to Shakespeare, this edited collection offers a wide range of thinking about the racialization of skin that contributes valuably to ongoing conversations about critical race studies, and particularly critical whiteness studies.

On the day before Halloween 2024, Donald Trump posed a haunting threat: 'I want to protect the women . . . whether the women like it or not' (qtd in Helmore).[12] Trump's vow to protect women from illegal immigrants performs several acts: erasing women's ability to consent, situating women within inescapable victimhood, villainizing immigrants (coded as primarily Black and Hispanic) as sexually violent, and enabling his own access (and the access of white men everywhere) to women. Such a rhetorical feat accomplishes many other goals, such as minimizing and excusing the sexual violence of white men, as well as diminishing the potential sexual victimhood of men, boys and non-binary people. And the women themselves, stuck in Trump's particular brand of white supremacist misogyny, are assumed to be white and cisgender. Trump's election comes with the promise

of redefining consent within a specific nationalistic framework to uphold American white supremacy.

But as Amanda Bailey's book *Shakespeare on Consent* reminds us, such strategizing is hardly new. 'Consent has long served as a mechanism of domination' (6) she argues, and considers 'what consent means when it is calibrated by race, ethnicity, class, sexuality, disability, and gender' (2). Bailey argues for understanding the construction and purposes of consent, questioning the binary of victim/perpetrator and the network of particularly racial and national power within which it is imbricated. Over six chapters that address rape and nationhood, shame and sexual subjectivity, incapacity and consent, the centrality of the bed, desire in relation to consent, and the conflict between personal desire and that of others, Bailey skilfully and virtuosically interrogates the uses and problems of consent. Reading transhistorically between contemporary political moments (Bill Clinton and Monica Lewinsky, the storming of the Capitol, the Jerry Sandusky scandal, the Steubenville rape case) and Shakespeare's plays, Bailey deftly ties together questions of sexual consent and reads new perspectives into both the plays and our modern moment.

Such readings feel more urgent than ever in the wake of Trump's re-election, which lingered over my reading of this work. In reading *The Rape of Lucrece*, Bailey emphasizes the state use of Lucrece's violated body, examining 'how the violation of an individual comes to register primarily as injury to the collective' (31). We must attend carefully to these identifications of how 'The mobilization of the threat to rape to gin up white supremacist sentiment is not unique to contemporary US political culture', in order to understand, strategize against, and resist these repeating paradigms and the violence they enable (39). In considering sexual shame, Bailey considers its stickiness and its transgressive nature, shifting from perpetrator to victim and eroding the boundaries of selfhood. After noting in the introduction how '*Hamlet* gestures toward procrastination as politics' (24), Bailey asks (but does not answer) 'What did this man [Hamlet Sr] do to his son?' (80) to prompt such terror in the Prince of Denmark. Against the rape of Lucrece, whose spectacular nature has always, for me,

---

[12] Helmore, Edward, 'Donald Trump vows to be protector of women "whether they like it or not"', *Guardian*, 31 October 2024, www.theguardian.com/us-news/2024/oct/31/donald-trump-women-protector-wisconsin-rally.

rendered it inauthentic to the experience of sexual violence, Hamlet's unaddressed debt to a father he fears who haunts him proposes a compelling new way into thinking about how we identify and relate to the after-effects of sexual trauma.

Chapter 3 turns to incapacity: intoxication and somnophilia. What is it that assailants find particularly arousing about lack of consent due to incapacity? While readings of Desdemona's death traditionally emphasize her passivity and subservience to her husband, Bailey reconfigures the pivotal moment to Othello's voyeuristic poring over her sleeping form, asking if it is 'the allure of Desdemona's incapacitated body' which 'propels Othello to follow through with his plan?' (93). She identifies too a crucial moment of audience response and consent in *A Midsummer Night's Dream*, where Puck's closing speech is reconfigured as an invitation to secure the audience in complicity with the play's non-consensual erotic happenings: 'if you are offended by having witnessed the imagined and threatened − if not actual − abduction and violation of incapacitated boys, lower rank men, and women, but did not protest . . . Then you too are in effect no different from the perpetrators you have watched' (99). In then examining the bed trick, Bailey's emphasis is on these intimate locations as sites of vulnerability and injury. Looking again to *A Midsummer Night's Dream*, Bailey asks 'what individuals and communities can and cannot remember about expropriation and sexual violence shows forgetting to be as active a process as remembering' (123). Chapter 5 puns on the once again exhaustingly familiar MAGA slogan: 'Make Sex Great Again'. *Romeo and Juliet* is positioned as the source of many modern Western cultural encounters with 'great sex' due to its prominence in high school classrooms, but it is the intertwining of sex with the civil that Bailey identifies as so crucial to these encounters. 'The play establishes a link between civility and rape culture as it shows male desire to be an uncontrollable force that overrides autonomy', she writes (141). Chapter 6 asks, 'Should the desires and fantasies you have allow you to ignore the way your personal intimacies are shaped by, shape, and move through and around institutions of which you are a part?' (173), and emphasizes non-performance as a strategy for survival.

If there is one difficult subject I wish this book could have treated in more depth it is the relationship between lack of consent and pleasure, which Fischler troubles so extensively in his work on *Screw Consent*. Through a feminist lens, we now fall easily into not only identifying the non-consent of Isabella and the Duke or Miranda and Caliban, but also their lack of sexual pleasure. A culture that casually erodes female sexual consent when in service to the state must also (however uncomfortably) consider where female pleasure may still be located in that world. These women's pleasure or lack thereof is one on which the plays are silent. And such questions can be posed of non-women victims in Shakespeare: Hamlet and his father, Ariel and Sycorax, Venus and Adonis.

Finally, I turn to *Shakespeare and Cultural Appropriation*, edited by Vanessa I. Corredera, L. Monique Pittman and Geoffrey Way. Writing this review on the day after Donald Trump was announced to have been elected once again president of the United States of America is a sobering task. Reading the book the day before the call, I heartily noted down Joyce Green MacDonald's condemnations of analyses of Trump voters: 'I mean, he's not even president anymore and people still want to talk to Trump voters. It's like, it's over, you need to move on' (218). This was, unfortunately, a book that needed to be evaluated within the framework that we have not been permitted to move on.

Over nine essays and four interviews, *Shakespeare and Cultural Appropriation* presents lightning flashes of critical and historical engagement with what it means to appropriate Shakespeare. Firstly, 'appropriation' here is defined with resistance to the idea as a binary mode − as one culture with total power over another, but one that is variably beneficial and exploratory as well as sometimes oppressive and dangerous. This draws on Richard A. Rogers's four types of appropriation: cultural exchange, cultural dominance, cultural exploitation and transculturation. The essays are concerned throughout with the nature of different domains of power and Shakespeare's relationship to authority, cultural identity and freedom. Such freedoms are those of entire peoples, of individuals deprived of education, of the ability to work in the academy.

In the first section, there are three diverse and compelling analyses of Shakespeare's role in constructing national identity in Europe, the USSR and Franco Spain. Ingrid Radulescu and L. Monique Pittman consider the translation of Romanian Hamlets and soft power, and how linguistic choices normalize through Shakespearian authority 'the gender inequalities of Romania's past and political present' (38). Elena Bandín turns to television adaptations in Franco's Spain, noting the use of Shakespearian authority as part of its 'propaganda regime' to 'fill the void left by the republican dramatists' (53). In the USSR, Natalia

Khomenko analyses stagings of *Othello* – the most popular Shakespeare play at this time by a wide margin – and the use of Othello's blackness to stage it 'as an anti-racist play . . . to serve the state's political ends by securing allies in its opposition to the capitalist West and by countering accusations of internal colonization' (78).

The next section considers three responses to Shakespeare: Tayeb Salih's *Season of Migration to the North*, Margaret Atwood's *Hag-Seed*, and Preti Taneja's *We That Are Young*. Ambereen Dadabhoy considers Salih's novel alongside Ira Aldridge's performance of *Othello*, where 'Aldridge's Black identity and subjectivity challenge the whiteness of both Shakespeare and the white actors who had, until that point, opened and determined the meanings of Othello and his Blackness' (95). Ultimately, Dadabhoy argues that the violence of the Other 'only matters in the context of a cross-cultural encounter, that it can be located and pathologized only within specific bodies deemed to be worthier of both social and scholarly attention' (107). Elizabeth A. Charlebois pushes against the popular reading of Atwood's work as subversive of patriarchal power and reads against postcolonial interpretations to instead emphasize Atwood's identification with Prospero, and how 'Rather than breaking free from them [racial stereotypes], she becomes their apologist and contemporary ventriloquist' (125). For Taarini Mookherjee, Taneja's work 'furthers an intersectional critique of the patriarchal attitudes underpinning both the Shakespeare play and contemporary India' (145). Together, these essays examine how Shakespeare is employed for both subversive and normative adaptation, even covertly.

Finally, on appropriation, reparation and the archive, the essays treat Aditi Brennan Kapil's play *Imogen Says Nothing*, the archives of the Shakespeare Birthplace Trust (SBT), and Caridad Svich's *Twelve Ophelias*. For Kathryn Vomero Santos, Kapil's play asks similar questions to Bachrach's book: 'How does it feel to be cut? What is a true story anyway? Truth for whom?' (162). The play, Santos argues, offers 'A rallying cry for the necessity to rethink how history is constructed from archives that are full of accidents, absences, and violent cuts' (172). For Bachrach, thinking from a literary-critical perspective, such issues are also paramount. Helen A. Hopkins considers 'How the SBT uses international gifts and Shakespeare's cultural capital to promulgate the ideal of a "universal" Shakespeare while also maintaining a clear sense of Stratfordian ownership' (177), and Katherine Gillen explores how Latinx theatre facilitates reparative work on Shakespeare in allowing 'characters, texts, and

even audience members – all unfinished, incomplete, fractured – to move forward toward fuller versions of themselves' (211).

In the first conversation, Sujata Iyengar asks questions of academic precarity and labour conditions, and the flexibility Shakespeare allows in connecting across so many strands of literature and culture. In the wake of another Trump victory that can anticipate future elaborations of the kinds of acts prompted by Ron DeSantis's Floridian 'Don't Say Gay' bill, which has led to the banning of *Romeo and Juliet*, *A Midsummer Night's Dream* and even *Paradise Lost* in some schools,[13] it remains to be seen what role Shakespeare will take, if any, in shaping America's national identity over the next four years – but it may well involve excising him altogether.

I want to conclude by considering two positions, one derived from Bailey's *Shakespeare on Consent* and one from *Shakespeare and Cultural Appropriation*. On 24 September, Donald Trump asked his crowd, 'Did you ever hear Shakespeare?' before following it up with a random idiom that had nothing to do with Shakespeare at all.[14] So, Trump, did we ever hear Shakespeare? Yes, we did once, and only time will tell what Shakespeare's role will be in the next four years of culture wars – but given Shakespeare's centrality to our 'woke leftist' English departments, his role might be in the garbage. For Iyengar, Shakespeare is 'my spaceship' (27): 'a way of knowing' (35) unfixed in space and time. As we confront the prospect of reliving four years that may force us to repeat and exacerbate the anxious havoc of 2016–2020, I hope that Iyengar's optimistic call will allow us some means to escape from this particular place and time. But I also turn to Bailey. We stand on the precipice of an era that promises to set back sexual consent and bodily autonomy to some nebulous, dreamy past (when America was 'great', when you could 'grab 'em by the pussy'), and this will become an inevitable reality for many Americans. What happens in the wake of Isabella's silence to the Duke? If we are to be required

---

[13] 'The Observer view on Ron DeSantis, Shakespeare and sex', *Guardian*, 13 August 2023, www.theguardian.com/commentis free/2023/aug/13/observer-view-on-ron-desantis-shakespeare-sex-censorship-florida-schools.

[14] Quoted in Myriam Page, 'Trump quotes Shakespeare at rally (but gets it wrong) and says he has bigger crowds than Churchill', *Independent*, 24 September 2024, www.independent.co.uk/news/world/americas/us-politics/donald-trump-rally-pennsylvania-shakespeare-crowd-sizes-churchill-b2617949.html.

to 'place your hands below your husband's foot', to 'Come on, and kiss me, Kate', what comes next (*The Taming of the* Shrew 5.2.175–8)? What writing and reinterpretation can we do? How should we try to continue to survive? Perhaps Shakespeare can be that spaceship to transport us to another time, or perhaps literature will be the way to keep us alive in the present. For 'The only thing worthwhile is literature', says Christine Angot, the author of *L'Inceste*: 'Justice, the police, it's nothing' (qtd in Wilentz).[15]

WORKS REVIEWED

Akhimie, Patricia, ed., *The Oxford Handbook of Shakespeare and Race* (Oxford, 2024)

Bailey, Amanda, *Shakespeare on Consent* (London, 2023)

Bachrach, Hailey, *Staging Female Characters in Shakespeare's English History Plays* (Cambridge, 2023)

Campana, Joseph, *Shakespeare's Once and Future Child: Speculations on Sovereignty* (Chicago, 2024)

Corredera, Vanessa I., L. Monique Pittman and Geoffrey Way, eds., *Shakespeare and Cultural Appropriation* (London, 2023)

Espinosa, Ruben, ed., *Shakespeare/Skin: Contemporary Readings in Skin Studies and Theoretical Discourse* (London, 2024)

Gordon, Colby, *Glorious Bodies: Trans Theology and Renaissance Literature* (Chicago, 2024)

Oakley-Brown, Liz, *Shakespeare on the Ecological Surface* (Abingdon, 2024)

Sparey, Victoria, *Shakespeare's Adolescents: Age, Gender and the Body in Shakespearean Performance and Early Modern Culture* (Manchester, 2024)

---

[15] Quoted in H. C. Wilentz, 'The challenge of *L'Inceste* and *The Incest Diary*', *New Yorker*, 15 February 2018, www.newyorker.com/books/page-turner/the-challenge-of-lincest-and-the-incest-diary.

reviewed by EMMA DEPLEDGE[1]

After a brief drought, 2024 saw the release of seven new single-play editions: *As You like It*; *Henry IV, Part I*; *Macbeth*; *Measure for Measure*; *The Merry Wives of Windsor*; *Romeo and Juliet*; and *The Tempest* – all published as part of the Oxford World's Classics New Oxford Shakespeare series. The texts, which are taken from *The New Oxford Shakespeare: The Complete Works*, overseen by Gary Taylor, John Jowett, Terri Bourus and Gabriel Egan in 2016, have now been furnished with compelling new introductions by Todd Andrew Borlik, Indira Ghose, Emma Smith, Emma Whipday, Callan Davies, Hannah August and Lauren Working, respectively, with more of the editions (twenty-eight in total) set to be released at the start of 2025.

New monographs included Ted Tregear's exploration of Shakespeare's position within the commonplace market in *Anthologizing Shakespeare, 1593–1603*, but the majority of work released in late 2023 and 2024 continued to mark the anniversary of the 1623 Folio: *The Library* issued James West's updates on the 'History of the Shakespeare First Folio' and the First Folio *Census*, and *Shakespeare Quarterly* offered a second anniversary issue, this one made up of essays guest edited by Holger Schott Syme. Further Folio-inspired publications that did not arrive in time for inclusion in this year's review include Matthias Bauer and Angelika Zirker's collection, *Shakespeare's First Folio 1623–2023: Text and Afterlives*, and *The Four Shakespeare Folios, 1623–2023: Copy, Print, Paper, Type*, edited by Samuel V. Lemley.

Crucial but often overlooked female contributions to the field of textual studies were celebrated in an essay by Claire M. L. Bourne that was published as part of Adam Smyth's *The Oxford Handbook of the History of the Book in Early Modern England*. Emma Smith and Lukas Erne contributed essays to *Liber amicorum H. R. Woudhuysen: A Bibliographical Tribute*, edited by Daniel Starza Smith and Hazel Wilkinson. Smith's essay focuses on the lost play 'Love's Labour's Won', while Erne examines the practice of scholarly editing. Journal articles included comparison of the cursive 'h' found in a newly discovered manuscript leaf with 'Hand D' of *Sir Thomas More* and – as an antidote to what Adam G. Hooks has termed (first) 'folio fatigue' – computational analysis of damaged and distinctive type to identify the printers behind all three sections of the fourth Shakespeare Folio of 1685.

EDITIONS

The fabulous introductory essays in the Oxford World's Classics New Oxford Shakespeare editions (OWC) are entirely new, but the textual work, attributions and notes are the work of the New Oxford Shakespeare (NOS) editors. It is a strange marriage, and the merging of the two series has advantages and drawbacks. A major event in the history of Shakespeare editing, the NOS (reviewed by Peter Kirwan in a previous issue of *Shakespeare Survey*) consisted of four related publications issued in 2016–2017: a *Modern Critical Edition* (*MCE*) that featured modernized spelling; a two-volume *Critical Reference Edition* (*CRE*), with original spelling; an *Authorship Companion*; and an accompanying website that combined aspects of the print volumes.[2] It should be noted that the textual work for *As You like It* was completed by Connor; *Henry IV, Part I*, by Anna Pruitt; *Macbeth*, by Jowett; *Measure for Measure*, by Bourus; *The Merry Wives of Windsor*, by Sarah Neville; *Romeo and Juliet*, by Connor; and *The Tempest*, by Rory Loughnane. Glosses – which are also provided by NOS editors – render the playtexts highly accessible.[3]

Paperback editions of individual plays cannot hope to contain all of the information provided in so many colossal volumes. Nonetheless, one problem with basing editions for a wide readership on the NOS's texts is that more explanation is needed than can be contained in the page and a half 'Note on the Text' its general editors provided for each of the OWC editions. As was much discussed at the time of its release, the NOS editors made controversial claims about the size and make-up of the Shakespeare canon and co-

---

[1] Sincere thanks to Simone Camponovo and Honor Jackson for their help in the preparation of this review section.

[2] An additional volume with 'Alternate versions' of the texts has long been promised but had yet to appear in print at the time of writing.

[3] *As You Like It* is the only edition released thus far said to also include 'a few notes and emendations' especially made 'for this edition' (52).

authorship, much of it supported by author attribution techniques, using computational stylistic approaches such as Word Adjacency Networks (WANs). A very positive upside of linking their canon to the OWC series is that *Arden of Faversham*, one assumes, is set to become available at a very low price in most high street bookshops. On the other hand, the same marketing that will be beneficial to lesser-known plays will also serve to cement conclusions embedded in the NOS in the minds of the general public.

It is debatable whether the short notes on textual choices do enough to prepare new readers for the potential shock of being told, in some instances, that what they hold in their hands is not a Shakespeare play but instead largely the work of Thomas Middleton. Concerning *Macbeth*, a folio-only play, Jowett's textual note restates the hypothesis that the folio text represents Middleton's adaptation of the play, with (unknowable) cuts made, and additions including 'the genre-bending passages presenting Hecate in 3.5 and part of 4.5' (37). The folio text has also been augmented by the addition of the full text of two songs (whereas the folio contains first lines only), and here it is explained that these come from Middleton's *The Witch*. Liable to create confusion is the apparent contradiction between statements that the text that readers have in front of them is 'Middleton's adaptation' and any attempt to reconstruct a pre-adaptation *Macbeth* would be 'speculative and incomplete', but that 'no continuous scene heading is provided for 3.5, because this scene is understood not to have appeared in Shakespeare's original version of the play' (38). The reader may be forgiven for asking what is 'understood' or known and what is 'speculation'. What is at stake here is not so much whether or not one agrees with the hypothesis but rather the fact that readers of the OWC editions are not privy to detailed accounts of the analysis, rationale or methodologies on which these conclusions are based.

Another case in point is Bourus's note on the text of *Measure for Measure*, where she does little to prepare the reader for the announcement that what they have in their hands is not an edition of Shakespeare's play but rather an adaptation. She refers to a performance of the play by the King's Men in 1604, states that the 1623 Folio is the only textual witness and that 'the play's text seems to have been significantly altered' in the interim. She dedicates a paragraph to the questionable nature of Shakespeare's authorship of the single-stanza song 'Take, oh take those lips away' (4.1), before confronting readers with the bald statement that 'the present edition

[of *Measure for Measure*] is based on Middleton's adaptation, probably written in late 1621' (48), without further explanation.

The General Editor's preface to the New Oxford Shakespeare is included in each OWC edition, but this sales pitch for the USP of the NOS, like other notes directing readers to its different volumes, risks stressing just how much is missing from the present editions. For example, Jowett's note on the text of *As You Like It* informs readers that the Folio is the first textual witness and provides helpful information about the play's songs, but readers of this and other editions are redirected to the *CRE* if they want to read 'a transcription and discussion of the original music manuscripts from this play', and the *MCE* if they wish to see 'a modern musical score' (52). To do so, they would need to shell out a lot more money than they did for their OWC edition: the NOS volumes retail for over £300.

Romeo and Juliet is exceptional among the editions released so far in that a genuine distinction is made between the texts found in the two series, but it does not result in the most resounding of endorsements for the OWC. Readers are told that the text of 'the New Oxford Shakespeare Complete Works and this Oxford World Classics edition' is based on the 1599 second quarto. However, whilst 'The New Oxford Shakespeare edition emphasizes the uninterrupted sequence of scenes, as presented in the play's first performances', the Oxford World's Classics volume instead features 'traditional act and scene numbers', which were 'conjecturally and anachronistically inserted by later editors' (46). Anachronism and conjecture will no doubt be real selling points for anyone browsing this edition in a bookshop but, sarcasm aside, Taylor's note on the text is worthy of praise as it stands out as being a particularly lucid, easy to follow stand-alone account of textual variants between the different quartos and the 1623 Folio edition of *Romeo and Juliet*.

A helpful 'Chronology of William Shakespeare' is included as a preliminary in each OWC edition and this is, happily, far more nuanced than the discussions of chronology and authorship found in the NOS *Authorship Companion*. Concerning the anonymously published *Arden of Faversham*, it is stated that 'many critics agree Shakespeare had a hand in scenes 4–8, and dispute scene 9' (55), a far less forceful assertion than the *Companion*'s claim that scenes 4–9 have been 'unequivocally' classified as Shakespeare's and that it is 'impossible' to believe that Shakespeare had no hand in the play (181, 193). There is also no reference to 'Love's Labour's

Won', included as part of the NOS 'canon', beyond quoting it as part of the list of Shakespeare plays given in Frances Meres's *Palladis Tamia* (c.1597). Users may, however, question why the timeline does not include reference to what Bourus says about the text of *Measure for Measure* having been written by Middleton in 1621, or even, more generally, why some of the editions are not accompanied by a chronology of Middleton's life and career in place of Shakespeare's.

The new chronology helpfully situates the writing of Shakespeare's plays, and their publication in different formats, in the context of Shakespeare's life and political developments, such as 'Elizabeth's proclamation for deportation of "blackamores"', plague closures and the founding of different colonies. Each individual edition is also accompanied by a select bibliography of 'General reading' and recommended reading on the play in question, and these do a good job of balancing classical studies, such as Stephen Orgel's *Impersonations: The Performance of Gender in Shakespeare's England* (1996) for *As You Like It*, with important recent scholarship, like Farah Karim-Cooper's *The Great White Bard: How to Love Shakespeare while Talking about Race* (2023).

Rather than full introductions to individual plays, the NOS *MCE* provided a 'sampling of the expanding universe of responses to Shakespeare', which was termed 'tapas Shakespeare' (iv). The OWC editions do a fabulous job of demonstrating how part of Shakespeare's 'timelessness is actually a serial topicality' and how his works 'continue to speak to issues of identity, politics, and culture in new ways' (Emma Smith, OWC General Editor's Preface). The texts may be (textually) based on a complete works edition from almost a decade ago, but the introductions are full of new ideas and readers will be pleasantly surprised by the extent to which these essays enable us to think afresh about some of the best-known plays in the Shakespeare canon.

Smith's introduction to *Macbeth* is a case in point, with its argument about the impact the play's opening stage direction – '*Thunder and Lightning*' – is likely to have had on the audience's bodies, their anxiety-levels, and their relationship to the villainous protagonist. Most likely produced by rolling a cannon ball, the sound of thunder is one that will have created both a loud noise and vibrations, eliciting 'a deep physical resonance, a sensation involving the spectator's whole body' (1). As Smith reminds us, the effect of this stage direction and 'one of the loudest noises ever experienced up close by early modern Londoners' is best understood in the

context of the Gunpowder Plot of 1605, which will have left them 'preoccupied by this breach of what would come to be known as homeland security' (12).

In a fascinating section on newly coined or newly topical terms within the play, Smith explains how *Macbeth* is replete with references to the Plot and the trials that followed in 1606. These include words that 'came to epitomize the Plot', like 'blow' and 'equivocate', a term 'associated with the language of political and ethical evasion and its Jesuit manipulators', which appears six times in *Macbeth*. We are also informed of the surprising fact that the play contains the first use of the word 'assassination' (1.7.2), an extension of the (known) word 'assassin', which was 'originally a word for Muslim fighters in the Crusades' (17). It will likely have both seemed and sounded 'strange'; it is 'an alienating term both in the sense that it implicitly likens Macbeth's plan to something done by exotic and distant people', and because it will have escaped the comprehension of the majority of the play's first audiences.

This example of opacity and obscuring fits Smith's (17) reading of Macbeth's first soliloquy (1.7), which she describes as a highly unusual example of such speeches in the Shakespeare canon in that the protagonist does not speak directly or clearly to the audience. In a passage full of beautiful close textual analysis, Smith details the evasive, solipsistic nature of Macbeth's speech, in which he never really says what it is that he is talking about. It is 'as if he cannot bring himself to tell us what he is really thinking' (15). It both does and does not prepare the audience for the crime Macbeth is about to commit and, with this confusion added to the play's startling, loud opening noise, Smith suggests that early audiences will likely have been as jumpy as Macbeth, who is 'morbidly susceptible to sound' (2), thereby aligning them with him as 'every noise' frightens and 'appals' (2.2.55). The overall result, as Smith terms it, is 'the absence of objective distance: we can only be, but never know Macbeth' (19).

Borlik's introduction to *As You Like It* is full of energy and enthusiasm and begins like a sales pitch detailing all that is great about the play, from the fact that it has the largest female role in all of Shakespeare and represents the most musical play in the canon, to its inclusion of a wrestling match 'for those who prefer hard-hitting sports', and even hints of an interest in animal rights (1). A long section is dedicated to Shakespeare's use of sources, particularly to Thomas Lodge's darker romance, *Rosalynde* (1590), and to the pastoral more generally, a genre which, Borlik reminds us, will already have seemed old fashioned to Shakespeare's audiences but will have held a sort of nostalgic, 'damnably quaint' rustic charm (4). A particularly strong subsection covers foresters and laws governing forests that appear to have influenced the play. Throughout, he provides a rich, celebratory handling of the play's treatment of gender, stopping just short of labelling it an Elizabethan version of Judith Butler's *Gender Trouble*.

Ghose provides a learned section on 'Histories' to open her discussion of *Henry IV, Part I*, and uses it to highlight both the context in which Shakespeare was writing and what sets him apart as a writer of histories. She covers the genre's appeal, be it in the public theatres, where there was 'a hunger for stories about the national past', or in the studies of Renaissance writers interested in historiography and – as with the given example of Polydore Vergil – fuelled by a desire to question received accounts of the past and demolish myths. Shakespeare, she argues, draws important distinctions between history and literature (2–3); in his history plays, Shakespeare 'avails himself of anachronism to heighten resonances with the present, and has no qualms reshuffling chronology for dramatic purposes' (8). The Tudor Myth is also explored, along with scholarship on and responses to the genre, ranging from E. M. W. Tillyard through Laurence Olivier's production of a film version of *Henry V* to support British efforts during World War II.

A compelling section entitled 'Shakespeare's Machiavellian Moment' explores the connection between Shakespeare's *Henry IV* and *The Prince*'s philosophy. Ghose's argument challenges conventional interpretations that align Machiavellian thought primarily with Shakespeare's villains. Instead, she positions Prince Hal as Shakespeare's most sophisticated embodiment of Machiavellian strategy. Ghose highlights Hal's soliloquy in 1.2 as a striking illustration of Machiavellian influence. Here, Hal demonstrates his mastery of 'suspense and wonder', skilfully revealing that his tavern escapades were an orchestrated façade (15). This revelation catches the audience off guard and signals the calculated 'surprise' he intends to spring on his peers, aligning with Machiavelli's account of Cesare Borgia's strategic use of shock-and-awe tactics to manipulate perception and consolidate power. Her analysis underscores Hal's deliberate and pragmatic approach, suggesting a ruler who will carefully manage his image and actions, embodying Machiavellian principles of political strategy and foresight. By portraying Hal as a tactician who shapes his destiny through calculated manoeuvres, Ghose offers an insightful reinterpretation of Shakespeare's character as one deeply informed by

Renaissance political thought, challenging the notion that his rise is driven solely by fortune or circumstance.

Another highlight is Ghose's analysis of characters as she asks whose history is told in the play, identifies Hotspur as one of the play's most memorable characters, and analyses the names 'Falstaff' and 'Oldcastle'. Drawing on the 'religious turn' in Shakespeare criticism to revisit censorship theories that have been proposed to explain these and other name changes in different versions of the play, Ghose shifts focus to a broader question: rather than fixating on whom Falstaff might represent, she asks why Shakespeare included him in the play and examines the function he serves. Her answer is that Falstaff is not merely a source of humour and wit but also a vessel through which Shakespeare celebrates the complexity of human nature. Falstaff embodies the contradictions of human life – its pleasures and its pains – allowing Shakespeare to present a nuanced vision of humanity in ways unparalleled in historical drama. Ghose concludes that Falstaff enriches the play by portraying human experience with a depth and vitality that transcends its historical framework, showcasing Shakespeare's innovative approach to character and narrative.

Whipday's introduction to *Measure for Measure* provides a fresh analysis of Isabella's interactions with Angelo, focusing on the 'dangerous game of imagination' she initiates. By asking Angelo to engage in 'a series of imaginative substitutions' to foster empathy and spare her brother's life, Isabella's actions, Whipday argues, closely mirror 'the act of performing a play' (3). This interpretation draws attention to the often-overlooked metatheatrical elements of *Measure for Measure*, highlighting how its structure encourages audiences and readers to confront moral dilemmas – asking themselves what they would do if they held Angelo's power or if 'their own kin were under his sentence' (4).

The play's concern with 'the act of shared imagination' (4), she argues, extends to its reliance on the audience's willingness to suspend disbelief, as seen when a mere cloak conceals the Duke's identity from all that know him and convinces others he is a friar. Whipday connects these self-aware depictions of performance and substitution to the political climate during the play's creation, reflecting on the transition of power as James I ascended the throne following Elizabeth I's reign. This alignment between theatrical representation and political change underscores the play's exploration of authority, identity and the shared illusions that sustain societal and dramatic structures. Other topics covered in this rich piece include the 'Monstruous Ransom', how the Duke can be seen as 'the most difficult to pin down' of the play's characters (14), treatment of *Measure for Measure*'s near obsession with women's maidenhead, and 'Marriage and Death'.

Davies presents a thorough and insightful introduction to *Merry Wives of Windsor*, exploring the play's status as a 'spin-off' and its relationship to the Henriad, as well as ways in which critics have responded to the Falstaff depicted in this play versus the character in the history plays. He also explores questions of genre and style, highlighting *Merry Wives* as a blend of domestic and city comedy, characterized by its heavy use of prose. He situates the play within its social and spatial context, discussing Windsor's representation and its implications for social status. His analysis extends to the themes of physical households and their dynamics, material culture (notably fabric and the iconic laundry basket) and the treatment of marriage and gender roles. One of Davies's most illuminating observations relates to the play's self-awareness in its exploration of role-playing and its engagement with 'social themes and contexts' (32). He offers a nuanced discussion of the play's reliance on physical comedy, unscripted moments, and its capacity to animate 'pre-modern ideas of fun' (37), showcasing *Merry Wives* as a vibrant, comedic work that is deeply connected to its cultural and theatrical milieu.

August uses the prologue to *Romeo and Juliet* to consider the play's structure and its interest in binaries. Noting how unusual it is for a prologue to give so many spoilers, she offers astute analysis of the impact it has on audiences. For example, it both anchors the Italian setting, with its associations with Petrarchan love and Catholicism, and ensures that 'subsequent action and dialogue is studded with painful moments of dramatic irony' (1). Attention is also paid to the play's genre and the way in which we are presented with paired scenes, whereby the first is comic and the second tragic, such as when Romeo and Mercutio's battle of wits (2.4) is revisited as a literal sword fight in 3.1, or in the case of Romeo and Juliet's two exchanges at her window, one of which ends in hope (2.1), the other with despair (3.5). Addressing the fallacy that this play constitutes the greatest love story of all time, she suggests that *Romeo and Juliet* instead 'explores the failure of both Petrarchan and platonic scripts of love to accommodate real world exigencies' (16).

Finally, in her account of *The Tempest*, Working presents the play as pastoral romance and travel story,

and as a critique of colonialism. She identifies traces of early modern literature proposing plantations in colonies in the play and contrasts this with critiques of imperialism, exemplified by lines spoken by Gonzalo (Shakespeare's 'most measured counsellor') which, for Working, echo Michel de Montaigne's defence of indigenous societies and reflect tensions the play stages between colonial ambition and utopian ideals. There is also a lovely account of the play's 'Language and Music', and a section on 'Books, Clothes, and Fragments' which illuminates the symbolic and thematic significance of material culture in the play. Further, she delves into the themes of 'Wonders, Illusion, and Intoxication', and explores the various forms of magic represented in the narrative in a segment titled 'Rejecting and Reclaiming the Witch'.

The different introductions show varying levels of interest in questions raised by the NOS. Some engage with textual decisions and authorship in detail (see, for example, Borlik, 34–9, and Smith, 23), and Davies reminds readers that 'Shakespeare and his audiences would have understood "the play" *Merry Wives* to be far more than the text presented in quarto or Folio, or in any modern edition, and to encompass elements that went beyond scripted dialogue' (2). Ghose's discussion of character names reflects a similar attitude to Davies, whilst others analyse their play without reference to early printed texts or the NOS.

Indeed, one of the greatest strengths of the OWC series is that the scholars introducing the plays have clearly been given the freedom to reflect their own interests and present the plays on their own terms. Concerning performance history, the result is that Smith's entire discussion of *Macbeth* is supported by helpful illustrative examples from past productions, films, and TV adaptations, most of which are still available to watch in one form or another (a thoughtful touch), whereas August pays focused attention to forms of performance, with separate sections on 'Early Modern Performances', 'Later Performance History', and on 'Altering and Augmenting the Text', from Restoration adaptations through recent productions that have 'explicitly embraced queer identities for the supporting characters' (43). Working has a closing section in which she charts adaptations and productions of *The Tempest*, from *The Sea Voyage* (1622) and John Dryden and William Davenant's *Enchanted Island* (1667), through postcolonial works, such as Aimé Césaire's *Une Tempête* (1969), to recent stage productions like Mohegan director and performer Madeline Sayet's solo performance of *Where*

We Belong at the Globe Theatre in 2019. Each approach to performance afterlives works equally well and it is refreshing not to have the same subheadings repeated for each play. Indeed, the varied structures contribute to the series' achievement in celebrating each play individually, on its own merits. It should also be noted that, in contrast to some of the notes on texts discussed above, the introductions each do a great job of balancing academic rigour and discussion of recent scholarship and debates with accessibility and an awareness of what it is that makes these plays 'classics'.

TEXTUAL STUDIES

Tregear's *Anthologizing Shakespeare* presents an exciting new perspective on Shakespeare's role as a literary author, portraying him as actively engaged in shaping the reception of his plays and poems. Tregear identifies what he terms Shakespeare's 'Anthologizing Period', a distinct phase in his early print career, from *Venus and Adonis* in 1593 to *Hamlet* in 1603. During this time, Shakespeare not only dominated anthologies but also embedded within his works 'conspicuously extractable passages' crafted to capture the attention of readers looking to select and extract material (25). Tregear argues that these passages were designed to do more than stand out to would-be commonplacers; they also invite reflection on the act of excerption itself – how it influences the meaning of a text, the voices it 'invests with authority', and the interpretations it enables or distorts (25). His study deepens our understanding of Shakespeare's print strategies in important ways, revealing his nuanced awareness of commonplace culture and ways in which his works could be curated, repurposed and consumed by contemporary readers.

Recent studies have explored commonplacing and anthologizing, but they tend to treat individual titles like the five anthologies considered by Tregear – *The Passionate Pilgrim* (1599), *England's Parnassus* (1600), *Bel-vedére* (1600), *Englands Helicon* (1600) and *Loves Martyr* (1601) – in isolation. This is understandable as there are notable differences between the form and contents of these collections and, as Tregear recognizes, they can be, and have been, classified under different generic labels. His rationale for grouping the five volumes together includes sensitive analysis of the floral metaphors running through them (including in their subtitles, e.g. *Bel-vedére* is a 'Garden of the Muses' and *Parnassus* a collection of 'choysest Flowers') and a reminder that 'although the word "anthology" had not yet passed into

English, the Greek *anthologia*, a compound of anthē legein, means a collection of flowers: anthology is choysest Flowers' (11). *The Passionate Pilgrim*, Tregear argues, ought thus to be seen as 'an anthology in disguise', and the contents may have been the work of a number of different writers but, with its title-page attribution, it 'singled Shakespeare out as representative of a whole style of 1590s poetry' (7).

Tregear breaks new ground by examining Shakespeare's role within the anthology genre as a whole, offering a more integrated perspective and an overview of the 'common problems' anthologies address (6). This yields significant insights, including statistical analyses that shed new light on the position and prominence of Shakespeare plays and poems across the corpus. For example, we learn that Shakespeare (cited 240 times) comes second only to Edmund Spenser in *Bel-vedére*, but is the most prominent dramatist in *Parnassus*, with 30 quotes from the plays and 65 from the poems.

The most frequently anthologized play in *Parnassus* and *Bel-vedére* is *Richard II*, and it is John of Gaunt's deathbed scene that seems to have most attracted the compilers. He contends that this selection highlights an inherent affinity between the play's structure and the anthology's form, and argues that the anthologies' focus on John of Gaunt's words in *Richard II* enhances, rather than diminishes, their connection to the emotional power of the dying scene. According to Tregear, Shakespeare uses the play to explore how historical drama can incorporate words that transcend their original spatial and temporal context – words that, through their potential for inclusion in anthologies, strive to establish an independent historical identity (35).

Lucrece is extracted more than any other Shakespeare text in *Parnassus*, with 39 extracts (ahead of *Venus and Adonis* with 26), and in *Bel-vedére*, with 97 extracts. We are told that these include many of the lines marked as *sententiae* in the 1594 edition of *Lucrece*, published by Richard Field, but they are 'not restricted to those lines alone' (109). Describing the 1594 *Lucrece* as 'an edition as likely to be authorized as anything Shakespeare issued', Tregear suggests plausibly that the inverted commas marking 'selected lines' in the margins may well have been Shakespeare's own additions (111). However, what strengthens Tregear's argument and enables him to push beyond previous accounts of typographical markers of literary *sententiae*, such as those in the 1603 quarto edition of *Hamlet*, is his identification of meta references to practices of excerpting and remembering across various Shakespearian texts. Lines like Adonis' calling Venus an 'over-handled theme', or his statement that 'the text is old, the orator too green', clearly comment on and invite commonplacing, as do many of Polonius's maxims, discussed in the chapter on tragedies. Further, he identifies thematic resonances between *Lucrece* and the anthologies that later featured Shakespeare's works, drawing attention to Lucrece's 'preoccupation with quoting: what it means to be quoted, misquoted, and to live on in quotations' (109). These examples cannot be mere printshop additions, they indeed seem to show Shakespeare engaging actively with the practices of excerpting and memorialization, embedding within his texts an awareness of their potential afterlives.

In sum, Tregear's monograph offers invaluable insights into Shakespeare's early reception, showing that he was not only read 'closely and enthusiastically', but also regarded as 'worthy of comparison with the best of his contemporaries' (6). The study also sheds light on the history of reading and book use through its analysis of manuscript annotations, including examples of readers amending excerpts to align with their sources. By bridging textual analysis with the broader cultural practices of anthologizing and reading, *Anthologizing Shakespeare* promises to significantly impact Shakespeare studies and the field of book history, offering a deeper understanding of how Shakespeare's works were consumed, adapted, and canonized in his own time and beyond.

One thing that Tregear was not able to shed light on is 'Love's Labour's Won', a play Emma Smith suspects might, if it was indeed ever printed or performed, be preserved within such anthologies, albeit without attribution. As mentioned above, Meres included the title in a list of Shakespeare plays given in *Palladis Tamia: wits Treasury*. A second reference to the title is found in a bookseller's accounts of 1603 (discovered in 1957, within waste papers used to bind a 1637 book), and these, plus other factors, are analysed by Smith in an essay within *Liber amicorum H. R. Woudhuysen*, to suggest that 'Won' likely once existed but is now lost. She shares an original hypothesis about 'Won's' relationship to *Love's Labour's Lost*, questioning assumptions that Won must be a sequel to *Lost* due to 'the syntactic parallel of their titles' (132).

Rather than view *Lost* as an incomplete play or one in need of a sequel – an interpretation grounded in the notion that its ending, where the lovers do not immediately marry, is an unsatisfying conclusion by conventional standards – Smith suggests a different possibility: what if 'Won' predated *Lost*? She challenges the assumption that 'Won' was merely a sequel by pointing out that it is often assumed that it would be 'comically restitutive', even though *Love's Labour's Lost* does not fully dramatize loss. This assumption, she rightly argues, overlooks the 'generic innovation' of *Lost*'s unresolved romantic ending. She gives evidence from across Shakespeare's works to show that phrases like 'won' and 'lost' appear in interchangeable order and, through comparison with other playwrights of the time, notes that it is rare to find pairs of plays with syntactical titles that genuinely form a cohesive narrative unit outside of history plays. This analysis offers a fresh perspective on Shakespeare's treatment of narrative structure and the interplay between his works, even if all we have – until a copy of 'Won' rears its head – is conjecture. Smith's essay is a fitting tribute to Woudhuysen, to whom the collection is dedicated, and who edited *Lost* for Arden 3 (1998).

In an effort to shed light on the often unnoticed or unacknowledged impact of editorial choices, Erne's essay in the same volume identifies thirteen significant types of editorial interventions. These range from decisions about the specific object of editorial recovery – especially critical in cases where multiple early modern versions exist – to elements like introductions, commentary, character lists, act and scene divisions, and approaches to spelling. While the list is not exhaustive, as Erne acknowledges, omitting aspects such as collation, collaboration and the commercial constraints of publishers, it serves as a valuable blueprint for editors and students of textual editing.

The essay enables Erne to make crucial points about 'perverse institutional practices' whereby 'the recognition bestowed on editions is rarely commensurate with the labour and expertise required from the editor' (145). Indeed, academic hiring committees too often choose to overlook the outputs of talented textual editors in favour of those who write monographs, even if, 'unlike academic monographs or journals, important Shakespeare editions are read by tens or even hundreds of thousands of people' (147). This critique underscores the urgent need to re-evaluate how editorial work is valued within academia, advocating greater recognition of the expertise and influence wielded by editors in shaping the reception and understanding of Shakespeare's works.

The topics of ghost copies and editing were also at the heart of a roundtable published as part of *Shakespeare Quarterly*'s second F1 anniversary issue of 2023. Speakers examined the centrality of the 1623 Folio and key trends in editing and textual criticism over the past two decades, thereby providing helpful points of reference for scholars and students alike. Additionally, the discussion (briefly) delved into the potential existence of 'ghost copies' of quartos predating F1. Eric Rasmussen referenced John Berkenhour's *Bibliographia Literaria* (1777), which lists a 1594 *Tempest* and a 1604 *Macbeth*, among others. This was supported by David McInnes, citing *The Beauties of the English Drama* (also 1777), and by reminders of Peter Blayney's estimate that a third of early books went unregistered (364).

Sonia Massai observed a shift in focus away from reconstructing authorial or theatrical intentions towards embracing the diversity of early textual sources. She emphasized the value of acknowledging the uneven quality of copies underlying both F1 and early quartos, suggesting that modern editors are increasingly free to adopt varied approaches (379). McInnes added to this the appealing suggestion that F1 should be viewed less as a first complete works, especially as it was no such thing, and more as a print 'festival' of Shakespeare's plays, 'compiled under tight deadlines and showcasing their variable states of readiness' (379). This perspective, he argued, allows contemporary editors to create editions that reflect 'multiple interpretative possibilities' (379). The session concluded with a forward-looking vision, articulated by Massai, who urged editors to critically reassess the authority traditionally accorded to F1. This 'unpicking' of F1's dominance, she argued, is essential for fostering a richer and more representative approach to editing Shakespeare's works 'that recognizes other types of authorities, including what more diverse editors can bring to Shakespeare' (380).

The special issue, entitled 'The Shakespeare First Folio as Source, Object, and Evidence' is less concerned with celebrating the F1 quatercentenary than it is with highlighting both the volume's status as 'a myriad-faceted brand' (304), and its many inconsistencies, so as to avoid them being 'theorized out of existence' or ignored altogether (304). A fabulous essay by Lucy Munro supports this aim by uncovering the roles played by members of Shakespeare's company whom F1's infamous 'Names of the Principall Actors' list sought to write out of history. Munro begins by detailing a list of books in folio-format owned by Henry Condell and his family that indicates both that actors were 'aware of the advantages of large-format publication' and, importantly, that the 1616 edition of Ben Jonson's *Workes* was 'not the only model available [to Condell] during the planning of the 1623 Shakespeare Folio' (315). But the books owned – which include a copy of Chaucer's works, *The Decameron* and the *Faerie Queen* – also

provide a reminder of just how wealthy and influential Condell was, a point that is made abundantly clear in the remainder of the essay.

Munro analyses the paratext to expose 'unstated rules of inclusion and exclusion', and makes key observations about the version of Shakespeare's company it seeks to represent: it is not only an inaccurate reflection of those who performed Shakespeare's plays, but also a carefully constructed document, one entirely composed of shareholders, that 'represents and is a product of, the company's elite' (326, 316). Indeed, as she goes on to show through careful attention to stage directions and speech prefixes in the playtexts of F1, 'references to hired players, apprentices, and musicians … implicitly acknowledge that there were actors' other than the company implied by the Folio list. This work is coupled with a breathtaking amount of evidence amassed from parish registers, wills and other legal documents which enables Munro to glimpse 'alternative lives and narratives' (316), and to bring to light 'the hierarchies and the invisible labor on which the work of the King's Men depended' (317).

The issue also contains a sub-section, put together by Bourne, which features short essays that address F1's existence as 'an object in the world', be it in the Bodleian library (Tara Lyons), Carl H. Pforzheimer's treatment of his copy, now held at the Harry Ransom Center, the University of Texas at Austin (Aaron T. Pratt), in the hands (or not) of two very different eighteenth-century collectors (Vanessa Braganza), or else by tracing the Auckland Free Library copy's movement from colonial-era donation to source of cross-cultural events (Jane Wild). The issue closes with Jason Scott-Warren's important reminder that petro-capitalism 'funded the establishment of some of the most prominent collections of Shakespeariana in the world' (305), a point which could have been further explored through detailed analysis of these collections and the extent to which they are and are not making efforts to recognize their varied legacies, but the essay instead ends up as an opinion piece rather than offering sustained consideration of the Folio as an object.

Lyons's brilliant chapter, by contrast, returns to sources to correct a narrative alleging that Sir Thomas Bodley banned playbooks from the public library he founded in Oxford in 1598, only to ease the ban in order to house the first Shakespeare Folio in 1624. The story has been repeated so often that it is considered fact. Lyons draws on manuscript library records to reveal 'a rich body of evidence of English playbooks in the pre-

1624 Bodleian collections' (387), and traces the story's rehashing and embellishments in modern scholarship from David-Scott Kastan's 2001 *Shakespeare and the Book* to Stephen Orgel's 2015 *The Reader in the Book*. Indeed, by analysing such 'counterfactual slippages', Lyons suggests that we are able to observe 'how the recirculation of conventional wisdom provided opportunities for scholars to bend the facts to aggrandize Shakespeare' (394). One cannot help but cringe for Douglas A. Brookes, whom Lyons also quotes as repeating the story, when re-reading his suggestion that Bodley 'had a change of heart' by 1623: as Lyons points out, Bodley died over a decade earlier. This essay also exposes scholarly tendencies to privilege the agency of wealthy, named owners and benefactors of repositories whilst overlooking the numerous agents who were responsible and continue to be responsible for the acquisitions, cataloguing, conservation and day-to-day smooth running of libraries and research institutes.

The truth of the matter, Lyons tells us, is that Bodley 'did direct his librarian to reject idle books such as plays in 1612' (388), but he also died shortly after penning that letter. The librarian, Thomas James, 'shelved and catalogued a wide range of English playbooks' as well as almanacs and other popular and small-format books, and did so before 1624 (388). Drama may not have been prioritized by James and his successor, John Rouse, but the library did house 'playbooks by Ben Jonson, George Chapman, Thomas Dekker, Thomas Middleton, Elizabeth Cary, Francis Beaumont, Robert Tailor, Thomas Heywood, and others' (388), as well as the 1616 Jonson Folio, and this long before the infamous Shakespeare Folio was added. These facts are clearly documented in library records, albeit in manuscript records that require persistence on behalf of the researcher. It seems that nobody has bothered to check until now. Or, to take Lyons's more cynical view, nobody has been inclined to check because the truth might disrupt convenient myths about Shakespeare and his Folio (388).

Another stand-out essay in the collection is Pratt's engaging discussion of a collector who, by masking the true make-up of his copy of F1, 'rather ironically obscured the very thing that most distinguishes it' (404). In a bid to raise the First Folio he purchased in the early 1920s to the top category of copies – based on condition and completion, as dictated by the likes of Sidney Lee in his Census of 1902 – Pforzheimer sought to complete and 'perfect' his copy by adding what at first appeared to be missing leaves. Having

consulted with Henrietta C. Bartlett, Pforzheimer had good reason to believe that his copy was not in fact imperfect but instead issued without the bifolium preliminary leaves 'containing Digges's verses and the list of actors' (398). Indeed, Pratt suggests, other surviving copies of F1 indicate that a handful of copies were probably issued without them.

Pforzheimer looks to have bowed to pressure exerted by Lee's system of classification and, having 'completed' his copy through the purchase of facsimile leaves, later felt able to describe his Folio (in the 1940 catalogue of his library) as follows: 'Since this copy was acquired the two preliminary leaves which had been lacking, at least since last bound, have been supplied with genuine originals, inlaid to size. This copy is listed in Lee's Census Class II, Division A. In its present condition it would be eligible for Class I, Division B' (398). He then went on, Pratt explains, to obtain 'a pair of restored originals, but they remain unbound and housed separately from his Folio', and he may well have instructed his cataloguer to downplay the theory of some copies of F1 being issued without the bifolium (398).

In essence, Pforzheimer was probably hedging his bets; 'Had the originals of the Digges and Actors leaves he acquired actually been inserted, he would indeed have earned himself a Class I First Folio', but by noting, even at the bottom of the catalogue page, 'that his copy appears to have been originally sold without them, he could still boast a copy that prompts insight into an untold aspect of [F1's] early circulation' (402). As it is, this case study about the combination of Lee's classification system and Pforzeimer's desire to own a 'perfect', complete copy indicates how collection habits at given moments in time can 'confuse, or even render forever uncertain, part of an entire edition's history' (398).

Further discussion of specific copies of F1 is also found in West's update to his 2003 *Worldwide Census of First Folios*, and in his survey of 'selected events in the story of the First Folio' since the publication of his 2001 *Account of the First Folio Based on Its Sales and Prices, 1623–2000*. To supplement the *Census*, he lists, in chronological order, all sales of Folios and all copies discovered since July of the year 2000. The *Census* listed 228 volumes and this has been taken up to 235. For each 'new' Folio, a new number has been assigned and details of provenance and the buyer, the bookseller or auctioneer, and the price are provided, along with comments related to each of these three categories. These are supplemented by guides for anyone hoping to find a copy: 'Pursuing Leads to "New" Folios', and

'Some Targets for First Folio Hunters'. Chief among the latter is a copy stolen from the Owens College (Christie Library), Manchester in 1972 (W218/Lee 63). It is perhaps worth noting that West records 'ghost' copies in his census, as well as known copies, whereas the online Shakespeare Census, managed by Zachary Lesser and Adam G. Hooks, only records copies whose survival has been confirmed.

West's updated *Account* consists of notes under a series of headings which include, but are not limited to, the project to digitize the Bodleian Library copy of F1, the Folger Shakespeare Library First Folio Exhibitions, sales of institutional copies, the Folio's worth and new record prices, how the Folger's holdings of copies of F1 increased, the theft and recovery of the University of Durham copy (W7), and Claire M. L. Bourne and Jason Scott-Warren's discovery that the manuscript annotations in the copy in the Free Library of Philadelphia (W179) were made by John Milton. It is helpful to have this update in article form, even if the listing feels a little dry in comparison to recent, engaging accounts of the history of copies of this iconic book.

Adam Smyth's refreshing collection, *The Oxford Handbook of the History of the Book in Early Modern England*, is packed with original essays, offering explanations of subjects from 'Ways of approaching the history of the book' and 'Making books', to 'Moving books: selling, circulating, borrowing, imagining' and 'Using books: reading and marketing, collecting and preserving'. It does not repeat the same material or approaches found in previous handbooks and companions, and one of the main strengths of the volume is its dedication to inclusivity and its questioning of 'how it is that book history has been created as a discipline that has perpetuated' inequalities and exclusions (14). This is illustrated (in relation to Shakespeare studies) in the essay discussed below, and in the inclusion of outstanding essays by conservationists, curators, librarians and cataloguers – the experts on whose knowledge all bibliographical and book-historical work depends. Many of the topics covered lie beyond the scope of Shakespeare textual studies and I regret that it is not possible to do justice to the full contents of the collection in this review. The volume as a whole contains vital reading for anyone with an interest in book history, bibliography and the origins, futures and alternate histories of the field.

Claire M. L. Bourne's essay in Smyth's collection, 'The handmaids' tale: book history, Shakespeare, and women's textual labour', investigates how women's bibliographic contributions have often been subsumed into male-dominated narratives of textual history, particularly concerning Shakespeare. She exemplifies this through Charlotte Lennox's *Shakespeare Illustrated* (1752), the first significant study of Shakespeare's sources; Evelyn May Albright, whose *Dramatic Publication in England, 1580–1640* (1927) critiqued foundational theories about Shakespeare's texts, including A. W. Pollard's 'good' and 'bad' quartos; and through the work of Alice Walker, who played a pivotal role in compositor studies in *Textual Problems of the First Folio* (1953), and whose unpublished old-spelling Oxford Shakespeare edition advanced understanding of the labour behind Shakespeare's texts. While Walker's work was recognized in her time, it has often been relegated to feminist critique, Bourne argues, rather than integrated into broader histories of the field. Her essay calls for a re-evaluation of bibliographic history that fully acknowledges the expertise and impact of these pioneering women, arguing that their work is essential for understanding the development of Shakespeare studies and textual editing.

Particularly illuminating is the essay's account of Henrietta C. Bartlett, known for her work on the *Census of Shakespeare's Plays in Quarto* (1916, 1939), but here lauded for her pedagogical innovations in book history and material bibliography. Bourne draws attention to Bartlett's teaching materials, preserved at the Beinecke Library, which include reverse-engineered quarto sheets and samples of early printing. As Bourne rightly summarizes, these resources reflect Bartlett's expertise and her effort to democratize access to bibliographic knowledge, just as Walker's insights into the relationships between compositors, copy and typesetting were transformative, marking a shift in how Shakespearian texts were approached and understood.

Walker also 'challenged the argument that the spelling of certain words written by Hand D in the *Booke of Sir Thomas Moore* manuscript pointed to Hand D being Shakespeare', suggesting that the spellings were 'too common in manuscripts of the period to have any significance' (34). This debate was revisited recently by Molly G. Yarn and Eric Rasmussen. They analysed a distinct scribal habit – 'in which the lower loop of a cursive *h* makes a high arch before connecting with an *a*' – previously thought unique to Shakespeare and Hand D in the *Sir Thomas More* manuscript (452). Their study included a newly discovered English manuscript leaf, dated *c.*1550, which displayed a similar *h-a* ligature. Comparative analysis led them to conclude that this hand differed from Hand D. Additionally, Heather Wolfe, Curator of Manuscripts at the Folger Shakespeare

Library, provided evidence of Robert Devereux, Earl of Essex, using a similar *h-a* form in a 1588 letter. Yarn and Rasmussen therefore understandably concluded that this ligature's presence across multiple examples 'challenges the uniqueness of the form' and may require a reassessment of its role as a link between Shakespeare and the *Sir Thomas More* manuscript (452). The article includes clear images and a diplomatic transcript, allowing readers to assess the evidence for themselves, without needing access to rare or distant archives.

It is always refreshing to see scholars return to old debates with fresh resources, as is also the case with a team of researchers investigating the printers of the fourth Shakespeare Folio of 1685. The 1685 collection was published by Henry Herringman, Richard Bentley, Edward Brewster and Robert Chiswell, whose names appear variously on different imprints, but no printer was named. We know, from George Watson Cole's 1909 work, that it was printed in three separate parts, with separate pagination, by three different printers and, until recently, only the printer of the first part had been identified. Fredson Bowers, writing in 1951, identified Robert Roberts as the printer of this section and, in doing so, corrected C. William Miller's 1948 suggestion that Thomas Newcombe Junior was behind it.

Equipped with the methodologies of computational analysis of damaged and distinctive type, the team – which consists of Christopher N. Warren, Samuel V. Lemley, D. J. Schuldt, Elizabeth Dieterich, Laura S. Deluca, Max G'Sell, Taylor Berg-Kirkpatrick, Kari Thomas, Kartik Goyal and Nikolai Vogler – have convincingly demonstrated that Robert Everingham printed the second section (spanning pages 1–328, sigs. BBBr–EEE8v) and John Macock printed the third section (from page 1 through 304, sigs. AA4–BBBB8v), along with the infamous error '*HAMLET / RPINCE of DENMARK*' echoed in the article's title. Further, their work corroborates Bowers's identification of Roberts as the printer of the first part, spanning signatures A1–Z4.

The approach consists of bringing Optical Character Recognition (OCR) to bear on digital facsimiles of copies of the 1685 Folio and publications with known printers, 'to identify and categorize all majuscule Roman-type pieces', before using 'a combination of computer-aided damage detection, visual inspection, and computational matching' to identify examples of distinctive or broken pieces of type (140, n. 5). In particular, the new attributions are linked to distinctive 'pica body type' and 'titling type matches', the latter of which shows that Macock was responsible for one of the title page's two settings and Roberts for the other (141). The article is accompanied by clear, convincing images to support these findings.

Comparing their methodology with that of Charlton Hinman, who consulted a minimum of three copies of F1 because he was analysing damaged type within a volume to attempt to determine the order in which sheets were printed, the authors note that their work 'requires consulting fewer copies because [they] rely on multiple, highly likely damage matches, for which any single one could conceivably be a phantom but which in toto represent a body of evidence in favor of a given printer' (141, n. 5). That makes good sense but what is lacking from their discussion is attention to the section of F4 that, according to Lara Hansen and Rasmussen, was reprinted in c.1700 by a printer working with Richard Wellington. Wellington inherited Bentley's copies and stock after his death in 1697 but discovered that he had been 'short sheeted' and therefore needed to commission the reprinting of seventeen sheets before he could sell complete copies of F4. The short sheeting can now be blamed on Everingham, as it came from the middle section of the edition, but it would be very interesting to know what further light the authors' study can shed on the printer who produced the reprinted sheets in c.1700.

The discovery is very exciting for Shakespeare studies and for analytical bibliography more generally, and the printers identified are very plausible contenders, given that they are known to have printed other projects for the publishers in question. To take one example, Everingham is known to have printed Bentley projects and even entered copies in the Stationers' Register on his behalf; and Macock, Everingham's former master printer, worked with Herringman on a number of publications. As the authors rightly note, Roberts seems the most unlikely of the three to be involved in the project but they add the fresh hypothesis that he may have stepped in to replace his 'longtime' partner, Anne Maxwell, who frequently worked with Brewster (the other publisher involved in F4), but who looks to have died at some point in 1685.

In sum, the year's work brought significant contributions, including fresh perspectives on seven plays, and critical reflections on the biases and assumptions underpinning Shakespeare editing and textual studies. A handful of scholars encouraged deeper interrogation of received knowledge and challenged the traditional narratives that shape accounts of book history, Shakespeare, the First Folio, and its compilers' enduring legacy. Material bibliographers advanced the field with innovative methodologies that uncovered new insights into textual production, and groundbreaking research on commonplace culture highlighted Shakespeare's strategic engagement with his reputation and works.

WORKS REVIEWED

August, Hannah, and Francis X. Connor, eds., *Romeo and Juliet*. The New Oxford Shakespeare Oxford World's Classics (Oxford, 2024)

Borlik, Todd Andrew, and Francis X. Connor, eds., *As You like It*. The New Oxford Shakespeare Oxford World's Classics (Oxford, 2024)

Bourne, Claire M. L., 'The handmaids' tale: book history, Shakespeare, and women's textual labour', in *The Oxford Handbook of the History of the Book in Early Modern England*, ed. Adam Smyth (Oxford, 2024), 20–46

Davies, Callan, and Sarah Neville, eds., *The Merry Wives of Windsor*. The New Oxford Shakespeare Oxford World's Classics (Oxford, 2024)

Erne, Lukas, 'Mediating Shakespeare: thirteen ways of looking at editorial agency', in *Liber amicorum H. R. Woudhuysen: A Bibliographical Tribute* (Oxford, 2024), 145–65

Ghose, Indira, and Ann Pruitt, eds., *Henry IV, Part I*. The New Oxford Shakespeare Oxford World's Classics (Oxford, 2024)

Rasmussen, Eric, and Molly G. Yarn, 'A newly discovered manuscript of Vincent of Lérins's *Commonitorium* and Shakespeare's Hand D in *Sir Thomas More*', *Papers of the Bibliographical Society* 118 (2024), 452–61

Schott Syme, Holget, ed., 'The Shakespeare First Folio as Source, Object, and Evidence', *Shakespeare Quarterly* 74 (2023)

Smith, Emma, '"Now I am in Arden: the more fool I": Love's Labour's Won and the Arden 3 series', in *Liber amicorum H. R. Woudhuysen: A Bibliographical Tribute* (Oxford, 2024), 125–44

Smith, Emma, and John Jowitt, eds., *Macbeth*. The New Oxford Shakespeare Oxford World's Classics (Oxford, 2024)

Smyth, Adam, ed., *The Oxford Handbook of the History of the Book in Early Modern England* (Oxford, 2023)

Starza Smith, Daniel, and Hazel Wilkinson, eds., *Liber amicorum H. R. Woudhuysen: A Bibliographical Tribute* (Oxford, 2024)

Tregear, Ted, *Anthologizing Shakespeare, 1593–1603* (Oxford, 2023)

West, Anthony James, 'Update of the Shakespeare First Folio *Census*', *The Library* 24 (2023), 445–64

West, Anthony James, 'Update of the history of the Shakespeare First Folio', *The Library* 25 (2024), 29–40

Warren, Christopher N., et al., 'Who rpinted Shakespeare's Fourth Folio?', *Shakespeare Quarterly* 74 (2023), 139–46

Whipday, Emma, and Terri Bourus, eds., *Measure for Measure*. The New Oxford Shakespeare Oxford World's Classics (Oxford, 2024)

Working, Lauren, and Rory Loughnane, eds., *The Tempest*. The New Oxford Shakespeare Oxford World's Classics (Oxford, 2024)

3. SHAKESPEARE IN PERFORMANCE
reviewed by MIRANDA FAY THOMAS

Preparing this review essay – a compilation covering the best of the last two years' publications – I have been reflecting on what I mean by 'Shakespeare in performance': what does this category permit, and what might it exclude? The connotations of 'performance' with 'liveness' and the here-and-now prompt an eagerness to review the latest studies about the latest performances, yet even as I do this is complicated by new light being shed on historical theatre practices and re-evaluations of adaptations in a variety of media (across TV, cinema and online platforms), let alone how digital and technological advances are forcing us to reconsider how we might conceive of 'liveness' at all. 'Performance studies', as a term, seems almost at odds with 'theatre history', the latter stuck in the past, the former thrillingly vital, yet both are on offer within Shakespeare studies; in fact, often, there is surprising continuity between theatre practices old and new (not to mention the building of new theatres, and new-old (replica or archetypal) theatres). And enough of the intentions of the performances: what of the reception? It is remiss not to also consider the focus of audiences, and their practices of decoding, reinterpretating and reappropriating. Does adaptation fall within the remit of performance? Does architecture? Does affect? 'Shakespeare in performance' – as the current state of the field stands – might be said to encompass all of the above and far more. My conclusion – for now at least – is to greedily devour up all such discourse, and present the very best of new research that augments rather than occludes performance possibilities.

Emma Whipday's latest edited collection, *Shakespeare/ Play: Contemporary Readings in Playing, Playmaking and Performance* is one of several new releases in Arden's Shakespeare Intersections series, described by the series editors as designed to 'actively question received critical formations' (xv). It is a publication that confirms Whipday's enviable talent for curating a wide selection of brilliant essays, innovatively organized: for *Shakespeare/ Play*, she structures the contributions into a format aimed at replicating the playgoing experience. Rather than sections, there are 'Acts' (each containing three essays on a related theme); these are interspersed with 'Act breaks' – shorter essays which consider the margins of public performance (such as David McInnis on lost plays, and Alison Findlay on domestic drama). The collection begins with

Whipday's own introduction – or 'playbill' – and Callan Davies's 'prologue'; it ends with Gina Bloom's 'jig' (a lively essay on using games to teach Shakespeare). Whipday introduces the book as one which 'aims to expose and explore the rich complexity of Shakespeare *slash* play: Shakespeare and play, the Shakespeare play, playing in Shakespeare, playing with Shakespeare, playing Shakespeare' (12). The result is a thoroughly engaging set of pieces, which open up all kinds of possibility for performance scholarship.

Davies's prologue is masterful, gorgeously interweaving quotations and details lifted from contemporary sources and using them, collage-like, to vividly place the reader into the excitement and bustle of a theatre-space before the show begins. It is a great example of how to write evocatively without sacrificing historical accuracy; in fact, it is strong evidence for the *necessity* of scholarship if such writing is to be truly effective. This is followed by 'Act 1', on 'Playing with Parts'. This opens with Laurie Maguire's contribution on doubling: while a term not in the English language until 1800 (31), it was nevertheless a necessary performance practice, more usually referred to as playing a second part. Described by W. J. Lawrence as 'drudgery' (32), this was a chore relegated to hired men rather than the company sharers. Yet Maguire notes how the meaning of 'the second part' seems to shift in the 1600s, in that it 'loses the sense of inferiority and subordination, of *second* as a value judgement' (28). Refuting Lawrence's value judgement of unrewarded labour, Maguire instead considers doubling as an inherent aspect of performance and its Protean roots. This essay is followed by Whipday's own work, which considers the absent character of Kate Keepdown in *Measure for Measure*. Kate is supposed to be married off to Lucio at the play's conclusion – one of the many couples created in the finale – but unlike the other betrotheds, she does not appear onstage. Whipday uses this absence to complicate 'the marital and sexual ideologies of the play's comic ending', and she uses examples of cue scripts from the play's other sex workers to make pertinent comparisons 'between the household and the brothel' (65). Emer McHugh acknowledges the provocative nature of asking the question 'Who is a Great Shakespearean?', using Kenneth Branagh as a case study. Rather than answering the question, she acknowledges that she poses it in order to prompt the reader into 'thinking about what it suggests'; she unpacks the over-simplified narrative of 'Great Shakespeareans', forged through 'concomitant mindsets' (69), in order to analyse how a working-class Protestant from Belfast became 'perhaps the most renowned Shakespearean of his generation' (70). McHugh's work impeccably situates Branagh's career within Irish theatre studies and Shakespearian performance history, implying the inseparability of the two. Her central contention – that 'Branagh's Irishness has been rendered invisible … through his actor training and the apparatus of British Theatre institutions' (72) – is a timely reminder that more complicated, more truthful and ultimately more interesting histories of Shakespearian acting are still much needed.

Act 2, 'Playing (with) Women', features scholarship from Chloe Kathleen Preedy, Eleanor Rycroft and Sally Barnden. Preedy examines *A Midsummer Night's Dream* and *The Merry Wives of Windsor* to demonstrate how Shakespeare 'connects play, childhood traditions and the dramatic presentation of arguably "wanton" or "airy" comedies in ways that recall, and potentially challenge, contemporary prejudices against the commercial theatre he wrote for' (96). She aligns Shakespeare's work with oral and folkloric traditions, and contends that the playwright implies a challenge to the gendered notion that 'both theatre and old wives' fables' are merely frivolous matter (111). Rycroft's essay on 'Women walking in Shakespeare' takes us on a journey that wanders around 'settings of femininity' (117), such as windows, woods and gardens, arguing that these places 'are a spatial shorthand for the punishment of women's mobile agency' (132). She writes with verve, and with a sharp sense of the need for social justice, noting how picturesque scenes can quickly become suffused with violence and violation: 'how quickly a window can become a display cabinet, a civilized garden can degenerate into a sex show or a verdant wood can transmute into a crime scene' (132). Barnden's focus is on some striking photographs of Victorian *tableaux vivants*: 'static performance[s] in which participants donned costumes, adopted poses and held them for a short period in front of an audience' (136). While such posed scenes – and the images that record them for posterity – may appear to consolidate the objectification of female characters and the actresses who embody them, Barnden questions the assumption that stillness always 'entails an abdication of subjecthood' (149), arguing instead that the

'indefinite duration' of such photographs 'disrupt[s]' the otherwise inevitable conclusions of these plays.

Act 3, 'Playing with Bodies and Minds', features topics such as disability, the ethics of comedy, and queer portrayals of Mercutio. Susan Anderson begins the section with a detailed analysis of Macbeth's fit during the banquet scene of 3.4, observing how 'framing strangeness through disability polices the boundaries of the normal' (168). Next, Urvashi Chakravarty writes a chapter on a topic I've long awaited new discussion on: the proximity of comedy to cruelty. She considers instances when the outcome of play is pain, rather than pleasure, by focusing on the gulling and ultimate incarceration of Malvolio in *Twelfth Night*, before briefly turning to the trick played on Bottom and Titania in *A Midsummer Night's Dream*. Building on Patricia Akhimie's work on racist humour, Chakravarty brilliantly argues that comedy can have a dangerous edge, 'operat[ing] as an agent of inclusion and exclusion' (188), concluding that plays such as *Twelfth Night* can underwrite social problems rather than simply depict or satirize them. Vanessa I. Corredera draws the act to a close by considering how Harold Perrineau's performance in Baz Luhrmann's *Romeo + Juliet* confirmed a trend in casting 'Minoritarian Mercutios' – characters with intersecting minority identities. Looking at two productions from 2021, she asserts that when a queer Mercutio dies almost directly after a heterosexual marriage, we are faced with the stark indication that 'the push towards heteronormative imperatives often comes at the expense of queer identities who pay the price to uphold a system that erases them' (220).

The final two acts – as many final two acts do – race by, but with no dip in quality.

Act 4, 'Playing with Stagecraft', covers the dramaturgy both of songs and of puppetry, and features a delicate and moving chapter from Hailey Bachrach about three productions of *The Merchant of Venice* and conversion, with particular emphasis on Jessica. After a brief act break, provided by the Box Office Bears research project, Act 5 brings matters towards a dénouement with three chapters on jests and games in *Henry VI*, *The Merry Wives of Windsor*, *Hamlet* and *Romeo and Juliet*. Whipday has curated an exceptional array of scholarship here, and like all the best moments of play, the reader is left enthralled, excited and eager for the next round.

The problem with the length of the average academic monograph is that we are taking what should be the mean and making it prescriptive. Something I often tell my students is 'not all ideas are the same size' (usually when, in consultation for a short essay, they pitch a topic that would take a lifetime to get a good crack at); but whether writing an article or a book-length study, almost all scholarly writers will have experienced the need to prune, or pad out, in order to meet a required word count. This is one of the reasons I'm so pleased by the success of Cambridge Elements, and recent publications in the Shakespeare and Performance series continue to offer detailed but concise scholarship within the size of a Mr Men book (three times the price point, but free online initially, which is outstanding value by the standards of academic publishing). Jennifer J. Edwards's *This Distracted Globe: Attending to Distraction in Shakespeare's Theatre* considers how the Bankside Globe's theatre space permits a phenomenologically productive lack of focus, and Paul Menzer's *Shakespeare Without Print* argues for a reconsideration of Shakespearian performance liberated from 'ink, paper, and movable type'. Both of these short books demonstrate serious knowledge lightly worn, their analyses making often profound statements with wit and erudition. Edwards's *This Distracted Globe* concedes straightaway that 'distraction gets a lot of bad press' (1), citing Michael Billington's frustration with all the elements a performance at the Globe competes with (noisy spectators, rain, et al.). Yet Edwards's central thesis is that to focus on the negatives of distraction misses the point. At the Globe, she argues, becoming distracted is 'an intrinsic aspect of this particular theatregoing experience' (1). Edwards reminds us of Lucretius' *De rerum natura* where the unpredictability of atoms is what generates new matter, new possibilities, new life. Her argument reminds me somewhat of Alice Leonard's *Error in Shakespeare: Shakespeare in Error* (2020) in that both see divergence from the expected path as a productive journey, prioritizing rather than punishing new or different ways of seeing. There's plenty of commentary currently discussing attention spans (although I could do without Edwards's citing of Johann Hari, whose book *Stolen Focus* misreads key studies to present attention-grabbing headline conclusions), and distraction is perhaps an inherent trait of the human condition. Perhaps what is different now is the extent of it, and also what might be at stake through lack of attention. There's a time and a place to let your mind wander aimlessly: a walk in the woods, fine; driving a bus, less so. But what is enjoyable about Edwards's book is that it reminds us not to equate distraction with an inherent lack of care or interest; rather, there is simply more to care about.

This Distracted Globe is divided into three sections. The first draws on archival material such as show reports and interviews with actors that detail the kinds of distractions experienced during performances at Shakespeare's Globe. This section is playfully interspersed with snippets from these archives, typographically aside from the main prose but sometimes still interrupting it mid-sentence. It's rare to see ergodic techniques used in academic writing, and it works beautifully as a way of reinforcing Edwards's thesis; it recalls the central material of Claire M. L. Bourne's *Typographies of Performance* (2020) in how printed material can work to replicate dramatic staging. Much of Edwards's material comes from 'End of Season Interviews' (EoSIs) with actors, who comment on their experience of audience distraction in performance. These anecdotal insights offer tantalizing details of the many 'you had to be there' moments which so often seem to epitomize the alchemical magic of theatrical experience; as Edwards so perceptively notes, 'happenstance unites actor and audience: theatrical form and pleasure come from chance' (32). Inevitably, some distractions will be unwelcome (audience members yawning; rainfall dampening the theatre's acoustic qualities, especially when landing on plastic raincoats); it's also true to say that some distractions (a pigeon eating Doritos, for example) will heighten the hilarity when a comedy is being performed, but totally puncture the tension of a tragedy.

Her second section explores how fainting spectators is another cause for distraction – but, nevertheless, a potentially fruitful one – at the Globe. The central case study here is Lucy Bailey's iconic *Titus Andronicus* (2006 and 2014). William Dudley's design for this production created 'a temple of death': a 'stifling, claustrophobic, edgy atmosphere' that had a palpable phenomenological effect on spectators (37). To be clear, Edwards is not arguing for theatremakers to consciously make their patrons as unwell as possible to demonstrate the impact of their work; what she notes is how certain circumstances create 'a form of emotional resonance not simply between actors and spectators ... but between spectators themselves' (44). Her focus is on the domino-effect of fainting during performances of this production, with many show reports noting audience members passing out in 'quick succession' (43). This section raises some truly pertinent questions that cannot be answered within the scope of the Element itself, such as 'how can feeling be shared when feeling is performed, and not authentic? How can we know how audiences feel, and how can we measure that felt experience?' (45). It would be fascinating to see Edwards tackle such issues in a longer study. Her final section considers the notion of distraction ('of being drawn apart') in relation to how the Globe adapted its theatremaking practices during the COVID-19 pandemic. It reveals the delightful detail that, in her 2018 and 2019 seasons as Artistic Director, Michelle Terry had an 'open door' policy during rehearsals, with all Globe staff encouraged to come and go as they pleased, to quite literally 'create distraction in the room' (52). In an interview Edwards conducted with Terry, the AD explains that 'You're doing it for a space you can't possibly pre-empt; no matter how much directors wish they certainly could control it, you really can't' (52). To learn that reacting to the unexpected was built-into the rehearsal process is evidence of Terry's own experience as an actor having a tangible impact on her leadership of Shakespeare's Globe. Edwards then details the practices introduced to enable the continuation of theatremaking even at times where social distancing was mandatory: again, what is most striking is how problems turn into artistic opportunities. For instance, Ola Ince, who directed *Romeo and Juliet* in 2021, noted how in scenes of violence, actors had to avoid physically roughing each other up, but could threaten each other with guns instead, or 'chas[e] each other with long machetes' (55).

By the Element's coda, it's clear that Edwards understands the age-old theatrical strategy of 'leave them wanting more': in sixty-or-so pages, the number of ideas covered makes me long for the deeper analysis of which she is surely capable. Perhaps this is an amuse-bouche for her future work; if so, I look forward to feasting on what follows. *This Distracted Globe* is a fabulous example of what a Cambridge Element should be, and places Edwards firmly at the exciting intersection between performance studies and Shakespeare studies. Her conclusion observes that much of the Globe Archive – the interviews in particular – have been underutilized, and she does what all good scholarship should do, which is prompt and encourage further analysis. It's almost a call-for-papers, promoting what the Globe has meticulously collected by way of anecdotal snapshots that nevertheless create a representative collage. Paul Menzer has already produced a book using a similar methodology – *Anecdotal Shakespeare* – but Edwards is right to highlight a resource that needs further exploration.

Menzer's own Cambridge Element takes as its central premise that 'Shakespeare's printed texts are everywhere

treated as the origin of meaning when they are the belated record of an event' (2). In *Shakespeare Without Print*, he describes print as being given an 'inflated pre-eminence', and he devotes his short book to taking the wind out of that particular balloon (3). There are certain academics who write for publication in a style that reveals just how good a teacher they must be. Paul Menzer is one of these. There are moments clearly indebted to Tiffany Stern's *Documents of Performance in Early Modern England* (2009), such as the evocative description of the many sheets of paper pinned up backstage at any theatre: 'music cues, costume-change-cues, and sound cues . . . prop lists, doubling charts . . . schedules, lists. Letters . . . By the end of every season, the backstage wall is absolutely plastered with text' (25). Despite being entitled *Shakespeare Without Print*, Menzer's central contention is that such a concept is impossible: 'Authors might lose the battle but they always win the war . . . Actors have to simultaneously remember the text and make the audience forget there ever was one. This is impossible, and so they fail' (35). He deploys 'affordance theory' – popularized by Don Norman – to consider how well-designed objects 'convey intrinsic "how-to-use" instructions' (37), and asks 'what performances do the modern edited texts of the plays of William Shakespeare afford and dis-afford?' (38). Interesting observations abound, such as how many audiences may not notice shared lines between characters; Menzer argues that lines, 'in performance, don't exist. They are a purely typographical phenomenon' (46). This is, I suspect, rather an issue for semantics; given that Menzer is such a fan of analogies (he describes footnotes as 'the cellar where editors keep their meanings' (50)), perhaps shared lines may be thought of as a 'serving suggestion' that the consumer is free to accept, or ignore, and still feast. He is optimistic about technological advances for Shakespeare in print, noting how the digital sphere may encourage possibility rather than procedure, and that the optionality for customization – user by user – will impact upon future performance. I remain somewhat sceptical about such a hypothesis: an actor's individual ownership of an alterable text will still be controlled by a dramaturg's edits and a director's preference. Acting performances will still be shaped by theatrical space and by audience expectation. That said, this is an Element fizzing with ideas, and while I may not agree with all of them, I found the book immensely helpful in provoking and testing my own assumptions.

Two exemplary monographs consider the process of race-crafting: one focusing on early modern England,

France and Spain (Noémie Ndiaye's *Scripts of Blackness: Early Modern Performance Culture and the Making of Race*); the other focusing on 21st-century America (Vanessa I. Corredera's *Reanimating Shakespeare's Othello in Post-racial America*). Ndiaye's *Scripts of Blackness* is one of the first titles in University of Pennsylvania Press's new series RaceB4Race: Critical Race Studies of the Premodern, and it is a book I have barely stopped mentioning to students and colleagues since its publication. It is utterly impossible to give full justice to the depth and breadth of the content of this monograph: it fizzes with ideas and connections, and contains more moments where I was left literally open-mouthed by its arguments, conclusions, and eloquence than many scholars would achieve in a lifetime. One of Ndiaye's central claims in her study of performative blackness is that 'racial impersonation . . . fashions what it claims to mimic' (2). She proves this contention through a rigorous exploration of various material practices and processes: 'black-up' (the use of cosmetics to construct a performance of blackness), blackspeak (the use of accent and voice modulation) and black dances (the use of kinetics as racialization). Racialization is not simple: Ndiaye conceives of it as a matrix, constituted of interconnected paradigms. Her introduction unpacks different understandings of race in the early modern period. Race-as-degree (that is to say, through aristocratic bloodlines) and race-as-religion (for instance, in Judaism and Islam, where blood was used to racialize religious difference and was considered hereditary) were understandings which dominated during the 1500s, but by the end of that century – 'stimulated by the age of discovery and the material incentives of colonization' – race-as-phenotype emerged (5). And while skin colour 'quickly became a shorthand' for this conceptualization (5), Ndiaye's work demonstrates that, while visible darkness was important, so too was accent and movement. In fact, the scant attention given to the latter two, she argues, is because 'the Western understanding of theatrical performance relies so heavily on the supremacy of the visual, or scopic, regime' (24). She focuses on not one, but three, countries – Spain, England and France – in order to show the interconnectivity of 'colonial drives' (9); in doing so, Ndiaye 'attempt[s] to grasp the stories Europeans told themselves through performative blackness' (3). This performative process becomes fundamental to her terminology: she consciously uses '*racecraft* as an allusion to *stagecraft*, to flag in no uncertain terms the role that performative practices played in shaping new racial formations' (17).

Chapters 1 and 2 focus on 'black-up', the first in terms of its demonizing effects, the second in terms of its sexualizing effects. 'The diabolical script of blackness', as she calls it in the first chapter (33), can be found in cosmetics practices that represent sub-Saharan Africans (for the specific purposes of Shakespearians reading this *Survey*, there is a virtuosic section on visual hermeneutics in *Othello* wherein Iago's character is described as 'the white male gaze at work' (55)). Chapter 2 – a 'herstory' to the previous chapter's 'history' – explores the sexualizing process at work in the performances/impersonations of black women; one section in particular focuses on the *mulata* as a stock character of Spanish theatre. Chapter 3, on 'Acoustic blackness and the accents of race', considers how blackspeak fashions identities that are infantilized and animalized. Beginning with a quotation from 2014's *An Octoroon* ('I don't know what a real slave sounds like. And neither do you'), Ndiaye explains how sonic difference (such as 'Africanese gibberish and black-accented European vernacular') is a racializing process. Her term, 'blackspeak', specifically conjures up similarities to George Orwell's 'Newspeak' in order to demonstrate how artificial linguistic constructions reshape and control perception (141), and she concludes that 'blackspeak framed those characters as childish, intellectually deficient, and excessively physical, three characteristics that made them particularly suited for slavery' (186). Chapter 4, on 'Dance, race, and power', demonstrates the processes of sexualization and animalization. Ndiaye demonstrates that 'dance was a particularly efficient medium for racializing Afro-diasporic people' – it had already 'triumphed across Renaissance Europe' in terms of shaping performances of both gender and class (188–9). Her chapter chronologically charts dance culture from the 1550s to the end of the seventeenth century: the first section shows how Afro-Spaniards used black dances 'to renegotiate the terms of their enslavement' (192); the second section focuses on how choreography in France which featured 'scripts of black animalization' resulted in Afro-diasporic people being 'downgraded . . . in the Great Chain of Being' (193).

An impressive appendix follows, which shows across a chart plays from Spain, England and France from the 1500s to the 1690s which feature black characters. Even a cursory glance at its various informational density and lacunae proves fascinating. The book is also furnished with high-quality colourplates, one of which is used as part of the cover design. Ndiaye's writing also takes into account her own subjectivity; indeed, her introduction begins with three scenes of examples of racialized performance, from 2008 to 2019. She uses these personal incidents to 'constitute the affective substrate' of her book (2), and while she certainly asks 'what did performative blackness do for early modern Europeans?' (3), Ndiaye also highlights what such conceptualizations – even 400-year-old ones – do for us today. Every once in a while, an early modernist scholar writes a book about the formation and conception of identity that becomes indispensable for generations to come. Stephen Greenblatt's *Renaissance Self-Fashioning* (1980) and Kim F. Hall's *Things of Darkness* (1995) are two such titles. Ndiaye's *Scripts of Blackness* will no doubt join them in becoming utterly indispensable to Renaissance studies, for it is a revelatory and revolutionary piece of scholarship.

Moments before his death, Othello implores of the onlookers: 'Speak of me as I am ... nothing extenuate'. Vanessa I. Corredera similarly urges such an approach to representations of Othello in his 21st-century afterlives. Her new monograph, *Reanimating Shakespeare's Othello in Post-racial America* (2023), 'takes up this question of re-telling Othello's story' through the exploration of a variety of media (4). Corredera uses 'reanimation' as her central term, rather than 'adaptation' or 'appropriation', although both are certainly present in her examples. However, the author's adoption of 'reanimation' formulates these afterlives as 'sites of concomitant identification', and, crucially, 'resistance to Shakespearean authority': their identity, distinctive from anything labelable as faithful or authentic, ensures 'the possibility of moving in a new direction regarding the ideological race work the play undertakes' (5). Furthermore, she argues that such reanimations, due to the breadth of their circulation, mean that the racial narratives disseminated by such memes, podcasts or comedy sketches have a far wider cultural impact. Corredera reminds us of the lost meaning of 'extenuate' in Renaissance parlance: to 'lessen in representation' (4). Accordingly, her book explores how the character of Othello has been diminished through particular representational choices – choices which may have originated as incidental, but which have had a profound effect upon contemporary reception. As Corredera herself acknowledges, 'reanimation' is a term which calls to mind Mary Shelley's *Frankenstein*, a text which 'reminds us, in the wrong hands and for the wrong purposes, that which is reanimated can and likely will be detrimental' (5).

It's impossible not to comment on the chronological scope Corredera sets for herself, especially in the current political moment. 'Post-racial America' limits her examples to 2008–2016, beginning with the election of President Barack Obama and ending with the election of President Donald Trump. Reviewing this book in late November 2024, the idea that the United States of America had overcome its genocidal roots and institutionally racist history to emerge as a full-on meritocracy is naive to the point of absurdity. But Corredera, like many anti-racist scholars, knew this long ago: as she argues in her book, 'post-racial' reanimations of Othello frequently 'reify the problems inherent in Shakespeare's tragedy', and in doing so 'troubl[e] the narrative of racial progress' (7). In six erudite chapters, she covers a variety of examples: the comic book series *Kill Shakespeare*, a modernized rap-adaptation entitled *Othello: The Remix*, and the phenomenally popular podcast *Serial* make up the first half. The second half of the book spotlights Keith Hamilton Cobb's *American Moor*, three plays about Desdemona (by Toni Morrison, Ann-Marie MacDonald and Paula Vogel), before a final chapter focuses on a Shakespearian comedy sketch by Keegan-Michael Key and Jordan Peele, and Peele's own debut feature film, *Get Out*. The opening three chapters offer case studies which illustrate anti-black reanimations, while the final three provide examples of how *Othello* can be reimagined for anti-racist purposes.

Particularly illuminating is her chapter on *Serial*, the podcast that was the first to be downloaded 5 million times on iTunes (119). The series uses investigative journalism to explore a criminal case from 1999, wherein Adnan Syed was accused of, charged with and imprisoned for the murder of his girlfriend, Hae Min Lee. In the first episode, creator Sarah Koenig introduces the story as a 'Shakespearean mashup', and implies similarities to both *Romeo and Juliet* and *Othello* by describing the couple as 'young lovers from different worlds thwarting their families', and Syed as 'not a Moor exactly, but a Muslim all the same' (120). Corredera observes how Koenig's tendency towards Othering creates a white racial frame, and notes how the podcaster has been accused of being a 'cultural tourist' (123). The chapter further argues that Koenig's curation of the case unintentionally aligns herself with 'Iago's strategies for endowing himself with narrative authority' (131), and while Corredera acknowledges the limits of such an interpretation, she maintains that Koenig is still ultimately responsible for Syed's 'racial representation' (132). Of similar analytical pertinence is chapter 6, which analyses the work of American comedian, screenwriter and director,

Jordan Peele. Where chapter 2's exploration of the Q-brothers' hip-hop adaptation of *Othello* draws critique from Corredera – a song in the production says of the story 'That's a tragedy ... yep, but there's comedy in it' (78) – the final chapter of Corredera's monograph circles back to the work of an artist initially best known as a comedian. Key and Peele's sketches were broadcast on Comedy Central between 2012 and 2015, and Corredera focuses on a single one, wherein two black men in early modern England visit the theatre to watch *Othello* for the first time. While initially delighted to see representation on the stage, they are angered and frustrated by the tragic ending; as Corredera argues: 'through these critiques of *Othello*, the men, and therefore the sketch, suggest that Shakespeare's engagement with and depiction of Blackness fails both then and now' (267). Corredera's thesis in this chapter is the necessity of resisting 'lobotomized Shakespeare', and refutes the still persistent claims of Shakespeare's universality as 'appealing' but ultimately 'just a fantasy' (271). She then turns her attention to Peele's first feature film, *Get Out*. Released in 2017, it falls outside of her 2008–2016 remit, but necessarily ends the study as a crucial case for revealing the failure of the imagined 'post-racial' America. In *Get Out* – which was miscategorized as a comedy at the Golden Globes – Corredera contends that Peele offers a remediation of the *Othello* narrative 'that no longer raises questions about a Black man's humanity but rather directs attention to the racist inhumanity directed against him through the shifting, potent tools of white supremacy' (277).

Corredera's work is at its most impressive when she unpicks America's racial habitus. Her conception of habitus – following Pierre Bourdieu – is that it 'functions most effectively through its hiddenness' (24); while such structures appear neutral, they invisibly shape and contort society while feigning naturalism and 'common sense'. Her case studies deftly dismantle such misleading and persistent ideologies. She astutely observes that Shakespeare's claim to universality is appealing because it becomes 'an easy shorthand to explain the purpose and significance of humanities scholarship' (298), and her epilogue proposes productive plurality, offering action points that can be committed to in order to 'pushback against the pervasiveness of colorblind racial denial' (307). *Reanimating Shakespeare's Othello* is a powerful and revelatory study, and its razor-sharp insights provide major ramifications for how Shakespearian narratives are used and reshaped.

D. J. Hopkins's 2024 Cambridge Element *'Sleep No More' and the Discourses of Shakespeare Performance'* has – unwittingly, as the author acknowledges – become 'the first retrospective on *Sleep No More*' (87). While initially conceived of as a tool and guide for audience members to approach the site-specific, immersive reimagining of *Macbeth*, by the time of its publication the production's closure had been announced. Running since 2011, Punchdrunk's iconic show is described by Hopkins as 'a *Macbeth*-themed haunted house' (1), and his short book unpacks the production's sophisticated engagement with not just Shakespeare, but also the cinematic work of Alfred Hitchcock.

The second half of Hopkins's title – 'and the Discourses of Shakespeare Performance' – allows him to situate his analysis of *Sleep No More* within far wider conversations, and he fundamentally identifies Shakespeare as a 'tool for critical inquiry, not only its object' (8). A particular obsession of this book, as one might expect, is theatrical ghosting, following in the theoretical footsteps of Marvin Carlson. As *Sleep No More* is mostly a wordless piece, Hopkins perceives that 'Shakespeare is disappeared, but not absent' (38), and that in performance the audience function 'as archive' who themselves bring 'the words that aren't spoken' (57). It's important to note that Punchdrunk themselves refrain from calling *Sleep No More* an adaptation (49), and Hopkins cites work from Julie Sanders, Barbara Hodgdon and M. J. Kidnie among others to focus not on 'what was done *to* Shakespeare', but 'what was done *with*' him (52). Ultimately, he argues that the production's non-linear form results in the source-text itself 'becom[ing] a navigational tool' (58), resulting in a three-hour-long rhizomatic approach to *Macbeth*. Hopkins's conception of theatrical ghosting also extends to the viewers, creating what he describes as 'an uncanny spectatorship' (43); indeed, Josephine Mâchon (referred to as Punchdrunk's unofficial scholar) describes the audience as 'witnesses, no longer spectators but *spectres* in the shadows' (27). It's worth noting that Hopkins describes Mâchon's work as scholarship, yet 'clearly partisan' (28), and such a statement necessitates comment: we need to face up to the fact that the idea of a detached, neutral academy is a myth – academic writing has always been used as a means of advocating (often for the status quo), and just because it might present itself as nonpartisan it doesn't mean that it actually is (see also my review above of Corredera's monograph).

The (mostly journalistic) criticism aimed at *Sleep No More* for its lack of adherence to a Shakespearian script, thus potentially rendering it illegible to those unfamiliar with the play, reveals what Hopkins calls a persistent 'literary bias' in Shakespeare performance (19). As a counter-narrative, he reframes 'immersive theatre as the extension of a history of long-standing if marginal theatre practices, not just an emerging trend' (23), and argues that immersive performances have traceable connections to ancient rituals. His most riveting sections offer detailed descriptions of his own experience of *Sleep No More* as an audience member, and these will offer a tantalizing window for those who now will not be able to experience it. His reportage of the vast site-specific space, filled with disorientating tunnels and a 'Secret Sixth Floor', utilize Gina Bloom's scholarship to conceive of the spectator's – or, rather, participant's – experience as one which can be gamified (56); indeed, given that Bloom's work reveals a strong tradition of theatre being a 'game space', Hopkins argues that 'gamification is part of what makes *Sleep No More* Shakespearean' (65). This Cambridge Element is often informal in style, but informative in substance, and while this long-running production has now closed, discussion of it seems far from over.

Performance studies has come a long way since the work of Peggy Phelan and Philip Auslander. 'Our understanding of what constitutes a theatrical performance', writes Aneta Mancewicz, 'has evolved over the centuries in terms of spatial set-ups and audience–actor configurations; however, it is the arrival of extended reality technologies that has brought a radical transformation of theatre's ability to give audiences the feeling of being present' (34). Three new publications engage with the topic of liveness and inventive performance practices: Mancewicz's own Cambridge Element, *Extended Reality Shakespeare*; Danielle Rosvally and Donovan Sherman's edited collection *Early Modern Liveness: Mediating Presence in Text, Stage and Screen*; and Robert Myles and Valerie Clayman Pye's *Innovation and Digital Theatremaking*. Mancewicz's *Extended Reality Shakespeare* considers recent adaptations of Shakespeare and their engagement with technology. Arguing that Shakespeare's predilection for including metatheatrical elements in his work creates additional layers of meaning when blending real and virtual environments, she defines extended reality as an 'umbrella term that currently covers augmented, virtual, and mixed reality . . . but might come to include future technologies as well' (1). There is a slight eeriness, for me, at least, in such a sentence, which outlines the remits of the book's key term while acknowledging that we don't fully know yet what else it will come to include. Yet Mancewicz's first section is primarily devoted to categorization, in order to ground her later examples within a spectrum of extended reality Shakespeares. Her key taxonomy has two extremes – physical and virtual – and along the scale she charts performances that are 'physical with some virtual elements' (such as *Hamlet's Lunacy*, CREW, 2019), 'physical and virtual balanced' (*Current, Rising*, Royal Opera House, 2021) and 'virtual with some physical elements' (*Dream*, RSC, 2021). As she herself acknowledges, creating such a taxonomy 'means deciding not only what we define as extended reality but also, and perhaps more importantly, what we recognise as theatre' (34). I do think perhaps some of these distinctions are somewhat arbitrary and subjective, but even if one does not necessarily fully agree with the individual categorizations, the attempt at such categorization itself creates a fruitful opportunity to consider the limits and ramifications of taxonomies as a structuring device.

Section 2, 'How Does It Work?', offers an engaging array of case studies, each representing a different point on Mancewicz's spectrum in order to 'demonstrate how Shakespeare's dramas can be used to advance our understanding of extended reality as a form of metatheatre' (41). To achieve this, she provides three in-depth examples. The first is *Hamlet's Lunacy*, created by the Belgian collective CREW. CREW have long experimented with new technologies in order to create theatrical innovations, and have been undertaking a practice-as-research project centred around *Hamlet* since 2016. The project's key question, 'How to act honourably in a conflicted world?', recognizes the temporal and emotional overlaps between Hamlet's world and our own: both ages are 'marked by dramatic paradigm shifts accompanied by a sense of uncertainty and insecurity' (44). Equipping audience members with items such as iPads and headsets, virtual reality blended with the immediate surroundings to create a hybrid space between the two. Participants were asked to use this technology to recreate the orbits of planets within the solar system, and in doing so it blurred the lines between spectator and spectacle. It created 'a hybrid choreography of physical bodies and digital images', and Mancewicz observes that this had the effect of 'recreat[ing] the pathos of *Hamlet*'s tragic ending' (49). Rather than 'representing the plot', the audience/participants were enabled to 'embody' it (50); instead of seeing an actor representing Hamlet's confusion, 'the protagonist's emotion becomes embodied by the participants' (51). The next case study, *Current, Rising*, was performed at the Royal Opera House in the summer of 2021. Taking *The Tempest* as its (loose) source, it was situated within 'an illuminated wooden box structure', the walls of which displayed commentary on the piece's themes and asked the primary question: 'What do we build from here?' (53). *Current, Rising* simultaneously used *The Tempest*'s location – an island of potentiality – and the audience's location of emerging from the pandemic lockdowns to consider the opportunities that both afforded. Performances were intimate – only four spectators at a time – with each audience member wearing headsets that transformed the others around them into avatars, while listening to Ariel's song 'Full Fathom Five'. The experience was 'dizzying and disorientating', and Mancewicz, who experienced the production, found her sense of proprioception muddled. While it was an engaging production, Mancewicz critiques *Current, Rising* for not negotiating more distinctly with its source material, particularly given the pertinence of how illusion and reality are framed within the play. Her final major case study is *Dream*, produced by the RSC in 2021. Available to watch live, but remotely, during the pandemic, it featured live actors using motion-capture technology interacting in real time. This production arguably made more of the text: Pippa Hill, Head of Literacy at the RSC, 'went through the play and found every mention of a plant, a flower, a tree or a creature that appears in the wood' and gave it to the Visual Developers to create the forest environment (64). The production also created the Gestrument: 'an interactive music device ... which allowed the performers to generate music with their movements in real time yet in harmony with the pre-recorded orchestral score' (64). While the performance was free, audiences could choose to pay for a more interactive experience, and were able to 'launch fireflies and plant seeds' (65); however, this element was not deemed especially successful, with several participants commenting that the experience was akin to 'witnessing someone else play a computer game' (65). Overall, Mancewicz concludes that 'the future of extended reality performance lies not so much in competing with cinema and gaming industries as in establishing its own identity and modus operandi' (74). It will be fascinating to see how future engagements between Shakespeare and extended reality demonstrate the latent potentialities of each.

Rosvally and Sherman's *Early Modern Liveness* – as one might expect from a multi-authored edited collection – takes a broader approach to the concept of performance and liveness. Following W. B. Worthen's contention

that 'the stage itself *is* a technology', they argue that theatre 'becomes the site of its own struggle with technology – and it does so *as* a technological implement itself' (3). Building on Sarah Bay-Cheng's concepts of digital performance, Rosvally and Sherman introduce their essay collection by conceiving of performance and liveness as 'everywhere, a filter we place on the raw material of experience that grants it legibility. We are always live – we always experience liveness – because we are always in the present' (4). Noting that case studies about liveness usually feature contemporary work, the editors here curate essays which negotiate how liveness was experienced in past eras of performance history. As such, they explore early modern theatre, both now and then, through the deceptively simple question: 'how does the early modern theatre produce a distinct sense of liveness?' (6). Their introduction concludes by offering a new way of conceiving liveness: one not restricted to physical, in-the-room presence, but instead as any experience of 'a feeling of copresence, which can be sparked at any moment when an audience encounters a piece of art' (9).

Part one, 'Proximity', considers the relationship between liveness and physical distance. Rebecca Bushnell focuses on interaction, and demonstrates instances of when 'versions of virtual Shakespeare have reflected or at least gestured towards the circumstances and interactive practices of early modern English theatre performance' (17). It's an engaging essay to kick off the collection, especially given that it takes historical theatre practices and pairs them with modern-day virtual technologies. Using examples from video games (such as *Elsinore*, wherein the player becomes Ophelia and must try and save the day before Hamlet's actions leave everyone dead) and virtual performances (such as a production of *The Tempest* ostensibly located in a virtual theatre named 'The Decameron'), Bushnell reflects that her experiences with such Shakespearian material in the pandemic and since have produced 'at least the illusion of close proximity' which is inseparable from liveness. Stephanie Shirilan then follows with an essay that starts by reflecting on the experience of teaching via Zoom: ostensibly synchronous, she meditates that the phenomenology is anything but, given the numerous delays and stutters of the technology, and the inability of the medium to replicate the nuances of in-person movement and body language. Her chapter asks the central question, 'what kind of shared experience of air and atmosphere is possible at a distance?' (38), and evocatively considers Cleopatra's 'breathless power' (50).

Next, Thomas Cartelli turns to two versions of *Macbeth*: Kit Monkman's 2018 film, and Big Telly's 2020 Zoom adaptation. Monkman's *Macbeth* was filmed entirely in front of a green screen, in doing so 'generat[ing] a dramatic/cinematic environment that is everywhere and nowhere at once' (63). Big Telly's production, by contrast, featured a cast of five who had never met, but who were morphed into proximity within virtual screens. He follows the work of Katherine Rowe by thinking in terms of medium specificity, and he draws a fascinating comparison between green screen / Zoom performance and much earlier practices, arguing that both productions 'turned upon challenges that were not dissimilar from those early modern actors faced in preparing to perform roles sketched out in character-specific scripts whose only concession to the whole cloth of a play were their entrance cues' (82). Cartelli rethinks liveness as, instead, *aliveness*, in doing so considering how 'distance or remoteness' can be overcome via methods of 'engagement with an audience of invisible lookers-on' (82).

Part two, 'Performance', begins with Aneta Mancewicz, whose recent book I have covered in depth above; her essay here offers something of a 'director's cut' from her Cambridge Element, in that it provides further case studies of virtual reality Shakespeare. Elizabeth E. Tavares contributes a fascinating essay on the role of the prompter in the Original Practice Shakespeare Festival (OPSF) in Portland, Oregon. Noting how the prompter would have been indispensable to early modern theatrical practices, she demonstrates how the use of a prompter at OPSF developed 'a dual role as part "shepherd" and part creative contributor' (131), able to simultaneously keep the script on track and provide moments of improvisatory joy that added keenly to the sense of liveness. Next, Murat Öğütcü explores three Turkish Shakespeare adaptations: *İkinci Katil* ('Second Murderer', 2017), *Kraliçe Lear* ('Queen Lear', 2019) and *Dream of Hamlet* (2020–2021), all of which reconceptualize possibilities for live theatre during the COVID-19 pandemic.

Part three, 'Premonition', features Kenneth Molloy, Gina M. Di Salvo and Jonathan Gil Harris. Molloy examines how life was conceived and imagined in early modern Islam; Di Salvo contributes a wonderful piece of theatre history by charting the theatrical effect of the blazing star. She reads the device as 'a technology of judgement' (197), noting how, while historical sightings of comets were seen as warnings for the nation, 'stage versions respond to individual experience' (200). In plays featuring Thomas Stukeley, she argues that the blazing star is 'a device of justice'; in *The Revenger's Tragedy* and *The Bloody Banquet* she contends that 'theatrical liveness transforms the blazing star into an authorization of righteous revenge' (206). A final chapter from Gil Harris asks 'what can prophetic apparitions' – in modern India and elsewhere – 'teach us about the "liveness" of the audience in the early modern English playhouse?' (219). I was touched by his conclusion that Shakespeare's theatres 'were less scenes of private scholarly reading than of ecstatic collective devotion': a heartful reminder of the power and catharsis of community, made possible through art. Offering a far-reaching approach, this edited collection will be useful reading for scholars of theatre history and performance studies curious about liveness and its implications.

Meanwhile, theatre practitioner Rob Myles and academic/practitioner Valerie Clayman Pye have joined forces to create an insightful guide which not only sheds light on the process of producing the digitally broadcast *The Show Must Go Online*, but on how any artists can find new ways to create work. *Innovation and Digital Theatremaking: Rethinking Theatre with 'The Show Must Go Online'* is explicitly not a retrospective – such analysis has already begun with *Lockdown Shakespeare* (ed. Gemma Kate Allred, Benjamin Broadribb and Erin Sullivan) – and its focus on being 'forward-facing' is a refreshing change from the traditional academic monographs published in the field of Shakespearian performance studies. Such an approach, focused on future work, is imperative. While acknowledging the success of the creative work that came out of the pandemic, Myles and Pye are unequivocal about the possibility of future global health crises ('we must stress: this will happen again' (4)).

The Show Must Go Online (TSMGO) had produced and broadcast its first play – *The Two Gentlemen of Verona* – a mere six days after COVID-19 was declared a pandemic by the World Health Organization. By the end of the year, it had covered the entirety of plays in the First Folio. Over time, their calling-card became 'Shakespeare for Everyone, For Free, Forever' (1). The company developed strong progressive values, focusing on egalitarian practices, race- and gender-conscious casting, and 'flattened hierarchies' (3), and these all run through the book, which they describe as 'a survival guide for making theatre in times of crisis' (3). It is structured via short but pithy sections, often making use of bullet-points and diagrams, and the work also contains 'asides', which function as a theatrically informed method of formatting print media with a knowing wink.

Chapter 1, 'Innovation and theatremaking', serves as a blueprint for best practice in theatre innovation. It puts pressure on what it calls 'pain points' (11) – in other words, 'what sucks about theatre and what sucks about lockdown' (see: unaffordable tickets, bad seats; lack of community, social distancing). It encourages readers to focus on these problems in order to imagine new possibilities, reminding us that 'failures are useful!' (28) because they indicate what to try next. Throughout, the book conceives of 'work' as a process, not just a product; work, for *The Show Must Go Online*, is a verb as well as a noun. QR codes in the printed book link to useful examples from *TSMGO*'s back catalogue; currently, this is a relatively fuss-free way of quickly bringing the reader face to face with clips that exemplify *TSMGO*'s practices. I have some trepidation about how sustainable this might be; there are also reference notes listing specific website pages, which will also be highly susceptible to 'link rot' (people reading this book in ten years – or even less! – may attempt to visit these pages and find they are no longer available). Linking to YouTube, as many of the QR codes do, might be a greater insurance against such loss, but it's still not a guarantee. But the links are great, for now at least: they allow us to see clips of AR/VR in action, such as the delightful use of a filter in their *A Midsummer Night's Dream* which superimposed the head of Donkey from *Shrek* onto the character playing Bottom.

Chapter 2 justifies the use of Shakespeare as their lockdown playwright, by arguing he's 'familiar', 'malleable' and 'resilient' (35). There is a slightly naive sentiment expressed in this section: 'If Shakespeare's works could survive 450+ years of pestilence, violence, and war and continue to thrive, perhaps we could, too' (38). I take their point, but Shakespeare's perpetuation had a great deal of help by being used as a colonial tool, and, lest we forget, he too has been used as part of violence and war (see Amy Lidster and Sonia Massai's *Shakespeare at War: A Material History*, reviewed later on in this article). More pertinently, Myles and Pye contend that Shakespeare worked so well for them because his work is 'economical in its production: it is a theatre of imagination' (36). Furthermore, 'Shakespeare's company needed to evolve, to create systems in order to produce regularly and rapidly' (36); of course, the Lord Chamberlain's Men needed to find ways to 'shortcut and systemize processes' (36) within a repertory system that demanded several different plays performed each week.

Chapter 3 is on community creation: 'with no financial resources or institutional support to draw on,

impassioned commitment and values-led practices were the only currencies' (42). The show-makers not only created community at a time when it was most needed, but also used it to help address problems of inequality, such as accent bias within the Shakespearian culture industry. 'We wanted to maximise the sound palette of the show' (48), they write, and they detail practices on casting and creating opportunities that opened up Shakespearian performance far beyond Received Pronunciation. This chapter also includes notes on safeguarding processes, and an interesting discussion of online community generated via the Live Chat function during broadcast, which gave rise to the wonderful phrase 'Digital Groundlings' (53). The remaining chapters focus on how to produce both 'rapidly' and 'regularly', how to direct for the digital medium, and highlight 'challenge areas' to focus on in the future. While this is not a traditional scholarly monograph, the knowledge contained within it will generate countless new artistic works – Shakespearian or otherwise – and its key achievements of pragmatism and genuine expertise should be applauded by academics and theatre-lovers alike.

Anyone still wondering what war might be good for has evidently underestimated its impact on Shakespearian entanglements. Amy Lidster and Sonia Massai's exhibition at the National Army Museum (2023–2024) is accompanied by a beautifully presented book, *Shakespeare at War: A Material History*. Featuring more than twenty-five essays and a similar number of images, all printed on extremely glossy paper, this edited collection is an impressive testament to their exhibition, and functions as a very well-informed catalogue. The editors begin with the observation that 'war is never simply eulogized or critiqued in Shakespeare', and their focus is on both material history and reception; that is to say, they reveal how Shakespeare's works – and the playwright's cultural dominance – are 'used at times of war, rather than how war is represented in Shakespeare' (3). The material objects explored in the book include photographs, newspaper cuttings, posters, manuscripts, leaflets, programmes and postcards, and between them they create a rich visual tapestry of Shakespearian engagements with the politics and practicalities of war.

There are too many essays in this collection to cover each in detail, so I will restrain myself and focus on a few key personal highlights. Lidster and Massai's collection is centred around conflicts 'that directly involved Britain' (2). This includes three chapters on Ireland, covering colonialism (Andrew Murphy), rebellion and revolution

(Katherine Hennessey) and the filming of Olivier's *Henry V* in Powerscourt, County Wicklow (Edward Corse). Five 'in conversation' pieces introduce pertinent practitioner voices: Maggie Smales, on her all-female *Henry V* in York; Julia Pascal on her *The Shylock Play* at the Arcola in London; Nicholas Hytner on his National Theatre *Henry V*; Maria Aberg on Roy Williams's *Days of Significance*; and Iqbal Khan on his RSC *Othello*. Ramona Wray contemplates the use of employing desert camouflage as costume in Shakespearian performance; Marius S. Ostrowski and Richard Ned Lebow consider Shakespeare and Germany in the World Wars I and II, respectively; and former commander of Allied Forces in Iraq, Jonathan Shaw, reflects on his role as military advisor to Hytner's 2013 *Othello*. It is an illuminating collection, offering a deep consideration of Shakespeare's many appropriations during wartime, which prompts powerful reflection on the ends to which Shakespeare is the means.

To conclude on what some may consider a superficial note, I have particularly enjoyed the innovative cover art enrobing some of the works reviewed above: special mentions go out to *Innovation and Digital Theatremaking* for its design of a lightbulb inside an Elizabethan ruff; *Reanimating Shakespeare's Othello* for its collage-style cover, featuring a quilt depicting Paul Robeson; and *Scripts of Blackness*'s arresting engraving of 'L'Afrique' from *Recueil de modes* (1750) – Ndiaye's reflections on this image conclude her book, so to close the volume and see the picture again on the cover was to view a familiar object completely anew (it is, of course, the very best scholarship that does precisely this). So I would like to take this moment to advocate for more interesting covers

beyond the generic, especially in an era when getting presses to provide physical books to review is increasingly difficult. Insisting on nicer covers reminds us of the beauty of these books as objects, much laboured-over treasures whose outsides celebrate the illuminating scholarship within.

WORKS REVIEWED

Corredera, Vanessa I., *Reanimating Shakespeare's Othello in Post-racial America* (Edinburgh, 2023)

Edwards, Jennifer J., *This Distracted Globe: Attending to Distraction in Shakespeare's Theatre* (Cambridge, 2023)

Hopkins, D. J., *'Sleep No More' and the Discourses of Shakespeare Performance* (Cambridge, 2024)

Lidster, Amy, and Sonia Massai, eds., *Shakespeare at War: A Material History* (Cambridge, 2023)

Mancewicz, Aneta, *Extended Reality Shakespeare* (Cambridge, 2024)

Menzer, Paul, *Shakespeare Without Print* (Cambridge, 2023)

Myles, Robert, and Valerie Clayman Pye, *Innovation and Digital Theatremaking: Rethinking Theatre with 'The Show Must Go Online'* (New York and Abingdon, 2024)

Ndiaye, Noémie, *Scripts of Blackness: Early Modern Performance Culture and the Making of Race* (Philadelphia, 2022)

Rosvally, Danielle, and Donovan Sherman, eds., *Early Modern Liveness: Mediating Presence in Text, Stage and Screen* (London, 2023)

Whipday, Emma, ed., *Shakespeare/Play: Contemporary Readings in Playing, Playmaking and Performance* (London, 2024)

ABSTRACTS OF ARTICLES
IN *SHAKESPEARE SURVEY 78*

LUKAS ARNOLD

'Necessity Has No Law': Justice and Affective Communities in *2 Henry VI*

This article re-examines the affective affordances of William Shakespeare's *2 Henry VI*, arguing that the garden scene did not necessarily lead spectators towards a specific conclusion on the issue of dearth. Instead, audiences were enabled to consider what constitutes justice through their collective emotional experience as an affective community.

BENJAMIN BROADRIBB

The BBC's Television Adaptations of *Henry VI* and Britain's National Identity Crises

This article explores *The Hollow Crown: The Wars of the Roses* through the lens of Brexit. It positions the series as the most recent in a line of BBC television adaptations of the *Henry VI* plays to capture the tensions and crises simmering within the changing national identity of Britain.

DAVID STERLING BROWN

Shakespeare under the Hood: Teaching, Researching and Learning Shakespeare from Within

Arguing for the value of being 'ratchetdemic' and engaging 'productive discomfort' – a defining feature of Brown's 'critical–personal–experiential' pedagogy – this article offers a retrospective examination of how the self matters in teaching, research and learning. Brown attends to the impact of personal trauma and suggests scholarly work is linked (un)consciously to healing.

RUI CARVALHO HOMEM

Reimagining the Community: A Transatlantic Tale of Two Scholars

This article discusses how two late nineteenth-century public intellectuals, based respectively in Portugal and Brazil, co-opted Shakespeare into discussions that involved reimagining the communities they addressed – at a crucial point in their social, political and constitutional histories.

CHARLES CATHCART

***Lucrece* and Leonard Becket, 1614–1633**

Leonard Becket's various publications insistently quote passages from *Lucrece* as illustrations for the subjects they explore. In developing this sustained afterlife for *Lucrece*, Becket's works exhibit a striking redactive agency, whilst the poem itself serves to illuminate a meditation on the fragility of life.

ABSTRACTS OF ARTICLES

SHEILA T. CAVANAGH

'Didst Thou Not Hear a Noise?': Shakespeare with Headphones
This article considers recent Shakespearian productions emphasizing sound, including Max Webster's acclaimed, yet controversial, London production of *Macbeth* with David Tennant and Cush Jumbo, and Knock at the Gate's entirely auditory Shakespearian presentations, created for listening in the dark with headphones. Binaural technology creates striking soundscapes in each instance.

ROCCO CORONATO

Some Deeper Thing: Visualizing Complexity in *Hamlet* through the Pyrrhus Speech
This article examines the sources behind the Pyrrhus Speech in *Hamlet*, demonstrating how Shakespeare's manifold interweaving of texts can be decoded through sequential procedures of complexity, and ultimately represented through networks.

PATRICK DURDEL

'By the Book': Source Study and the Plot of *Romeo and Juliet*
This article explores the role that notions of plot play in Shakespeare source study. Drawing on three moments of scholarly engagement with the sources for *Romeo and Juliet*, the article shows how plot structures critical inquiry by enabling some kinds of questions while precluding others.

CHLOE FAIRBANKS

'Here's Company': Fractured Englishness and Conflicted Communities in *The Merry Wives of Windsor* and *Henry V*
This article reconsiders Shakespeare's treatment of Englishness as far more provisional and divergent than has traditionally been understood. Attending to persistent inter-community conflicts in *Merry Wives* and *Henry V*, it presents Shakespearian history as defined as much by the lower and middle classes as by titled noblemen.

JOAN FITZPATRICK

War, Hunger and Gluttony in Shakespeare's English Histories: Sir John Oldcastle and Jack Cade
Shakespeare may have returned to his first tetralogy when writing the second tetralogy to develop connections between English bravery and hunger, as well as English cowardice and gluttony. Especially relevant are hitherto overlooked parallels between Sir John Oldcastle and Jack Cade in Shakespeare's treatment of dishonourable conduct and appetite.

NORA GALLAND

German Hermeneutics of Racecraft in Thomas Ostermeier's *Othello* (2010)
Challenging the general denial of race and racism in Europe, this article attempts to make visible the effects of German systemic racism by focusing on the archive version of Thomas Ostermeier's 2010 *Othello* tradaptation at the Schaubühne am Lehniner Platz in Berlin, in which Sebastian Nakajew, a white actor, played Othello in blackface.

JOSEPH P. HAUGHEY

'Strike Their Sounds Together': Radio and Television in the Teaching of Shakespeare in Twentieth-Century America
Radio and television were part of an ongoing narrative of technological innovation in the teaching of Shakespeare in the 1930s, 1940s and 1950s. This article examines the voices of NCTE's *English Journal* teachers in those decades who strived to weave the new technologies into student-centred, project-based curricula.

ABSTRACTS OF ARTICLES

GAVIN HOLLIS

'The New Map with the Augmentation of the Indies': Geographical Knowledge Communities at the Inns of Court and Shakespeare's *Twelfth Night*

This article examines the significance of geography at the Inns of Court in terms of community formation and its policing. It analyses *Twelfth Night* to explore how geographical references (especially to a 'new map') draw on the fraught atmosphere at the Inns in terms of ever-changing knowledge about the world.

MICHAEL P. JENSEN

Thomas Middleton on BBC Radio

This article surveys BBC radio broadcasts of ten plays by Thomas Middleton – both solely authored and collaborated plays. The sixteen productions broadcast between 1950 and 2009 received diverse story-telling approaches. Some are superb radio drama and some not. Also noted are news, documentary and discussion programmes with Middleton content.

PETER KIRWAN WITH TREEHOUSE SHAKESPEARE ENSEMBLE

(Grass)Root and (Tree)Branch: Building Community in the Early Modern Ensemble Training Model

This article introduces the artistic and community practice of Treehouse Shakespeare Ensemble (2022–2023) as emblematic of an ensemble-based MFA training model. Drawing on scholarship on community theatre, the article argues that a grassroots training model has the potential to bridge the theoretical division between university theatre and community partner.

DOMENICO LOVASCIO

'And Now Let Me Alone to End the Tragedy': *Othello*, Comedy and Candlelight in John Fletcher's *Women Pleased*

This article argues that Fletcher's *Women Pleased* features an overlooked response to Shakespeare's *Othello* in terms of dramatic structure, staging, setting, genre, characterization and thematic concerns that calls attention to some crucial aspects of Shakespeare's play in such a way as to make Fletcher emerge as an early critic of Shakespearian drama.

SHARON O'DAIR

Fat Ham and the Problem of Community

'Community' is a popular term often invoked by Shakespearians in ways that assume a clear meaning. To problematize community, this article briefly examines the literature on community in social science and history before turning to its use by Shakespearians. It concludes with a reading of community in James Ijames's *Fat Ham*.

REIKO OYA

Red Kabuki Actors Perform Shakespeare in Occupied Japan (1946–1952): Zenshinza's 'Theatre for Young People'

Immediately after World War II, a left-wing kabuki company called Zenshinza started the *seinen gekijo undo* ('Theatre for Young People'), performing four Shakespearian plays for young audiences throughout Japan. This article examines how Zenshinza's interpretations of Shakespeare first supported, and then later contradicted, the changing cultural policies of occupied Japan.

BENJAMIN S. REED

'Unrespective Boys': The Formation and Betrayal of Child Peer Communities in *Richard III*

Among *Richard III*'s child characters there are multiple moments of community building and disruption. In particular, Richard's pageboy undermines these communities by being culpable in his master's murderous plot. Rather than the pageboy being an 'anti-child', he exhibits self-preserving behaviours mirroring students in early modern grammar schools policing each other.

COURTNEY NAUM SCURO

Power, Horology and Imperial Doubt: Reimagining Time in Shakespeare's *A Midsummer Night's Dream*
In *A Midsummer Night's Dream*, competing approaches to timekeeping raise questions not only about the nature of time, but about who has influence over whom, why and when. This article explores overlooked intersections between time-practices and politics of place, empire, class and technology which preoccupy Shakespeare in *Dream*.

ROBERT SHAUGHNESSY

Mind's Eye: Audio-described Shakespeare
This article offers a critical account of audio description (AD) for Shakespeare performances. AD delivers visual information in verbal form for blind, visually impaired and partially sighted users, and the article addresses its mechanisms of composition, delivery and reception, as well as the issues that arise from its engagements with diverse casting.

ANDREA SMITH

John Gielgud on Air: 65 Years of Performing Shakespeare on Radio
Sir John Gielgud was a highly regarded Shakespearian performer on stage and screen. However, his prolific career playing Shakespeare on radio is far less celebrated. This article shows that he not only was one of the most important early radio actors, but continued to be influential throughout his life.

SIMON SMITH

Music and Drama at the Early Modern Inns of Court: *Twelfth Night* and *Hyde Park*
This article traces close links between professional musicians and acting companies at the early modern Inns of Court. It also explores two plays with documented Inns performances – Shakespeare's *Twelfth Night* and James Shirley's *Hyde Park* – considering how they may have been staged and received in this musically rich performance context.

MISHA TERAMURA

Hitchcock's Hamlet
This article discusses Alfred Hitchcock's plans to direct a modernized adaptation of *Hamlet* in the context of his filmography. While Hitchcock never completed any Shakespearian adaptations, his repeated allusions to Shakespeare in his films chart his thinking about the status of cinema and his own role as a directorial auteur.

VIRGINIA MASON VAUGHAN
AND ALDEN T. VAUGHAN†

'Say What Thou Seest Yond!': Music, Spectacle and the Actor's Voice in Audio Productions of *The Tempest*
This article discusses the ways audio versions of *The Tempest* convey the play's visual spectacles through language and sound effects; in addition, it examines the actors' voices, particularly the use of different accents and verbal tics that help the auditor visualize the characters and the action.

CHRISTINA WALD

'To Be or Not to Be in Ukraine': Ruining Shakespeare and Rebuilding Communities in *H-Effect* and *The Hamlet Syndrome*

This article focuses on a transmedial project that has become an important strand in a growing adaptational network in which *Hamlet* is being reactivated to explore the current situation in Ukraine. Exploring the adaptational principles of ruination and reconstruction, it discusses the fragility and promises of local, national and transnational community-building through Shakespeare.

HARVEY WILTSHIRE

'Bloody creditor[s]' and the Blood-Money Metaphor in *The Merchant of Venice*

This article explores *The Merchant of Venice* through the lens of developments in monetary, mercantile and medical knowledge at the turn of the seventeenth century, in order to demonstrate how and why Shakespeare thinks about blood in economic and peculiarly circulatory terms.

GILLIAN WOODS

A Lion, an Ass, a Dog, and a Wall: *A Midsummer Night's Dream*'s Ecological Theatricality

A Midsummer Night's Dream is one of Shakespeare's most environmentally explicit dramas. Exploring how the play stages the relationship between humans and the natural environment, this article argues that its comedically flawed attempts to represent nature unsettle any sense of human dominion over the wild, offering a new environmental epistemology.

INDEX

Footnotes are indicated by italic type. Unless otherwise stated, the works cited in the index are by (or are attributed to) Shakespeare.

INDEX